# Corporate Accounting
# Information Systems

Visit the *Corporate Accounting Information Systems*
Companion Website at **www.pearsoned.co.uk/boczko**
to find valuable **student** learning material including:

- Multiple choice questions to test your learning
- Revision notes and questions to help you check your understanding
- An online glossary to exaplain key terms

# Tony Boczko

# Corporate Accounting Information Systems

FT Prentice Hall
FINANCIAL TIMES

An imprint of **Pearson Education**

Harlow, England • London • New York • Boston • San Francisco • Toronto
Sydney • Tokyo • Singapore • Hong Kong • Seoul • Taipei • New Delhi
Cape Town • Madrid • Mexico City • Amsterdam • Munich • Paris • Milan

**Pearson Education Limited**

Edinburgh Gate
Harlow
Essex CM20 2JE
England

and Associated Companies throughout the world

*Visit us on the World Wide Web at:*
www.pearsoned.co.uk

_____

**First published 2007**

© Pearson Education Limited 2007

ISBN: 978-0-273-68487-9

**British Library Cataloguing-in-Publication Data**
A catalogue record for this book is available from the British Library

10  9  8  7  6  5  4  3  2  1
10  09  08  07

Typeset in 9.5/12pt Minion by 35
Printed and bound in China CTPSC/01

*The publisher's policy is to use paper manufactured from sustainable forests.*

For Janine, Christopher James, and
Jessica Leigh . . . and of course Max

# Brief contents

## Part 1    A contextual framework    1

## Part 2    Accounting information systems: a contemporary perspective    111

## Part 3    Transaction processing cycles    355

# Contents

## Part 1 A contextual framework 1

Contents

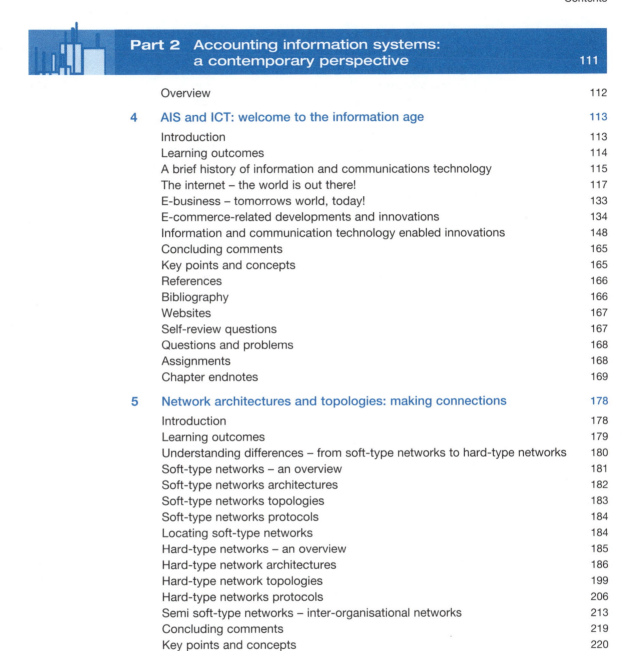

**Part 2    Accounting information systems:
a contemporary perspective                                111**

## Part 3 Transaction processing cycles

## Supporting resources

Visit **www.pearsoned.co.uk/boczko** to find valuable online resources

**Companion Website for students**
- Multiple choice questions to test your learning
- Revision notes and questions to help you check your understanding
- An online glossary to explain key terms

**For instructors**
- Complete, downloadable Instructor's Manual
- PowerPoint slides that can be downloaded and used for presentations
- Additional questions and assignments with suggested solutions

**Also:** The Companion Website provides the following features:
- Search tool to help locate specific items of content
- E-mail results and profile tools to send results of quizzes to instructors
- Online help and support to assist with website usage and troubleshooting

For more information please contact your local Pearson Education sales
representative or visit **www.pearsoned.co.uk/boczko**

# List of articles

# List of examples

# List of figures

# List of tables

# Introduction

## Aims of the book

To paraphrase an old Chinese proverb, we not only live in interesting, but in changing times. We live in an ever-changing world. A world dominated not by the changing nature of global politics, or by the international flows of goods and services, or indeed by the turbulent unpredictability of the global capital markets. We live in a world dominated almost exclusively by flows of knowledge and information – by technologies designed not only to sustain but also increase the socio-economic need and desire for more and more information.

This book offers an insight into the nature, role and context of accounting-related information within the competitive business environment, and explores how business organisations – in particular companies – use a range of theories and technologies not only to assist in the maximisation of shareholder wealth, but also in the management and control of organisational resources. It is concerned primarily with corporate accounting information systems – as an organisational arrangement of processes and procedures that employ both tangible and intangible resources to transform data – more specifically economic data – into accounting information. In doing so, such systems play an important role in four related areas of corporate activity:

- transaction processing management and the supporting of business operations,
- resource management and the fulfilment stewardship obligations,
- information management and the supporting of decision-making processes, and
- financial management and the fulfilment of legal, political and social obligations.

It is an understanding of each of these roles that informs the issues addressed by this book, a book which considers the following areas:

- systems thinking,
- control theories,
- accounting information systems and information and communication technology,
- architectures, topologies and networks,
- contemporary transaction processing cycles and systems,
- systems analysis, development and design,
- information systems and database management,
- e-commerce and the virtual economy,
- risk and fraud management,
- internal control and systems security, and
- accounting information systems audit.

The aims of this book are as follows, to:

- promote an understanding of the role of corporate accounting information systems in the maintenance, regulation and control of business-related resources,
- develop an appreciation and understanding of the practical issues and organisation problems involved in managing contemporary accounting information systems,
- promote an understanding of the political contexts of contemporary accounting information systems,
- deploy systems thinking, control theories and information theories as an integrated conceptual framework for understanding the contemporary nature of corporate accounting information systems,
- develop a recognition of the importance of information and communication technology in corporate accounting information systems management, development and design,
- promote an understanding of the importance of effective information management and transaction processing controls,
- provide a framework for the evaluation of corporate transaction processing cycles, systems and processes,
- identify the objectives and nature of internal control/security, and promote an understanding of the strategies a company could adopt to minimise exposure to corporate risk,
- promote an understanding of the internal control issues associated with alternative transaction processing architectures and system topologies, and
- provide an understanding of basic systems audit strategies.

 **Themes of the book**

### Practical orientation

Corporate accounting information systems are real-entities – they exist within a real-world environment. To provide a balanced overview this book not only provides an exploration of the practical and technical aspects of corporate accounting information systems but, more importantly, a consideration of the social, political and economic pressures that continue to shape the very nature of such systems.

### Accessibility

Where at all possible, a clear, informal linguistic style is used. The use of complex jargon and obscure terminology that seems to litter practical inter-disciplinary subjects such as corporate accounting information systems is, where possible, reduced to a minimum. Where this is inevitable, definitions and explanations of key terms and concepts are provided.

In addition, because much of the discussion on accounting information systems requires not only an appreciation of a range of theoretical ideas, but perhaps more importantly the understanding of a number of sometimes very diverse and very complex practical issues, an incremental approach is adopted in the presentation, analysis and development of such discussion.

### Integration with other disciplines

Corporate accounting information systems cannot be viewed in isolation. Whilst such systems are essentially created political structures whose primary role is seen as economic – as the processing of wealth-creating transactions, they function within the social fabric of the company, increasingly employing a wide range of information and communication technologies. Clearly, to understand fully such systems requires more than an understanding of accounting and finance – more than an understanding of information technology. It requires an appreciation of a wide range of business-related topics – from marketing to economics to organisational behaviour to management.

## Student learning features

Each of the chapters contains some or all of following elements;

### Introduction

This section presents a brief discussion of the relevance and importance of the issues discussed in the chapter.

### Learning objectives

This section presents a summary of expected competencies to be gained by the reader.

### Scenarios, case studies, examples and articles

Extracts from a range of publications are used to illustrate key arguments and demonstrate/highlight key issues within the chapter. The aim is to provide a 'real-world' context to the various aspects of corporate accounting information systems.

### Key points and concepts, references, bibliography and weblinks

At the end of each chapter a key points and concepts listing is provided. In addition, media-based and academic-based referencing to further relevant reading/research is also provided. Where possible the bibliography will provide alternative views on issues discussed in the chapter.

A list of useful websites is also provided.

### Self-review questions

At the end of each chapter a selection of short review questions are provided. These are designed to encourage the reader to review key issues presented in the chapter and, where appropriate, can be used as a review and revision aid.

### Questions and problems

At the end of each chapter a selection of questions and problems is provided. These are designed to provide an opportunity for the reader to demonstrate an understanding and appreciation of the key issues presented in the chapter.

### Assignments

At the end of each chapter a selection of assignments is provided. These assignments are larger case studies that require the reader to develop and examine a range of relationships between corporate accounting information systems and the larger corporate/business environment. These assignments integrate a range of theoretical ideas/practical issues and provide a real-world context to corporate accounting information system problems.

### Appendices

Where appropriate, appendices are included at the end of each chapter.

 **Support for lecturers**

### Website support

A website supporting this book is available and contains;

- powerpoint slides relating to each chapter,
- a selection of additional end-of-chapter questions, including multiple-choice questions, and
- links to useful websites.

### Lecturer's guide

An online lecturer's guide is available.

The guide contains supplementary material for each chapter including learning objectives, a key point listing and glossary, a selection of multiple-choice questions, and answers to all end of chapter questions and assignment questions.

### Target readership

Perhaps because of the increasingly volatile nature of financial/accounting regulation, the growing interconnectedness of both national and international markets, or indeed the increasing impact of information and communication technologies on accounting-related activities, it is only in the past 20 to 25 years that courses on corporate accounting information systems have begun to find their place not only on under-graduate degrees and professional accountancy courses but also increasingly on post-graduate MBA and MSc courses.

This book is aimed primarily at undergraduate students studying accounting/finance degrees, and intermediate-level professional students studying for ACCA, CIMA and ICAEW qualifications. It is, however, hoped that the critical underlying theme of the discussion in this book will also appeal to post-graduate MBA/MSc students studying accounting, finance and/or information systems.

# Topics covered

## Part 1   A contextual framework

### Chapter 1   Information systems in accounting and finance: a contemporary overview

Corporate accounting information systems represent an important link between the physical and often turbulent realities of economic activity, and the created representations – the financial reporting statements. This chapter provides an introduction to the nature and social context of corporate accounting information systems as a product of a complex, chaotic and ever-changing environment. It explores the role of corporate accounting information systems in supporting internal decision makers and how they contribute to the fulfilment of corporate obligations relating to issues of agency and stewardship.

### Chapter 2   Systems thinking: understanding the connections

This chapter introduces the notion of systems thinking and explores a range of systems ideas. It also provides a critical review of their implication on, and contribution to, understanding the contemporary role(s) of corporate accounting information systems. In particular this chapter considers the problematic issues inherent in the use of soft and hard systems methodology in the understanding of corporate accounting information systems.

### Chapter 3   Control theories: management by design

Companies are often complex entities often encompassing a range of not only interconnecting but very often conflicting aims and objectives. This chapter reviews the notion of the company as an interactive collection of interrelated sub-systems, and explores how in a contemporary context at least, the management and operations of such complex social entities is founded upon the notion of trust . . . in systems. It also explores the role of regulation, surveillance and control, and offers some insights into the need for and nature of systemic feedback and feedforward in socially constructed systems – in particular corporate accounting information systems.

## Part 2 Accounting information systems: a contemporary perspective

### Chapter 4  AIS and ICT: welcome to the information age

This chapter considers the changing context of corporate accounting information systems, and the increasing dependency of such systems on information and communication technologies. Commencing with a brief historical review of the development of corporate accounting information systems this chapter provides a critical review of the increasing importance of information and communication technologies, and considers the political context of such technologies in corporate accounting information systems.

### Chapter 5  Network architectures and topologies: making connections

Increasingly, corporate transaction processing cycles are becoming more reliant upon information and communication technologies to ensure the efficient and effective processing of such transactions. This chapter examine issues related to the development and control of alternative information system architectures and topologies. It also considers how information and communication technologies, and the adoption of alternative system architectures, have affected the computer-based transaction processing.

### Chapter 6  Contemporary transaction processing: categories, types, cycles and systems

Companies generate wealth through the temporal and spatial displacement of both tangible and intangible resources. However, because of the increasing complexity of such transactions, the growing fictitious nature of such transactions and, of course, the increasing separation between corporate management and corporate ownership, the need to ensure that adequate internal control procedures, authorisation protocols, recording procedures and management processes exist has become very important. Commencing with a review of the generic company types, this chapter provides an overview of four functional sub-systems normally encapsulated within corporate transaction processing cycles, namely;

- the revenue cycle,
- the expenditure cycle,
- the conversion cycle, and
- the management cycle.

### Chapter 7  Data management, data processing and databases: storage and conversion

Companies are complex entities whose survival depends on the active management of data/information flows. This chapter explores issues of data management, including data/information structures, data modelling and data flow management. It also explores the two main types of processing in contemporary use – batch processing and online processing.

Techniques such as dataflow diagrams, systems/document flowcharts and coding systems/charts of account are also considered in detail.

**Part 3 Transaction processing cycles**

### Chapter 8   Corporate transaction processing: the revenue cycle

Companies generate wealth through the temporal and spatial displacement of tangible and intangible resources. This chapter examines issues associated with the processing of revenue transactions (both debtor-based and non-debtor-based), and considers a wide range of issues relating to the management and internal control of revenue cycle transactions, and the consequences associated with the failure of internal controls.

### Chapter 9   Corporate transaction processing: the expenditure cycle

This chapter examines issues associated with the processing of expenditure transactions (both creditor-based and non-creditor-based), and considers a wide range of practical issues relating to the management and control of expenditure cycle transactions. This chapter also considers a range of issues associated with human resource management/payroll.

### Chapter 10   Corporate transaction processing: the conversion cycle

This chapter concentrates on production companies, and considers a wide range of issues related to product development, production planning/scheduling, manufacturing operations, production management, and cost management and control. It also explores issues related to the processing and management of conversion cycle data and the potential consequences associated with the failure of internal controls.

### Chapter 11   Corporate transaction processing: the management cycle

This chapter explores the issues associated with:

- financial management – the acquisition and management of long-term funds,
- fund management – the acquisition and management of short-term funds,
- assets management – the management and control of both fixed assets and current assets,
- liabilities management – the management and control of both long-term liabilities and current liabilities, and
- general ledger management – the management of financial information.

### Chapter 12   From e-commerce to m-commerce and beyond: ICT and the virtual world

The use of information and communications technologies, and the introduction and expansion of e-based commerce is in a corporate business context perhaps the single most important development of the late 20th century. This chapter examines the issue of e-commerce, in particular the problems and opportunities presented by its integration into corporate accounting information systems. It also explores issues related to e-advertisement, prospect generation, direct sales, business-to-business sales, customer support and education, and considers the particular problems/issues related to the use of e-money and the potential problems associated with internet-based finance/commerce.

## Part 4 Risk, security, surveillance and control

### Chapter 13 Risk and risk exposure: fraud management and computer crime

In a corporate accounting information systems context, risk cannot be eliminated, it can only be minimised by the use of appropriate control features and the establishment of an appropriate control environment. This chapter explores alternative sources and types of risk, problems associated with minimising the degree of risk exposure and the problems/conditions affecting exposure to risk. In particular it will examine issues of fraud, computer crime and computer viruses.

### Chapter 14 Internal control and system security: minimising loss and preventing disaster

This chapter considers issues associated with the notion of internal control – in particular general controls designed for application on a company-wide basis, and application controls designed for application on specific company systems, and explores alternative internal control procedures a company may adopt to minimise risk and ensure the physical security of resources, data/information and system networks.

### Chapter 15 Accounting information systems audit: towards a world of CAATs

Ensuring corporate accounting information systems function adequately is an essential pre-requisite for corporate survival. This chapter explores the underpinning rationale of audit, and considers the major issues and problems associated with auditing computer-based corporate accounting information systems. It also considers a number of alternative contemporary approaches to auditing computer-based corporate accounting information systems including auditing through, with and/or around the computer. The use of embedded audit facilities and the phasing of the audit process is also considered.

### Chapter 16 Accounting information systems development: managing change

The development of corporate accounting information systems often represents a huge but nonetheless necessary investment in both economic and social capital. Indeed, in today's ever-changing environment – an environment in which companies are increasingly engaged in a never-ending search for new markets, new customers and new products – in a never-ending pursuit for greater profitability and shareholder wealth, such developments are essential. This chapter examines:

- the importance of a corporate accounting information systems strategy,
- the problems related to *ad hoc* development, and
- the processes and problems associated with corporate accounting information systems development.

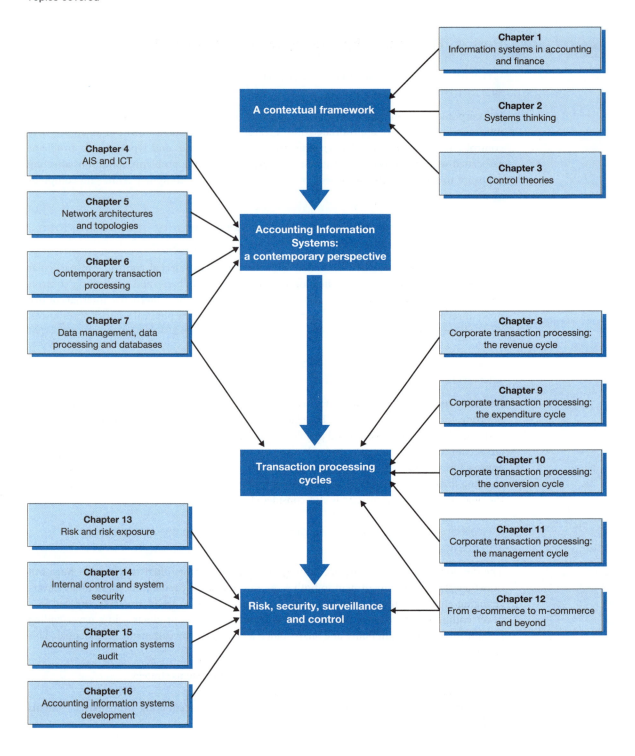

# Acknowledgements

My thanks to the following people for their assistance in the preparation of this book:

- Ron Hornsby for his inspiration, ideas and enthusiasm,
- Christopher James Boczko for his assistance and expertise on numerous technical aspects of this book,
- Matthew Smith at Pearson Education for his endless patience, professionalism and belief, and
- the various anonymous reviewers for their constructive and helpful comments.

We are grateful to the following for permission to reproduce copyright material:

Guardian News and Media Limited for the following articles 'Things fall apart' by James Meek published in *The Guardian* 1st March 2001, 'Quest to discover how hi-tech is changing Britain' by Stuart Miller published in *The Guardian* 16th March 2001, 'We'll sue illegal music downloaders, says BPI' by Dan Milano published in *The Guardian* 15th January 2004, 'Backlash as Google shores up great firewall of China' by Jonathon Watts published in *The Guardian* 25th January 2006. 'Big four bristle at claims that too much power rests in their hands' by Simon Bowers published in *The Guardian* 8th August 2006 and 'Inquiry launched after biggest ever credit card heist' by Rebecca Smithers and Bobbie Johnson published in *The Guardian* 31st March 2007 © Guardian News and Media Ltd; Stephen Timms MP for an article 'Every step of the way' published in *The Guardian* 29th May 2003; BusinessWeek.com for an extract 'Global capitalism – can it be made to work better?' by Pete Engardio and Catherine Belton, published on www.businessweek.com 6th November 2000; David Fickling for an article 'Court orders copyright filter on Kazaa' published in *The Guardian* 6th September 2005; Solo Syndication Limited for an article 'Boots to ban payment by cheque' published in *The Daily Mail* 11th September 2006; The Economist Intelligence Unit for an extract 'RFID Technology spreads beyond retail' published on www.electronicstalk.com 10th March 2006; The Economist Newspaper Limited for an article 'Do it yourself' published in *The Economist* 16th September 2004 © The Economist Newspaper Limited, London 2004; Telegraph Media Group Limited for an article 'Fraudsters hit Visa for a second time' by Danielle Rossingh published in *The Telegraph* 10th June 2003 © Telegraph Media Group; Computing.co.uk for an extract 'Banks double up on security' by Daniel Thomas published on www.computing.co.uk 23rd March 2006 © VNU Incisive Media; FosteReprints for an extract 'MyDoom worm spreads as attack countdown begins' published on www.cnn.com 29th January 2004; News International Syndication for an extract 'Sharp eyes of Laura Ashley captured massive fraud gang' by Lewis Smith, published in *The Times* 24th November 2004; and FT Syndication for an article

'Corporate character is not just a legal construct' by John Kay published in *The Financial Times* 13th December 2004; Booz Allen Hamilton Inc. for Figure 10.2; McGraw Hill Education for Table 13.4 by McClure/Scambray/Kutz, *Hacking Exposed*, 5th edition © 2005.

In some instances we have been unable to trace the owners of copyright material and we would appreciate any information that would enable us to do so.

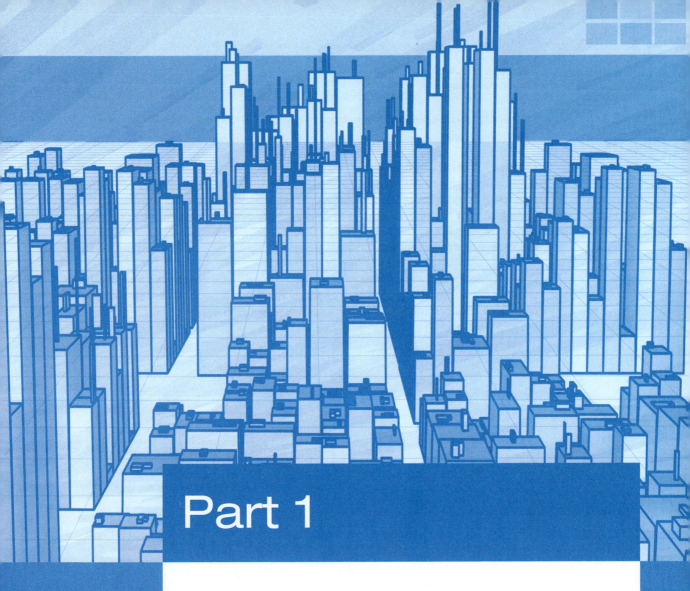

# Part 1

## A contextual framework

## Part overview

Part 1 of this book presents an introductory overview of corporate accounting information systems.

Chapter 1 provides an overview of the social, political and economic context of corporate accounting information systems, and considers their role in supporting organisational decision-making processes and the fulfilment of stewardship obligations and responsibilities. Chapter 2 explores the key features of contemporary systems thinking and considers why such thinking has become fundamental not only to the contemporary priorities of capital but, more importantly, business organisations and corporate accounting information systems.

Finally, Chapter 3 explores the issue of control – as a political construct dominated by the priorities of capital, and considers the application of control theory in the development and management of corporate accounting information systems.

# Information systems in accounting and finance: a contemporary overview

## Introduction

Corporate accounting information systems are significant inasmuch as they are socially created mechanisms through which symbolic forms of knowledge[1] that play an increasingly central role in portraying, evaluating and govern expanding domains of social and economic life are constructed. Symbolic forms of knowledge that have become a fundamental part of the struggle for corporate survival, as companies undertake economic transactions in a business world increasingly dominated by and concerned with a spatial context of 'oneness'. A business world in which the controlling mechanism of the marketplace has become pre-occupied with the notion of singularity – a single market, a single world society, a single global culture. With a single borderless society in which the once established cartography of political sovereignty continues to be reconfigured by a market dominated movement where the reduction of institutional and economic diversity is seen as paramount, and continuing socio-political heterogeneity is seen as increasingly unacceptable.

In a business world increasingly dominated by and indeed reliant upon information, corporate accounting information systems have become central to enabling social, political and economic activities to be rendered knowable, measurable, accountable and manageable. More importantly, such systems have become pivotal in the adjudication of rival business claims between competing social constituencies both inside and outside the company. Corporate accounting information systems are implicated not only in conditioning the global flows of capital investment and business resources, but also in assisting in determining/measuring the effectiveness of business institutions and organisations, institutions and organisations through which differing levels of social, political and economic power are expressed.

Clearly, the pervasive influence of corporate accounting information systems provokes many questions. Questions about how such accounting information systems develop; why particular accounting information systems and practices are adopted; and how such accounting information systems are regulated within business organisations. More importantly perhaps such influence provokes questions about how such corporate accounting information systems are utilised, and about the adequacy of the understandings distilled from the information such accounting information systems generate.

This chapter provides a critical review not only of the over-riding economic nature of corporate accounting information systems, but also considers their social and political context. Issues relating to the role of corporate accounting information systems in the supporting of organisational operations and decision-making processes, and the fulfilment of stewardship obligations and responsibilities, are also explored.

## Learning outcomes

This chapter covers a wide range of preliminary issues and provides an introduction to corporate accounting information systems in the context of an increasingly dynamic and hectic (some would say chaotic) business world. By the end of this chapter, the reader should be able to:

- describe the major influences that change the nature and context of corporate accounting information systems,
- describe the major characteristics of contemporary corporate accounting information systems,
- critically comment on the social, economic and political roles of corporate accounting information systems,
- illustrate an awareness of the role of accountants and accounting and finance related specialists in contemporary corporate accounting information systems, and
- demonstrate an understanding of the structure of corporate accounting information systems.

## Globalisation and a changing world – the need for information

Whatever chronology is imposed on understanding the nature and context of social and economic change, the very idea of globalisation is not only socially emotive but economically and politically divisive. In a 21st century world increasingly preoccupied with:

- the maintenance of local culture(s) and social identities,
- the securing of traditional political boundaries and democratic constituencies,
- the continued development of market arrangements and economic interrelationships, and
- the assessment of the social consequences of capital mobility,

globalisation remains a rich source of critical analysis, political rhetoric and economic debate. But a debate between whom? Between those who decry globalisation as a destructive process facilitating:

- the destruction of local traditions,
- the continued subordination of poorer nations and regions by richer ones, and
- the gradual elimination of culture and everyday life,

and those who support globalisation as a positive process facilitating:

- sustainable economic progress,
- social and cultural mobility,
- technological innovation,
- sustainable product and service development,
- information exchange, and
- increasing cultural freedom,

and those who suggest globalisation is an exploitative process concerned primarily with the economic commodification and political oppression.

Let's have a look at each of these views in a little more detail.

For conservatives traditionalists indoctrinated with notions of nationalism and territorial protectionism, globalisation represents at best a case of romantic idealism shrouded in liberal dogma, and at worst a baffling, bizarre and misunderstood phenomena. Whilst they recognise the inevitable rise of supra-territoriality, they nevertheless seek to defend notions of territorial sovereignty and the nation state, and the significance of globalisation as both a historical and contemporary process. Put simply, they consider globalisation to be both a utopian and an artificial condition of the post-Cold War world – a product of the delusional rhetoric of late 20th century contemporary society.

Liberalists however see globalisation as a progressive, benign and an inherently beneficial process – a release from the shackles of traditionalism and a realisation of the promise of modernity. In accommodating sentiments such as 'the end of geography', and 'the end of sovereignty' (O'Brien, 1992), and indeed the 'end of history', (Fukuyama, 1992) such liberalists treat notions of market economics, social democracy and political solidarity as timeless virtues of universal appeal and applicability. They see globalisation as an extension of an existing longer-term trend toward deeper international interdependency – as part of an ongoing corrective of the imperfections of a free world. More importantly, they contend that unrestricted market forces, western electoral democracy, scientific rationality, national self-determination and international cooperation can and ultimately will benefit all humanity.

In contrast, critics of globalisation recognise the rising tide of interconnectedness, but see the 'rise of supra-nationality' in terms of economic commodification[2] and social exploitation – an imposition of worldwide interrelationships and interdependencies by the increasing powers of market capitalism and modernist structures and organisations. Such critics see the rise of supra-nationality as a product of the uneven development of market capitalism and/or a product of socio-cultural oppression that is partially politically, but increasingly economically determined by the evermore controversial priorities of capital accumulation.

Clearly then, globalisation is by no means an unquestioned phenomenon. Indeed, as the ultimate expression of terrestrial universality, globalisation has been and indeed continues to be a highly contested notion: a notion of increasing interconnectedness, whose social, economic and political consequences continues to be seen as extremely unpredictable and increasingly unstable.

But an interconnectedness in what? In culture and behaviour, in social structures, in political institutions, in economic agencies?

For some, globalisation is synonymous with the incorporation of the people of the world into a single world society – a strengthening of a social appreciation of the global whole and a consciousness that the world is one place – synonymous with an increasing intensification of worldwide social relations. An acceleration of global interdependence through a continuing diffusion of western institutional arrangements across the world synonymous with a progressive fragmentation of traditional modes of social interrelationships, a continuing abandonment of established notions of territoriality and nationality, and an increasing commodification of culture, identity and consciousness.

For others, globalisation is predominantly social in nature: a 'cultural' westernisation of the world concerned primarily with the relocation of modes of socio-cultural awareness; an extension of western rationalism concerned primarily with the creation of a 'eurocentric' postcolonial culture of universality and standardisation. A global branding of modernist identities dominated by, and conditioned through, an increasingly global media, a progressively more volatile supply of westernised identities and a consumer demand for such identities circulating the globe at ever-increasing speeds. A global branding of modernist identities increasingly referred to as 'McDonaldisation' (Ritzer, 1993) or 'CocaColonisation' (Nederveen Pieterse, 1995).

And, for yet others, globalisation is predominantly political in nature. A process characterised by a changing context and structure of the nation state and the emergence of reformulated 'plurilateral' structures of regulation and authority (Cerny, 1995), in which the authority of the local is increasingly subsumed within the authority of the global. Globalisation is seen as a process wholly invested in the changing cartography of state sovereignty (Morgenthau, 1985) and the increasing marginalisation of national governments and their exercise of territorial power – a repositioning of international power in and between nation states in which the strong have become stronger and the weak have become weaker.

Whilst the social context of each of the above so-called 'engines of globalisation' (Riggs, 1998) provides a useful if somewhat limited insight into globalisation – it is by its very nature a product of human agency. A product primarily connected to and predominantly influenced by an evermore placeless and disembedded spread of market relations and business transactions. It is essentially economic in nature, (see Figure 1.1) and principally influenced by:

- a continuing deregulation of national and international markets,
- an increasing international transferability of both commercial and investment capital, and
- an increasing dependency on the mercantilisation of knowledge/information.

Globalisation is a process of commodification in which modern notions of geography, territoriality and nationality have become increasingly dominated by a singular systemic priority – capital accumulation and wealth maximisation. A priority founded on sustaining and extending interdependent and interconnected forms of market/business relations as politically neutral

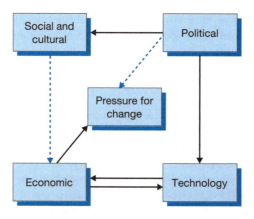

**Figure 1.1** Contemporary notions of globalisation

and socially detached from the economic consequences such global priorities seek to both encourage and promote.

Clearly, the increasing dominance of the global marketplace and associated flows of capital that today not only create (and recreate), but also sustain, contemporary forms of global interdependencies and interconnectedness represents one of the most wide-ranging (and for some) one of the most unsettling systemic trends in contemporary history (Scholte, 1995). Why? Because such trends encapsulate more than a process of reconstruction, reconstitution or global restructuring! They represent a transition, one dominated not by the chaotic flows of social identities and/or political ideologies, but by the erratic flows of commodity capital, investment capital and human capital.

Indeed, whether globalisation is regarded as constructive – that is facilitating positive social, economic and political change – or destructive – that is facilitating the elimination of local culture and local tradition – it clearly encapsulates a process of continuing radical change, of transition – of transformation. A transformation of modern society and the business environment in which the historical and contemporary settings of everyday social, economic and political activity have been shifted to what some have called a hyper-realism of a postmodern new world order (Luke, 1995). A new world order in which wealth maximisation and the search for competitive advantage have become central to the global logic of corporate capital and its desire to forge institutional interdependencies consistent with its continued survival and expansion. A new world order increasingly dependent upon the availability of evermore complex symbolic forms of knowledge, ephemeral technologies and knowledge based systems and on evermore transferable forms of information . . . on accounting!

## Competitive advantage and wealth maximisation

As suggested earlier, the continued dominance of capital mobility and freedom of accumulation (Surin, 1998) – of contemporary market capitalism and its interrelated notions of borderless private ownership, the free pursuit of profit and the existence of free (or at least a managed) market mechanism (McChesney, 1999) – remains a central feature of today's global business environment. A global business environment in which the primary aim of traditional market-based economic activity is the achievement and maintenance of competitive advantage and wealth maximisation. An environment in which success is measured and assessed, principally on the level of economic returns such activities generate for corporate stakeholders – in particular corporate shareholders (Rapaport, 1986). Clearly, the transformative consequences of global capital and the dominance of market economics in the late 20th and early 21st century have produced many social, political and economic benefits.[3] However, such benefits have been, and indeed continue to be, achieved at some cost. As suggested by Boczko (2000):

> *the often turbulent and erratic search for profit and gain – for new products and markets, new technologies, new spaces and locations, new processes of organisation and control – have increasingly produced the very market crises that such global competition and global change had sought to escape (2000: 139).*

The achievement and maintenance of competitive advantage, the development and maintenance of key success factors, the extending of product and service life cycles and the continued maximisation of product and service profitability, have all become evermore difficult to attain in a highly competitive global marketplace in which corporate success has become increasingly ephemeral. A global marketplace in which the traditional business philosophies that once formed the foundation of long-term financial survival have become subservient to highly competitive/ speculative strategies founded on notions of:

- emergent innovation,
- flexible accumulation, and
- freewheeling opportunism.

Speculative strategies that have become heavily dependent on information, on information and communication technologies and on intangible knowledge-based systems (specifically accounting information) to ensure the effective management of corporate resources, the accurate measurement of corporate performance and to provide a necessary determination of continued corporate survival.

Whilst the need for information is by no means a new phenomenon, in a global business environment increasingly shaped by the complex business transactions that have become evermore uncertain, compressed and increasingly lacking in transparency, corporate business activities have, out of necessity, become bound up with a growing dependency on networks of surveillance, on regulation and control and on the development of sophisticated systems for collecting, storing and processing information.

The need to know and the ability to control have not only become a central feature in the search for competitive advantage, profit and the maximisation of corporate wealth, but more importantly a central feature of a society increasingly dominated by the economics of gain and the need to know first. A society in which the politics of global competition and the economics of the marketplace have not only contributed to changing the structure, nature and context of contemporary society itself, but more importantly contributed to changing contemporary notions/perceptions of the company – the corporate entity. A company is no longer just a legal entity, a collection of rights or a collection of tangible and intangible assets and/or physical and virtual resources. Instead it is a complex social mosaic of people, systems and procedures. A complex interaction founded on the philosophy of agency, on the separation of ownership and control which requires trust,[4] not in people or in an abstract politicised legislative framework or market-based rules and regulations (although these are clearly important) but in procedures, information, technologies and systems.

## Business management and the need for information

The intimate relationship between:

- the corporate search for comparative advantage and the elimination of competitive threats and environmental disturbances,
- the development of market opportunities and the optimisation of the long-term rate of return,
- the management of social, political and economic change, and
- the maximisation of shareholder wealth,

and their dependency on information – specifically accounting/financial management information – is beyond doubt. This dependency is of course not a creation of 20th century capitalism and/or emerging late 20th century/early 21st century technologies but merely a redefining of needs and priorities that have existed since the dawn of commercial market activity. Indeed, as suggested by Lynch (2003): 'whether it . . . (a company) . . . needs to make a profit or not, every organisation needs information to survive' (Lynch, 2003: 402). Information that is not only used to:

- justify expansion and contraction,
- rationalise closure,
- defend closure and relocation, and
- justify increases in product/service prices,

but which can also be used to:

- control activity,
- compare performance,
- ensure accountability,
- facilitate surveillance and, perhaps most important of all,
- enforce regulations.

Such information (such symbolic forms of knowledge) can of course take many forms. From marketing information on customer relations and product pricing strategies, to human resources management information on organisational employment levels/policies and staff profiling/recruitment strategies, to operations management information on production timetable/schedules, to financial accounting/management information on corporate profitability, investment/financing strategies and dividend policies.

This book is however primarily concerned with accounting/financial management information, and with the systems, processes and procedures involved in its production and dissemination. Information such as:

- external financial reporting statements – for example the profit and loss account, balance sheet, and cash flow statement,
- internal management accounting statements – for example performance budgets, costing reports and activity reports, and
- financial management information – for example short-term working capital management, long-term investment strategies and dividend/debt policies.

Whilst the provision of such accounting/financial management information can and indeed does provide many benefits such as:

- the reduction of transaction uncertainty and business risk,
- the promotion of business confidence,
- the reduction of risk of financial loss, and
- the facilitation of organisational planning and control,

the central role of such information is one of governance – whether internal governance in terms of operational management processes and strategy development, or external governance in terms of corporate financial statements and corporate accountability. However, it is also important to recognise that information does not just facilitate business procedures and processes or business governance and accountability. Neither does it just assist in facilitating controllability. Its purpose is not merely the minimising of complexity and the promotion of maintainability – of survival. Information is a business resource. It is, as suggested by Vassen (2002), the fourth production factor.

Information has value. Whilst the measurement of this 'value' is an issue of continued heated debate – for example, for some, such value is normative (identifiable and measurable) so that it is based on realisable benefits, while for others such value is relative (indeterminate and ambiguous) and depends heavily on utility and context of use – information is nevertheless a valuable business resource. A marketable commodity that is not only political in context but, more importantly, social in construction, and as far as accounting/financial management information is concerned, economic in consequence.

But what do we mean by the term information?

## Information – toward a political context

There are many definitions of 'what' information is, some of which are complementary, others of which are contradictory. For example Stafford Beer (1979) suggested that information is that which changes us. Davis and Olsen (1984) extended this notion of change by suggesting that information is:

> *data that has been processed into a form that is meaningful to the recipient and is of real perceived value in current or prospective actions or decisions* (1984: 200).

This theme was also continued by Murdick and Munson (1986) who suggested that information can be defined as a coherent pattern of characters that can stimulate both action and reaction.

Blokdijk and Blokdijk (1987) however suggested that information is not merely concerned with action – process – reaction. They suggested a more value orientated definition, suggesting that information was what connects with man's consciousness being and contributes to his knowledge and ultimately his well being.

A common theme in all the above is the notion that information is data that have been processed in such a way as to be useful to the recipient. Such a theme suggests three separate but clearly interrelated contexts.

Firstly, 'data that have been processed' suggests a processing context – that is it implies that the value of information is associated with a notion of change, of transformation.

Secondly, 'in such a way as to be useful' suggests a structural context – that is the value of information resides not only in its component parts and their relationship but also in the underlying structure, the logical arrangement, the nature/context of the language/sets of symbols used.

Thirdly, 'to the recipient' suggests a communication context – that is it implies that the value of information is also associated with the notion of assembly, recording, transmission and communication using a shared symbol set designed to promote understanding. In other words, information is not information until it has been communicated and understood (see Figure 1.2).

Vaguely implied in all the above definitions is however the idea that information can in some way 'reflect' reality. That is, information possesses objective characteristics independent of the user and can therefore be processed like any other business resource. Such a 'reflectivist' perspective assumes that reality can be mirrored, more or less 'truly' or 'fairly', and that accounting/financial management information can not only provide a faithful picture of that economic reality, but as the nature of business transactions and economic activity evolves, refinements to accounting/financial management information and accounting systems and practices can be introduced to ensure their continuing faithfulness.

Clearly, this is not the case since information as, a 'body of knowledge' or as a 'set of rules and procedures' is created/designed for a purpose – to satisfy an 'assigned' role, for example to:

- promote order and control,
- reduce entropy and uncertainty,
- minimise waste, and/or
- maximise shareholder return.

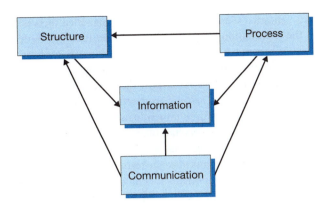

**Figure 1.2** The interrelated context of information

This assigned 'political' role is imposed by human agency. Interrelated notions of process, structure and communication are clearly dependent upon human agency and can therefore be neither politically nor socially neutral. They are embedded within social arrangements – within cultural and organisational contexts. The generation, management and application of information have social, political and economic consequences. Consequences often designed to sustain existing socio-political relationships and arrangements. In other words, information (or more appropriately the use of information) is not only intentional, it is perhaps more importantly politically constructive.

Such a 'constructivist' perspective contends that information communicated by a shared set of understandable signs and/or symbols can neither 'reflect' reality, nor neutrally express the intentions of those involved. Meanings communicated through the use of language(s) and/or a shared set of symbols are constructed within negotiated representational systems – representational systems that often conceal the social relations that not only comprise them, but more importantly construct them. What is capable of being known depends fundamentally on the social traditions/political contexts through which the world is rendered knowable.

Whilst the importance of information, especially accounting/financial management information, in the promotion of business efficiency and management effectiveness, and wealth maximisation cannot be understated, it is however important to recognise that the generation and communication of information is, contrary to the illusions of liberal economics anything but a neutral and unbiased technical activity (see Gray *et al.*, 1996). Such a political context, such a constructivist view of information clearly has implications on any assumed neutrality that the qualitative characteristics of information may appear to possess. Notions of relevance, reliability, understandability, validity, usefulness and timeliness are all 'imposed' characteristics, or more appropriately 'constructed' characteristics.

## Accounting information systems – nature, context and purpose

Above we considered the issue of information. Before considering the broad nature, context and purpose of corporate accounting information systems, it would be useful to consider first a broad introductory definition of the notion/idea of 'system'. (The notion of system and systems thinking will be considered in more detail in Chapter 2.)

So, what is a system? Harry (1994) suggested there was no universally accepted definition of the term/notion of system. True or false? Probably both!

Where as a biologist/medical scientist may use the term 'system' to define for example bodily parts or structures anatomically or physiologically related, a chemist may use the term to describe matter in which there exists more than one substance in a number of different phases. A geologist may use the term 'system' to describe a formation of rock strata created during a period of geological time, whilst a minerologist may for example use the term to define categories and/or divisions into which crystals may be placed on the basis of uniquely identifiable characteristics. Whereas an astronomer may use the term 'system' to describe a group of associated extraterrestrial bodies, an engineer may use the term to define any independent assembly of electronic, electrical or mechanical components forming a self-contained unit.

A sociologist may use the term 'system' to describe any scheme of economic classification, social arrangement and/or political stratification, whilst a psychologist may use the term to describe an individual's physiological or psychological makeup. And, finally, perhaps an economist may use the term 'system' to describe a group or combination of interrelated, interdependent or interacting elements forming a collective entity, whereas a political scientist may use the term to define opinions of thought, points of view or established doctrine(s) used to interpret a branch of knowledge.

Clearly, the notion or context of what a system is in each of the above definitions varies, depending on the nature of the knowledge/characteristics/components being considered. Yet they all nevertheless contain a number of similar themes – if sometimes by implication only.

Firstly, they all contain a common root meaning – that is there is a notion of methodical or coordinated assemblage. A collection or grouping of similar items, objects elements, and/or components.

Secondly, they all suggest that in general, stronger correlations (relationships) exist between one part of the system and another, than between one part of the system and parts outside the system. That is a system can broadly be regarded as a set of related objects/components whose relationship to each other is stronger than their relationship to their environment, a relationship resulting in the constitution (some would say 'perceived constitution') of an identifiable whole – separate from the environment (see Schoderbeck *et al.*, 1985).

Thirdly, as a complex of directly and/or indirectly related significant objects or elements, they all suggest that such components of a system operate together to attain a prescribed goal, aim or objective. Whatever professional perspective is adopted – whether a biologist/medical scientist, an engineer, a sociologist, an economist – they all imply, to a greater or lesser extent, that as a bounded set of objects/components, a system is capable of responding to external stimuli to undertake whatever function or change is required to achieve/maintain the system's objective.

For example the discovery of a new virus strain may cause biologists to review their understanding of medical physiology. The emergence/development of a new global economic cycle may cause economists to review understanding of how social and political interrelationships impact on economic institutions or the discovery of a new star cluster may cause astronomers to review their understanding of the universe as a developing system.

It should however be noted that such responses to new data/new conditions/new relationships are neither automatic nor apolitical. Such responses/interpretations are imposed by human agency – they are not only socially created, they are politically constructed.

So, what is a system? These core attributes of collection and commonality, relationship, and purpose, aim and response to change were perhaps best summarised by Beishon and Peters (1972), who suggested that a system was merely:

*an assembly of parts, where the parts or components are connected together in an organised way, . . . the parts or components are affected by being in the system and are changed by leaving it, . . . the assembly does something, . . . (and) . . . the assembly has been identified by a person as being of special interest (1972: 12).*

Gelinas *et al.* (2005) suggested that an accounting information system is merely:

*a specialised sub-system of the MIS . . . (Management Information System) . . . whose purpose is to collect, process and report information related to financial transaction (2005: 15).*

Such a definition is related to what are often described as the organisational/relational contexts of corporate accounting information systems.

Wilkinson *et al.* (2001) however suggested that an accounting information system is:

*a unified structure within a business entity such as a business firm that employs physical resources . . . to transform economic data into accounting information (2001: 7).*

Such a definition is related to what are often described as the procedural and/or functional contexts of corporate accounting information systems. (These alternative contexts will be explored later in this chapter.)

Whilst each of the above definitions do differ in some minor aspects, a common identifiable theme in each of the above definitions is the notion that an accounting information system is a cohesive organisational structure: a set of directly and indirectly interrelated processes and procedures, objects and elements, events and activities.

So, a collection of resources and other components designed for a purpose. But what purpose? Romney and Steinbart (2006) suggested that the purpose of an accounting information system is to process transaction data to provide users with information, a system that:

*collects, records, stores and processes data to produce information for decision makers (2000: 6),*

whereas Vaassen (2002) suggested that the purpose of an accounting information systems is to:

*provid(e) information for decision making and accountability to internal and external stake-holders, . . . provid(e) the right conditions for decision making, . . . (and) . . . ensur(e) that no assets illegitimately exit the organisation (2002: 3).*

Again a common theme in each of the above quotes is the notion that accounting information systems possess two common interrelated purposes:

■ to provide users with information, or a decision facilitating function – that is a function concerned with assisting decision making/decision makers by providing 'useful' information, and
■ to support decision making and facilitate control, or a decision influencing/mediating function – that is a function concerned with controlling and inducing alternative forms of behaviour in transacting parties where conflict exists and/or mediation is required.

## To provide users with information

There are of course many categories of accounting/financial management information, all with their own unique definition of role, purpose and nature. Whilst each category is by no means exclusive in terms of content and purpose, such information (such accounting/financial management information) can generally be categorised into three accepted categories.

Firstly, financial accounting information – that is information generally concerned with external performance reporting. Such information is often retrospective, historical in nature, very structured and often externally controlled. It is transaction orientated and concerned with the recording, classification and presentation of financial transactions in accordance with established concepts and principles, accounting standards and extant national/international legal requirements.

Secondly, management accounting information – that is information generally concerned with assisting in the formulation of corporate strategies and policies, with the planning and control of business activities, with decision making and with corporate governance – is often predictive, unstructured and internally controlled.

And, thirdly, financial management information – that is information generally concerned with processes associated with the acquisition of finance, and the efficient management and development of both long-term and short-term resources – is concerned primarily with financing and investment decisions made in pursuit of maximising the wealth of corporate shareholders and minimising risk associated with longer-term decision making.

## To support decision making and facilitate control

Here it is possible to identify four integrated purposes/objectives of an accounting information system:

- to sustain and reinforce organisational operations – that is transaction processing management,
- to support decision making by internal decision makers and ensure the objective transformation of economic/financial data into accounting information – that is information management,
- to discharge obligations relating to stewardship and control the acquisition, management and disposal of organisational resources – that is internal systemic control, and
- to fulfil legal, social and political responsibilities and encourage alignment with extant regulatory requirements – that is external systemic control.

Again, each of the above four purposes/objectives are closely interrelated.

Firstly, 'support organisational operations' suggests that corporate accounting information systems should facilitate the collection, recording and processing of business transactions. This is clearly related to the 'support decision making by internal decision makers and ensure the objective transformation of economic/financial data into accounting information', which implies that a corporate accounting information system should facilitate the generation of information not only for decision making purposes but also for purposes of accountability – to both internal and external stakeholders.

Second, 'fulfil obligations relating to stewardship and control the acquisition, management and disposal of organisational resources' suggests a corporate accounting information system should provide information/assurances to ensure assets do not enter or exit the company/ organisation without appropriate authority. Again this is clearly related to 'fulfil legal, social and political responsibilities and encourage alignment with extant regulatory requirements', which implies that a corporate accounting information system should not only seek to ensure and maintain the integrity of information generated, but also seek to maintain/ensure where possible the objectivity and validity of that information.

More importantly, from a functional business context, whilst information management activities are closely related to transaction processing management activities (as suggested earlier), such activities nevertheless have a clear defining impact on internal and/or external systemic control activities (see Figure 1.3).

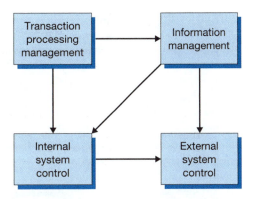

**Figure 1.3** The integrated nature of corporate accounting information systems

## Contemporary contexts of corporate accounting information systems

As suggested earlier, the basis of contemporary market-based capitalism concerns the notion of resource movement/exchange – that is the temporal and spatial displacement of resources[5] is the foundation of conventional economic activity, corporate profitability and wealth maximisation. (This issue will be explored further in Chapter 2.) More importantly, from a liberal economic perspective at least, such resource movement/exchange is also the foundation of continued corporate survival. Indeed, in today's highly competitive (some would say chaotic) global market-place companies must not only be flexible and adaptive, but also responsive to social, political and economic change. One consequence of this need/desire for continued flexibility/adaptability in an evermore hectic business environment, is that corporate accounting information systems as an essential part of a company's arsenal of competitive technologies have become increasingly complex – a complexity directly related to notions of security, control and risk reduction. A complexity directly influenced by:

■ ever-increasing volumes of accounting/financial management data and business data processing,
■ ever-increasing demands of internal and external users to reduce data processing times,
■ an evermore critical emphasis placed on correct processing,
■ an increasing importance on detail management,
■ ever-increasing computerisation of accounting/financial management transactions, and
■ an ever-increasing requirement/demand of market participants to minimise management/ regulatory intervention in competitive business activities.

However, despite such ever-increasing pressures, as suggested earlier, corporate accounting information systems are by their very nature created resource structures – that is they emerge from a need/desire to protect, control and manage resource activities and wealth creation processes. The purpose of such systems is to provide two clear functions:

■ a decision facilitating function, and
■ a decision influencing/mediating function.

Such a duality of function can and indeed often is interpreted in a number of alternative contexts (see Figure 1.4). Such contexts include:

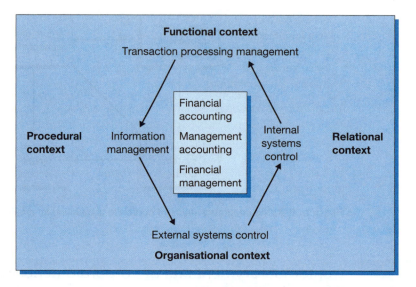

**Figure 1.4** Alternative context of corporate accounting information systems

- a procedural/processing context,
- an organisational and relational context, and
- a functional context.

## Procedural/processing context

From a procedural/processing context, corporate accounting information systems are essentially 'data transformation management systems'. That is such a contextualisation of corporate accounting information systems suggests that the purpose of such a system is to facilitate five key procedures (see Figure 1.5):

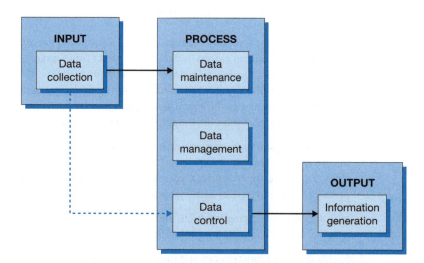

**Figure 1.5** Procedural context of corporate accounting information systems

- data collection,
- data maintenance,
- data management,
- data control, and
- information generation.

The procedural context is of course closely related to notions of input (data collection), process (data maintenance/data management) and output (data control and information generation), and is concerned primarily with ensuring the proper execution of a certain procedure and/ or series of procedures to guarantee appropriate processing – to ensure correct data storage, data maintenance and data/information retrieval and removal/disposal. Key issues within this procedural/processing context are often related to:

- limiting data redundancy (reliability)
- ensuring data consistency and standardisation (efficiency)
- promoting where possible data integration (spatial constraints)
- ensuring data accessibility (user control) and providing data flexibility (modification), and
- ensuring data security (integrity) by providing appropriate data capture and entry facilities (accuracy).

This generally involves ensuring:

- the provision of appropriate data capture and data input procedures, for example hard copy (physical) input or pre-formatted data-entry (virtual) input,
- the adoption of appropriate processing methodology, for example periodic (batch) processing, immediate processing, online processing, real-time processing and/or distributed processing,
- the development of appropriate maintenance procedures, for example data correctness, data accuracy, data relevancy, master file security and media access restriction, and
- the development and implementation of appropriate output procedures.

Clearly such a procedural contextualisation of corporate accounting information systems is closely related to decisions concerning the use of information and communications technology (software and hardware) and the development of physical and virtual (non-physical) information networks.

(This procedural/processing context will be explored further in Chapter 7.)

## Organisational and relational context

From an organisational context corporate accounting information systems are essentially hier-archical information systems (see Figure 1.6). That is they are designed to:

- assist in defining business strategies/policies,
- embed information into tactical decision-making processes, and
- provide useful information for operational control purposes.

From a relational context, corporate accounting information systems are essentially a component part of an integrated corporate information system (see Figure 1.7). That is they exist as an essential part/component of a company's overall management information system.

Such organisational and relational contexts are of course related to a range of internal/external factors such as:

- size of the company and the complexity of corporate structures/lines of accountability,
- organisation of the company and the intricacy of data/information flows,

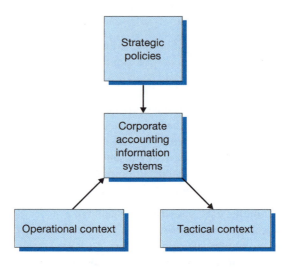

**Figure 1.6** Organisational context of corporate accounting information systems

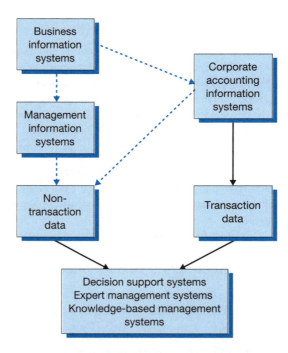

**Figure 1.7** Relational context of corporate accounting information systems

■ company maturity and the current stage of corporate evolution/development,
■ internal psychological factors and the underlying nature/philosophy of management behaviour/ activity (plus the related the attitudes of information users),
■ external environmental factors (including social/political/geographical factors) and the levels of risk and competition the company faces, and
■ company resources and the availability of financial resources for investment in systems development.

Key issues within this organisation and relational context are often related to:

- ensuring information standardisation,
- promoting where possible information consistency,
- ensuring appropriate levels of accessibility,
- ensuring appropriate levels of integration, and
- providing sufficient levels of information flexibility.

This generally involves ensuring:

- the provision of appropriate communication structures/procedures,
- the adoption of appropriate procedures of accountability, and
- the development of appropriate information models.

Clearly such an organisational and relational contextualisation of corporate accounting information systems is closely related not only to the development and maintenance of appropriate management decision support systems and strategic information systems, but, more importantly, to the development and maintenance of flexible knowledge-based information systems.

(This organisation and relational context will be explored further in Chapters 4 and 5.)

## Functional context

From a functional context, corporate accounting information systems are essentially transaction processing systems. That is they are designed to mirror a company's cycles of operation and/or business activity – the temporal and spatial displacement of resources founded on the following:

- tangible/intangible products and services absorb resource expenses,
- resources are bought and sold,
- resources are converted,
- equity is increased and/or diminished, and
- debts are incurred and/or liquidated.

Such activities can be analysed within the context of four functional sub-systems (see Figure 1.8):

- an expenditure cycle – generally consisting of an acquisition control system, a receiving and inspection system, and a purchasing and creditor system,
- a conversion cycle – generally consisting of a stock control system, a production control system, and a payroll system,
- a revenue cycle – generally consisting of a marketing system, a transportation system, and sales and debtors system, and
- a management – generally consisting of a cash receipts and payments system, a fixed assets and property system, and a general ledger system.

In general two categories of functional contexts can be identified.

## Category 1: Companies with a dominant flow of commodities
- Type 1(a)    Retail and distribution companies
            (i)   consumer-based retail
            (ii)  non-consumer-based retail
- Type 1(b)    Manufacturing and production companies
            (i)   continuous production
            (ii)  non-continuous production

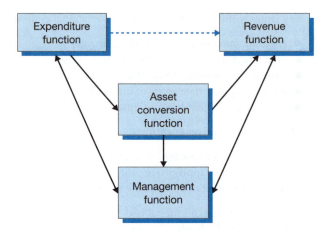

**Figure 1.8** Functional context of corporate accounting information systems

## Category 2: Companies with no dominant flow of commodities

- Type 2(a)    Companies with a limited flow of commodities
    (i)   limited owned commodities
    (ii)  limited non-owned commodities
- Type 2(b)    Time/space-based companies
    (i)   Specific time/space
    (ii)  Non-specific time/space
- Type 2(c)    Knowledge/skills-based companies
    (i)   Time-based specific knowledge/skills
    (ii)  Supply-based non-specific knowledge/skills

Each of the above will of course place different emphasis on different aspects of their transaction processing systems.

Key issues within this functional context are often related to the need to control, authorise and record the impact of resource movements. That is, issues related to internal control and the separation of administrative procedures and the separation of functional duties.

It generally involves ensuring;

- the provision of relevant control procedures,
- the adoption of appropriate custody procedures, and
- the development of accurate recording procedures.

Clearly such a functional context of corporate accounting information systems is closely related to:

- the development and maintenance of appropriate internal control procedures, and
- the development and maintenance of flexible audit and risk reduction/fraud management strategies.

(This functional context informs a range of corporate accounting information systems ideas and will be explored further in Part 3.)

# Corporate accounting information systems – social and political context

## Organisational context

As suggested earlier, corporate accounting information systems are created resource structures, political structures that possess a range of general characteristics:

- they are goal orientated – that is they are purposeful,
- they are generally comprised of a range of interacting components (sub-systems),
- they exist/function within a hierarchical context,
- as a system they have a defined boundary, and
- as a system they possess synergistic qualities.

Corporate accounting information systems have many users and involve many different groups of stakeholders. More importantly such systems are subject to a range of social, political and economic influences and controls – both internal and external to the company.

### Internal influences of corporate accounting information systems
Such influences include issues relating to:

- the size of the company,
- the knowledge base and intellectual capacity of the company (and its employees),
- the structure/organisation of the company and the complexity of information demands and requirements,
- internal management factors/features and, of course,
- the availability of company resources.

### External influences of corporate accounting information systems
Such influences would include issues relating to:

- political influences such as company law requirements and other legal/political requirements imposed by quasi-governmental organisations,
- social influences such as professional reporting standards requirements such as UK GAAP and other professional pronouncements,
- economic influences such as market regulatory requirements (London Stock Exchange requirements) and other industry standards/regulations and, of course,
- technological influences such as hardware/software technology constraints.

## Organisational users

Because of the vast range of influences affecting the functional nature/capacity of corporate accounting information systems, the continued survival and growth of a company increasingly depends on the supply of effective accounting information to a wide range of diverse stakeholder groups, both internal and external to the company (see Figure 1.9).

Clearly the nature, size, location and complexity of the company will have a direct impact not only on the range of corporate accounting information systems users, but also on the types of information various stakeholder groups may require. For example, a large, diversified, UK-based multinational company would have a greater range of accounting information systems users and information demand requirements than say a small, regional, single-purpose private limited company. So who uses corporate accounting information systems?

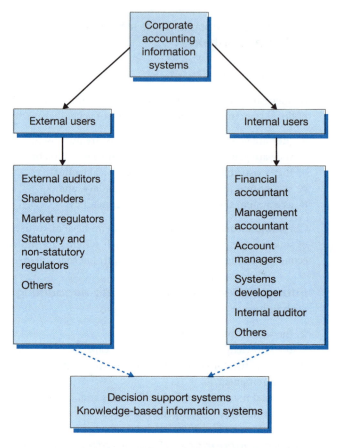

**Figure 1.9** Organisational users of corporate accounting information systems

### Internal users of corporate accounting information systems

The primary internal users of any corporate accounting information systems would be:

- financial accountant,
- account managers,
- management accountants,
- systems developers,
- internal auditors, and
- other departmental managers.

Many of these users would be generally concerned with outputs from the corporate accounting information system. For example outputs such as:

- profit and loss accounts,
- financial statements of affairs and balance sheets,
- cash flow statements,
- performance budgets/reports,
- costing and activity reports, and
- financial summaries.

Others would of course also be interested in:

- accounting information systems inputs, for example the collection/recording of relevant business transactions,
- accounting information systems processes, for example the processing and maintenance of proper accounting records, and
- accounting information systems controls, for example the application of appropriate regulatory requirements and standards.

Such users would for example include the financial accountant, internal auditor and perhaps the systems developer.

### External users of corporate accounting information systems

The primary external users of any corporate accounting information systems would be:

- shareholders,
- external auditors,
- potential lenders,
- markets regulators,
- government regulators,
- taxation authorities,
- suppliers and creditors, and
- other interest groups such as trades unions, employee groups and other social/political agencies.

As with internal users, many of these external users would be generally concerned with outputs from the corporate accounting information system. For example outputs such as:

- published profit and loss accounts,
- the balance sheet, and
- cash flow statements.

Again, as with internal users, some external users would of course also be interested in inputs, process and relevant controls. Such users would for example include the external auditor, government regulators, market regulators and, of course, taxation authorities, and their interest would generally derive from some legal and/or institutional requirement.

## Corporate accounting information systems – problems and fallacies

Like many created resource structures – often very bureaucratic ones – there are many problems and fallacies surrounding the effective use of corporate accounting information systems. Some of these problems and fallacies emerge from the narrow perspective and role assigned to such systems. Others emerge from misunderstandings over the nature, purpose and use of information.

### Problems with corporate accounting information systems

Two main problems exist. Firstly, corporate accounting information systems only represent a sub-set of a company's information system – a sub-set concerned primarily with data collection, data maintenance/management and data control. Consequently, corporate accounting information systems are only able to produce information in a limited context – mainly quantitative information. More importantly, such information is invariably historical in nature.

Secondly, such systems, because of the underlying political nature of information and information systems only generate information consistent with a particular perspective or 'world view' – a functional, liberal, economic/market-based view. The reason for this is purely historical.

Traditionally, corporate accounting information systems were, and to some extent still are, grounded in what has often been called a 'value driven approach' – that is an approach in which the management of financial outcomes such as profitability, levels of shareholder dividend, gearing and other financing issues often take priority over other issues. Such an approach – such an 'output driven approach' – whilst clearly supporting conventional liberal economic wisdom, that is the maximisation of shareholder wealth, unfortunately leads to:

- a rigid conceptual understanding/definition/model of the company,
- an over-emphasis of the 'procedural/process' context of corporate accounting information systems,
- an implicit faithfulness in outputs that is consistent with the 'reflectivist' contextualisation of information, and
- a 'single stakeholder' perspective of corporate accounting information systems that rejects any alternative perspective other than those consistent with wealth maximisation.

An alternative approach is an approach that has often been called an 'events based approach,' one which advocates that a company should focus on managing relevant business events or sequence of events as opposed to managing values in financial statements. Such an approach not only supports a business 'multi-stakeholder' view rather than the 'single-stakeholder' view, but also acknowledges the shortcomings of conventional notions of accounting and accounting information systems.

## . . . and some fallacies

There are many fallacies surrounding not only corporate accounting information systems in particular but also information systems in general.

Firstly, more is better – that is the greater the quantity of data processed, the greater the quantity of information produced, the more efficient and effective the company and/or organisation will become. False! Whilst clearly some relationship exists between information and corporate efficiency, there is no direct correlation between the quantity of processing and levels of corporate efficiency – such efficiency is normally related to the 'quality' of information produced.

Secondly, more communication means better performance. False! Improved performance is again related to the quality of information not the amount of times communication takes place. Although increased communication can provide some performance-related benefits, there is a level beyond which further communication can have a dysfunctional impact – that is, it can reduce efficiency and as a consequence decrease levels of performance.

In both the above it should however be noted that the term 'quality' is not only subjective but more importantly political in context.

Thirdly, providing users/managers with the information they 'need' will automatically improve decision-making procedures and processes. And, fourthly, users/manager know what they need, and need what they want. Both false!

Catering for individual needs and requirements whilst useful in a limited context may not only be excessively costly, but more importantly short sighted. Whilst many users/managers would like to believe they have a clear view of what they need, such users/managers generally function within a limited context – within their individual 'world view' – and as a consequence may not be fully aware of the bigger corporate picture.

# Corporate accounting information systems – a contextual framework

A key theme throughout the book is an acknowledgement that accounting[6] is a creative process – a social construct, designed to portray (in a particular way) the outcome of the temporal and spatial displacement of resources. It is an active 'political' technology of capital accumulation – wealth creation – directed towards preserving already dominant social structures and hierarchies, and is as such purposive rather than inherently purposeful.

More importantly, corporate accounting information systems as created resource structures – albeit increasingly virtual/intangible resource structures – are the 'practical embodiment' of this 'socially constructed' art form. Such systems are designed to maintain a particular set of processes consistent with the implied 'socio-political' purpose of accounting.

So, given the 'socio-political' nature of accounting/accounting information and the constructed political nature of corporate accounting information systems, is it possible to have a theory of corporate accounting information systems? Not really!

As with accounting/accounting information, the search for an underlying theory of corporate accounting information systems is the 'search for the holy grail'. An underlying theory of accounting/accounting information does not and will never exist.

Whilst some academics and some accountants may refer to the Statement of Principles issued by the Accounting Standards Board (1999) as a broad conceptual framework – a possible theoretical framework – such a view is mistaken and founded on misconceived notions of accounting/accounting information's neutrality and objectivity. Similarly an underlying theory of corporate accounting information systems does not and will never exist.

However, that is not to say a broad theoretical framework – or more appropriately a broad thematic context – cannot exist. It is this thematic context that forms the basis of discussion in Part 2 of this book – a thematic context founded on three interrelated notions/ideas/theories:

- systems thinking,
- control theory, and
- information theories.

See Figure 1.10.

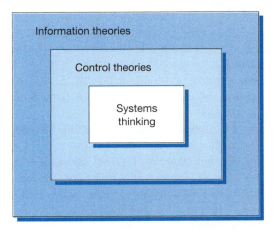

**Figure 1.10** Corporate accounting information systems – a thematic context

## Concluding comments

As we have seen, corporate accounting information systems are socially, politically and economically important. Not only do they affect all levels of management decision making and various internal and external groups of stakeholders, they are more importantly an enabling 'political' resource that plays a leading role in:

- obtaining and sustaining competitive advantage, and
- maximising the wealth of shareholders.

More importantly, they are without doubt an increasing critical success factor in the search for corporate survival.

## Key points and concepts

| | |
|---|---|
| Agency theory | Information management |
| Competitive advantage | Information theory |
| Corporate accounting information system | Internal systemic control system |
| | Management accounting |
| External systemic control | Systems thinking |
| Financial accounting | Transaction cost theory |
| Financial management | Transaction processing management |
| Globalisation | Transaction processing system |
| Information | Wealth maximisation |

## References

Accounting Standards Board (1999) Statement of Principles @ http://www.frc.org.uk/asb/technical/principles.cfm.

Beer, S. (1979) *The Heart of Enterprise*, Wiley, London.

Beishon, J. and Peters, G. (1972) *Systems Behaviour*, Harper Row, London.

Blokdijk, A. and Blokdijk, P. (1987) *Planning and Design of Information Systems*, Academic Press, London.

Boczko, T. (2000) 'A Critique on the Classification of Contemporary Accounting: Towards a political economy of Classification – the Search for Ownership', *Critical Perspectives on Accounting*, 11, pp. 131–153.

Cerny, P.G. (1995) 'Globalisation and the Changing Logic of Collective Action', *International Organisation*, 49(4), pp. 595–625.

Davis, G.B. and Olson, M.H. (1984) *Management Information Systems: Conceptual Foundations, Structure and Development*, McGraw-Hill, London.

Fukuyama, F. (1992) *The End of History and the Last Man*, Free Press, New York.

Gelinas, U.J., Sutton, S.G. and Hutton, J.E. (2005) *Accounting Information Systems*, South-Western College Publishing, Cincinnati.

Giddens, A. (1990) *The Consequences of Modernity*, Polity Press, Stanford, CA.

Gray, R., Owen, D. and Adams, C. (1996) *Accounting and Accountability*, Prentice Hall, London.

Harry, M. (1994) *Information Systems in Business*, Pitman, London.

Harvey, D. (1990) *The Condition of Post Modernity*, Basil Blackwell, London.

Luke, T. (1995) 'New World Order or Neo-World Order: Power, Politics and Ideology in Informalizing Glocalities', in Featherstone, M., Lash, S. and Robertson, R., (eds) *Global Modernities*, Sage, London, pp. 91–107.

Lynch, R. (2003) *Corporate Strategy*, Prentice Hall, London.

McChesney, R. (1999) 'The New Global Media: It's a Small World of Big Conglomerates', *The Nation*, 269(18), pp. 11–15.

Marx, K. (1976) *Capital: A Critique of Political Economy*, vol. 1., translated by Fowkes, B., Penguin, London. (Original 1867)

Morgenthau, Hans, J. (1985) *Politics Among Nations: the Struggle for Power and Peace*, Knopf, New York.

Mosco, V. (1996) *The Political Economy of Communication*, Sage, London.

Murdick, R.G. and Munson, J.C. (1986) *Management Information Systems: Concepts and Design*, Prentice Hall, London.

Nederveen Pieterse, J. (1995) 'Globalisation as Hybridization,' in Featherstone, M., Lash, S. and Robertson, R. (eds) *Global Modernities*, Sage, London, pp. 45–68.

O'Brien, R. (1992) *Global Financial Integration: The End of Geography*, Pinter, London.

Rapaport, A. (1986) *Creating Shareholder Value. The New Standard for Business Performance*, Free Press, London.

Riggs, F.W. (1998) Globalisation. Key Concepts @ http://www2.hawaii.edu/~fredr/glocon.htm.

Ritzer, G. (1993) *The McDonaldization of Society*, Pine Forge Press, Thousand Oaks, California.

Romney, M. and Steinbart, P. (2006) *Accounting Information Systems*, Prentice Hall, New Jersey.

Schoderbeck, P.P., Schoderbeck, C.G. and Kefalas, A.G. (1985) *Management Systems: Conceptual considerations*, Business Publications Inc. Plano, Texas.

Scholte, J.A. (1996) 'Beyond the buzzword: toward a critical theory of globalisation', in Kofman, E. and Youngs, G. (eds) *Globalisation: Theory and Practice*, Pinter, London.

Surin, K. (1998), 'Dependency's theory reanimation in an era of financial capital,' *Cultural Logic*, volume 1, Number 2.

Vaassen, E. (2002) *Accounting Information Systems – A Managerial Approach* Wiley, Chichester.

Wilkinson, J.W., Cerullo, M.L., Raval, V. and Wong-On-Wing, B. (2001) *Accounting Information Systems*, Wiley, New York.

## Bibliography

Bodnar, G.H. and Hopwood, W.S. (2001) *Accounting Information Systems*, Prentice Hall, London.

Hall, J.A. (2004) *Accounting Information Systems*, South Western, Cincinnati, Ohio.

Lucy, T. (2000) *Management Information Systems*, Letts, London.

Mosgrove, S.A., Simkin, M.G. and Bagranoff, N.A. (2001) *Core Concepts of Accounting Information Systems*, Wiley, New York.

## Websites

No specific websites are recommended for this chapter. However, you may find the following websites helpful in gaining an insight into some of the more business-related issues associated with corporate accounting information systems.

www.accaglobal.com
(Chartered Association of Certified Accountants)
www.cimaglobal.com
(Chartered Institute of Management Accountants)
www.cbi.org.uk
(Confederation of British Industry)
www.icaew.co.uk
(Institute of Chartered Accountants in England and Wales)
www.ft.com
(Financial Times)
www.economist.com
(Economist)
www.guardian.co.uk
(Guardian)
www.accountingweb.co.uk
(General accounting website)

## Self-review questions

1. Explain what is meant by 'engines of globalisation'.
2. Define the term 'comparative advantage' and explain its relationship to wealth maximisation.
3. Define information.
4. 'Information is the most valuable resource a company can possess.' Discuss.
5. 'The purpose of a corporate accounting information system is to provide information, and support decision making.' Discuss.
6. What role does accounting information play in the regulation of corporate activity?
7. Explain what is meant by the functional context of corporate accounting information systems and why the understanding of such context is important for corporate accounting information systems managers.
8. What are the main influences (internal and external) on corporate accounting information systems?
9. Who are the main internal users of corporate accounting information systems?
10. Who are the main external users of corporate accounting information systems?

## Questions and problems

### Question 1

The long-term financial objective of a company is often seen as being 'the maximisation of shareholder wealth'. Briefly describe how a company's accounting information system can assist in achieving this objective.

### Question 2

'Contemporary accounting information systems are ultimately political in nature.' Discuss.

## Question 3

'The increasing uncertainty and risk of organisational activity has resulted in an increasing dependency on trust systems.' Explain to what extent contemporary accounting information systems can be regarded as a trust system and illustrate how such a system is related to the changing nature of capital.

## Question 4

'All users of corporate accounting information systems are interested in one issue only – how profitable is the company/will the company be.' Discuss.

## Question 5

'Contemporary accounting information systems can be regarded the fundamental/core resource/asset of any corporate organisation.' Discuss.

# Assignments

## Question 1

Deltum Ltd is an established retail company located in the north east of England. The company has been operating successfully for over 50 years. In 2000, following a rather aggressive takeover bid Deltum Ltd finally acquired the company's only regional retail competitor, Hetmex Ltd.

Although the combined company did experience some early operating successes, the overall profitability and efficiency of the combined company has recently fallen sharply, market share and product quality are now at record lows with the combined company recording its first annual trading loss in 2003.

Despite attempts by the management of Deltum Ltd to combine the two companies' accounting information systems, a recent external consultants' report was highly critical suggesting that the core problems being experienced by the company have resulted from Deltum Ltd's management's inability to understand the nature, context and purpose of a company's accounting information system.

### Required

Provide a report for the management of Deltum Ltd explaining the nature, purpose and uses of a company's accounting information system, and offer reasons why Deltum Ltd has faced such significant problems.

## Question 2

Jeamer plc was an UK listed company that produced digital audio equipment for the retail market. The company's products were sold throughout Europe, North America, Australia and Canada, and were widely regarded as the best in the market. Indeed during the period 1995 and 2001 the company's digital audio equipment consistently won high praise from both consumer groups and retail critics.

In January 2003, however, Jeamer plc suddenly went into liquidation. The company failed with debts amounting to £125m. The failure of the company was headline news around the world with press speculation focusing on the possibility of large-scale financial reporting irregularities and potential management fraud. However in April 2003, following extensive enquiries, the company receivers published their findings. Their report indicated that whilst some unacceptable accounting irregularities had been evident in the company's published financial reports for a number of years, the principal cause of Jeamer plc's failure had been an inadequate accounting information system.

The company receivers' report concluded that:

*whilst accounting information was produced on a regular basis, this information was often out of date and of little use to managers.*

### Required

Describe the main function of an accounting information system for a company such as Jeamer plc and explain the possible risks associated with the failure of such a system.

## Chapter endnotes

[1] Such symbolic forms of knowledge include financial reporting statements such as profit and loss account, balance sheet and cash flow statement, and internal management accounting statements such as budgets, performance reports, costing reports, activity reports and investment appraisal reports.

[2] The term 'commodification' is used here in a Marxian context to describe the 'way capital(ism) carries out its objective of accumulating capital or realising value through the transformation of use values into exchange value' (Mosco, 1996: 140). In a conventional context this presumes an increasing use of competitive markets, an important issue in the accumulation process since the most common embodiment of capitalism is as 'an immense collection of commodities' (Marx, 1976: 126).

[3] Such benefits not only include macro benefits such as sustained national/international economic growth, national/international market stability, social and political security, but in a micro context, low investment risk, stable corporate growth and increasing market/product opportunities/development.

[4] Trust is a confidence in the reliability of a person or a system regarding a set of outcomes or events. The requirement for trust is not a lack of power but lack of knowledge. Trust in systems provide a means of understanding the causes of change, controlling the effects of change and regulating the impact of change.

[5] The term 'temporal and spatial displacement' is used here in the context of the increasing international movement of capital as a product of time-space compression (Harvey, 1990) or time-space distanciation (Giddens, 1990).

[6] The term accounting is used here to describe a 'regulated institutional process, a constructed model . . . for reporting and communicating the impact of temporal and spatial displacements on economic activity and associated regimes of accumulation' (see Boczko, 2000).

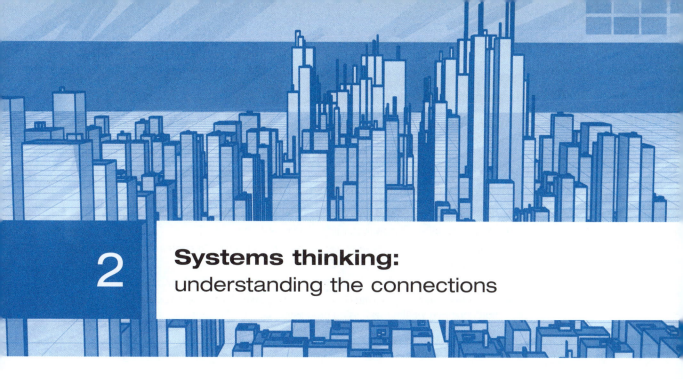

# 2

# Systems thinking:
## understanding the connections

## Introduction

The business environment is a complex and often chaotic collection of interrelated social institutions. A collection of social institutions that not only have an unpredictable and somewhat uncertain future but, more importantly, a complex and rather chaotic historical evolution – an evolution that has been overwhelmingly influenced by the changing patterns and nature of modern society, especially the emergence of contemporary capitalism as a dominant social force in the late 19th and early 20th centuries.

Characterised by a group of closely interrelated institutions/systems, modern society has (as suggested in Chapter 1) become (or at least is perceived to have become) increasingly global and as a consequence evermore risky, volatile, uncertain and unpredictable. Yet whilst it is important to realise that the business environment is an intrinsic product of modern society, and has as such become fashioned by the changing patterns of society, it is also important to recognise that society has itself become a product of the ever-changing whims and desires of the marketplace in the late 20th and early 21st centuries inasmuch as the constitutive dimension of nearly all social change has become market-based economic power, that is market-based capitalism.

This chapter provides a discussion of the changing nature and proactive involvement of regimes of capital accumulation/wealth maximisation and market-based economic power within a contextual review of systems thinking, and explores a range of systems ideas commonly assumed to be underpinning notions of contemporary accounting information systems. It provides a critical review of their implication on and contribution to understanding not only the function, nature and context of market-based corporate organisations, but also the contemporary role of corporate accounting information systems in the management of such organisations. In addition, problematic issues inherent in the use of soft and hard systems methodologies in conceptualising corporate accounting information systems are also explored.

The aim of this chapter is not only to ascertain the key features of systems thinking[1] but, more importantly, to explore why such thinking has become fundamental not only to contemporary capitalism but to business organisations.

## Learning outcomes

This chapter explores a wide range of issues related to contemporary systems thinking and provides an introduction to how systems thinking has been, and indeed continues to be, an increasingly important framework in understanding the evermore dynamic and chaotic business world.

By the end of this chapter, the reader should be able to:

- define a system and describe the main features of systems thinking,
- distinguish between soft systems and hard systems,
- critically comment on the importance of systems thinking to contemporary capitalism and wealth maximising organisations,
- illustrate an awareness and understanding of systems terminology, and
- describe and critically evaluate from a systems perspective the key socio-political factors that constrain wealth maximising organisations.

## Modernity – institutional dimension of modern society

Before we explore the main theoretical and somewhat abstract features of systems thinking, it would be useful to offer some context to our discussion – to explore the bigger picture so to speak, and provide some understanding of why such thinking has become central not only to a modern society entrenched within a market-based philosophy of competition and wealth accumulation, but more importantly corporate organisations in their search for profit and wealth maximisation.

Perhaps a useful staring point would be modern society or to use a more appropriate term often used by political economists, sociologists and other social scientists – 'modernity'.

So, what do we mean by modernity and why is it important?

### What is modernity?

This is one of those really big questions that has many possible answers. In its broadest sense, modernity refers to the modes of social organisation which emerged in western Europe from about the 17th century and which have subsequently developed throughout the world – the key forces in this global spread being the hegemonic social, economic and political power western Europe in the late 17th and early 18th centuries. At the core of modernity was, and still is (assuming we believe we live in a modern, and not as some sociologists would suggest, in a postmodern society), the prospect of limitless advancement in science and technology, of limitless improvement in moral and political thought, and of limitless rationalisation and economic gain.

Whereas a politician may view modernity or modern society from a purely institutional context, in terms of the changing cartographies of electoral power and increasing global democratisation, a liberal economist may view modern society as merely a combination of interrelated, interdependent, interacting marketable resources, a society governed by the supply of and demand for economic resources, and a sociologist may view modern society in terms of its social stratification, the distribution of cultural characteristics within society and/or the uneven distribution of political/economic power.

So what does the modern in modernity and modern society really mean? Berman (1982) suggested that to be modern and hence part of modern society (and modernity) was:

*to find ourselves in an environment that promotes adventure, power, joy, growth, transformation of ourselves and the world – and at the same time that threatens to destroy everything we have, everything we know, everything we are* (1982: 15).

What this illustrates is the contradictory nature of modernity – that modern society is not only fragmented, ephemeral and chaotic, but also enduring, complex and ever-changing – full of choice but also full of control – full of variety.

Given this complex multiplicity, we could clearly define modern society using a range of different criteria, for example in terms of cultural demographics, economic wealth, ecological sustainability, political arrangements/institutions, and/or territorial/geographical associations. For our purposes, however, we will simply define modern society (see Giddens, 1990), or modernity, as a collection of four fundamentally interrelated institutions/processes (to use systems terminology – but more of that later), these being:

- market capitalism – that is the market-based process of wealth accumulation in the context of competitive labour and product markets,
- state management – that is the governmental/legislative framework through which the control of social and organisational institutions is exercised,
- industrialism – that is the constructed institutional processes purposefully designed to develop and maintain a created environment, and
- surveillance – that is the process of information control and the concept of social supervision.

Whilst such sociological terminology may appear a little too abstract for what is essentially a discussion on systems thinking – perhaps a more business approximation of each of the above would be a form of PEST analysis, that is:

- the **p**olitical environment – the nation state,
- the **e**conomic environment – market-based capitalism,
- the **s**ocial environment – processes of surveillance, and
- the **t**echnological environment – industrialism.

Clearly, such a simplistic definition of modernity has many limitations.

Society is undeniably much more complex, undeniably much more obscure. In reality it cannot be sub-divided into simple semi-autonomous institutions/processes. Not only are such interrelated institutions/processes ephemeral and transitory, but their relationship is neither stable nor permanent. Modern society is always changing – for better or worse. It is both transient and chaotic. We live in a world in which social and institutional connections are continually being reorganised, in which relationships are constantly being reclassified, and, in which institutional expressions of power and control are frequently being redefined.

We live in society in which the only certainties in life are change and uncertainty (see Article 2.1).

## Change – for better or worse

It is this issue of change, not only in the structure and organisation of social and economic activity, in particular within market-based systems, but also in the interrelationships between institutions/processes, that is of importance. However, before we look at why this is the case, perhaps it would be useful to explore briefly why such changes occur and more importantly the possible consequences/effects of such changes.

## Article 2.1

# Things fall apart

Foot and mouth, savage blizzards and now a catastrophic train crash. Suddenly it seems our modern and apparently robust nation is as fragile as a house of cards. The trouble, says James Meek, is that we don't notice how complex our world is until things go wrong.

In their book *The Collapse Of Chaos*, Jack Cohen and Ian Stewart tried to explain that the apparent simplicities of our commonsense view of the world hid a teeming ocean of complexity. 'If our brains were simple enough for us to understand them,' they wrote, 'we'd be so simple that we couldn't.' Britain in the 21st century is a bit like that. If the web of electricity cables, microwaves, rails, roads, airways, computers, fibre-optic links, retailers, distributors, sewage systems, phone lines, warning systems, farmers and manufacturers was simple enough for us to understand it, it would be too simple to exist.

We only notice the complexity of the technology we have come to rely on when it stops working. We only marvel at smooth roads and cars travelling along them at 90 miles an hour when they are blocked by snow. We only realise the incredible level of mechanisation and international animal-shuffling of modern farming when a disease breaks out in livestock at opposite ends of the country and rural life shuts down.

We only remember that it is complicated to have hundreds of people and tonnes of goods, travelling in four different directions, on two levels, in two different kinds of transport, in all weathers, at combined speeds of hundreds of miles an hour, when they collide and people are killed.

Except that we don't marvel, we don't realise, and we don't remember. By entering a 'just-in-time' era of high-speed transport and communication, with high standards of health care and thousands of standard products available anywhere, anytime, we have only raised our thresh-hold of expectations. We think of technology and the fantastic degree of organisation and inter-linkage that makes Britain work, when we think of it at all, as making the country a more convenient place to live. Often it does. But convenient isn't the same as robust. When things go wrong, convenient Britain can turn out to be fragile Britain.

Cohen recalls the words of Arthur C Clarke: 'Any well-developed technology is indistinguishable from magic.'

'We've turned so much of our technology into magic that when it turns into something else it seems hard to comprehend,' he says. 'Like when getting into a room in Newcastle and walking out of the room a few hours later in London turns into a train, crashing into another train.'

'It's a lot to do with how complicated life is. We couldn't live the kind of complicated life we live if we had to deal with our own waste, build our own fires and generate our own electricity. It's only when things go wrong, when trains crash and sewage floods into the street that you remember the complexity is there.'

The piling-on of crises and disasters can give the impression that Britain stands on the brink of chaos. For once, the Queen spoke for many people yesterday [28 February 2001] when she said of the Selby train disaster: 'This is a particularly shocking tragedy coming on top of so much anxiety and loss from the foot-and-mouth outbreak and, before that, the recent floods.'

She could have added the autumn fuel crisis, the Hatfield disaster and its aftermath, and an unlucky bag of other mixed woes. It's tempting to invoke chaos theory; the notion that a small event, such as the flutter of a butterfly's wings, can produce huge consequences elsewhere, like a tropical storm.

But chaos theory is not involved. The common factor is the ugly sister of chaos – complexity. 'In the jargon of the mathematicians, this is complexity rather than chaos,' says Ian Stewart. 'A lot of people get them mixed up.'

Chaos theory, first developed by meteorologist Edward Lorenz in the 60s, involved unpredictable results emerging from minute changes in the data fed into a calculation. It was all about simple systems obeying simple rules – as the weather, for all its unpredictability, does.

Complexity produces unpredictable results from the interaction of a whole host of actions which, by themselves, seem simple. The fuel crisis, says Stewart, was a classic example – a protest outside a few oil refineries could shut down an entire country with astonishing swiftness. So are the paralysing effects of computer viruses, simple programs that can bring great institutions to their knees because of their complete reliance on technology.

'Complexity is the world we live in. People still think it isn't. People still think that when they go to a supermarket and buy a pound of meat it's exactly the same thing they used to do 30 years ago when they went to a shop up the road. In no respect is it the same. The meat has gone through the hands of 75 different people. It might be a French sheep, slaughtered in Belgium, butchered in Germany, part sent to Saudi Arabia and part sent here.

'I blame the training of today's managers. They've not been trained to think about robustness and stability. They've been trained to think about efficiency. Efficiency, to a modern manager, means that every conceivable component is just about to break down.

'The big problem here is reductionist managers operating with a complex system as if it was simple.'

In complex Britain, a problem can not only spread rapidly, as it has with foot and mouth disease, but problems can be compounded by other problems. In the Scottish Borders, where snowfalls have been so deep that they have been compared with the savage winter of 1947, many farmers postponed deliveries of feed and fuel and didn't clear the snow from their roads as normal because of fear of infection. Now, with electricity supplies cut off by the weather, many are in desperate need for fuel for emergency generators – but the snow is still blocking their roads.

The speed and efficiency of the rescue operation around the Selby crash was an example of complexity at its best. The reason why the car and its trailer came off the motorway are not yet known. But the conjunction of the country's fastest rail line and one of its major roads were ultimately summoned up by our demand for speed and efficiency, our impatience with delays and hitches.

'We're a very intolerant society nowadays,' says Andrew Porteous, professor of environmental science and technology at the Open University. 'We expect instant perfection. You see it everywhere. People have a fit when their computer crashes. They don't expect it to happen.'

In low-tech societies, such as Britain in the past, or parts of the developing world today, societies tend to take a more fatalistic attitude to disasters and crises. It doesn't protect them from destitution or suicidal despair. Nor does it stop them doing everything they can to put things right. If we have become impatient with technology which might as well be magic to us, people such as the cattle-herding Fulani of Nigeria and Cameroon make no distinction between magic and technology when they are seeking to cure their livestock.

The Fulani have a wealth of ancestral veterinary knowledge to fall back on – they practise a form of vaccination against foot and mouth disease in their cattle, for instance – but also go to wise men who, they believe, might cure their beasts by picking out good verses from the Koran.

Their low-tech world leaves them and their livestock vulnerable to a host of diseases such as rinderpest and HIV. They are at the mercy of the weather. At the same time, they are less reliant on technology they don't understand; they may have radios and bicycles, but they don't depend on them. The lack of a media blanket such as the one covering Britain means that a tragedy that affects one group has little impact on another 50 miles away. The lack of functioning African governments means that compensation and inquiries are not expected.

'Here there's the expectation of a safety net arrangement, of society owing something to them,' says Phil Burnham, professor of social anthropology at University College, London, who has worked with the Fulani. 'Out there, they may feel their kin owe them help in times of crisis, but there's no one else they can turn to, other than to pray.'

In spite of the small backlash from environmentalists and anti-globalism protesters, compared to the Fulani, we remain wedded to progress, demanding of efficiency, and condemning when something goes wrong. We're hooked on complexity.

'The classic difference between peoples like the Fulani and a modernist society like ours is that we believe things are going to get better, that we're going to continue to develop new technologies, knowledge and science,' says Prof Burnham.

'If something happens to suggest things aren't going to get better, somebody immediately starts blaming somebody, because there's a faith that science should be able to sort it. The idea that there are things we don't know about, or beyond our control – that's not a part of the modernist orientation. In so-called traditional societies, they think there are things you can't control. You can't just invest more money and get a breakthrough. Things aren't always going to get better tomorrow.'

Source: The *Guardian*, 1 March 2001,
**www.guardian.co.uk**.

In a societal context, the causes of social change, certainly in terms of modernity, can be divided into two distinct (but closely interrelated) groups, these being:

- the exercise of socio-political power through social/political domination, socio-economic imperialism, war or negotiation/agreement, and
- the social implications of technology – for example the 19th century industrial revolution or the 20th century IT revolution.

Clearly, whilst the latter has gained in importance, the former, although remaining significant, has nonetheless diminished in its consequence.

As suggested earlier, whilst the effects/consequences of such causes continue to remain both unpredictable and uncertain, some of the effects have been, (and indeed continue to be):

- a redefining of social/institutional relationships/organisations, for example the development of newer business structures such as from sole trader to partnership to company to group,
- a recharacterisation of territorial and social boundaries whether through political negotiation or the implication of international trade/business, to promote a greater international mobility, and
- a redefining of the nature of time and space as a consequence of technology, resulting in a move away from tangible products to intangible goods and services, and an increased imposition of political regulation and social surveillance.

This last point deserves further discussion.

In the medieval world, the concept of external space was appreciated only in a very broad context, often seen as an enigmatic teleological[2] force, beyond the comprehension of mere mortals. However, during the renaissance period, the emergence and institutionalisation of geographical knowledge of the world provided a powerful device for an increasingly profit-orientated society that radically reorganised general perceptions of time and space. Indeed, it was the renaissance revolution that provided the foundations not only for the conquest and rational ordering or commercialisation of geographical space, but also, in the course of exploring space, the discovery of the fundamental concept of the price of time.

In general then, change is often only achieved through:

- the development of new organisational/political forms of social relations (whether by negotiation or imposition), and/or
- the adoption and application of new technologies.

This is a notion/context of change or modernisation which is closely related to what some sociologists (e.g. Talcott Parsons (1937, 1951, 1966, 1971)) have referred to as 'structural differentiation' where change stimulated by technology and or changing social/political values results in processes that create increasingly more complex institutional arrangements. A process that has implications for:

- social space – that is the geographical area of business and trade, and
- social time – that is the speed, nature and context of business and trade.

It is therefore perhaps not surprising that the history of technological and organisational innovation has become synonymous with the search for increasingly more profitable regimes of wealth accumulation to such an extent that the singular, overarching motivating force in contemporary modern society has become market-based capitalism – that is the search for profit and the accumulation of capital (Harvey, 1990). See Articles 2.2 and 2.3.

## Article 2.2

### Every step of the way:

*Technology is changing the way the UK does business.*

Stephen Timms, junior minister at the Department of Trade and Industry, outlines how a sound IT strategy can improve customer relations and enhance productivity.

Today's ever-changing business environment presents UK companies with great opportunities and many new challenges. Growing global competition means that businesses increasingly need to broaden their market reach in order to maintain a competitive edge.

Businesses are already rising to the challenge and changing the way they work – most notably through the use of technology. Over a million households took up broadband access last year, making teleworking possible for many for the first time. And the introduction of terms such as 'e-procurement' into everyday business speak is a reflection of the fact that many companies are integrating technology into their business processes.

Technology really can transform the way we do business. It is no longer simply about adoption, having a website and using email – the rush to get online is over and businesses are now looking to make the most of new and emerging technologies. ICT (Information Communications Technology) belongs at the heart of business practices. And in the UK we are well placed to achieve this. A recent report from the Economist Intelligence Unit positioned UK businesses among the most 'e-ready' in the world.

Of course for any company the business case for adopting new technology must be compelling enough to justify new investment. Technology should not be implemented for implementation's sake. As with any investment, the decision to employ e-business technologies should meet the requirements of its overall business strategy.

For some businesses the case for investment may simply be the immediate opportunity to save money through fixed cost broadband internet access as opposed to the variable costs of a dial-up connection. On a wider scale, investment may lead to better relationships with customers and suppliers, plus better customer service.

E-commerce technologies are opening up new opportunities right across the supply chain. Companies can benefit from better and faster access to information, less paperwork and greater efficiency in all their business processes. For example stock control orders can be made automatically, systems can monitor levels of ordering and purchasing, allowing businesses to be much more flexible. Businesses can keep in touch with clients and suppliers and give customers more choice in how they communicate.

Earlier this month I called on Printoff, a Lancashire based printing firm employing 50 people, to officially switch on their broadband connection. They explained to me how broadband would transform their business, allowing them, for example, to transmit artwork to and from customers and between their own sites in seconds. In the past, it took hours to transmit via ISDN – or they just had to send it by car. Broadband has removed past constraints on developing the business.

Similarly, Skin Culture, a London-based company selling do-it-yourself skin treatments, invested in e-business technologies to improve communications with its customers. It set up an interactive website, designed to engage its customers, giving them the opportunity to browse through Skin Culture's catalogue of products, identify their skin problem and buy items through a secure online ordering system. The company now conducts over 75% of its business through the website and has branched out into international markets – the technology allowed it to tap into the growing internet-savvy shopper group.

In short, e-business can enhance the productivity, competitiveness and cost-efficiency of any business, whatever its size. But the question for many smaller businesses is how they take that first step. Integration of new technologies into existing business processes can seem a daunting task, but it does not need to be expensive or complicated. It could be as straightforward as ensuring one database of customer details is stored centrally on the business' system, rather than having two separate records for billing and delivery. When a customer's details change, only one entry then needs to be changed, saving time and money.

There are a number of support programmes available to businesses needing advice. There is a network already in place of several hundred UK Online for Business advisors, situated in Business Links and their equivalents across the country, who will work with companies on anything from building an effective website to getting the right purchasing software. UK Online for Business is also developing tools to help businesses take up and maximise the use of technology. The E-business Toolkit outlines e-business models and the Benchmarking Tool allows companies to measure their progress against similar companies. The planning tool, Be Online for Business, also offers practical and tailored advice on how to create and apply a realistic e-business strategy.

Many small and medium sized companies in the UK are already harnessing the benefits of new technologies. We are keen to reward that innovation. This year marks the fifth annual E-commerce Awards, set up to celebrate organisations that are successfully using new technologies to improve their business. Since their inception, we have seen rapid growth in the number of entrants; in 1999, 236 companies applied to the scheme. This grew to a massive 1,683 entries in 2002. As the awards have evolved to respond to changing business needs and new technologies, so the quality of entries has improved.

Back in 1999 the awards were focused on the use of internet and electronic trading applications. The 2003 awards will focus on the key ICT issues affecting organisations today. Truly e-enabled companies are those that have integrated ICT throughout their business.

E-business offers real benefits to small companies – allowing better and faster communication, improving efficiency and opening up new markets. With new technologies behind them, smaller businesses can succeed in an evermore competitive marketplace.

Source: The *Guardian*, 29 May 2003, **www.guardian.co.uk**.

## Article 2.3

### Quest to discover how hi-tech is changing Britain

A British research team is to embark on a quest for the definitive answer to 'the critical question' of the 21st century: how has new technology really affected the way we live?

Amid grandiose claims from the IT industry about the 'information revolution', the three year study claims to be the first independent, 'forensic' audit of the impact of computers, mobile phones, email, internet and the rest on the way we work, socialise and communicate.

Carried out by the Industrial Society – with the help of undisclosed but 'significant' sponsorship from the computing company Microsoft – the society project has already shed new light on the relationship between the British and new technology.

A preliminary survey published today indicates the extent to which technology is influencing everyday life. The most dramatic results were in the social sphere. Almost 50% of respondents believed technology had increased the number of friends they had, while 60% said they communicated more often with family and friends thanks to email, the internet and mobile phones.

A similar number believed computers were unfairly blamed for problems in society, while 20% thought the world would be a better place without computers and mobile phones.

But while 50% thought technology had reduced people's workloads, helped to fight crime and improved healthcare, 40% said it had increased inequality, and 70% blamed it for making life busier.

With the next generation of information and communications gadgetry about to be launched, there are already 10 microprocessors for every person on the planet, while email and mobile phone usage has exploded. In Britain there are around 40m mobiles.

Richard Reeves, the project's coordinator, said: 'If email is changing the nature of [people's] relationships with families, friends and work, that is extremely important for society.'

The involvement of Microsoft has raised doubts among some observers about the independence of the research.

However, Neil Holloway, managing director of the company's UK operation, said other companies would be brought on board as the project progressed. 'To understand the impact of technology, we have to get involved in this kind of project. The research will be available to all IT firms, allowing them to develop and market their products better.'

The rapid pace of change and the shifting nature of public attitudes has left question marks over whether the project will ever establish the true impact of technology.

But, Will Hutton, the Industrial Society's chief executive, said: 'We have to try. There is no doubt in my mind that the impact of information and communications technology over the next 10 to 15 years is the critical social and economic question of our age.'

## Most see benefit of innovation

- Around 50% said technology had actually increased the number of friends they had, and 60% said

email, the internet and mobile phone technology meant they communicated more often with friends and family.

- Almost 90% believed technology had increased opportunities.
- Around 50% of respondents said technology had helped fight crime and 50% said it had improved healthcare. But almost 40% said it had increased inequality and less than 30% said it allowed them more free time.
- Only 20% agreed that the world would be a better place without computers and mobiles, but over 70% said technology had made life busier and less than 30% said work had become more flexible.

Source: Stuart Millar, The *Guardian*, 16 March 2001, **www.guardian.co.uk**.

And there lies the problem! Whilst some parts of contemporary society have clearly benefited from the growth in market-based capitalism (e.g. some western European countries, the USA and commonwealth countries), other parts have not (e.g. some south-east Asian countries and many central and north African countries). The success of such change – the ongoing search from growth for profit and shareholder wealth – has often been achieved at some social and political cost. But why?

### A closer look at capitalism

Although capitalism (as a social system) is no more than an abstract social construct, it can nonetheless be defined in many ways. For our purposes we will define capitalism (see Chapter 1) as a system in which individuals or combinations of individuals compete with each other to accumulate wealth. More importantly, as a social system, we will characterise capitalism as a diverse construct comprising of a range of alternative forms of commodity/service exchange (that is production, distribution and exchange) within a market-based supply and demand economy, the key elements being:

- the existence of private property ownership – including the right to exclusive control, the right to benefit and the right to disposal,
- the right to free pursuit of profit/wealth accumulation, and
- the existence of a free market (or at least partially free) market mechanism for the determination of exchange prices.

But why is this relevant? Clearly, as a social process of commodity/service exchange in which all the advanced economies of the world have become implicated and involved, contemporary capitalism has been, and indeed continues to be, constrained by few discernible physical, political or technological boundaries. Nevertheless, as an invasive element capitalism is neither permanent nor stable. It is ephemeral, transitory and seemingly apathetic towards socio-culturally determined political, social or economic restrictions and regulations with a history which is less a predetermined timetable of predictable events and more an open contest of crisis and chaos.

It is, and perhaps has always been, a system founded on the speculative determination of profitable activities – new products and markets, new technologies, new spaces and locations, and new processes of organisation and control. Consequently, no matter how erratic, unstable, ambiguous, uncertain, and/or risky the process may appear to be, at the heart of capital's distinctive historical geography is the single-minded desire of its dominant market-based institutions, networks and alliances to accumulate further wealth in ever-increasing proportions.

More importantly it is this desire – the desire to ensure and maintain the deliberate transformation of the very society within which it is embedded – that charms and disguises, creates and destroys need and wants, exploits desires and fantasies, and transforms both time and space. Indeed, the social/economic history of market-based capitalism is littered with fraught attempts at identifying, minimising and where possible alleviating, if only temporarily, the causes of these crisis of wealth accumulation, not only on a corporate level, but more importantly on a national and international level.

Clearly, whilst history may seem to council caution, capitalism's inherent nature of speculative profitability – a process founded on the notions of opposition, rivalry and market competition – is responsible for generating its ever-present and ever-increasing crisis of accumulation; a crisis for which there exists but a few possible, albeit severely limited, responses. It is this central anathema of capitalism – the contradictory nature of its very substance – that is of great importance to the study of organisational systems generally, and corporate accounting information systems specifically.

The increasingly risky and turbulent search for profit seemingly produces the very crisis of accumulation it seeks to escape; a search in which contemporary accounting information systems as constructed organisational systems have been and indeed continue to be clearly implicated. Indeed, it is the inherent contradictions of capitalism, its expansionist nature, its endless and incessant reorganisation of regimes of accumulation, that companies have increasingly sought to proffer solutions and strategies that have become more and more dependent on the created representations generated from corporate accounting information systems. See Article 2.4.

## Article 2.4

### Global Capitalism – can it be made to work better?

It's hard to figure how a term that once connoted so much good for the world has fallen into such disrepute. In the past decade, globalisation – meaning the rise of market capitalism around the world – has undeniably contributed to America's New Economy boom. It has created millions of jobs from Malaysia to Mexico and a cornucopia of affordable goods for Western consumers. It has brought phone service to some 300 million households in developing nations and a transfer of nearly $2 trillion from rich countries to poor through equity, bond investments, and commercial loans. It's helped topple dictators by making information available in once sheltered societies. And now the Internet is poised to narrow the gulf that separates rich nations from poor even further in the decade to come.

It's little wonder then that, for many, the rage now being vented against globalisation is so perplexing. Even in this jittery autumn, as investors punish bourses and recession fears rise, many workers and government officials in nations such as China, Mexico, and Hungary still feel that the movement toward open markets has paid off. The tumultuous street theater of angry young middle-class Westerners vilifying multi-nationals and forming human chains to shut down meetings of bodies such as the World Bank, seems bizarrely detached from the real-life concerns voiced in countries that are supposed to be victims of global capitalism. Even in the toughest situations, there is little interest in returning to the past. 'The more open the Russian economy is to the rest of the world, the better,' says Yevgeny Gavrilenkov, an architect of President Vladimir Putin's economic plan.

RETHINKING. Yet it would be a grave mistake to dismiss the uproar witnessed in the past few years in Seattle, Washington, D.C., and Prague. Many of the radicals leading the protests may be on the political fringe. But they have helped to kick-start a profound rethinking about globalisation among governments, mainstream economists, and corporations that, until recently, was carried on mostly in obscure think tanks and academic seminars.

This reassessment is badly overdue. In the late 20th century, global capitalism was pushed by leaps in technology, the failure of socialism, and East Asia's seemingly miraculous success. Now, it's time to get realistic. The plain truth is that market liberalization by itself does not lift all boats, and in some cases, it has caused severe damage to poor nations. What's more, there's no point denying that multinationals have contributed to labor, environmental, and human-rights abuses as they pursue profit around the globe.

For global capitalism to move into the next stage will require a much more sophisticated look at the costs and benefits of open markets. To assess these increasingly important trade-offs, *Business Week* sent more than a dozen reporters around the world, from the deserts of Chad to the factories of Guatemala, to witness firsthand the effects of global capitalism. They met workers who toil 16 hours a day for miserly pay making garments sold in the U.S. as well as villagers who want oil companies off their land. But they also talked to factory laborers who have seen big gains in their standards of living as well as creative bureaucrats who have used markets to coax growth out of once moribund economies.

The overwhelming conclusion of this reporting is that there are many examples of where reckless investment has done harm – but there is no case where the hazards can't be addressed with better government and corporate policy. The real question isn't whether free markets are good or bad. It is why they are producing such wildly different results in different countries. Figuring out that answer is essential if businesses, government leaders, and workers are all to realize the benefits of global markets.

The extremes of global capitalism are astonishing. While the economies of East Asia have achieved rapid growth, there has been little overall progress in much of the rest of the developing world. Income in Latin America expanded by 75% during the 1960s and 1970s, when the region's economies were relatively closed. But incomes grew by only 6% in the past two decades, when Latin America was opening up. Average incomes in sub-Saharan Africa and the old Eastern bloc have actually contracted. The World Bank figures the number of people living on $1 a day increased, to 1.3 billion, over the past decade.

The downside of global capitalism is the disruption of whole societies, from financial meltdowns to practices by multinationals that would never be tolerated in the West. Industrialized countries have enacted all sorts of worker, consumer, and environmental safeguards since the turn of the century, and civil rights have a strong tradition. But the global economy is pretty much still in the robber-baron age.

If global capitalism's flaws aren't addressed, the backlash could grow more severe. Already, the once impressive forward momentum for new international free-trade deals has been stopped cold. An ambitious Multilateral Agreement on Investment, which would have removed all remaining restrictions on cross-border investment by corporations, fizzled last year. So have hopes for a new global trade round through the World Trade Organisation. In the U.S., Congress has refused to give the President fast-track authority to strike new trade deals.

The longer-term danger is that if the world's poor see no benefits from free trade and IMF austerity programs, political support for reform could erode. The current system is 'unsustainable,' says United Nations Assistant Secretary General John G. Ruggie, who, as a political economist at Columbia University, examined how previous golden ages of global capitalism, such as the one at the turn of the 19th century, unraveled. 'To survive,' says Ruggie, 'it must be imbedded in broader social concerns.'

NAIVETE. It all adds up to a breakdown of what was known as the Washington Consensus. The grandiose term refers to a world view pushed aggressively by the U.S. Treasury, the IMF, and the World Bank in the early 1990s. This dictum held that all countries should open their markets to trade, direct investment, and short-term capital as quickly as possible. The transition would be painful, but inevitably, markets would achieve equilibrium, and prosperity would result.

In hindsight, it was a naive and self-interested view. Free capital markets, which have proved the most disruptive part of the formula, were largely championed by Wall Street – which saw new trading opportunities

– over the objection of many economists. To be sure, developing nations badly needed to import capital and foreign financial knowhow to keep growing. But many nations simply couldn't handle the inflows. The results were huge white-elephant industrial and property projects that devoured funds and foreign-currency debt bombs that started exploding in 1994, first in Mexico and later in East Asia.

A more realistic view is now gaining hold. It begins with a similar premise: that trade and inflows of private capital are still essential to achieving strong, sustainable growth and to reduce poverty. But it acknowledges that multinationals – which account for the bulk of direct cross-border investment and one-third of trade – have social responsibilities in nations where the rule of law is weak. And it dispenses with the erroneous notion that open markets will magically produce prosperity in all conditions. Even the IMF now warns that a high degree of openness to global capital can be dangerous for some development. 'The IMF push for capital-market liberalization for all nations was driven by financial-market ideology,' says former World Bank chief economist Joseph E. Stiglitz, now a vocal IMF critic. 'They have conceded defeat, but only after the damage was done.'

Even the orthodoxy that developing countries should quickly lower import barriers and slash the state's role in industry is being challenged. Before trade and foreign capital can translate into sustainable growth, governments first must deliver political stability, sound economic management, and educated workers.

NOT SO FAST. East Asia's Tigers had many of these features when they began their export drives; most of Latin America and Africa did not. 'To get the benefits of trade and capital flows, you need a broader base of development,' says Dani Rodrik, a Harvard University economist whose research has raised hackles by suggesting that there is no automatic link between openness and growth in developing countries.

The search for a more intelligent approach to globalisation is most evident within the developing nations themselves. Russia is only now starting to recover from the massive corruption, capital flight, and economic collapse of the 1990s. Putin's government plans to continue market reforms and wants to join the WTO. But its blueprint also calls for strengthening the legal system and control of the financial sector. 'There's an emphasis on long-term plans for economic development instead of the haphazard, piecemeal policies of the pre-crisis years,' says Mikhail Zadornov, who was finance minister under Boris Yeltsin.

A similar view is forming in Romania, whose economy has contracted by 14% since 1996. The only way to achieve growth, says opposition Social Democracy Party legislator Adrian Nastase, is to make Romania more attractive to foreign investment, boost exports, and work with the IMF and World Bank. But he's also wary of importing pat formulas. 'We have been told that small is beautiful. We have been told to privatize as fast as possible. We have been told many things,' says Nastase, who is expected to be Romania's next prime minister. 'But the teachers are changing the contents of the schoolbooks.'

Some countries face such immense challenges that it could take a decade before they benefit from lifting trade and financial barriers. Despite considerable liberalization, growth in sub-Saharan Africa has fallen from 3.5% in the 1970s to 2.2% in the 1990s. And foreign investment is negligible. 'Companies have nothing against Africa,' says U.N. Development Program economist Salim Jehar. 'It's that stability, infrastructure, and skills are not there.' The only way for sub-Saharan Africa to begin digging out is for foreign creditors to forgive most of its debt, which consumes some 40% of export revenue. Then, it must somehow attract massive infusions of private investment.

Just as there are no one-size-fits-all policies for economic development, there also are no clear road-maps for corporate behavior. Balancing growth with environmental and labor regulations is wrenchingly complex in countries where people live on the margin. Many poor nations fiercely resist discussion of labor or environmental issues in the WTO because they fear the process will be hijacked by Western protectionists: The feeling is that Western unions will shield jobs at home by imposing standards that drive up labor costs in emerging markets to levels where developing nations can't compete. 'It's hypocrisy of the first sort for the West to talk about opening borders and then hide behind barriers,' says Indian economist Surjit Bhalla.

The result, however, is confusion. At a time when image is paramount, corporations are besieged with activists who harangue executives at shareholder meetings, organise consumer boycotts, smear their brand names on the Web, and pressure creditors and shareholders alike. To allay critics, companies such as Nike, Mattel, Levi Strauss, and Royal Dutch Shell Group have drawn up their own guidelines and invited monitors to ensure that they live up to them.

'People's expectations of the social and environmental role of businesses have absolutely changed in the past five years,' says Aron Cramer, vice-president of San Francisco's Business for Social Responsibility, which advises the Gap Inc., General Motors Corp., and other companies on their practices abroad. 'If there's a problem in a company's global supply chain, all it takes is one modem in Indonesia to alert the world about it.'

But altering business practices to appease pressure groups can also hurt more than help the impoverished if they are done hastily. For example, soon after a bill was proposed in the U.S. Congress in 1993 to ban imports from countries where children work in factories, garment makers in Bangladesh fired 36,000 workers under age 18, most of them girls. Studies by the International Labor Organisation and Unicef found that few of the fired workers ended up in school. Instead, many took more dangerous jobs or became prostitutes. 'Instead of just throwing children out of work, you first must address the underlying economic conditions,' says Nandana Reddy, director of India-based Concern for Working Children.

Partly to avoid having extremists set the agenda, efforts are now under way to clarify the rules. In May, the U.N. kicked off a program called Global Compact. The idea is to get multinationals to endorse a set of basic human rights, environmental, and labor principles, and allow private groups to monitor their compliance. So far, some 44 companies, including Shell and Nike, have signed up.

SANCTIONS. Because industry self-regulation schemes lack real teeth, critics dismiss them as merely public relations. But such pacts are beginning to form the basis of a kind of global capitalism with rules. There already are international agreements on intellectual-property rights, prison labor, and trade in endangered species that allow countries to bar imports from violators.

As the costs of consumer boycotts and monitoring rise, companies and their investors are likely to look toward more uniform standards of behavior. But make no mistake: It's unlikely that anyone would agree to an international central bank policing the capital markets or world legislatures and regulatory agencies enforcing good corporate behavior. The new rules of global capitalism will evolve slowly, in pieces, and with varying degrees of success.

A serious discussion on globalisation has begun. Until now, it has been dominated by extremists on both sides – anti-globalism radicals and dogmatic free-marketers. 'At each end of the spectrum are ideologues who are pushing agendas unrelated to reality,' says World Bank development research director Paul Collier. 'It has been a dreadfully silly debate.'

A decade ago, when much of the world was still clinging to various brands of wealth-destroying socialism, it may have made sense to push rigid doctrines. But the battle for market-driven economics has been largely won. And the flaws of trying to force every country into the same template have become clear. To take globalisation to the next level, it is time to forge a more enlightened consensus.

Source: Pete Engardio (Washington) and, Catherine Belton (Moscow), 6 November 2000, Business week online **www.businessweek.com**.

### Towards a framework of analysis

Whilst there are many alternative frameworks that could be used to analyse, explore and/or describe the consequences of capitalism's increasingly turbulent history – for example, the regulation school approach,[3] the neo-Smithian flexible specialisation approach,[4] the neo-Schumpeterian approach,[5] the disorganised capital thesis,[6] or the flexible accumulation approach,[7] there can be little doubt that the consequences of this increasing international mobility of capital has had a conscious impact on corporate organisations.

Because we are concerned with corporate accounting information systems as an integrated organisational structure/set of organisational structures that employs both tangible and intangible resources, and the role(s) such systems perform in both a business and organisational context, we will locate our discussion within a flexible accumulation context – that is the increasing mobility of capital, greater decentralization and increased global communications, and adopt as an underpinning analytical framework a regulation school approach.

The rationale for this choice is as follows. Firstly, the neo-Smithian flexible specialisation approach explores social and institutional change in the context of a close relationship between economics and politics, with the economic emphasis often reducing the political and institutional arrangements to contingent products of the dominant market mechanism. Secondly, the neo-Schumpeterian approach considers social and institutional change to be 'techno economic' where the evolution and effectiveness of social institutions rests on the development and adaptation of technologies. Although partially true, such a focus nonetheless reduces the impetus for social change to a form of technological determinism reminiscent of Kondratiev's 'long wave' theories. Thirdly, the disorganised capitalism thesis of Lash and Urry (1987), perceives transition as a growing disorganisation of contemporary capital emerging out of the material conditions associated with the powerful structure of class politics.

Contemporary regulation school thinking adopts a very systemic approach, contextualises change to be a consequence of interaction and perceives capitalism as being dependent on two interrelated institutions – regimes of accumulation, and modes of regulation.

Regimes of accumulation refer to set(s) of regularities at the level of the whole economy that enable rational processes of capital accumulation to occur, and include norms relating to production and management, forms of exchange, principles of wealth accumulation, and patterns of consumption and demand.

Modes of regulation refer to the social/institutional rules and regulations which ensure/secure capital accumulation. They consist of formal or informal rules that codify the main social relationships and include institutions and conventions which reproduce a given accumulation regime through law, state policy, political practices, codes of practice, rules of negotiation and bargaining, culture of consumption and social expectations.

Regulation school thinking perceives social markets to be institutions encompassed by other limiting institutions, in which interaction is subject to principles of reciprocity and cooperation. More importantly, regulation school thinking encapsulates a holistic view inasmuch as it insists any analysis explores the total package of relations and arrangements that contribute to the accumulation of wealth. It is therefore essentially a systemic framework of analysis that provides a useful mechanism for understanding:

- the complex nature of change in the context of a continuing crisis of accumulation, and
- the impact of that change on regulated social institutions.

Indeed, in explaining the paradox within capitalism, its tendency towards crisis and its ability to stabilise within the context of a set of institutional norms, regulation school thinking acknowledges the importance of historical processes, locating the systemic coherence of capitalist development on a number of key concepts. In characterising the development of market-based capitalism by specific forms of regimes of accumulation and modes of regulation, regulation school thinking views the hegemonic structure – the structure that describes the historical connection between regimes of accumulation and modes of regulation – as a result of a process of conflictual historical evolution, a process moulded by the social and economic impact of discrete phases of time–space compression or, more importantly, the impact of technology on society.

But what has all this to do with corporate accounting information systems?

## Modern society, the business environment and accounting information systems

Firstly, what the above clearly illustrates is that economic power, or market-based capitalism as the dominant social system, is extremely volatile, highly competitive and due to its inherent risk and instability, modulates from crisis to crisis. In so doing, it possesses a tendency to create 'protective' bureaucratic structures to surround the created processes of wealth accumulation. Indeed the company structure – the organisational structure at the centre not only of contemporary market-based capitalism but more importantly much of the discussion that follows in this book, primarily arose out of the social and political consequences of the changing nature of capital.

Secondly, as an increasingly complex social system, a social system populated by evermore complex and bureaucratic organisational structures, market-based capitalism (perhaps a more accurate description would be the institutions and organisations that comprise the marketplace) requires evermore complex regulation and socio-political intervention, not only to ensure increased accountability, transparency and control but, more importantly, to ensure market efficiency, especially pricing efficiency, although such intervention is also designed to promote both operational and allocational efficiency.[8]

Such demands, whether a product of government intrusion and/or market-based conscience, nonetheless promotes a greater dependency on systems – a trust in systems – in order that:

- governments ensure adequate regulatory control of an increasingly complex marketplace is maintained, and
- market regulators ensure an appropriate level of market confidence is maintained in extant regulatory procedures.

So what have been the main implications of this increasing trust in systems?

## From trust in systems to corporate accounting information systems

Because of the increasing complexity of business organisations, business transactions and business regulations, there has as a consequence been a comparative increase in the use of signs and symbols for information and communication purposes (Lash and Urry, 1993). Although the need and desire to communicate the financial consequences of business transactions undoubtedly has its roots in antiquity, and can be traced back to the ancient civilisations of Babylonia, Mesopotamia, Egypt and Central America, the influence of technological advancements and innovations, and the increasing global capitalistic spirit for wealth accumulation, has not only relocated but more importantly re-emphasised the use and role of such signs and symbols. That is, using the idea of systems (and more importantly a trust in systems) no longer merely provides a framework of communication between governments, market regulators and market participants, both in a national and international context, but is now a major influencing resource in the contemporary marketplace (see Figure 2.1).

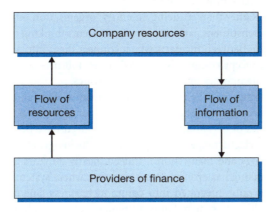

**Figure 2.1** Understanding the importance of systems thinking

In addition, the increasing complexity and associated business risk and uncertainty inherent within contemporary market-based capitalism has promoted an increase in the use of/demand for expert knowledge systems, and an increased emphasis on virtual/fictitious information – a demand for more and more intricate descriptions of the consequences of contemporary market-based decisions.

In combination, each of the above has resulted in a progressive increase in the use of:

- systems thinking – to understand how a business organisation operates within a changing business environment, and
- information models – to communicate how well the business organisation is operating in a relative sense compared to the rest of the business environment.

And because the key motivating force in contemporary society is market-based capitalism – wealth accumulation, with all its associated risks and uncertainties – what we can say with some degree of certainty is that the key system of knowledge in today's often chaotic business environment is accounting information – central to whose construction is an understanding not only of what inter-relationships exist, but more importantly how they interact.

## Systems thinking

Finally we have arrived, albeit with a few minor but nonetheless relevant diversions, at our consideration of systems thinking. So what is systems thinking?

Systems thinking is a contemporary interdisciplinary study – a study of organisation and relationship, independent of any substance, type, spatial or temporal scale of existence. Such thinking seeks to investigate:

- the principles common to all complex entities, and
- the models (often mathematical in origin) which can be used to describe them.

With its origins in biology, systems thinking was first proposed by the biologist Ludwig von Bertalanffy (1936) as a reaction to what von Bertalanffy viewed as the reductionism of contemporary science. Von Bertalanffy sought to emphasise the holistic nature of real systems. He sought to emphasise that real systems were open to, and interact with, their environments, and as such can acquire qualitative properties through processes of acquisition, adaptation and change – processes of emergent evolution.

Rather than reducing an entity, organisation or institution, or process, to the properties of its constituent parts or elements, systems thinking focuses on the arrangement of and relationships between the parts which connect them into a whole. This idea of looking at the whole is a concept commonly referred to as holism – a concept that has enormous consequence in contemporary financial reporting issues.

Since it is the particular set of relationships and/or organisation that determines a system, independent of the concrete substance of the system's elements, the same concepts and principles of organisation can be, and indeed have been, used to analyse and explore issues from an eclectic range of disciplines (e.g. sociology, economics, physics, biology, information technology and many more). Indeed, nearly 70 years after von Bertalanffy's proposition, systems thinking has evolved into a situation where systems thinking and its terminology has become not only integrated into common business language but everyday language – for example, health care system, family system, social system, human systems, information systems, banking systems, political systems.

## Hard system/soft system

Clearly whilst each of the above types of system possesses a range of common relational elements, they nonetheless represent an enormous diversity – a diversity founded on, for example, varying degrees of humanism (objectivity/subjectivity) and/or varying degree of predictability and stability. A diversity which can be categorised as 'hard systems' thinking and 'soft systems' thinking.

For our purposes we will use the framework developed by Burrell and Morgan (1979) which is constructed on two simple dimensions/criteria:

- an ontological dimension, that is a subjective/objective criterion, and
- an ethical/contextual dimension, that is a change criterion or a scale ranging from radical and chaotic change to regulation and stability.

Within the ontological dimension, a subjective view/assumption would perceive social reality/ system to be product of an individual and/or a shared consciousness, whereas an objective view/assumption would perceive social reality as having a hard objective, externally determined existence separate from the individual.

Within the ethical contextual dimension, a sociology of regulation would perceive social reality/system to be based on consensual agreement with stability achieved through discussion and cooperation, whereas a sociology of radical change would perceive social reality as containing widespread contradictions and conflict, with cohesion existing as a consequence of one group's domination over another.

Whilst such a framework neither implies nor distinguishes between:

- a social reality/system whose purpose/meaning is provided by society or an individual (or group of individuals) – that is a perpetuity/mechanistic explanation, or
- a social reality/system whose progress and purpose are externally imposed as a doctrine of final causes – that is a teleological explanation,

it does provide a structure within which two broad categories of systems (or views of social reality) can be identified:

- a hard systems view or hard systems thinking, and
- a soft systems view or soft systems thinking.

Within a hard systems context Burrell and Morgan (1979) identified two views (see Figure 2.2):

- the functionalist view perceives social reality/systems to be real, external to the individual, structured, purposeful and stable. (Individuals are regarded as no more than a component part, with understanding based on identifying relationships and regularities.)
- the radical structuralist view perceives social reality/social systems to be real, structured but generally unstable. (Again human intention is secondary, however understanding is based on identifying contradictions irregularities and conflict.)

Within a soft systems context Burrell and Morgan (1979) identified two further views of social reality/systems:

- the interpretive view which perceives social reality/systems to be humanist, interpretive in nature and based on consensual intention and free will, but nonetheless stable, and
- the radical humanist view which perceives social reality/systems to be humanist, creatively constructed and as such interpretive in nature, but generally unstable with arrangements and relationships as transient and subject to continuing change.

47

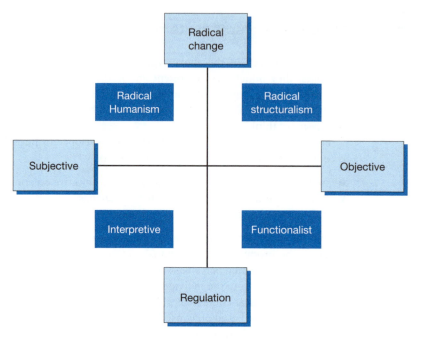

**Figure 2.2** Burrell and Morgan – four paradigms of analysis

But what is the importance and relevance of this distinction to corporate accounting information systems? Accounting in general, and accounting information systems in particular, are often viewed as hard systems, as functionalistic, structured, purposeful, specific and stable. However nothing could be further from the truth!

Clearly, financial statements are socially constructed and politically created statements. However, more importantly, the human interface that is ever present in corporate accounting systems, the choice, the flexibility, and the interpretive nature of accounting standards and regulations used in the preparation (and creation) of such financial statements, all result in unstable and sometimes contradictory, often unpredictable outcomes.

## What is a system?

As suggested in Chapter 1, there are a number of alternative definitions of a system. For example, a system can be defined as an entity which can maintain some organisation in the face of change from within or without, or more simply as a set of objects or elements interacting to achieve a specific goal.

For our purposes we will define a system as a complex of directly and indirectly related elements which operate to attain a goal or objective, in which the goal or objective is often used as the key controlling element, the function of the system being to convert or process energy, information or materials into a product or outcome for use inside the system, or, outside of the system (the environment) or both.

Furthermore, we will assume three key groups of ideas. Firstly, all systems, whether hard and/or soft, have a number of common elements (see Figure 2.3):

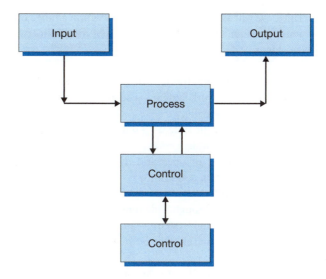

**Figure 2.3** A diagrammatic representation of a system

- input,
- throughput or transformation process,
- output
- an external environment and boundary,
- control,
- feedback and, where appropriate, feedforward, and
- a goal and/or objective.

Secondly, we will assume that all the systems possess the following fundamental, if somewhat generic, characteristics:

- all systems consists of a set of objectives and their relationships,
- all systems tend toward equilibrium (or balance),
- the constant interaction between systems results in a constant state of flux/change,
- all systems are composed of interrelated parts – that is a hierarchical system/sub-system relationship,
- where such sub-systems are arranged in a series, the output of one is the input of another; therefore, process alterations in one require alterations in other sub-systems,
- the parts of the system (sub-system) constitute an indissoluble whole,
- although each sub-system may be a self-contained system, it is nonetheless part of a wider and higher order,
- each sub-system works together towards the goal of the higher system.
- the system (and sub-system) must exhibit some predictability, but some systems are very complex and are impacted on by an infinite number of other systems, and as such can never attain total predictability of effects,
- the value of the system is greater than the sum of its parts (or individual sub-systems),
- to be viable, all systems must be strongly goal-directed, governed by feedback and have the ability to adapt to changing circumstances – that is exhibit properties of emergent evolution, and
- no system exists in isolation – a system interfaces with other systems that may be of a similar or different nature.

Third, we will assume that systems exist within a range of differing levels of complexity. As suggested by Wren (1994) alternative levels of complexity can be identified within systems thinking (see Figure 2.4), these being;

- level 1: a structural framework – a static, predictable and descriptive system,
- level 2: a clockwork system – a semi-dynamic, moving and predictable system that must be controlled externally,
- level 3: a cybernetic system – a semi-dynamic and predictable system capable of self-regulation within certain limits,
- level 4: a cell – an open and dynamic system, programmed for self-maintenance under changing external conditions,
- level 5: a plant system – an open, dynamic, and genetically determined system capable of self-regulation through wide range of changing external and internal conditions,
- level 6: an animal system – an open, dynamic and genetically determined system that adjusts to its environment by making internal adjustments and by forming simple social groups,
- level 7: a human being – an open, dynamic and self-regulating system, that is adaptive through wide circumstances because of the ability to think abstractly and communicate symbolically,
- level 8: a social system – a system more complex than an individual, more open to environmental influence and more adaptive to circumstance because of collective experience and a wider reservoir of skills, and
- level 9: a transcendental system – a system that is freely adaptable to circumstance and change because it rises above and extends beyond the boundaries of both individuals and social systems. May infer a teleological underpinning.

Clearly, in each of the above there are a number of distinguishing characteristics. Firstly, there is a distinction between a static system and a dynamic system. A static system is a system in which neither the system elements nor the system itself changes much over time in relation to the environment (e.g. level 1). A dynamic system is a system which is not only constantly changed by the environment, but also changes the environment in which it exists (e.g. levels 4 to 9). Levels 2 and 3 could perhaps best be described as semi-dynamic (or semi-static), since control and influence is generally external imposed/moderated.

Secondly, there is a distinction between an open system and a closed system.

An open system is one which is interactive with the environment, exchanging information, energy and/or raw materials for information, goods and/or services produced by the system. Such systems are generally self-regulating and capable of growth, development and more importantly, adaptation. Example of such systems would range from nature-based systems such as the human body and other plants and animals, to created organisational systems such as banks and financial institutions, manufacturing plants, governmental bodies, associations, businesses and many more.

A closed system is a system which is not interactive with its environment. Fixed and often automatic relationships exist between system components with no exchange with the environment. Such systems are generally incapable of growth or any form of development/adaptation and as such possess a limited life. Examples of such systems would range from nature-based systems, such as a rock as an example of the most closed type of system, to a mechanistic process, such as an autonomous piece of manufacturing machinery, to detached social systems such as families and/or communities that are isolated from the society and resistant to any outside influence.

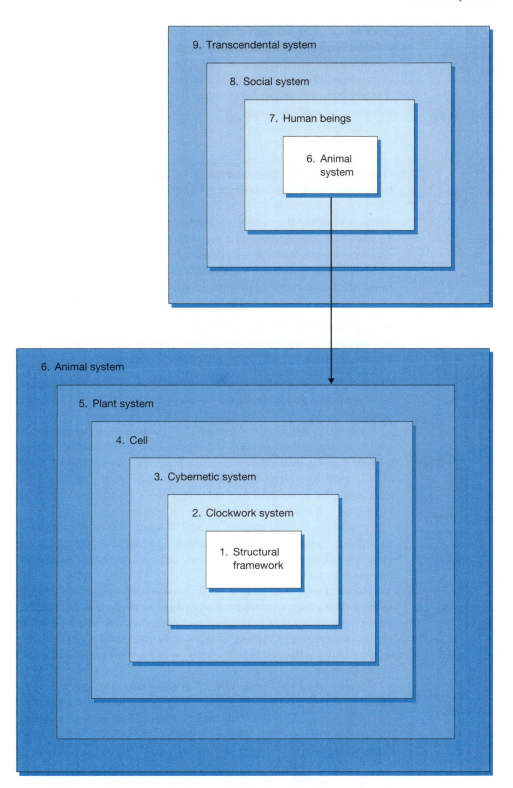

**Figure 2.4** Levels of complexity

This distinction between an open system and a closed system also encapsulates what is called the 'principle of equifinality'. We will discuss this principle later in the chapter but for the time being we can define the principle of equifinality as the capacity of an open system, because of its interactive nature, to reach its final state or achieve its goal(s)/objective(s) in a number of different ways, whereas a closed system can only achieve its final goal(s)/objective(s) or state based on its initial conditions.

## Understanding the context of systems thinking – systems thinking and the environment

Although some social systems (and institutions) may, in the short term, appear to be isolated and detached from their environment, such isolation is, in a system sense at least, limited. Prolonged detachment often results in either systems failure, that is the system becomes disorganised or entropic, or external influences intercede and the system becomes interactive with its environment, whether by choice or by imposition.

Clearly, then, the sustainability of a social system is dependent on its interactivity, that is:

- monitoring change in the environment,
- understanding the relationship between parts of the environment, and
- understanding the effects of change in the environment

However, because all social systems are created, constructed and artificial, their interactivity is often moderated and generally controlled, that is they exhibit characteristics of both open and closed systems – they are semi-open (or semi-closed) systems.

A semi-open system is a system which exchanges known or prescribed inputs and outputs with the environment: that is such systems are generally constructed and/or artificial processes and generally regulate interaction with the environment. As a consequence such systems are capable of sustainable growth and emergent development, where competition for limited resources may exist. Examples of such systems would of course be the business and financial environment (see Figure 2.5) and created social/organisational systems such as companies.

For example, for the company, prescribed inputs and outputs of resources and information are regulated not only by legal requirements and codes of practice, but more importantly, by market pressures of supply and demand, and internal resource constraints. Let's look at this notion of change a little closer.

Systems change because of an event or a series/sequence of events over time between or within systems. Such events can and often do cause multiple events (or change) in other systems. Where an event is a repetitive sequence, such a sequence is known as a cycle. From a system's perspective, cycle(s) or cycling, may be used either to retain and/or enforce balance within a system – that is to maintain equilibrium – or to stimulate growth – that is to attain a higher level of integration.

The attainment of a different level of integration through a series/sequence of events is often known as spiralling – that is where there is a sequential effect as a result of a series of events that magnifies the initial effect. Spiralling that has an increasing integrative effect is known as positive spiralling. Spiralling that has an increasingly disintegrative effect is known as negative spiralling.

Before we move on to a consideration of the key elements of a system, and systems thinking, perhaps it would be useful to provide some context to this notion of system and that of events, cycles and spiralling.

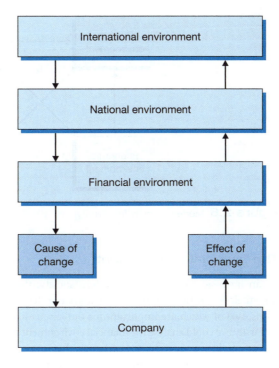

**Figure 2.5** The system view of the financial environment

 ## Applying systems thinking

### Modern society (modernity)

Earlier in this chapter we defined modern society as a complex (and often chaotic) arrangement of social, political and economic institutions – ever-changing, ever-evolving. More importantly, we described (somewhat simplistically) modern society as a composite of four interrelated environments:

- the political environment – the nation state,
- the economic environment – market-based capitalism,
- the social environment – processes of surveillance, and
- the technological environment – industrialism.

Whilst such an unsophisticated definition of modernity has many limitations it does nonetheless provide a framework of modern society by which we can locate and contextualise the main focus of our discussion – the corporate entity.

As a system, modern society – whilst open to continuous change and enormous environmental influence, the outcomes of which are often random and unpredictable – is nonetheless a controlled system, at least within the context of a regulatory and hopefully representative democratic political framework. It is in essence a semi-open system.

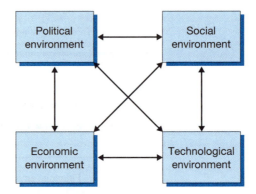

**Figure 2.6** Modern society (modernity)

## The financial environment

As an intrinsic component of modern society, the financial environment is a complex, but nonetheless constructed, institutional system that can be analysed on many different/distinct levels, two of which are important for our discussion.

Firstly, we could analyse the financial environment as an institutional system historically founded on commodity production and exchange: that is in a contemporary context, a socially constructed network through which processes of wealth accumulation are legitimated and through which the search for profit and gain takes place. It is an interconnected network/web of individuals, companies, commercial banks, government central banks and various quasi-regulatory agencies who buy and sell not only tangible but, increasingly, intangible assets and resources.

Clearly, whilst the activities of each group can, and indeed, do affect the overall functioning of the market, by far the most influential group are the corporate entities (the wealth creating entities) the companies.

Secondly we could analyse the financial environment as an integrated virtual network/web – a virtual information system whose physical reality is represented by a collection of geographically dispersed trading centres located around the world (e.g. London, New York, Hong Kong, Singapore, Frankfurt, Brussels and Amsterdam). In essence a global marketplace trading in financial instruments and corporate ownership that has grown considerably over the past 20 to 30 years – a virtual network independent of, but closely related to, commodity production and exchange.

The financial environment is represented in Figure 2.7.

## Company (cycles of operation)

At the core of modern society, and indeed the contemporary financial environment described above, is the company – a constructed social entity. But what do we mean by a company?

In a legal context a company is a 'corporation' – an artificial person created by law that not only has legal rights and obligations in the same way that a natural person does, but whose powers and duties (both of the company and those who run it), are closely regulated by the Companies Acts and by its own created constitution as contained in its Memorandum and Articles of Association.

In a financial context, this artificial person – this legal construct – is merely a collection of tangible and intangible resources and assets the management (and decision-making processes) which are designed not only to facilitate the safekeeping of capital invested in the company by

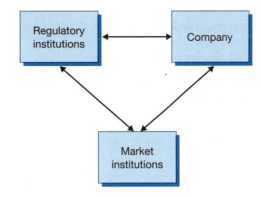

**Figure 2.7** Financial environment (capitalism)

corporate stakeholders (risk minimisation), but more importantly to maximise the wealth of its shareholders (wealth maximisation).

In a systems context, however, a company is (using a hierarchical decomposition context) merely a complex black box whose primary goal is a 'transformation process' – of inputs into outputs, of needs and desires into products and services, of market demand into market supply and, of course ultimately, wealth creation. A collection of systems, procedures and processes whose *weltanschauung* or 'world view' is clearly located within the latter financial contextualisation, but nonetheless limited by the former legal contextualisation.

As with modern society, and with the financial environment, we will take a fairly simplistic system's view of the company (whatever the nature of the business undertaken), and contextualise the company's activities/procedures/processes or more appropriately cycles of operation, as follows (see Figure 2.8):

- an expenditure system,
- a production (conversion) system,
- a revenue system, and
- a management system.

More importantly, we will consider the company to be a semi-open system seeking greater integration within its systemic environment – that is the financial environment and ultimately modern society.

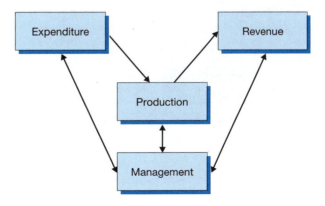

**Figure 2.8** Company (cycles of operation)

## Systems thinking – the full picture

### Key elements of a system

In the earlier discussion, a system was deemed to have a number of common elements, these being (see Figure 2.9):

- input – the data, energy and/or raw materials transformed by the system,
- transformation process – the function or purpose of the system, that is the process or processes used by the system to convert data, raw materials or energy from the environment into information, products and/or services that are usable by either the system itself or by the environment,
- output – the information, product and/or service which results from the system's transformation process,
- boundary – the functional barrier between systems (or sub-systems), that is the line or point where a system or sub-system can be differentiated from its environment or from other sub-systems: such a boundary can be rigid or permeable, tangible or intangible, physical or virtual,
- environment – the part of the environment external to the system,

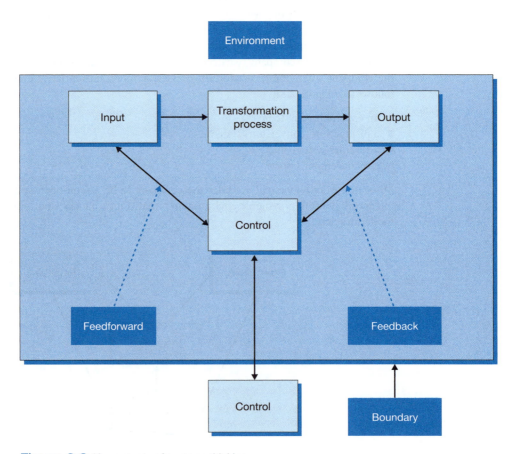

**Figure 2.9** Key aspects of systems thinking

- control – the mechanism for regulating performance to expectations, that is the activities, processes and procedures used to evaluate input, throughput and output in order to make corrections,
- feedback – information about some aspect of output that can be used to evaluate and monitor the system and to guide it to more effective performance,
- feedforward – information about some aspect of input that can be used to modify the system processing procedures and to guide it to more effective performance,
- goal/objective – the overall purpose for existence of the system, or the desired outcome of the system (that is its reason for being).

## Input

Input can be defined as the data, energy and/or raw materials transformed by the system. Input may be externalised, that is it is obtained directly from the system's external environment, or it may internalised, that is it can be the product of or output from another sub-system within the system's environment.

## Transformation process

The transformation process is the function or purpose of the system, that is the process or processes used by the system to convert data, raw materials or energy from the environment into information, products and or services that are usable by either the system itself or by the environment.

## Output

Output can be defined as the information, product and/or service which results from the system's transformation process. Output may be externalised, that is it generated for and delivered directly to the system's environment, or it may be internalised, that is it is the product/input of another sub-system within the system's environment.

## Boundaries

The system's boundary is a functional barrier that exists between systems (or sub-systems), a line or a point where a system or sub-system can be differentiated from its environment, or from another sub-system, or set of sub-systems. A system's boundary can of course take many forms – it may be rigid or permeable, tangible or intangible, physical or virtual. Nonetheless it is essentially a specified demarcation that enforces a limit within which the elements/components/attributes of a system and their interrelationships can be explained. That is the system's boundary is that which defines the system.

For example, in many biological, geological and created mechanical/physical systems, such system boundaries are often intangible and readily identifiable – a membrane surrounding a biological organism, a physical border between two countries or the body/shell of a motor vehicle. In many sociological and socio-political systems, however, such boundaries tend to be intangible and often virtual in nature, and as such often difficult to identify. More importantly, such systems may possess many alternative boundaries that may be in a constant state of flux as a result of changing environmental conditions. For example, what is the boundary of company – that is at what point does an employee enter the company in a systems context? Is it when the employee crosses the physical boundary that separates the company premises from the outside environment? Or is it when an individual became an employee of the company?

### Environment

The system's environment is that which is external to the system.

A system environment could be described not only as all those objects, elements, components and attributes not in the system, but more importantly, all objects, elements, components and attributes within specified limits, that may have influence on, or be influenced by, the operation of the system. That is a system environment does not only comprise of those external elements whose change may affect the nature, context, properties and functioning of the system, but includes all those elements that are themselves affected by the system's behaviour.

### Control

Although we will explore the issue of control in more detail in Chapter 3, for the time being we will define control as that which guides, directs, regulates and/or constrains the behaviour of a set of variables. It is a mechanism designed to regulate, monitor and/or compare performance to expectations – that is the activities, processes and procedures used to evaluate input, throughput and output and, where necessary, make appropriate corrections.

Such control can either be by means of feedback – where information about some aspect of output is used to evaluate and monitor the system and to guide it to more effective performance – or feedforward – where information about some aspect of input can be used to modify the system processing procedures and to guide the system to more effective performance.

### Objectives/goals

The ultimate objective/goal of a system or its *raison d'être* is dependent not only on the nature and context of the system, but more importantly on its hierarchical location. For example:

- for modern society it could be the reproduction and/or maintenance of existing social relationships and power structures,
- for the financial environment it could be the reproduction of exiting modes of regulation and regimes of wealth accumulation, and
- for the company it could be the accumulation of wealth by means of the temporal and spatial displacement of assets and resources.

## Systems thinking – other issues

### Equifinalty

Systems thinking recognises that semi-open systems and open systems can achieve their objective(s)/aim(s) in a variety of ways using varying inputs, processes, methods and procedures. As suggested by von Bertalanffy (1968):

> *the same final state may be reached from differential conditions and in different ways* (1968: 40).

### Systems adaptability

For closed systems the achievement of any objective/goal often requires little external intervention because such systems, by definition, require little or no environmental interaction to function. However for semi-open and open systems the achievement of any objective/goal,

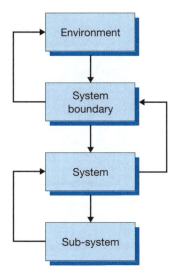

**Figure 2.10** System adaptability

almost certainly requires some on-going monitoring of the systems environment and systems adaptation where appropriate (see Figure 2.10). Why?

Because for such systems both input and output are affected by changes in the system environment and certainly in a business context where a system environment is rarely constant, stable and predictable, the successful achievement of any objective/goal or set of objectives/goals requires carefully planned change. A lack of monitoring and, where necessary, adaptation, may not only lead to increased disorganisation or *entropy* but, more importantly, a failure to meet ongoing objective(s)/aim(s).

## Shared and overlapping systems

One common feature of all systems, not only socially constructed open and semi-open systems, is that a system and/or sub-systems can belong to more than one system or sub-system: that is it is possible, and often common, for a system not only to possess multiple ownership/ membership of other systems and sub-systems, but also to interact at different levels with different systems/sub-systems.

Such multiple ownership/membership (see Figure 2.11) is particularly important where changes are made to systems.

## Interconnections

All systems are interconnected either by way of input and/or output or by processing relationship. Often systems/sub-systems will be connected to a number of systems/sub-systems simultaneously – interacting and exchanging data and information at various levels of activity. The number of interconnections can be calculated as:

$$(n\,(n-1))/2$$

For example, a system with four interrelated sub-systems would have $(5\,(5-1))/2 = 10$ potential interconnections (see Figure 2.12)

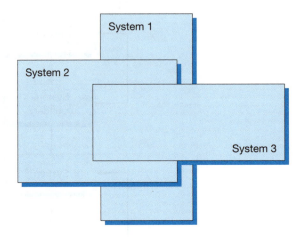

**Figure 2.11** Shared/overlapping systems

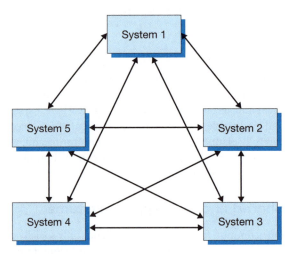

**Figure 2.12** System interconnections

As a system increases in complexity (number of sub-systems) the potential number of inter-connections also increases. For example:

- a system with 10 interrelated sub-systems would have $(10 (10 - 1))/2 = 45$ potential interconnections,
- a system with 50 interrelated sub-systems would have $(50 (50 - 1))/2 = 1,225$ potential interconnections, and
- a system with 100 interrelated sub-systems would have $(100 (100 - 1))/2 = 4,950$ potential interconnections.

## Decoupling

If sub-systems are interconnected, such interconnectivity implies not only spatial and temporal coordination but more importantly functional integration. Decoupling occurs where:

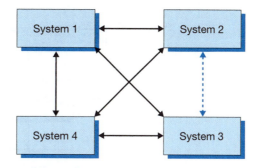

**Figure 2.13** System decoupling

- a number of systems (or sub-systems within a system) operate with a degree of independence, and/or
- an interconnection between two systems and/or sub-systems is suspended either temporarily or in some instances permanently.

Whilst many reasons can exist to justify/rationalise such decoupling (e.g. see the case study later in this chapter), such decoupling (see Figure 2.13) can nevertheless be difficult and problematic in terms of:

- the costs involved,
- the time period involved,
- the consequences of a loss of sub-systems connectivity and control, and
- the possibility that such decoupling could result in long-term sub-optimisation.

## Multiple and conflicting objectives

Large systems may possess a number of objectives or a hierarchy of objectives. Although sub-system objectives should contribute to achieving the objective of the system as a whole, in some instances such objectives may conflict (see Figure 2.14).

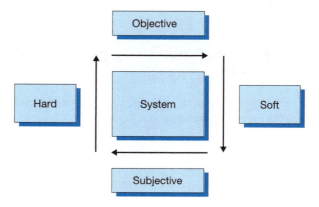

**Figure 2.14** Multiple/conflicting outcomes

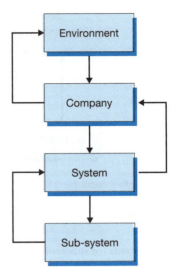

**Figure 2.15**  System constraints

## Systems constraints

Many systems, especially socially created systems, have constraints imposed upon them, for example operational limitations, resources shortages and/or structural difficulties.

Such constraints (see Figure 2.15) may well be temporary but can nonetheless severely restrict the system's ability to achieve its aim(s)/objective(s).

## Sub-optimality

Sub-systems should work towards the goal of their higher systems and not pursue their own objectives independently.

Where a sub-system seeks to pursue its own objectives/agenda to the detriment of higher objectives, or the decoupling of a number of sub-systems has reduced the overall efficiency of the system as a whole, or changes in a system's environment have not been correctly accounted for and as a consequence reduced the overall efficiency of the system, then a situation of sub-optimality may be said to exist.

## Systems thinking – using general systems theory as a framework

Let's look at some of these key elements of systems thinking in more detail in the context of the following case study scenario – Taj-a-Jac Ltd.

## CASE STUDY

### *Taj-a-Jac Ltd*[9]

### History and background

Taj-a-Jac Ltd is a UK-based hand-crafted furniture manufacturer, launched in the mid-1980s by Charles Wood. The business started its operations from one shop in York and has grown substantially so that by 2002 it had 48 shops located around the UK. In addition, in 1999, a seven-year contract with a national chain of leading department stores was signed which gave Taj-a-Jac Ltd wider market access in return for a flat fee and a precentage share of profits.

Originally, Charles Wood was the only full-time employee of Taj-a-Jac Ltd. He was responsible for the design, construction and marketing of the business's products as well as the day-to-day management of the firm. The business, which required £190,000 to start, was a partnership and in addition to his own investment, 50% of the required capital, was provided by Charles' brother-in-law, Thomas Heath. Thomas was an accountant by profession and acted in a part-time capacity as the company accountant and assisted Charles in certain aspects of management.

The company quickly expanded and problems emerged as supply could not keep pace with demand. It became necessary, therefore, to employ someone else to assist Charles in the construction of the furniture. As the business continued to grow, more people joined the company, so that by 1987, 21 people were employed by the firm. At the same time, further shops were opened and a separate workshop/warehouse was established. Taj-a-Jac Ltd's expansion was funded by a combination of reinvesting profits and medium-term bank loans.

The result of all these changes was that by 1987, Charles Wood's time was almost exclusively given over to the management of the business. The following year the decision was made that the company would become a private limited company and it was at this point that Thomas heath joined as full-time finance director. One of the first changes that Thomas brought about was the direct sourcing of the core materials used in the company's products. The pine now used is directly imported from Canada and Scandinavia.

On the 31 March 2003, after 19 years of trading, the financial statements of the company showed a turnover of £60m and a pre-tax profit of £14m.

### Strategic review

In 2002, external consultants were asked to identify the strategic options open to Taj-a-Jac Ltd. The review found that, although the middle/upper end of the furniture market was becoming increasingly competitive, there was still room for significant growth. Despite numerous store openings, the company was still very much a regional operator. Expansion of the market was predicted to continue for many years, although Taj-a-Jac Ltd's product and strategic positioning left the business vulnerable to changes in the business cycle. Indeed, the company had been affected quite significantly by a fall in turnover in the mid/late 1990s.

Aware of this, the consultants suggested a number of alternatives for the company. The first was for more stores to be opened – particularly in the south of England where the company had little presence. This option had implications for the management and organisational structure of the company as at least two additional workshop, warehouse and distribution centres would be necessary to provide the required infrastructure. Such a centre was opened in the latter part of 1997, as a programme of store openings had already been an idea that the management had been considering for some time. The company had previously considered franchising as a way to achieve this growth and the company did in 1999 enter into a seven-year contract that was signed with a large UK-based department store. However, subsequent market and business research regarding the UK market had suggested that franchising would not be an attractive/profitable propposition for a company like Taj-a-Jac Ltd and as a consequence the policy was abandoned.

A second alternative recommended was diversification. Significant experience of the import of quality pine from North America and Northern Europe was, the consultants suggested, not being exploited. The wholesale purchase of wood was therefore recommended. This had the added advantage of producing economies of scale which would have the effect of reducing unit costs. Charles and Thomas together with their senior managers had not previously considered this proposal and felt that so long as they were not supplying major competitors this was a proposition that could and should be pursued.

Thirdly, the consultants suggested the development of the 'lifestyle concept' store format – stores that not only sold furniture but also related accessories (such as soft furnishings) in a themed environment. Such stores had started to develop at the lower end of the market, but such a format had not yet been rolled out in the market sector that the company occupied. This proposal found immediate favour with some of the management board, although the size of each of the existing shops would not easily accommodate such a change. The movement to larger retail outlets or the opening of new additional stores that could accommodate this format would be necessary but costly.

Fourthly, the demand for English-designed quality furniture had always been popular in Asia. The region as a whole was becoming potentially a more significant market and the consultants argued that a gradual move into this market would in time reduce the company's dependence on UK demand. The consultants, concerned about the risk associated with this alternative, felt that expansion in this way should be via joint venture. This idea was one with which Charles, Thomas and their senior managers readily agreed.

The proposal suggested that, in the long-run, furniture should be manufactured in Asia using designs and templates from the UK. In the short and medium term, however, in order to establish the viability of the market, furniture should be exported – a practice that the consultants suggested should continue until the market was sufficiently mature – approximately five years hence.

As part of their review the consultants provided the following estimated summary costing for each of the alternatives.

### Alternative 1 – additional new stores
Initial investment cost        £86m
Potential annual income    £16m pa

### Alternative 2 – diversification
Initial investment cost        £23m
Potential annual income    £6m pa

### Alternative 3 – lifestyle concept
Initial investment cost        £57m
Potential annual income    £10m pa rising to £15m pa in four years

### Alternative 4 – move into the Asian market
Initial investment cost        £46m
Potential annual income    £6m pa rising to £14m pa in six years

Despite their caution, Charles and Thomas were keen to advance on each of the options identified by the external consultants. The question was how this growth should be financed. Financial advisors recommended a combination of possible financial strategies.

Since 1998 Taj-a-Jac Ltd had begun generating significant cash surpluses which, the financial advisors had suggested, should be used to partly fund the selected proposal/proposals. Another possibility, given the risks that expansion involved, was conversion to public limited company (plc) status so that a 'listing' might be sought. This, the consultants suggested, would raise an additional £40m.

In addition to this, the consultants suggested that debt instruments should be used to fund any remaining shortfall – given the current gearing ratio of the company. The company currently has a cost of equity of 12% and an after-tax cost of debt of 16%. In addition, it limits project life cycles to a maximum of 20 years. The company believes that if additional funds were raised through borrowing then its cost of equity would rise to 16%.

The following financial statements relate to Taj-a-Jac Ltd for the years 2001 to 2003.

## Balance sheets at 31 March

|  | 2001 £m | 2002 £m | 2003 £m |
|---|---|---|---|
| Fixed Assets | 36 | 47 | 75 |
| less Depreciation | 10 | 17 | 20 |
|  | 26 | 30 | 55 |
| Current Assets |  |  |  |
| Stocks | 16 | 16 | 20 |
| Trade Debtors | 28 | 47 | 57 |
| Debtors | 3 | 16 | 5 |
| Bank | 5 | 7 | 3 |
|  | 52 | 86 | 85 |
| Current Liabilities |  |  |  |
| Trade Creditors | 18 | 35 | 43 |
| Other Creditors | 15 | 7 | 15 |
| Taxation | 6 | 9 | 4 |
| Dividends | 3 | 4 | 3 |
|  | 42 | 55 | 65 |
| Total Net Assets | 36 | 61 | 75 |
| Long-Term Liabilities |  |  |  |
| Debentures | 2 | 14 | 20 |
|  | 34 | 47 | 55 |
| Capital |  |  |  |
| Share Capital | 20 | 32 | 40 |
| £1 Ordinary Shares |  |  |  |
| Accumulated Reserves | 14 | 15 | 15 |
|  | 34 | 47 | 55 |

## Profit and Loss Accounts for the years ending 31 March

|  | 2001 £m | 2002 £m | 2003 £m |
|---|---|---|---|
| Turnover | 40 | 60 | 80 |
| Cost of Sales | 12 | 20 | 38 |
| Gross Profit | 28 | 40 | 42 |
| Operating Expenses | 10 | 26 | 35 |
| Profit Before Taxation | 18 | 14 | 7 |
| Taxation | 6 | 9 | 4 |
| Profit After Taxation | 12 | 5 | 3 |
| Dividends | 6 | 4 | 3 |
| Retained Profit for the Year | 6 | 1 | 0 |

## Case study – discussion

Before we consider each component aspect of systems thinking, perhaps a summary of the key issues in the case study would be a useful starting point.

- Taj-a-Jac Ltd is an established and expanding business whose business environment is becoming increasingly competitive.
- The structure of the organisation has changed substantially over the past 20 years.
- Recent profits appear to be declining whilst turnover and demand for the company's products appears to be increasing.
- Many financial reasons could exist for this problem:
  - increasing cost of manufacture,
  - increasing revenue expenses,
  - over-capitalisation,
  - increased long-term debt, and
  - inconsistent working capital management.
- Each of these financial issues are merely products of a deeper process and/or systems problem – a problem recognised by the Taj-a-Jac Ltd management in their decision to undertake a strategic review with the aim of identifying an appropriate strategic plan/development not only to take the company forward but also to take advantage of an expanding marketplace.
- Four alternative strategies (and associate costs) have been identified each of which would have a significant impact on the functioning of Taj-a-Jac Ltd as a wealth maximising company.

### Input

Taj-a-Jac Ltd is clearly a manufacturing/retail company and as a result would attract/draw on an enormous range of both externalised and internalised inputs in order to function successfully. Some of the more important of these would be as follows:

- In terms of externalised inputs:
  - raw materials for the manufacture of specialist hand-crafted furniture,
  - human resources (skills of specialist trained woodworkers, etc. and other management and administrative staff),
  - financial resources,
  - data/information regarding resource availability, product demand, and changes in the marketplace regarding the structure of the market, prices and competitors.
- In terms of internalised inputs:
  - work-in-progress transferred between production processes, and
  - data/information regarding resource availability, internal production schedules and changes in operating procedures and management structures.

### Transformation process

As a complex manufacturing/retail company, Taj-a-Jac Ltd would have a number of interrelated transformation processes. At a superficial and somewhat generic level these transaction processes would include:

- acquisition transformation processes (expenditure cycle) – these would include converting/ transforming resource requirements into physical resources,
- conversion (manufacturing) transformation processes (conversion cycle) – these would include not only the conversion of raw materials to finished saleable products but also staff training (of employees from non-trained employees to specialist manufacturers),

- retail transformation processes (revenue cycle) – these would include the marketing and distribution of products and resources – converting potential demand to actual retail sales, and
- resource management transformation processes (management cycle) – these would include the conversion of sales into useable resources.

More importantly, each of the above transformation processes would also comprise of a number of self-contained but interrelated and interconnected transformation processes.

### Output

For Taj-a-Jac Ltd, externalised outputs would include, for example:

- finished products for sale,
- data/information about the company and its products, and
- financial performance information about the profitability of the company.

For Taj-a-Jac Ltd, internalised outputs (including data, information and resources) would occur at various stages of the transformation process, between the acquisition transformation processes, the conversion (manufacturing) transformation processes, the retail transformation processes, and the resource management transformation processes.

### Systems boundaries

Within Taj-a-Jac Ltd many functional boundaries would exist – some of which would be tangible and physically identifiable boundaries, others would be virtual and intangible. Whereas tangible boundaries would possibly act as barriers to prevent unauthorised access, for example:

- controlled access to manufacturing locations and retail locations outside normal retail hours, and
- security codes preventing access between different parts of the company, and
- password codes restricting access to the company's information database,

intangible or virtual boundaries would exist as a prescriptive demarcation, enforcing a limit within which the access to certain elements/components/attributes of the company and their interrelationships can be imposed. Such boundaries would include:

- the company organisational structure,
- work-related functional descriptors, which prescribe functions/duties within the company.

### Systems environment

For Taj-a-Jac Ltd (as a company), its systemic environment would comprise not only those external elements whose change may affect the nature, context, properties and functioning of the company, but also those elements which would themselves be affected by the company's behaviour. In essence the contemporary marketplace!

In such a marketplace key elements would include:

- shareholder pressure for increased value,
- supplier pressure,
- customer demand for greater value for money,
- market competitors,
- employees,
- debtors' demands for increase payment periods,

- creditor pressure for reduced payment times,
- directors,
- banks and other financial institutions, and
- government and other regulatory agencies.

Indeed, for Taj-a-Jac Ltd, changes to the nature and structure of the company's external environment, its increasing complexity and competitive nature is the source of both opportunity and concern. For example, whilst turnover has increased – clearly exploitation of market opportunities has occurred – profits have fallen, possibly due to a combination of operational problems resulting from external pressure/change.

Indeed, it is important to recognise that whilst the company as a whole has a systems environment outside its organisation boundaries, within the company individual sub-systems (e.g. conversion (manufacturing) transformation processes) would have an external systemic environment within the company governed to greater extent by internal management policy but nonetheless influenced by factors outside the company.

### Systems control

As a complex organisation functioning within a competitive but expanding business environment, it is perhaps important for the company not only to coordinate and regulate its activities, but also monitor efficiency and/or compare performance and activity to expectations. Such control would normally exist at a number of levels within Taj-a-Jac Ltd – at a strategic level, at a tactical level and of course at an operational level.

In a systems context, strategic control would normally be feedforward in nature, tactical control would be a combination of both feedforward and feedback, whereas operational control would almost entirely be feedback orientated:

- At a strategic level control issues would consider:
  - environmental pressures affecting the company,
  - the appropriate business focus for Taj-a-Jac Ltd, and
  - general financing requirements of the company.
- At a tactical level control issues would consider:
  - medium-term allocation of resource to company activities,
  - the quality policy of the company,
  - production management (including resource allocation) of the company, and
  - organisation facilities required to meet corporate objectives.
- At an operational level control issues would consider:
  - short-term allocation of resource to company activities, and
  - day-to-day management of operational resources.

### Systems objectives/goals

In a commercial competitive context, a company has two primary objectives/goals. Objective one is survival! Objective two is the maximisation of shareholder wealth, that is maximising the value of the company as expressed as follows;

$$v = (i, f, d, m)$$

where:

$i$ = the investment decision

$f$ = the financing decision

$d$ = the dividend (or distribution) decision

$m$ = the management of corporate resources.

For Taj-a-Jac Ltd, both of the above objectives are clearly evident in the company's considera-tion of the alternative strategic options suggested by the consultants.

Clearly objective one is contingent upon successfully meeting objective two and for Taj-a-Jac Ltd the falling profits indicate that the company is experiencing some difficulty in achieving this.

### Equifinalty

Clearly corporate survival and wealth maximisation can be achieved in a number of different ways as illustrated by the proposals made by the consultants to the management of Taj-a-Jac Ltd.

For example:

- proposal 1 considers regional consolidation through corporate franchising,
- proposal 2 considers vertical diversification,
- proposal 3 considers horizontal diversification and development of a lifestyle concept, and
- proposal 4 considers market/geographical relocation and a move to the Asian market through a joint venture arrangement.

Although each of the of the above proposals appear viable (in a purely financial (NPV) context):

- proposal 1:   $(-£86m) + (£16m \times 5.9288) = £8.86m$
- proposal 2:   $(-£23m) + (£6m \times 5.9288) = £12.57m$
- proposal 3:   $(-£57m) + ((£10m \times 2.7982) + (£15m \times 3.3106)) = £17.94m$
- proposal 4:   $(-46m) + ((£6m \times 3.6847) + (£14m \times 2.2441)) = £7.52m,$

they each nevertheless possess varying degrees of associated systemic risk (both internal and external), with perhaps proposal 3 being the least risky, then proposal 1, then proposal 2, and finally proposal 4 is the most risky.

Whilst such risk assessment is clearly very subjective, it can, in a very broad sense, be analysed from a purely systemic context in terms of systems adaptability, which is itself dependent upon:

- the degree of integration – that is shared and overlapping systems,
- the extent to which systems are interconnected,
- the need for systems decoupling,
- possible existence of multiple and conflicting objectives,
- existence of systems constraints, and finally
- the possibility of sub-optimality.

### Systems adaptability

For Taj-a-Jac Ltd, as a semi-open system, both the company's inputs and outputs (and therefore its transaction processing system(s) are clearly affected by changes in the company's environment, an environment that appears to be increasingly competitive, uncertain and unpredictable.

Of course regular strategic monitoring of the company's environment can clearly assist in minimising the impact of such environmental change. Indeed, and as indicated in the case study scenario, such monitoring has revealed an urgent need for adaptation/change. The success of any of the proposals identified by the consultants appointed by the management of Taj-a-Jac Ltd would of course be conditional upon the company's ability to adapt/change. Identifying/knowing what needs to be done is only part of the solution. Structuring that knowledge and successfully implementing a strategy based on that knowledge are the keys to future survival – both of which are dependant upon the company's flexibility and adaptability.

So what about Taj-a-Jac Ltd? Does the company appear to be sufficiently adaptable? Whilst there is no direct evidence – the answer (intuitively perhaps) is probably yes!

The very fact that such monitoring takes place would suggest that the management of the company are more than aware of the marketplace within which they operate; more than aware of the possible consequences to the company of a lack of adaptability, a lack of flexibility, a lack of reflexivity.

### Shared and overlapping systems

One common feature of all commercial entities, including Taj-a-Jac Ltd, is that they are composite systems – they are systems that are themselves comprised of a number of smaller sub-systems each of which can belong to, be accountable to or indeed be managed by more than one system or sub-system.

Consider the following. In Taj-a-Jac Ltd we earlier identified four transformation processes or functional cycles (sub-systems),

- an acquisition transformation process (or an expenditure cycle),
- a conversion (manufacturing) transformation process (or a conversion cycle),
- a retail transformation process (or a revenue cycle), and
- a resource management transformation process (or a management cycle).

Within each of these functional cycles[10] (or sub-systems) a number of sub-systems will exist, for example:

- An expenditure cycle would contain:
  - a procurement control system,
  - a receiving and inspection system, and
  - a purchasing and creditor system.
- A conversion cycle would contain:
  - a stock control system,
  - a production control system, and
  - a payroll system.
- A revenue cycle would contain:
  - a marketing system,
  - a transportation system, and
  - a sales and debtors system.
- A management cycle would contain:
  - a cash receipts and payments system,
  - a fixed assets and property system, and
  - a general ledger management system

It is possible, indeed probable, that within each of the above cycles and sub-systems some sharing/overlap will exist. Such overlap may be in terms of:

- sharing of data/information,
- interrelated activities, and
- shared resources, including staffing.

For example the cash receipts and payments system (management cycle) will clearly be related and connected to the purchasing and creditor system (expenditure cycle) and the sales and debtors system (revenue cycle). Whilst such sharing/overlapping does provide some benefit in terms of organisational rationalisation and potential cost saving, excessive sharing/overlapping can if unmonitored lead to:

- the emergence of highly politicised bureaucracies,
- an increased lack of trust between system members, and
- a failure of systems control and ultimately systemic failure.

More importantly for Taj-a-Jac Ltd, is the need not only to understand, but also appreciate the possible outcomes, implications and any emergent problems that may arise as a result of any organisational change (from implementing any of the four proposals) on shared/overlapping or multiple-owned systems.

### Interconnections

As a company, the systems (and sub-systems) that operate within Taj-a-Jac Ltd would not only be interconnected by way of input, output or by processing relationship but would also be interdependent upon one another – interacting and exchanging data and information at various levels of activity.

As with shared/overlapping systems and sub-systems, interconnectivity provides a number of benefits, in terms of control and accountability, but also problems if such connections are not appropriately managed. The result often excessive procedural bureaucracy and deficient time management.

Taj-a-Jac Ltd does appear to have some problems in this area – a problem substantiated by the existence of significant problems in working capital management. The source of this problem could exist at two distinct levels:

- systems/sub-systems interconnections may not be functioning adequately because of internal/external change, or
- systems/sub-systems have become decoupled.

### Decoupling

Although in a business context systems decoupling is part of the systems/sub-systems life cycle and occurs periodically – for example at year-end close down in terms of not only stock control, separating production from the stock management systems, but also in terms of financial accounting systems and the preparation of year-end statutory financial reports – the case study does not indicate whether direct activity decoupling exists on an operational level. However, there is some circumstantial evidence to suggest that some (at least partial) decoupling exists in:

- the expenditure cycle – within the procurement control system, and the purchasing and creditor system,
- the conversion cycle – within the stock control system,
- the revenue cycle – within the sales and debtors system, and
- the management systems – within the cash receipts and payments system, and the general ledger management system.

### Multiple and conflicting objectives

Earlier we suggested that Taj-a-Jac Ltd has two key objectives – survival, and once that is achieved, the maximisation of shareholder wealth. However, within each of these somewhat holistic objectives there exist a number of subsidiary (sub-systems) objectives:

- In the expenditure cycle:
  - procurement control system – to obtain the best quality raw materials at competitive prices,
  - receiving and inspection system – to ensure all materials are inspected within a specified time period and all sub-standard materials identified and appropriate action taken, and

- a purchasing and creditor system – to ensure all payments are made in accordance with supplier/company requirements.
- In the conversion cycle:
  - stock control system – to maintain sufficient stock to meet production requirements
  - production control system – to ensure appropriate quality standards are maintained,
  - payroll system – to ensure payments are made in accordance with company/legal requirements.
- In the revenue cycle:
  - marketing system – to ensure products are appropriately advertised/marketed,
  - transportation system – to ensure all sales are securely transported to customer location, and
  - sales and debtors system – to ensure products are appropriately priced, and all receipts are received in accordance with company requirements.
- In the management cycle:
  - cash receipts and payments system – to ensure adequate records and controls are maintained, and
  - fixed assets and property system – to ensure all assets are properly accounted for and legal titles securely maintained.

Whilst each of these appears appropriate conflict could arise between, for example, the need for best quality materials (procurement control system), the pricing of products (sales and debtors system) and the overall objective of maximising shareholder wealth. Why? Quality materials may incur substantial costs. Unless passed on to the customer such costs could reduce overall profits and therefore shareholder wealth.

Clearly the existence of such multiple objectives is not uncommon but conflicting objectives can, if not appropriately managed, result in the inefficient use of resources and in a systems context entropy and ultimately systems failure.

### Systems constraints

For Taj-a-Jac Ltd a number of internal and external constraints, or in a more accounting context, limiting factors, may exist. These are elements that not only constrain current activity, but may also limit the possible success of the proposals identified by the consultants. Such constraints could include:

- possible lack of raw materials,
- lack of specialist manufacturers,
- lack of financial resources to fund current and future activities,
- uncertainty of future demand, and
- possible legal restrictions.

### Sub-optimality

For Taj-a-Jac Ltd there is clearly some sub-optimality – a simple financial analysis of the company's profit and loss account and balance sheet clearly indicates the existence (in 2003 at least) of increasingly significant problems regarding working capital management especially debtor management and creditor management. Whilst it is unclear as to whether such sub-optimality is a result of:

- a lack of coordination with the business as a whole, for example individual employees working towards a set of personal objectives/agenda to the detriment of the company as a whole, or
- generic inefficiency increasingly endemic within the company's operations, or
- a failure of the management of the company to respond/adapt to environmental turbulence,

its existence is nevertheless worrying and perhaps a contributing factor in the management of Taj-a-Jac Ltd seeking the advice of a consultant.

## Concluding comments

General systems theory arose out of a generic interest in finding a general theory of similarity between different systems – a fundamental theory that could address problems associated with, and related to:

- order,
- structure, and
- organisation.

The aim of such a general systems theory is to provide a set of unifying principles of organisation that could be applied to all organisations at all levels of complexity (von Bertalanffy, 1968).

In essence, general systems theory addresses a number of structural and relational issues that are common to a vast range of interdisciplinary studies (including accounting and finance). Perhaps, more importantly, general systems theory, or systems thinking, provides a framework – a conceptual model – that can be applied to a diverse range of scientific and business areas. Indeed business practitioners and management scientists have learned a great deal about organisations and how they work by utilising a systems perspective, the benefits of which have been:

- more effective problem solving,
- more effective leadership,
- more effective communications,
- more effective planning, and
- more effective organisational development.

However, despite such benefits, as a conceptual framework, general systems theory and systems thinking do nonetheless possess a number of major limitations, including:

- general systems theory is by its very nature 'general' and as such is often accused of being ineffective in explaining anything,
- general systems theory adopts a somewhat hard structured analytical approach, and rejects/ignores the human factor or the behavioural context of systems and, perhaps more importantly,
- general systems theory imposes a very prescriptive mechanistic framework that necessitates the use of an overly functional analytical context.

So, if systems thinking possesses so many limitations – why is it used? Firstly, in the context of contemporary capitalism, general systems theory and systems thinking provides an assessable (if somewhat limited) framework that can be used not only to monitor but more importantly control business activity. Secondly, as a broad conceptual model general systems theory provides an acceptable conceptual version of how the physical aspects of capital move within the business environment.

And third, general systems theory provides a rational (if again somewhat limited) basis on which conceptual models of organisational structures (including those of a company) can be constructed.

## Key points and concepts

Closed system

Decoupling

Dynamic system

Entropy

Equifinality

Hard system

Modernity

Open system

Semi-open system

Soft system

Static system

System adaptability

System boundary

System optimality

Systems environment

Trust system

## References

Aglietta, M. (1979) *A Theory of Capitalist Regulation*, New Left Books, London.

Andre, C. and Delorme, R. (1982) *L'Etat et l'économie*, Seuil, Paris.

Berman, M. (1982), *All That is Solid Melts into Air: The Experience of Modernity*, Simon and Schuster, New York.

Burrell, G. and Morgan, G. (1979) *Sociological Paradigms and Organisational Analysis: Elements of the Sociology of Corporate Life*, Heinemann, London.

Dosi, G., Freeman, G., Nelson, R., Silverberg, G. and Soete, L. (1988) *Technical Change and Economic Theory*, Francis Pinter, London.

Freeman, C., Clark, J. and Soete, L. (1982) *Unemployment and Technological Innovation: A study of Long Waves in Economic Development*, Francis Pinter, London.

Freeman, G. and Perez, C. (1988) 'Structural Crisis of Adjustment, Business Cycles, and Investment Behaviour', in Dosi, G., Freeman, G., Nelson, R., Silverberg, G. and Soete, L. (eds) *Technical Change and Economic Theory*, Francis Pinter, London.

Giddens, A. (1990) *The Consequences of Modernity*, Polity Press, Cambridge.

Harvey, D. (1987) 'Flexible Accumulation through Urbanisation: Reflections on Post Modernism in the American City', *Antipode*, 19(3), pp. 260–286.

Harvey, D. (1990) *The Condition of Post Modernity*, Basil Blackwell, London.

Harvey, D. (1991) 'Flexibility: Threat or Opportunity', *Socialist Review*, 21(1), pp. 65–77.

Harvey, D. and Scott, A.J. (1988) 'The Practice of Human Geography: Theory and Empirical Specificity in the Transition from Fordism to Flexible Accumulation', in MacMillan (ed.) *Remodelling Geography*, Blackwell, Oxford.

Hirst, P. and Zeitlin, J. (1989) 'Flexible Specialisation and the Failure of UK Manufacturing', *Political Quarterly*, 60(3), pp. 164–178.

Hirst, P. and Zeitlin, J. (1991) 'Flexible Specialisation vs. post Fordism: Theory, Evidence and Policy Implications', *Economy and Society*, 20(1).

Jackson, M.C. (1991) *Systems Methodology for the Management Sciences*, Plenum, London.

Katz, D. and Kahn, R.L. (1966), *The Social Psychology of Organisations*, Wiley, New York.

Lash, S. and Urry, J. (1987) *The end of Organised Capitalism*, Polity Press, Cambridge.

Lash, S. and Urry, J. (1993) *Economics of Signs and Space: After Organised Capitalism*, Sage, London.

Lipietz, A. (1985) *The Enchanted World: Inflation, Credit and the World Crisis*, Verso, London.

Lipietz, A. (1987) *Mirages and Miracle: The Crisis of Global Fordism*, Verso, London.

Lucy, T. (2000) *Management Information Systems*, Letts, London.

Offe, C. (1985) *Disorganised Capitalism*, Polity Press, Cambridge.

Parsons, T. (1937) *The Structure of Socialisation*, McGraw Hill, New York.

Parsons, T. (1951) *The Social System*, Chicago Free Press, Chicago.

Parsons, T. (1966), 'The Political Aspect of Social Structure and Process', in Easton, D. (ed.) *Varieties of Political Theory*, Prentice-Hall, Englewood Cliffs, New Jersey.

Parsons, T. (1971), 'Action Systems and Social Systems', in *The System of Modern Societies*, Prentice-Hall, Englewood Cliffs, New Jersey.

Piore, M.J. and Sabel, C.F. (1984) *The Second Industrial Divide*, Basic Books, New York.

Sabel, C. (1982), *Work and Politics: The Division of Labour in Industry*, Cambridge University Press, Cambridge.

Sabel, C. and Zeitlin, J, (1985), 'Historical Alternatives to Mass Production: Politics, Markets, and Technology in 19th Century Industrialisation', *Past and Present*, no. 108, pp. 133–176.

Schumpeter, J. (1987) *Capitalism, Socialism, Democracy*, Allen and Urwin, London.

von Bertalanffy, L. (1936) 'A quantitative theory of organic growth', *Human Biology*, 10, pp. 181–213.

von Bertalanffy, L. (1968) *General System Theory: Foundations, Development, and Application*, George Braziller, New York.

Wren, D.A. (1994) *The evolution of management thought*, Wiley, New York.

## Bibliography

Ackoff, R.L. (1971) 'Towards a systems of systems concepts', *Management Science,* 17(11).

Checkland, P. (1981) *Systems Thinking, Systems Practice*, John Wiley, London.

Harry, M. (1994) *Information Systems in Business*, Pitman, London.

Kim, D.H. (1999) *Introduction to Systems Thinking*, Pegasus Communications, London.

Laszlo, E. (1996) *Systems view of the world*, Hampton Press, London.

O'Connor, J. and McDermot, I. (1997) *The Art of Systems Thinking*, Thorsons, New York.

Wienberg, G. (2001) *Introduction to General Systems Theory*, Dorset House, London.

## Websites

www.systemsthinkingpress.com
Chaos Theory – Critical Thinking, Organisational Development Portal

http://pespmc1.vub.ac.be/
Principia Cybernetica webpage

Other websites you may find helpful in gaining an insight into more accounting related discussion and systems thinking include:

www.accaglobal.com
(Chartered Association of Certified Accountants)
www.cimaglobal.com
(Chartered Institute of Management Accountants)
www.ft.com
(Financial Times)
www.economist.com
(Economist)

www.guardian.co.uk
(Guardian)
www.accountingweb.co.uk
(general accounting website)

## Self-review questions

1. Briefly explain the concept of 'trust in systems'.
2. What are the key features of the systems approach?
3. Distinguish between a soft system and a hard system.
4. What is sub-optimality?
5. What is the transformation process and why is knowledge of organisational boundaries important?
6. Why are systems boundaries so important?
7. What are the key features of a closed system and an open system?
8. A sales system has 14 sub-systems. How many possible connections could there be?
9. What is entropy?
10. Distinguish between a closed system and an open system.

## Questions and problems

### Question 1

Classical systems theory often considers a company to be a 'hard' closed system, whereas contemporary systems theory often considers a company to be a 'soft' open system.

#### Required

Define the 'hard' and 'soft' systems.

With the aid of diagrams, comment on and discuss the difference between these two theoretical approaches and their implications on designing computer-based accounting information systems.

### Question 2

Read the following extract:

*Management do not always know what information they need and information specialists often do not know enough about management in order to produce relevant information for the managers they serve. An example given by Professor Kaplan graphically illustrates this point. He reported that a group of American industrialists visiting Japan found that their counterparts were regularly supplied with information on the proportion of products which pass through the factory without re-working or rectification. They found that a typical percentage of products that needed no re-working was 92%. The American managers found that this information was not available to them at their factories at home but on investigation it was found that their ratio was 8%. They then worked on this factor for 6 months at which point the ratio had moved up to 66% and, more importantly, productivity was 25% higher (Lucy, 2000: 3).*

Assume that you are the Information Systems Director of Test Kits Ltd. This is a growing company that produces a range of chemical test kits for a wide range of products and markets. Currently the company is experiencing a boom in demand for its BSE test kit for beef.

You were planning a presentation to the Board of Directors entitled 'The accounting information system – an abstract representation of the company', when your Managing Director hands you the above quotation. He asks you to address those issues raised in the quotation in your presentation and also how they affect lower, middle and senior management.

Draft out the main points of the Information Systems Director's presentation. Ensure that you include a definition and diagram of a system and its principal components, explain the main systems concepts and address the practical problems raised in the quotation.

## Question 3

Read the following extract:

> *Sociological systems theory contributed a profound understanding of the nature and role of organis-ational sub-systems in meeting organisational needs. . . . The inspiration came in the form of a rigorous working out of the idea that organisms – and other types of complex systems – were* **'open systems'** (Jackson, 1991: 48).

*Required*

Explain, with the aid of a diagram, the relevance to an understanding of the accounting information system of '*open systems*'.

## Question 4

Katz and Kahn in *The Social Psychology of Organisations* (1966) cite five generic types of sub-system to meet an organisation's functional needs:

- The *production* or technical sub-system, concerned with the work done on the throughput.
- The *supportive* sub-system, concerned with obtaining inputs and disposing of outputs.
- The *maintenance* sub-system, which ensures conformance of personnel to their roles through selection, and through rewards and sanctions.
- The *adaptive* sub-system, ensuring responsiveness to environmental variations.
- The *managerial* sub-system, which directs, coordinates and controls other sub-systems and activities through various regulatory mechanisms.

*Required*

Identify these sub-systems in accounting terms and give an example of how the accounting information system obtains and supplies information for each of these sub-systems.

## Question 5

Using general systems theory as your analytical framework, identify and describe the main control elements of a medium-sized fast-moving consumer goods company's accounting system. In your description you should identify how each of the component parts of the accounting system are connected together and the related information requirements of each component part.

## Assignments

### Question 1

In December 2002, ERT plc, an established retail company located in the north-east of England, merged with PLR plc, an Edinburgh-based company that had been operating successfully for over 45 years and who had over the past seven years become a major competitor of ERT plc. In December 2002, the combined companies began trading as GBI plc.

Both ERT plc and PLR plc had enjoyed record profits during 2000 and 2001.

Although market reaction to the acquisition was positive with GBI's share price rising dramatically, the overall profitability and efficiency of the new merged company fell sharply during 2003, with GBI recording an annual trading loss in January 2004.

In March 2004, the management of GBI appointed consultants to identify why such a fall in the company's fortunes had occurred. The consultants' report was highly critical, suggesting that the core problems being experienced by GBI had resulted from an incompatibility of the ERT and PRT accounting information systems. In particular, the consultants identified an inability of GBI's management to understand the nature of systemic functional cycles of operation and the implications of systems theory in the management of corporate activity.

#### Required

(a) Describe and diagrammatically represent the main functional cycles of operation that may exist in a retail company such a GBI plc.
(b) Explain briefly why in the context of the above scenario the ERT's and PRT's cycles of operations may have been incompatible.
(c) Explain how a knowledge of systems theory may have assisted the management of GBI in their attempt to reverse the decline in the new company's financial fortune.

### Question 2

GHS Ltd is a small local company that sells motor car accessories. The company has 26 small retail outlets located throughout the UK. Each retail outlet employs five people: a sales assistant, a receptionist/secretary, two technical advisors and a manager.

The company operates a networked EPOS (electronic point of sale) system for all sales.

Sales are:

- through the companies website,
- by mail order, or
- over-the-counter cash/credit card sales.

Internet sales are handled by the company's head office and despatched from the company's main distribution centre in Crawley.

Mail order and over-the-counter sales are handled by the sales assistant at each individual retail outlet.

Over-the-counter sales can be for cash, credit card payment or payment by cheque. The sales assistant records the sale using the company's EPOS system and issues a sales receipt to the customer.

Mail order sales are only accepted from authorised customers. These customers are authorised by the retail outlet manager and are allowed 30 days' credit.

All mail order sales are recorded as a deferred sale using the company's EPOS system.

A list of these sales is held by the sales assistant until the payment is received when payment is recorded. Payments not received within the 30-day period are referred to the manager.

The receptionist/secretary opens all incoming mail and passes any payments to the manager for review. The manager passes these back to the sales assistant for recording in the company's EPOS system, and for the issue of a receipt which is sent back to the customer.

The sales assistant passes all cash and cheques back to the manager, in time for them to be banked each day, when the manager leaves to pick up his children from school. The manager also prepares the bank deposit slip.

The manager is solely responsible for any discounts and verifies these before payments are recorded in the company's EPOS system. The manager is also responsible for writing off any bad debts after seeking and receiving approval for these actions from head office.

### Required

Describe the system from a systems perspective, including suggestions for improvements.

## Chapter endnotes

[1] The term 'systems thinking' is used in preference to systems theory and/or general systems theory.

[2] Teleology is the supposition that there is purpose or directive principle in the works and processes of nature and society.

[3] For the neo-Marxist regulation school's socio-political account and its emphasis on the increasing tension between social modes of regulation and regimes of accumulation see Aglietta (1979), Andre and Delorme (1982) and Lipietz (1985, 1987).

[4] For the neo-Smithian flexible specialisation account and its emphasis on the structural relationship between dominant economic and political institutions see Sabel (1982), Piore and Sabel (1984), Sabel and Zeitlin (1985) and Hirst and Zeitlin (1989, 1991).

[5] For the neo-Schumpeterian approach, based predominantly on the premise of technological determinism reminiscent of Kondratiev's long wave theory, see Freeman *et al.* (1982), Dosi *et al.* (1988), Freeman and Perez (1988) and Schumpeter (1987).

[6] For the disorganised capitalism thesis and its emphasis on an increasing disorganisation of regimes of accumulation emerging out of the material conditions associated with the powerful structure of class politics see Lash and Urry (1987, 1993) and Offe (1985).

[7] For the flexible accumulation approach and its increasing emphasis on the impact of time–space compression and the increasing dominance of fictions in regimes of accumulation see Harvey (1987, 1990, 1991) and Harvey and Scott (1988).

[8] Pricing efficiency refers to the notion that prices should reflect in an unbiased way all available information. Operational efficiency refers to the level of costs of carrying out transactions within the marketplace, whereas allocational efficiency refers to the extent to which capital is allocated to the most profitable enterprise.

[9] Based on a case study developed by Geffory Firth, University of Lincoln.

[10] We will consider these functional cycles in Part 3 of this book.

# 3 Control theories:
## management by design

## Introduction

There can be little doubt that in the latter part of the 20th century and indeed the early part of the 21st century, market-based corporate activity has become overwhelmed by a social and political typology increasingly dominated by the economics of the 'free' marketplace. This has come about by an emphasis on reducing social diversity, minimising political prejudices, and eliminating economic asymmetries; by a push toward a single market, a single borderless society, a single global culture, a single homogenous polity.

Yet, although this seemingly unstoppable force – this immovable drive toward 'singularity' – toward a global oneness (in a commercial sense at least!) has produced many benefits, it has done so at some considerable cost. Whilst for some it has produced larger choice and greater freedom, and for others it has resulted in increased wealth and amazing prosperity, for yet others it has resulted in social poverty, economic destitution and political isolation. Whilst consideration of such issues is clearly beyond the scope of this book it is important to acknowledge that this relentless and often inescapable global pursuit of gain and profit – this inevitable push toward a single global marketplace – has become synonymous with a much more subtle if somewhat disconcerting trend. A trend encapsulating a conscious desire to minimise risk, reduce uncertainty, increase efficiency and maximise return. A covert trend of increasing bureaucracy, of greater regulation and of increased surveillance – a trend towards greater and greater control!

But what is control? A simple and obvious, yet deceptively difficult question to answer. Why? Because unfortunately, control is many things – to many people.

In a socio-cultural context the concept of control is sometimes 'individualised'. It is often defined and associated with adroitness, with the ability to illustrate great discipline and specialty and the capacity to exercise and demonstrate skilfulness and knowledge. Although we will not discount this notion of control completely, for the present we will restrict our discussion on control (and control theory) to what can be described as the 'group' or the 'entity' contextualisation – to the corporate perspective. For example, in a transactional/ commercial context control can be associated with the capacity to direct or determine a function and/or outcome, with the ability to regulate and manage, with planning and standard setting, and with comparison, evaluation, verification and validation, whereas in a governance/regulatory context control is normally associated with notions of power, surveillance and regulation, and with the imposition of authority and the capacity to exercise restraining commanding power, determine regulatory context and impose absolute exclusivity.

What is important here is to recognise that in the group or the entity contextualisation, control is an 'imposed' construct – a construct whose regulatory technology is neither objective nor neutral. It is a political construct – a construct dominated by the demands of the economic. Whether such control is in the form of polite informal restraint, passive formal guidance, or indeed an imposed authoritative regulation, its underlying context is rarely concerned with merely maintaining stability and order – it is rarely concerned with social conscience. There can be little doubt that as society treads warily into the early part of the 21st century, control has become undeniably market-based and unquestionably profit-orientated.

The aim of this chapter is to ascertain the key features of control theory and explore how and why control (and control theory) has become fundamental to contemporary capitalism. It has become fundamental not only to:

- ensuring the efficient and effective use of corporate resources,
- facilitating cooperation in the achievement of corporate objectives/goals, and
- minimising the impact of unpredictable disturbances on corporate activities,

but more importantly, for our purposes, to ensuring the reliability and relevance of information – in particular accounting information.

## Learning outcomes

This chapter explores a wide range of issues relating to control theory and its application in the development and management of accounting information systems and provides an introduction to how control theory has been, and indeed continues to be, increasingly relevant to understanding the complex nature of 21st century corporate activity.

By the end of this chapter, the reader should be able to:

- explain the contextual nature of control,
- understand the importance of control in complex systems,
- describe the basic elements of control,
- critically evaluate the relevance of environmental factors on control, and
- distinguish between feedback and feedforward, explaining their importance in control.

## Capital, control[1] and a trust in systems

As indicated earlier, there can be little doubt that today's global market is a product of many forces and influences. From an evermore disembedded spread of companies, to an increasing use of fictitious capital,[2] to an escalating growth in the marketability of technology and information.

Indeed, many business commentators and academics suggest we now live in what some term a 'global village', in which the increasing marginalisation of state power and territorial sovereignty have become secondary to the unremitting push towards a borderless society/polity – a push towards a global marketplace.

From colonial capitalism of the 16th century, to entrepreneurial capitalism and so-called international capitalism of the late 19th and early 20th century, to multinational/global capitalism of the late 20th century, to perhaps now the derivative/fictitious capitalism of the late 20th and early 21st century (further details are available on the website accompanying this text www.pearsoned.co.uk/Boczko), we now live in a global marketplace synonymous with:

- a continuing deregulation of markets,
- an increasing international transferability of capital, and
- an increasing dependency on, and evermore global commodification of knowledge and information systems.

Clearly, markets have changed/grown, technologies have developed and societies (well parts of some societies at least!) have embraced the new world order and the unstoppable force of commercialisation, of marketisation and globalisation. Today, capital is intrinsically global – all the advanced economies of the world are involved. Increasingly, political social and technological innovations develop subordinate to the needs of wealth accumulation and profit maximisation. Global capital flows are thus politically dynamic and technologically deliberate. Whilst some believe such global capital flows have helped to enhance social mobility and consumer sovereignty, others believe that such flows have helped to undermine territorial autonomy, national stability and cultural self-sufficiency (Amin, 1994; Lipietz, 1994). They have resulted in social exploitation, economic subordination, political volatility and environmental commodification, and have continued to promote economic polarisation and financial instability (Savage and Warde 1993). The heated debate continues!

But what has this all meant for the 'company' – the corporate entity? Well, as part of this 'global village', this increasingly technology-driven 'information society', this global marketplace now dominated by virtual trading and fictitious (derivative) capital (Harvey, 1990; Cerny, 1994), companies have become increasingly bound up with or, perhaps more appropriately, increasingly dependent upon:

- virtual systems for collecting, storing, and processing data and information,
- technology-based networks of surveillance, and
- systems of organisational control.

There are a number of reasons for this. Firstly, market-based capitalism is an institutional system founded on commodity production and exchange (Palloix, 1975, 1977; McChestney, 1999) and as suggested in Chapter 1 seeks to sustain a liberal ideology of the 'dominance of capital' and 'freedom of accumulation'. Consequently, the need to know and the ability to control internalised activity, not only to:

- coordinate business activity and resource utilisation, and
- the socialisation of people and procedures,

but also to monitor the impact/consequences of an ever-changing business environment in order to:

- ensure environmental fit,
- reduce the impact of environmental disturbances,
- provide a framework of conformity,

are now a central feature of the competitive market-based activity.

Secondly, the competitive nature of market capital and the increasing implications of technology have altered the 'perceived' structure and nature of business activity – of the corporate entity. They are no longer regarded as just collections of tangible assets and resources. Companies are now seen as complex 'social' arrangements of interacting intangible systems or procedures – of connections and interconnections. The contemporary framework of analysis of corporate activity has clearly moved from 'what do we do' – that is from being output driven – to 'how do we do it' – that is to being process driven.

Thirdly, the increasing complexity of the so-called 'global market' and the increasing uncertainty competition brings to those operating in such markets has resulted in a growing notion of agency and governance – of separation between ownership and control. Clearly such a notion of separation is by no means a contemporary phenomenon. Formally, such an enduring notion has probably existed since the creation of joint stock companies in the mid-19th century. Informally however, it has probably existed since the dawn of civilization and commercial trade, although its expression has, certainly during the latter part of the 20th century and early 21st century, manifest itself with much more clarity and urgency.

Such separation – between ownership and control – and indeed notions of agency and governance require at the very least not only an acknowledgement of the concept of accountability, but more importantly an acknowledgement of the notion of trust – in particular a trust in systems.

We will return to the notions and concepts of agency and governance, in particular corporate governance, later in this chapter. For the moment however, let's have a look at this notion of trust – of trust in systems!

Historically (in a corporate context at least) trust was in the majority of cases placed in, or assigned to people, as representatives, as sentient expressions of the business entity, of the corporate entity. Physicality it appeared ruled! Today however, trust is no longer merely placed in people or individuals – if at all. It is placed in systems and information – in the networks and the procedures and the interconnections that exist within and between corporate entities.

Consider the following.

*Imagine you are an elderly customer entering a bank to deposit money into your current account. At the bank counter you are greeted by a counter clerk who will deal with your transaction. As an elderly customer you may well believe that as the transaction that takes place there is trust relationship (however limited) between you as the customer and the counter clerk – a trust that is founded on the assumption that the correct procedures will be followed, the transaction will be properly processed and the money will be paid into the correct current account – your account.*

*In reality, however, this is not the case. As a customer you have (in the majority of cases at least) often no knowledge of the bank clerk apart from, say, a name badge and evidence that the bank clerk actually works for the bank. (We will discount here any possibility that the bank clerk may be an impostor or villain waiting to defraud the bank.) The customer's trust is not placed with the individual bank clerk, but in the system that the bank clerk represents and more importantly the systems that actually facilitated the bank clerk's presence at the counter to deal with customers in the first place!*

So trust is an important characteristic of contemporary corporate activity – both customer-based activity and corporate-based activity – but exactly what do we mean by trust?

Trust is essentially a belief – a firm belief in the reliability, honesty, veracity, justice, strength, etc of a person or thing. Trust is historically a product of human nature – a human construct designed to protect. A construct designed to minimise uncertainty and risk. In an anthropological context trust was, and indeed continues to be, associated with notions of cultural kinship and community, with notions of hierarchy and deference, with respect and responsibility, and with locality. However, contemporary society, or modernity, has, with all its complex processes and interconnections, detached social relations from their local contexts, their communities and their local hierarchies, and restructured them often across infinite spans of time and space.

Such complex processes are often referred to as 'disembedding mechanisms' (see Giddens, 1990). Disembedding mechanisms are those aspects of contemporary society that allow individuals and/or organisations such as companies to create and develop distance relations.

Whilst such disembedding mechanisms can be varied, and will undoubtedly have their roots in antiquity, in a contemporary context – or at the very least in a market capital context – there are perhaps two key and important disembedding mechanisms, these being:

- a trust in the use of symbolic tokens (e.g. money), and
- a trust in expert systems (e.g. a body of reflexive knowledge).

Have a look at the following.

*In contemporary society, as individuals we cannot produce or manufacture everything we need, want or desire. We live in an exchange environment in which we trade our services for a 'variable' financial reward depending on our skill/knowledge/abilities. A financial reward which we then use to acquire the things we need, want or desire. More importantly, we cannot know everything we need to know.*

*The world is too complex and because of this complexity we depend on others to help us navigate through the complexity – to demystify it and to make it less complex. This process of demystification however is far from straightforward and rarely apolitical!*

*Obviously there is again a price attached to such knowledge, information and demystification, and so again we are intrinsically associated with and/or connected to the exchange environment – the market process. And, as we enter the 21st century, our trust in the use of these symbolic tokens (of these expert systems) has been given further urgency by the impact of technology. Just think of a modern society without credit and debit cards, e-commerce, e-banking and everything else 'e'-based!*

In a contemporary context at least then, trust is no longer 'just' a confidence in the reliability of a person or persons. It is more importantly a confidence in the reliability of a system or a set of procedures and/or process(es) – on a particular outcome or an event. Indeed, contrary to popular belief, the requirement for trust – for the existence of a trust based interrelationship is not a lack of power. It is a lack of knowledge or understanding, a lack of ability, a lack of information.

And, here it seems that market-based capitalism is not without a sense of irony. Why? Because as the changing dynamic of the global market becomes evermore complex and individuals become increasingly dependent on symbolic tokens and expert systems – as companies become evermore integrated, interconnected and interdependent, evermore technology orientated and virtual – they become evermore disembedded and spatially remote. Evermore dependent on continual recreation and the development of distance relations.

Think of some of the world's largest companies and consider their spatiality! For example:

- BP plc[3] is one of Britain's biggest companies and one of the largest oil and petrochemicals groups in the world. The company has operations in over 70 countries. During 2003 it employed 103,700 employees and generated revenues of $233bn.

- HSBC plc[4], the world's 'local bank,' was founded in 1865 and had (at the start of 2004) 9,500 offices world wide, with 223,000 employees in 79 countries. The company now processes over 13 billion customer transaction annually including 87 million internet transactions.
- Time Warner[5] Inc is the world's leading media and entertainment company, whose businesses include filmed entertainment, interactive services, television networks, cable systems, publishing and music. For the year 2004 the company had approximately 80,000 active employees throughout the world and generated revenues of approximately $39.6bn.

So, we have three very diverse, very global companies.

In a broad context, as companies such as Time Warner Inc, HSBC plc, and BP plc expand and grow – as they become evermore spatially remote – they become increasingly dependent on systems and procedures, on interconnectivity and on the creation and development of boundaries. Not only interconnectivity internally between companies within the group but, more importantly, externally with other companies outside the group structure or group boundary: between companies as 'bounded' systems and between the commercial environment (the marketplace) as a higher 'bounded' system. So the need for a trust in systems and procedures becomes an evermore entrenched component within the marketplace and the market structure. Such trust becomes manifestly hierarchical, increasingly virtual and evermore essential (see Figure 3.1).

It is perhaps important to note that this trust in systems can be both explicit – that is through formally agreed contractual agreements – or implied – that is through the development of informal indirect dependencies/relationships.

More importantly, as a system or set of systems evolves and expands (or more appropriately as 'political' participants within or responsible for the system or systems facilitate such an evolution), they do so not only by creating more and more interconnections but also by eliminating redundant systems and inert connections. For example, a company can enter a new market by either:

- the development of a new range of products and/or services, or
- the acquisition of an existing company.

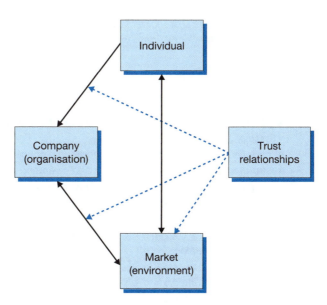

**Figure 3.1** Understanding the relationship – trust systems

Whichever strategy is adopted, the expanding company will create and seek to sustain new interconnections and new interdependencies whilst at the same time possibly destroying and/or relinquish others. And so?

Well, as these changing interconnections become evermore complex – as the level of inter-connectedness and interdependency rises – so boundaries become evermore difficult to monitor and control. Such boundaries become increasingly more porous – and their effectiveness becomes increasingly more unpredictable. As a consequence, the level of risk and inherent uncertainty within the system or systems rises, increasing the potential for entropy, chaos or failure. (Remember we are talking here about semi-open 'created' systems, whose environment is at best volatile and at worst extremely erratic, and where interconnections and interdependencies are created and destroyed in an often chaotic and random manner.)

As the potential for risk and inherent uncertainty rises – as the risk of possible failure and the level of insecurity rises – so the level of trust in the system or systems rises up to a point, a point at which the cost of such trust in systems outweighs the possible benefits to be gained.

Have a look at the following

*DFL plc is a large, established, international company seeking to expand its business activities into a third world country. Clearly risks will exist – certainly in terms of country risk. For example country risk could arise out of a country's government actions/policies that seek to either expropriate corporate assets and/or profits, impose discriminatory pricing intervention policies, enforce restrictive foreign exchange currency controls, and/or impose discriminatory tax laws.*

*On a more socio-political level such country risk can also arise out of a country's government actions/policies that seek to impose social/work-related regulations that offer preferential treatment to domestic companies, restrict the movement of corporate assets and resources, and/or impose regulations that restrict access to local resources.*

*Clearly then, the influence of such government actions/policies on a company's commercial activities can be substantial, with the impact of any one of the above producing considerable fluctuations in a company's short-term ability to generate profits and therefore maintain/maximise shareholder value. Moreover, in the long-term, the impact of such policies can dramatically affect a company's ability to repatriate and/or reinvest such profits for future growth.*

*To minimise such risk and uncertainty the company would most likely hope to develop, create and foster a range of risk minimising strategies that could, for example, include:*

- *obtaining insurance against the possibility of any potential expropriation of the company's assets,*
- *negotiating with host governments potential concessions and/or guarantees,*
- *structuring the company's financial and operating policies to ensure they are acceptable to and consistent with regulatory requirements,*
- *maintaining high levels of local borrowing to cover against the possibility of government action adversely affecting exchange rates,*
- *encouraging the movement of surplus assets from host country companies to the home country companies,*
- *developing close social/political relationships with host country institutions,*
- *internationally integrating production to include host and home country companies to ensure the former are dependent on the latter,*

- *locating research and development activities and any proprietary technology in the home country to reduce the possibility of expropriation,*
- *establishing global trademarks for company products and services to ensure such rights are legally protected domestically and internationally, and*
- *encouraging local participation in company activities and inviting local shareholders to invest in the company's activities.*

*Each of the above would invariably involve developing interconnections and interdependencies with a range of organisations – the greater the perceived risk the more intense these become, essentially to minimise any possible boundary incursion and protect the company from possible risk of loss and/or adversity.*

There is however a second important issue to consider. That is as the level of interconnectedness and interdependency rises – as the level of trust in the system or systems rises – so does the 'imposed' level of monitoring and control. In fact, as complexity and uncertainty within a system or interconnected systems rises, so the systems themselves become less concerned with the underlying context/rationale for such trust and a means of efficient operation, and more concerned with governance and control, an adaptation process that during the 20th century we have come to call bureaucracy.

But why does this so-called adaptation occur? In a corporate context at least, this silent conversion – this almost velvet revolution – occurs as systems within a hierarchy attempt to minimise at best any possible loss or at worst complete failure, not only of the company but the market as a whole!

In essence, as lower-level systems become increasingly more interconnected and more integrated into higher level systems, so the higher-level systems can and do exert greater influence and control on the lower-level systems. At best, this can be good because in a corporate/market sense at least, it can lead to the creation of a so-called 'level paying field', a fair, albeit competitive, marketplace. However, at worst it can lead to excessive surveillance and regulation, and thus lead to unfair competition and potential abuse. Indeed an endemic attribute of the ever-expanding influence of the marketplace – of market capitalism – is that features and system characteristics that often start out as 'facilitators' of commercial activity can (and very often do) eventually end up as conduits of 'economic politicalisation' and 'bureaucratisation'.

Why? Because such endemic risk and uncertainty – as emergent features from the ever changing interconnections and inter-dependencies, result in:

- an increasing need for environmental surveillance to monitor how these ever changing interconnections and inter-dependencies may cause potential failure and possible loss, and
- an increasing use of regulation and control to minimise the impact of such ever-changing interconnections and inter-dependencies.

Why? Because such thinking not only lies at the foundation of liberal economic thought it is (in a contemporary context at least) now the dominant ideology within the contemporary global marketplace!

So now that we have a general context for control let's have a look at how control is a key component of the so-called corporate governance triad:

- the framework of governance – regulation,
- the process of governance – surveillance, and
- the context of governance – control.

## Regulation, surveillance and control

As suggested earlier, in a superficial context (albeit an often overly emphasised context) the hierarchical nature of the marketplace provides a contextual mechanism through which companies not only exchange goods and services, but generate income and profit, and thus provide a context for their future survival. It is, however, also a highly integrated and dynamic systemic framework. A socio-political framework through which companies seek to:

■ interpret and understand the context of environmental change, and
■ manage and where appropriate minimise/maximise the consequences of such environmental change.

More importantly, it is a framework through which contemporary notions of corporate governance – of accountability and of responsibility – are both articulated and operationalised.

Corporate governance is, as suggested by Cadbury (2000), concerned with holding a balance between the economic, social (and political) goals of individuals and of the community. A (pro)active corporate governance framework is essential to:

■ encourage (and ensure) the efficient and effective use of resources, and
■ require accountability for the stewardship of those resources.

Thus, the aim of corporate governance is to align as closely as possible the interests of individuals, of companies and of society, and involves a control framework founded on regulation, surveillance and on control.

Although an in-depth discussion on corporate governance is beyond the scope of this book, an understanding of the component aspects of corporate governance, that is:

■ regulation,
■ surveillance, and
■ control,

is not.

### Regulation

Regulation relates to the provision of prescribed rules of operation and codes of practice that are designed to provide a framework for not only uniformity of action, but also accountability/responsibility for such action. Consequently, such prescribed rules of operation/codes of practice are normally process and/or procedure related – that is they define, they facilitate and they constrain not only what can be done but more importantly, how it can be done, where it can be done and when it can be done.

Whilst in a corporate context, modes of regulation/rules of operation/codes of practice may be seen as 'democratically negotiated' they are:

■ often imposed – whether internally and/or externally,
■ often hierarchical in content – that is they operate at different socio-political levels, and
■ generally pluralistic in context – that is they may not only have multiple origins, they may also impact on different levels within an organisation in different ways.

Indeed, in a 'free' market context, regulations generally evolve from a combination of pressures from the state, the market and the community – although invariably the levels of pressure exerted in the struggle to manage/enforce regulatory pronouncements is not necessarily reflective of that order.

## Surveillance

Surveillance is synonymous with notions of supervision – of close observation – and relates to any process or mechanism through which information on, or knowledge of the efficiency and effectiveness of extant modes of regulation/codes of practice/rules of operation can be obtained. Whilst in a societal context, surveillance is often associated with contemporary notions of a 'big brother' type imposed control and overly invasive bureaucratic monitoring of social and economic activities and processes, it is (in a corporate context at least) essentially an economically driven political process – a process concerned primarily with appropriating information and knowledge as both a current and future basis of power, of control, of gain. Thus in a corporate context, surveillance processes exist to assist companies in:

- seeking out opportunities and managing competition,
- understanding and controlling change (political and technological),
- mediating disputes,
- making decisions, and ultimately
- enforcing regulations.

## Control

Whilst there are many definitions of control (see the introduction to this chapter), for our purposes, we will define control as two distinct but interrelated activities.

Firstly, we will define control as the processes/mechanisms through which compliance with extant modes of regulation/codes of practice/rules of operation are monitored and enforced.

Secondly, we will define control as the power/ability to influence either directly or indirectly another's (either individual and/or corporate entity) activities.

In a broad sense, notions of control encapsulate an ability to determine, facilitate, and/or constrain such activities by enforcing adherence to and compliance with approved systems, policies and procedures – to ensure the maintenance of hierarchical responsibilities and accountabilities.

Although control may be:

- internal/external,
- direct/indirect,
- formal/informal,
- voluntary/statutory,
- facilitating/constraining, and
- mechanistic/organic,

the socio-political context of control as an organisational mechanism, is neither socially neutral nor economically impartial. Control is a political process at the centre of which is the need for access to, and use of, information and knowledge.

But what is the purpose of control? In a corporate context at least, as a 'constructed artificial process', the purpose of control is designed to assist a company in:

- promoting environmental fit,
- minimising the impact of environmental (socio-economic) disturbances,
- providing a framework of conformity (organisational isomorphism),
- promoting the coordination of action and resource utilisation, and
- promoting the socialisation of people and procedures.

In essence, control operates on three economically determined but nevertheless socio-political levels.

Firstly at a symbolic level in which controls are designed to further corporate/organisational value beliefs. The focus of such controls is the corporate community with the primary purpose of such controls concerned with the values embedded in a company's/organisation's action(s).

Secondly at a behavioural level in which controls are designed to monitor and evaluate process/procedure outcomes. The focus of such control is the company/organisation member, with the primary purpose of such control concerned with directing and coordinating behaviour towards specific outcomes.

Thirdly at a resource allocation level in which controls are designed to measure and evaluate the conduct of exchange-based mechanisms. The primary focus of such controls is the transacting party and/or parties, with the primary purpose of such controls concerned with providing an efficient mechanism for conducting exchanges.

In a broad sense, the symbolic and behavioural levels of control are perhaps closely associated with market-based notions of effectiveness, whereas the resource allocation levels of control are closely associated with the notion of efficiency. And perhaps herein lies the interesting political divide that continues to dominate contemporary UK political and economic thought. Why? Because in a traditionalist context:

- a more right-wing notion of economic activity would tend to favour a more 'marketplace' driven rationalisation of control and thus prioritise the notion of efficiency over effectiveness, for example control based on determining value-for-money measures and/or resource usage and wealth creation, whereas
- a more left-wing orientated notion of economic activity would tend to favour a more socially inclusive rationalisation of control and an agenda emphasising the notion of effectiveness over efficiency.

However whilst UK political and economic thought has (certainly during the latter part of the 20th century and the early part of the 21st century) become less differentiated politically the alternative perceptions/notions of control still persist.

## Corporate context of control

As we saw earlier in this chapter, in a corporate context, control is fundamentally an artificial construct – a construct whose increasing importance is directly correlated with the endemic risk and uncertainty associated with:

- the increasing complexity of the global marketplace, and
- the evermore controversial nature of market capitalism.

Whereas control's very existence – as an imposed socio-political function – is founded on the need to:

- monitor and regulate the influence of environmental disturbances (macro influences), and
- minimise the impact of incorrect/inefficient internal systems (micro influences),

its effectiveness is essentially determined firstly by the existence of:

- adequate information,
- effective channels of communication, and
- efficient organisational structures,

and secondly – and perhaps more importantly – by the socio-political context through which such controls are politicised and operationalised – that is whether controls are:

- coercive,
- mimetic, and/or
- normative.

For the moment however it would perhaps be useful to recap on a number of key control contexts identified in the discussion so far:

- control is a primary management task – as part of the wide corporate governance ethic,
- control processes and procedures exist/function as a facilitator of organisational action,
- control mechanisms are socially constructed political processes designed to ensure that operations/activities proceed and/or comply with extant modes of regulation/codes of practice/ rules of operation,
- **control is necessary because unpredictable environmental disturbances occur that can result in actual performance deviating from expectations, and/or a failure (whether passive or active) to comply with extant modes of regulation/codes of practice/rules of operation.**

To illustrate the basic elements of control, for the remainder of this chapter we will consider control as a mechanism for the identification and management of deviations from expectations – the description in the last point above.

## Basic elements of the control cycle

In a broad context, a systemic control cycle will consist of the following:

- an expectation – a standard and/or requirement specifying expected/anticipated performance, that is a performance plan and/or a resources budget,
- a measurement process in which actual results are quantitatively determined – usually by the use of an organisational sensor,
- a comparison in which actual results are compared to requirements/expectations to determine a quantitative estimate of performance – usually by the use of an organisational comparator,
- feedback – in which deviations and variations between expectations and actual performance are reported to a higher level control unit, and
- action – outcome and/or instruction activities resulting from the control process – usually by the use of an organisational effector.

The control cycle may also include feedforward – in which action is taken in anticipation of possible deviations and/or variations (see Figure 3.2).

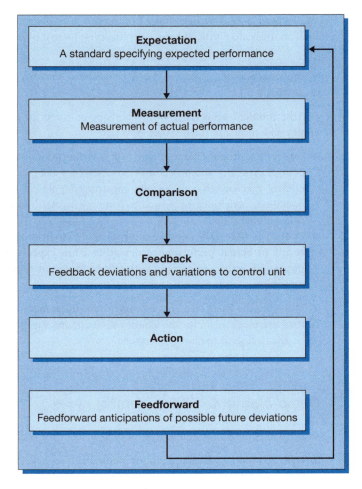

**Figure 3.2** The basic control cycle

 ## Understanding systemic control

### Feedback and feedback loops

In cybernetics and control theory, feedback is a process whereby some proportion of the output signal of a system is passed (fed back) to the input. Often this is done intentionally, in order to control the dynamic behaviour of the system. In corporate systems, control is generally exercised by the use of feedback loops. The term 'feedback loop' refers to a 'systemic connection' and can comprise of any mechanism, process, procedure and/or action, either physical (that is manually orientated) or virtual (that is essentially computer orientated), which gathers data on past performance from the output side of a system or set of interconnected systems.

These data are used to direct future performance by adjusting the input side of a system or set of interconnected systems. The component parts of a feedback loop would be:

- a sensor – an organisational system(s) for measuring actual outcomes,
- a comparator – an organisational system(s) for comparing actual outcomes with expectation,
- an effector – an organisational system(s) used to issue instructions based on comparisons,

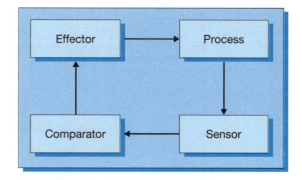

**Figure 3.3** Control cycle components

and of course the process.

A feedback loop can have many levels, for example single-loop feedback (one level – see Figure 3.4), double-loop feedback (two levels – see Figure 3.5) in which a higher-order control facility is introduced, or multi-loop feedback, in which a number of higher-order control facilities exist.

It is perhaps important to note that where more than one feedback loop exists within a control function such loops may be (and indeed often are) temporally, spatially and hierarchically differentiated. That is individual feedback loops – whilst a component part of a single control function – may occur at different times (or different intervals), at different places and at different organisational levels.

For example, within double-loop and/or multi-loop feedback arrangements, the initial loop (at say, for example, an operational/tactical level) may consider small variations between expectations and outcomes so where appropriate, action can be taken to adjust outcomes.

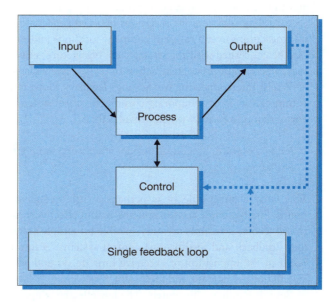

**Figure 3.4** A single-loop feedback

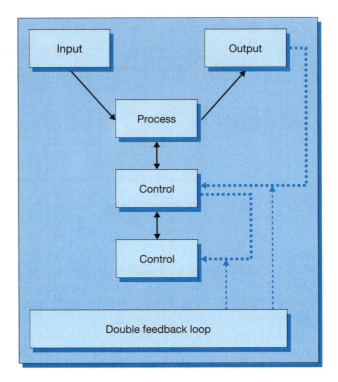

**Figure 3.5** A double-loop feedback

Since control is exercised within the system – that is there is no interaction with the external environment – such a control function would normally be regarded as a closed system, and would be fairly mechanistic and more than likely automated, and in contemporary corporate accounting information systems probably computer-based. A higher-level loop (or loops) may consider large or excessive variations between expectations and outcomes, and/or consistency of expectations over a range of company locations and/or reporting periods, and would therefore be concerned with the strategic or 'big picture' view. Such a higher-level loop (or loops) may, where appropriate, take action to revise/review plans/expectations.

Whilst interconnecting (or nesting) feedback loops to create multi-level loops has become commonplace in contemporary corporate control systems, it is perhaps worth considering the law of requisite variety[6] which provides that:

> *for full control . . . a control system should contain controls at least equal to the system it is wished to control.*

This fairly abstract rule (it is perhaps a little excessive to call it a law) provides two key points. Firstly, simple control systems cannot effectively control large complex systems – that is closed feedback systems are only suitable for simple systems. Complex systems require open-loop feedback and feedforward control systems. Secondly, increasing levels of control may result in the imposition of excessive time delays and additional costs which may render the system both redundant and inefficient.

Sounds familiar – absolutely! The law effectively operationalises the notion of bureaucracy as excessive levels of control.

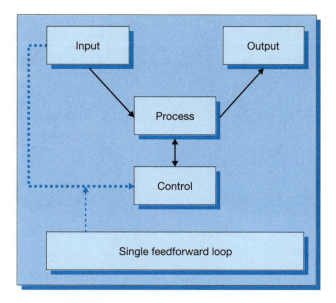

**Figure 3.6** A single feedforward loop

## Feedforward and feedforward loops

A feedforward loop is designed to react to immediate or forthcoming deviations and/or variations by making adjustments to a system or set of interconnected systems. As with feedback loops, feedforward loops can and often do exist at many levels – as single feedforward loops (see Figure 3.6), double feedforward loops (see Figure 3.7) or indeed multiple-level feedforward loops.

Examples of feedforward would include:

- advance news of a potential industrial dispute,
- probable increases in the prices of raw material used by a company,
- information regarding political unrest in a country in which a company has a number of production and/or retail facilities, and/or
- news regarding the emergence of a new market for a company's products.

In many instances, such events are beyond the control of the company, and as such all that the management of the company can do is to attempt to minimise/maximise the possible adverse/favourable consequences of such environmental disturbances by the active maintenance of feedforward procedures, processes and mechanisms.

It is perhaps important to note that the two types of control explored above – namely 'feedback' and 'feedforward' – are not mutually exclusive. Feedforward control systems are often combined with the feedback control systems. Why?

Firstly, feedforward control systems facilitate a rapid response to any environmental disturbance and feedback control systems correct any error in the predetermined adjustment made by the feedforward control system. Secondly, feedforward control systems do not have the stability problems that feedback control systems can and often do have, especially in feedback control systems that require some human intervention. Feedforward needs to be pre-calibrated whereas feedback does not: that is feedforward control applies to disturbances with known effects. So, the management of a company can only react to forthcoming disturbances if it is able to assess the potential effect of such disturbances.

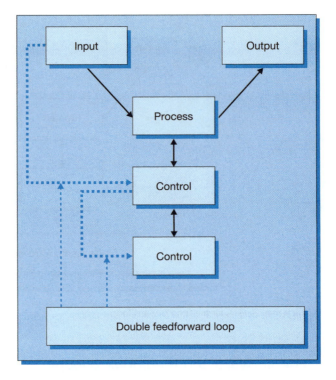

**Figure 3.7** A double feedforward loop

## Closed/open loop systems

A closed loop system is a system of feedback loops where control is an integrated part of the system – that is feedback, based on output measurement, is 'returned' back into the system to facilitate appropriate modification to the system's input. For example, an internal quality control cycle within a company's production process would be a good example of such a system.

An open loop system is a system where no feedback loop exists and control is external to the system and not an integral part of it. Control action is therefore not automatic and may be made without monitoring the output of the system.

It is also important to note that, in general, feedforward is an open loop inasmuch as it does not 'return' through the process as would feedback.

## Types of feedback

Before we consider some of the problems that can emerge within a control system and explore the issues of feedback and feedforward within the context of a case study scenario, it would perhaps be useful to define alternative types of feedback and feedforward.

### Positive feedback

Positive feedback is feedback which causes a system to amplify an adjustment result – that is positive feedback acts in the same direction as the measured deviation and thus reinforces the direction in which the system is moving.

### *Negative feedback*

Negative feedback is feedback which seeks to reduce/minimise fluctuations around a standard or an expectation – that is negative feedback acts in the opposite direction to the measured deviation and thus the corrective action would be in the opposite direction to the error.

### Types of feedforward

Whilst it is not customary to distinguish between positive or negative feedforward, it is possible for each variant to exist.

## Control systems – a reality check

In the real word, complex business organisations will invariably possess integrated control systems that consist of both feedback and feedforward, possibly at a double if not greater multiple nested levels (see Figure 3.8).

The reason for this is that:

- companies are invariably hierarchical and comprised of many interconnecting systems and sub-systems,
- relying on single-loop feedback may result in action being taken too late which may increase the possible risk of failure,
- relying on single-loop feedback may result in incorrect action being taken which may also increase the possible risk of failure,

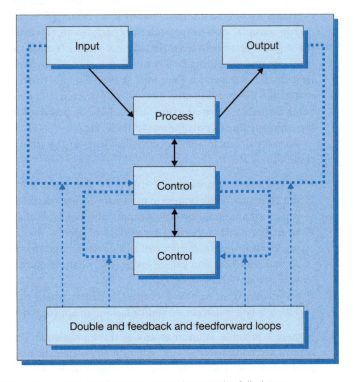

**Figure 3.8** Feedback and feedforward control loops – the full picture

- relying only on feedback may not alert the company to environmental changes that may have a significant impact of future activity, and
- feedforward, whilst important, would not on its own be able to instigate the appropriate corrective action where inefficiencies exist.

## Problems with control action

There are many issues that have an impact on the effective and efficiency of a control system. Such factors include:

- timing of the control action,
- delays in the control cycle,
- internal contradiction,
- political nature of management control systems,
- behavioural aspects of control systems, and
- organisational uncertainty.

Clearly this is not an exhaustive list, but merely illustrative of the possible problems a company could face.

### Timing of control action

There can be little doubt that control action is most effective when the control time lag is short – that is when the time difference between the determination/measurement of a deviation from expectations and the implementation of action to redress the divergence is minimised.

For example, monitoring budgetary performance is commonplace in many large companies. If a large deviation between expected performance (budget) and actual performance was to occur in a large manufacturing facility of a national company, in month 2 or 3 of the financial year – let's say the overspend is the result of excessive raw material wastage due to poor quality raw materials – then waiting until month 5 or 6 or even later could result not only in excessive losses being carried by the production facility, but also possible losses being incurred in other areas of the company due to possible loss of trade, etc.

But why do such delays occur? Problems in the timing of control action can occur as a result of:

- an inefficient organisational structure – that is excessive levels of management (e.g. where the company requires information concerning possible deviations from expectations to be processed and monitored by a number of managers at a number of different levels),
- an inappropriate reporting period/lack of speed – that is excessive waiting periods between the identification/measurement of a deviation and the making of that information available so that control action can be taken (e.g. where budgetary performance in May is not made available until June), and/or
- an ineffective information content – that is where the information available for control action is either inaccurate and/or lacking in appropriate detail.

Is there a possible solution to any of these problems? Difficult to say, but as a general rule control decisions/action should, where at all possible, be made at the lowest possible hierarchical level – that is as close to the event (the source of the deviation) as possible.

## Delays in the control cycle

Whilst eliminating:

- inefficient and out-of-date organisation structures,
- inappropriate reporting periods, and
- ineffective and redundant information content,

may improve the effectiveness of the control action, it is also important that corporate control systems should seek to ensure that:

- control action is taken as soon as possible after any deviation has been identified/measured,
- environmental disturbances are recognised and acted upon as soon as possible, and
- the concentration of control action is correctly focused on those areas of greatest potential risk

Nevertheless, and often despite the best actions of corporate managers, delays in control action can and indeed do arise at various stages of a control cycle. Such delays would, for example, include;

- collection delays,
- assessment delays,
- decision making delays,
- implementation delays,
- impact delays, and
- control delays.

## Internal contradiction

Internal contradiction or 'push/pull' problems arise from conflict resulting from the existence of multiple control factors within a system and/or group of interconnected systems. In a corporate environment such internal contradiction can arise where a system's and/or subsystems' boundaries are ill defined and its objectives/goals are contradictory. For example, a company whilst seeking to maximise shareholder wealth may nevertheless possess a range of secondary objectives that may – at least in the short term – result in contradictory pressures existing within the company. These could be, for example, seeking to maximise high-quality product specifications or attempting to maintain high levels of employee development whilst seeking to minimise/reduce overall costs.

Whilst the existence of such multiple objectives is clearly not uncommon, the role of corporate strategic managers to ensure that such conflicting objectives are prioritised and accommodated as painlessly as possible (i.e. with as little financial loss as possible) since such conflicting objectives can, if not appropriately managed, result in the inefficient use of resources and, in a systems context at least, possible entropy and ultimately systems failure.

## Corporate control – using control theory as a framework

Let's look at some of these key elements of control theory in more detail in the context of the following case study scenario: Westelle Ltd.

# CASE STUDY

## *Westelle Ltd*

Westelle Ltd is a large, UK-based, machine component manufacturing company that has been trading successfully for approximately 45 years. The company has a number of production facilities and wholesale retail outlets throughout the UK. The sales of Westelle's products currently account for approximately 18% of the total market for machine components in the UK.

Anthony Fisher is production manager of Westelle's Newcastle production facility. The company has five other production facilities located in Glasgow, Birmingham, Leeds, Swindon and Bristol, and four wholesale retail outlets located in Manchester, Bradford, Sheffield and Cambridge. The company's head office is in York.

The Newcastle production facility is a specialist non-trading division of the company. The production facility has limited contact with outside agencies (apart from contacting suppliers) and has no retail staff. Transactions at each of the six production facilities are internal in nature – that is with other production facilities and/or wholesale retail outlets within the company.

For accounting purposes, all the company's production facilities are treated as cost centres rather than an income generating revenue or profit centres.

### Senior managers committee meeting Tuesday 17 August 2004

Because of the company's somewhat dispersed geography, both wholesale retail managers and production facility managers meet on a regular basis but usually only every two months at the company's head office in York. They discuss management issues relating to the company's activities. It is also common practice for head office managers including the company accountant, the company personnel manager and the company operations manager to attend these meetings.

The chairmanship of the senior committee is rotated on an annual basis. This year the chairmanship is in the hands of John Lightman-White, Westelle's operations manager.

Although the August 2004 meeting agenda was unremarkable and similar to those of previous numerous meetings, the final agenda item – proposed by Anthony Fisher – was somewhat unusual and bound to raise the ambient temperature of the meeting. The agenda item concerned the ineffectiveness of the company's budgetary system as a corporate control mechanism.

The meeting commenced at 10:15 am in the board room at the company's head office in York. After nearly 1½ hours of rather mundane pleasantries, bureaucratic idiosyncrasies and tedious committee protocol, at approximately 11.45 pm John Lightman-White, in his role as chairman, looked at Anthony Fisher, and said, 'I believer this final item is your agenda item Anthony – the meeting is yours.'

With that Anthony looked around at the other members of the committee and took a deep breath. He began: 'As you may well know, I have been at Newcastle production facility of Westelle Ltd for a little over 18 months and have during that time become increasingly concerned about the ineffectiveness and inefficiency of the company's budgetary control system. In my opinion, and may I add an opinion supported by many of you around this table, the company's corporate accounting department – its accounting information system and in particular its budgetary control system – provides little useful information for either production managers or wholesale retail managers. The historical emphasis of the accounting information system – the historical nature of the budgetary control statements issued monthly to production and wholesale retail managers – continues to have a negative motivational impact on managers because the statements fail to reflect adequately on how efficiently and effectively both production and wholesale retail managers are in their day-to-day managerial activities. Indeed, despite repeated representations to the company head office by many of the productions facility managers and repeated attempts to discuss/explore these concerns with the company accountant, over the past 12 months little has changed.

'In my opinion, the budgetary control statements produced by corporate head office not only lack any realism, they are ambiguous, confusing, disingenuous and misleading.

'Over the past year the Newcastle production facility – and may I also add, the Birmingham, Leeds and Swindon production facilities – have all exceeded their budgeted production targets. Yet for the past 12 months the budgetary control statements continue to show Newcastle, Birmingham, Leeds and Swindon production facilities as carrying excessive costs. This despite the Newcastle and Leeds production facilities making substantial improvements in raw materials used in the production process, and the Birmingham and Swindon production facilities making vast improvements to man-hour output levels – none of which has been, nor will be to my knowledge, ever reflected in the production facilities budgetary control statements. It appears that any information provided by production and wholesale retail managers to head office – and in particular the company accountant – is continually ignored as irrelevant.

'Looking back over the past two years' budgetary control statements, all six of the production facilities have shown negative total variances for 20 out of the 24 months – and there appears little that either the production and/or the wholesale retail managers can do.

'It is clearly time for the accounting information system – and the budgetary control statements – to reflect what is actually happening at the various production and wholesale retail facilities and not some abstract notion created by head office accounting staff of what "might" be happening.

'Perhaps the company accountant would like to comment using the June 2004 budgetary control statement for the Newcastle production facility and explain why, as in the previous 15 months, actual head office costs have exceeded the budgeted head office costs.'

Anthony distributed a copy of the report to each of the committee members.

**Newcastle Production Facility: Budgetary Control Statement, June 2004**

|  | Allocation £000 | Actual cost £000 | +/(−) £000 |
|---|---|---|---|
| Materials |  |  |  |
| Potassium ethnolitrate | 2,000 | 1,980 | (20) |
| Abelithium | 1,980 | 1,970 | (10) |
| Zinctricate | 460 | 408 | (52) |
| Labour |  |  |  |
| Skilled | 1,200 | 1,200 | 0 |
| Technician | 1,180 | 1,090 | (90) |
| Semi-skilled | 3,040 | 3,010 | (30) |
| Manual | 560 | 540 | (20) |
| Head office costs | 100 | 534 | 434 |
| Total | 10,520 | 10,732 | 212 |

Throughout Anthony's presentation, most of the company's productions facility managers nodded in agreement, whilst the wholesale retail managers voiced an occasional word of support.

The company accountant, Alun Wayle, however sat quietly as he listened attentively to Anthony's critique.

'Alun, would you like to respond,' asked the chairman. After a brief pause, Alun Wayle rose to his feet and began his response. 'Firstly, I think it would be inappropriate for me to respond to the specifics in terms of levels of head office expenditure at each of the outlying production/wholesale retail facilities as raised by the Newcastle production facility manager.'

'That's a surprise,' whispered Anthony.

Whilst the other production facility managers smiled at Anthony's witty rhetoric – the company accountant scornfully ignored the comment, treating it with the contempt he believed it deserved. 'However,' he continued 'what I think is important is that we must not lose sight of the bigger picture. The accounting information system and the budgetary reporting system are a component part of a larger corporate information system that has operated successfully in the company for a number of years. Whilst the past few years has seen some change – the introduction of the company's new "online" accounting system and increased network facilities – the core accounting system has remained generally unchanged and in my opinion rightly so. The budgetary reporting systems have, and indeed continue, to operate and satisfy all the reporting requirements as laid down in the company's operation procedures guidelines issued some two years ago – and may I add agreed and ratified by this committee. More importantly, to undertake changes alluded to by the Newcastle production facilities manager would require substantial investment – funds which the company does not have available at its disposal.

'Whilst the budgetary control statements, produced by the budgetary reporting system are the basis for:

- evaluating the efficiency of both production facilities and wholesale retail facilities, and
- determining whether managers have compiled with the company's longer-term strategy and performed in accordance with set targets,

both production and wholesale retail managers should not worry too much. None of you have been sacked – yet!'

At this Anthony became extremely annoyed and agitated by the truculent attitude and arrogant demeanour of the company accountant. From discussions with other production managers, in particular Jessica Lee, the production manager of the Swindon facility, Anthony was certain that the company accountant was incorrect. He was aware for example, that over the past few years, because of the introduction of new computing technology, some rather substantial changes to the financial reporting systems of other non-production and non-retail facilities had been made.

As the company accountant retook his seat, Anthony rose to his feet without invitation, and started his reply. 'May I say that I find the egotistical attitude of the company accountant both naïve and insulting! I am sure that Alun is aware that the staff turnover of production managers at the company continues to be extremely high even though "few" managers have ever been sacked. Most managers seemed to resign – usually in disgust because of the belief that they are not being fairly evaluated – a point I'm sure the company personnel manager could confirm from his personnel records.

'The following are typical comments of production managers who have left Westelle Ltd over the past year:

- 'The company accountant may well be able to justify the numbers they use – but they know nothing about production. I just used to ignore the budgetary control statements entirely and pretend they didn't exist.' *Len Chapman ex Production facilities manager Leeds*
- 'No matter what they say about firing people, negative budgetary control statements mean only one thing – negative evaluations.' *Bryn Robson ex Production facilities manager Swindon*

- 'the company head office in York has never and probably never will listen to production facility managers. They see us as inconsequential – as a blot on the landscape. All the head office bureaucrats are concerned with are those wretched misleading budgetary control statements.' *Jim Barnes ex Production facilities manager Bristol*

'The market we operate in is a select and highly specialised market. Of the five managers who have left the company over the past year, four of them – including the three I have quoted – have taken posts of a similar nature with companies in direct competition with Westelle. Surely that cannot be good for the company – can it!'

'Absolutely not,' said Herald Bosse, company personnel manager 'but may I point out . . .'. 'Perhaps you could point it out at a later date,' said John Lightman-White, chairperson. 'Unfortunately we have run out of time. As you are all aware head office imposes a time limit on our meetings of two hours and we have just about reached that time limit. Perhaps we can carry the discussion on item 12 over to our next meeting – on 9 October 2004. Agreed?'

'Looks like we have no alternative,' said Anthony disdainfully. 'Yes – it does look as if we have no alternative, doesn't it,' replied the chairman. There were no further dissenting voices. The meeting was adjourned.

## Case study – discussion

Before we consider control theory aspects of the case study company, perhaps a summary of the key issues in the case study would be a useful starting point.

- Westelle Ltd is a large, UK-based, machine component manufacturing company that has been trading successfully for approximately 45 years. The company has a number of production facilities and wholesale retail outlets throughout the UK.
- Transactions of each of the six production facilities are internal in nature and, for accounting purposes, all the company's production facilities are treated as cost centres rather than an income generating revenue or profit centres.
- Wholesale retail managers and production facility managers meet on a regular basis.
- Whilst both production facilities managers and wholesale retail managers are concerned about the ineffectiveness of the company's budgetary system as a corporate control mechanism, the company's head office managers appear unwilling to accept criticisms.

Figure 3.9 provides a summary representation of Westelle Ltd's budgetary system.

Let's look at the key protagonists in the case study.

### The protagonists

Anthony Fisher is a highly qualified and experience production facilities manager, who appears competent and both accommodating and flexible inasmuch as he willing to accept and adopt new procedures. He also appears to care about the quality of his production facilities' output. However, currently he appears frustrated and perturbed at the reluctance of the company's head office to consider what he believes are important control issues and thus feels demotivated and under-valued.

Alun Wayle is an accountant of many years' experience who appears to care very little about departmental issues outside the confines of the head office. He is rather unsympathetic to concerns expressed by production facilities and wholesale retail managers, and unwilling (or even perhaps unable) to change. He is very much a bureaucrat in the traditional sense, and

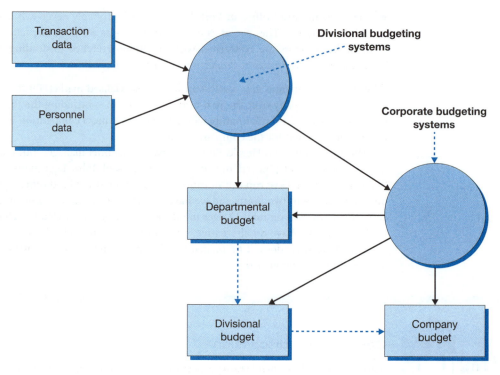

**Figure 3.9** Westelle Ltd

appears to have an extremely negative attitude towards criticism often treating it with rancour and contempt. He also appears to reject any advice – without any constructive discussion – despite such advice clearly being well-founded and appropriate.

But what are the key problems/control issues? Before we look at these it would be useful to consider the key sources and/or factors underpinning these problems/control issues.

### Key sources of problems/control issues

Firstly, we have the attitudes of the company's head office staff who seem more concerned with maintaining a 'closed-system' approach to management and consequently are overtly reluctant to answer questions over quality and procedure. They appeared blinkered by head office protocol and administrative bureaucracy. Moreover they not only appear unwilling to accept that change is inevitable and that as head office staff they may not possess all the correct answers but, more importantly, they appear wholly insensitive to shop floor issues and concerns.

Secondly, the nature of the control information – the budgetary control statements. Whereas the company head office staff, and in particular the company accountant Alun Wayle, appear to have few concerns over the information produced for wholesale retail managers and production facilities managers, the users of the control information (the wholesale retail managers and production facilities managers) consider the budgetary control statements to be:

■ short sighted,
■ inflexible,
■ management biased,
■ of limited usefulness, and
■ structured towards highlighting negative issues.

### Problems and control issues

In terms of systems thinking/control theory the Westelle Ltd case study raises a number of related issues of which the following are perhaps the most significant:

- the behavioural implications and political nature of control – that is the imposition of a reporting structure whose characteristics are dictated by head office bureaucracy and managerial politics rather than information efficiency and system effectiveness,
- problems related to contradictory system objectives – that is system participants all have alternative perceptions of what purpose the budgetary control statements serve,
- the impact and consequences of the inappropriate use of feedback and feedforward control loops – that is whilst superficially feedback and feedforward loops appear to exist their effectiveness and functionality leaves much to be desired,
- issues related to delays in the control cycle and the possible organisational consequences – that is information for control purposes is not only produced in a format that possesses few qualitative characteristics for the users of the information but it is produced after considerable time delay, a delay that is an inherent part of the system.

In essence the problems within the case study relate directly to the imposed nature of the company's organisational structure and the negative behavioural consequences that have emerged for it.

### Possible solutions to problems/control issues

There can be little doubt that Westelle Ltd is experiencing severe 'control' problems especially in its budgetary control systems and the statements that system produces. Part of these problems are clearly due to 'internal politics' and part are due to systemic failures – for example:

- feedback and feedforward problems,
- timing and delay issues, and
- internal systems conflict.

There are of course many possible solutions that could be proposed, including the following:

- redesign the corporate information structure – that is ensure feedback information highlights positive as well as negative issues, and more importantly highlights qualitative as well as quantitative issues,
- develop multi-level control loops to provide greater access and prevent sub-systems – this would probably mean greater integration between head office staff and regional production facilities and wholesale retail managers,
- improve communications between head office staff and regional production facilities and wholesale retail managers and reduce boundary interference,
- develop systemic ownership through, for example, the use of performance-related remuneration, and
- minimise timing delays in control information flow between head office staff and regional production facilities and wholesale retail managers.

## Concluding comments

Control, trust in systems, feedback, feedforward and control loops are now an endemic part of corporate activity. They are a product of:

- the evermore virulent spread of 'market-based' competitive capitalism, and
- the increasing 'public/media' demands for greater corporate responsibility and accountability, i.e. for more effective corporate governance.

The need to:

- undertake surveillance of corporate systems and activities,
- regulate and monitor corporate activities,
- control and monitor corporate procedures and processes,

is now a paramount preoccupation of many corporate managers – a preoccupation conditioned only by a single overarching objective – to maximise shareholder wealth, again and again, year after year! Indeed, such notions of control, of trust (in systems not people), of feedback and of feedforward have become commonplace not only in financial accounting, but also management accounting and financial management.

In a corporate context, if the possession of information and knowledge is the fundamental component for the exercise of management power, then the 'corporate system and/or inter-connected sub-systems' are the conduit(s) through which that management power is exercised and control in the mechanism through which that management power is maintained. This is management not only through design but, more importantly, management by design!

## Key points and concepts

| | |
|---|---|
| Closed-loop system | Feedforward loop |
| Coercive control | Mimetic control |
| Comparator | Negative feedback |
| Control | Normative control |
| Corporate governance | Open-loop system |
| Disembedding mechanism | Positive feedback |
| Effector | Regulation |
| Environmental fit | Sensor |
| Feedback | Socialisation |
| Feedback loop | Surveillance |
| Feedforward | Trust in systems |

## References

Amin, A. (1994) 'Models, Fantasies, and Phantoms of Transition', in Amin, A. (ed.) *Post Fordism*, Blackwell, London.

Ashby, W.R. (1956) *An Introduction to Cybernetics*, Chapman & Hall, London (available @ http://pcp.vub.ac.be/books/IntroCyb.pdf.

Cadbury, A. (2000) in 'Global Corporate Governance Forum', World Bank.

Cerny, P.G. (1994) 'The dynamics of financial globalisation – technology, market, and policy response', *Political Sciences*, 27, pp. 319–342.

Giddens, A. (1990) *The Consequences of Modernity*, Polity Press, Stanford, CA.

Harvey, D. (1982) *The Limits to Capital*, Blackwell, Oxford.

Harvey, D. (1990) *The Condition of Post Modernity*, Basil Blackwell, London.

Lipietz, A. (1994) 'Post Fordism and Democracy', in Amin, A. (ed.) *Post Fordism*, Blackwell, London.

McChesney, R. (1999) 'The New Global Media: It's a Small World of Big Conglomerates', *The Nation*, 269(18), pp. 11–15.

Parsons, T. and Shils, E. (1951) *Towards a Theory of Social Action*, Harvard University Press, Cambridge, MA.

Palloix, C. (1975), 'The Internationalisation of Capital and the Circuits of Social Capital', in Radice, H. (ed.) *International Firms and Modern Imperialism*, Penguin Harmondsworth, London.

Palloix, C. (1977) 'The Self Expansion of Capital on a World Scale', *Review of Radical Political Economics*, 9, pp. 1–28.

Savage, M. and Warde, A. (1993) *Urban Sociology, Capitalism and Modernity*, MacMillan, London.

## Bibliography

Bertalanffy, von, L. (1975) *Perspectives on General Systems Theory*, Braziller, New York.

Bertalanffy, von, L. (1976) *General Systems Theory*, Braziller, New York.

Checkland, P. (1981) *Systems Thinking, Systems Practice*, John Wiley, London.

Harry, M. (1994) *Information Systems in Business*, Pitman, London.

Kim, D.H. (1999) *Introduction to Systems Thinking*, Pegasus Communications, London.

Laszlo, E. (1996) *Systems view of the world*, Hampton Press, London.

Lucy, T. (2000) *Management Information Systems*, Letts, London.

Wienberg, G. (2001) *Introduction to General Systems Theory*, Dorset House, London.

## Websites

www.systemsthinkingpress.com
(Chaos Theory – Critical Thinking, Organisational Development Portal)
http://pespmc1.vub.ac.be/
(Principia Cybernetica webpage)

Other websites you may find helpful in gaining an insight into more accounting-related discussion and systems thinking include:

www.accaglobal.com
(Chartered Association of Certified Accountants)
www.cimaglobal.com
(Chartered Institute of Management Accountants)
www.ft.com
(Financial Times)
www.economist.com
(Economist)
www.guardian.co.uk
(Guardian)
www.accountingweb.co.uk
(General accounting website)

## Self-review questions

1. What is control?
2. Why is control necessary in any type of social organisations?
3. What are the basic elements of a control cycle?
4. What is a feedback loop?
5. What are the key components of a feedback loop?
6. What is a feedforward loop?
7. What are the key components of a feedforward loop?
8. Distinguish between negative feedback and positive feedback.
9. Why is the law of requisite variety important in control systems?
10. Why is control often regarded as a political process?

## Questions and problems

### Question 1

Control is a fundamental issue for any company seeking to function efficiently and maximise the wealth of its shareholders. Describe the basic elements of control and explain why it is necessary in corporate organisations?

### Question 2

One component aspect of control theory is surveillance. Identify and describe the systems of 'surveillance' you would expect to find in a large manufacturing organisation and describe the likely impact of constant surveillance on employees within an organisation.

### Question 3

Control systems can generally be divided into three levels:

- operational accountability,
- tactical control, and
- strategic management.

Explain how the increasing use of computer technology and information management has affected processes and procedures at each of the above three levels of control.

### Question 4

(a) Why is the timing of control important and what delays could exist in a company's control cycle?
(b) What would be the possible consequences of excessive delays in a company's control cycle?

### Question 5

Does the control function differ between soft systems and hard systems?

# Assignments

## Question 1

You have recently been appointed as systems accountant for KLW Ltd, an established FMCG company located in Newcastle. The company has retail outlets throughout the UK and has been operating successfully for approximately 35 years. During 2003, KLW Ltd's turnover was £102m with after-tax profits of approximately £26.5m.

The company currently operates a networked computer-based accounting information system with a growing percentage (currently approximately less than 3% of annual turnover) of its transactions occurring through its web-based e-commerce facility.

At a recent board meeting the managing director of the company presented the following extract taken from Tesco's annual review and summary financial statements:

*Tesco.com is the largest e-grocer and most profitable e-retail business in the world. Tesco.com sales for the year ended 22 February 2003 have increased by 26% on last year. This year (year ended 22 February 2003) our turnover reached £447m. Each week in the UK we deliver over 110,000 orders. We have 65% share of the UK internet grocery market.*

*We are the only UK supermarket to offer a nationwide service, covering 96% of the population. (2003: 26)*

The managing director's only comment was:

*In my opinion the future strategy of our retail activity should seek to fully embrace an increasing e-commerce facility. With potential growth opportunities in excess of 25%, we should aspire to use the available technology in all our retail activities. Although we cannot compete directly with companies like Tesco we should nonetheless seek to embrace the competitive advantage e-commerce offers companies like KLW Ltd.*

After protracted discussion and despite some reservations, following the managing director's somewhat brief presentation, the board made the following three resolutions;

- **Resolution 1:** to develop an e-commerce facility and aim for an overall turnover of approximately 25% of total sales by 2006.
- **Resolution 2:** to develop financial and accounting controls to ensure the efficient and effective operation of such an e-commerce facility.
- **Resolution 3:** to appoint a sub-committee (to be chaired by the managing director) to monitor the development of the company's e-commerce facility.

Following the sub-committee's first meeting in December 2003, you received the following internal memorandum;

---

**KLW Ltd    E-Commerce Sub Committee**

---

**Internal Memorandum**

---

From:    Chair
         E-commerce sub-committee
To:      Systems Accountant
Date:    05 January 2004

---

### E-commerce – a strategy for the future

The next meeting of the above committee will be on 2 April 2004 in the company board room KLW Ltd head office. As you may well be aware, following a recent board meeting, the company resolved to develop a company-wide e-commerce facility within the context of a secure financial accounting environment. As a consequence,

→

the members of the e-commerce sub-committee have requested a formal presentation on a range of issues related to the development of an extended e-commerce trading platform.

As part of the above discussion, the members of the e-commerce sub-committee would like you to provide a description and evaluation of the control-related activities you would expect to find for such a facility to operate efficiently and effectively.

### Required

Prepare a discussion document for the chairman of the e-commerce sub-committee in which you cover all the issues raised in his internal memorandum dated 5 January 2004.

## Question 2

Learn-a-lot Ltd is a small but expanding Leeds-based retail company that provides computer-based educational facilities and equipment for a range of public and private sector colleges and universities specialising in postgraduate professional IT courses. As a result of a recent increase in demand for the courses offered by universities and colleges, the company is considering expanding its current retail facilities.

The company is seeking to establish a presence in both Hull and York in order to benefit from the high number of undergraduate university students studying IT and computer science related degrees.

The company is, however, aware that such an expansion would require not only a substantial capital investment, but also a significant change in the company's accounting information systems procedures, especially those concerned with the recording of sales income.

### Required

As their recently appointed systems accountant, prepare a report for the management of Learn-a-lot Ltd on the importance for a company like Learn-a-lot Ltd to possess a cohesive control structure within its accounting information systems and the possible consequences of a failure of such controls.

## Chapter endnotes

1 The general context of control will be discussed within an 'equilibrium-based theory' or a 'stable state theory' of organisation in which the tendency is towards consensual explanations pointing towards norms and values as a basis for mutual coordination (e.g. see Parsons and Shils, 1951).

2 The term 'fictitious capital' was historically used to describe capital that did not productively employ labour: however in a contemporary context it has become increasingly associated with an escalating use of credit. Indeed, as Marx put it, fictitious capital is 'some kind of money bet on production that does not yet exist' (Marx quoted in Harvey, 1990: 107). In this context it is perhaps best described as any financial instrument (including derivative instruments) other than the tangible commodity of money. In a contemporary context such instruments are often associated with schemes of risk reduction and risk diversification (see also Harvey, 1982: Chapter 9).

3 For further information see www.bp.com

4 For further information see www.hsbc.com

5 For further information see www.timewarner.com

6 See Ashby (1956). This is commonly referred to as Ashby's law.

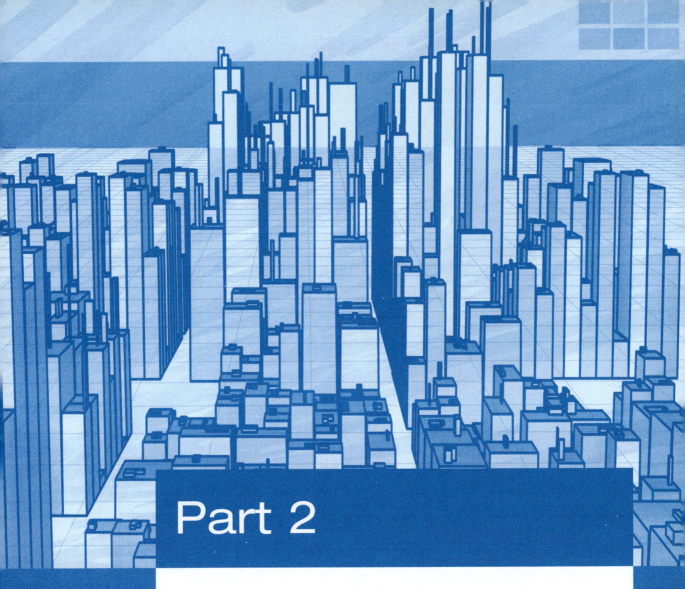

# Part 2

Accounting information systems:
a contemporary perspective

## Part overview

Part 2 of this book provides a contemporary perspective on corporate accounting information systems.

Chapter 4 explores a range of information and communication technology enabled innovations, and considers the impact of such technologies on the operations and management of corporate accounting information systems. Chapter 5 explores the role of alternative network architectures and topologies in corporate accounting information systems.

Chapter 6 provides a contextual typology of contemporary transaction processing cycles, and explores why such transaction processing cycles have become central to the maximisation of shareholder wealth. Finally, Chapter 7 explores issues relating to data management, data processing systems and databases, and considers the importance of effective data management and accurate data processing.

# 4

# AIS and ICT:
## welcome to the information age

## Introduction

*Technology is society* (Castells 1996: 5).

As you are probably aware the late 20th and early 21st centuries have seen what some would describe as an unrestrained explosion of technological innovation – innovation that has revolutionised the nature and context of social relations and transformed the very fabric of social life. A self-accelerating process of technological innovation and development whose pervasive, integrative and reflexive capacity to facilitate operations and communications in *real time* has clearly contributed to a reconfiguration of:

- the socio-economic relationships of production,
- the political notions of power and control, and
- the social contexts of knowledge and experience.

For some, the impact of such technological innovation and development has enabled/facilitated the creation of new global interdependencies and interrelationships – new global interconnections characterised by the emergence of:

- the new global informational economy,[1]
- a new integrated global network or a *space of flows*,[2] and, of course,
- the new network enterprise[3] increasingly dependent on information and communication technology to contribute to and participate in the increasingly volatile flows of information now at the heart of contemporary capitalism.

For others, however, such technological innovation and development has merely fragmented the very foundations of social life[4] and has not only become: intertwined with rising inequality and social exclusion throughout the world (Castells, 1998: 70), but has more importantly, contributed to the resulting increase in economic regionalisation, political territoriality and social segmentation (Castells 1996: 106). Why? Because of what has become known as the 'social paradox of technology'!

Clearly in a socio-economic context, the technological innovation and development over the past 20 or so years has opened up many new possibilities – many new opportunities. It also presented many social, political and economic challenges. Such technological innovation and development has not only challenged (and continues to challenge) the political landscape of socio-economic interrelationships, it has also changed (and continues to change) the economic context of those interrelationships. That is, it has not only changed the focus of power within the so-called new global network – it has also reinforced the concentration and flow of wealth within the new global network – especially between the corporate entities[5] that contribute to and participate in the new integrated global network.

What is important here is to recognise/understand that in a contemporary context at least the impact of recent information and communication technology enabled innovations have been and will undoubtedly continue to be neither impartial nor neutral. Their selection is invariably dominated by the demands and necessities of economics. They are, as such, rarely concerned with social consequences of their adoption. Such issues are often peripheral to the priorities of capital accumulation – and the marketplace. A fair price to pay? Only time will tell!

Commencing with a brief historical review of information and communication technology development and innovations, this chapter:

- considers the social, political and economic impact of information and communication technology enabled innovations on corporate activities, services and facilities – in particular corporate accounting information systems,
- examines the increasing dependency of corporate accounting information systems on information and communication technology enabled innovations, and
- explores how and why the selected adoption of such information and communication technology enabled innovations has become fundamental to the future of contemporary capitalism.

## Learning outcomes

This chapter explores a wide range of issues relating to information and communication technology enabled innovations and their implications on the functioning and management of corporate accounting information systems and provides an introduction to e-business and the virtual world. (These issues are discussed in detail in Chapter 12.)

By the end of this chapter, the reader should be able to;

- describe the major development stages of information and communication technology,
- consider and explain the impact of information and communication technology enabled innovations on corporate accounting information systems, and
- demonstrate a critical understanding of the social, political and economic aspects/consequences of information and communication technology enabled innovations.

# A brief history of information and communications technology

Despite illusions to the contrary, there are two constants in business:

- evolution is inevitable, and
- change is always chaotic.

Whilst the history of information and communications technology clearly has its roots in antiquity, a heritage that can be traced back to the ancient civilisations of Babylonia, Mesopotamia and Egypt, it would perhaps be negligent to consider innovation and development to be progressive and linear, to believe that the *new* is always accepted over the *old* and to assume that change (especially technological change) is apolitical and neutral. Nothing could be further from the truth. Why?

Because change emerges from, or perhaps more appropriately is a reflexive product of, the interaction of a vast array of influences and forces that coexist within an imposed hegemonic framework – a framework that is neither isolated from nor immune to the social, political and economic conflict and turmoil that continues to populate many of the institutional arrangements that comprise its very essence.

In an increasingly uncertain and unpredictable world, a world in which the priorities of organisational technologies, political bureaucracies and social hierarchies are constantly reupholstered, reconfigured and redistributed by:

- the complex territoriality of inter-state politics, and
- the chaotic global priorities of capital accumulation,

change is the one certainty that binds the past to the present, and the present to the future.

All change is connected and all change has consequences, however eclectic random or arbitrary! So, let's have a look at a brief (and very selective) history of information and communications technology.

## From the beginning . . . a selected history

### Pre-AD

- 5000 BC (approximately) the Sumerians of Mesopotamia devise cuneiform.[6]
- 4000 BC the Babylonians adopt the cuneiform script and devise symbols to represent syllables and/or parts of words.
- 3300 BC Sumerian temple officials use wet clay tablets and stylus as an input technology to maintain permanent inventory records.
- 3100 BC the Sumerians begin to keep the earliest books (actually large collections of dried clay tablets).
- 3000 BC the Egyptians write using a fine reed scribe to make marks on a smooth papyrus scroll.
- 2900 BC (approximately) Egyptians begin to collect and bind together a number of papyrus scrolls, a practice adopted and further developed by the Greeks.
- 2000 BC the Phoenicians devise the syllabic writing system and of course the Phoenician alphabet.
- 1700 BC (approximately) the Greeks restructure the Phoenician writing system.
- 1270 BC the first known encyclopaedia is written in Syria.
- 1000 BC the Greek writing system is adapted by the Romans and goes on to form the basis of our contemporary alphabet.

- 900 BC the first recorded use of a postal service, in China.
- 500 BC (approximately) the first portable and light writing surfaces using papyrus rolls and parchments of dried reeds are made.
- 530 BC the Greeks develop the first library.
- 500 BC the first messenger services are developed in both Egypt and China.
- 150 BC (but could be considerably earlier) the Chinese make paper from rags, a process which forms the basis of contemporary papermaking.
- 105 BC contemporary paper invented, in China.

### Pre-1940

- 14 AD (approximately) the Romans establish a postal service.
- 37 AD the first recorded use of mirrors to send messages (Roman Emperor Tiberius).
- 305 AD the first wooden printing presses are invented, in China.
- 1049 the first moveable clay type is invented, in China.
- 1450 newspapers appear in Europe.
- 1455 Johann Gutenberg invents the movable metal-type printing process.
- 1622 William Oughtred invents the slide rule, an early example of an analog computer.
- 1623 Wilhelm Schickard develops the calculating clock, the first calculator.
- 1642 Blaise Pascal invents/develops the Pascaline, a mechanical calculator.
- 1650 the first daily newspaper (Leipzig).
- 1674 Gottfried Wilhelm von Leibniz develops the Step Reckoner.
- 1714 Henry Mills obtain a patent for a typewriter.
- 1801 Joseph Marie Jacquard's invents a programmable mechanical loom.
- 1821 Charles Babbage develops the difference Engine No. 1 and Charles Wheatstone reproduces sound in a primitive sound box.
- 1831 Joseph Henry develops the first electric telegraph.
- 1835 Samuel Morse develops Morse code.
- 1843 Alexander Bain patents the first fax machine.
- 1861 Pony Express postal service commences.
- 1876 Alexander Graham Bell develops the telephone.
- 1880 Herman Hollerith developed a system for recording and retrieving information on punched cards (and also starts a company that eventually became IBM).
- 1887 Emile Berliner invents the gramophone.
- 1894 Guglielmo Marconi invents the radio.
- 1906 Lee Deforest invents the electronic amplifying tube (or triode) improving all electronic communications.
- 1923 Vladimir Kosma Zworykin invents the television or iconoscope.
- 1925 John Logie Baird transmits the first experimental television signal.

### 1940 to the present

- 1944 Howard Aiken and Grace Hopper design the MARK series of computers at Harvard University, USA.
- 1946 John Mauchly and J. Presper Eckert develop ENIAC (Electronic Numerical Integrator and Computer), the first high-speed, general-purpose computer using vacuum tubes.
- 1948 Geoff Tootill and Tom Kilburn co-invent The Manchester University Mark I, the first stored program computer.
- 1949 Maurice Wilkes develops EDSAC (Electronic Delay Storage Automatic Calculator) which became the first stored programme computer in general use.
- 1951 the first commercial computers are sold.

- 1951–58 first generation computers are developed with the following features:
  - vacuum tubes are used as the main elements within the computer,
  - paper-based punch cards are used to input data and store data externally,
  - rotating magnetic drums are used for internal storage of data and programs, and
  - computer programs written in machine code and composed using a compiler.
- 1959–63 second generation computers are developed with the following features:
  - vacuum tubes are replaced by individual transistors as the main element within the computer,
  - magnetic tape and magnetic discs are used to store data externally,
  - magnetic core memories are developed, and
  - high-level computer programming languages are developed, for example languages such as COBOL[7] and FORTRAN[8].
- 1964–79 third generation computers:
  - individual transistors are replaced by integrated circuits (silicon-based chips) as the main element within the computer,
  - magnetic tape and magnetic discs replace punch cards as external storage devices,
  - metal oxide semiconductor (MOS) memory replaces magnetic core internal memories,
  - advanced programming languages like BASIC are developed, and
  - the computer floppy disc is invented.
- 1975 Bill Gates and Paul Allen create Microsoft Inc.
- 1979 to the present, the fourth generation computers are developed with the following features:
  - large-scale and very large-scale integrated circuits (LSIs and VLSICs) are developed,
  - micro-processors containing ROM and RAM memory, logic and control circuits (an entire CPU on a single chip) are developed, and
  - MS-DOS (Microsoft Disk Operating System) debuts.
- 1981 IBM introduces the PC.
- 1983 GUI (graphical user interface(s)) for the PC arrive.
- 1984 Apple Mac is released.
- 1985 CD-ROMs in computers.
- 1990 MS Windows version 3 is released.
- 1991 WWW launched to the public.
- 1994 US government releases control of the internet.
- 1995 MS Windows 95 released.
- 1998 MS Windows 98 released.
- 1999 DVDs in computers.
- 2001 Apple Mac OSX released.
- 2001 MS Windows XP released.
- 2005 number of internet sites between 45 and 50 million.
- 2007 MS Windows Vista released.

And the rest will be history!

## The internet[9] – the world is out there!

### A brief history of the future

There can be little doubt that the idea for, and indeed the development of, an international computer network intended to facilitate communication between geographically dispersed computer users was neither the brainchild of a single individual nor a single group of individuals.

Its cultivation, sponsorship and promotion was the product of applied research and development undertaken by a vast number of unrelated yet inventive and forward thinking individuals and organisations, located not only throughout the USA, but more importantly throughout the world. Indeed, whilst the very existence of this so-called 'internet' is perhaps made more remarkable by the episodic and fragmented context of its history, and the contentious and conflict-ridden controversies associated with its early development, there can be little doubt that in a contemporary context, as an information and communication facility the internet has revolutionised the very fabric of polity, society and indeed economy. But what exactly is the internet?

In a technical context, the term 'internet' (as an abbreviation of the term internetwork – see below) refers to a publicly accessible worldwide system of interconnected computer networks that are connected by internetworking[10] and transmit data by packet switching[11] using a standardised internet protocol (IP)[12], and/or other agreed protocols/procedures. The internet is a created structure, a composed architecture, an interconnected configuration comprising of thousands and thousands of smaller networks. What types of networks? Some academic, some commercial, some domestic and some government based – all of which carry a vast array of information and communication services, including for example e-mail messages, electronic data, online chat and the interlinked webpages and other documents that comprise the world wide web.

Surprisingly enough the general foundations of the internet can be traced back to the late 1950s and early 1960s. Indeed, it was as a result of:

- the increasing frustration and dissatisfaction with contemporary communication facilities, and
- the growing realisation of the need for more efficient and effective communication between an increasing number of users of computers networks and information and communications systems,

that resulted (according to many academics) in the creation and development of the ARPAnet[13] in the USA – a quasi-military/academic network which for many, is inextricably associated with the birth of the contemporary internet.[14]

For many the ARPAnet was not only the core network in the early collection/group of networks that formed the original internetwork, it was and indeed remains the intellectual predecessor of the internet – as the first packet switching network. More importantly the ARPAnet, or more specifically its developers and researchers, was fundamental in the development of a number of innovative networking technologies – including open architecture networking[15] – technologies responsible for facilitating internetworking across not only limited regional networks, but across vast geographically dispersed computer networks irrespective of underlying characteristics and location.

As suggested earlier, the early internet, based around the ARPAnet, was:

- restricted to non-commercial uses such as military/academic research,
- government-funded, and
- limited (initially) to network connections to military sites and universities.

It was however the transition of ARPAnet from NCP to TCP/IP as a network standard that enabled the sharing of the ARPAnet internet technology base and resulted initially in the partitioning of its use between military and non-military use, and eventually the complete removal of the military portion of the ARPAnet to form a separate network, the MILnet. Indeed, by 1983, network connections to the ARPAnet had expanded to include a wide range of educational institutions/organisations and a growing number of research-related companies.

In 1986, the US National Science Foundation (NSF) initiated the development of the NSFnet, a university network backbone which coincided with the gradual decommissioning of the ARPAnet during the 1980s. Continued research and development during the late 1980s (e.g. the development of a domain naming system (1984)) and early 1990s (e.g. the arrival of the first commercial provider of Internet dial-up access (world std.com)) promoted an increasing public awareness and interest in the internet: an interest that resulted in the emergence and development of a number of commercial networks both in the USA and in Europe. And so the commercial use of the internet was born – although not, it should be said, without heated and often confrontational debate!

By 1994 NSFnet had lost its status as the 'backbone' of the internet with other emerging competing commercial providers in the USA, in Europe, and indeed further afield, creating their own backbones and network interconnections. Indeed by 1995 the main backbone of the internet was routed through interconnected network providers, commercial restrictions to access and use of the internet were removed, NSF privatised access to the network they had created and developed . . . and the internet took off!

By 1996/97 the word 'internet' had become common public currency.

So how big is the internet? That's an extremely problematical question to answer for two reasons. Firstly, the internet is neither owned nor controlled by any one person, company, group, government and/or organisation. Consequently accurate empirical data regarding the internet – its size and usage – are not only difficult to obtain, but more importantly difficult to substantiate and validate.

Secondly, the internet is an organic, ever-changing structure, an ever-evolving entity and an ever-developing network whose exponential rates of growth (certainly in the past five years) continue to belittle even the most optimistic of approximations.

In a general context however, estimates suggest that there are (as at 2005):

- approximately 350 million internet hosts,[16]
- nearly 77 million internet domains (see Article 4.1),
- a global internet universe of 934 million users (as at September 2005),[17] of which approximately 25.5 million are in the UK (as at September 2005)[18], and
- approximately 45 to 50 million websites.

It should nevertheless be noted that the internet is not a global network, irrespective of much of the commercial and political hyperbole surrounding its emergence into the global economic psyche. There still remain many parts of the world (e.g. some countries within the African continent, some parts of Asia and some parts of South America) where access to the internet continues to be severely restricted, not only for social and technological reasons, but increasingly for political and economic reasons.

## Controlling the internet: names, standards and regulations

Perhaps due to the fragmented nature of its development or the very nature of its underpinning technology, the internet as a social phenomenon has developed a significant cultural ethos. An ethos predicated on the notion of non-ownership – the idea that the internet as a virtual social network is not owned or controlled by any one person, company, group or indeed organisation.

Nevertheless, the need for some standardisation, harmonisation and control is necessary for any social network – especially a communication/information exchange network established on the ever-shifting foundations of technological innovation, development and change.

## Article 4.1

### Number of domain names approaching 77m

The number of unique internet domain names has almost topped 77 million, according to a new report.

Research by domain registration company VeriSign found that worldwide domain name registrations reached a record high of 76.9 million domain names in the first quarter of 2005; eight per cent up on the fourth quarter of 2004 and 22 per cent higher than the first three months of 2004.

VeriSign claims that more than 6.7 million new domain names were registered in all top-level domains (TLDs) during the first three months of this year, the highest increase in domain name growth to date.

The report reveals that the fastest recent growth in internet services and domain registrations has been in the Far East – China, Japan and South Korea. The domain registration firm suggests that the growth of new domain name registrations was a result of a strengthening global economy, increasing numbers of regular internet users and the continued growth of online advertising.

According to VeriSign, bundled product and services continue to drive growth and domain name registrars and resellers created more packages for registrants in the first quarter of 2005.

'Historically, an indicator of the health and growth of the internet has been the number of domain names registered and renewed,' said Raynor Dahlquist, vice president of VeriSign's Naming Services. 'Given VeriSign's role as operator of the .com and .net infrastructure, we are uniquely positioned to see the trends and factors driving domain name growth, and ultimately, internet growth.'

Source: 10 June 2005,
**www.weboptimiser.com/
search_engine_marketing_news/**.

### Names

Because a global unified namespace is essential for the internet to function properly, in September 1998 the Internet Corporation for Assigned Names and Numbers (ICANN), a non-profit making organisation, was created as the sole authority to: 'coordinate the assignment of unique identifiers on the internet, including domain names, internet protocol addresses, and protocol port numbers' (see www.icann.com).

ICANN's headquarters are in California, USA, and although its operations are overseen by a board of directors representing both commercial and non-commercial communities, there continues to be little doubt that the US government continues to play a pivotal role in approving changes to the domain name system. Recent years have seen a number of attempts not only to reduce the influence of the US government on the activities of ICANN, but also reduce the influence of ICANN. At a November 2005 World Summit on the Information Society (WSIS) in Tunis, Tunisia, ICANN retained a firm grip on its role as the key internet naming authority but many critics fear that the possible privatisation of ICANN will lead to the ultimate commercialisation of the internet (see Article 4.2).

### Standards and regulations

In a contemporary context, broad control of internet development and innovation is now exercised through a series of documents referred to as RFCs (Request For Comments). These are a series of numbered internet informational documents and standards widely followed by all those involved in developing internet-related/internet-based technologies.

## Article 4.2

# US wins net governance battle

### Retains control over main arms

The United States has won its fight to retain control over the internet, at least for the foreseeable future.

The world's governments in Tunisia finally reached agreement at 10.30pm last night, just hours before the official opening of the World Summit this morning. In the end, with absolutely no time remaining, a deal was cut.

That deal will see the creation of a new Internet Governance Forum, that will be set up next year and decide upon public policy issues for the internet. It will be made up of governments as well as private and civil society, but it will not have power over existing bodies.

Equally, there will be no new oversight body for ICANN, or no new ICANN come to that. Instead, all governments have agreed to work within existing organisations. Effectively that will mean within the Governmental Advisory Committee (GAC) of ICANN. Note the word 'advisory' because, again, the GAC has no powers of control over ICANN.

However, head of ICANN Paul Twomey promised delegates that ICANN was happy for the GAC to recreate itself as it saw fit. Twomey later pointed out to us that although the ICANN Board has to approve any GAC decision, there has yet to be an occasion when it hasn't gone along with it. A special meeting of the GAC will be convened at ICANN's conference in Vancouver in a fortnight's time.

The deal represents a remarkable victory for the United States and ICANN: only a month ago they were put on the back foot by an EU proposal that turned the world's governments against the US position.

But following an intense US lobbying effort across the board, the Americans have got their way. Countless press articles, each as inaccurate as the last, formed a huge public sense of what was happening with internet governance that proved impossible to shake.

Massive IT companies – again, mostly US and thanks to intense US government lobbying – came out publicly in favour of the status quo. And the EU representative, David Hendon, confirmed to us last night that in political and governments circles – at every level – the US had pushed home its points again and again.

A letter from US secretary of state Condoleezza Rice sent to the EU just prior to the Summit also had a big impact. Hendon said the UK's position was pretty much set by then, but that it may well have had an impact on other EU members. The exact wording of the letter has yet to come out but it is said to be pretty strong stuff.

And so without the EU forcing the middle ground, and with the US backed by Australia, the brokering – pushed in no short measure by chairman Massod Khan – was led by Singapore and Ghana. The result was that Brazil, China, Iran, Russia and numerous other countries were stymied.

Because of the extremely short timetable, the only deal possible was consensus. And every radical proposal was simply shot down. Today will see a jubilant US ambassador David Gross, a resigned EU (and one that may well learn some lobbying lessons in future) and a depressed Brazil.

Everyone of course claims victory but the reality is that the US has won out by shouting loudest. Expect to read numerous press articles that claim the United States has saved the Internet from a fate worse than death. That was never true, and there were never any good real reasons why the US should not cede some control to an international formation of governments. But reality and politics have never been good bed-fellows.

The shift to an international body will still happen but it will now be at least five years down the line.

The plus point of all this great theatre however is that the world, and its governments, are now infinitely more aware of how this internet thing really works.

Source: Kieren McCarthy, *The Register*, 16th November 2005, **www.theregister.co.uk/2005/ 11/16/us_wins_net_governance**.

As a series of documents, the RFC series began in 1969 as part of the original ARPAnet project. Whilst the first RFC[19] (surprisingly called RFC1) was written and published in April 1969, as at 2005 there are:

- over 4400 published RFCs (some now obsolete) describing every aspect of how the internet functions, and
- over 70 internet standards (STDs) standardising every aspect of how the internet functions.

Today, such RFCs are the official publication channel for the Internet Engineering Task Force (IETF)[20] the Internet Architecture Board (IAB)[21] and the wider internet community. RFCs are published by an RFC Editor,[22] who is supported by the Internet Society (ISOC)[23], but account-able to the IAB.

It is perhaps important to note that once published and issued, an RFC is never de-published,[24] but is rather superseded by the publication of a new RFC. An official list of RFCs which are currently active, or have become adopted internet standards (see below) and/or have been superseded is regularly published by the RFC editor.[25]

So how are RFCs produced and how does an RFC become an internet standard? Whilst RFCs can be promoted through a variety of processes and procedures, the majority of RFCs are now produced by working parties of technical experts. Such working parties/groups would publish what the IETF refers to as an internet draft[26] to:

- facilitate comment and review, and
- promote discussion and critique,

prior to submission to the RFC editor for publication. And such an information procedure works? Surprisingly, it does!

In managing to avoid both the ambiguities sometimes found in informal regulatory pro-nouncements, and the bureaucracy always found in formal regulatory pronouncements, the widespread adoption and acceptance of RFCs continues to define the workings of the internet.

(For more details about RFCs, and the RFC process, see RFC 2026 The Internet Standards Process, Revision 3 (1996).[27])

The acceptance of an RFC by the RFC Editor for publication does not automatically make the RFC a standard. Promotion to, and recognition of, an extant RFC as an internet standard (with the prefix STD) by the Internet Engineering Task Force (IETF) occurs only after many years of experimentation and use and when widespread acceptance has proven an extant RFC to be worthy of the designation 'internet standard'.

And yet even after being designated an internet standard, many RFCs are still commonly referred to by their original RFC number. For example, STD1 Internet Official Protocol Standards[28] is still frequently referred to as RFC 3700, its original designation prior to becom-ing an internet standard.

Clearly, the internet regulatory process, the issue and promotion of internet drafts, the adoption and publication of RFCs, and the development of internet standards, is an evolving and developing standardisation process; a control procedure whose informality has perhaps been its greatest success. Whether such informality will remain will have to be seen . . . but let's hope so.

## The internet today

In a contemporary context, the internet is more than just a complex arrangement of hard-wired physical connections or a growing collection of wireless interconnections. It is more than just the sum of its infrastructure. The internet – as a communication and information exchange network – is an interconnected series of:

- multi-lateral agreements/commercial contracts (e.g. peering agreements which are legal contracts that specify exactly how internet traffic is to be exchanged), and
- technical specifications or communication protocols that describe how data are to be exchanged over the network/the internet.

Indeed, the internet protocol suite[29] was consciously and deliberately designed to be autonomous of any underlying physical medium. As a consequence, any communications systems/network – whether hard-wired or wireless – that can carry two-way digital data can be used for the transmission of internet traffic.

Some of the most popular services and uses of the internet are:

- electronic mail (e-mail),
- file sharing,
- media streaming,
- VoIP (Voice over IP),
- internet relay chat (IRC),
- newsgroups, and
- the world wide web.

Of the above, clearly e-mail and the world wide web are the most used, with many other services being dependent upon them. Let's look at each of these in a little more detail.

### E-mail

Electronic mail (or e-mail) is a method of composing, sending and receiving messages, together with any associated attached files of text data, numeric data and/or images, via an electronic communication system/network, usually the internet. (We will discuss the nature and context of e-mail later in this chapter.)

### File sharing

File sharing is the activity of making a file of data/information, or files of data and/or information available to others, a sharing that can be accomplished in many ways, for example:

- data/information file(s) can be e-mailed to another user(s) as an e-mail attachment,
- data/information file(s) can be uploaded to a website and/or an FTP[30] server for download by another user(s), and
- data/information file(s) can be placed into a shared location or onto a file server using a peer-to-peer (P2P) network[31] for instant access/use by another user(s).

Clearly one of the key benefits of any network (especially the internet) is the ability to share files stored on a server with many other users. Whilst all of the above represent adequate mechanisms for this task, where a vast amount of file sharing occurs between many users, such traffic – such file sharing – may best be served/facilitated by the use of:

- a website and/or
- an FTP server, or
- a peer-to-peer (P2P) network.

Confused? Consider the following.

Many companies operate websites/FTP server facilities from which product catalogues, service information and/or corporate literature can be downloaded, for example, see:

■ Tesco plc @ www.tesco.com
■ HSBC plc @ www.hsbc.com
■ British Airways plc @ www.britishairways.com or
■ BP plc @ www.bp.com.

Many professional associations use secure FTP facilities to provide information to members only, for example, see:

■ Association of Chartered Certified Accountants @ www.accaglobal.com
■ Institute of Chartered Accountants of England and Wales @ www.icaew.co.uk
■ Chartered Management Institute @ www.managers.org.uk
■ Chartered Institute of Marketing @ www.cim.co.uk or
■ Chartered Institute of Management Accountants @ www.cimaglobal.com.

Many educational institutions – schools, colleges and universities – now use secure FTP facilities to provide student access to data/information files, with many schools, colleges and universities using blackboard[32] to facilitate and control/restrict student access. For example, see:

■ University of Hull @ http://blackboard.hull.ac.uk
■ University of Leicester @ http://blackboard.le.ac.uk
■ University of Teesside @ http://blackboard.tees.ac.uk or
■ Bournemouth University @ http://blackboard.bournemouth.ac.uk.

So what about file sharing using peer-to-peer (P2P) networks.

Although file sharing is a legal technology with many valid and legal uses (as indicated earlier) there remains nonetheless several major problems/concerns surrounding file sharing, especially file sharing[33] using peer-to-peer (P2P) networks. Why? For two reasons: firstly because of the anonymity of such file sharing; and secondly because of the questionable legality of such file sharing, especially where copyright concerns exist.

Whilst there can be little doubt that the popularity of anonymous internet file sharing grew with the increased availability of high-speed internet connections and the decreasing size (in a relative sense) of high-quality MP3 audio files (e.g. Napster,[34] the first major – albeit illegal – file sharing facility was launched in 1999). Today a vast array of file sharing programs are available (e.g. Gnutella[35]) which allow users to search for and share almost any type of file – copyright or not! Clearly, this situation has not gone unnoticed with those media companies who hold the legal copyright to the material being shared. Indeed the latter part of the 20th century and early part of the 21st century has been replete with media reports surrounding the attempts by companies to track down illegal file sharing, close down illegal file sharing facilities and prosecute those participating in the illegal file sharing of copyright material.

Whilst some successful prosecutions have been brought before the courts in an attempt to close down and/or force those responsible for the development and management of peer-to-peer (P2P) file sharing networks to legitimise their facilities/activities (see Articles 4.3, 4.4, and, 4.5), it would nonetheless appear that such companies may well be fighting a losing battle.

Why? For two reasons. First because the on-going development of new second generation decentralised peer-to-peer (P2P) protocols (e.g. Freenet[36] – see 'What is Freenet?' available @ http://freenetproject.org/index.php?page=whatis) are severely restricting the potential effectiveness of court action for file sharing and copyright infringement. Secondly, because of the growth of groups supporting the use of file sharing technology and questioning the legitimacy

## Article 4.3

### We'll sue illegal music downloaders, says BPI

The trade body for the British record industry stepped up the pressure on users of illegal internet music sites yesterday by warning that legal action against web pirates is 'increasingly likely'. The British Phonographic Industry said it would follow the lead of its counterpart in the United States, the Recording Industry Association of America, if illegal downloading escalated. Its main target will be consumers who trawl file-sharing services such as Kazaa and Grokster for free tracks, bypassing conventional retail outlets and legal internet sites.

'The disturbing increase in the illegal copying and distribution of unauthorised music files over the internet is making legal action increasingly likely. Nobody should be in any doubt that such uses of file-sharing networks are illegal and are harming the health of British music. We will take legal action if we are forced to,' said a BPI spokesperson.

BPI lawsuits are not imminent, however. The body is concerned that illegal downloads will take off in this country as broadband penetration increases from its present level of more than 3m homes. If use of illegitimate sites increases significantly as broadband rolls out across the UK, the BPI is expected to launch legal action.

Worldwide sales of recorded music fell 10.9% to $12.7bn (£6.8bn) in the first half of last year, a fall blamed on file-sharing and commercial piracy. Another concern for the BPI is the negative publicity that could be created by suing individuals. The RIAA has claimed that its controversial legal campaign against users of file-sharing networks has proved a successful deterrent against would-be pirates. It served writs against 341 consumers last year, and use of the Kazaa site dropped from a high of 16 million visitors in March last year to 8.2 million in October, a month after the first lawsuits were filed.

But the RIAA was accused of heavy-handed behaviour after it emerged that a writ had been served against Brianna LaHara, a 12-year-old schoolgirl. Ms Lahara's mother eventually settled the copyright infringement lawsuit for $2,000.

Using file-sharing networks is banned under UK copyright law but legal experts say the Crown Prosecution Service is unlikely to take on the added burden of pursuing consumers who use illegal sites.

Andrew Hobson, a partner at Reynolds Porter Chamberlain, a commercial law firm, said civil cases had a greater chance of success. 'You have a lower standard of proof. All you have to do is prove that there has been unauthorised copying,' he said. But that could bring the BPI into conflict with service providers, who would have to release the names of customers who have been using file-sharing sites. A spokesperson for ISPA, the trade body for British-based ISPs, said the BPI would not be able to demand information under the Regulation of Investigatory Powers Act, which allows law agencies and authorised bodies to access communications data. 'If it wishes to take any action it should have to do it via law enforcement or a recognised authority,' he said.

Source: Dan Milmo, 15 January 2004,
The *Guardian*, **www.guardian.co.uk**.

## Article 4.4

### Court orders copyright filter on Kazaa

Internet file-swapping was dealt a fresh blow yesterday after the Australian federal court ordered the world's largest file-sharing service to filter out copyrighted material from its network. Kazaa, a program estimated to be used for four out of five internet file-swaps, will have to include copyright filters in future editions of its software and the company behind the program must put pressure on current users to upgrade to the new version.

More than 317 million people have downloaded Kazaa – which allows users to swap music, film and digital information over the web – and several million are believed to be using it at any one time. The Sydney court found file-sharing copyrighted material over the network was illegal. 'Both the user who makes the file available and the user who downloads a copy infringes the owner's copyright,' the ruling stated.

The judgment against Sharman Networks, Kazaa's Sydney-based owners, is a further blow to internet file-swapping and follows a series of adverse rulings in recent months. Although Australian courts do not have jurisdiction overseas, their rulings customarily influence the development of law in other Commonwealth countries, including Britain.

Yaman Akdeniz, the director of Cyber-Rights and Cyber-Liberties, said the judgment would simply increase the exodus of users to alternative file-sharing applications. 'The number of users on Kazaa is already going down ever since it started to be targeted,' Mr Akdeniz said. 'If you put a successful copyright filter on it, there won't be anything left because most of the swapping done there is illegal.'

However, he said the ruling was unlikely to stop file-swapping altogether, adding: 'The legal system is slow and always lagging behind the software development.' In June, the US supreme court ruled that makers of peer-to-peer software could be held liable for the copyright infringement of their users. The peer-to-peer pioneer Napster was shut down in 2001 after a US court ordered it to stop users swapping copyrighted files. Napster has since been relaunched as a paid-for music file download service.

The music industry blames the growth of file-sharing software for its poor performance in recent years. CD sales have fallen by 25% since file-sharing began to take off in 1999. Kazaa, which moved to headquarters in Australia and a registration in the Pacific tax haven of Vanuatu after a similar court case in the Netherlands in 2001, was developed by the Swedish internet pioneer Niklas Zennström.

Mr Zennström has since become known for writing the software for the internet telephony service Skype.

Sharman and the five other defendants will also have to pay damages and 90% of the costs incurred by the record labels – including Universal, EMI, Sony BMG, Warner and Festival Mushroom – which brought the case.

Source: David Fickling, 6 September 2005, The *Guardian*, **www.guardian.co.uk**.

## Article 4.5

### Grokster file-sharing site in talks to go legitimate

Grokster, the file-sharing service used by tens of millions of people worldwide to illegally swap music and films, could be about to become legitimate.

The business is said to be in takeover talks with Mashboxx, a young company trying to establish a legal peer-to-peer service. The talks, reported in the *Wall Street Journal*, follow a US supreme court ruling in June that suppliers of file sharing software could be liable for its misuse.

The case was seen as a landmark in the music industry's fight against piracy. Mashboxx, based in Virginia, is run by former Grokster president Wayne Rosso.

Source: David Teather, 20 September 2005, The *Guardian*, **www.guardian.co.uk**.

of the so-called 'corporate witch hunt' for illegal file sharers – for whatever socio-political reason. See, for example, the Electronic Frontier Foundation[37] (EFF) and perhaps also the openDemocracy website @ www.openDemocracy.net.

### *Media streaming*

The delivery of media can be classified into two categories:

- delivery systems through which media can be delivered for concurrent consumption[38] – for example, television and radio, and

- delivery systems through which media can be delivered for deferred consumption – for example, DVDs, books, video cassettes and audio CDs.

The term 'media streaming' is often used to describe delivery systems for concurrent consumption, that is delivery systems and/or facilities through which the simultaneous delivery and consumption of online and real time media occurs, and is invariably applied to media that are distributed over computer-based networks. However, as we shall see, delivery systems for deferred consumption are now increasingly dependent on online media streaming, although some would categorise it as file sharing!

Although the basic concepts of media streaming had been well established as early as the 1970s, and the technical questions and problems regarding the feasibility of computer-based media streaming delivery systems[39] had been resolved as early as the 1980s, it was not until the mid/late 1990s and:

- the establishment of standard data/information protocols and formats,
- the development of reliable networking technologies,
- the growth in network capacity and usage, especially the internet, and of course,
- the increased processing capacity of the modern PC,

that dependable computer-based media streaming became a reality.

Today, not only do many of the existing radio and television broadcasters provide live internet media streams of programme broadcasts, see for example:

- www.bbc.co.uk for BBC media-streamed video and audio programming,
- www.sky.com/skynews/home for media-streamed news/current affairs video programming, and/or
- www.virgin.co.uk for media-streamed contemporary audio programming,

but a new breed of internet only broadcasters have emerged that provide a range of audio and video programming, from technical live web casts, to specialised video and audio programming, much of which are often unlicensed and uncensored!

Increasingly – certainly since the early part of the 21st century – media streaming has become an important mechanism in the delivery of media (audio and increasingly video) for deferred consumption – that is consumption in another place and/or another (later) time. For example, the availability of legal downloadable online music (see Napster @ www.napster.co.uk/index and/or Apple itunes @ www.apple.com/itunes) and the increasing availability of downloadable online movies (see ezMovies @ www.ezmovies.net and/or Movieflix @ www.movieflix.com), a market in which the major movie studios have only recently entered (see Movielink @ www.movielink.com and Cinemanow @ www.cinemanow.com).[40] (See also Article 5.6.)

There can be little doubt that media streaming has and indeed will continue to revolutionise corporate activity – not only those aspects associated with product delivery, but perhaps more importantly those aspects associated with service/process management: for example, media streaming (in particular web-cam-based media streaming technologies) for intra-company video conferencing where the technology brings with it many social, economic, and legal issues, many of which remain unresolved.

### VoIP (Voice over IP)

Voice over Internet Protocol (also known as VoIP, IP telephony, internet telephony, and digital telephony) is the routing of audio – in particular voice conversations – over the internet and/or any other IP-based network (e.g. a local area network and/or a corporate intranet). Essentially it is the use of internet protocol networks to carry voice phone calls inasmuch as voice data

## Article 4.6

### More online movie stores on the way

*Film industry plans to start offering download services to battle piracy and counterfeiting.*

LONDON (Reuters) – The film industry is working to launch online movie download services to avoid the same fate as the piracy-ridden music industry, NBC Universal Chairman and Chief Executive Bob Wright said Tuesday.

'It's something we have to do, but it has to be done well,' Wright said 'These movies are so expensive we have to be careful . . . We're pretty close. Hopefully by the end of this year we'll be able to do that.'

Wright was speaking at the launch of an anti-piracy and counterfeiting initiative with senior executives from media, software, pharmaceutical and food industries known as 'Business Action to Stop Counterfeiting and Piracy' (BASCAP).

Other participants included Microsoft's Chief Executive Steve Ballmer, Nestle's Peter Brabeck-Letmathe, Vivendi Universal's Jean-Rene Fourtou and EMI Group's Eric Nicoli.

'The problems are spreading and no one is immune,' Wright said. 'In my business we're just looking over the shoulder of the music industry, which has gone through a very difficult time.'

The global music industry has been decimated by physical piracy and online file-trading networks. It has stemmed some of the losses by aggressively targeting illicit file-sharers with lawsuits while also offering legal online alternatives like Apple's iTunes Music Store.

Movies are increasingly vulnerable to online piracy due to the spread of high-speed Internet connections and file-sharing technologies like BitTorrent. Eight people were charged last week for stealing a copy of 'Star Wars: Episode III – Revenge of the Sith' and posting it online before the movie appeared in theaters.

There are already at least two fledgling online movie stores: Movielink, which is a venture of five major Hollywood studios, and CinemaNow, which is jointly owned by Lions Gate Entertainment, Microsoft, Blockbuster and several private equity firms.

Wright also spoke about the battle over next-generation DVD technology. Universal Studios, a unit of NBC Universal, and Warner Bros Studios have endorsed the HD DVD format, while Paramount, Sony Pictures, Walt Disney Co. and Twentieth Century Fox have backed the rival Blu-ray format.

'You'd always rather have one standard – that's going to happen eventually,' he said. 'Hopefully this won't go as far as (the) Betamax-VHS (video tape format battle).'

Source: 4 October 2005, CNN,
http://money.cnn.com/2005/10/04/news/
fortune500/movies_piracy.reut/.

flows over a general-purpose packet switched network instead of traditional, dedicated, circuit switched voice transmission lines.

So what are the advantages and disadvantages of VoIP? The main advantages are:

- faster innovation – product innovation and development is dictated by the market, resulting in faster adoption of new or advanced features,
- lower cost[41] – a telephony service using VoIP costs less than the equivalent service from traditional sources, and
- increased functionality/portability – calls are always routed to a recipient's VoIP phone and calls can be made/received anywhere without additional cost.

The main disadvantages are:

- lack of reliability – power supply disruption/failure could significantly affect performance,
- geographical anonymity – some VoIP systems do not yet provide e999 facilities for emergency calls and consequently it can be difficult to route callers to appropriate emergency centre/facilities,

- integration into the global telephone number systems – although in the UK telephone numbers are regulated by OFCOM[42] in some countries there is no widely adopted number standard for the allocation of numbers for VoIP, unlike traditional telephone systems and mobile phone networks which comply with a common global standard E.164.[43]

Will VoIP replace contemporary mobile phones? Probably not – well not for the present at least. Why? For three reasons.

Firstly, because in an already saturated telecommunications market, demand for VoIP among both corporate clients and individual consumers will continue to remain weak and uncertain, unless and until wireless network coverage achieves a similar geographical exposure to contemporary mobile phone network coverage, thereby enabling a great usage of mobile VoIP phones (often called WiFi phones).

Secondly, because problems still remain with regard to VoIP systems' ability/capability to service adequately the requirements of a vast range of devices that depend wholly or in part on access to a quality voice-grade telephony for some or all of their functionality. Such devices would include, for example:

- fax machines,
- conventional modems,
- FAXmodems,
- digital satellite television receivers that require a permanent telephone connection (e.g. Sky+ (see www.sky.com)), and
- burglar alarm systems which are connected to the regional call centre through which a link (sometime automated) is provided to the emergency services.

Thirdly, the regulatory framework for VoIP is still in its infancy and whilst both EU and UK telecommunications regulators are now drafting appropriate codes of practice for providers, much still needs to be done.

As a consequence whilst some EU, UK and indeed US-based telecommunications providers do use IP telephony – often over secure and dedicated IP networks – it remains unlikely that the corporate office environment or the consumer home of the near future will use anything remotely like pure VoIP.

### Internet Relay Chat (IRC)

Internet relay chat is a form of instant communication over the internet. Originating in Finland,[44] IRC is essentially a huge multi-user live chat facility designed primarily for group (many-to-many) communication in discussion forums called channels, although it can and sometimes is used for non-group (one-to-one) communication.

With a number of interconnecting internet relay chat servers located around the world, internet relay chat allows people all over the world to participate in real-time conversations. It is therefore perhaps unsurprising that for many users, internet relay chat is where the internet becomes a living thing!

So how does internet relay chat work? To use IRC (apart from a PC and an internet connection) users need:

- a web browser like Netscape (available @ www.netscape.com), MS Internet Explorer (available @ www.windowsdownloads.com) or Mozilla Firefox (available @ http://www.mozilla.org/products/firefox) to use the world wide web, and
- an IRC client program, for example mIRC (available @ www.mirc.com).

Once an IRC client program has been installed, users can log onto an available IRC server, select an appropriate channel,[45] log into a chat session, and after learning a few basic commands and text protocols, converse by typing messages to other chat session participants that are instantly sent.

Surprisingly, many companies (especially IT companies) now hold regularly scheduled, secured chat sessions – between company representatives, customers and clients – not only to provide technical information and advice on products and services offered by the company, but also to gain feedback on product/service developments and enhancements, and opinions on possible future developments/innovations.

So, far from being merely a chat facility for the lost and the lonely hearted, internet relay chat can be a valuable and important business/marketing tool. Yet whilst internet relay chat as a communication facility clearly has many advantages it nonetheless has its seedier side! Indeed following a number of high-profile cases in the late 1990s and early 2000s, in October 2003 MSN and Microsoft closed MSN Chat, issuing the following statement:[46]

> *as part of an overall effort by MSN and Microsoft to provide consumers with a safer, more secure and positive overall online experience, MSN has decided to no longer offer MSN Chat in the UK as of October 14, 2003. This change is intended to help protect MSN users from unsolicited information such as spam and to better protect children from inappropriate communication online.*

### Newsgroups

Newsgroups are often referred to as repositories[47] although those which exist within the Usenet[48] system, are perhaps more appropriately referred to as discussion groups since they are used primarily for the distribution of messages posted from many users at many different locations.

Within Usenet, newsgroups are arranged into a number of hierarchies, as follows:

- comp.* – for discussion related to computer-related issues/subjects,
- humanities.* – for discussion related to humanities (e.g. literature, culture, philosophy),
- misc.* – for the discussion of miscellaneous issues/subjects not appropriate to any other hierarchy,
- news.* – for discussion on or about Usenet,
- rec.* – for discussion related to recreational activities/undertakings,
- sci.* – for discussion related to scientific issues/subjects,
- soc.* – for discussion related to social issues/subjects, and
- talk.* – for the discussion of contentious issues (e.g. religion/politics).

There are also a number of alternative newsgroup hierarchies:

- alt.* – for the discussion of 'alternative' issues/subjects,[49]
- gnu.* – for the discussion of issues related to the GNU project of the Free Software Foundation (see http://www.gnu.org), and
- biz.* – for discussion on business related issues/subjects.

(Note in all the above * is referred to as a wildcard extension.)

A number of newsgroups exist within each of the above hierarchies, for example:

- within the comp.* hierarchy – comp.ai for general discussions on artificial intelligence,
- within the news.* hierarchy – news.admin.net-abuse.email for discussion of abuse of e-mail by spammers and other parties, news.groups for discussion on the creation and deletion of newsgroups,
- within the rec.* hierarchy – rec.sport.soccer for general discussion of world football, and
- within the sci.* hierarchy – sci.geo.earthquakes for general discussion on earthquakes, volcanoes, tsunamis and other geological and seismic events.

Briefly, for a new newsgroup to be created, it must be introduced and discussed within news.groups (see above) and a resolution for adoption be voted upon. If two-thirds of those voting are in favour (and there are 100 more votes in favour than against) the resolution is passed and the new newsgroup can be created.[50]

So how do newsgroups work? Newsgroup servers are hosted by various companies, organisations and academic institutions, with many ISPs (internet service providers) hosting their own, or at least renting a news server for the use of their subscribers. See for example Google news groups available @ http://groups.google.com.

There are two ways to access the Usenet newsgroups:

- with the use of a newsreader program (most of the popular web browsers (Internet Explorer, Netscape, and Mozilla) provide integrated free newsreader facilities), or
- with the use of a web-based Usenet service, for example:
  - Google – see http://groups.google.com
  - Interbulletin – see http://news.interbulletin.com
  - Mailgate – see http://www.mailgate.org
  - News2Web – see http://services.mail2web.com/FreeServices/Usenet
  - WebNews-Exchange – see http://www.webnews-exchange.com.

### The world wide web

There can be little doubt that the one internet application most people are familiar with is the world wide web (WWW or simply the web). But what is the world wide web? The web is a portion of the internet, albeit a large one, which is a service that operates over the internet and is essentially a multi media information space into which information and resources are placed and made available to other users. The web facilitates access to information and other resources over the medium of the internet using the HTTP protocol (see below) to transmit data and allow web-based applications and services to communicate with each other. In essence the web is an eclectic collection of interlinked[51] multimedia web documents (usually referred to as webpages) that are accessible using a wed browser.[52]

Whilst the underlying ideas of the web can be traced back to 1980 and ideas initially proposed by Tim Berners-Lee[53] and Robert Cailliau, it was not until November 1990[54] that Tim Berners-Lee published a formal proposal for the web. In August 1991 he posted a summary of the web project on the alt.hypertext newsgroup[55] which effectively marked the debut of the web as a publicly available service on the internet.

So how does the web work? It is essentially comprised of three basic standards:

- the Uniform Resource Identifier (URI),[56] which is a universal system for referencing resources on the web, such as webpages,
- the HyperText Transfer Protocol (HTTP) which specifies how a web browser and a network server communicate with each other, and
- the HyperText Markup Language (HTML) used to define the structure and content of hypertext documents.

A webpage or other resource on the web can be accessed (using a web browser) in two different ways, by either:

- using the URL (uniform resource locator) or web address of the webpage required, or
- following a hypertext link on an existing webpage.

The server name aspect of the URL is converted into an IP address using the domain name system (DNS) – a global, distributed internet database. A HTTP request is then sent to the web server working at that IP address for the webpage that has been requested. The HTML text, graphics and any associated files that comprise the requested webpage are then returned to the user making the request. The user's web browser renders the webpage as instructed, incorporating where required any images, links and/or other resources as necessary. It is this rendering that produces the webpage the user will see.

So what are the social implications of the web? In a contemporary context there can be little doubt that the web has revolutionised the global interpersonal exchange of information on a scale that was unimaginable even a few years ago. It has allowed/enabled a sudden and extreme decentralisation of information and data unprecedented in history. Unfettered by the demands of the physical world, the virtual nature of the web and the digital nature of its content have presented an unparalleled opportunity for people separated by geography and time to mutually develop and to share/exchange:

- social/cultural experiences,
- political ideologies,
- cultural ideas and customs,
- advice, and
- literature and art.

A sharing that appears to know no boundaries!

In August 2001, the Google search engine (www.google.com) index held over 1.3 billion webpages. By early March 2004, Google's index held over 4 billion pages, whilst by November 2004 the number of indexed pages was a little over 8 billion. In August 2005 Yahoo (www.yahoo.com) announced that its online search engine index contained more than 20 billion web documents and images.

## The internet . . . the good, the bad and the great divide!

As an emergent phenomenon of the late 20th and early 21st centuries, the internet is an elaborate and intricate socio-technical system, a large-scale, highly engineered, highly complex system, whose growth and expansion has continued to astound and amaze even the most optimistic of users, developers and commentators.

And yet, whilst there can be little doubt that in a technical context the internet (and its component services) has provided facilities/services that were once deemed to be the stuff of science fiction, the socio-political impact of internet technology (or indeed – lack of internet technology) has often reinforced traditional socio-cultural differences and related socio-economic disadvantages. As suggested by Lu (2001), there exists,

> 'great disparities in opportunity to access the internet and the information and educational/ business opportunities tied to this access . . . between developed and developing countries' (2001:1).

Disparities which continue to reinforce the global digital divide in which the technologically rich get richer, and the technologically poor get poorer – perhaps not in absolute terms but certainly in relative terms.

Indeed, whilst the internet has undoubtedly revolutionised contemporary processes of communication and dismantled once traditional (almost sacred) spatial and temporal boundaries, it has more importantly enabled a greater socio-cultural sharing of ideas, knowledge and skills, and facilitated greater economic trade and the global movement of goods and services – any time, any place, any where. Yet, the rewards and benefits from these changes – these opportunities – have been and indeed continue to be shared by the very few!

Far from:

- facilitating greater knowledge/information access,
- encouraging greater social mobility,
- stimulating greater political democracy, and
- promoting sustained economic growth,

the contemporary internet (with its western-influenced internet culture[57]) has, for some, merely:

- exacerbated historical politico-economic differences,
- re-entrenched socio-cultural prejudices and inequalities, and
- reinforced the so-called 'north-south divide'[58].

Whilst many problems remain, for example ADSL[59] and broadband access remain rare even non-existent in many less developed/developing countries, it is hoped that developing internet technologies, for example wireless internet access and satellite based internet access, will help to equalise the distribution and availability of internet technologies and (hopefully) help to reduce the ever growing digital divide.

## E-business – tomorrow's world, today!

E-business[60] or, electronic business, is any business process that is empowered by an information system – which in a contemporary context invariably means the utilisation of information and communication technology enabled innovations, including of course web-based technologies. It enables companies/organisations to:

- connect both internal and external processes with greater efficiency and flexibly, and
- operate more closely with suppliers and/or related companies/organisations to better satisfy the needs and expectations of customers and clients.

Effective e-business involves:

- the development and introduction of new revenue streams through the use of e-commerce (see below),
- the enhancement of information and communication relationships with customers, clients and related companies/organisations, and
- the development of efficient, effective and secure knowledge management systems.

Whether conducted over the public internet, through the use of internal intranets (internal internet-based networks) or through the use of secure private extranets, e-business is clearly more than just e-commerce. Why? Because, in facilitating the integration of both intra- and inter-company/organisation business processes and procedures, e-business now encapsulates the whole range of business functions, activities and services, from:

- the functions central to a company/organisation's value chain, to
- the activities central to a company/organisation funding cycle, to
- the services that support both the commercial and non-commercial operations of a company/organisation.

Indeed, as indicated in the European e-business report (2004)[61]:

- the increasing migration towards broadband internet connections,
- the increasing use of business-to-business (B2B) online trading,
- the increasing business-to-consumer (B2C) online trading, and
- the increasing integration/adoption of information and communication technologies,

all suggest that within the European Union (and in particular within the UK) e-business has come of age and now represents an important aspect of corporate business and its never-ending search for profit.

For our purposes, we will explore e-business in the context of the following categories:

- e-commerce-related developments and innovations including:
  - websites,
  - electronic data interchange (EDI),
  - electronic funds transfer (EFT), and
  - electronic mail (e-mail),
- information and communication technology enabled innovations in accounting/finance, management and manufacture, and other innovations.

## E-commerce-related developments and innovations

Although we will explore the functional business aspects of web-based e-commerce in Chapter 12, it would perhaps be useful to provide a brief historical and contemporary context to e-commerce.

E-commerce or electronic commerce is often defined as the buying and selling of goods and services and, the transfer of funds, through digital communications via the internet, especially the web, but is perhaps more appropriately defined as a paperless inter-company/organisation and/or intra-company/organisation exchange of business information using a range of related information and communication related technologies. It can involve:

- electronic data interchange,
- electronic funds transfer,
- value chain activities,
- online transaction processing,
- supply chain activities,
- automated inventory management systems,
- automated data-collection systems, and
- electronic communication systems (e.g. e-mail).

In a historical context the term e-commerce originally meant the undertaking of commercial transactions electronically, using information and communication-related technologies, for example:

- electronic data interchange – to send and receive commercial documents electronically, and
- electronic funds transfer – to send and receive funds electronically.

In a contemporary context, however, the term e-commerce has become synonymous with a wide range of interrelated activities associated with the sale/purchase of goods and services via the internet-based world wide web.[62]

Whilst during the early/mid 1990s, many business and economic analysts forecast that internet-based e-commerce facilities would become the major retail vehicle of the late 1990s, it was not until the late 1990s/early 21st century that a number of US-based/Europe-based companies/organisations began to develop fully their web-based services including the integration of e-commerce facilities. And, despite the early 21st century witnessing the spectacular demise of a large number of so-called pure e-commerce companies during the dot com[63] collapse in

2000 and 2001, many established companies and organisations have continued to recognise the enormous added value (wealth creating opportunities) of increasingly sophisticated but user friendly e-commerce capabilities/facilities.

So is e-commerce a global phenomenon? No, not really. As suggested earlier, e-commerce (as with the internet) continues to remain very much a geographically focused phenomenon. Indeed, as at the end of 2005, whilst e-commerce has become well-established across much of North America, Western Europe and parts of Australasia, for a number of African, East Asian, and South American countries it still remains:

- a slowly emerging facility/capability in some industrialised countries, and
- an almost non-existent facility/capability in many third world countries, including many African countries.

More on this later – including the increasing use and availability of m-commerce[64] facilities (see Chapter 12).

Let's look at the core constituents of e-commerce, that is the key requirements for effective e-commerce:

- a website,
- electronic data interchange (EDI) facilities,
- electronic funds transfer (EFT) facilities, and
- electronic mail (e-mail) facilities.

## Websites

A website is merely a collection of related webpages or, more appropriately a collection of related HTML[65]/XHTML[66] documents accessible via HTTP[67], on the internet, using a web browser. Remember the web is merely a term used to describe all the publicly accessible websites in existence on the internet.

The related pages of a website are accessed from its homepage located at its web address or, more appropriately, its URL.[68] Whilst it is the URL of the related webpages that arranges and organises them into a related hierarchy, it is the hyperlinks[69] between the pages that:

- control how the website reader/visitor understands and comprehends the overall structure, and
- determine how the web traffic[70] (amount of web users) flows between the different aspects of the website.

No longer restricted to the PC domain, website pages are increasingly accessible and indeed viewable through the use of a range of portable media devices (e.g. PDAs and mobile phones) that possess internet browsing capabilities, internet functionality and, of course, internet connectivity.

So what types of websites exist? There are many different types, some of which allow free access, some of which require a subscription to access part of their content and others which require a subscription to access all of their content.

Some examples of website types would include:

- a company/business website – a website used for the promotion of a company, business and/or service (e.g. www.tesco.com) and www.lloydstsb.com,
- a commerce site (or e-commerce site) – a website used for purchasing goods and services,
- a community site – a website where persons with similar interests communicate with each other,

- an archive website – used to preserve valuable electronic content threatened with extinction,
- a database website – a website whose main use is the search and display of a specific database's content,
- a directory website – a website that contains varied contents which are divided into categories and subcategories (e.g. www.google.co.uk and www.yahoo.com),
- a download website – a website used for downloading electronic content, such as software, games, etc.,
- a professional website – a website designed specifically for members of a professional association (e.g. www.accaglobal.com and www.icaew.co.uk),
- a game website – a website that is itself a game or 'playground' where many people come to play,
- an adult website – a website dedicated to the provision of pornographic literature, images and movies,
- an information website – a website that contains content that is intended merely to inform visitors, but not necessarily for commercial purposes (e.g. www.dti.gov.uk),
- a news website – a website dedicated to dispensing news and commentary (e.g. www.ft.com.and and www.timesonline.co.uk),
- a search engine – a website that provides general information and is intended as a gateway to other websites (e.g. www.google.co.uk and www.yahoo.com),
- a web portal – a website that provides a starting point, a gateway or portal to other resources on the internet or an intranet,

and of course many websites would invariably fall into more than one of the above categories/ types!

### Electronic data interchange (EDI)

Electronic Data Interchange (EDI) is the exchange of structured and pre-defined information using agreed message standards and transmission protocols from one computer application to another by electronic means and with a minimum of human intervention. Perhaps, more appropriately, EDI is the specific interchange methods agreed upon by national or international standards bodies for the transfer of business transaction data.

There are in fact three major sets of EDI standards:

- UN/EDIFACT (United Nations/Electronic Data Interchange for Administration, Commerce, and Transport),
- ANSI ASC (X12)[71] (American National Standards Institute Accredited Standards Committee X12), and
- UCS (Uniform Communications Standard).

UN/EDIFACT is an international standard and the United Nations recommended standard and is predominant in all areas outside of North America, whilst ANSI ASC (X12), and UCS are popular in North America. These standards prescribe which pieces of information are mandatory for a particular document and which pieces are optional, and give the rules for the structure of the document/content, including:

- the document format,
- the allowable character sets, and
- the data elements,

that can be used in the exchange/transmission of documents and forms.

So what type of business transaction data is EDI used for? EDI can/is used to:

- transmit documents such as invoices, purchase orders, receipts, shipping documents, and other standard business correspondence electronically between companies, organisations and/or business partners, and
- transmit financial information in electronic form, and
- transfer financial payments and/or funds (usually referred to as electronic funds transfer (EFT)).

EDI is now widely employed in a variety of business-related industries, including:

- banking and financial services,
- manufacturing, and of course
- retailing.

So, why is EDI used as opposed to traditional, paper-based systems? For obvious reasons really.

Firstly, traditional paper-based systems are:

- invariably slow and often extremely bureaucratic,
- often labour intensive and costly,
- increasingly suffer from low levels of accuracy and high levels of human error, and
- often subject to processing delays resulting in often excessive uncertainty.

Secondly, EDI-based systems are:

- less bureaucratic and less paper-based – and therefore environmentally friendly,
- flexible and simpler to use – usually allowing one-time data entry,
- time efficient – promoting the speedier, more-efficient flow of information, and
- very accurate – reducing possible handling errors due to less human interface.

So how does EDI work? Within a typical EDI transaction between two trading partners (a source company and destination company), the following steps would normally take place:

- preparation of EDI documents by the source company – the collection and storage of data/ information into electronic files or a database;
- outbound translation by the source company – translation of electronic files/database into a standard, pre-determined, structured and formatted document according to an agreed specification;
- communication by the source company – transmission and routing of each file to the appropriate client destination e-mail box (via the internet) according to the destination set in the file;
- inbound translation by the destination company – retrieval of the data file from its e-mail box and translation of the data file from the pre-determined, structured and formatted document into the specific format required by the company's application software; and
- processing of EDI documents by the destination company – processing of the received data file by the client company's internal application system.

Historically, the transmission/communication of EDI involved using a value added network (or VAN) – a third party network performing services beyond the transmission of data (see Figure 4.1).

In recent years, however, there has been (as we have all witnessed) a dramatic growth in the use of e-commerce via the internet and, consequently, the use of such networks has become increasingly rare, although some high-security VANs are still in operation. It was the

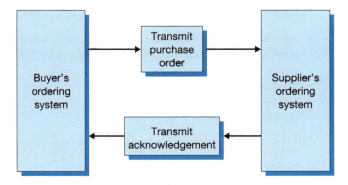

**Figure 4.1** Traditional information interchange using EDI

development of Multipurpose Internet Mail Extensions (MIME) as an enhancement to internet e-mail that enabled e-mail to carry a wide variety of alternative types of traffic – colloquially known as MIME types – including of course the sending of EDI transactions[72] using the internet.

In a broad sense, the sending of EDI transactions using the Internet[73] is fairly straightforward and merely involves:

- translating the transaction document into MIME format, and
- transmitting the message using e-mail from the source company to the destination company.

See Figure 4.2.

So what are the advantages/disadvantages of using the internet to transmit EDI transactions? The main advantages are:

- low transaction cost,
- low cost of transmission,
- ease of use – no need for a dedicated private system/network, and
- reduction in the need for/use of physical documentation.

The main disadvantages are:

- bandwidth may not be guaranteed and therefore transmission speeds may be affected, and
- security may be compromised by using the internet (as a public network) for the transmission of EDI information.

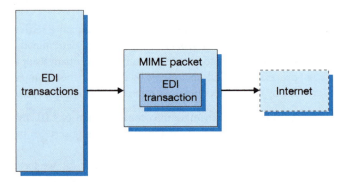

**Figure 4.2** Information interchange using EDI over the Internet

In general, the benefits of EDI can be categorised as either:

- (internal) value chain benefits, or
- (external) supply chain benefits,

with the potential value chain benefits including:

- a more efficient flow of resources,
- an increased overall competitiveness,
- a reduction in net operating cycle times/procedures,
- a lower overall operational costs and, as a consequence,
- an improved cash flow.

The potential supply chain benefits include:

- an increase in potential suppliers and/or customers, and
- an expansion of the corporate trading activities and the possibility of greater market access.

There are, of course, many risks arising out of the use of the EDI systems, in particular:

- risks associated with transmission, for example:
  - data completeness,
  - data accuracy, and
  - data authenticity,
- risks associated with verification, for example
  - data authorisation,
  - data access, and
  - error detection and correction.

The risks of EDI (and associated controls) are discussed in detail in Chapter 14.

### Electronic Fund Transfer (EFT)

Electronic Fund Transfer (EFT) is a generic term describing the transfer of funds between accounts by electronic means rather than conventional paper-based payment methods or, more appropriately, the transfer of money initiated through an electronic terminal, an automated teller machine (ATM), a computer, and/or a telephone. The term also applies to credit card payments, debit card payments and all automated payments including direct debits, standing orders, direct credits and/or other inter-bank transfers using BACS.[74]

So, what types of EFT are there? Three broad categories of EFT can be identified:

- CHAPS-based EFT,
- BACS-based EFT, and
- point of service-based EFT[75] or EPOS EFT.

Both CHAPS-based EFT, and BACS-based EFT would generally be used for business-to-business electronic funds transfer (known as B2B-EFT) whereas BACS-based EFT may in addition be used for:

- business-to-consumer electronic funds transfer (known as B2C-EFT), and
- consumer-to-business electronic funds transfer (known as C2B-EFT).

Within the point of service-based EFT there are two categories, these being:

- card-based systems, and
- non-card-based systems.

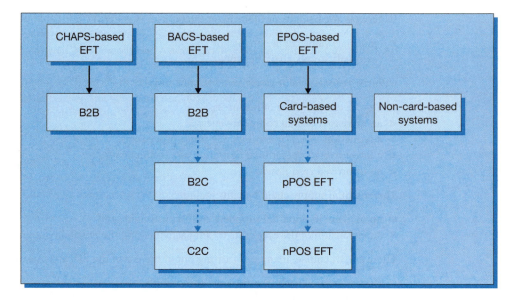

**Figure 4.3** Alternative types of electronic funds transfer

Card-based point of service EFT, or card-based EPOS EFT, can be divided into the following categories:

- cardholder 'present' transactions (known as pPoS-EFT), and
- cardholder 'not present' transactions (known as nPoS-EFT).

See Figure 4.3.

We will look at CHAPS-based EFT, and BACS-based EFT in more detail later in this chapter and EPOS EFT in more detail in Chapter 8.

### CHAPS-based EFT

The Clearing House Automatic Payments System (CHAPS) is an electronic bank-to-bank, UK-only, payment system. It is used by both banks and building societies where money is required to be transferred from one bank/building society to another on the same day: that is where a customer/client requires a secure, urgent, same-day payment. Under the auspices of APACS,[76] CHAPS Clearing Company Ltd:

- administers and manages the payment scheme(s), and
- provides the central infrastructure for same-day payment services.

Primarily for high-value transactions, the company processes RTGS (real time gross settlement) payments in both sterling and in euros.[77]

The main users of CHAPS are:

- banks and building societies – for inter-bank transfers and the movement of funds within the financial system, and
- companies and business – for the transfer of funds from one company's/business's bank account, to another company's/business's bank account.

It is very rare for private individuals to make personal CHAPS payments.

So, how are CHAPS payments/transfers made? Most of the UK banks and a majority of the larger UK building societies are *direct members* of CHAPS, with approximately 400 of the smaller UK banks and building societies being *indirect members*,[78] only having access to the CHAPS payment systems through a direct member.

Payments/transfers are made electronically and should start and finish on the same day. CHAPS payments/transfers can commence at 6.00 a.m. each day and payments/transfers usually have to commence before 4.00 p.m. for same-day settlement, although there is a facility to make late payments at up to 5.00 p.m. Payment/transfer instructions can be made electronically, usually using internet or other secure/private electronic banking facilities, often the case for regular users, although a substantial number of instructions for CHAPS payments/transfers are still – somewhat unbelievably – made by customers manually filling in forms.[79]

Within a CHAPS payment/transfer, the various stages would be as follows:

- a company requests (probably electronically) and authorises its bank to make a CHAPS payment/transfer out of its account,
- the paying bank (the bank of the company making the CHAPS payment/transfer request) validates, verifies and authenticates the request,
- the payment/transfer request is submitted/forwarded to a central processing centre,
- the payment/transfer request is cleared through the inter-bank payment and settlement system via the Bank of England,
- the payment/transfer is forwarded via a central processing centre to the recipient's bank, and
- the payment/transfer amount is credited to the recipient company account.

See Figure 4.4.

Clearly, whilst there exists a vast range of CHAPS procedural/security protocols designed to ensure that CHAPS payments/transfers are authorised, verified, authenticated and validated

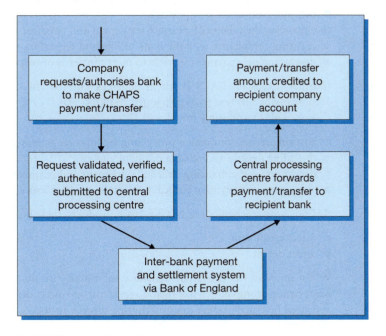

**Figure 4.4** CHAPS payment/transfer systems

prior to the payment/transfer taking place, very occasionally procedural protocols are violated and payments/transfers can go wrong. How? That's a difficult one to answer.

In general, the vast majority of problems tend to be associated with the provision of incomplete, faulty and/or incorrect payment instructions which, in exceptional circumstances, results in the occurrence of one or more of the following:

- a timing delay – the payment/transfer is not actioned as requested and the payment/transfer is not completed on the same day,
- payment errors – funds are either transferred to an incorrect account, and/or
- value errors – the incorrect value of funds is transferred.

Clearly for such payments/transfers, given the often high-value nature of the payment/transfer, the consequences of such a failure can be extensive, wide-ranging and extremely damaging, both legally and financially.

### BACS-based EFT

The Bankers Automated Clearing Services (BACS) was formed in 1971 (having previously been known as the Inter-Bank Computer Bureau) and its main task is to provide a central clearing function for bulk automated payments. In 1985, BACS changed its name to BACS Ltd and expanded its membership to include building societies. Following a corporate governance review during 2003, BACS Ltd was separated into two companies:

- BACS Payment Schemes Limited (BPSL) – to govern and administer the scheme, and
- BACS Ltd – to process payments and develop/enhance processing technologies.

In October 2004, BACS Ltd was rebranded as Voca Ltd.[80]

Currently, BACS processes approximately 4.5 billion financial transactions a year and up to 65 million payment transaction a day. BACS Payment Schemes Limited (BPSL) is responsible for:

- administering the scheme's payment rules and standards,
- providing advice on best practice,
- enhancing the quality of clearing, settlement and payment services,
- ensuring compliance with the Bank of England regulatory requirements, and
- developing new payment services to meet the needs of corporate customers and consumers.

(Further details on BACS Payment Schemes Limited (BPSL) are available on the website accompanying this text www.pearsoned.co.uk/boczko.)

Voca Ltd is responsible for:

- ensuring secure transaction processing facilities are provided,
- providing flexible and reliable payment engines,
- developing and enhancing clearing, settlement and payment services, and
- developing new payment services to meet the needs of both corporate and personal customers.

BACS Payment Schemes Ltd has two main products, these being:

- direct credit, and
- direct debit.

Whilst many of the above payments are submitted directly to BACS, currently over 50% of organisations/companies make their direct credit and direct debit payment submissions through approved bureaux[81] rather than submitting directly to BACS. Why? For a number of reasons, for example:

- the organisation/company may only make a small number of direct credit and/or direct debit payment transactions per month, or
- the organisation/company may be unable to fulfil all of the criteria to be able to make submissions itself direct to BACS (e.g. a newly established SME with a low turnover).

### Direct credit

Direct credit is a secure transfer service which enables organisations to make EFT directly into bank and/or building society accounts.[82] They are mainly used for paying wages and salaries,[83] although they are also used for a wide variety of other applications such as supplier payments, payments of pensions, payments of employee expenses, insurance settlements, payments of dividends and/or interest, and payment refunds.[84]

For the paying organisation/company, the main benefits of direct credits are:

- payments are prompt and cleared on arrival into the customer/recipient account,
- the payment transfer process is safe and secure, and
- the payment process is time efficient and inexpensive.

### Direct debit

A direct debit is an instruction from a customer to their bank or building society to authorise a third party organisation/company to collect varying amounts from their account.[85] In the UK, approximately 60,000 organisations/companies and approximately 45% of the UK paying population use direct debit services to collect a variety of regular and/or occasional payments including utility payments, insurance premiums, council tax payments, mortgages and/or loan repayments and subscription payments.

For the paying customer/client, the main benefits of direct debits are:

- payment is automatic,
- a direct debit payment is often cheaper than a cheque payment (although not always),[86]
- the payment process is convenient, and
- the payment process is safeguarded/guaranteed.[87]

### BACSTEL-IP

Unlike the CHAPS payment/transfer system which has a same day processing cycle, the BACS payment systems has a three-day processing cycle, that is a minimum of three UK bank working days, from the submission of a payment instruction to BACS for processing to the time that payment reaches the destination/recipient account.

Historically, direct access to the BACS payment services was through BACSTEL[88] a simple but effective telecoms-based payment service. However, in 2003 as part of a major renewal programme, a technology upgrade was launched and a whole-scale migration to BACSTEL-IP commenced.[89] Although the transition was far from smooth (see Article 4.7), BACSTEL-IP effectively replaced the dated telecoms-based customer delivery channel with an IP-based facility/technology incorporating both a public key infrastructure (PKI)[90] and public key cryptography (PKC)[91] and providing:

- online payment tracking and status monitoring,
- real time access to payment/transfer records,
- online electronic reporting, and
- automated receipt of payment and payment confirmation.

We will consider public key cryptography in greater detail in Chapter 13.

## Article 4.7

### UK firms drag heels over BACS transition

*Problems forecast if companies delay move until the last minute.*

Some 40,000 UK organisations have yet to make the transition to the internet-based version of the Bacs payment system. The industry deadline is now only a little more than six months away. Failure to make the transition before the end of the year could leave companies unable to pay employees or collect customer payments.

As of this week, 60,000 organisations had made the switch to Bacstel-IP, the internet-based version of the widely-used payments service, according to Bacs.

Bacstel-IP marketing manager Mike Hutchinson says problems could arise if all the remaining firms leave moving until the last minute. 'Sixty thousand firms made the transition in the past 18 months, and now another 40,000 need to move over in the next six months, so there will be a potential bottleneck if everyone leaves it until October,' he said. 'If a company doesn't change, they won't be able to use Bacstel-IP come January 2006.

'With 90 per cent of UK salaries paid by Bacs, they need to start planning now,' he added. Hutchinson

says the bulk of the companies that have not yet made the switch are smaller businesses, with most of the larger users and utility providers having made the change already. He has also ruled out any possibility of an extension to the deadline.

A survey of 22 existing Bacs users, published last week, shows that while 17 of these firms are in the process of migrating to Bacstel-IP, only one has not encountered any difficulties. The survey, conducted by specialist payments provider PSE Consulting, says a common theme to the problems being encountered is the technical and logistical complexity involved in dealing with multiple bank relationships.

In 2004, Bacs processed more than 4.5 billion direct debit, direct credit and standing order trans-actions in the UK.

Source: James Watson,
15 June 2005, *Computing*,
**www.vnunet.com/computing/news**.

To use the facilities offered by BACSTEL-IP (e.g. to submit payment/transfer requests and/or obtain activity reports), a company/business *must* be either:

- an approved/registered direct submitter, or
- a BACS approved bureaux.

To access the facilities offered by BACSTEL-IP, a company/business *must*:

- possess an appropriate and approved BACSTEL-IP software interface,[92] and
- satisfy the minimum hardware/software requirements[93] necessary to run the BACSTEL-IP application.

Whilst connectivity to the BACSTEL-IP application can be established through one of the following:[94]

- the internet,
- dial-up Extranet,
- broadband direct,
- DSL connect, and
- fixed Extranet connect,

for access management purposes BACSET-IP requires all approved users to use either:

- a smartcard-based security process/protocol,[95] or
- a hardware security module (HSM) solution/protocol.[96]

(Further information on BACSTEL-IP connectivity is available on the website accompanying this text www.pearsoned.co.uk/boczko.)

User verification/validation is achieved using two alternative security protocols:[97]

■ a PKI (digital certificate and digital signature) credentials which allows an approved BACSTEL-IP user to:
  ● sign in,
  ● send submissions (make payments/transfers),
  ● collect and view reports, and
  ● maintain reference data, or
■ an Alternative Security Method (ASM) which allows an approved BACSTEL-IP user to access the BACS payment services website, using a contact ID and password, to:
  ● collect reports, and
  ● view and update certain contact details.

So exactly how does the BACS payment system (using BACSTEL-IP) work?

The BACS processing is a four-stage processing procedure (arrival, input, process and output) within a three-day processing cycle (see Figure 4.5) comprising of:

■ arrival day (arrival/input stage) – the receipt of a company's/organisation's payment/transfer file at BACS Payment Schemes,
■ processing day (input and processing stage) – the acceptance and processing of all data through BACS Payment Schemes and transfer onto the paying banks, and
■ entry day (output stage) – requested payments/transfers are simultaneously debited and credited to the relevant bank and/or building society accounts.

Note: the three days must always be three consecutive processing days.

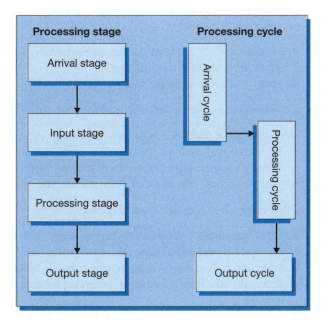

**Figure 4.5** BACS payment/transfer cycle

## Electronic mail (e-mail)

As suggested earlier, e-mail is a method of composing, sending, and receiving messages, together with any associated attached files of text data, numeric data and/or images, via an electronic communication system. In a contemporary context the majority of e-mail systems today are interconnected via the internet using the simple mail transfer protocol (SMTP),[98] facilitating the flow of e-mail to anywhere in the world – almost instantaneously.

### A brief history of e-mail

As suggested earlier, e-mail systems not only predate the internet but were both essential to and instrumental in the creation and development of the internet as we know it today.

The exact history of e-mail is at best vague, at worst ambiguous and frequently the source of heated academic debate. However, what is generally acknowledged is that the use of e-mail emerged in the mid/late 1960s as a simple communication resource for users of single 'stand alone' mainframe computer systems to allow them to send and receive messages, a facility that was rapidly developed and extended to users of networked computer systems, allowing them to transmit messages to and receive messages from different computers within a network.

Again, the history of precisely how the migration of e-mail from standalone mainframe computers to networked computer systems occurred is unclear. However, it is recognised by many academics and practitioners that the ARPAnet was one of the main contributors not only to the development and evolution of contemporary e-mail, but also to its exponential growth in popularity – from geek technology to killer application![99] Indeed, it was the widespread recognition (especially by those without access to the ARPAnet) of the benefits and advantages of e-mail as a means of communication that stimulated the development of a number of alternative protocols for the delivery/routing of e-mail among users on groups of time-sharing computers on different networks including ARPAnet, BITnet[100] and NSFnet.[101]

### Contemporary internet-based e-mail

Firstly, what is an e-mail message? An internet-based e-mail message would normally comprise of two major components:

- a header – which contains the message summary, sender details, receiver details and other information about the e-mail, and
- a body – which contains the message itself (with a signature block[102] at the end of the message).

A header would usually contain at least four defined fields:

- From: – the e-mail address of the sender of the message,
- To: – the e-mail address of the receiver of the message,
- Subject: – a brief summary of the contents of the message, and
- Date: – the local time and date when the message was originally sent.

Other common header fields would include:

- Cc: – sometimes referred to as carbon copy (old typewriting terminology) but is more appropriately defined as copy correspondence,
- Bcc: blind carbon copy – or more appropriately blind copy correspondence,[103]
- Received: – tracking information generated by mail servers that have previously handled a message,
- Content-Type: – information about how the message has to be displayed, usually a MIME type.[104]

Secondly, how do you send/receive e-mail messages? To send and/or receive e-mails a user must have:

- an active internet connection, and
- access to an active e-mail system.

Access to an e-mail system may be through the use of either:

- a standalone e-mail client like Outlook Express and/or Pegasus, or
- a web-based e-mail client (webmail), for example Hotmail or Yahoo, that uses an e-mail service appearing on a webpage and allows users to read and write e-mails using a web browser.

The e-mail system itself merely consists of a number of different interconnected servers, for example:

- a SMTP server – to deal with outgoing mail,
- a DNS[105] server – to locate domain names, and
- a POP3 server or an IMAP server – to deal with incoming mail.[106]

See Figure 4.6.

So how does e-mail work? Consider the following:

*Christopher (e-mail address – christopher@James.com) wants to send an e-mail to Jessica (e-mail address – Jessica@Leigh.com).*

The (simplified) procedure would be as follows:

- Christopher composes the e-mail message using his e-mail client. He types in Jessica's e-mail address and presses 'send e-mail' to send the e-mail message.
- Christopher's e-mail client uses the simple mail transfer protocol (SMTP) to send the e-mail message to the SMTP server.
- The SMTP server examines the destination address (or more appropriately the domain address). (Note: A contemporary internet e-mail address is a string of the form local@domain.xxx. The part of the address before the @ sign is the local part of the address, usually the username of the recipient, and the part of the address after the @ sign is a domain name of the address.)

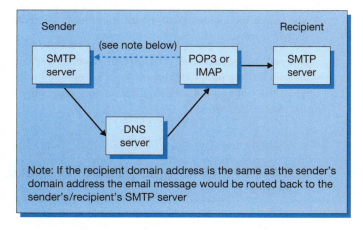

**Figure 4.6** Contemporary e-mail

- The SMTP server looks up the relevant destination domain name (Leigh.com) in the Domain Name System/Server to find the SMTP server accepting messages for that domain.[107]
- The SMTP server accepting messages for that domain name (Leigh.com) responds with a message exchange record.
- The message is delivered to the SMTP server for the domain name (Leigh.com).
- The SMTP server recognises the domain name for Jessica and forwards the e-mail message to a POP3 server (or IMAP server) and the e-mail message is placed in the mail box of the user Jessica.
- Jessica presses the 'get e-mail' to open her e-mail client and read the e-mail message.

In the above example, both Christopher (e-mail address – christopher@James.com) and Jessica (e-mail address – Jessica@Leigh.com) are using standalone e-mail clients.

Many people (and companies) are however choosing to use web-based e-mail, otherwise known as webmail.[108] Why? For many reasons, perhaps the most important being:

- e-mail messages can be accessed and/or used anywhere, providing the user has access to a web browser and an active internet connection, and
- webmail service providers offer a range of add-on features/facilities, for example:
  - e-mail filtering,
  - address book facilities,
  - e-mail spam detection,
  - mail retrieval,
  - anti-virus checking of mail attachments,
  - dictionary, thesaurus and spelling checking facilities . . . and many more.

However, there are some disadvantages, for example:

- users must stay online to access e-mail messages,
- some commercial webmail service providers limit individual user e-mail storage capacity, and
- access to webmail services can be affected by slow network/internet connections.

So, will e-mail usage continue to rise? More than likely!

Whilst recent problems have questioned the usefulness and security of e-mail, for example:

- the increasing occurrences of e-mail spam or spamming, that is the unsolicited mass distribution of e-mail messages,
- the growing threat from malicious intruders (hackers and crackers, see Chapter 13), and
- the increasing incidences of e-mail transmitted computer viruses or, more appropriately, e-mail worms,

recent years have nonetheless seen not only an enormous increase in the volume of e-mail traffic – in the UK (September 2005) there was 23.2 million e-mail users[109] – but has, perhaps more importantly, witnessed a widening dependency especially of companies on e-mail messaging and e-mail related services.

## Information and communication technology enabled innovations

There can be little doubt that information and communication technology enabled innovations, including for example:

- the availability and increasing sophistication of computer hardware,
- the growth of evermore advanced communication facilities,
- the adoption of increasingly complex networking technologies, and
- the widespread development of application specific computer software – especially, for our purposes, computer-based accounting software,

has, in a corporate context at least, revolutionised contemporary accounting, finance, and management-related activities.

We will discuss the wide ranging impact of developments in computer hardware capabilities, communication facilities and networking technologies on corporate accounting information systems in Chapter 5.

For the moment however what about computer-based accounting software? Computer-based accounting software is a generic term – a term used to describe application software that as an integral component of a company's and/or organisation's accounting information systems. It facilitates:

- the recording and processing of accounting transactions data, and/or
- the production and provision of financial information for:
  - internal management reporting – for the coordination and management of business activities, and/or
  - external stakeholder reporting – in accordance with regulatory requirements (e.g. the Companies Act 1985).

Because such computer-based accounting software can have many diverse origins, for example, it can be:

- developed in-house by a company/organisation,
- purchased 'off-the-shelf' from an external third party supplier by a company/organisation, or
- purchased 'off-the-shelf' from an external third party supplier by a company/organisation and modified for local settings applicable to the company/organisation,

it can vary enormously in:

- complexity,
- adaptability,
- flexibility,
- functionality, and of course
- cost,

often depending on the type and nature of the computer-based accounting software.

For example:

- Low-end computer-based accounting software would generally comprise of inexpensive application software that provides a range of basic business accounting functions with perhaps limited security and/or audit facilities. Whilst such software products would possess considerable functionality and transaction processing capabilities they would nonetheless be considered to be UK GAAP (UK Generally Accepted Accounting Practice), and/or IFRS (International Financial Reporting Standards) non-compliant.
- Mid-market computer-based accounting software would generally comprise of a wide range of accounting/finance-related software capable of serving the needs and requirements of UK GAAP, and/or IFRS. Such software products would, in addition to facilitating accounting in multiple currencies and providing integrated security facilities and transaction audit facilities, generally allow for the integration/incorporation of additional management information functions/modules.

■ High-end computer-based accounting software would generally comprise of an integrated suite of software products to service a full range of accounting/finance and management-related functions/activities. Compliant with all the needs and requirements of UK GAAP, and/or IFRS's, such software products would generally provide a suite of highly integrated transaction processing and information management facilities/capabilities, and would perhaps also include accounting software designed for specific business types.

Clearly, computer-based accounting software has existed for many years (certainly since the early/mid 1970s) and indeed has been widely available from an extensive range of suppliers certainly since the mid/late 1970s. However, whilst the late 1970s did witness an enormous increase in the number and variety of accounting software providers, the late 1980s and early 1990s saw not only widespread merger and acquisition activity between computer-based accounting software suppliers, but also the increasing consolidation/integration of computer-based accounting software functions. Why? Possibly for two reasons!

Firstly, the macro economic reason. During the late 1980s and early 1990s the market for computer-based accounting software became saturated with a vast range of low-end/mid-market accounting software products from an even greater range of software providers. Intense rivalry and competition for a limited market stimulated demand-side pressures within an already competitive/price orientated marketplace resulting in what many spectators referred to at the time as the 'supply side slaughter'.

Secondly, the technology reason. During early 1990s advances in information technology, including innovations and developments in computing capabilities and improvements in communication systems, had a significant impact on customer/user demands for greater functionality, integration, inter-product compatibility and product utility. The inability of the small/medium-sized accounting software suppliers to meet these ever-growing demands resulted in many small/medium-sized suppliers merging with or being acquired by the larger, more capable and more resource wealthy suppliers.

So what types of computer-based accounting software are there? In a contemporary context, there are of course several types/varieties available, some of which would consist of single, independent functional modules servicing specific accounting/finance requirements and others of which would consist of a range of integrated functional modules servicing an assortment of accounting/finance requirements. For our purposes we will classify these types into two categories:

■ accounting/finance-related software, and
■ management-related software.

Accounting/finance-related software is typically composed of various (sometimes integrated) modules, servicing a range of accounting/finance/management-related functions, and would include the following:

■ sales ledger management software,
■ sales order processing system software,
■ purchases ledger management software,
■ purchase order processing system software,
■ general ledger management software,
■ fixed asset management software,
■ cash book management software,
■ inventory management control software, and
■ payroll and human resources management software.

Such computer-based accounting software is often activity orientated.

Management-related software is typically process related, generally designed for decision-making purposes and would include the following:

- product/process costing software (including activity-based, costing-related software),
- budgeting and budgetary control software,
- resource planning/management software (including just-in-time (JIT) software, materials requirements planning (MRP-I) software and manufacturing resource planning systems (MRP-II) software),
- manufacturing and design management software (including computer-aided engineering (CAE) software, computer-aided design (CAD) software, computer-aided manufacturing (CAM) software and computer integrated manufacture (CIM) software),
- enterprise resource planning software, and
- business process re-engineering software.

In addition to the above computer-based accounting software there has also been a number of generic software innovations, perhaps the two most important being:

- spreadsheets, and
- databases.

Let's look at each of these categories in a little more detail.

## Accounting and finance-related software

Most contemporary, computer-based accounting software provides:

- fully integrated general ledger, sales ledger and purchase ledger systems,
- integrated transaction audit services,
- performance evaluation facilities,
- report writing solutions (e.g. VAT reporting), and
- financial statement preparation facilities.

For example, see:

- Sage Line 100 and/or Sage Line 200 (available from Sage (UK) Ltd @ www.sage.co.uk), and/or
- Access Horizons and/or Access Dimensions (available from Access Accounting Ltd @ www.access-accounts.com).

In addition, many of the high-end computer-based accounting software specifications provide:

- real-time online transaction processing facilities,
- customisation and connectivity facilities (for integration with other software applications),
- multi-currency consolidation software (for multi-company groups), and
- fully integrated e-business solutions (for web-based transaction processing).

Now let's look at the main features of each of the software modules that would comprise a mid-range/high-end computer-based accounting package.

### Sales ledger management software

The aim of sales ledger management software and sales order processing system software is to ensure:

- the acceptance of authorised orders only,
- adherence to sales processing procedures and company/organisation credit policies,
- adherence to company/organisation invoicing procedures,

- adherence to company/organisation pricing and discounting policies, and
- the proper management of customer (debtor) accounts.

Sales ledger management software is therefore designed to:

- manage sales transactions, and
- maintain customer accounts (debtor accounts).

The main features would include:

- online maintenance of individual customer (debtor) accounts,
- online transaction history,
- multi-currency processing facilities,
- online customer account analysis (using a range of categories)[110],
- online credit management facilities,[111]
- online customer (debtor) payment history analysis,
- online invoicing procedures,
- flexible discount facilities, and
- multi-presentational/flexible communication facilities.

### Sales order processing system software

Sales order processing system software is used to process customer orders. Such a system is normally integrated with a company's/organisation's stock management system and would control the processing of sales orders from:

- the initial recording of an order to,
- the despatch of goods, and
- the update of stock control and accounting modules.

The main features would include:

- multi-pricing facilities/options,
- online management of repeat orders for the same customers,
- online goods return/credit note management facilities,
- multi-currency processing facilities,
- flexible customer account details,[112]
- online order acknowledgement facilities,
- customer prioritising facilities,
- order consolidation facilities (that is consolidating a number of orders into a single invoice),
- inventory tracing facilities (from inventory to order to despatch to invoice), and
- flexible invoicing procedures.

### Purchases ledger management software

The aim of purchase ledger management software and purchase order processing system software is to ensure:

- adherence to purchase processing procedures and company/organisation payment policies,
- that all goods and services are ordered as needed,
- that all goods and services are verified and safeguarded until needed,
- that all invoices are verified and validated before payment,
- that all transaction records are accurately maintained,
- the proper management of supplier (creditor) accounts, and
- the acceptance of authorised orders only.

Purchase ledger management software is therefore designed to:

- process purchase transactions, and
- maintain supplier accounts (creditor accounts).

The main features would include:

- online maintenance of individual supplier (creditor) accounts,
- online transaction history,
- multi-currency processing facilities,
- online supplier account analysis (using a range of categories),[113]
- payment list creation and editing facilities,
- automated payment processing,
- online debtor payment history analysis, and
- multi-presentational/flexible communication facilities.

### Purchase order processing system software

Purchase order processing systems software is used to process orders for goods and services from suppliers.

Such a system is normally integrated with a company's/organisation's stock management system and would control the processing of purchase orders, including:

- the production of supplier documentation, and
- the update of stock control and accounting modules.

The main features would include:

- online matching of purchase invoice to delivery notes and purchase orders (including multiple delivery notes and purchase orders),
- online management of goods returned to suppliers for credit or replacement,
- multi-currency processing facilities,
- online authorisation of orders,
- online order prioritising facilities, and
- inventory tracing facilities (from inventory to order to despatch to invoice).

### General ledger management software

General ledger management software is designed to record and summarise all nominal account transactions accurately so that timely and useful financial reports may be generated.

The main features would include:

- online maintenance of individual nominal accounts,
- online creation of memorandum accounts in the nominal ledger,
- online nominal account analysis using a range of categories,
- batch journal entry facilities,
- pre-payment and accrual facilities, and
- multi-presentational facilities.

### Fixed asset management software

Fixed asset management software is used to record details of a company's/organisation's fixed assets, both tangible and intangible. The main features would include:

- online maintenance of individual asset records, including acquisition and disposal, and
- online maintenance of depreciation/amortisation records.

### Cash book management software

Cash book management software is designed to provides control of all bank-related activities (receipts and payments), including cash, cheques, credit cards, standing orders and direct debits.

The main features would include:

- online maintenance of individual bank account records,
- multi-currency processing facilities,
- batch data entry facilities,
- online creation of automatic direct debits and standing orders,
- online bank reconciliation facilities, and
- multi-presentational facilities.

### Inventory management control software

Inventory management control software is designed to record and control inventory movement in relation to:

- raw materials and components,
- work in progress, and
- completed products.

The main features would be:

- online maintenance of individual inventory records,
- active inventory level management facilities (using specified minimum and maximum inventory level controls),
- multiple location inventory management facilities,
- alternative inventory valuation facilities,
- online inventory tracking facilities,
- inventory source information (e.g. suppliers),
- automated stock-taking procedures, and
- multi-presentational facilities.

Inventory management control software may also integrate purchasing and production/manufacturing systems activities, and may involve, for example, the use of:

- just in time (JIT),
- materials requirement planning (MRP-I), and/or
- manufacturing resource planning systems (MRP-II).

### Payroll and human resources management software

The aim of sales ledger management software and sales order processing system software is to ensure:

- all legal and statutory requirements are complied with,
- employees are appropriately qualified,
- employee are remunerated at appropriate levels, and
- all statutory deductions are correctly made.

Payroll and human resources management software is therefore designed to:

- record and control employee movements/changes, and
- calculate and manage payroll payments to employees.

The main features would be:

- online maintenance of statutory personnel files,
- online maintenance of employee status changes,
- periodic verification of employee records and status,
- calculation and payment of statutory deductions, and
- online preparation of payroll, and pay advices.

## Management related software

### Product costing/process costing software (including ABC-related software)

### Product costing/process costing software

Whereas product costing systems are designed to accumulate cost data related to the production/manufacture of individual product units/service units, process costing systems are designed to accumulate costs for an entire production/manufacturing process.

An accurate assessment of product/process costs is important for:

- the valuation of product inventory (including both complete and part complete products),
- the planning of production/manufacturing activity,
- the measurement of product/service profitability,
- the management and control of production/manufacturing activity,
- the measurement of activity performance, and
- other related management decision-making purposes.

Product costing/process costing software is invariably used to maintain both financial and non-financial data related not only to completed but part-completed customer products and/or client services. Such software may be integrated with/connected to:

- the sales order processing system,
- the purchase order processing systems,
- the inventory management systems, and/or
- the budgeting/budgetary control systems.

### Activity-based costing (ABC) software

As a cost management system, activity-based costing was developed[114] primarily for use by companies/organisations:

- whose product range is diverse,
- whose operating overheads are generally high, and
- whose industry/market sector is highly competitive.

Proposed as an alternative methodology to the traditional cost management systems, its development was seen as an attempt to address two key issues:

- the inability of traditional systems/approaches to determine accurately the 'actual' cost of a product and/or a service, and
- the failure of traditional systems/approaches to provide relevant and appropriate information for management decision-making purposes, at both the strategic and tactical/operational level.

As a methodology for allocating costs to products and services, activity-based costing is generally used for planning, controlling and measuring the cost and performance of activities, resources and cost objects. As a methodology, activity-based costing recognises the cause–effect relationships of so-called 'cost drivers' to 'activities', inasmuch as:

■ cost objects (either consumer products and/or client services) consume activities,
■ such activities (in the process of producing such cost objects), consume resources, and
■ the resources (consumed in the performance of such activities) drives costs.[115]

Whilst a vast range of generic activity-based costing software is available (e.g. Acorn Systems Inc. @ www.acornsys.com, ALG plc @ www.algsoftware.com or Sage Group @ www.sagesoftware.com), as with traditional product costing/process costing software, activity-based costing software requires:

■ the identification of major processes/activities that occur within a company/organisation, and contribute to the production, manufacture and distribution of customer products/client services, and
■ the development and maintenance of a database of customer products and/or client services produced/manufactured and sold by the company/organisation.

Activity-based costing systems are often integrated into:

■ asset management systems (e.g. company/organisation inventory systems) to provide data/information on the valuation of inventory items,
■ budgeting systems and/or performance measuring systems to provide information on resource usage/efficiency, and
■ simulation, modelling and decision-making systems to provide information for product/service pricing and other decision making.

### Budgeting and budgetary control software

In a broad context:

■ budgeting as a planning process/procedure can be defined as the activity of translating corporate decisions into specific financial plans, usually short-term plans (within the context of longer-term financial plans of course), and
■ budgetary control as a controlling process/procedure can be defined as a reactive (after the event) financial control process in which actual performance and/or results for a defined period of time are compared with expected performance/(flexed) budgeted results.

The aim of the former is to provide a financial framework within which corporate/organisational activities may occur, whereas the aim of the latter is to identify deviations (or variances) from the agreed financial framework, and where appropriate recommend suitable remedial action (where required).

For many companies/organisations, budgeting and budgetary control systems are merely integrated software modules within existing financial accounting software, usually linked to (part of) the general ledger management systems. They assist in:

■ the development of annual budgeted financial statements (profit and loss account, balance sheet and cash flow statement), and
■ the periodic monitoring of actual income and expenditure in comparison with budgeted expectations.

What are the advantages of such integrated budgeting/budgetary control systems?
Such integration provides:

■ the ability to transfer financial transaction data directly from the general ledger management system to the budgeting/budgetary control system thereby reducing the timescale of budgeting/budgetary control activities,

- the ability to transfer financial transaction data to other integrated data manipulation/data analysis software packages and thereby facilitate scenario modelling/simulation,
- the ability to secure and control the transfer of financial transaction data thereby minimising the possibility of potential errors, and
- the ability (with the more sophisticated budgeting/budgetary control systems software) to integrate not only quantitative financial data, but also qualitative non-financial data.

### *Resource planning/management software*

### Just-in-time software

Although some consider that the origins of just-in-time methodology can be traced back to the early 1920s [116] the common view/consensus is that just-in-time as a manufacturing technique was first adopted and publicised by the Toyota Motor Corporation in Japan in the early 1950s.

Whether as a response to the impact of:

- the ever-changing/ever-reducing product life cycles, and/or
- the ever-increasing demands from clients and customers,

just-in-time is a methodology designed to smooth manufacture/production and minimise product and supply inventories by fulfilling material requirements as close as possible to the actual time of need/use, thereby:

- reducing inventory management costs (in-process inventory costs and associated carrying costs),
- improving product/service quality and delivery, and
- improving (in theory) company/organisation return on investment.

Just-in-time is, in essence, a demand orientated *pull system* of production and/or purchasing in which activities are organised and timetabled according to customer/client demand, as opposed to a supply orientated *push system*, in which inventories are used as a buffer to smooth out fluctuations in purchasing, manufacturing/production and sales.

In a contemporary context, the key requirements for an effective just-in-time system are:

- the active integration of production and inventory purchasing systems/procedures – that is purchase order processing systems (POPS) procedures and sales order processing systems procedures (SOPS),
- the continual monitoring of production/distribution processes and materials demand,
- the use of effective and identifiable signalling procedures,
- the existence of dependable and reliable suppliers, and
- the development and maintenance of good internal (and external) coordination,

all of which can, certainly within a large multi-product/multi-service company/organisation, require the use of increasingly sophisticated information and communication technology. Why?

Because, in seeking to:

- reduce waste within the manufacturing/production process,
- expose problems and bottlenecks within the manufacturing/production process, and
- identify and eliminate excess set-up times, production lead times and inventory,

just-in-time operations rely heavily not only on a methodology of continuous improvement, a focus on quality assurance and quality control, or the existence of a strong cohesive supply chain but also, certainly within a contemporary context, almost exclusively on the availability of accurate up-to-date inventory, production and customer/client data.

### Material requirements planning (MRP-I) software

Material requirements planning is based on a simple/commonsense principle:

*what you need, less what you have got, equals what you need to get!*

Developed in the mid/late 1960s, material requirements planning systems (MRP-I) are essentially proactive inventory management systems which seek to:

- reduce overall inventory levels,
- reduce production and delivery lead times, and
- improve coordination and increase efficiency.

They are essentially manufacturing/production scheduling systems, and are used by many manufacturing companies and/or organisations to:

- control the types and quantities of stocks required and ensure materials are available for production and finished products are available for delivery to customers/clients,
- plan/schedule manufacturing/production activities, delivery schedules and purchasing activities,
- ensure product demand/customer requirements are fulfilled, and
- minimise inventory levels and manufacturing/production costs.

So how do material requirements planning systems work? Essentially a materials requirements planning system schedules production on the basis of anticipated future demand. This is based on a master production schedule which is normally based on orders to be fulfilled and/or forecasted demand from which a stock requirements list (bill of materials) is prepared. Existing stock is deducted to establish net purchasing requirements (including any provision for production waste/scrap) and allowing for established lead times, purchase order and delivery schedules as well as production/manufacturing commencement times/dates are established.

Because the production/manufacturing process will invariably be hierarchical (i.e. occurs in a number of predetermined stages) the above process may be undertaken a number of times until the requirements for all production/manufacturing stages have been satisfied.

In general, material requirements planning software would essentially use:

- the bill of material data,
- the stock data, and
- the master production schedule,

to calculate requirements for materials, and make appropriate recommendations:

- to reorder materials, and
- to reschedule open orders when order due dates and production/manufacture requirement dates are not 'in phase'.

### Manufacturing resource planning (MRP-II) software

Although widely adopted throughout the 1970s and 1980s the main problem with materials requirements planning systems was that such systems operated as closed-looped systems and therefore lacked integration with other business activities. In the mid-1980s the need for greater integration resulted in the evolution of an integrated manufacturing management system – manufacturing resources planning (MRP-II) being a direct product and extension of materials requirements planning (MRP-I).

Manufacturing resource planning systems (MRP II) can be defined as systems designed to promote and ensure the effective planning of *all* the resources of a manufacturing company. As such, manufacturing resource planning systems (MRP II) normally comprise a variety of interrelated planning/activity functions, for example:

- business planning,
- master (or production) planning,
- master production scheduling,
- material requirements planning, and
- capacity requirements planning,

the output from which would be integrated into other operational activities within the company/organisation, for example:

- purchasing activities,
- inventory management activities, and
- manufacturing/production activities.

In essence, manufacturing resource planning systems (MRP II) are essentially materials requirements planning systems (MRP-I) together with capacity requirement planning and control procedures for both the short and long term.

In addition to the operational parameters/procedures required for materials requirements planning (MRP-I) systems, manufacturing resource planning systems (MRP II) software would also consider issues/data related to:

- the routing of manufacture/production,
- the operational times of each manufacturing/production activity,
- the activity/process capacity of manufacturing/production work centres, and
- the capacity of the manufacturing/production process.

Note: For many manufacturing companies/organisations, the term manufacturing resource planning (MRP-II) has been replaced/superseded by the term enterprise resource planning (ERP) – see below.

### Manufacture and design management software

Over recent years, many software tools have been developed that not only undertake activities related to, but also assist in the management of, the design, development and manufacture of products.

### Computer aided engineering (CAE)

Computer-aided engineering (CAE) is the application of computer software 'tools' in engineering to analyse the performance of components and assemblies, and encompasses simulation, validation and the optimisation of products and manufacturing equipment and resources.

Such software tools are widely used in many manufacturing industries, especially the car manufacturing industries, where their use has enabled many car manufacturers to not only reduce product development costs, but more importantly reduce product manufacturing times whilst improving the specifications of the cars/vehicles they produce.

### Computer aided design (CAD)

Computer-aided design (CAD) is the use of a wide range of computer-based software tools to design and develop both intermediate products[117] and/or end users products.

### Computer aided manufacturing (CAM)

Computer aided manufacturing (CAM) is the use of software tools to programme, control, and monitor manufacturing assets, processes, and procedures. Although the first commercial application of computer aided manufacture was in the car manufacturing industry (Renault in the 1970s), such software tools were also widely used in the aerospace industry.

### Computer integrated manufacture (CIM)

Computer-integrated manufacturing is a software application linking:

- just-in-time (JIT) software,
- materials requirements planning (MRP-I) software,
- manufacturing resource planning systems (MRP-II) software,
- computer-aided engineering (CAE) software,
- computer-aided design (CAD) software, and
- computer-aided manufacturing (CAM) software,

into a single application to provide direct monitoring and control of all production related operations and promote a flexible and adaptive manufacturing environment.

A simplified version of a computer integrated manufacturing system is provided in Figure 4.7.

For a manufacturing company/organisation, the use of computer integrated manufacturing can assist in:

- improving the scheduling of production activities,
- improving the sharing of manufacturing data/information and the availability of planning and control related information,
- reducing excessive stock levels,
- improving product quality,
- improving the usage of conversion cycle assets and resources,
- reducing wastage,
- reducing conversion cycle times,
- reducing production costs,
- increasing flexibility, and
- improving monitoring of production activities.

#### Enterprise resource planning software

Enterprise resource planning systems are essentially management information systems that seek to integrate and automate operations related and production related business practices/activities. Such practices/activities can include manufacturing, logistics, stock management and inventory, selling and distribution, and finance and accounting. Indeed because enterprise resource planning software can and often is used to manage and control a diverse range of business activities, from production and inventory management, to sales and delivery management, to invoicing

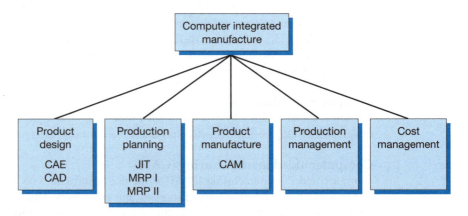

**Figure 4.7** Computer integrated manufacture

and credit management, to human resource management, it is often intimately connected to supply chain management systems.

So what is the aim of an enterprise resource planning system? The main aim of an enterprise resource planning system as an information system/process seeking to integrate all related processes, procedures and protocols, is to maximise the use of all the resources within an organisation, and thereby improve resource efficiency and operational effectiveness . . . and of course profitability.

Such resources would include:

■ all infrastructure processes and procedures (including organisation relationships),
■ all resource-based activities (including business support systems – for example, information technology and related communication systems), and
■ all human resource capabilities, skills and competencies.

Essentially enterprise resource planning systems are multidisciplinary/multifunctional workflow management systems, the key to which is:

■ the migration of control procedures from the execution phase to the implementation stage,
■ the integration of measurement points into the enterprise resource planning system, and
■ the concentration of responsibility within system procedures.

Although the enterprise resource planning vision is a single coordinated company/organisation wide integrated database and user interface, in reality – mainly for pragmatic organisational reasons – many enterprise resource planning systems and applications are only loosely integrated with the possibility of a number of interrelated databases and user interfaces existing, each sharing data/information within pre-defined security protocols/parameters.

There are of course many problems and risks associated with the implementation of an enterprise resource planning system. For example, employees may view the development and implementation of a company/organisation wide enterprise resource planning system as a down-sizing exercise leading inevitably to a reduction in employee numbers and may therefore resist its implementation. In addition, culture clashes/management problems may result from inconsistencies between enterprise resource planning system requirements, corporate/organisational capabilities and management expectations.

So what are the advantages of implementing an enterprise resource planning system? For many companies/organisations the benefits of such a system include:

■ lower inventory management costs (e.g. reduced ordering and carrying costs),
■ reduced selling, distribution and transport costs,
■ more flexible production processes and reduced production costs,
■ reduced financial accounting and record-keeping costs,
■ greater operational efficiency resulting in lower investment in assets, and
■ more efficient production coordination and scheduling resulting in reduced production down-times and stock-outs,

all of which increase operational transparency and production efficiency, allowing for greater product/service customisation (where required), which together with lower overall costs may increase market share and of course profitability.

The main disadvantages are:

■ systems may not only be expensive to acquire/develop, install and maintain but difficult to use/implement,
■ systems may distort/fragment systems boundaries, accountabilities and lines of responsibility, and as a result adversely affect employee morale,

■ internal management politics may resist the sharing of internal data/information, and

■ centralising system procedures and processes may result in high organisation risks (e.g. a potential failure could have widespread implications).

In addition, because of the integrated nature of such systems, once the systems are established, switching cost may be very high thus reducing future flexibility and strategic control.

And what of the next generation? Fully integrated, fully interactive, browser-based, platform independent, IP technology enabled, enterprise resource planning system software.

### Business process re-engineering software

Business process re-engineering is essentially a fundamental analysis and radical redesign of everything. From business processes, to management systems; from organisational structures and operational procedures and process; from corporate culture and belief systems to employee-related activities and behaviour. The aim being to increase efficiency and improve business performance by transforming and modernising business processes and procedures to meet contemporary business requirements.

But what is a business process? A business process is essentially a collection/arrangement of logically related tasks/procedures whose performance is designed to achieve a specific business outcome. Such processes, which are normally identified in terms of process input, process output and process interface, generally operate across system/organisational boundaries, under the ownership of either an internal and/or external client, and can be classified as follows:

■ entity-related processes – that is processes that occur/arise between two or more companies/organisations entities,

■ object-related processes – that is processes that effect the manipulation, movement and/or management of objects (physical or virtual, for example information), and

■ activity-related processes – that is processes related to either managerial activities and/or operational activities.

Business process re-engineering is often customer centred, multidisciplinary, and holistic in approach, and is commonly seen as a high risk 'final option' for a company/organisation facing an uncertain future (possibly a terminal situation) due to significant social, political and economic change.

So what are the stages involved in a business process re-engineering project? The main stages are:

■ develop a mission statement, a business vision and establish/prioritise process objectives,

■ develop a clear business strategy and identify processes that required redesigning/re-engineering,

■ define business process structure and assumptions,

■ identify trade-offs between business processes,

■ define activities and processes that will enable the company/organisation to achieve its aims and objectives,

■ identify key performance criteria and measure existing processes,

■ identify key information and communication technology factors,

■ design and prototype redesigned/re-engineered business processes,

■ coordinate the re-engineering activities, and

■ review and implement redesigned/re-engineered business processes.

And do business process re-engineering projects succeed? Not really! Approximately 70% of business process re-engineering projects fail, because of:

■ a lack of management commitment,

■ unrealistic expectations,

- narrow technical and/or financial focus, and
- a general resistance to change.

For a successful business process re-engineering project there needs to be:

- a clear management commitment and project support,
- a clear strategic context,
- a shared vision, and
- realistic and unambiguous expectations.

There are an increasing number of eclectic software tools available to assist with business process re-engineering projects, for example:

- static modelling software (e.g. flowcharting software),
- dynamic modelling software (e.g. forecast modelling and simulation software),
- workflow and process analysis tools/software, including online analytic processing (OLAP), and
- data mining software (e.g. data collection/database interrogation software),

and many more, with the selection software tools depending on a range of interrelated variables, not least:

- the nature of the company's/organisation's business, and
- the overall objective of the business process re-engineering project(s).

## Other generic innovations and developments

As suggested earlier, two of the most important generic innovations over recent years have been:

- spreadsheets, and
- databases.

### Spreadsheets

A spreadsheet is a computer program that displays – in rows and columns – a group of interrelated cells in a two-dimensional arrangement, a program that allows for the entering, editing, and manipulating of alphabetic and numeric data, and the undertaking of complex mathematical operations.

There are, of course, many versions/types of spreadsheet available, perhaps the most widely known being:

- Microsoft's Excel (part of the Microsoft Office suite – available @ www.microsoft.com),
- IBM's Lotus 1-2-3 (part of IBM's Lotus Smart suite – available @ www.lotus.com),
- Corel's Quattro Pro (part of the WordPerfect Office suite – available @ www.corel.co.uk), and
- StarOffice Calc (part of the StarOffice suite – available @ www.sun.com).

Whilst it is generally recognised that the inventors of the spreadsheet are Dan Brinklin and Bob Frankson who created/developed the VisiCalc spreadsheet using, as suggested by Brinklin 'a blackboard/spreadsheet paradigm to view the results of underlying formulas,' it was Mitchell David Kapor (the founder of Lotus Development Corporation in 1982) and Jonathan Sachs who designed the Lotus 1-2-3, a spreadsheet released in January 1983 that became the 'killer application'[118] of the 1980s and:

- revolutionised the use of PC's, and
- contributed significantly to the success of IBM PCs in the corporate environment.

However, market domination by Lotus 1-2-3 was short-lived!

Originally marketed as a spreadsheet program called Multiplan,[119] in 1982 the first version of Microsoft Excel was released for the Apple Mac in 1985, with the first Windows version being released in November 1987. By mid-1988, Microsoft Excel had begun to outsell Lotus 1-2-3, elevating Microsoft Inc. to the position of leading PC software developer – a position the company has maintained (not without a number of legal, commercial and technical battles) ever since. It also, perhaps more importantly, augmented the profile of spreadsheets from merely interesting add-on software technology to indispensable business tools so much so that in a contemporary business context the term spreadsheet has now become synonymous with accounting and finance. Indeed, in providing:

- user defined data input facilities – increasingly integrated into either other spreadsheets and/or other software applications to facilitate direct input,
- user defined data editing and data manipulation facilities – including facilities to perform complex iterative calculations using user defined processes (macros) and input variables and to link related spreadsheets and create multi-dimensional spreadsheets, and
- user defined data output using a range of textual and graphical features facilities,

spreadsheets have become an indispensable 'everyday' tool in accounting and finance, and are now widely used in many diverse areas, for example:

- in financial accounting for:
  - performance analysis, and
  - accounting adjustment calculations (e.g. depreciation and doubtful debt provisions),
- in management accounting for:
  - break-even analysis,
  - cost apportionment,
  - sensitivity analysis,
  - scenario analysis (including limiting factor analysis),
  - pricing,
  - budgeting, and
  - variance analysis,
- in financial management for:
  - capital investment appraisal,
  - risk assessments, and
  - finance scenario analysis.

### Databases

A database can be defined as an organised body of related data, or perhaps more appropriately as *a logical and systematic collection of interrelated data managed and stored as a unit*. A key feature of a database is the structural relationship between the objects represented in the database (called data elements), often referred to as a database schema. There are of course a number of ways of organising a database schema – that is alternative ways of organising the relationships between data elements stored in a database. Such alternative ways are often referred to as database models (or data models), the most common being:

- the flat data model,
- the hierarchical data model,
- the network data model,
- the relational data model, and
- the object-oriented data model.

So which database model is the best? That depends on a range of factors including the type and amount of data to be processed and stored.

There are of course many alternative databases available, perhaps the most widely known being:

- Microsoft's Access (part of the Microsoft Office suite – available @ www.microsoft.com),
- Corel Paradox (part of the WordPerfect Office suite – available @ www.corel.co.uk),
- Cracle (available @ www.oracle.com), and
- Microsoft SQL Server (available @ www.microsoft.com).

We will look at databases in more detail in Chapter 7.

## Concluding comments

There can be little doubt that the impact of information and communications innovations and developments on both social and economic activity over the past 20 years has been enormous, changing (as we have seen) not only:

- the content of corporate activity (that is *what* is undertaken), but also
- the context of that corporate activity (that is *how* it is undertaken), and perhaps more importantly
- the nature of that corporate activity (that is *where* it is undertaken).

And yet, as we enter the 21st century and before we congratulate ourselves on the success of this global technological revolution, it is perhaps important to recognise the socio-political consequences and ephemeral nature of the paradise we have created. Indeed, there can be little doubt that growing economic regionalisation, rising political territoriality and increasing social segmentation – whilst clearly products of early times – nonetheless provide iconic testimony to the late 20th and early 21st century information technology revolution.

## Key points and concepts

ARPAnet
BACS (Bankers Automated Clearing System)
BACSTEL-IP
Business Process Re-engineering
CHAPS (Clearing House Automated Payments System)
DNS (Domain Name Server)
E-business
E-commerce
EDI (Electronic Data Interchange)
EFT (Electronic Funds Transfer)
E-mail
Enterprise Resource Planning
File sharing
First generation computers

Flat file database
Fourth generation computers
FTP (File Transfer Protocol)
HTML (HyperText Markup Language)
HTTP (HyperText Transfer Protocol)
IETF (Internet Engineering Task Force)
IMAP (Internet Mail Access Protocol)
Internet
Internet relay chat
ISOC (Internet Society)
JIT (Just-in-Time)
Media streaming
MIME (Multipurpose Internet Mail Extension)
MRP-I (Materials Requirements Planning)
MRP-II (Manufacturing Resource Planning)

Newsgroups
Peer-to-peer network
POP3 server (Post Office Protocol 3 server)
Relational database
Request for comments
Second generation computers
SMTP (Simple Mail Transfer Protocol)
TCP/IP
Third generation computers

UN/EDIFACT (United Nations/Electronic
  Data Interchange for Administration,
  Commerce, and Transport)
URI (Uniform Resource Identifier)
URL (Uniform Resource Locator)
VAN (Value Added Network)
Voice over IP (VoIP)
Website
WWW (world wide web)

## References

Castells, M. (1996) *The Rise of the Network Society, The Information Age: Economy, Society and Culture*, volume I, Blackwell, Oxford.

Castells, M. (1998) *The end of millennium (The information age, economy, society and culture, volume III)*, Blackwell, Oxford.

Lu, M. (2001) 'Digital divide in developing countries', *Journal of Global Information Technology Management* 4:3, pp. 1–4.

Stadler, F. (1998) 'The Network Paradigm: Social Formations in the Age of Information', *Information Society* 14:4.

## Bibliography

Aglietta, M. (1979) *A Theory of Capitalist Regulation*, New Left Books, London.

Boyer, R. (1988) 'Technical Change and the Theory of Regulation', in Dosi, G., Freeman, G., Nelson, R., Silverberg, G. and Soete, L. (eds) *Technical Change and Economic Theory*, Francis Pinter, London.

Freeman, G. and Perez, C. (1988) 'Structural Crisis of Adjustment, Business Cycles, and Investment Behaviour', in Dosi, G., Freeman, G., Nelson, R., Silverberg, G. and Soete, L. (eds) *Technical Change and Economic Theory*, Francis Pinter, London.

Harvey, D. (1990) *The Condition of Post Modernity*, Basil Blackwell, London.

Jessop, B. (1991) 'Thatcherism and Flexibility, the White Heat of the Post Fordist Revolution', in Jessop, B., Kastendiek H., Nielsen, K. and Pedersen, O. (eds) *The Politics of Flexibility*, Edward Elgar, Aldershot.

Lipietz, A. (1985) *The Enchanted World: Inflation, Credit and the World Crisis*, Verso, London.

Lipietz, A. (1987) *Mirages and Miracle: The Crisis of Global Fordism*, Verso, London.

Piore, M.J. and Sabel, C.F. (1984) *The Second Industrial Divide*, Basic Books, New York.

Webster, F. (1995) *Theories of the Information Society*, Routledge, London.

## Websites

www.bacs.co.uk
Bankers Automated Clearing Systems
www.eff.org
Electronic Frontier Foundation
www.financial-ombudsman.org.uk
Financial Ombudsman Service
www.iab.org
Internet Architecture Board (IAB)
www.ietf.org
Internet Engineering Task Force (IETF)
www.irtf.org
Internet Research Task Force (IRTF)
www.isoc.org
Internet Society (ISOC)
www.rfc-editor.org
Request for Comments editor
www.voca.co.uk
Voca Ltd
www.voipproviderslist.com
VoIP provider list
www.w3.org
World Wide Web Consortium

## Self-review questions

1. Briefly explain the contribution APRAnet made to the development of the internet.
2. Distinguish between the internet, and the web.
3. Define the term RFC, and explain the role of RFCs in developing internet standards.
4. Define and explain what is meant by the term 'file sharing'.
5. Define and explain two of the following internet services/facilities:
   - e-mail,
   - file sharing,
   - media streaming,
   - VoIP (Voice over IP),
   - internet relay chat,
   - newsgroups.
6. Define and briefly explain the role of the Internet Society (ISOC).
7. Identify and describe the main categories of electronic funds transfer (EFT).
8. Define and distinguish between direct credit and direct debit.
9. Briefly explain the difference between card-based, and non-card-based EPOS EFT.
10. What are the major types of computer-based accounting software?

## Questions and problems

### Question 1

'The internet is a global phenomenon started by the Russians!' Discuss.

### Question 2

'The internet is a global phenomenon managed and controlled by the Americans!' Discuss.

### Question 3

Computer-based accounting software can be classified into two categories:

- accounting finance-related software, and
- management-related software.

#### *Required*

Describe and explain the three types of software within each of the above categories.

### Question 4

The BACSTEL payment service was withdrawn at the end of December 2005 and replaced by BACSTEL-IP.

#### *Required*

Briefly describe the four stage processing procedure of BACSTEL-IP and explain the main advantages of the new service.

(Note: Before answering the question have a look at the information available @ http://www.bacs.co.uk/bpsl/bacstelip).

### Question 5

There are many different types of websites, some of which allow free access, some of which require a subscription to access part of their content and some of which require a subscription to access all of their content.

#### *Required*

Describe (with examples) eight types of website available on the web today.

## Assignments

### Question 1

KDS Ltd is a UK-based services company. The company provides a range of secure delivery services for NHS hospitals in the south-east of England. Currently the company operates a fleet of 62 vehicles and is investigating the possibility of using VoIP for communication between the company's head office and the various delivery vehicles.

*Required*

Describe the advantages and disadvantages of using VoIP for a company such as KDS Ltd and the possible uses/benefits such a system could have in relation to the company's accounting information perspective.

## Question 2

At a recent accounting information systems conference in London, a guest academic speaker completed his lecture on 'the impact of information and communication technology on corporate accounting information systems' with the following statement:

*and remember, there are only four golden rules in corporate accounting information systems management, these being:*

- *information is money – protect it,*
- *trust is not a form of control,*
- *technology is paradox, and*
- *the cost of security can never be too high.*

*Required*

Critically assess the validity and appropriateness of the guest speaker's four golden rules.

## Chapter endnotes

[1] As suggested by Stadler (1998), the new economy is 'informational because the competitiveness of its central actors (firms, regions, or nations) depends on their ability to generate and process electronic information. It is global because its most important aspects, from financing to production, are organised on a global scale, directly through multinational corporations and/or indirectly through networks of associations.'

[2] Such space of flows comprises of a vast range of interconnected elements/networks through which socially constructed organisations (such as companies) constitute/(re)constitute themselves and organise their activities. For Castells (1996) such a space of flows comprises of three interrelated aspects:

- technology – the infrastructure of the network,
- places – the topology of the space formed by the links and connection within the network, and
- people – the segregation of people within such networks.

[3] For Castells the network enterprise is 'that specific form of enterprise whose system of means is constituted by the intersection of autonomous systems of goals' (1996: 171), and is a phenomenon arising from and comprising of changing patterns of both internal and external competition and cooperation.

[4] For Castells such increasing fragmentation is the result of 'societies . . . (being) . . . increasingly structured around the bipolar opposition of the Net and the Self' (1996: 3). For Castells, the Net metaphor relates to/symbolises the new emergent organisational formations and structures based on the pervasive use of networked communication media – formations and structures that are now characteristic of many companies, communities and social movements. The Self metaphor relates to/symbolises the activities through which individuals attempt to reaffirm their identities under the conditions of structural change and instability – structural change and

instability that is symptomatic of the organisation and (re)organisation of social, political and economic activities into dynamic networks.

[5] Or as described by Castells (1996) as 'network enterprises'.

[6] Cuneiform is a pictographic writing system used by many languages over several empires in ancient Mesopotamia and Persia. Cuneiform is derived from Latin meaning 'wedge shaped'.

[7] COBOL (COmmon Business Oriented Language) was developed in the 1960s as a programming language designed for and used primarily in business-related applications.

[8] FORTRAN (FORmula TRANslator) was developed by IBM in the late 1950s and was one of the first high-level program languages, used primarily for scientific calculations.

[9] In formal usage, the word Internet was traditionally written with a capital first letter, whilst in less formal usage, the capital letter was often dropped (internet). Up to 2000 the former dominated the media and the published press. However since 2000 a significant number of publications have adopted the latter less formal usage. It is this latter version that is used in this text.

[10] Internetworking involves connecting two or more distinct computer networks together into an internetwork, using devices called a router (a computer network device that forwards data packets across an internetwork through a process known as routing) to connect them together and allow traffic to flow between them.

[11] In computer networking, packet switching is the dominant communications procedure in which packets (units of information carriage) are individually routed between computer network nodes (devices).

[12] The Internet Protocol (IP) is a data-oriented protocol that is used by source and destination hosts for communicating data across a packet switched internetwork.

[13] The Advanced Research Projects Agency Network (ARPAnet) developed by ARPA (Advanced Research Projects Agency) of the US Department of Defense.

[14] For some, the urgency afforded to the development of the ARPAnet by the US government authorities was a direct consequence of the scientific success illustrated by the Russian Sputnik programme, especially Yuri Gagarin's successful spaceflight on 12 April 1961.

[15] In an open-architecture network, the individual networks may be environment specific – that is separately designed and developed with their own unique interface which they may offer to users and/or other providers, including other internet providers.

[16] See: www.zakon.org/robert/internet/timeline.

[17] Source: Computer Industry Alamanac – see www.i-level.com/resource-centre/statistics.asp.

[18] Source: BMRB Internet Monitor – see www.i-level.com/resource-centre/statistics.asp.

[19] RFC1 was written by Crocker, S., University of California, Los Angeles. It was published in 1969 and was entitled 'Host Software'.

[20] The Internet Engineering Task Force (IETF) is responsible for the development and promotion of internet standards. It is an open, all-volunteer organisation. It possesses neither formal membership nor any formal membership requirements. For further information see www.ietf.org.

[21] The Internet Architecture Board (IAB) (see www.iab.org) is responsible for overseeing the technical and engineering development of the internet by the Internet Society (ISOC) (see below). The board oversees a number of task forces, of which perhaps the most important are:

- the Internet Engineering Task Force (IETF), and
- the Internet Research Task Force (IRTF) – see www.irtf.org.

[22] The RFC Editor is:

- the publisher of RFC documents,
- responsible for producing the final editorial review of the RFC documents, and
- responsible for maintaining a master file of RFC documents called the RFC Index.

The RFC index is available at www.rfc-editor.org/rfcsearch.html. Currently the RFC Editor is a small group funded by ISOC. For further information on the RFC Editor see www.rfc-editor.org.

[23] The Internet Society (ISOC) is an international organisation responsible for promoting internet access and use, and to 'assure the open development, evolution and use of the Internet for the benefit of all people throughout the world'. ISOC membership is comprised of individuals, companies, non-profit-making organisations, government agencies, and educational institutions such as colleges and universities. For further information see www.isoc.org.

[24] For some the major advantage of the tradition of never de-publishing obsolete RFCs is that as a series of documents they form a continuous historical record of the development and evolution of internet standards.

[25] Current RFCs are available as an RFC index @ www.rfc-editor.org/rfc-index.html.

[26] A list of extant internet drafts is available @ www.rfc-editor.org/idsearch.html.

[27] The full text of RFC 2026 is available @ ftp.rfc-editor.org/in-notes/rfc2026.txt.

[28] The full text of STD 1 is available @ ftp.rfc-editor.org/in-notes/std/std1.txt.

[29] The Internet protocol suite (sometimes called the TCP/IP protocol suite) is the set of communications protocols that implement the protocol stack on which the internet is established and on which it effectively operates. A protocol stack is a hierarchical arrangement of layers in which each layer solves a set of problems involving the transmission of data. Higher layers within the protocol stack are logically closer to the user and deal with more abstract data. Lower layers within the protocol stack are more distant from the user and deal with the translation of data into forms that can eventually be physically manipulated.

[30] File Transfer Protocol (FTP) is a software standard for transferring computer files between computer and/or networks of computers which possess widely different operating systems. FTP belongs to the application layer of the internet protocol suite.

[31] Peer-to-peer (or P2P) networks are typically comprised of large informal connections and are useful for many purposes, including:

- file sharing data/information files especially where such files contain audio and/or audio data, and
- real time data transmision such as telephony traffic.

We will discuss P2P networks in greater detail in Chapter 5.

[32] For information on blackboard see www.blackboard.com.

[33] File sharing is distinct from file trading inasmuch as downloading files from a peer-to-peer (P2P) network does not require uploading files.

[34] Napster (www.Napster.com) was launched in 1999 by Shaun Fanning and was the first major file sharing facility – a centralised system which popularised file sharing for the mass public or at least internet users. Napster was a localised index for MP3 files. Following legal challenges to its activities, Napster was forced to close down its file sharing activities in July 2001. In 2002 the Napster brand and logo were acquired by Roxio Inc. The company subsequently used them to rebrand the Pressplay music service which it acquired in 2003. In 2005 Roxio Inc. changed its name to Napster Inc.

[35] Gnutella (www.Gnutella.com) is a 'decentralised' peer-to-peer (P2P) file sharing network operating without a central server. Files are exchanged directly between users. It is used primarily to exchange music, films and software. Gnutella is now one of the most popular file sharing networks in the internet, closely following the established favorites of eDonkey2000 (www.eDonkey2000.com), BitTorrent (www.BitTorrent.net), and the three FastTrack-based networks: Kazaa (www.Kazaa.com), Grokster (www.Grokster.com) and iMesh (www.iMesh.com).

[36] Freenet was, and indeed continues to be, developed as open source software, and is fundamentally different from other peer-to-peer networks. Freenet is primarily intended to combat

censorship and allow people to communicate freely and with near-total anonymity. More information on Freenet is available @ http://freenetproject.org.

[37] Founded in 1990 the Electronic Frontier Foundation (EFF) is a US-based, non-profit-making organisation whose main aims are to 'educate the press, policymakers and the general public about civil issues related to technology,' in the context of today's digital age. More information on the Electronic Frontier Foundation is available @ http://www.eff.org.

[38] The term 'consumption' is used here to mean any or a combination of the following:

- reading – if the media is text based,
- hearing – if the media is audio based, and
- viewing – if the media is video based.

[39] For example, protocol issues/requirements, data corruption issues, data recovery procedures and transmission guarantees.

[40] Movielink is a venture jointly owned by Paramount Pictures, Sony Pictures Entertainment, Universal Studios and Warner Bros Studios, and CinemaNow is a venture jointly owned by Lions Gate Entertainment, Microsoft, Blockbuster and several private investment companies.

[41] Although an IPS (internet service provider) will clearly charge for connection to the internet, the use of VoIP over the internet does not usually involve any extra/additional charges. Consequently VoIP users often view any calls as free. Example VoIP providers include Free World Dialup @ www.freeworlddialup.com and/or Skype www.skype.com.

For a comprehensive list of VoIP providers see VoIP provider list available @ www.voipproviderslist.com.

[42] UK Office of Communication.

[43] E.164 is a global standard which defines the international telecommunications plan that among other provisions defines the format of telephone numbers. Further details are available @ www.comm.disa.mil/itu/r_e0.html.

[44] Internet relay chat was created by Jarkko Oikarinen (nickname 'WiZ') in August 1988 to replace a program called MUT (Multi User Talk) on a bulletin board system called OuluBox, in Finland. The prominence and profile of internet relay chat grew enormously during 1991 when it was used extensively by many Kuwaitis to report on the Iraqi invasion of Kuwait in August 1990 and the consequential Gulf War in 1991, and by many Russians to report on the Soviet coup attempt – the August Putsch, in August 1991. Interent relay chat was also used in a similar way during the coup against Boris Yeltsin in September 1993. (See www.wikipedia.org.)

[45] It is not uncommon for an IRC server to have dozens, hundreds or even thousands of chat channels open simultaneously – some channels are more or less permanent, others less so.

[46] Available @ http://groups.msn.com/Editorial/en-gb/Content/chat.htm.

[47] A central location where data are stored and maintained.

[48] Usenet is a distributed discussion system through which users (or more appropriately usenetters), can access and distribute messages (often called articles) to a number of distributed newsgroups. The functionality of the system is maintained through a large number of interconnected servers, which store and forward messages from each other. And the difference between Usenet and the Internet is? The internet is the worldwide network of computers communicating to each other with the use of a specific communications protocol (TCP/IP) used by a vast range of applications. Usenet is essentially an application – a multi-user BBS (bulletin board system) that allows people to talk to each other on various subjects/issues.

[49] The alt.* hierarchy contains a vast number of sub-hierarchies/newsgroups for the discussion of a wide range of topics – some geographically orientated, some culturally determined – and many in a language other than English.

[50] The procedure/criteria for the creation of a new group within the alt.* hierarchy should be discussed in <u>alt.config</u>, and its adoption is not subject to the strict rules/voting procedures required for other hierarchies.

[51] Using a hyperlink, which is essentially a reference in a hypertext document to another document or other resource.

[52] A web browser is a software application that enables a user to access, display and interact with HTML documents (webpages) either:

- hosted by a web server, or
- held in a file system.

The most popular web browsers for personal computers (PC and Mac) include:

- Microsoft Internet Explorer (see <u>www.microsoft.com/windows/ie/default.mspx</u>),
- Mozilla Firefox, (see <u>www.mozila.org</u>),
- Opera (see <u>www.opera.com</u>), and
- Safari (see <u>www.aple.com/safari</u>).

[53] Tim Berners-Lee now heads the World Wide Web Consortium (W3C) – see <u>www.w3.org</u> – which develops and maintains standards that enable computers on the web to effectively store and communicate different forms of information.

[54] This document (Berners-Lee, T.M. and Cailliau, R. (1990) 'World Wide Web: Proposal for a hypertext project') is available @ <u>http://www.w3.org/Proposal</u>.

[55] See <u>http://groups.google.com/group/alt.hypertext/msg/395f282a67a1916c</u>.

[56] A URI (Uniform Resource Identifier) identifies a particular resource – a URL (Uniform Resource Locator) not only identifies a resource, but indicates how to locate the resource. That is the URL functions as a document/web page address.

[57] For example the most prevalent language on the internet is English (approximately 60%).

[58] A disparity in technological progress and development between those developed nations/countries able to develop and invest in information and communication technologies, and those less developed/developing nations/countries unable to develop and invest in information and communication technologies, continues to reinforce and indeed widen existing economic differences and inequalities, between:

- the most developed nations/countries of the world (e.g. the USA, Canada, Japan and those countries that comprise the EU), and
- the less developed and/or developing nations/countries of the world (e.g. many African and Latin American nations/countries and some South-East Asian nations/countries).

A global divide often characterised as the north–south divide – between the northern, wealthier nations/countries and southern, poorer nations/countries.

[59] Asymmetric Digital Subscriber Line (ADSL) is a data communications technology that enables faster data transmission over conventional telephone lines than a conventional modem can provide.

[60] The term e-business is often attributed to Louis V. Gerstner, Jr., Chairman of the board and Chief Executive Officer of IBM Inc. from April 1993 to December 2002.

[61] *The European e-business report: a portrait of e-business in 10 sectors of the EU economy* (2004) is available @ <u>www.ebusiness-watch.org/resources/documents/eBusiness-Report-2004.pdf</u>.

[62] Some commentators refer to such activities as web commerce.

[63] Dot com companies were the collection of mainly start-up companies selling a range of products and/or services using a range of information and communication-related vehicles – in particular the internet. Their exponential proliferation during the late 1990s dotcom boom was matched only by their spectacular decline in 2000/01.

[64] M-commerce can be defined as the buying and selling of goods and services through wireless (handheld) devices such as mobile telephone and www enabled personal digital assistants.

[65] HyperText Markup Language (HTML) is a markup language designed for the creation of webpages and other information viewable with a web browser. HTML is used to structure information identifying text, for example headings, paragraphs, lists, etc.

[66] Extensible HyperText Markup Language, or XHTML, is a markup language with the same semantic context as HTML but with a much stricter syntax.

[67] Hyper Text Transfer Protocol (HTTP) is the primary method used to convey information on the web.

[68] Uniform Resource Locator, or web address, is a standardised address name layout for resources (such as documents or images) on the internet.

[69] A hyperlink is merely a link or a reference in a hypertext document to another hypertext document and/or other resource.

[70] Web traffic can be analysed by viewing the traffic statistics found in the web server log file, an automatically-generated list of all the pages served or 'hits'.

[71] X12 refers to the version/generation.

[72] The sending of EDI transactions, using the Internet, involves translating the transaction document into MIME format and then using e-mail to transmit the message from the source company to the destination company.

[73] EDI on the internet is also-called 'open EDI' because the internet is an open architecture network.

[74] BACS (Bankers Automated Clearing System) is operated by BACS Payment Schemes Limited. The organisation is a membership-based industry body established and owned by the major UK banks to provide the facility for transferring funds (via direct debit, direct credit and/or standing order). Its role is to:

- develop, enhance and promote the use and integrity of automated payment and payment-related services, and
- promote best practice amongst those companies who offer payment services.

For further details see www.bacs.co.uk.

[75] Also known as point of sale.

[76] The Association for Payment Clearing Services (APACS) is a non-statutory association for those involved in providing payment services. The principal aim/task of APACS is to administer, coordinate supervise and manage the major UK payment clearing schemes through three operational clearing companies:

- BACS Ltd (now Voca Ltd),
- CHAPS Clearing Company Ltd, and
- Cheque and Credit Clearing Company Ltd.

[77] CHAPS Clearing Company Ltd currently has 22 direct members of which 14 are members of CHAPS Sterling and 20 are members of CHAPS Euro.

[78] See Ombudsman News issue 42 (December 2004/January 2005) published by the Financial Ombudsman Service available @ www.financial-ombudsman.org.uk/publications/ombudsman-news/42/42.htm.

[79] Although the payment/transfer will be made electronically, the sending bank will need to undertake a range of authorisation, verification, authentication and validation checks prior to the payment/transfer.

[80] For further information on Voca Ltd see www.voca.co.uk.

[81] Approximately 600 BACS approved bureaux exist throughout the UK. They each carry the BACS seal of approval and are inspected at least once every three years to assess the technical

competence and operational integrity of the bureaux in accordance with the requirements of the BACS Approved Bureaux Scheme. The following areas are normally assessed:

- physical security,
- computer operations, and
- applications and systems support.

[82] Note: The control of a direct credit payment normally resides with a payer's bank.

[83] During 2005 approximately 90% of the UK workforce was paid using direct credit – approximately 5 million wages every week and nearly 25 million salaries every month. However, direct credit can be used for a wide variety of other applications.

[84] During 2005 nearly 200,000 organisations used BACS for supplier payments, payments of pensions, payments of employee expenses, insurance settlements, payments of dividends and/or interest and payment refunds.

[85] Note: The bank and/or building society holding the payer's account is both responsible and answerable for all payments (including those made by direct debit) made for that account.

[86] Some organisations/companies sometimes levy an additional (interest) charge on customers for paying by direct debit.

[87] All direct debit payments are protected by three safeguards:

- an immediate, money back guarantee from the bank or building society if an error is made,
- advance notice from the recipient company/organisation if the date and/or the amount of the direct debit changes, and
- the right to cancel.

[88] BACSTEL payment service was withdrawn at the end of December 2005.

[89] Conversion/transfer of all direct submitters and BACS approved bureaux was completed by late 2005/early 2006.

[90] Public key infrastructure (PKI) is an arrangement which provides for third-party vetting of, and vouching for, user identities. It also allows binding of public keys to users. This is usually carried by software at a central location together with other coordinated software at distributed locations. The public keys are typically in digital certificates.

[91] Public key cryptography (PKC) is a type of cryptography in which the encryption process is publicly available and unprotected, but in which a part of the decryption key is protected so that only a party with knowledge of both parts of the decryption process can decrypt the cipher text.

[92] The software interface can be either:

- an acquired/purchased software interface from a BACS approved solution supplier – a company that provides BACS Payment Schemes approved software solutions to businesses that wish to access the BACS Payment Schemes service, including BACSTEL-IP software and hardware packages, mailbox services for BACS Payment Schemes reports and total management solutions to handle and run direct debit and direct credit systems, or
- an in-house corporate developed software interface which *must* conform to the technical and quality specifications of BACSTEL-IP and be subject to the conditions and testing protocols mandated under the BACS Approved Software Service.

[93] Currently, a company/business will need:

- WINDOWS 98 SE, WINDOWS NT4, WINDOWS 2000 or XP (all versions), or
- Linux & AS400, or
- Internet Explorer 5.01 and above, 128 bit SSL encryption; Netscape Navigator 4.7 and above, 128 bit SSL encryption, and
- zipping software (WinZip), and
- the ability to connect a smartcard reader (USB (preferred) or serial interface).

[94] For further details on each of these connectivity types see www.pearsoned.co.uk/boczko.

[95] A smartcard-based security process requires an operator to insert the card into a reader and key in a PIN each time a digital signature is required. Such a security process is normally used/best suited to a PC or other interactive-based system.

[96] A hardware security module (HSM) solution can be an external module connected to or an internal module integrated within the computer system to:

- store secret keys and other security-related material,
- provide a secure and controlled production of digital signatures, and
- provide different levels of security to prevent unauthorised access to the secret material.

Such a module is normally used/best suited for a mainframe or server environment, and/or where:

- unattended operations are performed,
- remote and/or secure computer environment is required, and/or
- physical access is limited.

[97] Sponsoring banks are responsible for (in agreement with the user's primary security contacts):

- setting up each user and contact point on BACSTEL-IP, and
- assigning relevant access levels for each contact point.

[98] Simple Mail Transfer Protocol (SMTP) is the standard for e-mail transmission across the internet. It is a simple, text-based protocol, where one or more recipients of a message are specified (and in most cases verified to exist) and then the message text is transferred.

[99] A 'killer application' is the term used to describe a computer (software) program that is so useful that people will buy a computer hardware and/or operating system simply to run the program.

[100] BITnet was a cooperative US university network founded in 1981 at the City University of New York.

[101] US-based National Science Foundation network (NSFNet) which formed a major part of the central network/core of the internet.

[102] A signature block is a block of text automatically appended at the bottom of an e-mail message that essentially signs off the message. Information usually contained in a signature block may for example include:

- the sender's name,
- the sender's email address, and
- other contact details where appropriate, for example website addresses and/or links.

[103] Here the recipient of this copy will know who was in the To: field, but the recipients cannot see who is on the Bcc: list.

[104] Multipurpose Internet Mail Extensions (MIME).

[105] The Domain Name System (or DNS) is a system that stores information about hostnames and domain names in a type of distributed database on networks, such as the internet. Of the many types of information that can be stored, most importantly it provides a physical location IP address for each domain name and lists the mail server accepting e-mail for each domain.

[106] POP is an abbreviation of Post Office Protocol, and IMAP is an abbreviation of Internet Mail Access Protocol.

[107] If the recipient address had been another user at James.com the SMTP server would merely transfer the e-mail message to the POP3 server for James.com (using what is called a delivery agent). However, because the recipient is at another domain, the SMTP server needs to communicate with that other domain.

[108] The market for webmail has two main competitors: Hotmail with approximately 33% of the market and Yahoo Mail with approximately 30% of the market. Gmail (Google mail) has approximately 4% of the market. The remaining 33% of the market is held by smaller providers.

[109] Source: BMRB Internet Monitor, See www.i-level.com/resource-centre/statistics.asp.

[110] For example, customer analysis by:

■ geographical location,
■ volume of trade, and/or
■ payment history.

[111] For example:

■ sending out debtor letters, payment reminders and statements of account,
■ making provisions for doubtful and bad debts, and
■ holding/closing accounts.

[112] For example, multiple delivery addresses for each customer.

[113] For example, supplier analysis by:

■ geographical location,
■ account type, and/or
■ credit terms.

[114] Activity-based costing was first defined in 1987 by Robert Kaplan and Robin Cooper (Kaplan, R. and Cooper, R. (1987) *Accounting and Management: A Field Study Perspective*, Harvard Business School Press, Harvard Business School).

[115] Where a cost object (product and/or service) uses and/or shares common resources differently (in different proportions or at different rates), the measure of the use of the shared activity by each of the cost object (product and/or service) is known as the cost driver. Note that an activity can have multiple cost drivers.

[116] See article @ http://www.ct-yankee.com/lean/mlw/jit.html.

[117] These are products integrated into other products.

[118] See note 99.

[119] Multiplan was an early spreadsheet program developed by Microsoft in 1982. It was initially developed for computers running operating systems such as CP/M, MS-DOS and Apple II, with the Apple Mac version being Microsoft's first GUI (graphical user interface) spreadsheet.

# 5

# Network architectures and topologies: making connections

## Introduction

*Information technology and business are becoming inextricably interwoven. I don't think any-body can talk meaningfully about one without talking about the other* (Bill Gates, Microsoft).

The history of any society (or group/organisation within a society) is a history littered with uncertainties and ambiguities. A history in which political and economic pressures often necessitate the frequent modification of organisational boundaries, and in which social and cultural pressures often require the imposition of new and/or redefined existing social structures, social arrangements and organisation interrelationships.

A history of change perhaps? But how do we know? We don't . . . well not with any degree of certainty, because history – especially the social history of a group, organisation and/or institution is often written/re-written through the eyes of the present!

However, that said, what we do know (if perhaps only intuitively) is that our species is socially interactive with an almost unconscious need/desire for collectiveness, connectivity and belonging. A need/desire that has perhaps existed since the dawn of time! From:

- the emergence of small self-sufficient groupings (small, self-sustaining social networks founded on the need for mutual survival), to
- the development of larger local assemblies and urban alliances/networks founded on the need for mutual protection and security, and the coordination of activity, to
- in a contemporary context, the establishment of large national and international democratic societies founded on the need for socio-political governance, economic management and wealth creation,

the need for belonging, for connectivity and for socially structured networks has remained a common feature/theme – a theme that perhaps unsurprisingly has continued to play an increasingly important role in the ever-changing cartography of modern 21st century society.[1] A society that is neither isolated nor protected from the consequences of inter-state politics, cultural territoriality and the ever increasing mobility of capital. One that possesses neither permanence nor stability, and is neither a static nor unchanging product of antiquity. Indeed, there can be little doubt that as an ever-changing, ever-complex network of socio-cultural arrangements, economic rationales and socio-political relationships, that society (and the groups, institutions and organisations of which it is comprised) are constantly being reupholstered, reconfigured and/or reconstructed by a vast array of often conflicting social, economic and increasingly political pressures.

Consider, for example, the past social conflicts that have punctuated the history of many of the worlds' societies, nations, and states,[2] or indeed the many political/democratic changes that have scarred many a social landscape and resulted in a redefining of individual societies, nations and states. Most (if not all) of these conflicts and changes have arisen/emerged from the desire of one social group (or indeed, one nation, or one state) – sometimes in collusion with others – to impose its world view, its idea of collectiveness (of belonging/connectivity), its *Weltanschauung*,[3] onto another social group (or indeed nation or state) – for better or worse![4]

There can also be little doubt that today – within western contemporary society, certainly during the latter part of the 20th century and the early part of the 21st century – much of the growing demand for greater interconnectivity and greater organisational/institutional networking has resulted from the increasing dominance of an almost singular economic philosophy.[5] A philosophy:

- whose foundation lies within the social politics of economic liberalism and the free pursuit of wealth accumulation, and
- whose organisation and continued success is dependent upon a structure of defined economic networks and socio-political interconnectivity.

An interconnectivity necessitated by:

- the ever-increasing numbers of market-based participants,
- the ever-increasing complexity of market-based interrelationships, and
- the ever-increasing geographical diversity of market-based activity.

Indeed, from the earliest social networks to the emergence of complex interrelated institutional networks (e.g. the limited liability company), to the development of virtual networks, the purpose of such networks – their *raison d'être* – has remained unchanged. To provide an interconnectivity of trust through which the use of data, information, assets and resources can be managed, coordinated, organised, structured and, perhaps most importantly, controlled.[6]

## Learning outcomes

This chapter considers a range of issues related to soft-type networks, hard-type networks and semi-soft-type networks, and explores the implications of such networks on corporate accounting information systems. It examines issues relating to the development and control of alternative network architectures and topologies, and considers how information and communication technology, and the adoption of alternative network architectures and topologies, have affected the computer-based processing of transaction data.

By the end of this chapter, the reader should be able to:

- describe the major characteristics of, and inter-relationships between, soft-type networks, hard-type networks and semi soft-type networks,
- consider and explain the socio-political context of networking, and
- demonstrate a critical understanding of the implications of alternative network architectures and topologies on corporate accounting information systems.

## Understanding differences – from soft-type networks to hard-type networks

All networks whether they are physical, social or indeed virtual possess three important characteristics:

- an architecture – that is a specific design for the inter-operation of the components that comprise the network,
- a topology – that is a specific shape or relational map that describes the network, and
- a protocol – that is a set of rules that prescribe and govern access to, engagement with, and communication within, the network, and/or between a network and other interrelated networks.

Remember Chapter 2 and the discussion on soft systems/hard systems? We will adopt a similar, albeit slightly extended, framework for our discussion on networks and distinguish between the following network types:

- soft-type networks – or social networks
- hard-type networks – or physical networks, and
- semi-soft-type networks[7] – or logical (virtual) networks.

See Figure 5.1.

### Soft-type networks

In a social context, a network can be described as a set of relationships and/or interconnections between individuals and/or groups of people, and refers to the interassociation between individuals and/or groups of individuals, designed to:

- share commonalities,
- form communities (or expand existing communities), and
- exchange information, knowledge and/or resources.

We will refer to these networks as soft-type networks, that is networks in which the dominant feature is mutual communication, social interaction, and exchange within a politically constructed, framework/arrangement.

Such soft-type networks can be divided into two categories:[8]

- a social network or socio-political network – often referred to as self-focused network which is created, developed and sustained for the benefit of the self, and

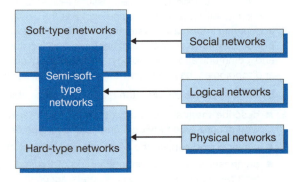

**Figure 5.1** Types of networks

- a business network or socio-economic network – often referred to as entity-focused network which is created, developed and sustained for the benefit of the entity (e.g. the company or mutual association).

We will only consider the latter category of entity-focused soft-type networks.

## Hard-type networks

In a structural context, a network can be described as a physical construct and defined by the components that comprises its underlying physical structure. For example, using an information and communication technology context, a network can be defined as:

- a group of devices connected by a communications facility, the primary use of which is the exchange of data and/or information, or
- a configuration of data processing devices and software programs connected for data and/or information interchange, or
- a group of computers and/or computer-related devices (e.g. a server) connected by a communications facility and/or telecommunications link that share data, and/or information and/or resources/facilities.

We will refer to these as hard-type networks, that is networks in which the dominant feature is a structured interconnectivity. Such hard-type networks (in particular, information and communication technology-based networks) may be either:

- permanent – for example a structure defined by physical interconnections and communications links, such as Ethernet cabling and/or fibre optic cabling, or
- temporary (on intermittent) – for example using non-physical wireless interconnections and communication links, such as digital links and/or satellite facilities.

Furthermore, given the highly structured (some would say mechanistic) nature of such networks, outcomes and performance are generally seen as certain and predictable, with performance often measured in quantifiable terms.

## Semi-soft-type networks

From a process context, a network may also be defined as an abstract organisational construct, a construct that is superimposed on all or part of one or more interrelated physical networks, and through which data/information is made available and/or resources and activities are coordinated and managed.

Such networks are sometimes referred to as logical networks[9] – a good example of which is of course the internet, and its associated derivatives, the intranet and extranet.

We will refer to these networks as semi-soft-type networks, that is networks in which the dominant feature is representational interconnectivity, or more appropriately a conceptual description/constructed representation concerned only with the interconnections and pathways that comprise the network.

Let's look at each of these alternative types of networks in a little more detail.

## Soft-type networks – an overview

As suggested earlier, an entity-focused soft-type network is in essence a social network that exists within a political framework – an interconnected assembly of network actors[10] who are linked by mutual interrelationships and interdependencies[11] which, whilst social in nature, are often political in context and invariably economic in origin. It is the interaction (directly or indirectly) of these network actors that influences the ongoing social, political and economic activities of the network and, as a consequence, determines:

- how effectively data/information flows within the network,
- how efficiently data/information is used within the network, and
- how patterns of trust and mechanisms of control are developed, established and fostered within the network.

Such interactions are determined by the interaction/interface of a range of factors/characteristics, the most important being:

- architecture-related structural characteristics – normally influenced by, for example:
  - the nature and purpose of the network, and
  - the nature of the social connectedness within the network,
- topology-related functional characteristics – normally influenced by, for example:
  - the type of relationships/links possible within the network, and
  - the frequency of social contact within the network, and
- protocol-related control/management characteristics – normally influenced by, for example:
  - the proximity of individuals within the network, and
  - the risk profile/nature of network activities.

Let's have a brief look at each of these characteristics.

 ## Soft-type network architectures

In a soft-type network context, the architecture provides the structure/framework through which aims and objectives of the network are realised. Whilst such architectures can vary enormously between networks, they can nonetheless be located on a somewhat subjective scale between:

- a formal and highly structured architecture, and
- an informal/casual architecture.

### Formal

A network with a formal type architecture can be loosely defined as a regulated social arrangement/ network of people and/or groups of people designed to facilitate interaction, communication and the exchange of both knowledge and resources.[12]

### Informal

A network with an informal type architecture can be loosely defined as a social arrangement/ network of people and/or groups of people designed to facilitate casual interaction – without a formal regulated framework.

In reality, of course most soft-type networks are rarely ever completely formal (i.e. rule-bound) or rarely ever completely informal (i.e. rule-less). Instead, such networks tend to be a combination of both formal and informal types, that is they tend to be a complex layering or blending of both formal and informal architectures,[13] a blending that historically has, in a corporate context at least, been associated with/dominated by the ever-changing demands of the marketplace and the priorities of capital accumulation.

## Soft-type network topologies

In a soft-type network context, a topology provides the specific shape or the relational map of the organisation/network. Again, whilst such topologies can vary enormously between networks, they can (again) be located on a somewhat subjective scale between:

- a bureaucracy[14] or bureaucratic topology, and
- an adhocracy or adhocratic topology.

### Bureaucracy

A bureaucracy can be defined as a form of social network/organisation exemplified by a hierarchical division of labour, a formal chain of command and a prescriptive (and often imposed) framework of anonymity, and is a (socio-political) network structure often associated with (and championed by) the German sociologist Max Weber,[15] but highly criticised by Karl Marx[16] in his theory of historical materialism.[17]

As artificial/created social networks typified by the existence of highly structured and highly standardised processes and procedures, in a contemporary context bureaucracies are (within varying degrees) the most common type of topology employed within the UK corporate sector.[18] And whilst many alternative types of bureaucracies exist, for example:

- mechanistic,[19]
- organic,[20]
- functional,
- process-based, and/or
- matrix (or mesh) orientated,

they are (despite their inherent problems[21]) designed primarily to promote stability, and equality, and provide for the allocation of:

- jurisdiction and responsibility,
- processes, procedures and resources, and
- hierarchical authority/control.

### Adhocracy

An adhocracy can be defined as a non-bureaucratic networked organisation or perhaps more appropriately as an organisation/social network in which there is an absence of hierarchy and/or formal constitution, and were developed (or emerged) in the mid 1940s, and early 1950s for soft-type networks in which autonomy, flexibility and creativity were considered to be the core requirements for sustained survival and continued success.

Providing for greater flexibility, greater adaptability and greater responsiveness to change – especially in periods of uncertainty and continuous change – adhocracies are exemplified by:

- the absence of formal rules and regulations,
- the absence of hierarchical structures of authority, and
- the absence of procedural standardisation and/or formal organisation.

In addition, they are typified by a core desire to maintain – at all costs – the autonomy and sovereignty of network actors/participants.[22]

## Soft-type network protocols

In a soft-type network context, the protocols provide the regulatory context of the organisation/ network, that is the management framework within which the network functions and undertakes its activities. Protocols are designed primarily to:

- reduce network variability,
- minimise possible instability,
- moderate the impact of future uncertainty and unpredictability, and
- secure future sustainability.

Such protocols (i.e. rules and regulations) are invariably a product of an often complex and highly politicised process, the outcome of which is invariably determined by the type of architecture and topology adopted by/imposed upon the network.

## Locating soft-type networks

As suggested earlier, we can locate a soft-type network on two distinct scales, based on:

- the type of network architecture – ranging from formal to informal, and
- the type of network topology – ranging from bureaucratic to adhocratic.

Using the former (network architecture) as a vertical scale, and the latter (network topology) as a horizontal scale, we can create an intuitive representation – albeit a somewhat simplistic representation – on which to locate alternative soft-type networks. This representation provides four categories, from:

- formal bureaucracy, to
- formal adhocracy, to
- informal bureaucracy, to
- informal adhocracy.

See Figure 5.2.

An established retail/distribution company, a manufacturing/production company or indeed a time/space-based company would, because of:

- the nature and interconnectivity of their activities,
- the hierarchical complexity of their activities, and
- the dependency on routine formalised processes and procedures,

tend to adopt a more formalised (more bureaucratic) structure, and would perhaps be located within the formal bureaucracy region of the model (see area A in Figure 5.2).

An established knowledge/skills-based company or profession-based company, dependent not on routine formalised activities but on:

- individual (or group) skills,
- individual professional knowledge and competence, and/or
- individual (or group) creativity and inventiveness,

would, for example, tend to adopt a less-formalised (more adhocratic) structure, and would perhaps be located within an area that overlaps a number of regions (see area B in Figure 5.2).

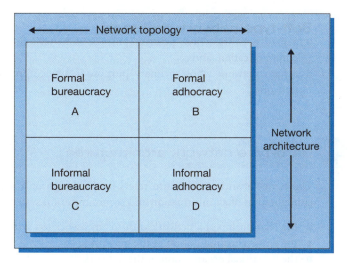

**Figure 5.2** Soft-type networks

A non-established company, or indeed a newly developed/emerging company, may well adopt a less-formalised (though nonetheless) bureaucratic structure, to accommodate:

■ the need for entrepreneurial flexibility, and
■ the need for accountability,

and would perhaps be located within an area that overlaps both the formal bureaucracy and informal bureaucracy regions of the model (see area C in Figure 5.2), although eventually as the company becomes more established, the priorities of accumulation and the pressure of the marketplace may well force such a company into either area A or area B (or out of business!).

Non-corporate-based soft-type networks, for example a charity or mutual association, would – depending of course on its size and range of activities – adopt a less formalised/more adhocratic structure, and perhaps be located within an area that overlaps a number of regions (see area B), although larger more established networks may well adopt a more corporate orientated bureaucratic structure, and perhaps move into the formal bureaucracy region of the model (see area D in Figure 5.2).

## Hard-type networks – an overview

For our purposes, we will define a hard network as an information and communications system that interconnects computer systems at different locations, and:

■ facilitates the transfer and exchange of data and/or information, and
■ allows the sharing of software, hardware (e.g. other peripheral information and communications devices) and/or processing power.

Such a network may be fixed, cabled and permanent, and/or variable (flexible), wireless and temporary.

There are essentially two categories of hard network:

- a hard network whose primary purpose is to facilitate interpersonal (person-to-person) communication, and
- a hard network whose primary purpose is service provision: for example, a bank ATM network.

## Hard-type network architectures

The term network architecture refers to the design of a network that is the basic layout or configuration of an information and communication system/computer system, and includes:

- the relationship of a network with/to any associated system,
- the physical configuration of the network,
- the functional organisation of the network,
- the operational procedures employed in the network, and
- the data formats utilised in the network.

There are many alternative types of hard-type network architectures, the most common being:

- wide area network (WAN),
- metropolitan area network (MAN),
- local area network (LAN),
- personal area network (PAN)
- client/server network, and
- peer-to-peer network.

Note that:

- computers and/or other information and communication devices within a network are called *nodes*,[23] and
- computers and/or other information and communication devices which allocate resources are called *servers*.[24]

Before we look at each of these alternative types of networks in a little more detail, it would perhaps be useful to consider/explain some of the components that comprise a hard network.

### Connecting components of hard-type networks

A hard-type network is the physical reality of the network and comprises a range of connected components and equipment necessary to:

- perform data processing activities, and
- provide communication management,

within a network. This would include:

- a computer workstation – to connect users to the network (the network human interface),
- a file server – to manage the flow of data/information between nodes of the network,
- a network interface card – to provide for communication within the network,
- a repeater – to amplify and rebroadcast signals in a network,
- a hub (multi-port repeater) – to interconnect network nodes,

- a bridge – to separate large networks into smaller more efficient networks or sub-networks,
- a switch (multi-port bridge) – to select network pathways/links within a network for the flow of data/information, and
- a router – to forward data packets to their network destinations.

Of course, all of these network components (or nodes) will require connecting using either:

- a wired connection, and/or
- a wireless connection.

Let's look at each of these network components in a little more detail.

### Computer workstation

All user computers connected to a network are called workstations or computer workstations and are referred to as network nodes. The phrase 'connected to a network' means a computer workstation that is configured with:

- a network interface card,
- appropriate networking software, and
- the appropriate physical cables if the network is hard wired, or the appropriate transmission/receiving devices if the network is wireless.

Whilst a computer workstation does not necessarily need/require independent storage capacity, because data files can be saved on the network file server, most computer workstations do possess storage capacity if only for use as a back-up facility in the event of network problems.

### File server

A file server stands at the centre of most networks and is, in essence, a computer that:

- stores and manages data files and software (e.g. end users' files),
- manages the use and availability of shared resources,
- provides network users with data, information and access to other network resources, and
- regulates communications between network nodes.

A file server may be dedicated – that is the computer workstation used as a file server is used *only* as a file server – or non-dedicated – the computer used as a file server is also used for other network-related tasks (e.g. it may also be used, simultaneously, as a network workstation). Any computer workstation can function as a file server. Whilst the characteristics and specifications of a file server would depend on the size and nature of the network served, the functionality of a computer workstation as a file server is dictated by the network operating systems (NOS) – whether it is a Novell Netware System, a Windows Server System or a UNIX Server System.

### Network interface card

The network interface card (also called network adapter or network card) and abbreviated to NIC, is a piece of computer hardware that is designed to provide for computer communication within a network. It is the physical connection between the computer workstation and the network. The vast majority of network interface cards are internal (i.e. within the computer workstation) and are built into the computer workstation motherboard,[25] although some older computer workstations may require the network interface card to plug into an expansion slot inside the computer workstation.

The network interface cards used in a network are a major factor in determining:

- the speed of the network, and
- the performance of a network.

Put simply, the network interface card implements a range of specific physical layer[26] and data link layer[27] protocols that are required for effective communication across a network.

### Repeater

A repeater is an OSI layer 1 device. In hard-wired networks, communication signals can lose strength as they pass across the network. Consequently, it may sometimes be necessary to boost the communication signal with a device called a repeater – usually where the total length of cable used in a network connection exceeds the standard set for the type of cable being used. A repeater merely amplifies the signal (the data/information message) it receives and rebroadcasts it across the network.

A repeater can be a separate device or it can (and often is) incorporated into a hub or switch.

### Hub

A (standard) hub – also known as a concentrator – is a networking component (an OSI layer 1 device) which acts as a convergence point of a network allowing the transfer of data/information. Put simply, a hub merely duplicates data/information received via a communications port and makes it available to all ports, allowing data/information sharing between all network nodes connected to the hub.

There are three types of hub:

- a passive hub – which allows the data/information to flow,
- a manageable hub – which allows data/information transfers to be monitored, and
- an active hub – which allows the data/information to flow but regenerates/amplifies received signals before transmitting them along the network.

### Bridge

A bridge is an OSI layer 2 device that facilitates:

- the connecting of a new network (or network segment) to an existing network (or network segment), and/or
- the connecting of different types of hard-type topologies.[28]

The purpose of a network bridge is to ensure that only necessary data/information flows across both sides of the network. To achieve such an aim a bridge can be used to:

- monitor the data flow/information traffic across both sides of the network, and
- manage network traffic to maintain optimum performance across the network.

### Switch

A switch, or more appropriately a switching hub (an OSI layer 2 device) is a device which filters and forwards data/information across a network. Whilst a standard hub simply replicates the data/information received, a switching hub keeps a record of the MAC addresses (media access control addresses) of the network nodes attached to it. When the switch receives data/information for forwarding, it forwards the data/information directly to the recipient network node identified by the MAC address attached to the data/information.

Most switches are active: that is they amplify the signal (the data/information message) as it moves from one network node to another. They are often used in a star topology and/or a star ring topology (see later).

### Router

A router (an OSI layer 3 device) is a networking component which transfers data/information from one network to another; and in a simple context is very similar to an intelligent bridge, inasmuch as a router can/will:

- select the best network path to route a message – using the destination address and origin address,
- direct network traffic to prevent head-on collisions – using the topology of the network and, where necessary,
- prioritise network paths and links when particular network segments are busy.

### Wired connections

Physical cabling is the medium from which a majority of network connections are created and through which data/information is transmitted across a network from one network node to another. There are, of course, several types of cabling currently in use and the choice of cable is dependent on:

- the size of the network,
- the topology of the network, and
- the network protocol.

Consequently, whilst some networks may utilise a single type of cabling, others may utilise many types of cabling.

The main types of cabling used in (computer) networking are:

- twisted pair cabling,
- coaxial cabling, and
- fibre optic cabling.

## Twisted pair (TP) cabling

There are essentially two main types of twisted pair cabling:

- unshielded twisted pair cabling, and
- shielded twisted pair cabling,

with a number of associated variants.

**Unshielded twisted pair (UTP) cabling** is a very popular (probably the most popular) cabling. Its quality may vary substantially from low-grade telephone cabling to high-grade, high-speed cabling. [29] Unshielded twisted pair cabling is not surrounded by any shielding and is comprised of four pairs of wires inside the cable jacket, with each pair of wires twisted with a different number of twists per centimetre. This twisting is to help eliminate possible interference from adjacent pairs of wires, and/or other communication and information technology-based devices.

Essentially, the closer/the tighter the twisting:

- the higher the potential data/information transmission rate and, of course,
- the greater the cost of the cabling per metre.

The advantages of unshielded twisted pair cabling are:

- it is cheap (relatively speaking),
- it is widely available,
- it is very flexible,

- it is commonly used – especially in temporary network connections and, most importantly of all,
- it is reliable.

The disadvantage of unshielded twisted pair cabling is that due to its lack of shielding, it is susceptible to radio and electrical frequency interference.

**Shielded twisted pair (STP) cabling** consists of four shielded pairs of wires twisted around each other. Such cabling is suitable for networks situated in environments where possible electromagnetic intrusion may occur and as a consequence interfere with network communications. However, such cabling can be fairly bulky and somewhat awkward to use because of its shielding.

The advantage of shielded twisted pair cabling is that it offers protection against electromagnetic interference and possible network crosstalk.[30]

The disadvantages of shielded twisted pair cabling are:

- it is costly (relatively speaking) due to the additional shielding,
- it is often bulky and very inflexible, and therefore
- can be difficult to use.

Shielded twisted pair cabling is commonly used in Ethernet networks and often on networks using star ring topology.

Associated variants of twisted pair cabling are:

- **foiled twisted pair cabling (FTP)** – unshielded twisted pair cabling surrounded by an outer foil shield thereby increasing protection from external interference,
- **screened unshielded twisted pair (S/UTP)** – unshielded twisted pair cabling surrounded by an outer braided shield,
- **screened foiled twisted pair (S/FTP)** – a combination of screened unshielded twisted pair and foiled twisted pair cabling (with a combined braided and foil shielding), and
- **screened shielded twisted pair (S/STP)** – shielded twisted pair cabling but with an extra outer braided or foil shield similar to coaxial cabling offering improved protection from external interference.

## Coaxial cabling

Coaxial cabling consists of a round, central conducting wire surrounded by an inner insulating spacer (also called a dielectric[31]), a cylindrical conducting shield[32] and an outer insulating layer. The cable is designed to carry a high-frequency or broadband signal and is widely used in wired computer networks, such as Ethernet,[33] and the cable television industry.

Coaxial cabling can be either rigid (sometimes known as thicknet[34]) or flexible (sometimes known as thinnet[35]). Whereas rigid coaxial cabling has a solid shield, a flexible coaxial cabling has a braided shield. In addition the dielectric may be solid or perforated.

The advantages of coaxial cabling are:

- it is highly resistant to signal interference, and
- it can support greater cable lengths between network devices than, for example, twisted pair cabling.

The disadvantages of coaxial cabling are:

- it can be costly,
- it can be inflexible (especially thicknet), and
- it can be difficult to install (again, especially thicknet).

## Fibre optic cabling

Fibre optic cabling consists of a glass or plastic central core surrounded by several layers of cladding materials and a protective layer (usually made of Teflon or PVC). Fibre optic cabling transmits light rather than electrical signals, thereby eliminating the problem of electrical interference, and can therefore carry data/information at vastly greater speeds over much greater distances. This capacity broadens communication possibilities to include services such as video conferencing and interactive services.

There are two types of fibre optic cabling:

- single-mode cabling which allows only a single mode (or wavelength) of light to be transmitted through the fibre – it is often used for long-distance connectivity, and
- multimode fibre cabling which allows multiple modes of light to be transmitted through the fibre – it is often used for workgroup applications and intra-building network applications.

The advantages of fibre optic cabling are:

- it is immune to signal interference,
- it can transmit signals over much longer distances than twisted pair cabling and/or coaxial cabling, and
- it is efficient (higher data transfer rates) – that is there is less loss of signal between network devices than, for example, twisted pair cabling and/or coaxial cabling.

The disadvantages of fibre optic cabling are:

- it can be costly (although comparable to, for example, copper wire cabling), and
- it can be difficult to install.

It is perhaps worth noting that fibre optic cabling is often used in the hard wiring of Tier 1 internet backbone networks.

### Wireless connections

The term wireless networking refers to technology that enables two or more computers/computer networks to communicate using standard network protocols, but without wired connections – for example, a wireless local area network (LAN).

For connectivity, such a wireless network may, for example, use:

- high-frequency radio signal connections,
- infrared connections, or
- laser connections,

to communicate between the network nodes, network file servers and other information and communication network devices. It may be:

- line of sight broadcast-based – in which a direct, unblocked line of sight must exist between source and destination, or
- scattered broadcast-based – in which transmission signals are transmitted in multiple directions (which can then bounce off physical objects to reach their destination).

For long-distance wireless networks, communications can also take place using:

- mobile telephony,
- microwave transmission, or
- satellite.

There are two kinds of wireless networks:

- an ad-hoc wireless network – that is an improvised and/or temporary impromptu network, and
- a peer-to-peer wireless network – that is a defined network of computers/terminals each equipped with a wireless networking interface card.

Within each of these a computer/terminal can communicate directly with all of the other wireless enabled computers to share data/information files and network resources. A wireless network can also use an access point (single and/or multiple) to provide connectivity for the wireless computers and connect (or bridge) the wireless network to a wired network allowing wireless networked computers to access wired network resources.

An access point can be hardware based, software based or both, and will of course vary:

- the wireless network distance (all access points have a finite distance), and
- the number of computers that can be linked wirelessly.

The advantages of wireless networks are that they are simple to develop and install, and relatively cheap to install and maintain.

The disadvantages of wireless networking are that:

- such networks are susceptible to external interference and signal interception, and provide limited security, and
- such networks are generally slower than wire-based networks.

Now we move on to look at the alternative types of network architecture.

## Wide area network

A wide area network is a network which covers a wide geographical area, often involving an array of computer and/or information and communication devices.

Typically, a wide area network would consist of two or more interconnected local area networks (LANs), connected using either:

- public communication facilities (e.g. the telephone system), or
- private communication facilities (e.g. leased lines and/or satellite-based communication facilities).

The best example of a wide area network would be the physical network underpinning the internet. We can distinguish between two types of wide area network:

- a centralised wide area network, and
- a decentralised (or distributed) wide area network, which is essentially a wide area network comprising of two of more interconnected local area networks.

### Centralised wide area network

The main distinguishing feature of a centralised wide area network is that there is no (or very little) remote data/transaction processing. All processing is controlled and managed centrally. Such an arrangement is useful where data transactions are homogenous, for example:

- a bank ATM system,
- a hotel central booking facility, and
- an airline booking facility.

The advantages of a centralised wide area network are that:

- it provides for a concentration of computing power,
- it provides economies of scale,
- it facilitates a database approach (or a standardisation approach) to data/transaction processing and data management, and
- it promotes greater security and control.

However, the disadvantages of a centralised wide area network are:

- it can be inflexible and change can be difficult to implement,
- it can be/may be unresponsive to user needs,
- network software can be costly, and
- centralisation may increase vulnerability to disaster.

### Decentralised (distributed) wide area network

The main distinguishing feature of a decentralised wide area network is that there is intelligent remote data/transaction processing: processing is decentralised within the network. Such an arrangement is useful where data transactions are heterogeneous, that is individual data transactions may possess unique characteristics that require local processing.

The advantages of a decentralised wide area network are:

- it is an efficient and effective means of sharing information, services and resources, and
- it is flexible, responsive and adaptive to user demands/requirements.

The disadvantages of a decentralised wide area network are:

- it can be difficult to maintain operationally, especially when a large number of local area networks (each with a large number of users) make up the decentralised wide area networks
- it can be difficult to manage and control data transactions and processing activities, especially peer-to-peer type local area networks, and
- security can be difficult to implement effectively.

## Metropolitan area network

A metropolitan area network (MAN) is in terms of geography an intermediate form of network – a network covering a geographical area (e.g. a city/metropolitan area) larger than the area covered by a large local area network, but smaller than the area covered by a wide area network. It is a term used to describe the interconnection of local area networks into a single larger network, usually to offer a more efficient connection to a larger wide area network.

A metropolitan area network typically uses a wireless infrastructure or an optical fibre connection for inter-site connection.

The advantages of a metropolitan area network are:

- it can provide an efficient connection to a wide area network,
- it can facilitate the sharing of regional resources, and
- it can be used to provide a shared connection to other networks.

The disadvantages of a metropolitan area network are:

- it can be inflexible, and
- it may be unresponsive to user needs.

## Local area network

A local area network (LAN) is a network of computers and/or information and communication devices, usually privately owned and within a limited area. The network is often at the same physical location, for example within a company or organisation that shares:

- a common communications link,
- a common group of interrelated resources, and/or
- a common processing facility/network operating system,

the purpose being to facilitate the exchange and sharing of information and resources.

In a wider, less-restricting context, a local area network may comprise of a number of smaller interconnected local area networks within a geographically compact area (e.g. within a large corporate office and/or university campus), usually connected using a high-speed local network communications backbone.

In smaller local area networks, workstations may act as both client (user of services/resources) and server (provider of services/resources). Such a network is sometimes called a peer-to-peer network because each node (workstation) within the network possesses equivalent responsibilities.

In larger local area networks, workstations may act as the client only and may be linked to a central network server. Such a network is sometimes called a server network because clients (individual workstations) rely on the servers for resources, data, information and processing power.

The advantages of a local area network are:

- it is an efficient and effective means of sharing information, services and resources, and
- it is flexible, responsive and adaptive to user demands/requirements.

The disadvantages of a local area network are:

- it can be difficult to maintain operationally – especially when a local area network has many users,
- it can be difficult to control – especially peer-to-peer type local area networks, and
- security can be costly.

A local area network is distinguished from other kinds of network by three characteristics:

- size,
- transmission technology, and
- topology.

## Personal area network

A personal area network (PAN) is a computer/information and communication network used for communication between computer and information and communication technology devices close to one person. Typically, the coverage area of a personal area network will usually be only a few square metres, with such a network used for either:

- intra-personal communication – that is communication with/between different technologies/devices, and/or
- up-linking – that is higher-level technology networking (e.g. connecting to the internet).

A personal area network may be:

- wired using a computer bus (e.g. a USB[36] or FireWire[37]), or
- wireless using wireless networking technologies such as IrDA,[38] Bluetooth[39] and/or Skinplex.[40]

## Client-server network

A client[41]-server network is a computer architecture which provides a convenient way to inter-connect and distribute software programs, and hardware resources and facilities, efficiently and effectively across different locations. A computer architecture in which each computer on a network is either a client[42] or a server inasmuch as:

- clients are PCs or workstations on which users runs applications,
- servers are computers and/or processes dedicated to managing and allocating network resources, and
- clients rely on servers for access to network resources and/or processing facilities.[43]

Such client-server architecture is sometimes referred to as a two-tier architecture – that is client-server architecture in which the user interface runs on the client and the resource is held by/stored on a server. The application logic can run on the client and/or the server. Alternative, newer, and increasingly popular, client-server architecture is called a three-tier architecture – that is client-server architecture in which:

- the client's computer/workstation runs the user interface – the first tier,
- the functional modules for the processing of data run on an application server – the second tier, and
- the database management system that stores the data required by the second tier runs the database server – the third tier.

The advantages of the three-tier client-server architecture (and the reasons for its increasing popularity) are:

- the separation between application server and database server facilitates easier modification and/or updating,
- the separation between application server and database server facilitates the easier replacement of one tier without affecting the other tiers within the network, and
- the separation of application functions from database management functions/systems facilitates more effective load balancing.[44]

Client-server networks can be both WAN-based and/or LAN-based, and tend to be the norm for most corporate-based systems. Indeed, the client-server network architecture has become one of the central ideas of computing and information systems, with most computer-based business-related applications using the client-server model.

In a client-server environment, files are stored on a centralised, high-speed file server, with appropriate access made available to clients – usually with the use of a username and password. Because nearly all network services (e.g. printing services, e-mail and FTP services) are routed through a file server it is designed to:

- allow clients/users access to their own directory,
- allow clients/users access to a range of public or shared directories in which applications and data are stored, and
- allow clients/users to communicate with each other (via the file server).

The file server can be used to:

- supervise network traffic,
- identify and detect inefficient network segments/facilities, and
- monitor client/user activities.

The main advantages of client-server architecture are:

- it is a cost-effective way to share data, information and resources between a large number of clients,
- it provides improved scalability[45] – that is it allows the number of network connections (and the number of clients/users) to be increased/decreased as needed,
- it supports modular applications inasmuch as software applications can be separated into identifiable modular portions on specific identifiable servers, and
- network/application upgrades can be stored on the file server, rather than having to upgrade each client/user's PC.

The main disadvantages of client-server architecture are:

- it can be difficult to ensure configuration information is up-to-date, current and consistent over all the network devices,
- it can be difficult to synchronise upgrades – especially on very large client-server networks, and
- redundancy and network failure procedures/protocols can be expensive and difficult to implement.

## Peer-to-peer network

A peer-to-peer network (often abbreviated to P2P) is a network architecture in which each workstation (or PC) within the network has equivalent responsibilities and capabilities.

In essence, a peer-to-peer network facilitates the connection of a number of workstations (or PCs), so that network resources may be pooled together. For example, individual resources connected to a workstation (or PC), such as various disk drives, a scanner, perhaps even a printer, become shared resources of the network and available to/accessible from any other workstation (or PC) within the network.

Unlike a client-server network in which network information is stored centrally on a centralised file server and made available (subject to security protocols, of course) to client workstations (or PCs), within a peer-to-peer network data and information is stored locally, on each individual workstation (or PC) within the network. In essence, each workstation (or PC) within a peer-to-peer network acts as:

- a client or user node, and
- a server or data/information store.

Structurally, there are three categories of peer-to-peer network, these being:

- a pure peer-to-peer network,[46]
- a hybrid peer-to-peer network, and
- a mixed peer-to-peer network.

In a pure peer-to-peer network, a peer acts as both client and server. Such a network would possess neither a central server nor a central router.[47]

In a hybrid peer-to-peer network, a central server maintains information on individual peers and responds to requests for information about peers. The central server would not normally store process/transaction files. Individual peers would normally be responsible for:

- hosting the information,
- informing the central network server which files they require, and
- downloading and/or transferring any shareable resources to other peers within the network as requested.

A mixed peer-to-peer network would of course possess characteristics of each of the above.

Functionally (based on the network application) there are also three categories of peer-to-peer network, these being:

- collaborative computing,
- instant messaging, and
- affinity computing.

### Collaborative computing

Collaborative computing, also referred to as distributed computing, is a peer-to-peer networking application through which idle, unused or spare CPU processing power and/or disk space on a workstation (or PC) can be utilised by (an)other workstation (PC) within the network.[48] Collaborative computing is most popular with science-based research organisations where research projects may require vast amounts of computer processing power.[49]

### Instant messaging

Instant messaging (internet relay chat) is perhaps the most common type of peer-to-peer networking application used and allows users to chat using text messages in real time.

We discussed internet relay chat in some detail earlier in Chapter 4.

### Affinity computing

Affinity computing is the use of peer-to-peer networking to build/create so-called 'affinity communities' or peer-to-peer networks facilitating the sharing of data and/or media files. Such affinity communities are based on mutual collaboration – that is peer-to-peer network users allowing other peer-to-peer network users to search for and gain access to information and computer files held on their PCs.

Although all affinity computing requires users to possess a peer-to-peer networking utility/software program together with an active internet connection, there are essentially two alternative options/models:

- index-based peer-to-peer file sharing, and
- non-index-based peer-to-peer file sharing.

## Index-based peer-to-peer file sharing

Index-based peer-to-peer file sharing requires the use of a central indexing server. This server does not host, store or manage any of the data and/or media files that are available for downloading. The server merely stores an index of all clients (users) currently logged onto the peer-to-peer network. Peer-to-peer clients will themselves provide areas where a file search for a specific data/media file can be undertaken.

Once a client (user) logs onto a peer-to-peer network and launches the peer-to-peer search utility, the utility queries the index server to find other connected users with the data/media file that has been requested. When a match, or number of matches, are located, the central index server informs the client requesting the search where the requested files can be found. If the client selects a result location returned by the central index server, the utility attempts to establish a connection with the client's PC hosting/storing the file requested. If the connection is successful the selected file will be downloaded, i.e. copied from the hosting client's PC to the requesting client's PC. Once the file download is complete the connection is terminated.

## Non-index-based peer-to-peer file sharing

Non-index-based peer-to-peer file sharing works in a similar way to index-based peer-to-peer file sharing but without a central indexing server. Once a client (user) logs onto a peer-to-peer network the peer-to-peer utility actively seeks out other online clients using the same peer-to-peer utility program and informs them of the user's presence online, effectively creating the network as individual clients log-on/log-off.

Clearly the size of the peer-to-peer network depends on the availability of the peer-to-peer software utility – as the number of clients with the utility software increases, so does the potential size of the network.

When a client launches a search for a specific data/media file, and:

- a match or number of matches are located, and
- the client selects the location of one of the returned matches,

the utility attempts to establish a connection with the client's PC hosting/storing the file requested. If the connection is successful the selected file will be downloaded – copied from the hosting client's PC to the requesting client's PC. Once the file download is complete the connection is terminated.

The advantages of a peer-to-peer network are it is:

- simple to create,
- easy to build, and
- inexpensive to maintain.

There are also additional advantages:

- an increase in network users creates increased network capacity – that is since one of the underlying concepts of peer-to-peer networks is that all clients provide resources such as bandwidth (communication capacity),[50] storage capacity and computing power, then as the number of nodes (clients/users logging-on) increases, and demand on the system increases, so the total capacity of the system increases in turn,[51]
- increased operational resilience (i.e. the distributed nature of peer-to-peer networks and the replication of data over multiple peers) increases the robustness of the network, thereby reducing the possibility of failure, and
- there is no single point of failure[52] – especially in non-index-based, pure, peer-to-peer networks, which enable peers to locate data and/or media files without reliance on a centralised index server.

The disadvantages of a peer-to-peer network are:

- there is no central store for files and applications, and as a result such networks can become fairly insecure,
- maintaining software on individual computers within a peer-to-peer network can be time consuming, and
- speed and performance can be poor – especially within large peer-to-peer networks.

As we saw in Chapter 4, there remain several major problems/concerns surrounding file sharing, especially file sharing using peer-to-peer networks, particularly for companies. The most important of these problems/concerns is network protection and security – a problem which emerges from the very architecture of the network itself. Why?

Firstly, because anonymous peer-to-peer networks allow for distribution of material with little or no legal accountability across (potentially) a wide variety of jurisdictions, and secondly, peer-to-peer networks are (increasingly) the subject of malicious attack. Examples of such attacks are:

- poisoning/insertion of virus attacks – providing corrupt and/or infected data files,
- denial of service/filtering attacks – inserting malware[53] (or spyware[54]) to reduce network efficiency,

- defection attacks – using network resources without contributing to the network capacity,
- identity attacks – harassing network users,
- spamming attacks – sending vast amounts of unsolicited data/information across the network.

The most appropriate defence – to minimise possible security threats – is to introduce:

- access policies to monitor network access – a protocol-based approach to monitor and prevent intrusive network traffic being received through the P2P clients, and
- content policies to monitor/control the files – a surveillance-based software solution approach to actively search for files based on their type, their name, their signature or even their content.

## Hard-type network topologies

The term network topology refers to the shape/map of a network and to:

- how different network devices are connected to each other, and
- how each of these network devices communicate with each other.

Topologies can be either:

- physical – that is relating to hard-type networks, and/or
- logical – that is relating to semi-soft type networks.

Whereas a physical topology would describe the physical connectivity of a network, that is how network devices are physically connected, a logical topology would describe how data and information flows within a network. For the moment we will consider physical (hard-type network) topologies.

So, what types of physical (hard-type network) topologies are there? The most common types of physical (hard-type network) topologies are:

- bus topology,
- ring topology,
- star topology,
- mesh topology, and
- hybrid topology.

Note: The star topology and the tree topology are often referred to as centralised topologies, whereas the mesh topology is often referred to as a decentralised topology.

Before we look at each of these topologies in a little more detail it is useful to consider the key factors that would dictate the design/selection of a network topology. These main factors would include:

- the financial cost of installing the network topology,
- the technical viability of the network topology (e.g. maintenance and faultfinding/ troubleshooting),
- the potential scalability of the network topology and the potential for future expansion,
- the required capacity of the network topology, and
- the physical nature/constraints of the network topology (e.g. the geographical distances involved).

## Bus topology

A bus topology (also known as a linear bus topology) is a topology in which a set of clients are connected through a shared communications line or a central cable, often called the bus or the network backbone.[55]

There are two alternative types of bus (or connection lines):

- a regular bus – in which each network node is directly attached to the network backbone by means of a shorter cable connection (see Figure 5.3), or
- a local bus – in which each network node is attached directly to the network backbone in a daisy-chain configuration[56] (see below).

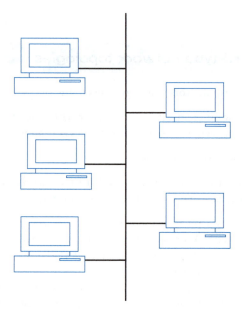

**Figure 5.3** Bus topology

Within a bus topology, communication signals are broadcast to all nodes on the network. Each node on the network inspects the destination address of the signal as it travels along the bus or the communication link. Remember, every node that comprises a network will have a unique network address, either a data link control address (DLC), or a media access address (MAC). If the signal's destination address matches that of the node, the node processes the signal. If the address does not match that of the node, the node will take no action and the signal travels along the bus.[57]

In general, a bus topology is regarded passive[58] inasmuch as the nodes situated on the bus simply listen for a signal, they are not responsible for moving the signal along the bus or communication link.

However, whilst such a topology is perhaps the simplest and easiest method to use to connect multiple clients, at multiple nodes, operationally, such a network topology can nonetheless be problematic. Why?

Consider the situation where two or more clients using two or more different network nodes want to communicate at the same time, using the same bus/network connection. To minimise the consequences of such a situation, a bus topology would employ:

- a scheduling protocol – to queue network traffic and prioritise communication, and
- a collision avoidance protocol – to monitor and control access to the communication link, or more appropriately, the shared bus – often using a media access control protocol, technically referred to as a carrier sense multiple access.[59]

The advantages of a bus topology are:

- they are easy to build and implement,
- they are simple to extend, and
- on a small scale, they are relatively cheap to set up.

More importantly, a network employing such a topology is generally more resilient to failure inasmuch as failure at one node does not affect the operational capacity of other nodes on the network.

The disadvantages of a bus topology are:

- they can be difficult to administer – especially for larger networks,
- they can be slow operationally, inasmuch as network performance may reduce as additional nodes are added, and
- maintenance costs can be higher, certainly in the longer term.

In addition:

- the size of such networks may be limited – that is limited cable length means limited number of nodes, and
- such networks are generally regarded as fairly insecure and easy to hack into, and a single virus infection at a node within the network will often affect all nodes within the network.

As indicated earlier, using a local bus to connect/attach each network node directly to a network backbone creates a daisy chain configuration – a topology in which each network node is connected in a series to the next network node.

Within a daisy chain configuration, communication signals are broadcast to all nodes on the network. Each node on the network inspects the destination address of the signal as it travels along the bus or the communication link. If the address does not match that of the node, the node will take no action and the signal is bounced along the communication link – in sequence, from network node to network node – until it reaches the destination address. Once the signal reaches the destination address, the destination node processes the signal.

## Ring topology

A ring topology is a topology in which a network node is connected to two other nodes, thus creating a closed loop ring. It is a topology in which every network node has two connections to it, and in which only two paths between any two network nodes exist.

See Figure 5.4.

In a ring topology there are no terminated ends and each network node on the ring network topology has equal rights and access, but only one network node can communicate at any time.

When a network node issues a message, the sending network node passes the message to the next network node. If this network node is not the destination node, the message is passed to the next network node, until the message arrives at its destination node. If, for whatever reason, the message is not accepted by any network node on the network, it will travel around the entire network and return to the sending node.

In a single-ring topology the signal travels around the circle in a single direction, usually clockwise. In a double-ring topology (sometimes known as a counter-rotating ring topology) the

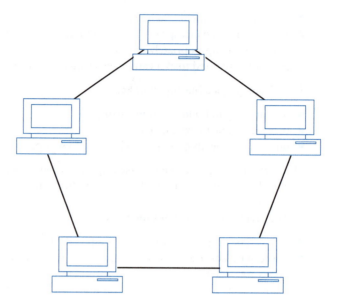

**Figure 5.4** Ring topology

signal travels in two directions, both clockwise and anti-clockwise, the intention being to provide fault tolerance in the form of redundancy in the event of a cable failure. That is if one ring fails, the data messages can flow across to the other ring, thereby preserving the integrity of the network.

Unlike a bus topology, a ring topology is an active topology, inasmuch as each network node repeats or boosts the message signal before passing it on to the next network node.

The advantages of a ring topology are:

- high data transmission speeds are possible because data messages flow in one direction only (for a double ring topology in the first ring the data message would flow in a clockwise direction, and in the second ring the data message would flow in an anti-clockwise direction – that is in the opposite direction);
- growth/expansion of a network employing a ring topology normally has a minimal effect on overall network performance;
- each node on the network has equal rights and access; and
- each node on the network acts as a repeater and allows a ring topology to span distances greater than other hard-type topologies.

The disadvantages of a ring topology are:

- it is often the most expensive topology to implement,
- as a network topology, it requires more connections than a linear bus network topology and, perhaps most importantly,
- the failure of a single network node will impact on the whole network.

## Star topology

A star topology is a topology in which all network nodes are connected to a central network node called a hub, which acts as a router for transmitted messages (see Figure 5.5).

Because the central network hub offers a common connection for all network nodes – that is every network node will have a direct communications connection/link to the central network

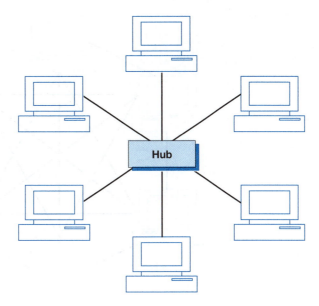

**Figure 5.5** Star topology

hub – communication between peripheral network nodes across the network occurs by passing data messages through the central network hub. In essence, peripheral network nodes may only communicate with all other peripheral network nodes by transmitting messages to and/or receiving messages from the central network hub only. The star topology is probably the most common form of network topology currently in use.

The advantages of a star topology are:

- it is easy to implement and extend, even in large networks,
- it is simple to monitor and maintain and, perhaps most importantly,
- the failure of a peripheral network node will not have a major effect on the overall functionality of the network.

The disadvantages of a star network topology are:

- maintenance/security costs may be high in the long run,
- it is susceptible to infection – if a peripheral network node catches a virus the infection could spread throughout the network, and
- failure of the central network hubs can disable/cripple the entire network.

## Mesh topology

A mesh topology (also known as a complete topology) is a topology in which there is a direct link between all pairs of network nodes within a network, resulting in multiple paths/links connecting multiple network nodes (see Figure 5.6).

In a fully-connected network with $n$ nodes, there would be $n(n-1)/2$ direct links. For example:

- a mesh topology with 10 network nodes would have $10(10-1)/2 = 90/2 = 45$ potential direct links, whereas
- a mesh topology with 100 network nodes would have $100(100-1)/2 = 9900/2 = 4950$ potential direct links, and

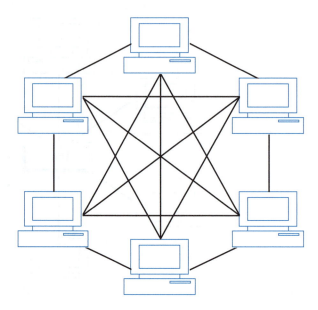

**Figure 5.6** Mesh topology

■ a mesh topology with 1000 network nodes would have $1000(1000 - 1)/2 = 999,000/2 = 499,500$ potential direct links.

Because of the possible complexity, especially in large mesh topologies, a router is often used to search the multiple paths/links between two network nodes and determine the best path/link to use for the transmission of data messages. The choice of path/links between two network nodes will be determined by, for example, factors such as cost, time and performance.

The advantages of a mesh topology are:

■ small ones are easy to create and maintain,
■ such a topology allows for continuous connections and reconfiguration around blocked paths/links by hopping from network node to another network node until a connection can be established, and
■ they offer stability, safety and reliability inasmuch as a mesh topology allows communication between two network nodes to continue in the event of a break in any single communication link between the two network nodes. That is the redundant connections make the mesh topology very reliable even in networks with high-volume traffic.

The disadvantages of a mesh topology are:

■ larger ones can be expensive and costly to install,
■ they can be difficult reconfigure, and
■ they can be difficult to administer, manage and troubleshoot.

Mesh topologies are most often employed in wide area networks (WANs) to interconnect smaller local area networks (LANs).

## Hybrid topology

A hybrid topology is a topology in which there is a combination of any two or more topologies and results when two different basic network topologies are connected.

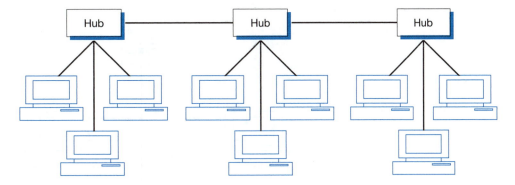

**Figure 5.7** Hybrid topology (star–bus topology)

Examples of such hybrid topologies would be:

- star–bus topology (also known as tree topology), and
- star–ring topology.

### Star–bus topology

A star–bus topology (also known as a tree topology) is a topology in which a collection of star networks are arranged in a hierarchical relationship and connected to a linear bus backbone.

See Figure 5.7.

A star–bus topology has three key characteristics:

- individual peripheral network nodes (sometimes referred to as leaves) are able to transmit messages to and receive messages from only one other network node,
- peripheral network nodes are neither able nor required to act as message repeaters and/or signal regenerators, and
- the function of the central network node (often a network switch,[60] sometimes referred to as an intelligent hub) may be, and indeed often is, distributed along the network.

The advantages of a star–bus topology are:

- it is easy to extend,
- simple to maintain, and
- resilient – if an individual peripheral network node fails then the failure will not have a major effect on the overall functionality of the network.

The disadvantages of a star–bus topology are:

- it can be difficult to configure (and physically wire), consequently maintenance costs may be high,
- failure of a network switch can disable a large portion of the network, and
- if the network backbone link breaks, an entire network segment may be affected.

### Star–ring topology

A variant of a ring topology is a star–ring topology or token ring network. A star-wired ring topology functions as ring topology, although it is physically wired as a star topology (see Figure 5.8), with a central connector called a Multistation Access Unit (MAU) which facilitates the movement of messages from one network node to another in a circular or ring fashion.

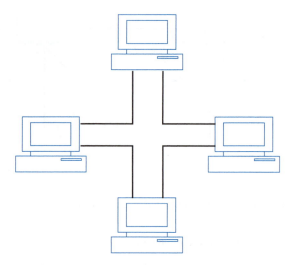

**Figure 5.8** Hybrid topology (star–ring topology)

Within a token passing network, signals are communicated from one network node to the next network node – sequentially using a token or small data frame. When a network node wants to transmit a message, it catches the token, attaches the data and a destination address to it, and then sends it around the ring. Note that each node can hold the token for a maximum period of time.

The token travels along the network ring until it reaches the destination address. The receiving network node acknowledges receipt with a return message – attached to the token – to the sending node. Once the sending network node has received the reply, the sending node releases the token for use by another network node.

In essence token-passing configurations are deterministic inasmuch as it is possible to calculate the maximum waiting and transmission times. In addition, such configurations can:

■ use prioritising protocols to permit and prioritise transmissions from designated, high-priority network nodes, and
■ employ fault-detecting protocols to identify and compensate for network fault: for example, selecting a network node to be the active network monitor.

## Hard-type network protocols

For communication and networking purposes, a protocol can be defined as a convention or standard that controls the connection, and enables the communication and transfer of data and information between two computers and/or network nodes. In a more technical context, a protocol can perhaps more appropriately be defined as a uniform/formalised set of rules that govern the syntax, semantics and synchronisation of communication. In essence, without protocols, networks would not exist!

In hard-type networks, protocols may be implemented by hardware, by software or by a combination of both, with all but the most basic of protocols being layered together or hier-archically arranged into so-called protocol stacks. A collection of protocols within a protocol stack is known as a protocol suite. Although the terms are often used interchangeably, in a strict technical sense, a protocol suite is the definition of the protocols and the protocol stack is the software implementation of them.

There exist many different types/collections of protocols, with the number and variety of protocols continually changing as new protocols emerge and old ones are abandoned in the name of information and communication technology development.[61] Clearly, the changing nature of hard-type network protocols makes it very difficult to generalise about different protocols/protocol suites because of their differences in purpose, sophistication and target audience/technology. For example, some protocols may be defined as proprietary protocols[62] – that is they are 'dedicated' protocols which are only recognised by or used in computer networks or information and communication applications from a particular manufacturer. They are therefore generally not publicly documented – at least not officially! Others may be defined as generic protocols, that is protocols which seek to provide a common structure, framework or platform on which future computing and/or information and communication technologies may be developed.

Nevertheless, despite such differences, most protocols/protocol suites – because of their underlying *raison d'être* – will, at the very minimum, seek to specify at least one (if not more) of the following activities:

■ the detection of network connections (wired or wireless),
■ the existence of other network nodes,
■ the nature of the network connection characteristics,
■ the structure and formatting of data/information messages,
■ the correction of network and/or data/information transmission problems,
■ the detection of unexpected problems and/or network failure, and
■ the termination of network/session connections.

We will consider two of the most important generic protocol stacks in contemporary information and communication technologies applicable to networking and internetworking (or more appropriately the internet) these being:

■ the seven-layer reference model known as the OSI reference model or OSI protocol stack (see Figure 5.9), and
■ the four-layer reference model known as the internet model and/or the TCP/IP model (see Figure 5.10).

## OSI reference model

As introduced earlier, the OSI model (or, more appropriately, the Open Systems Interconnection reference model) is a layered abstract description, a conceptual mapping of communications and computer network protocols. The seven layers are as follows, with the lowest level first and the highest last:

■ the lower layers:
  ● the physical layer (1),
  ● the data link layer (2),
  ● the network layer (3),
  ● the transport layer (4), and
■ the upper layers:
  ● the session layer (5),
  ● the presentation layer (6), and
  ● the application layer (7).

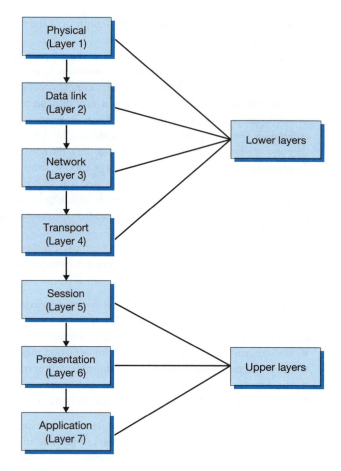

**Figure 5.9** OSI reference model (OSI protocol stack)

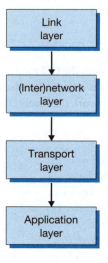

**Figure 5.10** Internet model (TCP/IP model)

In essence:

- the lower layers (physical layer, data link layer, network layer and transport layer) provide/perform the more basic network-specific functions like routing, addressing and data flow control, and are also known as the device layers, and
- the upper layers (session layer, presentation layer and application layer) provide/perform the more advanced application-specific functions like data formatting, encryption and connection management.

Let's look at each of the layers in a little more detail.

### Physical layer

The physical layer (layer 1) relates to the network hardware, and defines the physical characteristics of the transmission medium and the specifications for network devices, with the major functions and services performed by/within the physical layer being:

- the establishment of a connection to, and the termination of a connection to, a communications medium,
- the control and management of resource sharing, and
- the conversion of data to transmittable signals.

At the physical layer, design issues are normally concerned with the context, nature and timing of hardware interconnectivity.

Examples of layer 1 protocols would include:

- ISDN (Integrated Services Digital Network), and
- FDDI (Fibre Distributed Data Interface).

### Data link layer

The data link layer (layer 2) provides the functional and procedural means for the transfer of data between network entities and is concerned with transferring data across a particular link/medium. The data link layer:

- arranges data into data frames for transmission to other network nodes using the physical layer, by adding frame type information, destination address information and error control information to the data frame,
- controls the timing of data transmission over the network,
- receives acknowledgements that data frames have been correctly transmitted, and
- performs error detection and correction procedures, retransmitting data frames not correctly received.

The data link layer acts as an interface between the lower physical layer and the higher network layer, and in a practical context is the layer in which network bridges and network switches operate (see the earlier discussion on connecting components on page 188).

The data link layer can be divided into two sub-layers, an upper sub-layer – the logical link control (LLC) – and a lower sub-layer – the media access control (MAC). The logical link control is used to maintain the link between two computers/network nodes by establishing service access points (SAPs), with the media access control (MAC) used to coordinate the transmission of data between computers/network nodes.

Examples of layer 2 protocols would include:

- PPP (Point-to-Point Protocol),
- Token Ring, and
- ATM (Asynchronous Transfer Mode).

### Network layer

The network layer (layer 3) defines the end-to-end delivery of data frames and provides the functional and procedural means for transferring data frames from source to destination using one or more networks while maintaining a required quality of service.[63] The network layer is responsible for:

- undertaking network routing processes,
- maintaining data flow control processes, and
- performing error control functions.

In a practical context, network routers operate at this layer – determining how data is routed from the source to the destination.

Examples of layer 3 protocols would include:

- IP (Internet Protocol),
- AppleTalk, and
- ARP (Address Resolution Protocol).

### Transport layer

The transport layer (layer 4) provides the mechanisms for the reliable and cost-effective transfer of data between network nodes/users. The transport layer is responsible for:

- accepting data from upper layers,
- segmenting data (if necessary) before transmission,
- forwarding data to the network layer,
- ensuring that all data (and its associated components) arrives at the correct destination, and
- providing error control and data flow management control.

Some transport layer protocols also track the movements of data packets and where necessary retransmit those data packets that have failed to arrive at their desitination address.

Examples of layer 4 protocols would include:

- TCP (Transmission Control Protocol), and
- RTP (Real-time Transport Protocol).

### Session layer

The session layer (layer 5) provides the facilities for managing the dialogue, or more appropriately prioritising transmission, between application processes. The session layer is essentially the user's interface to the network and determines:

- when the application session has commenced,
- how long an application session is used, and
- when an application session is closed.

The session layer also:

- enables computers/nodes on a network to locate each other,
- allows network nodes/users located over the network to establish/set up application sessions, and
- controls the transmission of data during the session.

Examples of layer 5 protocols would include:

- SQL (Structured Query Language),
- NetBios names, and
- AppleTalk.

### Presentation layer

The presentation layer (layer 6) defines the way that data is formatted, presented, converted and encoded, and is responsible for the delivery and formatting of information to the application layer for further processing and/or display. In essence, the presentation layer provides:

- data translation/conversion facilities,
- data encoding/decoding,
- data encryption/decryption services, and/or
- data compression/decompression mechanisms,

so that different types of systems can exchange data/information. That is, the presentation layer makes the data transparent to surrounding layers and provides services to the (higher) application layer in order to:

- enable the application layer to interpret the data exchanged, and
- structure data messages to be transmitted.

Examples of layer 6 protocols would include:

- JPEG (Joint Photographic Experts Group) – an image formatting/compression mechanism,
- MPEG (Moving Picture Experts Group) – a video/music formatting/compression mechanism, and
- MIDI (Musical Instrument Digital Interface).

### Application layer

The application layer (layer 7) provides a direct interface with application processes and describes the way that programs interact/communicate with a network's operating system. The application layer establishes communication rights, initiates connections between applications and:

- provides the services software applications require to operate, and
- facilitates user applications interaction with the network services such as file transfer, file management, e-mail, and many more.

Examples of layer 7 protocols would include:

- HTTP (HyperText Transport Protocol) – used on the web,
- FTP (File Transfer Protocol),
- SMTP (Simple Mail Transfer Protocol),
- IMAP (Internet Message Access Protocol), and
- WWW browsers.

### . . . and finally

Clearly, the OSI reference model, with its layered approach, has many advantages and provides many benefits, for example it:

- promotes understanding by reducing complexity,
- encourages standardisation, and
- promotes interoperability.

However, it has many disadvantages, for example:

- real-world protocol suites often do not precisely correspond with the seven-layer OSI reference model, and
- in a practical context the distinction between each layer is often unclear and imprecise.

It is also worth noting that many computer network developers often (somewhat cryptically) use the phrase 'a layer 8 OSI reference model problem' to mean a problem associated with the 'human' end user and not with the network!

### Internet model (TCP/IP reference model)

The internet model or TCP/IP reference model specifically applies to internetworked systems, and has four layers:

- the link layer,
- the (inter)network layer,
- the transport layer, and
- the application layer.

Let's look at these in a little more detail.

#### Link layer

The link layer (also known as the network access layer) maps to/corresponds with the physical layer and the data link layer of the OSI reference model. Although not technically a part of the internet model, the link layer (or the network access layer) defines the method/process used to pass data packets from the internet layer of one network node/device to the internet layer of another network node/device, a process that can be controlled by either software, hardware, firmware or a combination of some or all of them.

At the sending network node/device, the link layer would, for example:

- prepare data packets for transmission (by adding a packet header to the data packets), and
- transmit the data frames (collections of data packets) over the connecting medium.

At the receiving network node/device, the link layer would:

- receive data frames,
- remove the packet headers, and
- transfer the received data packets to the (inter)network layer.

#### (Inter)network layer

Originally known as the network layer, the (inter)network layer corresponds to the network layer of the OSI reference model and manages the movement of data packets across a network. It is responsible for ensuring data packages reach their destinations. Two important components of this layer are:

- the internet protocol (IP), and
- the internet control message protocol (ICMP).

Whilst the internet protocol (IP) is the primary protocol within the TCP/IP (inter)network layer inasmuch as it provides the mechanism to address and manage data packets being sent to nodes/devices across a network, the internet control message protocol (ICMP) provides management and error reporting facilities to assist in managing the process of transmitting and routing data packages between nodes/devices across a network. A data packet with an IP header is called a datagram.

### Transport layer

The transport layer, which corresponds to the transport layer of the OSI reference model, provides the mechanism for network nodes/devices to exchange data packets with regards to software. In a TCP/IP reference model, there are two transport layer protocols:

- the Transmission Control Protocol (TCP), and
- the User Datagram Protocol (UDP).

The Transmission Control Protocol (TCP) is a connection-oriented mechanism in which network nodes/devices establish a connection before data packets are transmitted and transmissions are monitored to ensure that:

- data packets are received complete,
- data packets are received undamaged,
- data packets are received in the correct sequence,
- data packets that are faulty and/or undelivered are retransmitted, and
- communication connections are terminated once a transmission has been successful.

The User Datagram Protocol (UDP) is a connectionless mechanism in which network nodes/ devices are not required to establish a connection prior to data packet transmission, and in which speed is more important than accuracy of delivery.

### Application layer

The application layer which corresponds to the session layer, the presentation layer and the application layer of the OSI reference model is the layer that most common network-aware programs use to communicate across a network with other network-aware programs and would contain, for example, higher-level protocols such as:

- HTTP (HyperText Transport Protocol) for the web,
- FTP (File Transfer Protocol) for file transfer,
- SMTP (Simple Mail Transfer Protocol), POP3 (Post Office Protocol 3),
- IMAP (Internet Message Access Protocol), for electronic mail, and
- NNTP (News Network Transfer Protocol) for Usenet newsgroups.

### . . . and finally

There can be little doubt that the development and widespread acceptance of the internet model or TCP/IP reference model has provided many benefits and promoted the development/ introduction of many key information and communication technologies/features, for example:

- packet-switching[64] (see below),
- logical addressing[65]
- dynamic message routing[66]
- end node verification,[67] and
- name resolution.[68]

## Semi soft-type networks – inter-organisational networks

There are three types of interrelated semi-soft-type networks:

- the internet,
- an intranet, and
- an extranet.

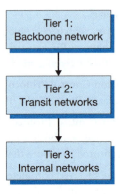

**Figure 5.11** Three-tier network hierarchy

## The internet

As suggested earlier, the internet is the largest internetwork in the world – a network comprised of many thousands of independent hosts/networks that use TCP/IP to provide worldwide communications – an internetwork that operates within a three-tier network hierarchy (see Figure 5.11).

At tier 1 is a collection of backbone networks interconnected to form a decentralised mesh network. A collection of core backbone networks that:

■ link the parts of the internet together, and
■ provide the primary data/information carrying lines of the internet.

Many of these backbone networks are now commercially owned, with some of the large multi-national companies – including MCI,[69] British Telecom,[70] AT&T[71] and Teleglobe[72] – acting as backbone network providers and therefore providing backbone connectivity.

At tier 2 (also called downstream tier 1) is a collection of mid-level transit networks,[73] for example:

■ **Network Service Provider** (NSP) – an international, national or regional service provider which provides bandwidth and network infrastructure facilities such as transit and routing services, and
■ **Internet Service Provider** (ISP) – a local service provider which provides customers with internet access and customer support services.

These mid-level networks connect the stub networks at tier 3 (see below) and to the backbone networks at tier 1.

At tier 3 is a collection of stub or internal networks (usually local area networks) and sometimes referred to as an intranet (see below) which carry data packets between local hosts (that is nodes within a local area network).

These so-called stub networks include:

■ commercial networks – for example .com or .co.uk. networks,
■ academic networks – for example .edu or .ac.uk. networks – and
■ other organisations/networks – for example .org.uk or .net. networks.

And of course many other diverse, worldwide physical networks both wired and wireless.

Put simply, the internet is a packet-switching network[74] with:

- a distributed mesh topology,[75]
- a client-server architecture, and
- a hierarchical interconnection scheme.

That is:

- national/international NSPs are responsible for developing, constructing, maintaining and managing national or international networks, and sell bandwidth to regional NSPs,
- regional NSPs purchase bandwidth from national/international NSPs and sell on the bandwidth (and other network services/facilities) to local ISPs, and
- local ISPs sell bandwidth and other internet services/facilities to end users (e.g. individuals, companies and other organisations).

However, in order to function as an internetwork, individual networks (as autonomous systems[76]) must interact/communicate with one another, that is individual networks must exchange data/information. To exchange data/information backbone networks must be connected.

Individual networks can be connected using either:

- an internet exchange point[77] (a convergence of many backbone networks interconnecting at a single point), or
- a private connection (a convergence of a few backbone networks interconnecting at a single point).

But how do individual networks exchange data/information?

The exchange of data/information between individual backbone networks is undertaken using a process known as peering. Peering is the exchanging of internet traffic between networks using different tier 1 backbone network providers and normally requires:

- a contractual agreement or mutual peering agreement,[78]
- a physical interconnection between the different networks (normally called a peering point), and
- technical cooperation to facilitate the exchange of traffic.

Most peering points (peering via the use of internet exchange points) are located in collocation centres[79] (sometimes called carrier hotels) – a data centre where tier 1 backbone network providers co-locate their points of presence[80] or connections to one another's networks. That is a peering agreement can only exist between tier 1 backbone network providers.

However, where individual tier 1 backbone network providers are interconnected using a private connection it is also possible for a private peering connection between only a few networks to exist.

So, how does the internet work? Have a look at the following example.

Imagine an administrative assistant at Tajajac Ltd (www.tajajac.co.uk) a UK-based retail company wants to access the website of Damacasae Inc. (www.damasacae.com) a US-based supplier. Since the internet is simply a network of networks, essentially Tajajac Ltd (as a local area network) will connect to the internet using a local ISP with whom the company has a contractual agreement. When connecting to the local ISP, the company Tajajac Ltd would become part of the ISP's network. The local ISP may then connect to a larger NSP's network and would therefore become part of their larger network.

When the administrative assistant types in www.damasacae.com into the internet browser, the browser contacts the domain name server to get the IP address.

Note: Remember the IP address is unique to every webpage and computer and makes it possible for computers to 'recognise' each other.

Once the IP address has been acquired, the computers can 'communicate' with each other using TCP/IP.

In essence, the TCP (Transmission Control Protocol) is responsible for acquiring the data to be sent over the internet and breaking data into small packets that can include, for example, programming instructions, text, pictures, sound and/or video in variety of combinations. The IP (Internet Protocol) is responsible for routing these packets of data through the network from the source computer to the destination computer. When the data packets arrive at the destination computer, the TCP reassembles them into a viewable webpage.

## Intranet

An intranet can be defined as a network based on TCP/IP protocols (essentially an internet) that is contained within and belongs to a company and/or organisation – a network which is accessible only by authorised company/organisation members, employees and/or agents, although the term intranet is sometimes used as a reference to the visible aspects of a company's/organisation's internal website.

As the fastest-growing segment of the internet, secure intranets are increasingly used to:

■ provide secure inter-company/inter-organisational communication (e.g. video conferencing),
■ facilitate the sharing/dissemination of data and information (e.g. policies, procedures and company/organisational announcements), and
■ provide access to company/organisational resources.

Why? For two reasons!

Firstly, because the development of a secure intranet is simple and inexpensive, and once operational is easy to manage, maintain and update. Secondly, because an intranet has three features normally lacking on the internet – speed, security and control.

Typically, an intranet will include connections to the internet using a gateway[81] and firewall[82] to:

■ provide access to networks outside the company/organisation (e.g. the internet),
■ allow access to the company/organisation intranet from outside the company/organisation, and
■ facilitate the monitoring and control of intranet use (e.g. websites and/or other networks accessed using the company/organisation intranet).

When (part of) an intranet facility is made available to external agents outside the company/organisation, that part of the intranet becomes part of an extranet.

So what types of activities are intranets used for? Today, companies and organisations use intranet facilities or, more appropriately, intranet portals to provide a wide variety of resources and services. These can be:

■ secured and available to authorised users only,
■ unsecured and available to all users – that is open access, or indeed
■ a combination of both.

Intranets have become an essential corporate/organisational tool by:

■ reducing operational costs,
■ improving organisational efficiency and effectiveness, and
■ gaining strategic corporate advantage over competitors.

Some of the main activities for which intranets are used include:

- Information systems and communications management – providing information on:
  - user facilities,
  - technical support and helpdesk facilities,
  - network resources,
  - resourcing schedules (e.g. system updates),
  - information systems security polices and procedures,
  - software training courses,
  - information systems and communications FAQs (frequently asked questions);
- Financial services management – providing information on:
  - financial regulations, policies and procedures,
  - income receipting and expenditure payments procedures,
  - e-commerce facilities,
  - requisitioning systems and asset management procedures and policies,
  - financial reports,
  - budgeting procedures, policies and timetable,
- Human resources management – providing information on:
  - employee conditions of employment,
  - health and safety regulation,
  - organisational/management structure,
  - employee training facilities and courses, and
  - recruitment;
- Increasingly companies/organisations use intranet facilities to provide a company/organisation newsletter;
- Sales and marketing management services – providing information on:
  - marketing data (e.g. regional sales and customer demographics),
  - customer feedback,
  - marketing press releases,
  - sales/marketing training facilities, and
  - market competitor research;
- customer services – providing information on:
  - customer order tracking,
  - available product and services, and
  - customer FAQs (frequently asked questions); and
- corporate/organisational management services – providing information on:
  - company/organisation history,
  - corporate/organisational strategic plans,
  - management meeting minutes,
  - market analysis – including, where appropriate, company share price tracking,
  - company/organisation calendar tracking – highlighting important events/activities, and
  - newsgroup facilities.

Whilst initial set-up costs may be high, for a company/organisation the benefits of an intranet cannot be underestimated. Not only does it provide for:

- more effective use of company/organisational resources, and
- more efficient communication between internal and external agents,

it also facilitates:

- more effective time management, and
- provides for more secure data/information management.

## Extranet

In a broad context, an extranet can be considered part of a company's/organisation's intranet – a part that is extended to authorised external users/agents and can be defined as a network based on TCP/IP protocols that facilitates the secure sharing of corporate/organisational information and/or resources with external agents such as product/service suppliers, customers, corporate/organisational partners and/or other businesses.

That is, it is an internet-based communication facility designed to support business to business (B2B) activities.

In essence:

- an intranet provides various levels of accessibility to people who are members of the same company/organisation, whereas
- an extranet provides various levels of accessibility to people who are *not* members of the same company/organisation or, more appropriately, outsiders.

In general, for both security and privacy purposes, access to a company/organisation extranet is normally controlled using a two-level access protocol – a valid username and password, and/or the issuance of digital certificates. The use of such an access protocol:

- validates/authenticates the user as an authorised user of the company/organisation extranet,
- determines which elements/facilities of the company/organisation extranet the authorised user has right of access to, and
- decrypts any secured encrypted elements/facilities of the company/organisation extranet the authorised user has right of access to.

There is little doubt that since the late 1990s/early 2000s[83] extranets – as a business to business (B2B) facility – have become a popular means for companies/organisations to exchange information ranging from:

- generic data/information such as price lists, inventory schedules and reports, delivery schedules and ordering/payment facilities, to
- product/service specific data/information such as detailed product/service specifications.

The main benefits of an extranet[84] include:

- better supply chain management by the use of online product/service ordering, order tracking facilities, and product/service management,
- reduced costs by providing technical documentation online to trading partners and customers,
- increased operational flexibility by allowing remote access by company and/or organisation staff to core business information/facilities,
- improved communication and customer service by enabling the sharing of common documentation online, and providing customers with direct access to product/service information, and
- improved security of communications – by controlling access to/use of extranet facilities.

## Blended networks and the pull effect of semi-soft-type networks

As suggested earlier, historically, entity-focused soft-type networks, or socio-economic networks, have been and continue to be heavily influenced by the priorities of capital and demands of the marketplace. An influence that has invariably promoted a soft-type network model founded upon bureaucratic notions of hierarchical responsibility and structural accountability, and informed many of the hard-type networks – especially information and communication technology-related hard-type networks – that have become a major part of many socio-economic networks. However, to paraphrased Dylan; 'the times they are . . . (most certainly) . . . a changing.'

The emergence of semi-soft-type networks and the widespread adoption by many entity-focused soft-type networks (or corporate organisations) of internet-based technologies (e.g. intranets and extranets), and other related information and communication technologies has prompted the emergence of what have become known as blended networks. That is the emergence of soft-type networks (traditionally of a highly-structured and formal bureaucratic nature) whose structures are increasingly blended with and in some cases dominated by online elements, creating alternative virtual inter-relationships that operate and exist outside the 'traditional' bureaucracy of entity-based soft-type networks. New blended networks that whilst increasingly informal and adhocratic, are nonetheless playing an increasing central role in the wealth accumulation process (see Article 5.1.)

## Article 5.1

### Eight out of ten shoppers turn to the web

*US consumers intend to be on the road less and on the web more.*

In the run up to Christmas more than eight out of 10 holiday shoppers will go online for holiday gifts, and 80 per cent are likely to purchase gifts online from small businesses, according to a poll published today. The survey, commissioned by Yahoo Small Business and conducted by Harris Interactive, predicts a 'significant increase' in online shopping this holiday season. Nearly a third (30 per cent) of shoppers polled will do at least half of their holiday shopping online. In addition, nearly two thirds (63 per cent) said that online 'speciality' or 'niche' retailers are the 'best places' to shop for unusual or hard-to-find gifts.

The nationwide survey of 1,813 US adults suggested that holiday shoppers look to small online retailers for unique, distinctive gift items, and a large majority are likely to buy gifts online from small companies. 'Holiday shoppers are ready and willing to buy gifts online from small businesses that offer variety and value,' said Rich Riley, vice president and general manager of Yahoo Small Business.

'The results are an encouraging confirmation that small business e-commerce has become an integral part of the holiday shopping experience for many consumers.'

Nearly four out of five holiday shoppers would change their shopping habits if petrol prices remain high or climb higher during the holiday buying season. Asked how they might change, many shoppers indicated that they would be on the road less and on the web more. Almost three in five holiday shoppers said it was important that their favourite speciality or gift stores have an online presence. Seventy per cent said they had no preference between shopping online with small versus large businesses.

Shoppers stated that the key reasons they would shop for holiday gifts online with small businesses include convenient hours, avoiding crowded car parks and the ability to find the 'right gift'. Greg Sterling, an analyst at Kelsey Group, said: 'This data confirms that small business retailers need to be in front of online consumers as they use the internet to shop for products during the hectic holiday season. Consumers clearly want what small retailers have to offer and those who can't be found online are missing a significant potential opportunity.'

Source: Robert Jaques, 18 November 2005,
**www.vnunet.com**.

## Concluding comments

Soft-type, semi-soft-type and hard-type networks now dominate *all* business-related activities from the departmental structure of companies/organisations, to the hierarchical allocation of duties and responsibilities, to the use of information and communication technologies in the processing of business transactions, and to the development and establishment of business-related/accounting-related information systems. Indeed, understanding not only how such networks operate, but perhaps more importantly how such networks can be managed and controlled, has become vital to 21st century market-based companies.

## Key points and concepts

| | |
|---|---|
| Adhocracy | Mesh topology |
| Affinity computing | Metropolitan area network (MAN) |
| Bridge | Network architecture |
| Bureaucracy | Network interface card |
| Bus topology | Network operating system |
| Centralised WAN | Network protocol |
| Client-server network | Network topology |
| Coaxial cabling | OSI reference model |
| Collaborative computing | Peer-to-peer network |
| Computer workstation | Personal area network (PAN) |
| Data link control address | Repeater |
| Decentralised WAN | Ring topology |
| Extranet | Router |
| Fibre optic cabling | Semi-soft-type networks |
| File server | Soft-type networks |
| Hard-type networks | Star topology |
| Hub | Switch |
| Hybrid topology | TCP/IP model |
| Internet | Twisted pair cabling |
| Intranet | Wide area network (WAN) |
| Local area network (LAN) | Wired network |
| Logical network | Wireless network |
| Media access address | |

## Bibliography

Mintzberg, H. (1979) *The Structuring of Organisations*, Prentice-Hall, New York.

## Self-review questions

1. In relation to soft-type networks, briefly explain the difference between a bureaucracy and an adhocracy.
2. Distinguish between:
   - a hub,
   - a bridge,
   - a switch, and
   - a router.

3. In relation to hard-type networks, define the term 'network topology' and distinguish between two types of topologies.
4. Explain the advantages and disadvantages of a peer-to-peer network.
5. Distinguish between collaborative computing and affinity computing.
6. Distinguish between the OSI reference model and the TCP/IP reference model.
7. Describe the advantages and disadvantages of a client-server network.
8. Briefly explain why the internet is often referred to as a three-tier network.
9. What are the major differences between:
   - an internet,
   - an intranet, and
   - an extranet.
10. Define and describe the advantages and disadvantages of:
   - a bus topology,
   - a ring topology, and
   - a star topology.

## Questions and problems

### Question 1

Distinguish between:

- a wide area network (WAN),
- a metropolitan area network (MAN),
- a local area network (LAN), and
- a personal area network (PAN).

### Question 2

Intranets are now an essential corporate/organisational tool.

*Required*

Explain why the use of intranets has become so important and describe the main activities intranets are used for.

### Question 3

The OSI model is a seven-layer reference model used as a template for the mapping of communications and computer network protocols.

*Required*

Briefly describe the content and importance of each of the seven layers, and describe the advantages and disadvantages of using such a reference model.

### Question 4

Soft-type networks can be categorised as:

- formal bureaucracy,
- formal adhocracy,
- informal bureaucracy, or
- informal adhocracy.

In which of the above categories would the following be located:

- an advertising and marketing consultancy,
- a privately funded medical research institute,
- an accounting/audit partnership,
- a large UK-based retail company,
- a public utilities company,
- a local council authority,
- a small family-owned manufacturer, and
- a newly established, publicly funded, monitoring authority

## Question 5

An extranet exists when the intranets of two or more companies/organisations are linked together.

### *Required*

Describe the main benefits that can accrue from a company/organisation linking its intranet with:

- the intranet(s) of its suppliers/service providers, and
- the intranet(s) of its customers/clients

## Assignments

## Question 1

Making whatever assumption you feel necessary, explain what type of network (i.e. a centralised wide area network, a decentralised wide area network or a local area network) would each of the following types of companies/organisations be likely to adopt:

- a financial institution with numerous offices located throughout the UK,
- a specialist retailer based in York with three retail outlets located in North Yorkshire,
- a bus company with a head office in Edinburgh and bus stations located in a number of cities throughout the UK,
- a manufacturing company with a head office and factory located in Hull,
- a regional water authority with automated monitoring offices in Bristol and the surrounding area,
- a travel agent with three outlets in Manchester, and
- a local departmental store,

Explain and justify your selection.

## Question 2

Clare Barber is an internal auditor with IQC, a large, London-based, consulting company. For the last financial year, IQC generated income of £200m from its consulting activities. In February 2007 the management committee of IQC decided to restructure the company's accounting and finance information systems. The management committee have decided to migrate all accounting and finance-related applications currently run on the company's centralised mainframe to eight local-area networks with the migration to be complete by March 2008. Clare is the audit department's representative on the company's systems committee responsible for designing and implementing the new system.

## Chapter endnotes

1 The term society is used here to denote a complex arrangement made up of people, groups, networks, institutions, organisations and systems, and includes local, national and international patterns of relationships.

2 Considerable literature exists that argues that nation and state are not identical, but inter-dependent collective associations/structural arrangements that sometimes combine, coalesce or fissure. This results in the possibility that not only may individual states arguably include/comprise of many different nations, but also individual nations may include/comprise of many different states. Whilst it is perhaps valid to suggest that in a small number of cases nation may well equate with state, in most cases such a collective notion merely over-generalises the relationship between territoriality, sovereignty and community. Moreover it over-simplifies the changing context and structure of the nation and state as increasingly reformulated 'plurilateral' structures of regulation and authority emerge as a condition of capitalist priorities and increasingly marginalise extant territorial power and state sovereignty.

3 *Weltanschauung* means to look onto the world. It refers to the framework through which an individual and/or society interprets the world and interacts in or with it.

4 Not convinced? Consider for example, the German invasion of Poland in 1939, the Russian annexation of Estonia, Latvia and Lithuania in 1945, the American involvement in Vietnam in the late 1960s, the British/Argentinean Falkland Island conflict in 1982 and, perhaps more recently, the American-led invasion of Iraq in 2003. Also the demise of the 'Soviet Bloc', the fall of the so-called 'Iron Curtain', the creation of the UN and NATO, the development of the WTO and the development and expansion of the EU. In all the above, the common denominator is the desire of one social group (or indeed one nation or state) to create, either through forceful intervention, mutual imposition and/or open negotiation, greater interconnectivity – whether socially, politically and/or economically.

5 That is not to say that socio-political and socio-religious groups will not continue to arise and seek to impose their will, either directly or indirectly, on the fabric of many modern societies. On the contrary: for example, consider the continuing social conflicts in Africa, the almost ever present socio-religious confrontation(s) in Afghanistan, the escalating political turmoil in Iraq and the growing unrest in the Middle East, and their impact on the interrelationships between social groups within the UK, the USA, Europe and indeed all the other western democracies.

6 The term control is used here in the context of promoting accountability and traceability.

7 Or semi hard-type networks.

8 Although such a distinction could be accused of ignoring the reciprocal nature of soft-type networks, that is the extent to which the market capital and its associated 'entity focused networks' influence (directly and/or indirectly) the nature and existence of 'self-focused networks', which in turn influence 'entity focused networks', which in turn feedback and influence 'self-focused networks', etc.

[9] A logical network is concerned with the connection pathways within a network and are deemed to exist independently of the physicality of the network.

[10] Actors within a social network can be a range of entities – from an individual, to a small local association, to a large multinational corporate organisation.

[11] Such relationships/dependencies may be directed (formal), undirected (informal) or mixed.

[12] An example of such a network – a network often characterised by the existence of an imposed external regulatory framework – would be a limited company (either public or/private), externally regulated by the requirements of the UK Companies Act 1985 (as amended).

[13] Sound familiar? Of course it does! It's the general systems theory notion that all systems are comprised of small sub-systems!

[14] The term bureaucracy is derived from the word bureau, used to refer to 'an office . . . a place where officials worked'. The Greek suffix *kratia* or *kratos* means 'power or rule' thus the term bureaucracy means office power/office rule, or more appropriately 'the rule of the officialdom'.

[15] Max (Maximilian) Weber (1864–1920), German political economist and sociologist, and pioneer of the analytic method in sociology.

[16] Karl Heinrich Marx (1818–83) – an influential philosopher, political economist and social activist, most famous for his critique of capitalism.

[17] Historical materialism or the materialist conception of history as an approach to the study of history and society that contextualises changes in human history not only in terms of economic and technological factors, but more importantly in terms of social conflict, and is generally considered the intellectual basis of Maxism.

For Marx, the historical origin of the notion of bureaucracy was to be found within interplay of four historical sources:

- religion,
- the formation of the state,
- commerce, and
- technology.

[18] Bureaucracies tend to proliferate in periods of economic stability and growth, and somewhat unsurprisingly, diminish in periods of economic instability and decline.

[19] A highly-structured, well-defined hierarchy, generally appropriate to conditions of relative stability.

[20] A flexible, adaptable network structure, generally appropriate to conditions of relative instability and change.

[21] Bureaucracies as a form of (socio-political) network structure suffer from a number of inherent defects, the main problems being:

- overly political lines of authority,
- overly complex organisational structures,
- excessive anonymity, and
- unclear areas of responsibility.

[22] Although, over time, they may well eventually become overly complex, extremely unpredictable and difficult to manage.

[23] A node is a processing location and can be a computer or some other information/communication device (e.g. a printer). Every node that comprises a network will have a unique network address, either a data link control address (DLC), or a media access address (MAC).

[24] A computer and/or information and communication device that manages network resources, for example:

- a file server is computer (or collection of computers) that is dedicated to storing files,
- a print server is a computer that manages one or more printers,
- a network server is a computer (or collection of computers) that manages network communications traffic, and
- a database server is a computer dedicated to processing database queries.

[25] A computer motherboard is the central or primary circuit board within a computer.

[26] The physical layer is layer one in the seven-layer OSI model of computer networking and refers to network hardware, broadcast specifications, network connection type and collision control and other low-level functions. It performs services requested by the data link layer – the major functions and services performed by the physical layer being:

- communications administration connection,
- network resources management, and
- data conversation.

[27] The data link layer is layer two of the seven-layer OSI model. The data link layer:

- responds to service requests from the network layer, and
- issues service requests to the physical layer.

The data link layer is designed to:

- ensure that data is transferred correctly between network nodes,
- provide the functional and procedural means to transfer between network entities and monitor, detect and correct (where possible) errors that may occur in the physical layer.

The data link layer is comprised of two components:

- a logical link control which determines where a frame of data ends and the next data frame starts, and
- a media access control (centralised or distributed) which determines who is allowed to access the media at any point in time.

[28] Although different topologies, a bridge must, however, be used between networks with the same network protocol.

[29] Unshielded twisted pair (UTP) cabling can range from:

- Category 1 UTP: voice only,
- Category 2 UTP: data – up to 4 Mbps,
- Category 3 UTP: data – up to 10 Mbps,
- Category 4 UTP: data – up to 20 Mbps, and
- Category 5 UTP: data – up to 100 Mbps.

[30] Crosstalk occurs when a transmitted signal across a network creates an undesired effect elsewhere on the network.

[31] A dielectric or electrical insulator is a substance that is resistant to flows of electric current.

[32] Designed to minimise electrical and radio frequency interference.

[33] Ethernet is a computer networking technology for local area networks (LANs), and defines:

- wiring and signalling for the physical layer, and
- data frame formats and protocals for the media access control (MAC)/data link layer.

It is (at present) the most widespread LAN technology in use and has largely replaced all other LAN standards.

[34] Thin coaxial cable is also referred to as 10Base2 which refers to the specifications for thin coaxial cable carrying Ethernet signals. The name 10Base2 is derived as follows:

- 10 refers to its transmission speed of 10 mbits/s (megabits per second),
- BASE is an abbreviation for baseband signalling, and
- 2 stands for the maximum segment length of 200 metres – although the actual maximum segment length is 185 metres.

[35] Thick coaxial cable is also referred to as 10Base5 which refers to the specifications for thick coaxial cable carrying Ethernet signals. The name 10Base5 is derived as follows:

- 10 refers to its transmission speed of 10 mbits/s (megabits per second),
- BASE is an abbreviation for baseband signalling, and
- 5 stands for the maximum segment length of 500 metres.

Thick coaxial cable has an extra protective plastic cover.

[36] Universal Serial Bus (USB) provides a serial bus standard for interconnecting computer and information and communication devices, usually to another computer and/or other devices for example:

- television set top boxes,
- game consoles, and
- personal digital assistants (PDAs)

[37] FireWire (also known as iLink or IEEE 1394) is a PC and digital video serial bus interface standard that provides high-speed communications and isochronous real-time data services. Up to 63 devices can be connected to one FireWire port.

[38] Infrared Data Association (IrDA) defines physical specifications, communications protocol and standards for the short range exchange of data using infrared light for uses such as personal area networks (PANs). For information and communication devices to communicate using IrDA devices must have a direct line of sight. Further information on infrared based networking and the IrDA is available @ www.irda.org.

[39] Bluetooth is an industrial specification for wireless personal area networks (PANs) and provides a way to connect and exchange data and information between information and communication devices such personal digital assistants (PDAs), mobile phones, laptop computers, PCs, printers and digital camera using a secure, low-cost, short-range radio frequency.

It is primarily designed for low power consumption, with a short range. Products are available in three different power classes:

- class 3 – allows transmission of between 10 centimetres and 1 metre,
- class 2 – allows transmission of up to a distance of 10 metres, and
- class 1 – allows transmission of up to a distance of 100 metres.

[40] Skinplex is a personal area network technology using the capacitive near field of human skin. Skinplex systems can detect and communicate up to 1 metre from a human body and are already in use in:

- access control systems,
- building management systems,
- integrated security and protection systems,
- anti-trapping/anti jamming systems,
- electronic locking systems, and
- alarm systems.

Further information is available @ www.skinplex.net.

41 In a computing context a client is a system/user that accesses a remote service/facility located on another computer within the same and/or related network to the client.

42 As part of a client server network architecture, a client can be defined as an application that runs on a PC and/or workstation, and relies on a server to facilitate access to and/or management of the performance of a processing operation(s). For example, an e-mail client is an application which facilitates the sending and receiving of e-mails.

43 Indeed, servers on a client-server network may also perform some of the processing work for client machines – processing which is often referred to as back-end processing.

44 Load balancing is the distribution of processing and communications activity evenly across a network so that no single computer and/or information and communications device is overwhelmed. Such balancing is important for networks where service demand is difficult to predict.

45 As compared to the now ancient and monolithic mainframe computing systems.

46 In a technical context, pure peer-to-peer networks/network applications are rare. Most networks and network applications described as peer-to-peer often contain and/or rely upon some non-peer elements.

47 A router is a computer networking device that forwards data (packets) toward their destinations. In essence, a router acts as a junction between two networks to transfer data (packets) between them. A router differs from a switch which merely connects network devices (or network segments) to form a network.

48 Most distributed computing networks are created by users volunteering to release, or make available to others any unused computing resources they possess.

49 An example of collaborative computing or distributed computing can be found at www.grid.org. United Devices hosts a number of projects, for example research into smallpox, anthrax, cancer and, most recently, human protein structure, on its Grid MP platform.

50 Bandwidth is a measure of frequency range and is a key concept in information and communication fields. Bandwidth is closely related to the capacity of a communication channel – the greater the bandwidth the greater the capacity. Issues of bandwidth and capacity are related by the Shannon-Hartley theorem, which is concerned with the maximum amount of error-free digital data that can be transmitted over a communication link with a specified bandwidth in the presence of noise interference.

51 This is clearly not the case for a client-server architecture-based network with a fixed set of servers, in which increasing the clients/users would reduce capacity, and potentially mean lower data transfer rates for users.

52 The term single point of failure is used to describes any part, link and/or component of system/network that can, if the part, link, and/or component fails, cause an interruption of the service – ranging from a simple service interruption or processing delay to complete network failure.

53 **Malicious software** that is designed to destroy, disrupt and/or damage a computer system/network.

54 Spyware is malicious software that covertly gathers user information through an internet connection without the user's knowledge and/or consent.

55 In networking, a bus is a collection of wires that connects nodes within a network and through which data and information are transmitted from one computer in a network to another computer in the network. Whilst the term 'backbone' is often substituted for the term 'bus', in a contemporary context it is a term often used to describe the main network connections that comprise the internet.

56 Peer-to-peer networks are often configured as a local bus.

57 Terminator connections are situated at the end of the bus – the communication links are designed to absorb the signal once it has reached the end of the network topology and prevent the signal from being reflected back across the bus.

[58] Although most wired networks tend to be regarded as non-passive, almost all wireless networks are regarded as examples of passive bus networks.

[59] Carrier Sense Multiple Access (CSMA) is a non-deterministic media access control (MAC) protocol in which a node verifies the absence of other traffic before transmitting on a shared physical medium (e.g. a bus).

[60] A network switch is a computer networking device which connects network segments (a portion of a computer network that is separated by a computer networking device – for example, a router, a bridge or switch, and/or a repeater or hub). It is often used to replace a central network hub. A switch is also often referred to as an intelligent hub.

[61] Details of all extant protocols are outlined in Request for Comments (RFCs). For further details on RFC's see Chapter 4.

[62] For example, the Token Ring protocol was a network protocol developed by IBM in the 1980s, whereas LocalTalk was a network protocol developed by Apple Computer Inc. for Macintosh computers.

[63] Quality of Service (QoS) refers to ensuring that data packets reach their destination. Such assurances are important, because:

- data packets may be dropped – that is the network routers fail to deliver,
- data packets may be delayed – that is data packets may take a long time to reach their destination,
- data packets may jitter – that is a group of related data packets may reach their destination a different times,
- data packets may be delivered out of order – that is the data packets arrive in a different order to the one with which they were sent, and
- data packets may be corrupted – that is packets may be misdirected or incorrectly combined.

A traffic contract, a quality of service contract or a service level agreement specifies/defines the quality of service required – thereby minimising the possibility of network problems/errors.

[64] That is the segmentation and transmission of data packets over a network – possibly by different routes.

[65] That is the use of uniform hierarchical addresses to provide any network node/computer connected to the internet with a unique identifying address.

[66] That is the use of different network routes for data packets – from source to destination.

[67] That is decentralised initiation, monitoring and termination of communication links.

[68] That is the mapping of domain names to numeric addresses.

[69] See www.mci.com.

[70] See www.groupbt.com.

[71] See www.att.com.

[72] See www.teleglobe.com/en.

[73] A transit network is a network which passes traffic between other networks in addition to carrying traffic for its own hosts, and must have pathways to at least two other networks.

[74] That is data is transmitted in packets across an internetwork that is comprised of multiple interchangeable pathways from source to destination.

[75] Which facilitates pathway redundancy – that is if a pathways fails an alternative pathway can be used.

[76] Autonomous Systems (AS) are the managed networks that comprise the internet. Often operated by a NSP or an ISP, such networks act as both management domain and routing domain, and are identified by a number assigned by ICANN (the Internet Corporation for Assigned Names and Numbers).

⁷⁷ An internet exchange point (IXP) is a physical infrastructure that allows different ISPs to exchange internet traffic between their respective networks. These were originally known as network access points (NAPs).

⁷⁸ A mutual peering agreement (MPA) is a bilateral agreement which facilitates the exchange of internet traffic between ISPs and/or NSPs without cost.

⁷⁹ There are currently a little over 300 peering points worldwide.

⁸⁰ A point of presence (PoP) is a physical point at which a network meets a higher level or even primary data/information carrying line of the internet, and are mainly designed to allow ISPs to connect into NSP networks.

⁸¹ A gateway is a computer and/or network node that acts as an entrance to another network or another internetwork (e.g. the interet).

⁸² A firewall is a set of related software programs located at a network gateway and designed to protect the resources of a intranet/private network from users from other networks.

⁸³ Although some academics argue that the term 'extranet' is merely used to describe what companies/organisations have been doing for many years – creating/developing interconnecting private networks for the sharing of data/information – it was during the late 1990s/early 2000s that the term 'extranet' began to be used to describe a virtual repository of data/information accessible to authorised users only – over the internet.

⁸⁴ The Extranet Benchmarking Association (see www.extranetbenchmarking.com) provides a forum for business to identify the best practices of extranet initiatives through benchmarking, allowing companies and organisations employing extranet facilities to:

- compare content,
- evaluate performance, and
- identify problem areas.

Membership is free to corporate members who have installed extranets or are planning to do so.

# 6

# Contemporary transaction processing: categories, types, cycles and systems

## Introduction

In an environment in which corporate success continues to be measured and assessed principally on the level of economic returns generated for corporate shareholders, there can be little doubt that failure to accommodate contemporary notions of freedom of wealth accumulation and to offer unreserved support for the free pursuit of profit is often seen as tantamount to committing corporate suicide – a ticket to ride on a solitary journey to the corporate graveyard. Indeed, in today's extremely volatile and highly competitive market, a central feature of the search for this *nirvana* of:

- sustainable wealth accumulation,
- long-term stability,
- constant economic growth, and
- continued market advantage,

is of course the temporal and spatial displacement of both tangible and intangible assets and resources: or put more simply, the buying and selling of ideas, commodities and symbols, people and identities, and goods and services.

As a fusion of political bureaucracies, social hierarchies, economic resources and organisational technologies that comprise contemporary corporate entities, transaction processing systems play a pivotal role in the portrayal, evaluation and governance of the expanding domains of corporate economic activity. Such systems not only enable social and economic activities to be rendered knowable, measurable and accountable by homogenising, categorising and classifying economic events and activities, they also enable the politicisation of wealth accumulation – in a specific and very particular way. It is the *constructed* processing of *real world* transactions that facilitates the creation of the now familiar (and sometimes misleading) *pictures/descriptions* of profitability and wealth accumulation whose continued residency within the financial pages of the business media (and thus their supposed/sustained believability) often appears to be beyond question.

Clearly of central importance to such transaction processing systems is of course the need to ensure that:

- adequate internal control procedures exist,
- appropriate authorisation procedures and protocols are in place, and
- effective recording procedures and management processes exist.

This chapter provides an overview and classification of the transaction processing systems normally found within a company's transaction processing cycles, namely:

- the revenue cycle,
- the expenditure cycle,
- the conversion cycle, and
- the management cycle.

## Learning outcomes

This chapter analyses the key features of contemporary transaction processing, but more importantly, it explores how and why such systems have become central to wealth creation and the maximisation of shareholder wealth.

It provides:

- a contextual typology for the analysis and categorisation of contemporary transaction processing, and
- an analysis and extended discussion on how such a contextual typology can be used both to understand and control the increasingly complex and dynamic operations of such companies.

By the end of this chapter, the reader should be able to:

- describe the main features of contemporary transaction processing,
- distinguish between different transaction processing categories, types (and sub-types), cycles and systems,
- critically comment on the importance of such a contextual typology for understanding wealth maximising organisations, and
- describe and critically evaluate the key transaction processing factors that both enable and constrain wealth maximising organisations.

The reader should also be able to consider the implications of the Data Protection Act 1998 on contemporary transaction processing – especially transactions which result in the generation and storage of information covered by the requirements of the Act.

## Contemporary transaction processing – an overview

Clearly there can be little doubt that today's 'global' society is sustained through and increasingly dominated by the global priorities of capital. A marketplace in which the company as a created entity can and often does exercise both enormous power and enormous influence. Just think of the power and influence exercised by companies such as Microsoft Inc., Time Warner Inc., HSBC Ltd, Shell plc, and many other multi-listed, multinational companies.

And yet whilst the company (as a created entity) has clearly become an important servicing component of the increasingly speculative logic of the competitive marketplace and thus inseparable from the social, political and economic interests they serve, it is neither isolated nor protected from the international mobility of capital and the temporal and spatial consequences of globalisation. Company priorities are constantly reupholstered, reconfigured and redistributed by not only the complex territoriality of inter-state politics or the social pressures of the labour market processes, but more crucially by the competitive and often chaotic global priorities of an ever-changing marketplace.

There can be little doubt then that companies are increasingly conditioned by a vast array of competing social, economic and political constituencies. Indeed whilst companies have undoubtedly become central to the globalising logic of capital as a vehicle through which once established social and economic sovereignties are reconfigured, redesigned and reinstalled, they have perhaps more importantly become a mirror of the dominance of the socio-cultural baggage associated with western capitalism and the marketisation of wealth, its desire to forge interrelationships and inter-dependencies and impose norms consistent with a self-image. A self-image founded on a distinctive historical geography in which social technologies are increasingly developed subordinate to the needs of a marketplace which is constantly changing and evolving, and in a state of constant instability and unrest. A marketplace which as a competitive forum for trade and exchange remains the primary mechanism through which profits are generated and share-holder wealth is maximised – a mechanism whose inherent volatility continues to ensure its outcomes are random, chaotic and unpredictable. But always entertaining!

So what has all this got to do with contemporary transaction processing? Well – remember the key elements of systems thinking in Chapter 2? Clearly, for purposes of growth and indeed survival, companies (as semi-open systems) need to/have to interact with other companies and organisations – with other semi-open systems within the environment or, more appropriately, within the marketplace. No matter how chaotic, unstable or unpredictable the market may be, such interaction is fundamental and lies at the very heart of market-based competition, wealth creation and profit maximisation. Interaction more often than not is achieved through a company's operations, its market-based activities, its transaction processing systems and the movement and/or exchange of both tangible and intangible assets and resources.

How? Consider the following. A company acquires products, services and resources through a process of exchange for:

- other products, services and/or resources, or
- legal title to other products, services and/or resources, or
- a legally enforceable promise to transfer legal title of other products, services and/or resources (e.g. a promise to exchange assets) at a future agreed date.

When a company acquires products, services and resources:

- sometimes such acquired products, services and resources are consumed internally to create other products, services and resources that can be exchanged externally (sold to other external organisations);
- sometimes such acquired products, services and resources are converted and exchanged externally without any internal consumption; and
- sometimes such acquired products, services and resources are merely stored (without any conversion – without any change) and then exchanged externally.

Clearly the acquisition, consumption and/or disposal of such products, services and resources results in either a present and/or future flow of funds. A flow of funds which inevitably impacts on either:

- short-term financing such as working capital, and/or
- long-term financing such as equity or debt.

Sound familiar? Of course it does!

Contemporary transaction processing cycles and their related systems are merely a contextual representation – a physical expression of:

- what company accountants have for many years commonly referred to as the corporate financing cycle or corporate funding cycle, and
- what company managers have for many years commonly referred to as the value cycle and/or the value chain.

See Figure 6.1 below.

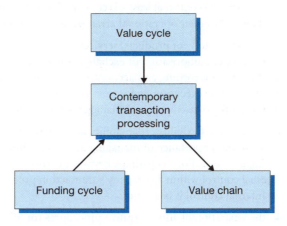

**Figure 6.1** Contemporary transaction processing and the business cycle

Before we consider the relationship between the corporate funding cycle, value chain, value cycle and a company's transaction processing cycles and system, it would perhaps be useful to a consider a few generic, albeit extremely important, characteristics of contemporary trans-action processing cycles and systems; characteristics often regarded as the 'fundamentals' of transaction processing cycles and systems.

Such characteristics include:

- flexibility,
- adaptability,
- reflexivity,
- controllability, and
- purposive context.

## Flexibility, adaptability and reflexivity[1]

In a marketplace that is rarely constant, stable or predictable, the achievement of any objective/goal – for example, increased market share, increased profitability and/or increased shareholder wealth – almost certainly requires not only flexibility and adaptability but more importantly reflexivity. Whereas flexibility can be defined as the ability of a company's processes and sys-tems to respond quickly to changes in the business environment, adaptability can be defined as the ability to alter corporate structure, function and/or processes in response to changes in the environment. In relation to contemporary transaction processing cycles and systems, reflexivity can perhaps be best defined as movement, activity and/or change performed automatically and without conscious decision.

For contemporary transaction processing cycles and systems, such flexibility, adaptability or reflexivity should seek to ensure that:

- changes to operating structures, functions and/or processes are relevant and appropriate, but more importantly,
- fundamental functions and processes continue to cope with and operate within an increasing unstable and uncertain environment.

## Controllability

There can be little doubt that a central feature of success, a key component to continued survival – in a corporate context at least – is control. Contemporary transaction processing systems should contain within their operational arrangements, appropriate structures to ensure;

- the safe custody of products, services, and resources,
- the proper authorisation of exchange transactions,
- the correct recording and accounting for exchange transactions,
- the accurate execution and proper completion of exchange transactions, and
- the appropriate control and management of exchange transactions.

Clearly, whilst flexibility, adaptability and reflexivity are essential prerequisites for continued survival, the importance of managing and controlling the impact of resource movements and exchange transactions is perhaps beyond question, with such control often operationalised as internal control within a company's transaction processing system.

Internal control is based on:

- the separation of administrative procedures (or SOAP), and/or
- the segregation of duties (or SOD).

The issue of control was introduced in Chapter 3. We will return to a brief but more functional consideration of internal control later in this chapter, and a more in-depth critical evaluation of internal control and systems security in Chapter 14.

## Purposive context

Purposive context refers to the need to ensure that contemporary transaction processing cycles and systems remain not only *input focused* but more importantly *output orientated*. That is contemporary transaction processing cycles and systems should not be process driven. Their present functions should not be determined solely by the histrionics of past activities/successes. In a commercial context, such a dependency on past glories/successes would be tantamount to long-term economic suicide. Why?

Put simply, in terms of contemporary transaction processing cycles and systems, purposive context means inherent corporate structures, functions and/or processes must be purposeful. They must exist and function for reasons other than the bureaucracy of self-survival or self-propagation.

Okay – so now that we have a broad understanding of the fundamentals of contemporary transaction processing cycles and systems, what about the relationship between contemporary transaction processing cycles and systems and:

- the corporate funding cycle,
- the value chain, and
- the value cycle.

**Contemporary transaction processing and the funding cycle**

The corporate funding cycle is shown in Figure 6.2.

In a simplistic context, corporate funding can be divided into:

- short-term sources and applications of funds (or working capital), and
- long-term sources and applications of funds.

Whilst this division may not always be as clear as some business commentators and finance academics would suggest (some sources/applications of funds may well be categorised as both short-term and long-term), the aim of any corporate funding policy is to ensure that a company possesses an adequate level of funds (both cash and non-cash funds) appropriate to its level of activities and suitable to the supply and demand requirements for such resources within the business.

Clearly on a day-to-day basis, working capital is essential, and the importance of balancing levels of stocks, debtors, creditors and of course cash is beyond question. However, working capital or short-term funding is not the only aspect of funding that has an impact of a company's operational capabilities and its abilities to generate shareholder wealth. Long-term funding or long-term sources and applications of funds also have a major impact, mainly because of their

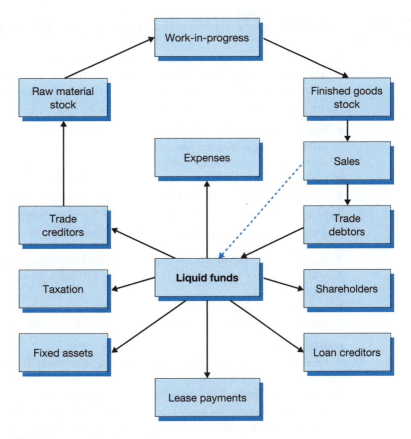

**Figure 6.2** Corporate funding cycle

size and timing – that is many of these 'non-working capital' sources and applications tend to be large-value items that either

- occur/reoccur regularly say weekly, monthly or even annually (e.g. tax payments, lease payments, dividends, interest and, possibly, the acquisition and disposal of fixed assets),
- occur irregularly as one-off events (e.g. new equity and loan finance and/or redemption of old equity and loan finance).

At the heart of the corporate funding cycle is of course contemporary transaction processing – that is the *practice of business* and the *activity of commodity exchange* through which funds are acquired, profits are generated and wealth is created. Indeed any redefining of a company's funding/financing policies and/or objectives, for example:

- decreasing the level of investment in stocks to increase cash flow,
- amending sales and debtor policies to increase cash flow, and/or
- the acquisition of additional resources to increase production – to increase sales and consequently cash flow,

will require (at the very least) perhaps a reconfiguring of a company's contemporary transaction processing systems and activities and/or a redefining of its management/administrative control procedures.

## Contemporary transaction processing and the value chain

The value chain is a model which analyses an organisation's strategically relevant activities, activities from which competitive advantage is derived. Porter (1985) suggested a value chain model composed of two distinct groups of activities – primary activities and support activities. Porter suggested primary activities could be divided into:

- inbound logistics – the receiving and warehousing of raw materials and their distribution to manufacturing as they are required,
- operations – the processes of transforming inputs into finished products and services,
- outbound logistics – the warehousing and distribution of finished goods,
- marketing and sales – the identification of customer needs and the generation of sales, and
- service – the support of customers after the products and services are sold to them.

And support activities could be divided into:

- infrastructure – organisational structure, control systems, company culture,
- human resource management – employee recruiting, hiring, training, development and compensation,
- technology development – technologies to support value-creating activities, and
- procurement – purchasing inputs such as materials, supplies, and equipment.

See Figure 6.3.

Clearly the stages and components within the value chain should not be viewed in isolation but considered in a holistic systemic sense – that is considered within a wider context to include the interactions and relationships not only within processes but between stages. Indeed, for Porter (1985), competitive advantage, profitability and shareholder wealth maximisation could only be achieved through the effective and efficient performance and management of not only primary value chain activities but more importantly value chain support activities.

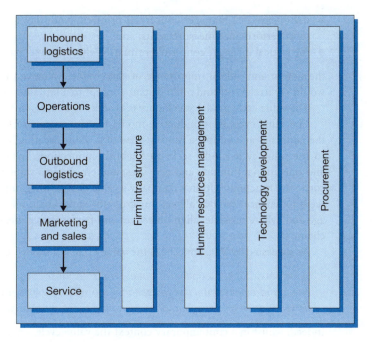

**Figure 6.3** Porter's generic value chain

So, what is the relevance of the value chain to contemporary transaction processing? The value chain model continues to remain a useful (if often criticised) analytical model for:

- articulating a company's core competencies,
- defining a company's fundamental activities, and
- identifying essential relationships and processes,

on which the company can plan its pursuit of competitive advantage and wealth maximisation through:

- cost advantage[2] – through either reducing the cost of individual value chain activities or by reconfiguring the value chain, and/or
- differentiation[3] – through either changing individual value chain activities to increase product/service uniqueness or by reconfiguring the value chain.

Clearly, there are many ways in which a company can reconfigure its value chain activities to either reduce costs and/or create uniqueness – all of which rely fundamentally on a redefining, rearranging and/or reconfiguring of the contemporary transaction processing activities within relevant value chain activities.

## Contemporary transaction processing and the value cycle

There can be little doubt that the responsibility for value management and for wealth creation is no longer merely the responsibility of the financial manager. The obligation to pursue and adopt wealth maximising strategies and procedures now extends to all levels of tactical and operational decision making. And yet, for:

- the operational manager concerned primarily with day-to-day service delivery and short-term performance measurements, and
- the tactical manager concerned primarily with resource management and accountability,

the notion and indeed importance of shareholder value can be an elusive, vague (and some would say irrelevant) and often distant concept to adopt and/or even comprehend.

The value cycle model (see Figure 6.4) seeks to address this shortfall.

The value cycle is an inductive model that in essence seeks to provide a 'system view' of the company and adopts a holistic view of a 'value creating' organisation/company. In doing so the value cycle model seeks to establish connections/linkages between strategic, financial and operational thinking and activities, and emphasises value relationships between different corporate functions within a company's value chain. More importantly, the value cycle model seeks to balance resource allocation across the value chain for sustainable competitive advantage and, where possible, align objectives and performance measures across a company's value chain.

As suggested by Vaassen (2002) the value cycle is a model that enables:

*visualisation of segregation of duties, the clear description of the coherence between positions and events within organisations, the relationship between flows of goods and cash flows, and the classification of any firm in a typology of organisations (2002: 34).*

Indeed, whilst in a contemporary context the value cycle – and value cycle management – has become synonymous with the efforts to:

- introduce and integrate more technology into transaction processing activities and procedures, and
- synchronise processes and procedures across the corporate transaction processing activities,

its *systemic approach* has more importantly resulted in an increasing acknowledgement of the cyclical nature of wealth creation and a movement away from the notion of *linear* value chain activities and inherent transaction processing activities. That is a rejection of the notion that business activities follow a linear path in the form of a supply/value chain of goods and services – a chain with a beginning and an end – and the adoption of a more dynamic, holistic, nonlinear approach. An approach embracing the idea of the business and indeed value creation as a continuous cycle, a cycle of interrelated systems and activities, exchange processes and procedures, and management and administrative control devices and mechanisms.

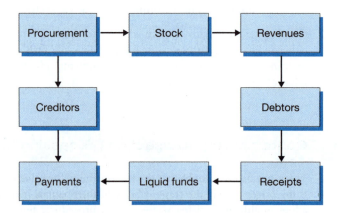

**Figure 6.4** Value cycle

Whilst clearly this is nothing new – it is really just a repackaged version or restructured application of systems thinking (see Chapter 2), it does provide a suitable functional context – incorporating the funding cycle and the value chain into a framework within which the holistic nature of contemporary transaction processing activities and related systems and procedures can be appropriately considered.

Now that we have a *context* within which to locate contemporary transaction processing activities, let's have a look at them in a little more detail.

## Contemporary transaction processing – toward a classification[4]

Why do we need a classification? Consider the number of active trading companies registered not only in the UK but in Europe, the USA, in Asia or indeed globally! In addition consider the following facts:

- No two companies are the same.
- No two companies operate in the same way.
- No two transaction processing systems are the same!

Understand the problem? Sound familiar. Of course it does! It's the same problem you may have come across when evaluating the comparative performance of two companies using, for example, financial performance analysis or financial/management ratios.

All companies possess a distinctive uniqueness – a corporate disposition based on a vast range of interrelated and interconnected characteristics and qualities particular to the company. Characteristics and qualities founded upon an ever-changing chronicle of past, current and future events and occurrences that reveal themselves in the existence of differences, for example in:

- degrees of geographical diversification,
- management hierarchies and decision-making processes,
- financing and funding policies,
- levels of organisational technology, and/or
- operational policies and procedure.

Clearly, because of the vast number of trading, registered public and private companies, and indeed the varied nature of their activities (for plcs just look at the variety of companies included in the FTSE 100, FTSE 250 or FTSE 350 indices[5]) it is perhaps important to provide a rational context/framework – a general classification – if only to bring some sense of order and understanding to what superficially appears to be a seemingly infinite array of chaotic variety and diversity. A classification of company types and sub-types – of transaction processing cycles and systems – into an ordered arrangement based on a defined range of characteristics, relationships and/or distinctive differences/similarities.

Indeed, whether inductive[6] and/or deductive[7] the purpose of any such classification of transaction processing systems is:

- to enable a description of the structure and relationship of such transaction processing systems to other similar transaction processing systems, but more importantly,
- to simplify relationships to facilitate discussion and the construction of general statements about such classes of transaction processing systems.

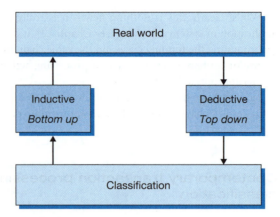

**Figure 6.5** Classification – inductive/deductive

Adapted and extended from Davis *et al.* (1990) (after Wilkinson *et al.* (2001) and Starreveld *et al.* (1998) (after Vaassen (2002)), this typology of transaction processing systems – see Figure 6.5 – is an inductive classification.

Indeed, inasmuch as its foundation is empirical observation, this taxonomy of transaction processing systems is a generalised hierarchical classification (see Figure 6.6): one developed from specific facts and observations over many years by many academics (certainly too many to list or identify individually). Nevertheless despite its celebrated history it is perhaps important to recognise that this classification is neither neutral nor unbiased. It is a classification developed upon a number of classic liberal economic assumptions such as:

- commodity/service exchange is the foundation of corporate wealth generation,
- all companies are wealth maximising, and
- all (or at least most) companies are free to enter (and exit) markets without constraint and/or penalty.

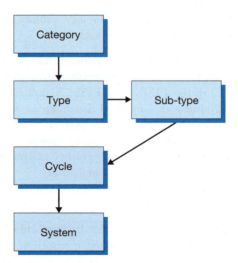

**Figure 6.6** Hierarchical classification of transaction processing systems

For the purposes of this typology, the following terminology will be used:

- the term *categories* will be used to refer to a group/sub-set of companies possessing common characteristics and/or sharing common attributes,
- the term *types* will be used to refer to the company business type/sub-type within a category,
- the term *cycles* will be used to refer to the cycles of operation within the company business type/sub-type, and
- the term *systems* will be used to refer to the systems within a company's cycle of operations.

## Contemporary transaction processing – categories

In general two broad categories of companies[8] can be identified, these being:

- Category 1 – companies with a dominant flow of commodities, and
- Category 2 – companies with no dominant flow of commodities.

Clearly this initial stage classification is intuitive which perhaps accounts for its rather vague superficiality and simplicity. Nevertheless it is an appropriate starting point and perhaps important to recognise that whilst in an empirical context such a distinction exists (or appears to exist) it is also important to acknowledge that the two categories are:

- by no means definitive, and
- by no means exclusive.

A company may well diversify its functions/activities and undertake transactions:

- within both of the above categories, and/or
- within different types within a single category.

This is because diversification within business activities does, according to contemporary portfolio theory at least, minimise business risk and the possibility of financial loss. Look for example at the following companies:

- HBOS plc,
- Tesco plc, and
- Legal and General plc.

All of the above three companies are established, well-known and, highly respected FTSE 100 companies. All three are fairly well diversified (geographically, operationally and strategically), and all three not only enjoy the benefit of substantial market confidence in their business activities (albeit that such confidence is sometimes unpredictable and often temperamental), they are all, without any doubt, extremely profitable.

For example, for the year 2004, HBOS plc announced profits of £4592m,[9] Tesco plc announced profits of £1600m[10] and Legal and General plc announced profits of £1222m.[11]

(QED?[12] – perhaps!)

## Contemporary transaction processing – types

Within the above two categories, five types of contemporary transaction processing structures can be identified (each with two sub-types), as follows.

## Category 1: Companies with a dominant flow of commodities

- Type 1(a)   Retail and distribution companies
  - (i)   consumer-based retail
  - (ii)  non-consumer-based retail
- Type 1(b)   Manufacturing and production companies
  - (i)   continuous production
  - (ii)  non-continuous production

## Category 2: Companies with no dominant flow of commodities

- Type 2(a)   Companies with a limited flow of commodities
  - (i)   limited owned commodities
  - (ii)  limited non-owned commodities
- Type 2(b)   Time/space-based companies
  - (i)   specific time/space
  - (ii)  non-specific time/space
- Type 2(c)   Knowledge/skills-based companies
  - (i)   time-based specific knowledge/skills
  - (ii)  supply-based non-specific knowledge/skills

Let's look at each of these in a little more detail

### Category 1: Type 1(a) Retail and distribution companies

Consumer-based retail and distribution companies are companies that *mainly* sell to high street customers and clients, and would include, for example:

- supermarkets and food retail-based companies (e.g. Asda plc, Tesco plc and Sainsbury plc),
- generic commodity retail companies/groups (e.g. Marks and Spencer plc, Boots plc and Kingfisher plc),
- specific commodity retail companies (e.g. Comet plc, Dixon's Group plc (electrical retail) and United Utilities plc (energy and water management)),
- online retail stores (e.g. Amazon.co.uk[13] (online entertainment and educational goods and services)).

Trade-based retail companies are retail companies that *mainly* sell to other companies and organisations – that is the majority of their trade activities is trade-to-trade business within the so-called *product supply chain*. Although many large manufacturing companies may well act as wholesale retailer – for example, Associated British Foods plc (food manufacturer) and Cadbury Schweppes plc (soft drinks manufacturer) – such companies are included in category 1 type (b) below. Companies in this category/type would not normally manufacture/produce the goods/commodities they sell, but would merely facilitate the product exchange process – that is from manufacturer to supplier to retailer to customer. Such companies would include wholesale retail companies in all market sectors – from groceries to electrical commodities to household utilities.

### Category 1: Type 1(b) Manufacturing and production companies

Continuous production companies are mass production companies (normally supply focused) that manufacture commodities, extract resources and/or produce energy for either the trade (corporate) markets and/or the retail (consumer) markets, and would include for example;

- constructive industry-based companies such Ford plc (car manufacturer), Hitachi Ltd (electrical goods manufacturer), Vodafone Group plc (mobile phone manufacturer), Carlsberg UK Ltd (brewery), Diageo plc (drinks manufacturer), Associated British Foods plc (food manufacturer) and British American Tobacco plc (cigarette manufacturer),
- extractive industry-based companies such as BP plc (oil extraction and petroleum production) and UK Coal plc (coal mining and extraction),
- agrarian industry (farming and agriculture)-based companies,
- energy production and distribution industry-based companies such as Npower plc (energy supplier) and BG Group plc (gas production/distribution).

Non-continuous production companies are contract production companies (normally demand focused) that develop/construct/manufacture commodities 'on demand' or more appropriately 'on contractual agreement' and would include, for example:

- house building/property development companies (such as Barrett Developments plc and George Wimpey plc),
- aircraft development and construction companies (such as BAE Systems plc),
- engineering manufacturing companies (such as Wolseley plc), and
- shipbuilding companies (such as Harland and Wolff Heavy Industries Ltd).

## Category 2: Type 2(a) Companies with a limited flow of commodities

Limited owned commodity companies are companies that are services orientated, but nevertheless have a limited flow of owned (either purchased and/or manufactured) commodities – commodities whose legal title (property) and ownership resides with the company. Such companies would include:

- restaurants (from fast-food outlets to the traditional high street brasserie to the Michelin Star restaurants) – for example from MacDonalds through to Le Gavroche,
- public bars and night clubs – for example from Scottish and Newcastle plc Public Bars (52 throughout the UK) to Stringfellows,
- publishing and media – from Guardian Newspapers Ltd (newspaper publishing) to Pearson Publishing plc (book publishing) and BSkyB plc (satellite broadcaster).

Limited non-owned commodity companies are companies that are essentially service-based, but have a limited flow of commodities whose legal title (property) and ownership resides with a third party. Such companies would include, for example, repair and/or retail orientated companies:

- repair companies – companies that provide services related to the repair and maintenance of specific commodities/assets (e.g. local garage and/or local electrical repairs), and
- retail companies – companies that provide retail facilities such as auction houses (e.g. Sotheby's New Bond Street, London) and/or estate agencies.

## Category 2: Type 2(b) Time/space-based companies

Specific time/space companies are ones that provide identifiable and specific time facilities and/or space capacity for customers and clients. Such business types would normally provide an individualised service and would include, for example:

- hotel services companies, (such as Intercontinental hotels plc and Hilton hotels plc),
- airline services companies, (such as BA plc and KLM Royal Dutch Airlines),

- rail services companies (such as Virgin Rail Group Ltd and, GNER Holdings Ltd),
- postal services companies (such as DHL plc, Interlink plc and Post Office Ltd (owned by Royal Mail Group plc)),
- security services companies (such as Group 4 Securicor plc).

Non-specific time/space companies are companies that provide non-specific time facilities and/or space capacity for customers and clients. Such business types would generally offer fee-based services *en masse* and would include, for example:

- cinema services (such as Odeon Cinemas Ltd, UGC Cinemas Ltd),
- leisure and sport facilities (such as David Lloyd Ltd),
- localised public transport operators (such as London Underground Ltd), and
- generic (UK-wide) public transport operators (such as Stagecoach Group plc).

## Category 2: Type 2(c) Knowledge/skills-based companies

Time-based knowledge/skills companies are companies that provide specific *profession-based* knowledge/skill services – services that are normally time-orientated and fee-based (usually by the hour). Although many of these business types tend to be Limited Liability Partnerships (LLP) especially the legal, financial and architectural services organisations (such as Gosschalks (legal services), KPMG, PricewaterhouseCoopers and Ernst and Young (accounting and accounting-related services), and Gelder and Kitchen (architectural and engineering consultants)), others remain as incorporated companies (such as ChemDry UK Ltd (cleaning services company)).

Supply based knowledge/skills companies are companies that provide non-specific knowledge/skill services for customers and clients. Such services would normally be facilities/services orientated and would generally be offered on a fee and/or subscription basis *en masse*, and would include a wide range of service/business types, for example:

- internet service provider companies (such as Pipex Communications plc),
- telephone service provider companies (such as BT plc, Motorola Ltd and Orange plc),
- banking and financial services companies (from high street banking services such as NatWest plc, LloydsTSB plc and Barclays plc, to merchant bankers such as Morgan Stanley International Ltd),
- insurance and related assurance services companies (such as Norwich Union and Aviva plc), and
- pension services companies (such as Prudential plc and Legal and General plc).

## A subjective classification

As you may have already recognised, the above classification of business types/sub-types is at best subjective. For example, whilst the distinctions between type 1(a) and 1(b), between type 2(b) and 2(c), and between type 1(a) and 2(a) are undoubtedly tenuous and certainly questionable, the distinction between some of the business sub-types, for example sub-types 1(a)(i), 2(b)(i), 2(c)(i) and 2(c)(ii) is also unquestionably problematic. In addition some of the example companies cited within the business sub-types can easily be included within another business sub-type – certainly those companies that are well diversified (see earlier).

For example, consider again Tesco plc. Included in type 1(a)(i) (see above) the company is not only the UK's largest food retailer (with approximately 30% of the market share for the year 2006), it now provides a wide range of:

- non-food retail services (including brown[14] and white[15] goods),
- restaurant and café facilities,

- financial services (including loans and credit cards),
- insurance services (including car and property insurance), and
- telecoms facilities (including home, mobile and broadband facilities),

which would probably place Tesco plc in business sub-types 1(a)(i), 2(a)(i), 2(c)(i) and 2(c)(ii).

So why include the company in business sub-type 1(a)(i)? Simple – Tesco plc's market share of non-food items (all those listed above) is only a mere 7% for the year 2004.[16]

So now we have a typology within which companies are separated into two broad categories, categories which are themselves divided into five business types, each with two business sub-types, let's complete our typology by introducing the notion of transaction processing cycles and transaction processing systems.

## Contemporary transaction processing – cycles

Whatever the company business type/sub-type, within that company a number of transaction processing cycles or cycles of operation will exist, although the exact nature and character of such cycles of operation will differ from company to company, mainly due to structural and/or functional issues.

Structural issues emerge from differences in:

- management practices,
- decision-making procedures,
- operational processes, and
- levels of technology.

Functional issues emerge from differences in degrees of integration. For example, whilst in some companies the cycles of operation may be distinct and clearly identifiable, in others such cycles of operation may be combined and/or merged or amalgamated together for either:

- operational reasons – for example to make the cycles more efficient by reducing processing procedures and increase processing effectiveness, or
- financial reasons – for example to reduce costs and promote financial efficiency (and of course maximise shareholder wealth).

Clearly, whatever the precise nature and character of a company's transaction processing cycles and/or systems its underlying rationale will remain the same – to ensure the expedient, efficient and effective processing of transactions and (as a consequence) the maximisation of shareholder wealth.

So exactly what are these cycles of operation? Within a company four functional cycles of operation (see Figure 6.7) – can exist, these being:

- the revenue cycle,
- the expenditure cycle,
- the conversion cycle, and
- the management and administrative cycle.

Before we look at each of these in a little more detail, it would be useful to note that it is at the cyclical and systemic level within a company's cycles of operation and transaction processing systems that control is operationalised, at least in a functional context. We will return to this issue later in the Chapter 14.

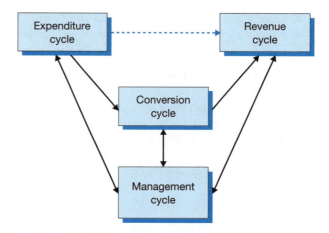

**Figure 6.7** Contemporary transaction processing cycles

## The revenue cycle

The term revenue means the earnings of a company before any costs or expenses are deducted. It includes all net sales of assets, commodities, services and/or facilities of the company together with any other revenue associated with the main operations of the business. (For our purpose we will not include dividends, interest income and/or non-operating income.)

Such revenue will result in an increase in net current assets, that is either:

- an increase in non-cash-based assets (debtor-based revenue cycles), or
- an increase in cash-based assets (non-debtor-based revenue cycles).

In general two types of corporate revenue cycles can be identified:

- debtor-based revenue cycles – these would include company-to-company credit sales and company-to-individual credit sales, and
- non-debtor-based revenue cycles – these would normally be concerned with either web-based transactions and/or EPOS-based transactions.

It is probable that:

- debtor-based revenue cycles would probably be employed by business types/sub-types 1(a)(ii), 1(b)(i), 1(b)(ii), 2(a)(ii), 2(b)(i), 2(b)(ii), 2(c)(i) and 2(c)(ii), and
- non-debtor revenue cycles would probably be employed by business types/sub-types 1(a)(i), 2(a)(i), 2(b)(i), 2(b)(ii), 2(c)(i) and 2(c)(ii).

It is however important to remember that some companies (especially well-diversified companies) may employ both alternatives depending on the service/activities being provided.

## The expenditure cycle

The term 'expenditure' (whether revenue or capital) is synonymous with the term 'cost', its purpose being to:

- acquire an asset, commodity, service, and/or
- obtain access to a facility.

Such expenditure requires the commitment of current and/or future net current assets, that is either:

- the incurrence of a liability (creditor-based expenditure cycles), and/or
- the reduction of current assets (non-creditor-based expenditure cycles).

In general, the majority of corporate expenditure cycles will be creditor-based expenditure cycles and would, for example, normally include:

- the purchase of commodities and services for production activities,
- the purchase of commodities and services for other operational activities,
- the purchase of capital assets,
- the purchase of financial securities, and
- the purchase of human resources and labour time (other than that of employees).

Non-creditor-based expenditure cycles would, for example, normally include:

- the purchase of small-value commodities and services for both production and other operations activities (normally paid in cash), and
- the purchase of employee labour time (payroll).

It is probable that all business types (and sub-types in) 1(a), 1(b), 2(a), 2(b) and 2(c) would use both creditor and non creditor cycles which would most probably co-exist as a single expenditure cycle.

## The conversion cycle

The term asset conversion means any process, procedure and/or event that results in a transformation and/or a change in the use, function, purpose, structure and/or composition of an asset to another use, function, purpose, structure and/or composition. In this definition an asset can be defined simply as anything owned by a company that has commercial value (that is, it can produce a stream of current and/or future incomes) or has a current and/or future exchange value.

Clearly then, the asset conversion cycle of operation is associated with physical modification – with a production process – with the conversion of unrelated raw materials/products/commodities into finished cohesive saleable products/commodities.

Such conversion/modification may of course vary from, for example;

- the refining of oil and the production of petroleum-based products (such as BP plc and Shell plc),
- the production/manufacture of cars (such as Ford plc),
- the construction of houses (such as Barrett Developments plc and George Wimpey plc),
- the production of brown goods (LG plc and Hitachi Ltd), and
- food and drinks manufacturing (Associated British Foods plc, Cadbury Schweppes plc and Diageo plc).

Clearly, as a part of the corporate exchange process, such a cycle of operation would exist and function as a connection between the corporate expenditure cycle and the corporate revenue cycle. As a consequence it is more than likely that some overlap in procedures and processes will exist and that considerable variation between business types/sub-types will also exist.

It is probable that business types (and sub-types in) 1(b), 2(a), 2(b) and 2(c) would utilise some form of asset conversion cycle.

## The management cycle

The management cycle is concerned not only with designing, developing, planning, programming and evaluating, but more importantly the control of business processes and procedures to ensure:

- the efficient implementation of company policy,
- the competent operation of company practices, and
- the effective utilisation of company resources.

Although the precise nature and context of each of the above system with be dependent on the company type/sub-type, for our purposes we will use the following distinction;

- fund management systems will refer to systems, procedures and processes concerned with the management of fund flows (cash and non-cash) within the business – normally at the operational and tactical management level,
- finance management systems will refer to systems, procedures and processes concerned with the management and control of financing requirements of the business – normally at the tactical and strategic level,
- asset management systems will refer to systems, procedures and processes concerned with the acquisition, retention, disposal and management of capital assets, and
- accounting management/control systems will refer to systems, procedures and processes concerned with general ledger management.

It is probable that all business types (and sub-types) would utilise some form of management and administrative cycle, although the level of importance and influence attached to each system would clearly depend on the business type/sub-type.

Although we will look at each of the systems in great detail later, for example:

- Chapter 8 will consider systems within the revenue cycle,
- Chapter 9 will consider systems within the expenditure cycle,
- Chapter 10 will consider systems within the conversion cycle, and
- Chapter 11 will consider systems within the management cycle,

it would nevertheless be useful to complete our typology and briefly consider the systems that would normally be present within each of the four cycles of operation discussed above.

## Contemporary transaction processing – systems

### Revenue cycle

Within a corporate revenue cycle of operation the following systems would normally exist:

- marketing systems,
- transportation/delivery systems, and
- receipting (sales and debtors) systems.

See Figure 6.8.

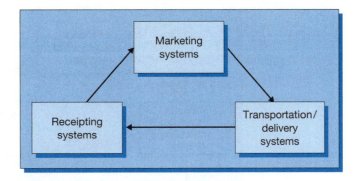

**Figure 6.8** Revenue cycle

## Expenditure cycle

Within a corporate expenditure cycle of operation the following systems would normally exist:

■ purchasing/acquisition systems,
■ receiving and inspection systems,
■ payment systems, and
■ payroll systems.

See Figure 6.9.

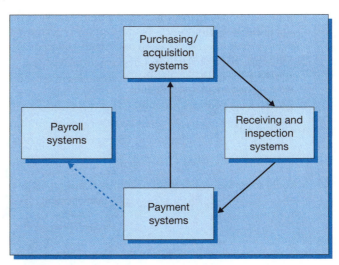

**Figure 6.9** Expenditure cycle

## Conversion cycle

Within an asset conversion cycle of operation the following systems would normally exist:

■ product development systems,
■ production planning/scheduling systems,
■ manufacturing operations systems,
■ production management systems, and
■ cost management systems.

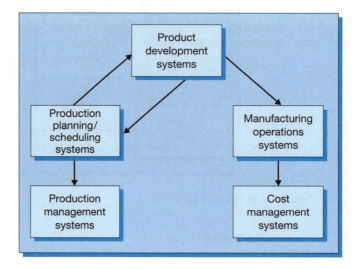

**Figure 6.10** Conversion cycle

See Figure 6.10.

## Management cycle

Within a corporate management and administrative cycle of operation the following systems would normally exist:

- fund management systems,
- finance management systems,
- asset management systems, and
- general ledger control systems.

See Figure 6.11.

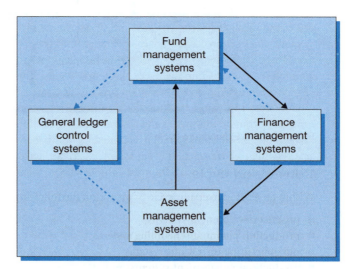

**Figure 6.11** Management cycle

## Transaction processing cycles and accounting information systems

So far we have developed a fairly comprehensive typology of transaction processing systems – a classification incorporating categories, types (and sub-types), cycles and of course systems. But, you may well ask, what is the relevance of this to accounting information systems? Before addressing this question it would perhaps be useful to revisit and reinforce two key points.

Firstly, the effective and efficient operations of a company's transaction processing systems is and perhaps always has been a significant factor in not only securing on-going business stability but, more crucially, ensuring corporate growth and possible future success. Why? Perhaps for two main reasons, although other reasons will undoubtedly exist:

- volume expansion – that is the ever-increasing volume of business transactions that companies now have to manage, and
- velocity compression – that is the growing social and economic demands to reduce transaction processing times.

Secondly, it is invariably the case that:

- it is the company type/sub-type that determines the precise nature of that company's transaction processing systems, but also
- it is the transaction processing system that determines – within certain structural and regulatory parameters/requirements – the nature, function and performance a company's accounting information system.

Remember (from Chapter 1) that an accounting information system should:

- provide users with information (a decision facilitating function), and
- support decision making and facilitate control (a decision influencing/mediating function).

Remember (also from Chapter 1) that whilst it may appear to be highly structured and closely regulated, all accounting information (in particular financial accounting statements) is politically and economically constructed. Accounting information is simply a constructed representation through which selected aspects of the exchange process can be measured, defined and legitimated (see Hines, 1988; Bryer, 1995; Cooper and Puxty, 1996). A constructed representation whose foundation resides within the data collected as a consequence of transaction events being processed within a company's transaction processing systems.

How does this work? Imagine the accounting information system as a reproduction of the company's transaction processing system – a virtual duplicate that is created using a specific rule set, one based upon generally accepted accounting concepts and conventions. That is, for data relating to a transaction event to enter – to be allowed access to a company's accounting information system – such data must comply with a specific set of rules, for example:

- data about transaction events must be expressed in financial terms – the money measurement convention,
- data about similar transaction events must be treated in the same way – the consistency convention, and
- the transaction events (which the data represents) must relate and be relevant to the company – the entity convention.

There are many other relevant examples available of how contemporary accounting concepts and conventions, such as:

- boundary rules – entity, periodicity and going concern,
- measurement rules – money measurement, historical cost, realisation, matching and accruals, duality, materiality and revenue recognition, and
- ethical rules – prudence, consistency and substance over form,

are used as the rule set to determine access to a company's accounting information system.

So what about transaction processing cycles and systems and a company's accounting information system? Within each of the cycles of operation discussed earlier – within each of the transaction processing systems identified earlier – there will exist a number of identifiable *contact points* at which:

- transaction data from individual transaction processing systems will be extracted and transferred to the accounting information system – an *exit point*, and
- transaction data from the accounting information system will be extracted and transferred to an individual transaction processing systems – an *entry point*.

Or put another way:

- an exit point is when an event is initiated within the relevant transaction processing system – that is exit from the relevant transaction processing system, and
- an entry point is when an event is initiated within the accounting information system – that is entry into the relevant transaction processing system.

An exit point will result in an accounting entry/event, whereas an entry point will result in a transaction processing event See Figure 6.12.

Do you recognise these exit points? They are the instances at which a transaction event becomes an accounting event – an entry in a company's accounting records – the point at which the bookkeeping accounting entries occur!

Consider the following examples.

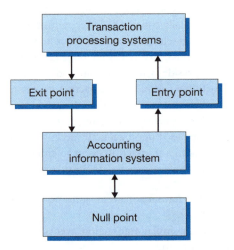

**Figure 6.12** Transaction processing systems/accounting information systems interface

## Exit point – the sale of goods/commodities on credit

Essentially a sale of goods and/or commodities on credit represents a transfer of legal title (property and possession) in exchange for a (legally enforceable) promise to pay at some future agreed time.

So, at what point does the transaction enter a company's accounting information system? When the order is received from the customer? When the goods/commodities are despatched to the customer? Or, when the invoice is despatched to the customer?

The answer is of course when the invoice is sent to the customer, which is often at the same time as the goods/commodities are despatched. It is at that point – the point at which legal title is exchanged for a future promise to pay – that the accounting entry occurs and the debtor (the legally enforceable debt) is created. This is the *contact exit point* – from the sales system within the corporate revenue cycle to the accounting information system.

We will look at how this works in more detail in Chapter 9 but for the moment it is useful to consider what the accounting entries would be.

When a debtor is created using double-entry bookkeeping traditionalists would suggest the following:

- Dr debtor account
- Cr sales.

Unfortunately, this is not strictly correct! Remember that in contemporary financial accounting there are three ledgers:

- the general ledger,
- the sales (or debtors) ledger, and
- the purchases (or creditors) ledger.

These ledgers are essentially databases – databases in which data is stored in a particular format according to particular, specific and highly structured rules. It is the general ledger from which a company's financial statements (the profit and loss account, the balance sheet, the cash flow statement) are prepared. The sales (or debtors) ledger and the purchases (or creditors) ledger are really memorandum ledgers which exist merely to store and maintain detailed information about individual debtors and creditors. However, all individual debtor and creditor balances also appear in the general ledger in total – within either the debtors control (or total) account and the creditors control (or total) account.

So the accounting entries would really be:

- Dr debtor control (or total) account
- Cr sales

in the general ledger, but also memorandum entries in the sales (or debtors) ledger in the individual debtor's account, that is:

- Dr debtor's individual account.

So, in reality, perhaps it is not double-entry bookkeeping but triple-entry bookkeeping!

## Exit point – the purchase of goods/commodities on credit

As with the above example on the sale of goods/commodities on credit, the purchase of goods and/or commodities on credit also represents a transfer of legal title (property and possession) in exchange for a (legally enforceable) promise to pay at some future agreed time.

As with the above, the creditor is recognised at the point at which legal title is exchanged for a future promise to pay: when the invoice is sent by the supplier, the accounting entry occurs and the creditor (the legally enforceable debt) is created. Again this is the *contact exit point* – from the purchases system within the corporate expenditure cycle to the accounting information system.

Again the accounting entries would be:

- Dr purchases
- Cr creditors control (or total) account

in the general ledger, but also a memorandum entry in the purchases (or creditors) ledger in the individual creditor's account, that is:

- Cr creditor's individual account.

We will look at how this works in more detail in Chapter 9.

## Exit point – payments from debtors/payments to creditors

As with the creation of a debtor and/or creditor, as some point in the future the debt will be discharged – that is payment will be received from the debtor and payment will be made to the creditor. Again these are both contact exit point events – that is the event is initiated within the relevant transaction processing system:

- for debtors – the sales and debtors system within the corporate revenue cycle, and
- for creditors – the purchases and creditors system within the corporate expenditure cycle.

When payment is received from the relevant debtor (through whatever agreed means – cash, cheque, and/or BACS[17]), the accounting entries would be:

- Dr bank
- Cr debtors control (or total) account

in the general ledger, but also a memorandum entry in the sales (or debtors) ledger in the individual debtor's account, that is:

- Cr debtor's individual account.

And as payment is made to the relevant creditor, the accounting entries would be;

- Dr creditors control account
- Cr bank

in the general ledger, but also a memorandum entry in the purchases (or creditors ) ledger in the individual creditor's account, that is:

- Dr creditor's individual account.

Clearly, payment, either received in full from the debtor and/or paid in full to the creditor, will result in the debt being (fully and) legally discharged!

## Entry point – debtors

As suggested earlier, a contact entry point occurs when an event is initiated within the accounting information system – that is entry into the relevant transaction processing system. Such a contact entry point will result in a transaction processing event.

Consider for example the case of a debtor who has failed correctly to discharge their outstanding debt. Clearly any sale on credit would be made under pre-agreed terms of delivery and payment – for example payment within 30 days of the invoice date. Failure to pay will require an outstanding debt reminder being despatched to the debtor. After all the debt cannot simply continue to exist. Not only would that constitute bad financial management practice and severely impact on corporate cash flow – especially where the levels of such debtors are high – the continuing existence of such a debtor within a company's accounting information system would (where the debt appears unlikely to ever be paid) also contravene the prudence concept/convention.

So, how would a debtor reminder be generated? A simple review (and increasingly automatic review) of the debtors accounts within the sales (debtors) ledger (within the accounting information system) would of course reveal any outstanding balances – not only the financial amount but also the time period that such a debt has been outstanding. It is based on the information that:

- any reminder would be despatched to relevant debtors, and/or
- any further transactions with the debtor would be prevented until the outstanding debt has been fully discharged, or if the debtor had a trading account, the balance of the account had been sufficiently reduced to allow further trading and, where necessary,
- any legal action for the recovery of the legally enforceable debt would be initiated, especially where a debtor has failed to pay despite a number of *polite* reminders.

## Null contact points

There will also be so-called null contact points. A *null point* occurs when transaction event data is not extracted and transferred between the accounting information system and an individual transaction processing system, but extracted and transferred either:

- within and/or between transaction processing cycles – for example between a number of transaction processing systems within the same transaction processing cycle, or between a number of transaction processing systems within different transaction processing cycles,
- within the accounting information system – for example between individual accounts as an accounting adjustment/amendment/transfer.

An example of the former (transfers between transaction processing system) would be the transfer of stock from work-in-progress stock to finished goods stock.

Examples of the latter (transfers within the accounting information system) would be:

- the creation of provisions – for example provision for depreciation and/or provision for doubtful debts,
- the creation of reserves – for example appropriation of revenue profit to a specific asset reserve,
- the writing off of irrecoverable debts, and/or
- the correction of accounting errors.

Recognise this latter group? In a financial accounting context these would constitute journalised entries and/or adjustments.

## Transaction processing cycles – control

Clearly the importance of operational efficiency and effectiveness within a company's transaction processing systems cannot be overstated; nor can the need for control, more specifically internal control. Internal control can be defined as management processes designed to provide reasonable assurance that the objectives of reliable financial reporting, effective and efficient operations, and compliance with laws and regulations are achieved.

Such internal control includes all procedures, processes and protocols, financial and otherwise, established by the management in order to ensure:

- business activities of the company are undertaken in an orderly and efficient manner,
- compliance with management policies and adherence to extant regulatory requirements,
- the safeguarding of all assets, and
- as far as possible, the accuracy and completeness of accounting records and financial information.

Securing effective internal control requires:

- an understanding and appreciation of the *control environment*,
- an understanding of relevant *control activities*,
- an understanding, identification and *analysis of the risk*,
- an assessment of *information and communication* channels both within the company and within the environment, and finally
- an appreciation and understanding of *monitoring* transaction processes.

We will discuss/evaluate each of the above issues in more detail in Chapter 14.

## Transaction processing systems and the Data Protection Act 1988

The Data Protection Act 1998[18] (DPA 1998) protects personal information held about individuals and regulates the processing of data relating to individuals or, more appropriately, data subjects.[19]

DPA 1998 applies to information held on or obtained from computers and to certain manual records. It gives rights to the individual data subject and imposes responsibilities on:

- the individual data subjects,
- the organisations holding the data, and
- the employees of those organisations who use the information.

DPA 1998 implements part of the European Convention on Human Rights. It applies only to information about individuals (such as names, addresses, personal reference numbers, income, entitlement to benefits). It does not apply to non-personal data, such as that relating to businesses and limited companies. Remember DPA 1998 only protects personal data about people who are alive.

DPA 1998 applies to every company/organisation that maintains lists, databases or files (paper or electronic) containing personal details of:

- staff – for example personnel information such as home address and date of birth,
- clients – for example account details, agreements, contact details and BACS payment details,
- customers – for example account details, contact details, credit card details, and/or
- other related parties.

All companies are required to:

- comply with the provisions of DPA 1998,
- comply with guidelines and interpretations of DPA 1998 issued by the Information Commissioner, and
- be registered with the Information Commissioner.

Failure to do so can result in:

- the imposition of substantial fines, and
- if deemed appropriate by the Information Commissioner, closure of the company/organisation.

DPA 1988 gives effect in UK law to EC Directive 95/46/EC and it replaces the Data Protection Act 1984: it was brought into force on 1 March 2000.

DPA 1998 provides the following definitions:

- *Data subject* – an individual who is the subject of the personal information (data) and who must be living for the provisions of the Act to apply.
- *Data controller* – a person who determines the purposes for which, and the manner in which, personal data are, or are to be, processed. (This may be an individual or an organisation, and the processing may be carried out jointly or in common with other persons.)
- *Data processor* – a person who processes data on behalf of a data controller. However the responsibility for correct processing under DPA 1998 remains with the data controller.

DPA 1998 also contains eight data protection principles which are designed to ensure data is properly handled:

- First principle – personal data shall be processed fairly and lawfully.
- Second principle – personal data shall be obtained only for one or more specified and lawful purposes, and shall not be further processed in any manner incompatible with that purpose or those purposes.
- Third principle – personal data shall be adequate, relevant and not excessive in relation to the purpose or purposes for which they are processed.
- Fourth principle – personal data shall be accurate and, where necessary, kept up-to-date.
- Fifth principle – personal data processed for any purpose or purposes shall not be kept for longer than is necessary for that purpose or those purposes.
- Sixth principle – personal data shall be processed in accordance with the rights of data subjects under the Act.
- Seventh principle – appropriate technical and organisational measures shall be taken against unauthorised or unlawful processing of personal data and against accidental loss or destruction of, or damage to, personal data.
- Eighth principle – personal data shall not be transferred to a country or territory outside the European Economic Area, unless that country or territory ensures an adequate level of protection of the rights and freedoms of data subjects in relation to the processing of personal data

DPA 1998 also gives rights to individuals in respect of personal data held about them by others. The rights are:

- right to subject access,[20]
- right to prevent processing likely to cause damage or distress,[21]
- right to prevent processing for the purposes of direct marketing,[22]
- rights in relation to automated decision taking,[23]
- right to take action for compensation if the individual suffers damage by any contravention of the Act by the data controller,[24] and
- right to take action to rectify, block, erase or destroy inaccurate data.[25]

Further details on the provisions of the Data Protection Act 1998 are available on the website accompanying this text.

In addition, the complete text of the Data Protection Act 1998 is available @ www.opsi.gov.uk/ACTS/acts1998/19980029.htm, with the UK Information Commissioners guidance available @ www.ico.gov.uk/what_we_cover/data_protection.aspx.

## Concluding comments

Contemporary transaction processing systems are socially, politically and economically significant. Not only do they play a leading role in ensuring that the exchange process at the heart of contemporary wealth maximisation is efficient and effective, they are without doubt a crucial factor in the search for corporate sustainability and indeed future success.

Whilst the nature, structure and functional efficiency of a company's transaction processing systems will invariably be the product of a enormous diversity of interrelated and interconnected characteristics and qualities, some commonality between the vast range of wealth maximising companies does nonetheless exist, as suggested by the inductive typology present in the main discussion.

## Key points and concepts

Contemporary transaction processing –
   categories
Contemporary transaction processing –
   cycles
Contemporary transaction processing –
   systems
Contemporary transaction processing –
   types
Control activities
Control environment
Conversion cycle
Data Protection Act 1998
Entry point
Exit point

Expenditure cycle
Funding cycle
Knowledge/skills-based companies
Management cycle
Manufacturing and production
   companies
Monitoring
Null point
Purposive context
Retail and distribution companies
Revenue cycle
Time/space-based companies
Value chain
Value cycle

## References

Bryer, R.A. (1995) 'A political economy of SSAP 22: Accounting for goodwill', *British Accounting Review*, 27, pp. 283–310.

Cooper, C. and Puxty A. (1996) 'On the proliferation of accounting (his)tories', *Critical Perspectives on Accountancy*, 7, pp. 285–313.

Davis, J.R., Alderman, C.W. and Robinson, L.A. (1990) *Accounting Information Systems: A Cycle Approach*, Wiley, New York.

Hines, R.D. (1988) 'Financial accounting: in communicating reality we construct reality', *Accounting, Organisations, and Society*, 13(3), pp. 256–261.

Porter, M.E. (1985) *Competitive Advantage: Creating and Sustaining Superior Performance*, The Free Press, New York.

Starreveld, R.W., De Mare, B. and Joels, E. (1998) *Bestuurlijke Informatieverzorging*, Samson, Alphen aan den Rijn.

Vaassen, E. (2002) *Accounting Information Systems – A Managerial Approach*, Wiley, Chichester.

Wilkinson, J.W., Cerullo, M.L., Raval, V. and Wong-On-Wing, B. (2001) *Accounting Information Systems*, Wiley, New York.

## Bibliography

Bodnar, G.H. and Hopwood, W.S. (2001) *Accounting Information Systems*, Prentice Hall, London.

Gelinas, U.J., Sutton, S.G. and Hutton, J. (2005) *Accounting Information Systems*, South Western, Cincinnati, Ohio.

Hall, J.A. (2004) *Accounting Information Systems*, South Western, Cincinnati, Ohio.

Lucy, T. (2000) *Management Information System*, Letts, London.

Mosgrove, S.A. Simkin, M.G. and Bagranoff, N.A. (2001) *Core Concepts of Accounting Information Systems*, Wiley, New York.

## Websites

The following websites may be helpful in providing:

- an insight into more accounting-related discussion of transaction processing systems, and
- practical examples of problems that may occur if transaction processing systems fail.

www.accaglobal.com
(Chartered Association of Certified Accountants)

www.cimaglobal.com
(Chartered Institute of Management Accountants)

www.ft.com
(Financial Times)

www.economist.com
(Economist)

www.guardian.co.uk
(Guardian)

www.accountingweb.co.uk
(General accounting website)

www.bbc.co.uk/news
(BBC Online)

www.vnunet.com
(VNUNET)

www.theregister.com
(The Register)

## Self-review questions

1. What are the key features of contemporary transaction processing?
2. Distinguish between transaction processing cycles and transaction processing systems.
3. What is meant by the term 'purposive context'?
4. What is meant by, and what are the key differences between, each contemporary transaction processing type/sub-type?
5. What transaction processing systems are normally found within a company's expenditure cycle?

6. What transaction processing systems are normally found within a company's revenue cycle?
7. Distinguish between the following contact points: exit point, entry point and null point.
8. Explain the main requirements for the securing of effective control within a transaction processing system?
9. In relation to the Data Protection Act 1998 define the following terms:
   - data subject,
   - data controller, and
   - data processor.
10. Describe the eight key principles contained within the Data Protection Act 1998.

## Questions and problems

### Question 1

Ergon plc was a Cambridge-based UK listed company. During the late 1990s the company produced digital positioning equipment for the global transportation sector, especially the merchant navy. The company's products were sold throughout Europe, North America, Australia and Canada, and were widely regarded as the best in the market. Indeed during the period 1993 to 2003 the company's digital positioning equipment consistently won high praise for both its design and capabilities.

In January 2004, however, Ergon plc went into liquidation, with reported debts of £230m. In March 2005, after extensive investigation, the company receivers, Hopwind LLP, published its findings on the failure of Ergon plc. The report suggested that the principal cause of Ergon plc's failure had been inadequate internal control within the company's revenue cycle operations, in particular the management of debtor payments.

#### Required

Describe the primary function of a revenue cycle for a company such as Ergon plc and explain how a lack of internal control could lead to the eventual collapse of the company.

### Question 2

Louis P. Lou is managing director of Ann de-Pandy Ltd an established female lingerie retail company located in the north and the south-west of England. The company has been operating successfully for many years with the period between 1998 and 2004 being one of exceptional growth both in market share (customer numbers and sales) and overall profitability.

Over the past three years the company has continued to enhance its accounting information system and has recently upgraded its computer network, and will from August 2006 introduce an extensive web-based e-commerce facility. Louis P. Lou is however concerned that the accounting information system development – especially the development of a web-based e-commerce facility could potentially reduce the company's level of control over its business operations.

#### Required

As the company's systems accountant prepare a brief report for the managing director of Ann de-Pandy Ltd addressing the managing director's concerns.

### Question 3

Lantern plc is a growing UK company which produces a range of biochemical products for the agricultural sector in the UK and the USA. Because of recent problems regarding the purchasing of raw chemical products, you have been asked by the managing director to make a presentation to the Board of Directors entitled *The importance of contemporary transaction processing system in wealth maximising companies.*

### Required

Draft out the main points of the presentation.

## Question 4

The Data Protection Act 1998 contains eight data protection principles which are designed to ensure data is properly handled. The data protection principles are listed on page 257.

### Required

Critically evaluate the eight data protection principles contained in the Data Protection Act 1998 and explain their relevance to a company that stores personal data on clients and debtors.

## Assignments

## Question 1

*Microsoft Engineer Charged With Fraud – FBI says he resold $9 million in software, bought cars, jewellery, and yacht.*

*Sales of Microsoft's high-end software were brisk last year – at least for one employee who was charged on Wednesday 11 December 2002 with illegally pilfering and selling $9 million worth of it for his own profit.*

*Daniel Feussner, a mid-level Microsoft engineer who headed up one of Microsoft's .Net technology projects, was arrested after an FBI probe uncovered his scheme. Feussner allegedly ordered products through Microsoft's internal purchasing programme and sold them on the street. According to a complaint filed a day before his arrest with the US District Court in Seattle, federal authorities say Feussner used his earnings to acquire a lavish car collection, a $172,000 yacht, expensive watches and diamond jewellery. He is charged with 15 counts of fraud and could face a maximum of five years in prison and a $250,000 fine for each charge, according to a spokesman for the US Attorney's Office in Seattle.*

*Microsoft released a statement on the matter, raising an issue that prompted some analysts to say that most companies should worry about internal control. 'We take employee theft very seriously and realize the effects it can have on the value we provide our customers and shareholders,' it said in the written statement. 'We have a number of internal measures in place to identify theft and work very closely with the appropriate authorities on these matters.'*

*While working as a manager of a speech-recognition project out of Microsoft's .Net development group, among other positions, Feussner used internal purchase orders to buy high-end server software, which he then sold for cut-rate prices while keeping the proceeds, the complaint alleges. Orders passed through a New York software vendor called ClientLogic, which would mail products to Feussner. He then sold the software out of a Seattle-area parking lot for cash, as well as through a middleman company called Cybershop Inn, court records indicate. Some 1700 products filtered through the scam, including development software, and copies of Microsoft's Windows operating system, beginning in late 2001, authorities said. The FBI said that Feussner's arrest is part of a larger probe into illegal use of Microsoft's internal purchasing programme. Matt Berger, IDG News Service, 13 December 2002, Available @ www.pcworld.com/news*

*Post Script – Microsoft Engineer Charged With Fraud – found dead*

*A former Microsoft manager facing federal fraud charges dies unexpectedly at a Bellevue hospital while out on bail. The circumstances surrounding the death of Daniel Feussner, 32, remain under investigation. Following the submission of Daniel Feussner's death certificate to Assistant US District Attorney's office in Seattle, prosecutors closed the case. Ian Ith, Seattle Times, 17 February 2003, Available @ www.seattletimes.nwsource.com*

### Required

(a) Describe the main functional cycles of operation that may exist in a company such as Microsoft Inc.
(b) Critically assess the key objectives of control within the transaction processing cycles of a company such as Microsoft Inc.
(c) Based on the information above, explain:
- what control activities appear to have failed,
- why the control activities appear to have failed, and
- how Daniel Feussner took advantage of such failures.

## Question 2

*The Enron collapse*

*Enron left behind $15bn of debts, its shares become worthless, and 20,000 workers around the world lost their jobs. Many banks were exposed to the firm, from lending money and trading with it. JP Morgan admitted to $900m of exposure, and Citigroup to nearly $800m. Former high-ranking Merrill Lynch bankers have been charged with fraud in connection with Enron transactions. Andersen, which failed to audit the Enron books correctly, collapsed with the loss of 7500 jobs in the US, and 1500 in the UK. BBC News Online, 08 July 2004, Available @ www.bbc.co.uk/news*

*Ebbers guilty of Worldcom fraud*

*Former Worldcom chief executive Bernie Ebbers has been convicted of conspiracy and fraud in connection with the 2002 collapse of the telecoms giant. Mr Ebbers, 63, who is to appeal against the verdict, was also found guilty of seven counts of filing false documents. Shareholders lost about $180bn (£94bn) in Worldcom's collapse – the largest bankruptcy in US history – and 20,000 workers lost their jobs.*

*Mr Ebbers could face up to 85 years in prison when he is sentenced on 13 June 2005.*

*Worldcom emerged from bankruptcy last year and is now known as MCI. A federal jury in Manhattan had spent eight days deliberating before returning their verdicts. BBC News Online, 15 March 2005, Available @ www.bbc.co.uk/news*

### Required

Whilst very different companies, both the Enron Inc. and Worldcom Inc. collapses have significant similarities. The source of their respective failures rests almost entirely on a lack of control.

Research the above corporate collapses and answer the following:

(a) What were the key objectives of control within Enron Inc. and Worldcom Inc.?
(b) What control activities appear to have failed in Enron Inc. and why did the control activities appear to have failed?
(c) What control activities appear to have failed in Worldcom Inc. and why did the control activities appear to have failed?
(d) How have the Enron Inc. collapse and the Worldcom Inc. collapse affected:
- contemporary notions of control (especially internal control), and
- the regulatory framework managing/controlling those responsible/accountable for the existence of internal control/corporate governance

## Chapter endnotes

[1] The terms 'reflex' and 'reflexivity' can be defined in many ways, for example an involuntary action and/or reaction, and/or an automatic response to an external stimulus/input, and/or an involuntary movement or response.

[2] Porter (1985) identified 10 cost drivers related to value chain activities:

- economies of scale,
- learning,
- capacity utilisation,
- linkages among activities,
- interrelationships among business units,
- degree of vertical integration,
- timing of market entry,
- firm's policy of cost or differentiation,
- geographic location, and
- institutional factors.

[3] Porter (1985) identified several drivers of uniqueness:

- policies and decisions,
- linkages among activities,
- timing,
- location,
- interrelationships,
- learning,
- integration,
- scale, and
- institutional factors.

[4] This typology is adapted and extended from Starreveld *et al.* (1998) after Vaassen (2002).

[5] The FTSE 100 is made up of the UK's 100 largest companies by market capitalisation, representing approximately 80% of the UK market. It is used extensively as a basis for investment products, such as derivatives and exchange-traded funds, and is the recognised measure of the UK financial markets. The FTSE 250 is made up of mid-capitalised companies, representing approximately 18% of UK market capitalisation. The FTSE 350 is made up of the UK's large capitalisation and mid-capitalisation companies (FTSE 100 + FTSE 250 indices).

[6] An inductive approach is when the specific observations are used to determine a rule and/or relationship. Consequently an inductive approach to classification is often called a *bottom-up* approach because using such an approach a classification is derived from specific observations – that is generalisations are developed from specific facts.

[7] A deductive approach is when the rule is given first and is then followed by examples of the rule. Consequently a deductive approach to classification is often called a *top-down* approach because using such an approach a classification is developed from generalised assumptions – that is specific conclusions from generalised assumptions.

[8] Although the term 'company' is used throughout this discussion on contemporary transaction processing categories, types, cycles and systems, such discussion may well also apply to other organisational configurations.

[9] See www.hbosplc.com/investors/includes/05-03-02_RNS.pdf.

[10] See www.tesco.com/corporateinfo.

[11] See http://lgen.client.shareholder.com/downloads/2004_Full_Year_Results.pdf.

[12] *Quod erat demonstrandum* meaning (in English) 'which was to be shown'.

[13] Amazon.co.uk is the trading name for Amazon.com International Sales, Inc. and Amazon Services Europe SARL. Both companies are subsidiaries of Amazon.com, the online retailer of products that inform, educate, entertain and inspire. The Amazon group now has online stores in the USA, Germany, France, Japan and Canada. Amazon.co.uk has its origins in an independent online store, Bookpages, which was established in 1996 and acquired by Amazon.com in early 1998.

[14] The term used to describe appliances such as computers, televisions, radios and other home electronics. The terminology originates from the time when many televisions and radios had wood or fake wood cabinets.

[15] The term used to describe large appliances such as refrigerators, washers and dryers. The terminology was derived from the standard white colour of these appliances that existed until recent years.

[16] http://www.tescocorporate.com.

[17] Bank Automated Clearance System – allows for the electronic transfer of monies into bank accounts.

[18] Further details on the provisions of the Data Protection Act 1998 are available on the website accompanying this text www.pearsoned.co.uk/boczko.

In addition, the complete text of the Data Protection Act 1998 is available @ www.opsi.gov.uk/ACTS/acts1998/19980029.htm, with the UK Information Commissioners guidance available @ www.ico.gov.uk/what_we_cover/data_protection.aspx.

[19] See the main text below for a definition of a data subject.

[20] Data Protection Act 1998 s7, s8 and s9.

[21] Data Protection Act 1998 s10.

[22] Data Protection Act 1998 s11.

[23] Data Protection Act 1998 s12.

[24] Data Protection Act 1998 s13.

[25] Data Protection Act 1998 s12(a), s14 and s62.

# Data[1] management, data processing and databases: storage and conversion

## Introduction

*Data are worthless . . . but information is priceless!* (Anon)

The purpose of a data processing system, in particular a transaction-based data processing system, is to ensure the accurate conversion/transformation[2] of data into information. Whilst such a conversion/transformation can of course be accomplished using a wide variety of methodologies and an ever-expanding range of processing technologies, such a conversion/transformation would invariably involve a number of integrated activities/functions, these being:

■ a development function – for the creation of data records/data files to act as a repository of data or to store data;
■ a maintenance function – for the amendment of, addition to, and/or deletion of data records/data files held within the data store;
■ a retrieval function – for the interrogation and manipulation of data records/data files held within the data store;
■ a disposal (or archiving) function – for the removal of data records/data files from the data store (subject to any extant legislative restrictions); and
■ a management function – for the coordination and control of the above development, maintenance, retrieval and disposal functions.

Commencing with a brief review of the nature of data and data management, this chapter explores a range of issues related to:

■ data processing,
■ data storage,
■ data flow analysis, for example:
   ● dataflow diagrams,
   ● entity-relationship diagrams,
   ● systems/document flowcharts,
   ● decision tables, and
   ● organisational coding systems/charts of account, and
   ● databases – in particular relational databases.

## Learning outcomes

By the end of this chapter, the reader should be able to;

- explain the contextual importance of data management,
- distinguish between and critically evaluate the effectiveness of alternative types of data processing,
- describe the main aspects of a file orientated approach and a data orientated approach,
- describe the main components of a database, and
- critically evaluate the relevance and usefulness of a range of data analysis techniques.

## Data management

As suggested earlier, data are worthless . . . but information is priceless. To be useful, data requires processing. More importantly, it requires processing in an organised and controlled manner. Such processing – whether it is manual-based processing or computer-based processing, or indeed a combination[3] (we will look at these in a little more detail later in this chapter), would normally comprise of a number of mutually interdependent stages, these being:

- data selection,
- data conversion,
- data capture,
- data input,
- data storage,
- data maintenance,
- data processing, and
- data output (or more appropriately information generation).

Let's have a look at each of these stages in a little more detail.

### Data selection

The term data selection can be defined as a process of filtering or, more precisely, a process of determining the appropriateness and relevancy of data. Such data selection would normally be based on pre-determined criteria as necessitated by end user needs/requirements, for example:

- the content of the data,
- the structure/format of the data, or
- the context/relevance of the data.

Consider the following:

*On 28 July 2007, KLU Ltd, a UK-based manufacturing company, received an invoice from HKL plc, a UK-based supplier, for products that were not received until 3 August 2007. KLU Ltd's year end is 31 July 2007. Because the products were not received until 3 August 2007, the invoice would not be relevant for 2006/07, but would be relevant for 2007/08.*

## Data conversion

Data conversion can be defined as a process or group of processes which convert(s) data from one data format to another. Data conversion is usually necessary where the data is relevant but presented in a structure/format that is inconsistent with the requirements.

Consider the following:

*On 30 March 2007, MGA Ltd, a UK-based retail company, received an invoice from GHF GmbH,[4] a German-based supplier, for services received during February 2007. MCA Ltd's year end in 31 March 2007. It is likely that the invoice received from GHF GmbH would be priced in euros. Consequently before the invoice can be processed the monetary value of the invoice would need to be converted to sterling.*

## Data capture

Data capture can be defined as the acquisition of data. Where data is selected for processing it is important to ensure all such data is processed. Data capture is therefore often considered to be a controlling process/function designed to ensure the full and complete processing of all selected data.

Note: In many data processing systems, data selection, data conversion and data capture are viewed as a single stage.

## Data input

Data input can be defined as the entry of data into a processing system. Broadly speaking, there are two types of data input:

- physical data input, and
- non-physical data input.

### Physical input

Physical data input is data input in which the source of the data is hard copy document. Such input is normally associated with offline data entry and is generally used in batch processing – that is where data are collected perhaps over a period of time before being processed.

Examples of such physical input/batch processing would be:

- time-cards completed by individual employees on a daily basis, which are then collected by payroll personnel and used to calculate individual employee weekly wages; or
- invoices received on a daily basis from product suppliers/service providers which are collected and processed for payment at the end of a week.

We will look at batch processing in more detail later in the chapter.

### Non-physical input

Non-physical data input is data input in which the source of the data is not a hard copy document. Such input is normally associated with online data entry. Such non-physical data input is often referred to as paperless data input or virtual data input.

There are two types of non-physical input, these being:

- automated non-physical input, or
- manual non-physical input.

### Automated non-physical input

Automated non-physical input is non-physical input which requires no human intervention, an example of which would be digital data input using Radio Frequency IDentification (RFID) technologies and/or chip and PIN technologies.

The benefit of such input systems it that input data can be encrypted at source.

### Manual non-physical input

Manual non-physical based input is non-physical input which requires human intervention and can be either:

- manual data capture/data entry – for example, keyboard-based data input[5] using web-based ordering/purchasing, or
- semi-manual/semi-automatic data capture/data entry – for example, optical character recognition (OCR) data input.[6]

Perhaps somewhat unsurprisingly, for many business/accounting related transactions, such manual non-physical data input has become the norm.

## Data storage

Data storage can be defined as the structured accumulation of data.

Within manual-based processing such data storage would perhaps be limited to physical paper-based systems, for example a hard copy file system. Pre-computer, data storage also used paper tape and punch cards.

Within computer-based processing, such data storage could be:

- magnetic storage – using different patterns of magnetisation on a magnetically coated surface to store data;
- semiconductor storage – using semiconductor-based integrated circuits to store data;
- optical disc storage – using tiny pits etched on the surface of a circular disc to store data; data are read by illuminating the surface with a laser diode and observing the reflection; and/or
- magneto-optical disc storage – using optical disc storage in which the magnetic state on a ferromagnetic surface stores data; the data are read optically and written by combining magnetic and optical methods.

There are many future data storage technologies in development, perhaps the most promising being:

- holographic storage – using crystals or photopolymers to store data, and
- molecular storage – using electrically charged polymers to store data.

## Data maintenance

Data maintenance can be defined as the preservation of data integrity, and generally involves the development of processes and procedures that not only ensure the correctness, accuracy and validity of all stored data, but more importantly maintains the relevance of all stored data. As such, data maintenance processes and procedures would be concerned with monitoring and controlling access to stored data – in particular authorising access related to the addition, deletion, amendment and/or removal of data from the data store.

## Data processing

Data processing can be defined as any process and/or procedure, or series of processes and/or procedures, that converts data into information.

We will look at two alternative approaches to data processing in more detail later in this chapter.

## Data output

Data output can be defined as the exit of data out of a processing system. Broadly speaking, there are two types of data output:

- physical output, and
- non-physical output.

### Physical output

Physical data output is produced in the form of a hard copy document – for example, a debtor invoice, or an employee pay slip.

Whilst historically physical data output was regarded as the norm, in contemporary computer-based processing – especially computer-based accounting information systems – such physical data output is perhaps now the exception rather than the rule and is becoming increasingly rare day by day owing to cost and efficiency factors.

### Non-physical output

Non-physical data output is data output in the form of a virtual (and increasingly) web-based document. For many business/accounting-related transactions such non-physical output has become increasingly the norm; a contemporary example of which would be providing customer statements/invoices using a secure password protected website.

## Data: the need for structure

In a literal sense, the term data[7] means that which is given, however in a more general context, the term data (sometimes referred to as data element) is often used to mean a representation of facts, concepts or instructions in a formal and organised manner, more specifically as a representation of the attributes of an entity. So what is an entity . . . and what are attributes?

Put simply, an entity can be defined as something that possesses a distinct and separate existence, though not necessarily a material or physical existence. For example, an entity can be:

- an object – for example, a product/service, or
- a person – for example, a customer/client or supplier/provider, or
- an event – for example, the sale of a product or the provision of a service,

An attribute can be defined as a characteristic of an entity, that is:

- the value or cost of a product/service,
- the location of a product supplier/service provider, and/or
- the name of a customer/client.

When data are collected they need to be stored and maintained. Whilst there are a number of alternative media that can be used some are more efficient than others. For example:

- in a manual-based system/process the storage medium would more than likely be a physical storage medium – for example, a paper file-based facility or a microfiche/microfilm-based facility,[8] whereas
- in a computer-based system/process such a medium could be a virtual storage medium – for example, a digital file-based facility.

In terms of storage[9] structure, data storage can categorised as either:

■ random data storage, or
■ organised data storage.

Random data storage, perhaps unsurprisingly, means data storage without any predictable or systematic pattern. Such data storage is designed to allow data to be:

■ stored in any location, and/or
■ accessed in any order,

with all storage locations being equally accessible.

Organised data storage means data storage with a predictable and systematic pattern. Such data storage is designed to allow data to be stored and/or accessed in a structured pre-determined order – whether sequentially or hierarchically. Although some virtual storage media use a random storage structure for the purposes of temporarily storing data and/or processing instructions,[10] the vast majority of storage media (both physical and virtual) use an organised storage structure for the purposes of permanent data storage. Why?

Put simply, using an organised data storage structure – whatever the storage medium used – provides for a more effective maintenance of data records/data files: for example, the creation, deletion and/or amendment to data records/data files and a more efficient management of such file changes such as the verification, coordination, validation, integration and control of data records, whether such records are in data files or data tables (or indeed data sets).

So what types of organised data storage structures are there? Organised data storage can take several approaches, perhaps the two most common approaches being:

■ data storage using a file orientated approach (or the applications approach), and
■ data storage using a data orientated approach (or the database approach).

## File orientated approach

A file orientated approach (sometimes referred to as a flat file approach) is based on a simple flat structure in which data files are 'owned' by particular application specific groups within a company/organisation, usually with such groups being able to dictate, for example:

■ the nature and structure of data capture procedures,
■ the content and structure of the data records/data files,
■ the timing of data maintenance issues, and
■ the nature and structure of data retrieval operations.

See Figure 7.1.

Before we look at the organisation of a file orientated approach, it is useful to consider how data would be structured using such an approach.

Within a file orientated approach, data would normally be stored within data files. A data file can be defined as an organised collection of data records, with a data record being a group or collection of data fields/data elements.

A data field can be defined as a specific area/portion of a data record allocated for a specific data element and a data element[11] can be defined as a stored attribute or stored characteristic. It is the term 'data element' that is often abbreviated to the term 'data'.

Consider the following:

*LKT plc is a Newcastle-based manufacturing company. The company sells its products worldwide and currently has 25,000 customers in 72 countries.*

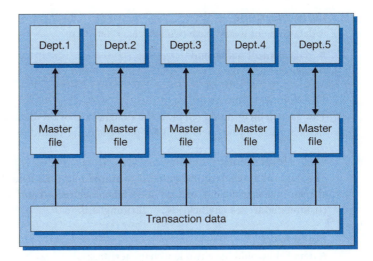

**Figure 7.1** File orientated system

*The record layout for each customer contains 99 characters, as follows:*

| *Field* | *Data element* | *Characters* |
|---|---|---|
| 1. | Customer reference number | 01–05 |
| 2. | Customer name | 06–21 |
| 3. | Customer address – street | 22–33 |
| 4. | Customer address – city | 34–43 |
| 5. | Customer address – postcode/zip code | 44–50 |
| 6. | Customer address – country | 51–52 |
| 7. | Opening balance | 53–60 |
| 8. | Transaction type | 61–68 |
| 9. | Transaction date | 69–74 |
| 10. | Transaction reference | 75–83 |
| 11. | Transaction amount | 84–91 |
| 12. | Closing balance | 92–99 |

*The current customer record for Potremic Inc is as follows:*

| *Field* | *Data element* | *Data* |
|---|---|---|
| 1. | Customer reference number | 18823 |
| 2. | Customer name | Potremic Inc |
| 3. | Customer address – street | 234 35th Street |
| 4. | Customer address – city | Birmingham |
| 5. | Customer address – post code/zip code | 35260 |
| 6. | Customer country | 13 |
| 7. | Opening balance | 1578.90 |
| 8. | Transaction type | Cr Sale |
| 9. | Transaction date | 050507 |
| 10. | Transaction reference | 98676 |
| 11. | Transaction amount | 1300.00 |
| 12. | Closing balance | 2878.90 |

### Data element

A data element would have two key characteristics:

- data element name, and
- data element value.

## Data element name

The data element name refers to the designation of the data. In the above example, the data element name of, say, field 4 of LKT plc's customer record is . . . customer address – city.

## Data element value

The data value refers to the actual data stored in a data field. In the above example the data element value of field 4 of LKT plc's customer record for the customer Potremic Inc (the customer address – city field) is . . . Birmingham.

### Data field

A data field would have two key characteristics:

- field length, and
- data type.

## Field length

The field length of a data field refers to the number of continuous positions (or characters) required within a particular data field to store a specific data element type. In the above example the field length of field 7 of LKT plc's customer record is 8 positions (or characters).

## Data type

The data type refers to the class or category of data stored in a particular data field. Such data types can vary from:

- an alphabetic data type – that is alphabetic characters only (e.g. a name),
- a numeric data type – that is numeric characters only (e.g. a customer reference number),
- an alpha-numeric data type – that is a combination of alphabetic and numeric characters (e.g. a customer address),
- a time and/or date numeric type data – that is a point in time data (e.g. 050507 (5 May 2007)),
- value data – that is a numeric value using either a fixed or floating decimal point (e.g. £1300.00), to
- a raw type data – that is graphic and/or audio/visual data.

In the above example, the data type of each of the 12 field's of LKT plc's customer record is as follows:

Field    Data type
  1.     Numeric type data
  2.     Alphabetic type data
  3.     Combined numeric and alphabetic type data
  4.     Alphabetic type data
  5.     Combined numeric and alphabetic type data[12]
  6.     Numeric type data
  7.     Numeric type data – (fixed decimal point)
  8.     Alphabetic type data
  9.     Numeric type data – (date type data)
 10.     Numeric type data

11.    Numeric type data – (fixed decimal point)
12.    Numeric type data – (fixed decimal point)

### Data record

As suggested earlier, a data record can be defined as a group or collection of data fields/data elements. In the above example, the data record for Potremic Inc is the complete customer record containing all 12 data fields and all 99 data characters.

### Data file

A data file is an organised collection of data records. In the above example, one type of data file would be a data file containing all 25,000 records of each of the customers of LKT plc. Such a customer record data file would – as we will see – be considered a master file.

Within a data file, data records can be organised sequentially or non-sequentially.

Whereas a sequentially ordered file is a file in which data records are stored in an organised manner according to a specific data record, for example debtor records in a debtor file may be organised in debtor number order or debtor name, a non-sequentially order file is a file in which data records are stored in a random unorganised manner.

We will return to the issue of sequential/non-sequential data files later in this chapter.

So, are there different types of data files? Yes there are! In general, within a file orientated approach, two specific categories/levels of files would be used, these being:

■ primary files or source files – because such files contain original source data derived from the system environment, or
■ secondary files or derivative files – because such files contain duplicate data derived from the transaction file.

## Primary files

The main types of primary files within a file orientated approach would be:

■ a master file,
■ a transaction file, and
■ a reference file.

A master file would contain data related to or concerned with a specific entity or group of entities. In an accounting information systems context, the general ledger, the creditor ledger, or indeed the debtor ledger would be regarded as a separate and individual master file.

A transaction file would contain data related to or concerned with a specific current event. In an accounting information systems context such events would be, for example, accounting transactions such as sales, purchases, the payment of an invoice, the receipt of payment from a debtor, etc.

A reference file would contain data related to or concerned with a specific group of attributes: attributes required to complete a transaction event or group of transaction events. In an accounting information systems context such attributes could be, for example, a product listing, a price listing or a customer/client listing, or a product supplier/service provider listing.

## Secondary files

The main types of secondary files within a file orientated approach would be:

■ a history file,
■ a report file, and
■ a back-up file.

A history file, sometimes referred to as an archive file, would contain data related to or concerned with specific past events. In an accounting information systems context such events would be, for example, completed accounting transactions. Such data would be derived from the transaction file.

A report file would contain data derived from the master file and/or the transaction file, and would be generated for a specific purpose. In an accounting information systems context such reports would include, for example, a stock status report, a doubtful debt listing or a creditor payment listing, etc.

A back-up file would contain data derived from the transaction file and would be generated for security purposes to ensure that a copy of all source data is available. Because transaction file data is frequently changing as transactions are processed, the back-up file would require frequent revision to ensure its contents reflected all processed transactions.

### File orientated approach: data records and data files . . . design considerations

In designing data files – in particular the arrangement and structure of data records within individual data files – it is important from a data management context to consider:

- who will use the data file(s),
- when the data file(s) will be used,
- what purpose the data file(s) will be used for,
- how the data file(s) will be accessed, and
- where the data file(s) will be accessed.

Why? Put simply . . . for efficiency and security purposes.

Firstly, identifying who will use the data file(s) will provide an indication of how data records within individual groups of data files should be organised – for example:

- how should creditor files within the creditor ledger be structured,
- what data records should the creditor file contain, and
- how should those data records in the creditor file be arranged.

Secondly, determining the purpose for which a data file(s) will be used will provide an indication of how long data records and data files should be retained – for example should data records/files be retained for a month, six months, a year or six years.[13]

Thirdly, establishing the degree of commonality required between data records in different data files – that is the extent to which data records in different data files should be capable of consolidation and/or shared by different users – will provide an indication of what security arrangements should be used to maintain the integrity of individual data records/data files and prevent the unauthorised addition, deletion and/or alteration to data records/data files.

So what are the advantages and disadvantages of a file orientated system?

### Advantages and disadvantages of a file orientated approach

The advantages of a file orientated approach are that:

- it is simple to use, and
- it can be extremely cost effective – especially if only small amounts of data are stored.

In addition, if well-designed, such an approach can handle large volumes of data very efficiently.

The disadvantages of a file orientated approach is that it can become very cumbersome (lots of duplication of data files), very complex, difficult to manage, overly bureaucratic and highly politicised, often resulting in the limited sharing of data. In addition, it can result in the excessive

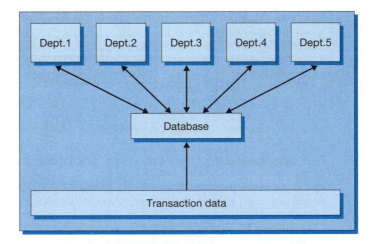

**Figure 7.2** Data orientated system/database system

duplication of data and high levels of data inconsistency due to the limited enforcement of data standards. More importantly, such system can be difficult to update and/or change – especially where extensive structural change to data content and/or file organisation is required.

## Data orientated approach/database system

A data orientated approach/database system (see Figure 7.2) is a structural approach in which data are considered a company/organisation asset or more appropriately a shared resource for all authorised organisational users and their respective applications. Such a resource is commonly referred to as a database: an organised collection of data elements within which data elements are organised into collections of record-like structures often referred to as data tables (or data sets).[14]

There are a number of alternative structural approaches that can be used within the data orientated approach, the main ones being:

- a flat data model,
- a hierarchical data model,
- a network data model, and
- a relational data model.

We will consider each of these in more detail later in this chapter. For the time being let's have a look at the advantages and disadvantages of a data orientated approach/database system.

### *Advantages and disadvantages of a data orientated approach/database system*

Whilst there can be little doubt that a database system can provide a powerful, centralised coordinating facility to manage the movement of large volumes of data, the main advantages are that:

- it provides an efficient means of managing data,
- it provides an effective means of controlling data access,
- it promotes greater data integration and improved data independence,
- it limits the need for data duplication,
- it provides for efficient data sharing and greater reporting flexibility, and
- it minimises data redundancy and limits data inconsistency.

The disadvantages of a data orientated system/database system are that:

- it can be extremely complex,
- there may be organisational resistance – implementation may require substantial organisation change,
- data may possibly be vulnerable, and
- the cost can be high.

So which one is best – a file orientated system or a data orientated system?

## File orientated systems v. data orientated system

File orientated systems are undoubtedly simple to develop, easy to maintain and of course simple to use. However the lack of integration within such systems often results in a high degree of inflexibility, imposing:

- significant limitations on user accessibility, and
- severe restrictions on data sharing opportunities.

And what of data orientated systems/database systems? Whilst such systems clearly increase user accessibility and promote improved flexibility, they are very costly to develop and can be very complex to maintain.

So which is the most popular? Pre-1980s the file orientated approach was probably the most popular, but since the mid/late-1980s (and certainly since the early 1990s), the data orientated approach/database system has become the most popular. Why?

Whilst there can be little doubt that the increasing availability of information and communication technologies (certainly since the early 1990s) and the ever-reducing cost of database-related technologies has clearly contributed to the increasing popularity of the data orientated approach and its increasing integration into a wide range of information and communication related applications, its widespread adoption – especially in business-related/accounting-related information systems – has perhaps more to do with the increasingly 'in vogue' view that data should be regarded as an organisational resource, whose efficient management (and use) is central to the development and maintenance of shareholder wealth. Certainly this is true in today's ever-more sensitive and competitive information dominated marketplace.

So what do we mean by the efficient management of data? Put simply, this means not only establishing efficient and effective facilities for the accurate capture and release of data, it also means developing and maintaining appropriate and acceptable levels of:

- data redundancy,
- data consistency,
- data integration,
- data accessibility,
- data flexibility,
- data security, and
- data integrity.

### Data capture (entry)/data release (exit)

Perhaps unsurprisingly, whilst data capture is concerned with the processes and procedures through which primary data is selected and acquired from the real-world, data release is concerned with the processes and procedures through which secondary data is issued to the real-world. Clearly, the more efficient the data capture/data release facilities, the more accurate the data and the more cost effective the data capture/data release facilities.

Using a file orientated approach may require data to be entered more than once, especially where the same data is duplicated within a company/organisation.

Consider the following.

*PLT Ltd is a Coventry-based manufacturing company. The company has six departments. Because PLT Ltd uses a file orientated approach to store and maintain product/service data, each department holds it own separate master file of product/service details. To update the data record of a particular product/service, it would be necessary to determine on which of the master files a copy of the product/service data is maintained (remember the product/ service data may be held in each master file), access the relevant master file and then update the relevant master file. This could mean that each of the six master files may need to be updated separately.*

Using a data orientated approach/database system, this multiple updating would not be necessary. Why? Because only a single product/service master file would be maintained within PLT Ltd, as a company-wide/organisation-wide resource accessible by each of the six departments within the company. To update the product/service master file would therefore only require a single data entry/data update.

### Data redundancy

Data redundancy is concerned with the usability of data or more appropriately the likelihood that data may become defective and unreliable. Clearly, levels of data redundancy are negatively correlated to levels of efficiency – that is the higher the levels of data redundancy, the lower the levels of efficiency.

So what types of data redundancy are there? There are two types, these being:

- direct redundancy, and
- indirect redundancy.

Direct redundancy occurs where data in a data file (using a file orientated approach) or data in a data table (using a data orientated approach/database system) is a *copy* of data held in another file or database record. Indirect redundancy occurs where data in a data file (using a file orientated approach) or data in a data record (using a data orientated approach/database system) can be *derived* from data held in another data file or data record.

Using a file orientated approach creates opportunities for both direct and indirect data redundancy to occur. Indeed, as demonstrated in the PLT Ltd illustration above, using a file orientated approach can lead to significant levels of direct data redundancy in stored data: that is the existence of many copies of the same data, resulting in not only the inefficient use of data storage space but perhaps more importantly the possibility of data inconsistencies.

Using a data orientated approach/database system, data are integrated as an amalgamation of several otherwise distinct data files. Whilst such an amalgamation clearly minimises (but not eliminates) the possibility of direct data redundancy – that is the likely existence of multiple copies of the same data within the database system – the possibility of indirect data redundancy nonetheless remains.

Using a data orientated approach/database system, incidences of data redundancy – whether direct or indirect – can be greatly reduced by normalisation. Normalisation is a series of techniques that make up a process which seeks to convert complex data structures into simple, stable data structures by organising data to reduce the possibility of data anomalies/data inconsistencies emerging.

We will look at normalisation later in this chapter.

### Data consistency

Data consistency is concerned with uniformity, and the standardisation of data within either a file (or series of files) and/or a database.

Clearly, improved levels of data consistency and data uniformity are positively correlated to levels of reliability – that is the higher the levels of data consistency, the higher the level of data reliability.

Consider the following.

*TLE Ltd is a new Leeds-based retail company. The company will commence trading in the next few months in seven retail outlets located throughout the north-east of England. Although the majority of company staff will be work in only one retail outlet, because of the eclectic nature of some of its products TLE Ltd expects some specialist staff will work at more than one retail outlet.*

*The company uses a file orientated approach to store and maintain personnel data with the manager of each retail outlet holding a separate master file of the staff employed at the retail outlet they manage.*

For those specialist staff working at more than one retail outlet, such an approach would result in the excessive duplication of personnel data. More importantly using a file orientated approach could also result in:

■ a high level of data inconsistency – for example, changes to specialist personnel staff data may be incorrectly documented or completely omitted, and (perhaps more importantly)
■ a low level of standardisation – personnel data may be stored differently by each manager at each retail outlet

Using a data orientated approach/database system to store and maintain personnel data centrally in the company's head office in Leeds would of course not only reduce the opportunity for data inconsistencies to occur, it would also – almost certainly – eliminate any possible standardisation issues.

### Data integration

Data integration is concerned with the opportunity to combine two or more data sets for the purposes of either:

■ data sharing between different users and/or different applications, and/or
■ data analysis for information provision purposes.

Clearly, effective data integration not only reduces possible data duplication, it also moderates the requirement for excessive data storage capacity and, of course, improves data availability/accessibility.

Using a file orientated approach can limit the possible levels of data sharing. Why? Sometimes for economic reasons, for example, the cost/time required to process data for data sharing purposes may be prohibitive; sometimes for technical reasons, for example, data sharing may be difficult because of data inconsistencies and/or a lack of data standardisation between data files; and sometimes for political reasons, for example, a manager may refuse and/or may make it difficult to gain access to data which they manage/control.

Using a data orientated approach/database systems of course eliminates some, if not all, of the above problems and allows for a higher degree of monitored data sharing and controlled data integration.

### Data accessibility

Data accessibility is of course concerned with the practicality and suitability of facilities used to provide users with access to data/data files and, whilst there can be little doubt that data use is clearly related to user accessibility, determining the suitability of data access facilities/opportunities can be problematic. Why? Because when determining the appropriateness of user access facilities/opportunities, issues of data security and data integrity must also be considered. For example, whilst unrestricted and/or unmonitored access may well promote high levels of user activity, such potential 'open access' could adversely affect data integrity/security: that is potential users may steal, fraudulently alter and/or even corrupt data. Conversely, constraining accessibility – for example, imposing severe restrictions on user access – may well help to maintain the integrity and security of the data, but could also adversely affect both the numbers and levels of user activity.[15]

Using a file orientated approach clearly constrains accessibility inasmuch as data may exist in separate data files owned by different users/different applications. Conversely, using a data orientated approach/database system improves accessibility due to the centralisation of data storage.

### Data flexibility

Data flexibility is concerned with the ease and cost effectiveness with which data can be modified. Using a file orientated approach, flexibility is often very low. Why?

Because data is often defined and organised by the individual (within the company/organisation) who effectively *owns* the data. More importantly, because multiple copies of the same data may be owned by different individuals within the company/organisation and stored in different locations within the company/organisation, amendment to or modification of any such data may be difficult and expensive.

Using a data orientated approach/database system, flexibility is often very high because the data are held in a single location. Indeed, such flexibility is often seen as the prime advantage of a data orientated approach/database system.

### Data security

Data security is concerned with ensuring that data are kept safe from corruption and that access is suitably controlled. Data security is closely related to data privacy and data confidentiality.

Using a file orientated system, because data may be maintained separately in a number of different locations, there may always be a chance that *some* data may be lost. Using a data orientated approach/database system, because data is maintained in the same location, *all* or most data may be vulnerable to loss especially if back-up copies are not routinely maintained. Of course, using a data orientated approach/database system does allow for a the imposition of a comprehensive data security system although such security systems can be expensive to implement and difficult to manage/monitor.

### Data integrity

Data integrity is concerned with minimising possible data inconsistencies and ensuring that data within a data file (using a file orientated approach) or data table (using a data orientated approach) is accurate. Levels of data integrity can be monitored using a range of integrity checks. Such integrity checks can be categorised as follows:

- type checks,
- redundancy checks,
- range checks,
- comparison checks, and
- constraint (or restriction) checks.

Type checks are designed to ensure that the data type within a data field in a data record is correct – for example, checking whether a data type within a numeric data field is numeric.

Redundancy checks are designed to ensure that the data within a data file, data table or data set is useable. (If you recall – we discussed direct and indirect redundancy earlier.)

Range checks are designed to ensure that a data item's value occurs within a specified range of values – for example, in a data field recording an employee's age such a check could ensure that an employee's age is, say, >16 and <75.

Comparison checks are designed to compare data within a data field and/or group of data fields, or with data within another data field and/or group of data fields: for example, comparing the salary of a group of employees is within the salary range/salary scale for those employees.

Constraint checks are designed to ensure that any constraint, condition or restriction imposed on data within a data field, data table or data set are complied with – for example, to ensure legal constraints over the deletion of data within a data field – especially data of a personal nature – are complied with.

Whilst both the file orientated approach and the data orientated approach/database system provide opportunities for the application of all of the above integrity checks, using the data orientated approach/database system helps not only to centralise the imposition of such integrity checks, but also minimises the cost of such checks whilst maximising their effectiveness.

 ## Data processing

As suggested earlier, data processing can be defined as any process and/or procedure, or series of processes and/or procedures, that converts data into information.

There are two alternative types of data processing approaches:

- manual-based data processing, and
- computer-based data processing.

### Manual-based data processing

Broadly speaking, manual-based data processing can be defined as the processing of data using, primarily, human-based resources. It does not necessarily signify the complete absence of information and communication technologies, but merely that the use of such resources whilst important is nonetheless of a secondary nature. Such data can loosely be categorised as either:

- routine business-related transaction data, or
- non-routine business-related transaction data.

#### Manual processing of routine business-related transaction data

Routine business-related transaction data are data relating to or referring to socio-economic events/transactions[16] which occur as part of the normal day-to-day wealth generating activities of a company/organisation, examples of which would be the purchase of products and services, the payment of creditor invoices or the payment of employee wages and salaries.

Although a small minority of companies/organisations continue to use manual-based data processing for the processing of routine business-related transaction data, the popularity of such manual-based data processing has declined significantly over the past 20 years. Why?

For a number of reasons – perhaps the most important being that such manual-based processing is:

- generally very slow,
- often very costly, and
- invariably an inefficient use of company/organisation resources.

The last is particularly the case where an individual manual-based process becomes politicised and seen as being owned by a group and/or department within a company/organisation.

Note: Where manual-based data processing is used for the processing of routine business-related transaction data, such processing would normally involve:

- the collection of transaction data into groups or batches (into a transactions data file), and
- the processing/updating of the master file when either:
  - a predetermined processing limit or batch size has been reached, or
  - a timetabled processing deadline has expired.

So how would the updating of the master file – that is the updating of the master file data with the data accumulated within the transaction file – take place?

There are two alternative approaches, these being:

- sequential file updating, and
- non-sequential (or random access) file updating.

Using sequential updating, the data in the transaction file would be validated, edited where appropriate and then sorted into the same order as the master file. The master file would then be updated in master file order.

Using non-sequential updating, the data in the transaction file would be validated, edited where appropriate and the master file would then be updated in transaction file order.

Whichever approach is used, an updating report would be produced for audit trail purposes.

Although non-sequential updating is much simpler, it can and generally does tend to be much more time consuming, especially where a large volume of data records require updating. As a consequence, manual-based processing generally uses a sequential updating approach.

### Manual processing of non-routine business-related transaction data

Non-routine business-related transaction data are data relating to or referring to socio-economic events/transactions that are not part of the normal day-to-day wealth generating activities of a company/organisation. Such events/transactions are normally characterised as being infrequent and/or unique transactions of a high value, examples of which would be the purchase of fixed assets or the investment of surplus funds.

Because of the unique nature of such non-routine business-related transactions it is likely that any related data would be processed using a non-sequential approach.

### Computer-based data processing

Computer-based data processing can be defined as the processing of data using communication and information technologies. Again, this does not necessarily signify the complete absence of human input, but merely that the use of such resources is minimal.

Such processing is generally used where large volumes of data are regularly processed, in particular where:

- the data processing is routine, continuous and/or repetitive,
- the data processing involves complex data selection, data capture, and/or data storage procedures, and/or

- the data processing is temporally and spatially separated – that is it occurs at different times and/or in different places.

Why? Put simply, computer-based processing can process transactions at great speed and with great accuracy. More importantly it can process transactions at a very low unit cost and offers a wider choice of secure storage facilities and processing alternatives.

So, what types of computer-based processing alternatives are there? There are essentially two:

- computer-based processing in which data is processed periodically (with either sequential updating or non-sequential updating) – usually referred to as batch processing, and
- computer-based processing in which data in processed immediately – usually referred to as online processing (although it is sometimes referred to as online real-time processing).

### Batch processing (or periodic processing)

Batch processing is data processing in which data are collected and processed in groups or more appropriately batches of data, and as such batch processing of data normally consists of four stages:

- stage 1 – a *collection* stage where individual data are collected into 'controlled' batches of data,
- stage 2 – an *input* stage where the controlled batch of data is input,
- stage 3 – a *processing* stage where the master file is updated based on the controlled batch of data, and
- stage 4 – an *output* stage.

See Figure 7.3.

Companies/organisations tend to use batch processing where it is necessary to:

- process and store large amounts of homogenous data on a regular basis, and
- produce large volumes of output regarding a large number of data entities (e.g. customers, clients, product suppliers, service providers, employees).

More importantly, it is used where:

- processing consists of the same sequence of pre-established procedures for *all* data, and
- processing responses times whilst significant, are not usually of critical importance providing the batch processing cycle[17] timetables are adhered to.

It is perhaps unsurprising that batch processing remains popular for the processing of, for example:

- payroll data for the payment of employee wages and salaries,
- creditor invoices for the payment of products and/or services received, and
- debtor invoices for the payment for products and/or services provided.

Consider the following example.

### Batch processing – payroll

*BLF Ltd is a small local manufacturing company with an annual turnover of £5.6m and an annual net profit of approximately £1.6m. The company currently employs a factory workforce of 65 full-time employees and an administrative/management workforce of 18 full-time employees. For the year ending 31 March 2007, the company's wages/salaries cost was £2.8m. An extract of the payroll procedure use by BLF Ltd for the payment of wages for the full-time factory workforce is as follows:*

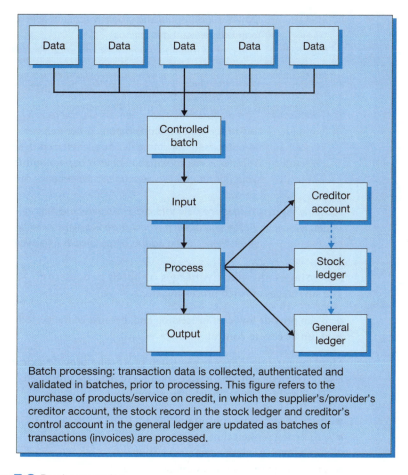

Batch processing: transaction data is collected, authenticated and validated in batches, prior to processing. This figure refers to the purchase of products/service on credit, in which the supplier's/provider's creditor account, the stock record in the stock ledger and creditor's control account in the general ledger are updated as batches of transactions (invoices) are processed.

**Figure 7.3** Batch processing

Friday:    At the end of each working week payroll clerk no. 1 reviews the payroll department files (updated by the personnel department) to determine the employment status/number of full-time factory employees. The payroll clerk then prepares a bar code-based timecard for each full-time factory employee and delivers these to the factory foreman on Friday at 4:30 pm. At the same time the payroll clerk collects the current week's completed timecards. The factory foreman confirms the validity of each timecard, and places it in a wall mounted open storage unit near the clocking-in/clocking-out facility at the entrance to the factory. Each full-time employee is required to clock-in using the timecard on arrival and clock-out using the timecard on departure. The factory week commences on Monday 7:00 am and ends on Friday 4:00 pm. The collected timecards are returned to the payroll office and securely stored until Monday 9:00 am.

Monday:    Using a bar code reader, payroll clerk no. 2 calculates the attendance times of each factory employee from the timecards and calculates the payable hours. A list of the payable hours for each factory employee is passed to payroll clerk no. 1. Using the updated payroll data provided by the personnel department each week, from the personnel master file payroll clerk no. 1 prepares a *payroll register containing details for each employee of the total net pay (gross pay less relevant deductions).*

*Tuesday:* *The payroll manager authorises and approves the payroll register and forwards the payroll register to the creditor department for review. The creditor department manager reviews the payroll register, authorises the payment and issues a disbursement voucher.*

*Wednesday:* *The disbursement voucher and payroll register are forwarded to the cashier's office for review/reconciliation. A file transfer for the payment of the wages is authorised and the BACS payment approved and processed. The payroll register is returned to the payroll department for filing and the disbursement voucher returned to accounting for processing and entry into the accounting system.*

*Thursday:* *Wages are paid into individual full-time factory employee bank accounts.*

*Friday:* *At the end of each working week payroll clerk no. 1 reviews the payroll department files . . . and so the batch processing cycle begins again.*

### Advantages and disadvantages of batch processing

The advantages of batch processing are:

- it can provide low-cost processing and, because of the periodic nature of the processing,
- it can be easy to control.

More importantly, not only can batch processing provide a clear processing audit trail, it can also be very efficient where large volumes of data are processed.

The disadvantages of batch processing are:

- it can be very time consuming,
- processing is often time constrained,
- it can involve lengthy data preparation,
- processing response times can be slow, and
- changes to processing procedures can be difficult to implement

### Online processing (or immediate processing)

Online processing can be defined as data processing in which data are input and processed as soon as complete data become available and is often used to signify the processing of data immediately upon receipt. As such the online processing of data consists of three stages:[18]

- an *input* stage where individual data are input,
- a *processing* stage where the master file is updated immediately on data input, and
- an *output* stage.

See Figure 7.4.

Companies/organisations tend to use online data processing where it is not only necessary to support a large and unpredictable number of concurrent users and transaction types and ensure the continuous availability of secure, high-performance data processing, but more importantly where:

- the majority of transactions are executed in a short period of time – possibly fractions of a second in some cases, and
- the majority of interactions between the user and the online system are for a short period of time.

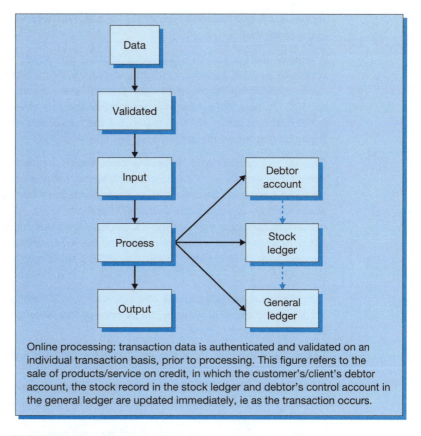

Online processing: transaction data is authenticated and validated on an individual transaction basis, prior to processing. This figure refers to the sale of products/service on credit, in which the customer's/client's debtor account, the stock record in the stock ledger and debtor's control account in the general ledger are updated immediately, ie as the transaction occurs.

**Figure 7.4** Online processing

More specifically, where:

- a small amount of data is input per transaction,
- a small number of a stored records are accessed and processed per transaction, and
- a small amount of data is output per transaction.

As such, online processing remains popular for the processing of, for example:

- ATM transactions,
- stock receipts/issues,
- quotations/reservations requests such as insurance quotations/airline reservations,
- EPOS transactions, and
- credit card/debit card verification/validation.

Consider the following example.

### Online processing example – ATM transactions

*An Abbey plc customer wishes to withdraw cash from a HSBC plc ATM. How would the transaction be processed?*

*Remember an ATM[19] is simply a remote data terminal with two input devices[20] and four output devices.[21] All ATMs are connected to, and communicate with, a host processor[22] which acts as a gateway through which all the various ATM networks in the UK become available to the cardholder.*

*In general, the transaction would be processed as follows. When a cardholder wishes to undertake an ATM transaction they must provide the necessary input/authorisation information by means of the card reader and keypad – that is an appropriate debit card/credit card and PIN. On receipt of a matching card and PIN, the ATM forwards the encrypted information to the host processor, which simply routes the transaction request to the bank or financial institution that issued the card – in our example Abbey plc.*

*Because the cardholder is requesting cash, the host processor would generate an electronic funds transfer from the cardholder's account to the host processor's account. Once the funds have been transferred to the host processor's bank account, the host processor would send an approval code to the ATM authorising the ATM to dispense the cash. The host processor would then transfer the cardholder's funds into the merchant's bank account (the bank account of the company operating the ATM) – in our example HSBC plc – usually the next bank business day. In this way, HSBC plc is reimbursed for all funds dispensed by its ATM.*

*Note: Most UK banks impose a limit on how much a cardholder can withdraw from their account using the ATM network in a 24-hour period, although the amount does differ substantially from bank to bank.*

In the above example there was no charge for the cash withdrawal. However, where an ATM is owned and operated by a company other than a bank/financial institution, for example Link (see http://www.link.co.uk), it is common for a nominal charge to be incurred by the cardholder, usually between £1.50 and £2.50 per cash withdrawal.

## Advantages and disadvantages of online processing

The advantages of online processing are:

- the speed at which data can be input,
- the low cost of data processing,
- immediate error correction,
- an immediate update of all files, and
- human interaction/interference is minimised.

The disadvantages of online processing are:

- set-up costs can be very high,
- data input and data processing controls can be costly,
- access authority levels may require constant monitoring,
- the system hardware may be costly,
- the system software may require extensive integration, and
- data audit trails may be difficult to locate.

### Centralised data processing v. distributed data processing

First two definitions:

- centralised data processing is data processing performed in one computer or in a cluster of coupled computers – at a single location, and
- distributed data processing is data processing performed by several separate computers/ computer networks, at several locations, linked by a communications facility.

Historically, when mainframe computers were measured not by the size of their memory capacity/ processing capability, but by the number of rooms they occupied, centralised processing was the norm. It was a processing approach adopted by the vast majority of companies/organisations – an approach in which *all* data was processed at a single head office location. Why?

For three reasons: Firstly, because of the high cost of data processing technologies, centralised data processing was viewed as the most cost-effective means of processing large amounts of data – a way of reducing data processing infrastructure costs. Secondly, because of the ever-changing complexities of using such data processing technologies, centralising data processing was seen as the most effective means of minimising possible duplication. Thirdly, because of the need for coordination, control and accountability, centralising data processing technologies were seen as the most efficient means of ensuring uniformity in the enforcement of processing standards and the imposition of data/processing security requirements. So why the demise?

Put simply, all forms of imposed bureaucracy – all forms of controlled centralisation – inevitably fail, whether as a result of internal pressure generated by ever-increasing inefficiencies[23] and inflexibilities, or external pressure associated with environmental innovation and change. Indeed, it was:

- the increasing demand for faster processing,[24]
- the increasing need for improved mobility, and
- the growing desire for greater flexibility,

excited by the ever-changing demands of the business environment, and fuelled by the ever-more dramatic advancements in information and communication technologies/capabilities that perhaps somewhat inevitably resulted in the demise of centralised processing. So what are the advantages and disadvantages of distributed processing?

The advantages of distributed processing are:

- it promotes greater flexibility in the use of data processing facilities,
- it promotes better resource sharing and greater user involvement,
- it increases location independence and therefore data processing efficiency, and
- it is more responsive to user needs.

The disadvantages of distributed processing are:

- the initial set-up costs can be very high, and
- the risk of data duplication, possible data incompatibility, processing error, and/or operational/ communication failure, can be high where there is an inadequate level of management and coordination.

### Centralised data processing v. distributed data processing – variation in degrees

Although we often discuss notions of centralised data processing and distributed data processing as if they were absolute terms, in reality such a distinction is perhaps best visualised as a sliding scale on which companies/organisations exhibit differing degrees of centralisation.

However, as with all qualitative assessments, measuring/determining degrees of centralised data processing/distributed data processing can be problematic. As a broad principle, where a company/organisation operates at a number of geographically dispersed locations the degree of distributed processing utilised by the company/organisation would generally be positively correlated with the degree of autonomy exercised at/by each geographically dispersed location.

See Figure 7.5.

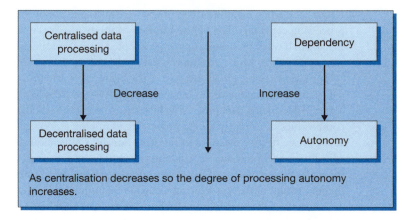

**Figure 7.5** Centralised data processing v. decentralised data processing

Such correlation would of course be affected by:

- the management structure of the company/organisation,
- the context type[25] of the company/organisation,
- the processing requirements/demands within the company/organisation, and
- the connectivity constraints within the company/organisation.

Consider for example Tesco plc and Sainsbury plc, or BP plc and Royal Dutch Shell plc, or indeed HSBC plc and LloydsTSB plc. Would the degree of centralised data processing/distributed data processing be the same? Of course not.

## Describing data processing systems

Within a company/organisation context – specifically within an accounting information systems context – there will always be a need to document and record information on:

- what system, flows and processes exist,
- how such system, flows and processes are related,
- what functions such system, flows and processes perform,
- how each system, flow and/or process is managed/controlled,
- what resources are allocated to each system, flow and process, and
- what added value each system, flow and/or process produces.

Why? Because accounting information systems and processes are continually changing and evolving. Whether such change occurs as a result of internal management policies, for example the restructuring of organisational activities, or indeed as a consequence of external environmental pressure, for example the development and introduction of new information and communication technologies, such change is – as we will see in Chapter 16 – inevitable, with often unpredictable and uncertain consequences.

There is a wide range of 'documenting' techniques used to describe and analyse the systems, flows and processes that comprise a company's/organisation's accounting information system, the most common being:

- data flow diagrams,
- flowcharts,
- entity-relationship diagrams, and
- decision tables.

In addition, as part of this discussion on describing techniques, we will also consider the coding system – that abstract framework of alpha numeric symbols – which lies at the heart of every computer-based accounting information system.

## Data flow diagrams

There are broadly speaking two types of data flow diagram:

- logical data flow diagrams, and
- physical data flow diagrams.

Whilst a logical data flow diagram focuses on the content of data flow, a physical data flow diagram focuses on the context of the data flow. A logical data flow diagram describes *what* data flows and a physical data flow diagram describes *how* data flows. The emphasis of both types is on identifying:

- the system/process boundaries that surround the data flow,
- the external entities involved in the data flow,
- the data involved in the data flow,
- the activities/events that occur within the data flow,
- the rules used to process the data and manage the data flow, and
- the data stores/files created and/or maintained as part of the data flow.

So, what notation is used in data flow diagrams? Although there are a number of variations concerning data flow diagram notation[26] for our purposes, we will use the following:[27]

- a square to indicate an entity,
- a circle to portray a process,
- two parallel lines to indicate a data store/file, and
- an arrow to portray the direction of a dataflow.[28]

See Figure 7.6.
Briefly:

- an entity (also referred to as external source/external destination) can be either an object and/or a subject which contribute data to and receive data from a process,

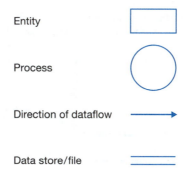

| Entity |
| Process |
| Direction of dataflow |
| Data store/file |

**Figure 7.6** Data flow diagram – symbols

- a process is an activity or event and/or procedure which transforms and/or manipulates data,
- a data store/data file is a location at which data is retained either temporarily or permanently,[29] and
- a named data flow arrow depicts the flow of data either to a process or from a process – that is data flow arrows must either start or end at a process, and cannot occur directly between:
  - data stores and/or
  - external entities and/or
  - a data store and an external entity.

### Logical data flow diagrams

A logical data flow diagram provides – independent of any physical information and communication technology that may be utilised in the data flow – a representation of the flow of data through a transaction system within a company/organisation and documents the relationship between data and data processing.

What does a logical data flow diagram look like? Broadly speaking, it is a component aspect of a data flow model which is merely a hierarchical collections of interrelated logical data flow diagrams, each representing a different level of detail within a data flow of a system/process.

## Context level data flow diagram

A context level data flow diagram is a data flow diagram that provides a holistic representation of the major data flows within a system/process. Where the system/process to which the context level diagram relates is composed of lower level sub-system/sub-processes, such a context diagram is sometimes referred to as the *level 0 data flow diagram*.

The main aim of a context level data flow diagram is to provide a simplified *single cycle* overview of the data flow within a system/process.

The context level diagram will generally indicate:

- the source entity within the data flow,
- the destination entity within the data flow,
- the process involved in the data flow, and
- the direction(s) of the data flow(s).

To construct a level 0 (context diagram) it is important to identify:

- all the data flows (e.g. documents) used in the system/process, and
- all the source entities and destination entities that interact within the system/process.

See Figure 7.7.

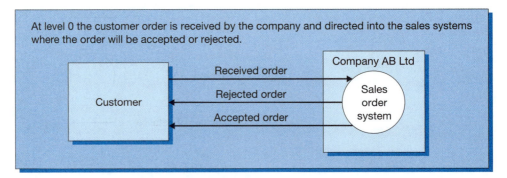

At level 0 the customer order is received by the company and directed into the sales systems where the order will be accepted or rejected.

Customer — Received order → Company AB Ltd / Sales order system
Customer ← Rejected order
Customer ← Accepted order

**Figure 7.7** Context level data flow diagram (level 0)

## Level 1 data flow diagram

Clearly, as on overview diagram, the context level data flow diagram provides very little detailed information. To analyse the system further it is necessary – in a metaphorical sense – to decompose the system identified in the context level data flow diagram, to provide greater detail on:

- what data flows occur, and
- what processes exist within the systems.

Such a data flow diagram is known as a *top level* or *level 1 data flow diagram*, and is designed to provide a description of the internal structure of the system or, more appropriately, a description of the component data flows and processes that comprise the system. See Figure 7.8.

Because there are of course no clear rules to determine what is or is not a level 1 process it can be difficult to know where to start. There are three optional analytical approaches that can be used to identify a practical starting point, these being:

- resource flow analysis,
- organisational structure analysis, and
- document flow analysis.

The resource flow analysis approach is useful when the system consists largely of the flow of resources. Such resources are traced from their input into the system, to their processing, and their output from the system. The rationale behind this method is that data normally flows in the same direction and on the same pathways as such resources.

The organisational structure analysis approach considers the main roles that exist within the organisation, rather than the goods or information that flow around the system, the aim being to identify the key processes and determine which functional areas are relevant and which are not. Why? Because the data flows between such processes (and relevant external entities).

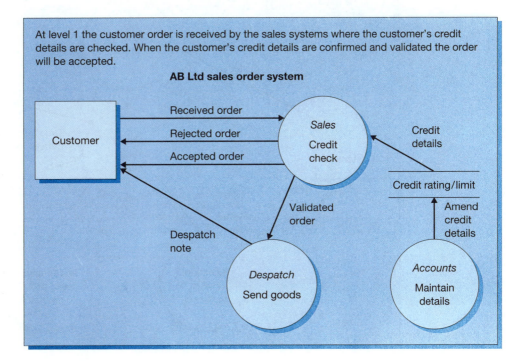

At level 1 the customer order is received by the sales systems where the customer's credit details are checked. When the customer's credit details are confirmed and validated the order will be accepted.

**AB Ltd sales order system**

**Figure 7.8** Top level data flow diagram (level 1)

The document flow analysis approach considers flows of data in the form of documents or computer input and output, the key stages in the approach being:

- determine the process/system boundary,
- list the major documents and their sources and recipients, and
- identify major data flows such as telephone and computer transactions.

## Level 2 data flow diagram

Where a process or a number of processes identified in a level 1 data flow diagram are composed of lower-level sub-processes, then each such sub-process may itself be decomposed into its component data flows and processes. Such a data flow diagram is known as a *level 2 data flow diagram* and is designed to provide a description of the component data flows and processes that comprise the sub-system detailed in the top level (level 1) data flow diagram. See Figure 7.9.

Clearly, where a sub process at a second level decomposition is itself comprised of separate data flows and sub-processes, such sub-processes may also be decomposed to a third, fourth or indeed even further depending on the complexity of the process/processes identified in the level 1 data flow diagram. So at what point will this decomposition process stop?

The sub-process decomposition will only stop when a sub-process can be described using an elementary process description – that is using a brief textual description of the process. Such an elementary process description would contain, for example, a description of:

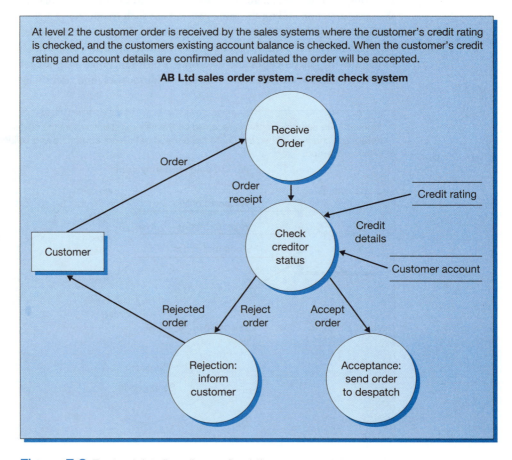

At level 2 the customer order is received by the sales systems where the customer's credit rating is checked, and the customers existing account balance is checked. When the customer's credit rating and account details are confirmed and validated the order will be accepted.

**AB Ltd sales order system – credit check system**

**Figure 7.9** Top level data flow diagram (level 2)

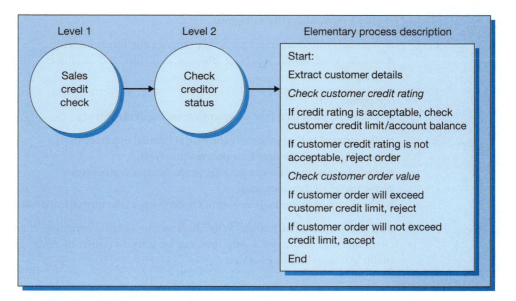

**Figure 7.10** Elementary process description

- how the data is accessed,
- the business constraints which dictate the process,
- the circumstances under which the process is invoked, and
- the constraints imposed upon the use of the process.

See Figure 7.10.

So how many levels of decomposition would there be? That's difficult question to answer. However, whilst in a broad context:

- a small simple system/process would normally contain two to three levels,
- a medium fairly complex system/process would normally contain between three and six levels, and
- a large complex system/process would normally contain six or more levels,

it is important to remember that not only must decomposition levels within a data flow model (that is a collection of hierarchically related data flow diagrams) be consistent with each other – that is the data inputs and data outputs at a higher level data flow diagram must correspond to those of all the constituent sub-processes at the next lower level data flow diagram – but that whilst a system may comprise of a number of processes and lower level sub-processes, the number of decomposition levels (that is levels of sub-processes) may differ, indeed will often differ between the individual constituent sub-processes of a system.

### Physical data flow diagram

A physical data flow diagram seeks to identify, specify and describe the physical environmental context of a data flow, that is specify within an information and communication technology context:

- *what* activities and/or processes occur, and
- *how* such activities and processes are carried out.

Within a physical dataflow diagram:

- a process would represent physical programs and functions, and
- a data store would represent physical data files and databases – both permanent and temporary.

See Figure 7.11.

Whilst physical data flow diagrams are useful in identifying:

- the physical nature of the data flow (e.g. manual or automatic),
- the sequence of the data flow process/processes,
- the nature of the data storage (e.g. permanent or temporary),
- the names of data files, and
- the names of individuals/departments involved in the movement of data,

their use is somewhat limited. Why? Because the same information concerning the physical environmental context of a data flow can be provided often in much greater detail using a traditional flowchart (see below).

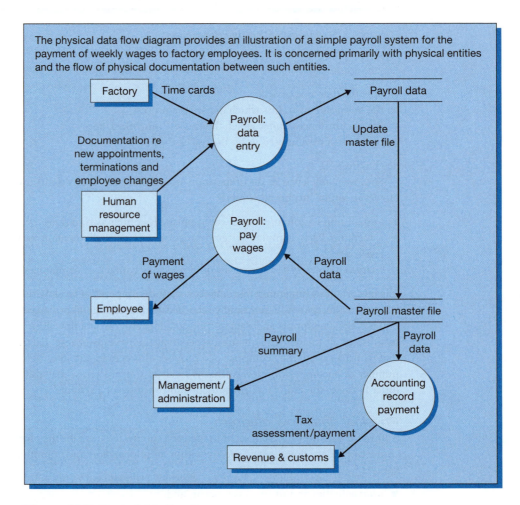

The physical data flow diagram provides an illustration of a simple payroll system for the payment of weekly wages to factory employees. It is concerned primarily with physical entities and the flow of physical documentation between such entities.

**Figure 7.11** Physical data flow diagram

## *Drawing a data flow diagram*

The main stages in drawing a data flow diagram would be:

- draw a context flow diagram to represent the entire system, and identify and add any external entities, resource flows and/or data flows,
- draw a level 1 diagram to illustrate the main functional areas of the system under investigation and, where necessary,
- draw a level 2 diagram to illustrate processes not fully explored in the level 1 diagram.

Of course, where appropriate, further decomposition of the level 2 data flow diagram into lower level(s) may be useful.

To ensure data flows are clearly presented, it is important – where possible, to:

- combine processes,[30]
- exclude minor data flows,[31]
- combine external entities, and
- combine data stores.

So, are there any general dataflow diagram conventions? Essentially there are five key conventions, these being:

- *the entity rule* – that is an entity must be either a source of data inputs or a destination for data outputs,
- *the process rule* – that is a process must have both input flows and output flows,
- *the data store rule* – that is data stores must have both input flows and output flows,
- *the data from rule* – that is data flows from a source entity and/or a data store and must flow into a process, and
- *the data to rule* – data flows to a destination entity and/or a data store must flow out of a process.

Remember, when drawing a data flow diagram:

- think logical, not physical, and
- think data flow, not control process.

## *Assessing the flow within a data flow diagram*

Once a data flow diagram has been prepared then as a representation of a system/process it is of course necessary to assess the appropriateness and effectiveness of the data flow. Why? Put simply, to identify any possible data flow inefficiencies and/or weaknesses.

In general, such an assessment would involve posing the following questions:

- Are all data flows sufficiently analysed?
- Are all processes decomposed to an appropriate level?
- Are all processes appropriately labelled?
- Do all decomposed processes in lower level data flow diagrams portray the same net inputs and outputs as their higher-level representations – that is, is there consistency between higher-level and lower-level data flows?
- Does all data travelling in the same data flow travel together? If not, why not?
- Do all data stores have an input data flow? If not, why not?
- Are there any *black holes* – that is are there any processes with only input data flows?
- Are there any *miracles* – that is are there any processes with only output data flows?
- Are there any *grey holes* – that is does every process possess an appropriate/matching level of inflows/outflows?

■ Are all data flows connected to two elements – a process and a terminator, or a data store or another process? If not, why not?

■ Does any data flow to a process where it is not used and/or is not required? If it does, why does it?

### Advantages and disadvantages of data flow diagrams

The advantages of data flow diagrams are:

■ they are simple and easy to understand,

■ they are a powerful technique for defining the parameters/boundaries of a system/process,

■ they provide a dynamic representation of a system/process from the viewpoint of data flows/movements, and

■ they can be used to represent/analyse a system/process at different levels of detail.

The disadvantages of data flow diagrams are:

■ they can be time consuming to create/develop,

■ they can become overly complex, and

■ they can sometimes be difficult to revise.

## Flowcharts

A flowchart is essentially a picture – a map of a process, a flow or a system. More precisely it is a diagrammatic representation of a system, a computer program or a document flow, and as such can be used for a variety of purposes, for example:

■ to identify the logic of a system, computer program or document flow,

■ to identify and/or define a system, computer program or document flow boundary,

■ to identify system, computer program and/or document flow redundancies and/or delays,

■ to identify possible areas of improvement, and

■ to develop a common understanding about a system, computer program or document flow.

So what symbols are used in flowcharting? There are a vast number, the most common being:

■ an oval – to indicate both the start and end of a process, flow or system,

■ a box – to represent an individual activity within a process, flow or system,

■ a diamond – to illustrate a decision point,

■ a circle – to indicate the connection of a particular activity within a process, flow or system to another activity within another process, flow or system,

■ a triangle – to indicate a file or store of data/information,

■ a document – to indicate the source of data,

■ a flow line – to indicate the directional path of a process, flow or system.

See Figure 7.12 for some examples.

We can distinguish flowcharts in two ways:

■ by level of detail, or

■ by type/category.

### . . . by level of detail

There are essentially three different levels of detail, these being:

■ a macro level flowchart,

■ a midi level flowchart, and

■ a micro level flowchart.

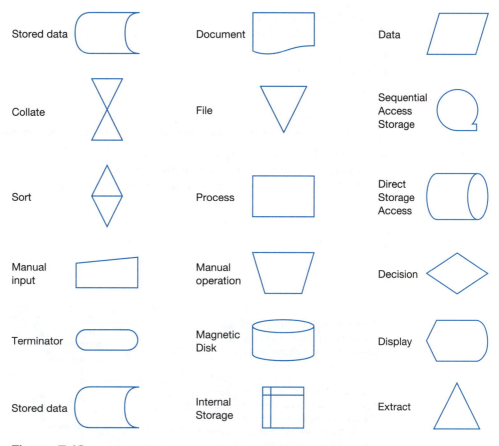

**Figure 7.12** Flowchart – symbols

### Macro level flowchart

A macro level flowchart is, in a management context, a strategic level flowchart. It is designed to show the big picture or, more appropriately, the organisational context of a system, computer program and/or document flow. For example, such a flowchart may be used to document/record a company's transaction processing system.

### Midi level flowchart

A midi level flowchart is a tactical level flowchart and typically focuses on a single part/segment of the macro level flowchart. For example, such a flowchart may be used to focus on the document flow within the revenue cycle of a company's transaction processing system.

### Micro level flowchart

The micro level flowchart is essentially an operational level flowchart designed to illustrate/provide a very detailed picture of a specific portion/segment of system, computer program or document flow, its aim being to document/record every action, flow and decision. Such flowcharts are commonly used when assessing levels of internal control within a system, process and/or document flow. For example, such a flowchart may be used to focus on the internal controls within the debtors systems of a company's revenue cycle.

### . . . by type/category

There are essentially three different types/categories of flowchart:

- a systems flowchart,
- a document flowchart,
- a program/computer flowchart.

## Systems flowchart

A systems flowchart provides a logical diagram of *how* a system operates and:

- illustrates the system in a step-by-step fashion,
- illustrates the conversion process from input to output, and
- indicates which functions are manual and/or computer-based.

A systems flowchart is:

- vertical,
- linear, and
- procedural.

See Figure 7.13.

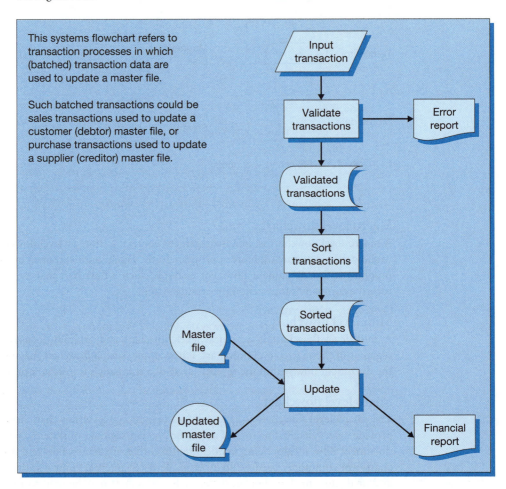

This systems flowchart refers to transaction processes in which (batched) transaction data are used to update a master file.

Such batched transactions could be sales transactions used to update a customer (debtor) master file, or purchase transactions used to update a supplier (creditor) master file.

Input transaction → Validate transactions → Error report
Validate transactions → Validated transactions → Sort transactions → Sorted transactions
Master file → Update ← Sorted transactions
Update → Updated master file
Update → Financial report

**Figure 7.13** Systems flowchart

## Document flowchart

A document flowchart illustrates the flow of documentation and information within a system – from origin to destination – and is concerned with:

- *how* the document flow occurs,
- *what* documents flow, and
- to *whom* the documents flow to and from.

A document flowchart is:

- horizontal,
- columnar, and
- documentary.

See Figure 7.14.

## Program/computer flowchart

A program/computer flowchart provides an illustration of the processing stages within a computer-based system, for example a batch processing system or an online processing system.

A program/computer flowchart is:

- vertical,
- linear, and
- procedural.

See Figure 7.15.

In accounting information systems, the most commonly used flowcharts are:

- a systems flowchart (also known as a procedural flowchart), and
- a document flowchart.

Such flowcharts can be used to illustrate/record the flow of resources and/or information within a system and/or process – an important aspect of which is an indication as to whether a set of procedures or a flow of documents within a system/process incorporate appropriate:

- authorisation procedures,
- custody procedures,
- control procedures, and
- recording procedures.

### Drawing a flowchart

Whilst there are many alternative ways in which a system, document, and/or a program/computer flowchart can be constructed, and indeed a vast range of software programs available with which to draw such a flowchart (e.g. see Smartdraw7 available @ www.smartdraw.com), it is nonetheless important that a clear understanding of each activity that takes place within the system/flow and/or process is developed/obtained, and that each decision stage within the system/flow and/or process is correctly identified. The main stages in flowcharting a system, a document flow and/or a computer program/process would be:

- where possible observe the system, document flow and/or the computer program/process to establish the context and boundaries of the system/flow/process,
- prepare a detailed record of the activities/decision stages observed/identified,
- sequence/arrange the activities/decision stages observed/identified, and finally

This document flowchart (based on a small York-based manufacturing company) refers to a sales transaction process in which:

1. A customer order is received
2. A sales order is prepared
3. A customer credit check is performed
4. A sales invoice is issued (if the credit check is successful) and authorised
5. Stock records are updated
6. A dispatch order is issued and, where necessary
7. A bill of lading is prepared.

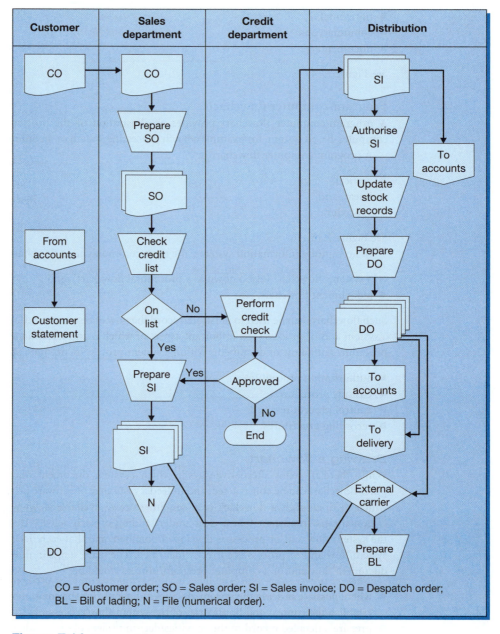

CO = Customer order; SO = Sales order; SI = Sales invoice; DO = Despatch order; BL = Bill of lading; N = File (numerical order).

**Figure 7.14** Document flowchart

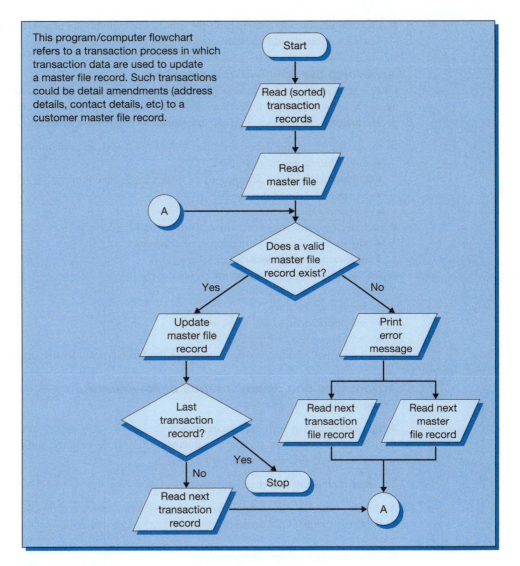

**Figure 7.15** Program/computer flowchart

- design/draw the flowchart, representing the system, document flow and/or the computer program/process exactly as observed/identified, recorded and sequenced/arranged.

There are a number of general flowcharting conventions. For our purposes, the most important conventions/rules are:

- *the direction rule* – that is within the flowchart, flows should generally commence on the top-left corner and flow from left to right and from top to bottom,
- *the consistency rule* – that is all flowcharting symbols should be used consistently throughout the flowchart and where appropriate a legend should be provided,
- *the sandwich rule* – that is all processing symbol should be sandwiched between an input symbol and an output symbol,
- *the narrative rule* – all flowcharting symbols should contain a brief descriptive label, and

■ *the multiple copy rule* – where multiple copies of documents are used in a system, flow and/or a process, these should be shown as overlapping symbols.

### Assessing the flow within a flowchart

Once a flowchart of a system/flow/program has been developed, it is of course important to assess the appropriateness of the flows described within the flowchart and identify any potential problems/issues/weaknesses. Such an assessment would involve an examination of:

■ the data/information/document flows within the flowchart to identify:
  ● any redundant activities/flows,
  ● any processing obstructions and/or weak processing connections,
  ● any poorly defined flows, and
  ● any non-value-adding flows,
■ each decision-making event within the flowchart to identify:
  ● any irrelevant decision-making events, and/or
  ● non-value-adding decision-making events,
■ each activity within the flowchart, to identify:
  ● any unnecessary activities,
  ● any repeat activities,
  ● any poorly defined activities, and
  ● any cost-only activities, and
■ each activity/decision-making loop within the flowchart to identify any redundant loops.

### Advantages and disadvantages of flowcharts

The advantages of flowcharts are:

■ they can be drawn with little experience,
■ they record the system, program or document flow in its entirety, and
■ they eliminate the need for extensive notes.

The disadvantages of flowcharts are that:

■ they are generally only suitable for standard systems/processes/flows, and
■ they are generally only useful for dynamic systems/processes/flows.

## Entity-relationship diagram

The entity-relationship diagram is a diagrammatic representation of what is commonly referred to as an entity-relationship model, an approach to data modelling developed in 1976 by Peter Chen, which uses two logical criteria:

■ an entity, and
■ a relationship.

### An entity

An entity[32] is essentially something that exists in the form of resources, events and agents. That is something that can be identified by means of its attributes – the unique characteristics that distinguish one entity (or an entity set/type)[33] from another entity.

An entity can be classified as:

■ an independent (or strong) entity – that is an entity that does not rely on another entity for identification,

- a dependent (or weak) entity – that is an entity that does rely on another entity for identification, or
- an associative entity (also known as an intersection entity) – that is an entity used to associate two or more entities in order to reconcile a many-to-many relationship (see below).

## Attributes

An attribute describes the entity to which it is associated – attributes which apply to all occurrences of the entity/entity type. Attributes can be classified as either an identifier or a descriptor. Whereas an identifier – more commonly referred to as a key – uniquely identifies an entity, a descriptor describes a non-unique characteristic of an entity. A given attribute belonging to a given entity occurrence can only have one value.

The primary key is the attribute (or group of attributes) that serve to identify uniquely an entity. Where two or more data items are used as the unique identifier this is referred to as *compound key*. If several possible primary keys exist, such keys are referred to as *candidate keys*, and where an attribute of one entity is a candidate key for another entity, it is termed a *foreign key*.

### A relationship

A relationship is an association between two entities and/or entity types. Such relationships are classified in terms of degree, connectivity, cardinality and existence.

## Degree of a relationship

The degree of a relationship can be defined as the number of entities associated with the relationship.

A binary relationship exists where an association between two entities exists.[34] A recursive binary relationship exists where an entity is related to itself: for example, a company employee may be married to another company employee. A $n$-ary relationship exists where an association between more than two entities exists.[35] Such relationships are generally composed of two or more interacting binary relationships.

## Connectivity and cardinality

The connectivity of a relationship describes the mapping of an entity-relationship. The basic types of connectivity are:

- one-to-one – referred to as (1:1),
- one-to-many – referred to as (1:$n$), or
- many-to-many – referred to as ($m$:$n$).

The cardinality of a relationship defines the maximum number of entities/entity types that can be associated with an entity/entity type.

A one-to-one (1:1) relationship occurs when entity A is associated with entity B and entity B is associated with entity A. An example of a one-to-one relationship would be where the managers of a company/organisation are allocated to an individual personal office. For each manager there exists a unique office and for each office there exists a unique manager.

A one-to-many (1:$n$) relationships occurs when for entity A, there are 0, 1 or many instances of entity B, but for entity B, there is only 1 instance of entity A. An example of a 1:$n$ relationships would be where a department within a company/organisation has many employees but each employee can only be employed by/in a single department.

A many-to-many ($m$:$n$) relationship occurs when for entity A, there are 0, 1 or many instances of entity B, and conversely for entity B there are 0, 1 or many instances of entity A. An example of a $m$:$n$ relationship would be where an internal auditor can be assigned to no more

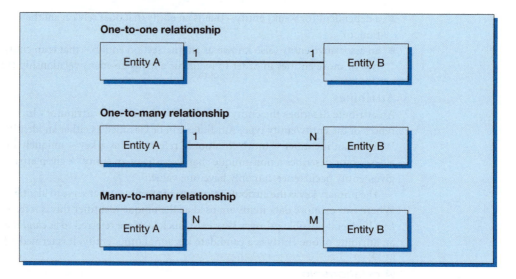

**Figure 7.16** Entity relationships

than three audit projects at the same time and where individual audits projects are required to have at least four assigned internal auditors. That is an individual internal auditor can be assigned to many audit projects and an individual audit project can have many internal auditors assigned to it. Here the cardinality for the relationship between internal auditors and audit projects is 3 and the cardinality between audit projects and internal auditors is 4.

Each of the above types of connectivity can be represented diagrammatically (see Figure 7.16).

### The direction of a relationship

The direction of a relationship indicates the originating entity of a binary relationship. The entity from which a relationship originates is often referred to as the *parent entity* and the entity at which the relationship terminates is, somewhat unsurprisingly, often referred to as the *child entity*.

An identifying relationship is a relationship in which the child entity is also a dependent entity, whereas a non-identifying relationship in which both entities are independent.

The direction of a relationship is determined by its connectivity. For example:

- in a 1-to-1 relationship the direction of the relationship would be from the independent entity to a dependent entity,[36]
- in a 1-to-many relationship, the entity occurring once is the parent entity and the direction of the relationship would be from the parent entity to the other children entities, and
- in a many-to-many relationship the direction of the relationship would be arbitrary.

### Existence

Existence denotes whether the existence of an entity is dependent upon the existence of another entity. The existence of an entity in a relationship can be defined as either optional or mandatory.[37] For example:

- if an entity must always occur for an entity to be included in a relationship, then the relationship is considered mandatory, or
- if an entity is not required, then the relationship is considered optional.

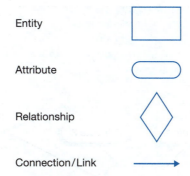

**Figure 7.17** Entity-relationship diagram – symbols

### Drawing an entity-relationship diagram

Although there is wide variation in the notation used in entity-relation diagrams, the most common notation used is:

■ a square – to indicate an entity,
■ a diamond – to portray a relationship,
■ an oval – to represent an attribute, and
■ an arrow – to portray a connection/link.

See Figure 7.17.

The main stages in drawing an entity-relationship diagram would be:

■ establish and identify the entities,
■ determine the relationships between the entities,
■ determine cardinality,
■ determine the attributes for each entity,
■ select and define the primary key for each entity,
■ compose an entity-relationship diagram, and
■ test the relationships and the keys.

Figure 7.18 provides an illustration of a generic entity-relationship diagram.

### Test the relationships and the keys

Once an entity-relationship diagram has been drawn, it is of course important to test the relationship and keys, and assess its appropriateness. Such an assessment/test would involve an examination to determine if, for example:

■ all entities have been correctly identified,
■ all attributes have been correctly identified,
■ all attributes have been associated with the correct entity, and
■ all cardinality pairs are appropriate.

### Advantages and disadvantages of entity-relationship diagrams

The advantages of entity-relationship diagrams are:

■ they are a simple and easy to understand, and
■ they are a powerful technique for defining the relationships within a system.

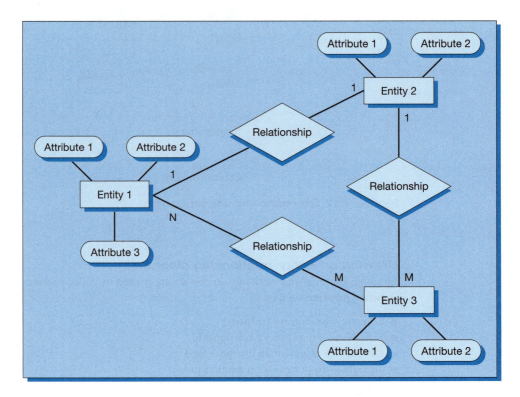

**Figure 7.18** Entity-relationship diagram

The main disadvantages are:

- they can become overly complex,
- they can be difficult to interpret, and
- they can sometimes be difficult to revise.

## Decision tables

As we have seen, whilst flowcharts – in particular program flowcharts – can be used to provide a representation of a system, procedure or process, such a descriptive technique may not always be suitable, especially when attempting to describe a complex decision process. An accepted alternative to flowcharting a system, procedure or process is to construct a decision table, although such tables are often used in addition to, as opposed to instead of, such flowcharts.

A decision table is a table designed to represent the logic of an activity and illustrate the possible combinations of available outcomes. Such tables are typically divided into four quadrants, these being:

- conditions,
- condition alternatives,
- actions, and
- action entries.

See Figure 7.19.

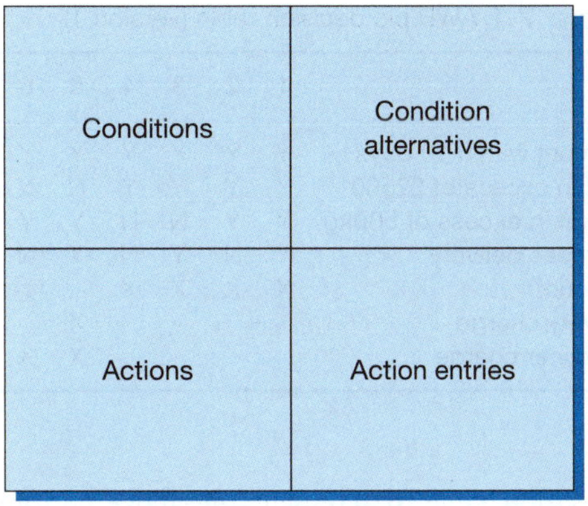

**Figure 7.19** Decision table

In the decision table:

- each condition corresponds to a variable whose possible values are listed among the condition alternatives, and
- each action is a procedure or operation to perform, with each action entry specifying whether and/or in what order the action is to be performed.

### Constructing a decision table

To construct a decision table, it is important to determine the maximum size of the table, eliminate any improbable situations, contradictions, inconsistencies or redundancies, and simplify it as much as possible. That is:

- determine the number of conditions that may affect the decision – the number of conditions becomes the number of rows in the top-half of the decision table,
- determine the number of possible actions that can be taken – the number of actions becomes the number of rows in the lower-half of the decision table,
- determine the number of condition alternatives for each condition,[38] and
- calculate the maximum number of columns in the decision table by multiplying the number of alternatives for each condition: for example, if there were four conditions and two alternatives for each of the conditions (yes or no) there would be 16 possibilities.

Have a look at the following example.

*ABW plc is a UK-based company supplying specialised building materials to the UK building industry. ABW plc allows customers 30 days' credit and calculates customer discounts and charges as follows:*

- *if the total value of the order is in excess of £2500 and the invoice is paid within 10 days of the invoice date a discount of 5% is received – payments made after day 10 do not attract a discount,*
- *if the total weight of the order is in excess of 500kg special delivery containers are used for which a charge is made – if the value of the building materials order is in excess of £2500 no charge is made for the special delivery containers,*
- *if the customer requests delivery outside the UK an additional charge is imposed – if the value of the building materials order is in excess of £2500 and the invoice is paid within 10 days no charge is made for the overseas delivery.*

**Table 7.1** AWB plc decision table (version 1)

| | 1 | 2 | 3 | 4 | 5 | 6 | 7 | 8 | 9 | 10 | 11 | 12 | 13 | 14 | 15 | 16 |
|---|---|---|---|---|---|---|---|---|---|---|---|---|---|---|---|---|
| Payment within 10 days | Y | Y | Y | Y | Y | Y | Y | Y | N | N | N | N | N | N | N | N |
| Cost in excess of £2500 | Y | Y | Y | Y | N | N | N | N | Y | Y | Y | Y | N | N | N | N |
| Weight in excess of 500kg | Y | Y | N | N | Y | Y | N | N | Y | Y | N | N | Y | Y | N | N |
| Overseas delivery | Y | N | Y | N | Y | N | Y | N | Y | N | Y | N | Y | N | Y | N |
| Discount | X | X | X | X | | | | | | | | | | | | |
| Delivery charge | | | | | X | | X | | X | | X | | X | | X | |
| Container charge | | | | | X | X | | | | | | | X | X | | |

A decision table to represent the above customer policy could be constructed as follows. Because this is a simple binary decision table in which the decision rule is yes (Y) or no (N), the number of possible conditions is: [(2 alternatives for condition 1) × (2 alternatives for condition 2) × (2 alternatives for condition 3) × (2 alternatives for condition 4)] or = $(2^4)$ = 16.

See Table 7.1.

In the above decision table:

- the possible conditions are:
  - payment within 10 days,
  - cost in excess of £2500,
  - weight in excess of 500kg, and
  - overseas delivery,
- the condition alternatives (of which there are 16 possibilities) are indicated with a Y (yes) or N (no),
- the possible actions are:
  - discount,
  - delivery charge, and
  - container charge, and
- the possible action entries are indicated with an X.

To simplify the above decision table, firstly we can eliminate column 8, column 10, column 12 and column 16 – there are no actions to be implemented. Secondly, we can apply the dash rule to columns where existing pairs can be merged – that is where an alternative does not make a difference to the outcome. The dash (–) signifies that a condition can be either yes (Y) or no (N), and action will still take place.

The revised decision table would look like Table 7.2.

**Table 7.2** AWB plc decision table (version 2)

| | 1, 2 | 3, 4 | 5, 13 | 6, 14 | 7 | 9 | 11, 15 |
|---|---|---|---|---|---|---|---|
| Payment within 10 days | Y | Y | – | – | Y | N | N |
| Cost in excess of £2500 | Y | Y | N | N | N | Y | Y |
| Weight in excess of 500kg | Y | N | Y | Y | N | Y | N |
| Overseas delivery | – | – | Y | N | Y | Y | Y |
| Discount | X | X | | | | | |
| Delivery charge | | | X | | X | X | X |
| Container charge | | | X | X | | | |

**Table 7.3** AWB plc decision table (version 3)

|  | 1, 2, 3, 4 | 5, 13 | 6, 14 | 7 | 9, 11, 15 |
|---|---|---|---|---|---|
| Payment within 10 days | Y | – | – | Y | N |
| Cost in excess of £2500 | Y | N | N | N | Y |
| Weight in excess of 500kg | – | Y | Y | N | – |
| Overseas delivery | – | Y | N | Y | Y |
| Discount | X |  |  |  |  |
| Delivery charge |  | X |  | X | X |
| Container charge |  | X | X |  |  |

We can apply the dash rule again to produce a further simplified and final decision table – see Table 7.3.

### Advantages and disadvantages of decision tables

The advantages of using decision tables are:

- they provide a simple and understandable summary of the processing tasks/actions for a large number of conditions, and
- they can be easily amended when changes in organisation policies/procedures result in the development/emergence of new tasks/action for existing conditions.

The main disadvantages are:

- they do not provide details of the order in which tasks/actions and conditions can/do occur, and
- whilst they can be easily amended, they can become overly complex and difficult to interpret.

## Coding system

A code can be defined in many ways, for example, it can be defined as:

- a collection of rules or principles or law, for example a legal code, or
- an organised collection of instructions, for example a computer code, or
- an arbitrary compilation of symbols and/or characters, for example a security/access code, or
- a structured arrangement of alpha-numeric characters, for example an information code.

For our purposes, we will use the last option above and define a code as a system of alpha-numeric characters used to represent a data/information set.

Where such codes are used to facilitate the accumulation, storage and transfer of data and/or information, such use is referred to as *encoding*. Where such codes are used to control, protect or restrict access to data and/or information, such use is referred to as *encryption*.

We will consider the issue of encryption later in Chapter 13. For the moment we will use a coding system for encoding purposes.

In accounting information systems, a code/coding system may be:

- numeric (or number-based) – for example a credit card/debit card number or a network IP address,
- alphabetic (or letter-based) – for example a computer network user name and/or password, and/or
- alpha-numeric (or letter and number-based) – for example a customer reference number and/or an employee's payroll reference number.

In a commercial/business context, the use of a coding system – for encoding purposes – can be classified as either:

- a chart of account-based codes, or
- a non-chart of account-based codes.

Before we look at each of these in detail, consider the following question: What are the characteristics of a good coding system? In general, the characteristics of a good code and/or coding system are:

- a coding system must have a clearly defined structure,
- a coding system must be sufficiently flexible to cope with expansion,
- a coding system must be adaptable to user needs,
- a coding system should be meaningful,
- each individual code within the coding system must have a unique identity,
- each individual code within the coding system should be sequential,
- each individual code must be universal and standard (within a company/organisation), and
- each individual code should be as short as possible (where human interface is expected).

### Chart of account-based codes

A chart of accounts is the coding system (structure) adopted within a company and/or organisation for the purposes of processing accounting related data. The purpose of such a coding system is to provide a means of:

- classifying income and expenditure,
- classifying capital and revenue transactions, and
- managing/controlling the recording of accounting transactions.

More importantly, a chart of accounts should provide a structured framework for:

- the interpretation and analysis of transaction-based/accounting-related information (a financial accounting function),
- the management of transaction-based/accounting-related resources (a financial management function), and
- the determination and allocation of transaction-based/accounting-related responsibilities (a management accounting function).

So what does a chart of accounts look like? Have a look at Appendix 7.1. This contains an example chart of accounts for a fictitious company called HUBS Ltd.[39]

So who determines the structure of a company's/organisations chart of accounts? Although in some countries there is a formally imposed chart of accounts used by all companies/organisations[40] – for example the French *plan comptable* or the Spanish, *plan general de contabilidad* – in the UK and many other Anglo-Saxon countries (see Nobes and Parker (2004)) there is no such imposed formal requirement. In such countries, charts of accounts tend to be developed independently – on a company by company and/or an organisation by organisation basis. As a result, the nature and structure of a company's/organisation's chart of accounts are often determined by internal management policy – albeit with significant input from the financial accountant. Such a chart of accounts generally seeks to match/combine:

- the organisational/operational structure of the company/organisation, and
- the regulatory structure of the company's financial statements.

It is for this latter reason that many company/organisation charts of accounts appear to be very similar.

All companies within the European Union (EU) are bound by and required to adopt extant directives which comprise the EU company law regulatory framework. In particular, all countries within the EU have adopted the EU Fourth Directive which provides prescribed formats for company profit and loss accounts and balance sheets. For example:

- in the UK the required formats were adopted via the UK company law framework – currently Schedule 4 of the Companies Act 1985,
- in Germany the required formats were adopted via the German commercial code (the *Handelsgesetzbuch (HGB)*), and
- in France the required formats were adopted via the French accounting plan (the *Plan Comptable*)).

In addition, as of 2005, listed companies on many of the largest stock exchanges (including all the major EU-based exchanges) are required to adhere to additional reporting requirements as prescribed by IASC International Financial Reporting Standards – in particular IFRS 1.

Consider the example chart of accounts for HUBS Ltd in Appendix 7.1. The chart of accounts for HUBS Ltd is hierarchically structured into three levels – see the summary codes – as follows:

- the geographical locations of the company,
- the internal (departmental) structure of the company, and finally
- the structure of the company's financial statements – that is the balance sheet and the profit and loss account.

Have a look at the following.

*Decode the following codes:*

- *50-51-0402/3*
- *10-11-0900-3-3-2-10*

*For the code 50-51-0402/3 the narrative would be:*

- *Hull – Production department – Plant and Machinery – Cost – Assets acquired during the year.*

*For the code 10-11-0900-3-3-2-10 the narrative would be:*

- *Company – All departments – Waged staff – Managers – Senior – Monthly paid – PAYE*

*Encode the following narratives:*

- *Rent paid for premises used solely by the accounting department in Manchester,*
- *Overtime paid to hourly paid part-time production staff in Southampton*

*For the narrative: Rent paid for premises used solely by the accounting department in Manchester, the code would be: 40-71-1000-1.*

*For the narrative: Overtime paid to hourly paid part-time production staff in Southampton, the code would be: 20-51-900-1-6-0-02.*

### Non-chart of account codes

Of course, companies/organisations use a range of codes other than those we have referred to above for a variety of different purposes. For example, a company/organisation may use a code:

- as a unique identifier – for example a product bar code or an employee's payroll number,
- for the compression data – for example an abbreviated product/service name,
- for the classification of data/collection of transactions – for example a debtor/creditor reference, and/or
- for the communication of a special meaning – for example access/security codes.

## Databases

Although a database can, broadly speaking, be defined as an organised collection of data or perhaps, more appropriately, as a logical and systematic collection of interrelated data that is managed and stored as a single unit (as we saw in Chapter 4), in general, a collection of data is only considered to constitute a database if:

- the data is *managed* to ensure data integrity and maintain data quality,
- the data is *organised* into an accepted and agreed schema,
- the data can be *accessed* by a shared community of approved users/user applications, and/or
- the data can be *interrogated* using an appropriate query language.[41]

So why have databases become so important in the management of transactions related data? There are many reasons, perhaps the most important being:

- the increasing volumes of transaction-related data,
- the complexity and interconnectedness of such data,
- the inherent business value of accurate transaction-related data, and
- the security and privacy restrictions imposed on the management of transaction-related data.

### Databases . . . a (very) brief history

Although the collection of data in the form of lists and/or tables can be traced back to the Sumerians of Mesopotamia, the earliest known use of the term 'data base' (as two words) was in the early 1960s.[42] Use of the term database (as a single word) did not become commonplace in the UK and Europe until the early 1970s.

During the latter part of the 1960s, two key data models arose:

- the network model – based on the work and ideas of Charles Bachman,[43] and
- the hierarchical model – used and developed by Rockwell Industries.

It was at about the same time that Charles Bachman began development of the first database management systems.

The relational model was first proposed by Edgar F Codd in 1970[44] and although research prototype databases using the relational model were announced as early as 1976,[45] the first commercial products did not appear until the early 1980s.[46]

During the latter part of the 1980s research activity focused on distributed database systems, with the 1990s seeing attention shift toward object-oriented databases. The early 21st century has witnessed a consolidation of databases technologies together with extensive development research in the increasingly fashionable area of XML[47] databases.

### Databases . . . alternative data models

As suggested above, there are a number of alternative data models developed for, and used to, structure data within a database. A data model is simply an abstract description of *how* data is represented/related in a database. Such alternatives include:

- the flat data model,
- the hierarchical data model,
- the network data model,
- the relational data model, and
- the object-oriented data model.

## Flat data model

Using the flat file data model, data in a database is stored in a two-dimensional table – a single database record per line, with data divided into fields using delimiters or fixed column positions with no relationships or links between records and fields except the database table structure.

Although databases using the flat data model data are simple and easy to maintain, and ideal for small amounts of data, it can be difficult to store complex data, with often multiple copies of the same data being stored, and costly to process and collate large amounts of data.

An example of a flat file database would be a table and/or list of debtor names and addresses.

## Hierarchical data model

Using the hierarchical data model, data within a database is organised into a tree-like structure using a parent/child arrangement inasmuch as data are related to each other using a one-to-many ($1:n$) relationship. Although the hierarchical data model was widely used in early database systems it is now rare, mainly because of its inability to accurately model real-world relationships.

Consider the following example.

*GHK Ltd is a small Manchester-based retail company specialising in children's games and toys. The company maintains personnel records on all employees. In addition, it also maintains records of any children the employees may have. That is there is:*

- *a collection of employee details as a record type called Employees, and*
- *a collection of children details as a record type called Children.*

Using a hierarchical data model, the Employees would represent the parent segment of the hierarchy and the Children would represent the child segment of the hierarchy. That is an employee may have many children, but each child can only have one parent.

But what if both the mother and the father of the child were employees of GHK Ltd? That would mean the one-to-many ($1:n$) relationship central to the hierarchical data model would be violated, because not only can an employee have more than one child, a child can have more than one parent! The relationship is therefore a many-to-many ($m:n$) relationship and, effectively, the hierarchy becomes a network.

## Network data model

Conceived and developed by Charles Bachman (the standard specification was published in 1969 by CODASYL[48]), the network model[49] allows an entity type to have multiple parent and child relationships – that is many-to-many ($m:n$) relationships – forming what is often referred to as a lattice type structure. At the foundation of the network model is the so-called 'set construct' – a set consists of an owner record type, a set name and a member record type, with a member record type able to belong to more than one set, hence the multi-parent concept. An owner record type can also be a member or owner in another set.

Although the network data model was widely implemented, it failed to gain popular support and become the dominant data model, perhaps for two reasons. Firstly, many companies/ organisations elected to use the hierarchical model in their products rather than the network data model (e.g. IBM Inc. and its Information Management System) and secondly the capabilities of the network model were eventually surpassed by development and widespread acceptance of the relational data model.

## Relational data model

Using the relational data model, data within a database is organised and accessed according to the relationships between data. Such relationships are expressed by means of two-dimensional tables,[50] which can be used to store data without reference to and/or consideration of any other physical orientation and relationship.

We will look at the relational data model and its use/application in relational databases in a little more detail later in this chapter.

### Object-oriented data model

A key problem with each of the above data models is their limited ability to store only alpha and/or numeric text-based data. Using the object-oriented data model, complex data types such as video graphics, pictures and three-dimensional representations can be stored, often using a traditional hierarchical arrangement in which lower class objects (called sub-class objects) are related to and can inherit attributes from higher-class objects (called super-class objects).

So which database model is the most popular? In a contemporary context, by far the most popular data model is the relational data model, despite the clear advantages offered by the far superior object-oriented data model. Why?

For two reasons: firstly, the costs associated with the practical implementation of the object-oriented data model and secondly, the limited availability (in an accounting information systems context) of appropriate functional applications.

To understand how a database works it is important to understand its various elements – elements often referred to as the components of a database environment.

## Elements of a database environment

Within a database environment, there are five separate elements, these being:

- the database schema,
- the database audience,
- the database management system (DBMS),
- the database administration system (DBAS),[51] and
- the physical database.

### Database schema

A database schema is essentially a structural narrative describing the logical structure of the database, that is:

- the type of data held within a database, i.e. the objects/facts represented in the database, and
- the structure/organisation of data stored within a database, i.e. the relationships between each of the objects/facts represented in the database.

Whilst, there are, as suggested earlier, a number of alternative approaches (or data models) that can be used to structure/organise data within a database, there are essentially three levels to any data model/schema, these being:

- the external level schema,
- the conceptual level schema, and
- the internal level schema.

See Figure 7.20.

The above three-level architecture is often referred to as the ANSI-SPARC architecture,[52] its objective being to maintain a so-called 'separation of views' of how data is stored within the database. That is a separation of views between:

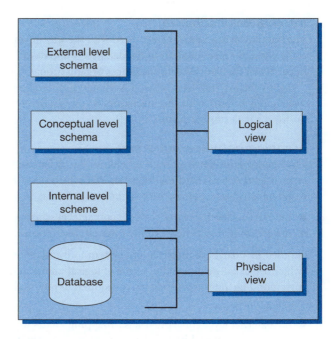

**Figure 7.20** Database schema

- the 'logical view' of the data within a database, and
- the 'physical view' of the data within a database.

Whereas the logical view considers how the users and/or user applications understand/perceive data within the database – that is how data appears to be stored – the physical view considers how the data are physically arranged and stored within the database.

Why is such a separation of view important? Firstly, it allows independent customised user views – that is each user within the database audience is able to access the same data, but has a different customised view of the data: changes to one user's view does not impact on another user's view. Secondly, it hides the physical storage details from users and therefore allows the database administrator within the database administration system to change the database storage structures without impacting on the users' view of the database.

### External level schema

The external level schema is concerned with the way in which individual users view portions of the data within the database – sometimes referred to as *sub-schema*. Such an external level schema can, and indeed will, consist not only of a number of different views of the database – one view for each user/user application, describing that portion of the database relevant to a particular user with such user views – but also different views of the same data for different users/user applications.

### Conceptual level schema

The conceptual level schema is concerned with the company-wide/organisation-wide view of the data within the database – independent of any storage considerations. That is the conceptual level schema describes:

- what data are stored in the database, and
- what relationships exist among the data within the database.

It is, in essence, a complete view of the data requirements of the company/organisation.

### Internal level schema

The internal level schema is concerned with the way in which the data are actually stored – that is the physical representation of the database – and describes how data are stored and accessed, in particular in terms of data structures/organisation.

Below the internal level schema is the physical level managed by the database management system and it deals with the mechanics of physically creating, storing and/or retrieving data on/from a data storage device.

### Mapping between schemas

The relationships between each schema – that is between the external level schema, the conceptual level schema and the internal level schema (see Figure 7.20 above) are referred to as mapping between schemas. Such mappings between:

- the external level views to the conceptual level schema, and
- the conceptual level items to the internal descriptions,

are used in a database management system to translate user/user application requests for data (which are usually expressed in terms of logical names and data relationships) into equivalent/corresponding indexes and addresses required to physically access the data within the database.

Put simply:

- the external level/conceptual level mapping charts a particular external view to its corresponding conceptual item – that is mapping a user/user application's view onto the relevant part of a conceptual level schema, and
- the conceptual level/internal level mapping charts a particular conceptual item to its corresponding internal level description – that is between a conceptual record to its stored corresponding item.

## Database audience

There are three broad classes of users within the database audience, these being:

- the application programmer – responsible for creating, altering, amending and managing the database,
- the database administrator (via the database administration system) – responsible for controlling all operations within the database, and
- the end-user, who access the database via the database management systems using either:
  - a pre-defined user program, and/or
  - a direct query using an appropriate query language.

## Database management system (DBMS)

The database management system is the interface which coordinates the various data transactions between the database and users/user applications. The database management system provides a link between the way data are physically stored and each user/user application's logical view of the data, and as such is responsible for:

- controlling the organisation of data[53] within the database,
- monitoring the storage, and retrieval of data from the database,
- managing the transfer/movement of data between the database and authorised users/user applications, and
- applying appropriate authorisation checks and validation procedures to maintain the security and integrity of the data within the database.

See Figure 7.21.

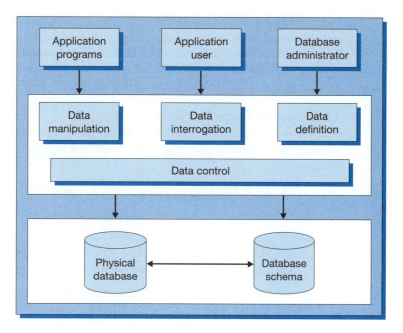

**Figure 7.21** Database management system

Such database management systems are often classified according to the database schema/ data model they are designed to support – for example, a network database management system, a relational database management system, or an object orientated database management system. Why?

Put simply, some database management system functions/activities are data model independent, that is they are not determined by the data model adopted within the database. Such data model independent functions/activities would include, for example, processes and procedures associated with:

- managing database performance,
- providing authorisation services,
- maintaining data integrity,
- ensuring functional concurrency, and/or
- monitoring data security.

Many database management system functions/activities are data model dependent – that is they are determined by the data model adopted within the database. Such data model dependent functions/activities would include, for example, processes and procedures associated with:

- accessing data within the database, and/or
- interrogating/querying data within the database.

Put simply, a database management system provides a means of performing a series of basic procedural functions often classified as:

- data control functions – using a data control language,
- data definition functions – using a data definition language,
- data manipulation functions – using a data manipulation language, and
- data interrogation functions – using a data query language.

Note: Although there are many types of data definition languages, data manipulation languages and data query languages available, currently the most popular 'all encompassing' language is SQL (structured query language) which is used to retrieve and manipulate data in a relational database. SQL is a fourth generation non-procedural language.

We will look at SQL in a little more detail later in this chapter.

### Data control language (DCL)

The data control language is used for controlling access to data within the database. In the case of SQL,[54] data definition functions are defined by a series of commands such as 'grant' and 'revoke'.

### Data definition language (DDL)

The data definition language allows the database administration system to:

- initialise/create the database,
- define and describe the logical structure of data within a database, and
- construct a data dictionary for the data within a database.

In the case of SQL, data definition functions are defined by a series of commands such as 'truncate', 'create' and 'alter'.

## Data dictionary

A data dictionary is a key component of the database management system and contains definitions and representations of all data elements stored within the database. Its purpose is to:

- specify the attributes of the data within the database, and
- stipulate user access limitations and/or security constraints imposed on specific data fields/ data records within the database.

For example, a company/organisation may use a database to store data on its customers – one aspect of which could be the customer number/reference. Information on the structure of the customer number/reference would be held in the data dictionary – information such as:

- the name of the data element,
- a description of the data element,
- data records which contain the data element,
- the source of the data element,
- the data field length, and
- the data field type.

In addition, the data dictionary would provide details on:

- which data processing procedures/programs can use the data element,
- which process outputs will contain the data element, and
- which users are authorised to create, amend and/or delete such a data element.

Figure 7.22 provides an illustration of the structure of an example data dictionary.

| Data element name | Description | Data records | Field length | Field type | Access level | Data element source | Data element output | Authorised user |
|---|---|---|---|---|---|---|---|---|
| | | | | | | | | |

**Figure 7.22** Data dictionary

So what are the advantages of using a data dictionary? Firstly, it ensures data consistency and promotes data integrity. For example, a company/organisation may use a database containing several tables which hold the same data elements (e.g. customer name and address). Using a data dictionary would ensure that the format of data elements would be consistent throughout the database. Secondly, it facilitates expansion. For example, where additional tables are required to be added to a database, tables which will contain data elements already held in other existing tables, it is not necessary to define each of those data elements again.

Perhaps the most significant disadvantage of using a data dictionary is that without proper management, such a data dictionary could become out-dated and irrelevant – especially where additions to, deletions of, and amendments to, data elements in the data dictionary are not properly monitored/controlled.

### Data manipulation language

The data manipulation language is used for data maintenance purposes, in particular to:

- update data within the database,
- insert data into the database, and
- delete data from the database.

In the case of SQL, data manipulation capabilities defined by a series of commands such as 'insert', 'delete' and 'update'.

There are essentially two types of data manipulation languages, these being:

- a procedural data manipulation language which allows the user/user application to define *how* the data within the database should be manipulated, and
- a non-procedural data manipulation language (or declarative data manipulation language) which allows the user/user application to define *what* data within the database is needed rather than how the data should be manipulated/retrieved.

### Data query language

The data query language allows users/user applications to interrogate data within the database. Whereas the data manipulation language is designed to facilitate change to or amendment of data within a database, the data query language is designed to select, retrieve, order and present sub-sets of data from within the database.

In the case of SQL, data interrogation functions are defined by the command 'select'.

### Database management system . . . as a control facility

The database management system provides two types of control often referred to as:

- transaction control, and
- concurrency control.

## Transaction control

One of the key control functions of a database management system is to enforce database transaction models/processes that possess appropriate data integrity properties. To do so, most database management systems enforce what are often referred to as ACID rules, these being:

- Atomicity – all the tasks in a transaction must be performed completely or cancelled,
- Consistency – every transaction must preserve the integrity of the database: that is all transactions must leave the database in a consistent state,
- Isolation – transactions cannot interfere with each other,
- Durability – completed transactions cannot be aborted or the results of the transaction discarded.

In practice, however, many database management systems allow the selective relaxation of some of the above rules where to do so would have a positive affect/impact on overall performance.

## Concurrency control

In a database management system concurrency control is concerned with the management of database transactions and is used to:

- ensure transactions are executed in a safe and secure manner,
- ensure transactions are not lost when recovering failed and/or aborted transactions,
- ensure transactions follow the above ACID rules, and
- ensure simultaneous users cannot edit/amend/delete the same data record, at the same time.

### Database management system . . . an operational context

In general, the processing of a user/user application access request can be viewed as a series of six sequential stages, as follows:

- Stage 1: request – using an appropriate data manipulation language, a user/user application issues an access request (sometimes referred to as an access call) for specific data (data elements) within the database.
- Stage 2: analysis – the database management system receives and analyses the access request (access call) by matching the requested (called) data (data elements) against the user view and conceptual view. If the data request is a match (that is the data is available within the database *and* the user/user application is authorised to access the requested (called for) data), the data request is approved and processed. If the data request does not match (that is either the data is not available within the database *and/or* the user/user application is not authorised to access the requested (called for) data), the data request is denied.
- Stage 3: retrieval – the database management system determines the appropriate access method for retrieval of the requested (called for) data and passes the instructions to the operating system (more specifically an operating system utility program) which performs the data retrieval.
- Stage 4: access – the operating system utility program accesses the data storage device and retrieves the requested (called for) data from the physical database.
- Stage 5: location – the operating system utility program initially locates the requested (called for) data in a memory buffer area managed by the database management system and then transfers the requested (called for) data to a location accessible by the user/user application issuing the access request.
- Stage 6: restore – once the access request has been completed the retrieval, access and location steps would be reversed to restore the requested data into the database.

## Database administration system (DBAS)

The database administration system is responsible for the overall control of the database system/resource. Where there is sharing of a common database between communities of multiple users, the database administration system – in particular the database administrator – plays a vital role in:

- the planning, design and implementation of the database environment,
- the maintenance of all database facilities, and
- the management and coordination of database-related activities.

Why? Because such sharing requires control. More specifically, such sharing requires:

- the establishment of rules and regulations for the supervision of user/user application access,
- the development of operational guidelines and procedures for the coordination of user/user application access, and
- the creation of appropriate processes and protocols for the management of database change,[55]

in order to protect the integrity and ensure the security of the database resource.

## Physical database

Whilst it is of course necessary for a database to possess an identifiable physicality, it is important to note that, in reality, the physical database will often bear little relation to the logical structure of the database. Why? Because as new and more efficient storage technologies and media develop so the physical structure/physical nature of the database will change. Such change will not necessarily affect the logical structure of the database.

The physical database would comprise of two components:

- a physical structure in which to store the data – for example sequential, non-sequential, indexed, etc., and
- a physical medium on which to store the database (e.g. disc, tape).

## Relational databases – understanding the components

By far the most popular type of database in use – at least within a business/commercial context – a relational database is simply a database whose structure is defined by the relational data model in which data is organised as a collection of tables logically associated with each other by common shared attributes.

A relational database consists of two interrelated components:

- a structural component – that is a set of tables (also-called relations)[56] in which data elements are stored, and
- a manipulative component – that is an interrogative facility with which to create, amend, question, and/or manipulate data and tables.

### Structural component

Within a relational database, data elements are organised into collections of record-like structures, with the relationships between data elements expressed by means of tables[57] which are used to represent[58] artificial and/or real-world objects (or more appropriately entities), with each data field within a table representing a selected attribute. That is:

- each row within the table contains data about a specific type of entity represented within the table, and
- each column within the table contains data about a specific attribute of that entity.

A table can be defined as an un-ordered collection of rows each of which consists of one or more un-ordered attributes (columns).

Where a database consists of more than a single table, it is likely that some commonality between a number of the tables would exists: that is some of the data elements and/or data attributes would be repeated in more than one of the database tables. This is an important feature of tables within a relational database.

As such, we can distinguish between three types of keys:

- A *primary key* is a data element/attribute within a data field of a data record that enables a database to uniquely distinguish one data record in a database from another data record within a database table.
- A *secondary key* is a data element/attribute within a data field of a data record that is not unique and cannot be used to distinguish one data record in a database from another data record within a database table.
- A *foreign key* is a data element/attribute within a data field of a data record within a database table that is a primary key in another database table.

Consider the following example.

*MKPH Ltd is a medium-sized retail company based in Scotland. The company sells a range of electrical products for the home. The following tables have been taken for MKPH Ltd's database:*

- Table 7.4 contains sample data extracted from MKPL Ltd's sales database,

**Table 7.4** MKPL Ltd sample data extracted from a sales database

| Sales invoice | Date | Product | Product number | Unit sales price | Total price | Customer reference number | Customer name |
|---|---|---|---|---|---|---|---|
| 32165 | 10.10.06 | CD player | RA3254 | 25 | 250 | 4933ED | Edwards, T.T. |
| 33812 | 12.11.06 | DVD player | SB3474 | 30 | 300 | 3100HE | Helman, L.P. |
| 34286 | 06.03.07 | Digital radio | RJ3570 | 65 | 130 | 6353ST | Stockman, L. |
| 36116 | 16.03.07 | Television | LH3172 | 125 | 500 | 8842SI | Simpson, O.S. |
| 37147 | 04.04.07 | DVD player | BM3606 | 42 | 840 | 1011JA | Jarvis, N. |
| 38642 | 15.04.07 | iPod | DO3849 | 72 | 360 | 3331CA | Cahill, R. |
| 39533 | 16.05.07 | CD player | AS3332 | 67 | 670 | 6353ST | Stockman, L. |
| 39756 | 21.06.07 | Radio | BJ3862 | 18 | 360 | 3100HE | Helman, L.P. |

- Table 7.5 contains sample data extracted from MKPL Ltd's stock database, and

**Table 7.5** MKPL Ltd sample data extracted from a stock database

| Product number | Description | Colour | Quantity | Unit cost price | Total cost | Supplier reference number | Supplier name |
|---|---|---|---|---|---|---|---|
| AS3332 | CD player | Silver | 10 | 50 | 500 | 36598/1 | Marshall Ltd |
| BC3678 | Digital receiver | Black | 11 | 35 | 385 | 65829/6 | Steinway plc |
| BJ3862 | Radio | Red | 12 | 12 | 144 | 26453/4 | Smithson Ltd |
| BM3606 | DVD player | Black | 25 | 25 | 625 | 78453/2 | PDP Ltd |
| DO3849 | iPod | White | 11 | 65 | 715 | 32491/7 | Apple Inc |
| LH3172 | Television | Silver | 18 | 98 | 1764 | 58943/6 | Benson plc |
| MU3989 | Television | Black | 12 | 195 | 2340 | 65845/8 | Zhu plc |
| RA3254 | CD player | Black | 24 | 19 | 456 | 66451/9 | Robson Ryan plc |
| RJ3570 | Digital radio | White | 25 | 52 | 1300 | 45821/1 | Bright Ltd |
| SB3474 | DVD player | Silver | 12 | 23 | 276 | 59731/6 | Reeves plc |

- Table 7.6 contains sample data extracted from MKPL Ltd's customer database.

**Table 7.6** MKPL Ltd sample data extracted from a customer database

| Customer number | Customer name | Customer address | Customer postcode | Customer credit limit |
|---|---|---|---|---|
| 4933EA | Edwards, T.T. | 70 Hutchinson Road, High Stile. | HI62 5XY | 3,000 |
| 3331CA | Cahill, R. | 593 Upton Street, Low Bridge. | LO15 6BA | 2,000 |
| 4030DA | Davison, B. | 36 Fowler Street, High Stile. | HI01 3CD | 4,000 |
| 5682SI | Simon, L.M. | 767 Howitt Close, Low Bridge. | LO6 5LX | 2,000 |
| 1011JA | Jarvis, N. | 75 Worman Street, High Stile. | HI17 8ML | 6,000 |
| 3010HE | Helman, L.P. | 87 Austin Close, High Stile. | HI17 5YY | 9,000 |
| 7803DE | Derwert, N.U. | 67 Newbold Street, Low Bridge. | LO8 7BJ | 3,000 |
| 8233LE | Lewis, E.K. | 371 Bashaw Road, Midshire. | MI16 4HK | 3,000 |
| 6535ST | Stockman, Y. | 136 Dullea Road, Midshire. | MI12 7MO | 7,000 |
| 5003RO | Rogers, R.T. | 573 Graley Street, Low Bridge. | LO7 7DE | 4,000 |
| 8841SI | Simpson, O.S. | 251 Hawkswood Street Low Bridge. | LO19 8YH | 4,000 |

Within each of the above tables, there is a data element/attribute unique to each table – that is a primary key, for example:

- within the sales database table (see Table 7.4) – the sales invoice number,
- within the stock database table (see Table 7.5) – the stock item number, and
- within the customer database table (see Table 7.6) – the customer reference number.

Note: In each of the above, the primary keys are a single data element/attribute (within a data field). It is not uncommon for a primary key within a table to be a combination of data elements/attributes.

Also, within each of the above tables, there is a data element/attribute not unique to each table – that is a secondary key, for example:

- within the sales database table (see Table 7.4) – the transaction date of the sales, and
- within the stock database table (see Table 7.5) – the stock description.

Foreign keys are used to link database tables. Two examples within the sales database table (see Table 7.4) would be:

- the customer reference number – this would link the sales database table to the customer database table in which the customer reference number is a primary key, and
- the product item number – this would link the sales database table to the stock database table.

To maintain the integrity of the database, there are four basic regulatory requirements, these being:

- every column in a row must be singled valued – that is there can be only one value in a cell,
- all non-key attributes in a table should describe a characteristic of the object identified by the primary key,
- a primary key value in a table cannot contain a *null* (blank) value – often referred to as the entity integrity rule, and
- for every foreign key value in a table there must be a corresponding primary key value in another table in the database – often referred to as the referential integrity rule.

### Manipulative component

Within a relational database it is important to be able to manage the data contained within the database. Perhaps one of the most popular computer languages used to create, modify, retrieve and manipulate data within a relational database is SQL.

During the 1970s, a group of researchers at the IBM Inc. research centre in California developed a database system that became known as 'System R'. The design was partially based on the ideas explored by Edgar F. Codd in his 1970 seminal paper.[59] Structured English QUEry Language (SEQUEL) was designed to manipulate and retrieve data stored in System R. The acronym SEQUEL was later condensed to SQL.[60]

Although the late 1970s saw IBM Inc. develop a number of commercial products based on the System R prototype that implemented SQL, it was not until 1979 when Relational Software, Inc. introduced Oracle (version 2) that the first commercial implementation of SQL became available.

SQL was adopted as a standard by ANSI (the American National Standards Institute) in 1986 and by ISO (the International Organisation for Standardisation) in 1987, although it has subsequently undergone a number of major revisions/additions.

Note: SQL is not a conventional computer programming language in the normal sense that Visual Basic, C++, Java are. SQL is a language used exclusively to create, manipulate and interrogate databases, and is concerned with data and results. Each SQL statement produces a result, whether that result is an update to a record, a deletion of a record, a query, or the creation of a database table.

Let's have a look at some of the SQL keywords we introduced earlier in our discussion on database management systems. For this we will use the following brief scenario:

*Rockpool plc is a UK-based book retailer. The company owns and operates 392 high street bookshops located throughout the UK and Europe. The company has estimated that it currently holds approximately 1.2 million English language books, and 900,000 non-English language books on a diverse range of subjects.*

*The company maintains a database of all books held at all 392 retail locations, and all 22 of its major storage depots located in the UK, France, Germany, Norway and Spain.*

## SQL keywords[61]

To create a database, the SQL command would be:

CREATE DATABASE database_name;

To create a database called Books, that is a register of all the books held by Rockpool plc (essentially a stock register), the SQL command statement would be:

CREATE DATABASE Book_Register;

To create a table within a database, the SQL command statement would be in the generic form:

CREATE TABLE name (col1 datatype, col2 datatype, col3 datatype, etc . . . );

To create a table called Books, the SQL command statement would be:

CREATE TABLE Books (Product Item Number INTEGER, Book Title TEXT,[62] Publisher TEXT, Author TEXT, ISBN No, INTEGER, Price CURRENCY, Year of Publication DATE, Location INTEGER);

To create a table called Users, the SQL command statement would be:

CREATE TABLE Users (Last Name TEXT,[63] First Name TEXT, User ID TEXT, Location TEXT, Department TEXT, Employee Number INTEGER, Access Level INTEGER);

Note: It is important to remember that once a database table is created the structure is not necessarily fixed. As requirements change, the structure of the database is likely to evolve to ensure all requirements are fulfilled.

**Table 7.7** Rockpool Ltd Books database table

| Product item number | Book title | Publisher | (first named) Author | ISBN | Price | Year | Location |
|---|---|---|---|---|---|---|---|
| 198201 | Accounting Information Systems | Prentice Hall | Romney | 0-13-196855-6 | 47.99 | 2006 | New Jersey |
| 119897 | Corporate Financial Management | Prentice Hall | Arnold | 0-27-368726-3 | 44.99 | 2005 | London |
| 152463 | Business Accounting and Finance | McGraw Hill | Davies | 0-07-710809-4 | 35.99 | 2005 | Maidenhead |
| 115267 | Organisational Behaviour | McGraw Hill | Buelens | 0-07-710723-3 | 40.99 | 2005 | Maidenhead |
| 192817 | Principles of Marketing | Prentice Hall | Brassington | 1-40-584634-8 | 42.99 | 2006 | London |
| 112768 | Company Law | Longman | Griffin | 0-58-278461-1 | 34.99 | 2005 | London |

**Table 7.8** Rockpool Ltd User database table

| Last name | First name | User ID | Location | Department | Employee number | Access level |
|---|---|---|---|---|---|---|
| James | Christopher | CJames | York, England | Retail | 66878 | One |
| Smith | Allan | ASmith | Paris, France | Administration | 63877 | Five |
| Brookes | Peter | PBrookes | Berlin, Germany | Finance | 75321 | One |
| Chapman | Julie | JChapman | Madrid, Spain | Retail | 52335 | Three |
| Baker | Mary | MBaker | Bergen, Norway | Retail | 41967 | Five |
| Simons | Rebecca | RSimons | Edinburgh, Scotland | Administration | 67876 | Four |

Now that we have created our database and two tables (Books and Users), which would appear as shown in Table 7.7 and Table 7.8 above, let's have a look at the SQL keywords we introduced earlier.

Note: For illustration purposes, both the Books table, and the Users table have been populated with example data.

### Data control

The first group of SQL keywords is the data control language (DCL) which manages the authorisation aspects of data and permits the user/user applications to control who has access to view and/or manipulate data within the database.

The most common keywords are:

- grant – this authorises one or more users/user applications to perform an operation or a set of operations on an object, and
- revoke – this removes or restricts the capability of a user/user application to perform an operation or a set of operations.

Such granting and/or removal of privileges can occur on a number of levels, for example

- a global level,
- a database level, and
- a table level.

### Global level

For example:

```
GRANT ALL ON *;
REVOKE ALL ON *;
```

The asterisk (*) means show all.

### Database level

For example:

> GRANT ALL ON Book_Register
> REVOKE ALL ON Book_Register

where *Book_Register* is the name of a database (see example below).

### Table level

For example:

> GRANT ALL ON Locations;
> REVOKE ALL ON Locations;

where *Locations* is the name of a table (see example below).

#### Data definition

The second group of SQL keywords is the data definition language (DDL) which allows the database administration system to:

- initialise/create the database,
- define and describe the data within a database,
- construct a data dictionary for the data within a database,
- specify the attributes of the data within the database, and
- stipulate user access limitations, and/or
- impose security constraints on specific data fields/data records within the database.

The most common keywords are:

- create – this causes an object to be created within the database,
- truncate – deletes all data from a table but not the table (a non-standard, but common SQL command), and
- alter – this modifies an existing object in various ways, for example:
  - add – this causes an existing object to be added within the database, and
  - drop – this causes an existing object to be deleted within the database . . . usually irretrievably.

For example, to create a table called Locations, the SQL command would be:

> CREATE TABLE Locations (Location ID INTEGER, Location Name TEXT, Location Address TEXT Location Country TEXT, Location Telephone Number INTEGER);

To remove all rows from a table, the SQL command statement would be:

> TRUNCATE TABLE Locations;

To add an e-mail address column to the Users table, the SQL command statement would be:

> ALTER TABLE Users
> ADD COLUMN eMail Address BOOLEAN;

The revised User table would look like Table 7.9.

To delete the department column added to the Users table, the SQL command would be:

> ALTER TABLE User
> DROP COLUMN Department;

The revised User table would look like Table 7.10.

**Table 7.9** Rockpool Ltd amended User database table

| Last name | First name | User ID | Location | Department | Employee number | Access level | E-mail address |
|---|---|---|---|---|---|---|---|
| James | Christopher | CJames | York, England | Retail | 66878 | One | CJames@Rockpool.co.uk |
| Smith | Allan | ASmith | Paris, France | Administration | 63877 | Five | ASmith@Rockpool.co.uk |
| Brookes | Peter | PBrookes | Berlin, Germany | Finance | 75321 | One | PBrookes@Rockpool.co.uk |
| Chapman | Julie | JChapman | Madrid, Spain | Retail | 52335 | Three | JChapman@Rockpool.co.uk |
| Baker | Mary | MBaker | Bergen, Norway | Retail | 41967 | Five | MBaker@Rockpool.co.uk |
| Simons | Rebecca | RSimons | Edinburgh, Scotland | Administration | 67876 | Four | RSimons@Rockpool.co.uk |

**Table 7.10** Rockpool Ltd amended User database table

| Last name | First name | User ID | Location | Employee number | Access level | E-mail address |
|---|---|---|---|---|---|---|
| James | Christopher | CJames | York, England | 66878 | One | CJames@Rockpool.co.uk |
| Smith | Allan | ASmith | Paris, France | 63877 | Five | ASmith@Rockpool.co.uk |
| Brookes | Peter | PBrookes | Berlin, Germany | 75321 | One | PBrookes@Rockpool.co.uk |
| Chapman | Julie | JChapman | Madrid, Spain | 52335 | Three | JChapman@Rockpool.co.uk |
| Baker | Mary | MBaker | Bergen, Norway | 41967 | Five | MBaker@Rockpool.co.uk |
| Simons | Rebecca | RSimons | Edinburgh, Scotland | 67876 | Four | RSimons@Rockpool.co.uk |

### Data manipulation

The third set of SQL keywords are the standard data manipulation language (DML) elements. The most common key words are:

- insert – used to add zero or more rows to an existing table,
- update – used to modify the values of a set of existing table rows, and
- delete – used to remove zero or more existing rows from a table.

For example, to insert an object into a database table, the SQL command statement would be in the generic form:

INSERT INTO target (field1, field2, field3, etc . . . )
VALUES (value1, value2, value3, etc . . . );

To insert a book record for the book titled Corporate Accounting Information Systems, into Books, the SQL command would be:

INSERT INTO Books (Product Item Number, Book Title, Publisher, Author, ISBN number, Price, Year of Publication, Location)
VALUES (119282, Corporate Accounting Information Systems, Prentice Hall, Boczko T, 0-27-36848-76, £42.99, 2007, London);

To insert a user record for user Jonathan Fisher, the SQL command statement would be:

INSERT INTO Users (Last Name, First Name, User ID, Location, Department, Employee Number)
VALUES (Fisher, Jonathan, JFisher, Hull, Finance, 68965)

The revised User table would look like Table 7.11.

**Table 7.11** Rockpool Ltd amended User database table

| Last name | First name | User ID | Location | Employee number | Access level | E-mail address |
|---|---|---|---|---|---|---|
| James | Christopher | CJames | York, England | 66878 | One | CJames@Rockpool.co.uk |
| Smith | Allan | ASmith | Paris, France | 63877 | Five | ASmith@Rockpool.co.uk |
| Brookes | Peter | PBrookes | Berlin, Germany | 75321 | One | PBrookes@Rockpool.co.uk |
| Chapman | Julie | JChapman | Madrid, Spain | 52335 | Three | JChapman@Rockpool.co.uk |
| Baker | Mary | MBaker | Bergen, Norway | 41967 | Five | MBaker@Rockpool.co.uk |
| Simons | Rebecca | RSimons | Edinburgh, Scotland | 67876 | Four | RSimons@Rockpool.co.uk |
| Fisher | Jonathan | JFisher | Hull, England | 68965 | Three | JFisher@Rockpool.co.uk |

To update an object in a database table, the SQL command statement would be in the generic form:

UPDATE table,
SET new value,
WHERE criteria;

For example, to move user Jonathan Fisher from Hull to York, the SQL command statement would be:

UPDATE User
SET Location 'York'
WHERE Employee Number 68965;

Note: The Employee Number is used to set the criteria because the it is unique to each individual employee.

The revised User table would look like Table 7.12.

**Table 7.12** Rockpool Ltd amended User database table

| Last name | First name | User ID | Location | Employee number | Access level | E-mail address |
|---|---|---|---|---|---|---|
| James | Christopher | CJames | York, England | 66878 | One | CJames@Rockpool.co.uk |
| Smith | Allan | ASmith | Paris, France | 63877 | Five | ASmith@Rockpool.co.uk |
| Brookes | Peter | PBrookes | Berlin, Germany | 75321 | One | PBrookes@Rockpool.co.uk |
| Chapman | Julie | JChapman | Madrid, Spain | 52335 | Three | JChapman@Rockpool.co.uk |
| Baker | Mary | MBaker | Bergen, Norway | 41967 | Five | MBaker@Rockpool.co.uk |
| Simons | Rebecca | RSimons | Edinburgh, Scotland | 67876 | Four | RSimons@Rockpool.co.uk |
| Fisher | Jonathan | JFisher | York, England | 68965 | Three | JFisher@Rockpool.co.uk |

To delete an object in a database table, the SQL command statement would be in the generic form:

DELETE FROM table
WHERE criteria;

For example, to delete user Christopher James, the SQL command statement would be:

DELETE FROM USER
WHERE Employee Number 66878;

Note: The Employee Number is again used to set the criteria because the Employee Number is unique to each individual employee.

### Data interrogation/data query

The fourth set, and perhaps the most frequently used SQL keyword, is select. Select is used to retrieve rows from one or more tables in a database and is sometimes viewed as a data manipulation command.

In using select it is necessary to specify a description of the desired result set. The most commonly used keywords relating to select are:

- from – used to indicate from which table(s) the data is to be taken,
- where – used to identify which rows are to be retrieved,
- group by – used to combine rows with related values into elements of a smaller set of rows,
- having – used to identify which of the combined rows are to be retrieved, and
- order by – used to identify which columns are to be used to sort the resulting data.

For example, to retrieve records from the Books table that have a price greater than £30.00, with the result sorted alphabetically by the author, the SQL command statement would be:

SELECT * FROM Books, WHERE price > £30.00, ORDER BY author;

Using the sample data introduced in Table 7.7 (as amended), this would produce the following data – see Table 7.13.

**Table 7.13** Rockpool Ltd List of books (by author)

| Author (first named) | Product item number | Book title | Publisher | ISBN | Price | Year | Location |
|---|---|---|---|---|---|---|---|
| Romney | 198201 | Accounting Information Systems | Prentice Hall | 0-13-196855-6 | 47.99 | 2006 | New Jersey |
| Arnold | 119897 | Corporate Financial Management | Prentice Hall | 0-27-368726-3 | 44.99 | 2005 | London |
| Boczko | 119282 | Corporate Accounting Information Systems | Prectice Hall | 0-27-36848-76 | 42.99 | 2007 | London |
| Davies | 152463 | Business Accounting and Finance | McGraw Hill | 0-07-710809-4 | 35.99 | 2005 | Maidenhead |
| Buelens | 115267 | Organisational Behaviour | McGraw Hill | 0-07-710723-3 | 40.99 | 2005 | Maidenhead |
| Brassington | 192817 | Principles of Marketing | Prentice Hall | 1-40-584634-8 | 42.99 | 2006 | London |
| Griffin | 112768 | Company Law | Longman | 0-58-278461-1 | 34.99 | 2005 | London |

# Developing a database – using a relational data model

Designing and developing a database can be an expensive, often political, and invariably a time-consuming task, requiring input from a wide diversity of individuals/professionals. However, a well-designed, properly developed database can provide enormous benefits, some of which would include:

- improved data efficiency,
- improved data consistency,
- enhanced data integration,
- simplified data management,
- improved data access,
- improved data ownership, and
- reduced data redundancy.

So, what are the key stages in the development of a database? These would be:

- database planning,
- database design,
- database design evaluation,
- database testing, and
- database implementation (including database maintenance).

## Database planning

The purpose of the database planning stage is to:

- define the scope of the planned database,
- ensure the development is consistent with the company's/organisation's information and communications technology strategy and, perhaps more importantly,
- ascertain the viability/feasibility of such a database – that is the costs and/or benefits of developing and using such a database.

Database planning would include, for example:

- defining the database environment,
- determining an adequate storage structure – that is the physical database,
- determining a valid back-up/recovery strategy,[64]
- establishing an appropriate access strategy – who can use what and when, and
- defining data requirements and extending/amending the existing data dictionary.

## Database design

The purpose of the database design stage is to determine the data content of the database – that is develop a conceptual level schema. Although the precise nature of the design stage would differ from company to company and from organisation to organisation, in general there are two approaches that can be used in designing a relational database, these being:

- a bottom-up approach to database design, and
- a top-down approach to database design,

of which the latter is by far the more common.

### Bottom-up approach to database design . . . using normalisation

When designing a database, tables must comply with a number of rules – rules referred to as normal form. Applying the normal form to collections of data is called normalisation. This is a process designed to reduce data redundancy and minimise data inconsistency – that is ensure data dependencies make sense and produce a database design that ensures the efficient access and storage of data and the maintenance of data integrity. Put simply, normalisation seeks to eliminate:

- the duplication of data – where the same data is listed in multiple lines of the database,
- the insertion of anomalies – where data about an entity cannot be inserted into a table without first inserting data about another entity,[65]
- the deletion of anomalies – where data cannot be deleted without deleting data about a related entity,[66] and
- the updating of anomalies – where data cannot be updated without changing related data in a number of other places.[67]

So what are the guidelines?[68]

There are six levels of normal form, which are numbered, perhaps unsurprisingly, from 1 (the lowest form of normalisation – referred to as 1st normal form or 1NF) to 6 (the highest form of normalisation – referred to as 6th normal form or 6NF).

Note: For database applications it is generally only necessary to normalise to the 3rd normal form.

An un-normalised table is a table that contains repeating data/attributes within the rows in the table – that is the same data may be stored in a number of places within a table which could lead to possible data inconsistencies.

### 1st normal form (1NF)

The 1st normal form (1NF) provides a set of simple guidelines for the creation of an organised database – these being:

- all duplicate columns/repeating groups of data from the same table should be eliminated,
- separate tables for each group of related data should be created, and
- unique columns or sets of columns should be identified as primary keys.

To be in the 1st normal form a table should contain no repeating groups.

### 2nd normal form (2NF)

The 2nd normal form (2NF) addresses the issue of duplicated data, and provides that a table should contain no repeating groups and no partial key functional dependencies. A partial functional dependency occurs when the value in a non-key attribute of a table is dependent on the value of some part of the table's primary key (but not all of it).

To be in 2nd normal form, a table should:

- satisfy all the requirements of the 1st normal form (contain no repeating groups),
- remove sub-sets of data (or partial data) that apply to multiple rows of a table and create a separate table for them, and
- create relationships between the newly created tables and their predecessor tables through the use of foreign keys.

### 3rd normal form

The 3rd normal form provides that a table should contain no repeating groups, no partial functional dependencies and no transitive functional dependencies. A transitive functional dependency occurs when an attribute is dependent on another, non-key attribute(s) in a table.

To be in the 3rd normal form, a table should:

- satisfy all the requirements of the 1st normal form (contain no repeating groups), and
- satisfy all the requirements of the 2nd normal form (contain no partial functional dependencies), and
- eliminate columns that are not dependent upon the primary key of the table.

Consider the following example:

*GPV Ltd is a UK-based company supplying engineering components for specialist car manufacturers. At present, the company has a single database table containing all transaction data relating to sales orders.*

*The data fields included in the original 'single' data table are currently as follows:*

- *sales order number,*
- *sales order date,*

- *customer number,*
- *customer name,*
- *customer address,*
- *customer postcode,*
- *sales advisor name,*
- *sales advisor ID,*
- *stock item number,*
- *stock item description,*
- *quantity ordered, and*
- *unit price.*

Normalising the above database table would involve the following.

## Normalising: 1st normal form

This would require separating repeating groups of data into a new table, creating a new table for the repeating groups of data and identifing the primary key.

First, remove the repeating groups of data. The revised new table would contain the following:

*Table 1*
- sales order number,
- stock item number,
- stock item description,
- quantity ordered, and
- unit price.

Second, create a new table containing the repeating groups of data. The new table would contain the following:

*Table 2*
- sales order number,
- sales order date,
- customer reference,
- customer name,
- customer address,
- customer postcode,
- sales advisor name, and
- sales advisor ID.

We now have two tables and a database in the 1st normal form.

## Normalising: 2nd normal form

This would require removing partial dependencies and creating a separate table for:

- the functionally dependent data, and
- the part of the key on which it is dependent.

The new tables would contain the following:

*Table 1*
- stock item number, and
- stock item description.

*Table 2*

All the above groups of data (except for the primary key) would be removed from the original 1st normal form table 1 (see above). The revised table would contain the following:

- sales order number,
- stock item number,
- quantity ordered, and
- unit price.

Note: stock item number is the primary key.

*Table 3 (unchanged 1st normal form table 2)*
- sales order number,
- sales order date,
- customer reference,
- customer name,
- customer address,
- customer postcode,
- sales advisor name, and
- sales advisor ID.

We now have three tables and a database in the 2nd normal form.

## Normalising: 3rd normal form

This would require removing transitive dependencies and creating a separate table containing the attributes and the data that are functionally dependent on it.

The new tables would contain the following:

*Table 1*
- customer reference,
- customer name,
- customer address, and
- customer postcode.

*Table 2*
- sales advisor name, and
- sales advisor ID.

*Table 3*

All the above groups of data (except for the primary key) would be removed from the original 2nd normal form table 3 (see above). The revised table would contain the following:

- sales order number,
- sales order date,
- customer reference, and
- sales advisor ID,

together with the unchanged tables:

*Table 4 (unchanged 2nd normal form table 2)*
- stock item number, and
- stock item description,

and

*Table 5 (unchanged 2nd normal form table 3)*

- sales order number,
- stock item number,
- quantity ordered, and
- unit price.

These tables make up the database in 3rd normal form.

The completed tables in the 3rd normal form would therefore be as follows:

- customer reference, customer name, customer address, customer postcode – called *CUSTOMERS*
- sales advisors: sales advisors ID, sales advisor name – called *SALES ADVISORS*
- stock item number, stock item description – called *STOCK ITEMS*
- sales order number, sales order date, customer reference, sales advisor ID – called *SALES ORDERS*, and
- sales order number, stock item number, stock quantity, and unit price – called *SALES ORDER DETAILS*.

## Top-down approach to database design . . . using entity-relationship models

In the above bottom-up approach, we started with a broad collection of data arranged into a single un-normalised data table and gradually refined the data table – using a process of normalisation – to end up with five tables in 3rd normal form.

Although it is possible to develop a workable database design using a bottom-up approach it is rarely used. Most designers tend to prefer the top-down approach in database design because it tends to produce more efficient and effective designs. The bottom-up approach is useful, however, to confirm/check the database design.

The top-down approach is essentially a data modelling approach in which a data model is created to represent user needs and requirements for the data stored in the database. Although there are a number of data modelling techniques that can be used, by far the most popular technique is entity-relationship modelling. Entity-relationship modelling involves:

- identifying all relevant entities about which data will be accumulated and stored in the database,
- determining how such entities are related to each other, and
- developing a relational representation of such relationships – a representation often referred to as an entity-relationship diagram.

(We looked at entity-relationship diagrams earlier in this chapter.)

For the remainder of the discussion, we will use the top-down approach. Consider the following brief scenario:

*AKL Solutions Ltd is a Manchester-based IT services provider offering a range of IT-related training programmes for corporate clients in the Greater Manchester area. All training programmes are provided by the company's in-house consultants. The company is currently designing a database for the sale of its training programmes.*

*Using the top-down approach, the design process would include some, if not all, of the following stages:*

- *identify all relevant entities,*
- *determine entity relationships,*
- *determine relevant data,*

- *construct database tables and columns,*
- *identify the primary keys,*
- *identify foreign keys and determine linking columns, and*
- *identify possible relationship constraints.*

### Identify all relevant entities

For AKL Solutions Ltd, relevant entities would be, for example:

- the corporate client,
- the training programme,
- the training consultant, and
- the invoice/account.

### Determine entity relationships

Once the relevant entities have been identified, it is necessary to determine the relationship between each of them. It is however important to remember that not all entity relationships are of importance. Only those relationships which reflect real-world flows are of relevance.

Consider the following:

*For the AKL Solutions Ltd database, we are modelling real-world flows concerned with sales transactions – that is transactions associated with the provision/sale of training programmes. Consider for example the following two entities: the entity called corporate client and the entity called training programme. Although there would of course be a relationship between the entity called corporate client and the entity called training programme, in terms of a sales transaction – which is after all our primary concern – the entity called corporate client is only related to the entity called training programme when a sales transaction occurs (i.e. when a training programme is (successfully) provided). As a result, in terms of entity relationships, we could say that:*

- *the entity called corporate client is related to the entity called invoice/account, and*
- *the entity called invoice/account is related to the entity called training programme.*

If you recall (from our previous discussion on entity-relationship diagrams), entity relationships can be categorised as either:

- one-to-one – referred to as (1:1),
- one-to-many – referred to as (1:$n$), or
- many-to-many – referred to as ($m$:$n$).

Figure 7.23 provides an entity-relationship diagram for AKL Solutions Ltd.

### Determine all relevant data

For each of the above entities, there will of course be a substantial amount of data associated with/related to it. For example, for AKL Solutions Ltd we could identify the following relevant data elements:

- for the corporate client – client reference, client name, client address and postcode,
- for the training programme – programme type, training programme catalogue number, programme cost,
- for the training consultant – consultant last name, consultant first name, consultant ID, consultant grade, date of birth, marital status, and
- for the invoice account – invoice number, invoice date, training programme, catalogue number, price, VAT.

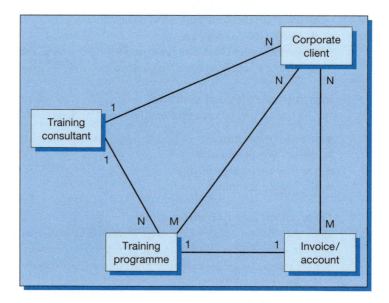

**Figure 7.23** Entity-relationship diagram for AKL Solutions Ltd

Remember: It is only necessary to identify data that are relevant now, or will be relevant in the near future, to the real-world flows being modelled.

### Construct/design tables and columns

Put simply:

- an entity will automatically become a table, and
- data about the entity will automatically become a column in the entity table.

It is important to ensure that all newly created data elements conform to the existing requirements of the company's/organisation's data dictionary, and therefore important to determine the characteristics of each data element – that is establish:

- a data element description – what the data will represent,
- a data element name – what the data will be known by,
- a data element type – what the data is,
- a data element length – how large the data element and the data length are.

For AKL Solutions Ltd such characteristics could be as shown in Tables 7.14 to 7.17.

**Table 7.14** Corporate client

| Data element description | Data element name | Data element type | Data element length |
|---|---|---|---|
| Unique client identifier | Client number | Numeric | 10 |
| Complete name of customer | Client name | Alpha | 20 |
| Number, street, town/city, postcode, county | Address | Alpha-numeric | 30 |
| Clients' business activities | Business | Alpha | 20 |
| Clients' current balance | Account status | Alpha-numeric | 10 |

## Table 7.15 Training product

| Data element description | Data element name | Data element type | Data element length |
|---|---|---|---|
| Training product unique identifier | Number | Numeric | 10 |
| Training product name | Name | Alpha | 20 |
| Nature of training delivery | Delivery type | Alpha | 10 |
| Period/length of training | Length | Alpha | 15 |
| Location of delivery | Location | Alpha-numeric | 30 |
| Cost of training product | Cost | Numeric | 10 |

## Table 7.16 Training consultant

| Data element description | Data element name | Data element type | Data element length |
|---|---|---|---|
| Training consultant unique identifier | Number | Numeric | 10 |
| Training consultant complete name | Name | Alpha | 20 |
| Street, town/city, postcode, county | Address | Alpha | 30 |
| Training consultant area of expertise | Specialism | Alpha | 15 |
| Current employment status of consultant | Current status | Alpha | 10 |
| Working location of training consultant | Location | Alpha | 15 |
| Current cost of training consultant | Cost | Numeric | 10 |

## Table 7.17 Invoice/account

| Data element description | Data element name | Data element type | Data element length |
|---|---|---|---|
| Date of invoice | Invoice date | Numeric | 10 |
| Number of invoice | Invoice number | Numeric | 10 |
| Unique client identifier | Client number | Numeric | 10 |
| Complete name of customer | Client name | Alpha | 20 |
| Number, street, town/city, postcode, county | Address | Alpha-numeric | 30 |
| Date(s) of training delivery | Delivery dates | Numeric | 10 |
| Training product unique identifier | Training product number | Alpha-numeric | 10 |
| Training product name | Training product name | Alpha | 20 |
| Location of delivery | Delivery location | Alpha-numeric | 30 |
| Cost of training product | Cost | Numeric | 10 |

### Identify primary keys

Because text-based names are not usually unique – for example a corporate client, and/or training programme could have the same (or a very similar) name – it is useful, where possible, to ensure the primary key is a sequential numeric value: in many cases, an internally developed/designed unique identifier.

For the entities we have identified in AKL Solutions Ltd, it is likely that:

- the primary key for the corporate client would be the corporate client ID,
- the primary key for the training programme would be catalogue number of the training programme,

- the primary key for the training consultant would be the consultant's employee ID, and
- the primary key for the invoice/account would be the invoice/account number.

### Identify foreign keys and determine linking columns

When primary key data in a table is replicated in another table (referred to as a foreign key), such replication can act as a link between columns in different tables. For example, in the previous discussion we suggested that the primary key for the entity called training programme would be the training programme catalogue number. This data element is also a data element for the entity called invoice/account – that is a foreign key creating a link between two columns in two different database tables.

As with entity relationships, such links can be categorised as either:

- one-to-one (1:1),
- one-to-many (1:$n$), or
- many-to-many ($m$:$n$).

### Identify any relationship constraints

Relationship constraints exist to ensure the integrity of the data within the database.

For example:

> If AKL Solutions Ltd were to create an invoice, a corporate client must exist. An entry in the corporate client table must therefore exist before the invoice can be raised – that is a relationship constraint must exist on the invoice/account table to ensure that prior to any invoice/account being created, a corporate client exists.

Such relationship constraints can be implemented in many ways, perhaps the most common being:

- as part of the data entry procedures, or
- as part of a monitoring protocol in the database management system.

## Database design evaluation

Whatever design approach is adopted – whether top-down, or bottom-up – once the design stage has been completed it is necessary to evaluate the design to identify any design faults that could cause data and/or data records to become unreliable, unstable and/or unusable.

Such a design evaluation would consider questions like:

- Do all of the tables in the database have a single defined theme – if not why not?
- Do all of the tables in the database have a defined primary key – if not why not?
- Have all relevant entities been identified correctly?
- Have all the dependencies within the database been recognised correctly?
- Have all the relationship constraints within the database been appropriately acknowledged?

## Database testing

Once the database design has been evaluated (with any design faults corrected) and approved, the database requires testing and assessment. Such testing could comprise of:

- testing individual database components – both software and hardware components,
- testing the whole database – for stability and connectivity,
- testing user acceptance of the database,

- testing database integrity,
- testing database security, and
- testing database performance.

## Database implementation

Once a suitable design has been evaluated and approved, and testing has not revealed any significant problems, the database would – subject to company/organisational requirements – be implemented. In doing so, it is important to:

- establish a suitable entry policy – to control user access,
- establish adequate security controls – to prevent possible data theft,
- establish a regular testing/assessment programme – to monitor and validate database context, and
- establish appropriate database maintenance procedures to:
  - monitor database performance,
  - where appropriate, reorganise user needs/requirements,
  - review database procedures, and
  - evaluate the use of new technologies.

## An alternative – the REA model

To overcome the limitations of a traditional, 'events-based' transaction processing approach, for example:

- the over-reliance on recording 'what' a transaction is as opposed to 'how' the transaction affects the company/organisation, and
- the excessive orientation of transaction processing toward a specific user/stakeholder perspective – invariably an economic-based shareholder perspective,

McCarthy (1979) proposed the REA data model, specifically for use in accounting information system-related databases.

As an 'events-orientated' data model, the REA data model proposed three basic classes of entities,[69] these being:

- resources – that is those things that have an economic value to a company/organisation,[70]
- events – that is those activities for which information is required,[71] and
- agents – that is those people and organisations that participate in events and about whom information is required for planning and controls purposes,[72]

with the basic template that:

- every event entity must be linked to at least one resource entity,
- every event entity must be linked to at least one other event entity, and
- every event entity must be linked to at least two participating agents.

Although the REA has become a source of much debate its adoption and use has been and indeed continues to be limited, mainly because its use would require a substantial change and move away from the traditional double-entry events-based approach that is used in the vast majority of accounting information systems.

## Concluding comments

In a 21st century business context, data have become a vital resource with data acquisition and management now dominated by technologies that regularly facilitate the accumulation, processing and transfer of volumes of data that were unimaginable a generation ago. Indeed, there can be little doubt that the increasing availability and use of computer-based data capture, online processing and computer-based data management (in particular database systems) has revolutionise contemporary understanding of the economic and political value of data.

## Key points and concepts

| | |
|---|---|
| ACID | Database design |
| Batch processing | Database implementation |
| Bottom-up approach | Database maintenance |
| Centralised data processing | Database planning |
| Coding system (chart of accounts) | Database testing |
| Computer-based data processing | DBAS (database administration system) |
| Data accessibility | DBMS (database management system) |
| Data capture | DCL (data control language) |
| Data consistency | DDL (data definition language) |
| Data conversion | Decision table |
| Data dictionary | Distributed data processing |
| Data element | Document flowchart |
| Data field | Entity-relationship diagram |
| Data file | File-orientated approach |
| Data flexibility | Foreign key |
| Data input | Logical data flow diagram |
| Data integration | Macro level flow chart |
| Data integrity | Manual-based data processing |
| Data maintenance | Micro level flowchart |
| Data manipulation language | Midi level flowchart |
| Data model | Normalisation |
| Data-orientated approach | Online processing |
| Data output | Physical data flow diagram |
| Data processing | Primary file |
| Data query language | Primary key |
| Data record | Program flowchart |
| Data redundancy | REA data model |
| Data security | Relational database |
| Data selection | Secondary file |
| Data storage | SQL |
| Database | Systems flowchart |
| Database design evaluation | Top-down approach |

## References

Chen, P.P. (1976) 'The entity-relationship model: toward a unified view of data' in *ACM Transactions on Database Systems*, 1(1), pp. 9–36.

Coad, P. and Yourdon, E. (1991) *Object-Oriented Systems Analysis*, Prentice Hall, New Jersey.

Codd, E.F. (1970) 'A Relational Model of Data for Large Shared Data Banks' in *Communications of the ACM*, 13(6), pp. 377–387.

Gane, C. and Sarson, T. (1979) *Structured System Analysis*, Prentice Hall, New Jersey.

McCarthy, W.E. (1979) 'The REA Accounting Model: a Generalised Framework for Accounting Systems in a Shared Data Environment' in *Accounting Review*, 57(3), pp. 554–578.

Nobes, C. and Parker, R. (2004) *Comparative International Accounting*, 8th edition, FT Prentice Hall, London.

## Self-review questions

1. Distinguish between physical data input and non-physical data input.
2. Describe the main advantages of the data-orientated approach to data storage.
3. Define data redundancy and distinguish between direct redundancy and indirect redundancy.
4. Distinguish between a data flow diagram and an entity-relationship diagram.
5. What are the main stages involved in constructing a decision table?
6. In an accounting information systems context, what is the purpose of a coding system/ chart of accounts?
7. Explain the difference between a flat file data model, a hierarchical model, a network data model and a relational data model.
8. In terms of a database management system, what is the role of a data dictionary?
9. What is the difference between a primary key, a secondary key and a foreign key?
10. In terms of database design, distinguish between the bottom-up approach and the top-down approach.

## Questions and problems

### Question 1

To be converted into useful information, transaction data requires processing. In an accounting information systems context, such processing requires the data to be structured and organised using file orientation and/or data orientation.

#### Required

Distinguish between a file-orientated approach and a data-orientated approach, and critically evaluate the advantages and disadvantages of each type, and the organisational characteristics that often determine which type will be adopted.

### Question 2

'Computer-based data processing is inherently risky.' Discuss.

→

## Question 3

Because of the increasing volume and complexity of business transactions, various system of processing data have emerged. In a contemporary context, such systems include batch processing and online processing.

### Required

Briefly describe the key characteristics of each of the above types of processing systems and discuss the advantages, disadvantages and uses of each type.

## Question 4

Distinguish between the following types of flowcharts:

- systems flowchart,
- document flowchart, and
- program flowchart,

and explain the advantages and disadvantages of using such flowcharts as analysis tools.

## Question 5

The increasing use of information technology has necessitated the need for increasingly sophisticated coding systems and charts of accounts.

### Required

Describe the qualities and characteristics of a good coding system and explain how a company would devise a chart of accounts relevant to its current and potential commercial activities.

# Assignments

## Question 1

ELF Ltd is an Edinburgh-based company that has been under the control of the same family for the past 50 years. During that time the company has been run on a friendly, informal basis with little reference to the principles of internal control and/or formal documentation. As a result of a recent fraud by a purchasing assistant, just over two years ago the directors of the company reorganised the company's purchasing and receiving procedures in order to guard against a recurrence of the purchase fraud. The directors have asked you to review the current system of internal control and the functions of the documents in the company's purchasing and receiving of goods for resale. In particular, the directors have asked you to prepare a system flowchart of the current purchasing/receiving system.

Following discussions with the company directors, you are aware that the company operates the following departments:

- a requisitioning department,
- a purchasing department,
- a receiving department,
- a stores department,
- a purchasing ledger (accounts) department,
- cashier/treasury department.

The general purchasing procedures are as follows. The requisitioning department raises a purchase request. This purchase request is forwarded to the purchasing department. The purchasing department then obtains a quotation from an approved supplier. Once the quotation has been received and approved, the purchasing department raises a purchase order (four copies). Two copies of the purchase order are sent to the supplier, one is sent to the receiving department and one to the purchase ledger department.

Prior to delivery the supplier is requested to send one copy of the purchase order back to the purchasing department as acknowledgement of the purchase order receipt. When the goods are delivered a goods received note (GRN) (three copies) is received. One copy is filed in the receiving department, one is kept by the stores department and one is sent to the purchase ledger department, where it is matched and filed with the appropriate purchase order. The supplier retains a delivery note – authorised (signed) by an appropriate member of staff from the receiving department. When the invoice is received from the supplier the purchasing department matches the purchase order, GRN and invoice, and authorises payment. All payments are made by cheque and require authorisation from the company cashier.

### Required

Prepare a document flowchart of the above purchasing system and comment on any problem areas.

## Question 2

There are essentially three optional types of computer-based processing, these being:

- periodic processing with sequential updating,
- periodic processing with non-sequential updating, and
- immediate processing.

### Required

For each of the following applications, specify (with reasons) which of the above processing alternatives is likely to be the most suitable:

- the reservation of a seat on a scheduled airline flight,
- the preparation of weekly payroll,
- the preparation of monthly statements for credit customers,
- the posting of journal entries
- the preparation of payments to suppliers/service providers,
- the preparation and submission of purchase orders to suppliers,
- the assessments of debtor balances and the preparation and distribution of payment reminders, and
- amendments to employee payroll details.

 **Chapter endnotes**

[1] For the purposes of our discussion we use the term 'data' in a very specific context: we will use it as a term referring to business-related transaction data.

[2] The term 'conversion' is used where no change in the structure and/or composition of the data occurs. The term 'transformation' is used where a change in the structure and/or composition of the data occurs.

[3] Such processing is sometimes referred to as hybrid processing.

[4] GmbH – *Gesellschaft mit besrankter Haftung* – meaning company with limited liability is the German equivalent of the UK private limited company (plc).

[5] Using an appropriate GUI (Graphical User Interface).

[6] Source data could include for example:

- text-based documents (printed or handwritten) such as internal memoranda, letters, surveys, reports, instruction manuals, business cards, index cards, etc.,
- number-based documents such as financial statements, payroll records, time sheets,
- forms-based documents such as questionnaires, application forms of any kind (credit cards, loans, product registration, etc.),
- image-based documents such as photographs, charts, and graphs, and
- mixed-format documents such as bank statements, credit card statements.

[7] As a plural of the term 'datum'.

[8] Microfiche/microfilm are both compact analogue storage media that are still used in many research/library institutions.

[9] The term 'storage' is sometimes used (somewhat incorrectly in the author's opinion) interchangeably with the term 'memory'. Where both terms are in use, the term memory is generally used for the faster forms of storage and the term storage is generally used for the slower forms of storage.

[10] For example RAM (Random Access Memory).

[11] In a limited sense, the terms 'attribute' and 'data element' can be, and indeed often are, used interchangeably.

[12] Although the example data value is only numeric it is also possible that the data value could be a combination of numeric and alphabetic characters (e.g. a UK postcode).

[13] Remember for some types of data, specific legal requirements may apply – for example the Data Protection Act 1998 and the Limitations Act 1980.

[14] Data set can be defined as a set of data elements bearing a logical relationship which is organised in prescribed manner.

[15] Indeed, a number of anecdotal studies on users of computer-based information systems have suggested that severe access restrictions can also adversely affect data integrity as users often attempt to find alternative means of access and/or alternative sources of data.

[16] Usually in the form of an exchange of economic consideration.

[17] The processing cycle can be defined as the throughput processing period – from input to output. Such a throughput processing period can commence when:

- a specified batch content limit has been reached – for example, a batch of say 100 invoices,
- a specific time period has expired – for example every seven days or every 14 days, or
- a specific date/time has been reached – for example the 19th day of each calendar month.

[18] Whilst it is of course possible for online processing to consist of four stages, for example:

- stage 1 – an *input* stage where individual data are input,
- stage 2 – a *collection* stage where individual data are collected into a secure temporary data file,
- stage 3 – a *processing* stage where the master file is updated based on input of the controlled data file, and
- stage 4 – an *output* stage,

the use and popularity of such online processing has declined significantly over recent years.

[19] Contrary to popular belief ATMs are not an American invention. The ATM was actually invented by John Shepherd-Barron in the early 1960s. He installed the world's first ATM at a branch of Barclays Bank in Enfield, North London, in 1967.

[20] The two input devices are:

■ a card reader which captures the account information stored on the magnetic stripe and/or chip on the back of the debit/credit card. The host processor uses this information to route the transaction to the appropriate bank/financial institution, and
■ a keypad which allows the cardholder to:
  • identify him or herself as the cardholder by entering the appropriate PIN, and
  • inform the bank/financial institution what kind of transaction is required – for example a cash withdrawal, an account amendment, an account balance request or a change of PIN, etc.

[21] The four output devices are:

■ a speaker which provides the cardholder with auditory feedback when the keypad is used,
■ a display screen which provides the cardholder with a menu of transaction options,
■ a receipt printer which provides the cardholder with a paper receipt of the transaction (if requested), and
■ a cash dispenser which consists of a secure vault, a cash-dispensing mechanism which consists of an electric eye that counts each note as it exits the cash dispenser and a sensor which tests the thickness of each note to ensure:
  • two or more notes are not stuck together, and
  • issued notes are not excessively worn, torn or folded.

[22] The host processor may be owned by a bank or financial institution, or it may be owned by an independent service provider.
[23] For example the inefficient/inequitable allocation of resources and/or distribution of information.
[24] Because distributed systems provide dedicated resources for user processes, response times can be greatly reduced.
[25] See Chapter 6.
[26] Two common variations to the data flow diagram notation are, for example, the Gane and Sarson (1979) notation and, the Coad and Yourdon (1991) notation.
[27] This notation is based on the Coad and Yourdon (1991) data flow diagram notation.
[28] Alternatively, the Gane and Sarson (1979) data flow diagram notation provides the following:

■ a square to indicate an entity,
■ a rounded square to portray a process,
■ an open box to indicate a data store/file, and
■ an arrow to portray the direction of a dataflow.

[29] In a physical data flow diagram there can be a number of alternative types of data stores, for example:

■ permanent computerised data store/file,
■ temporary (or transient) computerised data store/file,
■ permanent manual data store/file, and
■ temporary (or transient) manual data store/file.

[30] As a general rule, no data flow diagram should contain more than 12 process boxes.
[31] For example, where data is retrieved from a data store, it is not necessary to show the selection criteria used to retrieve it.

[32] A regular entity is an entity of independent existence – that is any physical object, event, and/or abstract concept on which factual data can be obtained. A weak entity is an entity of dependent existence – that is an entity whose existence is dependent on another entity.

[33] An entity set (or entity type) is a collection of similar entities.

[34] This is the most common type of relationship.

[35] Often referred to as a General Entity-Relationship Model (GERM).

[36] Where both entities are independent, the direction of the relationship is arbitrary.

[37] Such relationships are often referred to as a relationship's *ordinality*.

[38] In the simple decision table, there would be two condition alternatives – that is a yes or a no for each condition. In an extended-entry decision table, there could be many alternatives for each condition.

[39] This chart of accounts was originally developed by Ron Hornsby, University of Lincolnshire and Humberside (now University of Lincoln) with whose kind permission it has been reproduced.

[40] Such a chart of accounts is often imposed for macro economic purposes – for the collection of statistical data by national governments.

[41] A query language is a computer language used to make enquiries into databases and/or information systems. Such query languages can, broadly speaking, be classified as either database query languages or information retrieval query languages. For example:

- SQL (Structured Query Language) is a well-known query language for relational databases, and
- DMX (Data Mining eXtentions) is a query language for data mining models.

[42] For example in the early 1960s the System Development Corporation (based in California, USA) sponsored a conference on the development of computer-centred databases. See http://www.cbi.umn.edu/collections/inv/burros/cbi00090-098.html.

[43] Charles W. Bachman was a prominent computer scientist/industrial researcher in the area of databases. He received the Turing Award in 1973 for his work on database technologies and was elected as a Distinguished Fellow of the British Computer Society in 1977 for his pioneering work on database systems.

[44] Codd, E.F. (1970) 'A Relational Model of Data for Large Shared Data Banks' in *Communications of the ACM*, 13(6), pp. 377–387.

This paper is available @ http://www.acm.org/classics/nov95/toc.html.

[45] For example the System R project at IBM.

[46] For example Oracle and DB2.

[47] eXtensible Markup Language – a special purpose markup language capable of describing many different kinds of data.

[48] CODASYL (Conference on Data Systems Languages) was an IT industry consortium formed in 1959 to guide the development of a standard programming language that could be used on many computers. Its discussions eventually resulted in the development of COBOL. Although some derivative CODASYL committees continue to the present day, CODASYL itself no longer exists with interest in CODASYL fading in the early 1980s due to growing interest in relational databases.

[49] As defined by the CODASYL specification.

[50] Using the relational data model, a table can be defined as a collection of records, with each record in a table containing the same fields.

[51] In some smaller companies/organisations database administration is sometimes undertaken by a single individual – the database administrator – whereas in larger companies/organisations such database administration is often undertaken by a department of technical personnel.

[52] The American National Standards Institute (ANSI) Standards Planning And Requirements Committee (SPARC) architecture (1975).

[53] Including data fields, data records and data files.

[54] Because terminology can differ, for our discussion we will use the terminology used in Microsoft SQL Server 2005 edition.

[55] Such change could of course relate to:

- structural change – that is change to the database schema,
- technological change – that is change to the physical database, and/or
- definitional change – that is change to either user access to the database resource and/or user rights to use the database resource.

[56] Hence the term 'relational database'.

[57] Such tables are – in a technical context – more appropriately referred to as relations; hence the term 'relational database'.

[58] Remember such tables only describe how the data appear within both the conceptual level schema and the external level schema. The data are actually stored in the manner described in the internal level schema.

[59] See note 42 above.

[60] Because the word SEQUEL was a trademark held by Hawker-Siddeley Ltd in the UK. Hawker-Siddeley Ltd eventually merged into British Aerospace (BAe) in 1977.

[61] For a complete listing of the keywords available for Microsoft SQL Server 2005 Edition, have a look @ http://msdn2.microsoft.com/en-us/library/ms189822.aspx.

[62] In some database management systems the keyword TEXT may not be supported, in which case a specific string length has to be declared – for example: CHAR(x), VCHAR(x) or VARCHAR(x), where x is the string length.

[63] As note 62.

[64] For example, establishing the periodic dumping of the database on to backup tape and, where necessary, establishing secure recovery procedures for the reloading of the database from the backup tape.

[65] For example, where a customer cannot be created without a sales order.

[66] For example, where a sales order cannot be deleted without deleting all the customer data.

[67] For example, where to update customer data, it must be updated for each sales order the customer has placed.

[68] It is important to note that these are only advisory guidelines.

[69] Some REA data models include a 4th entity of locations, defined as physical objects and/or spaces not owned by the company/organisation. The use of this 4th entity is by no means widely accepted.

[70] Resources are the assets of a company/organisation used to generate revenue. However resources do not include some traditional accounting assets, for example debtor accounts.

[71] There are three classes of events:

- operating events – that is what happens,
- information events – that is what is recorded, and
- decision/management events – that is what is done (as a consequence).

Only operating events are included in the REA model.

[72] Such agents can be people, departments, and/or companies/organisations that can participate in events and affect company/organisation resources.

## Appendix 7.1: Hubs Limited Chart of Accounts

### Summary codes

| LOCATION: | DEPARTMENT: | FINANCIAL LEDGER SUMMARY |
|---|---|---|
| 10 COMPANY | 11 ALL DEPARTMENTS | 0100 CAPITAL |
| 20 SOUTHAMPTON | 21 PURCHASING/SALES | 0200 LOANS |
| 30 LONDON | 31 RECEIVING/DESPATCH | 0300 CURRENT LIABILITIES |
| 40 MANCHESTER | 41 STOCK[1] | 0400 FIXED ASSETS |
| 50 HULL | 51 PRODUCTION | 0500 STOCK |
| 60 NEWCASTLE | 61 SERVICE | 0600 DEBTORS |
| 70 GLASGOW | 71 ACCOUNTING | 0700 CASH |
| 80 BRISTOL | 81 PERSONNEL | 0800 MATS COST OF SALES |
| | 91 ADMINISTRATION | 0900 WAGES COST OF SALES |
| | | 1000 OCCUPANCY |
| | | 1100 ADMINISTRATION |
| | | 1200 COMMUNICATIONS |
| | | 1300 FINANCIAL |
| | | 1400 TAX |
| | | 1500 SALES |

### SUBSIDIARY CODES, CAPITAL and LOANS

| ORD'Y SHARE CAP & RES, SUMM'Y CODE 0100 | PRIOR CHGE CAP, CODE 0200 |
|---|---|
| 0100/0 ORDINARY SHAREHOLDERS FUNDS, TOTAL | 0200/0 ALL LOANS & PREF SH |
| 0100/1 -do-, AUTHORISED SHARE CAPITAL | 0200/1 AUTH PREF SHARES |
| 0100/2 -do-, ISSUED SHARE CAPITAL | 0200/2 ISSUED PREF SHARES |
| 0100/3 -do-, CAPITAL RESERVE | 0200/3 LOANS |
| 0100/4 -do-, GENERAL RESERVE | |
| 0100/5 -do-, REVALUATION RESERVE | |
| 0100/6 -do-, PROFIT & LOSS ACCOUNT | |

### CURRENT LIABILITIES, SUMMARY CODE 0300

0300/0000/00 CURRENT LIAB, ALL TYPES
0301/0000/00 -do-, GEN LEDG, MISC CRED BAL (inc. accruals), TOTAL
0301/0000/XX -do-, -do-, -do-, INDIVIDUAL ACCOUNTS [01 to 99]
0302/0000/01 -do-, -do-, CREDITORS LEDG CONTROL ACCT, BAL B/FWD
0302/0000/02 -do-, -do-, -do-, CURRENT PERIOD, INVOICES
0302/0000/03 -do-, -do-, -do-, -do-, CASH PAID
0302/0000/04 -do-, -do-, -do-, -do-, DISCOUNTS RECEIVED
0302/0000/05 -do-, -do-, -do-, -do-, CREDIT NOTES RECEIVED
0302/0000/06 -do-, -do-, -do-, -do-, CONTRA DEBTORS LEDGER
0302/0000/07 -do-, -do-, -do-, -do-, BALANCES WRITTEN OFF

[1] Includes Raw Materials and Finished Goods.

0302/0000/08 -do-, -do-, -do-, -do-, MISCELLANEOUS CREDITS
0302/0000/09 -do-, -do-, -do-, -do-, MISCELLANEOUS DEBITS
0302/0000/10 -do-, -do-, -do-, -do-, BALANCE CARRIED FORWARD
0302/0000/11 -do-, -do-, -do-, -do-, ONE MONTH OLD OR LESS
0302/0000/12 -do-, -do-, -do-, -do-, TWO MONTHS OLD
0302/0000/13 -do-, -do-, -do-, -do-, THREE MONTHS OLD
0302/0000/14 -do-, -do-, -do-, -do-, FOUR MONTHS OLD OR MORE
0303/0000/01 -do-, -do-, DOUBTFUL CREDITORS PROVISION, BAL B/FWD
0303/0000/02 -do-, -do-, -do-, ADJUSTMENT
0303/0000/03 -do-, -do-, -do-, BALANCE CARRIED FORWARD
0304/0000/XX        CREDITORS LEDGER BALANCES, XX, CODING STRUCT AS ABOVE
0304/A:ZXXX/XX   INDIVIDUAL SUPPLIERS' ACCOUNTS, CODING STRUCT AS ABOVE

EACH INDIVIDUAL CUSTOMER IS ALLOCATED A UNIQUE ALPHA-NUMERIC
ACCOUNT NUMBER WHICH BEGINS WITH THE FIRST LETTER OF THEIR NAME, IN
THE SERIES XO01 to X999. THIS NUMBER IMMEDIATELY FOLLOWS THE SUMMARY
CODE No. [e.g. 0304/H486/14 HARRIS LTD, BAL C/F, 4 MONTHS OR MORE]

## FIXED ASSETS, SUMMARY CODE 0400

0400/1    ALL CLASSES OF FIXED ASSET, ORIGINAL COST, BALANCE BROUGHT FWD
0400/2    -do-,   -do-, CURRENT PERIOD, ASSETS DISPOSED OF
0400/3    -do-,   -do-,   -do-, ASSETS ACQUIRED
0400/4    -do-,   -do-,   -do-, ASSETS HELD, BALANCE CARRIED FORWARD
0400/5    -do-, DEPRECIATION, BALANCE BROUGHT FORWARD
0400/6    -do-,   -do-, CURRENT PERIOD, ON ASSETS DISPOSED OF
0400/7    -do-,   -do-,   -do-
0400/8    -do-,   -do-, BALANCE CARRIED FORWARD
0400/9    -do-, WRITTEN DOWN VALUE, BALANCE CARRIED FORWARD

## DIFFERENT CLASSES OF FIXED ASSET

0401/1 to 0401/9    FIXED ASSETS, LAND & BUILD'GS, CODING STRUCT AS ABOVE
0402/1 to 0402/9    -do-, PLANT & MACHINERY, CODING STRUCT AS ABOVE
0403/1 to 0403/9    -do-, FIXTURES & FITTINGS, CODING STRUCT AS ABOVE
0404/1 to 0404/9    -do-, MOTOR VEHICLES, CODING STRUCT AS ABOVE

## CODES AVAILABLE FOR COUNTS OF NUMBERS OF ASSETS [e.g. MV]

04XX/10 NUMBER BROUGHT FORWARD
04XX/11 NUMBER DISPOSED OF IN PERIOD
04XX/11 NUMBER ACQUIRED IN PERIOD
04XX/12 NUMBER CARRIED FORWARD

## CODES FOR INDIVIDUAL FIXED ASSETS WITHIN CLASSES

EACH ITEM OF FIXED ASSET IS ALLOCATED A UNIQUE REFERENCE NUMBER IN THE
SERIES 0001 to 9999. THIS REFERENCE NUMBER IS APPENDED TO THE CLASS
CODE NUMBER. [e.g. 0404/9/4789 = £ WDV OF VAN REG No R 123 AAT]

## STOCK, SUMMARY CODE 0500

| | |
|---|---|
| 0500/0000/6/4 | ALL ITEMS, TOTAL STOCK VALUE, LCM RULE, £ MILLIONS |
| 0501/XXXX/1 | ITEM REF No 5XXX, QUANTITY IN HAND |
| 0501/XXXX/2 | -do-, TOTAL COST ATTRIBUTED |

[Attributed cost of quantity in hand after latest issue

PLUS actual cost of subsequent receipts]

| | |
|---|---|
| 0501/XXXX/3 | -do-, AVERAGE COST PER UNIT |

[TOTAL COST as above divided by QTY IN HAND as above]

| | |
|---|---|
| 0501/XXXX/4 | -do-, CURRENT MARKET VALUE PER UNIT [CMVPU] |
| 0501/XXXX/5 | -do-, TOTAL MARKET VALUE [QTY IN HAND times CMVPU] |
| 0501/XXXX/6 | -do-, TOTAL STOCK VALUE, LOWER OF COST OR MARKET RULE |
| 0501/XXXX/X/1 | -do-, -do-, DENOMINATION, UNITS |
| 0501/XXXX/X/2 | -do-, -do-, DENOMINATION, HUNDREDS |
| 0501/XXXX/X/3 | -do-, -do-, DENOMINATION, THOUSANDS |
| 0501/XXXX/X/4 | -do-, -do-, DENOMINATION, MILLIONS |

NOTE: EACH ITEM OF STOCK IS ALLOCATED A UNIQUE REFERENCE NUMBER IN THE SERIES 0001 to 9999. [THIS NUMBER IS IN THE SECOND POSITION i.e. FOLLOWING THE SUMMARY CODE NUMBER]

## DEBTORS AND PREPAYMENTS, SUMMARY CODE 0600

| | |
|---|---|
| 0600/0000/00 | DEBTORS AND PREPAYMENTS, ALL TYPES, BALANCE C/FWD |
| 0601/0000/00 | -do-, GEN LEDG, MISC DEBIT BAL (incl P/PAYTS), TOTAL |
| 0601/0000/XX | -do-, -do-, -do-, INDIVIDUAL ACCOUNTS [01 to 99] |
| 0602/0000/01 | -do-, -do-, DEBTORS LEDGER CONTROL ACCT, BAL B/FWD |
| 0602/0000/02 | -do-, -do-, -do-, CURRENT PERIOD, INVOICES |
| 0602/0000/03 | -do-, -do-, -do-, -do-, CASH RECEIVED |
| 0602/0000/04 | -do-, -do-, -do-, -do-, DISCOUNTS GIVEN |
| 0602/0000/05 | -do-, -do-, -do-, -do-, CREDIT NOTES GIVEN |
| 0602/0000/06 | -do-, -do-, -do-, -do-, CONTRA CREDITORS LEDGER |
| 0602/0000/07 | -do-, -do-, -do-, -do-, BALANCES WRITTEN OFF |
| 0602/0000/08 | -do-, -do-, -do-, -do-, MISCELLANEOUS CREDITS |
| 0602/0000/09 | -do-, -do-, -do-, -do-, MISCELLANEOUS DEBITS |
| 0602/0000/10 | -do-, -do-, -do-, BALANCE CARRIED FORWARD |
| 0602/0000/11 | -do-, -do-, -do-, -do-, ONE MONTH OLD OR LESS |
| 0602/0000/12 | -do-, -do-, -do-, -do-, TWO MONTHS OLD |
| 0602/0000/13 | -do-, -do-, -do-, -do-, THREE MONTHS OLD |
| 0602/0000/14 | -do-, -do-, -do-, -do-, FOUR MONTHS OLD OR MORE |
| 0603/0000/01 | -do-, -do-, DOUBTFUL DEBTS PROVISION, BAL B/FWD |
| 0603/0000/02 | -do-, -do-, -do-, ADJUSTMENT |
| 0603/0000/03 | -do-, -do-, -do-, BALANCE CARRIED FORWARD |
| 0604/0000/XX | DEBTORS LEDGER BALANCES, XX, CODING STRUCTURE AS ABOVE |
| 0604/A:ZXXX/XX | INDIVIDUAL CUSTOMERS' ACCOUNTS, CODING STRUCTURE AS ABOVE |

EACH INDIVIDUAL CREDIT CUSTOMER IS ALLOCATED A UNIQUE ALPHA-NUMERIC ACCOUNT NUMBER WHICH BEGINS WITH THE FIRST LETTER OF THEIR NAME, IN THE SERIES XO01 to X999. THIS NUMBER IMMEDIATELY FOLLOWS THE SUMMARY CODE No. [e.g. 0602/M296/03 MOORE & SON, CASH RECEIVED FROM]

## CASH, SUMMARY 0700

| | |
|---|---|
| 0700/0 | TOTAL BANK AND CASH |
| 0700/1 | PETTY CASH |
| 0700/2 | CASH IN HAND |
| 0700/3 | NATWEST BANK PLC |
| 0700/4 | BARCLAYS BANK PLC |
| 0700/5 | HSBC BANK PLC |
| 0700/6 | LLOYDSTSB BANK PLC |

## MATERIALS COST OF SALES, SUMMARY CODE 0800

| | |
|---|---|
| 0800/0 | TOTAL MATERIALS COSTS |
| 0800/1 | MATERIALS COST: TYPE X |
| 0800/2 | MATERIALS COST: TYPE Y |
| 0800/3 | MATERIALS COST: TYPE Z |

## WAGES, SUMMARY CODE 0900     SALARIES, SUMMARY CODE 1100

| | | | |
|---|---|---|---|
| 0900/0 | ALL WAGED STAFF | 1100/1/0 | ALL SAL'D STAFF |
| 0900/1 | OPERATIVES | 1100/1/1 | CLERKS |
| 0900/2 | SUPERVISORS | 1100/1/2 | SECTION HEADS |
| 0900/3 | MANAGERS | 1100/1/3 | MANAGERS |
| 0900/X/0 | ALL SERVICE LENGTHS | 1100/1/X/0 | ALL SERV LENGTH |
| 0900/X/1 | PROBATIONERS | 1100/1/X/1 | PROBATIONERS |
| 0900/X/2 | JUNIOR | 1100/1/X/2 | JUNIOR |
| 0900/X/3 | SENIOR | 1100/1/X/3 | SENIOR |
| 0900/X/4 | SUB CONTRACTORS | 1100/1/X/4 | SUB-CONTRACT |
| 0900/X/5 | TEMPORARY | 1100/1/X/5 | TEMPORARY |
| 0900/X/6 | PART-TIME | 1100/1/X/6 | PART-TIME |
| 0900/X/X/0 | HOURLY PAID | 1100/1/X/X/0 | HOURLY PAID |
| 0900/X/X/1 | WEEKLY PAID | 1100/1/X/X 1 | WEEKLY PAID |
| 0900/X/X/2 | MONTHLY PAID | 1100/1/X/X/2 | MONTHLY PAID |
| 0900/X/X/X/00 | TOTAL GROSS PAY | 1100/1/X/X/X/00 | TOT GRSS PAY |
| 0900/X/X/X/01 | BASIC PAY | 1100/1/X/X/X/01 | BASIC PAY |
| 0900/X/X/X/02 | OVERTIME | 1100/1/X/X/X/02 | OVERTIME |
| 0900/X/X/X/03 | COMMISSION | 1100/1/X/X/X/03 | COMMISSION |
| 0900/X/X/X/04 | HOLIDAY PAY | 1100/1/X/X/X/04 | HOLIDAY PAY |
| 0900/X/X/X/05 | OTHER REMUNER'N | 1100/1/X/X/X/05 | OTHER REMUNER |
| 0900/X/X/X/06 | NAT INS, EE'S DED | 1100/1/X/X/X/06 | NI, EE'S DED |
| 0900/X/X/X/07 | -do-, ER'S CONTRIB | 1100/1/X/X/X/07 | NI, ER'S CONTR |
| 0900/X/X/X/08 | PENS FND, EE'S DED | 1100/1/X/X/X/08 | PF, EE'S DED |
| 0900/X/X/X/09 | PENS FND, ER'S CONT | 1100/1/X/X/X/09 | PF, ER'S CONTR |
| 0900/X/X/X/10 | PAYE | 1100/1/X/X/X/10 | PAYE |
| 0900/X/X/X/11 | MISC DEDUCTIONS | 1100/1/X/X/X/11 | MISC DEDUCT |
| 0900/X/X/X/12 | TOT CST(WGES,NI,PF) | 1100/1/X/X/X/12 | TOT CST(SAL,NI,PF) |
| 0900/X/X/X/13 | NET WAGES BAL | 1100/1/X/X/X/13 | NET SALARY BAL |

## WAGED STAFF [CODE 0900]: NUMBERS IN DIFFERENT OCCUPATIONAL GROUPS

| | | |
|---|---|---|
| 0901/X to 0901/X/X/X | CODE STRUCT AS ABOVE, No IN GROUP AT BEGINNING |
| 0902/X to 0902/X/X/X | -do-, | CURRENT PERIOD, No OF LEAVERS |
| 0903/X to 0903/X/X/X | -do-, | -do-, No JOINING |
| 0904/X to 0904/X/X/X | -do-, | -do-, No IN GROUP AT END |

## CODES FOR INDIVIDUAL MEMBERS OF STAFF

EACH INDIVIDUAL MEMBER OF STAFF IS ALLOCATED A UNIQUE REFERENCE NUMBER IN THE SERIES 0001 to 9999. THIS REFERENCE NUMBER IS APPENDED TO THE BASIC CODE NUMBER. [e.g. 0900/X/X/X/XX/0653 = MARY SMITH]

## SALARIED STAFF [CODE 1100]: NUMBERS IN DIFFERENT OCCUPATIONAL GROUPS

| | | |
|---|---|---|
| 1101/X to 1101/1/X/X/X | CODE STRUCT AS ABOVE, No IN GROUP AT BEGINNING |
| 1102/X to 1102/1/X/X/X | -do-, | CURRENT PERIOD, No OF LEAVERS |
| 1103/X to 1103/1/X/X/X | -do-, | -do-, No JOINING |
| 1104/X to 1104/1/X/X/X | -do-, | -do-, No IN GROUP AT END |

## CODES FOR INDIVIDUAL MEMBERS OF STAFF EACH INDIVIDUAL MEMBER OF STAFF IS ALLOCATED A UNIQUE REFERENCE NUMBER IN THE SERIES 0001 to 9999. THIS REFERENCE NUMBER IS APPENDED TO THE BASIC CODE NUMBER.
[e.g. 1100/1/X/X/X/XX/1844 = HENRY JONES]

**OCCUPANCY, SUMMARY CODE 1000**

| | |
|---|---|
| 1000/0 | OCCUPANCY, ALL COSTS |
| 1000/1 | -do-, RENT PAID |
| 1000/2 | -do-, RATES |
| 1000/3 | -do-, LIGHTING |
| 1000/4 | -do-, HEATING |
| 1000/5 | -do-, REPAIRS & REDEC |
| 1000/6 | -do-, CLEANING |
| 1000/7 | -do-, INSURANCE |
| 1000/8 | -do-, DEPRECIATION |

**ADMINISTRATION, SUMMARY CODE 1100**

| | |
|---|---|
| 1100/0 | ADMINISTR'N, ALL COSTS |
| 1100/1 | -do-, SALARIES |
| 1100/2 | -do-, PROF FEES |
| 1100/3 | -do-, OTHER COSTS |

**COMMUNICATIONS, SUMMARY CODE 1200**

| | |
|---|---|
| 1200/0 | COMMUNICATIONS, ALL COSTS |
| 1200/1 | -do-, TELEPHONE |
| 1200/2 | -do-, POSTAGE |
| 1200/3 | -do-, PRINTING, STATIONERY |
| 1200/4 | -do-, ADVERTISING |
| 1200/5 | -do-, MOT VEH, RUN'G CSTS |
| 1200/6 | -do-, MV, DEPREC |

**FINANCE COSTS, SUMMARY CODE 1300**

| | |
|---|---|
| 1300/0 | FINANCE CSTS, ALL |
| 1300/1 | INT ON LOANS |
| 1300/2 | BAD DEBTS W/OFF |
| 1300/3 | DISCOUNTS GIVEN |
| 1300/4 | DISCOUNTS REC'D |
| 1300/5 | PREF DIVIDENDS |
| 1300/6 | ORDINARY DIVS |

### *TAXATION, SUMMARY CODE 1400*

1400/0   TAXATION, ALL TYPES
1400/1   -do-, ADVANCE CORPORATION TAX
1400/2   -do-, MAINSTREAM CORPORATION TAX

# Part 3

Transaction processing cycles

## Part overview

Part 3 of this book provides a detailed review of the major corporate transaction processing cycles.

Chapter 8 explores the corporate revenue cycle – both debtor-based sales systems (including where appropriate web-based sales systems) and non-debtor-based sales systems (including electronic POS systems and web-based sales systems), and considers the impact of information and communication technology enabled innovations on revenue cycle related activities. Chapter 9 explores the corporate expenditure cycle – both creditor-based expenditure related systems and non-creditor-based expenditure related systems. It also considers payroll related systems.

Chapter 10 concentrates on production companies and explores issues related to product development, production planning/scheduling, manufacturing operations, production management and cost management and control. Chapter 11 explores the corporate management cycle – in particular issues associated with the acquisition and management of funds, and the management and control of both assets and liabilities.

Finally Chapter 12 explores the practical aspects of e-commerce, in particular the uses of e-commerce innovations and technologies in transaction related activities, the problems and opportunities presented by the integration of e-commerce facilities into corporate accounting information systems and the regulatory issues related to the use of e-commerce.

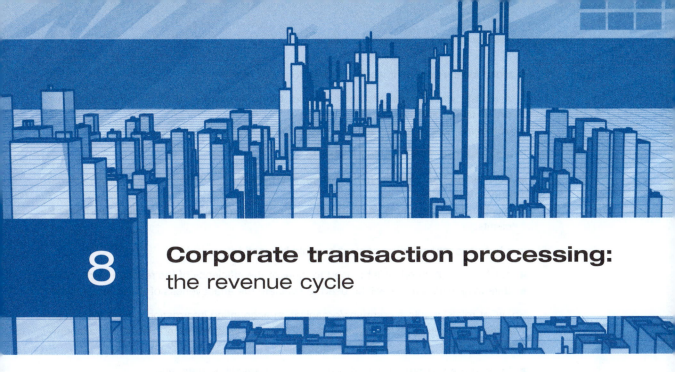

# 8

## Corporate transaction processing:
the revenue cycle

## Introduction

In a broad sense, the revenue cycle can be defined as a collection of business-related activities/resources and information processing procedures, concerned with:

- the provision and distribution of products/services to customers/clients, and
- the recovery of payment from customers/clients for those goods/services.

Inasmuch as the primary objective of the revenue cycle is to maximise income (and of course profits), by providing customers/clients with the right product, at the right price, at the right place and at the right time, the revenue cycle is indelibly linked to and closely integrated with a company's/organisation's marketing model.[1] That is to function efficiently and maximise retailing income it is important for the company/organisation to be able to:

- identify customer/client requirements,
- satisfy customer/client needs,
- maintain an appropriate level of product/service flexibility, and
- ensure an adequate level of product/service quality.

So what would such an integrated 'market-based' revenue cycle be used for? In a marketing context it would be used to:

- ascertain what products/services should be provided for customers/clients, and
- determine how the products/services should be offered to customers/clients.

In a selling (retailing) context it would be used to:

- determine what pricing policy should be adopted by the company/organisation, and
- identify what credit terms the company/organisation should offer customers/clients.

In a distribution context it would be used to:

■ establish what levels of stock should be retained/maintained by the company/organisation, and
■ determine how products/services should be delivered to customers/clients.

In a payment context it would be used to:

■ determine what credit limits the company/organisation should allow customers/clients, and
■ identify what payments facilities the company/organisation should allow customers/clients.

In a business management context it would be used to:

■ establish what criteria will be used to monitor the efficiency of the revenue cycle, and
■ determine what criteria will be used to evaluate the effectiveness of the revenue cycle.

So, what role(s) would a company/organisation accounting information system play in an integrated 'marketing-based' revenue cycle? Whilst in an operational context, the accounting information system would be used to assist in:

■ the capture and processing of revenue cycle transaction data, and
■ the organising, storing and maintaining revenue cycle transaction data,

in a more strategic context, the accounting information system would be used to safeguard revenue cycle resources and ensure:

■ the reliability of revenue cycle transaction data, and
■ the integrity of revenue cycle activities.

## Learning outcomes

This chapter explores a wide range of issues relating to the corporate revenue cycle, in particular:

■ debtor-based sales systems (including where appropriate web-based sales systems), and
■ non-debtor-based sales systems (including electronic POS systems and, of course, web-based sales systems).

By the end of this chapter, the reader should be able to;

■ describe the major activities and operations contained within the corporate revenue cycle,
■ explain the key decision stages within the corporate revenue cycle,
■ demonstrate an understanding of the key internal control requirements of a corporate revenue cycle,
■ demonstrate a critical understanding of the potential risks and threats associated with inappropriate internal control, and
■ consider and explain the impact of information and communication technology enabled innovations on the corporate revenue cycle.

## Revenue cycle and revenue income: an integrated 'market-based' context

### Revenue cycle and revenue income

The revenue cycle is concerned with the inflows of assets and/or resources into the company/organisation – in particular income/earnings generated from, or more appropriately by, business-related activities. In an accounting context, such income can be classified as either:

- capital income – that is income generated from the disposal of either tangible or intangible fixed assets, or
- revenue income – that is income generated from:
  - the sale of current assets,
  - the delivery of customer services, and/or
  - the provision of other non-trading activities/services (e.g. rental income from the leasing of surplus property).

We will look at additional issues/requirements associated with capital income later in this chapter. For the moment, we will consider revenue cycle issues/requirements associated with income/earnings generated from the sale of products/provision of services – that is revenue income/earnings. Why?

Because whilst the source of such revenue income may vary from company to company or organisation to organisation, for example:

- for context type 1(a) and 1(b)[2] companies/organisations such revenue income would more than likely be product orientated/related, and
- for context type 2(a) companies/organisations, such revenue income would be partially product orientated/related and partially services orientated/related, and
- for context type 2(b) and 2(c) companies/organisations such revenue income would more than likely be service orientated/related,

such income will – in terms of volume (and possibly value) – invariably constitute the majority of the income received by a company/organisation.

Consider the following. During 2005:

- Tesco plc revenue income from continuing operations/turnover was £37,070m (see www.tesco.com),
- Sainsbury plc revenue income from continuing operations/turnover was £16,364m (see www.jsainsburys.co.uk),
- Marks and Spencer plc revenue income for continuing operations was £7,710m (see www.marksandspencer.com).

### Revenue cycle: an integrated 'market-based' context

As we saw earlier, in an organisational context, the revenue cycle can be described as an integrated collection of income-related business systems, processes, procedures and activities (see Figure 8.1) indelibly connected to a company's/organisation's marketing function/activities.

Indeed, unless a company/organisation occupies a monopoly position within a market-place and is capable of enjoying or is allowed to enjoy all the benefits associated with such a position, all revenue cycle transactions (or at least, the vast majority of revenue cycle transactions) will be market driven or, more appropriately, demand orientated. That is the demand for a

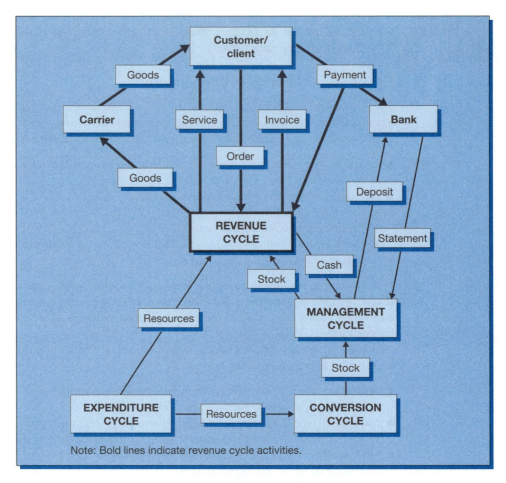

**Figure 8.1** Revenue cycle

company's/organisation's product/services will be influenced by the combination of a range of market-based factors, for example:

- the degree of competitive rivalry in the marketplace,
- the power of suppliers in the marketplace,
- the power of buyers in the marketplace,
- the availability of or the threats posed by substitute products/services, and
- the possible threat of new entrants/new competition within the marketplace.

Such market-based factors are often referred to as the Five Forces (Porter, 1980).

### Competitive rivalry in the marketplace

Competitive rivalry within the marketplace will be high where:

- it is easy for a competitor company/organisation to enter the marketplace,
- it is easy for a customer/client to move to a substitute product/service,
- there is little differentiation between the products/services sold to customers/clients, and
- marketplace exit barriers are high.

Competitive rivalry within the marketplace will be low where:

■ it is both difficult and costly for a company/organisation to enter the marketplace,

■ it is difficult for a customer/client to move to a substitute product/service,

■ there is substantial product/service loyalty by customers/clients within the marketplace, and

■ marketplace exit barriers are low.

### Power of suppliers in the marketplace

The power of suppliers will be high where:

■ there are very few product/service suppliers in the marketplace,

■ there are no product/service substitutes available in the marketplace, and

■ it is expensive for a company/organisation to move from one supplier to another, i.e. significant switching costs exist.

The power of suppliers will be low where:

■ there are a substantial number of product/service suppliers in the marketplace,

■ there are a number of product/service substitutes available in the marketplace,

■ switching costs from one supplier to another supplier are low (or non-existent).

### Power of buyers in the marketplace

The power of customers/clients will be high where:

■ there is little differentiation between product/services in the marketplace,

■ substitute products/services are widely available,

■ substitute products/services can be easily found,

■ customers/clients are price sensitive, and

■ switching to/from substitute products/services is simple and cheap.

The power of customers/clients will be low where:

■ there is substantial differentiation between product/services in the marketplace,

■ substitute products/services are not available,

■ substitute products/services are difficult to locate,

■ customers/clients are not price sensitive, and

■ switching to substitute products/services is difficult and/or expensive.

### Availability of product/service substitutes in the marketplace

Where an alternative/substitute product/service is available that offers customers/clients the same benefit for the same or lower price, the threat of product/service substitutes is high where:

■ it is simple and easy for a customer/client to switch to a substitute product/service, and

■ customers/clients are prepared to trade off price and performance.

The threat of product/service substitutes is low where:

■ it is difficult and expensive for a customer/client to switch to a substitute product/service, and

■ customers/clients are not price sensitive.

### Threat from new entrants to the marketplace

The threat from new companies/organisations entering the marketplace is high where:

■ entry barriers to the marketplace are low, and

■ economies of scale are easily achievable.

The threat from new companies/organisations entering the marketplace is low where:

- entry barriers to the marketplace are high, and
- economies of scale are difficult to achieve.

So what is the relevance of such factors on a company's/organisation's revenue cycle? Put simply, it is the combined impact of the above factors that invariably determines the strategic context of company's/organisation's revenue cycle transactions – that is how the company manages the threats presented by and opportunities offered by the collective impact of such market-based factors/forces. For example, a company/organisation may elect to pursue a cost leadership strategy – that is to provide its products/services at a price lower than any of its competitors, and use it product/service price structure to:

- deter potential market entrants, and
- defend against the development of a substitute product/service.

Alternatively, a company/organisation may elect to pursue a differentiation strategy – that is to provide a unique product or service or a unique brand of customer service, and use customer/client loyalty to:

- discourage potential entrants, and
- reduce the threat of possible competition

Finally, a company/organisation may elect to pursue a segmentation (or focus) strategy – that is concentrate on a specific regional market, a specific range of products or a specific group of services, or indeed a specific group of customers/clients.

## Revenue cycle

There are two possible alternative types of revenue cycles:

- a debtor-based revenue cycle, and
- a non-debtor-based revenue cycle.

In a debtor-based revenue cycle the property of an asset/service (i.e. the legal title to an asset/service) and the possession of an asset/service (i.e. the physical custody of an asset/service) are exchanged for a legally binding promise to pay at some predetermined future date or within a predetermined future period. Such transactions are often referred to as credit sales.

In a non-debtor-based revenue cycle, such property and possession of an asset/service is exchanged for the legal title to (property) and custody of (possession) another asset. Whilst such an asset will usually be cash or a cash equivalent it can, in both a legal and business context, refer to any mutually agreed asset. Such transactions are often referred to as cash/cash equivalent sales.

Before we discuss each of the above types of revenue cycle in a little more detail, first some clarification.

Whilst we often refer to the debtor-based revenue cycle and the non-debtor-based revenue cycles as separate (independent) revenue cycles they are, in essence, interdependent cycles. Whilst some systems, processes, procedures and protocols will be shared by both revenue cycles, some will invariably be unique to the debtor-based revenue cycle and some to the non-debtor-based revenue cycle. Have a look at Figure 8.2.

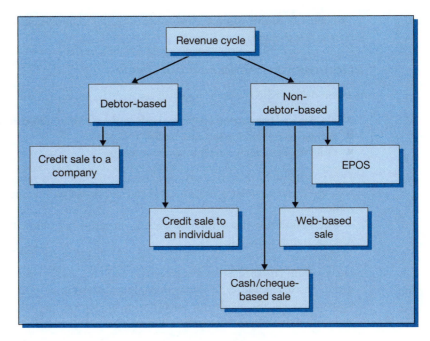

**Figure 8.2** Debtor-based system/non-debtor-based system

## Debtor-based revenue cycles

A debtor-based revenue cycle will generally be concerned with:

- company to company credit sales, and/or
- company to individual[3] credit sales,

that is revenue transactions in which the customer/client is authenticated, validated and approved before the transaction occurs. An agreed/authorised credit limit is always established for each customer/client prior to the acceptance and completion of any revenue transaction.

The debtor-based revenue cycle is therefore a subject (or customer/client) orientated revenue transaction cycle.

Generally such debtor-based revenue cycle transactions will occur within companies/ organisations classified as context type 1(a), and 1(b), and perhaps also 2(b) and 2(c). The processing of such transactions invariably involve/incorporate some information and communication technology-based interface/component whether at the retailing (customer order) stage, the distribution stage or the payment stage. Indeed, in a contemporary context, it is now likely that such debtor-based revenue cycle transactions (or some part) will be web-based.

For example a company/organisation may provide:

- the use of web-based catalogue to allow customers/clients to obtain detailed information on available products/service online,
- the use of secure extranet facilities (see Chapter 4) to allow customers/clients to order products/service online,
- the use of web-based stock-in-transit tacking/monitoring facilities (with the use of RFID[4] technologies) to allow customers/clients to monitor the movement of order products/services, and/or
- the use of a secure BACS-IP facility (see Chapter 4) to allow customers/clients (in particular corporate-based/organisation-based customers/clients) to submit payments online.

(We will discuss the uses and implications of RFID technologies on revenue cycle transactions later in this chapter.)

## Non-debtor-based revenue cycles

A non-debtor-based revenue cycle will generally be concerned with:

- EPOS-based transaction systems – both card-based and non-card-based systems,
- web-based transaction systems, and/or
- cash-based/cheque-based transaction systems.

That is, with revenue transactions in which the transaction is validated and authorised so that it is agreed and payment is authenticated and authorised prior to the completion of the revenue transaction.

The non-debtor-based revenue cycle is therefore an object (or transaction) orientated revenue transaction cycle.

Generally such non-debtor-based revenue transactions will occur within companies/organisations classified as context types 1(a) and 1(b), and perhaps also 2(a) and 2(b). As with debtor-based revenue cycle transactions, the processing of such non-debtor-based revenue transactions will also involve the use of a wide and increasingly integrated range of information and communication technologies – most of which are now web-based.

## Debtor-based revenue cycle

As we saw earlier a debtor-based revenue cycle will generally be concerned with:

- company to company credit sales, and/or
- company to individual credit sales.

Such a debtor-based revenue cycle can be divided into four component systems:

- the marketing system,
- the retailing (or customer/client ordering) system,
- the distribution and delivery system, and
- the payment management system.

See Figure 8.3.

## The marketing system

The purpose of the marketing system is to identify an appropriate market and/or customer/client base for the company's/organisation's goods/services.

See Figure 8.4.

It is in effect the company/organisation interface with the 'outside' world in both:

- a macro or market-based context, and
- a micro or product/service-based context.

## Macro-based context

In terms of the market, the system would be used to assist in determining:

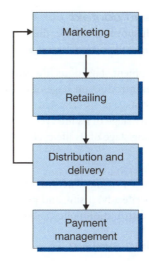

**Figure 8.3** Revenue cycle components

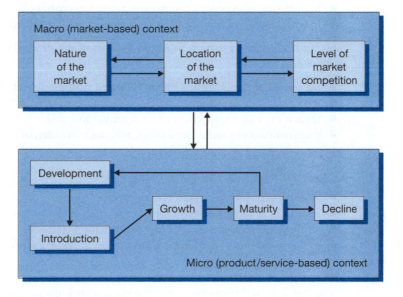

**Figure 8.4** Marketing system

- the nature of the market – for example, is the market a person-based one where the products/ services are aimed at individual customers/clients or a company-based one where the products/services are aimed at corporate customers/clients,
- the location of the market – for example, is the market a UK-based domestic/national one and/or is it an overseas-based international one, and
- the level of market competition within the market – for example, is the market competition aggressive and proactive or is it competition passive and reactive,

and in doing so establish a potential customer/client base for the company's/organisation's products/services.

### Micro-based context

In terms of the product/service, the system would be used to assist in determining the life cycle stage/position of the product/service – for example, is the product/service at:

- the development stage of its life cycle,
- the market introduction stage of its life cycle,
- the growth stage of its life cycle,
- the maturity stage of its life cycle, or
- the declining stage of its life cycle,

and in doing so establish:

- an acceptable pricing structure for the product/service,
- an appropriate advertising and promotion strategy for the product/service, and
- a suitable distribution policy and delivery system for the product/service.

## The retailing system

The purpose of the retailing (customer/client ordering) system is:

- to ensure the acceptance of only authorised orders,
- to maintain adherence to company/organisation credit policies, and
- to ensure adherence to company/organisation pricing policies.

Such a retail system generally functions as series of pre-determined sequential events/activities as follows:

- the receipt of an authenticated and validated customer/client order,
- the validation of a customer's/client's available credit/credit limit,
- the issue of a customer/client order confirmation, and
- the generation of a stores requisition, a production order, or a service/knowledge requisition.

See Figure 8.5.

The key documentation of such a retailing system would be:

- an approved customer/client order,
- a credit limit approval/amendment,
- an approved customer/client order confirmation, and
- an approved stores requisition, a production order or a service/knowledge requisition.

### Receipt of customer order

The first stage event/activity of the retailing system is the receipt of the customer/client order. Such orders can be received:

- in person at a retail store outlet,
- by mail,
- by telephone to a callcentre-based retail facility,
- using a web-based e-commerce facility, or
- in person using a sales representative.

Recent trends in the processing of customer/client orders have been for companies and organisations to allow the customer/client to complete the order whether as a paper-based document to be submitted my mail or in person, or increasing as a non-paper-based electronic document to be submitted using e-mail or a secured web-based e-commerce facility (most probably an intranet facility).

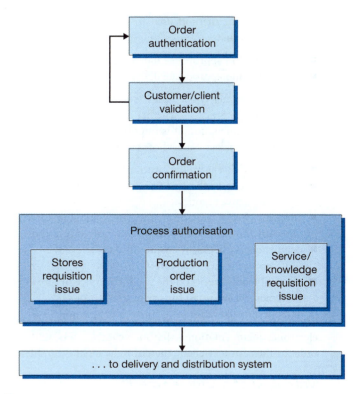

**Figure 8.5** Retailing system

Indeed, where a company/organisation receives paper-based documents, it is very likely that such documents will be scanned and converted into electronic, computer storable documents.

So what are the advantages/disadvantages of using customer/client originated, non-paper-based electronic documentation for the submission of customer/client orders? The advantages are:

- they assist in reducing the levels of errors,
- they assist in minimising the overall cost of the ordering process, and
- the use of such documentation generally increases the efficiency and effectiveness of the customer/client ordering process.

Put simply, this method eliminates, almost entirely, the need/requirement for human involvement in the customer/client ordering process. In addition, using electronic documentation – especially web-based facilities – is often viewed as being much more user-friendly since:

- it allows the customer/client ordering experience to be customised to meet specific customer/client requirements (see for example Dell Premier facilities @ www.dell.co.uk),
- it allows the customer/client to complete the order at a time convenient to them, and
- it allows the customer/client to customise the products/services required to their own specification.

The disadvantages of using customer/client originated electronic documentation are:

- poorly designed documentation – for example confused/unclear requirements and/or excessive information requirements may dissuade some customers/clients from using this method, especially web-based documentation, for ordering products/services, and
- poorly designed security system may result in the loss or theft of confidential customer/client information and/or customer/organisation assets and resources.

Irrespective of the method used to receive the customer order, it is however important to ensure/confirm that:

- all relevant and appropriate data is accurately collected, and
- all relevant and appropriate data is correctly recorded,

before the customer/client order is accepted/processed. That is within any customer/client order submission process – whether using a paper-based documentation process or non-paper electronic documentation, it is important that as part of the submission process, a number of checks are undertaken. Such checks would include, for example:

- authenticity checks on the customer/client to ensure they are who they say they are,
- validity checks on the customer/client account to ensure the customer/client account is a legitimate active account,
- authority checks using a signature (or digital signature/certificate for web-based submission) to ensure the customer/client order is correctly authorised,
- completeness checks to ensure all data relevant to the customer/client and the product/service order is received, and
- reasonableness checks on the product/service ordered to ensure that it is consistent with the customer's/client's past history of transactions.

Clearly, the benefit of non-paper-based electronic documentation, especially web-based online electronic documentation is that such checks can be undertaken prior to the submission of the order by the customer/client, thereby reducing the number of erroneous customer/client orders.

### Validation of customer credit

Once a valid customer/client order has been received, the second stage event/activity is the validation of the customer's/client's available credit/credit limit – that is a credit approval and/or credit limit check.

## For existing customers/clients

For customers/clients that have an existing and current credit approval rating, *and* an existing payment history (e.g. for the past 12 months), such a credit assessment would normally involve confirming:

- the customer's/client's current existing credit limit, and
- that the customer's/client's new order for products/services will not exceed the customer's/client's existing credit limit.

Where the customer's/client's credit limit is satisfactory and the new order placed by them will not exceed their current existing credit limit, it is likely that the order will be accepted – unless of course there are other (non-finance-related) reasons for the company/organisation not to do so.

Where a customer/client submits an order for products/services which if accepted would exceed their current existing credit limit, it would normally be necessary for additional approval to be obtained. Whilst such an approval would nominally mean obtaining authorisation from an appointed individual, for example an authorised credit manager, the credit assessment process for such an approval is in a contemporary context likely to be computer-related and based on:

- the transaction history of the customer/client – that is what level of trade has been undertaken with them,
- the payment history of the customer/client – that is how often have they made payment for outstanding invoices and have such payments been received within the approved credit period, and

- the assessment history of the customer/client – that is have they sought to extend their credit facilities in the past and have such applications been approved/rejected.

Where after such an assessment some doubt still remains over the customer's/client's suitability for extended credit facilities, it may be necessary to obtain an external third-party assessment of the customer's/client's current risk status – possibly from an online credit assessment agency, for example:

- Equifax @ www.equifax.co.uk,
- Experian @ www.experian.co.uk,
- Callcredit @ www.callcredit.co.uk, and/or
- CheckSURE @ www.checksure.biz.

### For new customers/clients

For new customers/clients, that is those that have not undertaken any transactions with the company over, say, the past 12 months and therefore do not have a valid credit rating and/or trading record/payment record with the company/organisation, it would be necessary, prior to the acceptance of any customer/client order, to:

- substantiate the identity of the customer/client, and
- authenticate the customer/client.

Once the identity of the customer/client has been confirmed, it would be necessary to establish their credit risk, possibly with an external agency where a large amount of credit is being requested. An example credit check report produced by CheckSURE on British Airways plc is available on the website accompanying this text www.pearsoned.co.uk/boczko.

If the customer's/client's credit risk/credit rating is acceptable – that is within a range approved by the company/organisation – the company/organisation can then:

- authorise a credit limit for the customer/client, and
- impose payments terms for the customer/client.

It is at this stage that the customer/client would be provided with:

- a debtor reference number/account number,
- information on the payment terms relating to the account (e.g. payment periods, payment conditions, penalties for late payment, applicable discounts for early payment),
- information on the payment process,
- information on the account limit/credit limit, and
- information on the use of customer/client-based data.[5]

### Issue of a customer order confirmation

Once the customer/client order has been validated and the credit limit confirmed and/or approved, the third stage event/activity is the issue of an order confirmation.

Where:

- the products ordered by the customer/client are available in stock and ready for immediate distribution,
- the products ordered by the customer/client require manufacture and the production resources are currently available for their immediate manufacture, or
- the services ordered by the customer/client are available for immediate provision,

then the customer/client order can be completed and confirmed.

Where products and or services are not available – either as completed stock or as manufactured products and/or deliverable services – due to a lack of immediately available resources to manufacture the products and/or provide the service, the customer/client order will need to be suspended and the customer/client offered the opportunity to:

- confirm either acceptance of the delayed delivery,
- order alternative products, or
- cancel the order.

### Generation of a stores issue request, a production order request or a service/knowledge request

As we saw above, once the customer/client order has been confirmed, it is important that:

- a stores issue request,
- a production order request, or
- a service/knowledge provision request,

is issued to ensure the appropriate products/services are supplied.

Whereas the generation of such requests is considered to be the fourth stage event/activity within the retailing system, the receipt of such requests is, broadly speaking, considered to be the first stage of the delivery and distribution system. This is the sub-system interconnectivity issue we came across in our discussion on system thinking in Chapter 2: that is the requests act as a systemic connection between the retail system (generation of the requests) and the distribution and delivery system (receipt of the requests).

Remember, the output from a sub-system within a system will always be the input to another sub-system either within the same system or another sub-systems within another system.

## The distribution and delivery system

The purpose of the distribution and delivery system is to identify any transportation requirements and, where necessary, initiate, monitor and manage the transportation and routing of the products, and the delivery of services. That is to ensure that not only is an appropriate distribution and delivery mechanism selected for all products/services but, more importantly, to ensure the prompt despatch/delivery of the right product/service, to the right customer/client, at the right place and at the right time.

Again, as a series of sequential events/activities, such a distribution system would generally function as follows:

- the receipt of stock issue request, production order request or service/knowledge provision request,
- the issue of a distribution/delivery order (for products) or a service provision order (for services),
- the selection of a product delivery/service provision mechanism, and
- the issue of a bill of lading (where required).

See Figure 8.6.

The key documentation linked to such a distribution and delivery system would be:

- an approved stock issue request or production order request (where a product requires manufacturing), or service/knowledge provision request (where a service requires scheduling for delivery),
- an authorised distribution/delivery order (for products),
- an approved distribution/delivery schedule (or transportation schedule) and, where necessary,
- an authorised bill of lading.

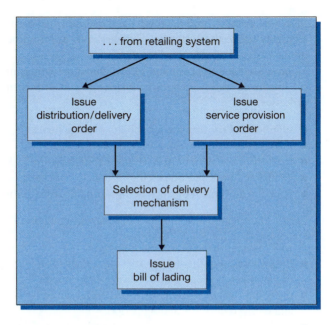

**Figure 8.6** Distribution and delivery system

### *Receipt of stores issue request, production order request or service/knowledge provision request*

The receipt of a stock issue request, production order request or service/knowledge provision request is essentially the point at which a virtual transaction becomes a physical reality: a real and tangible transaction involving the movement of physical assets and resources.

Remember, in many contemporary revenue cycle retail systems, the receipt and processing of a customer/client order (including the customer/client credit check and the generation of a stores issue request, production order request or service/knowledge provision request) is often undertaken using a range of integrated IT-based/web-based systems, involving little (if any) human and/or real-world interaction.

### Stores issue request

Where the products ordered by the customer/client are available in stock and the customer/client order can be completed, a stores requisition would be generated for the products to issue them from the stores.

Once a customer/client order has been accepted, in a revenue cycle context it should mean that:

- the products are in stock and need to be issued to satisfy/complete the transaction, or
- the products are not in stock and need to be ordered in to satisfy/complete the transaction.

Remember, a customer/client order for non-production items/products should never be confirmed unless the products ordered by the customer/client are in stock or will be in stock: that is the availability of the products for delivery to the customer/client is not in doubt. Why?

Put simply, to confirm a customer/client order and then fail to deliver the products within a reasonable period of time could have significant consequences. For example, in a financial context, it could result in the company/organisation incurring additional costs where a replacement product needs to be supplied to the customer/client, or suffering a loss of revenue income where a customer/client chooses to purchase the products from another company/organisation.

In a legal context it could result in the company/organisation facing a claim for damages, especially where the customer/client has entered into other third-party agreements/contracts on the basis of the order confirmation.

To minimise the possibility of the above occurring, many companies/organisations now use integrated store/warehousing systems as part of their in-house supply chain management processes, to:

- monitor and confirm the availability of stock items,
- manage the ordering and receipt of store items,
- track the movement of stock items within the store,
- control the issue and despatch of products from the store, and
- track the movement of stock items during delivery to the customer/client.

Clearly, the operational nature of a company's/organisation's warehousing system would depend on a number of factors, for example:

- the location(s) of the stores – that is whether stock items are held in a single secure location or a number of geographically dispersed locations,
- the volume of the stock items issued and received – that is how many stock items are issued and received during a trading period,
- the nature of stock turnover – that is whether stock items are issued/received on a cyclical basis, a seasonal basis or at a similar level throughout the year,
- the value of the stock turnover – that is whether store items are generic and of a low retail value, or unique and of a high retail value,
- the nature of the systems used to record the issue of receipt of stock items – that is what issuing system is used (paper-based, IT-based, web-based or a combination) and,
- the nature of the technologies used to manage and control the movement of stock items – that is are stock items bar coded or RFID tagged.

Nevertheless, whatever the procedures and processes used by the company/organisation to coordinate, manage and control revenue cycle systems, whatever the information and communication technologies used by the company/organisation to integrate revenue cycle system(s)/sub-system(s) into the company's/organisation's supply chain and provide an operational configuration for the store/warehousing system, it is important to ensure:

- all stock items are securely stored,
- the movement of *all* stock items, whatever the value, is closely monitored,
- all access to the store/warehouse facilities is restricted and controlled, and
- an accurate and up-to-date record of stock items within the store is maintained and reconciled to the physical stock on a regular basis.

We will discuss the management of current asset stocks and the use of store/warehousing systems in the issue and receipt of stock items in detail in Chapter 11. Here we will just provide a brief outline.

Consider, for example, a web-based ordering facility. Once the customer/client has submitted an order and it is confirmed by the company/organisation (and subsequently accepted by the customer/client), an approved stock issue request would be generated in the store/stock warehouse for the issue of the products from the company/organisation store/stock warehousing facility. The unique reference number generated on confirmation of the customer/client order would correspond directly with the number of the stock issue request generated in the store/warehouse, thereby creating a traceable connection between the customer/client and the physical stock items. The stock item references (or catalogue reference) used by the customer/client during the product selection process and by the company/organisation to confirm the availability of the products to the customer/client, would also be used to identify the location of the stock items within the company's/organisation's store/stock warehouse facilities.

Where all the products ordered by the customer/client (and included in the store issue request) are issued and forwarded to despatch for delivery to the customer, the store issue request would be electronically marked 'completed' to indicate a completed product issue. In some stores/stock warehousing systems, such a marking would generate a customer/client notification to inform them that the products they ordered have been despatched (with such notifications, where they are used, being increasingly e-mail-based).

Where some of the products ordered by the customer/client (and included in the store issue request) are not issued (e.g. a stock item/product may not be currently in stock), the store issue request would be electronically marked 'to be completed' to indicate a partially completed product issue. Again, such marking would generate a customer/client notification to inform them of which products have been despatched and provide a likely delivery date for the remaining products. Such a 'to be completed' store issue request would be monitored on a regular basis with the undelivered products checked to stock items/products received in store. Once the outstanding/undelivered products arrives from the supplier, the products would be recorded as a store receipt and immediately issued. The 'to be completed' store issue request would then be electronically marked 'completed' to indicate all the order products have been despatched. Again, a customer/client notification would be generated to inform the customer/client that the remaining outstanding/undelivered products have been despatched.

### Production order request

Where a customer/client orders a product or a group of products which require manufacture, for example where the customer/client has requested:

- a specific set of aesthetic characteristics (e.g. related to the colour and/or design of the product), and/or
- a specific group of technical features (e.g. related to product operability and performance),

it is necessary to confirm the availability of sufficient production resources/capabilities for the immediate manufacture of the products. To do so, a production order request would be generated for manufacture of the products either as part of an in-house manufacturing process or as part of an outsourced manufacturing process.

Where the products ordered by the customer/client require manufacture and the production resources are available for their immediate manufacture, the order can be completed and the customer/client order confirmed. A production order request would be generated to start the manufacturing process, either as part of an in-house process or as part of an outsourced one. Where an in-house manufacturing process is used, the production order request would be forwarded to manufacturing management who would be responsible for:

- the planning of the manufacturing process,
- the acquisition of resources for the production,
- the scheduling and commencement of the manufacturing process, and
- the completion and delivery into store of the completed product.

An example production order request is provided in Example 10.3 (p. 503).

Where an outsourced manufacturing process is used, the production order request would be used to generate a purchase order request to start the purchase process. Where, due to a lack of immediately available production resources to manufacture the products ordered by the customer/client, the order cannot be completed it will need to be suspended and a production schedule established to determine the future date at which the manufacturing resources required to produce the ordered products will be available either internally as part of the in-house manufacturing process or externally as an outsourced manufacturing process. The customer will need to be informed of the anticipated availability/delivery of the products.

We will look at purchase order requests in a little more detail in Chapter 9 and production order requests issues in a little more detail in Chapter 10.

### Service/knowledge provision request

Where the customer/client order is for services, it is necessary to confirm the availability of such services – that is to confirm that such services are available. The customer/client order can then be completed and confirmed. Where such a confirmation is issued, a service/knowledge provision request would be generated for the provision of the services, and the customer/client would be informed of the anticipated provision date.

Where, perhaps because of resource constraints and/or scheduling constraints such services are not available, and the order cannot be completed, it will need to be suspended and the company/organisation will need to determine the future date at which such services will be available and the order can be fulfilled. The customer/client will of course need to be informed of any delay.

So what types of services could they be? That would of course depend on the company/organisation, but generally such services could, for example, range from:

- profession-based services such accountancy services, IT consulting services, legal services, and/or architectural services,
- skills-related services such domestic maintenance and/or improvement services (e.g. domestic plumbing repairs, carpentry and electrical maintenance and improvement), to
- manual-related services such gardening/landscaping services and refuse collection/disposal.

### Issue of a distribution/delivery order

When the products are available for delivery, whether as a result of a store issue request or a production order request which has been satisfied (that is the products have been manufactured and are available for delivery) and received by the store, an authorised distribution/delivery order (for the products) would be created.

Remember, a distribution/delivery order would only be issued where it can be matched to a store issue request. This essentially means that where products are manufactured – whether in-house or outsourced to an external manufacturer – such products should be received into store *before* they are issued and available for distribution/delivery to the customer/client. Such a receipt into store, however, need not necessarily be represented by the physical movement of the products. In some instances, such a receipt into store would be a nominal representation of the movement of the products rather than a representation of the physical movement of the products themselves. Why?

Because in some instances products manufactured to order by an external manufacturer may be delivered directly to the customer/client, especially where such an action would reduce overall distribution/delivery costs. For example, it would be ridiculous for a company/organisation located in Edinburgh, to outsource the manufacture of a product to a company in Manchester, for a customer/client in Southampton and then for the company/organisation to require the products to be physically delivered into store in Edinburgh before they can be delivered to the customer/client in Southampton.

Once a distribution/delivery order has been raised, and the distribution/delivery number matched to the sales order request, the distribution/delivery orders would be used to generate a distribution/delivery schedule – often referred to as a transportation schedule. Whilst many distribution and delivery systems produce such transportation schedules at the end of a trading period (e.g. at the end of the day), in reality such schedules are updated in real-time to minimise the possibility of distribution/delivery errors.

So what would a transportation schedule contain? Put simply it would contain a list of product deliveries to be made to customers/clients during a particular period, for example during a working day say between 9:00 am and 5:00 pm. Where distribution/delivery is an in-house service, such transportation schedules would generally be date orientated, vehicle specific and location/area-based.

Consider the following example:

*KPO Ltd is a York-based electrical supplier. The company supplies household electrical products to companies/organisations throughout the UK from its store/warehouse facility in York. The company operates an in-house product distribution/delivery service, using a fleet of 15 vehicles, for the transportation of products to UK-based customers/clients.*

*On 18 May 2007, vehicle L459 (registration number YY06 YTL), was provided with a transportation schedule containing five scheduled deliveries in the York/Harrogate area.*

*Until recently, most companies/organisations would – prior to the delivery – contact the customer/client (either by telephone, text message or e-mail) and inform them of the expected delivery time of their ordered products. Increasingly, however, a significant number of companies/organisations are now using an automated company/organisation-based information service which the customer/client can contact – usually 24 hours before the due delivery date – to obtain a precise delivery time. Why?*

*Not only is it more cost effective for the company/organisation, it also places the obligation on the customer/client to obtain the information.*

*KPO Ltd provides customers/clients with a delivery hotline number and a web address for them to contact up to 24 hours before the delivery to obtain conformation details.*

So, what happens next? Because:

- the customer/client order is linked to a stores issue request, and
- the stores issue request is linked to a distribution/delivery order, and
- the distribution/delivery order is linked to a transportation schedule of deliveries,

to complete the retail/distribution and delivery process it is important for the customer/client to authorise and acknowledge receipt of the products.

Back to our example:

*Vehicle L459 (registration number YY06 YTL) has the following scheduled deliveries:*

- *delivery 1 is to a small company in Thirsk at approximately 10:00 am,*
- *delivery 2 is to a retail outlet in Ripon at approximately 11:30 pm,*
- *delivery 3 is to a high street retailer in Harrogate at approximately 1:30 pm,*
- *delivery 4 is to a medium-sized company in Wetherby at approximately 3:00 pm, and*
- *delivery 5 is to a small retail company in York at approximately 4:30 pm.*

*For scheduled deliveries 1, 2, 4, and 5, the deliveries were successful.*

*For each delivery, on receipt, the customer/client (or their assigned representative) authorises the receipt of the products.*

Whilst historically, transportation schedules were often multiple copy, paper-based schedules with authorisation merely a signature from an authorised signatory, today such transportation schedules are often electronic documents stored on an IT-based, hand-held device (probably a notebook, tablet or PDA[6]) often with web-based capabilities. At each point of delivery/delivery location, the products are scanned using an RFID tag (see later), to confirm the product details and the product delivery, and the receipt authorised by the customer/client by signing and dating a customer/client receipt, usually using a notebook, tablet or PDA-based document.

The delivery is now complete. The legal title to the products (that is ownership of the property), and possession of the products have been transferred to the customer/client – and a legal debt now exists for payment for the products. For the customer/client a copy distribution/delivery order is included with the products. On completion of each delivery, confirmation details are stored on the hand-held device.

Back again to our example:

*For delivery 3, for whatever reason, no customer/client was available to authorise and acknowledge receipt of the products. The products were retained and a notice of delivery was provided for the customer/client informing them of the time of the attempted delivery, giving contact details for re-arranging the delivery.*

*On completion of all of the above scheduled deliveries, confirmation details (including delivery-specific details – for example delivery times) are downloaded from the vehicle using a secure online weblink to KPO Ltd. Undelivered products are returned to the store/warehouse facility in York where they are returned into an 'in transit store'. Here the products remain for a period of no longer than 48 hours. If the customer/client does not contact the company to reschedule the failed delivery, the goods are returned into the main store and appropriate action taken.*

So, why is this important from an accounting information perspective? Because the receipt of the delivery confirmation is used certainly in a post-invoicing system (see later) to generate the invoice and of course create the accounting entries.

### Issue of a service provision order

Where the provision of a service is ordered by the customer/client, such a service provision would, depending on the type of service provision requested, be provided as either:

- a remote off-site service provision, or
- an on-site service provision.

Profession-based services (e.g. accountancy/auditing services, IT services, legal services and/or architectural services) are generally provided as a remote, off-site service provision. Whilst some on-site service provision may occasionally be necessary it will often be limited, although there are exceptions, for example the year-end audit undertaken by the external auditor(s).

Skills-related services (e.g. domestic maintenance and/or improvement services) and manual-related services (e.g. gardening/landscaping services and refuse collection/disposal services) are generally provided as an on-site service provision.

As we saw earlier, when a customer/client order for the provision of a service is received and a confirmation is issued, a uniquely numbered service provision request is created and, where required, appropriate employees would be scheduled to provide the service for the customer/client. Whilst the nature and content of such a service provision request would differ, depending on the company/organisation and the type of the service requested, they would, in essence, serve a similar purpose, as follows:

- where the service requested by the customer/client is a fixed-priced service, the service provision request would be used to identify the cost, and
- where the service requested by the customer/client is a variable priced service, the service request would be used to identify the resources required to complete the service provision for the customer/client (where the cost of the service is dependent on the resource used in its provision), and allocate the actual cost of, for example, staff time and of resources/assets used during the provision of the service requested by the customer/client.

Once the service has been provided and completed, the customer/client would be required to confirm their acceptance of, and satisfaction with, the service provided. For profession-based services, such confirmation would more than likely be in the form of an authorised completion document/certificate – possibly electronic, although it is still the case that such confirmation documents are often paper-based. For skill-based and/or manual-based services – especially where the service provider may have a number of customers/clients to visit during a delivery period (e.g. a day), customer/client confirmation of acceptance of, and satisfaction with, the service provided would probably be obtained by requesting the customer/client to sign an electronic document stored on an IT-based, hand-held device – probably a notebook, tablet or PDA.

Consider the following example:

*OPL Ltd is a Hull-based plumbing contractor providing a range of repair, maintenance and installation services. The company employs 15 qualified plumbers and has a fleet of 15 vehicles.*

*On 26 June 2007, Jon Simms (employee reference 389487) using vehicle C3P (registration number TH06 LUY), was provided with a service schedule containing four service deliveries in the Hull area, as follows:*

- *service 1 is to a small company in Hull,*
- *service 2 is to a retail hotel in Hessle,*
- *service 3 is to a high street retailer in Beverley, and*
- *service 4 is to a medium-sized company in Willerby.*

*Each vehicle carries a small store of items, which is restocked from the company's main store at the end of the week, with each plumber (service provider) using a Windows-based PDA to record service provision details. Each plumber's PDA is updated each day to provide details of the following day's service requirements.*

*On arrival the plumber opens the relevant service delivery request for the customer/client and the plumber's time at the customer/client commences. All store items used during the service provision are itemised and recorded. On completion, the customer/client confirms acceptance of and satisfaction with the service provided by signing an electronic document stored on the plumber's Windows-based PDA. The service plumber's time at the customer/ client then ceases as the service is now complete.*

*On completion of the final service provision for the day, Jon Simms sends confirmation details of all services undertaken and completed (including materials used in the provision of the requested services and the time taken to provide the requested services) from the vehicle using a secure online weblink to OLP Ltd.*

*Once a service delivery confirmation has been received by OPL Ltd, an invoice would be generated and, of course, the accounting entries created.*

### Selection of product delivery/service provision mechanism – to outsource or not to outsource?

In the above discussion, we assumed that the distribution/delivery of the product/service was in-house provided. Whilst such in-house provided services are used very successfully by many companies/organisations – including many established high street retailers – there are an increasing number of companies/organisations (especially those involved in the distribution/delivery of products) who choose to outsource to an external carrier some part, if not all, of their distribution/delivery services. This is especially the case where a company/organisation requires the use of a global distribution network for the secure transportation of products to customers/clients all over the world.

The selection of a distribution and delivery mechanism between:

- an in-house distribution and delivery service,
- an outsourced distribution and delivery service, or
- a combination of both,

depends on a number of factors, including, for example:

- the geographical location(s) of the company's/organisation's delivery/distribution centres,
- the geographical location of the customer/client,
- the physical characteristics of the product/service – for example the size of the product delivery, the structural composition of the product, the fragility of the product, the complexity of the service,
- the control/security requirements of the delivery and, of course,
- the cost of the distribution/delivery mechanism.

So what are the advantages and disadvantages of outsourcing the distribution and delivery of products? For the company/organisation, the advantages are:

- it avoids the need for companies/organisations to develop costly distribution and delivery infrastructures,
- it allows the company/organisation to focus on other core business aspects/areas,
- it provides access to specialist skills and experience which may not be available within the company/organisation, and
- it can provide significant cost savings for the outsourcing company/organisation.

For the company/organisation the disadvantages are:

- it may result in an excessive over-dependency on the external skills and experience of an external service provider/group of external service providers,
- it may result in a loss of service control,
- it may result in a possible loss of confidential information, and
- it may result in a loss of customer/client confidence if the external service provider fails to provide an efficient and effective distribution and delivery service.

### Issue of a bill of lading

Where an outsourced distribution and delivery service is used by a company/organisation for the delivery of products to customers/clients overseas, a bill of lading would normally be required. In addition, a company may also require an export licence if it is exporting:

- military products and/or technologies,
- paramilitary products and/or technologies,
- artworks,
- plants and animals,
- medicines, or
- chemicals.

For more details see www.dti.gov.uk/europeandtrade/strategic-export-control/licensing-rating/index.html.

In addition, where a company/organisation is exporting products that may be regarded as hazardous, it may also require a dangerous goods note (DGN).

A bill of lading is essentially a legal contract, a document that defines the responsibility for the transportation of products or more appropriately the carriage of products. Such a document serves a number of purposes, in particular it identifies:

- the company responsible for the transportation of the products – that is the carrier responsible for the carriage of the products,
- the source of the products – that is the company/organisation requesting the transportation of the products,
- the destination of the products – that is the customer/client address to which the products are to be delivered,
- the transportation instructions – that is the transportation mechanisms to be used to deliver the products to the customer/client, and
- the party or parties responsible for the products whilst they are in transit.

There are many different types of bills of lading the most common being as follows:

- a *straight bill of lading* is a document which provides that products are consigned to a specified customer/client, that is the carrier is required to provide delivery only to the named consignee in the document. Such a bill of lading is also known as a *non-negotiable bill of lading*.
- an *order bill of lading* is a document which provides that the company/person in possession of the bill of lading can reroute the products to a third party if so required. That is delivery is to be made to the further order of the consignee. Such a bill of lading is also known as a *negotiable bill of lading*.
- a *bearer bill of lading* is a document which provides that the delivery of products to which the bill of lading refers can be made to whoever has possession of the bill.

Wherever the type of bill of lading used, it serves three purposes. Firstly, it can serve as evidence that a valid contract of carriage exists. Secondly, it can serve as a receipt signed by the carrier confirming whether goods matching the contract description have been received in good condition. Thirdly, it can serve as a document of transfer governing the legal characteristics of physical carriage.

Further information on the documentation requirements for exporting products from the UK is available from SITPRO Ltd[7] @ www.sitpro.org.uk.

Note: Where a UK company/organisation undertakes trade[8] with a company/organisation in another European Union (EU) member state, the company/organisation is required to provide details of these transactions for statistical purposes. Intrastat is the system used to collect these statistics. Currently there are two main types of Intrastat declaration depending on whether the value of a company's/organisation's imports or exports is above or below a predetermined threshold. In 2006 the threshold limit was £225,000. For further details on Intrastat declarations, and the web-based submission of an Intrastat declaration see www.uktradeinfo.com/index.cfm?task=intrahome.

## The Payment management system

The purpose of the payment management system is to ensure:

- the correct assessment of the cost of products/services provided to customers/clients,
- the correct invoicing of *all* sales,

- the accurate management of customer/client accounts, and
- the adequate management of customer/client credit facilities and the recovery of outstanding debts.

Such a payment management system would – for internal control purposes – be divided into two sub-systems:

- the debtor creation (invoicing) sub-system, and
- debtor management sub-system.

See Figure 8.7.

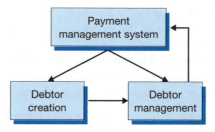

**Figure 8.7** Payment management system

### Debtor creation (invoicing)

As a series of sequential events/activities, such a debtor creation (invoicing) sub-system would generally function as follows:

- the generation of the customer/client invoice,
- the documentation of all transactions in the company's/organisation's accounting records, and either:
  - the creation of a debtor account for the customer/client, or
  - the amendment of an existing customer's/client's account.

See Figure 8.8.

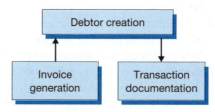

**Figure 8.8** Debtor creation

The key documentation of such a debtor creation sub-system would be:

- the invoice, and
- the debtor account.

### Generation of the customer/client invoice

As an activity, there can be little doubt that the generation of the customer/client invoice is a core activity within the debtor-based revenue cycle. However, before we discuss the invoicing process in a little more detail, it would perhaps be useful first to consider the three optional approaches used in invoicing, these being:

- the pre-invoicing approach,
- the on-demand invoicing approach, and
- the post-invoicing approach.

### Pre-invoicing approach

Using the pre-invoicing approach – sometimes referred to as 'before delivery' invoicing – the invoice is created and despatched/forwarded to the customer/client as soon as the customer/client order is approved: that is once a customer/client order conformation has been issued. The implicit assumption in using this approach is that once a customer/client order confirmation has been issued, the products/services *will* be delivered.

This is not a widely used invoicing approach because customers/clients may often receive the invoice before the products/services have been delivered/performed, a practice which some customers/clients may find objectionable.

### On-demand invoicing

Using the on-demand invoicing approach (sometimes referred to as 'on-delivery' invoicing), the invoice is created and despatched/forwarded to the customer/client with the products/services. Again, this is not a widely used invoicing approach although it is used by many online retailers.

### Post-invoicing

Using the post-invoicing approach (sometimes referred to as the 'after-delivery' approach), the invoice is created and despatched/forwarded to the customer/client once the products/services have been delivered and a customer/client authorised product/service delivery confirmation is available.

This is the most widely used invoicing approach – an approach which is often combined with payments procedures in which customers/clients pay on a statement of account basis (e.g. at the end of a calendar month). In such situations, the invoices received during a calendar month will usually be for information purposes only.

Where a customer/client pays, following any agreed period of credit, on receipt of an invoice, such a method is often referred to as the open invoice method. Where a customer/client pays, following any agreed period of credit, on receipt of a statement of account, such a method is often referred to as the balance forward method. (In our discussion, we will assume the post-invoicing approach is used.)

### Issue invoices – phased/cyclical invoice processing

In addition, where a company/organisation has a substantial number of customers/clients and uses a paper-based invoicing/statement of account system, such invoices/statement of accounts may be despatched to customers/clients on a phased or cyclical basis. That is customers/clients will be grouped (perhaps alphabetically by account name, or numerically by account number or geographically by customer/client location) and invoices/statements of account will be despatched to a particular group at a particular time during a collection period.

Consider the following:

*PeBoc plc is a Belfast-based large electrical component manufacturer. On average the company despatches 23,000 invoices a month. To distribute the work load efficiently, the company uses debtor names as a means of allocating the distribution of invoices and/or statement of accounts to customers/clients, as follows:*

- *customer/client account name between A–E: distribution – end of week 1:*
  - *invoice/statement of account date 1st of the month,*
  - *statement of account period – month ending 30th/31st of the previous month,*
- *customer/client account name between F–J: distribution – end of week 2:*
  - *invoice/statement of account date 8th of the month,*
  - *statement of account period – month ending 7th of the current month,*
- *customer/client account name between K–P: distribution – end of week 3:*
  - *invoice/statement of account date 15th of the month,*
  - *statement of account period – month ending 14th of the current month,*
- *customer/client account name between Q–Z: distribution – end of week 4:*
  - *invoice/statement of account date 22nd of the month,*
  - *statement of account period – month ending 21st of the current month.*

Of course, the need for such phasing of invoice/statement of account distribution or, more appropriately, cyclical billing can be eliminated by the use of electronic web-based/EDI-based invoicing – where the number of invoices/statement of accounts distributed is irrelevant. It is just a simple to distribute 10 invoices electronically as it is to distribute 10,000!

### The purpose and content of an invoice

The purpose of the invoicing sub-system is to summarise and reconcile selected information accumulated in:

- the retailing system – in particular the customer order, and
- the distribution and delivery system – in particular the delivery/packing order.

The purpose of the invoice is to advise the customer/client of:

- the amount(s) now due for payment (within agreed payment terms), or
- the amount(s) that will be added to the customer's/client's account.

So what information is required to produce an invoice and, perhaps more importantly, what type of information would an invoice contain?

The information required to create an invoice would include, for example, the following:

- the customer/client reference – to confirm the authenticity of the customer/client,
- the customer/client order number – to confirm the validity of the customer/client order,
- the quantity of the products/nature of the services delivered – to confirm the quantity of products delivered/services performed, and
- the price of the products/services delivered – to confirm the prices of products delivered and/or services performed.

Remember, all of the above will be available when the customer/client order is confirmed.

The information contained within an invoice would include, for example, the following:

- the supplying company/organisation name/address,
- the supplying company/organisation contact details (e.g. postal address, telephone number, e-mail address, website address),
- the supplying company/organisation VAT registration number,
- the invoice number – the reference number for the document,
- an invoice date (normally the tax point date for VAT purposes),
- the customer/client order number,
- the delivery date of the products/services,
- a description of the products/service supplied,
- details of the quantity of products/service supplied,

- details of the unit prices of the products/services supplied,
- details of the VAT applicable on the products/service supplied, [9]
- details of any trade/payment discounts offered and/or allowed,
- terms of payment – for example:
  - POD (Payment on Delivery)/COD (Cash on Delivery),
  - 30 days net (Payment within 30 days of the invoice date),
  - 3%/14 (A 3% discount is available if payment is made within 14 days), or
  - POA (Payable on Account – usually a calendar month end statement),
- the name and invoicing address of the customer/client, and
- the delivery address for products/services if different from the invoicing address of the customer/client

An example invoice is shown in Example 8.1.

| | INVOICE | |
|---|---|---|
| **AB plc**<br>1010 West Street<br>East Hampton<br>YY06 7RX<br><br>Tel ................<br>E-mail .................. | | Invoice No .............. |

| Customer address | Delivery address |
|---|---|
| | |

| Date ............... | Sales ref ............... | Terms of sale ............... |
|---|---|---|

| Delivery mode ............... | Delivery date ............... | Tracking ref ............... |
|---|---|---|

| Quantity | Item ref | Description | Unit price (£) | TOTAL (£) |
|---|---|---|---|---|
| | | | | |

| Condition on sale | | |
|---|---|---|
| | Sub total | |
| | Delivery charge | |
| | VAT | |
| | TOTAL | |

**Example 8.1** An invoice

It is perhaps worth noting that whilst paper-based invoices are still issued by a number of companies/organisations, a growing number are now using non-paper-based electronic invoices, either with a web-based extranet facility and/or a web-based EDI facility.

### Creation/amendment of debtor account

Once the invoice has been produced, the transaction will need to be recorded in the company's/organisation's accounting records.

Remember the bookkeeping entries for such a transaction? In an accounting context, the transaction would be recorded in the general ledger as follows:

- Dr debtor's control account
- Cr sales account.

A debit memorandum entry would also be made in the individual debtor's account in the sales ledger (also known as the debtors ledger).

Remember, however bizarre it may appear this is essentially triple entry, not double entry!

## New debtor

Where the transaction relates to a new debtor – the new debtor account will be debited.

Remember, the new debtor account would have been created during the initial credit check stage (see above). It is at the credit check stage that the customer/client would have been issued with a debtor reference (account number), and information about the payment terms and conditions relating to the account.

## Existing debtor

Where the transaction relates to an existing debtor, the existing debtor's account will be debited – that is amended and the balance increased. Remember, for an existing debtor it should not be possible to incur a debt greater than the current approved account limit/credit limit on the debtor's account. That is it should not be possible to increase the account balance over and above the current approved account limit/credit limit on the debtor's account. This is because the customer/client order and ultimate sale to which the invoice relates should have only been approved where:

- the customer's/client's account limit/credit limit is sufficient to allow the transaction/sale, or
- the customer's/client's account limit/credit limit has an amendment/increase to allow the transaction/sale.

So, how would the above accounting entries be processed and recorded?

## Recording debtor account transactions

Using an online (3 stage) accounting system such accounting entries would be recorded for each transaction as the transaction occurs and/or is approved. That is individual debtor accounts (in the sales ledger/debtors ledger) would be updated immediately. A summary sales journal would be created as a control record of all the transactions recorded during a particular period. Using an online (3 stage) accounting system, a sales journal would act as an 'after-the-event' control summary.

Using an online (4 stage) accounting system such accounting entries would also be recorded for each transaction. However, the debtor accounts would *not* be updated immediately. A sales journal would be created as a control record to summarise all the transactions recorded during a particular period and would be used to update the individual debtor's account (in the sales ledger/debtors ledger). That is the individual debtor's accounts would be updated as a batch of transactions. Using an online (4 stage) accounting system, a sales journal would act as a 'before the event' control summary.

Whilst 4 stage online processing has been, and indeed still continues to be, the preferred processing system for many companies/organisations (probably because of its similarity to the traditional hard-copy-based batch processing system), the increasing use and availability of the 3 stage online processing accounting systems has undoubtedly increased the popularity of real-time processing.

### Debtor management

Once the products/services have been supplied to the customer/client and an invoice or statement of account (where invoices are used for information purposes only) has been issued and presented to the customer/client for payment, it is important to ensure that all payments are collected. A failure to collect due payments can have significant and long-term consequences on a company's/organisation's working capital. Indeed, history is replete with examples of companies and organisations which have failed, not because of a lack of market opportunities, product/service demand or a lack of customer loyalty, but primarily because of a lack of pro-active working capital management.

So, what do we mean by a debtor management sub-system? As a series of sequential events/ activities, a debtor management sub-system generally comprises of four activities:

■ the collection and recording of payments made by customers/clients,
■ the reconciliation of customer/client account balances,
■ the assessment of doubtful debts, and
■ the write-off of bad debts/irrecoverable debtor accounts.

See Figure 8.9.

The key documentation of such a debtor management sub-system would be:

■ the debtor account,
■ a debtor account adjustment,
■ the debtor statement of account,
■ a debtor account payment reminder, and
■ an application to write-off.

### Collection and recording of payment receipts

As we saw earlier, a customer/client can pay:

■ on receipt of an invoice (the open invoice method), or
■ on receipt of a statement of account (the balance forward method),

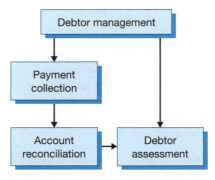

**Figure 8.9** Debtor management

with the choice of payment method used by the customer/client determined by the company/
organisation supplying the products/services. In general, for new customers/clients, a company/
organisation would normally use the open invoice method, with the balance forward method
used only for those customers/clients with an established trading relationship/payment record.

So how can a customer/client submit payment on receipt of an invoice or statement of
account? There are generally four methods a customer/client can use, these being:

- payment by bank transfer (BACS) using BACSTEL-IP (see Chapter 4),
- payment by EFT – using a debit or credit card,
- payment by cheque[10] – through the mail or by personal visit, and/or
- payment by cash – by personal visit.

Where at all possible, a company/organisation should dissuade customers/clients from using
payment methods that involve payment by cheque and/or payment by cash – simply because of
the cost.

Cheques and cash require processing, recording, secure storage, banking and periodic reconciliation, all of which can incur substantial additional costs for a company/organisation.

## Payment by BACS

Payment by BACS using BACSTEL-IP (see Chapter 4) would generally be used (although not
exclusively) by company/organisation-based customers/clients – more specifically in business-
2-business (B2B) transactions with repeat customers where regular automated payments are
made.

The advantages of using BACS as a payment method are:

- it reduces the time and the cost of administering payments and can assist in the management
  of cash flow and therefore improve financial control;
- it eliminates (almost totally) the need for human intervention in the payment process and
  therefore the possibility of human error;
- it reduces risk of loss, late payment and/or theft for customers/clients; and
- it allows for the automated settlement of payments between companies/organisations.

The main disadvantage is the costs involved in the setting up/using of the BACS payment by
BACSTEL-IP. Consequently, as a payment method it is suitable only for those companies/
organisations making more than, on average, 150 payments a month.

## Payment by EFT

Payment by EFT can be either:

- a card-based EFT – for example payment using a debit/credit card, or
- a non-card-based EFT – for example Pay-By-Touch (see later in this chapter).

Whereas card-based EFT is the dominant payment method and generally used by individual,
non-company or non-organisation-based customers/clients, non-card-based EFT whilst growing in popularity is (in the UK at least) currently restricted to individuals only.

So what are the advantages and disadvantages of accepting payment by card-based/non-
card-based EFT?

The advantages include:

- it allows a company/organisations to reach a wider customer/client base – for example it
  allows a company/organisation to accept payment by phone, by mail and/or online,
- it improves cash flow since payments by EFT usually clear more quickly than cheque payments,

- it can improve company/organisation security since less cash and less cheques are stored (however temporarily) on company/organisation premises, and
- it reduces administration costs and the need for the reconciliation of banked receipts.

The disadvantages include:

- the administrative and management costs involved in setting up agreements for process ETF-based payments,
- the costs involved in acquiring the technologies to process payments by EFT,
- the costs involved in developing the technical and administrative procedures to manage the acceptance and processing of EFT payments, and
- the costs associated with the possible increased in fraud as a result of accepting EFT payments, especially card-based payments.

We will look at the process of payment by card-based/non-card-based EFT later in this chapter.

## Payment by cheque or cash

Payment by cheque or cash could be used by both company/organisation-based customers/clients and individual, non-company/organisation-based customers/clients. Historically, payment by cheque was the preferred method of payment used by both company/organisation-based customers/clients and individual non-company/organisation-based customers/clients. Although its popularity has reduced considerably in recent years (certainly since the mid 1990s) it still continues to be a method of payment favoured by a small and declining number of individual, non-corporate customers/clients.[11]

We will look at the control issues associated with the receipt of customer/client payments – in particular the problems associated with the receipts of cheques and/or cash – in Chapter 11.

## Recording of payment receipts

Once payment has been received, it is of course important that the debtor account of the customer/client tendering the payment is correctly amended and updated to reflect the receipt of the payment.

Remember the bookkeeping entries for such a transaction? In an accounting context, the transaction would be recorded in the general ledger as follows:

- Dr bank account,
- Cr debtor's control account.

Where an early payment discount is allowed, the transaction would be recorded in the general ledger as follows:

- Dr discounts allowed,[12]
- Cr bank account,
- Cr debtor's control account.

A credit memorandum entry would also be made in the individual debtor account in the sales ledger (debtors ledger).

Again, remember it is essentially triple entry, not double entry!

So, how would the debtor account be updated? There are, of course, various ways in which a customer/client debtor account can be updated. A commonly used approach (although it is by no means universally accepted) is as follows.

Where the customer/client provides payment electronically – for example using payment by BACS or by EFT, the debtor account would be updated on receipt of the funds (especially where the debtor account reference is transmitted with the transfer of funds): that is the above triple entry – the updating of the general ledger and the sales ledger (debtors ledger) – would occur at the same time.

Where the customer/client provides payment manually, for example using payment by cheque and/or cash, it is likely that the debtor account would be updated by batch processing at the end of the day: that is the above triple entry – the updating of the general ledger and the sales ledger (debtors ledger) – would occur at separate times:

■ the general ledger would be up dated online on receipt of the payment, and
■ the sales ledger (debtors ledger) would be updated by batch processing, probably at the end of the trading day.

## Debtor account adjustments

Occasionally, it may be necessary to adjust a customer's/client's debtor account for three main reasons, these being:

■ errors in provision – for example products produced for, and sold to, the customer/client may be returned because they are defective or incorrect, or a service provided for a customer/client may have been incomplete or incorrect,
■ errors in pricing – for example products produced for, and sold to, the customer/client may have been inappropriately priced resulting in the customer/client invoice prices being either under- or over-stated, and
■ errors in payment – for example:
  ● an allocation error where payments received from a customer/client may have been recorded in, or allocated to, the wrong debtor account, or
  ● a transposition error where payments received from a customer/client may have been recorded incorrectly (wrong amount).

In an accounting context:

■ errors in provision would be recorded in the general ledger as follows:
  ● Dr sales account,
  ● Cr debtor's control account,
■ under-pricing errors would be recorded in the general ledger as follows:
  ● Dr debtor's control account,
  ● Cr sales account,
■ over-pricing errors would be recorded in the general ledger as follows:
  ● Dr sales account,
  ● Cr debtor's control account,
■ allocation errors would be recorded as a contra entry in the general ledger as follows:
  ● Dr debtor's control account,
  ● Cr debtor's control account,
■ transportation errors would be recorded in the general ledger as follows:
  ● Dr sales account,
  ● Cr debtor's control account.

Of course, in addition to the above, a debit and/or credit memorandum entry would also be made in the individual debtor's account in the sales ledger (debtors ledger).

From an internal control context, it is important that any adjustment is:

■ appropriately authorised – usually by a financial accounting manager, and
■ properly documented – using a journal to record the accounting entry.

## Reconciliation of customer/client accounts

Where a large volume of debtor-based transactions occur (where a large number of customer/client accounts exist), is it necessary periodically to reconcile the balance in the debtor's control account in the general ledger and the total of the individual debtor account balances in the sales ledger (debtors ledger) to:

- authenticate the outstanding balance on individual debtor accounts, and
- confirm the correctness of the balance of the debtor's control account in the general ledger.

It is important that a company/organisation identify and correct any errors that may exist between the debtor's control account in the general ledger and the total of the individual debtor account balances in the sales ledger (debtors ledger). This is because the existence of such errors could not only result in a loss of income – where debtor accounts in the sales ledger (debtors ledger) are understated – it could, more importantly, result in the qualification of the company's/organisation's financial statements.

In a practical context, the reconciliation between the debtor's control account in the general ledger and the total of the individual debtor account balances in the sales ledger (debtors ledger) is often an automated procedure. Indeed, many contemporary financial accounting packages not only allow user companies/organisations to select the frequency of such a reconciliation, they also allow user companies/organisations to determine – based on the nature of the error(s) discovered – the remedial action to be taken to correct the error(s).

Whilst such an automated reconciliation process does have many advantages, for example it minimises:

- the level of human intervention in the reconciliation process, and
- the overall cost of the reconciliation exercise,

it is important for management to be aware of the results of each reconciliation, since an excessive level of errors could indicate a serious information management/internal control issue. As a result many contemporary 'off-the-shelf' financial accounting systems allow user companies/organisations to create customised reconciliation reports, detailing for example:

- the accounting period covered by the reconciliation,
- the number of errors identified during the reconciliation,
- the value of the errors identified during the reconciliation,
- the debtors to which the errors relate,
- the nature of/reason for the errors identified, and
- the remedial action taken (if any) to correct errors identified.

## Assessment of doubtful debts

Whilst in an accounting context, a doubtful debt can be defined as a debt where circumstances have rendered its ultimate recovery uncertain, in a practical business context, determining the point at which a debt becomes doubtful can be much more problematic.

In a business context, a debt becomes doubtful where:

- a customer/client fails (for whatever reason) to make the appropriate payment(s) within an agreed period, and
- efforts to determine the reason(s) for such a failure to make payment (e.g. telephone calls and/or e-mails to the customer/client) have been unsuccessful.

In such circumstances, prudence would suggest that such an outstanding debt should be considered doubtful and action to recovery it commenced.

Although specific debt recovery procedures will differ from organisation to organisation, in general such procedures would involve some, if not all, of the following four stages:

- the issue of a formal reminder for payment,
- the issue of a formal demand for payment,
- the determination of legal judgment on the outstanding debt, and
- the collection of the outstanding debt.

During such a debt recovery process (especially during stages 1 and 2) it is likely that the company/organisation may also elect to use the services of a private debt collection agency. Whilst such an approach has become increasingly popular in recent years, it requires careful monitoring to ensure that the provisions of s40 Administration of Justice Act 1970 concerning harassment are fully observed.

### Stage 1 – a formal reminder for payment

Where a debt remains outstanding beyond its due payment date, a formal reminder for payment[13] would normally be sent to the customer/client, reminding them of the outstanding debt. Such a reminder would of course be produced automatically by the debt management sub-system of the revenue cycle if and when payment is not received from the customer/client by the due date.

### Stage 2 – a formal demand for payment

Where no payment and/or acknowledgement to the formal reminder to pay are received and/or the private debt collection agency has been unsuccessful in obtaining repayment of the outstanding debt, a formal demand for payment would be sent to the customer/client. Such a formal demand for payment would inform the customer/client that their failure to respond to the formal reminder to pay has resulted in legal action for the recovery of the debt commencing. Whilst the decision to use legal means to pursue the outstanding debt was historically a management decision – based on a range of business-related factors – many companies/organisations now pursue all outstanding debts above a predetermined limit – irrespective of the cost.

Note: Where a formal demand for payment is sent to a customer/client, the individual debtor account of the customer/client (in the sales ledger/debtors ledger) will normally be annotated to indicate a formal demand for payment has been sent to the customer/client. Any requests by the customer/client for the purchase of products/services following such a formal demand for payment should of course be refused.

### Stage 3 – a legal judgment

Legal action to recover an outstanding debt would normally take place at a local county court with the cost of such court action normally depending on the value of the outstanding debt. Where a county court determination is made, and judgment is awarded to the company/organisation, such a judgment (often referred to as a CCJ)[14] will allow the company/organisation to use a number of alternative mechanisms to recover the outstanding debts. It will also allow the company/organisation to recover all legal costs (including interest accrued at the statutory rate[15] commencing from the date of payment default)[16] incurred in pursuit of the outstanding debt from the customer/client. Such costs include, for example:

- interest charges (usually at the statutory rate of 8%),
- company/organisation administration costs and, of course,
- county court costs.

Note: Where judgment is awarded to the company/organisation against a customer/client, the individual debtor account of the customer/client in the sales ledger/debtors ledger will normally be annotated to indicate judgment has been awarded.

## Stage 4 – debt collection/debt recovery

On obtaining judgment, the company/organisation will need to decide how to pursue the outstanding debt – that is which mechanism to use. The company/organisation could, for example, ask the county court to issue a warrant of execution and/or a sequestration order to seize property/assets in payment of the outstanding debt or seek the imposition of a charge[17] on property/assets of the customer/client to recover payment for the outstanding debt at some future date. Whichever mechanism the company/organisation elects to use would depend on many factors, including:

- the legal status of the customer/client (e.g. is the customer/client an individual, a partnership, a limited partnership or a limited company),
- the nature of the outstanding debt, and
- the amount of the outstanding debt.

Note: Where a collection mechanism is selected by the company/organisation the individual debtor account of the customer/client in the sales ledger/debtors ledger will normally be annotated to indicate which mechanism is to be used and if/when any recovery is made.

### Write-off of bad debts/irrecoverable debts

An outstanding debt should only be written off where – based on available evidence – the outstanding debt (or part of the outstanding debt) is considered to be irrecoverable. Such a decision should be a management decision taken and approved by members of staff not directly involved in the debt collection and debtor management.

So, when would a debt be considered irrecoverable and the write-off of such a outstanding debt considered necessary? There are three circumstances, these being:

- zero recovery,
- partial recovery, and
- no recovery.

Zero recovery occurs where the company/organisation has pursued the outstanding debt (as above) without success. For example, during the debt recovery process evidence may have emerged that the customer/client would not be able to satisfy the outstanding debt – perhaps the customer/client has filed for bankruptcy (if an individual) or liquidation (if a company), in which case the whole of the outstanding debt will need to be written off.

Partial recovery occurs where the company/organisation has pursued an outstanding debt (as above), and recovered only part of the debt from the customer/client, in which case only part of the outstanding debt – the unrecovered balance – will need to be written off.

No recovery occurs where the company/organisation has *not* pursued an outstanding debt (as above), that is legal action has not been taken to recover the outstanding debt. This is simply down to cost. Some UK companies (including for example a number high street clothing retailers and utility service providers) do not pursue outstanding debts below a minimum amount,[18] although such companies/organisations do not make such debt collection/debt recovery policies publicly known.

In an accounting context, such a write-off would be recorded in the general ledger as follows:

- Dr bad debts account,
- Cr debtor's control account.

In addition, a credit memorandum entry would also be made in the individual debtor account in the sales ledger (also known as the debtors ledger).

At the end of the financial period, bad debts would be written off to the profit and loss account as an expense, as follows:

- Dr profit and loss account,
- Cr bad debts account.

Note: Where an outstanding debt (or part of an outstanding debt) is written off, the individual debtor account of the customer/client in the sales ledger/debtors ledger should be closed, to prevent any future transactions.

For the customer/client, such actions by the company/organisation – the legal pursuit of the debt, the imposition of a CCJ and, where necessary, the write-off of the debt would have significant consequences for the customer's/client's credit rating and would severely affect their ability to obtain credit in the future.

### Debt factoring

Debt factoring can be defined as a purchased service (often from a subsidiary of a major clearing bank)[19] in which a factor acquires the right to receive payment from a company's/organisation's debtors in return for an immediate payment of cash (of the face value of the debt less an agreed discount) to the company/organisation.

Although many variations exist, there are essentially two types of factoring:

- recourse factoring – where the risk of non-payment/non-recovery of the debt is borne by the company/organisation selling the debts, and
- non-recourse factoring – where the risk of non-payment/non-recovery of the debt is borne by the factoring company purchasing the debts.

So, how does debt factoring work? Procedures differ from company to company, but generally,

- 80 to 85% of the value of debts that are factored is paid to the company/organisation upon agreement with the factor, with funds usually transferred from the factor to the company/organisation during the next working day; and
- 15 to 20% is paid to the company/organisation when either the debt is paid to the factor (recourse factoring agreement) or it becomes due (non-recourse factoring agreement).

The cost will, of course, depend on the factoring company – but charges will normally comprise of:

- an administration fee – usually between 1 and 4% of the value of the debts factored, and
- a finance fee – usually 1 to 2% above the current base rate on the amount advanced.

The advantages of debt factoring are:

- it provides a company/organisation with more predictable cash flows, and
- it minimises, if not eliminates, the need for and costs associated with the internal management of debtors.

More importantly, because cash generated is linked directly to sales, potentially growth can be financed through sales, rather than having to resort to external funds.

The disadvantages of debt factoring are:

- it can be very costly with both administration and financial fees dependent on a number of factors, for example:
  - the volume of debtors,
  - the value of debtors,
  - the complexity of the accounts, and
- it can result in a loss of contact between the company/organisation and its customers/clients.

## . . . and finally customer/client relationship management systems

Customer/client relationship management can be defined as the implementation and co-ordination of processes and procedures designed to improve company/organisation interaction with customers/clients, the aim being to better serve the needs and demands of customers/clients and increase satisfaction and loyalty.

Emerging during the 1990s as part of a strategic movement to reflect the central role of customers/clients in determining the strategic positioning of a company/organisation, in a contemporary context such systems are essentially integrated databases. They seek to provide a coordinated analysis of information/knowledge relating to customer/client activity/behaviour, which can be used/exploited in determining the focus of market-based retail activity and ultimately the maximisation of company/organisation revenue income and of course profit.

So what information would such a customer/client relationship management system be concerned with? Such information – sometimes referred to as market cycle information – would include for example:

- customer profiling information,
- transaction activity information,
- market segmentation information, and
- customer response/behaviour prediction.

Whilst many critics of the trend for customer relationship management systems have suggested that the storage and use of such customer/client-related information is by no means a contemporary phenomenon, it is of course the use of information and communication technologies that has revolutionised the capabilities of such systems – especially in terms of the collection, processing and management of such information.

So what are the main operational problems of such systems? These stem from five issues:

- the technological issue – that is what information and communication technologies will be used for the collection, processing and analysis of customer/client information,
- the administration issue – that is what methodologies will be used for the integration of heterogeneous collections of customer/client information,
- the information issue – that is what internal data/information structure will be used, and how detailed the data/information will be (that is what levels of abstraction will be used),
- the acquisition issue – that is what knowledge discovery procedures and/or data/information acquisition processes will be used, and
- the security issue – that is who will be allowed access to the data/information and on what basis such access will be determined and approved.

Although there can be little doubt that such integrated customer/client relationship management systems have a number of company/organisation benefits, generally related to the 3Es (economy, effectiveness and efficiency), the commercialisation of customer/client information that occurs in the use of such systems has resulted in many questions being raised concerning the socio-political legitimacy of such systems – in particular the data protection issues associated with the collection and storage of confidential customer/client information.

However, despite such questions the astronomical growth in popularity that such customer/client relationship management systems have enjoyed over the past few years, is perhaps an indication that they are now a necessary feature of a company's/organisation's portfolio of business-related management systems and, given the evermore competitive nature of the business environment, perhaps here to stay.

## Debtor-based revenue cycle – risks

Clearly, any failure in processes and controls associated with the debtor-based revenue cycle could have significant consequences for the company/organisation and could result in:

- a loss of company/organisation assets,
- a loss of data/information,
- a loss of customers/clients and, perhaps most importantly,
- a loss of revenue income (and profits).

How? Have a look at the following.

### Marketing system

A failure within the marketing system of a company/organisation could result in:

- the inappropriate identification of marketing opportunities,
- the inaccurate assessment of market competition, and
- the ineffective marketing of products/services.

### Retailing system

A failure within the retailing system of a company/organisation could result in:

- the acceptance of incomplete customer/client orders,
- the acceptance of inaccurate customer/client orders,
- the acceptance of orders from customers/clients with excessive credit or poor credit rating,
- the acceptance of invalid and/or illegitimate orders,
- the loss or misplacement of customer/client orders,
- failure to fulfil legitimate customer/client orders, and
- the occurrence of repetitive stock-outs.

In addition, the failure of retailing system security procedures/access protocols could allow unauthorised persons to gain access to secure customer ordering systems and result in:

- the theft of confidential customer/client data,
- the misappropriation of assets, and/or
- the infection/corruption of customer/client files.

### Distribution and delivery system

A failure within the distribution and delivery system of a company/organisation could result in:

- the despatch of products/services to the wrong customer/client,
- the despatch of incorrect products/services to the customer/client,
- the despatch of incorrect quantities to the customer/client,
- the despatch of products/services at the wrong time,
- the delivery of products/service to an incorrect/unauthorised location, and
- the loss (or theft) of products/services in transit.

### Payment management system

A failure within the payment management system of a company/organisation could result in:

- a failure to invoice customers/clients,
- the incorrect invoicing of customers/clients,
- a violation of pricing policies,
- a failure to record transactions correctly (accounting entries),
- the theft and/or misappropriation of payment receipts,
- the fraudulent write off of debts,
- the creation of fictitious accounts for non-existent customers,
- the negligent and/or fraudulent management of credit refunds/reimbursements,
- the improper recording of customer/client transactions, and
- the possible overlapping of payment receipts.

In addition, the failure of payment management system security procedures/access protocols could allow unauthorised persons gaining access to debtor account records, and payment receipting systems resulting in:

- the theft of income,
- the illegal creation, amendment or deletion of debtor account records, and/or
- the corruption of debtor ledger files.

## Non-debtor-based revenue cycle

As suggested earlier, there are three main types of non-debtor-based systems:

- EPOS-based transaction systems,
- web-based transaction systems, and/or
- cash/cheque-based transaction systems.

Clearly, the last although still in use in many smaller companies/organisations is, as a revenue collecting system, very much in decline.

### EPOS (Electronic Point of Service) systems

As we saw in Chapter 4, there are essentially two types of EPOS systems:

- card-based EPOS systems, and
- non-card-based EPOS systems.

#### Card-based EPOS systems

For most individuals, point-of-service-based EFT is perhaps the most common of all EFT types – one which the vast majority of individuals will use on a regular basis, monthly, weekly even perhaps daily. There is an enormous (and ever-increasing) range of cards/card schemes available which can be divided into two categories/types:

- payment cards[20] which would include debit cards, credit cards, store cards (affinity cards and/or own brand cards), charge cards and stored value cards (e.g. an e-money smart card or an e-purse), and
- non-payment cards which would include loyalty cards, ATM cards, cheque guarantee cards and e-money smart cards.[21]

Our discussion will be restricted to payment cards.

First, however, some definitions:

- the cardholder – the customer/client with a payment card and an agreed amount of purchasing power,[22]
- the merchant – the business that accepts a payment card as a method of paying for goods or services,
- the acquirer (or acquiring bank)[23] – the bank and/or other financial institution acting as a payment processing company and a link between the merchant[24] and the card issuer, and
- the card issuer – the bank, building society or financial institution that issues a card to a cardholder and maintains the cardholder's account.

For completeness, we will discuss three types of EPOS processing:

- offline processing using a manual processing system,
- online processing using an EFT system – cardholder present, and
- online processing using an EFT system – cardholder not present.

Clearly, the first of the above is not an EFT-related system and is rarely used in everyday revenue cycle transaction-based activities. It is, however, included because it represents an important back-up processing system should technologies fail!

## Offline processing using a manual processing system

Manual processing normally entails the use of an imprint copy of the customer/cardholder card details onto a transaction slip, and normally involves three stages:

- a processing stage,
- an authorisation stage, and
- a settlement stage.

The procedure would be as follows:

*Processing stage:*
- the merchant takes an imprint of the customers card on a triplicate copy transaction slip,
- the merchant completes the transaction slip with details of service/sales,
- the customer/client cardholder checks and signs the transaction slip, and
- the merchant validates the cardholder signature on the sales slip against the cardholder payment card.

*Authorisation stage:*
- the merchant (may) obtain authorisation for the transaction by contacting (usually by telephone) the acquirer, who would contact the card issuer. If the transaction is approved by the card issuer an authorisation code would be returned to the merchant via the acquirer,
- the merchant writes the authorisation code on the sales slip,
- the merchant gives one copy of the transaction slip to the customer/cardholder,
- the merchant retains one copy of the transaction slip for its own records, and
- the merchant pays the other copy into its bank account for processing by the acquirer.

*Settlement stage:*
- the acquirer processes the transaction slip, forwarding the transaction slip to the card issuer for payment and reimbursing the merchant for the transaction, less the merchant service charge, and
- the card issuer reimburses the acquirer and bills the cardholder on their monthly statement.

The settlement stage usually takes three working days, although it can take longer.

Clearly offline processing has a number of disadvantages:

- the processing procedure is labour intensive,
- the process can be time-consuming because:
  - every transaction (for some merchants) has to be approved by the acquirer, and
  - every card number has to be checked against a printed list of the card numbers of lost and/or stolen cards, and
- the process can be costly – high charges may be incurred because significant delays can occur between the merchant conducting the transaction and reimbursement.

## Online processing using an EFT system – cardholder present (pPoS EFT)

Online processing of cardholder present transactions normally involves four stages:

- a validation stage,
- an authorisation stage,
- a settlement stage, and
- a reconciliation stage,

with the key systems requirements being:

- an active online PoS terminal and secure communication link,
- appropriate card validation software and card authorisation software, and
- approved settlement software (acquirer and card issuer).

*Validation stage:*

- the merchant enters the customers card data into its system by either:
  - swiping the customer's card through the magnetic stripe reader (a PDQ machine)[25], or
  - inserting the customers card into a smart card reader (chip and PIN), or
  - keying in the customer's card details manually, and
- the authorisation software validates the customers card.[26]

*Authorisation stage:*

Following validation, the merchant needs to authorise the transaction to ensure that the customer/cardholder has sufficient funds to finance the purchase. If the transaction value is less than the agreed MSA[27] limit, the EFT system will authorise the transaction offline. If the transaction amount is equal to or above the MSA limit, the transaction details will be forwarded online to the acquirer for authorisation.

Where the transaction is authorised offline, the merchant will receive either a transaction authorised[28] or transaction declined[29] response. Where the transaction is sent online, the acquirer may return a transaction authorised, transaction declined or transaction referred[30] response.

If the transaction is authorised the merchant must either:

- obtain the customer/cardholder's signature or, more likely,
- request the customer/cardholder to input their PIN number into the smart card holder key pad.

For the former, if the signature on the transaction slip does not match the signature on the card the merchant *must* decline the transaction. For the latter, if the pin number entered remains incorrect following a number of attempts, the merchant *must* either:

- decline the transaction, or
- request a signature and further identification from the customer/cardholder to confirm their identity.

*Settlement stage:*

Details of all transactions marked for payment are sorted and forwarded to the appropriate acquirer for settlement (payment). The acquirer will acknowledge receipt of the file and confirm:

- the validity of the transactions, and
- the accuracy of the data.

Once all data checks have been satisfied the merchant will be reimbursed accordingly.

*Reconciliation stage:*

The reconciliation stage is essentially a feedback stage that provides the merchant with a range of transaction reports including:

- PoS source files,
- settlement files, and
- acquirer acknowledgement files,

to ensure that no settlements remain unpaid.

## Online processing using an EFT system – cardholder not present (nPoS EFT)

Cardholder not present transactions are normally associated with:

- mail order-based transactions,
- call centre-based transactions and, of course,
- web-based (e-commerce) transactions.

Such online processing is normally associated with so-called distance contracts,[31] that is a contract where there has been no face-to-face contact between the consumer and a representative of the company/organisation selling the goods and/or services, or someone acting indirectly on the business's behalf, such as in a showroom or a door-to-door sales person, up to and including the moment at which the contract is concluded.

(We will examine such transaction including web-based e-commerce transactions later in this chapter and in more detail in Chapter 12.) For the moment let's look at the process.

The validation stage and the authorisation stage are more or less the same whether the customer/cardholder is present and/or the customer/cardholder is not present. Clearly, however, when the customer/cardholder is not present there are a number of problems, for example:

- the merchant cannot view the card to assess and/or confirm its authenticity, and
- the merchant cannot obtain objective authorisation via either the customer/cardholder's signature or the customer PIN.

In addition, for mail order/call centre-based transactions card details may need to be keyed in manually increasing the risk of possible data entry errors.

Clearly the use of online processing (pPoS EFT and nPoS EFT), and indeed to some extent offline processing, also presents many risks – perhaps the greatest being that of fraud resulting from:

- employee skimming – that is the copying of customer/cardholder card details onto a blank card (using either a magnetic card reader and/or computer software), and increasingly
- hacking (or more appropriately cracking)[32] – that is either forced entry to non-secure computer systems or the interception of information designed to obtain confidential (for our purposes, credit card) information.

To assist in the prevention of fraud an increasing large range of anti-fraud measures can and indeed are used to minimise the possibility of fraud, some of the more popular being:

- the use of forced online protocols,[33]
- the use of floor limits,[34]
- the use of 'one-in-$n$'checks – that is sample random transactions checks,
- the use of multiple transaction checks,
- the use of hot card files,[35]
- the use of encryption,
- the use of Secure Sockets Layer (SSL),[36]
- the use of card security code (CSC),[37]
- the use of address verification services (AVS),[38] and
- the use of payer authentication.[39]

For a review of card processing and the procedures a merchant should adopt if card fraud is suspected, have a look at the following HSBC plc website: www.hsbc.co.uk/1/2/business/needs/card-fraud.

### Finally

To facilitate point-of-service EFT (for both offline and online payments), a company/organisation must have a merchant account (and ID)[40] issued by an acquiring bank. In addition, to process online payments a company/organisation must also have:

- an internet merchant account (and ID), and
- an approved Payment Service Provider (PSP).[41]

We will look at both these in greater detail in Chapter 12.

### Non-card-based EPOS systems

A point-of-service-based EFT non-card based system is any point-of-service EFT system that operates without the need for a debit/credit card *and* external authentication such as a signature match or PIN. Whilst a wide range of biometric[42] technologies using behavioural and/or physiological characteristics, for example:

- voice recognition,
- signature recognition,
- fingerprint recognition,
- iris recognition,
- face recognition, and
- hand geometry recognition,

are now widely used in a range of security sensitive/identification sensitive areas – for point-of-service EFT systems, as at end 2006, the current favoured technology appears to be pay by touch[43] using fingerprint recognition. This is a biometric-based payment service which enables consumers to pay for the purchase of goods and/or services with the touch of a finger without the need for debit or credit cards, cheques or indeed cash, essentially using a finger scan to authorise the point-of-service EFT transaction (see www.paybytouch.com).[44]

Before we look at pay by touch in a little more detail, it would perhaps be useful to provide some general context to our discussion on biometric systems.

Biometric identification technologies are essentially pattern recognition systems and generally involve four stages:

- enrolment – that is a record associating a specific identifying biometric feature with a specific individual is created,
- accumulation – that is storing a record of the biometric feature either in a permanent, non-movable facility (e.g. a centralised database) or on a decentralised portable storage module (e.g. on a smart card),
- acquisition – that is when identification is required, a new sample of the biometric feature is acquired (e.g. a new iris scan and/or a new fingerprint scan), and
- matching – that is the newly acquired sample is compared to the stored sample and if the newly acquired sample matches with the stored sample, there is a positive identification.

In the above we have assumed that only a single biometric measurement is used for identification purposes. Such a system is referred to as an *unimodal* (or *monomodal*) biometric system: that is a biometric system which relies on a single source of biometric data, information or evidence for identity authentication. Where two or more biometric measurements are used concurrently for identification purposes, such a system is referred to as a *multimodal* biometric system: that is a biometric system which relies on multiple sources of biometric data, information and/or evidence for identity authentication. Finally where a single biometric measurement is used for identification purposes but is used concurrently with another form of variable input (e.g. a number, word or phrase), such a system is referred to as an *unimodal+* (or *monomodal+*) biometric system: that is a biometric system which relies on a single source of biometric data, information or evidence *and* an additional input variable for identity authentication.

Because biometric identification technologies used in point-of-service EFT systems are used to not only establish but also confirm the identity of an individual,[45] such biometric identification technologies tend to be unimodel+ (or monomodal+) systems, that is:

- the initial biometric measurement establishes/determines the identity of the individual, and
- the additional input variable confirms the identity of the individual.

## Pay By Touch

Whilst the use of biometric identification technologies in point-of-service EFT systems have been gradually increasing in the USA since 2002, the Pay By Touch scheme currently being piloted by the Midcounties Co-operative stores in Oxford (see Article 8.1) is the first of its kind in the UK.

To participate, a customer/client must enrol, usually online. Once enrolment is complete the customer/client is provided with a Pay By Touch wallet (www.paybytouch.com), which essentially stores the customer's/client's direct debit details/bank account information. As part of the enrolment process the customer must create a *search number* and a *password*.

The search number (usually a six to eight digit number of the customer's/client's choosing) is required to access the customer's/client's Pay By Touch wallet each time they use the Pay By Touch facilities. The password is required by the customer/client to manage their Pay By Touch wallet online. The Pay By Touch wallet can be amended and updated as often as the customer/client deems necessary.

Once the online enrolment is complete and the direct debit account is approved (the customer/client is informed by e-mail on approval) the customer/client must finalise the process (at a participating store) within 60 days of the registration date, by presenting:

- a bank authorisation mandate form,
- a copy of a bank account statement,
- a Pay By Touch search number created during the online registration,

## Article 8.1

### Pay By Touch goes live in the UK

Shoppers and members at The Midcounties Co-operative now have the option of quickly and securely paying for their groceries using a finger scan linked to their bank account.

This is the first UK implementation by Pay By Touch, the global leader in biometric authentication, personalised rewards, membership and payment solutions.

The new service is an innovative payment system which enables consumers to pay for their purchases using their finger rather than a card, cheque book or cash. The payment service will be available in three Midcounties Co-operative supermarkets in and around Oxford.

Bill Laird, Chief Operating Officer – Retail, at Midcounties Co-operative said, 'Initial response from our members to this new service has been very encouraging and we are delighted to be the first UK retailer to offer a more secure and convenient way to pay and receive dividend points. Our customers are embracing Pay By Touch because it helps them get through the checkout faster without having to hunt for cards, cheques, wallets or purses.'

The Pay By Touch system uses a simple method of finger imaging, making it both secure and highly convenient. The shopper uses a simple finger scan for identification and in doing so, a payment is made directly from his or her bank account, while members' dividend points are automatically awarded. The initial sign up process is quick and simple and can be completed either at home on the internet, or in-store. The service is then activated when the consumer visits a participating store. Enrolment in Pay By Touch is free to consumers and is free to use.

John Rogers, Chairman, Founder and Chief Executive of Pay By Touch said, 'In the US, over 2.3 million shoppers are already using Pay By Touch to pay, access frequent shopper programmes and cash cheques at over 2,000 retail locations. This reflects the enormous interest consumers have shown in a faster, more convenient and secure way to pay for their shopping.'

Tom Fischer, Vice President of Pay By Touch, commented, 'The Midcounties Co-op has a reputation for successfully deploying new technologies that enhance customer convenience. Pay By Touch is already proving popular and we are confident this will continue as the system is more widely adopted.'

Source: 10 March 2006,
www.cooperatives-uk.coop/live/cme913.htm.

- identification (either a photo-card driving licence or passport), and
- a finger (for scanning purposes).

Once stage two is complete and approved the facility is activated and the customer/client can use the Pay By Touch point-of-service EFT systems.

It is important to note that all personal details (e.g. the customer's/client's Pay By Touch wallet contents) and all biometric measurements/information is encrypted and stored in a centralised database at a secure UK-based IBM data centre.

To use Pay By Touch at a checkout facility of a participating store, the customer/client simply places their finger on the fingerprint reader and enters their search number. Once the customer's identity is authenticated, the total value of the purchases is approved and funds are transferred from the customer's/client's bank account to the company's bank account using a standard direct debit facility.

So what are the advantages and disadvantages of biometric-based payment systems – in particular fingerprint recognition systems.

The main advantages are:

- easy to use,
- customer/client convenience,
- eliminates the need for passwords, and
- reduces the possibility of fraudulent transactions.

The main disadvantages are:

- noise – that is the possibility of so-called 'non-recognition' – for example, the finger may be injured and/or scarred,
- non-universality – that is some individuals may not be able to use the system (for example they may lack a cohesive fingerprint due to the nature of their work such as a manual worker), and
- non-acceptance – that is some individuals may view biometrics as an invasive, anti-privacy technology and may refuse to use such a system.

Clearly, whilst the use of biometric identification technologies in point-of-service EFT systems remains in its infancy, there can be little doubt that the development of such systems does signify a significant challenge to the dominance of the traditional card-based point-of-service EFT systems. It is, however, far too early in the development cycle of such systems to allow us to speculate with any degree of certainty as to how significant this challenge will be.

### The advantages EPOS EFT systems

The advantages of using EPOS EFT systems are:

- the increased speed and accuracy of such funds transfers,
- the reduced costs of such transactions, and
- the improved efficiency of such transaction processing.

### The disadvantages EPOS EFT systems

The disadvantages of using EPOS EFT systems are:

- the increased lack of transaction transparency,
- the investment cost required to enable such a system, and
- the substantial in-house management required to ensure such systems continue to operate efficiently and effectively.

## Web-based sales system

We will look at web-based sales systems (or more appropriately web-based e-commerce systems) in detail in Chapter 12. For the moment, a brief outline.

For a company using a web-based e-commerce facility for revenue cycle-based transactions, such a facility would normally comprise of a portal interface to provide access to a retailing resource. Such a portal interface would compromise of:

- a web-based storefront,
- a web-based catalogue,
- a virtual shopping cart,
- a check-out system, and
- a payment processing system.

For example, have a look at the following:

- Tesco plc @ www.tesco.com,
- Sainsbury plc @ www.jsainsburys.co.uk,
- Marks and Spencer plc @ www.marksandspencer.com,
- Comet Group plc @ www.comet.co.uk,
- Debenhams plc @ www.debenhams.com, and
- Matalan plc @ www.matalan.co.uk.

Whilst each of the above web-based e-commerce facilities may appear to be very different such differences are merely aesthetic and generally exist as a result of a desire by the company/organisation (and the web designer(s)) to maintain the company's/organisation's brand image online. In essence, all such web-based e-commerce facilities both function and operate in the same way – processing similar types of transaction data, using similar types of internal controls/system security procedures, and interacting within similar external agents.

So what are the advantages and disadvantages of a web-based sales system?

### The advantages of web-based sales systems

For a company/organisation providing the e-commerce facility, the advantages include:

■ immediate access to a global customer base,
■ immediate access to non-stop retailing,
■ improved opportunity to enter/create new markets, and
■ improved communications with customers.

For a customer/client using the e-commerce facility, the advantages include:

■ increased access to a 'world of stores',
■ increased choice,
■ greater availability of a larger and broader selection of products and services,
■ greater convenience,
■ increased speed, and
■ increased ease of use.

### The disadvantages web-based sales systems

Although the advantages of web-based sales systems – for both the company/organisation providing the facility and the customer/client using the facility – are significant, such advantages are not without consequence. Disadvantages can be categorised as:

■ issues relating to the social costs of e-commerce,
■ problems associated with the political consequence of e-commerce, and
■ concerns relating to the economic costs of e-commerce.

(We will discuss these in more detail in Chapter12.)

On a more functional/operational level the main disadvantages are:

■ the increased possibility of electronic fraud, and
■ the increased possibility of illegal access.

It is course not possible for a company/organisation to completely eliminate electronic fraud. However, it is possible to minimise its occurrence by adopting a few simple procedures, for example:

■ never accept incomplete customer/client orders,
■ always request additional information where 'despatch to address' differs for 'payment address',
■ always request additional information where an order is received from a 'free' e-mail service,
■ periodically sample check large value orders – especially next day delivery orders,
■ always validate and confirm all international orders, and
■ always validate and confirm all credit card transactions.

To minimise the possibility of illegal access a company/organisation could use:

- system firewalls,
- intrusion detection systems (or intrusion detection software),
- data/information encryption facilities,
- digital certificates, and/or
- authentication and authorisation software.

For more information on each of the above see Chapter 13.

## Cash-based/cheque-based sales system

Despite the technological advances made in recent years, in particular the increased use/availability of card/non-card EPOS payment systems, and of course web-based payment systems, there still remains, and perhaps always will remain, a small number of transactions and customers/clients for which payment in cash or by cheque will still remain the preferred option. Why?

Perhaps for three reasons, these being:

- transaction-related attributes – that is the nature of the product/service and/or value of the transaction may preclude the use of a non-cash payment system (e.g. the value of the transaction may be very small, say less that £5)[46],
- customer/client-related demographics – that is the customer/client may not be able to use non-cash payment system (e.g. they may choose not to have or use, or indeed may not be able to use, a debit/credit card),[47] and/or
- company/organisation-related characteristics – that is the company/organisation may prohibit the use of non-cash payment systems (e.g. the company/organisation may have an insufficient level of transactions to warrant the investment in a EPOS system).

So, where are cash-based/cheque-based sales systems used?

In recent years many companies/organisations have attempted to minimise the use of cash-based/cheque-based sales systems by, for example, offering indirect incentives to some card-based paying customers/clients. (Many retail companies offer cash withdrawal facilities/cash back schemes at retail check-outs to customers paying by debit card and using chip and PIN facilities.) Cash-based/cheque-based sales systems have continued to remain in common use, especially in the retailing of relatively low-cost, high-turnover products (e.g. food/clothes retailing) although the popularity of cash-based/cheque-based sales systems has continued to decrease at an ever-increasing rate.

Although we will discuss the internal control/systems security issues of cash-based systems in detail in Chapter 11, for the moment let's have a brief look at revenue cycle-related issues of cash-based/cheque-based sales systems in context type 1(a)(i) companies/organisations: that is for example in town/city-based supermarkets such as Tesco, Asda, Sainsbury and Morrisons, or town/city-based departmental stores such as Marks and Spencer, Bhs and Debenhams, or indeed in high street retail/clothing outlets such as Next, Burtons, Monsoon and many others.

So, how would a cash-based/cheque-based sales system operate? Consider for example a supermarket check-out facility.

As we have seen above, a customer purchasing a small number of products would usually have a number of alternative payment options – payment by debit and/or credit card (card-based EPOS payment), Pay By Touch (non-card-based EPOS payment), or payment by cash or cheque. Suppose the customer decides to pay by cash or cheque. What would happen?

Currently, each product would be scanned separately at an EPOS terminal linked to a cash receipting facility. The bar codes on each of the individual products would probably be scanned and read by a static bar code reader. (This will also deactivate any security tagging on the product.)

Using a central management facility, the EPOS terminal would update the stores stock records for each individual product purchased by the customer. Where appropriate the stores facility would also up link – probably using a intranet facility for internal regional stores and/or an extranet facility of external suppliers, detail of stock requirements for products/product lines which have fallen below the economic reorder quantity level. Finally, the EPOS terminal would check the product register database and identify the current price of each product presented for purchase by the customer. Once all products have been scanned, the EPOS terminal would present – as a single value – the total value of all the customer's purchases.

Where payment by cash is offered, a receipt would normally be printed and presented to the customer in exchange for the appropriate cash payment. However, before accepting the cash payment, it is likely that any paper cash tendered by the customer (e.g. £5, £10 and especially £20 and £50 notes) would be scanned and checked for authenticity, usually using an ultra violet light scanner to identify any possible forgeries. All authenticated cash would then be placed in the EPOS terminal cash receipting lock box facility, the products and receipt presented to the customer, together with an appropriate amount of change if relevant. Once the transaction has been completed the lock box facility would be closed and opened only at the end of the next transaction.

Where payment by cheque is offered, again a receipt would be printed and presented to the customer in exchange for payment. However payment would only be authorised and accepted where a payment guarantee is provided – usually by means of a valid signed debit card acting as a cheque guarantee card with, where necessary, additional appropriate identification. Where such a guarantee is not provided by the customer, the cheque payment should be refused and the sale transaction terminated or an alternative payment method requested. All valid cheques would normally be placed in the EPOS terminal cash receipting lock box facility. Once the transaction has been completed the lock box facility would be closed and opened only at the end of the next transaction.

Clearly, the number and the value of cash-based/cheque-based payments received would determine how an individual EPOS terminal cash receipting lock box facility would need to be emptied – that is how often the EPOS terminal cash facility lock box should be removed and replaced with an empty lock box.

It is of course important, for both safety and security reasons, that individual EPOS terminal cash receipting lock boxes are regularly removed and securely transported to a protected and access controlled environment (away from the shop floor) where cash and cheques can be removed, counted, reconciled to individual EPOS terminal receipting records and prepare for banking (if possible on the same day to minimise the need for expensive safe storage facilities). Where limited cash/cheque deposits are received such deposits may be transported by company/organisation staff. However, where a substantial amount of cash and cheques are received on a regular basis it may be necessary to employ a security company (e.g. Group 4 Securicor (www.g4s.com), for the transportation of deposits to the company's/organisation's bank.

The advantages of cash-based/cheque-based sales systems are:

- the transaction process is simple and visible,
- there is no need for an invoice (only a cash receipt), and
- on completion of the sales transaction there is an immediate receipt of liquid funds (cash sales) and near cash funds (cheque-based sales).

The disadvantages are:

- the additional costs associated with the need for additional investment in cash receipting facilities. In a large supermarket, such investment could be substantial, especially where the use of an integrated network of cash register/till is required,

■ the need for increased security (including perhaps the appointment of security staff and/or an external security agency) to manage the movement of cash and prevent possible theft,

■ the costs associated with the requirement to count, record, account for and control the movement of cash, and the resulting cost of such activities, and

■ the need to regularly bank all cash receipts and separately reconcile cash receipts banked with cash receipts received from the sale of products.

Note: Many retail companies, for example Tesco plc, Asda plc and now Boots plc, actively discourage the use of cheques (see Article 8.2). Could the use of cheques as a method of payment soon disappear completely?

## Article 8.2

### Boots to ban payment by cheque

Cheques are to be banned by Boots as high street stores move to kill off the traditional method of payment within five years.

The health and beauty giant is launching a trial ban in 46 stores in the south of England this month with a view to rolling it out across all 1,500 outlets within weeks. The decision follows a total ban by Shell, introduced a year ago, and similar trials or restrictions on cheque use by Asda and Tesco. The move against cheques will be a blow to those aged over 65, who are the biggest users of this traditional method of payment.

Help the Aged said it was concerned that a ban on cheques would make it more difficult for older people to do their shopping. Boots has seen a sharp fall in the use of cheques following the introduction of the chip and PIN regime for debit and credit cards earlier this year. Cheque use has plummeted by 35 per cent compared to last year and they now account for just two purchases in every 1,000 – 0.002 per cent.

Some of its stores currently only take 40 or 50 cheques a week.

Boots claims the use of cheques increases queueing times because of the time it takes to write and process them at the tills. Stores fear that cheques are also more open to fraud, for which they have to pick up the bill, than plastic cards authorised with a four digit PIN. A memo sent to Boots' staff suggests that fraud losses associated with cheques will reach around £1 million this year alone. There is also a drain on time because they have to be sorted and shipped to banks. The four-week trial will start at 46 stores in Surrey and Sussex on September 26. Notices are going up in the outlets now.

A memo to staff states: 'The purpose of the trial is to gauge customer reaction to this change. If there is no or little negative response from our customers this change will be implemented across all shops in early November.' It adds: 'The ability to accept cheques will still be available at the till. This will be removed at a later date should we decided to stop accepting cheques nationally.'

A company spokesman said: 'Cards are a faster method of payment and more secure. If the trial is successful, we would expect to roll out this change to all our stores quite quickly.' A pilot scheme by Asda at 21 stores within the M25 actively discourages the use of cheques. Shoppers are allowed to pay by cheque on one occasion and then told they will need to find an alternative in future.

Tesco is running a trial in some stores where shoppers paying by cheque cannot spend above their cheque card guarantee limit. This is an anti-fraud measure. Asda said: 'We are trying to give customers the best service at check-outs. Queues are a bugbear and paying by cheque takes more time than paying by debit card or cash. We would like to try it elsewhere depending on how the pilot goes.' However, a spokesman for Help the Aged warned against a rush to kill-off cheques. 'This would not be welcome,' he said.

'A lot of older people do not have access to credit and debit cards. Most prefer to use cash, while there is a significant proportion who like to use cheques. Consequently, if there are bans on cheques that significantly reduces their ability to do their shopping.' The Association for Payment Clearing Services (APACS), which represents the banks on payment methods, said the cheque is losing out to the debit card. The big banks put the total amount of consumer spending on the high street and via the internet at £240 billion in 2005. Cheques accounted for less than 4 per cent of this. The value of cheque purchases fell 14 per cent compared to the year before to around £9 billion. By contrast debit card spending rose 9 per cent to £89 billion.

APACS communications chief, Sandra Quinn, said: 'Most people cannot remember the last time they wrote a cheque and would not know where their cheque-book is. You are seeing a transition where cheques have moved from being a mass-market product to a niche product. Cheques are a traditional part of our lives, but people have moved on to debit cards, which have now been around for almost 20 years.

'The rate of decline of the cheque has speeded up dramatically over the past two years, they could be gone from the high street within five years. People find chip and PIN cards easier and more secure. It is interesting that retailers are leading the way on this. They find dealing with cheques, particularly if it is a low number, is a real drain on their resources.'

Source: 11 September 2006,
www.dailymail.co.uk/pages/live/articles/news/
news.html?in_article_id=404708&in_page_id=1770.

## Non-debtor-based revenue cycle – risks

Whilst there can be little doubt that the use of non-debtor-based revenue cycle sales systems – especially EPOS-based and web-based sales systems – are now an essential feature of the revenue cycle activities of many high street retailers, the use of non-debtor-based revenue cycle sales systems is not without risk.

The main risk associated with an EPOS-based sales system is the acceptance of fraudulent transactions – that is payments made by customers/clients using a stolen debit/credit card.

The main risks associated with web-based sales system, include:

■ the infection of web-related information systems,
■ the theft of customer/client-related data,
■ the unauthorised access/viewing of confidential data, and
■ the misappropriation of assets and/or resources.

And the main risks associated with cash-based/cheque-based sales system, include:

■ the misappropriation of cash, and/or
■ the misappropriation of cheques.

## Revenue cycle – internal control and systems security

As we have seen, the key processing requirements of a company's/organisation's revenue cycle, in particular the debtor-based revenue cycle but also where appropriate the non-debtor-based revenue cycle, is to ensure:

■ the existence of adequate operational policies, procedures and controls,
■ the adoption of appropriate customer selection and approval procedures,
■ the existence of adequate assessment procedures for the establishment of price and payment terms,

- the existence of accurate and up-to-date product/service availability information,
- the accurate processing of all transactions,
- the correctness of transaction-based activity reports,
- the accuracy of customer/client statements and accounts,
- the appropriate authorisation of customer/client debtor account adjustments/amendments,
- the regular reconciliation of revenue transactions and customer/client accounts (e.g. the use of control accounts),
- the receipt of all payments in accordance with customer/client credit terms,
- the regular monitoring of *all* customer/client debtor accounts, and
- the recovery of *all* outstanding debts.

The key control requirements are to ensure, where at all possible:

- the appropriate use of control documentation,
- the existence of appropriate authorisation procedures for the movement of resources, the collection of data and the dissemination of information,
- the existence of adequate internal control procedures and internal security procedures to safeguard assets and resources, and
- the existence of adequate structures of responsibility and accountability.

But how do these key control objectives translate into real-world activities – into practical internal controls, not only general controls but also applications controls?

## General controls

General controls applicable to the revenue cycle can be categorised as:

- organisational controls,
- documentation controls,
- access controls,
- asset management controls,
- management practice controls, and
- information system controls.

### Organisational controls

Organisational controls generally refer to the separation or segregation of duties. Within the revenue cycle such controls should ensure that there is an organisational separation between:

- activities concerned with authorising functions,
- activities concerned with custodial functions, and
- activities concerned with recording functions.

That is for example, a separation of duties between those involved in:

- activities related to the authorising of revenue transactions – for example the acceptance of a new debtor, the authorising/amendment of a debtor's credit limit and the acceptance of a customer/client order,
- the distribution and delivery of a products/service to customers/clients,
- activities related to invoicing,
- activities related to the collection of payments from customers/clients,
- the management of debtor accounts, and
- the recording of financial transactions.

In addition, there should also be a separation of duties between:

■ systems development personnel, and
■ systems operations personnel.

That is between:

■ those involved in the creation and/or modification of revenue cycle programmes, and
■ those involved in the day-to-day revenue cycle activities and processes.

### Documentation controls

Complete and up-to-date documentation should be available for all revenue cycle procedures. Such documentation should include, for example:

■ organisational charts detailing the responsibility structure within the revenue cycle and the separation/segregation of duties within each of the revenue cycle systems,
■ procedural descriptions of all procedures and processes used within the revenue cycle,
■ system flowcharts detailing how functions/activities within the revenue cycle operate,
■ document flowcharts detailing what documents flow within revenue cycle systems,
■ management control/internal control procedures detailing the main internal controls within the revenue cycle – in particular the credit approval process and the debtor write-off process,
■ user guides/handbook providing a broad overview of the main functions/activities within the revenue cycle, and
■ records of recent internal/external audits undertaken on individual revenue cycle systems.

### Access controls

For all revenue cycle systems it is necessary to ensure that all tangible physical assets – for example stocks held within company/organisation stores and/or cash/cheques temporarily held within the company/organisation finance office – and all intangible information assets – for example customer/client data/information – are protected and securely stored, with access to such assets closely monitored.

Where information and communication technology is used as an integral part of the revenue cycle systems and activities, it is important for both internal control and security purposes to ensure that:

■ assigned user names and passwords are used to authenticate users and authorise access to revenue cycle transaction data and customer/client information,
■ location and/or terminal restrictions are used, where appropriate, to control access to revenue cycle-based data/information (e.g. confidential debtor account information should only be accessible by appropriate staff (finance staff) at approved locations, such as within the finance office), and
■ transaction data/information is securely stored with access to both current transaction files/master files and back-up copies of all transactions files/masters files restricted.

### Asset management controls

Assets management controls refer to processes and procedures designed to ensure that assets are properly managed, suitably controlled and, appropriately valued. Such controls generally involve:

■ the use of appropriate control records – for example a debtor's control account or a stock control account,
■ the periodic reconciliation of such records underlying physical assets – often referred to as a reconciliation and, where necessary,

- the periodic review and assessment of the condition and value of the underlying asset – for example the physical condition of individual stock items or the determination of the recoverability of an outstanding debt.

Such reconciliations would include, for example:

- debtor reconciliation – a reconciliation of the balance in the debtor's control account in the general ledger and the total of the debtor account balances in the sales ledger (debtor ledger),
- stock reconciliation – a reconciliation of the balance in the stock account (or individual stock accounts if different classes of current assets are stored) in the general ledger and the physical stock(s) held in the store(s)/warehouse(s),
- bank reconciliation – a reconciliation of the balance in the bank account (or bank accounts if a number of different accounts are used) in the general ledger and the bank statement for each account,
- movement reconciliation – a reconciliation/record of assets prior to any movement/transfer – for example a mail room assistant listing all cheques received in the post prior to the transfer of such cheques to the finance/cashier's office.

### Management practice controls

Whilst management practices controls can be categorised as either:

- passive management practice controls – that is controls concerned with the recurring operational procedures, or
- active management practice controls – that is controls concerned with systems/procedural change,

in general, such management practices controls would include, for example:

- regular employee training on revenue cycles systems/procedures,
- regular personal checks/assessments, and
- the use of internal audits in monitor revenue cycle activities.

### Information systems controls

Information systems controls are designed to ensure:

- the efficient scheduling of data processing activities relating to retail sales and the recording of income receipts, and
- the effective management and use of information and communication systems resources.

## Application controls

As with all application controls, those applicable to the revenue cycle can be categorised as input controls, processing controls or output controls.

### Input controls

Revenue cycle input controls are designed to ensure the validity, appropriateness and correctness of revenue cycle specific input data.

Such controls would include, for example:

- appropriateness checks, for example:
  - data matching checks – comparing the customer/client order with either the stock issue request, production order request (where a product requires manufacturing) or the service provision schedule (where a service requires scheduling for delivery), and the customer/client invoice,

- data entry checks – comparing the customer/client order with product/service price lists, and
- data validity checks – comparing payment receipts with the customer/client order and invoice,

■ authorisation procedure checks – for example customer/client identification checks and credit approval checks/credit limit checks, and price list checks, to ensure the validity of transactions,

■ conversion controls tests, record count checks and/or completeness checks – for example batch control totals, sequence totals and/or hash control totals, to ensure *all* data is processed, and

■ error tests/error correction procedure checks to ensure all incorrect data is identified appropriately and dealt with.

Where input data is transmitted from a source origin to a processing destination electronically, additional supplementary input controls would normally be required.

Such additional input controls would include, for example:

■ transmission tests – to ensure the completeness of the transmission,

■ security checks – to ensure the authenticity of the customer/client and the legitimacy of the transmission, and

■ validity checks – to ensure/confirm the completeness of the transaction data.

### Processing controls

Revenue cycle processing controls are designed to ensure only authorised revenue cycle transaction data are processed and all authorised revenue cycle transaction data are processed accurately, correctly and completely.

Such controls would include, for example:

■ file maintenance checks – to ensure that both debtor file records and transaction records are efficiently maintained,

■ file labelling checks – to ensure all revenue cycle data files are correctly labelled,

■ verification checks – to ensure all revenue cycle transaction data are validated and approved prior to processing,

■ processing logic checks – to ensure that the actual processing steps by which data are transformed or moved are consistent with defined procedures/protocols,

■ limit checks – to ensure that all revenue cycle transaction data exist within defined processing parameters (e.g. value of transaction, date of transaction),

■ reasonableness checks – to ensure that revenue cycle transaction data are consistent with processing expectations,

■ sequence checks – to ensure that no interruptions or gaps exist in the sequence of transaction data processed,

■ audit trail controls – to ensure that a visible trail of evidence and/or chronology of events is available to enable the tracing of transaction events,

■ control totals checks – to check that revenue cycle transaction file control totals are consistent with the contents of the transaction file to which they relate, and

■ data checks – to check for the existence of duplicate and/or missing data.

### Output controls

Revenue cycle output controls are designed to ensure all revenue cycle output is authorised, accurate and complete, and distributed to approved and authorised recipients only. Such controls would include, for example:

- distribution controls to ensure the debtor statement of accounts are sent to the correct customer/client,
- verification control to ensure the validity and accuracy of output information (e.g. invoices/ statement of accounts),
- reconciliation checks to ensure all transaction numbers are accounted for, and
- review/audit trail checks.

Where output data is transmitted from a processing origin to a user destination electronically, additional supplementary output controls would normally be required.

Such additional output controls would include, for example:

- transmission tests to ensure that data are transmitted correctly,
- recipient identifier checks/controls to authenticate the recipient before the delivery of data/ information,
- security checks/controls to ensure data/information is delivered completely, and
- validation checks/controls to ensure data/information is received and accessed by the authorised recipient only.

## Revenue cycle and capital income

In broad accounting terms, capital income can be defined as income receipts relating to the disposal of capital assets and/or investments. As we saw earlier, the receipt of revenue income, and the revenue cycle activities related to income generated from the sale of products and services generally, commences with an external consumer/client activity or a series of related activities (e.g. the submission of a customer/client order). The receipt of capital income from the disposal of capital assets/investments, however, generally commences with an internal management action/decision or series of related decisions/activities. For example, the receipt of such capital income may result from:

- an internal management decision to raise additional capital funds for investment in other capital projects/assets, or
- an internal management decision following a speculative request for an external agent to purchase existing company/organisation assets, or
- a recurring asset replacement cycle decision.

We will look at capital income – in particular issues related to capital income resulting from the disposal of company/organisation assets and investments – in more detail in Chapter 11.

## Revenue cycle information requirements

As we saw earlier, the primary objective of a company/organisation revenue cycle – whether debtor-based or non-debtor-based, is to maximise income (and of course profits) by providing customers/clients with the right product, at the right price, at the right place and at the right time.

To do so successfully, however, requires more than just an appropriate level of resources or collection of processes, procedures and protocols, it also requires information to cope with market unpredictability and uncertainty.

Whilst the ever-changing and ever-expanding marketplace in which companies/organisations promote their products/services continues to provide almost limitless opportunities for increased trade, and of course increased profitability, such opportunities are often more than off-set by the ever-present threats posed by substitute products/services becoming available and/or new entrants/new competition entering the marketplace.

For a company/organisation operating in such a volatile and competitive environment, information is vital: in particular revenue cycle information that can be used to, for example:

- identify appropriate market segments for the company's/organisation's products/services,
- assess the cost(s) associated with revenue cycle activities,
- determine an appropriate product/service pricing policy/structure,
- establish a suitable customer/client credit policy,
- determine an appropriate customer/client payment policy,
- establish a suitable company/organisation stock policy, and
- determine an appropriate company/organisation sales returns/refund policy.

So, what type of revenue cycle information would a company/organisation require?

Whilst individual companies/organisations will invariably possess different internal structures, use different operating procedures/protocols, employ different degrees of information and communication technologies, market different products/services in different ways and sell to different types of customers/clients often in different markets, they will nonetheless require similar types of revenue cycle information. Ultimately, they will all possess the same objective: the maximisation of company/organisational income/profit.

So what type of revenue cycle information would a company/organisation require? Although there are many ways in which such information requirements can be categorised, for our purposes we will categorise such information as follows:

- period-based activity information,
- period-based performance information, and
- activity analysis information.

## Period-based activity information

Period-based activity information is operational level information related to specific systems/processes/activities during a particular week or month and would include, for example:

- the number of customer/client orders received,
- stock movement reports,
- the number of invoices raised,
- the number of credit notes issued and/or refunds made, and
- the number of payments received.

## Period-based performance information

Period-based performance information is tactical level information measuring the efficiency and effectiveness of revenue cycle processes and procedures during a particular week or month, and would include, for example:

- response times to customers requests,
- order fulfilment times,
- product/service delivery times,
- bad debt levels, and
- debt recovery rates.

### Activity analysis information

Activity analysis information is strategic level information measuring/assessing the relative success or otherwise of revenue cycle-related activities and would include, for example:

- customer requirement/satisfaction analysis,
- market share analysis,
- product/service profitability analysis,
- volume/value analysis, and
- retail performance analysis.

## Concluding comments

As we saw in the introduction, the revenue cycle is simply a collection of business-related activities/resources and information processing procedures whose primary objective is to maximise income (and of course profits) by providing customers/clients with the right product, at the right price, at the right place, and at the right time. It is therefore perhaps unsurprising – given the increasingly competitive/global nature of today's marketplace – that many business managers, accountants and academics consider the revenue cycle to be the lifeblood of the company/organisation. Stop the flow and the company/organisation dies.

It is for this reason that many companies/organisations have invested, and indeed continue to invest heavily, in revenue cycle-related information and communication technologies to improve the flow of products/services to customers/clients, to increase the flow of income to the company/organisation and to improve the collection and exchange of data/information.

And whilst there may be some uncertainty over how future changes in information and communication technologies will affect revenue cycle systems, processes and procedures, there can nevertheless be little doubt that the future will continue to see revenue cycle activities remaining at the very heart of many corporate/organisational activities.

## Key points and concepts

| | |
|---|---|
| Activity analysis information | Debtor account adjustment |
| Bad debt | Debtor-based revenue cycle |
| Bill of lading | Debtor management |
| Capital income | Debtor payment request |
| Card-based EPOS sales system | Distribution and delivery order |
| Cash-based/cheque-based sales system | Distribution and delivery system |
| Customer/client order | Doubtful debt |
| Customer/client order confirmation | EPOS |
| Customer/client relationship management | Formal demand |
| | Invoice |
| Debtor account | Marketing system |

Non-card-based EPOS sales system
Non-debtor-based revenue cycle
On-demand invoice approach
Payment management system
Period-based activity information
Period-based performance information
Phased/cyclical processing
Post-invoice approach
Pre-invoice approach

Production order request
Retail system
Revenue cycle
Revenue income
Service/knowledge provision request
Statement of account
Stores issue request
Transportation order
Web-based sales system

## Bibliography

Aseervatham, A. and Anandarajah, D. (2003) *Accounting Information and Reporting Systems*, McGraw Hill, Sydney.

Bagranoff, N.A., Simkin, M.G. and Strand N.C. (2004) *Core Concepts of Accounting Information Systems*, Wiley, New York.

Porter, M. (1980) *Competitive Strategy*, Free Press, New York.

Romney, M. and Steinbart, P. (2006) *Accounting Information Systems*, Pearson Education Inc., New Jersey.

Vaassen, E. (2002) *Accounting Information Systems – A Managerial Approach*, Wiley, Chichester.

Wilkinson, J.W., Cerullo, M.L., Raval, V. and Wong-On-Wing, B. (2001) *Accounting Information Systems*, Wiley, New York.

## Self-review questions

1. Distinguish between a debtor-based revenue cycle and a non-debtor-based revenue cycle.
2. Briefly explain the key processing requirements of debtor-based/non-debtor-based revenue cycles.
3. Describe the main stages of a debtor-based revenue cycle.
4. Where a debtor has failed to make payment within an agreed period, it may be necessary to take action to recover the debt. Briefly explain the main stages of a debt recovery process.
5. Distinguish between pre-invoicing, on-demand invoicing and post-invoicing.
6. Identify and describe the four main methods a customer/client can use for the submission of payment.
7. Describe the four stages normally involved in the online processing of a cardholder present transaction (pPoS EFT).
8. Briefly explain the three main types of payment cards.
9. What are the major differences between card-based EPOS payment systems and non-card-based EPOS payment systems.
10. Briefly explain the advantages and disadvantages of Pay By Touch payment systems.

## Questions and problems

### Question 1

BeTiCe Ltd is a newly formed, UK-based retail company. The company will specialise in street fashion accessories for both men and women, and will commence trading in three months, once a number of retail outlets have been refurbished. At a recent management meeting the company financial director proposed that the company should use a non-card payment system – particularly a Pay By Touch EFT system – for payments by customers. He was however unable to provide precise details of how such a system would work.

#### *Required*

Provide a brief report to the company's management committee and explain:

- how a Pay By Touch system would operate,
- the main stages involved in implementing a Pay By Touch system, and
- the main advantages and disadvantages of such a payment system.

### Question 2

RTY plc is a UK retail company with retail outlets in the south-east and north-west of England. In total the company has six retail outlets in the south-east and eight in the north-west. The company currently employs 195 staff.

The company has been trading successfully for a number of years.

For the year ending 31 December 2002 the company's turnover was £4.8m and its net profit for the year was £1.1m. As part of the company's information technology strategy, RTY plc is considering installing an Electronic Point Of Sale (EPOS) system for use in *all* its retail outlets.

The company is, however, aware that the acquisition and development of an EPOS system would require not only a substantial capital investment, but also a significant change in operating procedures at each of the retail outlets – possibly involving staff redundancies.

The management board of RTY plc have asked you, as their recently appointed Systems Accountant, to prepare a report on EPOS systems for presentation to the company's management board at its next meeting in June 2003.

#### *Required*

Prepare a report for the management board of RTY plc on the development and implementation of an EPOS system. Your report should provide;

- a brief description of how an EPOS system works,
- a review of the potential advantages and disadvantages of EPOS systems for the company, and
- an evaluation of the potential control problems RTY plc could face as a consequences of implementing a company-wide EPOS system for its retail operations.

### Question 3

ZKO Plc was an UK-listed company that produced digital audio equipment for the retail market. The company's products were sold throughout Europe, North America, Australia and Canada, and were widely regarded as the best in the market. Indeed, during the period 1995 to 2001, the company's digital audio equipment consistently won high praise from both consumer groups and retail critics.

In January 2002, however, ZKO Plc suddenly went into liquidation. The company failed with debts amounting to £105m.

The failure of the company was headline news around the world with press speculation focusing on the possibility of large-scale financial reporting irregularities and potential management fraud.

However, in April 2002 the company receivers published their findings. Their report indicated that whilst some unacceptable accounting irregularities had been evident in the company's published financial reports for a number of years, the principal cause of ZKO Plc's failure had been inadequate control within its revenue cycle operations – in particular the management of debtor payments.

The company receivers' report concluded that:

*whilst substantial profits were generated by sales transactions these profits were rarely converted into cash-based resources. Moreover, the company increasingly maintained an unhealthy and somewhat excessive level of debtors, many of which were clearly irrecoverable.*

### Required

Describe the main function of a sales system for a company such as ZKO Plc and explain the inherent risk associated with the failure of such a system.

Describe the primary function of debtor management and explain the separation of duties necessary for adequate debtor management in a company such as ZKO Plc. Indicate the problems that may occur in a debtor management system when such separation of administrative powers does not exist.

## Question 4

A company's sales system functions not only as part of the corporate marketing cycle, but also as part of the corporate asset interface/exchange process.

### Required

Describe the accounting controls you would expect to find in a sales system designed for the sales of electrical commodities and discuss how the failure of such accounting controls could potentially affect the valuation and security of company assets and the disclosure of company assets in the annual financial reports.

## Question 5

You have recently been appointed by the management board of JKL Ltd, a small electrical accessories company, to design a company-wide computer-based sales/debtors system. To date, the company has maintained a manual record system for its sales/debtors.

For the previous three financial year the company has had an average annual turnover of £18m (all sales are in the UK), and average annual profits of approximately £4.4m. The company has approximately 50 employees working at six locations throughout the UK: Manchester, which is the company's head office, Birmingham, Leeds, Swindon, Bristol and Newcastle. In Manchester, five staff are directly involved in sales/debtors system, whereas in the remaining five locations only 10 members of staff are directly involved – two at each regional location.

For the year ended 31 January 2007, approximately 95% of the company's sales were trade sales to UK retail companies, of which 88% of these sales were on credit. In addition, for the past three financial years, bad debts relating to trade sales have averaged approximately 5% of the company's turnover in each year, resulting in lost income over the three years of approximately £2.7m. It is this loss of sales income that has prompted the management board of the company to review its sales/debtors system.

The company purchases all its retail stock.

### Required

Making whatever assumptions you consider necessary, prepare a draft design for the management board of JKL Ltd indicating, where appropriate, the necessary control procedures you recommend in order to minimise the growing level of bad debts.

# Assignments

## Question 1

*UK card fraud has risen steadily over the past 10 years, from £83.3m in 1995 to £504.8m in 2004. Over the same period, card usage and the number of cards issued has risen, and continues to rise in the UK. With increasing card use comes an increased risk of exposure and . . . (companies) . . . should remain vigilant to the potential fraud risk (http://www.hsbc.co.uk/1/2/business/needs/card-fraud).*

### Required

To assist in the prevention of fraud (especially in relation to point of service EFT), a large number of anti-fraud measures are now available for retailers to use. Some of the more popular anti-fraud measures are:

- the use of forced online protocols,
- the use of floor limits,
- the use of 'one-in-*n*' checks – that is sample random transactions checks,
- the use of multiple transaction checks,
- the use of Hot Card files,
- the use of encryption,
- the use of Secure Sockets Layer (SSL),
- the use of Card Security Code (CSC),
- the use of address verification services (AVS), and
- the use of payer authentication.

Describe and critically evaluate each of the above anti-fraud measures.

## Question 2

BPL Ltd is a small local retail company. The company sells a branded clothing range for 18–30 year olds. During the past financial year (year ending 31 December 2005) the company had an annual turnover of £1.5m and an annual net profit of approximately £700,000.

The company has two retail outlets located in Manchester and Oxford, and employs five part-time sales assistants, one administrator and one manager.

Currently, sales are either over-the-counter sales at either retail location, or mail order sales from the company's annual catalogue. Over-the-counter sales can be for cash, credit/debit card payment or payment by cheque. Mail order sales can be for credit/debit card payment and/or cheque payment only. All mail order sales are processed at the company's Manchester retail outlet. Last year 42% of the company's turnover was from mail order sales.

For credit/debit card-related sales, the company operates a chip and pin-based ePOS (electronic point of sale) system. All over-the-counter sales are processed by the sales assistants. All mail order sales are recorded by the administrator.

Mail order sales are only accepted from authorised customers. These customers are authorised by the manager in advance and are allowed 45 days' credit. In the past financial year, however, the manager authorised the write-off of £86,000 for bad debts arising from non-payment by mail order customers. Estimates for the current financial year suggest that bad debt write-offs may exceed £100,000.

The manager has become increasingly concerned about the growing level of bad debts, and is exploring the possibility of developing an internet-based e-commerce facility to replace its catalogue-based mail order facility, and eliminate ever-increasing levels of bad debt.

### Required

Describe the main function of a sales system for a company such as BPL Ltd and explain the inherent risk associated with the failure of internal controls within such a system.

**Chapter endnotes**

[1] In a broad sense, marketing is concerned with identifying, anticipating and meeting the needs of customers in such a way as to make a profit. Inasmuch as marketing generally operates at two levels within a company/organisation:

- the strategic level – concerned with major long-term decisions that affect the whole organisation, and
- the tactical level – concerned with applying the marketing mix in the most appropriate way: that is organising promotions, setting prices, positioning the product/service, and organising distribution and delivery,

a company's/organisation's marketing model can be defined as the company's/organisation's unique combination of a marketing strategy and an appropriate selection of marketing tactics to create a customer-orientated, profit-making business.

[2] See Chapter 6.

[3] Whilst we will use the term 'individual', it can refer to any non-corporate entity/organisation.

[4] RFID (Radio Frequency IDentification) is a method of remotely collecting and/or retrieving data with the use of RFID tags/transponders.

[5] And the requirements of the Data Protection Act 1998.

[6] Personal Digital Assistant.

[7] SITPRO Limited, formerly The Simpler Trade Procedures Board, was set up in 1970 as the UK's trade facilitation agency. Reconstituted as a company limited by guarantee in April 2001, SITPRO is one of the non-departmental public bodies for which the Department of Trade and Industry has responsibility.

[8] Such trade between member states is referred to as either:

- arrivals or acquisitions (purchases or imports), and
- dispatches or removals (sales or exports).

[9] VAT-registered companies/organisations subject to extant VAT tax rules can offset VAT payments related to inputs (purchases) against VAT receipts on outputs (sales).

[10] These would also include payment by postal order and/or money order.

[11] Demographically, such a payment method is perhaps only favoured by the elderly.

[12] Where a cash discount is allowed – as an incentive to encourage customers/clients to pay early – it is important to ensure that any such payment requirement is fulfilled. In the UK, a number of companies have now discontinued the practice of offering early payment discounts as customers/clients frequently accept such discounts without submitting payment within the required period.

[13] A formal reminder for payment would normally contain a reminder to the customer/client for payment of the outstanding balance – usually within seven days – but also somewhat paradoxically, an apology to the customer/client if payment has already been made before the receipt of the formal reminder.

[14] County court judgment.

[15] Currently the statutory rate is 8% pa.

[16] See s69 County Courts Act 1984.

[17] Such a charge could be either:

- a fixed charge on specific assets/group of assets of the customer/client, or
- a floating charge on all the assets of the customer/client.

[18] For a number of well-known UK companies this minimum level is currently £50.

[19] Such companies often offer a range of debt management services, ranging from:

- sales ledger accounting, to
- credit insurance, to
- debt factoring/debt management.

[20] In the main card schemes are MasterCard and Visa which together account for nearly 90% of all the payment cards in circulation.

[21] See Chapter 12 for further details on e-money.

[22] For debit cards this will be the amount of money in the cardholder's account (together with any overdraft facility). For credit cards, this will be the amount of money that the card issuer is prepared to lend the cardholder (the credit limit).

[23] The acquirer (or acquiring bank) will be responsible for:

- forwarding transaction requests from the merchant to the card issuer so that the cardholder's identity can be verified and to ensure that the cardholder has sufficient funds available to support the transaction;
- acting on behalf of the card issuer and authorising transactions where a referred transaction requires further information from the card holder;
- collecting the settlement files from the merchant;
- forwarding settlement files to the appropriate card issuer;
- reimbursing the merchant with the funds payable on the transactions (less the merchant service charge); and
- maintaining a Hot Card File – a record of all cards reported as being either lost or stolen.

Examples of UK acquirers are:

- Royal Bank of Scotland,
- Barclays Merchant Services,
- NatWest Streamline,
- Lloydstsb Cardnet, and
- HSBC Merchant Services.

[24] It is possible and, indeed often the case, that a merchant has more than one acquirer.

[25] A generic term for the machine used to 'swipe' a debit and/or credit card.

[26] If the system has a Hot Card checking facility the customer's card number will be checked against a list of lost or stolen cards provided by the banks or other financial institutions/organisations. If the customer's card number matches a card number on the list, the merchant *must* decline the transaction and *retain* the customer's card.

[27] Merchant Service Agreement.

[28] The acquirer has agreed the transaction and has confirmed that the customer/cardholder has the funds available and the merchant will receive payment for the transaction.

[29] The acquirer has refused the transaction. No explanation will be offered by the acquirer: that is the merchant will not be informed why the transaction was declined.

[30] The acquirer has requested further information before deciding whether to authorise the transaction. For example, the acquirer may request the merchant to obtain further confirmation of the identity of the customer/cardholder before a decision on whether to authorise or decline the transaction is made.

[31] The Consumer Protection (Distance Selling) Regulations 2000 defined a distance contract as: 'any contract concerning goods and services concluded between a supplier and a customer under an organised distance sales or service provision scheme run by the supplier who for the purposes of the contract makes exclusive use of one or more means of distance communication up to and including the moment that the contact is concluded' (s3).

[32] See Chapter 13.

[33] Where a merchant is unsure about the validity of a customer/cardholder's identity or has suspicions about the transaction, the merchant can force the transaction to be authorised online.

[34] A floor limit is an agreed limit between the merchant and acquirer. If the transaction amount exceeds the floor limit, the transaction is forced online for authorisation.

[35] Hot Card files contain details of lost and stolen cards. Where Hot Card checking is installed, each time a merchant accepts a card as payment for a transaction, the system checks the card number against entries in the Hot Card file. Obviously if the card number is listed, the merchant *must* decline the transaction and retain the card.

[36] SSL provides a secure method of transmitting and authenticating data over a network via TCP/IP. Developed to enable the secure transmission of information over the Internet, SSL can be used to reduce the risk of credit card information being intercepted.

[37] Card Security Codes (CSC) were introduced as an anti-fraud measure for customer/cardholder not present transactions (nPoS EFT) where objective verification/validation is not possible. A CSC is a three-digit number (four-digit number for American Express) that is generated automatically on manufacture. The CSC is printed on the signature strip on the back of the card.

[38] Address Verification Services (AVS) were also introduced as an anti-fraud measure for customer/cardholder not present transactions (nPoS EFT) where objective verification/validation is not possible. AVS entails the checking information about the customer/cardholder's address.

[39] Specifically to reduce the incidence of fraudulent internet-based transactions payer authentication enables online merchants to authenticate customer cardholder's in real time.

[40] A merchant ID is a unique electronic ID assigned to a merchant by an acquiring bank.

[41] A Payment Service Provider (PSP) provides payment gateway services to enable a merchant to process, authorise, settle and manage credit/debit card transactions.

[42] The word 'biometric' is derived from the Greek words *bios*, meaning life, and *metrikos*, meaning to measure.

[43] It perhaps worth noting that the Pay by Touch service provided by paybytouch @ www.paybytouch.com, does not actually use fingerprints, but uses micro measurements of an individual's finger which are then converted into a mathematical equation, encrypted and stored on a secure database.

[44] Established in 2003, Pay by Touch currently services over 154,000 retail clients, manages personalised rewards programmes for more than 130 million opt-in consumers, and has more than 2.3 million shoppers using biometric authentication products and services at over 2000 retail outlets in the USA (and Europe).

[45] Biometric technologies are also used for identity verification and security screening purposes.

[46] For example, many small out-of-town food retailers (e.g. Costcutter, see www.costcutter.co.uk), often charge an additional fee for payment by debit and/or credit card if the value of the transaction is less than a minimum – often £5.

[47] Whilst the majority of customers/clients in this category may make a conscious decision not to use a debit/credit card to pay for the purchase of products, in some instances, a customer/client may be precluded from using such payment facilities. For example, recent personal bankruptcy and/or an excessive level of personal debt may result in an issuing bank/credit card company withdrawing access to debit/credit card facilities.

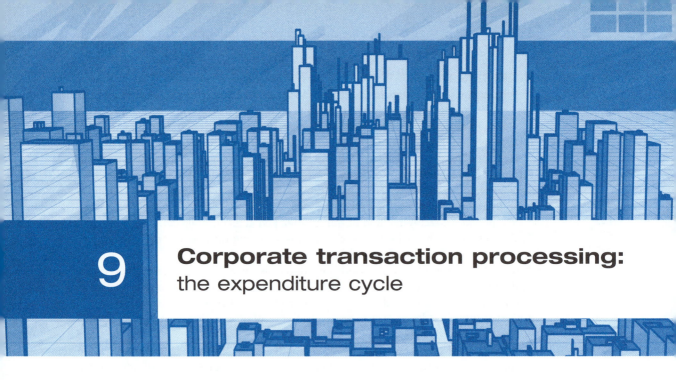

# 9 Corporate transaction processing:
## the expenditure cycle

## Introduction

The expenditure cycle can be defined as a collection of business-related activities/resources and information processing procedures, concerned with:

■ the acquisition of products/services from approved suppliers/providers, and
■ the payment to suppliers/providers for those goods/services,

with the primary objective of the expenditure cycles being to minimise the total cost of acquiring and maintaining the products/services required for the company/organisation to function effectively, whilst maintaining the good image of the company/organisation.
See Figure 9.1.
In general, three types or variations of expenditure cycle can be identified:

■ the revenue-related expenditure – that is the expenditure cycle concerned with:
  ● the purchase of current assets (e.g. stock) for production and/or retail purposes, and/or
  ● the purchase of services for use by or within the company/organisation,
■ the capital-related expenditure – that is the expenditure concerned with the purchase of fixed assets for retention and use within the company/organisation, and
■ the human resource-related expenditure (or the employee remuneration cycle) – that is the expenditure cycle concerned with the purchase of and payment for personal services via a payroll system.

It is perhaps worth noting that whereas both the revenue-related expenditure cycle and the capital-related expenditure cycle would utilise many of the same company/organisation procedures, process and controls (see later), the human resource-related expenditure cycle – although primarily concerned with revenue-related expenditure such as the payment of wages and salaries to employees – would utilise a number of procedures, processes and controls unique to that expenditure cycle.

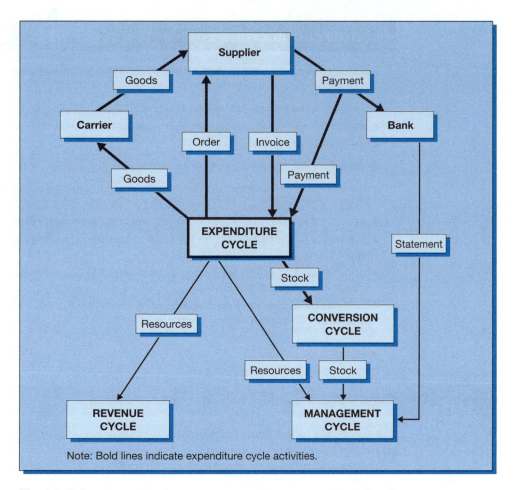

Note: Bold lines indicate expenditure cycle activities.

**Figure 9.1** Expenditure cycle

Why? Put simply, employee remuneration systems tend to be subject to very specific and often very complex statutory requirements and fiscal regulations.

So, what role(s) would a company/organisation accounting information system play in an expenditure cycle? Whilst in an operational context, the accounting information system would be used to assist in:

- the capture and processing of expenditure cycle transaction data, and
- the organising, storing and maintaining expenditure cycle transaction data,

in a more strategic context, the accounting information system would be used to safeguard expenditure cycle resources and ensure:

- the reliability of expenditure cycle transaction data, and
- the integrity of expenditure cycle activities.

## Learning outcomes

This chapter explores a wide range of issues related to the corporate expenditure cycle, in particular:

- creditor-based expenditure-related systems,
- non-creditor-based expenditure-related systems, and
- payroll-related systems.

By the end of this chapter, the reader should be able to;

- describe the major activities and operations contained within the corporate expenditure cycle,
- explain the key decision stages within the corporate expenditure cycle,
- demonstrate an understanding of the key internal control requirements of a corporate expenditure cycle,
- demonstrate a critical understanding of the potential risks and threats associated with inappropriate internal control, and
- consider and explain the impact of information and communication technology enabled innovations on the corporate expenditure cycle.

## Expenditure cycle – revenue expenditure

The expenditure cycle is concerned with the acquisition of assets, raw materials products and/or services for business-related purposes.

The main objectives of the revenue expenditure cycle are to:

- ensure that all products, services and/or resources are ordered as needed/required by the company/organisation,
- ensure all ordered goods are received,
- verify all products are received in an appropriate condition,
- safeguard products until required by the company/organisation,
- record and classify expenditure correctly and accurately,
- record and account for all expenditure cycle-related obligations/commitments,
- ensure that all disbursements/payments are for authorised and approved expenditure only, and
- record and account for all expenditure cycle-related disbursements to suppliers/providers to the correct account in the creditor's ledger.

In an accounting context, such expenditure can be classified as either:

- capital expenditure[1] – that is expenditure related to the acquisition and/or improvement of either tangible or intangible fixed assets, and
- revenue expenditure[2] – that is expenditure incurred as a result of
  - the purchase of current assets,
  - the repair and maintenance of fixed assets, and/or
  - the purchase of supplier/provider services.

Within the expenditure cycle, capital expenditure is sometimes referred to as high-value/low-volume expenditure whereas the revenue expenditure is sometimes referred to as low-value/high-volume expenditure.

We will look at additional issues/requirements associated with capital expenditure later in this chapter, and in more detail in Chapter 11. For the moment, we will consider expenditure cycle issues/requirements associated with revenue expenditure.

For revenue-based expenditure, because of the often high volumes of products/services involved, it is important for the company/organisation to be able to identify:

■ the optimal level of product stocks required for the company/organisation to function efficiently,
■ the most appropriate location(s) for the delivery of purchased products/services,
■ the optimal location for the storage of purchased products,
■ the most appropriate suppliers/providers to supply/provide the best quality products/services at the best prices,
■ the optimal procedure/process for making payments to suppliers/providers, and
■ the data/information required for the efficient and effective acquisition of products, services and resources.

Before we look at the expenditure cycle in detail, it would perhaps be worth noting that underpinning the following discussion is an assumption that all expenditure cycle purchasing activities, in particular expenditure cycle activities concerned with the purchase of revenue assets, are market orientated: that is no single company/organisation occupies a monopoly position within the market.

Why is this important? Put simply, by:

■ restricting the availability of a product/service and maintaining high product/service prices,
■ controlling market regulators and developing a socio-political monopoly – including, for example, the development of an economic cartel, and/or
■ acting in an anti-social/anti-competitive way – for example stifling technological progress and/or misallocating resources and reducing product choice/consumer choice,

such a company/organisation could adversely influence the supply of products and/or services to the marketplace.

What is the relevance of this to a company's/organisation's accounting information systems? Whether as a result of:

■ the existence of substantial economies of scale, or
■ the imposition of legal constraints preventing competition, or
■ the unrestricted collusion of two or more companies/organisations – that is the creation of a cartel type arrangement, or
■ the exclusive ownership of a unique resource or set of resources (e.g. the possession of copyrights, patents and/or licences),

the existence of such an anti-competitive monopoly within the marketplace would severely limit the effectiveness of the market mechanism to distribute wealth amongst market participants. It would also constrain the ability of other companies/organisations to maximise the wealth of their owners.

Perhaps, more importantly, it would limit the necessity for, and effectiveness of, some internal controls within other market-based companies/organisations, for example supplier/provider selection procedures.

It is therefore not surprising that legislative provisions exist within the UK, the European Union and indeed many of the WTO[3] membership countries to prohibit agreements, business practices and commercial conduct that may damage market competition and the free (or more appropriately regulated) flow capital.

For example in the UK, the Competition Act 1998 prohibits:

- the use of anti-competitive agreements – see Chapter 1 of the Competition Act 1998,[4] and
- the abuse of a dominant position in a market – see Chapter 2 of the Competition Act 1998.[5]

In addition, the Competition Act 1998 also established the Competition Commission (see www.competition-commission.org.uk), as an independent public body to 'conduct in-depth inquiries/investigation into mergers, markets and the regulation of the major regulated industries.'[6]

Because the Competition Commission has no power to conduct inquiries on its own initiative, every inquiry/investigation undertaken by it is in response to a reference made to it by another regulating/monitoring authority – usually the Office of Fair Trading (OFT), the Secretary of State or the regulator of a sector-specific industry, for example OFWAT (Office of Water Services) or OFCOM (Office of Communications).

## Expenditure cycle – types

As with the revenue cycle, there are two possible alternative types of expenditure cycle:

- a creditor-based expenditure cycle, or
- a non-creditor-based expenditure cycle.

So what is the difference? In a creditor-based expenditure cycle the property of an asset/service (i.e. the legal title to an asset/service and the possession/physical custody of an asset/service) are exchanged for a legally binding promise by the customer/client to pay at some predetermined future date or within a predetermined future period. Such transactions are often referred to as *credit purchases*.

In a non-creditor-based expenditure cycle, such property and possession of an asset/service is exchanged for the legal title to (property) and custody of (possession) another asset. Whilst such an asset will usually be cash, or a cash equivalent, it can – in both a legal and business context – refer to any mutually agreed asset. Such transactions are often referred to as cash or cash equivalent purchases.

### Creditor-based expenditure cycle

A creditor-based expenditure cycle will generally be concerned with:

- company-to-company credit purchases, and/or
- individual-to-company credit purchases.

That is expenditure transactions in which the supplier/provider is selected, and approved prior to the completion of any expenditure transaction. The creditor-based revenue cycle is therefore a subject (or supplier/provider) orientated revenue transaction cycle.

Generally, such creditor-based expenditure cycle transactions will occur within companies/ organisations classified as context type 1(a)[7] and 1(b), and perhaps also 2(b) and 2(c), with the processing of such transactions invariably involving/incorporating some information and communication technology-based interface/component. Whether this is at the supplier selection/approval stage, at the product/service ordering stage, at the product/service receiving stage or indeed at the payment stage, it is now likely that such creditor-based expenditure cycle transactions (or some part of them) will be web-based.

For example a company/organisation may use:

■ a supplier/provider web-based catalogue to obtain detailed information on available products/service online,
■ a secure extranet facilities (see Chapter 5) to order products/service online, from a supplier/provider,
■ web-based stock-in-transit tacking/monitoring facilities to monitor the movement of order products/services, and/or,
■ a secure BACS-IP facility (see Chapter 4) to submit payments online to suppliers/providers to allow customers/clients (in particular corporate-based/organisation-based customers/clients) to submit payments online.

## Non-creditor-based expenditure cycle

A non-creditor-based expenditure cycle will generally be concerned with expenditure transactions in which the transaction is validated and authorised. That is the transaction is agreed and payment is authenticated and authorised prior to the completion of the expenditure transaction.

The non-creditor-based expenditure cycle is therefore an object (or transaction) orientated revenue transaction cycle.

Generally such non-creditor-based expenditure transactions can be classified as either:

■ cash-based expenditure, or
■ card-based expenditure,

and will occur within companies/organisations classified as context types 1(a) and 1(b), and perhaps also 2(a), 2(b), and possibly 2(c) albeit to a very limited extent.

We will look at both cash-based, and card-based non-creditor expenditure later in this chapter.

## Creditor-based expenditure cycle

As we saw earlier, a creditor-based expenditure cycle will generally be concerned with:

■ company-to-company credit purchases, and/or
■ individual-to-company credit purchases.

Such a creditor-based expenditure cycle can be divided into four component system:

■ the supplier selection/approval system,
■ the product/service ordering system,
■ the product/service receiving system, and
■ the payment management system.

See Figure 9.2.

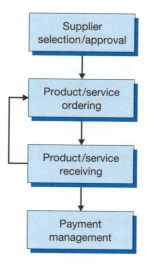

**Figure 9.2** Creditor-based expenditure cycle

## Supplier selection/approval system

The purpose of the supplier selection/approval system is:

■ to identify an appropriate supplier/provider for the product/service required, and
■ to determine an appropriate level of relationship with that supplier/provider.

See Figure 9.3.

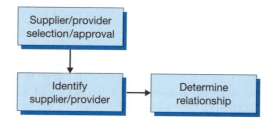

**Figure 9.3** Supplier selection/approval system

The key documentation of such a supplier selection/approval system would be:

■ a supplier approval/registration document,
■ an approved supplier/provider register (database),
■ a supplier/provider amendment document, and
■ a supplier/provider assessment and review document,

### Identifying an appropriate supplier/provider

Inasmuch as the identifying of an appropriate supplier/provider of a product and/or service is often regarded as a trade-off between product/service quality and supplier/provider performance, it is important that a company/organisation considers a range of issues when seeking to identify an appropriate supplier/provider. Such issues could include:

■ the price of the product/service,
■ the quality of the product/service,

- the product/service lead time – that is the time required for the product/service to be delivered,
- the terms of settlement offered by the supplier/provider, and
- the method of delivery used by the supplier/provider.

Remember, cheap is not necessarily best since a good supplier/provider may charge a higher price for:

- the provision of good-quality management/quality control and guarantee the delivery of defect-free product/services,
- the assured direct delivery of products/services to the right place, at the right time and in the right quantities, and
- the provision of simplified administrative processes and authorisation procedures/arrangements.

So, how would a company/organisation identify an appropriate supplier/provider? There are a number of possible ways, the most common being through:

- a formal tender process in which suppliers/providers are invited to submit a formal tender for the supply of products/services – usually for a fixed, defined period, or
- an informal invitation process in which suppliers/providers are invited to provide product/service details and specifications and information of supply/provider terms and conditions of supply.

The assessment of any supplier/provider would of course need to consider a range of issues such as:

- any past experiences/previous trading relationships with the supplier/provider,
- any negative press/media speculation concerning the supplier/provider – for example speculation regarding the financial stability of the supplier/provider,
- the quality/reputation of the supplier/provider, and
- the reliability and flexibility of the supplier/provider – for example the supplier's/provider's willingness and ability to comply with special orders/requests.

Where an appropriate supplier/provider is identified a supplier approval/registration document would be completed (electronically) – more than likely by an employee within the purchasing department.

For both quality control purposes and perhaps more importantly internal control purposes, many companies/organisations create and maintain what is often referred to as an approved supplier/provider register or perhaps, more appropriately, a supplier/provider database (since many of these are now computer-based). This register/database identifies those suppliers/providers whose supplier credentials have been validated and verified by the company/organisation.

So what information would such a register/database contain? Although the precise contents of such a register/database would differ from organisation to organisation, in general it would contain information such as:

- the supplier's/provider's reference,
- the geographical location of the supplier/provider,
- the type of products/service offered by the supplier/provider,
- the delivery mechanism used by the supplier/provider,
- the supplier/provider terms and conditions of supply/provision,
- the supplier/provider payment conditions including, for example, the availability of discounts and, where possible,
- the transactions (successful or otherwise) undertaken with the supplier/provider

Regarding this last point, increasingly, many companies/organisations now link the supplier/provider register/database to the company's/organisation's creditor ledger within the accounting information system, the benefit of this being that where a supplier/provider has provided products/services to the company/organisation, it allows financial information such as:

- the level of trade undertaken with the supplier/provider, and/or
- the recent payment histories with the supplier/provider,

to appear in the approved supplier register/database.[8]

Note: This link would of course only be possible where an approved product supplier/service provider had supplied products/provided services for which payment has been made: in other words where a financial transaction has occurred and there existed an *active* relationship between the supplier/provider and the company/organisation. In essence, all creditors *must* be either an approved product supplier and/or an approved service provider, and *must* appear in the supplier/provider register/database. However not all suppliers/providers will appear in the creditors ledger. Some product suppliers/service providers may be approved but have not yet supplied products to or supplied services for the company/organisation. Such suppliers/providers would be regarded as *inactive* and would neither possess a creditor account reference nor appear in the creditors ledger.

It is of course important that the performance of all active product suppliers/service providers is closely monitored and, where necessary, the approved supplier/provider on the register is regularly updated. In assessing a supplier's/provider's level of performance a company/organisation may consider the following:

- Does the supplier/provider provide good value for money?
- Does the supplier/provider provide good quality products/services?
- Does the supplier/provider delivery meet the expectations/requirements of the company/organisation?
- Are the products/services delivered accurately and on time?
- Does the supplier/provider offer competitive payment terms?
- Does the supplier/provider offer an appropriate level of after-sales support?
- How efficient is the supplier/provider in processing product/service orders?

For internal control purposes, such a review must be undertaken by employees not directly involved in the initiation and processing of purchase orders.

Finally, where a supplier's/provider's details change – for example change of address or change of account details – an amendment to the supplier/provider register/database would be required. All such supplier/provider amendments must be authorised and approved *before* a change to the supplier/provider register/database is permitted.

### Determining an appropriate level of relationship

Clearly, once a supplier/provider has been approved, it is necessary to determine what type of relationship/what level of commitment the company/organisation requires. Such relationships can be in the form of either:

- an informal relationship in which a supplier/provider is approved but no formal supply commitment is agreed, or
- a formal relationship in which a supplier/provider is approved and a formal contractual agreement is established.

Clearly, a formal relationship can vary substantially from organisation to organisation, and whilst many variations exist, the most common are:

- a fixed, long-term supply agreement/contract – for example a three-year supply agreement at fixed terms and conditions of the supply,

- a flexible/rollover, long-term supply agreement/contract – for example a three-year agreement in which the terms and conditions of the supply contract can be renegotiated/varied within agreed parameters,
- a fixed period, short-term supply agreement/contract – for example a three-month supply agreement at fixed terms and conditions of the supply, and
- a flexible, open-ended supply agreement/contract – for example a supply agreement without any termination date in which the terms and conditions of the supply contract can be renegotiated/varied within agreed/established parameters.

So, which is best? That depends on many factors, for example:

- the nature of the product/service provided by the supplier/provider,
- the requirements of the purchasing company/organisation and, perhaps most importantly,
- the prevailing conditions within the marketplace – for example the degree of volatility, flexibility and competition in the market.

Have a look at the following article relating to supplier contracts.

## Article 9.1

### Supplier contracts

If a purchaser is to get the best out of a potential supplier it is seen as a good move to lock yourself into a long-term contract. But will this not make the supplier complacent and monopolistic in the long run? And in a time of crisis, the purchaser will have no alternative options.

Christopher Barrat, director of the Greystone Partnership, writes: There are three questions here, and all of them go to the heart of issues that purchasers face.

First, I would challenge your initial assumption. 'Long term' as a concept is hard to defend in the more flexible and networked marketplace of today. However, if you do believe you have a great deal, then securing it with a contract is a good thing to do.

Contracts also force both parties to make sure they have agreed the key elements of the deal, and that alone has benefits. I agree that this could make suppliers complacent – although it rarely makes them monopolistic. Complacency comes because they don't have to fight for the business any more, so processes can get sloppy and service drops. This is a reactive response to stability, which is very different from a proactive response of behaving in a monopolistic way. Providing you were happy with the deal in the first place, then the contract helps to avoid monopolistic behaviour rather than encourage it.

If over the time of the contract the market forces have moved, then it will be these, rather than the attitude of supplier, that will determine whether they

can take a monopolistic attitude, or if you can take an opportunistic one. The skill is to constantly monitor how the balance of dependency is shifting. At one end both parties could be independent of any reliance on the other. In the middle you could have some dependency, and ultimately you could find you are totally interdependent. This will determine the degree to which you lock yourself in.

The third point is about market flexibility. If you have a long-term contract then it certainly should have strict definitions of how each party will behave if there is a crisis, and this should include your rights to seek alternative supplies. It is your duty as a purchaser to ensure you have some alternative suppliers who you are at least 'keeping warm'. Most suppliers are keen to break into customers who are linked to the competition, and what better time than when the incumbent supplier has let them down.

You will only be left with no alternatives if you too have become complacent and forget to keep your supply network interested. Remember this is not a marriage – it is a business relationship. You may have a partner at the moment, but don't let that stop you from the occasional flirtatious liaison: it can keep all parties fresh and interested in making things work.

Source: Advisor, 25 May 2006, *Supply Management*
http://www.supplymanagement.co.uk/EDIT/
CURRENT_ISSUE_pages/CI_adviser_item.asp?id=14894.

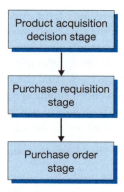

**Figure 9.4** Product/service ordering system

## Product/service ordering system

The purpose of the product/service ordering system is to ensure that products and services relevant to the business process are ordered by authorised employees only, and obtained/purchased from appropriately approved suppliers/providers. See Figure 9.4.

The key documentation for such a product/service ordering system would be:

- a purchase requisition,
- a purchase order and, where appropriate,
- a purchase confirmation.

Most companies/organisations separate the purchase/ordering system into three key stages:

- the purchase acquisition stage,
- the purchase requisition stage, and
- the purchase order stage.

Before we look at the purchase/ordering system in detail, it is worth noting that whilst the purchase price of a product/service is an important component in a purchasing decision it is only one of many costs that could occur as a consequence of expenditure cycle activity: that is the purchase price is only one component of the total purchase cost incurred during the purchase of a product/service.

So what are these other costs? Although some of these costs would apply to both products and services, and some to products only or services only, in general these other costs would include:

- ordering costs – the administration costs associated with the processing of purchase orders for products and/or services,
- delivery costs – the costs associated with the transportation of purchased products,
- payment costs – the administration and finance costs associated with the payment of invoices for purchased products/services,
- receiving costs – the costs associated with the secure receipt of purchased products and/or services,
- inspection costs – the costs associated with the quality assessment of purchased products,
- handling costs – the costs associated with the movement and administration of purchased products,
- storage costs – the costs associated with securely storing purchased products,
- disruption costs – the costs associated with or resulting from the non-delivery of products/services,

- wastage costs – the costs associated with the disposal of products,
- reworking costs – the costs associated with the reworking of poor-quality products, and
- opportunity costs – the costs resulting from the loss of custom owing to the receipt of faulty products and, in rare instances, services.

### Purchase acquisition stage

The purchase acquisition stage is concerned with three key issues:

- what products/services should be ordered,
- when the products/services should be ordered, and
- what volume, or more appropriately how much, of a product/service should be ordered.

For the moment, we will look at issues associated with the acquisition of purchased products only and consider issues associated with the acquisition of services later in this section.

### Products and the purchase acquisition stage

For products, the purchase acquisition stage is essentially concerned with stock management – that is determining an answer to a question which superficially appears to be simple and straightforward, but is in fact deceptively complex. So what is the question? The question is: how much stock should the company/organisation hold/possess?

There are essentially three possible answers to this question:

- retain/maintain a very small stock of products/no stock of products – that is as little stock as possible, or
- retain/maintain a large stock of products – that is hold as much stock as possible, or
- retain/maintain a moderate stock of products – that is a pre-determined/calculated level of stock.

So which is the correct answer? Well, that depends, perhaps somewhat unsurprisingly, on a range of factors which we will look at in detail in Chapter 11.

### Services and the purchase acquisition stage

Although cost benefits/cost efficiencies are often cited as important factors in the decision to 'buy in' a service from an external agent/service provider, in general a company/organisation would seek to acquire the provision of a service by an external agent/external service provider where:

- a legal requirement/contractual arrangement necessitates the use of an external agent/service provider, and/or
- an insufficient level of knowledge, skill, ability and/or experience is available within the company for internal employees to provide the required service.

So, what types of acquired services are there? In general, acquired services can be classified as either:

- a recurring acquired service, or
- a non-recurring acquired service.

## A recurring acquired service

A recurring acquired service can be defined as a service which is purchased to fulfil/satisfy either:

- a specific contractual obligation – for example an asset service agreement/maintenance agreement, or

■ a legal obligation – for example a health and safety assessment or a CRB (Criminal Records Bureau) check.[9]

The necessity for such a recurring service would normally occur as a consequence of a specific identifiable event or series of events, that is for example:

■ the purchase/acquisition of an asset or group of assets, or
■ the provision of a specific activity/service.

## A non-recurring acquired service

A non-recurring acquired service can be defined as a service which is required for:

■ a specific period – for example the outsourcing of a business-related function/activity such as payroll management or purchase order processing within the company/organisation for a fixed period, or
■ a defined assignment – for example a one-off commission for a specific purpose, for example the appointment of a consultant to review company/organisation procedures.

The requirement for such a non-recurring service would normally occur as a consequence of a specific management decision, for example:

■ a decision to restructure a specific business-related activity/function, and/or
■ a decision to reorganise and/or outsource an administrative process.

### Purchase requisition stage

The purchase of a product and/or a service by a company/organisation would normally be initiated by the issue of a purchase requisition, instigated within either:

■ a manual procedure, or
■ an automatic procedure.

Within a manual procedure the purchase requisition would be generated by the actions of/ through the intervention of an authorised employee. Such a procedure would normally be associated with a small company/organisation in which stock movement is monitored by assigned employees. Within an automatic procedure the purchase requisition would be generated by the actions of a system-based monitoring procedure. Such a system would normally be associated with a medium/large company/organisation in which high levels of turnover occur and stock management/movements procedures are computer-based.

So what is a purchase requisition? This can be defined as a physical and/or electronic document used to inform the purchasing department of a company/organisation that purchased products and/or services are required for business purposes. The purchase requisition would normally be prepared by the product/service user and duly authorised by the appropriate budget holder/cost centre manager, in accordance with company/organisational management policy. It would:

■ specify the products/services required – those which are not available internally from within the company/organisation,
■ authorise the purchasing staff to enter the company/organisation into a supply contract with an external company/organisation for the supply of the requested products/services, and
■ allocate/charge the cost of those products/services to a specified cost code or cost centre.

Example 9.1 provides a sample purchase requisition document.

| PURCHASE REQUISITION | | | | |
|---|---|---|---|---|
| Requisition no. .................... Requisition date .................. | | | | |
| Materials/ components | Quantity | Description | Unit cost (£) | Total cost (£) |
| | | | | |
| | | | | |
| Prepared by .................... Authorisation .................... Accounting .................... | | Notes | | |

**Example 9.1** A purchase requisition document

## Using a computer-based purchase requisition system

Where a computer-based purchase requisition system is used and the purchase requisition is issued and transmitted to the company/organisation purchasing department electronically – say using a secure intranet facility – it is very likely that a range of:

- content and format checks,
- document sequence checks,
- transmission checks,
- validity checks, and
- authorisation checks,

would be undertaken to ensure the legitimacy and authenticity of the purchase requisition.

Regarding the latter, such authorisation checks would be undertaken to verify the authority of the purchase requisition issuer to issue/generate purchase requisitions and allocate the cost to the cost code or cost centre specified on the purchase requisition. Why? Put simply, to prevent the overspending budget holder/cost centre manager allocating the purchase requisition cost to another budget holder's/cost centre manager's cost code or cost centre! In addition, on transmission to the purchasing department each purchase requisition would be assigned a unique reference number.

## Using a paper-based purchase requisition system

Where a paper-based purchase requisition system is used, it is likely that all such purchase requisition documentation would be regarded as 'controlled stationery' – that is all such documentation would be pre-formatted and sequentially numbered, with the issue and use of such documentation requiring appropriate authorisation.

So how would such a system operate? It is likely that such a system would be either a two-copy or a three-copy system.

Using a two-copy purchase requisition system, one copy of the completed purchased requisition would be sent to the purchasing department, via the internal mail system, and one copy of the completed purchase requisition would be retained within the requisitioning department.

Using a three-copy purchase requisition system, one copy of the completed purchased requisition would be sent to the purchasing department, via the internal mail system, (as above) and two copies of the completed purchase requisition would be retained within the requisitioning department. One copy would be retained by the requisitioning department's administration section and one would be retained by the individual section head/section leader generating/instigating the purchase requisition. Such a system would normally be used in larger companies/organisations where requisitioning departments are comprised of a number of individual semi-autonomous sections and the responsibility for the generation of purchase requisitions is delegated to individual section heads/section leaders within the requisitioning departments.

## Purchase requisitions and commitment accounting

Where devolved budgets are used within a company/organisation, and budget holders/cost centre managers are able to issue purchase requisitions, it is likely that such requisitions would also be required to include details of the actual cost or, if these are not known, an estimated cost of the product/service being requested. Such an amount would then be committed against the budget holder's/cost centre manager's budget and would be replaced with the actual cost once the invoice for the purchase has been received from the product supplier/service provider. Such a system – known as a commitment accounting system – is designed to prevent budget holders/cost centre managers from incurring expenditure above their allocated budget limit and is common in public service organisations.

### Purchase order stage

As suggested above, once an approved/authorised purchase requisition has been received by the purchasing department within the company/organisation, a formal purchase order would be raised – assuming of course that the total cost of the purchase requisition does not exceed company/organisation purchase limits. Where the cost of the products/services exceeds the purchase limits imposed by the company/organisation purchasing policy, it may be necessary – in accordance with company/organisation policy – for the purchasing department to obtain a number of tenders for the supply/provision of the products/services requested.

For example, a company/organisation may require all purchase requisitions in excess of, say, £15,000 to be submitted for competitive formal tendering requiring three or four suppliers/providers to submit sealed bids for the supply of products/the provision of services. Once the formal bids have been received, and the successful tender has been awarded, a purchase order would be issued to the successful supplier/provider.

So what is a purchase order? A purchase order can be defined as a commercial document issued by a buying company/organisation to a supplier/provider (the selling company/organisation) indicating:

- the types of products/services ordered,
- the quantities of products/services ordered, and
- the agreed prices of the products/services ordered.

In addition, a purchase order would also include:

- a unique purchase order number,
- a unique supplier reference number,
- a requested delivery date,

| | | PURCHASE ORDER | | |
|---|---|---|---|---|
| Purchase no. .................... | | | Income address .................. | |
| Supplier name .................... | | | .................. | |
| Supplier no. .................... | | | .................. | |

| Purchase requisition no. | Materials/ components | Description | Unit cost (£) | Total cost (£) |
|---|---|---|---|---|
| | | | | |
| | | | | |
| | | | | |
| | | | | |

Prepared by .................

Authorisation .................

Please deliver to invoice address

**Example 9.2** A purchase order document

- an invoicing address,
- a delivery address requested terms, and
- the terms of references of the purchase order.

Example 9.2 shows a sample purchase order document.

The issue of a purchase order by the buying company/organisation to a product supplier/ service provider constitutes a legal offer to buy products and/or services. Acceptance of a purchase order by the selling company/organisation forms a one-off contract between the buying company/organisation and the selling company/organisation for the products/services ordered. However, it is important to note that no legal contract exists *until* the purchase order has been accepted by the selling company/organisation. So, how would the purchase order be issued?

As we saw earlier, many companies/organisations use authorised suppliers and/or providers – that is purchase orders are only issued to suppliers/providers who have been approved as suitable and appropriate for the company/organisation. Within a small or even a medium-sized company/organisation the issue of purchase orders will often be undertaken, monitored and controlled by a small number of administrative employees within the so-called 'purchase office'. However, within a large production/retail company/organisation, where:

- a substantial number of purchase orders are issued – on a regular basis, and/or
- the products/services ordered are of a highly technical/high complex nature,

it is likely that the buying company/organisation may employ specific purchasing agents/ buyers to issue such purchase orders to approved suppliers/providers – that is specialists who are responsible for either a specific type of product/service or a specific group/range of suppliers/providers.

More importantly, where:

- a large number of purchase orders are issued on a regular basis, and
- pre-approved companies/organisations are used as product suppliers/service providers,

it is more than likely that an electronic purchase order system would be used – using perhaps a secure EDI (Electronic Data Interchange) facility[10] and/or B2B (Business-to-Business) extranet facility.[11]

Why? For three key reasons: security, speed and cost.

Firstly, such facilities can provide a level of security not achievable with the traditional paper-based purchase order systems – for example data encryption facilities, transmission confirmation facilities and many more – all of which can minimise, although not totally eliminate, the possibility of confidential data (in our case purchase order data) going astray. Secondly, unlikely the traditional paper-based purchase order system in which the purchase order has to be physically delivered to the supplier/provider and can take a up to a number of days, the transmission and delivery of the purchase order is instantaneous (well almost). And thirdly, whilst the initial set-up costs of such a facility may be high, the cost per transaction is very small, certainly compared to the cost of a transaction using the traditional paper-based purchase order system.

### Using a computer-based purchase order system

Where a computer-based EDI/B2B facility is used to issue purchase orders, a copy purchase order would be transmitted to the product supplier/service provider and a copy purchase order, together with copy details of the transmission, and a copy transmission receipt (received from the product supplier/service provider) would be retained within the purchase office.

Once the purchase order has been transmitted to the supplier/provider, a purchase order confirmation would be issued, internally, and transmitted to:

- the budget holder/cost centre manager (the receiving department),
- the stores department, and
- creditor management department.

The purpose of the budget holder/cost centre manager receiving a purchase confirmation is twofold. Firstly, to confirm that an authorised purchase order for the requested products/ services has been sent to/transmitted to an approved supplier/provider and secondly to inform the budget holder/cost centre manager – the originator of the purchase requisition – precisely what products/service have been ordered from the supplier/provider. This latter point is extremely important inasmuch as it confirms any variations that may have been made to the original purchase requisition.

For example, variations could be:

- some of the requested products/services may no longer be available so substitute products/ services may have been ordered by the purchase office, or
- some of the requested products/service may not be available immediately so a number of part deliveries may occur in order to fulfil the purchase requisition.

The purpose of the stores department receiving a purchase order confirmation would be to alert the stores department of the forthcoming delivery of products and the need to update/amend the stores records.

The purpose of the creditor management department receiving a purchase order confirmation would be to alert the creditor management department of the purchase order and the forthcoming invoice.

## Using a paper-based purchase order system

Where a paper-based purchase order system is used within a company/organisation it would be likely that instead of a purchase order confirmation being issued and/or generated multiple copies of the purchase order would be produced and distributed as follows:

- one copy to the supplier/provider,
- one copy for the purchase office,
- one copy for the budget holder/cost centre manager (the receiving department),
- one copy for the stores department, and
- one copy for the creditor management department,

with the paper copies serving the same purpose as described above within a computer-based purchase order system.

What different types of purchase orders are there? There are, of course many different types, the main ones being:

- the single-use (one-off) purchase order, and
- the multi-use (or blanket) purchase order.

## Single-use (one-off) purchase order

A single-use (one-off) purchase order is used where it is important to keep track of a single purchase order from a supplier/provider – that is until all products/services contained in the purchase order have been received. Once all products/services have been received, and the purchase order has been fulfilled, the purchase order number becomes invalid and can no longer be used – usually for a substantial period of time.

## Multi-use (or blanket) purchase order

A multi-use (or blanket) purchase order is often used by companies/organisations where it is important to:

- monitor spending within a particular department/location within the company/organisation,
- monitor/record transactions with a specific supplier/provider,
- limit expenditure on a specific project, and/or
- limit expenditure to a specific timeframe.

### Outsourcing the product/service order system

There can be little doubt that in a commercial context, the effective management of the purchase/service order system is an essential prerequisite for business stability and financial success. However, such systems can be expensive to develop and difficult to maintain – especially where large volumes of purchase orders are generated on a regular basis. One option is to outsource some or all of the product/service order function and/or the stock management function(s), and use an externally managed stock system, often referred to as a Supplier Managed Inventory (SMI) system.

Whilst specific outsourcing arrangements would differ from organisation to organisation, in general an externally managed stock arrangement would normally constitute a form of agreed cooperation between a customer (the buying company/organisation), and a product supplier (the selling company/organisation) – an arrangement in which the customer agrees to share information with the supplier. As part of the agreement:

- the customer agrees to transfer all purchase order functions, and
- the supplier accepts responsibility for replenishing the customer's stock to within agreed, pre-determined limits/levels – based on information supplied by the customer.

Where the customer's internal control systems require the production of a purchase order, such a document would be generated automatically by the supplier, based on the replenishment information provided by the customer.

So what if a company/organisation uses a number of product suppliers/service providers? There is no reason why it could not enter into an agreement with a number of product suppliers/service providers, with each agreement referring to a different range of products/services used by it.

For the customer – that is the buying company/organisation – the main benefits/advantages include:

- a reduction in stock levels,
- an improvement in stock replenishment rates/procedures,
- a decrease in ordering costs,
- a decrease in holding costs, and
- an elimination of product/service ordering activities.

For the supplier – that is the selling company/organisation – the main benefits/advantages include:

- an improved visibility of customer requirements,
- a reduction in customer returns, and
- a long-term commitment from the customer.

The main problems/disadvantages are:

- the cost – such arrangements can be very expensive,
- the controls – to function effectively such arrangements not only require accurate and up-to-date data/information but, more importantly, continuous monitoring and assessment, and
- the commitment – such arrangements may require the customer (the buying company/organisation) to enter into a long-term agreement with the supplier (the selling company/organisation) thereby reducing customer choice and flexibility,

## Product/service receiving system

The purpose of the product/service receiving system is to ensure that:

- all authorised purchases of products/services are appropriately receipted,
- all purchased products are securely stored,
- all purchased services are used in accordance with the purchase requisition/purchase order, and
- all purchases are appropriately accounted for.

See Figure 9.5.

The key documentation for such a product/service receiving system would be:

- a delivery note – generated by the supplier, and
- a goods received note – or receiving report.

Whilst it is possible for a company/organisation to receive products/services at any number of locations, for our purposes we will assume that:

- all products received and accepted from approved product suppliers will be receipted into a centralised store facility, and
- all services received and accepted from approved service providers will be receipted at an operational/functional location within the company/organisation as requested in the purchase requisition and the purchase order.

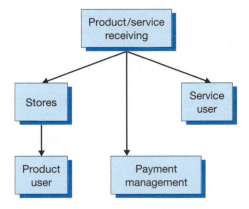

**Figure 9.5** Product/service receiving system

## Products received from approved product suppliers

Where products are received into a centralised store, such a store would – for security and control purposes – be comprised of a number of separate functions/activities. The most likely division/separation of duties within a centralised store would be:

- a store/stock receipting/issuing facility responsible for:
  - receiving products from the supplier/supplier's agent, and
  - issuing products to operational departments within the company/organisation as requested,
- a store/stock warehousing facility responsible for securely storing products within the store/stock warehouse, and
- a store/stock warehousing control facility responsible for recording and documenting the movement (the receipting and issuing) of products.

### Store/stock receipting/issuing facility

When receiving products from a supplier, the main function/responsibility of the store/stock receipt facility would be to confirm the quantity/quality of products and, where appropriate, accept the delivery of the products.

To confirm and accept the delivery of stock from a supplier/supplier's delivery agent, the store/stock receipting/issuing facility would need either:

- to access the purchase order to which the delivery relates if the purchase order system is computer-based, or
- to access a copy of the purchase order to which the delivery relates if the purchase order system in paper-based.

Primarily, the store/stock receipting/issuing facility would be responsible for:

- verifying that the purchase order number identified on the supplier's delivery note (the delivery note would be attached to/included with the delivery) is an appropriate and valid purchase order number,
- confirming that the supplier delivery note details correspond to the purchase order,
- checking the quantity of products received against the supplier delivery note, and
- assessing the quality of the products received from the supplier.

So, under what circumstances would the stock receipting facility reject a delivery? This would happen where, for example:

- the purchase order number identified on the supplier's delivery note does not correspond to a valid purchase order number, and/or
- a substantial number of the products delivered by the supplier/supplier's delivery agent have failed a quality inspection test[12] – that is the products are of an inferior quality, and/or
- a substantial number of the products delivered by the supplier/supplier's agent are damaged.

On rejection the delivery would be returned to the supplier via the supplier's delivery agent. However, where for example:

- an incorrect quantity of products have been received from the supplier/supplier's delivery agent,
- a small number of the products delivered by the supplier/supplier's delivery agent have failed a quality inspection test, and/or
- a small number of the products delivered by the supplier/supplier's delivery agent are damaged,

it is likely that – subject to the supplier's agreement – the delivery note would be amended to reflect the actual products accepted by the company/organisation and the incorrect products/damaged products would be returned to the supplier via the supplier's delivery agent.

Note: An adjustment note (often called a debit note) would need to be prepared to authorise the adjustment to be made to the supplier's invoice for the returned products (see the discussion below).

Once the products have been verified, approved and accepted from the supplier's delivery agent, and before the products are receipted into the central store within the store/stock warehousing facility, the store/stock receipting facility would allocate a product identification code/location marker for each of the products/groups of products received. Put simply:

- to manage and control the movement of stock into and out of the stock warehousing facility, and
- to monitor the movement of products within the stock warehousing facility.

Such product identification codes/location markers would of course vary from organisation to organisation and would primarily depend on:

- the size of the stock warehouse facility used by the company/organisation,
- the nature and type of products stored by the company/organisation and, of course,
- the degree of information technology used in the product/service ordering system and the product/service receiving system.

So what type of location markers could be used? These could vary from:

- a simple, hand-written or pre-printed product code/location marker, to
- a more sophisticated, pre-printed barcode-based product code/location marker, to
- a state of the art RFID tag (see Chapter 12).

Once the accepted products have been appropriately marked, coded or tagged, and routed into the central store, the store/stock receipting/issuing facility would prepare a goods received note (sometimes called a receiving report), listing and detailing the products accepted from the supplier/supplier's agent.

Where a computer-based purchase order/product receiving system is used, the purchase order would be authorised as complete, indicating the receipt of the products and the location of the products in the store/stock warehousing facility. This authorisation would automatically update the record of products in the store – often somewhat misleadingly referred to as the stores ledger.

Where a paper-based purchase order/product receiving system is used, a paper-based goods received note would be prepared, authorised and attached to the supplier delivery note and the purchase order. The documentation (the purchase order, the delivery note and the goods received note/receiving report) would then be forwarded to the store/stock warehousing control facility. This facility would be responsible for updating the record of products in the store (see below) and issuing products to operational departments within the company/organisation.

If you recall, we looked at the issue of store products to operational departments within the company/organisation in detail in Chapter 8 – in particular the use of store issue requests.

### Store/stock warehousing facility

Once in the central store of the store/stock warehousing facility, the products would be stored in the locations required by the product mark, code or tag. Where substantial numbers of products are received on a regular basis it would be normal for such a procedure to be substantially automated, with little or no human intervention.

We will look at the use of automation technologies – in particular RFID-related technologies – in managing and controlling the storage and movement of products in greater detail in Chapter 12.

### Store/stock warehousing control facility

The store/stock warehousing control facility would be responsible for:

- maintaining an appropriate and adequate record of products in store,
- ensuring the store ledger provides an up-to-date reflection of the movement of products into, and products out of, the store/stock warehousing facility, and
- undertaking a periodic reconciliation of the stores ledger and the actual products in the store/stock warehousing facility – that is undertaking a regular physical stock count/product audit.

Where a computer-based purchase order system/product receiving system is used as indicated earlier, confirmation of delivery and authorisation of the receipt of the products would automatically update the record of products in the store.

Where a paper-based purchase order system/product receiving system is used, the receipt of the delivery note *and* an authorised goods received note/receiving report *and* the copy purchase note would allow the store/stock warehousing control facility to amend stock records accordingly. The updating would of course be based on the goods received note/receiving report prepared by the store/stock receipting facility which reflects the products accepted from the supplier, and not the supplier's delivery note which merely reflects the products delivered to the company/organisation by the supplier's delivery agent.

Once the updating has been complete, the documentation (the delivery note and the goods received note/receiving report) would be forwarded to the creditor management department.

#### Services received from approved service providers

So far we have considered issues related to the receipting of products from product suppliers. What about services purchased for an external service provider? As we saw earlier, such acquired services can be classified as either:

- a recurring acquired service, or
- a non-recurring acquired service.

### Recurring acquired service

For a recurring acquired service it is likely that a single generic purchase requisition/purchase order would be issued for a specific set of contractual/legal obligations.

Why? Consider the following.

*Because of the services they provide, SKB Medical Ltd and PST Ltd are both legally required to ensure all prospective employees are CRB (Criminal Records Bureau) checked prior to their appointment. SKB Medical Ltd provides private medical services for the NHS in the Manchester area and PST Ltd provides supply teachers for primary and junior schools in the East Yorkshire area. During 2006, SKB Medical Ltd requested 72 CRB checks and PST Ltd requested 69 CRB checks.*

*Whilst it would clearly be feasible for both SKB Medical Ltd and PST Ltd to issue a new purchase order each time a CRB check is requested and a fee becomes payable,[13] given the likely numbers involved it would perhaps be much more practical to use a single generic purchase order number – probably issued by the personnel department under the auspices of the personnel department budget holder (probably the personnel manager/human resources manager).*

For some recurring acquired services, payment would be required on the submission of a service request in advance of the service provision. Such is the case for a CRB check. For other recurring acquired services, payment would be required on completion of the service – usually on submission of a service provider's invoice. In such instances, it is important to confirm, prior to the processing of the service provider's invoice/account, that:

- a valid purchase request/purchase order exists authorising the acquisition of the service provision, and
- an appropriate level of evidence exists to verify that the service provision requested/ordered has been appropriately provided and completed satisfactorily.

### Non-recurring acquired service

For a non-recurring acquired service it is likely that an individual specific purchase requisition/ purchase order would be issued for each particular appointment. Why? Because each particular appointment would occur as a consequence of a specific management decision and would therefore be unique.

For all non-recurring acquired services, payment would normally be required on the successful provision and completion of the service, although in some instances where the service is provided over a substantial period of time – for example a payroll outsourcing contract say over a period of four years – interim payments would often be made to the service provider during the service provision period, usually on submission of a service provider's interim invoice or statement of account.

Clearly, for all non-recurring acquired services, it is important to confirm – prior to the processing of the service provider's completion and/or interim invoice/account – that a valid purchase request/purchase order exists authorising the acquisition of the service provision.

For interim payments, it would be necessary to confirm that sufficient evidence exists to verify that the service provision for which the interim payment has been requested has been satisfactorily completed and that any such interim payment is in accordance with the service provision agreement (or service level agreement).

For completion payments, it would be necessary to ensure that sufficient evidence exists to substantiate that the service provision has been appropriately provided and satisfactorily completed.

### Payment management system

The purpose of the payment management system is to ensure:

- the correct payment of invoices, and
- the adequate management of creditor accounts.

Such a payment management system would – for internal control purposes – be divided into two sub-systems:

■ a creditor creation (invoice receipting) sub-system, and
■ a creditor management sub-system.

See Figure 9.6.

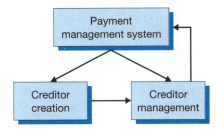

**Figure 9.6** Payment management system

### Creditor creation (invoice receipting)

The creditor creation (invoice receipting) sub-system is designed to ensure:

■ the verification and validation of the supplier's/provider's invoice, and
■ the documentation of all transactions in the company's/organisation's accounting records – that is either the creation of a creditor account for the supplier/provider or the amendment/updating of an existing supplier's/provider's account.

See Figure 9.7.

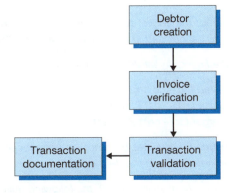

**Figure 9.7** Creditor creation (invoice receipting)

Essentially, the creditor creation (invoice receipting) sub-system would be responsible for all payment management aspects up to the payment of the invoice.

The key documentation of a creditor creation (invoice receipting) system would be:

■ an invoice, and
■ the creditor account.

### Verification/validation of the supplier's/provider's invoice

In general, the legal obligation to pay a product supplier/service provider for the supply/ provision of a product and/or service arises on the delivery, receipt and acceptance of the product and/or service – that is in a legal context a debt is created when the successful delivery of a product/service occurs. In practice, however, for the majority of business-related commercial transactions, such a debt is often only recognised when the invoice for the products and/or services is received from the product supplier/service provider because it is both easier and simpler to do so. More importantly, because the invoice date is often very close to the product/service delivery date – usually within a few working days, to use the invoice date for debt recognition purposes has very little impact, if any, on daily decision making. It must, however, be noted that where invoice-based debt recognition is used, adjustments are often required (for year-end accounting purposes) for purchases of products/services which occur shortly before the year-end date.

Consider the following.

*Aktil plc, is a UK-based manufacturing company whose accounting year end is 31 March 2007. The company receives deliveries of raw materials for use in its production process on a regular basis from a number of approved suppliers. During the last few days of March 2007/first few days of April 2007, the following transactions occurred:*

- *28 March 2007 a delivery of raw materials was received from Yeted Ltd, cost £13,670. The invoice was received on 31 March 2007.*
- *29 March 2007 a delivery of raw materials was received from Seltle Ltd, cost £30,450. The invoice was received on 5 April 2007.*
- *30 March 2007 a delivery of raw materials was received from Hargot Ltd, cost £16,960. The invoice was received on 4 April 2007.*
- *31 March 2007 an invoice was received from Telil Ltd for raw materials which were actually delivered on 2 April 2007. The cost of the raw materials was £2960.*
- *1 April 2007 a delivery of raw materials was received from Mecte plc, cost £9870. The invoice was received on 3 April 2007.*

*Which of the above deliveries should be included in the financial year 2006/07, and which should be included in the financial year 2007/08?*

*In the financial year 2006/07, the following deliveries would be included:*

- *Yeted Ltd – cost £13,670,*
- *Seltle Ltd – cost £30,450,*
- *Hargot Ltd – cost £16,960.*

*Although the invoices have not yet been received from the supplier, the raw materials have been delivered and the debt exists.*

*In the financial year 2007/08, the following deliveries would be included:*

- *Telil Ltd – cost £2960, and*
- *Mecte plc – cost £9870.*

The objective of the verification/validation process is to ensure that the payment of a supplier's/provider's invoice occurs only when the product(s) and/or service(s) have been received. Such verification/validation would normally involve a match between three documents:

- the purchase order (PO),
- the goods received note (GRN)/receiving report (RR), and
- the product supplier's/service provider's invoice.

Firstly, matching the invoice to the purchase order (PO) would:

■ verify the products/services were authorised and ordered from the product supplier/service provider, and
■ validate the cost and quantity of products/services included on the invoice.

Secondly, matching the invoice to the goods received note (GRN)/receiving report (RR) would:

■ verify the products/services have been received from the product supplier/service provider, and
■ verify the quantity/quality of products/services received from the product supplier/service provider.

This process is often referred to as the 'traditional three document' verification process.

So who would be responsible for undertaking such a verification process? Whilst the allocation would differ from organisation to organisation, it is common for such a verification process to be undertaken by an employee or a group of employees within the finance office – in particular within the purchase ledger section of the finance office. This would be for internal control purposes.

It is important to ensure that wherever possible the employee or employees undertaking the verification process are not involved in:

■ the product/service ordering process, or
■ the product/service receiving process.

### Creation/amendment of creditor account

Once the invoice has been verified and validated the transaction would need to be recorded in the company's/organisation's accounting records – that is the legally enforceable debt for the products/services would need to be established in the company/organisation accounting information system.

Remember the bookkeeping entries for such a transaction? In an accounting context, the transaction would be recorded in the general ledger as follows:

■ Dr purchases account,
■ Cr creditor control account.

A credit memorandum entry would also be made in the individual creditor's account in the purchases ledger (also known as the creditors ledger).

### New creditor

Where the transaction relates to a new creditor a new creditor account would need to be created. However, before a new creditor account can be created in the purchases ledger (creditors ledger) and the supplier/provider to which the account relates is assigned a creditor reference (account number), it is important to confirm that the supplier/provider is an approved product supplier/service provider for the company/organisation. This is because the use of unapproved product supplier/service providers could result in, for example:

■ the payment of higher than normal prices for products/services,
■ the loss of possible discounts,
■ the receipt of inferior quality products/services, and/or
■ the imposition of inappropriate settlement terms by the supplier/provider.

Put simply, if the supplier's/provider's details are not contained within the approved supplier/provider register/database (see earlier), it is important – for internal control purposes, systems security purposes, quality assurances purposes and, most importantly, fraud prevention purposes, to determine:

- how a transaction between an unapproved product supplier/service provider and the company/organisation occurred,
- why a transaction between an unapproved product supplier/service provider and the company/organisation occurred, and
- who authorised the transaction between an unapproved product supplier/service provider and the company/organisation.

Whilst possible explanations could range from:

- the obvious and the innocent – for example the supplier/provider register/database is not up-to-date, in which case procedures should be amended to ensure it is, to
- the sinister and the fraudulent – for example employees deliberately using unapproved suppliers/providers for their own personal gain and to the detriment of the company/organisation,

such transaction must, if at all possible, be eliminated.

Once established and verified, the new creditor account would be credited.

### Existing creditor

Where the transaction relates to an existing creditor, the existing creditor's account will be credited – that is amended to reflect the additional purchase – and the balance increased.

### Recording creditor account transactions

Using an online (3 stage) accounting system such accounting entries would be recorded for each transaction as it occurs or is approved. That is, individual creditor accounts (in the purchases ledger/creditors ledger) would be updated immediately. A summary purchases journal would be created as a control record of all the transactions recorded during a particular period. Using an online (3 stage) accounting system, a purchases journal would act as an 'after the event' control summary.

Using an online (4 stage) accounting system such accounting entries would also be recorded for each transaction. However, the creditor accounts would *not* be updated immediately. A purchases journal would be created as a control record to summarise all the transactions recorded during a particular period and would be used to update the individual creditor's account (in the purchases ledger/creditors ledger). That is, the individual creditor accounts would be updated as a batch of transactions. Using an online (4 stage) accounting system, a purchases journal would act as a 'before the event' control summary.

So, which is the preferred processing/recording option? As with the revenue cycle and the processing of debtor account receipts whilst online (4 stage) processing has been, and indeed still continues to be, the preferred processing system for many companies/organisations (probably because of its similarity to the traditional hard-copy-based batch processing system), the increasing use and availability of online (3 stage) accounting systems has undoubtedly increased the popularity of real-time processing.

#### Creditor management

The creditor management sub-system is designed to ensure:

- the processing of approved outstanding invoices,
- the payment of approved outstanding invoices,

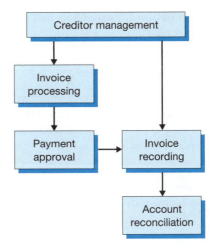

**Figure 9.8** Creditor management

- the recording of invoice payments,
- the adjustment/amendment of creditor accounts, and
- the effective and efficient management of creditor accounts – including the reconciliation of supplier/provider accounts.

See Figure 9.8.

Once the products/services have been supplied by/provided by the supplier/provider, and an invoice or statement of account (where invoices are used for information purposes only) has been received from the supplier/provider, it is important to ensure that payments are made in accordance with the terms and conditions agreed with the supplier/provider. This is because a failure to pay invoices at the appropriate time and in accordance with agreed conditions of payments could not only have a significant and long-term impact on a company's/ organisation's relationships with its product suppliers/service providers, it could also adversely affect its credit rating and therefore its ability to raise funds and/or obtain future finance/credit. More importantly, it could also result in financial loss where early payment discounts are available.[14]

The key documentation for such a creditor management system would be:

- a payment document and, where required,
- a debit memorandum (or refund note) – also known as a creditor account adjustment.

### Processing of approved outstanding invoices

There are generally two approaches that a company/organisation can use for the processing of approved invoices/statements of accounts, these being:

- a non-voucher system approach, or
- a voucher system approach.

### A non-voucher system approach

Within a non-voucher system each invoice as received and recorded (as above) would be stored in an open 'to be paid' file. (Remember invoices will be paper-based documents.) When the invoice is approved for payment, it would be removed from the open 'to be paid' file, processed for payment, marked paid and then stored in an invoice paid invoice file. Such a system is often used by smaller companies/organisations where a limited number of invoices are processed for payment.

## The voucher system approach

Within a voucher system, a disbursement voucher is prepared which lists the invoices to be paid, identifying the creditor account and the amount to be paid (after the deduction of applicable discounts and allowances). Such a system is often used by companies and organisations that process a large number of invoices for payment on a regular basis. Using a voucher-based system:

- reduces the number of payments to be made (invoices can be processed in batches), and
- provides a clear audit trail for the invoice processing and invoice payment procedures.

So how can a company/organisation submit payment to the supplier/provider on receipt of an invoice or statement of account?

### Payment of approved outstanding invoices

In a revenue cycle context, there are – as we saw in Chapter 8 – a number of alternative payment systems through which a company/organisation can receive payment from a customer/client. For example a debtor may submit payment in cash or by cheque (both of which are becoming increasingly rare), by EFT (electronic funds transfer) using a debit/credit card or indeed by bank transfer using BACSTEL-IP. Although the selection of the payment system is a customer/client decision, many companies/organisations now restrict the availability and use of cash-based and cheque-based systems by customers/clients.

In an expenditure cycle context, for purposes of administrative efficiency, internal control and, perhaps most importantly, financial security, the submission of payments to product suppliers/service providers should always be made by bank transfer (BACS) using BACSTEL-IP. This is especially the case where a company/organisation uses a voucher-based payment system to process payments to creditors.

Note: Payments to creditors using any other payment system – for example cheques, debit/credit card or cash – whilst clearly possible, should not normally be allowed because of internal and other costs.

Payment of creditor invoices by cheque whilst feasible is far too expensive. Remember, not only does the company/organisation have to pay for *each* cheque that it issues – incurring as a result a significant financial cost – it would also have to prepare, process and distribute each cheque it issues and reconcile the clearance of each cheque through its bank account – incurring a substantial administrative cost.

Payment of creditor invoices in cash whilst simple is clearly unrealistic, and from a security perspective far too risky. It is, as some companies/organisations suggest a zero benefit option! There are, put simply, no discernable benefits to either the paying company/organisation or the receiving company/organisation in using cash as a payment method – only risks!

Payment of creditor invoices by debit/credit card (using EFT) whilst possible is again unrealistic, with no significant benefits to either the paying or receiving company/organisation.

So how, using BACS, would an invoice payment be processed?

Let's assume a company/organisation uses a voucher system for the payment of invoices.

Once the disbursement voucher has been prepared, approved and authorised – usually by a senior manager within the creditor's department – to approve the transfer of cash funds from the company's/organisations bank account to the various product suppliers'/service providers' bank accounts it is then forwarded to the treasury department/cashier's office. The treasury department/cashier's office would review the content of the disbursement voucher. If no problems are identified, a senior manager within the treasury department/cashier's office would authorise the transfer of funds and electronically submit the payment file using the appropriate BACS protocols to the company's/organisation's bankers to enable the payments to be transferred to individual supplier/provider bank accounts. This file transfer would of course be encrypted and require authorisation by an assigned senior manager within the company/organisation.

Remember, the processing of payments is a four-stage processing procedure (arrival, input, process and output) within a three-day processing cycle,[15] comprising of:

- arrival day (arrival/input stage) – the receipt of a company's/organisation's payment/transfer file at BACS Payment Schemes,
- processing day (input and processing stage) – the acceptance and processing of all data through BACS Payment Schemes and transfer onto the paying banks, and
- entry day (output stage) – requested payments/transfers are simultaneously debited and credited to the relevant bank and/or building society accounts.

Once complete the disbursement voucher and associated documentation (e.g. BACS transfer receipt) would be forwarded to accounting for recording.

### Recording of invoice payments

Once payment has been made, it is of course important that the creditor account of the supplier/provider to which payment has been made is correctly amended and updated to reflect the payment. In an accounting context, the transaction would be recorded in the general ledger as follows:

- Dr creditor control account,
- Cr bank account.

Where an early payment discount is received, the transaction would be recorded in the general ledger as follows:

- Dr creditor control account,
- Cr discounts received,
- Cr bank account.

A debit memorandum entry would also be made in the individual creditor account in the purchase ledger (creditors ledger).

Where the submission of payments to product suppliers/service providers is made by bank transfer (BACS) using BACSTEL-IP, the creditor account could be updated online in real-time on payment of the funds (especially where the creditor account reference is transmitted with the transfer of funds): that is the above triple entry – the updating of the general ledger and the purchases ledger (creditors ledger) – would occur at the same time.

Where payment is made by cheque, the creditor account would be updated on the issue of the cheque and the payment of the funds – usually using an offline batch processing system.

### Creditor account adjustments/amendments

Occasionally, it may be necessary to adjust a supplier's/provider's creditor account. This is for three main reasons:

- errors in provision – for example products received from the supplier/provider may be returned because they are defective, incorrect or a service provided for a customer/client may have been incomplete or incorrect,

- errors in pricing – for example products received from the supplier/provider may have been inappropriately priced resulting in the supplier's/provider's invoice prices being either under- or over-stated, and
- errors in payment – for example:
  - an allocation error where payments made to a supplier/provider may have been recorded in or allocated to the wrong creditor account, or
  - a transposition error where payments made to a supplier/provider may have been recorded incorrectly (wrong amount).

In an accounting context:

- errors in provision would be recorded in the general ledger as follows:
  - Dr creditor control account,
  - Cr purchases account,
- under-pricing errors would be recorded in the general ledger as follows:
  - Dr purchases account,
  - Cr creditor control account,
- over-pricing errors would be recorded in the general ledger as follows:
  - Dr creditor control account,
  - Cr purchases account,
- allocation errors would be recorded as a contra entry in the general ledger as follows:
  - Dr creditor control account,
  - Cr creditor control account,
- transportation errors would be recorded in the general ledger as follows:
  - Dr creditor control account,
  - Cr sales account.

Of course, in addition to the above, a debit and/or credit memorandum entry would also be required in the individual creditor accounts in the purchase ledger (creditor ledger).

As with the revenue cycle and adjustments to debtor accounts, it is important – from an internal control context – that any adjustment to the creditor accounts is:

- appropriately authorised – usually by a financial accounting manager, and
- properly documented – using a journal to record the accounting entry.

### Creditor account management and the reconciliation of supplier/provider accounts

Where a large volume of creditor-based transactions occur or where a large number of supplier/provider accounts exist, periodically is it necessary to reconcile the balance in the creditor control account in the general ledger, and the total of the individual creditor account balances in the purchases ledger (creditors ledger) to:

- authenticate the outstanding balance on individual creditor accounts, and
- confirm the correctness of the balance of the creditor control account in the general ledger.

It is important that a company/organisation identifies and corrects any errors that may exist between the creditor control account in the general ledger and the total of the individual creditor account balances in the purchases ledger (creditors ledger).

In a practical context, the reconciliation between the creditor control account in the general ledger and the total of the individual creditor account balances in the purchases ledger (creditors ledger) is often an automated procedure. Indeed, many contemporary financial accounting packages not only allow user companies/organisations to select the frequency of such a reconciliation, they also allow user companies/organisations to determine – based on the nature of the error discovered – the remedial action to be taken to correct the error(s).

Whilst such an automated reconciliation process does have many advantages, for example it minimises:

- the level of human intervention in the reconciliation process, and
- the overall cost of the reconciliation exercise,

it is important that management is aware of the results of each reconciliation, since an excessive level of errors could indicate a serious information management/internal control issue. As a result, many contemporary 'off-the-shelf' financial accounting system allow user companies/organisations to create customised reconciliation reports, detailing for example:

- the accounting period covered by the reconciliation,
- the number of errors identified during the reconciliation,
- the value of the errors identified during the reconciliation,
- the creditors to which the errors relate,
- the nature of/reason for the errors identified, and
- the remedial action taken (if any), to correct errors identified.

### *Electronic invoicing and invoice-less payment processing*

### Electronic invoicing

To reduce administrative bureaucracy, streamline processing costs and improve invoice processing, some companies/organisations now receive invoices electronically using EDI. This allows the company/organisation to automate its invoice verification process and use computer-based verification for the matching of the purchase order (PO), the goods received note (GRN)/receiving report (RR) and the product supplier's/service provider's invoice. Only those invoices which fail the automated computer-based verification process would require manual verification – so-called manual verification by exception.

The advantages of electronic invoicing are greater efficiency, more effective invoice processing and, of course, substantially lower invoice verification costs.

### Invoice-less payment processing

A logical extension of electronic invoicing is of course invoice-less payment processing[16] – that is the total elimination of the invoice. The use of invoice-less payment procedures has become increasingly popular between companies/organisations which have a long-standing and successful trading relationship with product suppliers/service providers and have integrated processing cycles.

So, how does invoice-less invoicing work? Unlike the traditional three-document matching system, using the purchase order (PO), the goods received note (GRN)/receiving report (RR) and the product supplier's/service provider's invoice, invoice-less invoice processing is a two-document matching system – using only the purchase order (PO) and the goods received note (GRN)/receiving report (RR). And how does invoice-less payment processing work? Have a look at Figure 9.9.

For many of the purchases undertaken by a company/organisation, the prices of the products/services being purchased are already known with certainty. This is especially the case where an approved list of product suppliers/services providers is used. As a consequence, as soon as the

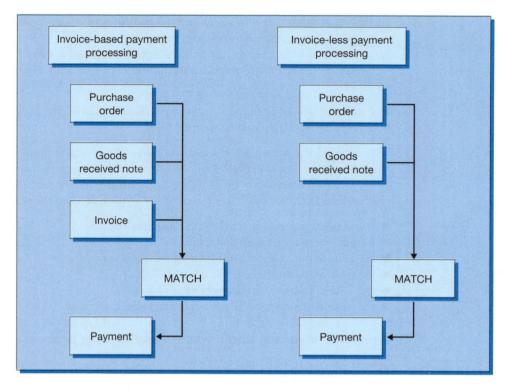

**Figure 9.9** Invoice-less payment processing – information flow

products have been received/the services have been delivered, and such receipt/delivery has been verified, payment can be made, with only those invoices failing the verification process requiring manual processing. Obviously for such invoice-less payment processing to function adequately, it is critical that:

- accurate and up-to-date product/service prices are available from suppliers/providers to ensure correct prices are quoted for the products/service ordered, and
- comprehensive receipting/inspection procedures are used by the purchasing company/ organisation to ensure products/service are delivered as requested.

The advantages of invoice-less payment processing are reduced documentation processing and therefore substantially lower administration costs.

## Creditor-based expenditure cycle – risks

As with the debtor-based revenue cycle, any failure in processes and controls associated with the creditor-based expenditure cycle could have significant consequences for the company/ organisation, and could result in:

- a loss of company/organisation assets,
- a loss of data/information,
- a loss of suppliers/providers and, perhaps most importantly,
- a loss of revenue income (and profits).

## Supplier selection/approval system

A failure within the supplier selection/approval system could result in:

- the purchasing of products/services from unapproved or unauthorised suppliers/providers,
- the purchasing of products at inflated prices, and/or
- the purchasing of inferior quality products.

In addition, the failure of supplier selection/approval procedures could allow unauthorised persons to gain access to the supplier or provider register/database, and result in:

- the creation of fictitious supplier/service provider profiles,
- the possible theft of confidential supplier/service provider data,
- the potential misappropriation of assets, and/or
- possible infection/corruption of data/system files.

## Product/service ordering system

A failure within the product/service ordering system of a company/organisation could result in:

- the issue of fictitious purchase orders,
- the issue of unauthorised purchase orders, and/or
- the issue of unnecessary orders – resulting in excessive stocks of products.

In addition, the failure of retailing system security procedures/access protocols could allow unauthorised persons to gain access to secure product/service ordering systems, and result in:

- the issue of fraudulent purchase orders, and
- the possible theft of assets.

## Product/service receiving system

A failure within the product/service receiving system of a company/organisation could result in:

- the under-/over-delivery of products/services,
- the early/late receipt of products/services,
- the loss or damage of products, and/or
- the theft of products.

## Payment management system

A failure within the payment management system could result in:

- the inefficient processing of payments to products/services,
- the inappropriate processing of product supplier/service provider documentation,
- the possible under-/over-charging by product suppliers/service providers,
- the incorrect accounting for purchase transactions,
- the possible omission of creditors liabilities,
- the inadvertent violation of supplier/provider settlement policies, and
- the unauthorised and/or fraudulent alteration of payment documentation.

In addition, the improper management of creditor accounts and/or the failure of payment management security procedures/access protocols could allow unauthorised persons to gain access to creditor account details resulting in:

- the possible amendment and/or alteration to creditor ledger files, and/or
- the corruption of creditor ledger files.

## Non-creditor-based expenditure cycle

As we saw earlier, non-creditor-based expenditure transactions can be classified as either:

- cash-based expenditure, or
- card-based expenditure.

### Cash-based expenditure

Cash-based expenditure is sometimes referred to as petty cash expenditure because such expenditure is often only concerned with small value purchases, for example office stationary items and employee-based expenses such as travel costs. Whilst such expenditure is perhaps inevitable – emergencies arise despite the best planning – for both internal control and, more importantly, cash flow/cash management purposes, the excessive use of cash-based expenditure should, where at all possible be:

- closely monitored,
- reduced to a minimum,
- restricted to very small value products and services.

Note: There are no legal restrictions on what a company/organisation can/cannot pay out of petty cash. However for Revenue and Customs purposes, wages and/or wage-related expenses should *never* be paid from the petty cash.

We will look at the use of petty cash systems – in particular petty cash imprest systems – in detail in Chapter 11.

### Card-based expenditure

The use of card-based expenditure has become increasingly popular in some companies/organisations – especially in B2B retailing. Why? For a number of business-related reasons/benefits, perhaps the most important being more efficient and effective financial administration.

So what is card-based expenditure? Such expenditure is normally employee-based expenditure – expenditure which occurs where an authorised employee, usually a mid-level manager, is allowed to incur expenses using a company/organisation charge or credit card.

So, what is the difference between a company/organisation charge card, and credit card? A company charge card account balance would be paid in full by the company at the end of the account period, usually by direct debit, and as such no interest is chargeable. With a credit card account, 45 days' interest-free credit is provided, with the flexibility for the company to decide how much will be paid. Of course, any balance which exists after the 45-day period will of course be subject to interest charges.

Charge/credit cards can be used for:

- business-related accommodation costs,
- business-related travel expenses, or, where appropriate,
- customer/client entertainment expenses.

Whilst many, if not all, companies/organisations which operate such card-based expenditure schemes impose fairly stringent limits/restrictions on:

- what can be regarded as legitimate expenditure, and
- how much an employee may spend (a card limit),

any card-based scheme which allows individual employees to incur/authorise expenditure on behalf of the company/organisation requires close monitoring for obvious reasons!

## Non-creditor-based expenditure cycle – risks

Whenever cash- or card-based expenditure is incurred, there are inevitably risks. Such risk would include:

■ the purchasing of unauthorised products/services,
■ the purchasing of non-business-related products/services, and
■ the misappropriation of cash assets.

## Expenditure cycle – internal control and systems security

As we have seen, the key processing requirements of a company's/organisation's expenditure cycle – in particular the creditor-based expenditure cycle but also, where appropriate, the non-creditor-based expenditure cycle, is to ensure:

■ all products and services ordered are needed/required by the company/organisation,
■ all invoices are appropriately verified and validated before payment is made,
■ all available discounts are identified and used/obtained if economically justified,
■ all purchase returns and allowances are authorised,
■ all payments are made for authorised expenditure only, and
■ all payments are recorded and classified promptly and accurately.

More importantly, it is to ensure:

■ the existence of adequate operational policies, procedures and controls,
■ the adoption of appropriate supplier/provider selection and approval procedures,
■ the accurate processing of all transactions,
■ the correctness of transaction-based activity reports,
■ the appropriate authorisation of payments to creditors,
■ the regular reconciliation of expenditure transactions and supplier/provider accounts – for example the use of control accounts,
■ all payments are made in accordance within supplier/provider settlement conditions/credit terms.

The key control requirements being to ensure, where at all possible:

■ the appropriate use of control documentation,
■ the existence of appropriate authorisation procedures for:
  ● the acquisition of products, services and resources,
  ● the collection of data, and
  ● the dissemination of information,
■ the adherence to supplier/provider payment policies and settlement conditions,
■ the existence of adequate internal control procedures and internal security procedures to safeguard assets and resources, and
■ the existence of adequate structures of responsibility and of accountability.

As with revenue cycle activities (see Chapter 8) in a practical context such internal controls can be categorised as either general controls or application specific (expenditure cycle specific) controls.

## General controls

General controls applicable to the expenditure cycle could be categorised as:

- organisational controls,
- documentation controls,
- access controls,
- liability management controls,
- management practice controls, and
- information systems controls.

### Organisational controls

Within the expenditure cycle such controls should ensure that there is a separation of duties between:

- those involved in activities related to the authorising of expenditure transactions,
- those involved in the receiving of products/services from suppliers/providers,
- those involved in storing purchased products – that is undertaking a custodial function,
- those involved in activities relating to the making of payments to suppliers/providers,
- those involved in the management of creditor accounts, and
- those involved in the recording of financial transactions.

In addition, as we saw with the revenue cycle, there should also be a separation of duties between:

- systems development personnel, and
- systems operations personnel.

That is between:

- those involved in the creation and/or modification of expenditure cycle programs, and
- those involved in the day-to-day expenditure cycle activities and processes.

### Documentation controls

Complete and up-to-date documentation should be available for all expenditure cycle procedures. Such documentation should include, for example:

- organisational charts detailing the responsibility structure within the expenditure cycle and the separation/segregation of duties within each of the expenditure cycle systems,
- procedural descriptions of all procedures and processes used within the expenditure cycle,
- systems flowcharts detailing how functions/activities within the expenditure cycle operate,
- document flowcharts detailing what documents flow within expenditure cycle systems,
- management control procedures/internal control procedures detailing the main internal controls within the expenditure cycle,
- user guides/handbook providing a broad overview of the main functions/activities within the expenditure cycle, and
- records of recent internal/external audits undertaken on individual expenditure cycle systems.

### Access controls

Where information and communication technology is used as an integral part of the expenditure cycle systems and activities, it is important – for both internal control and security purposes – to ensure that:

- assigned users' names and passwords are used to authenticate users and authorise access to expenditure cycle transaction data and supplier/provider information,

- location and/or terminal restrictions are used – where appropriate – to control access to expenditure cycle-based data/information – for example confidential creditor account information should only be accessible by appropriate staff (finance staff) at approved locations (e.g. within the finance office), and
- transaction data/information is securely stored with access to both current transaction files/master files and back-up copies of all transactions files/masters files restricted.

### Liability management controls

Such controls would generally involve the use of appropriate control records and the periodic reconciliation of such control records to underlying physical liabilities: for example a reconciliation of the balance in the creditor's control account in the general ledger and the total of the creditor account balances in the purchases ledger (creditors ledger).

### Management practice controls

In general, such management practices controls would include for example:

- regular employee training on expenditure cycle systems/procedures,
- regular personal checks/assessments, and
- the use of internal audit in monitor expenditure cycle activities.

### Information systems controls

In general, such information systems controls would include for example:

- the efficient scheduling of data processing activities relating to the purchase of products, services and/or resources and the recording of expenditure payments,
- the appropriate authorising of all data/information processing procedures, and
- the effective management and use of information and communication systems resources.

## Application controls

As with all application controls, those applicable to the expenditure cycle can be categorised as input controls, processing controls and output controls.

### Input controls

Expenditure cycle input controls are designed to ensure the validity, correctness and appropriateness of expenditure cycle specific input data.

Such controls would include:

- appropriateness checks – for example:
  - data matching checks to ensure the consistency of data (e.g. comparing payments with supplier/provider invoice/statement of account), and
  - data entry/data validity checks to confirm that input data is within expected parameters and in the correct format,
- authorisation procedure checks – for example supplier/provider identification checks,
- conversion controls tests, record count checks and/or completeness checks – for example batch control totals, sequence totals and/or hash control totals, to ensure all data is processed, and
- error tests/error correction procedure checks to ensure all incorrect data is identified and appropriately dealt with.

Where input data is transmitted from a source origin to a processing destination electronically, additional supplementary input controls would normally be required. Such controls would include for example:

- transmission tests – to ensure the completeness of the transmission,
- security checks – to ensure the authenticity of the customer/client and the legitimacy of the transmission, and
- validity checks – to ensure/confirm the completeness of the transaction data.

### Processing controls

Expenditure cycle processing controls are designed to ensure only authorised expenditure cycle transaction data are processed and such data are processed accurately, correctly and completely. Such controls would include for example:

- file maintenance checks – to ensure that both creditor file records and transaction records are efficiently maintained,
- file labelling checks – to ensure all expenditure cycle data files are correctly labelled,
- verification checks – to ensure all expenditure cycle transaction data is validated and approved prior to processing,
- processing logic checks – to ensure that the actual processing steps by which data are transformed or moved are consistent with defined procedures/protocols,
- limit checks – to ensure that all expenditure cycle transaction data exist within defined processing parameters (e.g. value of transaction, data of transaction),
- reasonableness checks – to ensure that expenditure cycle transaction data are consistent with processing expectations,
- sequence checks – to ensure that no interruptions or gaps exist in the sequence of transaction data processed,
- audit trail controls – to ensure that a visible trail of evidence and/or chronology of events is available enabling the tracing of transaction events,
- control totals checks – to check that expenditure cycle transaction file control totals are consistent with the contents of the transaction file to which they relate, and
- data checks – to check for the existence of duplicate and/or missing data.

### Output controls

Expenditure cycle output controls are designed to ensure all expenditure cycle output is authorised, accurate and complete, and distributed to approved and authorised recipients only. Such controls would include for example:

- distribution controls to ensure creditor payments are made to the correct supplier/provider,
- verification controls to ensure the validity and accuracy of output information,
- reconciliation checks to ensure all transaction numbers are accounted for, and
- review/audit trail checks.

Where output data is transmitted from a processing origin to a user destination electronically (e.g. payments to suppliers/providers), additional supplementary output controls would normally be required. Such controls would include for example:

- transmission tests to ensure that data are transmitted correctly,
- recipient identifier checks/controls to authenticate the recipient before the delivery of data/information,
- security checks/controls to ensure data/information is delivered completely, and
- validation checks/controls to ensure data/information is received and access by the authorised recipient only.

## Expenditure cycle – capital expenditure

Capital expenditure is concerned with the purchase of both tangible and intangible fixed assets for retention and use within the company/organisation. The objectives of the capital expenditure cycle/fixed assets management are to ensure, *inter alia*, that:

- all fixed asset acquisitions and disposals are properly planned, suitably evaluated, appropriately approved (with supporting documentation) and accurately recorded,
- all fixed asset transactions (including the allocation of depreciation expenses) are properly recorded, monitored and controlled,
- all fixed assets accounting records are accurately maintained and regularly updated,
- all acquired fixed assets are securely maintained (and periodically reconciled/reviewed), and
- all appropriate property titles/custody rights to such fixed assets are obtained, and securely stored.

We will look at capital expenditure/fixed assets management in more detail in Chapter 11.

## Expenditure cycle – information requirements

As we saw earlier, the primary objective of a company/organisation expenditure cycle – whether creditor-based or non-creditor-based, is to minimise the total cost of acquiring and maintaining the products/services required for the company/organisation to function effectively, whilst maintaining the good image of the company/organisation.

As with the revenue cycle in Chapter 8, to do so successfully requires more than just an appropriate level of resources or collection of processes, procedures and protocols: it requires information, in particular expenditure cycle information. This can be used to, for example:

- identify appropriate product suppliers/service providers,
- assess the efficiency of purchase ordering activities,
- assess the effectiveness of stock receipting procedures,
- verify the accuracy of supplier/provider invoicing, and
- determine the appropriateness and effectiveness of payment management procedures.

So what type of expenditure cycle information would a company/organisation use/require?

Although there are many ways in which such information requirements can be categorised, as with the revenue cycle we will categorise such information as follows:

- period-based activity information,
- period-based performance information, and
- activity analysis information.

### Period-based activity information

Period-based activity information is operational level information relating to specific systems/processes/activities during a particular week or month, and would include for example:

- the number of supplier/provider orders issued,
- the number of invoices received,
- the number credit notes received and/or refunds requested,
- the level of discounts claimed and received, and
- the number of payments made.

## Period-based performance information

Period-based performance information is tactical level information measuring the efficiency and effectiveness of expenditure cycle processes and procedures during a particular week or month, and would include for example:

- supplier/provider response times,
- supplier/provide credit periods,
- purchase order fulfilment times, and
- product/service delivery times.

## Activity analysis information

Activity analysis information is strategic level information measuring/assessing the relative success or otherwise of expenditure cycle-related activities and would include for example:

- supplier/provider characteristics analysis,[17]
- supplier/provider performance analysis,
- supplier/provider product/service quality analysis,
- payment trend analysis,
- expenditure cycle efficiency analysis, and
- stock movement/stock management analysis.

## Expenditure cycle – human resource management/payroll

As suggested earlier, the human resource-related expenditure cycle[18] (or payroll cycle) can be defined as a collection of business-related activities/resources and information processing procedures concerned with ensuring the timely and appropriate compensation of company/organisation employees. It is directly related to the company/organisation Human Resource Management (HRM) cycle (or personnel cycle) whose primary objective can be defined as the effective management and development of the company's/organisation's employee workforce, and would include procedures, processes and controls associated with:

- the recruitment of new employees,
- the training of current employees,
- the assignment of work-related tasks,
- the evaluation of employee performance and, of course,
- the voluntary and/or involuntary discharge of employees.

Whilst there can be little doubt that the employee workforce of a company/organisation – whatever its context type – represents an important, valuable and wealth creating asset/resource, its value is (quite rightly) only recognised when the asset/resource has been consumed/used. Because unlike other assets/resources within a company/organisation which are generally owned by the company/organisation, employees are not 'owned'. They are, in general, employed for the services/skills they can provide and the contribution and added value they can bring to the company's/organisation's activities. Although there are some categories of employees whose contractual obligations can be, and indeed often are, sold or transferred from one company/organisation to another such employees are the exception rather than the norm.

Perhaps the most common example of the sale of an employee would be the transfer of a professional footballer from one football club (e.g. AC Milan) to another (e.g. Chelsea). See Article 9.2 below.

## Article 9.2

### Shevchenko completes record £31m move as Mourinho gets his man

Jose Mourinho was last night celebrating 'a day when the dream became reality' as he finally signed Andriy Shevchenko from Milan.

Chelsea did not disclose the fee but it is understood to be a British record €45m (£30.8m) and ends the club's years-long pursuit of the Ukraine striker.

'Andriy has always been my first choice for Chelsea since I arrived,' Mourinho said. 'Before it was not possible, now it is for real. He has great qualities, ambition, discipline, tactical awareness and of course he is a great goalscorer.'

Source: Matt Scott and Jon Brodkin,
1 June 2006, The *Guardian*,
http://football.guardian.co.uk/News_Story/
0,,1787328,00.html.

Before we look at the HRM/payroll cycle in greater detail, it is useful firstly to identify the source of major inputs into, and the destination of its major outputs from, the HRM/payroll cycle, and, secondly to consider the role/function of a company's/organisation's accounting information systems in the efficient functioning of an HRM/payroll cycle.

The major sources of HRM/payroll cycle inputs would be:

- company/organisation departments (e.g. the HRM department) – information on recruitment/ appointments, conditions of employment, termination of employment and details on employee deductions, hours worked and/or products produced,
- government agencies – information on income tax and National Insurance deductions/ payments, employment laws, rules and regulations (including health and safety),
- other non-statutory bodies (e.g. trade unions) – information on conditions of employment, rates and pay, etc., and
- employees – information on/authorisation of voluntary deductions (e.g. savings schemes, charitable donations and/or pension contributions).

The major destination of HRM/payroll cycle outputs would be:

- company/organisation departments (including the HRM department) – information on staffing/employment levels and budget commitments,
- company/organisation departments (in particular accounting and finance) – information on both employee payments and payments to other statutory/non-statutory agencies,
- employees – payment of net pay,
- government agencies – payment of income tax and National Insurance, and the provision of statutory payroll information, and
- insurance companies/pension funds – payments of employee and, where appropriate, employer contributions.

Note: Whilst the above lists of sources and destinations are by no means exhaustive, they do however provide a representative sample of the main sources and destinations found in the majority of companies/organisations.

So what function(s) does a company's/organisation's accounting information system provide/ play in the efficient functioning of a company/organisation HRM/payroll cycle?

## The accounting information systems connection

In general, the precise nature of the functions provided and activities undertaken by a company/organisation accounting information system in relation to the HRM/payroll cycle would differ from company/organisation to company/organisation. Whilst companies and organisations may appear to be similar – their structure, composition and ownership may imply a degree of similarity, such similarities will often only exist at a very superficial level. As we have seen, companies/organisations are more than just a legal construct designed to manage the ownership of an abstract collection of resources and assets. They are a complex inter-relationship – a complex and unique combination of hard and soft systems. Irrespective of whether a company/organisation is:

- owned by another company/organisation and thus belongs to a specific group of companies/organisations,
- designed to provide a specific function/service and thus belongs to a particular industry/economic sector, or
- required to comply with and operate within a prescribed regulatory framework,

in terms of HRM/payroll, the nature and context of the functions/activities provided by the accounting information systems would invariably depend upon a number of key organisational features/characteristics, for example:

- the type of employees comprising the company/organisation workforce – for example professionally qualified employees, skilled technicians, semi-skilled operators or manual/unskilled employees,
- the payment process used by the company/organisation – for example employees may be paid in cash, by cheque or by BACS transfer,
- the basis on which employees are compensated/remunerated – for example time-based remuneration, production-based remuneration or a fixed rate remuneration,
- the frequency at which employees are paid/compensated – for example employees can be paid by weekly wages or by monthly[19] salary, and
- the nature of the payroll process – for example a positive payroll[20] or a negative payroll.[21]

That said, in an HRM/payroll context, certainly for companies/organisations operating within the UK, within Europe and indeed within much of the USA, the company's/organisation's accounting information system is seen as providing three basic functions/support activities, these being:

- the processing of transaction data relating to the remuneration of employees,
- assisting in the safeguarding of company/organisation assets, and
- the provision of payroll-related information for decision-making purposes.

## Processing of payroll transaction data

To fully understand the processing of payroll transaction data, it would perhaps be useful to understand:

- *who* is involved in the processing of payroll payments, and
- *what* is involved in the processing of payroll payments

### Departments involved in payroll

In general, the main company/organisation departments that are likely to be involved, either directly or indirectly, in:

- the maintenance of payroll data/information,
- the preparation of the weekly/monthly payroll, and
- the payment of wages and/or salaries to employees,

would include:

- the personnel (or HRM) department,
- the production department (or employing department),
- the payroll department,
- the treasury department/cashier,
- the (management) accounting department for cost control/budgeting, and
- the (financial) accounting department for general ledger control.

We will look at what each of these departments do and then consider the relevance of their activities to the functions/service support provided by the company's/organisation's accounting information system.

## Personnel (or HRM) department

The personnel (or HRM) department would be responsible for or involved in some, if not all, of the following:

- the advertising of staff/employee vacancies,
- the assessment/filtering of suitable applications,
- the arrangement of staff/employee interviews,
- the arrangement of induction training for new staff/employees,
- the arrangement and provision of training and education for existing employees,
- the management and coordination staff/employee evaluations and reviews,
- the maintenance of payroll master file data and, where appropriate,
- the provision of personnel/payroll data/information for both internal managers and approved external users.

## Production department (or employing department)

The production department (or employing department) would be responsible for:

- the issue of time cards and/or job cards to employees – where employees are paid by the hour or by the number of goods produced (normally associated with weekly paid staff),
- the issue of time sheets – where employees are paid a fixed salary (normally associated with monthly paid staff),
- the collection of employee time cards/job cards/time sheets, and
- the authorisation of hours worked/goods produced by employees.

## Payroll department

The payroll department would be responsible for:

- the preparation of the weekly/monthly payroll, including the calculation of:
  - employee gross pay based on hours worked/goods produced,
  - employee deductions (both statutory and voluntary deductions), and
  - employee net pay,
- the preparation of employee pay advices, and
- the issue of a payroll payment requisition, forwarded to the treasury department/cashier.

### Treasury department/cashier

The treasury department/cashier would be responsible for:

- the preparation of the payroll payments,
- the financing of the payroll payments, and
- the authorisation of payment transfers to individual employee accounts (assuming wages are paid to employees using the BACS payment system).

The treasury department/cashier would also be responsible for authorising the payment of income taxes, National Insurance Contributions and pension deductions to relevant third parties, in addition to any other voluntary deductions (e.g. an employee SAYE (Save As You Earn scheme)), and/or other statutory imposed deductions (e.g. County Court imposed attachment of earnings deductions).[22]

### Management accounting department – cost control/budgeting

The management accounting department would be responsible for:

- the profiling of payroll budgets (as agreed with departmental managers/budget holders,
- the allocation/posting of payroll payments to departmental payroll budgets,
- the comparison of departmental payroll budgets to actual payroll expenditure,
- the preparation of budgets statements for departmental managers/budget holders, and
- the distribution of budget statements (usually monthly) to departmental managers/budget holders.

### Financial accounting department – general ledger control

The financial accounting department would be responsible for:

- the creation of journal entries for the posting of the payroll payments (whether weekly or monthly) within the company's/organisation's financial accounting system,
- the authorisation of the financial accounting entries, and
- the reconciliation of actual payroll payments (as authorised by the treasury department/ cashier) and financial accounting entries.

So now we know who would be involved in the payroll process, how would the payroll be prepared?

#### Payroll procedures – general arrangements

Note: What follows is a description of a generic payroll procedure – a procedure that includes all the major stages one would normally expect to find within the payroll procedure of a medium-sized company/organisation. It does not necessarily represent a model payroll procedure. Remember the payroll procedures used by individual companies/organisations may well differ and whilst these differences may well appear substantial their occurrence cannot be used as a measure of the correctness of a particular system/procedure. Providing appropriate internal controls and system security measures are present within a company's/organisation's payroll procedures, the existence of such differences merely means they are just that and nothing else!

### Payroll – the last bastion of batch processing

Whilst many accounting-related information systems have, over the past 20 years, become online-based processing systems, the processing of payroll payments has continued to remain the last bastion of batch processing, inasmuch as their processing and the compensation of employees (that is the payment of wages and salaries) continues to be based on the collection/ batching of employee-based data (hours worked/goods produced).

The payroll procedure can be divided into three main stages:

■ the pre-payment stage, which would include:
  ● the maintenance and updating of payroll master file data, and
  ● the validation and allocation of departmental payroll budgets – including the determination of employee staffing levels,
■ the payment stage, which would include:
  ● the collection and validation of time/attendance data or goods produced data (depending on how employees are remunerated), and
  ● the preparation of the payroll and the validation of payroll deductions (both statutory and voluntary), and
■ the post-payment stage, which would include:
  ● the disbursement of payments to employees,
  ● the accounting for and reconciliation of payroll payments, and
  ● the disbursement of statutory and voluntary deductions.

See Figure 9.10.

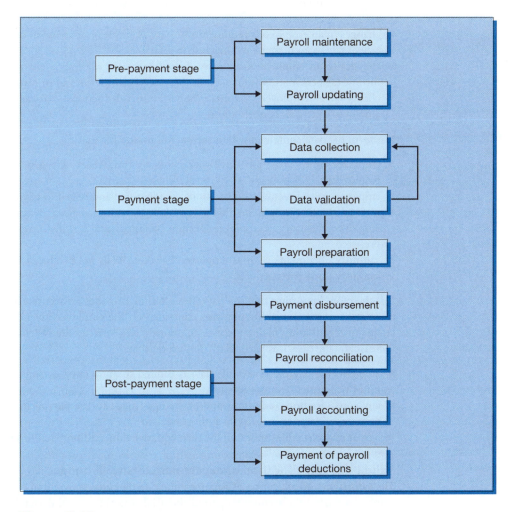

**Figure 9.10** Payroll

## Maintenance and updating of payroll master file data

The first activity in the HRM/payroll cycle is the creation of an employee personnel record – that is a permanent payroll master file record on each member of staff employed by the company/organisation. Such a permanent master file record would contain details such as:

- the employee reference number[23] – a unique number for each employee,
- the name and home address of the employee,
- the current remuneration rate of the employee,
- the current qualifications of the employee – if relevant,
- the current status of the employee (e.g. active, suspended or terminated),[24]
- the location of employment within the company/organisation of the employee – including where appropriate the employee title/reference currently assigned to the employee, and
- the current level of both statutory and non-statutory deductions to be made from the employee's wage/salary.

The payroll master file should be regularly updated to take into account:

- new appointments, terminations or status changes – for example employee promotions and/or relocations,
- changes to an employee's remuneration – for example an increase in an employee's hourly rate of pay or an incremental increase in salary,
- changes to an employee's statutory deductions – for example a change in an employee's income tax personal allowance, applicable rate of income tax and/or National Insurance, and
- changes to an employee's voluntary/non-statutory deductions – for example a change in an employee's pension contributions.

It is from the data contained within the payroll master file that:

- employee time cards, job card/work cards or time sheets are generated and issued to employees,
- employee pay adjustment notifications are identified and issued to payroll,
- internal documentation such as a cumulative earnings register, a company/organisation employee inventory, a employee location inventory and a skills/competencies register are prepared, and
- statutory documents such as employee P45s and P60s are produced in addition to other statutory third-party reports.

It is therefore important that the payroll master file provides an accurate and up-to-date representation of the status of employees contained on the employee inventory listing. Where a company/organisation maintains/uses an online payroll master file system, which is becoming increasingly the case, it is particularly important that:

- access to the payroll master file data is limited to authorised persons only – for example HRM department employees only,
- any edits, deletions, additions and/or changes made to the payroll master file are appropriately validated and correctly authorised, and
- a clear and verifiable audit trail for each edit, deletion, addition and/or change exists.

## Validation and allocation of departmental payroll budgets

The validation and allocation of departmental payroll budgets would of course be undertaken before the start of the accounting period/financial year as part of the overall budgeting process for the company/organisation, with any budget allocation being based on the approved employee location inventory[25] for each department/cost centre. Clearly, changes can and indeed some-times would be made to departmental payroll budgets. However such changes if significant[26] would of course not only require senior management approval, but more importantly detailed financial justification. For example, if additional employees are requested, would the additional number produce any added value to the company/organisation and/or any identifiable increase in company/organisation revenue? If so, when would the increased revenue be realised, how much revenue would be produced and would the increase in revenue exceed the cost of the additional employees?

## Collection and validation of time/attendance data or goods produced data

For each employee, time-based data (that is hours worked by the employee), or production-based data (that is goods produced and completed by the employee) would be supplied by individual employee departments. Although historically such data were often collected using hard-copy paper-based documents (e.g. a time card, time sheet or job card), many companies/organisations now collect and validate such data digitally[27] with the appropriate departmental manager/employee supervisor authorising the data (as a data transaction file) before submission to the payroll department.

Where a company/organisation has a number of sections/departments it is possible that individual departmental managers/employee supervisors would be responsible for submitting an authorised transaction file to the payroll department only after approval/authorisation by a higher level manager. It is therefore possible that the payroll department may receive a number of data transaction files over a short period of time.[28]

Once all the data transaction files have been received, the payroll department would:

- consolidate all received data into a single file, and
- organise the consolidated transaction file into employee number order – the same as for the payroll master file.

It is this consolidated/sorted data transaction file that would be used to prepare and calculate employee payroll payments.

The payroll master file data for each employee and the consolidated/sorted data transaction file content for each employee would be interrogated and matched, and the gross pay for each employee calculated as follows:

- for wage-based employees remunerated on a hours worked basis – the gross pay for the employee would be calculated by multiplying the hours worked by the employee (from the data transaction file) by the approved rate of pay for the employee (from the payroll master file) – with any overtime premiums and bonuses added as appropriate,
- for wage-based employees remunerated on a goods produced basis – the gross pay for the employee would be calculated by multiplying the goods produced by the employee (from the data transaction file) by the approved rate of pay for the employee (from the payroll master file) – with any bonuses added as appropriate, and
- for salary-based employees – the gross pay for the employee would be calculated as a fraction of the employee's annual salary with the fraction representing the period worked by the employee. For example 1/12th of an employee's annual salary would be paid where an employee is remunerated at the end of every calendar month, or 1/13th of an employee's annual salary would be paid where an employee is remunerated at the end of each four-week period (or lunar month). Where such employees are also entitled to payment for overtime work such payments are normally paid in the month following. That is overtime worked in April would normally be paid at the end of May.

### Preparation of the payroll and the validation of payroll deductions

Once the gross pay has been calculated for each employee, statutory and voluntary deductions (based on employee data in the payroll master file) would be totalled and subtracted from the employee's gross pay to calculate their net pay. The employee data in the payroll master file would then be updated to reflect the upcoming payroll payments – for example, employee data such as:

- gross pay to date,
- total deductions to date (including sub-totals for individual deductions to date), and
- net pay to date.

Finally, a payroll register would be produced. The payroll register is merely a listing or report containing details of each employee's gross pay, total deductions and total net pay. Historically it was at this point in the payroll procedure that employee pay cheques and pay advices were produced. However, these days, with the vast majority of payroll payments now being paid using BACS, only individual employee pay advices would be produced. These pay advices (or pay slips as they are often referred to) would normally be issued by the payroll department to individual employees on the day before payday.

Note: Because each employee of the company/organisation would be assigned to a specific product/function or located in a specific service department, the cost of the employee (in terms of gross pay) would be allocated to a specific cost centre/budget centre of the company/organisation. This means that often as part of the payroll register, a cost centre allocation would also be produced and reconciled to the total gross pay in the payroll register.

### Disbursement of payments to employees

Once the payroll register has been approved and authorised – usually by a senior manager within the payroll department – it would be sent to the creditor's department for approval and review by a senior manager, who would also authorise the issue of a disbursement voucher to approve the transfer of cash funds from the company's/organisation's bank account to its payroll bank account.[29] The disbursement voucher and payroll register would then be forwarded to the treasury department/cashier's office.

The treasury department/cashier's office would review, compare and reconcile the content of the payroll register and the value of the disbursement voucher. If no problems are identified, a senior manager within the treasury department/cashier's office would authorise the transfer of funds from the company's/organisation's bank account to its payroll bank account, and submit the payment file to its bankers to enable the net wage payments/salary payments to be transferred to individual employee bank accounts. This file transfer would of course be encrypted and require authorisation by an assigned senior manager within the company/organisation. Once complete:

- the payroll register would be returned to the payroll department for filing, and
- the disbursement voucher would be returned to accounting.

### Accounting for and reconciliation of payroll payments

It is the disbursement voucher, once returned to accounting, that would form the basis of the accounting entries. In terms of accounting for payroll payments, many companies/organisations use a payroll clearing account (within the general ledger) to record and account for such payroll payments. Such accounting would generally involve two stages:

- a financial accounting stage – stage 1, and
- a management accounting stage – stage 2.

The accounting entries for each stage would be as follows:

*Stage 1*

- Dr payroll control account – with the gross amount of pay,
- Cr cash account (payroll bank account) – with the payroll payments made to employees,
- Cr various liability accounts – with the amount of the deductions made from employee payroll payments. Such deductions would include, for example, income tax deductions, National Insurance Contributions, pension deductions and other statutory and/or voluntary deductions.

*Stage 2*

- Dr labour costs/gross payroll costs to various budget centre/cost centre accounts,
- Cr payroll control account.

For internal control purposes, each of the above accounting entries should of course be supported by appropriate journal vouchers acting as the source documentation for each of the accounting entries.[30] In addition, following the above set of accounting transactions, the balance of the payroll control account should be zero. As a result the internal control check associated with the above accounting entries is often referred to, somewhat unsurprisingly, as a *zero balance check*.

It would be the responsibility of the accounting department (more specifically the management accounting department) to produce the periodic financial statements/management statements for departmental managers – more appropriately cost centre/budget centre managers.

### Disbursement of statutory and voluntary deductions

The final activity in the payroll payment process would of course be the payment of payroll-associated third-party liabilities. Such payments would relate to the statutory and voluntary deductions made from employee wages/salary payments and would include (as suggested above) deductions relating to income tax, National Insurance Contributions, pensions and other statutory and/or voluntary deductions/payments. For some statutory deductions (e.g. income tax and National Insurance), fixed payment periods exist. That is the company/organisation is required to make payment of any deductions to the relevant agency (e.g. Revenue and Customs) within a fixed period of time. Currently, if a company's/organisation's combined income tax deductions (under the PAYE scheme) and National Insurance Contributions averages more than £1500 per calendar month, the company/organisation must make payments to Revenue and Customs on a monthly basis. If the total is, on average, less than £1500 per calendar month, then payments can be made on a quarterly basis.[31]

### Safeguarding of company/organisation assets and information

The second major function of a company's/organisation's accounting information systems in the HRM/payroll cycle is to ensure that adequate internal control exists to safeguard HRM/payroll cycle assets and information, and ensure that all HRM/payroll-related transactions:

- are efficiently processed, suitably authenticated, appropriately authorised and properly and accurately recorded, and
- comply with/adhere to extant rules and regulations.

Such internal controls are sometimes classified as either:

- asset-related controls, or
- information/data-related controls.

### Asset-related controls

Such controls are typically associated with maintaining the integrity and security of payroll-related assets and would include:

- the maintenance of statutory employee files within the HRM department including the regular verification of employee master file details and the periodic verification of employee status details,
- the application of detailed employee appointment procedures including the verification of applicant's skills and experience, references and employment history,
- the management and coordination of employee status changes through the HRM department, and
- the use of security procedures regarding the allocation and transfer of payroll payments. *All* payroll payments should be paid directly into the employee bank account using the BACS system. Payroll payments using cheques and/or cash should be prohibited . . . without exception!

For internal control purposes, it is also important that:

- within the HRM/payroll cycle a distinct separation exists between the pre-payment stage, the payment stage and the post-payment stage,
- *no* personal relationship exist between:
  - those employees responsible for the maintenance of employee personal records (within the HRM department),
  - those employees responsible for the preparation and calculation of payroll payments, and
  - those employees responsible for the processing and payment of wages and salaries to company/organisation employees, and
- where at all possible, employees involved in the preparation and calculation of payroll payments, and/or the processing and payment of wages and salaries to company/organisation employees, are rotated on a frequent basis to prevent potentially 'dangerous' employee relationships developing between payroll staff and other employees.

It is perhaps also important, if not essential, that appropriate education and training on:

- current developments in employment regulations and law, and
- information and communications technologies,

are also made available to relevant HRM/payroll staff. Where possible, such education and training should be combined with the use of work-based performance metrics to assess:

- the efficiency of HRM/payroll-based employees, and
- the relevance and effectiveness of the education and training programmes.

### Information/data-related controls

Such controls are typically associated with ensuring the integrity and validity of payroll transaction data and payment information, and would include:

- the use of secure online payroll data collection (in the place of physical documents such as time cards, job cards and/or time sheets),
- the use of both physical and logical access controls[32] to prevent unauthorised access to payroll data,
- the encryption of payroll data to ensure data security,

- the use of data transmission controls/protocols,
- the use of validity checks,[33] field checks,[34] and limit checks[35] to confirm the authenticity of payroll changes to the payroll master file,
- the use of authorisation checks to confirm the legitimacy of payroll changes to the payroll master file,
- the reconciliation of all statutory and non-statutory deductions made from employee wages and/or salaries,
- the use of a payroll clearing account,
- the use of batch control totals and hash control totals[36] in the processing of payroll data to ensure the completeness of data processed,
- the use of regular data back-up procedures and the existence/availability of a disaster recovery plan specifically for the HRM/payroll cycle, and
- the reconciliation of payroll payment totals (via the BACS system) to accounting entries.

## Payroll-related information for decision-making purposes

As we have seen, in the context of a company's/organisation's HRM/payroll cycle, the accounting information system fulfils three key roles. In an operational context it plays a major role in the processing of payroll transactions, whilst in a more tactical context it plays a vital role in the safeguarding of company/organisation assets and information. In a strategic context, however, the accounting information system plays a major role in the provision of information for decision-making purposes, for example regarding:

- the future employment requirements of the company/organisation,
- the current performance of employees, and
- the efficiency and effectiveness of the HRM/payroll cycle.

### Future employment requirements

It is important for those senior managers responsible for the development of the long-term strategic plans of the company/organisation to be aware of not only the variety and level of competencies and skills currently available within the company/organisation, but also the variety and level of competencies and skills that it will require to fulfil its future strategic plans. Such information will allow the strategic managers of the company/organisation to:

- Develop a range of employee redundancy policies to address any identified oversupply of skills and competencies within the company/organisation. Where redundancies are anticipated for whatever reason (e.g. a production facility closure, a product line closure or indeed a strategic redirecting of the company/organisation), it would clearly be important to ensure that employees' trade union representatives are appropriatly *consulted* prior to any redundancy decision being made by the company/organisation and not merely *informed* of the redundancy decision.
- Develop a range of employee recruitment policies to address any identified shortfall of skills and competencies within the company/organisation. Where an extensive recruitment of employees is anticipated – perhaps due to a growth in the demand for the company's/organisation's products/services – it would again clearly be important to ensure that suitable levels of remuneration/conditions of employment are offered to secure the recruitment of appropriately qualified employees.
- Design an appropriate portfolio of education and training programmes for both current and prospective employees not only to *maintain* the skills and competencies of employees, but also to *enhance* them.

### Current employee performance

It is of course important that the performance of current employees is regularly assessed. In some industries/sectors the regular assessment of employee skills/competencies is mandatory (e.g. commercial airline pilots, Department of Transport approved driving instructors), in others it is required for regulatory compliance purposes (e.g. health and safety purposes), and in yet others it is required for professional accreditation/licensing purposes (e.g. ICAEW and ACCA licensed practitioners/registered accountants and auditors).

Whilst there still remain a few industries/sectors in which externally imposed employee assessments are not required, many of the companies/organisations within these industries/sectors nonetheless undertake employee assessments:

- for internal quality assessment/quality control purposes,
- for internal comparison purposes – for example between different accounting periods (a temporal comparison) or different departments/sections within the company/organisation (a cross-sectional comparison), or
- for employee promotion purposes.

Such performance assessments – whether mandatory or voluntary – can of course be undertaken using a variety of means, the most common being either:

- a formal/direct performance metric – for example an employee skills/competency test, or
- an informal/indirect performance assessment – for example a measurement of an employee's error rates.

In addition to the above, overall employee performance (as well as individual employee performance) would be adversely affected by excessively high levels of unauthorised absenteeism and sickness. Where information provided by the payroll department indicates such levels appear excessive it is important to:

- determine the possible reasons for such high levels – for example are such high levels due to a health and safety issue, a managerial issue (within a particular section, department or location), an employee moral issue or simply a remuneration issue, and
- identify possible remedial action that could be taken to minimise such unauthorised absenteeism and sickness – for example by improving/offering fringe benefits to employees or by relocating disruptive employees and/or ineffective managers.

### Efficiency and effectiveness – the HRM/payroll cycle

There can be little doubt that the cost of providing an efficient and effective HRM/payroll cycle can be very high – not only in financial terms, but more importantly in staff commitment terms. Clearly, the cost of providing such an in-house facility is related to:

- the number of staff employed by the company/organisation,
- the types of staff employed by the company/organisation – for example the number/mix of skilled staff, semi-skilled staff and manual staff,
- the frequency of payroll payments made to employees – for example the number of weekly and monthly paid staff, and
- the nature of the payroll payments – for example the number of payroll payments made by cash, by cheque or by BACS transfer.

In a strategic context, it would nevertheless be important to evaluate the efficiency and effectiveness of any such in-house facility by assessing:

- the integrity of data acquired, stored and maintained within the HRM/payroll cycle,
- the accessibility and usability of information produced by the HRM/payroll cycle,

- the accuracy of payments made to employees by the HRM/payroll cycle and, in particular,
- the level of errors – fraudulent or otherwise – occurring in:
  - the maintenance of employee data, and
  - the processing of payroll payments.

Where information suggests that:

- the costs associated with the provision of such an in-house facility exceed the appreciable benefits of keeping such a provision within the company/organisation, or
- the effectiveness and efficiency of such an in-house facility has fallen below a level that would be regarded as acceptable – for example excessive levels of over-payments or frequent errors in the recording of payroll related data,

it would of course be a dereliction of their duty and responsibility to the shareholders/ stakeholders of the company/organisation for the strategic managers not to consider the possibility of outsourcing some, or indeed all, of the HRM/payroll cycle. Obviously, where such a decision is taken, its impact on the company/organisation – in particular on the staff employed within the in-house HRM/payroll facility, could be substantial. As a consequence, decisions to outsource part or all of an in-house facility can be controversial especially where possible redundancies may result.

We will have a look at outsourcing in a little more detail later in this chapter.

### Consequences of a failure of controls

There are of course a large number of possible consequences associated with the failure of payroll-related controls. For the purposes of simplicity, we will classify such consequences into the following categories:

- employee-related consequences,
- third-party-related consequences, and
- company/organisation-related consequences.

#### Employee-related consequences

Such consequences could include:

- the use of inappropriate recruitment procedures and the appointment of unqualified staff/ employees,
- a failure to recognise behavioural irregularities among employees – for example unusually high levels of absenteeism,
- a failure to identify possible employee conflicts of interest,
- the incorrect use of employee evaluation procedures,
- the improper application of employee remuneration packages, and
- the unauthorised deduction of funds from employee payments.

#### Third-party-related consequences

Such consequences could include:

- a failure to meet statutory fiscal obligations – for example the incorrect payment of income and National Insurance deductions,
- a failure to comply with extant employment laws,
- the violation of legal/statutory requirements, and
- a failure to comply with employee pension requirements.

### Company/organisation-related consequences

Such consequences would include:

- the incorrect/fraudulent disbursement of pay and/or deductions,
- the duplication of payments to employees,
- the fraudulent alteration of employee pay,
- the unauthorised amendment to payroll master file,
- the inputting of incorrect payroll data – for example hours worked/goods produced,
- the inaccurate processing/calculation of payroll payments,
- the possible theft of payroll payments,
- the loss, alteration and/or unauthorised disclosure of payroll data,
- the incorrect allocation of payroll expenditure, and
- the inappropriate withholding of payroll liabilities.

## Outsourcing

In our discussion so far, we have assumed that the HRM/payroll cycle operates as an in-house process/procedure, staffed and managed internally within the company/organisation. Many companies/organisation however now outsource some or all of their HRM/payroll services/ activities, using either:

- a payroll bureau, or
- a professional employer organisation.

### Using a payroll bureau

A payroll bureau is a company/organisation which specialises in the provision of some or all of a client company's/organisation's payroll-related activities. Whilst the use of a payroll bureau may clearly have many advantages, for example:

- it can reduce the overall cost of providing an HRM/payroll service/facility,
- it can free up resources for use elsewhere within the company/organisation, and
- it can provide access to wider range of benefits/facilities other than those that would be available with a limited in-house provision,

it may also have many disadvantages, for example it can result in:

- a loss of control over confidential personnel/payroll data, and
- a greater need for the monitoring of the outsourced service.

Despite such disadvantages, the use of payroll bureau services – especially in small and/or medium-sized companies/organisations has become increasingly popular.

Examples of such payroll bureau include:

- Wispay Payroll Bureau @ <u>www.wispaypayrollbureau.co.uk</u>,
- Compupay Bureau @ <u>www.compupaye.com</u>,
- PSC Payroll @ <u>www.pscpayroll.com</u>, and
- 1st Choice payroll @ <u>www.1stchoicepayroll.co.uk</u>.

In general, a payroll bureau would provide services[37] relating to:

- the processing and management of all payroll-related data – often using multi-media input,
- the processing of starter and leaver calculations (including P45 management services),

- direct communication with third parties (e.g. Revenue and Customs, pension administrators, etc.),
- the provision of a question and answer service – usually through a designated coordinator,
- the automatic processing of all regular payroll additions/deductions,
- the provision of client specified management reporting in alternative formats,
- the archiving of payroll output,
- the delivery of payroll output, and
- the provision of payslips – including self-service electronic payslips.

## Using a professional employer organisation (PEO)

A professional employer organisation is a company/organisation which specialises in the creation and maintenance of a three-way relationship between:

- the professional employer organisation (PEO),
- the client company/organisation, and
- the employees of the client company/organisation.

Essentially, the professional service organisation and the client company/organisation enter into a contract that apportions the traditional employer responsibilities between them. Although contracts can vary in terms of:

- the period of the contractual agreement – for example short-term (less than a year) to long-term (over a year and up to five years),
- the range of services to be provided by the professional employer organisation, and
- the cost of the services to be provided by the professional employer organisation,

in the majority of circumstances the professional employee organisation will (for a monthly fee) provide all employee payments and employee benefits packages, and assume administrative responsibilities for payroll, human resources and employment taxes, leaving the client company/ organisation to focuses on traditional growth areas and future directions for the business.

Note: Because the client company/organisation and its employees reside on the payroll of the professional employer organisation, the use of the professional employer organisation is sometimes, somewhat incorrectly, referred to as employee leasing. Examples of professional employer organisations include for example:

- Accord @ www.accordhr.com, and
- StaffPay @ www.staffpay.com.

So, for a client company/organisation, what would be the advantages and disadvantages of using a professional employee organisation? The advantages would include:

- a reduced HRM/payroll administrative workload for the client company/organisation,
- the immediate acquisition of HRM/payroll expertise, and
- the acquisition of big company/organisation benefits packages for employees (e.g. healthcare benefits, retirement benefits and insurance benefits).

The disadvantages would include:

- a loss of control over important business areas,
- a possible growth in employee dissatisfaction,[38]
- a possible increased subjection to business statutes,[39] and
- a potential loss of flexibility.

Regarding this last point – it is important to note that whilst the use of a professional employer organisation can relieve a client company/organisation of a vast range of administrative duties, and potentially provide employees with a range of benefits that may not otherwise have been available, such benefits/advantages may come at a price – for example:

■ a loss of control over the appointment and termination of employees within the company/organisation, and
■ a loss of control over the selection of employee benefits that should be made available to employees.

## To outsource or not to outsource . . . that is the question!

The answer, of course, would depend on:

■ management preferences,
■ employee capabilities,
■ resource availabilities, and
■ the potential impact of outsourcing on employees.

More importantly, because the decision to use either a payroll bureau or a professional employee organisation is a significant one for any company/organisation, it is important that the bureau/organisation is carefully assessed before any long-term contact is entered into. Such an assessment would consider a wide range of factors, perhaps the most important being:

■ the reputation of the payroll bureau or a professional employee organisation,
■ its financial stability,
■ its resource credentials, and
■ its services offered.

Firstly, given the significance of the choice, it is important to ensure that wherever possible references from current/past clients of the professional employee organisation are obtained, especially from those of a similar size and with similar service requirements.

Secondly, given that as part of its administrative tasks the professional employee organisation will pay taxes and disburse funds to company/organisation employees and creditors on behalf of the company/organisation – disbursements which will obviously be reimbursed by the company/organisation on an agreed basis – it is nevertheless the professional employee organisation that will assume ultimate responsibility for those payments/disbursements. It is therefore essential that the professional employee organisation has sufficient financial resources to meet any such financial obligations.

Thirdly, because the company/organisation will be relinquishing a substantial measure of control over some of the company's/organisation's confidential personnel/payroll data – at least in part – it is important that the professional service organisation possesses sufficient expertise and resources to ensure the provision of a secure and efficient service.

Finally, because the aim of any outsourcing arrangement is to reduce costs and improve the efficiency and effectiveness of a service/facility, it is important that the benefits derived from the range of services provided by the professional employee organisation will indeed result in a genuine relief from *all* the administrative concerns associated with the provision of the out-sourced service.

## Concluding comments

As we saw in the introduction, the expenditure cycle is simply a collection of business-related activities/resources, whose primary objective is to minimise the total cost of acquiring and maintaining the products/services required for the company/organisation to function effectively, whilst maintaining the good image of the company/organisation. Such systems, processes and procedures have – as we have seen – become increasingly computer based and, whilst there may be some uncertainty over how future changes in information and communication technologies will affect expenditure cycle systems, processes and procedures, there can be little doubt that the future will (as with revenue cycle activities – see Chapter 8) continue to see expenditure cycle activities remaining at the very heart of many corporate/organisational activities.

## Key points and concepts

Capital-related expenditure

Card-based expenditure

Cash-based expenditure

Competition Act 1998

Creditor account

Creditor-based expenditure cycle

Economic Order Quantity (EOQ)

Electronic invoicing

Goods received note (GRN)

Human resource-related expenditure

Invoice

Invoice-less payment processing

Just-In-Time (JIT)

Materials Requirements Planning (MRP)

Multi-use purchase order

Non-creditor-based expenditure cycle

Non-recurring acquired service

Non-voucher payment system

Payment management system

Payroll

Payroll bureau

Product/service ordering system

Product/service receiving system

Professional employer organisation (PEO)

Purchase confirmation

Purchase order

Purchase requisition

Receiving report

Recurring acquired service

Revenue-related expenditure

Single-use purchase order

Supplier selection/approval system

Voucher payment system

## Bibliography

Aseervatham, A. and Anandarajah, D. (2003) *Accounting Information and Reporting Systems*, McGraw Hill, Sydney.

Bagranoff, N.A., Simkin, M.G. and Strand N.C. (2004) *Core Concepts of Accounting Information Systems*, Wiley, New York.

Harris, F.W. (1915) *Operations Cost* (Factory Management Series), Shaw, Chicago.

Romney, M. and Steinbart, P. (2006) *Accounting Information Systems*, Pearson Education Inc., New Jersey.

Vaassen, E. (2002) *Accounting Information Systems – A Managerial Approach*, Wiley, Chichester.

Wilkinson, J.W., Cerullo, M.L., Raval, V. and Wong-On-Wing, B. (2001) *Accounting Information Systems*, Wiley, New York.

Wilson, R.H. (1934) 'A Scientific Routine for Stock Control', *Harvard Business Review*, 13, pp. 116–128.

## Self review questions

1. Distinguish between a creditor-based revenue cycle and a non-creditor-based revenue cycle.
2. Briefly explain the key processing requirements of creditor-based/non-creditor-based revenue cycles.
3. Describe the main stages of a creditor-based revenue cycle.
4. What information is likely to be stored in an approved supplier/provider register or database.
5. Distinguish between a recurring acquired service and a non-recurring acquired service.
6. Identify and describe the main activities within the product/service ordering stage of the creditor-based expenditure cycle.
7. Distinguish between period-based activity information and period-based performance information.
8. Briefly explain the role of the treasury/cashier's office in the processing of payroll payments.
9. What information is likely to be stored in an employee's permanent payroll master file record?
10. Briefly explain the advantages and disadvantages of using a payroll bureau.

## Questions and problems

### Question 1

The following documentation is commonly used in a creditor-based expenditure cycle:

- purchase requisition,
- purchase order,
- goods received note,
- receiving report,
- creditor invoice, and
- disbursement voucher.

#### *Required*

For each of the above, describe the purpose and function of the documentation within the expenditure cycle.

### Question 2

HLU plc is a UK-based retail company. During a recent systems review of its creditor-based expenditure cycle, you noted the following requirements:

- employees responsible for the receipting of products from product suppliers cannot be involved in the approving/authorising of invoices for payment to creditors,
- employees responsible for the approving/authorising of invoices for payment to creditors cannot be involved in the processing of payments to creditors,
- employees responsible for the processing of payments to creditors cannot be involved in the reconciliation of the company bank account, and
- employees responsible for the receipting of products from product suppliers cannot be involved in periodic stock checks of products in store.

*Required*

Explain:

- the purpose of each of the above requirements within a company such as HLU plc, and
- the problems which could occur should the above requirements not be complied with.

## Question 3

You have recently been appointed Systems Accountant at BHJ Ltd, a small electrical accessories company. Your main brief is to design a company-wide computer purchasing system. To date the company has maintained a semi-manual record system for all its purchases.

For the previous five financial years the company has made average annual purchases of £15m (all purchases are from UK suppliers) and average annual profits of approximately £9m. The company has 47 employees working at seven locations throughout the UK: York, Hull, Birmingham, Oxford, Swindon, Bristol and Portsmouth.

For the year ended 31 March 2007, approximately 95% of the company's purchases were on credit. The company is currently reviewing its purchasing system and is considering introducing a fully computerised purchasing system with the possibility of a web-based purchasing protocol linked to selected suppliers.

*Required*

Making whatever assumptions you consider necessary, prepare a draft report for the management board of BHJ Ltd, detailing the following:

- the control objectives of a company purchasing system.
- the general controls and application controls you would expect to find in a computerised purchasing system, and
- the control issues relevant to a web-based purchasing system.

## Question 4

Describe the accounting controls you would expect to find in the purchasing system of a high street retail company, and discuss how the failure of such accounting controls could potentially affect the valuation and security of company assets and the disclosure of company assets in the annual financial reports.

## Question 5

SEC Ltd, a small electrical accessories company, wants to design a company-wide computer purchasing system. To date the company has maintained a semi-manual record system for all its purchases.

For the previous three financial years the company has made average annual purchases of £34m (all purchases from UK suppliers) and average annual profits of approximately £10.6m. The company has approximately 350 employees working at six locations throughout the UK: Manchester, which is the company's head office, Birmingham, Leeds, Swindon, Bristol and Newcastle.

You have recently completed an audit of activities within the purchasing department within SEC Ltd. The department employs 15 buyers, seven supervisors, a manager and clerical personnel. Your audit has disclosed the following conditions:

- The company has no formal rules on conflicts of interest. Your analysis produced evidence that one of the 15 buyers in the department owns a substantial interest in a major supplier and that he procures supplies averaging £150,000 a year from that supplier. The prices charged by the supplier are competitive.

- Buyers select proposed sources without submitting lists of bidders for review. Your tests disclosed no evidence that higher costs were incurred as a result of that practice.
- Buyers who originate written requests for quotations from suppliers receive the suppliers' bids directly from the mail room. In your test of 100 purchases based on competitive bids, you found that in 55 cases the lower bidders were awarded the purchase order.
- Requests to purchase (requisitions) received in the purchasing departments in the company must be signed by persons authorised to do so. Your examination of 200 such requests disclosed that three requisitions, all for small amounts, were not properly signed. The buyer who had issued all three orders honoured the requests because he misunderstood the applicable procedures. The clerical personnel responsible for reviewing such requests had given them to the buyer in error.

### Required

(a) For each of the above, explain the risk, if any, that is incurred if each of the conditions described previously is permitted to continue and describe the control(s), if any, you would recommend to prevent continuation of the condition described.

(b) Explain the main function of a purchasing system employed by a company such as SEC Ltd, the risks associated with its failure and the controls that can be installed in order to minimise the impact of such risks.

## Assignments

### Question 1

OWS Ltd has been under the control of the same family Mr I and Mrs N Sane (who are now both 62 years old) for the past 30 years. During that time the company has expanded rapidly. Unfortunately it still operates a fairly simple manual-based/cheque-based purchasing system.

A document flowchart of the company's current purchasing system is provided in Figure 9.11 below.

### Required

Identify the major internal controls within the company's purchasing systems and, where appropriate, suggest possible improvements to the company's purchasing system.

### Question 2

You have recently been appointed as an accountant at LQOH, a Harrogate-based firm of certified accountants. You are currently reviewing the payroll system of PLT plc. The company is a small local manufacturing company with an annual turnover of £4.2m and an annual net profit of approximately £1.2m. The company currently employs a factory workforce of 56 employees and has an annual factory wage bill of £2.2m.

The following document flowchart (see Figure 9.12) of PLT's factory payroll system was prepared during the last systems audit of the company approximately three months ago.

### Required

Based on the above flowchart, identify and describe the weaknesses within PLT's factory payroll system and recommend possible areas for improvement.

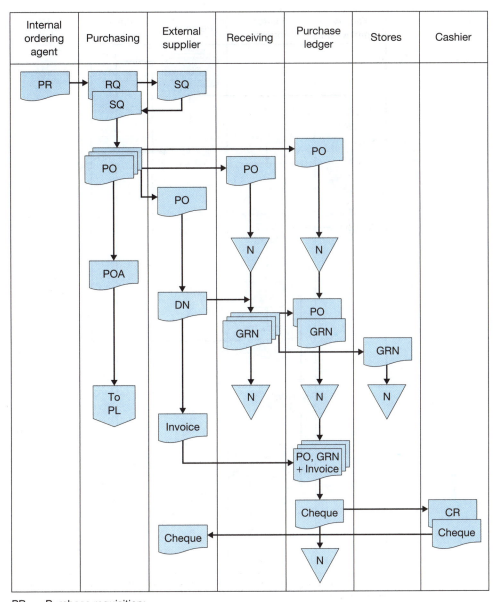

PR  = Purchase requisition;
PO  = Purchase order;
QR  = Quotation request;
SQ  = Supplier quotation;
N   = File (numerical order);
POA = Purchase order acknowledgement;
DN  = Delivery note;
CR  = Cheque register.

**Figure 9.11** OWS Ltd purchasing system – document flowchart

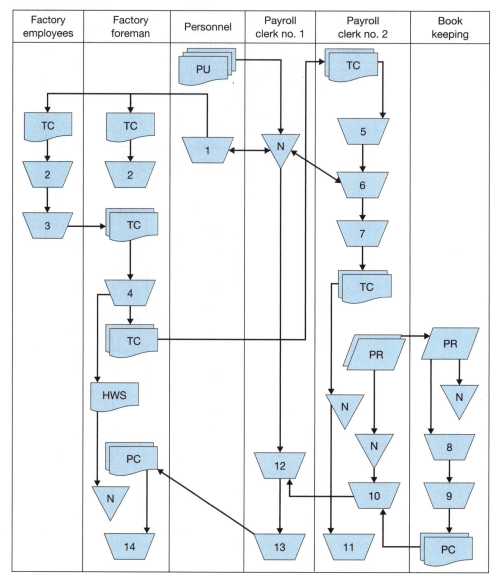

PU = Payroll update; TC = Timecards; PR = Payroll register; PC = Payroll cheque; HWS = Hours worked summary.

**Events/activities**

1. Personnel file reviewed and timecards prepared.
2. Timecards used to record hours worked.
3. Timecards submitted for approval on a weekly basis.
4. Timecards review and authorised – hours worked and overtime hours summarised.
5. Hours worked calculated and overtime hours worked noted.
6. Employee status checked and pay rate and deductions confirmed.
7. Gross pay and net pay are calculated and payroll register prepared.
8. Payroll register details checked and confirmed.
9. Sequentially numbered cheques are prepared for each employee.
10. Gross pay and net pay calculations are checked and the sequence of cheques confirmed.
11. Hours worked and overtime worked verified.
12. Employee's identity confirmed and all cheques signed (using automated cheque signing machine).
13. Chequessentto Finance for distribution to employees.

**Figure 9.12** PLT plc payroll system – document flowchart

## Chapter endnotes

[1] Capital expenditure is sometimes referred to as fixed assets expenditure.

[2] Revenue expenditure is sometimes referred to as current assets expenditure.

[3] The World Trade Organisation (WTO) is an international organisation concerned with: the rules of trade between nations. Consisting of a series of negotiated trade agreements ratified by the governments of individual member states, many critics blame the WTO for extending and reinforcing existing economic demarcations between the impoverished third world countries and the rest of the world's developed economies. As at December 2005, the WTO had 149 members. For more information see www.wto.int.

[4] This Chapter enacts Article 81 of the EC Treaty.

[5] This Chapter enacts Article 82 of the EC Treaty.

[6] The Competition Commission replaced the Monopolies and Mergers Commission (MMC) on 1 April 1999.

[7] See Chapter 6.

[8] Clearly, for Data Protection Act 1998 compliance purposes, access to such a database would need to be severely restricted to approved users only.

[9] The Criminal Records Bureau is an executive agency of the Home Office set up to help organisations make safer recruitment decisions. Its primary role is to reduce the risk of abuse by ensuring that those who are unsuitable are not able to work with children and vulnerable adults.

[10] See Chapter 4.

[11] We will discuss internet-based business-to-business (B2B) facilities in detail in Chapter 13.

[12] In some instances, the quality inspection test may only be carried out on a random sample of the products received. However, where a number of the randomly sampled products fail, then the whole delivery consignment would be rejected and returned to the supplier.

[13] With effect from 6 April 2006, a standard CRB check costs £31.00 and an enhanced CRB check costs £36.00.

[14] It is of course important to recognise that an early payment discount would only be taken where there would be a net benefit to the company/organisation. That is where the financial gain of the discount exceeds the financial costs associated with early payment – costs such as, for example, borrowing funds to make the payment.

[15] Remember also that the three days must always be three consecutive processing days.

[16] Invoice-less payment processing is often somewhat confusingly referred to as invoice-less invoicing.

[17] To identify any duplicate product suppliers/service providers.

[18] Also known as the employee remuneration cycle.

[19] Whilst the calendar month is by far the most common, many companies/organisations use a lunar month period – that is payment of salaries every four weeks.

[20] A positive payroll can be defined as a payroll in which employee remuneration is calculated each period based on hours worked and/or products produced/services provided. Such a payroll is normally associated with weekly paid wages.

[21] A negative payroll can be defined as a payroll in which employee remuneration is fixed each period and adjusted only where additional remuneration is approved – for example the payment of overtime and/or the payment for authorised expenses. Such a payroll is normally associated with monthly paid salaries.

[22] An attachment of earnings order is where a creditor has applied for, and the County Court has approved, an order to allow the creditor to take funds directly from an individual's wages

or salary. The individual's employer must by law deduct the monies from the employee's wages or salary and make payments to the creditor up until the time the debt is paid off.

[23] Although some companies/organisations use employee reference schemes which use a combination of both alpha and numeric characters, by far the most common employee reference schemes are those based on numeric characters only.

[24] It is likely that an employee whose employment is either terminated or who leaves voluntarily will remain on the payroll master file for at least the current financial year in which their employment ceased.

[25] An employee location inventory is merely a list of staff employed in particular sections/departments within a company/organisation.

[26] Significant in this context means a substantial change in the number of employees within a department/section, and excludes what could be regarded as normal or expected turnover in employee levels.

[27] For example see the Zeus Compact system (details available @ www.autotimesystem.co.uk) which comprises of a swipe terminal that records employee time-keeping and a software package that calculates hours worked/attended, and provides employee-based management reports.

[28] It is likely that submission deadlines for both weekly paid, and monthly paid employees would be agreed in advance at the start of the accounting period/financial year.

[29] As with payments to creditors – for which a separate creditor's payment bank account is used, for internal control purposes, a separate bank account should be used for the processing of payroll payments. Such payments should not be made from the company's/organisation's general bank account.

[30] Remember, all accounting entries must be supported by source documentation. Such source documentation can be categorised as:

- an invoice – for both sales and purchases,
- a cash voucher – for both payments and receipts, or
- a journal voucher – for all other accounting entries.

[31] Currently (late 2006), Revenue and Customs require payments to be received within 14 days of the end of each tax month or tax quarter.

Note: Tax months end on the 5th, so payments need to be received by Revenue and Customs by the 19th of the month/quarter – although if payments are made using the BACS system, they need to be received by the 22nd of the month/quarter. For Revenue and Customs purposes, tax quarters end on 5th July, 5th October, 5th January and 5th April.

[32] Whereas a physical access control could include for example the use of security/password protected entrance controls to the payroll department – to restrict the movement of employees into and out of the payroll department to authorised personnel only – a logical access control could include, for example, the use of security users' names and passwords for access to payroll data files.

[33] For example checking the validity of data fields such as employee reference numbers to ensure that only approved/recognised employee reference numbers are accepted and processed.

[34] For example checking the content of data fields such as employee reference number and/or the number of hours worked to ensure that the correct format of data is included.

[35] For example checking the content of data fields such as the number of hours worked and/or the gross amount of pay awarded to an employee to ensure maximum limits are not exceeded.

[36] A hash total can be defined as an otherwise meaningless control total calculated by adding together numbers (such as payroll or account numbers) associated with a data set – a total which is used to ensure that no entry errors have been made.

[37] Obviously the services provided by the payroll bureau would of course be price sensitive, that is, the larger the number of services required, the higher the cost of the service.

[38] The use of a professional employer organisation often requires the legal termination of employee contracts by the client company/organisation and re-appointment by the professional employer organisation which may – quite understandably – confuse or even upset some employees.

[39] A major advantage of small/medium company/organisation status is the exemption that can be claimed for many legal regulations. However, because many professional employer organisations are often very large companies/organisations such regulations may often apply to them resulting in a once exempt small/medium-sized company/organisation being subject to monitoring and legal regulations it may have otherwise avoided.

# Corporate transaction processing:
## the conversion cycle

*The beginning is the most important part of the work* (Plato, *The Republic*, 360BC).

## Introduction

The conversion cycle can be defined as a recurring collection of business related processes, procedures and activities (including information processing operations) associated with the production and manufacture[1] of products. That is all those operational events and activities within a company/organisation which contribute to the conversion of raw material inputs into finished product outputs.[2]

The objectives of the conversion cycle are to ensure:

- adequate conversion cycle resources are available to meet production requirements,
- appropriate conversion cycle assets are available to meet production requirements,
- conversion cycle resources and assets are appropriately utilised and properly controlled,
- stocks of raw materials and work-in-progress are efficiently converted into finished goods,
- appropriate levels of product quality are maintained, and
- production costs are accurately recorded, fully recovered and, where possible, minimised.

In essence, within a type 1(b) company/organisation – that is a manufacturing/production company/organisation (see Chapter 6), the conversion cycle is the link between the revenue cycle (see Chapter 8), and the expenditure cycle (see Chapter 9) inasmuch as:

- the revenue cycle provides information to the conversion cycle on levels of demand for the company's/organisation's products – information that can be used to budget production and where necessary stock levels of raw materials and finished products, and
- the conversion cycle provides information to the expenditure cycle on the requirements for the purchase/acquisition of raw materials, products and services based on budgeted production requirements/raw materials and finished goods stock levels.

So, what functions does a company's/organisation's accounting information system provide for the conversion cycle?

In an operational context, the accounting information system would be used to assist in:

- the capture and processing of conversion cycle transaction data,
- the organising, storing and maintaining of conversion cycle transaction data, and
- the provision of decision-making information relating to, for example:
  - production levels,
  - product mix,
  - resource allocation, and
  - production costs.

In a more tactical/strategic context, the accounting information system would be used to:

- safeguard conversion cycle assets and resources,
- ensure the reliability of conversion cycle transaction data, and
- maintain the integrity of conversion cycle activities.

## Learning outcomes

By the end of this chapter, the reader should be able to:

- describe the major activities and operations contained within the corporate conversion cycle,
- explain the key decision stages within the corporate conversion cycle,
- demonstrate an understanding of the key internal control requirements of a corporate conversion cycle,
- demonstrate a critical understanding of the potential risks and threats associated with inappropriate internal control, and
- consider and explain the impact of information and communication technology enabled innovations on the corporate conversion cycle.

##  Conversion cycle – key activities and processes

As suggested earlier, the conversion cycle is simply a collection of interrelated activities, all of which contribute to the creation of a saleable product. Such activities include:

- product development,
- production planning/scheduling,
- manufacturing operations,
- production management, and
- cost management.

Have a look at Figure 10.1.

Note: Although we have identified cost management as a separate aspect of the conversion cycle, in reality it is an integrated component of each of the individual conversion cycle activities.

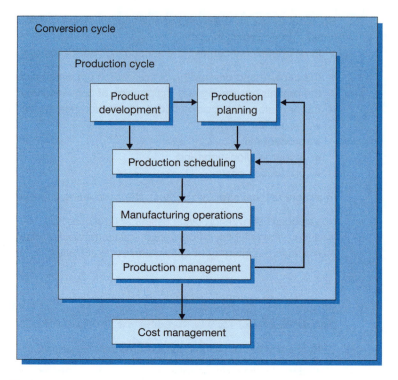

**Figure 10.1** Conversion cycle

 ## Product development

Product development can be defined as a conversion cycle process concerned with the conception, development, design and realisation of a new product. However, it is not only concerned with the identification of new development opportunities and the generation of new product ideas, but is, perhaps more importantly, concerned with establishing the feasibility/plausibility of any new product.

A new product can be classified as either:

■ a product that is new to the marketplace, or
■ a product that is new to the company.

This idea of categorising a new product according to either its newness to market, and/or its newness to the company was developed by Booz-Allen and Hamilton (1982)[3] who suggested that a product would be considered new to the marketplace where it was:

■ a *variation* of an existing product/product line, or
■ a *revision* or update of an existing product, or
■ an *augmentation/enhancement* of an existing product/product line.

A product would be considered new to the company where it was:

■ an *extension* to an existing product/product line,
■ a *repositioning* of an existing product/product line, or
■ a completely *new* product.

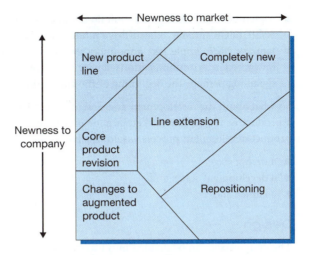

**Figure 10.2** Product development

Source: Booz Allen and Hamilton (1982), *New Product Management for the 1980s*,
Booz Allen Hamilton Inc., New York.

Have a look at Figure 10.2.

Consider for example the increasingly ubiquitous Apple iPod. Since the launch of the iPod by Apple Inc., in 2001, there have been a number of changes/improvements. How would each of these changes/improvements be classified using the Booz-Allen and Hamilton classification?

Have a look at the following timeline – after each date (and narrative), a possible (Booz-Allen and Hamilton) classification is presented – *in italics*. Do you agree with the classifications?

## Apple iPod – a development timeline

- October 2001: first generation iPod launched – all white model, monochrome screen, with a 5GB or 10GB hard drive, and scroll wheel (*new product*).
- July 2002: second generation iPod was launched – all white model with a 10GB or 20GB hard drive, monochrome screen, with touch wheel (*product revision*).
- January 2004: third generation iPod was launched – multi-function click wheel, available in silver, gold, pink, blue and green with 4GB hard drive (a 6GB hard-drive version was released in February 2005) (*product variation*).
- July 2004: fourth generation iPod launched with click wheel – all white model with monochrome screen, available in 20GB or 40GB hard-drive models (*product augmentation/ enhancement*).
- October 2004: iPod with colour display (iPod Photo) launched – all white, colour display, available in 40GB and 60GB hard drive models. Additional colour models were released in February 2005 – 30GB hard drive version – and July 2005 – 20GB and 60GB hard drive versions) – (*product augmentation/enhancement*).
- January 2005: first generation iPod Shuffle launched – all white model, no display, available in 512MB and 1GB hard drive versions with Flash memory (*product extension*).
- September 2005: iPod Nano launched – white or black body, with click wheel, flash memory (USB only), available with 1GB hard drive (2GB hard-drive and 4GB hard-drive models were released in February 2006) (*product extension*).
- October 2005: fifth generation iPod Video launched – black or white body with widescreen colour display, 30GB or 60GB hard-drive versions (USB only), (*product repositioning*).

- September 2006: sixth generation iPod launched – improved display music search function, 30GB, 60GB and 80GB hard-drive models (*product revision*).
- January 2007: Apple Inc. announces the arrival of the iPhone (available June 2007) – an integrated telecommunications device with multi-media capabilities (music and video) signalling perhaps the beginning of the end of the iPod (*new product*).

So what about the development and design process? Broadly speaking, irrespective of whether a product is new to the marketplace, or indeed, new to the company, it is very likely that the product development process would involve, at the very least, three key stages, these being;

- a design stage,
- a development stage, and
- a launch stage.

## Design

The design stage can be divided into three activities:

- design generation,
- design screening, and
- design testing.

### Design generation

Design generation is concerned with the identification and generation of new product designs. Often referred to as the fuzzy front end of product development – because of the general uncertainty surrounding the outcome of any proposed new product design – it is perhaps the most crucial aspect of any product development process, an aspect which whilst often time consuming, is generally viewed as being a relatively inexpensive activity (Smith and Reinertsen, 1998).

Okay, so where do such designs originate? From many sources, for example, from customers, competitors, employees, research and development groups internal and/or external to the company/organisation, management, internal focus groups and many more. And they should all be considered however bizarre they may appear to be. Remember, some of the most ridiculed and derided product designs have not only gone on to become hugely successful and highly profitable products but have, more importantly, gone on to become an essential aspect of modern society. Can you imagine 21st century society without for example the aeroplane, the motor car or the television!

### Design screening

Design screening is concerned with the analysis of the new product design ideas/concepts – that is the translation of a new product design into a business specific context and the elimination of those ideas which whilst conceptually feasible are nonetheless technologically/commercially doubtful.

It is generally concerned with four interrelated questions:

- Is the design of the product plausible? If so,
- is the manufacture of the product technically feasible? If so,
- is the target market for the product identifiable? And finally, and perhaps most importantly,
- is the production, distribution and retailing of the product likely to be profitable?

### Design testing

The design testing stage is concerned with assessing the qualitative characteristics of the design. In some industries – for example information and communication technology-related industries – such testing is sometimes referred to as alpha testing: an internal company/ organisation pre-production testing to identify and eliminate possible design defects and/or deficiencies. In essence, design testing represents the first critical assessment of the new product design, its purpose being to:

- consider the quality of the design,
- assess the functionality of the potential new product,
- determine the durability of the potential new product, and
- identify and make recommendations on the resource implications of manufacturing/ producing the new product.[4]

## Development

The development stage can be divided into two activities:

- product testing, and
- market testing.

### Product testing

Product testing is concerned with assessing the quantitative characteristics of the product. It generally involves two stages:

- producing a physical prototype of the new product – based on the approved design to identify any required alterations/adjustments, and
- producing an initial run of the product to test/determine customer acceptance of the new product.

This latter stage – the external testing of the product – is sometimes referred to as beta testing, the purpose of which is to:

- assess the performance of the product in a range of external customer-related situations and identify how the product performs in an actual user environment,
- determine any product defects/faults that are more likely to be revealed by the actual product, and
- provide recommendations for possible product modifications/corrections.

Unlike alpha testing which is undertaken in a controlled internal environment using company/ organisation employees, beta testing is undertaken in an unrestricted external environment using 'real' customers to perform the evaluation.

### Market testing

Once the design has been evaluated (alpha tested), and a product developed and appraised (beta tested), it may be necessary to consider the target market of the product. A gamma test (or in-market test)[5] is a product-based test that is sometimes used to determine/measure the extent to which a new product will meet the need/satisfy the requirements of the target customers. Such a test seeks to evaluate the product itself through a placement of the new product in a field setting – for example a target distribution within a geographically constrained area for a specific period of time. Such a test was recently used by the Midcounties Co-operative Society in its trial testing of Pay-by-Touch in early 2006.[6]

Gamma testing can be used not only to identify the advertising and promotional require-ments of the new product launch but, more importantly, to determine the likely selling price and potential sales volume of the new product.

## Launch

Whilst the product launch is of course the final stage of the product development process – a stage that is often by far the most publicly visible (consider, for example, the much publicised and very delayed product launch of Microsoft Vista[7] during the early part of 2007) – it is perhaps more importantly the first stage of the product life cycle.[8] Prior to any new product launch, whilst it is of course important to ensure that a new product launch plan/strategy has been prepared and agreed, it is perhaps equally important to ensure:

■ the new product has been successfully evaluated,
■ market receptivity has been tested,
■ all product documentation (including, for example, user documentation, operating manuals and maintenance instructions) have been completed and finalised,
■ all production processes have been validated and are fully operational,
■ all advertising, product brochures, marketing materials, press releases and website pages have been prepared,
■ appropriate sales and distribution channels and target markets have been identified and established, and
■ all sales, service and support personnel have been fully trained.

## Development and design – protecting new products

Once a product has been developed and successfully launched many legal questions can arise. For example, if it is necessary to protect the intellectual property of a product and preserve the new product from imitation, how would such protection be enforced? For example, would such protection be legally enforceable? If it would be, in which legal jurisdictions would it be enforceable, how much would such legal protection cost and, more importantly, how long will such legal protection last?

There are four main types of intellectual property, these being:

■ copyrights – these protect material, such as literature, art, music, sound recordings, films and broadcasts,
■ trade marks – these protect signs that can distinguish a company's/organisation's products and/or services from another company's/organisation's products and/or services,
■ design rights – these protect the visual appearance/aesthetic appearance of a product, and
■ patents – these protect the technical and functional aspects of product and/or service.

Each of these is regulated by different combinations of legislation. For example in the UK:

■ copyrights are regulated by the Copyright, Designs and Patents Act 1988 (as amended),
■ trade marks are regulated by the Trade Marks Act 1994 (as amended),
■ design rights are regulated by the Copyright, Designs and Patents Act 1988, the Design Right Rules 1989 and the Design Right (Amendment) Rules 1992, and
■ patents are regulated by the Patents Act 1977, the Copyright, Designs and Patents Act 1988, the Regulatory Reform (Patents) Order 2004 and the Patents Act 2004.

Note: Although copyrights, trade marks, and design rights are often only enforceable in very specific circumstances, they are nonetheless relatively cheap and fairly easy to obtain. Patents however tend to involve complex approval processes and are, as a result, much more difficult to obtain and even more expensive to defend and maintain.

The UK Patent office is responsible for intellectual property in the UK.[9]

**Production planning/scheduling**

## Production planning

Production planning can be defined as the planning of human and non-human resources for the purpose of producing products to accommodate customer/client requirements, and is used to ensure that an appropriate quantity of products is manufactured as efficiently and as economically as possible. Put simply, to ensure the right resources are available at the right time, and at the right place to enable the production of the right goods.

There are many factors driving the need for effective production planning, perhaps the most important of these being:

- the increasing complexity of both products and markets,
- the increasingly integrated nature of production processes and, perhaps most importantly,
- the increasing competition within the marketplace.

Although specific details and stages may differ from company to company or organisation to organisation, depending on for example the nature of the production process – that is whether products are manufactured to order or whether they are manufactured to stock, and the location of the manufacturing process – that is whether products are produced in-house or whether some of the manufacturing process is outsourced – in general, the development of a production plan would include some, if not all, of the following stages:

- the establishment of a production/manufacturing sequence,
- the generation of a processing procedure/structure,
- the identification of manufacturing centres' capacity/resource requirements,[10]
- the production of a Bill of Materials (BOM),
- the development of a master production schedule (see below), and
- the establishment of monitoring/control procedures to monitor the production/manufacturing sequence.

## Production scheduling

Production scheduling can be defined as the allocating of resources and the sequencing of activities to ensure the efficient production of goods and services, the aim of such a schedule being the management and coordination of resource flows within the manufacturing process, and the identification and, where possible, the elimination of possible resource conflicts. Accurate and effective production scheduling can not only improve the efficiency of production flows (and thereby increase productivity) and minimise average production time (and therefore operating costs), but perhaps more importantly maximise the utilisation of human and non-human resources, and minimise the need for excessive stocks of raw materials, production components and work-in-progress.

Note: Because production schedules will normally contain specific target start times/dates and completion times/dates they can – and indeed invariably are – used as a control mechanism to measure actual performance/achievements.

## Manufacturing operations

The key part of any conversion cycle is of course the actual manufacturing process – that is the physical creation of the product. Although the specifics of the manufacturing process(s) would differ from product to product, company to company or organisation to organisation, in general such manufacturing processes can be classified either by type or by orientation.

Have a look at Figure 10.3.

### Classification by type

From a functional perspective, manufacturing processes can be classified as:

- continuous manufacturing (or flow manufacturing),
- batch manufacturing (or intermittent manufacturing), or
- on-demand manufacturing

Continuous manufacturing is a method of manufacture in which homogeneous products are continuously produced through a series of standardised procedures. It is generally defined as the complete and uninterrupted manufacture of a product from the raw material components to the final product.

Batch manufacturing is a method of manufacture in which products are produced in discrete groups (or batches)[11] which require the same raw materials and production processing/operations. It is generally defined as the intermittent manufacture of a product.

On-demand manufacturing is a method of manufacture in which discrete products are produced in accordance with a customer's instructions/requirements.

### Classification by orientation

From an orientational perspective, manufacturing processes can be classified as either:

- push-based, or
- pull-based.

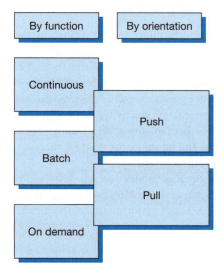

**Figure 10.3** Classification of manufacturing processes

## Push-based manufacturing

Continuous manufacturing and batch manufacturing are sometimes referred to as push-based manufacturing inasmuch as such manufacturing is normally supply orientated – that is the lower the levels of stock of a finished product the company/organisation possesses, the greater the levels of manufacture. A push-based manufacturing system possesses two key features:

- all products are manufactured in accordance with a pre-determined demand forecast, and
- all information flows in the same direction as the production, that is from the company/organisation to the customer.

## Pull-based manufacturing

On-demand production is normally referred to as pull manufacturing inasmuch as such manufacturing is normally demand orientated – that is the manufacture of a product only commences when a sales order is received from a customer/client. In a pull-based manufacturing system, information flows in the opposite direction to production – from the customer to the company/organisation.

## Changing nature of the manufacturing environment

Since the latter part of the 20th century, increasing market competition, the availability of new technologies and the ever-changing demands of customers/clients have resulted in the emergence of a number of alternative manufacturing environments to the traditional push-based manufacturing environment. Perhaps the most important of these have been:

- the lean manufacturing environment,
- the flexible manufacturing environment, and
- the adaptive manufacturing environment.

### The traditional manufacturing environment – it's all about push

The 1970s/early 1980s was the era of push manufacturing – an era in which production companies/organisations focused on building production capacity and, perhaps more importantly, maximising production throughput, with production almost exclusively based on demand-based forecasts. A manufacturing environment rooted in the post-Victorian industrial beliefs of the early 20th century, it was, and indeed still remains, an essentially supply orientated process, based on a simple philosophy of make as much as you can, as fast as you can – a manufacturing philosophy best suited to manufacturing environments in which:

- production complexity is relatively low, and
- product demand is fairly stable/fairly predictable.

Although many manufacturing companies/organisations have for various reasons now moved away from a dependency on the traditional manufacturing environment, variations of push-based manufacturing still continue to be used, especially by those manufacturers who have relocated their manufacturing operations to the so-called third world countries to exploit the low cost of human resources.

It is also still popular with many petrochemical companies/organisations.

### The lean manufacturing environment – from push to pull

Lean manufacturing has a long and distinguished history (see Womack *et al.*, 1991) – a history that can be traced back to Elias Whitney,[12] Frederick Winslow Taylor,[13] Frank Bunker Gilbreth,[14] Henry Ford[15] of the Ford Motor Company Inc., Alfred P. Sloan[16] of General Motor Company

Inc. and, of course, Taichii Ohno and Shigeo Shingo[17] of the Toyota Motor Company, co-inventors of the Toyota Production System[18] as immortalised in the writings of Norman Bodek.[19] It was, and indeed still remains, a management philosophy – a set of core values and beliefs whose *raison d'être* is to get the right things, to the right place, at the right time and in the right quantity, whilst maintaining flexibility and openness to change. Focusing on the reduction of over-production, the efficient use of transportation, the elimination of waiting, the elimination of excessive stocks, the minimising of motion and the elimination of production defects, lean manufacturing encapsulates three core concepts:

- reflective analysis,
- continuous improvement – often referred to as *kaizen*,[20] and
- mistake-proofing – often referred to as *poka-yoke*,[21]

to achieve its core objectives of:

- minimising waste,
- maximising the use of scarce resources,
- decreasing production times,
- improving product quality and, where appropriate, product diversity,
- promoting risk sharing – between the company and the customer/client, and
- reducing production costs.

Whilst lean manufacturing was introduced with varying degrees of success, by a wide range of companies/organisations during the late 1980s/early 1990s – especially US-based companies keen to replicate the high profit margins of their Japanese competitors – in general lean manufacturing and its various contemporary (re)incarnations has tended to work best in manufacturing environments in which:

- product demand is fairly stable, and
- product variability is relatively low.

Examples of industries in which the lean 'pull-based' manufacturing environment has been introduced and indeed continues to be used (with some success), include for example:

- the motor car manufacturing industry (e.g. Ford, General Motors, Toyota, Renault),
- the computer hardware production industry (e.g. Apple, IBM and Hewlett Packard), and
- the pharmaceutical industry (e.g. AstraZeneca).

### The flexible manufacturing environment – making lean leaner

In response to escalating global competition and increasing market volatility, the late 1980s/early 1990s saw the emergence of a new post-industrial manufacturing environment – a new 'flexible' manufacturing environment in which manufacturing responsiveness, operational flexibility,[22] product adaptability and, above all, product availability, became key factors in the battle to maintain product sales and market share. A new manufacturing environment in which the reflective questioning of the lean manufacturing environment – that is how can *we* do what *we* do better, was replaced with a more reflexive questioning of what do *you* want us to do.

Whilst there can be little doubt that in some companies/organisations flexible manufacturing clearly provided for better resource utilisation, lower direct labour cost, greatly reduced levels of stocks, better product quality, lower cost/unit of output and reduced errors – and as a result lower levels of rework, repairs and/or rejects – it was nonetheless found to be an expensive and very costly system to implement and operate. Indeed it was this issue of cost that prompted many companies/organisations who had embraced the new flexible manufacturing environment to search for and adopt alternative forms of flexibility. The most common alternative adopted by many of these companies was the relocation of manufacturing activities to economic agents located outside the company. So began the era of outsourcing[23] in the manufacturing industry.

### The adaptive manufacturing environment – using new technology

As the latter part of the 1990s came to a close and the early part of the 21st century arrived full of anticipation and hope, manufacturing companies again found themselves on the precipice of an uncertain future. Not only had the once-established logic of traditional push manufacturing found itself under increasing pressure, despite its many years of proven success, alternatives such as lean manufacturing and flexible manufacturing had failed to deliver a cost-effective response to the increasing competition within the global marketplace. What had been seen as the brave new world had become no more than a reincarnation of the same old nightmare – a nightmare in which the once key differentiating characteristics of product availability, cost efficiency and product quality had been replaced by demands for shorter product life cycles, speedier pull-based production and quicker delivery and response times.

It was in response to this increasingly time-sensitive environment that the adaptive manufacturing environment emerged. A manufacturing environment in which the key not only to sustaining production flexibility but also maintaining the product/service delivery velocity demanded by customers/clients was the close integration of information and communication technologies throughout the conversion cycle.

Note: Although the use of information and communication technologies within manufacturing operations had been widespread for many years, such use had often been disjointed and fragmented. It was the emergence of internet-based networking during the mid/late 1990s that provided for the wholesale integration of such information and communication technologies throughout the conversion cycle, allowing manufacturing companies to link product development and design to production planning/scheduling, to manufacturing operations, to production management and co-ordination and to cost control.

### Managing pull-based customisation

So what of the future? Whilst there can be little doubt that change over the past four decades to the manufacturing environment have helped to:

- improve conversion cycle response times,
- improve product quality, and
- improve conversion cycle visibility and product traceability,

perhaps the greatest challenge facing contemporary manufacturing is the issue of customisation: that is improving the use of adaptive manufacturing systems to produce individually customised output or, perhaps more specifically, improving the use of adoptive manufacturing systems to efficiently combine the low unit cost mass production with the flexibility of pull-based (or individual) customisation. So, what is pull-based (or individual) customisation?

Traditionally, customisation was categorised as:

- cosmetic customisation in which companies/organisations manufacture a standardised product which is marketed to different customers, in different geographic/demographic market segments, in different ways,
- transparent customisation in which companies/organisations provide customers with unique products without informing them that the product is customised, or
- collaborative customisation in which companies/organisations produce a standardised product, but the customer is able to customise the product within a pre-determined and often restricted menu.

Such customisation was generally referred to as push-based customisation inasmuch as it was imposed by/offered by the manufacturer to the customer – a process in which the customer was no more than a reactive recipient.

Increasingly however customers are requiring a greater direct input into and a greater influence on the manufacture of the products they wish to purchase. Such customisation has become known as pull-based (or individual) customisation: that is customisation in which the customer determines the precise nature of the product prior to manufacture, a process in which the customer is no longer a reactive recipient but a proactive contributor.

## Production management

Production management – sometimes referred to as operations management – can be defined as the coordination and controlling of all the activities required to make a produce a product, and encapsulates a range of strategic, tactical and operational issues. For example:

- at a strategic level production management would be concerned with:
  - determining the size and location of manufacturing operations,
  - deciding the structure of service or telecommunications networks, and
  - designing technology supply chains,
- at a tactical level production management would be concerned with:
  - plant layout and structure,
  - project management methods,
  - equipment selection, and
  - resources replacement cycles,
- at an operational level production management would be concerned with:
  - production scheduling and control,
  - stock management,
  - quality control and inspection,
  - traffic and materials handling, and
  - equipment maintenance policies.

Put simply, the aim of production management is to ensure all production-related processes and activities are organised efficiently, performed effectively and managed competently.

## Cost management

Within the context of the conversion cycle, the term cost management is a term used to describe a range of finance orientated planning and control techniques used for conversion cycle decision-making purposes. We will look at cost management in more detail later in this chapter.

## Conversion cycle – data input

Within the conversion cycle, irrespective of whether manufacturing is push-based (continuous and/or batch) or pull-based (on-demand) there would be a number of source documents (either paper-based or computer-based) that would be used to instigate, record and/or monitor the production/manufacturing of products.

Note: some of these documents, whilst relevant to the conversion cycle, originate within either the revenue cycle (see Chapter 8) and/or the expenditure cycle (see Chapter 9).

Such documents would include for example:

■ a sales forecast,
■ a production budget,
■ a product design schedule,
■ a customer order,
■ a sales order,
■ a bill of materials,
■ a production schedule,
■ a production order,
■ a materials requisition,
■ an equipment requisition,
■ a labour work record,
■ a movement record,
■ an inspection report,
■ a production completion document, and,
■ a production order cost assessment report.

## Sales forecast

A sales forecast is the expected demand for a company's/organisation's products based on market requirements. Such a forecast is extremely important where push-based continuous manufacturing or batch manufacturing is used to ensure over-production does not occur.

## Production budget

A production budget provides a financial limit to the costs – materials, labour and expenses – that may be incurred. Such costs would normally be established by reference to the product design, the bill of materials and the production plan/schedule.

Such a production budget could be:

■ process-based – where push-based continuous manufacturing is used,
■ batch-based – where push-based batch manufacturing is used, or
■ order/job-based – where pull-based on-demand manufacturing is used.

## Product design schedule

The product design schedule is the blueprint of the product and provides the basis for determining what assets and resources will be required to produce the product. Where push-based continuous manufacturing or batch manufacturing is used it is likely that the product design schedule will remain unchanged or will only change as a result of a company/organisation (internally generated) decision. Where pull-based on demand manufacturing is used, especially where customers/clients are able to customise the products/services they order, amendments to the product design specification may be required on a regular basis and as a result an amended product design schedule may be produced and matched with each customer/client order.

## Customer order

A customer order is an externally generated revenue cycle document submitted by the customer/client requesting the purchase of goods and/or the provision of services.

## Sales order

A sales order is an internally generated revenue cycle document used to approve the sale of products/services to a customer and/or client. It is generated in response to the receipt of a customer order. Where pull-based on-demand manufacturing is used such a sales order would initiate the manufacture of the product

## Bill of materials

A bill of materials specifies the types of raw materials/components and the quantities of raw materials/components to be used in the manufacture of a product. The bill of materials would be related to a specific product design specification. Where such a specification is amended – either as result of an internal company decision or customer/client demand – a revised bill of materials would need to be produced. An example bill of materials is provided in Example 10.1.

| BILL OF MATERIALS | | | |
|---|---|---|---|
| Product no. .................... Batch quantity .................... Authorisation no. .................... | | | |
| Material/ component | Description | Quantity per batch | Quantity required |
| | | | |

**Example 10.1** A bill of materials document

## Production schedule

A production schedule specifies the sequence and timing of operations to be used in the manufacture of the product. An example production schedule is provided in Example 10.2.

## Production order

A production order (sometime referred to as a work order) is generally used in pull-based on-demand manufacturing and is generated by the formal issue of a sales order to a client An example production order is provided in Example 10.3.

## Materials requisition

A materials requisition would authorise stores to issue raw materials/components to specific individuals and/or work locations. For control purposes, such requisitions would normally

| | | Order 1 | | Order 2 | |
|---|---|---|---|---|---|

**PRODUCTION SCHEDULE**

Department no.          ...................
Production period     ...................

Production schedule no.   ...................
Page                                    ....... of .......

| Production batch no. | Production quantity (units) | Commencement date | Completion date | Commencement date | Completion date |
|---|---|---|---|---|---|
| | | | | | |

**Example 10.2** A production schedule document

**PRODUCTION ORDER**

Product order no.          ...................
Product description     ...........................................................................................................

Product design ref          ...................
...........................................................................................................

| Production location | Operation | Description/ activity | Standard hours | | Actural units produced | Actual units scrapped | Inspection | |
|---|---|---|---|---|---|---|---|---|
| | | | Set-up | Production | | | Date | Insp. |
| | | | | | | | | |

**Example 10.3** A production order document

specify standard quantities – as indicated by the production design/bill of materials. An example materials requisition is provided in Example 10.4.

### Equipment requisition

An equipment requisition would authorise the use of production equipment as specified in the production schedule, and may require the relocation of existing equipment and/or the acquisition of new equipment. An example equipment requisition is provided in Example 10.5.

| MATERIALS REQUISITION | | | | | |
|---|---|---|---|---|---|
| Issue no. ...................        Authorisation ................... <br> Production order no. ................... <br> Production location ................... | | | | | |
| Materials/ components | Description | Stock ref. | Quantity issued | Units cost (£) | Total cost (£) |
| | | | | | |
| Distribution path ................... <br> Receipt ................... <br> Accounting ................... | | | | | |

**Example 10.4** A materials requisition document

| EQUIPMENT REQUISITION | | | | | | |
|---|---|---|---|---|---|---|
| Issue no. ...................      Period ................... <br> Production order no. ...................      Authorisation ................... <br> Production location ................... | | | | | | |
| Equipment Ref | Description | Number issued | Unit cost (£) | Total cost (£) | Comment | |
| | | | | | | |
| Distribution path ................... <br> Receipt ................... <br> Accounting ................... | | | | | | |

**Example 10.5** An equipment requisition document

## Labour work record

A labour work record would record the staff hours expended on a production order. For control purposes, the actual hours worked would be compared to the hours indicated within the production schedule.

## Movement record

A movement record is used to authorise the movement of a product during its various stages of manufacture and can be used not only to ensure production schedule timetables are adhered to/complied with, but also monitor the process of manufacture.

## Inspection report

An inspection report is used to ensure the quality of manufacture. Such quality inspections may occur at any stage of manufacture and are generally designed to confirm that all product manufacturing requirements are complied with.

## Production completion document

The production completion document signifies the end of the manufacturing process. On completion of all the various stages of manufacture, completed products would be transferred to stores awaiting their sale/delivery to the customer. Where pull-based on-demand manufacturing is used it is important to ensure that all manufacturing requirements have been complied with before the manufactured products are despatched to the customer.

## Production order cost assessment report

Where pull-based on-demand manufacturing is used, a production order cost assessment report would be produced on a regular basis to provide a comparative assessment of:

- the on-going cost of manufacturing the products as required by the production order, and
- the initial budgeted cost of manufacturing the products as required by the production order.

## Conversion cycle – data processing

Conversion cycle data/information is data/information specifically related to production/manufacturing orientated transactions. Such data/information can be processed using either:

- paper-based documentation, or
- computer-based documentation.

## Using paper-based documentation

Consider the following example.

*LOQ plc is a UK-based manufacturer. The company manufactures a range of signal processing components for use in the manufacture of HD televisions. Because of the high cost of the processing components and the specialist nature of the product, the company only manufactures to order. That is the company operates a pull-based manufacturing system.*

*On 5 February 2007, the company received a manufacturing enquiry from NeiChiO, a Taipei-based Taiwanese company for the manufacture of 60,000 NFC861 type 2 signal processors. Because NeiChiO required a number of alterations to be made to the basic design of the type 2 signal processor, extensive negotiations took place in Taipei and in London during late February 2007 and early March 2007 to clarify the precise nature of the amendments requested by NeiChiO. On 27 March 2007 LOQ plc submitted a fixed price bid for the supply of the type 2 signal processors. The bid price was £732,000.*

*Note: To submit a bid price LOQ plc prepared:*

- *a revised design specification based on NeiChiO's requirements, and*
- *a detail analysis/budget of the total cost of manufacturing and supplying the volume of signal processors required by NeiChiO.*

*On 5 April 2007 NeiChiO submitted an official order to LOQ plc for 60,000 NFC816 type 2 signal processors to be delivered in three equal batches in June 2007, September 2007 and December 2007.*

Assuming LOQ plc use paper-based documentation to process conversion cycle transactions how would the conversion cycle activities associated with fulfilling the above order be documented? Have a look at the following.

*Prior to the submission of the bid to NeiChiO, LOQ plc prepared:*

- *an order-related budget providing a detailed analysis/budget of the total cost of manufacturing and supplying 55,000 NFC816 type 2 signal processors, and*
- *a revised design schedule providing a detailed specification of the amended NFC861 type 2 signal processors.*

*Note: The preparation of these was coordinated by production planning in consultation with cost management and production design, with submission of the bid authorised by LOQ's production director.*

*On acceptance of the bid, NeiChiO submitted a formal customer order to LOQ plc. The customer order provided details of:*

- *the total number of goods ordered,*
- *the total price to be paid for the goods ordered,*
- *the time and date of delivery of the ordered goods, and*
- *the conditions of supply/manufacture.*

*On receipt of the customer order LOQ plc issued a sales order. The issue of the sales order was coordinated by revenue cycle sales management staff.*

*Note: As suggested earlier, in a pull-based manufacturing environment, the issue of the sales order effectively marks the commencement of the production/manufacture process.*

*On the issue of the sales order, the following documents would be generated:*

- *a bill of materials (based on the amended specification for the NFC861 type 2 signal processors as detailed in the revised design schedule), providing details of:*
  - *the types of materials and components required to satisfy the sales order, and*
  - *the quantities of materials necessary to complete the order,*
- *a production schedule providing details of:*
  - *the sequence of activities/operations required to manufacture the signal processors,*
  - *the operational centres to be used in the manufacture of the signal processors – that is which work centre(s) are within the manufacturing environment,*
  - *the human and non-human resource requirements for each activity/operation within the manufacturing process, and*
  - *the time duration for each manufacturing activity/operation required to manufacture the signal processors, and,*

- *a production order authorising the commencement of the manufacture of the order – the manufacture of 55,000 NFC816 type 2 signal processors.*

*Note: In a pull-based manufacturing environment, a production order would only be valid where an authorised customer order number/reference exists.*

*On the issue of a production order, the following documents (where necessary) would be generated:*

- *a materials requisition directing the stores department to issue materials and/or component parts to a specific location and/or an authorised individual,*
- *an equipment requisition allocating specific equipment/asset-based resources to the production order,*
- *a labour work record providing details of the hours worked/expended on the manufacture of the products,*
- *a movement record providing details of the movement of the production order from one location/work centre to another location work centre, and*
- *an inspection report providing details of quality assessments undertaken during the manufacturing process.*

*Note: Each of the above documents would only be valid where an authorised production order number/reference is used.*

*Once production is complete, the completed type 2 signal processors would be transferred to stores awaiting delivery to the customer. On completion of production a production completion document would normally be finalised.*

*Although the production of the 60,000 NFC816 type 2 signal processors was a fixed price, it would still be necessary – for both planning and control purposes – to identify any under/over-spending that may have occurred during the production/manufacturing of the processors.*

*The actual costs incurred in the manufacture of the signal processors for NeiChiO would be accumulated on a regular basis – probably using a batch approach. Such information would be obtained from the materials requisitions, equipment requisitions and labour work records related to the production order with the cost for each resource consumed derived by using a standard and/or average unit cost, with all such accumulated costs monitored against the original bid price to identify any potential under- and/or over-spending. Because the manufacture of the signal processors covers a number of reporting periods (approximately nine months) a production order cost assessment report would be produced monthly, based on the production schedule, to provide a comparative assessment of the on-going cost of the production order.*

Clearly, in a contemporary manufacturing environment the use of paper-based documentation to record/process production orientated transaction data/information can of course be problematic. Firstly, because of the physical nature of the documentation and the volume often generated, the use of such paper-based documentation can be very expensive – not only in an administrative/management context but perhaps, more importantly, in eco-environmental context.[24]

Secondly, because conversion cycle processes and activities are invariably document dependent, if the use, timing and flow of documentation is not properly monitored or controlled:

- conversion cycle processes and activities may be delayed resulting in possible loss of revenue, and/or
- internal controls may be compromised resulting in a loss of conversion cycle assets and/or resources.

Consider, for example, a failure by production planning to generate an approved material requisition for a new production order. Such a failure could result in required raw materials/components not being issued by the stores at the correct time and/or to the correct location, resulting in:

- a delay in the production of goods,
- a failure to achieve delivery deadlines, and
- the imposition of possible non-delivery penalties (if provided for in the conditions of supply).

Thirdly, because companies/organisations often adopt a file orientated system to store/maintain such documentation: that is completed documentation is returned to and therefore stored and located within the source department/function within the conversion cycle responsible for generating the documentation, it can result in the possible fragmentation of data management and, perhaps inevitably, the politicisation of data access.[25]

## Using computer-based documentation

Consider the following example.

*EFMM plc is a UK-based manufacturer making specialist computer components to order.*

*On 20 March 2007, the company received a manufacturing enquiry from JCN Inc., a US-based computer manufacturer, for the manufacture and supply of 45,000 combined GHP/SMN reflex multi-core processors for incorporation into JCN's new fourth-generation SMARTmap® notebook to be launched in March 2008.*

*The combined GHP/SMN reflex multi-core processor is a standard product that has been manufactured and supplied by EFMM plc to a number of US, European and Asia-based, computer manufacturers over the past 10 months.*

*On 2 April 2007 EFMM plc submitted a variable price bid for the supply of the above components. The bid price was £1,623,000.*

*On 15 May 2007 JCN Inc. submitted (using a secure web-based facility) an official order to EFMM plc for the supply of 45,000 combined GHP/SMN reflex multi-core processors for delivery by 30 September 2007.*

*Assuming EFMM plc operates computer-based online documentation how would the conversion cycle activities associated with fulfilling the above order be documented?*

Let's assume EFMM plc uses computer integrated manufacturing.[26] For internal control purposes:

- all computer-based facilities are password protected and access to computer-based facilities is restricted to relevant and appropriate departmental personnel,
- all production/manufacturing orientated transaction data are processed online and stored on preformatted documentation within a central relational database, and
- all documentation is maintained in virtual/electronic format only – paper documentation is only produced when requested/required.

In addition EFMM plc uses the following organisational functions/departments within its conversion cycle:

- production design,
- production planning/scheduling,
- manufacturing,

- production management,
- stock management, and
- cost management.

*On receipt of the manufacturing enquiry from JCN Inc., an enquiry was acknowledged and a formal response automatically generated. The enquiry would be routed via production management to the following three departments/functions:*

- *production design – to identify the product design specification and bill of materials for the combined GHP/SMN reflex multi-core processor,*
- *production planning/scheduling – to prepare a forecast production/manufacturing time-table, resource allocation and a detailed production schedule, and*
- *cost management – to prepare a cost estimate (based on standard costs) for the manu-facture of 45,000 combined GHP/SMN reflex multi-core processors.*

*On receipt of the above information, production management would prepare the variable price bid for JCN Inc. Production management would allocate a pending production order number.*

*Following review and approval by the production director the bid would be submitted to the prospective customer.*

*Note: In addition to the above, on receipt of the manufacturing enquiry, an automatic customer check would be undertaken to determine if JCN Inc. currently is or ever has been an existing customer of EFMM plc. The purpose of this is to identify any possible future issues that may arise.*

*On receipt of the customer order from JCN Inc., EFMM plc would issue a sales order – an automatic confirmation sales order receipt would be sent to JCN Inc.*

*Details of the issue of the sales order would be routed to production management who would activate the pending production order, which would now be regarded as an active production order. This would be made available to design management, production planning and cost management. On receipt of the production order:*

- *design management would issue and forward the revised design specification and revised bill of materials to production planning, and*
- *cost management would create/establish a 'live' budget for the sales order and forward the budget details to production planning.*

*On receipt of the above, production planning would allocate and schedule resources, both manufacturing resources and production staff requirements, for the completion of the pro-duction, and identify key inspection dates during the manufacturing process.*

*Notification (usually a copy of the production schedule) of material requirements would be routed to the stores systems – to inform stores management of the materials/components requirements. On receipt, stores management would issue the relevant materials/components to the work location(s) identified on the production schedule. Because all store materials/components are RFID tagged the stores ledger would be updated and the cost of raw materials would be automatically allocated to the production order on issue by stores management. Similarly, because all production staff use computer-based identification cards – time worked on a production order would also be automatically allocated to the production order.*

*Costs for the use of production equipment and other production overheads would be allocated by cost management based on the production schedule.*

*Note: Records of all time allocations would also be submitted to HRM/payroll for recon-ciliation with the individual production staff record of attendance.*

*All quality inspections would be undertaken by production management. A monthly produc-*
*tion order cost assessment would be prepared to monitor all costs being assigned to the*
*production order. On completion of the production a production completion report would*
*be completed. This would be routed to stores management, the stores ledger would be*
*automatically updated and a copy would also be routed to cost management.*

## Conversion cycle – the reality

Although the past few decades have seen information and communication technology having,
and indeed continuing to have, a major impact on a range of conversion cycle procedures
and activities, its practical implementation is often disjointed. In reality, many companies/
organisations continue to use production/manufacturing systems with little or no integration,
resulting in not only the inefficient management of assets and resources but, more importantly,
the inefficient management of data/information.

 ## Conversion cycle – data management

First we consider the file-oriented approach and then the data oriented approach.

### File orientated approach

#### *Primary files*
As in the other transaction processing cycles, conversion cycle primary files can be classified as
either:

- a master file, or
- a transaction file.

Although the specific data contained within each file would vary from company to company or
organisation to organisation, each file would nonetheless serve a similar purpose.

### Master files
Three possible master files may be used:

- a materials stock master file,
- a work-in-process master file, and
- a finished products/goods master file.

The materials stock master file would contain records of the raw materials, components and
other assemblies required by the company for the production process. The work-in-process
master file would summarise the materials, direct labour and overhead costs expended on
production orders currently in production, and the finished products/goods master file would
provide a record of completed stock items available for resale.

### Transaction files
Three possible transaction files may be used:

- a production order file,
- a materials issues file, and
- an operations or routing file.

The production order file would contain details relating to current production orders and data similar to the data elements contained in Example 10.3. An open production order file would also include details of the movement of production through its production process (especially where production occurs at different locations) to facilitate the monitoring of production orders as they move through the physical production operations.

The materials issues would contain details of materials issued to production orders in accordance with the approved bill of materials.

An operations file would contain details of production orders in progress.

### Secondary files

These would include for example:

- a location file,
- a history file, and
- an inspection file.

A location file would contain details of the status of a work centre, department or production location, and details relating to assigned production equipment and direct labour resources. A history file would contain details of past production orders, work centre performances and equipment utilisation. An inspection file would contain details of work centre, department or location quality assessments.

## Data orientated approach

Where a company/organisation uses a data orientated approach, although the contents of the conversion cycle database would be very similar to the contents of the files discussed above, the data would be organised differently, as structured records (usually in the form of a number of normalised tables).

So what function(s) does a company's/organisation's accounting information system provide to ensure the efficient functioning of a company/organisation conversion cycle?

## Cost management – the accounting information systems connection

Whilst the precise nature of the functions provided/activities undertaken by the accounting information system in relation to the conversion cycle would differ from company to company or organisation to organisation, in general the accounting information system would undertake a range of cost management-related activities concerned primarily with the collection of conversion cycle costs for two purposes:

- product costing – that is determining the total cost of a product/service, and
- performance measurement – that is assessing the performance of a function/activity within the company/organisation.

## Product costing

There are two stages to product costing:

- cost collection, and
- cost assessment.

### Cost collection

The collection or accumulation of production costs and the updating of production records would generally occur in concert with the actual physical production process, with the costs collected/accumulated on the same basis as the production methodology adopted by the company/organisation. For example, costs would be collected/accumulated on:

- a process basis – where continuous manufacturing or flow manufacturing is used (sometimes referred to as process costing),
- a job basis – where batch manufacturing or intermittent manufacturing is used (sometimes referred to as job costing), or
- a production order basis where on-demand manufacturing is used (sometimes referred to as contract costing or order costing).

Whichever process is adopted, the stages of the cost collection procedure would be as follows:

- the collection and assignment of all direct material costs, all direct labour costs and all direct expenses – with the amounts charged on the basis of standard unit costs,
- the accumulation and assignment of production overheads – with the amounts charged on the basis of a standard production overhead rate,
- the computation of the cost variances (for materials, direct labour, direct expenses and production overhead costs) based on differences between the actual costs (actual production × standard unit costs) and the expected costs (expected production × standard unit costs).

Note: Variances between actual unit costs and standard unit costs would not form part of the conversion cycle process.

When production is completed costs are transferred from the work-in-process file/record to the finished goods file/record, with the total costs posted to the stock control account in the general ledger.

### Cost assessment

For cost assessment purposes, the vast majority of companies/organisations in the UK use one of the following approaches (or an amended version) to determine the cost of a product and/or service:

- an absorption cost-based approach,
- a variable cost-based approach,
- an activity cost-based approach,
- a target cost-based approach, or
- a standard cost-based approach.

## Absorption cost-based approach

Absorption costing (also referred to as full costing) considers the total cost of manufacturing a product and/or providing a service: that is in addition to all direct costs, a proportion of production overhead costs are also apportioned (or more precisely absorbed),[27] with each product/service therefore charged with both fixed and variable production costs.

Using absorption costing, the production cost of a product (or the provision cost of a service) would therefore include:

- all direct material costs – that is those materials that have become a part of a product or have been used up in providing a service,

- all direct labour costs – that is those labour costs that can be easily traced to the manufacture of a product or the provision of a service,
- all direct expenses – that is those expenses directly applicable to the manufacture of a product or the provision of a service, and
- a proportion of indirect production overheads.

Have a look at the following:

|  | £ | £ |
|---|---|---|
| Sales |  | 150 |
| *Direct costs* |  |  |
| Direct materials | 50 |  |
| Direct labour | 40 |  |
| Direct expenses | 10 |  |
| *Prime cost* | 100 |  |
|  |  |  |
| Indirect costs: |  |  |
| Production overheads | 20 |  |
| *Product cost* | 120 |  |
|  |  |  |
| Period costs: |  |  |
| Non-production overheads | 10 |  |
| *Total product cost* |  | 130 |
| Net profit |  | 20 |

Note: Indirect production overheads (or non-production overheads) are considered a period cost and not a product cost/service cost – that is not until the product is sold and/or the service is provided do they take effect.

Consider the following example.

*XLT Ltd is a Hull-based company that manufactures desks. The company commenced trading on 1 January 2006. For the year ending 31 December 2006 production was expected to be 40,000 desks. However the company actually produced 50,000 desks but only managed to sell 45,000 desks.*

*The costs per desk are as follows:*

|  | £ |
|---|---|
| Direct materials | 40 |
| Direct labour | 5 |
| Variable overheads | 6 |

*Fixed costs for the period are:*

|  | £ |
|---|---|
| Production costs | 800,000 |
| Administration expenses | 100,000 |
| Selling costs | 140,000 |

*Sales commission is also paid at a rate of 5% of total sales revenue. All desks are sold at a retail price of £100.*

*Using an absorption cost-based approach we can prepare a profit statement for XLT Ltd for the year ending 31 December 2006 as follows:*

*Production overhead absorption rate would be: £800,000/40,000 = £20 per unit*

*Production costs would be: £40 + £5 + £6 + £20 = £71*

| | | £ | £ |
|---|---|---|---|
| Sales | 45,000 × £100 | | 4,500,000 |
| Production | 50,000 × £71 | 3,550,000 | |
| Minus closing stock | 5,000 × £71 | 355,000 | |
| | | | 3,195,000 |
| | | | 1,305,000 |
| Sales commission | 5% × 4,500,000 | | 225,000 |
| | | | 1,080,000 |
| Admin and sales costs | | | 240,000 |
| | | | 840,000 |
| Over-absorbed production overheads | | | 100,000 |
| Profit | | | 740,000 |

So what are the advantages and disadvantages of an absorption cost-based approach? The advantages are:

- it provides a summary total cost for a product and/or service,
- it can be used to identify the profitability of a product and/or service, and
- it complies with the valuation requirements of SSAP 9 for stocks and work-in-progress.

The main disadvantage of an absorption cost-based approach is it is a subjective approach, inasmuch as the allocation of fixed costs is arbitrary and can be politically motivated, leading (potentially) to the calculation of a misleading total cost for a product and/or service.

### Variable cost-based approach

Variable costing (also referred to as marginal costing), provides an alternative approach to the costing of products/services in which only the variable costs of production or service provision are charged to the product/service.

Fixed production costs are not considered to be the real costs of product production/service provision, but rather costs which enable product production/service provision to occur, and are therefore treated as period costs and charged to the period in which they are incurred. Stocks are valued on a variable production cost basis that excludes fixed production costs.

Using variable costing, the production cost of a product/the provision cost of a service would therefore include:

- all variable material costs – that is those materials that have become a part of a product or have been used up in providing a service,
- all variable labour costs – that is those labour costs that can be easily traced to the manufacture of a product or the provision of a service individual product, and
- all variable expenses – that is those expenses directly applicable to the manufacture of a product or the provision of a service.

Have a look at the following:

| | £ | £ | £ |
|---|---|---|---|
| Sales | | | 150 |
| *Variable costs* | | | |
| Direct materials | 50 | | |
| Direct labour | 40 | | |
| Direct expenses | 10 | | |
| *Total variable cost* | | | 100 |
| Contribution | | | 50 |
| *Fixed costs* | | | |
| Production overheads | | 20 | |
| Non-production overheads | | 10 | |
| *Total fixed costs* | | | 30 |
| Profit | | | 20 |

Note: All fixed overheads are considered a time cost and are expensed in the year incurred.
Consider the following example:

*RLK Ltd is a York-based company that manufactures chairs. The company commenced trading in 2003. For the year ending 31 December 2006 production was expected to be 60,000 chairs. However the company actually produced 55,000 chairs, but only managed to sell 50,000.*

*The costs per chair are as follows:*

|  | £ |
|---|---|
| Direct materials | 25 |
| Direct labour | 5 |
| Variable overheads | 7 |

*Fixed costs for the period are:*

|  | £ |
|---|---|
| Production costs | 300,000 |
| Administration expenses | 200,000 |
| Selling costs | 200,000 |

*Sales commission is also paid at a rate of 5% of total sales revenue. All chairs are sold at a retail price of £70.*

*Using a variable cost-based approach we can prepare a profit statement for RKL Ltd for the year ending 31 December 2006 as follows:*

*The variable cost would be: £25 + £5 + £7 = £37.*

|  |  | £ | £ |
|---|---|---|---|
| Sales | 50,000 × £70 |  | 3,500,000 |
| Production | 55,000 × £37 | 2,035,000 |  |
| Minus closing stock | 5,000 × £37 | 185,000 |  |
| Contribution |  |  | 1,850,000 |
|  |  |  | 1,650,000 |
| Sales commission | 5% × 3,500,000 |  | 175,000 |
|  |  |  | 1,475,000 |
| Fixed costs |  |  | 700,000 |
| Profit |  |  | 775,000 |

So what are the advantages and disadvantages of a variable cost-based approach? The advantages are:

- the contribution per unit is a useful indicator for management,
- there is no arbitrary allocation of costs,
- the recognition of cost behaviour provides better support for sales pricing and decision making, and
- it allows better control information.

The disadvantages of a variable cost-based approach are:

- it can be difficult to determine what are fixed costs and what are variable costs, and
- it does not comply with the valuation requirements SSAP 9 for stocks and work-in-progress.

## Activity cost-based approach

The activity cost-based approach (more commonly referred to as Activity-Based Costing (ABC)) provides yet another alternative approach to the costing of products and services. First defined by Kaplan and Bruns (1987) such an alternative arose primarily in response to criticisms aimed at the more traditional volume-based approaches.

Activity-based costing is founded on the understanding that costs arise because of the activities utilised, not because of the products and/or services produced, with the management and control of costs best achieved through the management of such activities.[28] Rather than levels/volumes of production, activity-based costing considers four different groups of activities giving rise to overheads, such as movement, production demand, quality and design, and requires all cost types to be identified and classified into:

- those costs which are volume-based,
- those costs which are activity-based, and
- those costs which may have some other basis.

Consider the following example:

*RTY Ltd has provided the following information on the production of two products, the Jet 203 and the Kite 402.*

| Activity | Overhead £ | Cost driver |
|---|---|---|
| Output related | 50,000 | machine hours |
| Material handling | 16,000 | kg of material |
| Production set-ups | 14,000 | production runs |
| Despatch | 20,000 | no. of customers |
| | 100,000 | |

| | |
|---|---|
| Cost of direct materials (per kg) | £6 |
| Cost of direct labour (per hour) | £5 |

| Production data | Jet 203 | Kite 402 |
|---|---|---|
| No. of units | 2,000 | 1,000 |
| Direct material per unit (kg) | 3 | 2 |
| Direct labour hours per unit | 2 | 1 |
| Machine hours per unit | 9 | 7 |
| Production runs in period | 20 | 50 |
| No. of customers in period | 4 | 16 |

*Using an activity-cost based approach the total cost of each product could be calculated as follows:*

**Output related based on machine hours (£50,000)**

| | Jet 203 | Kite 402 | Total |
|---|---|---|---|
| Total machine hours | | | |
| 2,000 units × 9hrs | 18,000 | | |
| 1,000 units × 7hrs | | 7,000 | 25,000 |
| | | | |
| Cost per hour £50,000/25,000 = £2 | | | |
| Cost per unit £2 × 9hrs | 18 | | |
| £2 × 7hrs | | 14 | |

**Material handling based on kg of material (£16,000)**

| | Jet 203 | Kite 402 | Total |
|---|---|---|---|
| Total material | | | |
| 2,000 units × 3kg | 6,000 | | |
| 1,000 units × 2kg | | 2,000 | 8,000 |
| Cost per kg £16,000/8,000 = £2 | | | |
| Cost per unit £2 × 3kg | 6 | | |
| £2 × 2kg | | 4 | |

**Production set-ups based on production runs (£14,000)**

| | | | |
|---|---|---|---|
| Number of production runs | 20 | 50 | 70 |
| Cost per run £14,000/70 = £200 | | | |
| Number of units per run 2,000/20 = 100 | | | |
| 1,000/50 = 20 | | | |
| Cost per unit £200/100 | 2 | | |
| £200/20 | | 10 | |

**Despatch based on number of customers (£20,000)**

| | | | |
|---|---|---|---|
| Number of customers | 4 | 16 | 20 |
| Cost per despatch £20,000/20 = £1,000 | | | |
| Number of units per despatch | | | |
| Jet 203      2,000/4 = 500 | | | |
| Kite 402     1,000/16 = 62.5 | | | |
| Cost per unit £1,000/500 | 2 | | |
| £1,000/62.5 | | 16 | |

| Cost of Product | Jet 203 | Kite 402 |
|---|---|---|
| | £ | £ |
| Materials   3kg × £6 | 18 | |
| 2kg × £6 | | 12 |
| Labour     2hrs × £5 | 10 | |
| 1hr × £5 | | 5 |
| Overheads | | |
| Output related | 18 | 14 |
| Materials handling | 6 | 4 |
| Production set-ups | 2 | 10 |
| Despatch | 2 | 16 |
| Total cost | 56 | 61 |

So what are the advantages and disadvantages of an activity cost-based approach? The advantages are:

- it focuses on activities and not production volumes;
- it can be used to identify loss-making products;
- it makes visible waste and non-value added, and
- it supports performance management and scorecards.

The disadvantages of an activity cost-based approach are:

- it is subjective,
- it is historical,
- it requires identification of cost drivers (activities),
- it requires the relating of activities to the production of a product/delivery of a service,
- it is an expensive and time-consuming exercise, and
- it does not comply with the valuation requirements of SSAP 9 for stocks and work-in-progress.

## Target cost-based approach

The target cost-based approach (more commonly referred to as target costing) is often considered to be a reversible cost accounting technique. That is rather than calculating the total cost of a product/service and then determining the market price of the product/service based on the total cost – for example, total cost plus a pre-determined profit margin – the target cost of a product/service is established by reference to the external marketplace. There are three alternative approaches to target costing these being:

- a price-based targeting approach,
- a cost-based targeting approach, and
- a value-based targeting approach.

Using a price-based targeting approach the target cost of a product/service is derived by subtracting the desired profit margin from a competitive market price of a similar and/or equivalent product/service.

Using a cost-based targeting approach the target cost of a product/service is derived by establishing a total cost for a product/service by reference to costs incurred by the company. The aim of this approach to seek to reduce, as far as possible, the costs incurred from the buying-in of goods and services from suppliers.

Using a value-based targeting approach the target cost of a product/service is determined by estimating the 'value' the market will place on the product/service (the value that the product/service would bring to the customer/client and how much the customer/client would be willing to pay) and then subtracting the desired profit margin.

Consider the following example.

*RD Ltd is a Hull-based manufacturing company. The company is currently developing a new product referred to in-house as L0L4. The market for the new product is extremely competitive with a number of similar, albeit inferior, products already available. The current average market price of the products similar to L0L4 is £300.*

*RD Ltd requires a profit margin of 25% on all products. Using a price-based targeting approach, what would the target cost of L0L4 be?*

*The target cost would be £300 – (£300 × 20%) = £240 and the profit per product would be £60, that is 25%.[29]*

Remember the target cost is merely an estimate and may well be considerably less than the initial/current costs of a product/service. In such cases, such a target cost is regarded as a product/service cost to be achieved over a period of time, hopefully before the product/service reaches the maturity stage of its life cycle.[30]

For obvious reasons, a target-based cost approach may not be suitable for all product/services. Such suitability would be determined by the nature of the product/service and perhaps most importantly the nature and structure of competition within the market. For example a price-based targeting approach can only be used where similar or equivalent products/services are already available within the marketplace and a cost-based targeting approach can only be used successfully where the company enjoys a significant position within the marketplace, and can therefore pressurise suppliers into reducing supply costs so that its target cost is achieved.

So, what are the advantages and disadvantages of a target based cost approach? The advantages are:

- it encourages the minimisation of total cost, and
- it eliminates cost overruns.

The disadvantages of a target-based cost approach are:

■ it can lead to excessive cost cutting, and
■ it can have a destabilising affect on the operations of a company.

## Standard cost-based approach

The standard cost-based approach is based on using pre-determined costs for materials, labour and expenses so that the standard cost of the product and/or service produced and/or provided in a period can be determined. Such costs are widely used in:

■ the valuation of work-in-progress and finished goods,
■ the establishment of product/service selling prices but, more importantly,
■ the measurement, assessment and control of business-related activities.

There are many types of standards of which the following are the most common:

■ a basic standard – that is a standard that is used unaltered over a long period of time and which is deemed achievable under *all operating conditions*,
■ an attainable standard – that is a standard that is achievable only under *normal operating conditions* and in which some allowance is made for possible delays/inefficiencies, and
■ an ideal standard – that is a standard that is achievable only under *perfect operating conditions* and which assumes no inefficiencies.

So what are the advantages and disadvantages of a standard cost-based cost approach? The advantages are:

■ it can be used to highlight areas of strength and weakness,
■ it can be used as a basis for stock valuation, and
■ it can be used in the evaluation of performance by comparing actual costs with standard costs and so assisting in identifying responsibility.

The disadvantages of a standard cost-based approach are:

■ it can be difficult to establish the standard, and
■ it can be difficult to administer.

## Performance measurement

Although a wide variety of both accounting and non-accounting performance measurement techniques are used by companies/organisations, perhaps the most widely used accounting technique not only for conversion cycle activities but also revenue cycle activities, expenditure cycle activities and, to a lesser extent, management cycle activities, is standard costing and the use of variance analysis.

### Flexible budgeting and variance analysis

Because of the ever-changing nature of the business environment, for control purposes budgets[31] – as a quantitative expression of management's belief of the costs (and revenues) that will arise on an activity and/or group of activities over a pre-defined future period – will often required revision. Such a revision is normally referred to as 'flexing' the budgets and is designed to enable the comparison of expected costs and revenues with actual costs and revenues, and the calculation and analysis of cost and revenue variances.

Consider the following example.

*KLP Ltd is a Sheffield-based manufacturer producing specialist conservatory roller blinds.*

*The following results are available for the month of March 2007:*

|  | Budget | Actual |
|---|---|---|
| Units of finished goods | 400 | 500 |
| Direct materials |  |  |
|    Total (kg) | 4,800 | 5,500 |
|    Cost per kg (£) | 0.50 | 0.55 |
|    Total cost (£) | 2,400 | 3,025 |
| Direct labour |  |  |
|    Total man hours | 10,000 | 13,000 |
|    Cost per man hour | 0.60 | 0.65 |
|    Total cost | 6,000 | 8,450 |
| Direct expenses | 500 | 700 |
| Indirect expenses (fixed costs) | 2,000 | 2,400 |
|  | £10,900 | £14,575 |

*We could prepare a flexed budget for KLP Ltd for March 2007 based on the production of 500 units as follows:*

|  | Budget | Actual |
|---|---|---|
| Units of finished goods | 500 | 500 |
| Direct materials |  |  |
|    Total (kg) | 6,000 | 5,500 |
|    Cost per kg (£) | 0.50 | 0.55 |
|    Total cost (£) | 3,000 | 3,025 |
| Direct labour |  |  |
|    Total man hours | 12,500 | 13,000 |
|    Cost per man hour (£) | 0.60 | 0.65 |
|    Total cost (£) | 7,500 | 8,450 |
| Direct expenses (£) | 500 | 700 |
| Indirect expenses (fixed costs) (£) | 2,000 | 2,400 |
|  | 13,000 | 14,575 |

*A statement of variances (often called an operating statement) is as follows:*

|  | £ |
|---|---|
| Direct materials |  |
| (3,000 – 3,025) | (25) |
| Direct labour |  |
| (7,500 – 8,450) | (950) |
| Direct expenses |  |
| (500 – 700) | (200) |
| Indirect expenses |  |
| (2000 – 2400) | (400) |
| Total variance (13,000 – 14,575) | (1,575) |

Such variances could be classified as either:

- price-related variances – for example, price variances, rate variances, and/or expenditure variances, or
- quantity-related variances – for example, usage variances, capacity variances and/or efficiency variances.

|  | £ | £ |
|---|---|---|
| Direct materials price variance | | |
| $(0.55 - 0.50) \times 5,500$ kg | (275) | |
| Direct materials usage variance | | |
| $(5,500\text{kg} - 6,000\text{kg}) \times 0.50$ | 250 | |
| | | (25) |
| Direct labour price (rate) variance | | |
| $(0.60 - 0.65) \times 13,000$ hrs | (650) | |
| Direct labour efficiency variance | | |
| $(13,000 \text{ hrs} - 12,500 \text{ hrs}) \times 0.60$ | (300) | |
| | | (950) |
| Direct expenses variances | | |
| $(500 - 700)$ | (200) | |
| Indirect expenses variances | | |
| $(2,000 - 2,400)$ | (400) | |
| Total variance $(13,000 - 14,575)$ | (1,575) | |

So why would such variances arise? For a number of reasons, for example:

■ direct material price variances could arise due to the purchase of higher/lower priced materials, possible price inflation, supplier discounts and/or foreign currency exchange rate fluctuations,

■ direct material usage variances could arise due to the purchase of inferior/superior quality materials, manufacturing efficiency, pilfering and/or ineffective stock control,

■ direct labour rate variance could arise due to the use of higher/lower skilled labour and/or wage inflation,

■ direct labour efficiency could arise due to the use of higher/lower skilled labour and/or inaccurate time allocation, and

■ direct/indirect expenses variances could arise due to price inflation, capacity efficiencies/inefficiencies (e.g. excessive wastage and/or idle time) and/or resource usage efficiencies/inefficiencies.

In using variance analysis, it is of course important to identify:

■ the controllability of variances, and
■ the responsibility for variances.

But should all variances be investigated? That depends! There are a number decision models that can be used to determine whether a variance should be investigated, perhaps the most common being:

■ a percentage rule – that is a variance should only be investigated if it is greater than a pre-determined percentage of the standard, and

■ a statistical significance rule – that is a variance should only be investigated if it is greater than the unusual occurrences using a normal statistical distribution.

## Conversion cycle – risks

Clearly, any failure in the processes and controls associated with the conversion cycle could have significant consequences for the company/organisation and could not only result in a loss of customers/clients, and as a consequence a loss of revenue income (and profits), but perhaps more importantly a loss of company/organisation assets including confidential conversion cycle information.

Such consequences may arise as a result of:

- poor development and design,
- over/under-production,
- an inappropriate investment in production resources/assets,
- the disruption of conversion cycle activities,[32]
- the theft/loss of raw materials, work-in-progress and/or finished products,
- the provision of inaccurate performance data/information, and/or
- the loss, alteration and/or unauthorised disclosure of confidential conversion cycle data.

## Poor development and design

Poor development and design could not only result in the inefficient use of production resources, for example inappropriate production scheduling, but perhaps more importantly could in the short-term result in an increase in the overall cost of a product/service because of higher warranty repair costs and, in the longer term, a loss of demand for the company's/organisation's products/services.

In extreme cases poor development and design could also result in loss/personal injury which may – in very serious cases – result in litigation and possible claims for damages.

So why does poor development and design occur? For many reasons, perhaps the most common being:

- the desire to be the first in the market,
- the desire to cut costs, or
- an inappropriate understanding/consideration of the consequences of poor development and design.

The solution:

- proper control of research and development activities,
- proper monitoring of product development and design, and
- regular review of customer/client feedback.

## Over/under-production

Whilst over-production could result in the supply of finished products in excess of market demand and therefore has an adverse impact on liquidity – for example, significant over-production could not only have a detrimental effect on working capital, but could also result in lower retail prices – under-production could result in loss of revenue and potentially a loss of customers/clients.

Over/under-production can occur because of:

- inappropriate management of production orders,
- inefficient use of production/manufacturing resources, and/or
- incorrect monitoring of stocks.

The solution:

- proper planning and scheduling,
- proper approval of production orders, and
- regular review of production budgets.

## Inappropriate investment in production resources/assets

Whilst any over-investment in production assets – that is production-related fixed assets – will increase overhead production costs and reduce profitability, any under-investment will impair productivity, reduce income and again reduce profitability. It is therefore important for a company/organisation to maintain an adequate level of useable production assets and balance the sometimes competing demands of greater productivity and higher profitability:

The solution:

- proper authorisation and approval of all fixed asset-related transactions,
- proper documentation and recording of all fixed asset-related transactions,
- proper custody and supervision of all fixed assets, and
- proper control of all fixed assets.

Note: We will look at the management of fixed assets in detail in Chapter 11.

## Disruption of conversion cycle activities

Events which may result in the disruption of conversion cycle activities – or unplanned interruption to conversion cycle activities, in particular manufacturing-related activities – can be broadly classified as either:

- a management-related event, or
- an environment-related event.

A management-related event is an event which occurs as a result of the improper use and/or incompetent administration of conversion cycle resources, examples of which would be:

- the inappropriate allocation of production resources – could result in excessive delays between the generation of a production order and the start of production operations,
- the inefficient management of raw materials – could result in the delay of manufacturing operations as a result of a lack of appropriate raw materials or, indeed,
- the recruitment of unqualified production staff – could result in the manufacture of faulty an/or sub-standard quality products.

An environment-related event is an event which occurs as a result of an external social, economic and/or political incident, examples of which would be:

- a labour dispute – could result in the reduced availability of production staff,
- a supply chain failure – could result in the limited availability of raw materials,
- a power supply failure – could result in the temporary failure of production processes,
- the accidental destruction of conversion cycle resources – could result in an adverse change in environmental conditions (e.g. flood damage, storm damage), and/or
- the deliberate sabotage to or destruction of conversion cycle assets/resources.

Although environment-related events are generally regarded as being 'externally generated,' very often the history of such events lies within the internal management activities of the company/organisation, for example:

- A labour dispute may well be precipitated by the actions of a trade union on behalf of its members. However such a dispute may well have emerged from a failure of management and staff representatives to negotiate an acceptable pay award for production-related staff.

■ A supply chain failure may result from a refusal by suppliers to supply and deliver raw materials. However such a refusal may have resulted from a failure of management to meet conditions imposed by raw material suppliers – for example payment conditions.

■ The accidental destruction of conversion cycle resources whilst perhaps resulting from an incidence of extreme weather (e.g. storm damage), could as a consequence have been exacerbated by a failure of management to provide adequate disaster recovery planning.

Clearly any disruption to conversion cycle activities is unacceptable since such disruptions can not only result in higher costs in the shorter-term but, more importantly, can adversely affect company/organisation relations with customers/clients in the longer-term. Whilst future uncertainties will always mean unplanned disruptions to conversion cycle activities will perhaps be inevitable, the consequences of such interruptions can be greatly reduced by:

■ the continuous monitoring of conversion cycle activities,
■ the proper securing of all conversion cycle assets, and
■ the appropriate management of all conversion cycle resources.[33]

The solution:

■ proper monitoring of all conversion cycle-related transactions,
■ proper custody of all conversion cycle-related activities,
■ proper custody of all conversion cycle-related assets and resources, and
■ proper disaster recovery planning.

### Theft/loss of raw materials, work-in-progress and/or finished products

The theft/loss of raw materials, work-in-progress and/or finished products is a major problem area for manufacturing companies/organisations. Not only can such theft/loss result in a permanent loss of current assets, it can also result in an over-statement of stock balances and, as a consequence, possible under-production.

The solution:

■ restricted access to stores of raw materials, work-in-progress and finished products,
■ proper authorisation of all stores-related transactions,
■ proper recording of all stores transactions,
■ regular physical stock checks, and
■ proper identification and location tracking of raw materials, work-in-progress and finished products.

### Inaccurate performance data/information

Whether as a result of:

■ the fraudulent charging of production costs,
■ the deliberate falsification of stores records or, simply,
■ the inadvertent and/or improper use of cost data/information,

the inaccurate collection, processing and management of cost data/information not only results in incorrect costs being charged to work-in-progress and/or finished goods and, as a consequence, the incorrect valuation of work-in-progress and/or finished goods, but can, more importantly result in the under/over-production of goods, the establishment of inaccurate product prices (where prices are determined by reference to costs), and/or the inaccurate assessment of production performance.

The solution:

- restricted assess to data/information, and
- periodic reconciliation of records with physical counts.

## Loss, alteration and/or unauthorised disclosure of confidential data

The loss, alteration and/or unauthorised disclosure (or theft) of confidential data can have enormous consequences – both legal and financial – for a company/organisation, especially where such data is customer/client/employee-related and regulated by the provisions of the Data Protection Act 1998.

The solution:

- proper use of data back-up facilities,
- proper access controls – for example passwords/security IDs,
- proper segregation of duties, and
- proper use of encryption technologies.

## Conversion cycle – internal controls and systems security

The key processing requirements of a company's/organisation's conversion cycle are to ensure:

- all conversion cycle activities are appropriately authorised and scheduled,
- all stocks of raw materials, work-in-progress and finished products are safeguarded,
- all valid conversion cycle transactions are properly and accurately recorded,
- all records are maintained and protected,
- all stocks of raw materials, work-in-progress and finished products are correctly valued, and
- all conversion cycle activities are performed effectively and efficiently.

The key control requirements are to ensure, where at all possible:

- the appropriate use of control documentation,
- the existence of appropriate authorisation procedures for:
  - the acquisition of products, services and resources,
  - the collection of data, and
  - the dissemination of information,
- the adherence to internal production/manufacturing policies,
- the existence of adequate internal control procedures and internal security procedures to safeguard assets and resources, and
- the existence of adequate structures of responsibility and accountability.

As with revenue cycle activities (see Chapter 8), and expenditure cycle activities (see Chapter 9) in a practical context such internal controls can be categorised as either general controls or application specific (conversion cycle specific) controls.

## General controls

The general controls applicable to the conversion cycle could be categorised as:

- organisational controls,
- documentation controls,
- access controls,
- authorisation controls,
- asset controls,
- management practice controls, and
- information systems controls.

### Organisational controls

Within the conversion cycle such controls should ensure that there is a separation of duties between:

- those involved in activities related to the management and coordination of production-related operations/activities,
- those involved in stores/warehouse-related activities and the management and control of raw materials, work-in-progress and finished products, and
- those involved in the provision of conversion cycle-related data/information, specifically, finance/accounting-based information.

### Documentation controls

Complete and up-to-date documentation should be available for all conversion cycle procedures. Such documentation should include, for example:

- organisational charts detailing the responsibility structure within the conversion cycle and the separation/segregation of duties within each of the conversion cycle systems,
- procedural descriptions of all procedures and processes used within the conversion cycle,
- systems flowcharts detailing how functions/activities within the conversion cycle operate,
- documents flowcharts detailing what documents flow within conversion cycle systems,
- management control procedures/internal control procedures detailing the main internal controls within the conversion cycle,
- user guides/handbooks providing a broad overview of the main functions/activities within the conversion cycle – especially the production and manufacturing-related activities, and
- records of recent internal/external audits undertaken on individual conversion cycle systems – for example an assessment of internal control procedures related to product development and design activities.

### Access controls

Where information and communication technology is used as an integral part of the conversion cycle systems and activities, for example as part of a computer integrated manufacturing system, it is important, for both internal control and security purposes, to ensure that:

- assigned users' names and passwords are used to authenticate users and authorise access to conversion cycle production data,
- production planning and control data/information is only accessible by approved management staff,
- location and/or terminal restrictions are used, where appropriate, to control/restrict access to conversion cycle-based data/information, and
- production data/information is securely stored with access to both current transaction files/master files and their back-up copies restricted to approved management staff only,

### Authorisation controls

It is important to ensure that all significant events and activities within the conversion cycle are appropriately authorised, for example:

- the issue of production orders,
- the issue of raw materials,
- the scheduling of production activities,
- the transfer of finished products to the stores, and
- the write-off of production waste/scrap raw materials.

### Asset controls

To ensure the continued protection of all assets, it is important that there is:

- regular reconciliation of physical stocks of raw materials, work-in-progress, and finished products to stores records and general ledger records,
- periodic reconciliation of production performance to standard production requirements and regular analysis of any significant variances, and
- a reconciliation of completed production orders to transfer orders authorising the movement of finished products from production to the stores.

### Management practice controls

In general, such management practices controls would include for example:

- regular employee training on conversion cycle systems/procedures, especially where improvements/changes to conversion cycle processes and procedures are made,
- regular personal checks/assessments of conversion cycle staff, and
- the use of internal audits to monitor conversion cycle activities.

### Information systems controls

In general, such information systems controls would include for example:

- the scheduling of data processing activities relating to the production of products/services,
- the authorising of all data/information processing procedures, and
- the management and control of all information and communication systems resources.

## Application controls

As with all application controls, those applicable to the conversion cycle can be categorised as input controls, processing controls and output controls.

### Input controls

Clearly, it is important to ensure that controlled documentation (either physical/paper-based documentation or virtual/computer-based documentation) is used for all production order requests, resource requisitions (both labour and materials), work-in-progress movements and finished goods transfers. It is important to ensure adequate controls exist to guarantee the validity, correctness and appropriateness of conversion cycle input data. Such controls would include for example:

- appropriateness checks – to ensure the consistency of input data,
- data validity checks – to confirm that input data is within expected parameters,
- data entry checks – to ensure input data is in the correct format,
- authorisation procedure checks – to confirm all data is appropriately authorised prior to input and processing, and

- error tests/error correction procedure checks – to ensure all incorrect data is identified and appropriately dealt with.

Where input data is transmitted from a source origin to a processing destination electronically, additional supplementary input controls would normally be required. Such additional input controls would include for example:

- transmission tests – to ensure the completeness of the transmission,
- security checks – to ensure the authenticity of the customer/client and the legitimacy of the transmission, and
- validity checks – to ensure/confirm the completeness of the transaction data.

### Processing controls

Conversion cycle processing controls are designed to ensure only authorised conversion cycle transaction data are processed and all such data are processed accurately, correctly and completely.
Such controls would include for example:

- file maintenance checks – to ensure that both production records and work-in-progress records are properly maintained,
- file labelling checks – to ensure all conversion cycle data files are correctly labelled,
- computational checks – to ensure all production orders and work-in-progress stock records are correctly calculated and approved prior to processing,
- processing logic checks – to ensure that the actual processing steps by which data are transformed or moved are consistent with defined procedures/protocols,
- limit checks – to ensure that all conversion cycle transaction data exist within defined processing parameters (e.g. value of transaction, data of transaction),
- monitor checks – to ensure any resubmitted transactions (production orders that have been rejected and require reworking) are correctly processed,
- reasonableness checks – to ensure that conversion cycle transaction data are consistent with processing expectations,
- reconciliation checks – to ensure all resources (both raw materials and labour) are accounted for and all production orders are consistent with the finished goods produced,
- sequence checks – to ensure that no interruptions or gaps exist in the sequence of transaction data processed,
- audit trail controls – to ensure that a visible trail of evidence and/or chronology of events is available to enable the tracing of transaction events,
- control totals checks – to check that conversion cycle transaction file control totals are consistent with the contents of the transaction file to which they relate, and
- data checks – to check for the existence of duplicate inconsistent and/or missing data.

### Output controls

Conversion cycle output controls are designed to ensure all conversion cycle output is authorised, accurate and complete, and distributed to approved and authorised recipients only.
Such controls would include for example:

- distribution controls – to ensure production orders are charged allocated to the correct cost code/budget holder account,
- verification controls – to ensure the validity and accuracy of output information,
- reconciliation checks – to ensure all transaction numbers are accounted for, and
- review/audit trail checks – to ensure that a visible trail of evidence exists to enable the tracing of conversion cycle output.

Where output data is transmitted from a processing origin to a user destination electronically – for example payments to suppliers/providers – additional supplementary output controls would normally be required.

Such additional output controls would include for example:

- transmission tests – to ensure that data is transmitted correctly,
- recipient identifier checks/controls – to authenticate the recipient before the delivery of data/information,
- security checks/controls – to ensure data/information is delivered completely, and
- validation checks/controls – to ensure data/information is received and accessed by the authorised recipient only.

## Conversion cycle – information requirements

As we saw earlier, the primary objective of a company/organisation conversion cycle is to transform raw materials into finished products and then saleable products. Whilst a key feature of an efficient and effective conversion cycle is the availability of an adequate and appropriate level/quality of assets and resources, the planning, scheduling and controlling of conversion cycle activities perhaps more importantly requires information: in particular, conversion cycle information that can be used to assess the efficiency and effectiveness of production and manufacturing-related activities.

So what type of conversion cycle information would a company/organisation use/require? As with the revenue and expenditure cycles, we will categorise such information as follows:

- period-based activity information,
- period-based performance information, and
- activity analysis information.

### Period-based activity information

Period-based activity information is operational level information relating to the specific availability of conversion cycle resources and would include for example:

- raw materials, work-in-progress and finished goods levels/status,
- work centre/location resource availability, and
- employee availability/production activity.

### Period-based performance information

Period-based performance information is tactical level information measuring the efficiency and effectiveness of conversion cycle processes and procedures, and would include for example:

- employee productivity reports,
- work centre/location performance reports,
- production status – production completion and production-in-progress,
- equipment usage, and
- material wastage/idle time.

### Activity analysis information

Activity analysis information is strategic level information measuring/assessing the relative success or otherwise of conversion cycle-related activities and would include for example:

- customer/client satisfaction measurements including quality, service and product availability assessments,
- conversion cycle performance – production cycle times, conversion cycle yield and location/work centre productivity,
- resource efficiency – for example stock turnover, employee productivity and resource efficiency, and
- production flexibility – for example changeover times and productivity/non-productivity days.

## World class manufacturing

The term world class manufacturer is increasingly being used in accounting and finance related texts – but what does it mean? Put simply, a world class manufacturer can be defined as a manufacturer that demonstrates the use of best practice and achieves a high level of competitiveness in the areas such as:

- product/service quality,
- product/service price,
- product/service delivery,
- reliability,
- manufacturing flexibility/adaptability, and
- production innovation.

Invariably, the term world class manufacturing has become synonymous with terms such as flexible manufacturing, adaptive manufacturing and the use of computer integrated manufacturing.

## Concluding comments

Over the past few years conversion cycle activities have undergone a radical transformation – a transformation that has not only resulted in an increasing abandonment of long-held, traditional, push-based manufacturing environments in favour of an increasingly pull-based manufacturing environment but, perhaps more importantly, the increasing integration of information and communication technologies into almost all aspects of the conversion cycle.

## Key points and concepts

| | |
|---|---|
| **Absorption cost** | **Cost management** |
| **Activity-Based Cost (ABC)** | **Financial planning** |
| **Adaptive manufacturing** | **Flexible manufacturing** |
| **Alpha testing** | **Gamma testing** |
| **Beta testing** | **Lean manufacturing** |
| **Budgetary control** | **Product development and design** |

Product manufacture

Production management and coordination

Production planning

Production scheduling

Pull manufacturing

Push manufacturing

Traditional manufacturing

Variable cost

Variance analysis

World class manufacturing

## References

Booz-Allen and Hamilton (1982), *New Product Management for the 1980s*, Booz-Allen and Hamilton, Inc., New York.

Kaplan, R., and Bruns, W. (1987) *Accounting and Management: A Field Study Perspective*, Harvard Business School Press.

Smith, P.G., and Reinertsen, D.G. (1998) *Developing Products in Half the Time*, (2nd Edition), Wiley, New York.

Womack, J.P., Jones, D.T., Roos, D. (1991) *The Machine That Changed the World: The Story of Lean Production*, Harper Business, London.

## Bibliography

Aseervatham, A. and Anandarajah, D. (2003) *Accounting Information and Reporting Systems*, McGraw Hill, Sydney.

Bagranoff, N.A., Simkin, M.G. and Strand N.C. (2004) *Core Concepts of Accounting Information Systems*, Wiley, New York.

Hermann, J.W. (2006), *Improving Production Scheduling: Integrating Organisational Decision-Making and Problem-Solving Perspectives*, Industrial Engineering Research Conference, Orlando, Florida.

Romney, M. and Steinbart, P. (2006) *Accounting Information Systems*, Pearson Education Inc., New Jersey.

Vaassen, E. (2002) *Accounting Information Systems – A Managerial Approach*, Wiley, Chichester.

Wilkinson, J.W., Cerullo, M.L., Raval, V. and Wong-On-Wing, B. (2001) *Accounting Information Systems*, Wiley, New York.

## Self-review questions

1. Briefly describe the main activities and processes that comprise the conversion cycle.
2. Distinguish between alpha testing, beta testing and gamma testing.
3. Distinguish between push-based manufacturing, and pull-based manufacturing.
4. Distinguish between continuous manufacturing, batch manufacturing and on-demand manufacturing.
5. Explain the role of a production order.
6. Explain the main problems associated with the use of paper-based documentation in the processing of production/manufacturing orientated transactions.
7. What are the advantages/disadvantages of using a target-based costing approach?
8. Identify the main risks associated with the conversion cycle.

9. Distinguish between period-based activity information and period-based performance information.

10. Explain the term 'world class manufacturing'.

## Questions and problems

### Question 1

'Excessive stocks can camouflage manufacturing problems and lead to overproduction of products.' Discuss.

### Question 2

Explain why it is important for the accountant to be involved in product development.

### Question 3

Briefly explain the internal control procedures that could be used to detect and/or prevent the following:

- the theft of work-in-progress by factory employees,
- the issue of a production order for products that are already overstocked in the company's stores,
- the theft of completed production by stores clerks,
- the incorrect recording of time worked by factory workers (100 hours was claimed instead of 10 hours),
- the theft of expensive production equipment by the factory production manager.

### Question 4

If the activity cost-based approach is seen as superior to the absorption cost-based approach and the variable cost-based approach, why is it still rarely used in practice?

### Question 5

You have recently been appointed as production accountant for a small manufacturing company that produces leather accessories and has recently been asked to explain the need for the following:

- the regular production of a master production schedule,
- the RFID tagging of materials, components and completed production,
- the use of passwords to control access to the management system responsible for generating production orders, and
- the documentation of all spoiled production and scrapped materials and components.

## Assignments

### Question 1

UKP plc is a UK-based shoe manufacturer producing a range of orthopaedic shoes. The company produces 12 different styles of orthopaedic shoes, based on NHS demand. The company operates a computer-based production planning/manufacturing systems as follows.

At the end of each production cycle (a production cycle is 10 days) the production planning department prepares a master production schedule for the next production cycle detailing the styles and quantities of shoes to be produced during the next production cycle. The master production plan is used to prepare a production operations list, for which a production order is generated for the production of each style of shoe. Each production order is added to an open production order master file.

At the end of each day, the store clerk reviews the open production orders and the master production schedule to identify the materials and components required to be issued for production purposes for the next day. All materials are RFID tagged.

The 12 different orthopaedic shoe styles are produced at eight different production locations in the company's factory. Materials and components received by the factory workers at each production location are scanned as they are used.

To operate the production equipment, factory workers use computer-based biometric fingerprint readers to both commence and terminate the production. This information is used to monitor production levels and determine remuneration levels. (All factory workers are paid a fixed basic wage plus a bonus based on levels of production.)

Once the shoes have been produced, each pair is RFID tagged and despatched to the company warehouse for safe storage. Every one in 50 pairs of shoes produced is quality checked prior to despatch to the warehouse.

### Required

Prepare a systems flowchart of the production system described above and describe the internal control procedures you would expect to be included in such a production process.

## Question 2

SCW Ltd is a small UK-based company that manufactures custom-made pine furniture. The company employs 12 specialist carpenters, four designers, one production scheduler, two administrators and a manager. Because of the high reputation enjoyed by the company only one sales person is employed since the quality of the company's furniture attracts sufficient orders to maintain production at full capacity. When a customer order is received, it is allocated to a designer who designs the product, manages the production process and approves the final result. The production scheduler assigns at least two specialist carpenters to each order, depending on factors such as complexity of the design and the requested date of delivery. Once the product is completed, the production price is determined by accumulating all related costs and a percentage mark-up is added to determine the sale price.

### Required

(a) Prepare a list of the data elements that would be required to be able to plan, manufacture and monitor the progress of a customer order.
(b) Explain what data elements would be required to calculate a sales price for a customer order.
(c) Prepare an systems diagram for the above production system – from the receipt of the customer order to the completion and delivery of the finished product.
(d) Describe several reports that will be useful to the production scheduler and carpenter in performing their duties.
(e) A customer order has recently been received, the details are as follows:

- Order No:             498983
- Order details:        One Cartier style dining room suite
- Customer No:          Clare Barber, Ardslave, Western Isles, Scotland
- Order Date:           1 April 2007
- Delivery date:        1 October 2007
- Assigned designer:    Jordon Reece-Spencer
- Assigned carpenters:  Tony Barber
                        Louise Ritter

Briefly describe the possible internal control problems that could arise in the processing of this order.

## Chapter endnotes

1  Although the terms are often used interchangeably we will adopt the following hierarchy – manufacturing process is a component aspect of the production system, which is a component aspect of the conversion cycle.

2  This chapter is primarily concerned with the production of tangible products.

3  Booz-Allen and Hamilton are US-based market research consultants.

4  Such recommendations would include, for example, a component specification for the new product and a summary of additional assets/resources required to produce/manufacture the new product including, where necessary, any possible staff training/development requirements.

5  In-market testing should not be confused with test marketing which seeks to determine the overall marketability/financial viability of a new product.

6  Have a look at Article 8.1.

7  See www.microsoft.com/windowsvista.

8  Remember the four stages: introduction, growth, maturity and decline.

9  Further information is available @ www.patent.gov.uk.

10  This could involve for example the acquisition of additional human/non-human resources, the relocating of existing human/non-human resources and, where necessary, the development of training programmes for new and/or relocated personnel.

11  To minimise costs, the numbers in such batches tend to be very high.

12  Elias (Eli) Whitney (1765–1825): American inventor and manufacturer – promoted the development of interchangeable parts in a manufacturing process.

13  Frederick Winslow Taylor (1856–1915): American engineer – promoted the use of standardised patterns.

14  Frank Bunker Gilbreth (1868–1924): proponent of scientific management – pioneered the use of motion studies.

15  Henry Ford (1863–1947): founder of the Ford Motor Company Inc. – promoted the use of the modern assembly line in mass production.

16  Alfred Pritchard Sloan, Jr. (1875–1966): long-time president and chairman of General Motors Inc. – also promoted the use of flow lines in the manufacturing process.

17  Shigeo Shingo (1909–90): Japanese industrial engineer and leading expert on manufacturing practices and the Toyota Production System.

18  It is perhaps worth noting that acronyms such as World Class Manufacturing (WCM), Stockless Production Systems (SPS), Continuous Flow Manufacturing (CFM) and many more are all essentially derivatives of the Toyota Production System.

19  Norman Bodek popularised many of the Japanese quality tools, techniques and technologies that transformed American and European industrial practices in the 1980s and the 1990s, including the work of Shigeo Shingo and Taiichi Ohno (Toyota Production System), Yoji Akao (Quality Function Deployment), and Hoshin Kanri and Seiichi Nakajima (Total Productive Maintenance). Norman Bodek is currently president of PCS Press, a publishing, training and consulting company.

20  *Kaizen* is a Japanese term meaning change for the better or improvement, the English translation being continuous improvement or continual improvement.

21  The concept was originated by Shigeo Shingo as part of the Toyota Production System.

22  Such operational flexibility was often divided into three categories:

■  input related flexibility – for example resource acquisition, usage and management,

■  process related flexibility – for example production volume/capacity, and

■  output related flexibility – for example market demand.

[23] We consider outsourcing in detail in Chapter 16.

[24] More paper, less trees!

[25] See Chapter 7 for more details on this issue.

[26] See Chapter 4 for further details on computer integrated manufacturing.

[27] The absorption rates used to absorb overhead costs would normally be calculated on the basis of expected production output and budgeted overheads. Since actual overheads and levels of production are unlikely to equal such budgeted amounts, an under- and/or over-absorption of overhead is likely to occur – for which a profit and loss account adjustment would be required.

[28] Such activities are often referred to as cost drivers.

[29] Remember, profit margin is profit expressed as a percentage of cost. Mark-up is profit expressed as a percentage of selling price. Where the profit margin of a product/service is 25%, expressed as a percentage of cost, the profit mark-up would be 20%.

[30] Remember the life cycle of a product/service can be characterised as four stages: introduction, growth, maturity and decline.

[31] Companies/organisations prepare budgets using a range of approaches, for example:

- an incremental approach – an incremental budget can be defined as a budget that is amended only for changes in the level of prices (inflation) and/or changes in levels of activity.
- a rolling approach – a rolling budget can be defined as a budget which once established is constantly updated and/or amended to take into account developing circumstances, and/or
- a zero-based approach – zero-based budgeting can be defined as an approach to budgeting which starts from the premise that everything to be included in a budget must be considered and justified.

This is for a variety of reasons, for example to:

- assist in the planning of business-related activities,
- provide a channel of communication for such plans,
- assist in the coordination of business related activities, and
- facilitate the control and evaluation of costs and revenues associated with such business activities.

[32] Such interruptions are unplanned and occur outside the normal down time used for the refurbishment and/or renewal of production resources.

[33] For example:

- ensuring the continuing availability of power supplies by maintaining on-site generators, and
- ensuring the continuing availability of production staff by undertaking active negotiations/consultations with trade unions and other workforce representatives where changes to workplace practices/rates of remuneration are proposed.

# 11

# Corporate transaction processing:
the management cycle

## Introduction

In a broad sense, the management cycle can be defined as a collection of business-related activities/resources and information processing procedures, relating to the efficient and effective management of *all* company/organisational resources.

Put simply, the corporate management cycle is concerned with:

- finance management – the acquisition and management of long-term funds,
- fund management – the acquisition and management of short-term funds,
- assets management – the management and control of both fixed and current assets,
- liabilities management – the management and control of both long-term and current liabilities, and
- general ledger management – the management of financial information.

See Figure 11.1.

So, what role(s) would a company/organisation accounting information system play in the management cycle? Whilst in an operational context, the accounting information system would be used to assist in:

- the capture and processing of management cycle transaction data, and
- the organising, storing, and maintaining of management cycle transaction data,

in a more strategic context, it would be used to safeguard management cycle resources, and ensure:

- the reliability of management cycle transaction data, and
- the integrity of management cycle activities.

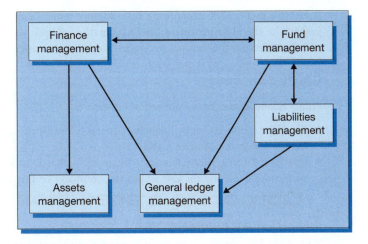

**Figure 11.1** Management cycle

## Learning outcomes

By the end of this chapter, the reader should be able to:

■ describe the major activities and operations contained within the corporate management cycle,

■ explain the key decision stages within the corporate management cycle,

■ demonstrate an understanding of the key internal control requirements of a corporate management cycle,

■ demonstrate a critical understanding of the potential risks and threats associated with inappropriate internal control, and

■ consider and explain the impact of information and communication technology enabled innovations on the corporate management cycle.

## Finance management

Finance management is concerned with the management of all forms of non-transactional financing, that is financing not directly associated with:

■ the revenue cycle activities of the company/organisation, and/or
■ the expenditure cycle activities of the company/organisation.

Such non-transactional finance would include, for example:

■ equity financing,
■ debt (loan) financing
■ convertible securities,
■ derivative instruments, and
■ transferable warrants.

Before we look at the accounting information systems aspects of each of the above would perhaps be useful to provide a brief explanation of each type of non-transactional financing and then consider the internal controls relevant to each one.

## Equity financing

Equity financing can be categorised as either:

- issued (or acquired) equity financing – that is finance 'provided' by the owners of the company for use within the company, and
- non-issued (or generated) equity financing – that is finance 'produced' by and retained within the company for use within the company or for distribution to the owners of the company.

### Issued equity financing

Within the UK, issued equity financing (or more appropriately share capital) can be categorised as:

- preference shares,
- ordinary shares, or
- redeemable shares.

Although different classes of shares can be issued by a company (subject of course to extant regulatory requirements), the vast majority of shares in issue within the UK at present are ordinary shares, whose associated rights include:

- the right to attend company meetings,
- the right to vote at company meetings,
- the right to receive dividends (see below),
- the right to receive a copy of the company's accounts or, at least, summary financial statement, and
- the right to transfer shares.[1]

## Preference shares

Preference shares are irredeemable shares which provide the shareholder with:

- a preferential entitlement to receive a share of the profits of a company (a dividend) before any payments are made to ordinary shareholders, and
- a legal right to receive a share of the company's assets in the event of the company's liquidation, before any payments are made to ordinary shareholders, but only after appropriate preferential creditor debts have been fully discharged.

In general, preference shares have a fixed dividend – that is a dividend which does not fluctuate with the levels of company profits. In addition, some preference shares are cumulative preference shares – that is dividends not paid in one year must be paid in a subsequent year (before any ordinary share dividend is paid); although the vast majority are non-cumulative preference shares – that is dividends not paid in one year are required to be paid in subsequent years.[2]

In a contemporary sense, the use of preference shares has become particularly popular in venture capital-related schemes – for example new business start-ups and management buy-outs.

## Ordinary shares

Ordinary shares are also irredeemable shares which provide the shareholder with:

- an entitlement to receive a share of the profits of a company (a dividend) but only after other demands have been met – including those of preference shareholders, and
- a legal right to receive any residual share of the company's assets in the event of the company's liquidation – that is a share of the company's assets after all creditor debts have been fully discharged and appropriate payments to preference shareholders have been made.

In addition, unlike preference shares, ordinary shares have a fluctuating dividend – that is a dividend which can change with the levels of company profits.

## Redeemable shares

Redeemable shares are limited life ordinary shares – that is ordinary shares which an issuing company can buy back from shareholders at some agreed future date. A company issuing redeemable shares must of course have other irredeemable shares in issue

Note: There is of course no maximum number to the shares a company can issue, and whilst there is no minimum value of shares for a private limited company, a public limited company must have an authorised (and issued)[3] share capital of at least £50,000.

### Non-issued equity finance

Non-issued equity finance is of course retained earnings – and not retained profits! Whereas 'retained earnings', which as a financial term can be defined as the finance generated by the company's/organisation's activities that is surplus to requirements – that is not required to meet operational expenses and/or outstanding liabilities – 'retained profits' as an accounting term, can be defined as profits that have not been distributed to company shareholders as dividends.

A subtle, but extremely important difference between retained earnings and retained profits is that within a company:

- the retained earnings will be represented by liquid assets within the company/organisation – that is cash or a cash equivalent (e.g. a balance in a bank account or a short-term investment), whereas
- the retained profits will be represented by the net movement of all assets/liabilities within the company/organisation (which of course may or may not include cash and/or cash equivalents).

Remember, retained profits are an accounting adjustment. They are a balancing figure – a product of the accruals basis of contemporary accounting and the duality of the accounting equation. They are perhaps the reason why a company may show substantial levels of retained profits within its financial statements, but may be unable to satisfy its immediate financial commitments and as a result be forced into liquidation and possibly cease trading.

Have a look at the following example.

*LMP plc is a UK retail company that has been trading successfully for a number of years. The management of the company has, however, become increasingly concerned because there has been a substantial reduction in the company's liquid funds (in particular the company's bank balances) for the year ending 31 December 2006, even though the company has continued to generate profits. Indeed, for the year ending 31 December 2006 the company's bank balance has fallen by £1,400,000 from 31 December 2005, even though the company's profits before tax for 2006 have increased on the previous year, and the company's retained profits for 2006 have increased on the previous year.*

*LMP plc financial statements for the years ending 31 December 2005 and 31 December 2006 are as follows:*

### Balance Sheet as at 31 December

|                          | 2005 £000s | 2006 £000s |
|--------------------------|-----------:|-----------:|
| Fixed assets             | 3,800      | 6,500      |
| less Depreciation        | 1,700      | 1,400      |
|                          | 2,100      | 5,100      |
| **Current assets**       |            |            |
| Stocks                   | 3,200      | 4,200      |
| Trade debtors            | 2,800      | 5,100      |
| Debtors                  | 900        | 500        |
| Cash and bank            | 1,500      | 100        |
|                          | 8,400      | 9,900      |
| **Current liabilities**  |            |            |
| Trade creditors          | 2,000      | 3,000      |
| Other creditors          | 500        | 500        |
| Taxation                 | 1,000      | 1,000      |
| Dividends                | 600        | 700        |
|                          | 4,100      | 5,200      |
| **Long-term liabilities**|            |            |
| Debentures               | 2,000      | 3,800      |
|                          | 4,400      | 6,000      |
| **Capital**              |            |            |
| Share capital            | 2,000      | 2,600      |
| Accumulated reserves     | 2,400      | 3,400      |
|                          | 4,400      | 6,000      |

### Profit and Loss Accounts for the year ended 31 December

|                           | 2005 £000s | 2006 £000s |
|---------------------------|-----------:|-----------:|
| Turnover                  | 7,000      | 9,000      |
| Cost of sales             | 3,500      | 4,200      |
| Gross profit              | 3,500      | 4,800      |
| Operating expenses        | 1,400      | 2,100      |
| Profit before taxation    | 2,100      | 2,700      |
| Taxation                  | 1,000      | 1,000      |
| Profit after taxation     | 1,100      | 1,700      |
| Dividends                 | 600        | 700        |
| **Retained profit for the year** | 500 | 1000      |

*The reduction in LMP's liquid resources (cash and bank) could be explained as follows:*[4]

|                             | £000s   | £000s   |
|-----------------------------|--------:|--------:|
| Profit before taxation (2006) |       | 2,700   |
| **Inflow of funds**         |         |         |
| Share capital               | 600     |         |
| Debenture                   | 1,800   |         |
|                             |         | 2,400   |
| **Outflow of funds**        |         |         |
| Fixed assets                |         | (3,000) |
|                             |         | 2,100   |
| **Changes in working capital** |      |         |
| Increase in stock           | 1,000   |         |
| Increase in debtors         | 1,900   |         |
| Increase in creditors       | (1,000) |         |
| Payment of 2005 taxation    | 1,000   |         |
| Payment of 2005 dividend    | 600     |         |
|                             |         | 3,500   |
| Decrease in bank            |         | (1,400) |
|                             |         | 2,100   |

Clearly, the company is generating profits, but much of the company's revenue from sales appears to be increasingly debtor-based. In addition, the company appears to be investing heavily in fixed assets with a substantial part of the investment being funded from revenue receipts.

## Debt (loan) financing

Debt financing can be defined as the borrowing from another person or persons (including another company/organisation) of purchasing power from the future and represents (in most circumstances) an obligation to repay a sum of capital, plus an agreed amount of interest.[5]

Such debt can be categorised as either:

- secured debt, or
- non-secured debt.

### Secured debt

Secured debt can be defined as debt (usually long-term) in which a lender (creditor) is granted a specific legal right over a borrower's property/assets.[6] The purpose of securing debt is to allow a lender (creditor) to be able to seize, or more appropriately, sequester[7] property/assets from a borrower in the event that the borrower fails to properly satisfy the repayment requirements of the debt, and/or adequately adheres to specific conditions imposed by the debt instrument.[8] Such secured debt is referred to as a debenture,[9] and any conditions attached to the borrowing would normally be identified in a debenture trust deed.[10]

There are many types of debenture, the most common being:

- a mortgage debenture – that is long-term debt (sometimes irredeemable debt) which is usually secured against specific property/assets of a borrower, and
- a floating debenture – that is long-term debt which is secured against a range of unspecified property/assets of a borrower.

### Non-secured debt

Unsecured debt can be defined as debt – usually short- to medium-term – that is not collateralised or not secured against any property/assets of the borrower. Such debt would include, for example, borrowing using:

- short-term overdraft facilities,
- short-term loans – for example a three- or six-month money market loan, and
- medium-term loans – for example a two-year bond.

### Overdraft

An overdraft is borrowing which is repayable on demand. The maximum overdraft allowed for a company/organisation on its current account(s) would normally be negotiated and agreed with the bank prior to the facility being made available. Charges would normally include a fixed initial setting-up charge together with interest calculated on a daily basis on the amount of the overdraft.

The vast majority of companies/organisation will, at some time, finance some of their activities with a short-term overdraft. Why? Because overdrafts are relatively cheap, very flexible and simple to arrange – although they can be somewhat risky inasmuch as overdrafts are, subject to legal conditions/obligations, essentially repayable on demand.

### Short-term loans

Short-term loans are essentially loans obtained from a bank or other financial institution which are repayable within a year. However such loans can, and indeed often do, last much longer – sometimes well in excess of a year. Borrowers will often renegotiate short-term loans at the end of the loan period and, if agreed with the lender, simply extend the loan for another three, six or nine months depending on the initial short-term loan agreement.

### Bonds

A bond can be defined as a negotiable debt instrument, normally offering a fixed rate of interest (coupon) over a fixed period of time, with an agreed redemption value (par). A debenture is therefore a specific type of bond!

As a negotiable debt instrument, there are three categories of bonds:

- a domestic bond,
- a foreign bond, and
- a eurobond.

A domestic bond is a bond issued in the country in which the borrower is domiciled. It is a negotiable debt instrument denominated in the home country currency and essentially available for domestic distribution only.

A foreign bond is a bond issued in the country other than that which the borrower is domiciled. It is a negotiable debt instrument denominated in the local currency of the issuer, but available for international distribution.

A eurobond is a bond issued outside country of its currency (see the section below). Such bonds are not only issued by borrowers domiciled in almost any country they can also be acquired by investors domiciled in almost any country.

In addition, there are within each of the above categories, many possible types of bond, the main ones being:

- a fixed rate bond,[11]
- a zero coupon bond,[12]
- a floating rate bond,[13]
- a sinking fund bond,[14]
- a rollover bond,[15] and
- a convertible bond (see below).

Theoretically a bond can be either:

- redeemable – that is with a fixed and/or negotiable redemption date, or
- irredeemable – that is a perpetual bond without a future redemption date, the vast majority of bonds in issue in the UK are redeemable.

### Convertible securities

Convertible securities[16] can – perhaps unsurprisingly – be defined as securities that can be converted into another security. Although there are many varieties of convertible securities,[17] the most common is a debt instrument such as a bond and/or a debenture that can, subject to certain terms and conditions, be converted into equity in the issuing company at:

- a pre-announced ratio – commonly known as the conversion ratio, and
- a pre-agreed time – commonly known as the conversion date.

Such convertible securities will generally have a lower coupon rate than corresponding non-convertible securities.

## Derivative instruments

Derivative can be defined as financial instruments that derive their value from the value of another financial instrument, underlying asset, commodity index or interest rate. The most common type of derivatives are:

- futures,
- forwards,
- options, and
- swaps.

### Futures

Futures are exchange-traded contracts[18] that are now traded on various currencies, various interest-bearing securities and various equity or stock indexes.

Futures are essentially binding obligations under which a person, a company or an organisation buys and/or sells a specified asset at a specified exercise price on the contract maturity date. The specified asset is not literally bought and sold but the market price of that contract at maturity compared to the contract price will determine whether the holder of the future will make a profit or a loss.

Unlike a forward (see later) which can possess a high degree of credit risk, futures are generally marked to market at the end of each trading day with the resulting profit or loss settled on that day. Where futures are not marked to market at the end of the trading day, exchanges will often seek to ensure that all participants are able to meet any claims arising from this continuous settlement process by requiring participants to undertake a performance bond as security for their obligations. Such a performance bond is known as the margin.

### Forwards

Forwards can be defined as agreements to buy or sell a given quantity of a particular asset (usually currency), at a specified future date at a pre-agreed price.

Forwards are 'over-the-counter' or OTC instruments that are traded not on organised exchanges but by dealers (typically banks) trading directly with one another and/or with other parties.

The use of forwards in terms of foreign exchange are generally restricted to large companies, governments and other major institutions who have access to extensive financial credit. Individuals, partnerships and small businesses/private companies will generally not participate in the forward market because of the costs involved in securing and maintaining the necessary credit.

### Swaps

There are essentially three types of swaps:

- currency swaps,
- interest rate swaps, and
- equity swaps.

## Interest rate swaps

Interest rate swaps are contractual agreements entered into between two parties under which each party agrees to make a periodic payment to the other for an agreed period of time based on a notional amount of principal/capital.

Although an amount of principal is required in order to compute the actual cash amounts that will be periodically exchanged, such an amount is notional inasmuch as there is no requirement to exchange actual amounts of principal in a single currency transaction.

The commonest form of interest rate swap is a fixed/floating interest rate swap, under which a series of payments is calculated by applying a fixed rate of interest to a notional principal amount is exchanged for a stream of payments similarly calculated but using a floating rate of interest. An alternative form of an interest rate swap is the money market swap, under which both series of cash flows are calculated using floating rates of interest based upon different underlying indices, for example LIBOR (London Inter-band Offer Rate) and a commercial paper rate, or a Treasury bill rate and LIBOR.

Commercial and investment banks, non-financial companies, insurance companies, investment trusts and government agencies, use interest rate swaps for several reasons including for example:

- to obtain lower cost funding,
- to hedge interest rate exposure,
- to obtain higher yielding investment assets,
- to create types of investment asset not otherwise obtainable,
- to implement overall asset or liability management strategies, and/or
- to take speculative positions in relation to future movements in interest rates.

## Currency swaps

Currency swaps can be defined as a combination of a spot foreign exchange transaction and a simultaneous forward foreign exchange contract reversing the initial spot transaction. However, used in its more general meaning, currency swaps are a combination of:

- a spot foreign exchange transaction in which one currency is bought and sold for another currency,
- a forward foreign exchange transaction in which, on a pre-determined future date, the initial spot transaction is reversed, and
- an exchange of payments calculated by reference to prevailing interest rates applicable to the swapped currencies. The payments exchanged may be floating rate payments in both currencies, fixed rate payments in both currencies or fixed rate payments in one currency and floating rate payments in another currency.

Transactions for which a company/organisation may use currency swaps would probably include the following:

- hedging currency exposure,
- accessing restricted markets,
- altering the currency of either payments and/or income, and/or
- reducing funding costs.

## Equity swaps

Equity swaps can be defined as an exchange in which one party exchanges a payment equal to the return on a specified equity index, a sub-index, a specified group or 'basket' of equities or even an individual share, for a series of payments based on a short-term interest index, such as LIBOR.

As with a interest rate swap, payments are calculated by reference to a notional principal amount that is not exchanged. In principle, the exchange mechanism covers both increases and decreases in the index, and transactions can be denominated in either the same currency or in different ones.

A company/organisation could use an equity swap for a number of reasons which would include for example:

- to permit rapid switching and diversification between international equity markets,
- to avoid transaction costs and market barriers that may make direct investment in an equity market either impossible or prohibitively expensive,
- to earn an enhanced coupon yield while retaining ownership of a portfolio of shares,
- to reduce the cost of a contested acquisition,
- to protect against share price falls, and
- to avoid exchange limits and restrictions imposed on trading in equities.

## Options

Options are perhaps the most difficult derivative financial instrument to discuss, because whilst they are essentially simple in concept, they can nevertheless be very complex.

The basic concept underlying an option is well known – quite simply it means choice. Any option agreement is a contract which gives the holder the right but not the obligation to buy (a call option)[19] or sell (a put option)[20] a specified underlying asset at a pre-agreed price[21] (the strike price) at:

- a fixed point in time (called a European option),
- a number of specified times in the future (called a Bermudan option), or
- a time chosen by the holder up to maturity (called an American option).

The holder of the option pays a premium to the writer of the option at the time the option contract is entered into, reflecting its value at that time. If the strike price of the option was such that if it were exercised today it would produce a profit for the holder, the option is said to be 'in the money'. If the reverse is true, the option is said to be 'out of the money'. And, if the strike price of the option is such that if it were exercised today it would produce neither a profit nor a loss for the holder, the option is said to be 'at the money'. Consequently, the more an option contract is in the money when it is entered into, the higher the premium that will be paid, or put another way, the more an option contract is out of the money when it is entered into, the lower the premium that will be paid.

Such a premium would however also be influenced by:

- length of time the option has to run to its maturity, since the longer the period the greater the possibility that a favourable price change could take place in the underlying asset making the option profitable for the holder, and
- the likelihood, based on historical experience, that the price of the underlying asset will be subject to frequent and volatile price variation.

As with other derivative financial instruments, traded options can be based on stock market equities, market indices, interest rates,[22] bonds and currencies.

## Transferable warrants

A warrant[23] can be defined as a security that entitles the holder to buy or sell a certain additional quantity of an underlying security, at an agreed price, within an agreed period of time.[24] The right to buy an underlying security is referred to as a call warrant, whereas the right to sell an underlying security is known as a put warrant. There are of course many alternative types of transferable warrants, the most common ones being:

- a traditional warrant – which is a warrant issued in conjunction with a bond (usually known as a warrant-linked bond), and represents the right to acquire shares in the company issuing the bond, and
- a naked warrant which is a warrant issued without an accompanying bond.

## Non-transactional finance – internal controls

From an internal control perspective, it is important to:

- ensure the safe custody of all non-transactional finance-related deeds/legal documents,
- ensure the appropriate authorisation of all acquisitions, transfers and/or disposals for all debt and equity-related financial instruments,
- maintain accurate accounting records for all acquisitions, transfers and/or disposals, and
- ensure the accurate monitoring of all debt-related commitments – including commitments relating to convertible securities, derivative instruments and transferable warrants.

### Equity

It is important to ensure that all share issues (whether by public offer, by placement, by introduction or indeed by rights issue) are appropriately approved/authorised and comply with all extant regulatory requirements.[25] In addition, the company must:

- ensure an up-to-date record of all existing shareholders – a company share register – is maintained,
- ensure all transfers of shares are appropriately documented, registered and certified,
- ensure the accurate preparation and payment of dividends to shareholders, and
- ensure the appropriate production of shareholder reports for Companies House.

All these tasks would normally be the responsibility of the company share registrar.[26]

For internal control purposes, it is important to ensure that adequate segregation of procedures/separation of duties exists between all authorities and responsibilities relating to:

- the recording and processing of share issues and/or transfers,
- the custody and control of share certificates,
- the processing, registration and certification of share transfers, and
- the accounting for, and payment of, shareholder dividends.

### Secured debt and convertible securities

It is important to ensure that all issues of debentures and/or convertible securities are closely monitored and appropriately approved.

(Remember, convertible securities are essentially a debt instrument until – subject to certain terms and conditions – they are converted into equity or redeemed.)

The company must:

- ensure an up-to-date record of all existing debenture holders/convertible securities holders – a company debenture register – is maintained,
- ensure all transfers, redemptions and/or conversions are appropriately documented, registered and certified,
- ensure the accurate preparation and payment of interest to debenture holders, and
- ensure compliance with any imposed financial requirements.

Again, for internal control purposes, it is important to ensure that adequate segregation of procedures/separation of duties exists between all authorities and responsibilities relating to:

- the recording and processing of debenture issues, transfers, redemptions and/or conversions,
- the custody and control of debenture certificates,
- the processing, registration and certification of debenture transfers,
- the accounting for all debenture redemptions, and
- the accounting for, and payment of, debenture holder interest.

### Non-secured debts

It is important to ensure an up-to-date record of all outstanding short-term loans, bond issues (usually a bond register) and overdrafts is maintained, and that all non-secured borrowing is appropriately approved and authorised. The company must:

- ensure all redemptions of short-term loans and/or bonds are appropriately documented, registered and certified,
- ensure the accurate preparation and payment of interest, and
- ensure compliance with any imposed financial requirement – in particular ensure that any agreed borrowing limit (e.g. on an overdraft facility) is not exceeded without prior agreement.

For internal control purposes, it is important to ensure that adequate segregation of procedures/ separation of duties exists between all authorities and responsibilities relating to:

- the recording and processing of bond issues, transfers and/or redemptions,
- the borrowing of short-term funds,
- the custody and control of bond certificates,
- the processing, registration and certification of bond transfers,
- the accounting for the redemption of bonds/prepayment of loans/overdrafts,
- the accounting for, and payment of, bond interest, loan interest and overdraft charges/interest.

### Derivative instruments

Where derivatives are regularly used to manage a company's/organisation's risk exposure then as part of its risk policy[27] the company/organisation must not only ensure that an up-to-date record of all commitments relating to futures, forwards, options and swaps is maintained but, more importantly:

- ensure the regular valuation and audit of *all* derivative transactions,
- ensure the regular monitoring of *all* derivative transactions to confirm compliance with extant policies, procedures and regulations, and
- ensure the regular monitoring of *all* derivative dealers' positions.

For internal control purposes, it is important to ensure that adequate segregation of procedures/ separation of duties exists between all authorities and responsibilities relating to:

- the determination of exposure requirements,
- the acquisition and disposal of derivatives, and
- the recording of, and accounting for, derivatives transactions.

### Transferable warrants

It is important to ensure that all warrant issues are appropriately approved/authorised and, where necessary, comply with all extant regulatory requirements, and an up-to-date record of warrants issued by the company is maintained – this is especially the case for traditional warrants. For internal control purposes, it is important to ensure that adequate segregation of procedures/separation of duties exists between all authorities and responsibilities relating to the authorisation, issue and recording of warrant issues.

## Fund management

Fund management is concerned with the management of all forms of transactional financing, that is financing that is directly related to or associated with:

- the revenue cycle activities of the company/organisation (inflows of funds), and
- the expenditure cycle activities of the company/organisation (outflows of funds).

Such transactional finance is, put simply, the life blood of a company/organisation and can, in a broad sense, be categorised as either:

- cash-based transactional finance, and
- cash equivalent transactional finance.

### Cash-based transactional finance

Cash-based transactional finance is – perhaps unsurprisingly – concerned primarily with cash as a physical medium of exchange. Theoretically, it should include all physical cash whatever the currency, however in the UK, whilst some UK retailers will (somewhat reluctantly) now accept payment in euros, the majority of companies/organisations continue only to accept cash payments denominated in UK sterling. So, in a UK context, accounting information systems are generally only concerned with UK sterling.

#### Cash-based revenue transactions

Although historically cash-based revenue transactions were extremely popular – both in volume and value terms – especially in:

- context type 1(a)(i) companies/organisations – consumer-based retail companies, and
- context type 2(a)(i) companies/organisations – companies with a limited flow of commodities (e.g. restaurants, bars and clubs),

the popularity of cash-based revenue transactions has, certainly over the past 20 years, declined quite dramatically, so much so that in value terms, cash-based revenue transactions now represent only a small portion of the total transaction-based revenue received by companies/ organisations. Consider for example the changes that have occurred in many of the major high street retailers over the past 20 years!

So, why has the decline in so-called 'hard cash' transactions occurred? Put simply, the availability, widespread acceptance and increasing use of alternative low-cost e-based payment technologies have made the use of hard cash as a medium of exchange not only unattractive but, more importantly, unacceptable due to the high risks[28] associated with accepting cash-based transactions.

There can be little doubt that the future of hard cash transactions is limited, inasmuch as the continuing development and acceptance of new and improved e-based payment technologies has all but resulted in the terminal decline of cash as a medium of exchange. And, whilst it is of course unlikely that cash-based revenue transactions will disappear from the economic landscape totally, recent survey trends would appear to suggest that within the next 10 to 15 years – certainly within the UK retail sector – it is likely that as little 3% of all non-debtor-based revenue transactions will be cash-based.

### Cash-based expenditure transactions

Although many companies/organisations use a controlled petty cash imprest systems for:

- the purchase of small value items, and/or
- the limited reimbursement of staff expenses,

it would of course be extremely unwise for any company/organisation to use cash as its major medium of exchange to discharge outstanding debts/commitments relating to expenditure cycle-related transactions, including payroll. This is for two reasons. Firstly, the costs associated with managing large volumes of cash within the company/organisation and, secondly, the high level of risk associated with possessing and securing large volumes of cash within the company/organisation. (We will look at the petty cash issue later in this chapter.)

## Cash equivalent transactional finance

Cash equivalent transactional finance includes:

- all e-money-based payments (e.g. debit/credit card payments),
- all BACS payments (see Chapter 12),
- all transferable payment documents (e.g. cheques, postal orders and money orders), and
- all tradable financial instruments.

For revenue cycle transactions, with the exception of a few small companies/organisations, the vast majority of consumer-based companies/organisations allow the use of:

- transferable payment documents (e.g. payment by cheque and/or postal order),[29] and/or
- e-money-based payments (debit/credit card payments),

with the majority of non-consumer-related companies/organisations favouring the BACS system.[30]

For expenditure-related transactions the vast majority of both consumer and non-consumer-based companies/organisations favour the BACS payment systems.

## Understanding the operational context of transactional finance

Before we look at fund management in a little more detail, it would perhaps be useful to consider briefly the operational context of transactional finance.

Put simply, the distinction between cash-based transactional finance and non-cash-based transactional finance is not the same as the distinction between debtor-based sales and non-debtor-based sales (introduced in our discussions in Chapter 9), or indeed creditor-based purchases and non-creditor-based purchases (introduced in our discussions in Chapter 10). Why not? Because, the debtor/non-debtor distinction (for revenue cycle transactions) and the creditor/non-creditor distinction (for expenditure cycle transactions) refers to the entry context/classification of a transaction, whereas the cash-based/non-cash-based transactional finance distinction refers to the exit context/classification of a transaction. See Figure 11.2.

Consider the following example.

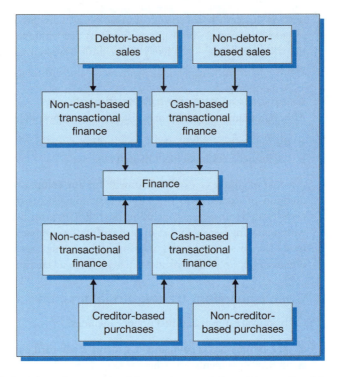

**Figure 11.2** Cash-based transactional finance/non-cash-based transactional finance

*SJK Ltd is a UK-based retail company. The company made the following sales during December:*

|  | £ |
|---|---|
| Debtor-based sales | 6,595 |
| Non-debtor-based sales | 4,700 |

*All debtor-based sales were fully discharged (paid in full) during December.*

*(The above represents the entry context/classification of the December transactions.)*

*In terms of payment profile, the debtor-based sales were paid as follows:*

|  | £ |
|---|---|
| BACS | 5,320 |
| Cash | 1,275 |

*and, the non-debtor-sales were paid as follows:*

|  | £ |
|---|---|
| Credit card/debit card | 2,460 |
| Cheque | 890 |
| Cash | 1,350 |

*(The above represents the exit context/classification of the December transactions.)*

*In terms of the above revenue-based transactions:*

- *the cash-based transactional finance received during December was £2,625 (that is £1,275 + £1,350), and*
- *the non-cash-based transactional finance received during December was £8,670 (that is £5,320 + £2,460 + £890).*

## Understanding fund management

Put simply, the purpose of fund management is:

- to ensure the proper management of all fund related balances (e.g. cash balances, bank balances),
- to ensure the adequate maintenance of all fund-related accounting records – including the periodic reconciliation of all fund balances, and
- to ensure the accurate supervision of all receipts and disbursements (including small cash receipts and disbursements).

In an organisational context, fund management can be divided into three levels, these being:

- operational fund management,
- tactical fund management, and
- strategic fund management.

Before we look at each of these in a little more detail, it is worth noting that in a Keynesian context:

- operational fund management is concerned with the transaction aspects/motives of fund management,
- tactical fund management is concerned with the precautionary aspects/motives of fund management, and
- strategic fund management is concerned with the speculative aspects/motives of fund management.

### Operational fund management

Operationally, fund management is concerned with the establishment of policies and procedures that ensure adequate and effective internal controls in the processing of cash/cash equivalent transactions, in particular the segregation of procedures[31] and the separation of duties[32] in the following areas:

- the authorisation of cash/cash equivalent transactions,
- the custody and physical movement of cash,
- the use of and access to cash/cash equivalent transaction processing facilities,
- the recording of and accounting for cash/cash equivalent transactions, and
- the reconciliation of cash/cash equivalent transaction records and banking records.

Any segregation of procedures/separation of duties should of course apply to:

- all cash/cash equivalent receipts,
- all cash/cash equivalent payments, and
- all cash/cash equivalent administrative/management procedures.

Operational fund management is often associated with Keynes's so-called 'transaction motive'.

### Tactical fund management

Tactically, fund management is concerned with the establishment of an adequate cash management model for the efficient matching of organisational funds and operational requirements to ensure adequate cash resources are available within the company/organisation as and when required.

Whilst there are many alternative cash management models available, two of the most popular are:

- the Baumol (1952) cash management model, and
- the Miller–Orr (1966) cash management model.

### Baumol cash management model

The Baumol model is an EOQ-based model and suggests the cost of meeting cash demand (that is the buying and selling of marketable securities to meet cash demand) is the cost of the transaction plus the opportunity cost of the interest foregone. If:

$t$ = annual transaction volume (assumed to be uniform over time)
$k$ = fixed cost per transaction
$i$ = annual interest rate
$c$ = size of each deposit

the cost could be expressed as $k(t/c) + i(c/2)$, where:

$k(t/c)$ is the cost of the transaction
$i(c/2)$ is the opportunity cost of interest foregone.

The Baumol cash management model suggests that the optimal deposit size is given by:

$$c = \sqrt{2kt/i}$$

The Baumol cash management model assumes:

- the company/organisation is able to forecast its cash requirements with certainty,
- the company/organisation will receive a specific amount at regular intervals,
- the company's/organisation's cash payments will occur uniformly
- the opportunity cost[33] of holding cash is known with certainty
- the opportunity cost of holding cash does not change over time, and
- the company will incur the same transaction cost[34] whenever it converts securities to cash.

As a consequence, the Baumol cash management model may only be relevant if the pattern of a company's/organisation's cash flows/transfers are uniform (same size), fairly consistent (occur on a regular basis) and are predictable (known with a degree of certainty).

Consider the following example.

*KLY plc is a UK-based retailer. The company regularly invests surplus funds in seven-day notice short-term deposits on the UK money market. Currently such short-term deposits pay an interest of 5% per annum. Also currently KLY plc has cash payments for each month totalling £1,250,000 per month or £15,000,000 pa.*

*Assume transactions costs are £15.40 per transaction.*

*Using the Baumol cash management model:*

$$c = \sqrt{2kt/i}$$
$$c = \sqrt{(2 \times 15.40 \times 15,000,000/0.05)}$$
$$= £96,125$$

*That is the most economic amount of cash that KLY plc should transfer to its bank account is £96,125 or, in an operational context, KLY plc should transfer cash three times a week (£15,000,000/£96,125).*

## Miller–Orr cash management model

Unlike the Baumol cash management model, the Miller–Orr cash management model allows cash flow to vary within two control limits. Using this cash management model, a company/organisation can allow its cash balance to fluctuate between:

- an upper control limit, and
- a lower control limit.

Put simply, when a company's/organisation's cash flow reaches the upper limit, the company/organisation buys sufficient marketable securities to reduce cash to a normal level of cash balance, known as the return point. When a company's/organisation's cash flow reaches the upper limit, the company/organisation sells sufficient marketable securities to increase cash back to the normal level.[35] If:

$r$ = the range between the upper and lower limits
$k$ = the £ cost for the sale of one security
$v$ = statistical variance of daily cash flows
$s$ = the daily interest rate cost of holding cash
$rp$ = return point
$l$ = lower limit

then the Miller–Orr model sets the range between the upper limit and the lower limit as:

$$r = 3[(0.75 \times k \times v/s)^{1/3}]$$

and the return point ($rp$) would be calculated as follows:

$$rp = (l + r/3).$$

Consider the following example.

*MTR plc is a UK-based retailer. The company regularly invests surplus funds in either Call or two-day notice short-term deposits on the UK money market. Currently such short-term deposits pay an interest of 4.5% per annum. Also currently MTR's cash flows are fairly erratic and daily cash flows currently have a standard deviation of £4000 (and therefore a variance of £16,000,000).*

*The finance director of the company has estimated that the minimum cash balance required by the company is £80,000.*

*Assume transactions costs are £15.40 per transaction.*

*Using the Miller–Orr cash management model:*

$r = 3[(0.75 \times k \times v/s)^{1/3}]$
$r = 3[(0.75 \times 15.40 \times 16,000,000/0.000123)^{1/3}]$
$\quad = 3 \times 11,453$
$\quad = £34,359$

*Therefore the upper limit would be £80,000 + £34,359 = £114,359 and the return point (rp) would be:*

$rp = (l + r/3)$
$rp = £80,000 + £34,359/3$
$\quad = £91,453$

### Comparison of models

So which model should a company/organisation adopt? Whilst the Baumol model is a simple and easy to implement cash management model, the Miller–Orr cash management model is perhaps more realistic inasmuch as it allows variations in cash balance within the upper limit and lower limit, and allows the lower limit to be set according to the company's/organisation's liquidity requirement.

If the Miller–Orr model is adopted, it is of course important that the lower limit cash requirement is regularly reviewed to ensure that it accurately reflects the timing and flow of funds into and out of the company/organisation.

#### Strategic fund management

Strategically, fund management is concerned with the development/establishment of an appropriate planning model and the determination of an appropriate lending/borrowing strategy to ensure not only that all the funding requirements of the company/organisation are satisfied, but also that all funding surplus to requirements is suitably invested. In essence, it is concerned with:

- the lending of surplus funds and, where necessary,
- the borrowing of short/medium-term funds.

Such lending and/or borrowing – undertaken using the UK Money Market – could be for example:

- overnight – lending/borrowing repayable the next day,
- two-day notice – lending/borrowing repayable on demand with a notice period of two days,
- seven-day notice – lending/borrowing repayable on demand with a notice period of seven days,
- one month period – fixed period lending/borrowing repayable in one month,
- three month period – fixed period lending/borrowing repayable in three months,
- six month period – fixed period lending/borrowing repayable in six months, or
- nine month period – fixed period lending/borrowing repayable in nine months.

Interest rates are usually fixed for the period, although negotiable interest terms (e.g. rollover interest terms using LIBOR) are available for fixed period lending/borrowing – at a premium.

Note: All lending/borrowing for notice periods, and/or fixed periods of less than one year, are colloquially known as temporary money, even though it is possible for two-day notice money and seven-day notice money to remain for periods in excess of one year.

Because of the possible value of funds that could be involved in such transactions (currently the minimum lending/borrowing amount is £250,000) it is important not only to ensure adequate written policies and procedures exist for *all* temporary lending/borrowing, and that senior finance manager/director approval is obtained before any such lending/borrowing is undertaken, but more importantly to ensure that an adequate segregation of procedures/separation of duties exists between all duties and responsibilities related to and associated with the lending and borrowing of temporary funds.

### Fund management – receipts

In general, such receipts would comprise of:

- receipts from revenue cycle-related transactions,
- receipts from the disposal of fixed assets,
- refund receipts from suppliers/service providers, and
- the borrowing (and/or receipt)[36] of temporary funds.

By far the largest volume of receipts would of course be related to revenue cycle-related transactions.

### Receipt of funds – internal controls

From an internal control perspective, it is important to ensure that:

- all receipt of funds amounts are received intact,
- all recorded receipts of funds represent the actual amounts received,
- all receipt of funds are deposited intact into the company's/organisation's bank account(s),
- all accounting entries are reconcilable to receipts and deposits, and
- all accounting records are accurately maintained and regularly updated.

To satisfy such internal control requirements, it is necessary to establish formal procedures/protocols for the processing and authorising of all receipting activities. In particular, it is important to:

- ensure the supervisory approval for all cash/cash equivalent receipts,
- ensure the existence of adequate processing internal controls, in particular an appropriate segregation of procedures/separation of duties between custody, management and recording/accounting activities,
- ensure an authorised internal listing of *all* cash/cash equivalent receipts is produced – in particular listings of cheques and cash received through the postal systems,[37]
- ensure the daily reconciliation of *all* cash/cash equivalent transactions,
- ensure all accounting records are updated regularly,
- ensure the secure storage and movement of cash and regular banking of cash receipts, and
- ensure no payments are made from undeposited cash – that is no teeming and lading.[38]

In addition, periodic and regular internal audits of all receipting activities should be undertaken to ensure the adequacy, relevancy, appropriateness and cost efficiency of all internal control procedures.

## Fund management – disbursements

In general, transactional financing payments/disbursements would comprise of:

- payments for expenditure cycle-related transactions,
- payments for the acquisition of fixed assets,
- refund payments to customers/clients, and
- the lending (and/or repayment) of temporary funds.

By far the largest volume of disbursements would of course be related to expenditure cycle-related transactions.

### Disbursement of funds – internal controls

From an internal control perspective, it is important to ensure that:

- all disbursements are appropriately authorised,
- all recorded disbursements of funds represent the actual amounts paid,
- all recorded disbursements represent only disbursements for actual goods and services,
- all disbursements are paid from the appropriate company/organisation bank account,
- all accounting entries are reconcilable to payments and withdrawals, and
- all accounting records are accurately maintained and regularly updated.

To satisfy such internal control requirements, it would be necessary to establish formal procedures/protocols for the processing and authorising of all receipting activities. In particular, it is important to:

- ensure supervisory approval for all cash/cash equivalent disbursements,
- ensure the existence of adequate processing internal controls, in particular an appropriate segregation of procedures/separation of duties between authorisation management and recording/accounting activities,
- ensure the daily reconciliation of *all* cash/cash equivalent transactions,
- ensure *all* expenditure cycle-related transactions – without exception – are paid using the BACS payment systems,
- ensure all cancelled transactions are properly authorised,
- ensure the daily reconciliation of *all* cash/cash equivalent transactions,
- ensure all accounting records are updated regularly,
- ensure no payments are made from undeposited cash – that is no teeming and lading,
- ensure an authorised internal listing of *all* cash disbursement is produced (e.g. petty cash disbursements), and
- ensure the secure storage and movement of cash and regular banking of cash receipts.

In addition, periodic and regular internal audits of all disbursement activities should be undertaken to ensure the adequacy, relevancy, appropriateness and cost efficiency of all internal control procedures.

## Fund management documentation – ensuring an audit trail

To ensure an adequate audit trail[39] exists for *all* cash/cash equivalent receipts and disbursements, the following traceable control documentation[40] is often used in fund management:

- a summary *remittance listing* – completed to record cash equivalent receipts received from customers/clients through the mail,
- a *receipt* – issued for all cash/cash equivalent funds received,
- a summary *disbursement voucher* – issued for all cash equivalent disbursements made,
- a *deposit slip* – completed for all cash receipts paid into the company/organisation bank account,
- a *journal voucher* – completed to record the receipts/disbursements in the company's/organisation's accounts, and
- a *reconciliation statement* – completed to match/reconcile cash/cash equivalent receipts and disbursements to bank account transactions

For internal control purposes it is important to:

- ensure that the preparation of the summary remittance listing is supervised by personnel not involved in or responsible for the recording/issuing of receipts or the depositing of funds, and
- ensure the reconciliation statement[41] is prepared on a regular basis by personnel not involved in the receipting or disbursement of funds.

## The issue of petty cash

If you recall, we introduced petty cash in Chapter 9. Because of the risks and moral hazards associated with maintaining a store, however small, of petty cash, the level of administrative care often required to remove the temptation for fraud and minimise the possibility of theft is frequently disproportionate to its financial importance. As a consequence – certainly in a contemporary context – some companies/organisations now take a very pragmatic cost-benefit approach to the provision of petty cash facilities. That is if the costs associated with providing and managing a petty cash facility are greater than the benefits accrued from such a facility, then such a facility will not be provided.

Although not universally the case, most companies/organisations that use/provide petty cash facilities tend to use a petty cash imprest system to monitor and control such expenditure. A petty cash imprest system is one in which a predetermined fixed amount is allowed, with the replenishment of petty cash based on authorised/approved expenditure incurred: that is at any time, the total of the cash together with any receipts will always equal the total amount allowed. In some companies/organisations the replenishment of petty cash is made by the finance department on a regular basis – say every two or four weeks. In others, it is undertaken by the finance office as and when requested by the spending department.

Clearly, the level of petty cash would of course differ from company to company or organisation to organisation. Indeed, it may well differ from department to department within the same company/organisation. However, as a general rule the amount of petty cash should be as low as is practically possible – based of course on the average amount of petty cash required over a reimbursement period. In practice, a departmental petty cash float of £100 is not uncommon.

### Managing a petty cash system

To ensure the efficient management of a petty cash facility, it is important to establish a company/organisation-wide policy and procedures which should:

- determine the levels of petty cash floats to be made available,[42]
- identify all allowable reimbursable expenses, and
- detail petty cash replenishment procedures and internal control requirements.

In a practical context, it is important to:

- ensure the replenishment of petty cash is appropriately documented and correctly authorised (usually by the finance department/treasury department within a company/organisation) and that a verifiable audit trail is available for all such transactions,
- ensure petty cash floats are stored in a locked, fireproof strong box or safe – this is especially important where multiple petty cash balances exist throughout a company/organisation,
- ensure access to petty cash is limited to authorised personnel only, and an accurate record of all petty cash reimbursements is maintained – where at all possible ensure vouchers are obtained for all expenditure,
- ensure *all* personnel (irrespective of status/position) provide evidence of appropriate expenditure before any reimbursement is made, and
- ensure a petty cash reconciliation is undertaken on a regular basis – reconciling petty cash documentation (replenishments and reimbursements) with actual cash balance(s).[43] Where petty cash is provided in several locations (e.g. different departments within a company/organisation) such petty cash balances should be checked simultaneously to avoid the possibility of petty cash being switched between locations.

Finally it is crucial that personnel are not allowed to use petty cash funds for personal purposes – to essentially borrow funds from petty cash.

## Fund management – risks

There are of course many risks associated with the failure of fund management procedures and internal controls. In particular, such risks would include:

- the possible theft and/or misappropriation of cash-based financial resources,
- the fraudulent misuse of cash-based financial resources,

- the possible need for excessive borrowing/overdrafts,
- the potential loss of business and trade,
- the potential loss of investment opportunities and, perhaps ultimately,
- the possible liquidation of the company/organisation.

Indeed, the business press is replete with examples of companies/organisations that have failed as a result of bad fund management. Recent examples in the UK would include the closure of MG Rover in 2005 and its eventual sale to the China-based Nanjing Automobile (Group) Corporation (see Article 11.1), and the collapse of Golden Wonder and its eventual sale to the Northern Ireland based Tayto Group in February 2006 (see Article 11.2).

## Article 11.1

### Nanjing Auto buys collapsed British MG Rover

Administrators for MG Rover Group Ltd. have said that the collapsed British automaker has been bought by Chinese carmaker Nanjing Automobile (Group) Corp. The announcement Friday ended months of speculation about the future of Rover, the country's last major automaker, but also raised questions about how much production Nanjing would retain in Britain – and how many jobs would be involved.

PricewaterhouseCoopers, which took over administration of Rover when the automaker filed for bankruptcy in April, said Nanjing had bought the assets of both MG Rover Group and its engine-producing subsidiary, Powertrain Ltd.

The terms were not disclosed. A person close to the deal, however, said Nanjing paid just over £50 million (US$87 million; €73 million).

Nanjing had faced two competitors in its bid to buy Rover's assets – a similar offer from China's state-owned Shanghai Automotive Industry Corp, which prompted the company's collapse earlier this year when it pulled out of talks about a merger, and an offer by British businessman David James to buy two parts of the company.

Tony Lomas, joint administrator at PwC, said in a statement that the 'level and conditionality of SAIC's bid left Nanjing's bid as the preferred way forward.' Unions had supported the SAIC deal because they believed it was the most likely to restart substantial production at Rover's Longbridge plant in central England, which was forced to close with the loss of 6,000 jobs when the company collapsed.

'Having viewed both the Nanjing and SAIC bids, there is no doubt in our mind that on first viewing the SAIC proposals appeared to suggest more jobs for Britain,' said Tony Woodley, general secretary of the Transport and General Workers Union. 'It's disappointing, therefore, that the administrators have not seen fit to allow SAIC to complete its bidding process.'

Woodley said the union will now seek talks with Nanjing to discuss jobs.

Lomas said Nanjing plans to begin hiring staff to implement its plan for the company, which includes relocating the engine plant and some of the car production to China, while retaining some production in Britain. It also plans to develop a research and development and technical facility here.

Rover had hoped the earlier deal with SAIC would generate cash to allow it to introduce new models and stem the falling sales of its current makes. The company, which turned out 40 percent of the cars bought in Britain in the 1960s, had not produced a new model since 1998 and held only a 3 percent share of the market at the time of its collapse.

The British government plowed millions of pounds in emergency loans into the company to keep it operating for a short time as its bankruptcy provided an embarrassing backdrop to the ruling Labour Party's election campaign, which was centered on the strength of the British economy.

PwC ended those loans and closed the factory when the prospects of a bidder for the entire group appeared to vanish.

Some intellectual property rights for Rover models were sold to SAIC in a £67 million deal last year, but the Chinese company does not hold the rights to produce the cars in Asia.

German car maker BMW AG has the rights to the Rover name, retaining them when it sold the company to Phoenix Venture Holdings for a token £10 in 2000. BMW gave MG Rover permission to use the name indefinitely for free under a licensing agreement and said it would consider letting another company use the name. BMW sold the rights to the MG name to Phoenix in the same deal.

The directors of Phoenix have been criticized for paying themselves significant salaries and pensions as the company was falling into the red. The so-called 'Phoenix Four' offered assets of up to £30 million to assist Rover as it tried to resuscitate talks with SAIC in April, but acknowledged that the assets on offer were subject to attack from creditors.

Source: 23 July 2005,
www.chinadaily.com.cn/english/doc/
2005-07/23/content_462703.htm.

## Article 11.2

## Tayto buys Golden Wonder crisps

Crispmaker Tayto is to buy most of its rival Golden Wonder, the company has announced. Tayto will take over the Golden Wonder brand name and the firm's major manufacturing plant in Scunthorpe. Last month, the County Armagh-based firm bought Golden Wonder's factory in Corby, which manufactures the Pringles Minis brand. Tayto, based in Tandragee, kept on 195 of Golden Wonder's Northamptonshire factory staff to make Pringles Minis. Last year, Tayto secured a major contract to supply own label crisps to the supermarket chain Tesco. About 350 people are employed at its Tandragee headquarters.

Last month, Golden Wonder went into administration, blaming falling sales and fierce competition in recent years. With the purchase of Golden Wonder, Tayto has also acquired the Ringos brand. It will sell two of Golden Wonder's brands – Nik-Naks and Wheat Crunchies – to United Biscuits, but will continue to manufacture those brands for United Biscuits. Golden Wonder employed some 820 staff prior to the bankruptcy.

Tayto chairman Raymond Hutchinson said the company had a clear vision of where it wanted to be in the future. 'Golden Wonder affords us the opportunity for a high growth strategy and that's where we wanted to be,' he said. 'Over the last five years we put in a management structure to enable us to do deals like this, and we are very confident with the management we have that we can make this work very well for us.' BBC NI business editor James Kerr said: 'Tayto has been looking to expand in recent years – this deal catapults it into a different league – with sales of £100m, a staff of 350 in Northern Ireland and 550 in England.'

Source: 26 February 2006,
news.bbc.co.uk/1/hi/northern_ireland/4732620.stm.

## Assets management

Assets management can be divided into two categories:

■ fixed assets management, and
■ current assets management.

## Fixed assets management

In a broad operational sense, fixed assets are essentially a foundation resource on which *all* other company/organisation operations depend. Indeed, inasmuch as such assets are acquired for retention and use within the company/organisation, and not for resale, they can – depending on the company/organisation context type – provide:

- a physical business framework – for example, land, office buildings and factory premises,
- the apparatus of production – for example, plant, machinery and related production equipment,
- an administrative infrastructure – for example, fixtures, fittings and other administrative-related equipment,
- a means of transportation and distribution – for example, motor vehicles,
- a legal right to produce and sell goods and/or provide services – for example, a trademark, copyright or patent, and/or
- a means of ownership (of another commercial entity) – for example, an investment in another company/organisation.

However, because the acquisition (and disposal) of such fixed assets can not only have a significant effect on the flow of funds within a company/organisation but, more crucially, exert considerable influence on a company's/organisation's ability to generate cash flows and profits, it is important – in a practical context, to:

- establish suitable company/organisation policies and procedures, and
- adopt appropriate company/organisation-wide internal controls,

to ensure that the acquisition, retention and disposal of fixed assets is managed in an efficient and effective manner.

Fixed assets management is concerned with maintaining a level of fixed assets within the company/organisation appropriate for and commensurate with its operational activities. The objectives are to:

- ensure all fixed asset acquisitions and disposals are properly planned, suitably evaluated, appropriately approved (with supporting documentation) and accurately recorded,
- ensure all fixed asset transactions (including the allocation of depreciation expenses) are properly recorded, monitored and controlled,
- ensure all fixed assets records (usually contained within a fixed assets register) are securely maintained and regularly updated,
- ensure all acquired fixed assets are securely maintained and periodically reconciled to fixed assets records, and
- ensure all appropriate property titles/custody rights to both tangible and intangible fixed assets are securely stored.

### Fixed assets management – allocation of duties/responsibilities

Although there are many alternative ways in which the duties and responsibilities related to the management of fixed assets can be allocated within a company/organisation – as a general rule, for internal control purposes, any such allocation must ensure an adequate and appropriate separation of duties/segregation of responsibilities between;

- the authorising of fixed asset-related transactions,
- the recording of fixed asset-related transactions,
- the custody of fixed assets, and
- the control of fixed assets.

For the remainder of our discussion on fixed assets management, we will assume an allocation of duties/responsibilities between the following:

- the facilities services director/manager[44] (and department),
- the ICT[45] director/manager (and department),
- the finance director/manager (and department),
- departmental/location personnel, and
- the internal audit department.

More specifically, the facilities services director/manager would be responsible for:

- the acquisition of non-ICT-related fixed assets,
- the regular inspection and maintenance of non-ICT-related fixed assets,
- the disposal of all redundant non-ICT-related fixed assets,
- the issue of all non-ICT-related fixed assets to company approved locations,
- the issue of guidance on the use of all non-ICT-related fixed assets, and
- the maintenance of a non-ICT fixed assets register.

The IT director/manager would normally be responsible for:

- the acquisition of ICT-related fixed assets,
- the regular inspection and maintenance of ICT-related fixed assets
- the disposal of all redundant ICT-related fixed assets,
- the issue of all ICT-related fixed assets to company approved locations,
- the regular checking of the company's/organisation's ICT fixed assets portfolio,
- the issue of guidance and the provision of training on the use of ICT-related fixed assets, and
- the maintenance of a ICT-related fixed assets register.

Both the facilities services director/manager and the ICT director/manager would also be responsible for:

- providing estimates of the useful economic life of fixed assets under their control,
- providing information on the impairment of, damage to, and/or the obsolescence of fixed assets for which they are responsible, and
- obtaining, where necessary, appropriate authorisation for the write off, disposal and sale of fixed assets for which they are responsible.

The finance director/manager would be responsible for:

- the determination of suitable fixed asset accounting policies,
- the (re)valuation of all fixed assets,
- the maintenance of fixed asset-related financial accounting records,
- the preparation of fixed assets-related financial accounting statements, and
- the authorising of fixed asset write off/disposals and, where appropriate, the determination of the method of sale.

As a general rule departmental personnel would be responsible for:

- ensuring all fixed assets are used in accordance with company/organisation policy/guidance,
- ensuring all fixed assets are not used without appropriate authorisation and, where necessary, appropriate training,
- ensuring all fixed assets are safeguarded from theft, loss and damage, and
- ensuring any theft, damage and/or loss is reported immediately.

Internal audit would be responsible for:

- evaluating the appropriateness and effectiveness of all fixed assets management internal control processes and procedures,
- identifying areas of weakness within fixed assets management internal control processes and procedures, and
- making appropriate recommendations for improvements to fixed assets management internal control processes and procedures.

## Acquisition of fixed assets

In general, the acquisition of fixed assets can be divided into three stages:

- an identification stage,
- an authorisation stage, and
- an acquisition stage.

Although the above stages would apply to the acquisition of all types of fixed assets, for obvious reasons it is likely that some procedural differences would exist between the acquisition of tangible fixed assets, the acquisition of intangible fixed assets and the acquisition of long-term investments.

For the following discussion we will restrict our discussion to the acquisition of tangible fixed assets only.

### Identification stage

The identification stage is, perhaps unsurprisingly, concerned with identifying fixed assets requirements within the company/organisation and ensuring appropriate approval is undertaken prior to the acquisition.

So, why would a company/organisation require new and/or additional fixed assets? For a number of reasons, for example:

- to expand and/or diversify company/organisation business activities,
- to reorganise and/or rationalise company/organisation business activities,
- to improve and/or reorganise the company's/organisation's portfolio of fixed assets, and/or
- to replace existing company/organisation fixed assets impaired or damaged by unexpected events/unpredicted occurrences.

In general, the acquisition of fixed assets can be categorised as either:

- a programmed/replacement cycle acquisition – that is the acquisition of a fixed asset or group of fixed assets as part of an agreed general fixed assets renewal/replacement programme – as determined by the company/organisation strategic plan, or
- a non-programmed/non-replacement cycle acquisition – that is the acquisition of a fixed asset or group of fixed assets as a result of damage caused to existing fixed asset(s) by an unpredicted event and/or an unexpected occurrence.

Where an acquisition is a programmed acquisition, authorisation would of course be routine – providing the acquisition request is consistent with the company's/organisation's strategic plan. However, where an acquisition is a non-programmed acquisition, special approval would need to be obtained. This is because any such non-programmed acquisitions could have a substantial impact on:

- the capital needs and requirements of a company/organisation – especially where significant capital rationing[46] issues exist within the company/organisation, and

- the revenue needs and requirements of a company/organisation – especially where significant working capital constraints exist within the company/organisation.

Once approval for the acquisition of the fixed asset is confirmed, the facilities director/manager or the ICT director/manager would be informed accordingly.

Note: A review of a number of evaluation techniques used to evaluate/review:

- a non-replacement decision – that is the purchase/acquisition of a new asset or a new group of assets,
- a replacement cycle decision – that is the replacing of an existing asset or an existing group of assets with the same (or similar) type of asset/assets,
- an investment timing decision – that is replacing of an existing asset or an existing group of assets with a different type of asset/assets,
- a life cycle decision – that is replacing a long-lived asset/assets with a short-lived asset/assets, and
- a financing decision – that is comparing a lease or buy.

is available on the website accompanying this text www.pearsoned.co.uk/boczko.

### Authorisation stage

Once approval for the acquisition of the fixed assets has been obtained, it would be necessary to identify an appropriate supplier. This would probably mean inviting suppliers to provide a tender for the supply of the fixed assets.

## Alternative forms of tender

Although there are many variations, the most common types of tender processes are:

- the open tender,
- the restricted tender, and
- the negotiated tender.

An open tender is a single stage tendering/bidding process in which all interested suppliers are invited to submit a tender, usually in response to a company sponsored advertisement. The advertisement would usually provide:

- details of where, and how interested suppliers can obtain authorised tender documents,[47]
- details of the tendering process, and
- the last date by which interested suppliers must submit their tenders.

A restricted tender is a two-stage tendering/bidding process in which all interested suppliers are invited to submit an expression of interest usually within a predetermined time period, again in response to a company sponsored advertisement. The advertisement would usually provide:

- details of what information must be submitted by the supplier,
- where and how interested suppliers can obtain authorised expression of interest documents, and
- the last date by which interested suppliers must submit their expressions of interest.

All suppliers submitting an expression of interest are then evaluated by the company and a short-list of appropriate suppliers invited to submit a tender. Such restricted tendering is often used where a large number of suppliers are expected to bid.

A negotiated tender is where, following a process of pre-qualification, a company negotiates with a small select group of companies/organisations for the supply of fixed assets. Such a negotiated tendering process is often used where:

- the fixed assets to be acquired are of a highly complex nature,
- the fixed assets to be acquired are of a highly technical nature, and/or
- there is some uncertainty over the precise nature/technical specification of the fixed assets to be acquired.

As with an open tendering process, all compliant tenders received by the due date from the short-listed suppliers would be anonymously evaluated and the contract awarded in accordance with the criteria set by the company/organisation.

### Evaluation and award

To ensure objectivity and consistency, and preserve the integrity of the tendering process, all tenders received (whichever process is used), would normally be evaluated by an evaluation team, against a pre-determined set of criteria – determined at the time the tender documentation was compiled. Whilst the main evaluation criteria will often be quantitative – usually price orientated – other qualitative criteria may also be used, for example supplier experience and supplier flexibility.

Once a supply contract has been awarded, a tender approval notice would normally be issued and the successful (and unsuccessful) suppliers informed accordingly. Where necessary legal contracts may also be exchanged.

#### Acquisition stage

This acquisition stage would of course be part of the company/organisation expenditure cycle, inasmuch as once an approved supplier had been identified, an authorised company/organisation purchase order would be issued and despatched. In some circumstances, for example where:

- the acquisition is of a substantial nature, and/or
- the acquisition may occur over a substantial period of time,

the supplier may require a formal legally binding contract of supply to be signed under seal before the supply of any fixed assets commences.

On the satisfactory receipt of purchased fixed assets a receiving report would be issued. Where fixed assets are supplied to geographically dispersed company/organisation locations such a receiving report would of course only be issued when appropriate evidence of satisfactory delivery has been received.

Once delivery has been completed and an invoice has been received, the payment would be processed. Again, where the supply is for substantial volume of fixed assets over a substantial period of time, it is common for interim payments to be made to the supplier either on achievement of agreed performance targets or at agreed dates over the life of the supply agreement/contract. On satisfactory completion, where appropriate, any legal titles/deeds of ownership (e.g. freehold property titles/vehicle ownership documents) for the fixed assets acquired by the company/organisation would be transferred from the supplier to the purchasing company/organisation.

On receipt of the invoice, the transaction would be recorded in the general ledger as follows:

- Dr fixed assets account,
- Cr creditor control account.

On payment of the invoice, the transaction would be recorded in the general ledger as follows:

- Dr creditor's control account,
- Cr bank account.

Appropriate creditor memorandum entries for receipt and payment of the invoice would also be made in the individual creditor's account in the purchases ledger.

Once the transaction has been complete – that is on the transfer of property ownership and asset possession, it would be necessary to enter the acquired fixed assets onto the company's/organisation's assets register.

## Retention of fixed assets

As suggested earlier, fixed assets are acquired for use within the company/organisation, and as such will generally be retained within it for a period in excess of a single financial year/accounting period. This continued retention raises a number of issues, not least the necessity to:

- maintain an accurate record of all fixed assets (including leased fixed assets) retained within the company/organisation – using for example a fixed assets register,
- regularly verify, and where appropriate adjust, the value of such fixed assets and, perhaps more importantly,
- periodically confirm the existence and legal ownership of all fixed assets in use within the company/organisation.

### Fixed assets register

Most if not all companies/organisations which possess a significant number of fixed assets now maintain a fixed assets register – usually in the form of a secure computer-based database, the purpose being to allow a company/organisation to:

- record details of all company/organisation fixed assets,
- monitor and record details of all acquisitions and disposals of fixed assets,
- record and amend as required the valuation of all fixed assets for depreciation, taxation and insurance purposes, and
- generate accurate information to satisfy both internal and external reporting requirements.

Whilst the precise nature and format of the information to be stored in the fixed assets register would differ from company to company or organisation to organisation, influenced by:

- the internal reporting requirements of the company/organisation and, perhaps more importantly,
- the external regulatory requirements/disclosure requirements imposed on the company/organisation by external companies/agencies (e.g. regulatory authorities, insurance companies, banks and taxation authorities),

such information would, in general, include details on:

- the nature, types and classes of each fixed asset maintained within the company/organisation,
- the acquisition profile of each fixed asset maintained within the company/organisation,[48]
- the value of each fixed asset[49] maintained within the company/organisation,
- the ownership of individual fixed assets maintained within the company/organisation,[50]
- the geographical location of individual fixed assets,
- the office/department/section responsible for the day-to-day use and management of individual fixed assets,
- the fixed asset identifier,[51] and
- the maintenance requirements/replacement requirements of individual fixed assets.

Access to the fixed assets register should of course be restricted to approved personnel only.

Where a company/organisation has a substantial land/property portfolio and/or a significant investment portfolio, it may also use a land and property register, and an investment register.

In addition to the above fixed assets register, where a company/organisation has a substantial land/property portfolio and/or a significant investment portfolio, the company/organisation may also use:

- a land/property register to record details of all land and property owned and/or leased by the company/organisation, and
- an investment register to record details of all equity and/or debenture investments held by the company/organisation.

## Disposal of fixed assets

All fixed assets whether they are tangible fixed assets such as buildings, fixtures and fittings, plant and machinery, and vehicles and equipment, or intangible fixed assets such as patents, copyrights, trademarks and brand values, have a limited useful life and will either become uneconomic and unable to generate revenue income over and above the cost of their continued use, or simply expire. This arises for many reasons, perhaps the most common being:

- physical deterioration (or wear and tear),
- technical obsolescence,
- physical impairment,
- the expiration of a legal right, and/or
- the loss of commercial value.

Where a fixed asset has some residual value, the disposal may of course result in the sale of the fixed asset to another company/organisation and a net inflow of funds. However, where the fixed asset has no residual value, the disposal (or perhaps, more appropriately, the write-off) may result in a net outflow of funds.

For some fixed assets, regulatory requirements may impose very specific conditions on their disposal, inasmuch as requirements may stipulate specific changes/alterations that must be made to a fixed asset before it is deemed suitable for disposal. For example, the European Council Regulation No. 2037/2000 on substances that deplete the ozone layer (October 2001), requires 'the removal of ozone depleting substances (including CFCs[52] and HCFCs[53]) from industrial, commercial and domestic refrigeration equipment/appliances before such equipment/appliances are scrapped.'

### The disposal process/procedure

Although specific procedures may well differ from company to company or organisation to organisation, in general any fixed assets disposal process/procedure would include:

- an identification/scheduling stage,
- an approval stage, and
- a recording stage.

### Identification/scheduling stage

For non-ICT-related fixed assets, the responsibility for identifying and scheduling the disposals would be that of the facilities services director/manager (and department) and for ICT-related fixed assets it would be the ICT director/manager (and department). We can, however, distinguish between two types of fixed asset disposals, these being:

- a programmed disposal – that is a disposal/write-off of a fixed asset or group of fixed assets as part of an agreed general fixed assets renewal/replacement programme, as determined by the company/organisation strategic plan,[54] and
- a non-programmed disposal – that is a disposal/write-off of a fixed asset or group of fixed assets as a result of damage caused by an unpredicted event and/or an unexpected occurrence.

### Approval stage

As suggested earlier, the responsibility for authorising the disposal/write-off of a fixed asset or group of fixed assets would be that of the finance director/manager (and department).

Where the disposal is a programmed disposal the authorisation would of course be routine, providing the disposal request is consistent with the company's/organisation's strategic plan. However, where the disposal is a non-programmed disposal, special approval would need to be obtained and, where necessary, appropriate funding identified, especially if – as would probably be the case – the disposal would also need to be matched with the acquisition of a replacement fixed asset. In addition, if the value of the fixed assets involved is substantial and/or such non-programmed disposal requests have become a regular occurrence (and their cumulative value is substantial), it is likely that an independent internal investigation (probably by internal audit) would also take place – to establish why!

Once approval for the disposal of the asset is confirmed, the facilities director/manager or the ICT director/manager would be informed accordingly, and the asset disposed of/written-off.

Note: It is also at this stage that the fixed assets register would be updated to reflect the disposal/write-off.

So, how would such a disposal/write-off be recorded in a company's/organisation's accounting information systems?

### Recording stage

For accounting purposes, the disposal/write-off would be recorded as follows. On approval, the disposal/write-off would be recorded in the general ledger:

- Dr fixed assets disposal account,
- Cr fixed assets disposal account,

and any accumulated depreciation transferred, as follows:

- Dr provision for depreciation account,
- Cr fixed assets disposal account.

Where a sale is involved, the sale would be recorded in the general ledger as follows:

- Dr debtor account,
- Cr fixed assets disposal account,

and, on receipt, the payment would be recorded in the general ledger as follows:

- Dr bank account,
- Cr debtor account.

If a profit on disposal is realised, the profit would be recorded in the general ledger as follows:

- Dr fixed assets disposal account,
- Cr profit and loss account.

Appropriate debtor memorandum entries for the sale and receipt of payment would also be made in the individual debtor account in the sales ledger.

If a loss on disposal is realised, the loss would be recorded in the general ledger as follows:

- Dr profit and loss account,
- Cr fixed assets disposal account.

## Fixed assets management – internal controls

For our purposes we will classify fixed assets management internal controls into the following categories:

- acquisition-related internal controls – that is internal controls designed to ensure all fixed asset acquisitions are properly identified, appropriately approved and correctly accounted for,
- retention-related internal controls – that is internal controls designed to ensure all fixed assets are securely maintained within the company/organisation,
- disposal-related internal controls – that is internal controls designed to ensure all fixed asset disposals are appropriately approved and correctly accounted for, and
- information management internal controls – that is internal controls designed to ensure appropriate management information is provided to enable the effective management of the company's/organisation's fixed assets resource.

### Acquisition-related internal controls

To ensure all fixed asset acquisitions are appropriately approved and correctly accounted for, it is important to:

- ensure adequate written policies and procedures exist for the acquisition of *all* fixed assets,
- ensure appropriate authorisation is obtained prior to the acquisition of *all* fixed assets, and
- ensure, where necessary, competitive tenders are obtained for *all* fixed asset acquisitions.

### Retention related internal controls

To ensure all fixed assets are securely maintained within the business, it is important to:

- ensure adequate written policies and procedures exist for the determination of fixed asset useful lives and the calculation of depreciation,[55]
- ensure appropriate arrangements are made for the regular independent inspection of all fixed assets,
- ensure adequate arrangements are made for the maintenance, safekeeping and security of all fixed assets,
- ensure, where necessary, access to and use of fixed assets is monitored and controlled,
- ensure appropriate procedures exist for the regular and, where necessary, independent valuation/revaluation of fixed assets, and
- ensure all authorities and responsibilities relating to the retention of fixed assets are appropriately allocated, and adequate segregation of procedures/separation of duties exists between, for example:
  - procedures/personnel involved in the physical verification/inspection of fixed assets and procedures/personnel involved in maintaining and updating the fixed assets register, and
  - procedures/personnel involved in authorising the transfer/movement of fixed assets and procedures/personnel involved in maintaining and updating the fixed assets register.

### Disposal-related internal controls

To ensure all fixed asset disposals are appropriately approved and correctly accounted for, it is important to:

- ensure adequate written policies and procedures exist for the disposal of fixed assets,
- ensure appropriate arrangements are made for the identification, assessment and authorisation of all fixed asset disposals,
- ensure all income receipts from the disposal of fixed assets are correctly accounted for,
- ensure adequate records are maintained of all fixed asset disposals, and
- ensure all authorities and responsibilities related to the disposal of fixed assets are appropriately allocated and adequate segregation of procedures/separation of duties exists between, for example:
  - procedures/personnel involved in identifying fixed assets for disposal and procedures personnel involved in the authorising of such disposals, and
  - procedures/personnel involved in identifying fixed assets for disposal and procedures personnel involved in maintaining and updating the fixed assets register.

### Information management internal controls

To ensure the appropriate management information is provided to enable the effective monitoring and control of fixed asset management policies and procedures, it is important to ensure:

- all procedures and financial regulations relating to fixed asset management are accurately documented and regularly updated,
- all authorities and responsibilities relating to fixed asset management activities are appropriately allocated and regularly reviewed, and
- all access to fixed asset-related data is monitored and controlled, and restricted to authorised personnel only.

## Fixed assets management – risks

Clearly, a failure to adequately manage the acquisition, retention and disposal of fixed assets could have serious consequences for a company/organisation.

Such a failure could result in, for example:

- the fraudulent misappropriation of fixed assets,
- the deliberate damage to or sabotage of company/organisation fixed assets, and/or
- the inappropriate retention of fixed assets beyond their useful economic life.

More importantly, any such failure could have a significant impact on the revenue earning capacity of a company/organisation.

## Current assets management

Current assets can be defined as assets acquired by and/or generated by the company/organisation for the purpose of resale and/or conversion into cash or cash equivalents, the management of which can, perhaps unsurprisingly, be divided into two categories:

- stock management, and
- debtor management.

## Stock management

Stock management is concerned with the insulation and, as far as possible, protection of product/service-related transaction processes from adverse changes in the external environment. That is the primary objective of stock management is to ensure that not only are appropriate levels of stocks available within the company/organisation to meet anticipated production requirements, possible legal requirements and/or predicted customer/client demands but, more importantly, that excessive working capital is not tied up in unwarranted/unnecessary stocks – stocks surplus to transaction processing requirements. Put simply, to ensure that the right amount of stock is available, at the right time, and in the right place.

So how would a company/organisation decide what levels of stocks to hold? Broadly speaking, it could adopt one of three possible positions:

- maintain very small levels of stocks, or indeed maintain no stocks,[56]
- maintain large levels of stocks,[57] or
- maintain pre-determined or calculated levels of stocks.[58]

Although the selection would of course be dependent on a vast range of interrelated company/organisation specific business factors, some of which would include, for example:

- the availability of stocks,
- the reliability of suppliers,
- the predictability/certainty of demand for stocks,
- the expectation of possible future price changes, and
- the availability of trade discounts for volume purchasing,

the selection would, perhaps more importantly, be influenced by:

- the costs associated with holding/storing products – stock holding costs, and
- the costs associated with ordering products – stock ordering costs.[59]

For our purposes we will define stock holding costs as all those costs associated with the holding/keeping of stock over a period of time and would include, for example:

- the rent and/or depreciation costs associated with maintaining storage facilities,
- the overheads costs associated with such storage facilities – for example heating costs, lighting costs, insurance costs and possible security costs,
- the administration costs associated with maintaining a stock of products raw materials,
- the opportunity costs associated with possible stock obsolescence and/or stock deterioration, and
- the costs associated with the loss and/or theft of stock.

Furthermore, we will define stock ordering costs as all those costs associated with the ordering and receiving of stock and would include for example:

- the administration costs associated with the processing of orders,
- the inspection costs associated with the receiving of stock,
- the financial costs associated with the return of poor-quality products,
- stock related transport costs, and
- stock related handling costs.

Whilst retaining large levels of stocks can simplify stock management procedures and ensure – at least theoretically – the availability of stocks, it can nevertheless unnecessarily tie up working capital, increase the possibility of stock obsolescence and result in high stock holding costs.

Conversely, retaining very small levels, or indeed, zero stocks can improve efficiency and flexibility, and of course minimise stock holding costs, but it can be a difficult and complex way of managing stock as it increases dependability on external suppliers and again results in high stock ordering costs.

Retaining moderate levels of stocks can – assuming the pre-determined/calculated level of stock is both adequate and appropriate for the needs of the company/organisation – not only minimise stock holding costs but also minimise stock ordering costs.

Clearly, it is important, especially where large volumes of relatively low-value stock items/ products are required, that an appropriate stock management model is adopted – as would be the case for say:

- a retail and distribution company (category type 1(a)),
- a manufacturing and production company (category type 1(b)) or, indeed,
- a company/organisation with a limited flow of commodities (category type 2(a)).

So what alternative stock management models are available? There are a number that can and indeed are used by companies/organisations not only throughout the UK but throughout the world, the most common of these being:

- the economic order quantity (EOQ) model,
- the just in time (JIT) model, and
- the materials requirements planning (MRP) model.

Before we look at each of these in a little more detail, it would perhaps be useful to consider who would be involved in the management of fixed assets.

### Stock management . . . allocation of duties/responsibilities

Although there are many alternative ways in which the duties and responsibilities related to the management of stock can be allocated within a company/organisation, as a general rule, for internal control purposes, any such allocation must ensure an adequate and appropriate separation of duties/responsibilities between:

- the authorising of stock-related transactions (the receipting and issuing of stock),
- the recording of stock-related transactions,
- the custody of stock, and
- the control of stock.

For the remainder of our discussion on stock management, we will assume an allocation of duties/responsibilities between the following:

- the store services director/manager[60] (and department),
- the finance director/manager (and department),
- departmental/location personnel, and
- the internal audit department.

The store services director/manager (and department) would be responsible for:

- the receipt and safe custody of stocks,
- the secure storage of stocks,
- the regular inspection and maintenance of stocks,
- the disposal/write-off of impaired/damaged stocks,
- the issue of stocks to company approved locations, and
- the maintenance of a stock register.

Where stocks are stored at a number of geographical locations, it would nonetheless remain the responsibility of the store services director/manager (and department) to ensure the safe and secure storage of all stocks.

The finance director/manager would be responsible for:

- the determination of suitable stock accounting policies,
- the (re)valuation of all stocks,
- the maintenance of stock-related financial accounting records,

- the preparation of stock-related financial accounting statements, and
- the authorising of stock disposals/write-offs.

As a general rule departmental personnel would be responsible for:

- ensuring all stocks are used in accordance with company/organisation policy/guidance,
- ensuring all hazardous stocks are not used without appropriate authorisation and where necessary appropriate training,
- ensuring all stocks are safeguarded from theft, loss and damage, and
- ensuring any theft, damage and/or loss is reported immediately.

Internal audit would be responsible for:

- evaluating the appropriateness and effectiveness of all stock management internal control processes and procedures,
- identifying areas of weakness within stock management internal control processes and procedures, and
- making appropriate recommendations for improvements to stock management internal control processes and procedures.

### Economic order quantity model

Often referred to as the traditional approach to stock management, the economic inventory model can be defined as a model used to determine the optimal quantity to order required to meet customer demand, that minimises ordering costs, holding costs and stock-out costs. Although the economic order quantity model was originally developed by Harris (1915) the in-depth analysis/development of the economic order quantity model was undertaken by Wilson (1934). This has resulted in many academic texts – perhaps somewhat unfairly – referring to the economic order quantity model as Wilson's EOQ.

The economic order quantity model is based on the following assumptions:

- the demand for the product is known with certainty,
- the lead time[61] of the product is fixed and known with certainty,
- the receipt of the product order occurs in a single instant,
- quantity discounts are not available, and
- product shortages or stock-outs do not occur.

Put simply, the economic order quantity model can be expressed as:

$$Q = \sqrt{2cd/h}$$

where: $Q$ = the quantity to order

$d$ = the number of product units required per annum (annual demand)

$c$ = the cost of placing an order

$h$ = the holding cost per product unit per annum

Note: You may also see the economic order quantity formula expressed as $Q = (2cd/h)^{0.5}$.

Consider the following.

*MJY Ltd, a Manchester-based company, has identified that its demand for product DR35 – a main component of its best selling product range – is 40,000 units per annum. This demand is at a constant rate throughout the year. If it costs the company £20 to place an order, and £0.40 to hold a single unit of DR35 for a year, determine:*

- *the order size to minimise stock costs,*
- *the number of orders to be placed each year,*

- *the length of the stock cycle, and*
- *the total costs.*

*The order size that would minimise stock costs would be:*

$$Q = \sqrt{2cd/h}$$
$$= \sqrt{(2 \times 20 \times 40,000/0.40)}$$
$$= 2,000 \text{ units}$$

*The number of orders to be placed each year would be:*

*40,000/2,000 = 20 orders.*

*The length of the stock cycle would be:*

*52/20 or every 2.6 weeks.*

*Total costs would be total ordering costs + total holding costs, that is:*

*h(Q/2) + c(d/Q) = 0.40(2,000/2) + 20(40,000/2,000) = £800 per year*

*So when would MJY Ltd order product DR35? It would be ordered every 2.6 weeks, because from the information contained in the question there appears to be no lead time. However suppose that the supplier of product DR35 operated with a lead time of one week. How often would MJY Ltd now have to order the product?*

*Assuming MJY Ltd consumes product DR35 evenly throughout the year, it would mean that the company would need to order the product when a minimum stock level of approximately 770 is reached – that is 40,000/52. It is this minimum level of stock that is often referred to as buffer stock – the stock that can be consumed whilst the ordered stock is awaiting delivery.*

Note: Whilst the economic order quantity model can of course be used to manage/control both raw material stocks and finished product stocks – that is it can be used by manufacturing and production companies/organisations and/or retail and distribution companies/organisations – in a practical context its application/use can differ substantially from company to company or organisation to organisation.[62] Nevertheless it is perhaps worth noting that the economic order quantity model is, in essence, a risk-averse stock management model inasmuch as the most significant implication of its use is it can, and indeed often does, result in companies/organisations holding significant amounts of stocks. In addition, buffer stocks may also be introduced to compensate for the uncertainty that often exists in the use of the model/formula – for example, supplier lead times may be difficult to determine with any degree of certainty. Why? Put simply, to minimise the possibility of any stock-outs[63] occurring which may result in unfulfilled/unsatisfied transactions and as a consequence the loss of revenue income.

### Just in time model

Just in time can be defined as a stock management strategy designed to improve the efficiency and effectiveness of a company/organisation by reducing in-process stock and its associated costs. Originating in Japan[64] in the early 1950s, the core philosophy of just-in-time is continuous review, continuous improvement, with the aim being to:

- eliminate waste – throughout a company's/organisation's supply/production chain,
- minimise ordering costs, and
- reduce, if not eliminate, holding costs by removing the 'security blanket' of holding stocks.

Essentially, within a just-in-time systems the existence of stocks, or more appropriately the holding of stocks to service a production and/or retail system, is viewed as a sign of sub-standard management.

Why?

Because the very act of holding stocks is viewed as a drain on the limited resources of a company's/organisation's production and/or retail system, with the holding of such stocks merely designed to conceal problems and inefficiencies within the production/retail system, such as an ineffective use of resources, a lack of flexibility in the use of employees and, perhaps most importantly, an inappropriate level of planning/capacity management.

Put simply, a just-in-time stock management system can – in a practical context – be summed up as small stocks/frequent deliveries, that is the right material, at the right time, at the right place, and in the exact amount, with new stock ordered when existing stock reaches its reorder level. So how does this differ from the economic order quantity model discussed earlier?

If you recall, from our earlier discussion, we suggested that the economic order quantity is essentially that which minimises total annual cost and is, on cost grounds, the quantity a company/organisation should order. The economic order quantity is determined by the following formula:

$$Q = \sqrt{2cd/h}$$

where: $Q$ = the quantity to order

$d$ = the number of product units required per annum (annual demand)

$c$ = the cost of placing an order

$h$ = the holding cost per product unit per annum

So, what about just-in-time with its underpinning philosophy of small/frequent orders and very low levels of stock? In the above formula, both $c$ the cost of placing an order, and $h$ the holding cost per product unit per annum, are fixed. However, if for example we can reduce the cost of ordering ($c$), and/or the holding cost per product unit per annum, then the EOQ would also fall.

Consider the following.

*NBC Ltd, a York-based company, has identified that the company's demand for product BB33 is 1280 units per annum. This demand is at a constant rate throughout the year. If it costs the company £5 to place an order and the cost of holding a single unit is £0.50, what order size would minimise total stock costs?*

*Using the EOQ formula, the order size that would minimise total stock costs would be:*

$$Q = \sqrt{2cd/h}$$
$$= \sqrt{(2 \times 5 \times 1{,}280/0.50)}$$
$$= 160 \text{ units}$$

*and the total holding cost would be:*

$$h(Q/2) + c(d/Q) = 0.50(160/2) + 5(1{,}280/160) = £80$$

*Say, for example, we could reduce c – the cost of placing an order – by 75% to £1.25, and at the same time reduce h – the holding cost per product unit per annum – by 20% to £0.40. What would the effect be on both the EOQ and the total costs?*

*The effect would be as follows:*

$$Q = \sqrt{2cd/h}$$
$$= \sqrt{(2 \times 1.25 \times 1{,}280/0.40)}$$
$$= 89.44 \text{ units (rounded up to 90 units)}$$

*and the total holding cost would be:*

$$h(Q/2) + c(d/Q) = 0.40(90/2) + 1.25(1,280/90) = £35.78$$

*Although the frequency of the orders would increase – that is the length of the stock cycle would fall from 6.5 weeks (52/(1,280/160)), to approximately 3.66 weeks (52/£1,280/90)), the quantity ordered would fall – resulting in lower stocks – and the total cost would fall.*

This is, in fact, one of the main ideas underpinning just-in-time – the continuous reduction of $c$ and $h$. As a consequence, if a company/organisation can not only develop close links with suppliers, but also identify, develop and sustain operational efficiencies within the company/organisation and thereby reduce the cost of ordering and the cost of holding products/items of stock, it becomes much more attractive to order small quantities (as we have seen). Indeed, if $c$ can be reduced to 0 – that is products/items of stock can be ordered free, without external and/or internal cost – then it becomes beneficial for a company/organisation to order products/items of stock as required (just-in-time so to speak).

The main benefits/advantages of just-in-time include:

- greater processing efficiency and higher productivity due to reduced product cycle times and lower production set-up times,
- improved product quality,
- reduced scrap/need for reworking,
- smoother production flow, and
- improved supplier relationships.

The main problems/disadvantages with just-in-time are:

- developing and implementing just-in-time stock management models can – both in management time and commitment – be very costly,
- determining reorder levels can be problematic (some companies/organisations now use a moving average based on the past two or three, months activity),
- establishing a workable/dependable relationship with external suppliers/providers can be complex, and
- maintaining, monitoring and assessing the efficient and effectiveness of just-in-time stock management models can be difficult

Note: Whilst many companies/organisations continue to develop and use just-in-time related stock management models, they nevertheless continue to hold some buffer stocks to compensate for the uncertainty/unpredictability of suppliers.

### Materials requirements planning model

Developed in the mid/late 1960s, materials requirements planning systems (MRP-I) are essentially proactive stock management systems which seek to:

- reduce overall stock levels,
- reduce production and delivery lead times,
- improve coordination, and
- increase efficiency.

They are essentially manufacturing/production scheduling systems and are used by many production companies and/or organisations to:

- control the types and quantities of stocks required and ensure materials are available for production and finished products are available for delivery to customers/clients,

- plan/schedule manufacturing/production activities, delivery schedules and purchasing activities,
- ensure product demand/customer requirements are fulfilled, and
- minimise inventory levels and manufacturing/production costs.

Essentially a materials requirements planning system schedules production on the basis of anticipated future demand. A master production schedule is prepared to establish an overall stock requirement. Existing and available stocks are deducted from the overall stock requirements and a net purchasing requirement (including any provision for production waste/scrap) established. Using this net purchasing requirement, purchase order and delivery schedules are established, and production/manufacturing commencement times/dates determined.

The main benefits/advantages of such systems are:

- they can reduce/eliminate the risk of under/over-stocking, and
- they can minimise the need for the duplication of stock/production data.

The main problems/disadvantages are:

- inaccurate forecasting can result in excessive costs being incurred, and
- inaccurate bills of materials and/or inappropriate production planning can result in the use of inaccurate stock reorder levels resulting in possible stocking problems.

### Just-in-time stock model and the materials requirements planning model – the key differences

Firstly, although both models can of course assist in reducing costs, eliminating waste and increasing efficiency/productivity, the just-in-time model tends to be used predominantly by retail-based companies (although production-based companies employ variations of the just-in-time model), whereas the materials requirement planning model tends to be used predominantly by production-based companies.

Secondly, the materials requirement planning model schedules production/stock requirements to meet an anticipated/forecasted demand level therefore *creating* stock, whereas the just-in-time model schedules production/stock requirements to meet a specific/defined customer/client demand, therefore *minimising* if not eliminating the need for stock.

Finally, the just-in-time model tends to be more appropriate for stocks which have an unpredictable/uncertain demand patterns, whereas the materials requirement planning model tends to be more appropriate for stocks which have predictable/certain demand patterns for which alternative production patterns exists and for which lead times are uncertain.

### Organisational context of stock

Whether it is because of supply-side uncertainty, demand-side unpredictability or a combination of both, many companies/organisations continue to hold some stocks, however small the volume or value.

Such stocks would include for example:

- stocks of raw materials and/or product components,
- stocks of unfinished products (often referred to as work-in-progress),
- stocks of finished products for resale, and
- stocks of consumables for use within the business,

all of which (as we have seen) play a vital role within the revenue cycle (see Chapter 8), the expenditure cycle (Chapter 9) and the conversion cycle (see Chapter 10) activities of the company/organisation. See Figure 11.3.

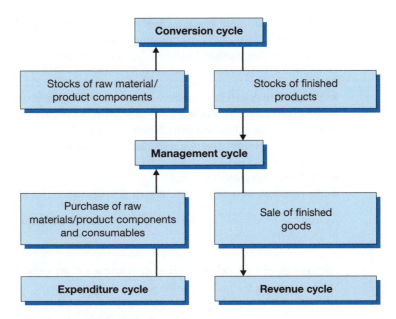

**Figure 11.3** Organisational context of stocks

It is of course important for a company/organisation to be able to accurately identify what stocks it possesses, where the stocks are located and how much they are worth. To do so, a company/organisation must:

- ensure an accurate record of all stocks retained within the company/organisation is maintained,
- ensure the secure storage of all stocks retained within the company/organisation,
- ensure the periodic confirmation of both the quantity and quality of the stocks retained within the company/organisation, and
- ensure appropriate adjustments are made to reflect any diminution in value.

### Stores records and the stock register

For internal control purposes, most if not all companies/organisations which maintain a stock of raw materials/components, unfinished products, finished products and/or consumables for use within their day-to-day transaction processing systems maintain a record of all stocks retained – a record often referred to as a stock ledger[65] or perhaps, more appropriately, as a stock register. The purpose of such a record is to:

- document details of all stocks retained within the company/organisation,
- record details of all receipts (purchases) and issues (sales) of stock,
- record, and amend as required, the valuation for all stock, and
- generate accurate information to satisfy both internal and external reporting requirements.

Note: Where a company/organisation maintains different types of stock – for example a raw materials/components stock, an unfinished products (or work-in-progress) stock, a finished products stock and/or a consumables stock, it is likely that a separate stock register would be maintained for each type.

Although historically stock register records were maintained using a variety of paper/card-based systems, the majority of companies/organisations now maintain their stock register(s) in the form of a secure computer-based database, containing information such as:

- the nature, type and/or the category of stock retained within the company/organisation,
- the acquisition profile of stock receipts – for example date of delivery, location of delivery,
- the value of each item of stock[66] retained within the company/organisation,
- the geographical location of each item of stock,
- the office/department/section responsible for the day-to-day use and management of individual items of stock,
- the stock item identifier,[67] and
- the replacement requirements of each item of stock – including its reorder level.

As with the fixed assets register (see above), access to the stock register(s) should be restricted to approved personnel only.

### Stores and the secure maintenance of stocks

Where stocks are maintained within a company/organisation, it is of course important to ensure adequate and appropriate storage facilities are provided to secure and protect stock items, and to minimise the risk of theft and/or damage. Such risks are especially high where:

- stock items are portable, easily resaleable and do not carry/feature a company/organisation logo/symbol,
- storage facilities are unsecured, regularly left unsupervised and are unmonitored (e.g. no CCTV), and
- stores personnel are untrained and regularly left unsupervised.

Remember, if something can go missing, it will go missing.

Whilst the precise nature of a company's/organisation's stores management/stores security policies and procedures would depend on a wide range of factors, for example:

- the type and variety of stock items stored,
- the volume of stock items stored,
- the value of the stock items stored,
- the location of the stores, and
- the turnover of stock items,

it would, nonetheless, be important for a company/organisation to:

- ensure all storage locations are secure and appropriate,
- ensure all stock items are coded/tagged,
- ensure access to store facilities (warehouses and stockrooms) is restricted to authorised personnel,
- ensure the appropriate surveillance of stores and surrounding areas, for example car parks, delivery area and other key locations, and
- ensure stores personnel are adequately trained, appropriately supervised and, where possible, frequently rotated to minimise the possibility of collusion.

### Physical verification of stock – quantity and quality

Periodically it is important to undertake a physical stock count – a physical verification of the stock(s) retained within the company/organisation. The primary objectives are to:

- confirm the existence of stocks held,
- verify the amount of stock held (by comparison with the stock ledger), and
- to identify/confirm the physical state of the stocks held.

There are of course many alternative types of physical stock counts or stocktakes, the most common being:

- periodic stocktaking – that is where a physical count of all stock items is undertaken, or
- continuous stocktaking – that is where a physical count of only a selected sample of stock items is undertaken.

Remember: For valuation purposes, a physical count of all stock items *must* be undertaken at the year-end date (or as close as possible).

For accounting purposes, the introduction of closing stock (based on the reconciled stocktake) into these financial accounts would be recorded as follows:

- Dr (closing) stock account,
- Cr trading account.

Remember: For accounting purposes, the introduction of any opening stock (based on the previous accounting period's closing stock – as adjusted) into these financial accounts would be recorded as follows:

- Dr trading account,
- Cr (opening) stock account.

Whilst the primary responsibility for the stocktake would be that of the store services director/ manager (and department), in some companies/organisations – especially retail companies which operate at a number of geographical locations – such responsibility may be delegated to the retail outlet manager, especially where stock ledgers are maintained by the store services department.

Have a look at the following extracts taken from stocktaking instructions (for the year ending 31 March 2006) recently issued to store managers of a UK-based retail company:

## Extract 1: Stocktake responsibilities

*The manager of the store is responsible for the co-ordination, control and completion of the physical stocktake. Before any physical stocktake commences, the manager of the store is responsible for:*

- *ensuring sufficient trained personnel are available to participate in the stocktake, and*
- *ensuring all personnel counting stock are issued with a written copy of the company's current stocktaking procedures/instructions.*

*The manager of the store is also responsible for informing the financial department and the internal audit department of the time and date of the physical stocktake. It is, however, the responsibility of the finance director/manager and, where appropriate, the internal audit manager to ensure finance and/or audit personnel are available to supervise/observe the physical stocktake.*

## Extract 2: Stocktake procedures

*On the day before the physical stocktake in-store stocks should be checked to ensure that all products received have been entered into the stock ledger prior to the commencement of the count.*

*On the day of the stocktake, personnel appointed to conduct the physical stocktake should be either assigned an area within the storage facility or allocated a type of stock within the storage facility. Where a manual method of stocktake is used, personnel appointed to conduct the physical stocktake should be issued with stock count sheets that identify details of the unit of measurement to be used in the stocktake (e.g. tin, box, carton) but does not include any data on stock levels. Where a scanner method of stocktake is used – for example where stock items are bar coded or RFID tagged – personnel appointed to conduct the physical stocktake should be issued with an authorised scanner. On completion of the stocktake scanned details should be downloaded (by authorised personnel only) to maintain a record of areas scanned.[68]*

### Extract 3: Responsibilities – personnel conducting the stocktake

*Personnel conducting the stocktake will be responsible for:*

- *ensuring all stocktake sheets are appropriately signed (manual stocktake), and/or all scanner data is correctly downloaded (automated stocktake),*
- *assisting financial department personnel in the supervision of the stocktake and the verification of quantities recorded,*
- *ensuring all counted stocks are marked to ensure stock items are not double counted,*
- *investigating discrepancies as directed by the store manager,*
- *undertaking, where directed by the store manager, the recount of stocks,*
- *ensuring that all stock items within their assigned area is included in the stocktake, and*
- *identifying damaged and/or obsolete stock.*

### Extract 4: Responsibilities – personnel supervising the stocktake

*Personnel supervising the stocktake will be responsible for:*

- *ensuring all personnel appointed to conduct the physical stocktake are properly instructed in relevant procedures,*
- *ensuring all stock quantities are recorded in the correct units, and*
- *investigating stock variances.*

*Staff supervising the stocktake will also be responsible for:*

- *supervising additional test checks on the physical stock,*
- *ensuring all proposed adjustments to stock are approved by the store manager and the finance department representative attending the stocktake, and*
- *ensuring that all procedures undertaken as part of the stocktake process – for example, additional test counts, the investigations of variances and the valuations and write-off of stocks, are adequately documented.*

### Extract 5: Variances and write-offs

*Once the stocktake has been completed, all physical stock counts should be compared to the stock ledger for the store. Where variances are identified, these should initially be investigated by the store manager. Where variances are significant (in excess of 5% of the total value of the stock) such variances should also be reported to the finance department and internal audit department for further investigation.*

*Where during a stocktake, obsolete and/or damaged stock is identified, such stock should be excluded from the physical count and appropriate arrangements made to dispose of the stock items. Where the value of such write-offs is significant (in excess of 5% of the total value of stock) such write-offs should be reported to the finance department and internal audit department for further investigation.*

## Extract 6: Audit function

*The internal audit department will be responsible for:*

- *undertaking sample comparisons of completed manual stock count sheets and/or automatic stock count listings to the physical stock within the store, and*
- *identifying, investigating and resolving any discrepancies identified.*

### Valuation of the stocks

SSAP 9 (stock and long-term contracts) provides that all stocks should be valued at: 'the lower of cost or net realisable value',[69] defining cost as 'that expenditure which has been incurred in the normal course of business in bringing the product or service to its present location and condition',[70] and net realisable value as the selling price of the stock item, less all further costs to be incurred *before* a sale can be completed.

Inasmuch as the determination of profit for an accounting period requires the allocation of all costs relating to stocks sold and/or consumed to the accounting period,[71] the cost (or net realisable value) of any unsold or unconsumed stocks can be carried forward to the period in which the stock is sold and/or consumed, and the income received – but only to the extent that it is believed that the cost (or net realisable value) of such unsold and/or unconsumed stocks is recoverable.

This requires not only an assessment of the value of individual items of unsold and/or unconsumed stocks but, more importantly, a matching of costs/net realisable values using for example a First-In First-Out (FIFO) basis, a Last-In Last-Out (LIFO) basis, an Average Cost (AvCo) basis, or any other reasonable approximation, to provide a realistic valuation of the cost of any unsold and/or unconsumed stocks.

(Remember: FIFO, LIFO, AvCo, etc., are merely methods of allocating costs and are not descriptions of the actual usage of stock.)

More importantly, any accounting policy adopted for the allocation of costs must be used consistently from year to year. This is for two reasons. Firstly, to prevent or at least minimise the possible fraudulent manipulation of reported profits[72] and secondly to ensure, where at all possible, comparability with both previous and future accounting periods.

For accounting purposes, any reduction in the value of stock would be recorded as follows:

- Dr profit and loss account,
- Cr (closing) stock account.

The reduction in value would be written off as soon as possible – that is in the accounting period in which it is identified.[73]

### Stock management – internal controls

For our purposes we will classify stock management internal controls into the following categories:

- movement-related internal controls – that is internal controls designed to monitor and control the movement of stock including the receipting and issuing of stock,
- security-related internal controls – that is internal controls designed to ensure the secure storage of stock,
- quality-related internal controls – that is internal controls designed to maintain the quality of stock, and

- information management-related internal controls – that is internal controls designed to ensure appropriate management information is provided to enable the effective monitoring and control of stock management policies and procedures.

### Movement-related internal controls

To ensure all stock receipts are monitored, appropriately controlled and correctly recorded, it is important to:

- ensure adequate written policies and procedures exist for the receipting of *all* stocks,
- ensure all stocks are appropriately coded/tagged and correctly located within the storage facility, and
- ensure stock records are accurately updated for *all* receipts of stock.

To ensure all stock issues are appropriately approved and correctly accounted for, it is important to:

- ensure adequate written policies and procedures exist for the issue of stocks,
- ensure appropriate authorisation is obtained for all issues of stock, and
- ensure stock records are accurately updated for *all* issues of stock.

In addition, it is important to ensure that all authorities and responsibilities relating to the movement of stock are appropriately allocated and adequate segregation of procedures/separation of duties exists between procedures/personnel involved in authorising the movement of stock and those involved in maintaining and updating the stock register.

### Security-related internal controls

To ensure all stocks are securely maintained within the business, it is important to:

- ensure adequate arrangements are made for the maintenance, safekeeping and security of all stocks,
- ensure all storage facilities used to store stocks are regularly assessed,
- ensure, where necessary, that access to storage facilities used to store stocks is monitored and controlled, with access granted to authorised personnel only, and
- ensure all authorities and responsibilities relating to the storage of stocks are appropriately allocated and adequate segregation of procedures/separation of duties exists between procedures/personnel involved in the physical verification/inspection of stock and those involved in maintaining and updating the stock register.

### Quality-related internal controls

Quality control is of course an essential aspect of any stock management system, however it is particularly important where, for example, the health and/or safety of company/organisation personnel, customers/clients and/or members of the public could be adversely affected by poor quality stock.

It is therefore important for a company/organisation to ensure that all stocks – especially stocks of completed products – are regularly assessed for quality. Where faults are identified, the source of any such faults should be determined and the problem(s) rectified as soon as possible. Indeed, whatever the origin of the faults, for example the purchase/supply of faulty components, a failure of production controls, or the deliberate sabotage by an employee for purposes of fraud and extortion, it is important, that:

- all unsold stocks are withdrawn from sale, and
- all sold stocks are recalled and either repaired and/or replaced.

Where appropriate, all withdrawn stocks should be disposed of/written off.

For accounting purposes, any disposal/write-off of stock would be recorded as follows:

■ Dr profit and loss account,
■ Cr (closing) stock account.

## Information management-related internal controls

To ensure the appropriate management information is provided to enable the effective monitoring and control of fixed asset management policies and procedures, it is important to ensure:

■ all procedures and financial regulations relating to the management of stock are accurately documented and regularly updated,
■ all authorities and responsibilities relating to the management of stock are appropriately allocated and regularly reviewed, and
■ all access to stock-related data is monitored and controlled, and restricted to authorised personnel only.

## RFID technologies and stock management

The history of Radio Frequency IDentification (RFID) technologies is a disputed one. Whilst the origins of RFID technologies can be traced back to Leon Theremin in 1945,[74] for many, the inventor of current RFID technologies is Mario Cardullo in 1973 and his development of a passive radio transponder with a memory.

In a contemporary context, RFID technologies are often referred to as automatic identification technologies, that is technologies which rely on the storing and remote retrieval of data/information using transponder devices. Such transponder devices are often referred to as an RFID tags.[75]

An RFID system consists of several components, for example:

■ RFID tags,
■ RFID tag readers,
■ processing hardware, and
■ application software.

It is designed to:

■ enable data/information to be transmitted from a RFID tag,
■ enable such data/information to be read by a RFID reader, and
■ facilitate the processing of such data/information according to the needs of a particular application/system.

In general, the data/information transmitted by a RFID tag can be categorised into three types:

■ location information – that is information about the geographical location of a subject and/or an object,
■ object information – that is information on object-related characteristics, for example product price, product colour, product date, or
■ subject information – that is information on the identity of a subject and/or the location of a subject.

### Types of RFID tags

There are essentially three types of RFID tags:

■ passive,
■ semi-passive (or semi-active), or
■ active.

### Passive RFID tag

A passive RFID tag is an RFID tag that does not possess an internal power supply. Such passive tags operate using a process often referred to as backscattering – that is the RFID tag antenna is not only designed to collect power from the incoming signal (the carrier signal from the reader), but also transmit an outgoing signal to the reader.

Passive RFID tags are often referred to as dumb tags.

### Semi-passive RFID tag

A semi-passive RFID tag is very similar to a passive tag except for the addition of a small battery. The battery allows the RFID tag to be constantly powered and therefore removes the need for the RFID tag antenna to collect power from the incoming signal.

Semi-passive RFID tags are generally faster and stronger compared to passive tags.

### Active RFID tag

Unlike passive and/or semi-passive RFID tags, active RFID tags possess their own internal power source, usually an internal battery, to generate and transmit an outgoing signal to the reader.

Active RFID tags are often referred to as beacon tags because such tags broadcast their own signal.

#### RFID tags – current use

The current areas in which RFID tags are now used include:

- supply chain management,
- product tracking and distribution management,
- product/asset security,
- transport management,
- revenue collection, and
- personal identification.

The advantages of using RFID technologies in stock management (and associated revenue cycle activities) can be categorised as either:

- company/organisation related, or
- customer/client related.

For the company/organisation the advantages/benefits associated with the use RFID technologies include:

- improved data management,
- increased data capacity,
- simplification of stock management processes,
- a reduction in operating costs,
- a reduction in stock management errors and inaccuracies,
- the more accurate and timely tracking of products and assets,
- greater supply chain visibility/supply chain management, and
- a possible reduction in product counterfeiting, fraud and theft.

For the customer/client the advantages/benefits associated with the use RFID technologies include:

- faster and simpler check-out procedures – for example there are no line-of-sight requirements for RFID tags,

- greater counterfeiting protection, and
- better product tracking/distribution management and therefore better matching of product availability and product demand.

For the company/organisation the disadvantages/problems associated with the use RFID technologies include:

- the costs associated with the implementation and use RFID-related technologies, and
- the possibility that RFID tags could be 'infected' with viruses and therefore their usability and integrity may be compromised.

For the customer/client, especially the individual customer/client, the major disadvantage/problem associated with the use RFID technologies is the privacy issue and the ability of such technologies not only to track product movement, but also profile customer purchasing activities. Whilst this is perhaps the major reason why RFID technologies have not yet enjoyed any major success in the retail sector, it would appear change is on the horizon (see Article 11.3).

## Article 11.3

### RFID technology spreads beyond retail

RFID technology is having a tangible impact on a wide array of industries across the globe, according to a new briefing paper by the Economist Intelligence Unit. Companies in the retail sector have been the fastest to adopt RFID, but programmes in consumer goods, logistics, life sciences, automotive and government are now delivering reduced costs, better inventory control and improved responsiveness to consumer demand. RFID (radio frequency identification) is a wireless technology consisting of tags and readers that can be used to exchange information about items, people or animals.

Although most commonly used to track and identify goods and materials within supply chains, the technology is also being used in applications as diverse as 'contactless payment' systems, passports and patient identification in hospitals.

Wider industry adoption will help grow the global market for RFID from $1.4 billion in 2003 to $10.9 billion by 2009, according to US market research firm ABI Research. The briefing paper's findings are published today in RFID comes of age, a report written by the Economist Intelligence Unit and sponsored by The North of England Inward Investment Agency (NEIIA), an organisation responsible for promoting direct business investment from North America.

The main findings include the following:

**RFID is gathering momentum.** The decision taken by leading global retailers to mandate use of RFID by their suppliers, aided by the emergence of global technical standards, have eliminated any doubt that the technology will be used on a broad scale. Pilot programmes in retail, consumer goods, logistics, life sciences, automotive and governments are under way and are already producing tangible benefits such as reduced costs, better inventory control and improved responsiveness to consumer demand.

**The supply chain is becoming smarter.** RFID has already made its mark on the supply chain, with companies like Wal-Mart, Tesco and Gillette using it to track inventory and improve stock replenishment. But to fulfil its potential, the technology needs to be integrated into operational management tools such as ERP (enterprise resource planning) software.

**RFID works for people as well as things.** Outside of the supply chain, a range of other applications are emerging, especially in applications that enhance customer convenience, such as 'contactless payment' systems.

Another growth area will be in identifying and authenticating people or items for safety or security purposes, such as within passports or to verify a patient's identity at the operating table.

Much work remains to be done. For all its promise, a range of technical, business and political barriers to RFID's development still exists.

Standards bodies and academic institutions need to harmonise hardware and software standards globally, while companies should lay out a framework that helps them understand and address the process changes required to get value from the technology. Privacy can be protected without killing RFID.

The use of RFID in consumer goods has sparked controversy about consumer privacy. Although some of the concerns raised overstate RFID's capabilities, there are genuine issues to be resolved, such as the ability for anyone with an RFID reader to track people by the items they wear or carry.

This report concludes that legislators should require that RFID tags be deactivated at point of sale to allay privacy concerns, but not require the permanent 'killing' of stored data, as this would limit users' ability to opt-in to interesting post-sale applications that benefit consumers as well as businesses.

'RFID is being used successfully in corporate supply chains, and there are a range of potentially valuable applications in the pipeline,' said Gareth Lofthouse, Director of Custom Research in Europe at the Economist Intelligence Unit. 'But for RFID to achieve its potential, the industry must address valid concerns over customer privacy.'

'NEIIA commissioned the report to help promote informed debate about the RFID industry,' commented David Allison, Chairman of The North England Inward Investment Agency. 'The report provides quality content that we believe will help RFID companies meet the broader challenges and opportunities confronting this burgeoning industry.'

Source: 10 March 2006,
www.electronicstalk.com/news/ecn/ecn100.html.

### Stock management – costs/risks

In a broad context, stock management is concerned with the trade-off between:

- the additional income and profit that may be generated as a result of holding stocks, and
- the administrative and financial costs and risks associated with holding such stocks.

The costs/risks associated with not holding (or holding low) stocks would include:

- a possible loss of customer goodwill when stock-outs occur,
- the dislocation/fragmentation of production dislocation,
- possible loss of flexibility due to increased dependency on suppliers, and
- possible increase in reorder costs.

The costs/risks associated with holding stock in trade would include:

- a possible lost of interest,
- an increased working capital cycle (see Article 11.4),
- increased storage cost, and
- increased insurance cost.

## Debtor management

Debtor management is concerned with ensuring that all debtor-based sales are promptly and correctly invoiced and all income relating to such debtor-based sales is efficiently collected. In a practical context, this means establishing effective company/organisation-wide internal controls to ensure the efficient management and administration of all debtor-related sales.

## Article 11.4

### Matalan given a dressing down

Matalan came under pressure yesterday after a leading broker cut its profit forecasts in the light of a year-end round-up meeting with the discount retailer.

After a disastrous Christmas, Matalan warned the City last month that it would make profits of only between £60m and £70m in the year ended February 28.

Yesterday, German bank Dresdner Kleinwort Wasserstein moved its estimate to the lower end of that range, citing concerns that Matalan had been unable to clear excess stock despite heavy discounting.

Dresdner said it had cut its pre-tax profit forecast by 8% to £60.4m and had advised clients to switch into JJB Sports, off 2.5p at 294.

'On our revised estimates, the stock trades on 13.9 times 2005 earnings. This looks expensive relative to the rest of the sector and we therefore maintain our reduce recommendation,' Dresdner said. The bank said it was concerned that the company might have to cut its dividend. Last year Matalan paid a dividend of 8.1p.

Other analysts were not so gloomy. Nick Bubb at Evolution Beeson Gregory said that although he had reduced his profit forecast by a couple of million pounds Matalan had made a good start to the new season. He believes it is possible that he will be upgrading his 2005 forecast when the company reports the full-year figures in May.

Matalan shares closed 7.25p lower at 164p – one of the biggest fallers in the FTSE 250.

Source: Neil Hume, 26 February 2004, The *Guardian*, **http://business.guardian.co.uk/story/0,,1156473,00.html**.

### Debtor management – internal controls

For our purposes we will classify debtor management internal controls into the following categories:

- pricing-related internal controls,
- order-related internal controls,
- invoicing-related internal controls,
- payment-related internal controls, and
- information management internal controls.

#### Pricing-related internal controls

To ensure appropriate charges are made for all products supplied to and services provided for customers/clients, it is important to:

- establish an official company/organisation-wide pricing policy and related customer/client discounting policy for all products supplied and services provided to customers/clients, and
- ensure all procedures and regulations related to such a company/organisation-wide policy are accurately documented and, where necessary, regularly updated.

It is also important to:

- ensure the company/organisation-wide price listing/discount listing is regularly reviewed and appropriately updated,[76] by authorised personnel only and, where appropriate, ensure that the official price listing (or a version of it) is made available to the prospective customers/clients,[77] and
- ensure all authorities and responsibilities relating to product/service pricing are appropriately allocated, and adequate segregation of procedures/separation of duties exists between procedures/personnel involved in raising invoices and those involved in establishing product/services prices and/or determining/authorising customer/client discounts.

### Order-related internal controls

To ensure products/services are only supplied to or provided for approved customers/clients it is important to establish clear criteria for the credit risk assessment of all new and existing customers/clients,[78] to ensure that products and services are not supplied to or provided for customers/clients with:

- an inappropriate credit rating, and/or
- a significant level of outstanding debt with the company/organisation.

It is also important to ensure all authorities and responsibilities relating to the processing and approval of customer orders are appropriately allocated and adequate segregation of procedures/separation of duties exists between procedures/personnel involved in determining credit risk and those involved in authorising the supply of products/provision of services to customers/clients.

### Invoicing-related internal controls

To ensure all debtor-based sales are promptly and correctly invoiced, it is important to establish an invoicing issuing procedure/timetable and ensure all such procedures and related financial regulations and controls are accurately documented and regularly updated. It is also important to:

- ensure all invoices are issued within a prescribed time period,
- ensure all invoices issued by the company/organisation are issued on official company/organisation documentation,
- ensure all amendments/adjustments to debtor accounts relating to invoices raised are authorised by appropriate staff and clearly documented, and
- ensure all authorities and responsibilities relating to customer invoicing are appropriately allocated and adequate segregation of procedures/separation of duties exists between, for example:
  - procedures/personnel involved in issuing invoices and those involved in collecting and/or recording debtor-related income,
  - procedures/personnel involved in receiving post (or complaints) and those involved in issuing invoices, and
  - procedures/personnel involved in issuing invoices and those who have access to and/or responsibility for the movement/allocation of products and/or services.

### Payment-related internal controls

To ensure all income relating to debtor-based sales is collected efficiently, it is important to establish an appropriate debt recovery policy and:

- ensure all outstanding debts (debtor account balances) are regularly monitored,
- ensure all debtor payments are correctly recorded,
- ensure that where debt write-off is deemed appropriate, such write-offs are authorised by approved senior personnel only, and
- ensure all authorities and responsibilities relating to payment processing are appropriately allocated and that an adequate segregation of procedures/separation of duties exists between, for example:
  - procedures/personnel involved in collecting debtor-related income and those involved in recording debtor-related income, and
  - procedures/personnel involved in issuing invoices and/or collecting debtor-related income and those involved in debt recovery procedures.

### Information management internal controls

To ensure appropriate management information is provided to enable the effective monitoring and control of debtor management policies and procedures, it is important to:

■ establish accurate activity or profit/cost centre-related budgets for all debtor related income, and
■ ensure that appropriate activity-related reports (including temporal[79] and/or cross sectional[80] comparative analyses) are produced for senior managers on a regular basis.

We discussed these in Chapter 8.

Within each of the above categories, it is of course important for data protection purposes (see the Data Protection Act 1998)[81] to ensure that access to confidential and/or personal debtor-related data is monitored and controlled, and restricted to authorised personnel only.

## Debtor management – costs/risks

In a broad context, debtor management is concerned with the trade-off between:

■ the additional income and profit that may be generated by providing and/or extending credit facilities to customers and/or clients, and
■ the administrative and financial costs and risks associated with providing/extending credit facilities to customers and/or clients.

The costs/risks associated with granting trade credit to customers/clients would include:

■ the loss of interest due to the deferred receipt of income,
■ the loss of purchasing power due to the deferred receipt of income,
■ the costs associated with debtor management-related administration, and
■ the risk (of consequential cost) of possible bad debts.

The costs/risks associated with denying trade credit to customers/clients would include:

■ the loss of customer goodwill,
■ the loss of sales income, and
■ the costs associated with a possible increase in cash/cash equivalent transactions.

## Liabilities management

Liabilities management can be divided into two categories:

■ gearing (or leverage) management, and
■ creditor management.

## Gearing (or leverage) management

Gearing is a description of the relationship between the levels of debt and equity within a company/organisation – a relationship often expressed in the form of a gearing ratio, that is:[82]

$$[(\text{Market value of debt/Market value of equity}) \times 100]$$

Inasmuch as the gearing ratio of a company/organisation can be used as a measure or indication of financial risk:

- a company/organisation with low levels of debt – that is a low-geared company/organisation – is generally considered to be of a low financial risk, and
- a company/organisation with high levels of debt – that is a highly-geared company/organisation – is generally considered to be of a high financial risk.

So, if debt increases financial risk, why do companies/organisations borrow? Because compared to equity, debt has a lower direct cost. It is generally perceived as being less risky to a lender/investor than equity for two reasons.

Firstly, in the event of a company liquidation and distribution of assets, secured lenders such as debenture holders will generally take priority over the shareholders of the company. Such security often results in lenders/investors requiring a rate of return lower than that normally required by shareholders. Secondly, all legitimate debt-related interest payments take priority and *must* be paid before any dividend payments are made, and are (in the UK at least) allowable as a tax expense whereas dividend payments to shareholders are not!

However, borrowing does have a number of disadvantages.

Firstly, increasing levels of debt within a company/organisation can increase the possibility of financial distress[83] and the risk of corporate/organisation failure, inasmuch as when combined with falling revenue incomes and/or high interest rates, excessive levels of debt within a company/organisation can increase the possibility of debt default – that is a company/organisation being unable to meet outstanding debt commitments. (See Article 11.5.)

Secondly, and perhaps more importantly, increasing the levels of debt within a company/organisation can adversely affect shareholder earnings inasmuch as higher levels of debt will normally require higher levels of interest (although not necessarily higher interest rates, see below). Such increases in interest – where they exceed any increases in earnings generated by the use of the additional debt funds within the company/organisation – will of course produce a reduction in profits available for distribution to shareholders as dividend payments. This, somewhat unsurprisingly, often results in shareholders demanding a higher rate of return in compensation and therefore increasing the cost of equity.

Consider the following.

*Assume that the value of a share can be approximated as follows:*

*d/r*

*where: d = current dividend, and*
*r = the expected rate of return.*

*Such a value is often known as the fundamental value of a share.*

*YHU plc is a UK-based retailer. The company has recently paid a dividend of 20p per share and the company expects the dividend to remain unchanged for the foreseeable future. Assuming an expected rate of return of 5%, the value of a YHU plc share would be:*

*0.20/0.05 = 400p or £4*

*Suppose the current dividend was increased to 22p, but because of additional debt the expected rate of return also increased to 6%. Then the value of a YHU plc share would be:*

*0.22/0.06 = 367p or £3.67*

# Article 11.5

## Rising debt levels place companies at risk

*FDs warned about rising levels of company debt and recent moves by debt holders to reduce their risk exposure.*

Financial directors need to start paying almost as much attention to the holders of their debt as they do to their shareholders, debt advisers have warned. Over the past year, debt trading has flourished in Europe, as the holders of debt have sought to reduce their risk exposure to particular sectors and regions. Executives, however, are unaware of the potential impact this phenomenon could have on their companies.

Low interest rates have seen companies carrying more debt on their balance sheets. According to the Centre for Management Buy-Out Research, more than 50% of UK buyouts were funded by debt in 2004.

Research by Close Brothers, meanwhile, found that FTSE250 companies were carrying higher levels of debt than five years ago. The merchant bank said that average gearing in the FTSE250 was 4.1 times earnings before interest, tax and depreciation (EBITDA), up on the 1.75 times the EBITDA figure revealed in a report in 2000.

In the report 'The growing importance of debt in European corporate transactions', Ernst & Young said that as long as interest rates remained low and trading conditions were healthy, companies with high gearing would remain safe. But if interest rates climbed from their historical lows and the economy slowed, these companies could find themselves in trouble.

Their shareholders, who are traditionally the focus of management's energy, would be replaced by the holders of their debt in the pecking order.

'As soon as a company runs into trouble, the balance of power shifts dramatically in favour of those holding its debt rather than its equity,' said an E&Y spokesperson, adding that many investors were aiming to take hold of a company by purchasing its debt rather than its equity.

Nick Hood, partner at corporate recovery specialists Begbies Traynor, said company directors, particularly in smaller plcs, were not aware of the growing importance of debt in their capital structure and the implications of their debt being traded. 'It is paramount that executives understand the importance of debt, because when your debt is traded you never quite know what you are dealing with. Unlike banks, the buyers of debt have varying agendas,' Hood said.

Neill Thomas, head of debt advisory at KPMG, said that private equity-backed companies were most likely to run into trouble because of high gearing. 'Generally speaking, quoted companies are sensibly geared. Private equity companies are the most vulnerable, especially if they operate in sectors where trading cracks appear,' said Thomas.

Source: 24 November 2005,
http://www.whatpc.co.uk/accountancyage/
news/2146588/rising-debt-levels-place.

*To maintain a share value of £4, the dividend would have to increase to:*

$$400 \times 0.06 = 24p$$

*or the expected rate of return would have to increase to:*

$$0.22/4 = 0.55 \text{ or } 5.5\%$$

So, how do the changes in the cost of equity affect the company/organisation? There are two alternative views as to how an increase in the levels of debt affect a company/organisation, in particular its overall cost of capital – that is its Weighted Average Cost of Capital (WACC),[84] these being:

- the traditionalist view, and
- the net operating income view (also known as the Modigliani–Miller theorem).

### The traditionalist view

The traditionalist view suggests that whereas the cost of equity will increase as the levels of debt increase, the cost of debt will remain unchanged up to a level beyond which the cost of debt will also increase. This results in a company's/organisation's weighted average cost of capital initially falling as the relative proportion of debt increases, and then increasing as the rising cost of equity and, perhaps more importantly, the rising cost of debt become increasingly significant.

*The traditionalist view therefore suggests that increasing levels of debt have, overall, an adverse impact on a company's/organisation's weighted average cost of capital.*

### The net operating income view

The net operating income view (as proposed by Modigliani and Miller in 1958) suggests that a company's/organisation's weighted average cost of capital remains unchanged regardless of the level of gearing. They suggest that the cost of debt remains unchanged as the level of gearing increases, with the cost of equity increasing in such a way as to keep a company's/organisation's weighted average cost of capital constant. Modigliani and Miller later adjusted their model suggesting that taxation relief on debt-related interest payments will reduce a company's/organisation's weighted average cost of capital which would, they claim, continue to fall up to a 100% gearing.

*The net operating income view (as amended) therefore suggests that increasing levels of debt have, overall, a favourable impact on a company's/organisation's weighted average cost of capital.*

So, which is correct? Whilst there can be little doubt that the latter view – the net operating income view (and its related propositions)[85] – has many theoretical merits, and some academic support, there is nonetheless substantial evidence (albeit much of which is anecdotal) in support of the traditionalist view.

### Gearing (leverage) management – costs/risks

Clearly, a failure to adequately monitor and control levels of gearing could have severe consequences, inasmuch as:

■ a high level of securitisation could impede a company's/organisation's ability to generate revenue, and
■ an excessive number of debt covenants could restrict a company's/organisation's use of assets – in particular fixed assets,

both of which could not only have a significant impact on the overall value of a company/organisation but, more importantly, severely affect the company's/organisation's future prospects.

## Creditor management

Creditor management is concerned with ensuring that all creditor-based purchases are correctly invoiced and all payments relating to such creditor-based purchases are efficiently disbursed.
In a practical context, this means:

■ determining an appropriate company/organisation-wide credit policy, and
■ establishing effective company/organisation-wide internal controls,

to ensure the efficient management and administration of all creditor-related purchases.

## Creditor management – internal controls

For our purposes we will classify creditor management internal controls into the following categories:

- invoicing-related internal controls,
- payment-related internal controls, and
- information management internal controls.

### Invoicing-related internal controls

To ensure invoices relating to creditor-based purchases are correctly processed, it is important to establish an invoice payment timetable in accordance with the creditor's payment instructions and ensure all payment processing procedures and related financial regulations are accurately documented and regularly updated. It is important to:

- ensure that all invoices processed for payment relate to authorised purchase orders issued by the company/organisation,
- ensure all products/services to which an invoice relates have been satisfactorily received from/performed by the company/organisation,
- ensure that the products/services to which an invoice relates are correctly identified and correctly priced (including appropriate taxes), and
- ensure all amendments/adjustments to creditor accounts (e.g. refunds for returned products) are clearly documented and appropriately authorised.

It is also important to ensure that all authorities and responsibilities relating to invoice processing activities are appropriately allocated and that an adequate segregation of procedure/separation of duties exists between, for example:

- procedures/personnel involved in receiving invoices and those involved in authorising and/or recording creditor-related payments, and
- procedures/personnel involved in processing creditor invoices and those that have access to and/or responsibility for the movement/allocation of products and/or services.

### Payment-related internal controls

To ensure all payments relating to creditor-based sales are disbursed efficiently, it is important to:

- ensure all outstanding debts (creditor account balances) are regularly monitored,
- ensure all creditor payments are correctly authorised, processed and recorded, and
- ensure all authorities and responsibilities relating to creditor management activities are appropriately allocated and that adequate segregation procedures/separation of duties exists between, for example:
  - procedures/personnel involved in authorising creditor-related payments and those involved in processing creditor-related payments, and
  - procedures/personnel involved in processing creditor-related payments and those involved in recording creditor-related payments, and
- ensure all invoices processed for payment are processed within the prescribed time period.

### Information management internal controls

To ensure that appropriate management information is provided to enable the effective monitoring and control of creditor payment processes and procedures, it is important to:

- establish accurate activity or profit/cost centre-related budgets for all creditor related payments, and

■ ensure that appropriate activity-related reports (including temporal[86] and/or cross sectional[87] comparative analyses) are produced for senior managers on a regular basis.

We discussed these in Chapter 9.

Within each of the above categories, it is of course important for data protection purposes (see the Data Protection Act 1998)[88] to ensure that access to confidential and/or personal creditor-related data is monitored and controlled, and restricted to authorised personnel only.

## Creditor management – costs/risks

In a broad context, creditor management is concerned with:

■ obtaining satisfactory credit from suppliers,
■ extending, where necessary, credit during periods of cash shortage, and
■ maintaining good relations with regular and important suppliers.

The costs/risks associated with taking trade credit from suppliers/service providers would include:

■ the possible price implications of taking credit,
■ the possible loss of product supplier/service provider goodwill,
■ the costs associated with creditor management-related administration, and
■ the potential restrictions of taking credit on other business-related activities.

The costs/risks associated with not taking trade credit from suppliers/service providers would include:

■ the possible loss of interest,
■ the inconvenience associated with not taking credit, and
■ published financial statements – that is the external issue of accounting information.

## General ledger management

As we have seen, the primary objective of a contemporary accounting information system is to generate reliable and relevant information for:

■ controlling and monitoring business-related activities,
■ safeguarding company/organisation assets,
■ accounting for company/organisation liabilities,
■ preparing annual financial statements, and
■ ensuring adherence to/compliance with extant statutory/regulatory requirements.

In a modern contemporary accounting information system (paper-based or computer-based) the general ledger is at the very heart of the accounting information system. Put simply, the general ledger *is* the accounting information system inasmuch as the general ledger is the *master file* of all company accounts, with the other subsidiary ledgers merely providing detailed analysis/ listings of balances within a general ledger account (e.g. debtor's control account and/or creditor's control account).

From an accounting information systems context, the main functions of the general ledger are:

■ to provide a framework for the recording of accounting adjustment entries – a data processing/ recording function,

- to provide a control mechanism for the management of accounting data – a controlling function, and
- to generate appropriate financial reports – an information generation function.

## The general ledger and the accounting process

The first function of the general ledger is a data processing/recording function. As you may remember, wealth – at least in a corporate/organisational context – is generated by transactions involving the movement of resources. All such transactions are, in an accounting information systems context, evidenced by a transaction event document – a document designed not only to provide data on, but more importantly provide an audit trail for, such resource-related transactions. There are essentially two types of transaction event documents both of which were discussed in Chapters 9 and 10, these being:

- the invoicing document – this includes invoices issued to customers/clients and received from suppliers/service providers, and refund vouchers issued to customers/clients (credit note) and received from suppliers/service providers (debit notes), and
- the payment document – these include cheques and BACS-related receipts received from customers/clients and cheques and BACS related-payments issued to suppliers/service providers.

What this means is that *all* resource-related transactions recorded in the general ledger *should* be represented by a transaction event document – that is either an invoicing document or a payment document.

What about transactions not involving a movement of resources? Non-resource-related transactions are sometimes referred to as post-transaction adjustments and are, in an accounting information systems context, evidenced by an adjusting event document – a document designed not only to provide data on, but more importantly an audit trail for, such non-resource-related transactions. Such an adjusting event document is known as a journal voucher, which is essentially a sequentially numbered control document whose purpose is to document/record authorised accounting adjustments or, more appropriately, to document/record amendments/alterations to *existing* accounting data within the general ledger.

Again, what this means is that *all* non-resource-based transactions recorded in the general ledger should be represented by an adjusting event document – a journal voucher – and an example journal voucher is shown in Example 11.1.

There are essentially six categories of accounting adjustments, these being:

- accruals adjustments,
- prepayment adjustments,
- provision adjustments,
- asset/liability revaluation adjustments,
- errors corrections, and
- control account entries.

### Accruals adjustments

An accruals adjustment is a year-end accounting adjustment where a commitment to pay funds (an accrued expense) or a right to receive funds (accrued income) exists, but for which no cash has yet been received or disbursed.

An example of an accrued expense would be employee wages due but as yet unpaid, whilst an example of accrued income would be outstanding interest and/or dividends to be received.

| JOURNAL VOUCHER | | | | | | |
|---|---|---|---|---|---|---|

| | Initial | Date | | Number |
|---|---|---|---|---|
| Prepared by<br>Authorised by<br>Input by | | | | Type<br>Narrative<br><br>Reference<br>Posting |

| Ledger | Account | Debit | Credit | Reference | Narrative |
|---|---|---|---|---|---|
| | | | | | |

Notes:

**Example 11.1** A journal voucher

### Prepayment adjustments

A prepayment adjustment is a year-end accounting adjustment where:

- a payment in advance of the acquisition and custody of a product and/or service has been made (a prepaid expense), or
- income in advance of the delivery of a product/provision of a service has been received (prepaid income).

An example of a prepaid expense would be where a company/organisation has paid for energy supplies for a period which exceeds the accounting year end, whilst an example of accrued income would be the receipt of an annual membership fee in advance of the year to which the fees relate.

### Provision adjustments

A provision adjustment refers to accounting entries that either increase or decrease an existing provision within a company's/organisation's balance sheet. In the UK, such provisions include, for example:

- the provision for depreciation, and
- the provision for doubtful debts,

although other EU countries (despite the harmonising affects of the fourth company law directive) still allow provisions to be created for other purposes.

### Asset/liability revaluation adjustments

Such revaluation adjustments refer to approved increases/decreases in the value of existing assets and/or liabilities and would include for example:

- the revaluation of both tangible and intangible fixed assets – for example increasing asset values to reflect the current market values of such assets,
- the revaluation of current assets – for example the write-off of stock due to obsolescence and/or losses identified by a physical stock count,
- the revaluation of current liabilities – for example to reflect an agreed reduction in an outstanding creditor account following a legal dispute, and
- the revaluation of long-term liabilities – for example the marking to market of a debenture/bond.

### Error corrections

Such entries relate to the correction of errors that have been identified in the general ledger and would include, for example, the correction of:

- errors of principle,
- errors of commission,
- errors of omission,
- errors of original entry,
- transposition errors, and
- compensating errors.

### Control account entries

Such entries would refer to the introduction of an event-related accounting value and would include, for example, the introduction of a closing stock value following a year-end stocktake/stock valuation.

## The general ledger – a control mechanism

The second function of the general ledger is a control function to ensure:

- all accounting transactions are recorded and processed accurately,
- all financial reports represent (as far as possible) a true and fair view of those accounting transactions, and
- all amendments/updates are appropriately authorised.

It is important that an effective framework of traceable/auditable control procedures exist. Such procedures would include, for example:

- the use of periodic trial balances before the preparation of interim financial reports and year-end financial statements,
- the use of appropriate accounting period close-down and start-up procedures,
- the monitoring and reallocation of *all* general ledger suspense account entries,
- the reconciliation of all general ledger control accounts,[89] fund-related accounts[90] and current asset-related accounts.[91]

## The general ledger and the generation of financial information

The final function of the general ledger is an information generation function, that is the provision of data/information for the preparation of financial reports/statements. Such financial reports/statements would include:

- internal management reports,
- interim financial statements, or
- year-end financial statements.

### Internal management reports

Such internal management reports would include, for example:

- turnover/activity reports,
- profitability reports, and
- efficiency analyses.

### Interim financial statements

Such interim financial reports would include, for example:

- a summarised profit and loss account,
- a summarised balance sheet,
- a summarised statement of changes in equity,
- a summarised cash flow statement, and
- explanatory notes.

Explanatory notes would provide details/information on, for example:

- changes to accounting policies,
- the issue or repurchase of shares,
- debt repayments,
- the acquisition or disposal of long-term investments,
- dividend payments,
- corporate/organisational restructuring,
- discontinuing operations,
- error corrections,
- the write-off of stock,
- impairment loss on property, plant, equipment, intangibles or other assets,
- litigation settlements, and
- related party transactions.

### Year-end financial statements

In the UK, all public and private companies are required to produce audited year-end financial statements, although Statutory Instrument 2004 No. 16 (SI 2004/16) provides an audit exemption for small companies which have an annual turnover of not more than £5.6m and gross assets of not more than £2.8m.

Such year-end financial statements would include:

- a profit and loss account, and a balance sheet, as required by the Companies Act 1985 (see Schedule 4),
- a statement of changes in equity,
- a cash flow statement (as required FRS1), and
- explanatory notes.

For an example of such year-end financial statements have a look at the following:

- Marks and Spencer plc 2006 financial statements,[92]
- Tesco plc 2006 financial statements,[93] or
- BP plc 2005 financial statements.[94]

In addition to the above, all UK listed companies are required to produce additional interim financial statements as required by London Stock Exchange listing rules and FSA regulations/requirements, with non-mandatory guidance available in IAS 34 Interim Financial Reporting.

### Financial statements and the EU Transparency Directive

Published on 31 December 2004, the EU Transparency Directive came into force on 20 January 2005 with an implementation deadline of 20 January 2007. The aim of the directive is to enhance transparency within EU capital markets by establishing rules for the disclosure of periodic financial reports for companies whose securities (either equity-based or debt-based) are traded on a regulated market within the EU, and in doing so:

- reduce the cost of capital, and
- improve corporate liquidity.

The key objectives of the directive are:

- to improve annual financial reporting of all listed companies,
- to increase the disclosure of periodic financial information of issuers of equity-based securities, using summary quarterly financial reports and more detailed half-yearly financial reporting,
- to introduce half-yearly financial reporting for issuers of only debt-based securities,
- to improve the disclosure of major changes in the shareholdings of listed companies, and
- to impose stricter disclosure deadlines.

## General ledger management – risks

Clearly, any failure in the processes and controls associated with the general ledger could have a significant impact on a company's/organisation's ability to accurately record business-related financial transactions, and could severely impair a company's/organisation's ability to produce financial statements that present a true and fair view of the company's/organisation's business activities for the accounting period/financial year. So, what are the main risks?

The main risks would include:

- errors in updating general ledger accounts – for example, errors of omission, errors of principle, errors of calculation/value and/or errors of transposition,
- unauthorised amendment to, and/or loss of, financial data, and
- errors in the generation of financial reports – for example, the incorrect use of year-end close-down procedures and/or the incorrect transfer of opening balances.

## Concluding comments

Whilst not directly involved in any value creating/revenue generating activities, the management cycle plays a important coordinating role in the organisation, supervision and control of *all* company/organisational resources: a role without which all other business-related activities would be meaningless.

## Key points and concepts

| | |
|---|---|
| Baumol cash management model | Non-cash-based transactional finance |
| Cash-based transactional finance | Non-issued equity finance |
| Convertible securities | Non-transactional finance |
| Debt | Open tender |
| Derivatives | Operational fund management |
| Economic order quantity model | Petty cash |
| Fixed assets register | Restricted tender |
| Gearing (leverage) | RFID |
| Issued equity finance | Stock register |
| Just-in-time model | Strategic fund management |
| Leverage (gearing) | Tactical fund management |
| Material requirements planning model | Transactional finance |
| Miller–Orr cash management model | Transferable warrant |
| Negotiated tender | Weighted Average Cost of Capital (WACC) |

## References

Baumol, W.J. (1952) 'The Transactions Demand for Cash: An Inventory Theoretic Approach', *Quarterly Journal of Economics*, 66(4), pp. 545–556.

Black, F. and Scholes, M. (1973) 'The pricing of options and corporate liabilities', *Journal of Political Economy*, 81(3), pp. 637–659.

Garman, M.B. and Kohlhagen, S.W. (1983) 'Foreign currency option values', *Journal of International Money and Finance*, 2, pp. 231–237.

Harris, F.W. (1915) *Operations Cost* (Factory Management Series), Shaw Chicago.

Miller, M. and Orr, D. (1966) 'A model of the demand for money by firms', *Quarterly Journal of Economics*, 80(3), pp. 413–435.

Wilson, R.H. (1934) 'A Scientific Routine for Stock Control', *Harvard Business Review*, 13, pp. 116–128.

## Bibliography

Aseervatham, A. and Anandarajah, D. (2003) *Accounting Information and Reporting Systems*, McGraw Hill, Sydney.

Bagranoff, N.A., Simkin, M.G. and Strand, N.C. (2004) *Core Concepts of Accounting Information System*, Wiley, New York.

Romney, M. and Steinbart, P. (2006) *Accounting Information Systems*, Pearson Education Inc., New Jersey.

Vaassen., E. (2002) *Accounting Information System – A Managerial Approach*, Wiley, Chichester.

Wilkinson, J.W., Cerullo, M.L., Raval, V. and Wong-On-Wing, B. (2001) *Accounting Information Systems*, Wiley, New York.

## Self-review questions

1. Distinguish between retained earnings and retained profits.
2. Briefly describe and explain the main types of internal controls you would expect to find in the management of derivative instruments.
3. Describe the functions of a share registrar.
4. What information would you expect to find in a fixed assets register?
5. Distinguish between an open tender, restricted tender and a negotiated tender.
6. Identify and describe the main differences between the Baumol cash management model and the Miller–Orr cash management model.
7. Describe the main functions of the general ledger.
8. Briefly describe and explain the following categories of internal controls normally found in a stock management system:

   - movement-related internal controls,
   - security-related internal controls,
   - quality-related internal controls, and
   - information management-related internal controls.

9. Briefly describe the alternative types of RFID tags available and explain how the use of such tags could improve the management of fixed assets and current assets.
10. Why is it important for a company/organisation to undertake a regular physical stocktake of all stock held?

## Questions and problems

### Question 1

The management of fixed assets can be divided into three stages:

- the acquisition stage,
- the retention stage, and
- the disposal stage.

#### *Required*

Briefly describe the main purpose of each stage and the internal controls you would expect to find in a medium-sized retail company.

### Question 2

You are an internal auditor working for Eketel plc., a UK-based retail company. The company has an in-house training policy that requires all graduate entrants to the company's finance department to work within the internal audit department for the first six months of their training contract. The chief internal auditor of Eketel plc has asked you to write an induction pack for the graduate entrants, explaining the importance and relevance of internal controls in the management of current assets.

#### *Required*

Prepare a report for the chief internal auditor, explaining the importance and relevance of internal controls in the management of current assets, and evaluate the types of internal controls you would expect to find in the management of stock *and* of debtors.

## Question 3

Kiley plc is a UK-based retailer. The company regularly invests surplus funds in seven-day notice short-term deposits on the UK money market. Currently, such short-term deposits pay an interest of 5% per annum. Also currently, Kiley plc has cash payments for each month totalling £1,250,000, per month (or £15m pa).

Assume transactions costs are £15.40 per transaction.

### *Required*

Using the Baumol cash management model calculate how much Kiley plc should transfer to its bank account and briefly explain the main assumptions that are made when using the Baumol cash management model.

## Question 4

One of the most important operational resources a company possesses is undoubtedly cash. Often regarded as the lifeblood of corporate activity, cash systems (especially cash receiving systems) are surrounded by elaborate internal control procedures, often based on the separation of operational duties between a range of company employees and the control of cash receiving documentation.

### *Required*

(a) Describe the documentation you would expect to find in an operationally controlled cash receiving system of a medium-sized retailer and briefly explain the purpose of the documentation you have described.
(b) With the aid of a columnar documentary flowchart illustrate how the separation of duties between company employees can be used to reduce the potential of cash fraud occurring. (In your flowchart you must use all the documentation you have described above.)

## Question 5

'In computer-based accounting information systems, the general ledger is no longer required and is, to all intent and purposes, redundant.' Discuss.

## Assignments

## Question 1

You have been appointed to audit GTH Ltd, a local restaurant that has recently opened. The owner and head chef of the restaurant is Helen Betts. Helen is a wonderful cook but possesses little knowledge of business and business practices. As a result she has a tendency to trust her employees . . . perhaps a little too much.

At the restaurant the waiters are given a note pad each day on which to take orders. The sheets are turned over to the kitchen to prepare the orders as instructed. The waiters then deliver the prepared meal to the customer. When the customers are ready to leave, the waiters merely sum up the total bill and take the cash. Since there is no cashier, the waiters tender change to the customers from sums they have received. The restaurant does not accept payment by cheque and/or credit cards.

At the end of the day the waiters tender their net cash receipts to Helen who then banks the cash.

Recently Helen remarked that even though she was always busy in the kitchen, daily sales have not been as high as expected. Indeed, because of the cash flow problems being experienced by the business, Helen is now considering closing it down.

*Required*

Explain to Helen what internal controls need to be implemented over cash sales and offer a possible explanation as to why the business is experiencing cash flow problems.

## Question 2

QLP plc is a UK-based delivery company. The company has 26 depots located throughout the UK with a head office in Birmingham.

At a recent board meeting the company discussed a proposal to replace part of its fleet of delivery vans. The replacement will entail the acquisition 14 vehicles and the disposal of 16 others of varying age and condition. Although such vehicle replacements have occurred in the past – the most recent being 18 months ago – problems have always arisen, in particular regarding the disposal of old vehicles.

*Required*

As the recently appointed chief internal auditor of QLP plc, the managing director of the company has asked you to prepare a report for the management board of the company describing the main stages and evaluating the key internal controls you would expect to find in the acquisition and disposal process.

## Chapter endnotes

[1] Subject of course to any restrictions imposed by the company's articles of association.

[2] There are a further five classes of preference shares, these being:

- Participating preference shares – entitles the shareholder to a fixed dividend and the right to participate in any surplus profits after payments of agreed levels of dividends to ordinary shareholders have been made.
- Zero dividend rate preference shares – the shareholders receive no dividends throughout the life of the shares.
- Variable dividend rate preference shares – the dividend is either agreed at a fixed percentage plus, for example, LIBOR (London Interbank Offered Rate), rather than receiving a fixed level of dividend, or is a variable dividend set at regular intervals to a market rate by means of an auction process between investors known as AMPS (Auction Market Preferred Stock). Auction market securities are money market financial instruments, created in 1984, which reset dividends at a rate that is fixed until the next auction date, when the securities adjust with a new yield to reflect market conditions.
- Redeemable preference shares – shares issued on terms which require them to be bought back by the issuer at some future date, in compliance with the conditions of the Companies Act 1985, either at the discretion of the issuer or of the shareholder.
- Convertible preference shares – shares which have terms and conditions agreed at the outset, which provide the shareholder with the option to convert their preference shares into ordinary shares at a future date.

[3] That is only if the public limited company is trading.

[4] You may recognise this as a Statement of Sources and Applications of Funds (as was required by SSAP 10 – now withdrawn).

[5] It is for example possible to have a zero coupon bond – that is a bond on which no interest is payable.

[6] Either a fixed charge on specific assets or a floating charge on a group of assets.

[7] Sequestration can be defined as the act of removing, separating or seizing property and/or assets from the possession of its legal owner for the benefit of a lender (creditor) or the state.

[8] For example, a lender (creditor) may impose:

- a minimum current ratio or quick ratio for the company/organisation,
- conditions relating to the disposal of fixed assets,
- restrictions on the issue of debt and/or equity,
- conditions regarding the maintenance of a specific level of financial gearing, and/or
- restrictions on amounts of dividends payable by the company/organisation.

[9] Note – somewhat confusingly, in the USA (and in many other countries) a debenture is defined as an unsecured debt with a fixed coupon (interest rate).

[10] The debenture trust deed would contain details relating to:

- period of the loan,
- security for the loan,
- power to appoint a receiver,
- interest rate and payment terms,
- financial reporting requirements,
- redemption options/procedures for the repayment of the debentures, and
- any restrictive covenants imposed by the debenture trust deed.

[11] A bond with an interest rate fixed to maturity.

[12] A bond which pays no interest (coupon) but is priced, at issue, at a discount from its redemption value. These are attractive to investors seeking capital gains rather than income from interest.

[13] A bond whose interest rate is linked to a specified market rate.

[14] A bond whose redemption is funded by a specific fund – a sinking fund – which is merely a pool of funds set aside by a company/organisation to help repay a bond issue.

[15] A bond whose interest rate is linked to another commodity index or interest rate, and whose interest rate is renegotiated at an agreed interval. For example, a rollover bond could be three-year bond with a coupon rate of $\frac{1}{2}\%$ above the three-month LIBOR. That is the interest rate would be renegotiated every three months and set at a rate of $\frac{1}{2}\%$ above.

[16] The conversion value of the convertible bond may be calculated as:

$$V_n = S \times (1 + g)^n \times N$$

where:

$g$ = the expected annual percentage growth rate of the share price,
$N$ = the number of ordinary shares that will be received on conversion,
$S$ = the estimated ordinary share price at the conversion date.

The current market value of the convertible bond ($V_o$) may of course be found by calculating the present value of future annual interest ($I$) plus the present value of the securities conversion value after $n$ years ($V_n$), using the market rate of return on bonds expected by investors ($R_d$), that is

$$V_o = I/(1 + R_d) + I/(1 + R_d)^2 + I/(1 + R_d)^3 \ldots \ldots + (I + V_n)/(1 + R_d)^n$$

[17] For example:

- an optional convertible security – in which the holder of the convertible security has the option to convert the debt into shares at a number of agreed futures dates, and/or

- an exchangeable convertible security – in which the shares underlying the debt are in a company other than the company issuing the convertible security.

[18] Such exchanges would include:

- the London International Financial Futures Exchange (LIFFE),
- the Chicago Board of Trade (CBOT),
- the Chicago Mercantile (CME),
- the Tokyo Stock Exchange, and
- the Paris Marche a Terme d'Instrument Financiers (MATIF).

[19] A call option is the right (not the obligation) to *buy* a specified number of securities at a specified price (the strike price) at or over a specified time.

[20] A put option is the right (not the obligation) to *sell* a specified number of securities at a specified price (the strike price) at or over a specified time.

[21] Option pricing is a complex issue, with the price of an option determined by many inter-related factors, such as:

- the current price of the security,
- the strike price (exercise price) of the security,
- the unexpired period to exercise date,
- the volatility of the underlying security,
- the risk free rate of return, and
- the exposure of the option writer.

The classic option pricing model is of course the Black-Scholes model (1973), with an adapted version for pricing currency options by Garman and Kohlhagan (1983) also widely used.

[22] Such options are sometimes referred to as swaptions.

[23] The intrinsic value of a warrant ($V_w$) can be calculated as the current price of the ordinary shares ($S$), less the exercise price ($E$), times the number shares ($N$) provided by each warrant, that is:

$$V_w = (S - E) \times N$$

[24] Such periods can range from a few months up to 15 years.

[25] A company seeking a full listing on the London Stock Exchange must comply with a number of important criteria contained within the so-called 'Purple Book' which sets out all the rules for securities on the Official List, covering both listing approval and continuing obligations. For example, a company seeking a listing must:

- issue a prospectus that includes financial performance forecasts and other information required by prospective investors,
- ensure that following the listing a minimum of 25% of the shares must be owned by the public,
- have made sales for at least three years up to the listing date from an independent business activity,
- have not had any significant changes in directors and senior managers of the business over the previous three years,
- have a minimum market capitalisation of £700,000, and
- have audited accounts for the previous three years.

[26] For cost and control purposes, many companies now outsource all share registrar activities to external agents/companies, such companies including for example:

- Capita @ www.capitaregistrars.com,
- LloydsTSB @ www.lloydstsb-registrars.co.uk, and
- Computershare Investor Services PLC @ www.computershare.com.

[27] Such a risk policy would include:

- the identification and measurement of possible risk exposures,
- the development of an appropriate foreign exchange rate and/or interest rate exposure strategy, and
- the selection of appropriate exposure techniques, hedging techniques and derivatives.

[28] The main risks associated with the use of hard cash as a medium of exchange are its volatility, its desirability, its usability and its general lack of traceability.

[29] Although to an increasingly limited extent.

[30] Although some will, in exceptional circumstances, accept payment using transferable payment documents and/or a tradable financial instrument.

[31] The term segregation of procedures refers to the concept of having more than one activity and/or procedure required to complete the task or process.

[32] The term separation of duties refers to the concept of having more than one person required to complete a procedure or task. Its objective is to ensure that duties (roles) are assigned to individuals in a manner so that no one person can control a process. It is sometimes referred to as segregation of duties.

[33] Cash holdings incur an opportunity cost in the form of opportunity foregone.

[34] Each transaction incurs a fixed and variable cost.

[35] The Miller–Orr model assumes that net cash flows are normally distributed.

[36] That is the receipt of previously invested surplus funds.

[37] Such activities should of course be supervised by personnel not directly involved in any other fund management activities.

[38] Also known as 'lapping' this is a type of fraud often used where an individual wants to cover up a theft. Sometimes known as 'robbing Peter to pay Paul' fraud.

[39] An audit trail can be defined as a sequence of records and/or documents (both physical or virtual) which contains evidence directly relating to and/or resulting from the execution of a commercial transaction, a business process or systems function.

[40] That is sequentially numbered documentation whose issue is subject to periodic supervisory reconciliation and whose use is subject to periodic internal audit reviews.

[41] That is a reconciliation using deposit slips and disbursement vouchers.

[42] The amount of a petty cash float should be decided by an appropriate senior officer in accordance with the company's/organisation's procedures. The levels of such petty cash floats should of course be reviewed on a regular basis with any review considering:

- the average amount of petty cash used each week/month over, say, the past year
- the maximum amount required over, say, the past year,
- the minimum amount required over, say, the past year, and
- the difficulties associated with the replenishment of cash.

[43] Within larger companies/organisations, such reconciliations are sometimes undertaken as part of the internal audit of petty cash facilities.

[44] Can also be referred to a property services director/manager or estates management director/manager.

[45] The term ICT (Information and Communications Technology) is used in preference to the term IT (Information Technology) because of the increased blurring between IT assets/facilities and ICT assets/facilities.

[46] Capital rationing exists where a company/organisation has a limit on the amount of funds available for investment in fixed assets.

47 Such documents would include:

- instructions to the tendering company/organisation detailing administrative procedures relating to the tender – for example a tendering timetable, details on alternative methods of tender return and an explanation of the tender evaluation criteria, and
- invitation to tender, including a detailed specification of the company's/organisation's supply requirement and pricing schedule.

48 For example the date of acquisition or the supplier.

49 Including any approved revaluations/devaluations.

50 For example assets acquired under a finance lease (see SSAP 21 Accounting for leases and hire purchase contracts).

51 For example with the use of an RFID tag. Such an identifier tag can not only be used to verify the existence and location of a fixed asset, it also assists in the programming/scheduling of fixed assets maintenance, and provides a communication framework.

52 Chlorofluorocarbons.

53 Hydrochlorofluorocarbons.

54 With all such fixed asset disposals normally matched to or identified with a recent or forthcoming acquisition.

55 For most companies/organisations depreciation is charged from the month of purchase to either the month of disposal or the end of the estimated life of the fixed asset, whichever is the earlier. An example of which would be:

| Asset | Number of months | Basis |
|---|---|---|
| Land | 0 | 0 |
| Building | 480 | Straight line |
| Fixtures and fittings | 120 | Straight line |
| ICT hardware | 36 | Reducing balance |
| ICT software | 24 | Reducing balance |
| Non-ICT equipment | 180 | Straight line |
| Motor vehicles | 60 | Straight line |

56 Appropriate only where the operating environment is fast-moving but predictable – in which:

- stock development is predictable but rapid,
- the stock are inexpensive to buy (low ordering costs),
- storage costs are high,
- stocks are perishable, and/or
- stock replenishment is simple, quick and easy.

57 Appropriate only where the operating environment is slow-moving and predictable – in which:

- stock development is restricted/limited,
- the stock is expensive to buy (high ordering costs),
- storage costs are low,
- stocks are not perishable, and/or
- stock replenishment is complex, time-consuming and difficult.

58 Appropriate only where the operating environment is unpredictable/uncertain – in which:

- stock development is uncertain,
- the stock is inexpensive to buy (low ordering costs),

- storage costs are low
- stocks are perishable, and/or
- stock replenishment is simple, quick and easy.

[59] We will also assume – for reasons of simplicity – that the products in stock are not time sensitive. That is the products do not degrade and will not (at least in the immediate future) become obsolete.

[60] Can also be referred to as stores controller or stock services manager.

[61] In a supply chain management context, the term lead time can be defined as the time between recognising the need for an order and the receipt of product from the supplier. Such a lead time can include, for example:

- order preparation time,
- queuing time,
- transportation time, and
- receiving and inspection time.

[62] For example, in some companies/organisations:

- for high cost/high turnover products all applicable stock ordering and stock holding costs may be included, whereas
- for low cost/low turnover products only a stock ordering and/or stock holding costs may be included.

[63] A stock-out can be defined as a situation where insufficient stock exists to satisfy the demand for a product/item of stock.

[64] The introduction of just-in-time as a recognised work-related technique/philosophy is generally associated with the Toyota motor company, with Taiichi Ohno of the Toyota motor company most commonly credited as being the father/originator of the just-in-time philosophy.

[65] Although in a conventional sense it is not an accounting ledger but merely a listing of items of stock.

[66] Including any approved revaluations/devaluations.

[67] For example with the use of an RFID tag. Such an identifier tag can not only be used to verify the existence and location of a fixed asset, it also assists in the programming/scheduling of a fixed asset's maintenance and provides a communication framework.

[68] Obviously where scanners have a limited memory capability such downloading may need to occur a number of times during a stocktake.

[69] As required by the prudence concept (see FRS 18 Accounting policies).

[70] For retail companies/organisations, the cost of a product available for sale would be the purchase price plus the cost of delivery to the retail store.

For manufacturing/production companies/organisations, the cost of any manufactured product available for sale would be the direct costs of labour, materials and expenses, including any production overheads absorbed into the product.

[71] As required by the accruals concept (see FRS 18 Accounting policies).

[72] Such fraudulent manipulation is often incorrectly referred to as creative accounting. Remember all accounting is creative: it's not a science but an art!

[73] As required by the concept of prudence (see FRS 18 Accounting policies).

[74] And his invention of a covert listening device for use by the Russian government during the late 1940s/early 1950s.

[75] An RFID tag is a small object that can be attached to or indeed be incorporated into an object (e.g. a product), or a subject (e.g. a person or an animal). Such tags generally contain digital

chips and antennas to enable them to receive and respond to radio frequency queries from an RFID transceiver.

[76] Any updating or amendment should of course be approved by appropriate senior managers, for example the board of directors and/or the senior management team.

[77] Increasingly companies/organisations publish such information on their websites as part of their product/service portfolios.

[78] It is of course important – especially where high inflation/high interest rates exist – that the credit rating of all customers is reviewed on a regular basis.

[79] That is between different time periods – for example the current year compared with the previous year.

[80] That is between different companies/organisations.

[81] Remember the requirements of the Data Protection Act 1998 do not apply to debtors which are incorporated organisations such as, for example, limited companies.

[82] Alternatively gearing can be calculated as [(Market value of debt/Market value of debt + Market value of equity) $\times$ 100].

[83] And the costs associated with managing such financial distress – that is the costs associated with activities/operations designed to limit the possibility of company/organisation failure, for example restructuring costs and/or re-financing costs.

[84] That is weighted average cost using market values.

[85] These propositions being:

- proposition 1 – debt irrelevancy proposition,
- proposition 2 – expected return proposition, and
- proposition 3 – optimal investment proposition.

[86] That is between different time periods, for example the current year compared with the previous year.

[87] That is between different companies/organisations.

[88] Remember the requirements of the Data Protection Act 1998 do not apply to creditors that are incorporated organisations such as, for example, limited companies.

[89] For example the debtor's control account and the creditor's control account.

[90] For example the bank account.

[91] For example the stock account.

[92] Available @ http://www2.marksandspencer.com/thecompany/investorrelations/downloads/2006/complete_annual_review.pdf.

[93] Available @ http://www.tescocorporate.com/images/tesco_review_SFS_2006.pdf.

[94] Available @ http://www.bp.com/liveassets/bp_internet/globalbp/globalbp_uk_english/secret_area/secret_investors/STAGING/local_assets/downloads_pdfs/bp_ara_2005_annual_report_and_accounts.pdf.

# 12 From e-commerce to m-commerce and beyond: ICT and the virtual world

## Introduction[1]

As we saw in Chapter 4, the term e-commerce has, in a contemporary context at least, become synonymous with web-based commercial activities,[2] in particular web-based activities associated with the sale and/or purchase of goods and/or services, using what increasingly appears to be an ever-expanding range of information and communication related technologies.

Although the early 1990s saw the dawn of a corporate realisation of the potential of the internet and the world wide web (the web), it was not until perhaps the late 1990s that a number of companies/organisations began to develop simple, effective, albeit rudimentary e-commerce related websites. Indeed, whilst a large number of pure e-commerce companies disappeared during the dotcom collapse in 2000 and 2001, it was the late 1990s/early 21st century that saw many traditional retailers – many of the so-called bricks and mortar retailers – beginning to recognise the commercial potential and added value benefits of e-commerce.

Yet surprisingly, whilst there can be little doubt that the emergence and continuing development of e-commerce-related technologies from the mid-20th century to date, and the widespread integration of e-commerce facilities into 21st century corporate consciousness, has revolutionised (and indeed continues to revolutionise) the nature of corporate business activities, especially those related to income generation, profit creation and, of course, wealth management, and have provided the platform for the worldwide expansion of e-commerce,[3] the origins of e-commerce lie in the history of other much older e-commerce related technologies. A history pre-APRAnet technologies and pre-internet technologies – in the information and communication technologies associated with Electronic Data Interchange (EDI) and Electronic Funds Transfer (EFT) used for the transfer of commercial documents and the secure transfer of funds, which predate the advent of the internet (as we know it today) by perhaps 15 to 20 years.

Today of course the ongoing development of related e-commerce technologies, and the continuing relocation by companies and organisations of much of their commercial operations and business-related activities to online facilities, continues to redefine the very nature of market competition by creating an 'omnipotent e-marketspace' in which companies and organisations compete for market share in an evermore volatile and unpredictable self-service economy. Indeed, with many UK, European and US-based companies and organisations now employing an extensive range of information and communication technologies to provide a wide assortment of so-called information society services[4] (including integrated e-commerce facilities), and facilitate what often appears to be an increasingly unconstrained flow of goods, services and information, corporate businesses are now overwhelmingly reliant upon *created* web-based environments that are no longer constrained by the physicalities of geography and the economic politics of international trade.

## Learning outcomes

This chapter continues the discussion on information and communication technologies introduced in Chapter 4 and explores the practical aspects of e-commerce, in particular:

- the uses of e-commerce innovations and technologies in product/service advertising, prospect generation activities, sales (Business-to-Business (B2B), Business-to-Consumer (B2C) and Customer-to-Customer (C2C)), customer support facilities, and education and research facilities,

- the problems and opportunities presented by the integration of e-commerce facilities into corporate accounting information systems, and

- considers the regulatory issues relating to the use of e-commerce, in general, and e-money, in particular, and the potential problems associated with web-based finance/commerce.

By the end of this chapter, the reader should be able to:

- consider and explain the impact of information and communication technology enabled innovations on e-commerce,

- describe the major aspects of B2B, B2C and C2C-based e-commerce,

- demonstrate a critical understanding of the advantages and disadvantages of e-commerce-related technologies, and

- consider critically the jurisdiction and implication of legislative and regulatory pronouncements on e-commerce and related activities/services.

## E-commerce and the changing world of business – towards a self-service economy!

We are constantly reminded that the world of business and commerce has changed, is changing or indeed will change! Whatever timeline you may choose to believe, there can be little doubt that the world of business and commerce of the late 20th century is but a dim and distant memory. This is owing to:

- the rapid development of evermore powerful information and communication technologies,
- the growing interconnectivity afforded by such technologies, and

■ the increasing importance of the internet and web in almost all business-related commercial activities.

This has all – some would say with increasing ease – promoted the development of an increasingly customer-centric, self-service, e-commerce economy. A self-service, e-commerce economy in which the conservative traditionalisms of contemporary capitalism and the historical conventionalities of wealth accumulation that dominated the world of business and commerce for more than 150 years continue to be swept away and are replaced by a postmodern, demand orientated, customer-led, *virtual* world of business and commerce.

Consider the following.[5] During 2004:

■ the total value of non-financial business web-based sales in the UK increased by 81% compared to 2003, totalling £71.1bn,
■ the total proportion of companies/organisations selling online increased by 24% to 6.7%, compared with 2003, and
■ nearly 34% of companies/organisations possessed and used a website (up by 10% on 2003) and for companies/organisations with over 1000 employees this percentage was 98%.

Although in total terms web-based sales by non-financial businesses for 2004 represented only 3.4% of the total sales of non-financial businesses, for 2003 this was a little under 2%, and in 2002 this was a little over 1%. This essentially means that from 2002 to 2004, total web-based sales by non-financial businesses has increased by a little over 200%. See Article 12.1.

## Article 12.1

### E-commerce growing as predicted

The Internet is finally showing some its enormous potential as predicted at the turn of the century. Value of sales over the Internet has risen 81 per cent year-on-year to touch a high of £71.1bn in 2004 (£39.3bn in 2003) according to the Office of the National Statistics.

The ONS did a survey covering 12,000 businesses excluding the financial sector. The largest of these, with 1000-plus employees, accounted for the biggest piece of the pie – £21.8bn – 43 per cent of total sales on the Web (although this is less compared to previous year's 51 per cent of total sales on the Internet).

Within this group, only 32 per cent did business over the Web while 70.3 per cent made purchases. The previous year – 2003 had shown only 6.7 per cent of this group doing business online and 35.3 made purchases. Online spending by this group also increased 84 per cent y-o-y suggesting growing acceptance of the Internet as the medium of tomorrow.

A rung lower than this group, yet no small achievers, were the medium-sized businesses with more than 250 but fewer than 1000 employees. They have taken the maximum advantage of the tremendous growth in ecommerce, raking in £15.3bn of total sales – an increase of 132 per cent y-o-y.

Following in their footsteps, were the small businesses (with fewer than 10 employees) that grew 127 per cent with their share of £3.4bn.

The total of sales value £71.1bn includes B2B transaction. Sales to households had grown 67.6 per cent y-o-y, rising from £10.8bn in 2003 to £18.1bn in 2004.

Despite the impressive numbers, business on the Internet still does not compare well with business done on the other media. In the same year, sales over other communications technologies were triple in value to that of sales over the Internet.

This was the fifth annual survey of the medium by the ONS.

Source: James Rowe,
6 November 2005, ABC money,
**www.abcmoney.co.uk/news/0620051277.htm.**

In addition, of the £71.1bn web-based non-finance business sales during 2004:

- 71% related to physical products – that is products ordered online for delivery offline, for example electrical products, stationery, computer hardware, CD-ROMS, DVDs and books,
- 26% related to services – that is products ordered online for delivery offline, for example hotel accommodation, air and/or rail travel tickets, and
- 2% related to digitised products – that is products ordered online for delivery online (in a digitised format), for example product information, computer software and audio and video recordings,

with:

- approximately 75% of the sales relating to B2B sales, and
- approximately 25% of sales relating to B2C sales.

It is perhaps worth noting that sales by non-financial businesses over non-web-based information and communication technologies (for example using EDI, automated telephone systems or e-mail), only fell by a little over 1% in 2004 to £198.1bn (from £200.6bn in 2003). However, as a percentage of total sales, sales over non-web-based information and communication technologies fell to 74% in 2004, a reduction of nearly 12% on 2003. Between 2002 and 2003 the percentage reduction was nearly 6%, perhaps a clear indication that customers and users are migrating in increasing numbers to web-based technologies from the more conventional non-web-based information and communication technologies.

Whilst there are clearly some critics who consider the ever-increasing migration to web-based information and communication technologies, and as a consequence the development of a more self-service e-commerce economy, a less than welcome change – perhaps with good reason (see Article 12.2) – such a repositioning of retailing activities is, given the current levels of migration, unlikely to slow down. Indeed, it is as some suggest (see Article 12.3) likely to increase. Why? Put simply – profit!

## Article 12.2

### Do it yourself: Self-service technologies, such as websites and kiosks, bring both risks and rewards

So you want to withdraw cash from your bank account? Do it yourself. Want to install a broadband internet connection? Do it yourself. Need a boarding card issued for your flight? Do it yourself. Thanks to the proliferation of websites, kiosks and automated phone systems, you can also track packages, manage your finances, switch phone tariffs, organise your own holiday (juggling offers from different websites), and select your own theatre seats while buying tickets. These are all tasks that used to involve human interaction. But now they have been subsumed into the self-service economy.

Many people complain about companies outsourcing work to low-wage economies: but how many notice that firms are increasingly outsourcing work to

their own customers? In theory, companies can save money by replacing human workers with automated self-service systems, while customers gain more choice and control and get quicker service. There is even talk of self-service doing for the service sector what mass production did for manufacturing, by enabling the delivery of services cheaply and on a massive scale. Surely the expansion of self-service into more and more areas is to be welcomed?

### Touch-tone torment

Not necessarily. When it is done well, self-service can benefit both companies and customers alike. But when done badly – who has not found themselves trapped in a series of endless touch-tone menus? – it can infuriate and alienate customers. In their desire to cut costs, many companies deliberately make it difficult to get through to a human operator; yet their phone or web-based self-service systems do not always allow for every eventuality.

In areas where self-service is only just starting to take hold, this is less of a problem: fuming customers can, after all, always take their business elsewhere. But if every bank were to adopt impenetrable self-service systems, disgruntled customers would no longer be able to express their discontent by voting with their feet. Such a scenario ought to provide an opportunity for some firms to differentiate themselves: some banks, for example, already promise that their telephone-banking services always offer the option of talking to a human operator. But in return for guaranteed access to humans, many firms will simply charge more.

As a result, people who prefer not to use self-service systems (such as the elderly) will be forced to pay higher prices. This is already happening: many travel firms offer discounts to customers who book online. Buy your tickets the old-fashioned way and you must pay more. Firms are, in effect, introducing penalty charges to persuade customers to use self-service systems. Some customers might resent this.

Another objection to self-service is that while it saves companies money, it does not always save their customers time. In the best cases, it does, of course: checking yourself in at the airport or tracking your own packages on a shipping firm's website can be quicker than queueing or making a phone call. But as more and more tasks are unloaded on to customers, they may start to yearn for the (largely mythical) days of old-fashioned service. Again, this ought to provide an opportunity for specialists (such as travel agents) who can offer a convenient, one-stop-shop service.

All of this suggests that there are limits to how far self-service can be taken. Companies that go too far down the self-service route or do it ineptly are likely to find themselves being punished. Instead, a balance between self-service and conventional forms of service is required. Companies ought to offer customers a choice, and should encourage the use of self-service, for those customers that want it, through service quality, not coercion. Self-service works best when customers decide to use a well designed systems of their own volition; it infuriates most when they are forced to use a bad system. Above all, self-service is no substitute for good service.

Source: 16 September 2004, The *Economist*,
**www.economist.com/opinion/**
**displayStory.cfm?story_id=3196309**.

## Article 12.3

### E-commerce in new growth spurt

New research from e-commerce software developer Actinic points to a sharp rise in internet adoption and ecommerce deployment among small British retailers.

According to Actinic's fifth annual e-commerce report, the proportion of small to medium businesses in the UK retail sector that own websites has risen sharply from 7% in 2004, and may be as high as 25%. In addition, the percentage offering an online ordering and payment facility has also increased. The figure stood at 3% in 2004 and is at 8% in 2005. However, it still remains low overall and lags behind the deployment of new business websites. There is a trend to using server-based/ASP ecommerce solutions with a growth over 2004 of 22 percentage points to 29%.

The survey also revealed rises in the number of companies planning to adopt ecommerce in the future (13%), and in the number of online traders planning

further development to their sites (48%). The findings confirm predictions by Gartner, of a second wave of internet adoption driven by the spread of broadband. Profitability among retail sites remains high at 70% (72% in 2004).

Chris Barling, CEO of Actinic, comments, '2005 may prove to be the year when ecommerce finally comes of age. But there is still a long way to go before the percentage of businesses trading online comes anywhere near the percentage of consumers who are shopping online. Many small businesses are still missing out on a huge opportunity – and at a time when traditional retail is under increasing pressure.'

Source: 17 October 2005, *Net4Now*,
**www.net4now.com/isp_news/**
**news_article.asp?News_ID=3286**.

## E-commerce – the success factors

Whilst the success of a company's/organisation's e-commerce facility will of course depend on the demand for its products/services, in many cases it will, more importantly, depend on two groups of interrelated factors, these being:

■ organisation/structure-based factors, and
■ function/process-based factors.

### Organisation/structure-based factors

Organisation/structure-based factors are those factors that have a direct influence on the business infrastructure of the company/organisation. Clearly, it is important for a company/organisation to ensure that there is an adequate level of activity and coordination of activities, and an appropriate level of resource(s) management within the company to ensure that the demands of the customer are met in full.

Such factors would include, for example:

■ the existence and adequacy of the company's/organisation's long-term strategy,
■ the appropriateness of the company's/organisation's business model and value chain,
■ the knowledge/resource capabilities within the company/organisation,
■ the use of technologies within the company/organisation, and
■ the adaptability/flexibility of the company/organisation.

### Function/process-based factors

Function/process based-factors are those factors that influence the functionality of a company's/organisation's website.

Clearly, it is also important for a company/organisation to ensure that the e-commerce provision must provide an enjoyable and rewarding experience for the customer. It is for example important for the customer to own the purchasing experience and be able to direct it. In doing so, it is important that the customer receives not only a responsive, personalised and user friendly service but, more importantly, a secure, reliable and value-for-money experience – an experience which the customer may want to repeat in the future. This can be achieved, for example:

■ by offering incentives to customers (by providing discount schemes and/or loyalty programmes),
■ by creating a sense of community (by developing affinity programmes), and/or
■ by providing access to information (by developing/creating social networks).

So, what makes a good website and what a bad one? That's difficult to say but broadly speaking a good website would be one in which:

■ presentation is clear and consistent,
■ navigation is simple,
■ navigation tools are easy to use,
■ features/page layouts are clearly designed,
■ video and audio is used in a relevant and appropriate manner,
■ information is grouped/arranged consistently and logically, and
■ language options are available where necessary/appropriate,

and a bad website is one in which:

■ colours are used in an inconsistent and unhelpful manner,
■ audio/video imagery/presentation is poor,
■ technology is used in a limited/ineffective manner,
■ navigation is difficult and/or navigation tools do not function adequately,

- page layouts are confusing and inconsistent, and
- presentation limits/restricts audience access.

So what are the key rules to good website design? Put simply – manageability and functionality.

It is also important to ensure that what is promised on the website is delivered. For example, if the website indicates/promises that daily updates will be available then it is important to ensure that such updates are available. It is also vital that the website is useable by customers/users. Sophisticated state of the art graphics may look good at the development stage, but if a large proportion of customers/users cannot access them properly they are – to all intent and purpose – useless.

## E-commerce – the failure factors

There are of course many companies/organisations whose e-commerce facilities have failed to produce the results initially expected. The most common reasons for such a failure being:

- an inadequate appreciation of the need and requirements of customers,
- an over-estimation of company/organisational skills and competence.
- an inadequate understanding of the competitive situation,
- an ineffective coordination of business-related e-commerce activities,
- an inability to manage the impact and consequences of change.
- a lack of organisational commitment, and/or
- a lack of organisational security.

In addition to the above, an e-commerce facility may fail because the product(s) and/or service(s) for sale may not be suitable for the e-commerce environment. For example, products that are generally considered suitable for e-commerce are:

- ones that have a high value-to-weight ratio,
- digital products/services,[6]
- component products (e.g. spare part components), and
- ones that have a high personal/erotic content (e.g. pornography and other sex-related products).[7]

In general the following products are generally considered unsuitable fore e-commerce:

- ones that have a low value-to-weight ratio,
- ones that have a smell, taste or touch component (e.g. perfume),
- ones that need trial fittings (e.g. clothing), and
- ones where colour appears to be important.

## Categories of e-commerce

As we saw earlier, e-commerce is essentially a sub-category of e-business. Its principal activity is (somewhat unsurprisingly) commerce, that is market-related retail and distribution activities or put another way the sale and/or purchase of goods and/or services using digital communications, including all inter-company and intra-company functions that enable such commerce.

Such e-based retail activities can be categorised into a number of alternative application types, these being:

- B2C e-commerce,
- B2B e-commerce,
- business to business to consumer (B2B2C) e-commerce,

- C2B e-commerce,
- C2C e-commerce, and
- customer to business to consumer (C2B2C) e-commerce.

Each of these use a portal interface to provide access to a retailing resource.[8]

In an internet/web context, a portal is essentially a virtual doorway – a gateway that provides the customer/user with information on and access to a range of company/organisation goods, services and facilities. Whilst the format of an access portal will depend primarily on the nature and image of a company/organisation (e.g. market location, market branding, corporate/organisation image/colour scheme), the structure of a portal will depend primarily on the range and diversity of the business activities undertaken by the company/organisation. A portal – as an access platform – can therefore vary from:

- a vertical platform on which specific information on and/or access to a single service/facility or single portfolio of services/facilities is provided, or
- a horizontal platform on which aggregate information on and/or access to a diversified portfolio of services/facilities is provided.

In addition a portal can, and indeed increasingly is, used as a security filter requiring customers/users to input a username and password before access to a retailing resource is permitted. This is especially the case for B2B e-commerce portals.

The retailing resource provides the facilities/resources for the customer/user to either:

- purchase goods and/or services, or
- sell goods and/or services.

This depends of course on the e-commerce application type and varies from:

- a static price platform in which the prices of goods, services and facilities are non-negotiable and determined by the retailer, to
- a dynamic price platform in which the prices of goods, services and facilities are negotiable using either:
  - a bid (or auction-based) facility, or
  - a discount (or activity-based) facility.

A bid (or auction-based) facility is a facility in which a customer/user can play a dual role as either a seller – offering to sell goods and/or services – or a purchaser – bidding to buy goods and/or services, and the prices of goods, services and facilities are dependent upon the levels of interest shown (or bids made) by potential purchasers.

A discount (or activity)-based facility is a facility in which the prices of goods, services and facilities are dependent upon the actions of customer/user – for example price discounting for large volume purchases or free delivery for large value purchases.

### A dotcom company (or a single-channel company)

This is a company/organisation that undertakes business activities primarily online using a URL that ends in *.com* although it also applies to URLs that end in *.co.uk*. Such companies have no high street presence. Examples of such dotcom companies would be:

- Amazon @ www.amazon.co.uk,
- eBay @ www.eBay.com,
- Google @ www.google.co.uk, and
- Yahoo @ www.yahoo.com.

Such companies are also referred to as *single-channel companies* or *pure e-tailers*.

## A dotbam company (or a dual-channel company)

This is a company/organisation that undertakes business activities in both the 'real-world' using a physical retail outlet and online, the 'bam' component of the name being an abbreviation of 'bricks and mortar' as a reference to the real, physical, world environment. Examples of such dotbam companies or *dual channel companies*[9] would be:

- John Lewis partnership[10] @ www.johnlewis.com,
- Dixons plc @ www.dixons.co.uk, and
- Debenhams plc @ www.debenhams.com.

Such companies are also referred to as 'clicks and mortar' companies, 'clicks and bricks' companies or *mixed e-tailers.*

## A dotbam+ company (or a tri-channel company)

This is a company that undertakes business activities using three retail channels, Examples are:

- online retailing facilities,
- physical 'real-world' retail outlets, and
- retail catalogues (e.g. mail order catalogues).

Examples of such tri-channel companies would be:

- Littlewoods Ltd @ www.littlewoods.co.uk, and
- Argos Ltd[11] @ www.argos.co.uk.

## B2C e-commerce

Business-to-Consumer (B2C) e-commerce (often called online trading or e-tailing) is the selling of goods, services and/or information by a company/organisation to a single individual customer. The most common example of such a B2B application is the retail website featuring/advertising/offering for sale a company's/organisation's goods and services which can be purchased by the consumer, commonly using:

- an imaginary 'shopping cart' facility,
- a virtual 'check-out' facility, and
- a payment processing facility.

There are many examples of such e-tailing websites, for example:

- Amazon @ www.amazon.co.uk,
- Play.com @ www.play.com,
- Tesco plc @ www.tesco.com,
- WHSmith plc @ www.whsmith.co.uk, and
- Marks and Spencer plc @ www.marksandspencer.com.

We will discuss B2C e-commerce in more detail later in this chapter.

## B2B e-commerce

Business-to-Business B2B e-commerce is the selling of goods, services and/or information by one company/organisation to another and are now common in a wide range of industries from traditional, so-called, bricks and mortar economy companies (e.g. manufacturing, wholesale distribution and retailing), to the increasingly important information society services-based companies. The majority of B2B e-commerce occurs between dotbam companies.

We will discuss B2B e-commerce in more detail later in this chapter.

### B2B2C e-commerce

Business-to-Business-to-Consumer (B2B2C) e-commerce is the selling of goods, services or information by a company/organisation to a single individual customer, using a company/organisation as an intermediary or a middleman. There are many examples of such e-tailing websites, from:

- online travel/accommodation agencies (e.g. www.travelocity.co.uk, www.travel4less.com, www.travelselect.com, all travel-related facilities provided by Last Minute Network Ltd),
- online banking (e.g. www.smile.co.uk, an online banking facility provided by The Co-operative Bank plc), and
- online insurance (e.g. www.morethan.com, an insurance service provided by Royal and Sun Alliance Insurance plc).

### C2B e-commerce

Consumer-to-Business (C2B) e-commerce is the purchasing of goods and/or services by an individual customer (or a collective of individual customers acting as a buying cartel) from a company/organisation (e.g. www.LetsBuyIt.com).

### C2C e-commerce

Consumer-to-Consumer (C2C) e-commerce is the selling of goods/services and the communication/transfer of information by a single individual/customer to another. Such e-commerce is normally associated with the retail of 'second-hand' or 'nearly new' products/commodities (e.g. www.ebay.co.uk).

### C2B2C e-commerce

Consumer-to-Business-to-Consumer (C2B2C) e-commerce is the selling of goods/services and/or the communication or transfer of information by a single individual customer to another, using a company/organisation as an intermediary. As with the above, such e-commerce is also associated with the retail of 'second-hand' or 'nearly new' products/commodities (e.g. www.autotrader.co.uk).

## Other e-commerce-related activities

There are of course many other e-business-related e-commerce activities, for which a company/organisation could use its website, the most common of these being:

- product/service advertising activities,
- prospect generation activities, and
- customer support activities.

### Product/service advertising activities

Advertising product/services using a website differs from traditional advertising inasmuch as the website is, in effect, hidden from the customer. To access a website the customer needs to find it using:

- a weblink from a search engine,
- a weblink on an existing webpage, or
- a web address.

In the first instance, most customers would find a website by surfing – that is scanning available websites using a search engine (e.g. www.google.co.uk) until the site is located. Because of the obvious limitations of such an approach, some companies/organisations use other company/organisation websites for advertising purposes. For example, it is increasingly common for a company to advertise its products/services on the website of another company within the same group (e.g. see www.virgin.com/uk) or indeed on the website of an unrelated company on a reciprocal *quid pro quo*[12] basis. Indeed, where retail outlets occupy a single or geographical area it has become increasingly common for such companies/organisations to advertise on so-called geographical shop front sites. See for example:

■ Trafford Centre, Manchester @ www.traffordcentreshopping.co.uk,
■ Princes Quay, Hull @ www.princes-quay.co.uk, and
■ McArthur Glen, @ www.mcarthurglen.com.

The advantages of using a website for product/services advertising activities are:

■ it is a low overall cost alternative – compared to other available alternative media (e.g. TV), and
■ such advertising can reach a 'global' audience and it not regionally and/or geographically restricted.

The disadvantage of using a website for product/services advertising activities is that such websites are hidden and therefore need to be 'found'.

## Prospect generation activities

Prospect generation activities relate to websites designed to:

■ provide information to prospective customers – for example by the use of online brochures, promotional material, company/organisation newsletter and catalogues, and/or
■ collect information on prospective customers – for example by the use of online data capture forms to collect names, addresses, phone numbers, email addresses, etc.

The advantages of using a website for prospect generation activities are:

■ it is cost efficient – for example it saves on printing, manufacturing and distribution costs, and
■ it can be very effective – for example an online brochure can reach hundreds/thousands of potential customers that may never have been reached using traditional hard-copy prospect generation activities.

The disadvantage of using a website for prospect generation activities is the possible restrictions that may exist on the collection and storage of personal data (see for example the Data Protection Act 1998).

## Customer support activities

In addition to prospect generation activities, another growth area in e-commerce has been the increasing use of websites for information provision purposes. That is for example using web-based facilities to provide:

■ technical product/service specifications,
■ support facilities – for example online diagnostic tools for troubleshooting purposes,
■ repair/maintenance manuals,
■ customer enquiry pages – for example FAQ (Frequently Asked Questions) pages, and
■ customer discussion forums.

The advantages of using a website for customer support activities are:

- it is a cost-efficient, highly effective method of providing product/service information, and
- may offer a source of competitive advantage for a company/organisation.

The disadvantage of using a website for customer support activities is the potential generic nature of support service activity made available to customers, for example 'one service for all enquiries'.

## Barriers to e-commerce

Whilst it would be very easy to believe the media rhetoric that now appears to surround almost every aspect of e-commerce – all is not well! Indeed whilst e-commerce-related activities have grown substantially over the past few years (as we have seen) in general, consumers continue to be unwilling to accept the online, self-service, e-commerce business model in numbers greater than many companies/organisations (and indeed many regulatory authorities) would have liked. There are perhaps several key reasons that may explain this slow uptake, the main ones being:

- concerns over control,
- concerns over issues of access, and
- concerns over issues of privacy, safety and security.

### Control concerns

As we saw in Chapter 4, ICANN (Internet Corporation for Assigned Names and Numbers) continues to retain firm control over the assignment of unique identifiers on the internet, including domain names, internet protocol addresses and protocol port numbers. It is also true to say that there has been, and indeed continues to be, very little (if any) control over *what is available* on the internet and the web – an issue which continues to be one of great concern for many people. Recent years have seen a growing number of attempts (some quite successful) to control/managed access to and use of the internet, mainly by regional governments (in collaboration with companies such as Google (www.google.com)), for example:

- the French government continues to restrict access to websites that stir up racial hatred,
- the German government continues to restrict access to websites that deny the Holocaust, and
- the US government continues to restrict access to websites that infringe commercial copyright agreements.

So, the issue of control still continues to worry many users of the virtual highway.

More recently, a number of governments have created task forces to actively pursue control and monitoring policies to enable authorities not only to police and restrict access to but also identify and locate users of websites containing inappropriate literature and/or images.[13] See for example:

- the Virtual Global Taskforce[14] @ www.virtualglobaltaskforce.com, and
- the Internet Content Rating Association @ www.icra.org.

Whilst many politicians, social commentators and media groups have welcomed such moves, some critics whilst accepting the need for a 'policing of the virtual highway' have suggested that the imposition of excessive restrictions could, in an extreme case/scenario, lead to excessive political censorship. Many commentators now cite Google's consent (albeit somewhat reluctantly) to requests by the Chinese government to restrict severely internet access to a range of websites (see Article 12.4).

## Article 12.4

# Backlash as Google shores up great firewall of China

Google, the world's biggest search engine, will team up with the world's biggest censor, China, today with a service that it hopes will make it more attractive to the country's 110 million online users.

After holding out longer than any other major internet company, Google will effectively become another brick in the great firewall of China when it starts filtering out information that it believes the government will not approve of.

Despite a year of soul-searching, the American company will join Microsoft and Yahoo! in helping the communist government block access to websites containing politically sensitive content, such as references to the Tiananmen Square massacre and criticism of the politburo.

Executives have grudgingly accepted that this is the ethical price they have to pay to base servers in mainland China, which will improve the speed – and attractiveness – of their service in a country where they face strong competition from the leading mandarin search engine, Baidu.

But Google faces a backlash from free speech advocates, internet activists and politicians, some of whom are already asking how the company's policy in China accords with its mission statement: to make all possible information available to everyone who has a computer or mobile phone.

The new interface – google.cn – started at midnight last night and will be slowly phased in over the coming months. Although users will have the option of continuing to search via the original US-based google.com website, it is expected that the vast majority of Chinese search enquiries will go through mainland-based servers.

This will require the company to abide by the rules of the world's most restricted internet environment. China is thought to have 30,000 online police monitoring blogs, chatrooms and news portals. The propaganda department is thought to employ even more people, a small but increasing number of whom are paid to anonymously post pro-government comments online. Sophisticated filters have been developed to block or limit access to 'unhealthy information', which includes human rights websites, such as Amnesty, foreign news outlets, such as the BBC, as well as pornography. Of the 64 internet dissidents in prison worldwide, 54 are from China.

Google has remained outside this system until now. But its search results are still filtered and delayed by the giant banks of government servers, known as the great firewall of China. Type 'Falun Gong' in the search engine from a Beijing computer and the only results that can be accessed are official condemnations.

Now, however, Google will actively assist the government to limit content. There are technical precedents. In Germany, Google follows government orders by restricting references to sites that deny the Holocaust. In France, it obeys local rules prohibiting sites that stir up racial hatred. And in the US, it assists the authorities' crackdown on copyright infringements.

The scale of censorship in China is likely to dwarf anything the company has done before. According to one internet media insider, the main taboos are the three Ts: Tibet, Taiwan and the Tiananmen massacre, and the two Cs: cults such as Falun Gong and criticism of the Communist party. But this list is frequently updated.

In a statement, Google said it had little choice: 'To date, our search service has been offered exclusively from outside China, resulting in latency and access issues that have been unsatisfying to our Chinese users and, therefore, unacceptable to Google. With google.cn, Chinese users will ultimately receive a search service that is fast, always accessible, and helps them find information both in China and from around the world.'

It acknowledged that this ran contrary to its corporate ethics, but said a greater good was served by providing information in China. 'In order to operate from China, we have removed some content from the search results available on google.cn, in response to local law, regulation or policy. While removing search results is inconsistent with Google's mission, providing no information (or a heavily degraded user experience that amounts to no information) is more inconsistent with our mission.'

Initially, Google will not use Chinese servers for two of its most popular services: Gmail and blogger. This is a reflection of the company's discomfort with the harsh media environment – and the subsequent risks to its corporate image.

In an attempt to be more transparent than its rivals, Google said it would inform users that certain webpages had been removed from the list of results on the orders of the government. But its motivation is economic: a chunk of the fast-growing Chinese search market, estimated to be worth $151m (£84m) in 2004. This is still small by US standards, but with the number of web users increasing at the rate of more than 20 million a year, the online population is on course to overtake the US within the next decade.

Julian Pain of Reporters Without Borders – a freedom of expression advocacy group that also has its website blocked in China – accused Google of hypocrisy. 'This is very bad news for the internet in China. Google were the only ones who held out. So the Chinese government had to block information themselves. But now Google will do it for them,' he said. 'They have two standards. One for the US, where they resist government demands for personal information, and one for China, where they are helping the authorities block thousands of websites.'

Local bloggers were already wearily resigned to the change. 'What Google are doing is targeting commercial interests and skirting political issues,' said one of the country's most prominent, who writes under the name Black Hearted Killer. 'That by itself is no cause for criticism, but there is no doubt they are cowards.'

## Forbidden searches

Words or phrases that can trigger pages to be blocked or removed from search results:

- *Tiananmen Square massacre* – the killing of hundreds, if not thousands, of civilians by the People's Liberation Army in 1989
- *Dalai Lama* – the exiled spiritual leader of Tibet, who is denounced as a splittist by the government in Beijing
- *Taiwanese independence* – the nightmare of the Communist party, which has vowed to use force to prevent a breakaway
- *Falun Gong* – a banned spiritual movement, thousands of whose members have been imprisoned and in many cases tortured
- *Dongzhou* – the village where paramilitary police shot and killed at least three protesters last month

Source: Jonathan Watts, 25 January 2006, The *Guardian*
http://www.guardian.co.uk/china/story/
0,,1694293,00.html.

Correction (Published January 28th 2006) attached to this article:

In an article about Chinese censorship of the internet, Backlash as Google shores up great firewall of China, page 3, January 25, we described Falun Gong as a cult. In doing so, we should have made clear that we were giving the Chinese government's official view of the movement.

## Access concerns

As we saw in Chapter 4, it is of course a fallacy to presume that the internet is a global phenomenon. There still remain many parts of the world where access to the internet continues to be severely restricted, not only for social and technological reasons, but increasingly for political and economic reasons. Indeed, far from creating equality, the internet has, as Table 12.1 illustrates, assisted in the creation of an even more divided world – a world in which the structural and technological deficit between those that have access and those that do not (or have severely restricted access) continues to become greater every day. Perhaps not so much global integration but rather imposed fragmentation!

Of a world population of approximately 6.5 billion, only 15.7% (a little over 1 billion people) use the internet, with the greatest concentration of internet users being found in:

- Asia (35.7% – approximately 364 million users),
- Europe (28.5% – approximately 290 million users), and
- North America (22.2% – 226 million users),

which together account for a total of 86.4% (approximately 880 million users) of the world population using the internet.

**Table 12.1** World internet usage and population statistics

| World region | Population (millions) | Population of the world (%) | Internet usage (millions) | Population penetration (%) | Internet usage of the world population (%) |
|---|---|---|---|---|---|
| Africa | 915 | 14.1 | 23 | 2.5 | 2.2 |
| Asia | 3,668 | 56.4 | 364 | 9.9 | 35.7 |
| Europe | 807 | 12.4 | 290 | 35.9 | 28.5 |
| Middle East | 190 | 2.9 | 18 | 9.6 | 1.8 |
| North America | 331 | 5.1 | 226 | 68.1 | 22.2 |
| Latin America/Caribbean | 554 | 8.5 | 79 | 14.3 | 7.8 |
| Oceania/Australia | 34 | 0.5 | 18 | 52.9 | 1.8 |
| Total (world) | 6,499 | 100 | 1,018 | 15.7 | 100 |

Source: Internet World Statistics, **www.internetworldstats.com**.

Perhaps more noticeably (and somewhat unsurprisingly) the lowest concentration of internet users is found in:

- Africa (2.2% – approximately 23 million users),
- Middle East (1.8% – approximately 18 million users), and
- Oceania/Australia (1.8% – 18 million users).

More importantly, of the top 10 languages used by internet users (see Table 12.2):

- 30.6% use English as the primary language,
- 13.0% use Chinese as a primary language, and
- 8.5% use Japanese as a primary language,

**Table 12.2** World internet users by language

| World region | Internet users by language | Percentage of all internet users | Population estimate of language use (millions) | Internet penetration by language (%) |
|---|---|---|---|---|
| English | 311 | 30.6 | 1,126 | 27.6 |
| Chinese | 132 | 13.0 | 1,341 | 9.9 |
| Japanese | 86 | 8.5 | 128 | 67.2 |
| Spanish | 64 | 6.3 | 392 | 16.3 |
| German | 57 | 5.6 | 96 | 59.2 |
| French | 41 | 4.0 | 381 | 10.7 |
| Korean | 34 | 3.3 | 74 | 45.8 |
| Portuguese | 32 | 3.2 | 231 | 14.0 |
| Italian | 29 | 2.8 | 59 | 48.8 |
| Russian | 24 | 2.3 | 144 | 16.5 |
| Top 10 languages | 810 | 79.6 | 3,972 | 20.4 |
| Rest of the world languages | 207 | 20.4 | 2,528 | 8.2 |
| Total (world) | 1,018 | 100.0 | 6,499 | 15.7 |

Source: Internet World Statistics, **www.internetworldstats.com**.

**Table 12.3** Countries with the highest number of internet users

| Country/region | Internet users | Population estimate of language use (millions) | Internet penetration by language (%) |
|---|---|---|---|
| United States | 204 | 299 | 68.1 |
| China | 111 | 1,307 | 8.5 |
| Japan | 86 | 128 | 67.2 |
| India | 51 | 1,112 | 4.5 |
| Germany | 49 | 83 | 59.0 |
| United Kingdom | 38 | 60 | 62.9 |
| Korea (South) | 34 | 51 | 67.0 |
| Italy | 29 | 59 | 48.8 |
| France | 26 | 61 | 43.0 |
| Brazil | 26 | 184 | 14.1 |
| Russia | 24 | 143 | 16.5 |
| Canada | 22 | 32 | 67.9 |
| Indonesia | 18 | 222 | 8.1 |
| Spain | 17 | 44 | 38.7 |
| Mexico | 17 | 105 | 16.2 |
| Australia | 14 | 21 | 68.4 |
| Taiwan | 14 | 23 | 60.3 |
| Netherlands | 11 | 16 | 65.9 |
| Poland | 11 | 38 | 27.8 |
| Turkey | 10 | 75 | 13.7 |
| Top 20 countries | 810 | 4,064 | 19.9 |
| Rest of the world | 208 | 2,435 | 8.5 |
| Total (world) | 1,018 | 6,499 | 15.7 |

Source: Internet World Statistics, **www.internetworldstats.com**.

despite the fact that in world population terms only 17.3% use English as a primary language. The most popular language (in world population terms) is Chinese with 20.6%. Japanese (perhaps unsurprisingly) is used as a primary language by only approximately 2% of the world population.

So, why the dominance of the English language on the internet? There are perhaps three reasons:

- the history/origin of the internet,[15]
- the management and control of access to the internet (see above), and
- the composition of the current dominant users of the internet.

In terms of the last issue, it is perhaps worth noting that of the top 20 countries in terms of internet users, a number (e.g. the USA, the UK and Australia) use English as a primary language, with others (e.g. India and Indonesia) recognising English as a secondary language (see Table 12.3).

## Privacy, safety and security concerns

Whilst concerns over controllability and accessibility continue to represent a significant barrier to the ongoing development of 21st century e-commerce in both the UK and the rest of the world, it is perhaps the issues of privacy and security that, nevertheless, dominate the minds of many companies, organisations, government agencies, regulators and of course customers/users. See Articles 12.5 and 12.6.

## Article 12.5

### UK leads the world in online spending . . . but security fears hold many back

UK consumers spend more online than than their counterparts in Europe or the US, according to a newly published survey of e-commerce in the US, UK, Germany and France.

The study, commissioned by RSA Security (see www.rsasecurity.com) found that Britons spent an average of €231 during September 2005, compared to the poll's average of €153. US consumers spent an average of €129 per capita.

But fears of online crime are still holding back spending. Some 16 per cent of respondents in the US, and 13 per cent in the UK, said that they are spending less than they used to, compared to six per cent in Germany and nine per cent in France.

'With this year's ongoing wave of publicity around US-based data breaches and online fraud, it should not be a surprise to anyone that the understanding of these threats is highest in North America,' said Art Coviello, president of RSA Security.

'What concerns me is that, while the industry is working hard to promote best practice and defence measures to our citizens, a high volume remain blissfully unaware of what identity theft is, leaving them exposed to potential exploitation.'

The survey did find very low levels of awareness about online fraud; fewer than half of those questioned were aware of what phishing means.

But it is a lack of confidence in electronic retailers that is holding many consumers back, the poll reported.

Nearly half of all the Americans questioned indicated that they had 'little confidence' or 'no confidence' that their personal information was being protected, and this also concerned two thirds of the French respondents.

Nevertheless the future for e-commerce looks good. Most people are buying more online than they did last year, and two thirds of respondents are buying 'a few more' or 'a lot more' items than last year.

Source: 18 October 2005, Iain Thomson,
www.vnunet.com./vnunet/news/2144097/
uk-leads-online-spending.

## Article 12.6

### Security fears still hurting e-commerce . . . many consumers reluctant to shop or bank online

Security fears are still preventing consumers from doing personal business over the internet, with one in four now cutting back on online shopping.

And according to research commissioned by RSA Security, (see www.rsasecurity.com) one in five consumers refuses to deal with their bank over the internet because of fears over identity theft and phishing attacks.

'Clearly there is a lot of work to be done if businesses want to build more online trust with consumers. While awareness of threats remains high, consumer confidence in dealing with those threats is low,' John Worrall, vice president of worldwide marketing at RSA Security, said at the RSA conference in San Francisco.

The survey of 1,000 consumers found that only 18 per cent of adults feel that personal information is safe online, and 23 per cent actually feel more vulnerable to identity theft compared to 2004. Some 25 per cent of respondents have reduced their online purchases in the past year.

Two out of five respondents refuse to give out personal information to online merchants, and more than half said that traditional user ID and password security is not enough.

Two thirds of respondents admitted to using fewer than five passwords for all electronic information access, and 15 per cent use a single password for everything.

'We have seen the beginnings of a trend toward the widespread replacement of passwords with better authentication methods. And its continuation will help bridge the gap between consumer awareness of identity theft and actual protection against it,' said Worrall.

Source: 16 February 2005, Steve Ranger,
www.vnunet.com./vnunet/news/2126767/
security-fears-hurting-commerce.

## Article 12.7

### Fraudsters hit Visa for second time

The credit card details of 'a large number' of Visa customers in America and Europe have been stolen from a US-based retailer, Visa said yesterday. It is the second time this year that the credit card giant has fallen victim to an attempt to illegally obtain card numbers. Last February, a computer hacker gained access to 5m Visa and Mastercard accounts in the US.

Visa yesterday said it was cooperating with the American authorities on the matter. It also said it had issued a fraud alert to its member banks after it was informed of an 'internal security breach' at the American retailer's database. Although Visa declined to comment on the exact number of cards compromised because of the investigation, a spokesman for Visa Europe said: 'Everyone who used a credit card at this US merchant could have been affected.'

Credit card numbers can be used to make payments, such as buying books on the internet, booking a flight or hiring a car. Visa operates a zero liability policy, which means card holders are protected from having to pay for any unauthorised or fraudulent charges. Peter Lilley, a fellow of the UK Chartered Institute of Banking and author of books on hacking and business crime, warned that someone gaining unwanted access to a large customer database could inflict serious damage.

Visa, which was running tips on fraud prevention on its corporate website yesterday, processes some 3.9m credit card transactions a day. There are currently more than a billion Visa-branded cards in use. The credit card company said the decision to reissue the compromised cards would be up to its numerous card issuers. Meanwhile, 2,000 Visa card holders in the Netherlands received a letter last Friday saying their cards had been blocked and would be reissued within a fortnight.

Source: Danielle Rossingh, 10 June 2003, Telegraph, **www.telegraph.co.uk/money/main.jhtml?xml=% 2Fmoney%2F2003%2F06%2F11%2Fcnvisa11.xml**.

With examples such as the Mastercard and Visa security breach (February 2003) in which 5 million credit card details were hacked (see Article 12.7), it is perhaps unsurprising that customers/users continue to feel apprehensive about providing personal financial information via a webpage, irrespective of how secure it may appear to be.

## Removing the barriers to e-commerce – protection schemes

Clearly, the above issues of privacy and security and of customer/user unease represent an enormous problem to companies/organisations engaged in e-commerce-related activities. So, what has been done to combat such problems?

There are a number of alternative schemes/technologies that have been, and indeed continue to be, used as a means of improving/enhancing the protection of all users. Such schemes/ technologies include:

- the establishment of a system/network firewall,
- the use of intrusion detection systems (or intrusion detection software),
- the use of data/information encryption facilities,
- the use digital certificates, and
- the use of authentication and authorisation software.

We will look at each of these technologies (and a few others) in detail in Chapter 13.

## B2C e-commerce

If you recall, we looked at point of service-based EFT for both card-based systems and non-card-based systems in Chapter 4 and in more detail again in Chapter 8. Briefly, within point of service-based EFT there are two sub-categories, these being:

- card-based systems, and
- non-card-based systems.

Point of service-based EFT card-based systems can be further sub-categorised as:

- offline processing using a manual processing system,
- online processing using an EFT system – cardholder present, and
- online processing using an EFT system – cardholder not present.

Online web-based e-commerce transactions are essentially classified as online processing – cardholder not present transactions. To process online cardholder not present transactions, a company/organisation has a choice of three methodologies, these being:

- using an internet merchant account facility,
- using a payment processing company facility, or
- using a shopping mall facility.

In general, the vast majority of private limited companies and perhaps all public limited companies use an internet merchant account facility. The payment processing company facility and/or the shopping mall facility are typically used by sole traders, small partnerships and/or very small private limited companies.

To use an internet merchant account facility, a company/organisation must have:

- an internet merchant account (and ID) from an acquiring bank, and
- an approved Payment Service Provider (PSP).

An acquiring bank is a high street bank that offers debit and credit card processing services. The acquiring bank acquires the money from the customer, processes the transaction and credits the company/organisation account. If a company/organisation wants to take debit and credit card payments, it will need a merchant service account (and ID) with an acquiring bank (as we saw in Chapter 8). In addition, where a company/organisation wants to undertake web-based online e-commerce, then it will also need an internet merchant account (and ID).

In the UK there are a number of banks that provide both merchant account facilities and internet merchant account facilities – these banks are often referred to as merchant acquirers or acquiring banks, and include, for example:

- Royal Bank of Scotland @ www.rsb.co.uk,
- Barclays Merchant Services, @ www.epdq.com,
- NatWest Streamline @ www.streamline.com,
- Lloyds TSB Cardnet @ www.lloydstsbcardnet.com, and
- HSBC Merchant Services @ www.hsbc.co.uk.

A payment service provider (PSP) is essentially a payment gateway. It is a virtual service/system that collects the debit/credit card details over the web and passes them to the acquiring bank. A payment service provider acts as an intermediary between the merchant's website (the retailing company/organisation) and all the financial networks involved with the transaction. These will include of course the customer's debit/credit card issuer and the company's/organisation's merchant account.

If a company/organisation wants to undertake transactions involving the use of online debit and credit card payments, it will need a payment service provider. Examples of current payment service providers include:

- SECpay @ www.secpay.com,
- Ogone @ www.ogone.com,
- Universal Gateway Payment @ www.securehosting.com,
- Worldpay @ www.worldpay.com, and
- Protx @ www.protx.com.

Note: Some payment service providers only operate with particular acquiring banks. For example, SECpay (see above) has operating agreements with Ulster Bank, NatWest Streamline, Paymentech, LloydsTSB Cardnet, HSBC, Euro Conex, Barclays Merchant Services, Bank of Scotland, Alliance and Leicester, American Express and Diners; whereas Protx (see above) has operating agreements with Lloyds TSB Cardnet, the Bank of Scotland, Barclays Merchant Services, HSBC, NatWest Streamline, American Express and Diners.

As a payment gateway, the payment service provider essentially:

- checks the validity of the debit/credit card,
- encrypts the transaction details and debit/credit card details,
- ensures that the encrypted details are transmitted to the correct destination,
- decrypts the response(s), and
- confirms the response(s) with the merchant's website or shopping cart/basket either as:
  - an authorised transaction,
  - a referred transaction, or
  - a declined transaction.

Many UK acquiring banks (including those above) offer PSP services as part of their product range – that is as part of their internet merchant services account facilities. For example, Worldpay is part of the Royal Bank of Scotland Group. In addition, where a payment processing company facility or a shopping mall facility is used, payment service provider-related services would normally form part of the service provision.

## Online and open for business

As suggested earlier in this chapter, a company's/organisation's e-commerce website normally comprises of two parts:

- a portal interface (or access portal), and
- a retailing resource.

For the following discussion we will use Marks and Spencer plc online shopping facility @ www.marksandspencer.com.

The portal interface used by a company/organisation would provide the customer/user with information on and access to a range of company/organisation goods, services and facilities. See Example 12.1.

**Example 12.1** Marks and Spencer – portal interfaces

The retailing resource would provide the customer/user with facilities to undertake a range of commercial transactions – in particular the purchase of products and/or services. Such a retail resource would normally comprise of:

- an electronic order-taking facility – using for example an imaginary 'shopping cart/basket' facility,
- a virtual 'check-out' facility, and
- a payment processing facility.

See Figure 12.1.

## Electronic order-taking facility

Most online retailers use the notion and image of a shopping cart/basket both to typify the electronic order-taking facility and exemplify the online shopping experience. Indeed, for a wide range of online retailers, the shopping cart/basket is now considered to be a standard

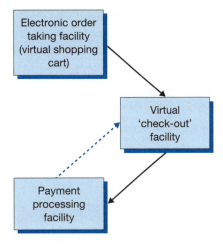

**Figure 12.1** E-commerce retailing resource

component of the online shopping process. But exactly what is a shopping cart/basket and what purpose does it actually serve?

In essence, the shopping cart/basket is simply a collection facility. It is an interface between the customer and the company's/organisation's product/services database. That is every time the customer selects a product/service to purchase the items are added to the shopping cart/basket.

In an information technology context a shopping cart/basket is simply a software program. However, in an operational e-commerce context a shopping cart/basket merely records the ongoing results of the customer's ordering process and is designed to allow the customer to view the details of all ongoing transactions or purchases – on request and at any time up to check out. See Example 12.2.

When the customer has completed all their transactions, they are invited to proceed to the virtual check-out facility to complete the purchasing process. See Example 12.3.

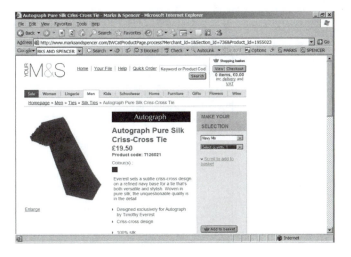

**Example 12.2** Marks and Spencer – shopping basket facility

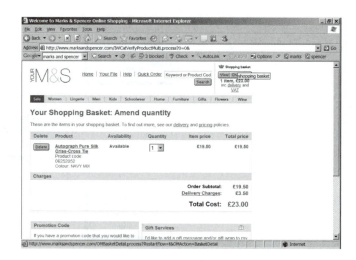

Example 12.3 Marks and Spencer – check-out facility

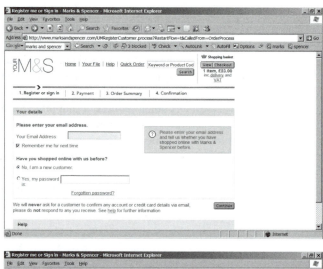

Example 12.4 Marks and Spencer – email and registration requirements

## Virtual check-out facility

An e-mail address is required so that confirmation can be e-mailed to the customer once the order process and payment procedure have been completed. Where the customer is a new customer further personal details are required. See Example 12.4.

However, where the customer is an existing customer all that is required is a customer password (which is linked to the e-mail address).

Let's assume that we are a new customer. As a new customer payment details (credit and/or debit card details) will be required. See Example 12.5.

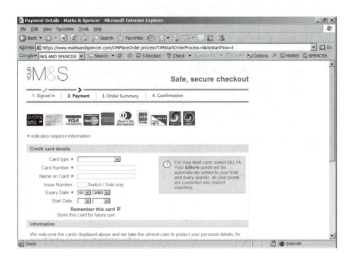

**Example 12.5** Marks and Spencer – payment details

Once these credit/debit card payment details have been verified, approved and authorised, a conformation e-mail (containing an order number) is e-mailed to the customer's e-mail address. The transaction (at least the online component of the transaction) is now complete. All that is required is delivery of the product purchased by the customer.

Although a small number of products and services may be distributed digitally most products (including those in the above example) will need to be physically delivered. Once a commitment to purchase has been made, some online retailers allow customers to select alternative delivery modes.

Some retailers offer free delivery of products when the total value of a purchase exceeds a predetermined limit or where delivery is to within a particular geographical area, but impose an additional charge where special distibution and delivery mechanisms are requested (e.g. next day delivery). Other retailers may impose a small nominal charge for all types of delivery irrespective of the purchase order value (e.g. Example 12.3 above). In reality, however, whatever the marketing or advertising rhetoric nothing is for free. The cost of any 'free' delivery is merely absorbed within the cost overheads of the product. The distinction between 'free' or 'unpaid for' delivery and 'paid for' delivery is merely a creative marketing tool designed to attract the interest of prospective customers/clients. In a marketing/advertising context, think of the word 'free' when used in relation to product delivery as a linguistic metaphor – one used to signify a concealed and hidden cost.

## Payment processing facility – accepting online payments

As suggested earlier, there are three alternative methods that can be employed to process/receive online payments, these being:

- using an internet merchant account,
- using a payment processing company, or
- using a shopping mall facility.

### Using an internet merchant account

Where a company/organisation currently accepts debt/credit card payments, that is face-to-face transactions or, more appropriately, online processing pPoS EFT (online cardholder present electronic funds transfer, see Chapter 4), then it will already possess a current merchant account. To accept online credit/debit card payments, such a company/organisation would need to acquire an internet merchant account facility. Such an account is useful where a company/organisation expects to undertake a high volume of fairly simple, low risk, online transactions.

The advantage of using an internet merchant account is that debit/credit card payments are available for use by the company/organisation within three to four working days after the transaction. The disadvantages are:

- application procedures can be complex – often merchant banks impose severe information requirements on companies applying for internet merchant account facilities,
- the technology costs – for example secure socket layer (SSL) technology is required to encrypt transaction data and to transmit the necessary customer and debit/credit card details to the acquiring bank for the transaction to be authenticated, and
- the administrative costs – for example all acquiring banks impose a set-up fee and day-to-day transaction charges (see Table 12.4 below).

**Table 12.4** The cost of an internet merchant account – HSBC Merchant Services

| Packaged product (turnover up to £50,000) | Individual quote (turnover in excess of £50,000) |
|---|---|
| £250 one-off set up charge | £150 set-up charge |
| 2% of every credit card transaction | £18 per month per standard terminal rental for each terminal, plus VAT |
| 25p for every debit card transaction | |
| No terminal rental for 12 months | Transaction charges negotiated on an individual basis |
| No minimum monthly service charge. | Minimum monthly service charge of £20 per month |

Source: http://www.hsbc.co.uk/1/2/business/cards-payments/card-processing.

In addition, the costs of any fraudulent transactions are borne by the company/organisation and not the payment processing company. That is if a fraudulent transaction occurs its value is recovered in full by the payment processing company from the company/organisation account.

### Using a payment processing company

Where a company/organisation:

- does not process a large number of online transactions,
- does not currently accept credit/debit card payments – that is the company/organisation does not currently possess a merchant account and, perhaps,
- does not have an established trading history,

it may consider using the facilities of a payment processing company (sometimes referred to as a payment bureau). Such payment processing companies obtain payment from the customers' credit and/or debit card issuer on behalf of the company/organisation. The advantages of using a payment processing company are:

- the reduced technology costs – that is there is no need to invest in a costly secure payment system,
- the reduced administrative costs – that is the payment procedures are managed by the payment processing company, and
- reduced application procedures – that is information requirements are less severe than those for an application for an internet merchant account.

The disadvantages of using a payment processing company are:

- it may hold payment receipts from customers for a minimum settlement period (the period depends on the payment processing company) before they are transferred to the company/organisation account, and
- customers are aware that their payments are being directed through a payment processing company.

In addition (as with an internet merchant account) the costs of any fraudulent transactions are borne by the company/organisation and not the payment processing company.

In general, payment processing companies offer a useful and relatively cheap alternative for companies/organisations that have limited debit/credit card transactions or who, for whatever reason, do not open a merchant account with an acquiring bank. Examples of such payment processing companies are Paypal @ www.paypal.com. For further examples, see www.electronic-payments.co.uk, a UK government agency sponsored information website

### Using an online shopping mall

An online shopping mall can be a good alternative for a small company/organisation which has a limited turnover of standardised products/services and does not currently offer debit/credit card facilities, but is seeking to establish an online presence.

Essentially an online shopping mall is a collection of online retail outlets on a single website in which:

- individual retailers are responsible for maintaining and updating their own retail outlets, and
- the shopping mall provider is responsible for managing the shopping mall facility including, for example, payment processing facilities.

Such shopping mall facilities are offered by many trade and industry associations. Indeed, some Internet Service Providers (ISPs) also offer online shopping mall facilities.

For a small company/organisation, the advantages of an online shopping mall facility are:

- such shopping malls provide an immediate online presence, and
- there is no need for the company/organisation to arrange/set up a internet merchant account or separate payment processing facilities.

The disadvantages are:

- the company/organisation joining the shopping mall will often be limited to a standard format presentation, usually with limited facilities, and perhaps more importantly
- such shopping mall facilities can be very expensive. For example a company/organisation joining a shopping mall may have to pay not only an arrangement/set-up fee, but also a percentage charge for each transaction undertaken through the facility and, in some instances, a monthly or annual management fee.

## B2C e-commerce – behind the screen

Below is a brief step-by-step guide to an online transaction using an internet merchant account and a payment gateway service provider.

Stage 1   The customer visits the retailer's website.

Stage 2   The customer selects items within the retailer's purchasing pages.

Stage 3   The customer's selection is added to the retailer's shopping cart.

Stage 4   Once at the 'checkout', the customer's personal and financial details are recorded on a secure form using a SSL (Secure Socket Layer) mode. It is at this stage that the retailer's website should switch to the SSL mode. As you may recall SSL is a widely used encryption technology which allows encrypted information to be transferred between the retailer's checkout page and the payment gateway service server. Usually a padlock symbol will appear on the web page/web browser (lower left-hand corner) to show that the page is secure.

Stage 5   The customer's details are transmitted to a payment gateway service, which is often separate from the shopping cart.

Stage 6   The gateway service securely routes the information through the relevant financial networks to gain authorisation.

Stage 7   The payment gateway service will provide notification of transaction status (authorised, referred or declined) to the retailer and then process the transaction through the banking system. If the transaction is successful, the customer's account is credited and the retailer's merchant account is debited with the value of the transaction, less the acquiring bank's commission and/or fees.

Stage 8   Once all funds have cleared, the retailer is able to transfer the money to its ordinary business bank account.

Stage 9   The payment gateway service would normally collect fees/charges for the transactions processed on a monthly basis – usually by direct debit.

## B2B e-commerce

Whilst variants of Business-2-Business (B2B) e-commerce have existed for many years – for example EDI (electronic data interchange) and more recently EFT (electronic funds transfer) – such activities were, in a business context, considered peripheral to the main supply chain activities of a company/organisation, and therefore often existed as fragmented and disjointed standalone processes/procedures, divorced from key retail and distribution activities. Although such fragmented processes/procedures did play, and indeed in some instances continue to play, a key role in retail-related business activities, it was perhaps the emergence of web-based information and communication technologies and capabilities that enabled the development of the infrastructure that we now know as B2B e-commerce.

In a contemporary context, B2B e-commerce has become synonymous with supply chain integration, and the use of extranet-based[16] facilities to provide access to a range of supply chain-based facilities. The aim is to improve the efficiency and effectiveness of business-related retail and distribution activities, by integrating a customer's network directly to a supplier's network.

Clearly the precise nature of the B2B e-commerce provision will differ from supplier to supplier but, in broad terms, a B2B e-commerce provision would normally include secure access to:

- online product/service catalogues,
- product/service synopses,
- product/service availability profiles,
- online (real-time) ordering facilities,
- real-time order-based tracking and transportation facilities,[17] and
- customer payment facilities.

## Using e-money

Although the term 'e-money' is often used interchangeably and somewhat incorrectly with terms such as electronic cash (e-cash) or digital cash, the term e-money has a specific meaning/definition. E-money, or an e-money scheme, is a scheme regulated by the FSA (Financial Services Authority) that involves the creation of digital value-based tokens (in a single currency or multiple currencies) that are stored on either:

- an electronic device (e.g. a PC and/or computer network), or
- a smart card[18] (also known as an e-purse),

that can be transferred from one person/company to another person/company, for example a consumer/buyer to a retailer/seller.

Consequently, e-money can be defined as monetary value which is stored on an electronic device, issued on receipt of funds and accepted as a means of payment by persons other than the issuer,[19] and can – as an electronic means of payment – be used to pay for either goods or services purchased:

- in the high street (e.g. see Article 12.8 below)
- by mail order, or
- via the web.

Structurally there are two types of e-money:

- identified and
- anonymous.

Identified e-money is e-money in which the identities of the parties to the transaction – in particular the payer (or consumer/purchaser of the goods/services) – are revealed in the payment operation. Anonymous e-money is e-money in which the identity of the payer (or consumer/purchaser of the goods/services) is not revealed in the payment transaction. It is the latter type of e-money which essentially operates like a cash exchange and can more accurately be described as e-cash or digital cash.

In addition, each of the above types of e-money exists in two varieties:

- online e-money – that is an e-money transaction in which a transaction can only be completed between a payer/customer once interaction with the originator of the e-money (or an appointed authorised institution) has occurred and the validity of the transaction verified (e.g. sufficient funds are available), and
- offline e-money – that is an e-money transaction that can be completed between a payer/customer without interaction with the originator of the e-money (or an appointed authorised institution).

So who can issue e-money? Banks and building societies that are already authorised by the FSA to provide high street banking services can issue e-money as a component part of their

## Article 12.8

### London transport targets Oyster 'e-money' trials in 2005

Trials of the Oyster card 'e-money' scheme that will allow millions of Londoners to buy everything from newspapers to parking time with their travel smartcards could begin before the end of the year. Transport for London (TfL) has just announced the shortlist of bidders for the e-money project and hopes to choose a partner by the end of the year. TfL announced plans earlier this year for the e-money project, which will allow the Oyster card to be used instead of cash for goods and services at news-agents, parking machines, fast-food restaurants and supermarkets.

The shortlist of companies and consortia invited to negotiate with TfL are alphyra; Barclays; BBVA, Accenture, MTR and Octopus; EDS and JP Morgan; Nucleus, Dexit, Ericsson, Hutchison 3G and Euroconex; PayPal; and Royal Bank of Scotland. Negotiations commence next month and TfL hopes to trial the technology and confirm its chosen partner by the end of 2005. Work on the development and delivery of e-money on Oyster cards will then start in January 2006.

Jay Walder, managing director of finance and planning at TfL, said in a statement: 'Oyster has the largest customer base of all smart cards in the UK, with 2.2 million users and a significant level of public trust. Extending Oyster to include low value payments is a natural progression which will make the smart card even more convenient.'

A similar scheme, called Octopus, already exists in Hong Kong.

TfL hopes Oyster e-money will provide greater convenience for passengers and generate additional revenue for the transport network.

Source: 21 July 2005, Andy McCue,
http://software.silicon.com/applications/
0,39024653,39150647,00.htm.

portfolio of banking-related activities. However, specialist e-money issuers[20] have to apply for FSA authorisation to issue e-money and provide e-money-related services.

At the heart of the regulatory framework lies two EU directives:

- Directive 2000/46/EC (the E-money Directive), relating to the taking up, pursuit of and prudential supervision of the business of electronic money institutions (September 2000), and
- Directive 2000/28/EC amending Directive 2000/12/EC (the Banking Co-ordination Directive) relating to the taking up and pursuit of the business of credit institutions.

The Directives' objectives are:

- to protect consumers and ensure confidence in e-money schemes through the implementation of rules for safeguarding the financial integrity and stability of e-money institutions, and
- to facilitate/provide for licensed e-money institutions to offer/provide cross-border services/facilities.

The above E-money Directive was introduced into the UK regulatory systems through a number of regulatory provisions/amendments, namely:

- the Financial Services and Markets Act 2000 (Regulated Activities) (Amendment) Order 2002,
- the Electronic Money (Miscellaneous Amendments) Regulations 2002, and
- the Financial Services Authority's ('FSA') Handbook of Rules and Guidance.

Consequently:

- the issuing of e-money is classified as a regulated activity under the Financial Services and Markets Act 2000 (as amended),[21] and

■ the issuers of e-money (including specialist issuers who are not an existing bank and/or building society) are regarded as credit institutions, and are regulated in a similar way to banks and building societies – although with less stringent requirements.

So who might want to use e-money? There are of course many potential uses for and users of e-money, for example:

■ those who feel more secure using e-money to purchase goods on the web rather than using debit and/or credit cards,
■ those who feel more secure carrying e-money on a plastic smart card rather than a wallet/purse full of notes and coins,
■ those who may need to carry multiple currencies and, perhaps most importantly,
■ those who for whatever reason do not have access to a bank account or debit/credit card.

The main advantages of e-money are:

■ it is a secure payment methodology,
■ it is very portable,
■ it has growing acceptability, and
■ is regarded as user-friendly.

The main disadvantage is that as a payment system e-money is still in its infancy and may take a number of years to develop fully.

## M-commerce

M-commerce or mobile commerce can be defined as electronic commerce undertaken with the use of a mobile device such as, for example, a mobile phone and/or a PDA.[22] Whilst the development and growth of m-commerce was perhaps inevitable given:

■ the increasing growth in internet and web use over the past 25 years,
■ the establishment and continuing development of web-based e-commerce technologies, and
■ the continuing development of portable WAP[23] communication technologies and devices,

as business and commerce tread warily into the 21st century, m-commerce was still in its infancy at the start of 2007. Perhaps it is a technology whose time has yet to arrive?

### M-commerce applications

The term 'm-commerce' was first used in the late 1990s during the so-called dotcom boom – the idea being to use broadband mobile telephony to provide on-demand services and applications.[24] Unfortunately the idea(s) disappeared gently into the twilight zone – along with many of the dotcom companies. Why? Put simply, the technologies available during the 1990s were insufficiently evolved to be able to deliver many of the applications and services promised. It was not therefore a lack of demand from customers/users – it was an inability to supply on the part of the companies.

In general, m-commerce applications can be categorised as either:

■ active m-commerce applications – that is m-commerce in which the customer/user is pro-active in the initiation of a service/application, or
■ passive m-commerce applications – that is m-commerce in which the service/application is self-initiating and the customer/user is merely a reactive recipient.

### Active m-commerce service/applications

Active m-commerce service/applications can be categorised as:

- transaction processing applications,
- digital services/applications, and
- telemetry applications.

## Transaction processing applications

Such applications essentially relate to e-commerce using a mobile wireless device (mobile phones and/or PDA) equipped with web-based capabilities. Whilst there are a number of high street retailers exploring the commercial possibilities of m-commerce activities, it is likely that the highest volume of m-commerce transactions using such devices will relate to micro transactions (or micro payments) – that is small value purchases, for example:

- car parking fees,
- cinema tickets, and
- vending machines purchases.

## Digital services/applications

Such services/applications, also known as 'digital content delivery', can be categorised as either:

- digital information services – for example receiving weather reports, bus/train timetables, news reports, sports scores, ticket availability, market prices, or
- digital applications and products – for example games, high resolution video and digital audio.

Both of these require the recipient to subscribe to and pay for the service, application and/or product received.

## Telemetry applications

Such applications would include, for example, using a mobile wireless device to manage/control and/or communicate with remote devices and/or a facility.

### Passive m-commerce services/applications

Such services/applications are self-initiating in that the customer/user is a reactive recipient. An example of such an application would be the collection of toll charges and or parking fees where simply driving pass a toll barrier/car park barrier would automatically charge a prescribed fee to the driver's mobile device.

## M-commerce – the practicalities

So how will m-commerce work? In essence the mobile device user would register with their network operator in advance for m-commerce services. The network operator (e.g. $O_2$, T-mobile, Vodafone or Orange, or any other network operator/provider) would manage the m-commerce Point-of-Sale transaction (mPOS transaction), with the cost of the service/application either:

- being charged to the customer's monthly account, or
- deducted directly from the customer's pay as you go account.

Whilst the network operator would process/manage all the transaction formalities including customer authentication, payment processing and response processing, the business retailing the application/service/product (the point of sale client) would process/manage the payment authorisation and refund management formalities.

## M-commerce – the regulations

Although m-commerce is, in a comparative context, a relatively new technology, it is – particularly those services that utilise micro-payments – regulated within the framework provided by the European Union E-money Directive – although its implementation (perhaps unsurprisingly) does differ between member states. This is because m-commerce micro payments are considered a form of e-money and are therefore subject to the regulations contained within the directive. As we saw earlier in our discussion of e-money, in the UK the FSA is responsible for the regulation of e-money/e-money-related schemes.

## The advantages and disadvantages of m-commerce

For companies/organisations, the advantages of m-commerce include better targeted service/application delivery and, as a consequence improved cost efficiency, and a more effective use of business resources. For mobile device users, the advantages include greater portability of and increased accessibility to services and applications – perhaps the reason why m-commerce devices are often referred to as 'anytime, anywhere' devices. In addition to such convenience, m-commerce provides increased personalisation of service/application provision – that is m-commerce transactions are often perceived as 'one-to-one' transactions.

For companies/organisations, the disadvantages of m-commerce include the possibility slow/interrupted data transmission, often resulting from a lack of (inter) network uniformity. For mobile device users the disadvantages include:

- limited processing power of mobile devices,
- limited display facilities of mobile devices, and
- limited technical capabilities of mobile devices.

In addition, there are only a limited number of payment methods available to pay for services used/applications purchased, the main ones being:

- use of premium-rate calling numbers,
- charging to the mobile device user's bill/account, or
- deducting the cost from the mobile device user's calling credit, either directly or using a reverse-charged SMS.

## What is the future of m-commerce?

Undoubtedly higher bandwidth facilities, more efficient processing/storage power, increased display/resolution capabilities and improved security facilities, will not only improve access to more advanced video/audio applications, it will also allow for the development and increased availability of a vast range of information-based storage/retrieval services and applications, including for example:

- mobile banking or m-banking facilities – that is m-commerce-based facilities to allow mobile device users to gain access to their personal accounts and allow the management of account-based transactions, the transfer of funds and the purchase of services,
- mobile trading/mobile brokerage – that is m-commerce facilities to allow a registered subscriber to react to market developments in a timely fashion and irrespective of their physical location, and
- mobile retail – that is m-commerce facilities to allow customers not only to purchase online but receive information on available discounts, etc.

## Benefits of e-commerce

The benefits of e-commerce can be categorised as:

- provider-related benefits, and
- customer/user-related benefits.

### Provider related benefits

For a company/organisation providing the e-commerce facility – whether it is a dotcom company, a dotbam company, or a dotbam+ company, the benefits include:

- immediate access to a global customer base – products and services supplied anytime, any-place, anywhere,
- immediate access to non-stop retailing – buying and selling 24 hours a day, seven days a week, 365 days a year,
- improved opportunity to enter/create new markets,
- improved communications with customers,
- improved inventory control,
- more efficient customer order processing and customer order tracking,
- reduced operational costs,
- reduced transaction costs, and
- more efficient information and resource management.

### Customer/user-related benefits

For a customer using the e-commerce facility, the main benefits include:

- greater competitive pricing of products and services,
- increased access to a 'world of stores',
- increased choice,
- greater availability of a larger and broader selection of products and services,
- increased flexibility,
- greater convenience, increased availability of more in-depth and up-to-date information on products and services,
- increased speed, and
- increased ease of use.

## Problems of e-commerce

Although the benefits of e-commerce are significant, such benefits have not come without consequence – that is without longer-term problems/costs. These can be categorised as follows:

- social costs of e-commerce,
- political consequence of e-commerce, and
- economic costs of e-commerce.

The social costs of e-commerce would include, for example:

- a reduction in (local) employment opportunities,
- the closure of local retail facilities, and
- a possible increase in social poverty and depravation,

as customers migrate from local retail facilities to online self service shopping.

In addition, such costs could also include the social costs associated with the socio-economic/socio-demographic division between those that have access to, and are able to use web-based services, and those that do not have access to and are therefore unable to use web-based services.

The political consequences of e-commerce would include, for example, the need to:

- monitor and ensure the legality of e-commerce operations,
- regulate the quality and safety of products supplied using e-commerce facilities (e.g. medical supplies), and
- control the purchase of restricted/banned products using e-commerce facilities (e.g. pornography, restricted drugs/narcotics).

The economic costs of e-commerce would include, for example, the costs associated with:

- an increasingly competitive marketplace,
- an increasingly uncertain business environment,
- a continuing reduction in business margins, and
- a continuing change in customer expectations.

Inasmuch as web-based e-commerce has provided and increased access to global markets it has also increased competition, in particular global competition, resulting in ever-growing pressures to maintain a low cost base whilst at the same time remaining flexible, adaptable and open to change.

## E-commerce – and the matter of regulation!

It is perhaps not surprising that:

- the continuing proliferation of e-commerce (and of course m-commerce)-based information and communication technologies, and
- the escalating use of e-commerce transactions (both web-based and non-web-based) during the latter part of the 20th century and the early part of the 21st century,

has not evaded the eagle eyes of European/UK legislators and regulators. Indeed, the past few years (certainly since 1998) have seen an enormous increase in regulatory pronouncements and the imposition of rigorous (some would say authoritarian) requirements – more specifically legislation-based.

So what are the main legislative pronouncements/regulatory requirements? For our purposes we will restrict our discussion to the following:[25]

- the Data Protection Act 1998,[26]
- the Consumer Protection (Distance Selling) Regulations 2000,[27]
- the Electronic Communications Act 2000,[28]
- the Electronic Signatures Regulations 2002,[29]
- the Electronic Commerce (EC Directive) Regulations 2002[30] and the Electronic Commerce (EC Directive) (Extension) (No. 2) Regulations 2003
- the Privacy and Electronic Communications (EC Directive) Regulations 2003,[31]
- the Disability Discrimination Act 1995[32] and the Code of Practice: Rights of Access to Goods, Facilities, Services and Premises 2002.[33]

## The Data Protection Act 1998

As we saw in Chapter 6, the Data Protection Act 1998 (the 1998 Act) applies to every company and organisation that maintains lists, databases or files (paper or electronic) containing personal details of:

- staff – for example personnel information such as home address and date of birth,
- clients – for example account details, agreements, contact details, BACS payment details,
- customers – for example account details, contact details, credit card details, and/or
- other related parties.

All companies are required to;

- comply with the provisions of the 1998 Act,
- comply with guidelines and interpretations of the 1998 Act issued by the Information Commissioner, and
- be registered with the Information Commissioner.

Failure to do so can result in;

- the imposition of substantial fines, and
- if deemed appropriate by the Information Commissioner, closure of the company/organisation.

### Data Protection Act 1998 and e-commerce

Where a company/organisation uses a website merely as a web-based facility to:

- provide advice and/or information, or
- advertise goods and services,

the provisions and requirements of the 1998 Act do not apply.

Examples of such websites include:

- a community site – for example www.leven-village.co.uk,
- an archive website – used to preserve valuable electronic content threatened with extinction.
- an information website – that contains content that is intended merely to inform visitors but not necessarily for commercial purposes (e.g. www.dti.gov.uk),
- a news website – one dedicated to dispensing news and commentary (e.g. www.ft.com and www.timesonline.co.uk),
- a search engine – a website that provides general information and is intended as a gateway to others (e.g. www.google.co.uk and www.yahoo.com), and
- a web portal – a website that provides a starting point, a gateway, or portal to other resources on the internet or an intranet.

However, if a company/organisation uses a website as an interactive web-based facility – that is a facility which provides for/allows for the exchange of personal information (e.g. user details and information such as name, address, credit/debit card details) then the provisions and requirements of the 1998 Act apply – in full!

Examples of such websites are:

- a company/business website – one used for the promotion of a company, business and/or service (e.g. www.tesco.com, www.marksandspencer.com, and www.lloydstsb.com),
- a download website – one used for downloading electronic content such as computer software,
- a professional website – one designed specifically for members of a professional association (e.g. www.accaglobal.com and www.icaew.co.uk), and
- a games website – one that is itself a game or 'playground' where many people come to play,

Essentially, all interactive e-commerce websites operated by and/or owned by UK-based companies/organisations *must* comply with the eight Data Protection Act Principles. Such companies/organisations must ensure that personal data acquired as a result of web-based activities must be:

- fairly and lawfully processed – 1st principle,
- used for specific purposes – 2nd principle,
- adequate, relevant and not excessive – 3rd principle,
- accurate and where necessary kept up-to-date – 4th principle,
- kept for no longer than necessary – 5th principle,
- used in accordance with the rights of individuals under the 1998 Act – 6th principle,
- kept secure – 7th principle, and
- not transferred to another country outside the EU without adequate protection – 8th principle.

Essentially, the provisions of the 1998 Act require that companies and organisations adopt appropriate technical and organisational measures to minimise the possibility of:

- unauthorised access to or unlawful processing of personal data,
- accidental loss of personal data,
- malicious corruption of personal data, and/or
- destruction of or damage to personal data.

Such technical and organisational measures would comprise of a range of internal control-based measures within three main areas

- systems security measures – including the use of:
  - hardware and/or software firewalls,
  - encryption procedures,
  - audit trails, user-based password/security protocols,
  - anti-virus software,
  - data backup facilities, and
  - physical location security,
- policy and procedures – including the use of:
  - up-to-date and relevant policies and procedures on internet use/abuse, and
  - appropriate separation of duties within data processing activities, and
- employee training – including the use of compliance training/testing.

Remember that companies/organisations engaging in e-commerce activities must ensure:

- the reliability of employees who have access to client/customer personal data where personal data is processed in-house, or,
- the compliance of the data processor with the requirements of the 1998 Act where data processing is outsourced.

In general, to comply with the provisions and requirements of the 1998 Act, companies and organisations should:

- appoint a data controller,
- identify and document how the company/organisation collects, processes and stores personal data, and
- produce a company/organisation-wide data protection/privacy policy.

In terms of web-based activities, companies/organisations should produce a detailed website policy – which should be available online:

- specifying the terms and conditions associated with use of the company/organisation website, and
- detailing company/organisation data protection/privacy[34] terms in relation to the company/organisation website.

The company's/organisation's data protection/privacy policy should contain details of:

- what data/information is collected,
- how the data/information is collected,
- how the data/information is stored,
- for what purpose the data/information is used and the purposes for which the data/information will not be used,[35]
- who the data/information will be shared with,
- whether the data/information collected will be transferred outside the EU,
- how a website user/visitor can verify (and if necessary update) the personal data stored, and
- how the website user/visitor can object to the use of covert data collection (e.g. the use of 'cookies').[36]

## The Consumer Protection (Distance Selling) Regulations 2000

The Consumer Protection (Distance Selling) Regulations 2000[37] (commonly referred to as DSRs 2000) were brought into force in October 2000 to implement the EC Distance Selling Directive in the UK, and imposed specific obligations on suppliers of goods and services, in particular for our purposes, web-based suppliers.

The DSRs 2000 give consumers certain rights and protection when they shop for goods or services at a distance. A distance contract[38] is one where there has been no face-to-face contact between the consumer and a representative of the company/organisation selling the goods and/or services, or someone acting indirectly on the business's behalf, such as in a showroom or a door-to-door sales person, up to and including the moment at which the contract is concluded.

Key features of the regulations[39] are:

- the consumer must be given clear information about the goods or services offered,
- after making/agreeing to purchase goods and/or services, the consumer must be sent confirmation, and
- the consumer must be granted a 'cooling-off' period of seven working days.

The DSRs 2000 apply to companies/organisations if they sell goods or services without face-to-face contact using an organised scheme, for instance via:

- the web (e-commerce),
- text messaging,
- phone calls,
- faxing,
- interactive TV,
- mail order catalogues, and/or
- mail order advertising in newspapers or magazines.

The DSRs 2000 neither apply to B2B transactions – that is non-consumer-based transactions nor to:

- financial services,
- the sale of land or buildings,
- purchases from a vending machine or automated commercial premises,
- the use of a public pay phone,
- auctions, including internet auctions, and/or
- rental agreements that have to be in writing (e.g. a lease for three years or more).

See s5(1) of the DSRs 2000.

There are also some partial exceptions, for example:

- accommodation, transport, catering or leisure services,
- package travel and timeshare,
- food and drink or other goods for everyday consumption delivered to the consumer's home or workplace by regular rounds-men (e.g. a milkman).[40]

See s6(2) of the DSRs 2000.

In brief, the DSRs 2000 provides that a company/organisation must always give clear and unambiguous information to prospective customers to allow them to make an informed decision as to whether or not to undertake a purchase. The information a business must give must include details about:

- the business,
- the goods or services,
- payment arrangements,
- delivery arrangements, and
- the customers' right to cancel their orders.

Companies/organisations must also provide customers with confirmation of the above details in writing or where appropriate by some other 'durable' medium.[41]


### Prior information

Section 7 of the DSRs 2000 provides that companies/organisations must supply prospective customers (before they agree to buy) with 'pre-contract' or 'prior' information. Pre-contract information is required prior to the conclusion of the commercial contract and must include:

- the company's/organisation's name,
- the company's/organisation's address – if payment in advance is required,
- a description of the goods or services being offered,
- the full price – including any taxes,
- for how long the price or any special offers remain valid,
- details of any delivery costs,
- details of how payment can be made,
- the arrangements for delivery or performance,
- when customers can expect delivery, and
- information about the customer's right to cancel.

Whilst such information can be provided by any method deemed appropriate by the company/organisation – in terms of the form of distance communication being used to conclude the contract – such information must be clear and comprehensible.[42]

If a company/organisation provides pre-contract information in a form that does not allow it to be stored and/or reproduced then it must confirm such pre-contract information in writing or, where appropriate, in some other durable medium. In addition a company/organisation must also provide customers with durable information[43] on:

- how to exercise the DSRs 2000 right to cancel, including how to return the goods following a cancellation – and who pays for their return,
- details of any guarantees or after-sales services,
- the geographical address of the company/organisation to which the consumer may address any complaints, and
- if a contract lasts for more than a year or is open-ended, the contractual conditions for cancelling it.

Finally, if a company/organisation intends to make a service non-cancellable once performance has commenced, then it must inform the consumer in advance of such performance commencing that performance will result in a loss of right to cancel.

### Written confirmation

When an order has been made the company/organisation selling the goods and/or services must send to the consumer confirmation of the prior information in writing or another durable medium, such as fax or e-mail, unless it has already been provided in writing (e.g. in a catalogue or advertisement). This should include information on:

- when and how the consumer can exercise the right to cancel,
- a postal address where they can contact the company/organisation, and
- details of any after-sales services and guarantees.

The company/organisation selling the goods and/or services must provide this confirmation at the latest by the time that they are delivered or, in the case of services, before or in good time during the performance of the contract.

If a company/organisation is providing a service with no specified end date or for a period of more than one year (e.g. a mobile phone, satellite or cable television or gas and electricity supply), it must also send details about when and how the consumer can terminate the contract.

### Cancellation periods

The DSRs 2000 require a company/organisation to inform customers before any contract is made, and then confirm in a durable medium that they can cancel their orders and get full refunds.

Consumers may change their minds and cancel their orders at any time from placing the order:

- for goods – seven working days from the day after either the customer received the goods or they received the written information, whichever is later, and
- for services – seven working days from the day after either the customer agreed to go ahead with the order or they received the written information, whichever is later.

If a company/organisation fails to provide consumers with written confirmation of all the required information, then the cancellation periods can be extended up to a maximum of three months and seven working days. If the missing information is provided during this time, then the cancellation period ends seven working days beginning with the day after the full written confirmation is received by the consumer.

Where a contract is cancelled, the consumer must ensure that reasonable care is taken of any goods received and 'restore' them to the company/organisation. This does not mean that they have to return them – unless the company/organisation selling the goods stipulates this in the contract – only that they make them available for the business to collect.

Section 14(3) of the DSRs 2000 provides that a company/organisation must refund the consumer's money as soon as possible and, at the latest, within 30 days of receiving the written notice of cancellation. Where a consumer returns goods at the expense of the supplying company/ organisation, the latter can – subject to the terms of the supply agreement – recover such costs.

If payment for the goods or services is under a related credit agreement, the consumer's cancellation notice also has the effect of cancelling the credit agreement.

The information and cancellation provisions do not apply to contracts for accommodation, transport, catering and leisure services, including outdoor sporting events, but only where the supplier agrees to provide these on a specific date or within a specific period.

In addition, the provisions do not apply to package travel, timeshare and contracts for the supply of food, drinks or other goods for everyday consumption supplied by 'regular roundsmen'.

Also the right to cancel does not apply to the following, unless agreed otherwise:

- personalised goods or goods made to a consumer's specification,
- goods that cannot, by their nature, be returned,
- perishable goods,
- unsealed/unopened audio or video recordings or computer software,[44]
- newspapers, periodicals or magazines,
- betting, gaming or lottery services,
- services that begin, by agreement, before the end of the cancellation period providing the supplier has informed the consumer before the conclusion of the contract, in writing or another durable medium, that they will not be able to cancel once performance of the services has begun with their agreement,
- goods or services the price of which is dependent on fluctuations in the financial market.

Where a customer wants to cancel an order, they must inform the business in writing or another durable medium, that they want to cancel. This includes by letter, fax or e-mail; a telephone call is insufficient. As soon as possible after the customer cancels, or within 30 days at the latest, the company/organisation must refund the customer's money, even if it has not yet collected the goods or had them returned to the business.

It is the customer's responsibility to take reasonable care of the goods.

If a company/organisation requires the customer to return the goods (e.g. at the end of a contract) it must make that clear in the contract and as part of the 'durable' information. If the customer fails to return the goods, the company/organisation can charge them with the direct costs of recovery.

If such details are not included in the agreement the company/organisation cannot charge anything and cannot require a consumer to pay the cost of returning substitute goods.

If the goods are faulty or do not comply with the contract, the company/organisation *must* pay for their return.

### Contract performance

A company/organisation must deliver goods or provide services within 30 days, beginning with the day after the consumer sent an order, unless it agrees otherwise with the consumer. If a company/organisation is unable to meet the deadline, it must inform the consumer before the deadline expires and, unless a revised date is agreed, the consumer must be refunded within a further period of 30 days.

The consumer cannot be obliged to agree to a revised date. If they do not want to agree a revised date, then the contract is cancelled and any money paid must be returned within 30 days.

If the company/organisation wishes to provide substitute goods or services, this must have been made clear in the prior information received by the consumer before entering the contract.

### Inertia selling

Although only indirectly relevant, the DSRs 2000 amended the Unsolicited Goods and Services Act 1971 and removed:

- any rights of a supplier in respect to the supply of unsolicited goods and services, and
- any obligations on the consumer in respect to the receipt of unsolicited goods and services.

As such, consumers can retain unsolicited goods or dispose of them as they wish. They are under no obligation to:

- keep them safe, or
- return them to the company/organisation from which they were received.

More importantly, s24(5) of the DSRs 2000 makes it an offence for the supplier of such goods and/or services to demand payment from consumers for unsolicited goods or services.

The complete text of the Consumer Protection (Distance Selling) Regulations 2000 is available at www.opsi.gov.uk/si/si2000/20002334.htm.

## The Electronic Communications Act 2000

The main purpose of the Electronic Communications Act 2000 (the 2000 Act) is to:

- regulate cryptographic service providers in the UK (Part 1, s1 to s6), and
- to clarify and confirm the legal status of electronic signatures (Part 2, s7 to s10),[45]

and is part of the legislative framework designed to support e-communications and e-commerce along with the Electronic Signatures Regulations 2002 and the Electronic Commerce (EC Directive) Regulations 2002 (see later in this chapter).

Whilst cryptography has been used by banks, financial institutions and government departments and agencies for many years, there can be little doubt that cryptography and the use of electronic signatures not only play a core role, but are an essential tool for electronic transactions.

Cryptography[46] encrypts documents or messages, and is a means of converting information from a normal, comprehensible format into an incomprehensible format, rendering it unreadable. It is a process designed to ensure secrecy and confidentiality in important communications[47] that can and indeed often are used as the basis of an electronic signature.

Electronic signature can mean either:

- a signature imputed to a document or a message by electronic means and designed to:
  - identify the person that appends the signature, and
  - indicate their agreement to the content of a document in the same way as a handwritten signature, or
- a cryptographic addition designed to add non-repudiation and message integrity features to a document and or message – often referred to as a digital signature.

Electronic signatures are used to confirm the authenticity and integrity of a document and/or message, with the owner of an electronic signature usually verified through the possession of a certificate provided by a cryptography service provider or, as they are commonly known, a trust service provider (see below).

### Cryptography service providers

Part 1 (s1 and s2) of the 2000 Act provided for the UK government to set up a voluntary approval scheme for the registration of companies and organisations providing cryptography support services[48] (such as electronic signature and confidentiality support services) to other companies and organisations, and the public. However, the UK government elected – in accordance with s3 of the 2000 Act – to delegate the approvals and monitoring function to an industry-led private sector scheme – the tScheme.[49] In addition, the Department of Trade and Industry has indicated that such a statutory scheme will only be introduced if an industry-led scheme fails.[50]

### Legal status of electronic signatures

Part 11 (s7) of the 2000 Act provides that in any legal proceedings:

- an electronic signature incorporated into, or logically associated with, a particular electronic communication or particular electronic data (s7(1)(a)), and
- the certification by any person of such a signature (s7(1)(b)),

shall each be admissible in evidence in relation to any question as to the authenticity of the communication or data, or as to the integrity of the communication or data.

That is electronic signatures, supporting certificates and the processes associated with the creation, issue and use of such signatures and certificates can be admitted as evidence in court – s7(3).

## The Electronic Signatures Regulations 2002

The UK Electronic Signature Regulations 2002 (the 2002 Regulations) impose a duty on the UK Secretary of State for Trade and Industry to:

- keep under review the carrying on of activities of certification service providers who are established in the UK and who issue qualified certificates to the public (s3(1)),
- to establish and maintain a register of certification service providers who are established in the UK and who issue qualified certificates to the public, (s3(2)), and
- record in the register the names and addresses of those certification service providers who are established in the UK and who issue qualified certificates to the public (s3(3)).

For the purposes of the regulations:

- a certificate is an electronic confirmation that an e-signature belongs to the named individual, that is an electronic attestation which links signature-verification data[51] to a person and confirms the identity of that person (s2), and
- a qualified certificate is a certificate which meets the requirements in Schedule 1 of the 2002 Regulations and is provided by a certification service provider who fulfils the requirements of Schedule 2.

Certification service providers who offer such certificates must ensure adherence to both the applicable standards for these certificates and those in respect of their own conduct.

Section 4 of the 2002 Regulations imposes a liability on certification service providers who issue or guarantee qualified certificates to the public for any losses suffered as a result of reasonably relying on such certificates, even though there is no proof of negligence unless the certification service provider in question proves they were not negligent. Furthermore, s5 of the 2002 Regulations imposes a duty on certification service providers to comply with specified data protection requirements – re the Data Protection Act 1998 – with any breach of duty of care potentially subject to a claim for damages, possible prosecution and, if successful, the imposition of a fine.

The Secretary of State is obliged to publicise any failure to meet the standards specified in Schedule 1 and Schedule 2 of the regulations (s3(5)).

## The Electronic Commerce (EC Directive) Regulations 2002

The Electronic Commerce (EC Directive) Regulations 2002 (the E-commerce Regulations) apply to companies/organisations that:

- undertake retail and distribution activities using a web-based facility and/or an e-mail facility,
- advertise the company's/organisation's goods and/or services using a web-based facility and/or an e-mail facility,
- provide, convey or store electronic content for use by other companies/organisations, and/or
- provide access to a communications network (e.g. a web hosting company/organisation or telecommunications provider).

### Purpose and scope

The E-commerce Regulations are primarily designed to:

- ensure the free movement of information society services, and
- encourage greater use of e-commerce,

and cover service providers[52] that provide either:

- paid-for services and information, or
- non-paid-for service and information (e.g. free search engines/research facilities).

Whilst the E-commerce Regulations apply to the provision of an information society service by a service provider established in the UK irrespective of whether that service is provided in the UK or in another member state (s4(1)), they specifically exempt the following fields/areas:

- taxation – s3(1)(a),
- information society services regulated by the Data Protection Act 1998 – s3(1)(b),
- information relating to agreements and practices regulated by competition law/cartel law[53] – s3(1)(c),
- activities of a public notary or equivalent professions – s3(1)(d)(i),
- activities relating to legal representation of a client in a court of law – s3(1)(d)(ii), and
- betting, gaming or lotteries – s3(1)(d)(iii).

### Main provisions

### Section 6

This section provides that a service provider must make available to the recipient of the service and any enforcement authority:[54]

- the name, registered address and details of the service provider (including company registration number and VAT registration number where appropriate),
- contact details of the service provider (including e-mail address),
- details of where the service provider is registered in a trade,
- the details of any relevant supervisory authority where the service provided is subject to an authorisation scheme, and
- where the service provider is a member of a regulated profession:
  - details of any professional body or similar institution with which the service provider is registered,
  - the service provider's professional title and where applicable professional registration number, and
  - details of the professional rules applicable to the service provider.

## Section 7

This section imposes a duty on a service provider to ensure that any commercial communications (including e-mails) which constitute or form part of an information society service:

- identify the communication as a commercial communication, (s7(a)),
- identify the person on whose behalf the commercial communication is made, (s7(b)),
- identify any promotional content/offer and the conditions which must be satisfied to qualify for the offer (s7(c)), and
- identify any promotional competition or game and ensure that conditions for participation are accessible and presented clearly and unambiguously (s7(d)).

## Section 8

This section imposes a duty on a service provider to ensure that any unsolicited commercial communication sent to prospective customers and/or clients are clearly and unambiguously identifiable.

## Section 9[55]

This section imposes a duty on a service provider to ensure that unless agreed[56] otherwise, where a contract is, or is to be, concluded by electronic means, the service provider must, prior to an order being placed by the recipient of a service, provide to that recipient in a clear, comprehensible and unambiguous manner the following information:

- the different technical steps required to conclude the contract (s9(1)(a)),
- whether or not the concluded contract will be filed by the service provider and whether it will be accessible (s9(1)(b)),
- the technical processes for identifying and correcting input errors prior to the placing of the order (s9(1)(c)), and
- the languages offered for the conclusion of the contract (s9(1)(d)).

Furthermore, unless agreed otherwise, a service provider must:

- indicate which relevant codes of conduct it subscribes to, and provide information on how such codes of conduct can be consulted electronically (s9(2)), and
- provide to the recipient – in a way that allows the recipient to store and reproduce them – terms and conditions applicable to the contract (s9(3)).

## Section 11[57]

This section imposes a requirement on a service provider to ensure that unless agreed otherwise, where the recipient of the service places their order through technological means, a service provider must:

- acknowledge receipt of the order to the recipient of the service without undue delay and by electronic means (s11(1)(a)), and
- make available to the recipient of the service appropriate, effective and accessible technical means allowing them to identify and correct input errors prior to the placing of the order (s11(1)(b)).

Furthermore:

- the order and the acknowledgement of receipt will be deemed to be received when the parties to whom they are addressed are able to access them (s11(2)(a)), and
- the acknowledgement of receipt may take the form of the provision of the service paid for where that service is an information society service (s11(2)(b)).

*Liability of the service provider*

## Section 13

This section provides that failure by a service provider to comply with the E-commerce Regulations could result in:

- a claim for damages, for breach of statutory duty,
- possible prosecution and, if successful,
- the imposition of a fine, and
- the imposition of an enforcement order.

There are however, three possible exemptions:

- when the service provider acts as a conduit,
- when the service provider provides a caching[58] service/facility,
- when the service provider provides a hosting service/facility.

## Section 17: Service provider acting as a conduit

Where an information society service is provided which consists of the transmission of information provided or the provision of access, s17 provides that the service provider will not be liable for damages or any criminal sanction as a result of that transmission/provision where it:

- did not initiate the transmission,
- did not select the receiver of the transmission, and
- did not select or modify the information contained in the transmission.

## Section 18: Service provider providing a caching service/facility

Where an information society service is provided which consists of the transmission of information provided or the provision of access, s18 provides that the service provider will not be liable for damages or any criminal sanction as a result of that transmission/provision where:

- information is the subject of automatic, intermediate and temporary storage,
- storage is for the sole purpose of making more efficient onward transmission of the information to other recipients of the service upon their request, and
- the service provider does not modify the information and:
  - complies with any conditions on access to the information,
  - complies with any rules regarding the updating of the information, specified in a manner widely recognised and used by industry, and
  - does not interfere with the lawful use of technology to obtain data on the use of the information.

## Section 19: Service provider providing a hosting service/facility

Where an information society service is provided which consists of the storage of information provided by a recipient of the service, s19 provides that the service provider will not be liable or subject to any criminal sanction as a result of that storage, where the service provider:

- does not have actual knowledge of unlawful activity or information,
- is not aware of facts or circumstances from which it would have been apparent that the activity or information was unlawful, and
- upon obtaining such knowledge or awareness, acts expeditiously to remove or disable access to the information.

In addition, the recipient of the service must not act under the authority or the control of the service provider.

The complete text of the Electronic Commerce (EC Directive) Regulations 2002 is available at www.opsi.gov.uk/si/si2002/20022013.htm.

## The Electronic Commerce (EC Directive) (Extension) (No. 2) Regulations 2003

Section 3(2) of the Electronic Commerce (EC Directive) Regulations 2002 provides that: 'these Regulations shall not apply in relation to any Act passed on or after the date these Regulations are made,' that is 30 July 2002.

The 2003 Regulations ensure the Electronic Commerce (EC Directive) Regulations 2002 apply to the legislation that was amended by the Copyright and Related Rights Regulations 2003.

The complete text of The Electronic Commerce (EC Directive) (Extension) (No. 2) Regulations 2003 is available at www.opsi.gov.uk/si/si2003/20032426.htm.

## The Privacy and Electronic Communications (EC Directive) Regulations 2003

The Privacy and Electronic Communications (EC Directive) Regulations 2003 (the 2003 Regulations) came into force on 11 December 2003 and superseded the Telecommunications (Data Protection and Privacy) Regulations 1999.[59]

The 2003 Regulations were designed to:

- promote uniformity among telecommunications networks and services, and
- guarantee the protection of personal data.[60]

In general, the 2003 Regulations cover issues relating to:

- the use of publicly available electronic communications services for direct marketing purposes, and
- the use of unsolicited direct marketing activities by:
  - fax (s19),
  - automated calling systems (s20),
  - telephone (s21),
  - electronic mail – or spam (s22), and
  - text, video and/or picture messaging.

The 2003 Regulations generally prohibit the distribution of unsolicited electronic commercial communication (e-mail) unless:

- the user/recipient has specifically 'opted in' – that is agreed to the communications (e.g. clicking on a website icon or requesting information by, say, e-mail), or
- there exists or existed a pre-existing customer relationship.[61]

They also cover issues relating to:

- the security of telecommunications services (s5),
- confidentiality of electronic communications (s6),
- the processing of electronic communications traffic data[62] (s7 and s8),
- the processing of electronic communications location data[63] (s14), and
- the use of cookie[64] type devices.

Briefly:

- traffic data can be defined as 'any data processed for the purpose of the conveyance of a communication on an electronic communications network and includes data relating to the routing, duration or time of the communication,' (s2(1)), and
- location data can be defined as 'any data processed in an electronic communications network indicating the geographical position of the terminal equipment of the user of a public communications service, including data relating to the latitude, longtitude or altitude of the terminal equipment, the direction of travel of the user, or the time the location information was recorded,' (s2(1)).

The 2003 Regulations provide that unless the user to whom the cookie (or other similar tracking device) is served is provided with:

- clear and comprehensive information about the purpose, the storage and access to such data/information being collected, and
- an opportunity to refuse the storage of, or access to, such data/information,

then the use of cookies or similar devices are specifically prohibited (s7 and s8).
In essence:

- users must be able to opt out of any disclosure of personal data/information,
- users must be advised who will be using the information,
- users must be informed to whom the information may be disclosed, and
- users must be advised of the usage of cookies and/or similar tracking devices.

### Failure to comply

If a company/organisation operates retail/distribution facility using an online presence, and it collects or stores information from prospective customers, clients and/or other users, then it *must* conform to the requirements of the above regulations. Failure to comply with the 2003 Regulations could result in:

- a claim for damages,
- possible prosecution and, if successful,
- the imposition of a fine, and
- the imposition of an enforcement order (issued by the UK Information Commissioner) compelling compliance.

## The Disability Discrimination Act 1995 and Code of Practice 2002

*The power of the web is in its universality. Access by everyone regardless of disability is an essential aspect,*[65] (Tim-Berners-Lee, Director W3C[66] and inventor of the web).

Currently (as at 2005)[67] it is estimated that there are:

- 610 million disabled people worldwide, of which 400 million disabled people live in the world's developing countries, and
- 39 million disabled people in Europe (compared to 49 million disabled people in the USA), of which 8.6 million disabled people[68] live in the UK.

In addition, it is estimated that disability affects between 10% and 20% of the population of every country in the world.

In the UK:

- the Disability Discrimination Act 1995 (DDA 1995) (as amended), and,
- the Disability Discrimination Act 1995 Code of Practice: Rights of Access to Goods, Facilities, Services and Premises (2002),

provide the broad legislative and regulatory framework in relation to disability issues and web-based e-commerce.

The DDA 1995, Part III, s19 provides that it is unlawful for a service provider,[69] including providers of 'access to, and use of information and communication services',[70] to discriminate against a disabled person:

- in refusing to provide, or deliberately not providing, to the disabled person any service[71] which it provides, or is prepared to provide, to members of the public (s19(1)(a)),
- in failing to comply with any duty imposed on it by s21 of the DDA 1995 in circumstances in which the effect of that failure is to make it impossible or unreasonably difficult for the disabled person to make use of any such service (s19(1)(b)),
- in the standard of service which the service provider provides to a disabled person or the manner in which service provider provides it to a disabled person (s19(1)(c)), or
- in the terms on which the service provider provides a service to a disabled person (s19(1)(d)).

A service provider discriminates against a disabled person if:

- for any reason which relates to the disabled person's disability, it treats a disabled person (due to their disability) less favourably than it treats or would treat other members of the public (s20(1)(a)), and cannot show that the treatment in question is justified (s20(1)(b), and/or
- it uses practices, policies or procedures which makes it impossible or unreasonably difficult for a disabled person to make use of a service which it provides or is prepared to provide to other members of the public, and fails to make reasonable adjustments or change to such practices, policies or procedures so that it no longer has that effect (s21(1)).

Such reasonable changes have been a legal obligation since October 1999 and although the DDA 1995 does not define 'reasonable', the Code of Practice: Rights of Access Goods, Facilities, Services and Premises (2002), s4.21, provides that reasonability[72] is dependent upon:

- the type of service provided,
- the nature of company/organisation providing the service,
- the resources available to the service provider, and
- the impact on the disabled person.

As of October 2004, the small company/organisation exemption was removed (as was the police and fire services exemption)[73] imposing a legal obligation on such companies/organisations to make all their services accessible to the disabled – including websites, intranet sites and extranet sites.

### Using a website – potential difficulties

For a disabled person, or more appropriately a disabled service user, there are of course many potential difficulties that could be encountered when using/accessing a website, all of which would depend on:

- the nature of the person's disability, and
- the severity of the person's disability.

For example:

- a person with a hearing disability may encounter difficulties where:
  - audio excerpts are used to provide instructions without appropriate text subtitling, and/or
  - video excerpts are used to provide information without appropriate text subtitling,
- a person with a sight disability may encounter difficulties where:
  - video excerpts are used without accompanying audio, and/or
  - non-contrasting text and background colours are used,
- a person with a physical disability may encounter difficulties where:
  - there is an over-reliance on a single navigation device – for example a pointing device such as a mouse, and/or
  - complex navigational commands require above average levels of dexterity, and
- a person with a mental disability may encounter difficulties where:
  - the language used is overly complex,
  - there is a lack of illustrative non-text-based content,
  - the website is relatively complicated to access,
  - the website is relatively complicated to use, and/or
  - the website uses excessive flashing, flickering or strobe effect designs.

For a service provider, a failure to comply with the provisions of the DDA 1995 and Code of Practice 2002 – for example a failure to make reasonable amendments to a website (without appropriate justification) when requested to do so, could result in:

- a claim for damages,
- possible prosecution and, if successful,
- the imposition of a fine and a court order compelling such reasonable amendments to be made.

It could also result in:

- substantial adverse publicity,
- a possible loss of customer goodwill, and
- a possible loss of business income.

Clearly then, compliance with the provisions of DDA 1995 and Code of Practice 2002 is not only morally correct, it is also economically and socio-politically expedient!

### Web Accessibility Initiative

The World Wide Web Consortium (W3C) was founded in October 1994 to oversee the development of the web. However, by 1997 the consortium had identified a core problem – as the web expanded so did the amount of inaccessible web content.[74] Pursuant to W3C's commitment to 'lead the web to its full potential . . . (including) the promoting of a high degree of usability for people with disabilities,' the Web Accessibility Initiative (WAI)[75] was launched in 1997 to 'work with organisations around the world to develop strategies, guidelines and resources to help make the web accessible to people with disabilities.'

The Web Accessibility Initiative (WAI) through its working groups[76] and in partnership with organisations from around the world[77] pursues its core objective of accessibility through five primary activities:

- ensuring that core technologies of the web support accessibility,
- developing guidelines for web content, user agents and authoring tools,
- facilitating development of evaluation and repair tools for accessibility,

- conducting education and outreach, and
- coordinating with research and development that can affect the future accessibility of the web.

## Web Content Accessibility Guidelines version 1.0 (WCAG 1.0)

In 1999 WAI published the Web Content Accessibility Guidelines version 1.0 (WCAG 1.0) a definitive set of international guidelines to be used for building accessible websites. The guidelines (WCAG 1.0) are available @ www.w3.org/TR/WCAG10/.

The guidelines comprise of 65 checkpoints categorised into three levels of priority assigned by the web content working group based on each checkpoint's impact on accessibility, and three levels of conformance, as follows:

- Conformance level A is a basic standard of accessibility. To achieve this standard company/organisation websites must comply with all of the priority 1 checkpoints.
- Conformance level AA is a medium level of accessibility. To achieve this standard, company/organisation websites must comply with all priority 1 and 2 checkpoints.
- Conformance level AAA is the highest standard of accessibility. To achieve this standard, company/organisation websites must comply with all priority 1, 2, and 3 checkpoints.

A complete list, in priority order, is available @ www.w3.org/TR/WCAG10/full-checklist.html.

Where a company and/or organisation claims conformance – at whatever level – such conformance *must* be indicated on the company/organisation webpage.[78]

## Web Content Accessibility Guidelines version 2 (WCAG 2.0)

WCAG 2.0 is currently a working draft. WCAG 2.0 addresses a wide range of accessibility issues and is comprised of 13 guidelines categorised under four principles of accessibility:

- perceivable – that is all content must be perceivable, for example providing text for non-text content,
- operable – that is interface elements in the content must be operable, for example access via a keyboard or keyboard interface,
- understandable – that is content and controls must be understandable, for example text should not be confusing or ambiguous, and
- robust – that is content must be robust and sufficiently adaptable to operate with current and future technologies, for example the content will work with old, new and potential future technology.

In additions WCAG 2.0 offers a number of recommendations for making web-based content more accessible.

The guidelines (WCAG 2.0) are available @ www.w3.org/TR/WCAG20/guidelines.html.

Conformance to the WCAG 2.0 working draft is based on three levels of success criteria – as assigned by the web content working group – with conformance defined as follows:

- conformance level A – to achieve this standard, company/organisation websites must meet all level 1 success criteria – assuming user agent[79] support for only the technologies in the chosen baseline,[80]
- conformance level AA – to achieve this standard a company/organisation websites must meet all level 1 and 2 success criteria – assuming user agent support for only the technologies in the chosen baseline, and
- conformance level AAA – to achieve this standard a company/organisation websites must meet all level 1, 2 and 3 success criteria – assuming user agent support for only the technologies in the chosen baseline.

## Concluding comments

Disregarding the many myths that continue to surround e-retailing and e-commerce (see Article 12.9) there is perhaps, as one would expect, a range of opinions regarding the costs, the consequences and the potential future impact of e-commerce on society.

## Article 12.9

### Top ten e-commerce myths

***You can advertise too much, apparently.***

Businesses are fooling themselves about how easy it is to shift to an online store, according to a new report.

The findings, by e-commerce company Digital River (www.digitalriver.com) uncover a number of myths surrounding the venture into e-commerce. These include the belief that a company is 'global' once it starts accepting credit cards and PayPal (www.paypal.com) and that e-commerce is 'something the IT department will handle'.

'Building an e-commerce site is not as simple as ABC,' said Digital River. 'By addressing these myths, companies will hopefully avoid landing themselves in hot water or losing unnecessary revenue.'

### The top 10 myths:

1. Building an e-commerce site enables businesses to trade with no complications.
2. The moment a businesses can accept credit cards and PayPal, it becomes global.
3. E-commerce will boost the finances of any business.
4. Customers will stumble on a company's site easily; there is no need to do additional marketing or merchandising.
5. Businesses cannot market products aggressively online if they sell their products through a reseller.
6. E-commerce is a project for the IT department and requires little outside input.
7. Aggressive marketing will create bad will with customers.
8. Ease of site navigation is not a major factor.
9. Potential customers will assume that a company's site is legitimate.
10. Companies cannot sell directly to the SMB market via websites.

The report also warned that, with an estimated £8.2bn spent online by UK shoppers in 2005, businesses had to be able to compete.

'Businesses with something to sell cannot afford to dismiss the potential boost to revenues offered by the internet,' said Digital River.

Source: 3 April 2006, Matt Chapman,
www.vnunet.com/vnunet/news/2153257/
top-myths-online-shops.

Whilst many of these opinions (perhaps unsurprisingly) reach very different conclusions on the social, political and economic costs and benefits associated with e-commerce and the emergence of the self-service economy, they all nonetheless agree that as a society – as an increasingly interrelated and interconnected global marketplace – we are, at the start of the 21st century, in the midst of an ongoing virtual revolution, a revolution whose final outcome has yet to be determined (or even invented).

Put simply, technologies – especially information and communication technologies associated with web-based activities – are (contrary to the naivety of popular belief) developed in a fragmented and often disjointed manner. Whilst we can speculate (perhaps with some degree of certainty) that future technologies will:

- improve internet security,
- increase user freedom and mobility,
- enhance internet usability and, hopefully,
- improve accessibility,

we have no way of knowing how such future technologies will impact on the demand for, and use of, e-commerce and m-commerce related services.

## Key points and concepts

Acquiring bank
Banking Co-ordination Directive
Business-to-Business (B2B) e-commerce
Business to Business to Consumer (B2B2C) e-commerce
Business-to-Consumer (B2C) e-commerce
Cipher
Code of Practice: Rights of Access Goods, Facilities, Services and Premises 2002
Consumer Protection (Distance Selling) Regulations 2000
Consumer to Business, (C2B) e-commerce
Consumer-to-Consumer (C2C) e-commerce
Customer-to-Business to Consumer (C2B2C) e-commerce
Data Protection Act 1998
Digital certificate
Disability Discrimination Act 1995
Dotbam company
Dotbam+ company
Dotcom company
E-commerce

Electronic Commerce (EC Directive) Regulations 2002
Electronic Communications Act 2000
Electronic Money (Miscellaneous Amendments) Regulations 2002
Electronic Signatures Regulations 2002
E-money
E-money Directive
Encryption
Financial Services and Markets Act 2000 (Regulated Activities) (Amendment) Order 2002
Financial Services Authority's Handbook of Rules and Guidance
Firewall
Internet merchant account
Intrusion detection system
M-commerce
Online shopping mall
Payment service provider
Privacy and Electronic Communications (EC Directive) Regulations 2003
Self-service economy
Shopping cart
Web accessibility initiative

## Bibliography

Consumer Protection (Distance Selling) Regulations 2000, HMSO, available @ www.hsmo.gov.uk.

Department of Trade and Industry (DTI) distance selling regulations summary available @ www.dti.gov.uk/ccp/topics/guide/distsell.htm.

Home Shopping Distance Selling Regulations (2004), Office of Fair Trading (OFT), available @ www.oft.gov.uk.

## Websites

Electronic payment information @ www.electronic-payments.co.uk.
Internet world statistics @ www.internetworldstats.com.
Virtual global task force @ www.virtualglobaltaskforce.com.

## Self-review questions

1. Explain what is commonly meant by the term 'self-service economy'?
2. What are the main factors that contribute to a good website design?
3. Distinguish between a dotcom company, a dotbam company and a dotbam+ company.
4. Describe and explain the three main component facilities of a Business-to-Business (B2B) e-commerce website.
5. Distinguish between a symmetric key algorithm and an asymmetric key algorithm.
6. Describe and briefly explain the main stages of a Business-to-Consumer (B2C) e-commerce transaction.
7. Distinguish between identified e-money and anonymous e-money, and briefly explain the main advantages and disadvantages of using e-money.
8. Distinguish between an active m-commerce service/application and a passive m-commerce service/application.
9. Briefly describe the main provisions of the UK Electronic (EC Directive) Regulations 2002.
10. Briefly describe the web accessibility initiative and distinguish between WCAG 1.0 and WCAG 2.0.

## Questions and problems

### Question 1

'Despite the rhetoric to the contrary, the internet-based "virtual shop" will never replace the traditional high street retail outlet.' Discuss.

### Question 2

Companies and organisations are increasingly using a range of alternative schemes/technologies to protect their information systems and e-commerce facilities.

Such schemes/technologies include the use of:

- system firewalls,
- intrusion detection systems,
- data/information encryption facilities,
- digital certificates, and/or
- authentication and authorisation software.

#### Required

Describe each of the above schemes/technologies and explain how each of them assists in protecting a company's/organisation's information systems and e-commerce facilities.

## Question 3

Whilst e-commerce-related activities have grown substantially over the past few years, in general, consumers are still unwilling and/or unable to accept the online self-service e-commerce business model.

*Required*

Explain why such a reluctance to accept the online self-service e-commerce business model continues to exist.

## Question 4

Retail companies/organisations increasingly use their websites for a range of activities other than e-commerce-based retail sales. Such activities include:

- product/service advertising activities,
- prospect generation activities, and
- customer support activities.

*Required*

Explain what is meant by each of the above activities, and the advantages and disadvantages of using a website for such activities.

## Question 5

'Although the benefits of e-commerce are undoubtedly significant, such benefits are not without social, political and economic cost/consequence.' Discuss.

# Assignments

## Question 1

BPL Ltd is a small local retail company. The company sells a branded clothing range for 18–30 year olds. During the last financial year (year ending 31 December 2005) the company had an annual turnover of £1.5m and an annual net profit of approximately £700,000.

The company has two retail outlets located in Manchester and Oxford, and employs five part-time sales assistants, one administrator and one manager.

Currently, sales are either over-the-counter sales at either retail location or mail-order sales from the company's annual catalogue. Over-the-counter sales can be for cash, credit/debit card payment or payment by cheque. Mail order sales can be for credit/debit card payment and/or cheque payment only. All mail-order sales are processed at the company's Manchester retail outlet. Last year 42% of the company's turnover was from mail order sales.

For credit/debit card-related sales, the company operates a chip and PIN-based ePOS.

All over-the-counter sales are processed by the sales assistants. All mail-order sales are recorded by the administrator.

At a recent management meeting the manager informed the administrator that he had appointed an external consultant to develop and design a web-based e-commerce facility to replace its catalogue-based mail order facility. The manager expected the new facility to be operational within the next two months.

*Required*

Critically evaluate the main advantages and disadvantages to the company of using a web-based e-commerce facility to replace its current mail order catalogue facility.

## Question 2

The business environment of the early 21st century continues to change with increased vigour. The growth of e-commerce and e-retailing, and the use of the internet for the movement of goods, services and information, has clearly promoted a greater interconnectivity. An interconnectivity that has not only opened up and created enormous business opportunities, but has also increased the exposure of UK businesses, in particular UK companies, to previously unknown levels of risks and security threats, the costs and consequences of which have been and indeed continue to be significant.

*Required*

With reference to e-commerce, select a company context type (see Chapter 6) and critically evaluate the type and nature of risk and security threats such a company faces and the control procedures and security strategy/measures that such a company might employ to protect itself against such risks and threats.

## Chapter endnotes

[1] This chapter is concerned primarily with distance selling web-based online transactions.

[2] Although it also encapsulates non-web-based activities – that is commercial activities undertaken over a private computer-based network connection, for example EPOS transactions using EFT. (See Chapter 5 for further details.)

[3] Some commentators have referred to this as the 'global e-revolution'.

[4] Information society services means 'any service normally provided for remuneration, at a distance, by electronic means and at the individual request of a recipient of services,' and includes a wide range of online activities including:

- online information services – for example newspapers, magazines, libraries, electronic databases, (re)search engines,
- e-commerce-related services,
- online consulting agencies – for example advertising/marketing services,
- online professional services – for example consulting services, translating services, designing services and IT-related services,
- online validation services – for example services relating to the certification of electronic signatures, user authentication and data/information recording,
- online services to consumers – for example interactive shopping services,
- online tourist information services, and
- online entertainment services – for example on-demand telecommunications services (videoconference, internet access, e-mail, newsgroups and discussion forum).

See: www.coe.int/T/E/Legal_affairs/Legal_co-operation/Information_Society_Services.

[5] See 'Information and Communication Technology Activity of UK Businesses 2004 (Amendment)' published February 2006, National Statistics, London. The publication is available @ http://www.statistics.gov.uk/downloads/theme_economy/ecommerce_report_2004.pdf.

[6] Such products/services would include for example:

- information and communication services,
- music,
- movies,
- software, and
- financial transactions.

[7] Perhaps unsurprisingly the provision of such products and services has become the largest and most profitable segment of e-commerce.

[8] Remember we are only concerned with e-commerce facilities which provide opportunities/facilities for the exchange of goods, services and resources.

[9] It would, of course, be feasible – albeit highly unlikely – for a dual channel company to operate without online facilities, that is with:

- physical 'real-world' retail outlets, and
- retail catalogues – for example mail order catalogues.

[10] The John Lewis Partnership is one of the UK's top 10 retail businesses with 27 John Lewis department stores and 173 Waitrose supermarkets, and is the country's largest worker co-ownership organisation in which all 63,000 permanent staff are partners in the business. See www.johnlewispartnership.co.uk.

[11] Argos Ltd, the UK's leading general merchandise retailer, is owned by GUS plc (originally Great Universal Stores plc) and part of the Argos Retail Group.

[12] *Quid pro quo* is a commonly used Latin phrase meaning 'something for something'.

[13] For example literature and images associated with terrorist activities, and/or child pornography.

[14] The Virtual Global Taskforce (VGT) was created in 2003 as a direct response to lessons learned from investigations into online child abuse around the world. It is an international alliance of law enforcement agencies working together to make the internet a safer place.

The mission of the Virtual Global Taskforce is:

- to make the internet a safer place;
- to identify, locate and help children at risk, and
- to hold perpetrators appropriately to account.

The Virtual Global Taskforce comprises:

- the Australian High Tech Crime Centre,
- the National Crime Squad for England and Wales,
- the Royal Canadian Mounted Police,
- the US Department of Homeland Security, and
- Interpol.

(For more information see www.virtualglobaltaskforce.com/aboutvgt/about.html.)

[15] See Chapter 4.

[16] See Chapter 6.

[17] Using RFID (Radio Frequency Identification) technology.

[18] In essence an e-money card/smart card looks and functions like a debit card, however the main difference is:

- the user does not need to have a bank account to use it, and
- losing an e-money card is equivalent to losing cash.

[19] Electronic means of payment that:

- can only be used to pay for an issuer's own goods/services, and
- are only accepted by the issuer in payment for such goods and service,

are not considered to be e-money schemes and are therefore not subject to FSA regulation.

[20] Note: Small e-money issuers that satisfy a number of strict criteria are not regulated by the FSA, but need to apply for an FSA certificate confirming that they meet the criteria. Such a certificate may be granted to a company/institution (other than a credit institution) with a UK-based head office if one of the following apply:

- the company/institution only issues e-money with a maximum storage of €150 on its e-money devices, *and* the company's/institution's total e-money liabilities will not exceed €5m, or
- the company's/institution's total liabilities with respect to its e-money scheme will not exceed €10m and the e-money issued by the firm is accepted as a means of payment only by other companies/institutions within the issuing company's/institution's group, or
- the e-money issued by the company/institution is accepted as a means of payment in the course of business by not more than 100 persons within a limited local area, all having a close financial/business relationship with the company/institution. (Such a company/institution is often referred to as a local e-money issuer.)

[21] See Article 9B of the Regulated Activities Order 2002.

[22] A Personal Digital Assistant is a hand-held computer device which manages personal information and can interact with other information and communication systems.

[23] Wireless Application Protocol (WAP) is an international standard for applications that use wireless communication – for example internet access from a mobile phone. WAP is now the protocol used by the majority of mobile internet sites, aka WAPsites. The Japanese I-MODE system is the other major wireless data/application protocol.

[24] Indeed, it was the idea that highly profitable m-commerce applications would be possible though the broadband mobile telephony provided by 3G mobile phone services which resulted in high licence fees (somewhat willingly) paid by mobile phone operators for 3G licences during 2000 and 2001.

[25] We are concerned only with legislative pronouncements/regulatory requirements of relevance to commerce-based companies/organisations and not with related legislative pronouncements/ regulatory requirements applicable to non-commerce-based companies/organisations, for example local/public authorities. Consequently, we will not consider, for example, the Freedom of Information Act 2000, details of which are available @ www.opsi.gov.uk/acts/acts2000/20000036.htm and the UK Information Commissioner @ www.informationcommissioner.gov.uk.

[26] Available @ www.hmso.gov.uk/acts/acts1998/19980029.htm.

[27] Available @ www.hmso.gov.uk/si/si2000/20002334.htm. In addition, the DTI Consumer Protection (Distance Selling) Regulations: Guide for Business is available @ www.dti.gov.uk/ccp/topics1/pdf1/bus_guide.pdf.

[28] Available @ www.hmso.gov.uk/acts/acts2000/20000007.htm.

[29] Available @ www.hmso.gov.uk/si/si2002/20020318.htm.

[30] Available @ www.legislation.hmso.gov.uk/si/si2002/20022013.htm. In addition the DTI Electronic Commerce (EC Directive) Regulations: Guide for Business is available @ www.dti.gov.uk/industry_files/pdf/businessguidance.pdf.

[31] Available @ www.opsi.gov.uk/si/si2003/20032426.htm.

[32] Available @ www.opsi.gov.uk/acts/acts1995/1995050.htm.

[33] Available @ www.drc-gb.org/open4all/law/Code%20of%20Practice.pdf.

[34] For further information – see the Information Commissioners' Data Protection Act 1998 Compliance Advice: Website FAQs, available @ www.informationcommissioner.gov.uk/cms/DocumentUploads/Website%20FAQ.pdf.

[35] A website user/visitor should be given the choice (that is to 'opt-in' or 'to opt-out') of how data/information is to be used – in particularly where the intention is to:

- use such data/information for direct marketing purposes, or
- share such data/information with other third parties.

[36] Cookies refer to information a web server stores on a user's computer when the user browses a particular website. See also note 64.

[37] The Consumer Protection (Distance Selling) Regulations (2000) are enforced by:

- the Office of Fair Trading,
- local authority trading standards departments in England, Scotland and Wales, and
- the Department of Trade and Industry.

These bodies are under a duty to consider any complaint received and have powers to apply to the courts for an injunction against any person, company and/or organisation considered responsible for a breach of the regulations.

[38] The Consumer Protection (Distance Selling) Regulations (2000) defines a distance contract as: 'any contract concerning goods and services concluded between a supplier and a customer under an organised distance sales or service provision scheme run by the supplier who for the purposes of the contract makes exclusive use of one or more means of distance communication up to and including the moment that the contract is concluded,' (s3).

[39] The regulations do not apply if a business does not normally sell to consumers in response to letters, phone calls, faxes or e-mails and/or does not operate an interactive shopping website.

[40] This exception does not apply to the growing market for home deliveries by supermarkets.

[41] For the purposes of the Distance Selling Regulations 2000 the term 'durable' medium includes e-mail, post and/or fax.

[42] Where a company/organisation uses 'cold calling' by telephone to sell to consumers, the caller (as a representative of the company/organisation) must clearly identify:

- the name of the company/organisation the caller represents,
- the address of the company/organisation the caller represents, and
- the commercial purpose of the call,

at the beginning of the conversation.

[43] Note – a business does not have to send its customers this durable information if they have already given it to them through a catalogue or advertisement.

[44] This includes CDs, video tapes and/or DVDs.

[45] Part 3 of the Act:

- Section 11 and s12 relate to telecommunications licences and are no longer in force. They have been replaced by Chapter 1, Part 2 of the Communications Act 2003.
- Sections 13 to 16 are supplemental sections concerning interpretation and commencement of the Act.

[46] Derived from Greek *kryptós* meaning hidden and *gráphein* meaning to write.

[47] For an interesting and entertaining historical review/exploration of cryptography and codes through the centuries see Singh, S. (2000) *The Code Book: The Secret History of Codes and Code-breaking*, Fourth Estate Ltd, London.

[48] Section 6 of the Act defines cryptography support services as: 'any service which is provided to the senders or recipients of electronic communications, or to those storing electronic data, and is designed to facilitate the use of cryptographic techniques for the purpose of:

- securing that such communications or data can be accessed, or can be put into an intelligible form, only by certain persons (s6(1)(a)), or
- securing that the authenticity or integrity of such communications or data is capable of being ascertained, (s6(1)(b)).

[49] The tScheme is a membership scheme for trust service providers designed to ensure minimum standards of approval and service. Further information is available @ www.tscheme.org/.

[50] See 'Achieving best practice in your business – Information Security: Guide to the Electronic Communications Act 2000' DTI available @ www.dti.gov.uk/bestpractice/assets/security/eca.pdf.

[51] Signature verification data means data which are used for the purpose of verifying an electronic signature – using a signature verification device.

[52] The Electronic Commerce (EC Directive) Regulations 2002 define a service provider as: 'any person providing an information society service' (s2(1)).

[53] The Electronic Commerce (EC Directive) Regulations 2002 define cartel law as: 'the law relating to agreements between undertakings, decisions by associations of undertakings, or concerted practices as relates to agreements to divide the market or fix prices' (s3(3)).

[54] The Electronic Commerce (EC Directive) Regulations 2002 define an enforcement authority as: 'any person who is authorised, whether by or under an enactment or otherwise, to take enforcement action' (s2(1)).

[55] The Electronic Commerce (EC Directive) Regulations 2002 (s9(4)) provides that the requirements of s9(1) and s9(2) do not apply to contracts concluded exclusively by exchange of e-mail or by equivalent individual communications.

[56] By parties who are not consumers.

[57] The Electronic Commerce (EC Directive) Regulations 2002 (s9(4)) provide that the requirements of s11(1) do not apply to contracts concluded exclusively by exchange of e-mail or by equivalent individual communications.

[58] A cache can be defined as: 'a local storage of remote data designed to reduce network transfers and therefore increase speed of download'.

[59] And also the Telecommunications (Data Protection and Privacy) (Amendment) Regulations 2003.

[60] The regulations specifically require that users of electronic communication be informed of the possible uses of personal data – in particular, the possible inclusion in publicly available directories.

[61] The Privacy and Electronic Communications (EC Directive) Regulations 2003 (s22) provide that three criteria must be satisfied, these being

- contact details must have been obtained in the course of business,
- the communication is regarding similar products and/or service, and
- the recipient can at any time – free of charge – refuse further communications.

[62] Traffic data means 'any data processed for the purpose of the conveyance of a communication on an electronic communications network and includes data relating to the routing, duration or time of the communication', the Privacy and Electronic Communications (EC Directive) Regulations 2003 (s2(1)).

[63] Location data means 'any data processed in an electronic communications network indicating the geographical position of the terminal equipment of the user of a public communications service, including data relating to the latitude, longtitude or altitude of the terminal equipment,

the direction of travel of the user or the time the location information was recorded', the Privacy and Electronic Communications (EC Directive) Regulations 2003 (s2(1)).

[64] The 'cookie' information (which can include a vast range of personal information) helps the web server track the user's activities and preferences.

[65] See: www.w3.org/WAI/.

[66] The World Wide Web Consortium (W3C) develops 'interoperable technologies (specifications, guidelines, software and tools) to lead the web to its full potential.' W3C is a forum for information, commerce, communication and collective understanding.

[67] Source: Employers Forum Disability Online Summary Report, available @ www.employers-forum.co.uk/www/pdf/DisabilityOnline.pdf.

[68] Aged 16 and over and self-declared as disabled.

[69] A person is 'a provider of services' if he or she is concerned with the provision in the UK of services to the public or to a section of the public (Discrimination Act 1995 (s19(2)(b)).

[70] Although the provision of web-based information services/facilities is not specifically cited in the Disability Discrimination Act 1995.

[71] The provision of services includes the provision of any goods or facilities (Disability Discrimination Act 1995 (s19(2)(a)). In addition, it is irrelevant whether a service is provided on payment or without payment (Disability Discrimination Act 1995 (s19(2)(c)).

[72] The Code of Practice: Rights of Access to Goods, Facilities, Services and Premises 2002 (s4.22) suggests the following as types of factors which may be taken into account when considering what is reasonable:

- whether taking any particular steps would be effective in overcoming the difficulty that disabled people face in accessing the services in question,
- the extent to which it is practicable for the service provider to take the steps,
- the financial and other costs of making the adjustment,
- the extent of any disruption which taking the steps would cause,
- the extent of the service provider's financial and other resources,
- the amount of any resources already spent on making adjustments, and
- the availability of financial or other assistance.

[73] The only organisation/service *still* specifically excluded from the provisions of the Disability Discrimination Act 1995 is the armed forces.

[74] See Dardailler, D. (1997) *Briefing package for project Web Accessibility Initiative (WAI)*, available @ www.w3.org/WAI/References/access-brief.html.

[75] See www.w3.org/WAI/.

[76] These working groups include:

- Authoring Tools Working Group (AUWG) – develops guidelines, techniques and supporting resources for web 'authoring tools' – which are software that create websites,
- Education and Outreach Working Group (EOWG) – develops awareness and training materials and education resources on web accessibility solutions,
- Evaluation Tools Working Group (ERT WG) – develops techniques and tools for evaluating accessibility of websites and for retrofitting websites to be more accessible,
- Protocols & Formats Working Group (PFWG) – reviews all W3C technologies for accessibility,
- Research and Development Interest Group (RDIG) – facilitates discussion and discovery of the accessibility aspects of research and development of future web technologies,
- User Agent Working Group (UAWG) – develops guidelines, techniques and supporting resources for web 'user agents' – which includes web browsers and media players accessibility, and

■ Web Content Working Group (WCAG WG) – develops guidelines, techniques and supporting resources for web 'content' – which is the information in a website, including text, images, forms and sounds.

[77] These include a wide range of public and private sector organsiations – for example companies, government agencies, education-based research organisations and many more.

[78] Indication of conformance can be presented in two alternative forms.

Form 1: Specify on each page claiming conformance:

■ the guidelines title: 'Web Content Accessibility Guidelines 1.0',
■ the guidelines URI: http://www.w3.org/TR/1999/WAI-WEBCONTENT,
■ the conformance level satisfied: 'A', 'Double-A' or 'Triple-A',
■ the scope covered by the claim (e.g. page, site or defined portion of a site).

An example of which would be: 'This page conforms to W3C's "Web Content Accessibility Guidelines 1.0", available at http://www.w3.org/TR/1999/WAI-WEBCONTENT, level Double-A'.

Form 2: Include on each page claiming conformance, 1 of 3 icons provided by W3C and linking the icon to the appropriate W3C explanation of the claim. Information about the WAI icons and instructions on how to insert them into a webpage is available @ www.w3.org/WAI/WCAG1-Conformance.html.

[79] A user agent is defined as 'any software that retrieves and renders web content for users'. Such software may include web browsers, media players, plug-ins and other program including assistive technologies – for example:

■ screen magnifiers,
■ screen readers,
■ voice recognition software,
■ alternative keyboards, and
■ alternative pointing devices.

See: www.w3.org/TR/WCAG20/appendixA.html.

[80] A baseline is defined as 'a set of technologies assumed to be supported by, and enabled in, user agents in order for web content to conform to these guidelines'. See www.w3.org/TR/WCAG20/appendixA.html.

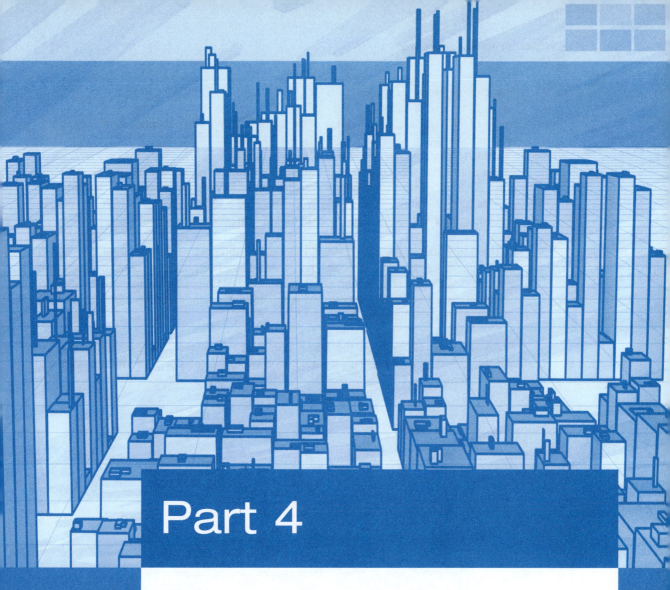

# Part 4

## Risk, security, surveillance and control

## Part overview

Part 4 of this book explores a range of issues associated with risk, security and control.

Chapter 13 explores the social and economic contexts of risk, and considers a range of issues associated with corporate accounting information systems related fraud and computer crime. Chapter 14 explores the socio-economic contexts of control – in particular internal control – and considers the implications of such internal control on information and communication technology enabled transaction processing systems.

Chapter 15 explores the underpinning rationale of audit, and considers the major issues and problems associated with auditing computer-based corporate accounting information systems. It also considers a number of alternative contemporary approaches to auditing computer-based corporate accounting information systems including auditing through, with and/or around the computer.

Finally, Chapter 16 explores the major stages of the systems development life cycle and explores the socio-political context of corporate accounting information systems development.

# 13 Risk and risk exposure:
## fraud management and computer crime

## Introduction

Risk can be defined in many ways. For example:

- the chance of bad consequence,
- an exposure to mischance,
- the probability of loss,
- the possibility of hazard and/or harm, or
- the uncertainty of present processes and/or future events.

Whatever way we seek to define or describe risk, assessing its implications and consequences has, in a business context[1] at least, become primarily associated with the determination and evaluation of outcomes – with the quantification of probabilities.[2] The probability that an event, or series of events, may occur that results in the emergence/expression of socially and economically harmful consequences – consequences that could have an undesirable impact on both the present and future stability and financial wellbeing of the company. Indeed, as suggested by Beck (1994), by quantifying unmanageable uncertainties we (including companies as created persons) can create manageable risks and in doing so make the 'incalculable calculable' (1994: 181),[3] and thus make the uncertain certain. Or at least provide a comforting (if perhaps misleading) perception of certainty that is bounded by a normalising assumption that all risks are not only discoverable, but more importantly measurable!

The contemporary notion of risk – in particular business risk – and its perceived emergence into the socio-economic consciousness of the marketplace is now closely related to the notion of *expected future return.* More importantly, perhaps, risk is indelibly associated with the nature and structure of market competition, and is accordingly, regarded by some as merely a generic product of the increasingly competitive demand-driven mechanism of capitalism – of global capitalism. Such risk – such expected risk – is an ever-present phenomenon of contemporary market-based capitalism and its inherent uncertainties – an ever-present and somewhat controversial phenomenon of increasing significance and consequence.

Clearly, in a corporate context, risk – whether it is social in origin, economic in nature and/or political in consequence – cannot be eliminated. It cannot be relegated to the division of *not-so-important irrelevancies*, nor can it be regarded as an ephemeral and inconsequential by-product of the contemporary marketplace, a merely irritating inconvenience.

So, what about corporate accounting information systems? There can be little doubt that information systems/information technology associated corporate activities – in particular corporate activities relating to and/or associated with corporate accounting information systems are neither impervious nor resistant to the potential ravages – the potential chaos and consequences risk (in all its possible manifestations) may manufacture.

Whether risk relates to:

- the likelihood of loss,
- the probability of mischance, and/or
- the possibility of hazard or harm,

it cannot be totally eliminated. Indeed, the significance and implications of risk (in particular exposure to socio-economic risk) cannot be diluted by the rhetoric of liberal economics, nor can its consequence be minimised by the merely acknowledging its being. The very existence of risk – the very existence of business/corporate risk – invites/requires explicit and unambiguous proactive management, the economisation of uncertainty[4] and the adoption (at least in a contemporary context) of the so-called *precautionary principle.*

We will return to, and indeed explore in greater detail, the nature and context of the so-called precautionary principle in the next section of this chapter, but for the moment it is worth noting that within a corporate context (and indeed an accounting information systems context) the incidence of risk can only be detected by the use of appropriate control features, such as:

- internal control procedures, and
- administration and management protocols,

whereas the occurrence of risk (and its associated consequences) can only be diminished by the establishment of appropriate control environments, such as:

- the timetabling of regular risk assessment,
- the development of structured control activities, and
- the regular and frequent monitoring of corporate activities – especially information systems/information technology-related corporate activities.

Clearly then, effective risk management (as guided by the so-called precautionary principle) relies on:

- identifying the nature and contexts of risk (risk identification),
- constructing an effective understanding of its origin and nature (risk assessment),
- developing an appreciation of its implications (risk evaluation), and
- designing effective strategies to manage its consequences (risk management).

This chapter considers:

- the alternative sources and types of risk a company may face,
- the issues and problems associated with minimising the degree of risk exposure,
- the problems and conditions affecting corporate exposure to risk, and
- the management of risk exposure and in particular risk issues associated with fraud, computer crime and computer viruses.

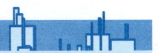

## Learning outcomes

This chapter presents an analysis of the key features of risk, risk exposure and fraud, and examines issues associated with fraud management and the risks associated with information systems and information technology – in particular computer crime. By the end of this chapter, the reader should be able to:

- describe the social and economic contexts of risk,
- distinguish between different types of sources and types of risk and then explain the control issues associated with minimising risk exposure,
- describe and critically comment on the problem conditions affecting exposure to risk, and
- evaluate the key issues associated with fraud and computer crime.

## Social and economic context of risk

As suggested earlier, risk is the chance or possibility of loss or bad consequence. It arises from a past, present and/or future hazard or group of hazards of which some uncertainty exists about possible consequences and/or effects. Put simply, whereas a hazard or group of hazards is a source of danger, risk is the likelihood of such a hazard or group of hazards developing actual adverse consequences/effects. In this context, uncertainty relates to the measure of variability in possible outcomes – the variability (whether expressed qualitatively or quantitatively) of the possible impact and consequence/effect of such hazards. Whilst such uncertainty can clearly arise as a result of a whole host of complex and often interrelated reasons, it does – in a corporate context at least – more often than not arise as a result of a lack of knowledge, a lack of information and/or a lack of understanding.

As with the never-ending variety that is symptomatic of modernity, there are many types of risk – many of which overlap in terms of definition and context. Have a look at the following definitions/examples of risk:

- social risk – the possibility that the intervention (whether socio-cultural, political and/or institutional) will create, fortify and/or reinforce inequity and promote social conflict,
- political risk – the possibility that changes in government policies will have an adverse and negative impact on the role and functioning of socio-economic institutions and arrangements,
- economic risk – the risk that events (both national and international) will impact on a country's business environment and adversely affect the profit and other goals of particular companies and other business-related enterprises,
- market risk – the risk of a decline in the price of a security due to general adverse market conditions (also called systematic (or systemic risk)), and
- financial risk – the possibility that a given investment or loan will fail to bring a return and may result in a loss of the original investment or loan, and
- business risk – the risk associated with the uncertainty of realising expected future returns of the business, (also known as unsystematic (or non-systemic) risk), and/or the uncertainty associated with the possible profit outcomes of a business venture.

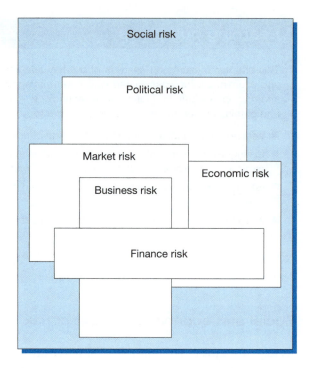

**Figure 13.1** Categorisations of risk

Clearly whilst there are many other definitions/examples of risk – many other categorisations of risk, especially within the context of socio-economic activities (see Figure 13.1) – they all possess a singular common feature.

Whatever way we seek to perceive or indeed conceptualise risk,[5] however we seek to define or describe it, at the core of any definition – any understanding of risk (including all of the above) – is the notion of uncertainty and the associated possibility of danger, hazard, harm and/or of loss. Harm and/or loss results from uncertain future events that may be social, cultural, economic, political, psychological and/or even physiological in origin.

Indeed, whether risk is viewed primarily in a qualitative context as:

- a social construction,[6]
- a product of reflexive modernisation,[7]
- a cultural[8] consequence of the growing economisation of society and polity, and/or
- a product of modern society's increasing interconnectivity but diminishing trust,[9]

or primarily in a quantitative context as:

- a quantifiable deviation from the norm,
- a statistical probability, or
- a calculable and determined measurement,

issues of uncertainty and of risk (from wherever they originate) now dominate contemporary understanding of corporate activity and its context and location within the macro economic framework of the so-called *global village*. Such issues not only influence and determine all forms, aspects and levels of corporate decision making, (especially, as we shall see, decisions related to corporate accounting information systems) but continue to be an authoritative influence on and pervasive (some would say insidious) feature of many (if not all) aspects of contemporary economy, society and polity.

Indeed, in today's evermore risk-averse world – a world bounded by the sociology of com-modification and constrained only by the politics of marketplace and economics of more social, economic and political activities are increasingly influenced by and indeed organised around a singular cautionary notion. A notion that it is better to be safe than sorry or, perhaps more appropriately, it is better to err on the side of caution.

Enshrined within this cautionary approach (some would say pessimistic approach) is an assumption of the worst case scenario. That is:

- when the outcomes of present or future actions and events are uncertain or unpredictable, and/or
- when information, knowledge or understanding is incomplete or uncertain,

such an approach provides that:

- where there are significant threats of serious or irreversible damage,
- where there are substantial uncertainties that could result in severe and permanent harm, and/or
- where critical hazards exist which could be potentially fatal,

a lack of certainty should not be used as a reason – as a justification – for postponing measures to prevent such damage and/or such harm.

It is this approach – this assumption of worst case scenario – that has in recent years become known as the *precautionary principle*. A principle whose origins are clearly linked to the German *vorsorgeprinzip*, or foresight principle, it is now increasingly used and is indeed widely embraced (both formally and informally) at various levels within society, economy and polity (that is not only at a societal/governmental level but also at a economic/market level), to deal with the various risks and uncertainties arising from:

- the imposition of new technologies,
- the development of new products, and
- the expansion and growth of new markets.

Primarily introduced to regulate and control hazardous environment-based activities, pre-vent environmental harm and control health-related issues/developments[10] the precautionary principle with its three variants – the weak form, the moderate form and the strong form (see Figure 13.2) – has subsequently been redesigned, repackaged, exported and indeed adopted into the decision-making processes surrounding a diverse range of socio-economic activities, none more so than corporate risk management – specifically information systems and information technology risk management.

In today's increasingly complex and uncertain world – for a corporate entity operating in a highly competitive and highly diversified environment, with a diversity of computer-based information systems technologies whose loss or failure could result in substantial damage (financial or otherwise) the adoption of the precautionary principle – the embracing of such a cautionary strategy – not only minimises risk, it also safeguards security and protects future stability. And, in the longer term (hopefully), it maximises shareholder wealth.

As indicated earlier, the precautionary principle operates at three levels. In a general corporate risk context, these three levels can be viewed as follows:[11]

- Weak form precaution (generic reactive intervention) – intervention only where there is general positive evidence of risk, the possibility for harm/damage and evidence that such

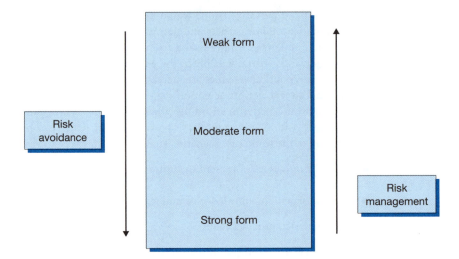

**Figure 13.2** Precautionary principle – variants

intervention would be effective and cost-efficient. The underlying presumption is one of risk management.

■ Moderate form precaution (specific reactive intervention) – intervention on a case by case basis where there is specific positive evidence of risk, the probability of harm/damage and evidence that such intervention would be effective and where possible cost-efficient. Again the underlying presumption is one of risk management.

■ Strong form precaution (proactive intervention) – intervention where a perceived risk of potential harm/damage exists and evidence that such intervention would be effective. Cost efficiency is not a concern. Because of the nature and severity of the risks, the underlying presumption is one of risk avoidance.

Whilst there is no widely accepted formal rule set (or criteria) by which the application of any of the above can be determined, in general and very informally, the potential application of each (separately or in combination) is often determined by:

■ the level of uncertainty in the consequences of the particular hazard, and
■ the level of uncertainty in the likelihood that the particular hazard will be realised.

See Figure 13.3.

That is the level of uncertainty and therefore the level of risk exposure associated with a particular hazard and/or group of hazards would not only determine the nature, the context and the focus of corporate precautionary activities, but more importantly the level of:

■ diagnostic monitoring,
■ remedial maintenance, and
■ preventative intervention,

that a company may engage in or undertake.

In other words, different corporate activities are subject/exposed to different hazards and threats, different risks, different uncertainties. As a consequence, for purposes of efficiency and the effective utilisation of corporate resources, such activities should be subject to different levels of precautionary activities (see Figure 13.4).

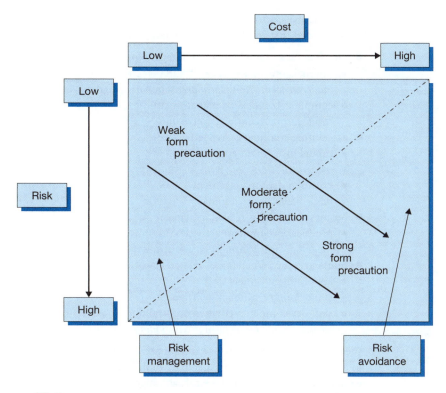

**Figure 13.3** Activities at each variant form of the precautionary principle (A)

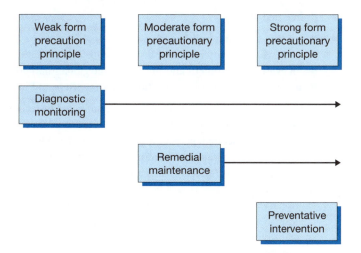

**Figure 13.4** Activities at each variant form of the precautionary principle (B)

Consider for example the following range of corporate activities (systems):

- information systems/information technology-related activities,
- accounting and finance-related activities,
- business/marketing-related activities,
- human resources/personnel-related activities.

Each of the above activities would contain a range of different but nonetheless risk-related activities (sub-systems) that would require different levels of precautionary management. For example:

- information systems/information technology-related activities:
  - internal control activities – fraud detection activities
    *moderate form/strong form precautionary activities*
  - computer-based virus management
    *strong form precautionary activities*
- accounting and finance-related activities:
  - capital investment appraisal
    *moderate form/strong form precautionary activities*
  - portfolio/debt management
    *moderate form precautionary activities*
- business/marketing-related activities:
  - product development activities
    *moderate form precautionary activities*
- human resources/personnel-related activities:
  - appointment of new staff
    *strong form precautionary activities*
  - staff development activities/staff training
    *weak form/moderate form precautionary activities.*

Clearly, whilst the precise nature and context of the precautionary activities differs from company to company and from business activity to business activity, the level of precautionary activities would nevertheless remain the same, although in a practical context such precautionary activities may well change over time.

Let's look at this issue in a little more detail. We live in an ever-changing world. A world dominated by:

- an ever-changing political landscape,
- an increasingly international flow of goods and services,
- an evermore turbulent and unpredictable global marketplace, and
- an increasing dependency on flows of knowledge and information.

Indeed, we live in an ever-changing world dominated by technologies designed not only to sustain but also increase the socio-economic need/desire for more of everything. A world founded on highly integrated interdependencies and interconnections in which even the smallest changes within a socio-political landscape, the economic marketplace or a company's resource structure may have a substantial impact/affect on the nature and source of risk, the type of risk and the degree of risk exposure a company may face. Such a change may well necessitate a change in the levels of precautionary activities associated with particular business activities undertaken by a company.

Now we have a broad socio-economic context of risk, we will focus on risk and risk exposure specifically associated with computer-based/information technology orientated information systems, in particular, corporate accounting information systems.

## Risk exposure

As suggested earlier, risk can be described in many ways, for example, as a hazard, a chance of bad consequence or exposure to mischance. And for a company, the measurability of such risk is directly related to the probability of loss.

Indeed, the very existence of uncertainty, unpredictability, randomness, change or a lack of knowing means that risk – the risk of loss – cannot be fully eliminated. It cannot be systemised or fully controlled: it can only be managed. It can only be minimised by the use of appropriate and adequate control features – precautionary features which are dependent on three key features:

- the nature and source of risk,
- the type of risk, and
- the degree of risk exposure.

Remember, we are now primarily concerned with risk exposure specifically associated with and/or related to computer-based/information technology orientated information systems – in particular, corporate accounting information systems.

## Source of risk

In an information systems context, in particular, a corporate accounting information systems context, we can distinguish between:

- two primary sources of risk, and
- four associated secondary sources of risk.

The primary sources of risk can be categorised (somewhat subjectively) as either:

- event/activity-based risk – that is risk associated with a particular event/activity and/or a group or series of events/activities, and a subsidiary primary source,
- resource/asset-based risk – that is risk associated with the possession and/or use of a resource/asset or group of resources/assets.

If you are not sure why we should consider resource/asset-based risk a subsidiary primary source then consider the following.

The foundation of all contemporary business activity – of contemporary capitalism – is movement. Capitalism is a *socially constructed event-based process*. That is all contemporary business activity is based ultimately on the buying and selling of goods and services, and/or the transfer of property and ownership in exchange for payment or promise of payment. Indeed, at the heart of any business transaction is an identifiable event and/or activity, one which ultimately results in the temporal and/or spatial displacement of assets and/or resources (the duality of which accountants record using the age old methodology of double-entry bookkeeping).

Associated with both of the above primary sources of risk are the following secondary sources of risk:

- authorised internal employee and/or external agent-based risk – for example risk of possible loss that may result from either unintentional mistake/oversight or premeditated, intentional or deliberate error, theft and/or acts of violence,
- unauthorised persons-based risk – for example risk of possible loss that may result, possible breaches of security and/or acts of violence resulting in the theft or misappropriation of assets, resources, information and/or identity, and
- (act of) nature-based risk – for example risk of possible loss that may result from geographical disaster, adverse meteorological conditions and/or created human catastrophes.

See Figure 13.5.

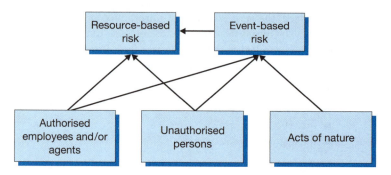

**Figure 13.5** Source of risk

## Types of risk

Clearly, as indicated above, within the secondary sources of risk identified above, there are many types of risk associated with computer-based/information technology orientated information systems, in particular corporate accounting information systems. Let's have a look at these in a little more detail:

- Unintentional errors – these relate to inadvertent mistakes and/or erroneous actions attributable to bad judgement, ignorance and/or inattention, and are neither deliberate nor malicious in intent.[12]
- Deliberate errors – conscious erroneousness and incorrectness whose occurrences are designed to damage, destroy and/or defraud a person, group of persons and/or organisation. Such errors are intentional and premeditated.
- Unintentional loss of assets – an undesigned loss whose incidence occurs without deliberate purpose or intent. Such (accidental) losses may occur due to bad judgement, ignorance and/or inattention.
- Theft of assets – the wrongful and criminal taking of property from another.
- Breaches of security – the successful defeat and/or violation of controls which could result in a penetration of a system and allow/facilitate unauthorised access to information, assets and/or system components whose misuse, disclosure and/or corruption could result in severe financial loss.
- Acts of violence – intentional, reckless and/or grossly negligent acts that would reasonably be expected to cause physical injury and/or death to another person, and/or cause the damage to and/or the destruction of valuable tangible/intangible assets.
- Natural disasters – events with catastrophic consequences whose origins lie beyond humankind and human activity. Such events can result in death, injury, damage and/or destruction to people and/or property and are dependent on many factors which themselves may not be natural in origin but created by human action/inaction.

### Degree of risk exposure

Clearly the degree of risk exposure is dependent on many factors, perhaps the most important being:

- the source and type of events/activities,
- the frequency of the events/activities,
- the vulnerability of the company to potential loss as a result of the events/activities, and
- the possible extent/size of the potential loss as a result of the events/activities.

So how can a company minimise risk exposure?

## Minimising risk exposure – ensuring information security

The need to identify security risks/threats and ensure the existence of adequate control procedures is paramount to:

- ensuring the effectiveness and efficiency of corporate operations, the continuity of business processes and the survival of the company,
- minimising unproductive time and effort, and reducing the cost of downtime and service outage,
- protecting the corporate brand name, the corporate image, any intellectual property rights and of course the company's market share and underlying share value, and
- ensuring compliance with applicable laws and regulations and avoiding any penalties and fines that may arise from a failure to comply with extant legislative requirements and regulatory pronouncements.

Consequently, minimising risk is indelibly associated with three aspects central to contemporary notions of information security, these being:

- the maintenance of confidentiality – that is protecting information from unauthorised disclosure,
- the preservation of integrity – that is protecting information from unauthorised modification, and
- the assurance of availability – that is protecting the availability of information.

Not only in a business context, but more importantly in a corporate context, maintaining confidentiality, preserving integrity and ensuring availability are dependent upon:

- establishing an appropriate control environment,
- undertaking regular risk assessment,
- developing and maintaining structured control activities,
- ensuring the existence of adequate information and communication systems and protocols,
- ensuring monitoring activities are regularly undertaken, and
- maintaining internal control and the separation of administrative functions.

Although we will consider issues of internal control and systems security in greater detail in Chapter 14, it would perhaps be useful to provide a brief review of the contemporary regulatory framework of information security management.

British Standard BS 7799 Part 1 provides a code of practice for information security management. Originally published in 1995 and revised in 1999, Part 1 became ISO/IEC 17799[13] in 2000, an international standard (code of practice) for information security management which provides, amongst other things, a comprehensive set of security controls/practices currently in use by businesses worldwide.

British Standard BS 7799 Part 2 (currently published as BS 7799-2:2002 Specification for Information on Security Management)[14] provides/defines a management framework for:

- the identification of security requirements, and
- the application of the best practice controls as defined in ISO/IEC 17799,

and specifies in some detail the key requirements of an Information Security Management System (ISMS).

Both of the above (ISO/IEC 17799 and BS 7799 Part 2) apply to all information regardless of where it is located, how is processed and/or how or where it is stored. They also outline a number of key principles[15] central to effective information security, these being:

- risk assessment – that is identifying and evaluating risks, and specifying appropriate security controls to minimise loss or damage associated with these risks,
- periodic review of security and controls – that is assessing and identifying any changes within the company/business activities that may result in new threats and vulnerabilities, and
- implementation of information security – that is designing, implementing, monitoring, reviewing and improving information security.

Annex A of BS 7799 identifies 10 relevant areas of control:

- the adoption/development of a security policy – to provide management direction and support for information security,
- the organisation of assets and resources – to assist in managing information security within the organisation,
- the classification and control of assets – to assist in identifying and appropriately protecting corporate assets,
- the provision of personnel security – to reduce the risk of human error, theft fraud and/or the misuse of corporate systems, networks and/or facilities,
- the existence of physical and environmental security – to prevent unauthorised access, damage and/or interference to or with business premises and information,
- appropriate communications and operations management – to ensure the correct and secure operation of information processing facilities,
- the installation of access control – to manage and control access to information,
- the existence of systems development and maintenance procedures – to ensure that security is built into information systems,
- appropriate business continuity management – to counteract interruptions to business activities and to protect critical business processes from the effects of major failures or disasters, and
- regulatory compliance – to avoid breaches of any criminal and civil law, statutory, regulatory or contractual obligations, and any security requirements.

Key to the effective implementation of the above principles is of course the development and implementation of an information policy – a corporate-wide information security policy. Although such a policy would clearly vary from business to business and company to company, in general such an information security policy should include most (if not all) of the following:

- a definition of the nature of 'corporate' information security – its scope, objectives and importance to the company,
- a statement of intent and an explanation of standards, procedures, requirements and objectives of the policy,
- a detailed explanation of the consequences of security policy violation and the legal, regulatory and possible contractual obligations for compliance,
- a definition of the general and specific roles and responsibilities, in terms of promoting security awareness and information security training and education, and ensuring the prevention and detection of viruses and other malicious software,
- a statement detailing the processes and procedures for reporting/responding to security incidents, and
- a statement detailing the location and availability of information security supporting documentation – for example corporate policy, operational procedures and implementation guidelines.

As indicated earlier, we will return to a more detailed discussion of internal control and systems security and the importance of information security in Chapter 14.

## Corporate accounting information systems – problem conditions and exposure to risk

As suggested earlier, there are many sources and types of risk and events/activities whose occurrences may result in the possibility of danger, hazard, harm and/or loss. In a corporate accounting information systems context, perhaps the most important problem conditions are:

- fraud, and
- computer crime (or more appropriately computer assisted crime).

## Fraud

Originating from the old French word *fraude* and the Latin *fraus* meaning deceit and/or injury, the word fraud is defined[16] as 'criminal deception, the use of false representation to gain unjust advantage', or 'a wrongful or criminal deception intended to result in financial or personal gain', or perhaps more appropriately 'the use of deception with the intention of obtaining an advantage, avoiding an obligation or causing loss to another party'.

Whilst there exists no single statutory offence of fraud in the UK, the Home Office (2004) provides examples of offences that would be classified as fraud (or fraudulent):

- false statements by company directors (Theft Act 1968 s19),
- fraudulent trading (Companies Act 1985 s458),
- false accounting and failure to keep proper accounting records (Theft Act 1968 s17 and Companies Act 1985 s221(5) and (6)),
- obtaining property by deception (Theft Act 1968 s15),
- obtaining services by deception (Theft Act 1968 s1),
- insider dealing (Criminal Justice Act 1993 s52),
- carrying on business with intent to defraud (Companies Act 1985 s458),
- unauthorised access to computer material (Computer Misuse Act 1990 s1),
- fraudulent misappropriation of funds (Proceeds of Crime Act 2002),
- evasion of liability by deception (Theft Act 1978 s3),
- conspiracy to commit cheque or credit card fraud (Theft Act 1987 s12),
- obtaining pecuniary advantage by cheque or credit card fraud (Criminal Justice Act 1987 s12), and
- misconduct in the course of winding up (Insolvency Act 1986).

The term 'fraud' clearly encompasses an array of irregularities and illegal acts which include:

- deception – providing intentionally misleading information to others,
- bribery – offering something (usually money) in order to gain an illicit advantage,
- forgery – the making or adapting objects or documents with the intention to deceive (fraud is the use of objects obtained through forgery),
- extortion – forcing a person to give up property in a thing through the use of violence, fear or under pretence of authority,
- corruption – the unlawful or improper use of influence, power and other means,
- theft (of assets and/or identity) – larceny or the act of taking something from someone unlawfully,

- conspiracy – undertaking secret agreement(s) to perform and/or carry out some harmful or illegal act,
- embezzlement – the fraudulent appropriation of funds or property entrusted to your care but actually owned by someone else,
- misappropriation – the illegal taking of property (includes embezzlement, theft and fraud),
- false representation – the fraudulent concealment of material facts, and
- collusion – agreeing (with others) to defraud another of property and/or rights, and/or obtain an object and/or property forbidden by law.

Whilst the more serious of the above illegal acts may be subject to possible Serious Fraud Office (SFO) investigation[17] such illegal acts can loosely be categorised as:

- an intentional perversion of truth, misrepresentation, concealment or omission of material fact perpetrated with the intention of deceiving another which causes detriment and/or injury to that person,
- a deceitful practice or device perpetrated with the intent of depriving another of property, and/or other rights, and/or
- a dishonest act designed to manipulate another person to give something of value.

They can be classified as follows:

- misrepresentation of facts and/or failure to disclose material facts,
- embezzlement – that is the misappropriation or misapplication of money or property entrusted to another's care, custody or control,
- larceny – that is the unlawful taking or carrying away of personal property with intent to deprive the owner,
- bribery – that is the practice of offering something (usually money) in order to gain an illicit advantage,
- illegal gratuity – that is an illegal reward to another in exchange for a service.
- forgery – that is the process of making or adapting objects or documents with the intention to deceive (fraud is the use of objects obtained through forgery),
- extortion – that is the forcing of another to give up property in a thing through the use of violence, fear and/or under the pretence of authority,
- corruption – that is the dishonest or partial behaviour on the part of a company official or employee.

Although there are many types of fraud, the following – although not exclusively restricted to technology-based issues – nevertheless rely heavily on remote communication (often via the internet) to further the aim of the fraud. Thus they are often referred to as computer *assisted* fraud rather that computer-*related* fraud.[18] See Article 13.1 on the growing level of computer *assisted* fraud.
Examples of computer assisted frauds would include:

- false billing,
- financial (funds) fraud,
- advanced fee frauds,
- identity theft, and
- phishing.

## False billing

These types of fraud are usually aimed at large corporate organisations with large, often automated, payments systems/sub-systems. They often involve an attempt to obtain funds/payments for goods and/or services that have never been provided.

## Article 13.1

### Online fraud hits record levels

**_Total amount stolen in the US last year estimated at $1.2bn._**

Nearly 10 million people suffered from some kind of online fraud last year, according to figures released today by Gartner at the RSA Conference in San Francisco.

The analyst firm's survey of US consumers estimated that fraudsters had hit 9.5 million people last year. The total amount was $1.2bn, the bulk of which was stolen by criminal gangs in eastern Europe and African states. 'You hear a lot of numbers but everyone agrees on that figure,' said Avivah Litan, research director of payments and fraud at Gartner. 'Banks do not move at lightning speed, but for the first time they are taking it seriously. They are losing money. They don't like to talk about it, but they are.'

Litan explained that, while levels of traditional fraud like stolen cheques had remained relatively constant, information theft was rising sharply. This was reflected in higher levels of fraudulent transfers of money from bank accounts.

The analyst praised the banking community for making credit card fraud much more difficult after monitoring unusual sales. But she stressed that more needed to be done to bring the same skills to the rest of the financial services sector.

These levels of fraud would drive investments in security technology, Litan added, which would include better authentication of users and a move away from passwords.

By 2007 she predicted that 75 per cent of US, and 70 per cent of worldwide, banks would no longer rely on passwords alone to protect online accounts.

Source: Iain Thomson, 16 February 2005,
RSA Conference in San Francisco, **www.vnunet.com**.

Many variants exist, including for example:

- frauds which attempt to obtain funds for placing an advert in a non-existent publication,
- frauds which attempt to sell space in a false and/or limited-distribution business directory, and
- frauds which attempt to gain payment for false invoices for non-existent goods and/or services.

### Financial (funds) fraud

These can range from:

- financial theft and the illegal transfer of funds from a company's bank accounts, to
- ATM-based frauds, to
- credit card/electronic fund-related crimes that normally involve obtaining goods/services for payment using stolen and/or illegally obtained financial information.

The most common types of financial (funds) frauds are:

- card-not-present frauds, and
- cash-back money transfer fraud.

### Advanced fee frauds

These often (but not exclusively) originate from parts of Africa. In particular, Nigeria is infamous as a source of this type of fraud. Indeed advanced fee frauds are often referred to as '419 schemes' after section 4:1:9 of the Nigerian government penal code.

The common characteristics of such advanced fee frauds are:

- a company receives a communication (e-mail, letter or fax) from a purported 'official' representative of a foreign government agency,

- the communication offers to transfer millions of pounds into the company's bank account (for a 'pay-off fee' which the company will receive on completion of the transfer) normally claiming that the funds are from over-invoiced projects or unaccounted excess funds from a previous political regime, or funds relating to property transfers/low-cost oil transfers, and

- the targeted company (or more appropriately victim company) is nearly always asked to provide blank company letter-headed paper, bank account details/information, confidential telephone/fax numbers, and sooner or later the payment of an up-front or advance fee payment to cover various taxes, legal costs, transaction costs and/or bribes.

A variation of such advance fee frauds is the dead relative variation or the current affairs/disaster variation. For example the December 2004 Tsunami disaster in South East Asia produced a plethora of fee fraud e-mails.

### Identity theft

Identity theft is the deliberate assumption of another's identity (either person and/or company), usually:

- to fraudulently obtain goods and/or services using that identity,
- to gain access to a source of finance and/or credit using that identity,
- to allocate/apportion guilt for a crime and/or fraud to that identity,
- to enable illegal immigration using that identity, and/or
- to facilitate terrorism, espionage, blackmail and/or extortion.

There are clearly many ways in which an identity can be assumed, from scouring local press/media to 'web spoofing' (setting up websites to elicit information as part of a seemingly legitimate transaction). See Article 13.2.

## Article 13.2

### Hackers pull off biggest ever credit card heist

*Security vulnerabilities allow theft of information on 40 million cards.*

Credit card provider MasterCard International has warned that hackers have stolen information for as many as 40 million cards.

The theft occurred at CardSystem Solutions, a third-party processor in Tuscon, Arizona, that handles payments on behalf of several credit card companies.

Hackers used security vulnerabilities in the company's systems to infiltrate its network and access customer data.

MasterCard's fraud-fighting tools pointed the card provider to the hack, and allowed it to trace the incident back to CardSystems Solutions.

The online security breach is almost certainly the largest ever case of identity theft, and is just another occurrence in a series of exposures of confidential information.

Last week CitiFinancial had to admit that several tapes holding information on 3.9 million customers were lost in transit to a credit bureau.

Other compromised companies this year included LexisNexis, ChoicePoint and the Polo Ralph Lauren retail stores.

Organisations in the US are obliged to disclose security breaches of customer information under local legislation including California's 2003 Security Breach Information Act and similar laws in Massachusetts.

The law forces hacked companies doing business in those states to reveal whether their security has been breached. They were previously allowed to keep quiet about such incidents.

Source: Tom Sanders, 20 June 2005, **www.vnunet.com**.

## Phishing

Phishing (and pharming) is the fraudulent acquisition, through deception, of sensitive personal information such as passwords and credit card/finance details by:

- masquerading as someone (either a person or company) with a legitimate need/requirement for such information, and/or
- using malicious/invasive software programs (e.g. a trojan horse – see later in this chapter) to obtain covertly confidential and highly sensitive information.

Phishing is in essence a form of social engineering attack – an attack designed to deceive users and/or managers/administrators at the target site or location. Historically such social engineering attacks were typically carried out through conventional telecommunication channels (e.g. telephoning users and/or operators and pretending to be an authorised user) to gain illicit access to systems. In terms of contemporary business activity however, in particular in terms of computer-based information systems and computer security, a social engineering attack can be defined as the practice of using information technology to deceive people into revealing sensitive information and/or data on a computer system, that is to gain personal and/or confidential information for the purposes of identity theft and/or funds fraud.

It is perhaps not surprising that the term is often associated with e-mail fraud in which an e-mail is sent to an end-user with the intent of acquiring personal and/or corporate information. It is perhaps worth noting that such phishing (and pharming) are no longer the sole domain of the external hacker/cracker – internal hackers/crackers (see Article 13.3) are increasingly regarded as a primary threat to corporate information security.

## Article 13.3

### Internal hackers pose the greatest threat – beware the enemy within

Internal hackers pose the greatest threat to the IT systems of the world's largest financial institutions, according to the 2005 Global Security Survey released today by the financial services industry practices of Deloitte Touche Tohmatsu.

Over a third of respondents admitted to having fallen victim to internal hack attacks during the past 12 months (up from 14 per cent in 2004) compared to 26 per cent from external sources (up from 23 per cent in 2004).

Instances of phishing and pharming, in which hackers lure people into disclosing sensitive information using bogus emails and websites, rocketed during the past year, underscoring the human factor as 'a new and growing weakness in the security chain'. The study noted that the shift in tactics to exploit humans, rather than technological loopholes, is explained by the improved use of IT security systems.

This includes the increased deployment of antivirus systems (98 per cent compared with 87 per cent in 2004), virtual private networks (79 per cent compared

with 75 per cent) and content filtering and monitoring (76 per cent compared with 60 per cent).

'Financial institutions have made great progress in deploying technological solutions to protect themselves from direct external threats,' said Adel Melek, a partner in the Canadian member firm of Deloitte Touche Tohmatsu.

'But the rise and increased sophistication of attacks that target customers, and internal attacks, indicate that there are new threats that have to be addressed. Strong customer authentication, training and increased awareness can play a significant role in narrowing this gap.' However, the survey results show that security training and awareness have yet to top the agenda of chief information security officers, as less than half of respondents have training and awareness initiatives scheduled for the next 12 months.

Training and awareness was at the bottom of the security initiatives list, far behind regulatory compliance (74 per cent) and reporting and measurement (61 per cent). The findings aligned with financial institutions' future investment plans in security, with 64 per cent of money set aside for security tools, compared with only 15 per cent for employee aware-ness and training.

Ted DeZabala, a principal in the security services group at Deloitte & Touche LLP, said: 'With threats such as identity theft, phishing and pharming on the rise, organisations should be implementing identity management solutions encompassing access, vulner-ability, patch and security event management. These solutions should be augmented by security training and awareness if organisations are to minimise the number of human behavioural threats. Clearly, con-tinued vigilance is needed to meet and exceed the requirements and truly protect corporate data from security threats.'

Source: Robert Jaques, 23 June 2005, **www.vnunet.com**.

## Fraud management – fighting fraud and minimising loss

There can be little doubt that the 21st century has seen an enormous increase in the number of frauds and illegal scams directed at both companies and individuals. Whilst the greater availability of information technology and the increased accessibility and use of the internet are often cited as the key reasons for this increase, such reasons clearly represent only part of the answer.

In recognising the increasingly complex threat posed by the use of improved technology by both national and international criminal elements in:

- modifying and adapting existing corporate frauds – that is supporting traditional crimes with the use of internet and information technology, crimes such as fraud, blackmail, extortion, identity theft and cyber-stalking, and
- developing, designing and executing new corporate frauds – that is using the internet and information technology not only to develop new crimes and further present new opportun-ities to both national and international criminal elements, but also challenge contemporary law enforcement – crimes such as hacking, viruse transmission, Denial of Service (DoS) attacks and spoof websites,[19]

the UK government – in April 2001 – created the National Hi-Tech Crime Unit (NHTCU)[20] to:

- combat national and trans-national serious and organised hi-tech crime which impacts upon and/or occurs within the UK,
- present sustained leadership and focus (nationally and internationally) in defining and dis-charging world class standards in the fight against organised crime,[21]
- provide a comprehensive database of information and advice on a range of technology-based frauds, and
- bring to justice and/or disrupt the activities of those involved in and/or responsible for serious and organised hi-tech crime.

There are perhaps a number of key practical steps a company can take to minimise the possible occurrence of fraud. Firstly, it could seek to identify potential reasons as to why it may/may not be susceptible to fraud. Possible reasons could for example include:

- a lack of internal control,
- a lack of internal audit,
- inadequate fraud risk management skills,

- poor data integrity and security,
- inappropriate authority levels,
- ineffective employee recruitment procedures, and/or
- a continuous and unrestricted abuse of separation of duties.

Secondly, undertake a company-wide risk assessment and establish a fraud management strategy group to:

- identify the key risk areas,
- assess the potential scale of risk,
- develop a (workable) fraud management protocol,
- allocate responsibilities to all management levels, and
- regularly monitor the effectiveness of corporate internal controls and fraud management protocols.

Finally, develop a fraud management control system, by:

- adopting and implementing a corporate code of conduct,
- implementing regular employment checks for potential and current employees
- ensuring the regular rotation of staff employed in risk areas,
- implementing appropriate internal control procedures,
- undertaking regular fraud audit,
- promoting regular ethics training to employees, and
- undertaking appropriate surveillance of employee activities.

In addition, on a more functional, computer-based transaction level, as part of a fraud management control system, a company may, where appropriate, also seek to:

- adopt an suitable level of cryptography to safeguard information,[22] and
- promote the use of electronic signatures for e-based transactions.[23]

The Electronic Communications Act 2000 (together with the Electronic Signatures Regulations 2002 and the Electronic Commerce (EC Directive) Regulations 2002) provides a regulatory framework for the use of cryptographic service and clarifies the legal status of electronic signatures.[24]

## Computer crime

Computer crime can be defined as a deliberate action to gain access to, and/or steal, damage or destroy, computer data without authorisation. It involves:

- the dishonest manipulation of computer programs and/or computer-based data,
- the fraudulent use/abuse of computer access and resources for personal gain, and/or
- the deceitful use of computer-based data/computer-based resources in the perpetration of fraud.

There are many reasons advanced by both academics and practitioners who seek to explain the exponential growth in computer crime over the past 10–15 years, perhaps the most common of these being:

- the increasing access to and concentration of contemporary computer processing in business (and in society),

- the increasing necessity for and use of highly integrated computer systems/networks in business and commerce, and
- the increasing dependency on computer-based decision-making processes in both personal and business/corporate activities.

See Article 13.4 below.

## Article 13.4

### Hacking and phishing soars in May (A)

*NHTCU figures put cost at £2.4bn in 2004.*

Computer crime cost UK businesses more than £2.4bn last year, according to figures from the National Hi-Tech Crime Unit (NHTCU). The organisation is warning firms to tighten their IT security after 89 per cent of UK businesses suffered from some form of computer crime in the past 12 months, an increase from 83 per cent last year (Computing, 26 February 2004 – available @ www.computing.co.uk).

Password stealing trojans, computer viruses and financial fraud are the greatest threats with organised crime syndicates looking to profit from insecure computer systems, says the National Opinion Polls survey, conducted for the NHTCU published this week. Some 83 per cent of the 200 firms interviewed for the NHTCU's Hi-Tech Crime: The Impact on UK Business 2005 report have been targeted by viruses, worms, trojans and keylogging software which steals financial data and passwords.

Some 15 per cent of companies have also had their corporate systems commandeered for criminal or illegitimate purposes, such as distributed denial of service attacks (DDoS). DDoS attacks which use thousands of compromised home and business computers to bring down corporate systems as part of a blackmail attempt also increased last year, affecting 13 per cent of businesses at a cost of more than £558m. Large and medium businesses, with over 1,000 employees, were hit hardest by computer crime gangs who cost them a minimum of £2.4bn, according to the report.

And businesses with less than 1,000 employees lost over £177m from hi-tech crimes. Financial services and telecoms firms were targeted the most, as criminals looked to steal customer databases, identities and sensitive passwords for financial gain. Malicious software, such as viruses, worms and trojans, caused the biggest losses for UK businesses, last year, creating more than £748m in damage. Financial fraud had the second biggest impact costing over £680m.

Source: Daniel Thomas, *Computing*, 05 April 2005,
**www.computing.co.uk**.

Nearly every UK business makes use of the internet, with 97% making regular use of the internet and 81% now possessing a website.[25] More importantly:

- 62% of UK businesses (for larger ones the figure was 87%) indicated that a security breach leading to substantial data corruption would cause significant business disruption, with
- 56% of UK businesses (for larger ones the figure was 74%) indicating that a loss of access to computer-based information would in itself significantly interrupt business activity.

And yet, in the UK, businesses (in particular corporate businesses), still only spend an average of 4.5% of their information technology budget on security, with only 40% of medium-sized UK businesses possessing a formally defined and documented information security policy. (For large UK businesses the figure was 73%.[26]

Clearly, the number of UK businesses that possess a security policy has continued to increase over the past 10 years, with virtually all UK businesses now implementing some form of anti-virus software. Nevertheless, as long as companies (or more importantly company managers) fail to recognise the importance of computer systems/networks as a fundamental/core wealth creating resource in contemporary corporate activity, and fail to invest in:

- better staff education,
- enhanced security protocols,
- improved security and protection procedures,
- better management control systems/security audits, and
- more effective contingency planning,

the army of potential threats that now exist within the socio-economic marketplace, ones ready to expose and indeed exploit any computer system/network security weakness, will only continue to grow – as will computer crime!

So, how common is computer crime? Here are some facts. For 2005:[27]

- 62% of UK businesses suffered a security breach (for larger UK businesses this figure was 87%),
- 29% of UK businesses suffered accidental systems failure and data corruption (for larger UK businesses this figure was 46%), and
- 52% of UK businesses suffered malicious incidents (for larger UK businesses this figure was 84%),

with the average cost to UK businesses of most serious security breaches being approximately £12,000. (For large UK businesses this figure was more than £90,000.) See Article 13.5.

Clearly then there can be little doubt that computer crime represents a contemporary and indeed continuing socio-economic problem not only for business and business organisations in general but for corporate organisations in particular. But who actually commits this so-called computer crime (including of course computer assisted fraud), and perhaps more importantly, why do they do it?

## Article 13.5

### Hacking and phishing soars in May (B)

**_Security firms cancel summer holiday plans._**

May saw a resurgence in the amount of viruses in circulation and the number of phishing attacks.

The latest monthly report from managed security vendor MessageLabs noted that virus attacks, and particularly Trojan attacks, increased by a third month on month, in part due to the Bagel virus.

Meanwhile phishing reached its highest level of all time, after declining since January. MessageLabs logged over nine million phishing attacks in May, over three times the number in April.

'As the financial stakes increase, criminals have become much more familiar with the use of IT in the commission of these types of fraud and criminal activities,' said Paul Wood, chief information security analyst at MessageLabs. He continues, 'Although any measure taken to update the law to address this trend is to be welcomed, the issue really needs to be tackled at source. Industry and government co-operation is essential to identify and shut down perpetrators, alongside a tighter legal framework and stronger enforcement powers. More specifically, ISPs should face up to their responsibility to protect their customers.'

Source: Iain Thomson, 21 June 2005, **www.vnunet.com**.

Whilst any demographic would clearly be an over-generalised and grossly simplified characterisation/depiction of those involved in computer crime – those committing computer crime (or at least those identified or found guilty of committing computer crime) often (but not always) tend to present one or more of the following characteristics:[28]

- they are often white Caucasian male, usually aged between 19–30 years old (computer crime) and 25–45 years old (fraud),
- they are often intelligent, generally well educated and like a challenge,
- they tend to be first-time offenders with what is often described as a modified Robin Hood syndrome,
- they identify with technology and are often employed in an information technology role and/or a financial/accounting role, and
- they generally feel exploited, underpaid and dissatisfied with their employer, but do not (generally) intend harm, seeing themselves as a borrower and not a thief.

The main reasons perpetrators of computer crime often offer as a defence for their actions/activities generally fall into one (or more) of the following areas:

- personal financial pressure,
- personal vices (drugs/gambling, etc.),
- personal lifestyle,
- personal grievances, due perhaps to increased stress/pressure relating to employment conditions, and/or
- personal vendetta against the business/company or one or more of its managers/owners.

There are many types and categorisations of computer crime of which the following are perhaps typical examples of contemporary computer crime (see Table 13.1 below):

- inappropriate use of corporate information technology,
- theft of computer hardware and/or software,
- unauthorised access and information theft,
- fraudulent modification of data/programs,
- sabotage of computing facilities, and
- premeditated virus infection and disruptive software.

**Table 13.1** Type of computer crime/security breach suffered by UK businesses in 2005

| Type of computer crime | All UK businesses (%) | Large UK businesses (250+ employees) (%) |
|---|---|---|
| Inappropriate use of corporate information systems | 21 | 32 |
| Theft of computer hardware | 8 | 45 |
| Unauthorised access and information theft, and/or the fraudulent modification of data/programmes | 17 | 44 |
| System failure | 29 | 45 |
| Premeditated virus infection and disruptive software | 43 | 35 |

Source: Information Security Breaches Survey 2006 Technical Report (April 2006), PricewaterhouseCoopers and Department of Trade and Industry, http://www.enisa.eu.int/doc/pdf/studies/dtiisbs2006.pdf.

## Inappropriate use of corporate information technology

Inappropriate use is not inadvertent (mis)use! By inadvertent we mean not on purpose or accidental and without intention. Inadvertent (mis)use of corporate information technology generally occurs as:

- a one-off/accidental event, and
- a consequence of a series of breaches of protocol and/or procedural controls which are not the responsibility of the person guilty of inadvertent (mis)use of corporate information technology facilities.

Such inadvertent (mis)use of corporate information technology facilities is often minor in consequence, and generally results in little or no loss of assets and/or resources.

Clearly, however, where such inadvertent (mis)use occurs repeatedly with increasing/escalating consequence, then it may indeed become inappropriate. So, what is inappropriate use?

Clearly such a term can cover a very wide range of activities ranging from:

- the use of corporate technology for personal reasons, for example:
  - employees shopping online during work hours, and/or
  - employees sending personal e-mails to internal and/or external individuals,
- the abuse of corporate information technology, for example:
  - the viewing, downloading and/or distribution of pornographic material, and/or
  - the viewing, downloading and/or distribution of racist material, to
- the misuse of corporate information technology for malicious criminal purposes, for example:
  - employees disclosing confidential corporate information, and/or
  - employees selling sensitive and confidential corporate information.

See Table 13.2.

The impact of such use, abuse and misuse of corporate information technology can have many consequences. Not only can external knowledge of such abuse and/or misuse be extremely embarrassing for the company, particularly where it is widespread, such activities can severely and, in some circumstances, irreparably damage a company's social/market reputation.

More importantly such activities could potentially result in:

- an increased risk of possible virus infection and/or the downloading of other invasive and potentially damaging software programs,

**Table 13.2** Type of inappropriate use of computer information technology suffered by UK businesses in 2005

| Type of inappropriate use of computer information technology | All UK businesses (%) | Large UK businesses (250+ employees) (%) |
|---|---|---|
| Misuse of web browsing facilities | 17 | 52 |
| Misuse of e-mail facilities | 11 | 43 |
| Unauthorised access to systems and/or data | 4 | 18 |
| Infringement of laws and/or regulations | 2 | 8 |

Source: Information Security Breaches Survey 2006 Technical Report (April 2006), PricewaterhouseCoopers and Department of Trade and Industry, http://www.enisa.eu.int/doc/pdf/studies/dtiisbs2006.pdf.

- a potential loss of revenue especially where such abuse and misuse of corporate information technology results in reduction in overall productivity
- a severe reduction and/or even loss of network bandwidth where significant inappropriate activities are occurring, and
- an increased risk of liability and legal action where such inappropriate activities result in, for example:
  - racial or sexual discrimination and harassment,
  - misuse of personal information in breach of the Data Protection Act 1998,
  - the propagation of libellous literature, and/or
  - the loss of goods, services and/or information.

Clearly, prevention is better than any cure. That is:

- the development of active employee screening and vetting procedures,
- the development of a clear policy/definition of what is and is not acceptable,
- the installation of an active and up-to-date virus defence,
- the use of e-mail content checking,[29] and
- the adoption of usage filtering and monitoring,[30]

can all assist in minimising inappropriate use. However, where inappropriate use of corporate information technology is detected, a corporate recovery strategy must be adopted – a strategy that would depend largely on a range of interconnected variables, for example:

- the nature and context of the inappropriate use,
- the period over which inappropriate use may have occurred,
- the extent to which potential losses may have been incurred,
- the degree (if any) to which the inappropriate use may have exposed the company to legal liability and, finally,
- the extent to which the inappropriate use may have been detected by and/or impacted on other (external) parties.

However, whilst the precise nature of the strategy may differ – the basic process would involve:

- qualifying the exact nature of the inappropriate use incident(s),
- establishing the potential threat posed to the company by the inappropriate use incident,
- assessing the impact of the inappropriate use incident and determining its extent,
- containing the impact of the inappropriate use incident, and
- adopting appropriate countermeasures, for example:
  - adopting software upgrades and/or installing software patches,
  - increasing network protection/security,
  - reviewing intrusion detection protocols and policies,
  - adjusting network server access,
  - review outsourcing agreements (as appropriate),
  - revising and/or negotiating liability clauses and warranties,
  - managing publicity issues and, where appropriate,
  - involving relevant external parties (e.g. the National High Tech Crime Unit (NHTCU)).

## Theft of computer hardware and software

There can be little doubt that where the opportunity rises due to negligent security controls and/or infrequent and ineffective security monitoring/surveillance – theft will occur. Not may occur or can occur, but *will* occur! Indeed, during 2005, 10% of UK businesses suffered from the physical theft of computer equipment (for larger UK businesses this figure was an astonishing 46%).

Clearly, the prevention of theft of computer hardware and/or software requires a commitment to security and investment in the provision of a wide range of measures and controls, which can be categorised as follows:

- preventative controls – that is controls designed to minimise and/or prevent opportunities for theft to occur,
- detective controls – that is controls designed to detect theft attempts, and
- recovery controls – that is controls designed to trace/track down stolen items and facilitate the recovery of such items and/or the possible prosecution of individual/individuals responsible for the theft/misappropriation.

Such controls would normally operate on three distinct hierarchical layers:

- physical security control layer,
- technical security control layer, and
- human security control layer.

### Physical security control layer
Physical controls can generally be divided into two types:

- physical controls designed to prevent/restrict resource access, and
- physical controls designed to prevent/restrict asset movement.

## Physical controls preventing/restricting resource access
The controls are generally designed to prevent/restrict access to a secure area/facility and invariably exist on a number of levels or at a number of different layers. For example, secure areas (such as those areas/buildings in which corporate computer facilities are located) may be monitored using CCTV cameras recording access to and from such secure areas. In addition, access may be restricted to authorised personnel only by the use of entry control facilities. Such entry controls could range from:

- the use of ID badges,
- the use of hardware/software tokens,
- the use of smart cards,
- the use of security passwords, to
- the use of personalised biometric measurements.

A combination of such entry controls may of course be used in concert – especially where the consequences of any theft or misappropriation of computer hardware/software may result in substantial financial distress. For example, primary perimeter controls may be used to restrict access to a secure area/facility, whereas secondary internal controls may be used to restrict movement/access within the secure area/facility.

## Physical controls preventing/restricting asset movement
The controls are generally designed to minimise the possibility of unauthorised misappropriation of assets, facilitate the traceability of stolen items of computer hardware/software and can range from:

- the security tagging of both computer hardware and software,
- the registration and regular audit of computer hardware, to
- the secure storage of software programs and applicable registration licences and security passwords.

Clearly, security tagging and, registration and audit are of major importance where computer assets are sited in remote locations (not necessarily networked), away from the company's main computing facilities: for example, where employees are geographically dispersed and use portable computing facilities as part of their daily activities/duties.

### Technical security control layer

Whereas physical security controls are designed to prevent/restrict resource access and asset movement, technical security controls are generally designed to restrict/control the user privileges.

There are of course a number of possible security controls available, of which the most common appear to be:

- the use of access controls to define profile user rights and prevent the unauthorised appropriation or accidental removal of software programs and data files, and
- the use of cryptographic facilities to encode sensitive software programs and data files, to restrict access and ensure the security and integrity of any such programs and files.

Technical security controls may also be used to monitor use and survey access by:

- the use of penetration testing[31] to evaluate the effectiveness of technical security of a computer system or network in protecting software programs and data files – often by simulating an attack by an unauthorised and malicious hacker/cracker, and
- the use of intrusion detection systems/programs designed to detect inappropriate use and/or unauthorised access. (These are discussed in greater detail below.)

### Human security control layer

People-based controls or, more appropriately, the human security control layer is within any business system – especially within a computer-based information system – and is perhaps the most important control feature.

No matter how virtual the commercial business process becomes, or how computerised business information systems become, or how fictitious payment methodologies become, at some point in the business process (however fleeting and/or insignificant it may appear to be), the physical world becomes an important and relevant feature and human interaction becomes inevitable. Indeed, whilst technologists would have us believe that humankind is now a redundant and less than activity participant in the contemporary business process, the human touch remains a key feature of the materiality that lies at the heart of contemporary capitalism.

So what do we mean by human security controls? Such controls can range from informal control in terms of promoting security consciousness and creating a control culture through awareness training, education programmes and in-house training, to the imposition of formal contractual obligations that enforce restrictions on the activities employees can undertake.

### Unauthorised access and information theft

As indicated earlier, the DTI Information Security Breaches Survey (2006) illustrates that 62% of UK businesses (87% of large UK businesses) had suffered a premeditated or malicious security breach. Perhaps, more importantly, nearly 22% of UK businesses report some form of probing attempt – that is an attempt to:

- probe, scan or test the vulnerability of a system, server or network and gain access to data, systems, servers or networks, and/or
- breach security or authentication measures and gain access to confidential information,

without the express authorisation of the owner of the system, the server and/or the network. See Table 13.3 below.

**Table 13.3** Type of unauthorised access attempts suffered by UK businesses in 2005

| Type of unauthorised access attempt | All UK businesses (%) | Large UK businesses (250+ employees) (%) |
|---|---|---|
| Attempts to probe the internet gateway or website | 13 | 30 |
| Unauthorised attempts to connect to wireless network | 3 | 5 |
| Actual penetration into the systems by an outside agent | 4 | 6 |
| Unauthorised disclosure or theft of confidential information | 2 | 8 |

Source: Information Security Breaches Survey 2006 Technical Report (April 2006),
PricewaterhouseCoopers and Department of Trade and Industry,
**http://www.enisa.eu.int/doc/pdf/studies/dtiisbs2006.pdf.**

The DTI Information Security Breaches Survey (2006) also found that:

■ 66% of UK businesses who had suffered an unauthorised access breach regarded the unauthorised access breach as very serious (compared with 34% who regarded the unauthorised access breach as serious), and
■ 16% of UK businesses who had suffered a confidentiality breach regarded the confidentiality breach as extremely serious (compared with 22% who regarded the confidentiality breach as very serious, and 49% who regarded the confidentiality breach as serious).

There can be little doubt that 21st century connectivity has clearly proved to be a vivid paradise not only for the world's hackers but also the world's crackers.

Originally, the term hacker was used to describe any amateur computer programmer seeking to make software programs run more efficiently and computer hardware perform more effectively. However, in a contemporary context, the term hacker is often used misleadingly (especially by the media) to describe a person who breaks into a computer system and/or network and destroys data, steals copyrighted software, and/or performs other destructive or illegal acts. That is a computer vandal.

This is perhaps unfortunate since such a definition is more appropriate for a person known as a cracker[32] – that is an individual who breaks (or cracks) the security of computer systems in order to access, steal or destroy sensitive information. In essence a cracker is a malicious hacker – and contrary to popular belief, the term cracker is not synonymous with the term hacker.

There are many reasons why an individual would attempt to breach a computer system/network security protocols to gain unauthorised access and the damage caused by such a breach could include, for example:

■ the theft of confidential and sensitive corporate information,
■ the theft of protected information,
■ the disruption of a corporate service and/or facilities (e.g. payment systems), and/or
■ the infestation of a computer system and/or network.

So, how exactly would a hacker/cracker gain access to a computer system? Look at Table 13.4, an edited version of McClure et al.'s (2005) *Anatomy of a Hack*.

There are of course a number of prevention strategies that a company can adopt in order to prevent and/or manage unauthorised access to a computer system/network and/or data, these being:

■ the development and adoption of a corporate defence protocol,
■ ensuring user vigilance,

**Table 13.4** Anatomy of a hack

| Objective | Methodology | Example technique |
| --- | --- | --- |
| Foot printing | Target source<br>Gather information essential for a surgical attack | Open source search |
| Scanning | Undertake a target assessment and identify the most promising avenues of entry | Ping sweep |
| Enumeration | Begin intrusive probing and identify valid user accounts | List user accounts<br>List file shares<br>Identify applications |
| Gaining Access | Once sufficient data collected make an informed attempt to access the target | Password eavesdropping<br>File grab |
| Escalating privileges | If target system access obtained, escalate user privileges | Password cracking |
| Pilfering | Gather system information and identify mechanisms/processes to gain/enable access to trusted systems | Evaluate trusts |
| Covering Tracks | Once target system ownership is obtained . . . hide | Clear logs<br>Hide tools |
| Creating a back door | Create trap doors to ensure privileges and access cannot be denied | Create rogue user accounts<br>Infect start up files<br>Plant remote control devices<br>Install monitoring mechanisms<br>Replace application file with Trojans |
| Denial of service | If access attempts to target system denied . . . seek to disable target system from future use | ICMP techniques<br>DDOS |

Source: McClure, S., Scambray, J. and Kutz, G. (2005) *Hacking exposed: Network Security, Secrets, and Solutions,* McGraw-Hill, San Francisco. Reproduced with permission of The McGraw-Hill Companies.

- the adoption of appropriate training and education and, perhaps most important of all,
- the use of information and communication technologies.

Let's look at this final issue in more detail. There are many security tools and computer-based technologies that can be used to manage access, control use and, where appropriate, prevent unauthorised entry. Such tools and technologies include:

- the use of system/network firewalls,
- the use of information and communication technologies,
- the use of data encryption facilities,
- the use of digital certificates,
- the use of authentication and authorisation software, and
- the use of scanners, patches and hotfixes.

Some of the above were briefly discussed in Chapter 12.

### *Firewall*

Often referred to as border protection device, as we saw in Chapter 12 a firewall is essentially a system gateway designed to prevent unauthorised access to or from either a personal computer and/or a private network. They are frequently used to prevent unauthorised internet users from accessing private networks connected to the internet, especially intranets. They can be in the form of:

- an hardware appliance and/or network device,
- a feature of another network device – for example a network router,
- a software package installed on a server/host system, and/or
- a combination of some or all of the above.

A firewall is designed to ensure that only approved network traffic of:

- an authorised nature and/or type, or
- from prescribed applications,

is allowed to move in and between a network or networks according to an approved security protocol thereby preventing unauthorised access and the possible risk of an security breach.

The basic task of a firewall is to control traffic between areas or regions of different levels of trust.[33] That is provide controlled connectivity through:

- the enforcement of a security/access policy, and
- an connectivity model based on the least privilege principle.[34]

and as such, can be used to:

- control and record network connection attempts and network traffic,
- authenticate users trying to make network connections,
- inspect network packets,
- monitor network connections,
- inspect application traffic, and
- protect internal networks.

There are essentially two access denial criteria used by firewalls, these being:

- to allow all traffic unless it meets certain criteria, or
- to deny all traffic unless it meets certain criteria.

The criteria used by a firewall to determine whether traffic should be allowed through it will depend on:

- the type of firewall,
- the concern of the firewall (e.g. to control/restrict access by traffic type, source address types or destination address type), and
- the network layer/operational location of the firewall – that is the layer within the OSI and TCP/IP network model.

Firewalls can broadly be classified into four categories, these being:

- a packet filter,
- a circuit level gateway,
- an application level gateway, and
- a multilayer inspection firewall.

## Packet filtering

A packet filter firewall operates at the network layer of the OSI model or the IP layer of TCP/IP, and is usually part of a router. In a packet filtering firewall each packet is compared to a set of criteria before it is forwarded. Depending on the packet and the criteria, the firewall can reject the packet, forward the packet or send a message to the packet originator. Rules can include source and destination IP address, source and destination port number and protocol used.

Packet filtering firewalls are a low-cost firewall option that tend to have a relatively low impact on the performance of the system/network on which they are used.

### Circuit level gateways

A circuit level gateway operates at the session layer of the OSI model or the TCP layer of TCP/IP, and monitors TCP handshaking between packets to determine whether a requested session is legitimate.

Whilst circuit level gateways are also a relatively inexpensive option they cannot be used to filter individual packets.

Packet filtering and circuit level gateways are often referred to as network layer firewalls.

### Application level gateway

Application level gateways – also referred to as proxies – are essentially application specific circuit level gateways that filter packets at the application layer of the OSI model. That is incoming and/or outgoing packets will be denied access to services for which there is no proxy. For example, an application level gateway configured as a web proxy will only allow web-based traffic through: all other traffic will be rejected. Because application level gateways can be used to filter application specific commands and can also be used to record log-ins and log user activity, they offer a high level of security, but can have a significant impact on system/network performance.

### Multilayer inspection firewalls

A multilayer inspection firewall generally combines aspects of each of the above types of firewalls, inasmuch as they:

- filter packets at the network layer,
- determine whether session packets are legitimate, and
- evaluate the contents of packets at the application layer.

Multilayer inspection firewalls are often referred to as a state-full firewall (as opposed to a stateless firewall)[35]. Because such a firewall can:

- monitor/track the state of a system/network connection, and
- distinguish between legitimate packets and illegitimate packets for different types of connections.

they can provide a high level of security and transparency. However such a firewall can be expensive and insecure if inappropriately managed.

### *Intrusion detection systems*

An Intrusion Detection System (IDS) acts as a system/network security service, its primary aim being to monitor and analyse system events for the purpose of detecting, identifying and providing real-time warning of attempts to access system/network resources in an unauthorised manner.[36] They can be used to:

- protect key internal network servers,
- identify internet-based attacks, and
- monitor network access points.

An example of an open source network intrusion and detection system is Snort – this combines signature-based, protocol-based and anomaly-based inspection methods.[37]

An intrusion detection system is composed of three key components, these being:

- a sensor(s) which monitors activity and generates security events,
- a console which monitors the security events and control the sensors, and
- an control device which records the security events recorded by the sensor(s) in a database and uses pre-established rules to generate alerts from security events received.

A system can be categorised by location, nature or type.

By location, intrusion detection systems can be categorised as either:

- network-based systems – where the intrusion detection system monitors traffic, identifies malicious packets and prevents network intrusion, and reports on suspicious and/or atypical activity, or
- host-based systems – where the intrusion detection system is installed on network servers to identify activity and anomalies and report on server specific problems or activity.

By nature, intrusion detection systems can be categorised as either:

- passive detection systems – where the system detects a potential security breach, logs the information and signals and alert, or
- reactive detection systems – where the system responds to the suspicious activity by either:
  - logging off a user to prevent further suspicious activity, or
  - reprogramming the firewall to block network traffic from the suspected malicious source.

By type, intrusion detection systems can be categorised as either:

- misuse detection systems – where the intrusion detection system analyses the information gathered and compares it to large database of attack signatures; that is the intrusion detection system monitors for specific known attacks which have already been documented, or
- anomaly detection systems – where the intrusion detection system uses a pre-defined baseline or normal state of a network's traffic load, breakdown, protocol and typical packet size, and monitors network segments to compare their state to the normal baseline to detect anomalies.

### Encryption

Cryptography[38] is the study of alternative means of converting data/information from a comprehensible format into an incomprehensible format, the aim being to render the data/information unreadable to anyone without a special knowledge of the conversion process. It is this conversion process that is known as encryption – a process designed not only to ensure secrecy but, in a contemporary context, ensure and maintain security, especially in the communication of confidential, sensitive and highly valuable data/information where it is important to be able to verify both the integrity and authenticity of a message.

In a contemporary context, there are two different types of encryption:

- symmetric key algorithm[39] (or secret key cryptography), and
- asymmetric key algorithm (or public key cryptography).

In a symmetric key algorithm (or secret key cryptography) both the sender of the message/communication and the receiver of the message/communication possess a shared secret key – the same shared secret key. The sender uses the secret key to decrypt the message/communication, whereas the receiver uses the secret key to decrypt the message/communication. Many of the early classical ciphers[40] used a symmetric key algorithm (or secret key cryptography), examples of which would include:

- a substitution cipher,[41]
- a transposition cipher,[42]
- a product cipher,[43]
- block cipher[44] and/or
- a stream cipher.[45]

In an asymmetric key algorithm (or public key cryptography) there are two separate keys:

- a public key which is published and available to the public and therefore enables any sender to encrypt a message/communication, and
- a private key which is kept secret by the receiver and enables only the receiver to decrypt the message/communication.

Common asymmetric algorithms include:

- RSA (Rivest-Shamir-Adleman) encryption, and
- elliptical curve cryptography.

Examples of the current uses of an asymmetric key algorithm (or public key cryptography) in e-commerce would include for example:

- Secure Sockets Layer (SSL) encryption, and
- Secure Electronic Transactions (SET) encryption.

### Digital certificates

Digital certification is a security technique that encrypts a digital certificate containing a unique key onto a client computer system/network.

A digital certificate is an electronic file that can be used as a means of identification and authentication. Such certificates are the digital equivalent of positive identification and are based on public key cryptography which, as we have seen, uses a pair of keys (private and public) for encryption and decryption.

In essence, the digital certificate contains 'the public key linked to the personal identification (ID) of the certificate holder,' (Slay and Koronios, 2006: 149). To be valid, such digital certificates require the digital signature and the endorsement of a certification authority, for example:

- Verisign Ltd @ www.verisign.co.uk, or
- Comodo Group @ www.comodogroup.com.

### Authentication and authorisation systems

Authentication can be defined as the process of proving an identity, for example of a user: that is determining who they are. Authorisation can be defined as the process of permitting or denying access to a system, resource and/or facility to an authenticated user: that is determining what they are allowed to do.

The are many alternative methods of authentication which can be categorised as:

- attribute-based – that is authentication based on something unique to the user, for example a biometric characteristic/identifier (DNA sequence/fingerprint/retinal scan) or biological trait (voice pattern recognition),
- possession-based – that is authentication based on something the user possesses, for example an identification card or a security token/card, and

■ knowledge-based – that is authentication based on something the user knows, for example a password, phrase or a Personal Identification Number (PIN).

Such authentication procedures/systems are increasingly used where it is important to control user access. For example authentication systems are commonly used for controlling ATM transactions and/or managing/controlling access to internet banking facilities, with many authentication systems often involving a combination of attribute/possession/knowledge-based authentication methods. See Article 13.6.

## Article 13.6

### Banks double up on security

*Two factor authentication is helping UK banks to cut online fraud*

Last week the UK's seventh largest bank, Alliance & Leicester, issued all of its one million online banking customers with extra security technology designed to stamp out internet phishing scams. The two-factor technology is the firm's response to banking-related online identity theft and fraud, which according to industry group Apacs, cost the UK £23.2m last year. The software identifies the customer's computer and assures them they are not entering a phishing website. While Alliance & Leicester is adopting its own form of two-way, two-factor customer authentication from vendor PassMark , other UK banks are taking a different approach, using physical devices to identify customers. Earlier this month, Lloyds TSB revealed that it has eliminated online banking fraud among some 23,500 customers who have been testing the key-ring sized devices over the past five months (*Computing*, 10 March). HSBC is also working on developing two-factor authentication technology for internet banking customers, which it will issue to customers later this year. It is already rolling out passcode generating devices from supplier Vasco in the Asia-Pacific region. 'The solution will provide extra protection against fraudulent activities such as phishing, keylogger trojans and remote hacking,' said an HSBC spokesman. The token devices generate a unique passcode for each user every 30 to 60 seconds.

Even if a criminal manages to intercept an online banker's user ID and password via keystroke logging software, spoof sites or phishing emails, they would not be able to access the bank account or transfer money. 'Fraud has adapted over time and spyware is more sophisticated. This is something we needed to tackle,' said Matthew Timms, director of internet banking at Lloyds TSB. 'Customers will use the device once to log in, and again to make transfers, standing orders or person-to-person payments.' But because many people in the UK hold several bank accounts with various financial services organisations, a proliferation of different physical authentication devices could become inconvenient or confusing.

For this reason Apacs has developed an industry standard device to authenticate online transactions, and card-not-present purchases made online or by telephone (*Computing*, 5 January 2006). Alliance & Leicester and Lloyds TSB say they will move to this form of authentication device when they feel the time is right. 'Tokens secure the transactions, but the Apacs industry standard covers a greater spectrum, including one-time, log-in passwords; card-not-present transactions; and person-to-person transfers,' said Timms. Martha Bennett, research director at analyst Forrester Research, agrees that a common approach within the banking industry will boost user acceptance. Lloyds TSB and Alliance & Leicester's existing investments will be transferable, she says. 'Lloyds TSB has chosen a back-end system that will work with the Apacs standard. The only non-reusable technology will be the tokens,' she said. 'And what Alliance & Leicester is doing is something that can be used in conjunction with it.'

But Bennett says rather than putting the responsibility on the customer to authenticate themselves, the bank should be investing more in back-end systems and transaction analysis databases to curb financial losses.

'In the US they will do almost anything to avoid using two-factor authentication, so they are adding more sophistication to back-end systems. Whereas in Europe financial services are taking the opposite

→

approach of strengthening the front door,' she said. By using software to analyse where a customer is physically logged-in and by identifying behavioural usage patterns, banks should be able to detect anomalies and spot criminals trying to access accounts from other countries, she says. Timms agrees: 'The Access Code Device is one part of our overall strategy; we are also doing a lot with transaction monitoring and that has already been very successful for us.' But online fraud is still less of a concern to the industry compared with the potential financial losses if worried internet customers switch back to more costly high-street and telephone banking services. So long as this concern remains prevalent, banks are likely to stay focused on high-profile, public-facing security projects, rather than just behind the scenes intelligence systems.

## Anti fraud . . . in 30 seconds

How does two-factor authentication work?

Banks are developing two-factor authentication technology to tackle identity theft and internet fraud. Although approaches vary from bank to bank, the technology relies on two things: something you know, such as a password or PIN, and something you have, such as a computer or token. Some 15 million Bank of America customers in the US authenticate themselves using the PassMark system adopted by Alliance & Leicester. In Brazil and the Asia-Pacific region, HSBC has been testing key-ring sized tokens that generate a unique code for users to enter when they log in. In Sweden, the government is working with the banking industry to develop BankID, a digital signature system to verify transactions. Thales' SafeSign technology is currently used by nine banks and more than 600,000 people. In the UK, three technologies are being explored: Alliance & Leicester is using the computer as the authenticator; Lloyds TSB is testing key-ring sized tokens; and industry group Apacs is developing a card reader. In Finland, Nordea Bank issues customers with sheets of paper containing one-off passcodes that consumers scratch off each time they log on.

Source: 23 March 2006, Daniel Thomas, *Computing*, www.computing.co.uk/computing/analysis/ 2152546/banks-double-security.

### Scanners, patches, and hotfixes

Scanners remain a popular type of virus/hacking defence software. Virus scanners (see also later in this chapter) are software programs designed to identify and eradicate 'known' viruses. They are simple to install and generally easy to use. However they require constant maintenance inasmuch as they need to be frequently updated (using approved patches and/or hotfixes) with the latest virus information in order to remain effective. A number of virus scanners exist, including:

- McAfee virus scanner @ http://us.mcafee.com,
- AVG anti virus scanner @ http://www.grisoft.com, and
- Symantec Anti Virus scanner @ http://www.symantecstore.com.

Vulnerability scanners are software programs designed to test for 'known' security defects. Because such scanners can only test for existing and 'known' faults – much like virus scanners – such vulnerability scanners require constant updating with the latest version. A number of vulnerability scanners exist, including:

- ISS (Internet Security Scanner) @ http://www.b2net.co.uk,
- Nessus @ http://www.nessus.org, and
- CyberCop @ http://www.cybercop.co.uk.

### The Computer Misuse Act 1990

The Computer Misuse Act 1990 provides for three distinct offences:

- unauthorised access to computer material,
- unauthorised modification of computer material, and
- unauthorised access with intent to commit or facilitate the commission of further offences.

Issues relating to the unauthorised modification of computer material and the unauthorised access with intent to commit or facilitate the commission of further offences will be discussed later.

In relation to unauthorised access to computerised material, s1 of the Act makes it an offence for any person and/or persons to cause a computer to perform any function with intent to secure unauthorised access to any program or data file held in a computer. That is the Act makes it a criminal offence to access a computing system/network unless authorised to do so. The Act clarifies the term 'unauthorised access' as including the altering, erasing, copying and/or moving of programs and/or data files to another storage medium other than that in which it is held (s17(2)).

Section 1 of the Act (and following the Computer Misuse Act 1990 (Amendment) Act 2005) makes the activity of hacking and/or cracking a criminal offence and a person found guilty of such an offence is liable:

- on summary conviction, to imprisonment for a term not exceeding six months or to a fine not exceeding the statutory maximum or to both, and
- on conviction on indictment, to imprisonment for a term not exceeding two years or to a fine or to both.

## Fraudulent modification of data/programs

In an information technology/information systems context, the fraudulent modification of data/programs means the dishonest and deceitful variation, alteration and/or adaptation of software programs and/or data files. Examples of such actions would include:

- the destruction of data files,
- the creation and/or introduction of a virus, and/or
- the deliberate generation of data/information to promote a computer system/network malfunction.

Section 3 of the Act makes it an offence for a person and/or group of persons to undertake the unauthorised modification of computer programs and/or computer-based data files that will:

- impair the operations of a computer system/network,
- prevent or hinder access to computer programs and/or data files, and
- impair the integrity of any computer programme and/or data file.

This offence also covers the introduction of harmful worms and viruses to a computer network/system.

Section 17(7) of the Act provides that a modification occurs if by the operation of any function of any program on a computer system/network

- any program or data file held in the computer system/network is altered or erased, or
- any program or data file in the computer system/network is added to.

In addition, s17(8) of the Act provides that a modification is unauthorised if the person and/or group of persons promoting the modification is:

- not entitled to determine whether the modification should be made, and/or
- does not possess the requisite consent/authority to undertake the modification

For s3 of the Act to apply there must be:

- intention to cause and/or promote modification, and
- knowledge and understanding that the intended modification was/is unauthorised.

In addition, any person and/or persons found guilty of an offence under s3 of the Act is, following the Computer Misuse Act 1990 (Amendment) Act 2005 liable:

- on summary conviction, to imprisonment for a term not exceeding six months or to a fine not exceeding the statutory maximum or to both, and
- on conviction on indictment, to imprisonment for a term not exceeding five years or to a fine or to both.

## Sabotage of computing facilities

In its broadest sense, the term sabotage means the wilful, malicious and/or deliberate destruction or damage of resources, assets and/or property to hinder the legal activities of a person, group of persons and/or organisation, and adversely affect the reputation and/or safety of a business and its employees.

In an information technology context or perhaps more appropriately in an information systems context, however, the term sabotage means the interference with computer processes by causing deliberate damage to a processing cycle and/or to computer equipment, (Audit Commission, 2001:3). That is any invasive, deliberate and/or malevolent act motivated by either revenge and/or malicious intent that results in:

- the loss and/or destruction of data files,
- the corruption/destruction of software programs,
- the theft /misappropriation of resources /assets, and/or
- the complete failure of a computer system/network.

The DTI Information Security Breaches Survey (2006) found that 5% of systems failures/data corruptions suffered by UK businesses were due to sabotage.

Clearly, sabotage (whether promoted by an employee, an ex-employee, and/or an external agent) can take many different forms, including:

- the damaging of key computer hardware,
- the damaging of network activity,
- the altering or deleting data files,
- the theft of computer hardware and/or software,
- the distribution of unauthorised and/or abusive and/or offensive literature, and
- the unauthorised disclosing of confidential information to competitors.

Whilst at a corporate level, the consequences of any invasive act of sabotage can be extremely damaging and financially costly, at an industry/market sector level detecting sabotage, collecting empirical evidence of its occurrence, and/or estimating with any degree of accuracy the frequency of such attacks against corporate computer-based information technology systems continues to be almost impossible. Why? Because many corporate victims choose not to disclose such events/occurrences:

- companies often see very little benefit for themselves (as the victim companies) inasmuch as the damage is done and the law is often unlikely to be able to undo the damage caused by the saboteur(s),
- companies often view the possible cost of collecting evidence and launching possible legal action against the saboteur(s) as prohibitive (although recently this is increasingly not the case), and

- companies often believe the potential adverse publicity surrounding the disclosure of such events/occurrences could have disastrous commercial consequences and harm the future prospects of the company.

Section 2 of the Computer Misuse Act 1990 makes it a criminal offence for any person and/or persons to gain unauthorised access to a computer system, network, program and/or data file held in a computer with the intention of:

- promoting a denial of service, and/or
- committing or facilitating the commission of further offences.

Any person, and/or persons found guilty of an offence under s2 of the Act is, following the Computer Misuse Act 1990 (Amendment) Act 2005, liable:

- on summary conviction, to imprisonment for a term not exceeding six months or to a fine not exceeding the statutory maximum or to both, and
- on conviction on indictment, to imprisonment for a term not exceeding two years or to a fine or to both.

## Premeditated virus infection and disruptive software

For our purposes we will categorise computer infections and disruptive software/programs into five main categories:

- viruses,
- worms,
- trojan horses,
- spyware, and
- addware.

Before we look at each of these in more detail, it is worthwhile noting that the DTI Information Security Breaches Survey (2006) found that:

- 72% of UK businesses (for larger UK businesses the figure was 83%) had received e-mails and/or data files containing a virus,
- 50% of UK businesses (for larger UK businesses the figure was 67%) had been infected by a virus, and
- 7% of UK businesses (for larger UK businesses the figure was 12%) had suffered a denial of service attack.

### Viruses

A computer virus is a computer program which invades, replicates and/or attaches itself to a program or data file. It is essentially a software program capable of unsolicited self-reproduction/self-replication that can disrupt, modify and/or corrupt data files and/or other program files without human assistance, causing substantial damage to a computer system. The two key aspects of a virus are self-execution and self-replication.

Although many types of viruses exist they can be categorised into perhaps six main (although by no means definitive) categories:

- A macro virus – these viruses normally attach themselves to features within standard computing applications to perform unexpected tasks, for example moving data and/or inserting text and numbers – recent examples include DMV, nuclear and word concept.
- A file virus/program virus – these viruses normally attach themselves to files and affect the operations of program files[46] which are stored in the

computer memory during execution. The virus becomes active in memory, making copies of itself and infecting files in the system memory – recent examples include Sunday and Cascade.

■ A boot sector virus – these virus infections normally lie dormant and become active when a particular system/computer operation is started – recent examples include form, disk killer, michelangelo and stone virus.

■ A multipartite virus – these are hybrid of program and boot viruses, which initially infect program files that when executed infect the boot record – recent examples include invader, flip and tequila.

■ A stealth virus – these viruses actively seek to conceal themselves from discovery or pro-actively defend themselves against attempts to analyse or remove them – recent examples include frodo, joshi, whale.

■ A polymorphic virus[47] – these alter their codes to avoid being detected by anti-virus pro-grams. Such viruses encrypt themselves differently every time they infect a system/network, making it harder to track and prevent them – recent example include stimulate, cascade, phoenix, evil, proud, virus 101.

### Worms

A worm is a virus-like program that is designed to replicate and spread throughout a computer system/network. Such programs usually hide within application-based files (e.g. Word documents/Excel files), and can:

■ delete and/or amend data,
■ migrate rapidly through a computer systems/network, and/or
■ incapacitate particular data files and software programs,

normally resulting in a significant drain on computer resources, memory availability and, where appropriate, network access.

Because this type of infection/infestation is self-propagating, worms can have a devastating impact on a computer system/network. See Article 13.7.

## Article 13.7

## MyDoom worm spreads as attack countdown begins

*Variant emerges, targets Microsoft.*

For a fourth consecutive day, Internet service providers and corporations were bogged down by a crush of infected e-mails.

Security experts said as many as one in three e-mails in circulation was triggered by MyDoom.A, making it the fastest spreading Internet contagion ever.

'We are seeing companies struggling with this as they cannot clear the viruses quickly enough,' said Graham Cluley, technology consultant for anti-virus and anti-spam firm Sophos Plc. 'This one will be with us for a while.'

Meanwhile, sleep-deprived security experts said they were largely powerless to stop the virus's coordinated digital attacks, timed to hit Websites for SCO on Sunday and Microsoft on Tuesday, security officials said.

'It's very difficult for anti-virus firms to react in these scenarios. We're always going to be on the back foot,' said Paul Wood, chief information analyst for British-based e-mail security firm MessageLabs.

## Machines turned into zombies

Since appearing this week, the MyDoom.A worm, also dubbed Novarg or Shimgapi, has infected computers across the globe by enticing users to open a file attachment that releases a program capable of taking over a victim's computer.

Once hit, the program scours the Web for more computers to infect. MyDoom.A is programmed to send spam e-mails to spread the infection further and marshal an army of infected machines to knock SCO's Website offline on Sunday.

On Wednesday, a second variant dubbed MyDoom.B, appeared. It spread less quickly, but carried a program timed to unleash attacks on SCO and Microsoft. Also, it prevented access to anti-virus sites where patches for the bug are available.

Computer security companies continued to warn people not to open any suspicious attachments in e-mail messages.

Since the worms often appear as error messages from 'Mail Administrators' and other official-looking addresses, many people inevitably open the attachment after finding minimal information in the message.

Computers running any of the latest versions of Microsoft's Windows operating system are at risk of being infected, although the worm doesn't exploit any flaws in Windows or software.

Instead, MyDoom is designed to entice the recipient of an e-mail to open an attachment with an .exe, .scr, .zip or .pif extension.

## In the firing line

The financial damage from the outbreak – from network slowdown to lost productivity – is difficult to measure, but is assumed to be billions of dollars, according to experts.

For the ordinary computer user, MyDoom's toll will be measured in bounced e-mails and an inability at times to enter your inbox as ISPs seek to filter out bogus traffic.

For Microsoft and SCO, their Websites are once again in the firing line.

SCO, a small Utah-based software maker suing International Business Machines Corp. over the use of code for the Linux operating system, has been the target of denial-of-service attacks in the past by apparent pro-Linux protesters.

Last year, Microsoft's site for software upgrades was permanently moved to a new Web address to avert a similar onslaught triggered by the Blaster worm.

SCO this week issued a $250,000 bounty for information leading to the arrests of the authors of MyDoom. In November, Microsoft offered two $250,000 rewards for tips leading to the arrest of the Blaster and SoBig virus writers.

Some security experts theorized that the MyDoom variants were written by the same individual or group, but had no solid clues on their whereabouts.

Source: CNN, 29 January 2004, **www.cnn.com**.

### Trojan horses

A trojan horse is a malicious program (often hidden and/or disguised), which when activated can result in the loss, damage, destruction and/or theft of data. Unlike a worm, (or indeed any other virus) a trojan horse cannot self-replicate. However, such relative impotence does not minimise the destructive impact a trojan horse can have on a computer system/network. Some common features/consequences of trojan horse program infection include:

- amending payments (changing payment values),
- initiating unauthorised payments (causing illicit payments to be activated),
- instigating network/system-wide configuration changes,
- distributing confidential security information to external third parties (e.g. user names and access passwords), and
- providing unauthorised access pathways to external third parties (usually known as backdoors and trapdoors).

See Article 13.8.

## Article 13.8

## UK infrastructure under Trojan attack

*Firewalls and antivirus software useless, warns UK security agency.*

The UK's key computer systems are being targeted by Trojan software apparently originating from the Far East, according to the National Infrastructure Security Coordination Centre (NISCC).

Both the UK government and private companies are being targeted, and an NISCC bulletin lists 76 Trojan programs that have been detected. The organisation claims that the IP addresses on the emails often come from the Far East.

'Trojan capabilities suggest that the covert gathering and transmitting of otherwise privileged information is a principal goal,' stated the bulletin. 'The attacks normally focus on individuals who have jobs working with commercially or economically sensitive data.'

The bulletin also warned that firewalls and antivirus software do not protect against the Trojans as they can be modified by security code to avoid signature traces.

'We see more than a dozen new pieces of malware capable of stealing highly valuable and sensitive information every day,' said Carole Theriault, security consultant at Sophos.

'Trojans which allow unauthorised remote access to a computer pose a serious risk to all businesses.' The malware gets onto systems via spam emails containing .exe, .chm, .rar or .zip files at target systems. The recipient is then tricked into opening the attachment and the code either logs keystrokes and send them to a third party or allows complete remote control of the infected PC. 'Because of the nature of the threat we only get to see a small part of what's there,' said Steve Withers, managing director at networking security company Radware. 'If you call up Barclays bank they're not going to tell you they got hacked. It's predominantly a government problem but it's something that affects us all at the end of the day.'

Source: Iain Thomson, 16 June 2005, **www.vnunet.com**.

Perhaps worthy of note here is the term 'logic bomb'. This term is derived from the malicious actions such a program can effect when triggered. A logic bomb is, in effect, a type of trojan horse, one which is placed within a computer system/network with the intention of it executing a predetermined set of actions when some triggering condition occurs. Such a triggering condition could be, for example:

- a change in the content of a file,
- the input of a particular data sequence,
- the execution of a particular computer program, or
- the input of a particular time and/or date.

Usually viruses/infections are often disguised as, and/or attached to, something else. For example:

- a software update/release,
- an e-mail and/or e-mail attachment, and/or
- an internet download.

Whilst the impact of any virus and/or infection can and will vary depending on its origin and nature, the consequences of any infestation can range from:

- mild system irritation – for example computer crashes, unauthorised movement of data and/or files, and/or overloaded network servers,

- temporary loss of data integrity – for example changing data fields and file content and/or the unauthorised release of data files,
- complete loss of computing resource – for example loss of systems partitions (organisation of disc space), to
- significant loss of corporate assets – for example theft of financial resources.

There are many ways a company/organisation can seek to minimise the potential risk of virus infection. These strategies include:

- promoting environment security and user vigilance, and
- adopting and using appropriate and up-to-date virus defence software and, where appropriate, software security patches and/or hotfixes.

It is also important for a company to possess a clear and definitive virus defence strategy detailing:

- the deployment of virus software,[48]
- procedures/mechanisms for updating virus defence software,[49]
- isolation procedures/policies if an infection event occurs,
- the post-event recovery procedures.

Whilst the above can represent a substantial cost, there can be little doubt that whatever the cost(s) incurred for virus prevention, such costs are in the long-term small compared to the possible costs and associated consequences of dealing with and recovering from a virus infection. They include costs relating to:

- the eradication of the virus and/or infection,
- the organisation of any clean-up operation, and
- the installation of procedures to ensure no potential re-infestation.

### Spyware

Spyware can be defined as any malicious software that covertly gathers user information through an internet connection without the user's knowledge and/or consent. It is similar to a trojan horse inasmuch as it is usually packaged as a hidden component of, for example:

- a downloaded freeware and/or shareware program,[50] and/or
- a downloaded peer-to-peer file.

Once downloaded and installed, such spyware can:

- monitor keystrokes,
- scan files on a computer hard drive,
- invade and/or monitor other software applications,
- install other spyware programs,
- read cookies,[51]
- use internet bandwidth and computer memory,
- monitor internet activity and change the user settings,
- amend web browser specifications, and
- transmit confidential information to a third party – information which could include for example:
  - information about e-mail addresses,
  - security usernames and passwords, and
  - credit card/debit card numbers.

So, can the existence of spyware be detected? Indirectly, yes! For example:

- the frequent malfunction of computer processes – including computer crashes,
- the occurrence of unauthorised changes to a web browser specifications,
- the appearance of extra toolbar facilities,
- the frequent appearance of pop-up advertisements – usually adult-related, and
- the failure of established internet links (hyperlinks),

all suggest (although not conclusively) the existence of a spyware.

Anti-spyware software is now crucial to maintaining the security of a system/computer network. It searches for evidence of spyware within a computer/computer network and deletes any spyware detected. A wide range of anti-spyware software is now available, for example:

- Windows anti-spyware – available @ www.microsoft.com/athome/security/spyware/software/default.mspx, and
- Spybot: search and destroy – available @ http://www.safer-networking.org/en/download.

### Adware

Adware (or **ad**vertising-supported soft**ware**) is a software program which automatically plays, displays or downloads pop-up advertising material to a computer/computer system.

There are essentially two types of adware:

- passive adware – that is adware attached to a legitimate software program, the purpose being to promote and advertise other legitimate software programs and/or related products, and
- active adware – that is adware which takes the form of either:
  - spyware which tracks user activity, often without consent, or
  - malware which interferes with the function of other software applications.

As with spyware, the solution is to use anti-adware software, for example Ad-Aware SE available @ www.lavasoft.de/ms/index.htm.

### Concluding comments

There can be little doubt that as businesses (in particular corporate businesses) seek to employ a growing arsenal of computer-based technologies in the name of corporate efficiency and the never-ending search for greater profitability and increased competitive advantage, the potential risk of fraud (especially computer assisted fraud), and the threat of computer crime in terms of:

- the increasing incidence of security breaches, virus infections and disruptive software,
- the growing occurrences of information systems misuse,
- the increasing frequency of unauthorised access attempts,
- the growing incidence of theft and fraud involving computer systems/networks, and
- the increasing levels of systems/network failure/data corruption,

remain both a growing and ever-present danger, whose consequence can range from:

- minor business disruption and damage to business reputation, to
- substantial data corruption, major loss of business capabilities and significant direct financial loss.

See for example Article 13.9.

## Article 13.9

### Tesco's call centre staff sacked for massive online fraud

Fourteen staff at Tesco's main UK call centre in Dundee have been sacked or suspended after auditors uncovered a massive fraud involving false discount vouchers used to buy groceries, alcohol, cigarettes and DVDs over the internet. Last week investigators removed computers to search hard drives in a bid to discover the true extent of the fraud, which is believed to run well into six figures.

Instead of answering calls from customers, crooked employees spent hours on the office internet purchasing thousands of pounds worth of groceries, drink, cigarettes and DVDs for pennies by inputting codes for VIP discount vouchers into online orders – which were then delivered to their home by Tesco deliverymen.

Some internet shopping bills were slashed from £200 to just £10 and it is understood that a manager at one of the large Dundee Tesco superstores has been suspended for not spotting the transactions.

One woman involved is said to have defrauded more than her £13,000-a year salary. Another is understood to have offered to repay the value of the goods stolen.

According to the company, four workers have been sacked and ten have been suspended pending disciplinary action following the discovery of fraud by auditors.

Source: Kurt Bayer, 27 February 2006,
**http://business.scotsman.com**.

Perhaps there is no single solution – no single correct strategy – but merely a series of alternative (some would say commonsense) practices and procedures that can be adopted to protect and secure assets, resources and technologies from abuse and/or misuse.

Clearly, the ever-changing technology demands of the business environment/marketplace requires/demands:

■ an increasing understanding of technology and technology management but, more importantly,
■ a greater awareness of the importance of security and of course willingness to invest in system/network security.

Implicit in each of the above requirements is the need for businesses, and in particular companies, to ensure that:

■ adequate employee training regarding fraud and computer crime is available/undertaken,
■ appropriate updated anti-virus software and other hardware and/or software protection technologies are used,
■ appropriate write/protect procedures and protocols are adopted,
■ data/file back-ups of all essential data and programs are maintained,
■ access to computer systems/networks is appropriately monitored and controlled, and
■ Common sense is applied.

Even the most elaborate frauds/business scams have been revealed by nothing more than employee intuition and basic common sense. See Article 13.10.

## Article 13.10

# Sharp eyes of Laura Ashley captured massive fraud gang

A highly sophisticated multimillion-pound fraud ring that operated throughout Britain has been smashed by a Laura Ashley shopworker. The woman store manager's suspicions about an Algerian customer led to a huge police operation that found scores of fake bank accounts and £1.5 million of stolen property. Louise Large, who works in Stratford-upon-Avon, became suspicious about the man's behaviour as he tried to get a refund for an £80 Laura Ashley floral print dress bought in Dundee. She alerted security and the man was followed as he trawled other high street stores to seek refunds on clothes and electrical products. When the police arrested him they discovered £3,500 of clothes and electrical goods, with their receipts, in the boot of his car.

The police then organised a big surveillance operation that involved regional police forces and the anti-terrorist squad. A watch was kept on other suspects in Northampton, Southampton and Stratford.

Last year a number of arrests were made and 80 bank accounts, all said to be in false names, were revealed, which led the police to recover £400,000 and trace a further £400,000.

In a container pointed out to officers in Stevenage, Hertfordshire, the police discovered a further £1.5 million of clothes and electrical goods, again all bought from high street stores and with receipts attached.

The scam had been running for at least 18 months until last November. Even so, detectives believe that they have recovered only a small percentage of the total amount of property that was stolen. Detective Sergeant Stephen Gregory, of the Metropolitan Police, said: 'We believe we've found only a very small proportion, the tip of the iceberg of the fraud.'

However, the authorities are still unable to say for sure what happened to the money that had been siphoned off, probably to bank accounts overseas.

All members of the gang who had been arrested were living on benefits and in frugal circumstances.

Ms Large said yesterday that at the time she did not imagine that her routine security alert could have led to such a haul for the police. 'I remember a man trying to get a refund. He looked a little Arabic and was very smartly dressed in a leather jacket,' she said.

'It was gut instinct that made me suspicious. Something told me there was something not quite right about it, so I alerted the radio link we have between stores here to warn each other of suspicious customers.'

At Middlesex Guildhall Crown Court in London yesterday, Paul Taylor, for the prosecution, said: 'This was a well organised, persistent fraud. At the time of the final arrests in this case there were 60 active bank accounts and 20 accounts going through a period of gestation.'

Gang members, all Algerian asylum-seekers or of Algerian descent, operated by opening bank accounts in false names and built a stockpile of chequebooks and cards. They would go into high street stores in a co-ordinated 'blitz' across the country, all on the same day, to buy items using cheque guarantee cards.

A day or two later, before the cheques could be rejected, they went to a different branch to demand a refund.

Bank accounts would be opened either by using false names, supported by fake passports or fake French or Italian identity cards, or by taking over a previously legitimate account of someone who was returning to Algeria.

Source: Lewis Smith, 24 November 2004,
**www.timesonline.co.uk**.

## Key points and concepts

| | |
|---|---|
| Advance fee fraud | National Hi-Tec Crime Unit |
| Business risk | Patches |
| Computer crime | Pharming |
| Cracker | Phishing |
| Denial of service | Physical security control layer |
| Diagnostic monitoring | Political risk |
| Economic risk | Precautionary principle |
| False billing | Preventative intervention |
| Financial fraud | Reflexive modernisation |
| Financial risk | Remedial maintenance |
| Firewall | Risk exposure |
| Fraud | Scanner |
| Hacker | Serious Fraud Office |
| Hotfix | Social risk |
| Human security control layer | Spyware |
| Identity thief | Technical security control layer |
| Intrusion detection system | Trojan horse |
| Malware | Virus |
| Market risk | Worm |

## References

Abercrombie, N., Hill, T. and Turner, B. (1984) *Dictionary of Sociology*, Penguin, Harmondsworth.

Audit Commission (2001) *yourbusiness@risk: an update on IT abuse 2001*, Audit Commission publications, Wetherby.

Beck, U. (1992) *Risk Society – Towards a new modernity*, Sage, London.

Beck, U. (1994) 'The reinvention of politics: towards a theory of reflexive modernization', in Beck, U., Giddens, A. and Lash, S. (eds) *Reflexive Modernization – Politics, tradition and aesthetics in the modern social order*, Stanford University Press, Stanford.

Beck, U., Bonss, W. and Lau, C. (2003) 'The Theory of Reflexive Modernization: Problematic, Hypotheses and Research Programme', *Theory, Culture and Society*, 20(2).

Beck, U., Giddens, A. and Lash, S. (1994) *Reflexive modernization: Politics, Tradition and Aesthetics in the Modern Social Order*, Stanford University Press, Stanford.

Berger, P.L. and Luckmann, T. (1966) *The Social Construction of Reality: A Treatise in the Sociology of Knowledge*, Anchor Books, New York.

Department of Trade and Industry and PricewaterhouseCoopers LLP (2004) *Information Security Breaches Survey 2004 Technical Report*, DTI, London.

Home Office (2004) *Counting Rules for Recording Crime*, HMSO, London.

McClure, S., Scambray, J. and Kutz, G. (2005) *Hacking exposed: Network Security, Secrets, and Solutions*, McGraw-Hill, San Francisco.

Slay, J. and Koronios, A. (2006) *Information Technology security and risk management*, Wiley, Milton, Queensland.

Weyman, A. and Kelly, C. (1999) *Risk Perception and Communication: a review of the literature*, Health and Safety Executive, Research Report 248/99.

Zinn, J. (2004) *Working paper 2 Literature Review: Economics and Risk*, Social Contexts Responses to Risk (SCARR) Network, University of Kent, Kent.

## Bibliography

Bishop, M. (2002), *Computer Security: Art and Science*, Addison-Wesley, London.

Brown, A., Doig, A., Summers, G. and Dobbs, L. (2004), *Practically Fraud*, Tolley Publishing, London.

Chirillo, J. (2001), *Hack Attacks Encyclopedia – A Complete History of Hacks, Cracks, Phreaks and Spies Over Time*, John Wiley, London.

Department of Trade and Industry, *Information Security: A Business Manager's Guide*, DTI, London.

Department of Trade and Industry, *Information Security: BS 7799 and the Data Protection Act*, DTI, London.

Department of Trade and Industry, *Information Security: A Business Guide to Using the Internet*, DTI, London.

Department of Trade and Industry, *Information Security: Guide to the Electronic Communications Act 2000*, DTI, London.

Mitnick, K.D. and Simon, W.L. (2004), *The Art of Deception: Controlling the Human Element of Security*, Hungry Minds, New York.

Mitnick, K.D. and Simon, W.L. (2005), *The Art of Intrusion: The Real Stories Behind the Exploits of Hackers, Intruders, and Deceivers*, Hungry Minds, New York.

## Websites

### General information websites

www.dti-bestpractice-tools.org/healthcheck/
DTI information security health check tools

www.dti.gov.uk/industries/information_security/downloads.html
DTI information security publications

www.dti.gov.uk/bestpractice/infosec
DTI information security business advice pages

www.sfo.gov.uk
Serious Fraud Office

www.iso.ch.
International Organisation for Standardisation

### Websites of virus defence software companies

F-Secure: www.f-secure.com
Finjan: www.finjan.com
Frisk Software International: www.f-prot.com

McAfee: www.mcafee.com
Messagelabs: www.messagelabs.com
Mimesweeper: www.mimesweeper.com
Network Associates: www.networkassociates.com
Sophos: www.sophos.com
Symantec: www.symantec.com
TrendMicro: www.trendmicro.com
Vmyths: www.vmyths.com

### Websites for hotfixes and patches

Microsoft: http://windowsupdate.microsoft.com.
Solaris Fixes: www.sun.com/software/security

### Other websites

Other websites on which you may find helpful articles about risk, fraud and computer crime include:

www.isc.sans.org
Internet storm centre
www.computerweekly.com
*Computer Weekly* news and reports
www.theregister.co.uk
Computer news
www.ft.com.
*The Financial Times*
www.guardian.co.uk.
*The Guardian*

## Self-review questions

1. Briefly explain the precautionary principle and distinguish between weak form precaution, moderate form precaution and strong form precaution.
2. Distinguish between event/activity-based risk and resource/asset-based risk.
3. What are the three main factors that determine the degree of risk exposure a company may face?
4. What is the purpose of BS7799 Part 1 and IOS/IEC 17799?
5. Define the term 'fraud' and describe/explain the illegal acts normally associated with the term.
6. Briefly explain the main differences between a virus, a worm and a trojan horse.
7. Distinguish between preventative controls, detective controls and recovery controls.
8. What are the main categories of computer crime?
9. What is meant by the term 'phishing'?
10. Why would a company normally deploy virus defence software at three hierarchical levels – the internet gateway level, the network server level and the desktop/workstation level?

## Questions and problems

### Question 1

During a recent computer system/network review of HaTiMu Ltd, the following issues were identified:

- computer staff are allowed unrestricted and unmonitored access to the internet,
- all company staff are allowed free access to the offices in which the main computer facilities are located,
- access to software programs is restricted by the use of a company password which is posted on the company's intranet site (for security purposes the password is changed every three months),
- all e-mails are monitored for key words (attachments to e-mails are not monitored).

#### Required

Identify a risk exposure that each of the above issues present. For each of the above, give an example of the security procedure/control protocol that should exist and list one or more factors that could cause the risk exposure to be relatively high.

### Question 2

The business environment of the early 21st century continues to change with increasing vigour. The growth of e-commerce and e-retailing and the use of the internet for the movement of goods, services and information has clearly promoted a greater interconnectivity. An interconnectivity that has not only opened up and created enormous business opportunities, but has also increased the exposure of UK businesses, in particular UK companies, to previously unknown levels of risks and security threats, the costs and consequences of which have been and indeed continue to be significant (see DTI (2004)).

#### Required

For a UK-based retail company, critically evaluate (with specific reference to the company's **accounting information system (and related systems),** the type and nature of risk and security threats such a company faces and the control procedures and security strategy/measures that such a company might employ to protect itself against such risks and threats.

### Question 3

Sentel plc is a UK financial services company with offices in the south-east and north-west of England. In total the company has five offices in the south east of England and six in the north-west. It currently employs 97 staff. The company has been trading successfully for 17 years. For the year ending 31 December 2005 the company's fee income was £18.4m and its net profit for the year was £10.1m. During 2006, however, Sentel's computer system/network was targeted by a number of UK-based groups attempting to gain unauthorised access to the company's system/network and steal confidential client information. During May 2006 the company computer system/network was severely infected by a polymorphic virus and on 6 May 2006 the computer system/network suffered a complete systems failure resulting in company losses of approximately £655,000.

#### Required

Explain the main prevention strategies and technology tools a company like Sentel plc could adopt/use to prevent or at least manage unauthorised access and virus infection.

### Question 4

You have recently been appointed as a trainee chartered accountant at Shuster Whitehouse LLP, a Manchester-based accounting partnership. Following your induction, a senior partner has asked you to undertake a risk review of the computer-based accounting information system of Bepolo Ltd. The company is a small local electrical retail company with an annual turnover of £1.2m and an annual net profit of approximately £700,000.

### Required

Describe and explain:

- the primary and secondary sources of risk, and
- the main types of risk,

a small local retail company such as Bepolo Ltd would be subject to.

## Question 5

Fraud can be defined as the use of deception with the intention of obtaining an advantage, avoiding an obligation or causing loss to another party.

Although there are many types of fraud, the following – although not exclusively restricted to technology-based issues – nevertheless rely heavily on remote communication (often via the internet) to further the aim of the fraud.

### Required

Distinguish between computer *assisted* fraud and computer *related* fraud, and describe and explain each of the following types of fraud:

- false billing,
- financial (funds) fraud,
- advanced fee frauds, and
- identity theft.

Briefly explain the strategies a company could adopt to minimise the potential impact of fraud on its commercial and business-related activities.

## Assignments

## Question 1

Biloce Ltd is an established retail company located in the south-east of England. The company has been operating successfully for over 35 years with the late 1980s and early 1990s in particular being a period of rapid growth and expansion both in market share and profitability. The company is currently in the process of consolidating its market position and is seeking to enhance its accounting information system by the introduction of an upgraded computing network and an extensive web-based e-commerce facility.

The managing director of Biloce Ltd is, however, concerned that the proposed accounting information system development may introduce an unacceptable level of risk into the company's operations. His concerns have been aroused by recent press articles and academic studies that have alluded to a dramatic growth in computer crime in the retail sector over the past 10 years. He is particularly concerned about potential exposure to computer virus infection.

→

*Required*

Prepare a brief report for the managing director of Biloce Ltd addressing his concerns. In your report you must:

- Clearly define the term 'computer crime' and describe the various categories of computer crime.
- Describe the main types of computer virus and describe risks such computer viruses present to a retail company such as Biloce Ltd.
- Explain the possible courses of action Biloce Ltd could take to minimise risk exposure to computer crime, in particular risk exposure to computer virus infection.

## Question 2

Jessica Leigh and Christopher James were both undergraduate students at the University of Hull studying for a BSc in Computing. Not only were Jessica and Christopher potential first class honours students, they were also highly skilled computer hackers, collectively known among their friends as 'Matrix'.

At a recent high-profile trial, both Jessica and Christopher were found guilty of six offences of corporate espionage and extortion. In January 2002 they were both sentenced to eight years in prison.

Their illegal activities began shortly after Jessica and Christopher had both completed a six-month undergraduate work placement during 2001. They were both employed at Dia-gen UK Plc, a computer software developer. By accident, they both came across confidential information containing software codes for an advanced computer operating system which Dia-gen Plc was developing with Intec Inc. an American-based development think tank.

In order to profit from this information, Jessica distributed the stolen software codes on the black market and Christopher placed a trojan horse, designed to trap and save passwords, in the software code's log-on procedure. They also made modified codes available to other hackers by setting up a home page on the web.

Finally, Christopher inserted the modified code into Dia-gen's computer system and obtained a range of passwords relating to sensitive development files, using them to access information in the files, information which Jessica then sold via the web.

Over a four-month period Jessica and Christopher sold confidential information about Dia-gen Plc and Intec Inc. products for approximately £1.5m.

*Required*

(a) Discuss the nature of the risk exposure illustrated by this situation.
(b) What are the similarities and differences between a trojan horse and a computer virus?
(c) Identify in broad terms several control procedures and security measures that a company might employ to protect itself against such activities.

 **Chapter endnotes**

1 Businesses are concerned with a narrow and somewhat absolutist perception of risk – a perception bounded by the need for technical assessment and statistical analysis.
2 The term 'probability', derived from the Latin word *probare* (to prove or to test) is used in preference to possibility or possibilities. Informally, the word probable is one of several words applied to uncertain events or knowledge, being more or less interchangeable with likely, risky, hazardous, uncertain and doubtful, depending on the context.

[3] See also Beck (1992).

[4] The term 'economisation of uncertainty' is used here to emphasise how economic literature presupposes that 'there is an objective (potentially) measurable risk and assumes that the decision on how to reduce this risk can be made rationally on the ground of statistical methods . . . (or) . . . the objective statistical reduction of risk' (Zinn, 2004: 3).

[5] There is a range of approaches used to conceptualise risk. For example whereas the actuarial approach would seek to use past data to extrapolate and forecast future trends, the epidemiological approach would use modelling to explore causality and attempt to identify and quantify the relationship between exposure to a hazard and outcome. Likewise where the engineering approach would seek to use probabilistic analysis to identify cause and consequence, the economic approach would use cost-benefit analysis and seek to balance possible gains with possible risks whilst assuming that participants are rational, economic actors interested solely in maximising gains. And finally, whereas, the psychological approach would use heuristics (rules of thumb) to focus on personal preferences and seek to identify alternative perceptions of risk, the cultural approach would seek to view risk as a social construct and explore responses to and perceptions of risk as determined by cultural belief patterns and/or social imposed filters.

[6] Social constructionism is an idea/notion that reality is constructed uniquely by each person and/or group of persons – that reality is an invention or artifact of a particular culture or society (see Berger and Luckmann (1966)).

[7] The theorists of reflexivity suggest that modernity has begun to modernise its own foundations. It has become directed at itself (see Beck *et al.* (2003)), thus the term 'reflexive modernisation' means 'the possibility of a creative (self-)destruction for an entire epoch – that of industrial society . . . (with) . . . the subject of this creative destruction not the revolution, not the crisis, but the victory of western modernisation,' (Beck *et al.*, 1994: 2).

[8] The term 'cultural' is used here to define the symbolic and learned processes which generate and sustain norms and values between members of a social group (for example see Abercrombie *et al.*, 1984: 59).

[9] In a contemporary context, trust has emerged as an area of major significance in understanding risk perceptions and responses and, as suggested by Weyman and Kelly (1999), serves as a zone of convergence between psychological and socio-cultural approaches to risk.

[10] See UNEP (United Nations Environment Programme), Declaration on Environment and Development, Rio de Janeiro, June 1992.

[11] Adapted from Annex 1 Precautionary Principle: Policy and Application, United Kingdom Interdepartmental Group on Risk Assessment (UK-ILGRA) available @ www.hse.gov.uk/aboutus/meetings/ilgra/pppa.htm.

[12] Where unintentional errors occur regularly then they may well hide a deliberate intention to defraud and/or cause harm or damage.

[13] The full text of ISO/IEC 17799 Code of Practice for Information Security can be obtained @ www.iso.ch.

[14] The full text of BS 7799-2: 2002 Specification for Information on Security Management can be obtained @ www.bsi-global.com.

[15] See Information Security: BS 7799 and the Data Protection Act (2004) Department of trade and Industry – available @ www.dti.gov.uk.

[16] Oxford English Dictionary (1991) Edmund S. Weiner, and Simpson, J. (eds), Oxford University Press, Oxford.

[17] In the UK the SFO is an independent government department responsible for investigating and prosecuting serious or complex fraud. The key criterion used by the SFO in deciding whether to accept a case is that the suspected fraud should appear to be so serious or complex

that its investigation should be carried out by those responsible for its prosecution. The factors generally considered are:

■ Does the value of the alleged fraud exceed £1 million?
■ Is there a significant international dimension?
■ Is the case likely to be of widespread public concern?
■ Does the case require highly specialised knowledge, for example of financial markets?
■ Is there a need to use the SFO's special powers, such as s2 of the Criminal Justice Act?

The SFO does not have jurisdiction over Scotland, the Isle of Man and/or the Channel Islands.
[18] Although the distinction is by no means widely accepted, in a broad context, a computer *assisted* fraud is a fraud and/or fraudulent act in which the use of a computer and/or a computer system/network is central to the fraud, whereas a computer-*related* fraud is a fraud and/or fraudulent act in which the use of a computer and/or a computer system/network is coincidental.
[19] DoS attack is a type of cyber crime – it prevents a target computer, computer systems and/or computer network from accessing a network resource. See www.mynetsec.com/html/security.htm.
[20] The National Hi-Tech Crime Unit, part of the National Crime Squad, was created in April 2001. The NHTCU works to combat national and transnational serious and organised hi-tech crime both within, or which impacts upon, the UK. A multi-agency unit, it has staff seconded from:

■ the National Crime Squad (NCS),
■ the National Criminal Intelligence Service (NCIS),
■ Her Majesty's Customs and Excise Law Enforcement and Investigation (HMC&E),
■ the Intelligence Agencies, and
■ the military armed forces.

The work of the unit is broadly divided into six key disciplines:

■ tactical and technical support,
■ intelligence,
■ operations,
■ digital evidence recovery,
■ crime reduction, and
■ industry liaison.

Crimes targeted include:

■ fraud,
■ denial of service attacks,
■ blackmail and extortion,
■ online child abuse,
■ hacking and virus attacks,
■ software piracy, and
■ class A drug trafficking.

[21] See www.nhtcu.org.
[22] Cryptography encrypts documents or messages and seeks to ensure they remain confidential and such encryption can be used as a basis for an electronic signature.
[23] An electronic signature is associated with an electronic document and seeks to confirm the authenticity of the document/communication.
[24] See *Information Security: Guide to Electronic Communications Act 2000* (2004) Department of Trade and Industry – available @ www.dti.gov.uk.

[25] See *Information Security Breaches Survey 2006 Technical Report* (April 2006), Pricewaterhouse-Coopers and Department of Trade and Industry – available @ http://www.enisa.eu.int/doc/pdf/studies/dtiisbs2006.pdf.

[26] *The Information Security Breaches Survey 2006 Technical Report* (April 2006), categorises UK businesses as follows:

- a small UK business is a business with 1–49 employees,
- a medium UK business is a business with 50–249 employees, and
- a large UK business is a business with 250+ employees.

Available @ http://www.enisa.eu.int/doc/pdf/studies/dtiisbs2006.pdf.

[27] See *Information Security Breaches Survey 2006 Technical Report* (April 2006), Pricewaterhouse-Coopers and Department of Trade and Industry – available @ http://www.enisa.eu.int/doc/pdf/studies/dtiisbs2006.pdf.

[28] KPMG Fraud Survey available @ www.us.kpmg.com.

[29] A content checker filters incoming and outgoing e-mail messages and attachments for specific words and phrases to ascertain whether given file types are present. Messages can also be filtered to limit the size of e-mails.

[30] Monitoring staff usage of corporate information technology is a controversial issue with a fine balance being struck between the corporate need to prevent crime and the employee's human rights. The following legislation must be considered where the monitoring of employee e-mails is being considered:

- the Human Rights Act 1998,
- the Data Protection Act 1998 (specifically the Data Protection Monitoring at Work section and Part 1 (Vetting & Personnel)),
- the Regulation of Investigatory Powers Act 2000,
- the Telecommunications (Lawful Business Practice) (Interception of Communications) Regulations 2000.

[31] Penetration testing is often characterised by simulating an attack by an unauthorised and malicious hacker/cracker to identify security weaknesses.

[32] Crackers often like to describe themselves as hackers. Cracking normally relies on persistence and repetition of a handful of fairly well-known tricks to exploit the security weaknesses of target computer systems/networks. See www.infosec.gov.hk/engtext/general/glossary.htm.

[33] For example an external network such as the internet may be regarded as a region of little or no trust, whereas an internal network may be regarded as a region of high trust.

[34] In an information and communication technology context, the principle of minimal privilege (also known as the principle of least authority) requires that in granting privileges, authority, and/or access, only that level of privileges, authority and/or access which will permit legitimate and effective action to occur should be granted. That is, excessive privileges, authority and/or access should not be granted to an individual, and/or group of individuals where they are not required for that individual and/or groups of individuals to undertake their duties and activities effectively and efficiently.

[35] A stateless firewall is a firewall that treats each packet in isolation and as such is not able to determine if a packet is part of an existing connection or part of an attempt to establish a new connection, or merely an illegitimate rogue packet. Modern firewalls are state-full firewalls inasmuch as they are connection-aware (or state-aware).

[36] See for example Honeynet available @ http://www.activeworx.org/programs/hsc/index.htm.

[37] Snort (available @ ww.snort.org is the most widely deployed intrusion detection and prevention technology worldwide and has become the *de facto* standard for the industry.

[38] From Greek *kryptós* meaning to hide and *gráphein* meaning to write.

[39] An algorithm is a procedure or a finite set of instructions for accomplishing a particular task/procedure.

[40] A cipher is an algorithm for performing the encryption and decryption process – that is the series of defined procedures that must be followed during the encryption and decryption process.

[41] A substitution cipher is a cipher in which data (e.g. a word or character) are replaced with other data (e.g. another word or character) in a prearranged manner (Slay and Koronios, 2006: 133).

[42] A transposition cipher (sometimes known as a route cipher) is a cipher in which plaintext is first written out in a grid of given dimensions, then read off (or transposed) in a predetermined pattern. Variants include columnar transposition, double transposition and disrupted transposition.

[43] A product cipher is a cipher in which a combination of other kinds/types of ciphers is used.

[44] A block cipher is a cipher in which the data is divided into defined blocks each of which is then encrypted independently of other blocks – although in reality often there is some commonality in the encryption of blocks of data.

[45] A stream cipher is a cipher in which data items are encrypted as single data items – one data item at a time. A substitution cipher is an example of a steam cipher.

[46] Such as those with extensions like .BIN, .COM, .EXE, .OVL, .DRV (driver) and .SYS (device driver).

[47] See www.antivirus-software.net/glossary.shtml.

[48] In a contemporary context the deployment of virus defence software normally occurs at three distinct levels:

- the internet gateway level,
- the network server level, and
- the desktop/workstation level.

[49] There are three common types of virus defence software:

- scanners,
- check-summers, and
- heuristics.

[50] Although not all freeware and/or shareware is infected with hidden spyware!

[51] A 'cookie' is a message given to a web browser by a web server which is then stored by the web browser as a text file.

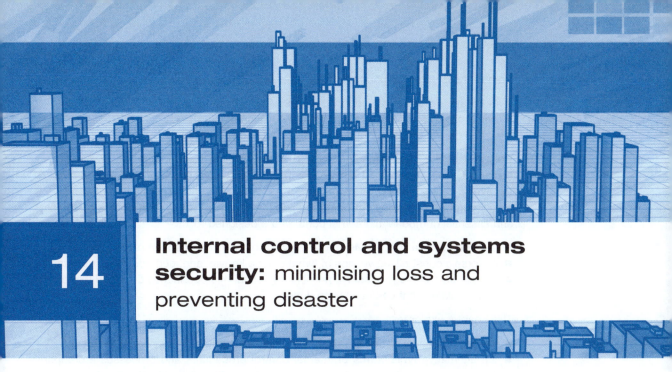

# 14

# Internal control and systems security: minimising loss and preventing disaster

## Introduction

As with any socially constructed corporate activity, economically designed procedure/process or politically imposed protocol, internal controls (as a series of processes and procedures) are neither objective nor neutral. That is all aspects, procedures and processes associated with the notion of internal control are coloured by an unacknowledged affinity with the legitimation of what we have previously characterised as the priorities of capital, whose primary *raison d'être*[1] is sustaining the tradition of economic liberalism as the dominant regime of truth.

What is internal control? As suggested in Chapter 6, internal control comprises of all the management processes designed to provide reasonable assurance that the objectives of reliable financial reporting, effective and efficient operations, and compliance with laws and regulations are achieved.

Such internal control includes all procedures, processes and protocols – financial and otherwise – established by the management of a company or indeed any organisation, to ensure that:

- business activities of the company/organisation are undertaken efficiently,
- management policies and procedures are complied with,
- all assets and resources are appropriately safeguarded, and
- all accounting records and financial information is accurate and complete.

Although we will explore the notion/definition of internal control in more detail later in this chapter, clearly the term internal control is an *enclosing* definition. It is a term used to signify a variety of processes and procedure designed to perpetuate a precept of perceived authority which is actively managed through:

- the creation of system boundaries and
- the imposition of a politically selected bounded rationality.[2]

Both of these – in a corporate context – serve to:

- delineate the power of economic authorities,
- demarcate the capacities for corporate decision making, and
- define the influence/identities of component social constituencies.

Coloured by the understanding/belief that the (contemporary) priorities of capital are and indeed will continue to remain compatible with, supportive of and sympathetic to the ever-growing plurality of institutional structures and cultural/norms that comprise the global corporate environment (and of which the corporate entity is of course an intrinsic and essential component), internal controls are designed to:

- promote/allow a specific vision of reality – a particular perception of 'what is',
- endorse a constraining version of 'what can be known' and, perhaps more importantly,
- impose an anthology of social, political and economic boundaries designed to manage and regulate 'what can/cannot be done'.

This chapter explores:

- the socio-political issues associated with internal control (and systems security),
- the alternative types/forms of internal control procedures and processes a company may adopt to minimise systems risk and ensure the physical security of resources, data/information and system networks,
- the on-going reciprocal relationship between information and communication technologies on internal control (and system security), and
- the problems and issues associated with information and communication enabled business processes and procedures.

## Learning outcomes

By the end of this chapter, the reader should be able to;

- describe the socio-economic contexts of control,
- distinguish between alternative classifications of control and the issues associated with system security,
- describe and critically comment on the impact of information and communication technologies on internal control (and systems security), and
- evaluate the internal control and systems security implications of information and communication technologies enabled business processes.

## Internal control and systems security – a contemporary context

As suggested earlier, internal control comprises the processes and/or procedures within a company designed to provide reasonable assurances that business objectives – primarily the maximisation of shareholder wealth – will be achieved and any undesired events, unwelcome occurrences and/or unfavourable incidences will be prevented and/or detected and corrected.

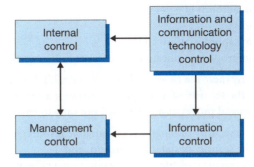

**Figure 14.1** Internal control and related control types

Internal control is of course closely related to:

- management control – which can be defined as a diverse range of activities designed to conduct, direct and control business activities and ensure consistency with corporate business objectives, and
- information control – which can be defined as a diverse range of activities undertaken by or on behalf of a company's management, designed to ensure the proper and appropriate operation of underlying information systems and the consistency, reliability and relevance of information provision – for both internal and external use and, of course,
- information and communication technology (ICT) control – which can be defined as all those activities employed by or on behalf of a company's management designed to ensure the reliability of a company's information systems.

See Figure 14.1.

As an enclosing definition or, perhaps more appropriately, an encompassing expression, the term 'internal control' includes all those imposed management procedures and processes designed to ensure:

- the reliability and integrity of both financial and non-financial information,
- the economic, effective and efficient use of business resources,
- compliance with management policies and adherence to extant regulatory requirements,
- the safeguarding of all business assets and resources, and
- the accomplishment of established corporate/organisational goals and objectives:

The provision of effective internal control requires:

- an understanding and appreciation of the *control environment*,
- an understanding of relevant and appropriate *control activities*,
- an understanding, identification and *analysis of (internal and external) risk*,
- an assessment of the efficiency and effectiveness of *information and communication* channels used both internally within the company and externally within the environment and, finally,
- an appreciation and understanding of need for effective and appropriate *monitoring* of transaction processes and procedures.

We will return to these issues and discuss each of these in more detail later in the chapter.

For the moment however what about systems security? For our purposes we will classify systems security as a specific albeit increasingly important component aspect of internal control and as such we will define systems security as the deployment of a range of procedures, processes, policies and protocols to protect assets, resources, data and/or information against:

- unauthorised access,
- loss,
- misappropriation, and/or
- improper modification, deletion and/or alteration.

Clearly there is a close symbiotic relationship between a company's internal control procedures and the security of a company's operational systems inasmuch as such system security procedures and processes are designed not only to ensure:

- the security of tangible/non-tangible resources,
- the security of data/information, and
- the security of company/organisational networks,

but also ensure proper and adequate protection from possible systems failures/disasters.

Indeed, as a legitimate and (some would say) necessary corporate expense, system security procedures should seek to maintain:

- the integrity of corporate operations,
- the confidentiality of corporate data and/or information, and
- the protection of corporate assets and resources.

Perhaps before we explore the more technical issues associated with contemporary internal control (and systems security), it would be useful to provide a background context – a socio-economic perspective/framework – to our discussion and, in particular, consider albeit briefly, the powerful influence of the priorities of capital on the designing and shaping of the operational aspects of corporate internal control.

## Internal control and the priorities of capital

In a contemporary context, the increasingly chaotic realities of the global marketplace, the evermore uncertain realities of corporate activities and the increasing possibility of corporate failure and financial loss are often upheld as a defence for:

- the imposition of greater regulatory constraints,
- the development of increasingly hierarchical control systems,
- the creation of evermore complex socio-economic boundaries, and
- the imposition of progressively more proactive internal control systems.

There can be little doubt that such increasing regulation and control has also contributed to:

- sustaining the priorities of the marketplace or, more appropriately, the priorities of capital as the singular dominant socio-economic force,
- preserving the tradition of economic liberalism as the dominant regime of truth, and
- justifying its ever-increasing influence on the very social processes and institutional structures which not only shape but govern corporate activities.

Indeed, by imposing a way of thinking or understanding, such market orientated priorities effectively determine the social and institutional nature and context of internal control processes and procedures as a consequence of:

- the enforcement of a structured series of boundary parameters – that is determining what can/cannot be done and who can/cannot do it,
- the imposition of a series of what are often called threshold limits – that is establishing what is/is not material, and

■ the establishment of a series of what are often called relevance limits – that is determining what can/cannot be included and/or omitted.

Such priorities continuously (re)socialise and (re)legitimate the ongoing imposition and adoption of the internal control processes and procedures onto the operational cartography of corporate activity – a cartography which in a contemporary context lies at the very heart of modern societal activities and comprises the very fabric or essence of what we regard as contemporary corporate society. How? Through a process we will refer to as *context filtering*

## Context filtering – an imposed hierarchical context

Context filtering is a complex and often unpredictable filtering process whose outcomes are contingent upon the interaction of a vast array of interrelated social, political, and economic factors and characteristics – *Macro level* factors and characteristics such as:

■ international level pressures and characteristics, and
■ national (territorial) factors and characteristics,

and *micro level* factors and characteristics such as:

■ industry/sector level factors,
■ corporate/organisational characteristics, and
■ personal/individual level factors and characteristics.

See Figure 14.2.

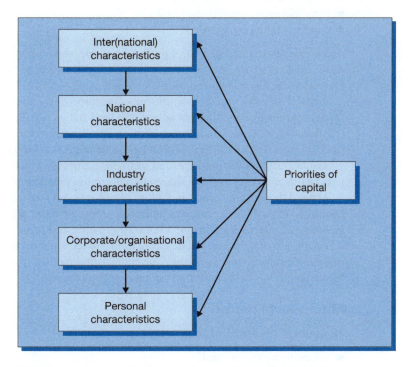

**Figure 14.2** Socio-economic filtering – an imposed hierarchical context

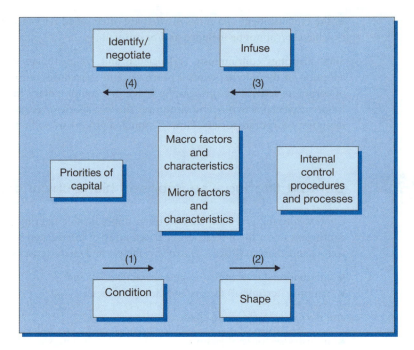

**Figure 14.3** Internal control and the priorities of capital

It is through the interaction of such factors and characteristics that:

- system boundaries are identified,
- threshold limits are endorsed, and
- relevance limits are approved.

As a consequence internal control processes are imposed – often through the sanctioning and enforcement of a vast assortment of management procedures and operational protocols. How? Have a look at Figure 14.3 and consider the following.

Arrow 1 denotes the mechanisms/processes/procedures through which the priorities of capital continually condition not only macro level factors (e.g. international level and national (territorial) level factors and characteristics), but also micro level factors (e.g. industry/sector level, corporate/organisational level and personal/individual level factors and characteristics).

Arrow 2 denotes the processes and procedures through which such macro level and micro level factors and characteristics shape internal control procedures and processes.

Arrow 3 denotes the formal and informal contexts and mechanisms through which internal control procedures and processes reflexively infuse or more appropriately act/impose upon national and international institutional arrangements, and social and cultural values/norms.

Finally, arrow 4 denotes the influence of macro level and micro level factors and characteristics in identifying and negotiating the contexts/mechanisms through which the influence of the marketplace – the priorities of capital – will be exercised.

## Macro level factors

These macro level factors comprise of:

- international factors, and
- national or territorial factors,

both of which affect all companies within a nation state, geographical region and/or territorial domain. Such factors are systematic in nature and, whilst in the past the impact of adverse national (territorial) factors/characteristics on corporate activity may have often been minimised or even eliminated by geographical/territorial relocation, the effectiveness of such relocation has, in recent years, become increasingly limited. Why? Mainly because international pressures/characteristics have – in the name of global capitalism – become evermore invasive and dominant in reinventing, redesigning and reupholstering national (territorial) structural factors and characteristics – all in the global rush toward homogeneity, singularity and that nirvana a single global marketplace!!

### International level factors

These international level factors consist of all those social, political and economic factors and characteristics which either directly or indirectly impact on the activities of all companies in all – or at least most – national/territorial domains. Such factors and characteristics would include:

- in an economic context:
  - the increasing mobility of capital and its impact on traditional conceptions of sovereignty, and
  - the growing power of the 'western' market ethic and the increasing dominance of the 'multi-national' company,
- in a political context:
  - the increasing global nature of interstate relations, territorial democracy and global politics, and
  - the continued growth of supra-national organisations such as the UN, WTO, and NATO, and
- in a social context:
  - the growth of global ICT and its continuing impact on local culture, community and tradition, and
  - the increasing global social anxiety over the depletion of ecological resources and environmental sustainability.

Invariably such international factors and characteristics are national (territorial) in origin.[3] Their migration and elevation beyond national territoriality, whether by chance, design or through the exercise of socio-political/economic power, has of course become the dominant feature of contemporary society, and in particular late 20th century/early 21st century society. Not convinced? Then just consider the power, role and influence of the USA in contemporary global society.

### National (territorial) level factors

These are factors/characteristics associated with a specific territoriality and/or geographical domain. Whether such a specific territoriality/geographical domain is:

- an identifiable country and/or nation state (e.g. England, France or Germany),
- a regional grouping and/or association (e.g. the European Union), or
- a tightly controlled federation (e.g. the Russian federation of states),

such factors often exist as an agreed, albeit a sometimes imposed, common framework through which:

- international level factors/pressures/characteristics are interpreted, accommodated and operationalised, and
- socio-economic activities are authorised, approved and permitted to take place.

Such national (territorial) factors and characteristics would, for example, include:

- the nature, power and influence of extant cultural norms and social interrelationships,
- the context and authority of current socio-political arrangements and institutional relationships,
- the sovereignty of law and the requirements of extant legislative/regulatory pronouncements,
- the socio-political importance of environmental/technological issues, and
- the influence of contemporary liberal economic thought and the authority/power of the marketplace and the market mechanism.

They would of course not only differ from country to country, regional grouping to regional grouping or federation to federation, but may also differ within a country, regional grouping or federation of countries. Just consider the variety that still exists not only within the European Union but, more importantly, within most member state countries – despite the endless years of social, political and economic change.

## Micro level factors

These micro level factors only affect companies and/or individuals within:

- a specific industry/sector, and/or
- a company/organisation.

Such factors are unsystemsatic in nature and, whilst some characteristics can be eliminated by inter-industry/sector and/or inter-company/organisation relocation, as with macro level factors the effectiveness of such relocation has, in recent years, become increasingly limited.

### Industry/sector level characteristics

These would include a wide range of industry/sector specific characteristics associated with:

- the nature and context of social and economic interrelationships within the industry/sector,
- the nature and context of the industry/sector specific regulatory arrangements and requirements,
- the influence/importance of the market mechanism within the industry/sector, and
- the social, political and economic importance of environmental/technological issues within the industry/sector.

Clearly, whilst all companies within a sector/industry would be affected (although perhaps not equally) by a combination of the above factors/characteristics, slight variation in the importance/implication of each of the above factors/characteristics would invariably exist between different sectors/industries.

Whilst all active trading companies would clearly be subject to the chaos that is symptomatic of the contemporary marketplace they may nevertheless prioritise certain factors, for example:

- a retail and distribution type company *may* prioritise the competitive nature – the social and economic interrelationships within the marketplace,
- a manufacturing/production type company *may* prioritise the influence of environmental and/or technological issues within its respective industry/sector,
- a time/space-based type company *may* prioritise the importance of competition within the industry/sector, and
- a knowledge/skills-based company *may* prioritise the importance/influence of industry/sector specific regulatory arrangements and requirements.

### Corporate/organisational level factors and characteristics

These would include corporate/organisational specific characteristics relating to the creation and development of a corporate/organisational identity – a corporate/organisational personality.

There are of course many who would argue that a company/organisation is merely:

- a collection of tangible and intangible resources,
- an artificial compilation of systems, procedures and protocols, or
- a nexus of social, legal and economic obligations,

with any notion of a company/organisation possessing a personality and/or an identity being mere sentimental nonsense (see Article 14.1). And, of course, there are many others who would argue that the notion of corporate/organisational personality – a corporate/organisational identity – is not mere emotive anthropomorphisation.[4] They would argue that a company/organisation is more than a legal construct – more than the sum of its constituent parts. Corporate organisations are sentient entities whose very existence is the foundation of contemporary capitalism. Indeed whilst a company/organisation may possess no immortal soul, like human beings, they live and die . . . and whilst they live, their wealth and prosperity (their profitability and commercial success) is founded on a single composite attribute – their corporate personality.

## Article 14.1

## Corporate character is not just a legal construct

Companies have no immortal soul but live and die like human beings – prosperous by the attributes of their personality. This week, John discusses the many faces of corporate personality.

Can an organisation learn or forget? Can it have integrity or lack it? Can it laugh or be angry? Does a company have a soul? The film and book of The Corporation degenerate into tedious rants against modern business, but they raise a serious issue. Is there such a thing as corporate personality?

Treating companies as if they were people is not simply a conceit of management gurus. Some people ascribe the concept of corporate personality to the Supreme Court, which determined in 1819 that Dartmouth College was an entity distinct from its current members. During the 19th century, judges and legislators elaborated this idea. The modern company can sue and be sued; its assets and liabilities are its own, not those of the people who manage or invest in it.

But can a company have thoughts, knowledge or intentions? The British government proposes to create an offence of corporate manslaughter. The definition of this crime, however, rests on the ability to make analogies between the behaviour of a business and that of an individual. What does it mean to say that an organisation was negligent? Is it possible to ascribe a state of mind to an abstraction?

Many economists and business people think this anthropomorphisation of the company is sentimental tosh. A company is a nexus of contracts defined by its charter or articles of association. Lawyers have tried to resolve the issue in a different way. They search for a 'directing mind', whose thoughts and desires can be detected in everything the organisation does. Many chief executives would happily cast themselves in the role of directing mind, and business journalists often write as though everything that happened at General Electric happened because Jack Welch willed it.

But neither the nexus of contracts nor the directing mind describes the reality of modern corporate life. If a business was no more than a nexus of contracts, you could establish an equally successful business by reproducing the nexus of contracts. You cannot, because an effective organisation relies on the social context surrounding its nexus of contracts. Customers might put their trust in contracts but generally prefer to rely on the reputation of the business and to deal with people they know. Workers may aspire to be part of a profitable nexus of contracts, but also look for a working environment in which they can take pride.

The personalisation of large companies is equally mistaken. Mr Welch was the product of a management system that ensured the chief executive of General Electric was always the most admired chief executive in America; that shows it is the company, not the individual, that really matters. The successful business is necessarily more than an aggregate of agreements or

→

people; just as the unsuccessful business is less than the aggregate of agreements or people.

The issue of corporate manslaughter arises precisely because sloppy businesses, such as Railtrack, have no directing mind: their failures were not the product of bad people, but of an arrogant and complacent corporate culture. In the truly dreadful organisation, everyone has positioned themselves not to be responsible when something goes wrong. The horror of Enron was not just that it was home to some corrupt people but that the environment encouraged their corruption.

So in both good and bad companies, corporate personality is a commercial reality, not just a legal construct. And if the company has its own distinctive character, like an individual, that refutes the claim that the company is necessarily amoral, that it has no ethics, only interests. This is the one nice point made in The Corporation: a personality devoid of moral sense, which is instrumental in its treatment of stakeholders, generally would be diagnosed by psychologists as psychopathic. Society punishes psychopathic personalities, through social ostracism and imprisonment, and it punishes psychopathic companies through the market and political action. That was the fate of Enron and Andersen, IG Farben and Japanese zaibatsu. Companies have no immortal soul but, like human beings, they live and die. While they live, they prosper by the attributes of their personality.

Source: John Kay, 7 December 2004, The *Financial Times*, **www.ft.com**.

Consider the following diverse range of companies:

- retail-based companies such as Asda, Tesco, Sainsbury and Marks and Spencer,
- extractive industry-based companies such as BP and Shell,
- energy production and distribution companies such as Npower and BG Group,
- publishing and media companies such as Pearson Publishing and BSkyB,
- hotel services companies such as Intercontinental Hotels and, Hilton Hotels,
- airline services companies such as BA and, KLM Royal Dutch Airlines,
- postal services companies such as DHL, Interlink and Post Office Ltd (owned by Royal Mail Group),
- security services companies such as Group 4 Securicor,
- telephone service provider companies such as BT, Motorola and Orange,
- banking and financial services companies such as NatWest, LloydsTSB and Barclays.

Do any of the above companies possess a corporate personality – a corporate identity? Of course they do!

In an advertising/marketing context such a corporate personality/identity is often associated with/depicted as the corporate brand or the corporate brand name. Indeed, in a financial reporting context, some companies actually give this corporate personality, corporate brand or corporate brand name a value. And it is included on the balance sheet under intangible assets.

### Personal/individual level characteristics

These would include person specific characteristics relating to an individual's needs, wants and desires. Perhaps the most cited framework for such needs and wants is Maslow's Hierarchy (see Maslow 1943 and 1987). Maslow proposed a hierarchy of needs:

- a self-actualization need[5] – that is the quest to reach one's full potential as a person,
- ego/esteem needs[6] – that is the need for self-respect, for personal worth and for autonomy,
- social needs – that is the need for love, friendship, comradeship and belonging,
- security needs – that is the need to be protected from danger and to feel safe, secure and free from the threat of physical and emotional harm, and
- physiological needs[7] – that is the need for the fundamentals required to sustain life such as warmth, shelter and food.

So, what is the importance of such personal/individual level characteristics? Although there is little evidence to:

- support Maslow's strict hierarchy of needs, and
- support the view that people are indeed driven by the same needs – at the same time,

there are nonetheless some important sociological implications of Maslow's hierarchy in terms of the impact of such personal/individual level characteristics on:

- workplace motivation/performance,
- management style and, perhaps most importantly for our purposes,
- the operationalisation and effectiveness of internal control.

Remember, despite the enormous advances made in:

- information processing technologies,
- information and communication technologies,
- management information systems, and
- computer-based accounting information systems,

most (if not all) internal control processes, procedures and/or protocols eventually involve some form of human interface – whether at:

- the planning/design stage,
- the implementation stage,
- the operational stage, and/or
- the monitoring stage.

Consequently, a failure to:

- provide adequate levels of remuneration (physiological need),
- provide a controlled working environment (safety need),
- reinforce the need for team dynamics and accountability (social need),
- recognise achievements and ensure employees are valued and appreciated (esteem/ego need), and
- provide work which enables innovation, creativity and progress according to long-term goals (self actualisation need),

could all have significant adverse consequences/implications on:

- the appropriateness of a company's/organisation's control environment,
- the effectiveness of a company's/organisation's control activities,
- the relevance of a company's/organisation's risk minimising procedures,
- the efficiency of a company's/organisation's information and communication channels, and
- the operational suitability of a company's/organisation's monitoring of control activities.

## Internal control – a composed framework

If you remember, in Chapter 6 we suggested that the securing of appropriate and effective internal control required:

- an understanding and appreciation of the *control environment*,
- an understanding of relevant and appropriate *control activities*,

- an understanding, identification and *analysis of (internal and external) risk,*
- an assessment of the efficiency and effectiveness of *information and communication* channels used both internally within the company and externally within the environment, and finally
- an appreciation and understanding of need for effective and appropriate *monitoring* of control activities.

Indeed, it is the combination of each of these five interrelated components that is commonly referred using the generic and enclosing term 'internal control'.

## Control environment

The imposition/identification of a control environment is the foundation for all other components of internal control within the company. It provides:

- discipline – within business procedures,
- structure – within business processes.

The term control environment refers to the (imposed) norms and values – or more appropriately the actions, policies and procedures – imposed by the company management and seek to reflect the overall attitudes of the company management, directors and owners (shareholders) about control (specifically internal control) and its importance to the company.

The creation/determination of a control environment in effect seeks to impose – within an operational environment – a control consciousness. A control consciousness imposed by but derived from the norms and values that form the central character of the company's organisational culture. Such norms and values would include:

- ethical values enshrined within the company procedures,
- the company management commitment to competence and best practice,
- company management operating philosophy,
- company structure and organisational accountability,
- assignment of authority and responsibility within the company, and
- company human resource policies and procedures.

An effective control environment is an environment within which individuals and participants are aware of:

- the activities/procedures and/or processes for which they are responsible,
- the limits of their authority and role(s) within the company, and
- the controls imposed upon them and their activities within the company.

It is clearly within the context of the control environment that control activities exist.

## Control activities

These are the policies and procedures used by management to meet its objectives – within the framework of the norms and values imposed by the control environment. They are the activities and actions which when undertaken in a proper and considered manner and supported by appropriate and relevant policies and procedures facilitate the management (and hopefully reduction) of risk.

Such control activities can be categorised into the following groups:

- adequate segregation of duties,
- appropriate separation of administrative procedures,

- relevant and appropriate authorisation procedures,
- appropriate documentation and records,
- appropriate physical security of assets and records, and
- relevant and proper direct and indirect supervision of business procedures and business performance.

Within a control environment such control activities must be implemented/applied consistently and, of course, cost effectively.

Whereas minor lapses in control activities could result in:

- possible loss of assets/resources, and/or
- possible interruption/suspension of business activities and the financial losses associated with such disturbance,

substantial failure of such control activities could lead to:

- significant adverse publicity, and/or
- significant fluctuations in share values and ultimately corporate collapse.

Have look at Articles 14.2 to 14.5.

Clearly, central to the existence of adequate control activities is:

- an understanding of the risk associated with a failure of internal control,
- the existence of adequate communication channels and flows of information, and
- the effective monitoring of both company processes and procedures, and control activities.

We will look at alternative classification of controls later in this chapter.

## Article 14.2

### Inquiry launched after biggest ever credit card heist

*Raids on fashion retailer TK Maxx in US and UK*
*45 million at risk on both sides of Atlantic*

British authorities yesterday launched an inquiry into how computer hackers who targeted the cut-price fashion retailer TK Maxx were able to steal information from more than 45 million credit and debit card holders on both sides of the Atlantic.

As the extraordinary scale of the biggest credit card heist unravelled, internet security experts urged all businesses and banks to tighten up their computer security systems to protect their customers.

TK Maxx shoppers were advised to check their credit and debit transactions for irregularities amid warnings that the criminals involved could even use the data to commit identity theft. Internet fraud is now one of the fastest growing areas of illegal activity in the UK.

TK Maxx's US parent company, TJX, revealed the extent of the 'unauthorised intrusion' in its annual report on Thursday, claiming that someone had used sophisticated software to access its data centres in Watford, Hertfordshire, and in Framingham, near Boston, Massachusetts.

Names, card numbers and personal data were stolen – and in the US, social security numbers – over a 17-month period and covering transactions dating as far back as December 2002. The firm said it did not know how many of the cardholders affected were shoppers at TK Maxx's 210 stores in Britain and Ireland, although more of them were likely to be American. Canadian shoppers have also been affected. The company disclosed in January that it had a problem but suggested the volume of information stolen was not on a large scale.

The government's information commissioner, Richard Thomas, was said to be extremely concerned. A spokesperson for his office said yesterday: 'The information commissioner's office takes breaches of privacy extremely seriously. The Canadian privacy commissioner is investigating this matter and is working with the federal trade commission in the US. We are liaising with them on this. It was brought to our attention today that information may have been hacked from the company's data centre in Watford. We are therefore contacting the company in the UK today. To date we have not received any complaints arising from this breach.'

Crime of this type is common, and £210m was lost to credit card fraud during the first half of 2006, according to figures from the payment industry body Apacs. But some experts say fraud and hacking is at far greater levels than realised.

'We see a couple of commercial thefts at a very serious level each week,' said Dan Hagman of 7 Safe, which specialises in so-called intrusion forensics. 'Credit card details are being stolen in huge numbers – and the problem is that if you're hacked you don't necessarily know.'

Although it remains unclear how many of TK Maxx's customers have been defrauded as a result of the security failure, Mr Hagman said the impact of an investigation by the information commissioner would be unprecedented: 'This is not a little site, it's a big, well-respected player and I think this case is going to have a profound effect on how the industry deals with security.'

David Hill, ID theft specialist at the personal security company red24, said: 'People should most definitely be concerned, and if they have shopped in TK Maxx they should go back through their credit card and bank statements to make sure no fraudulent transactions have taken place. Criminals carrying out credit card fraud will often make small purchases as these are less likely to stand out and may go undetected. If people do spot suspect transactions . . . they should immediately shut down their accounts and any linked accounts and register with a credit reference agency.'

New legislation coming into force in June will impose tough penalties and sanctions on companies that fail to safeguard their customers' card information.

British consumers should ring **0800 779 015** and those in the Republic of Ireland **0044 800 77915**. The homepage at www.tkmaxx.com has a customer alert with updated information.

## FAQ: TK Maxx

### When did this happen?

According to TK Maxx, the intrusions began in July 2005 and cover credit and debit card purchases stretching back to 2003. The hacking activity ended in December 2006, which is likely to be the first time the company became aware of a problem. It admitted the breach in January, but it was only this week that the full extent of the problems was revealed.

### Why did the problems last so long?

In most cases, a company discovering a security breach will act to close down the loophole that lets hackers in immediately. However, it is quite possible that criminals could have been operating invisibly for almost 18 months before being discovered.

### Why did they keep details on file?

There are no strict rules on how long transaction data can be held, and guidelines from Britain's privacy watchdog suggest it can be kept for as long as there is a 'business use'.

Source: Rebecca Smithers and Bobbie Johnson
31 March, 2007 The *Guardian*
**www.guardian.co.uk**.

## Article 14.3

### AIB fraud 'going on for years'

Allied Irish Banks (AIB) says the alleged fraud dis-covered earlier this month at its US subsidiary had been going on for five years. 'The periods in which the losses arose extend back to 1997,' said chief executive Michael Buckley. The revelation came as the bank reported its results for 2001 and finalised the losses it incurred as a result of the fraud at $691m (£484m). This is less than the initial estimate of the losses, which amounted to $750m. But the company was also hit by the news that it had suffered another loss in the US, although the £7m loss was not the result of fraud, but poor trading. However, it will raise more questions about the bank's risk management and control mechanism.

The bank's management, meanwhile, is still com-ing to terms with the huge losses at its Allfirst sub-sidiary. 'The suspected fraud has been a substantial blow to all AIB stakeholders,' said Mr Buckley. 'I am determined to spare no effort in repairing the damage we have suffered.'

Pre-tax profits during 2001 fell 47% to 612m euros (£374m; $535m).

Austin Hughes, chief economist with rival IIB bank in Dublin, told the BBC's World Business Report that it was a big hit for AIB. 'But at the same time it shows that the bank is still fairly strong in as much as it can absorb it,' he said. Without the $691m loss, the bank would have seen its pre-tax profits rise 10% to €1.4bn.

The bank has blamed the alleged fraud at its subsidiary Allfirst on the actions of currency trader John Rusnak. Mr Rusnak's lawyers have insisted that he did not steal money from the bank. Allfirst has reported a net loss of $36.8 for 2001, down from its restated net profits of $47.3m. Following the revela-tions of the loss, questions were asked about AIB's internal controls and risk management processes. The FBI and AIB are both currently investigating the circumstances behind the loss.

Source: BBC News, 20 February 2002,
**www.bbc.co.uk/news**.

## Article 14.4

### Satellite TV card details posted on pirate websites

A 19 year-old student has been charged with steal-ing details of satellite television smart cards and posting them on the internet. Los Angeles resident Igor Serebryany was hired to scan technical papers needed by satellite TV provider DirecTV as part of a lawsuit. But prosecutors claim that he sent hundreds of digital documents to three satellite pirate websites. According to *The New York Times*, this could help pirates develop hacks for DirecTV's smart cards.

Federal prosecutors explained that Serebryany would be charged under the rarely used 1996 Economic Espionage Act and faces a maximum sentence of 10 years in prison and a $250,000 fine.

The documents contained technical specifications for DirecTV's Period 4 generation of satellite smart cards. The technical details were valuable because the three previous generations of DirecTV access cards have already been hacked by pirates, costing the company a fortune in lost revenues.

The company has 11 million paying subscribers in the US, but industry analysts estimate that an additional million or more households illegally receive DirecTV signals.

Source: Nick Farrell, 3 January 2003,
**www.vnunet.com**.

## Article 14.5

### Citigroup pays $75m to end action

Citigroup is to pay $75m (£39.2m) to settle a class-action suit over its role in the collapse of telecom network provider Global Crossing. The US banking giant had been accused of issuing inflated research reports and failing to flag up conflicts of interest in the three-year-old case.

Citigroup denied wrongdoing, saying it made the settlement to end the expense and uncertainty of further litigation. The terms of the settlement need to be approved by a US district court.

New York-based Citigroup added that the pay-out resolves claims of investors in Global Crossing and its Asian affiliate between 1999 and 2003. In March last year Global Crossing's founder Gary Winnick and some former officers and directors at the firm agreed to pay $325m to settle investor lawsuits. The Citigroup settlement will help to 'compensate Global Crossing stock holders who lost a tremendous amount of money,' said Jay Eisenhofer, the plaintiffs' lead lawyer. 'Hopefully, we'll be able to obtain more from the remaining defendants.'

Other defendants in the ongoing case include the Canadian Imperial Bank of Commerce unit CIBC World Markets Corporation, US financial services company JP Morgan Chase and the now defunct auditor Arthur Andersen. The investors accused Global Crossing, former officers and directors, and advisers of falsifying financial filings to hide losses.

The Public Employees Retirement System of Ohio and the State Teachers Retirement System of Ohio, two of the main claimants in the case, alleged that they lost more than $110m as a result of alleged accounting fraud. Global Crossing filed for Chapter 11 bankruptcy protection in January 2002 as it struggled with huge debts and amid questions about its accounting practices. The company had built a 100,000 mile (160,900km) network of fibre optic cables around the world, but crashed when the internet and telecoms bubble burst. The group emerged from bankruptcy in December 2003 under the control of Singapore Technologies Telemedia.

Source: BBC News Online, 3 March 2005,
**www.bbc.co.uk/news**.

### Analysis of internal and external risk

The analysis of risk, or risk assessment/evaluation, is the study of the weaknesses and threats and

- the likelihood of such threats materialising,
- the possible loss and/or impact of such threats, and
- the theoretical effectiveness of security measures/internal control procedures.

That is a risk assessment is concerned with:

- the identification and analysis of risks relevant to the achievement of operational objectives, financial reporting objectives and/or compliance objectives,
- the determination of expected losses, and
- the establishment of the degree of risk acceptability to system operations.

Such an assessment seeks to answer three simple questions:

- What can go wrong?
- How likely is it to occur? and
- What would the consequences be?

The issue of risk analysis and risk exposure was explored in Chapter 13 but such analysis and assessment is also designed to assist in:

- the formulation of appropriate control strategies/policies that can be incorporated into the company/organisation control environment, and
- the implementation of relevant procedures and processes that can be incorporated in the company's/organisation's range of control activities.

## Information and communication

Appropriate and relevant information, and efficient, cost-effective and well-organised communication channels are essential prerequisite for effecting adequate control. Information about a company's:

- strategic plans,
- control environment,
- internal and external risks,
- control activities,
- current operational activities, and
- current performance,

must be communicated up, down and of course across the company's management structure/hierarchy.

Clearly relevant information must be:

- appropriately identified,
- captured,
- transmitted, and
- communicated,

not only in an understandable form/context but, more importantly, in a relevant and appropriate timeframe to enable recipients to carry out/undertake their activities and associated responsibilities effectively and efficiently.

Clearly such information (structured and/or unstructured) may be:

- information concerning internal operations – based primarily on internally generated data, and/or
- information concerning external conditions and events – external activities or operations are required to adequately inform internal business decision-making/management processes and procedures.

Such communication channels may be:

- formal – within a predetermined and regulated hierarchical structure, and/or
- informal – within an undefined and unregulated social framework.

## Monitoring

Monitoring refers to the collection and analysis of financial and non-financial information on a regular basis in order to evaluate performance on control activities. It includes regular management and supervisory activities, and other control associated actions undertaken by other personnel in the performance of their duties and in the exercising of their responsibilities.

It is, in essence, the assessment of control activities either:

- over period of time, or
- over a range of corporate activities.

Such monitoring is usually accomplished through:

- the continuous monitoring/evaluation of all control activities within a control environment, and/or
- the separate evaluation of specific pre-identified control activities/internal control procedures/processes within a control environment,

through the use of:

- internal self-assessments,
- internal/external peer reviews, and/or
- internal audits.

Clearly the scope and frequency of separate evaluations will depend primarily on the risks associated with a particular control activity and the effectiveness of continuous ongoing monitoring procedures.

Whilst the monitoring of control activities is often seen as an internal activity – that is such monitoring is normally concerned with inputs, activities and outputs – it can also be an external activity.

The purpose of monitoring control activities – whether as a continuous process or a series of separate evaluations – is to assess the quality of such control activities/internal control systems (usually over time) and:

- ensure the regular collection and analysis of information,
- assist in timely decision making,
- promote accountability, and
- provide the basis for organisation learning.

## And internal control?

Clearly, internal control – as a composed framework of five interrelated components – is an ever-changing, ever-evolving, ever-developing collection of related processes, procedures and activities. However whilst the existence of an appropriate internal control framework can clearly assist a company in:

- ensuring the reliability of its financial reporting,
- ensuring compliance with extant laws and regulations,
- maintaining long-term wealth creation/maximisation,
- minimising all possible losses, and
- ensuring corporate survival,

it is nevertheless important to realise that the existence of an adequate internal control framework does not in any way provide any absolute guarantee and/or any unqualified assurance as to a company's future success.

For example individual component aspects of internal control may operate efficiently but poor and/or faulty management decision-making procedures may reduce the effectiveness of such internal control. In addition, internal control activities whilst appropriate may be circumvented through:

- the conscious collusion of one or more individuals, and/or
- inappropriate management activities.

Finally, the effectiveness of internal controls may be adversely affected by management imposed resource constraints. Remember – the benefit accrued from the imposition of any internal control procedure/process must outweigh the cost of imposing that internal control.

## Classification of controls

There are many ways of classifying different types of controls that comprise internal control, the most commonly used being:

- classification of controls by function, for example:
  - preventative controls,
  - detective controls,
  - corrective controls, and
- classification of controls by type/scope, for example:
  - general controls, and
  - application controls.

Before we look at each of the above in more detail, it would perhaps be useful to note that whether controls are classified by function or type/scope, there is – perhaps somewhat predictably – a degree of commonality or overlap between the types of controls included in each of the two classifications. As illustrated by Figure 14.4:

- application controls essentially comprise of either preventative and detective type controls, whereas
- general controls essentially comprise of preventative, detective and, in some instances, corrective type controls.

### Classification by function

#### Preventative controls

Preventative controls are proactive controls designed to prevent and/or deter the occurrence of adverse events and the loss of assets and/or resources. Examples of such controls would be:

- the segregation of management/administrative duties,
- segregation of transaction processing duties,
- the existence and use of appropriate and adequate formal documentation,
- the existence and use of proper authorisation procedures/processes,

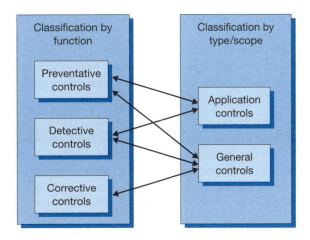

**Figure 14.4** Classification of controls – by function and by type/scope

- the formal controlling of access to assets/resources/facilities, and
- the existence and use of defined policies/procedures/processes.

### Detective controls

Detective controls are passive/reflexive controls or 'after the event' controls. They are designed to detect undesirable consequences of events which may have already occurred. Examples of such controls would be:

- the duplicate checking of calculations,
- the preparation of monthly accounting trial balances,
- the review of policy procedures and controls,
- periodic physical stock takes,
- periodic reconciliations of balances (e.g. debtors, creditors and bank), and
- periodic internal audits.

### Corrective controls

Corrective controls are active controls designed to eliminate and/or remedy the causes of adverse threats and/or undesirable events.

Examples of such controls would be:

- the creation and retention of backup copies of transaction data/information,
- the creation and retention of backup copies of master files,
- adherence to data protection policies, and
- the existence and use of adequate data processing correction procedures.

Put another way, although there is some overlap, in a control context:

- approvals procedures are generally preventative in nature,
- reconciliation and review processes tend to be detective in nature,
- asset/resources management procedures are typically corrective in nature,
- asset/resource security procedures tend to be both preventative and detective in nature, and
- segregation of management/administrative duties and the segregation of transaction processing duties are often viewed as preventative in nature although they are sometimes regarded as corrective.

## Classification by type/scope

### General controls

General controls relate to all activities involving the company's/organisation's resources, assets and facilities (including accounting information systems resources).

They are designed to:

- ensure that a company's/organisation's control environment remains stable and secure,
- maintain the integrity of corporate functions/activities (including accounting information systems processing functions/activities) and associated systems and networks,
- preserve the on-going reliability of the company's/organisation's control environment *and* enhance the effectiveness of application controls,
- maintain appropriate levels of physical security practices and environmental protection measures to minimise the possible risk of vandalism, theft and/or sabotage, and
- ensure the adoption of appropriate disaster planning and recovery protocols to ensure continuity of systems, networks and processing procedures.

In an accounting information systems context, general controls seek to ensure that:

- all appropriate data is correctly processed,
- all systems applications and network functions and processes are operated in accordance with established schedules and protocols,
- all processing errors are identified, traced and resolved,
- appropriate recovery procedures are established for processing failures,
- data/information file backups are maintained and updated at periodic intervals,
- systems/network development and change control procedures are applied, and
- all related human resources activities are monitored and reviewed.

General controls are generally classified into the following categories:

- organisational controls,
- documentation controls,
- access controls,
- asset management controls,
- management practice controls, and
- information systems controls.

## Organisational controls

Organisational controls usually exhibit a preventative control focus and/or a detective control focus and comprise of all those controls that are derived from and/or related to the structural composition of a company. They are inevitably political in nature and are invariably associated with:

- the hierarchical nature of the company, and
- the structural relationship between company personnel – their duties, activities and responsibilities.

In a social context, such controls normally manifest themselves in the form of:

- a functional separation of management/administrative processes, procedures and protocols – a preventative control focus,
- a segregation of duties, activities and responsibilities between company/organisation personnel – also a preventative control focus, and
- the independent monitoring/reviewing of processes, procedures and protocols – a detective control focus.

The purpose of organisational controls is to establish *organisational autonomy* or, more appropriately, *function/activity independence*, with the primary objective being to ensure the complete separation of incompatible functions and activities. As such organisational controls normally seek to ensure a separation between:

- procedures concerned with the *authorisation* of transactions,
- activities associated with the *custody* of assets/liabilities,
- processes connected to the *recording* of transactions, and
- functions related to the *controlling* of assets/liabilities.

Whilst there can be little doubt that the principal activities of the company and its associated (externally imposed) regulatory requirements, and the internal management/organisational structure of the company/organisation and its associated internal politics, will clearly influence:

- 'how' such a separation of management/administrative processes and procedures is realised, and
- 'how' such a segregation of duties and/or activities is implemented,

it is the composition and availability of resources within the company that will, perhaps more importantly, determine the balance between a preventative control focus and a detective control focus.

Consider first, the issue of a small/medium-sized company. For such a company – a company with limited financial assets and often limited personnel resources – the existence of organisational controls established upon the separation of management/administrative processes and procedures, and the segregation of transaction processing duties/functions, may not only be impractical and unrealistic, but more importantly unfeasible and perhaps inappropriate. Where resource constraints exist that not only impose limitations on the scope of such organisational controls but also restrict the effectiveness of such controls, the emphasis of control activities – as a component of internal control – often migrates from organisational controls with a preventative control focus (separation of processes and procedures and the segregation of duties/activities) to organisational controls with a detective control focus (independent management monitoring/internal audit – usually 'after the event monitoring' of processes and procedures).

A short-term resource led solution that is – certainly in the longer term – a particularly risky internal control strategy.

Consider next the issue of information technology and computer-based transaction processing. For many large companies – and to an increasing extent also small/medium-sized companies – computer-based transaction processing has become the norm, with many companies now (as a matter of general business practice) employing a wide range of information systems technologies. For example, in 2005 89% of UK businesses used transaction websites that allow customers to initiate transactions (for larger UK businesses this figure was 93%).[8] Within such companies a number of important transaction processing functions/controls are often integrated/automated, for example:

- customer credit approval (where appropriate),
- customer order authorisation, and
- customer payment approval.

More importantly, information systems technologies have become a key controlling feature in an array of transaction processing system activities – an array of transaction processing activities in which the apparent complete separation of control activities appears no longer possible! To maintain/ensure some degree of control – some degree of accountability within such companies – a separation of administrative responsibilities or segregation of functions and activities must exist, for example, between:

- information systems development activities,
- data management/processing procedures,
- information and communications services functions, and
- information systems administration activities.

In other words, within such companies' transaction processing systems the preventative control focus remains – integrated within the information systems management, design and implementation.

## Documentation controls

Documentation[9] controls are all those controls associated with managing the format and content of all corporate documentation utilised in processes and procedures connected to:

- the acquisition and recording of data and/or information,
- the storage of data and/or information, and
- the distribution of data and/or information.

Such data/information can be *permanent* in nature – for example data/information relating to:

- established policies and procedures,
- management hierarchy,
- responsibility structures,
- administrative procedures, and/or
- operational protocols,

and/or *transactional* in nature – for example data/information relating to:

- all source input documentation,
- all documentation relating to processing procedures, and
- all output-based documentation.

Documentation controls should ensure that:

- all documentation is controlled,
- all documentation (including changes to existing documentation) is approved prior to use, and
- all (details and examples of) approved documentation is properly secured within a documentation library.

In addition to the above permanent and/or transaction data/information-related documentation, where information systems technologies are used extensively in transaction processing then additional documentation controls would exist, for example:

- system documentation – including documentation relating to:
  - systems management and development policies,
  - information technology operations procedures and policies, and
  - security and disaster recovery procedures and policies,
- systems application documentation – including documentation relating to:
  - application procedures (systems flowcharts and narrative descriptions),
  - data format and file descriptions,
  - input/output documentation (format descriptions and details),
  - charts of accounts (relationship schedules), and
  - control and error correction policies and procedures,
- system program documentation – including documentation relating to:
  - program procedures (program flowcharts and narrative descriptions),
  - input/output documentation (format descriptions and details),
  - change procedure and policies,
  - program content and listings,
  - test procedures and policies, and
  - error reporting policies and procedures,
- data documentation – including documentation relating to:
  - data elements/format descriptions, and
  - data element relationships,
- operating documentation – including documentation related to:
  - performance and management instructions,
  - set-up policies and procedures,
  - recovery and restart policies and procedures, and
  - report distribution lists and procedures,

- user documentation – including documentation related to:
  - data input/entry policies and procedures,
  - input accuracy/completeness checks,
  - reports formats, and
  - error correction policies and procedures.

## Access controls

Access controls exhibit a preventative control focus and are all those controls associated with ensuring:

- the security of company/organisation assets and resources,
- the integrity of corporate/organisational operations and activities, and
- the confidentiality of corporate data and/or information,

and minimising the risk of:

- unauthorised/undetected access,
- loss,
- misappropriation, and/or
- improper modification, deletion and/or alteration.

We will consider access controls later in this chapter.

## Asset management controls

Asset management controls are all those controls associated with ensuring:

- assets are properly managed, suitably controlled and appropriately valued,
- assets are properly recorded and appropriate control registers/records are maintained of all asset acquisitions, transfers and disposals,
- periodic reconciliations are undertaken to confirm asset values and corroborate asset balances, and
- periodic reviews and assessments are undertaken to determine the ongoing condition of and relative value of the assets.

Asset management controls seek to minimise possible financial loss associated with:

- accidental loss/damage,
- deliberate impairment,
- larceny,
- incorrect valuation, and/or
- bad management decision making.

They are closely associated with access controls and their role in maintaining/protecting the security of assets (discussed later).

## Management practice controls

Management practice controls are all those controls associated with minimising management-related risks which may arise from:

- inadequate and/or unsatisfactory management decision making,
- deficient and/or incompetent management practices, and/or
- dishonest and/or fraudulent management activities.

Indeed, as history has repeatedly revealed, for example with financial scandals concerning BCCI, Barings Bank, Enron and Parmalat, bad management activities and practices, or perhaps more appropriately *the activities and practices of bad management*, often lie at heart of many of the most spectacular corporate collapses – certainly many of the major corporate failures during the latter part of the 20th century and the early part of the 21st century.

Management practice controls comprise of not only the general controls discussed so far but also include all controls associated with the management, administration and development of application systems, and include all those controls associated with systems management and development, in particular:

- amendment/modification controls, and
- development management controls.

Although we will explore the above controls in more detail in Chapter 16 when we discuss issues relating to systems development and design, such controls would include all those controls associated with the planning, analysis, design and implementation of new and/or amended application systems.

## Information systems controls

Information systems controls are all those controls associated with:

- information technology management, and
- information systems administration.

Information technology management controls seek to ensure the protected custody of computer hardware and related peripheral equipment, and the security and integrity of software programs. Such management controls are clearly related to access issues (and related security issues) and will be discussed later in this chapter.

Information systems administration controls seek to ensure the correct and appropriate processing of data and information, through:

- the scheduling of data collection activities,
- the continuous monitoring of data processing activities, and
- the management of data/information output activities.

### Application controls

Application controls – sometimes called transaction controls – are controls that relate to specific aspects of a company's/organisation's processes, procedures, resources, assets and/or facilities (including accounting information systems resources).

They are designed to:

- prevent and detect transaction processing errors,
- identify transaction processing discrepancies, and
- correct transaction processing irregularities.

In an accounting information systems context, application controls (or application specific controls) seek to ensure that:

- only authorised transaction data appropriate to the specific systems is processed,
- all transaction processing is efficient, effective, appropriate, accurate and completed in accordance with established systems, specific procedures and protocols,
- system-specific transaction processing procedures and transaction processing programs are secure, and
- all system-specific transaction processing errors are identified and corrected, and accounted for when a error occurs.

Application controls are generally classified into the following categories:

- input controls (e.g. undertaking editing tests),
- process controls (e.g. ensuring appropriate record counts), and
- output controls (e.g. maintaining error catalogues/listings).

## Input controls

Input controls are designed to ensure the validity, appropriateness and correctness of system/application specific input data, for example:

- payroll input data (e.g. hours worked, hourly pay rates) are processed by the payroll system,
- purchasing input data (e.g. payment of invoices) are processed by the purchasing system, and
- sales input data (e.g. the issue of sales invoices) are processed by the sales system.

They would, for example, include the use of:

- appropriateness checks (e.g. data matching checks),
- authorisation procedures checks,
- conversion controls tests (e.g. batch control totals and/or hash control totals),
- record count checks,
- error identification tests/checks,
- error correction procedure checks, and
- completeness checks (e.g. sequence totals and/or control totals).

In addition to the above, where input data is transmitted (from a source origin to a processing destination), additional supplementary input controls would normally be required and would for example include:

- transmission tests (e.g. echo checks and/or redundancy checks),
- security checks (e.g. verification checks), and
- validation checks.

## Processing controls

Processing controls are designed to ensure that:

- only authorised system/application specific input/transaction data are processed,
- all authorised transaction data are processed accurately, correctly and completely,
- all appropriate program files/system procedures are used in the processing of transaction data,
- all processing is validated and verified, and
- an appropriate audit trail of all transaction processing is maintained.

They would, for example, include the use of:

- file maintenance checks,
- file labelling checks,
- verification checks,
- processing logic checks,
- limit checks,
- reasonableness checks,
- sequence checks,
- audit trail controls,

- control totals checks, and
- data checks (e.g. checks for duplicate data and/or missing data).

## Output controls

Output controls are designed to ensure that:

- all output is validated, verified and authorised,
- all output is accurate, reliable and complete, and
- all output is distributed to approved and authorised recipients.

They would, for example, include the use of:

- distribution controls,
- verification checks,
- reconciliation checks,
- review checks (e.g. source data/document comparisons), and
- reconciliation of totals.

In addition to the above, where output data is transmitted (from a processing origin to a user destination), additional supplementary output controls would normally be required and would for example include:

- transmission tests,
- recipient identifier checks,
- redundancy checks,
- security checks, and
- validation checks (e.g. continuity checks).

## Alternative classifications of control

Although the classification of controls by function and/or by type/scope tends to dominate much of the academic and professional literature on internal control, auditing and accounting information systems (indeed for the remainder of this chapter we will adopt the classification of internal control by type/scope), many alternative classification schema exist.

For example:

- a spatial/directional classification – between direct and/or indirect controls,
- a temporal classification – between proactive and/or reactive controls (or *before the event* and *after the event* controls),
- a social classification – between formal and/or informal controls,
- an objective classification – between facilitating and/or constraining controls,
- a regulatory classification – between voluntary and/or statutory controls, and
- an environmental classification – between mechanistic and/or non-mechanistic controls.

So which classification system is best? All of them . . . and none of them! Remember, a classification is a purposeful socio-political creation, a socially constructed discrimination. It is a distribution in accordance with a set of established criteria and no more than a conscious differentiation based on a selected variable and/or group of variables. Not only is:

- the content of classification – that is what is included and what is not included in the classification – constrained by the social functionality imposed by the classifier but, more importantly,
- the context of a classification – that is what is the purpose and what is not the purpose of a classification – constrained by the political structure imposed by the classifier,

## Systems security and internal control – purpose and scope

Systems security is indelibly linked to internal control, the aim of such security measures/ protocols being to provide an appropriate level of protection from:

- unauthorised and/or undetected access to corporate systems,
- unauthorised use and/or acquisition of corporate assets, resources and facilities,
- improper deletion and/or alteration of systems data, information and/or procedures,
- systems breakdown and/or processing interruptions, and
- systems failure.

Such security measures/protocols can be classified into four categories, these being:

- internal control procedures and processes designed to maintain the security of tangible/ non-tangible resources – (see also Chapter 16),
- internal control procedures and processes designed to maintain the security of data/ information – (see also Chapter 6 in particular issues regarding the Data Protection Act 1998),
- internal control procedures and processes designed to maintain the security and integrity of company/organisational networks (including computer-based networks) – (see also Chapters 5 and 6), and
- internal control procedures and processes designed to assist in the retrieval, recovery, and/or reconstruction (where necessary) of any:
  - lost assets, resources and/or facilities, and/or
  - corrupted data/information,
  as a result of an adverse incident/event and/or systems failure. (Such measures are often referred to as disaster contingency and recovery procedures.)

## Internal control and the security of tangible/non-tangible resources

Such security measures/protocols would normally consist of (internal) controls designed to:

- validate and verify the existence (or otherwise) of all assets and resources,
- monitor and control access to assets and resources, and
- restrict/control the privileges of users who have a legitimate right of access to assets and resources.

The primary aim of any such security measures being to:

- ensure the accountability/traceability of all assets and resources,
- minimise and/or prevent opportunities for the misappropriation and/or theft of assets and resources, and
- facilitate the detection and recovery of any misappropriated assets and resources.

To ensure accountability/traceability, such security measures could include:

- the use of asset registers to record the location/valuation of company assets,
- the use of regular asset audits (including physical stock-checks and, where appropriate, valuation checks),

- the use and maintenance of appropriate control procedures for the acquisition and/or disposal of assets,
- the maintenance of appropriate records of, and procedures for, the movement of assets, and
- the use of security tagging of valuable assets.

To minimise and/or prevent opportunities for the misappropriation and/or theft of assets, such security measures could include:

- the use of access controls (e.g. ID badges, smart cards, security passwords, and/or personalised biometric measurements) to define/restrict access to assets, and
- the use of surveillance controls (e.g. the use of intrusion detection systems and procedures) to detect inappropriate use and/or unauthorised access.

## Internal control and the security of data/information

Such security measures/protocols would normally consist of (internal) controls designed to:

- validate and verify the existence (or otherwise) of all data and/or information files,
- monitor and control use of, access to and transfer of data and/or information files, and
- restrict/control the privileges of users who have a legitimate right of access to data and/or information files.

The primary aim of any such security measures being to:

- prevent the dishonest acquisition of data and/or information files,
- prevent the deceitful misuse of data and/or information files,
- restrict the fraudulent variation, alteration and/or adaptation to data and/or information files,
- prevent the deceitful infection and/or destruction of data and/or information files, and
- minimise the deliberate and fraudulent reproduction and transfer of data and/or information files.

In addition, for companies whose activities require the collection, storage and use of personal data/information, such security measures should also ensure compliance with the requirements/provisions of the Data Protection Act 1998 (see also Chapter 6).

## Internal controls and the security of company/organisational networks

Such security measures/protocols would normally consist of (internal) controls (often technology-based) designed to:

- validate and verify all access to company/organisational networks, and
- monitor and control the use of company/organisational networks.

The primary aim of any such security measures being to:

- ensure the continued security of company/organisational networks and related programs and files, and/or
- maintain the integrity of company/organisational networks and related programs and files,

to prevent:

- the unauthorised appropriation of company/organisational network programs,
- the malicious removal (accidental or otherwise) and/or destruction/sabotage of company/organisational network programs,
- the deliberate and/or malevolent infection of company/organisational networks,
- the misappropriation and misuse of confidential and sensitive corporate information,
- the theft of protected information, and/or
- any other adverse events that could lead to the possible disruption of a corporate service and/or facilities.

Such security measures will invariably (although not exclusively) comprise of computer-based technologies used to:

- manage access,
- control permission and, where appropriate,
- monitor use.

Such tools and technologies would include:

- the use of ID protocols,
- the use of hardware and/or software firewalls, and
- the use of intrusion detection systems.

(See Chapter 13 for further details.)

So, in terms of systems security, especially computer-based systems (including of course computer-based accounting information systems), what are the most common, security-based vulnerable areas?

McClure *et al.* (2005)[10] suggested the following top 14 key areas:

- inadequate router access control,
- unsecured and unmonitored remote access,
- information leakage,
- host running unnecessary services,
- weak, easily guessed and/or reused passwords,
- excessive user privileges,
- incorrectly configured internet servers,
- incorrectly configured firewall and/or router,
- out-of-date an/or unpatched software,
- excessive file and/or directory access,
- excessive trust relationships,
- unauthenticated services,
- inadequate logging, monitoring and detection capabilities, and
- lack of accepted/promulgated security policies.

## Disaster contingency and recovery planning

The term 'systems failure' is a generic term, one that can and often is used to describe the adverse consequences of a wide range of incidents and events which may affect a company's ongoing operational capacity. Such incidents/events could range from:

- minor incidents – such as:
  - the failure of a network server,
  - the temporary failure of power supply,
  - the partial flooding of administration offices, to
- major events – such as:
  - the failure of online payment/receipting facilities,
  - long-term industrial action by key employees,
  - significant industrial accident, to
- company-wide disaster/crises – such as:
  - the total failure of core facilities (e.g. IT services/processes),
  - the complete destruction of key operational assets/resources and loss of personal resources.

All of which can be caused by or result from a wide variety of factors including:

- external environment-based factors – such as earthquakes, floods and fire,
- socio-economic-based factors – such as power supply problems, infra-structure failure and industrial action,
- socio-political factors – such as social unrest, bombings and war, and/or
- internal environment-based factors – such as corporate sabotage and user error.

In today's highly volatile and decidedly unpredictable environment in which the only certainty is uncertainty, adverse incidents and events occur all the time. Whilst some of these incidents and events will be minor in nature and their potential impact limited, some will inevitably be major in nature and their potential impact both serious and wide-ranging – perhaps in extreme situations, even fatal. Clearly then, it is important for a company to possess an appropriate and up-to-date plan of action not only to manage but to limit the impact of such incidents/events. An appropriate and up-to-date disaster contingency and recovery plan (DCRP) is needed to provide a cohesive collection of approved procedures, guidelines and protocols. It provides a formal incident/crisis management framework to assist in:

- minimising the overall impact of any adverse incident/event, and
- ensuring the continuity of business activities and other related operational capabilities.

A comprehensive DCRP would normally consist of two defined (albeit interrelated) protocols:

- a prevention protocol, and
- a recovery protocol.

See Figure 14.5.

A prevention protocol (or 'before the event' protocol) would normally comprise of:

- a disaster contingency management (DCM) system designed to maintain the relevance and appropriateness of the company's DCRP (especially where substantial organisational change has occurred),
- disaster contingency backup (DCB) procedures designed to secure and maintain the safe storage of company assets, resources, data and information, and
- a disaster contingency testing (DCT) protocol designed to test, using mock disaster scenarios, the suitability and effectiveness of a company's DCRP.

A recovery protocol (or after the event protocol) would normally comprise of:

- a disaster contingency emergency (DCE) protocol designed to provide procedures and guidelines to be followed during and immediately after an incident/disaster, and
- a disaster contingency recovery (DCR) protocol designed to restore/re-establish full operational capacity.

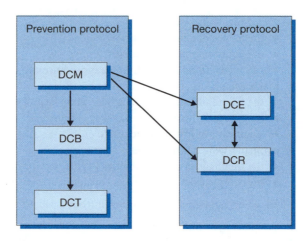

**Figure 14.5** Disaster contingency and recovery plan

Remember, there is no magic answer, off-the-shelf solution or generic step-by-step reference guide to managing such adverse incidents/events. The key to a company's recovery from any adverse incident/event and/or corporate-wide crisis/disaster is prioritisation – that is the *determination of criticality* and the identification of those aspects of the business (its assets, resources, processes and services) which are critical to its continuing survival and those which are not.

Put simply, for even the most well-prepared of companies, the ability to recover all affected assets and resources – to restore all affected business processes, services and facilities – immediately after a traumatic adverse incident/event, even from a minor isolated event, can be severely impeded by the ambiguity of past events, the uncertainty of future events and the irrationality of management!

Criticality is the ascertainment of importance or, perhaps more appropriately, a question of significance, founded on a determination of how long a company/organisation can survive without a set of business assets and/or resources, a collection of processes and/or procedures or a group of essential services and/or facilities. Clearly, whilst some assets and resources, etc. may require/necessitate immediate recovery, others may not. It is actually quite surprising what a company/organisation can survive without – at least in the short term!

## Prevention

Whether an imposed regulatory requirement, or merely a commercial/financial consideration, it is important (if not essential) for a company/organisation:

- to identify and prioritise the importance of each of its corporate systems/systems element, and
- to determine the possible consequences of such systems/system elements failing as a result of an adverse incident/event.

A prevention protocol would seek to determine and review (on a regular basis):

- the existence, relevance and appropriateness of existing systems and procedures,
- the existence of any local/regional threats[11] to operational capabilities,
- the existence of any potential single points of failure with the company's system/procedures,[12] and
- the existence of relevant and appropriate licences, warranty agreements and relevant support contracts.

And as a consequence:

- identify possible adverse changes within the company's environment,
- assess the possible consequences of such environmental changes,
- eliminate or at least reduce corporate dependency on any single service source, asset and/or resource,[13] and
- minimise the disruption that may be caused by any potential adverse incident/event.

How? Through the development and existence of appropriate security measures/internal control procedures that would include, for example:

- appropriate staff appointment procedures, staff education and crisis awareness training,
- the maintenance of regular backups of data and information and the storage of such backups away from company premises,
- the use of mutual support agreements with other unrelated companies and/or organisations,
- the existence of backup resource facilities and/or incident support premises and equipment, and
- the regular testing of disaster contingency measures and procedures.

Although prevention is better than cure, unfortunately no matter how well informed the company/organisation may be – no matter how up-to-date, appropriate and effective its prevention protocols – adverse incidents/events will still occur.

## Recovery

A recovery protocol would normally consist of four key stages:

- qualification of the incident/event,
- containment of the incident/event,
- assessment of the impact of the incident/event, and
- application of countermeasures.

### Qualification of the incident/event

For qualification purposes, the key issue is the determination of:

- the size of the incident/event,
- the possible causes of the incident/event, and
- the possible consequences of the incident/event – both short and long-term.

For minor incidents it is probable that recovery, containment and assessment procedures would take place within the established management hierarchy of the company/organisation. The approval of countermeasures may well require higher level management approval. For major incidents however (including company-wide disasters/crises) most companies would assemble a pre-designated/pre-arranged incident response team which would, for example, include:

- for operational issues – managers from the company areas affected by the incident/event,
- for staffing and employment issues – human resource representatives/managers,
- for asset/resource issues – appropriate facilities/utilities managers and/or representatives, and
- for Public Relations (PR) issues – PR/corporate communications managers and/or representatives.

Clearly the size of the incident response team would depend on the nature and impact of the incident/event.

### Containment of the incident/event

For containment purposes the key issue is damage limitation – the minimising of consequences of any adverse incident/event by ensuring:

- affected systems, services, assets and/or resources are isolated (certainly if the incident is ongoing),
- appropriate human resources policies are implemented, and
- relevant and appropriate internal/external regulatory bodies are informed.

Such containment procedures must be:

- timely,
- relevant,
- appropriate and, of course,
- effective.

### Assessment of the impact of the incident/event

For assessment purposes it is essential not only to establish the extent of the potential damage of the incident/event but, more importantly, determine both the short- and long-term impact of the incident/event on the company and its business activities – commercially, financially and operationally.

Clearly, an essential aspect of such assessment procedures will be a determination of the source(s)/cause(s) of the incident/event. If malicious intent is suspected then:

- appropriate evidence must be collected, and
- relevant regulatory authorities (including the police) will need to be informed.

### Application of countermeasures

Once the nature of any incident/event has been qualified, once containment procedures have been introduced and once an appropriate assessment of the impact of the incident/event has been performed, a determination of appropriate countermeasures needs to be made. This is a formal active response to:

- alleviate the adverse consequences of an incident/event,
- mitigate any potential undesirable effects of such an incident/event, and
- minimise the possibility of future threats and/or vulnerabilities.

The determination and application of such countermeasures should of course be a collective decision either by the incident response team (should such a team exists) or by management in consultation with appropriate managers. More importantly such countermeasures should be applied in risk priority order and their effectiveness monitored to ensure predicated outcomes are achieved. Where appropriate – where the incident/event is of a major nature and one which may adversely affect the company's/organisation's future business activities – media and PR exercises may also be required as part of the countermeasures to alleviate any potential unfavourable market reactions resulting from possible speculation regarding the future viability of the company/organisation.

## Information and communication technology enabled innovations – internal control and systems security issues

As discussed in Chapter 4, information and communication technology innovations and developments – in particular those related to transaction processing systems such as:

- electronic data interchange (EDI), and
- electronic funds transfer (EFT),

continue to have a major, some would say revolutionary impact, on many of the functional aspects of corporate finance and accounting information systems.

Indeed, there can be little doubt that in a contemporary business context at least, the relationship between such enabling innovations and developments and accounting information systems – in particular internal control and systems security – continues to be an intimate if somewhat volatile and complex relationship. A relationship in which the processing and management opportunities presented by the evermore creative capabilities of information and communications technology continues to be tempered by the often overly pessimistic, some would say conservative, realism of the caretakers of contemporary capitalism – corporate management. A conservative realism in which the increasingly powerful 'push effect' of information and communication technology enabled innovations and developments have been, and indeed continue to be, frequently countered by the 'pull effect' of greater accountability and transparency – of greater internal control and systems security. See Figure 14.6.

So what are the push and pull effects? Rather than identifiable, cogent, rational and coherent forces – consider both the push and pull effect as generic terms – as expressions representing the opposing/balancing sides of a SWOT[14] matrix, with:

- the push effect representing the possible strengths and opportunities offered by what sometimes appears to be an almost never-ending progress and advancement in information and communication technology, and
- the pull effect representing the possible weaknesses and threats posed by information and communication technology innovations and developments.

## The push effect

So what have been and indeed continue to be the implications of the so-called push effect? Whilst the push effect of information and communication technology innovation and development on corporate finance and accounting information systems has been, and indeed continues to be, associated with the evermore complex integration of once diverse technologies or once unrelated procedures and processes, in a broad sense it can be sub-divided into four interrelated themes:

- the ever-increasing use of programmed processes and procedures to replace once established but increasingly redundant manual control procedures and processes,

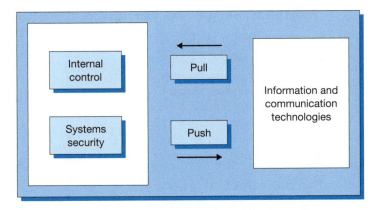

**Figure 14.6** Push/pull – internal control and information and communication technologies

- the increasing use of information and communication technology/computerised processes and procedures in data collection, data processing, data storage and data transfer procedures and processes,
- the growing use of information and communication technology/computerised processes and procedures in information provision and related services/facilities, and
- the ever-increasing transfer of control processes and procedures from the system process/procedure stage (or the execution stage) to the system development stage.

There can be little doubt that there are, and indeed continue to be, many benefits (strengths and opportunities) associated with some of the above themes, benefits such as:

- increased processing flexibility,
- increased application consistency,
- enhanced processing speeds and power,
- increased resource efficiency, and
- greater processing homogeneity.

For example:

- the increasing use of programmed processes and procedures forces users to follow the same fixed sequence of steps in the same fixed way in order to fulfil a specific task, and
- the increasing computerisation of data management procedures and information provision services/facilities promotes the homogenisation of data/information management activities and avoids many control problems associated with manual processing.

However, there can also be little doubt that there are many problems (weaknesses and threats) associated with some of the above themes, problems such as:

- decreased processing transparency,
- reduced visibility of processing control/measurement points, and
- increased risk of processing failure.

For example:

- the transferring of control processes and procedures to the development stage forces measurement points to be integrated within system processes and procedures and thus obscures the visibility of such measurement points and the transparency of system processes/procedure, and
- the ever-increasing integration of once diverse technologies and related procedures and processes whilst increasing operational capabilities also necessitates the use of a growing arsenal of control and security measures to mitigate the risks associated with the ever-present threats from use of information and communication technologies.

Threats that may:

- impair processing capabilities,
- compromise information confidentiality,
- damage information integrity,
- adversely affect control procedures,
- inhibit access to processing facilities,
- corrupt information authenticity, and
- prohibit access to and/or the availability of information.

## The pull effect

As suggested earlier, the pull effect is a generic expression referring to all those pre-emptive information and communication technology controls designed and implemented (within the company's/organisation's internal control and systems security framework) to minimise the risks and threats associated with/arising out of the increasing use of information and communication technology enabled innovations.

For some, the use of such information and communication technology controls represents a rational, prudent and coherent risk-averse approach to dealing with the weaknesses and uncertainties inherent within and the possible threat posed by such technology innovation and development, and is therefore good. For others, the use of such information and communication technology controls is symptomatic of the excessive bureaucracy that appears to characterise much of contemporary corporate management and its lack of understanding of and appreciation for the opportunities offered by such information and communication technology innovation and development, and is therefore bad.

In reality of course whilst it is important to grasp the opportunities offered by such information and communication technology innovation and development, it is also important to eliminate or at least minimise the impact of any associated threats and ensure that appropriate information and communication technology controls exist. So both sides are a bit right and a bit wrong!

What do we mean by pull effect information and communication technology controls? Information and communication technology controls are all those activities employed to ensure the proper functioning of a company's/organisation's information systems. Such controls are:

- a component aspect of a company's/organisation's information and communication technology infrastructure, and
- an essential element of a company's/organisation's internal control/system security measures,

and can, in a broad sense, be sub-divided into four interrelated themes:

- controls associated with process management controls,
- syntactic[15] controls associated with message/transmission structure,
- protocol management controls, and
- security controls/measures,

within which a variety of protection/security methods are often used, including:

- encryption,
- event logging,
- access control,
- routing control,
- physical security measures,
- fall back/backup systems,
- data recovery protocols,
- data and time stamps,
- confirmations,
- priority and pre-emption,
- authentication,
- digital signature, and
- message authentication codes.

Let's look at the above information and communication technology controls and associated protection/security methods in relation to:

- EDI (Electronic Data Interchange) and
- EFT (Electronic Funds Transfer).

## EDI and EFT

Electronic Data Interchange (EDI) and Electronic Funds Transfer (EFT) were discussed in detail in Chapter 4.

Essentially, EDI is the exchange of structured and pre-defined information using agreed message standards and transmission protocols from one computer application to another by electronic means and with a minimum of human intervention, or perhaps more appropriately it is the specific interchange methods agreed upon by national or international standards bodies for the transfer of business transaction data.

EFT is the transfer of funds between accounts by electronic means rather than conventional paper-based payment methods. It is a computerised system that processes:

- financial transactions, and
- information about financial transactions,

that affect an exchange of value between two parties and includes the transfer of money initiated through:

- an electronic terminal,
- an automated teller machine,
- a computer (via the internet), and
- a telephone.

EFT also applies to credit card and automated bill payments.

### Risks in EDI and EFT systems

Despite the overwhelming popularity of EDI and EFT systems, their use is clearly not without its problems and associated risks that include:

- the loss of physicality and the elimination of source documentation (e.g. purchase orders, invoices and payment documents),
- the loss of signatures of authorisation, and
- the loss of an audit trail.

Clearly, the use of EDI and EFT requires:

- procedural interdependence, and
- process integration,

founded not only on a reciprocal trust but more importantly a mutual reliance and understanding of security, a failure of which could result in:

- the unauthorised initiation and/or alteration of transactions,
- the potential corruption of transaction files and data, and
- the fraudulent alteration of application procedures, processes and protocols.

So what can be done? Below we discuss some possible solutions/answers.

### Controls in EDI and EFT systems

To minimise the possible problems and risks that may arise within an EDI and/or an EFT system, attention should be focused on four key areas:

- process management controls,
- syntactic controls,

- protocol management controls, and
- security controls.

### Process management controls

Process management controls are concerned with maintaining the validity of EDI and EFT processing, and ensuring the accuracy and completeness of transactions and transaction data.

Such controls should seek to ensure that:

- adequate and appropriate separation of duties exists within the EDI/EFT process,
- appropriate and where possible the most current version of EDI/EFT software is used,
- effective message authentication codes and encryption protocols are used, and
- appropriate system/network virus protection procedures/firewall protocols are in place.

### Syntactic controls

Syntactic controls are concerned with ensuring that appropriate outbound translation, communication and inbound translation protocols are effective. Such controls should ensure that:

- there are effective reciprocal acknowledgements confirming the occurrence of an EDI/EFT transaction, and
- appropriate translation headers and trailers are used during translation to ensure transaction completeness.

In addition, appropriate integrated test facilities could be used to monitor EDI and EFT transactions continuously.

### Protocol management controls

Protocol management controls are concerned with ensuring all applicable regulatory procedures and pronouncements are complied with.

Such controls should ensure that:

- appropriate user/operator identification codes and passwords are used,
- all EDI and EFT transmissions are authenticated and approved prior to internal processing, and
- all EDI and EFT processes and procedures comply with approved regulatory standards.

### Security controls

Security controls are concerned with maintaining the physical integrity of the EDI system. Such controls should ensure that:

- appropriate restrictions on physical access to EDI and EFT facilities are in place,
- appropriate constraints on authorisation exist,
- EDI and EFT backup files are maintained and securely stored,
- appropriate system/network intrusion detection protocols are in place, and
- approved EDI/EFT-related disaster contingency recovery protocols are in place.

## Concluding comments

There can be little doubt that:

- the increasingly chaotic realities of the global marketplace,
- the evermore uncertain realities of corporate activities, and
- the increasing demands of greater corporate responsibility and accountability,

have been responsible for promoting the need for more effective corporate governance and greater corporate accountability. Corporate management needs not only to understand the relevance of corporate control activities but, more importantly, regulate, monitor and control corporate procedures processes and activities. The existence of appropriate control processes and procedures within a company are needed to:

- provide reasonable assurances that business objectives – primarily the maximisation of share-holder wealth – will be achieved, and
- ensure any undesired events, unwelcome occurrences and/or unfavourable incidences will be prevented, and/or detected and corrected.

Clearly, whilst internal control and system security measures cannot directly influence the creative processes of wealth development/maximisation, they nonetheless play an important role in:

- maximising the utility of corporate processes and procedures,
- optimising the utility of corporate assets and resources, and
- sustaining the operational capability of the company.

## Key points and concepts

Application controls

Context filtering

Control activities

Control environment

Corrective controls

Detective controls

Disaster contingency and recovery plan

Disaster contingency backup procedures

Disaster contingency emergency protocol

Disaster contingency management
   system

Disaster contingency recovery protocol

Disaster contingency testing protocol

General controls

Information and communication
   technology control

Information control

Internal control

Macro level factors

Management control

Micro level factors

Monitoring

Preventative controls

Prevention protocol

Process management controls

Protocol management controls

Pull effect

Push effect

Recovery protocol

Relevance limits

Syntactic controls

Systems boundary

Systems security

Threshold limits

## References

Maslow, A.H. (1943) 'A Theory of Human Motivation', *Psychological Review*, 50, pp. 370–396.

Maslow, A.H. (1987) *Motivation and Personality* (3rd edn), HarperCollins, London.

McMlure, S. Scambray, J. and Kutz, G. (2005) *Hacking exposed: Network Security, Secrets, and Solutions*, McGraw-Hill, San Francisco.

## Self-review questions

1. Describe the five interrelated components that comprise the term 'internal control'.
2. Distinguished between preventative controls and detective controls.
3. Define the term 'corrective control' and describe four examples of such a corrective control relevant to a computer-based accounting information system.
4. Distinguished between general controls and application controls.
5. Define, describe and evaluate the following general controls:
   - organisational controls,
   - documentation controls,
   - access controls, and
   - asset management controls.
6. What are the main purposes of application controls?
7. What are systems security measures designed to ensure?
8. Define and describe the concept of business process re-engineering.
9. Describe the risks associated with:
   - EDI, and
   - EFT.
10. In relation to information and communication technology innovation and development, distinguish between:
    - the push effect, and
    - the pull effect.

## Questions and problems

### Question 1

In January 2006, Jessica Leigh (finance director) and Stephanie Dodsworth (sales director) both resigned from the management board of Deeport plc, a large UK retail company, following a critical report by the company's auditors, Barber LLP. The company's auditors found that insufficient internal controls and a lack of systems management had resulted in the fraudulent misuse of funds and resources. For the first time in its 22-year history, the company declared a loss of £26m (for the year ending 31 March 2006).

#### Required

Distinguish between general controls and application controls, and identify in broad terms only, the general control procedures and security measures that could be employed by a company such a Freeport plc to protect against the activities indicated in the above situation.

### Question 2

During a recent information systems review of HTM Ltd, the following internal control procedures were identified:

- Assigning different employees to maintain physical stock in the warehouse and the stock records.
- Storing high-value stock items within a secure area with authorised/restricted access.
- Requiring all payments for sales to be made by cheque/credit or debit card.
- Counting stock periodically and comparing the count of each item to the stock records.
- Requiring all returns of sold goods to be listed on a special credit form that is prepared and signed by a manager.
- E-mailing a monthly statement to each customer, showing the details of all transactions and the balance owed.

→

*Required*

Identify a risk exposure that each of the following control procedures or practices is intended to prevent or detect. For each of the above, provide an example of what might occur if the control were not in place and list one or more factors that could cause the risk exposure to be relatively high:

## Question 3

The business environment of the early 21st century continues to change with increasing vigour. The growth of e-commerce and e-retailing, and the use of the internet for the movement of goods, services and information has clearly promoted a greater interconnectivity. An interconnectivity that has not only opened up and created enormous business opportunities, but has also increased the exposure of UK businesses, in particular UK retail companies, to previously unknown levels of risks and security threats, the costs and consequences of which have been and indeed continue to be significant.[16]

*Required*

Critically evaluate the type and nature of risk and security threats such a company faces and the internal control procedures and security strategy/measures that it might employ to protect itself.

## Question 4

VeTel Ltd is a well-established industrial cleaning company with a turnover of approximately £30m. The company has 15 regional offices throughout the UK and its head office is in Beverley.

Five days ago, the company's head office suffered severe fire and the IT services and facilities department is completely destroyed. The cause of the fire has yet to be determined, but deliberate sabotage is not suspected. The company has activated its DCRP (last reviewed six months ago) and is currently at the qualification stage of recovery.

*Required*

Define and explain the main stages and contents of a DCRP and, making whatever assumptions you believe necessary, comment on VeTel Ltd's progress so far in recovering from the severe fire.

## Question 5

'The impact of innovations and developments in information and communication technology on corporate accounting information systems has removed the need for excessive internal control.' Discuss.

# Assignments

## Question 1

SEC Ltd, a small electrical accessories company, wants to design a company-wide computer purchasing system. To date the company has maintained a semi-manual record system for all its purchases.

For the previous three financial years the company has made average annual purchases of £34m (all purchases from UK suppliers) and average annual profits of approximately £10.6m. The company has approximately 350 employees working at six locations throughout the UK: Manchester, which is the company's head office, Birmingham, Leeds, Swindon, Bristol and Newcastle.

You have recently completed an audit of activities within the purchasing department within SEC Ltd. The department employs 15 buyers, seven supervisors, a manager and clerical personnel. Your audit has disclosed the following conditions:

- The company has no formal rules on conflicts of interest. Your analysis produced evidence that one of the 15 buyers in the department owns a substantial interest in a major supplier and that he procures supplies averaging £150,000 a year from that supplier. The prices charged by the supplier are competitive.
- Buyers select proposed sources without submitting lists of bidders for review. Your tests disclosed no evidence that higher costs were incurred as a result of that practice.
- Buyers who originate written requests for quotations from suppliers receive the suppliers' bids directly from the mail-room. In your test of 100 purchases based on competitive bids, you found that in 55 of 100 cases, the lower bidders were awarded the purchase order.
- Requests to purchase (requisitions) received in the purchasing departments in the company must be signed by persons authorised to do so. Your examination of 200 such requests disclosed that three requisitions, all for small amounts, were not properly signed. The buyer who had issued all three orders honoured the requests because she misunderstood the applicable procedures. The clerical personnel responsible for reviewing such requests had given them to the buyer in error.

### Required

(a) For each of the above explain the risk, if any, that is incurred if each of the conditions described previously is permitted to continue and describe the internal control(s), if any, you would recommend to prevent continuation of the condition described.

(b) Explain the main function of a purchasing system employed by a company such as SEC Ltd, the risks associated with its failure and the controls that can be installed in order to minimise the impact of such risks.

## Question 2

You have recently been appointed by the management board of Bepelear Ltd, a small electrical accessories company, to (re)design the company-wide computer purchasing system. To date the company has maintained a semi-manual record system for all its purchases. For the previous five financial years the company has made average annual purchases of £18m (all purchases from UK suppliers) and average annual profits of approximately £9m. The company has approximately 50 employees working at six locations throughout the UK: Manchester, which is the company's head office, Birmingham, Leeds, Swindon, Bristol and Newcastle. For the year ended 31 March 2006, approximately 95% of the company's purchases were on credit. The company is currently reviewing its purchasing system and is considering introducing a fully computerised purchasing system with the possibility of a web-based purchasing protocol linked to selected suppliers

### Required

Making whatever assumptions you consider necessary, prepare a draft report for the management board of Bepelear Ltd detailing the following:

(a) the control objectives of a company purchasing system,

(b) the general controls and application controls you would expect to find in a computerised purchasing system, and

(c) the control issues relevant to a web-based purchasing system.

## Chapter endnotes

1  *Raison d'être* is used here to signify motivation, rationale and/or basis of existence.

2  Bounded rationality is used here to signify behaviour that is rational within the parameters of a simplified model and/or imposed understanding, or a form of behaviour associated with uncertainty where individuals do not examine every possible option open to them, but simply consider a number of alternatives which happen to occur to them.

3  Remember we live in a socially constructed world – a world in which all social, political and economic systems, processes and procedures are invented and/or constructed.

4  To anthropomorphise means to ascribe human features to something and/or to infer humanist characteristics to an artifical construct.

5  Unlike lower level needs, this need is rarely – if ever – fully satisfied. That is a person rarely achieves their full potential since as a person matures and grows, psychologically new and challenging opportunities continually arise. Maslow suggested that self-actualised people tend to have virtues/values (he called these virtues B-values) such as order, truth, justice and wisdom . . . and many others.

6  Maslow classified such needs as either internal or external. Internal esteem needs are those related to self-esteem such as self-respect and achievement, whereas external esteem needs are those such as social status, recognition and reputation.

7  According to Maslow's theory, if these fundamental needs are not satisfied then a person will be motivated to satisfy them. Higher needs such as social needs and esteem/ego needs will not be recognised by a person until that person has satisfied the needs basic to existence.

8  See 'Information Security Breaches Survey 2006 Technical Report' (April 2006), Pricewaterhouse-Coopers and Department of Trade and Industry – available @ http://www.enisa.eu.int/doc/pdf/studies/dtiisbs2006.pdf.

9  The term 'documentation' does not relate solely to *physical documentation* but includes all formatted media (including virtual media, for example computer screen, webpage, database page) through which data/information can be collected, stored, analysed and communicated.

10  See Appendix B (page 657 of McClure, S., Scambray, J. and Kutz, G. (2005) *Hacking exposed: Network Security, Secrets, and Solutions*, McGraw-Hill, San Francisco.

11  Such external threats would include, for example, the existence of:

- adverse environmental conditions,
- neighbouring companies that may be a source of high-risk, or
- neighbouring companies that may be the source of civil unrest.

12  Such single points of failure would include, for example:

- communication links,
- source of accommodation,
- power supply,
- transport links/facilities, and
- computer system/network,

13  Such as using possible alternative service providers/supplementary resources suppliers or seeking insurance against the failure of such providers/supplies.

14  SWOT – Strengths, Opportunities, Weaknesses and Threats.

15  The word 'syntax' originates from the Greek words *syn*, meaning 'together', and *taxis*, meaning 'sequence/order'.

16  See note 8.

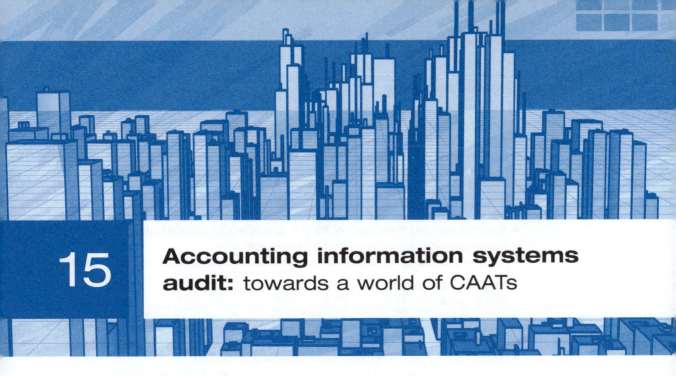

# Accounting information systems audit: towards a world of CAATs

**15**

## Introduction

> *Accounting information is power . . . it's as simple as that!* (Anon)

Why? Because, not only is it used to communicate representations of the life-world,[1] it is also used to signify, identify, categorise, conceptualise and (re)construct understandings and experiences of the life-world – to create realities. Indeed, in a contemporary market context, accounting information – as a series of politically constructed representations[2] – continues to be used to:

- classify and categorise activity,
- rationalise understanding and experience, and
- simplify and abbreviate reality.

It thus forms the basis of all business/market-related choice – the basis of all corporate decision making.

Indeed, the components of contemporary accounting information – not only as 'created' figures of thought, but also as politically motivated intellectual constructions – have become the established story-telling machinery and the accepted image creating technology through which:

- the received wisdom of liberal economic thought is communicated,
- the regulatory politics of contemporary market capitalism are imposed, and
- the chaotic socio-economic priorities of corporate capital are inadvertently obscured if not purposefully concealed.

Clearly then, the use of accounting information, whilst offering a landscape of enormous explanatory power, nonetheless provides avenues for distortion and misrepresentation. Indeed, in today's highly competitive, fast moving, ever-changing, technology-based contemporary global marketplace – a marketplace in which accounting information has become an essential prerequisite for corporate survival, such a palate for ambiguity and confusion not only results in the propagation of misleading optimism and disingenuous certainty, but also promotes the proliferation of false idealism.

More importantly, in a market orientated society increasingly dependent on abstract visualisation, evermore preoccupied with alternative modes of representation and increasingly absorbed with the reification of often 'false' objectivity, the biased politicisation of accounting information has become (some would say) an invasive and somewhat insidious aspect of contemporary society – of contemporary capitalism with its ever-growing pathology of corporate failure.

It is within this ever-changing and uncertain socio-economic context that:

- the contemporary framework of audit and auditing (in particular the audit of financial statements and accounting information systems), and
- the ever-increasing role and function of the auditor – in particular the external auditor,

has developed – and indeed continues to develop.[3]

This chapter:

- explores the underpinning rationale of an audit – in particular an accounting information systems audit,
- evaluates the role of the internal and external auditor, and
- considers the major issues and problems associated with auditing computer-based corporate accounting information systems.

It also considers a number of alternative contemporary approaches to auditing computer-based corporate accounting information systems including the use of Computer Assisted Audit Techniques (CAATs).

## Learning outcomes

This chapter explores a wide range of issues related to the audit of corporate accounting information systems.

By the end of this chapter, the reader should be able to:

- define the term 'audit' and describe the main alternative types of audit a company may be or choose to be subjected to,
- distinguish between CAAT-based and, non-CAAT-based auditing,
- critically comment on the importance of accounting information systems audits to contemporary capitalism and the management and shareholders of wealth maximising organisations, and
- describe and critically evaluate from a system's perspective the key features and aspects of a corporate accounting information systems audit.

## The role of the auditor

Like much of contemporary English language, the word 'audit' has its roots in Latin – meaning to hear or to perceive a sound. Consequentially, an auditor is, literally one who hears or someone who listens attentively. So, the role of an auditor is quite literally to audit!

The term 'audit' can be defined in many ways. In a broad context, an audit is an inspection, examination and verification of a company's financial and accounting systems, supporting documents, records and financial statements. This rather broad definition can be further divided (somewhat subjectively) into two separate, albeit highly interrelated, definitions. An audit is either:

- a review and examination of records and activities to assess the adequacy of system controls to:
  - ensure compliance with established policies, procedures and pronouncements, and
  - recommend appropriate changes in controls, policies, procedures, or
- a professional assessment and verification of a company's accounting documents and supporting data for the purpose of rendering an opinion as to their fairness, consistency and conformity of the financial statements with UK GAAP.[4]

The former would normally be associated with the role of an internal auditor, whereas the latter would normally be associated with the role of an external auditor.

For our purposes – that is from an accounting information systems perspective – we will define an audit as an independent examination[5] that seeks to evaluate the reliability of corporate accounting information and the efficiency and effectiveness of corporate accounting information systems. An independent examination by a competent and authorised individual – an auditor, a qualified accountant[6] – whose role – in a contemporary corporate context – can accordingly be defined as:

- the inspection of the accounting systems, records and practices of a company[7] and, where required, and/or appropriate
- the provision of an independent report to a company's members as to whether its financial statements have been properly prepared.[8]

## Types of auditor

So what about the different types of auditors? There are, in essence, two types of auditors:

- an internal auditor, and
- an external auditor.

### Internal auditor

An internal auditor is an employee of the company, responsible and accountable to the senior management within the company and independent of any functional activity/procedure within the company. The role of an internal auditor in:

- appraising the efficiency of operational activities of the company,
- assessing the effectiveness of internal administrative and accounting controls, and
- evaluating conformance with managerial procedures and policies,

would generally involve undertaking a wide range of audits/examinations/reviews, including:

- systems-based audits,
- internal control evaluations,
- risk appraisals,
- governance reviews, and
- security audits (especially regarding computer-based information systems).

The Institute of Internal Auditors suggests that the primary function of an internal auditor is to:[9]

- examine and evaluate how organisations are managing their reputational, operational or strategic risks,
- provide the company (audit committee and/or the board of directors) with information about whether risks have been identified, and how well such risks are being managed,
- offer an independent opinion on the effectiveness and efficiency of internal controls (extant operation protocols, policies and procedures),[10]
- review accounting information system developments to ensure that appropriate internal control policies and procedures are maintained and, where appropriate,
- provide consultancy services and/or undertake special reviews at the request of management.

There can be little doubt that:

- issues of corporate governance and the development of the Combined Code of Practice in 2000,[11]
- the increasing role and influence of non-executive directors in company affairs,
- the growing use of corporate audit committees, and
- the increasing occurrence of large corporate failures/collapses – not only in the UK but worldwide,

have all contributed to:

- enhancing the prominence of internal audit within corporate activities, and
- ensuring its continued presence in 21st century corporate activities.

## External auditor

An external auditor is:

- independent of the company (or organisation),[12] and
- appointed /reappointed annually at the company (or organisation) AGM (Annual General Meeting).[13]

In a corporate context, the role and duties of an external auditor are – in the UK – regulated by provisions of UK corporate legislation. The external auditor's primary functions/duties are provided in the Companies Act 1985 (s235 and s237). Under these provisions, an external auditor is – as part of a statutory annual audit – required to report to the company shareholders stating whether in their opinion:

- the company's financial statement provides a true and fair view[14] of the company's state of affairs as at the end of the financial year, and its profit and loss accounting for the year, and
- that such financial statements have been properly prepared in accordance with the requirements of the Companies Act 1985 (as amended).

However as Article 15.1 suggests, even such a long-standing, well-established Anglo-Saxon notion of 'true and fair view' may well be under threat.

An external auditor is required *prime facie* to ensure that:

- the company has maintained proper underlying accounting records, and
- the financial statements are in agreement with the underlying accounting records.

Specific requirements exist regarding the appointment, removal and/or replacement of an external auditor.

## Article 15.1

## 'True and fair' view of British audits is in jeopardy

The 'true and fair view' assessment of a company's state of affairs has been a cornerstone of UK accounting. It is now in jeopardy. Britain and Europe are moving dangerously close to a weak, narrow and limited US-style audit based on technical compliance.

While in recent weeks the debate on protecting auditors from negligence claims has re-emerged, for investors it is a sideshow to the main event. Our worry is about the nature and quality of the audit itself and the potential for reduced shareholder protection.

The audit is a key safeguard in the relationship between management and the owners of their company, the shareholders. Under the current regulatory framework, an auditor has to make qualitative judgments about whether a company's accounts present a true and fair view of a business's state of affairs – not simply an arithmetic compliance with the letter rather than the spirit of accounting standards.

Technical benchmarks of compliance can never hope to be flexible enough to capture all the issues that arise in a company's affairs. The dangers can be seen in such cases as Enron. Before it collapsed, the energy trading group regularly received a clean bill of health under the more restricted focus of US audits.

The threat to the UK approach arises from two factors.

The first is the unilateral imposition of the International Auditing Assurance Standards Board's US-derived international standards of auditing (ISAs). These process orientated standards create a significant shift in the emphasis and focus of the audit which could undermine the current overriding principle that audit opinions must encompass the 'true and fair view' of a business's state of affairs as enshrined by the UK Companies Act of 1985. Under these ISAs, we would move to a much narrower US-style technical compliance-based audit, which gives priority to rules at the expense of robust judgment and common sense.

Second, their impact will be compounded by proposals to give these standards a legislative footing. Under the European Union's proposed eighth company law directive, ISAs could change the application and interpretation of existing auditing principles. We believe this will significantly reduce the scope and rigour of UK audits.

As the Association of Certified Chartered Accountants said in its submission to the Department for Trade and Industry on directors' and auditors' liability: 'US-influenced audit standards are heavily influenced by the "tick box" approach which has the aim of demonstrating that the auditor has not been negligent. In our view, this reduces the essential quality of an audit.'

Here it is worth recalling why we have audits. Their purpose is to act as a safeguard and check on 'agency problems and costs' that arise from the separation of ownership and control in companies. The risk is that management may not always act in the best interests of the shareholders. There may also be an imbalance in the availability and control of information that can affect the quality of reporting.

Auditors act for and in the interests of shareholders. To this end, they are given privileged rights of access to a company. The purpose is to protect the company itself from the consequences of undetected errors or, possibly, wrongdoing and, in particular, to provide shareholders with 'reliable intelligence'. Investors rely on the auditors' professional and independent judgment, based on the exercise of skill, care and caution.

There is a broad and talented pool of audit practitioners across Europe. We need to decide whether we want the focus to be on ensuring that they are properly empowered to carry out substantive audits or whether we subordinate them to a US-style, process-based framework. Meanwhile, any protection against negligence claims must be put on hold. Investors have reiterated a long-standing position that any further limitation of auditor liability for audit failures must be specifically linked to addressing audits' shortcomings.

We recognise that some scope exists to adjust auditor liability as a trade off for improved audit quality. But that does not mean there is a pressing need for change to be rushed through regardless of the wider issues.

There is no sense in introducing further safe harbour provisions for those who carry out audits when there are serious concerns about the nature of the audit itself. In short, the auditor liability regime should not be changed until the quality of the audit has been ensured. To do otherwise is to put the cart before the horse.

Source: Keith Jones, 6 July 2005, *The Financial Times*, **www.ft.com**.

Section 385(2) of the Companies Act 1985 provides for company shareholders to appoint an external auditor on an annual basis. Similarly, resolutions to remove and/or replace an external auditor must also be made at a company's annual general meeting. However, s319A provides that:

- 28 days' notice of the resolution to remove and/or replace an external auditor must be provided to both shareholders and existing auditors, and
- the existing external auditor is provided with an opportunity to make representations to the shareholders on the intended resolution to remove and/or replace them.

So, how effective are external auditors in discharging their statutory duties? Although the evidence on their effectiveness is contradictory and less than conclusive, it is worth noting that in 2005, in the UK, of the FTSE 100 companies:

- 43 were audited by PwC,
- 22 were audited by KPMG,
- 17 were audited by Deloitte, and
- 17 were audited by Ernst and Young.

And of the FTSE 250 companies:

- 82 were audited by PwC,
- 64 were audited by KPMG,
- 54 were audited by Deloitte, and
- 142 were audited by Ernst and Young.

See Article 15.2.

## Article 15.2

### Big four bristle at claims that too much power rests in their hands

The creeping global dominance of the 'big four' auditing firms is in danger of compromising the independence of UK regulators and hampering disciplinary actions, according to one of Britain's most powerful shareholder groups.

The Association of British Insurers, whose members control almost 20% of the shares on the London stock market, says the four multinational auditing groups – KPMG, PricewaterhouseCoopers, Ernst & Young and Deloitte – have a stranglehold on the market for auditing work and too much influence over regulators. It has called for regulators and competition authorities to show their teeth.

Peter Montagnon, head of investment affairs at the ABI, said: 'The acid test is whether the regulators feel they have to have a different approach to disciplinary processes in the case of the big four firms than they do for smaller audit companies. If they do feel this, there is clearly something seriously wrong.'

In Britain, the big four audit all but one of the FTSE 100 companies and 97% of midcap firms and their dominance of big business auditing is similar in other leading markets. Mr Montagnon said: 'If there are very few firms doing audits, they can influence too heavily the way auditing is organised and implemented.'

His comments echo widespread concern among policymakers that too much power rests in the hands of the four accountancy firms. Many fear they are too big to fail, which makes it difficult to regulate them strictly.

Backed by the Department of Trade and Industry, accountancy watchdog the Financial Reporting Council has been conducting a review of the auditor choices available to British businesses. It is this ongoing review that yesterday prompted the ABI to publish its damning assessment of the audit market. Its views have been submitted to the FRC review but its claims that regulators may be compromised by the power of multinational audit firms have begun to ruffle feathers. Paul Boyle, FRC chief executive, said: 'It is a rather curious suggestion that the FRC, which has embarked on this project looking at the dominance of the big four firms, could be corrupted by the same big four firms.'

Peter Wyman, a partner at the largest of the big four, PwC, said: 'I think the ABI is on a different planet. Our regulator is Sir John Bourn [chairman of an FRC committee]. He is the most independent person you will come across. The suggestion that we have somehow captured him is just nonsense. It is like suggesting BT had been able to capture Ofcom.'

The FRC's committees, which oversee every element of accountancy, are well populated by senior figures from the big four. While Mr Boyle recognises the potential conflict, he argues against the US model, where a ban on audit groups holding regulatory posts occasionally leaves the watchdog looking out of touch.

In its submission to the regulators, the ABI said: 'We are not comfortable with a position where large firms could determine the shape of regulation by threatening to withdraw from the audit market.' Some industry experts said this was a reference to the heated debate in recent years over whether audit firms should have their liability limited in the event of a substantial audit failure.

The big four – which make only a fifth of their profits from statutory auditing work – effectively demanded their liabilities be capped, insisting they were no longer prepared to operate under unlimited liability, risking the same fate as Andersen, the auditing firm that imploded after the Enron scandal.

The government is pushing a company law reform bill through parliament to provide the four with much of the comfort demanded.

The four are sending last-minute submissions to the FRC before all position documents are published on the watchdog's website this week. All are thought to play down suggestions of a crisis. Ernst & Young recognises 'concentration of auditor choice is an important matter', but claims 'the current state of the market is not causing significant problems for most large public companies and there appears to be ample choice in the market for other companies'.

Mr Wyman puts it more strongly: 'We don't think that the market is anything other than fiercely competitive. There are many, many, many markets where four suppliers would be considered an absolute luxury. I'm sure BA would love to have four plane suppliers.'

Ernst & Young tells the FRC: 'The salient question in this debate is how to avoid the collapse of a large firm.' While all agree this would be calamitous, the ABI suggests steps must be taken to prevent auditors using this scenario as a threat. 'Moral hazard considerations must be weighed up against the expectations of large audit firms that they will be protected by special regulatory treatment because they are too important to fail.'

An FRC meeting, scheduled for next month, is expected to be a lively affair. While some will suggest the spectre of Enron should be left to fade in the memory, many others point to a catalogue of recent cases that could threaten another blue chip auditor.

Among them is a tax avoidance scheme sold by KPMG to super-rich individuals in the US in the late 1990s that resulted in a £250m settlement and the imminent trial of 16 former employees. A dark shadow was cast over PwC's future after its Japanese affiliate signed off the fraudulent accounts of cosmetics group Kanebo, leading to a £100m fine and string of client defections. Both firms survived, but another Andersen may not be far away.

Source: Simon Bowers, 8 August 2006, *The Guardian*, http://business.guardian.co.uk/story/0,,1839332,00.html.

Now we know what types of auditors there are – what types of audit exist? Porter *et al.* (2003) have suggested that based on the primary audit objective, three main categories of audits may be recognised, namely:

- 'financial statement audit,
- compliance audit, and
- operational audit' (2003: 4).

Porter *et al.* define each of the above as follows:

- a financial statement audit is 'an examination of an entity's financial statements, which have been prepared ( . . . ) for shareholders and other interested parties outside the entity,' (2003: 4),

■ a compliance audit is '(designed to) . . . determine whether an individual or entity has acted (is acting) in accordance with procedures or regulations established by an authority such as the entity's management or a regulatory body,' (2003: 6), and

■ an operational audit is 'the systematic examination and evaluation of an entity's operations which is conducted with the view to improving the efficiency and/or effectiveness of the entity,' (2003: 6).

Whilst the above does provide an insight into the alternative categories of audit and a basis on which to distinguish between the role of an internal auditor and the role of an external auditor (see Figure 15.1), we can – in a more functional context – further subdivide each category and identify and distinguish between a number of alternative types of audit[15] (see Figure 15.2).

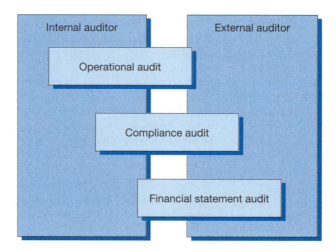

**Figure 15.1** Role of the internal auditor and external auditor

**Figure 15.2** Alternative types of audits

So what types of audits exist within each category? Types of audit within the financial statement audit would, for example, be:

- a balance sheet audit,
- a profit and loss account audit, and
- a cash flow statement audit.

Types of audit within the compliance audit would, for example, be:

- an internal control audit
- a management audit, and
- a corporate governance audit.

Types of audit within the operational audit would, for example, be:

- a risk audit,
- a social audit,
- an environmental audit, and
- a value for money audit.

Before we have a look at each of these types of audit in more detail, it would perhaps be useful to note that in the UK, since 1991, it has been the responsibility of the Auditing Practices Board (APB)[16] to issue pronouncements (see Scope and Authority of APB pronouncements (Revised) 2004), that can be categorised as follows:

- Statements of Auditing Standards (SASs),
- practice notes – to assist auditors in applying Auditing Standards of general application, and
- bulletins – to provide auditors with guidance on new emerging issues.

Statements of Auditing Standards (SASs) contain:

*the basic principles and essential procedures with which external auditors in the United Kingdom and the Republic of Ireland are required to comply* (Scope and Authority of APB pronouncements 1993: para 1).

Compliance with the basic principles and essential procedures identified within extant auditing standards (SASs) is mandatory and failure to comply with such auditing standards may result in disciplinary action by the Recognised Supervisory Body (RSB) with which the auditor is registered.

In addition, the International Auditing Practices Committee, (IAPC) a committee of the council of the International Federation of Accountants (IFAC)[17] issues:

- International Standards on Auditing (ISAs), and
- International Auditing Practice Statements (IAPSs).

The aim of these is to improve the degree of consistency, uniformity and homogeneity in auditing practices throughout the global marketplace. Whilst the pronouncements of the IFAC are usually welcome and accepted without to much debate, occasionally such tacit acceptance is not the case (see Article 15.3).

It should however be noted that whilst member bodies of the IFAC[18] – which include the UK and Irish professional bodies – are required to endeavour to ensure compliance with extant IASs, where inconsistencies exist between IASs issued by the International Auditing Practices Committee (IAPC) and national/local SASs issued by the UK Auditing Practices Board (APB), such IASs do not override local/national SASs. Such inconsistencies are however rare! A list of extant SASs and IASs is available on the website accompanying this text www.pearsoned.co.uk/boczko.

## Article 15.3

### IFAC under fire over audit standards

*Investment community claims international standards threaten to undermine audit practice in the UK.*

Later this month, the government is expected to announce its crucial decision on whether auditors will be allowed to negotiate proportionate liability with clients. Hopes of success had been high, but the chances of it happening now look somewhat remote after a change of heart from investors, who have withdrawn their support en mass. Concerns have been growing within the investment community over recent and forthcoming changes in the regulatory environment that, they believe, will reduce auditors' exposure to risk and at the same time reduce audit quality. At such a time, they feel it would be unwise to further diminish an auditor's risk profile without some concrete and substantial improvements in audit quality.

The main target of their ire is global accountancy body the International Federation of Accountants, which is responsible for the creation of international standards on auditing. It is these standards, investors claim, that threaten to undermine audit practice in the UK. Ian Richards at Morley argues that these ISAs would 'harmonise audit standards under a US derived framework that suits the approach of the US side', reduce the scope of UK audits and the rigor

and tests applied in these audits. He also claims that should such standards, already in force in the UK through the Auditing Practices Board, become enshrined in European law, it would mean 'the end of true and fair view audit as we know them'.

Current IFAC president and Pricewaterhouse-Coopers partner Graham Ward says the criticism was 'unjustified' and that the body 'is not beholden to any individual nation'. He adds that it 'issues high-quality, principles-based standards on auditing and quality control that require the exercise of responsible judgement by auditors. It is determined to support first-class auditing and an investment climate of trust'. Investors are unconvinced and continue to pressurise government to hold back on proportionate liability. Whether they have been successful should be revealed soon. But whichever way the government decides to go, it is unlikely that the arguments over audit standards, and their impact on quality will go away any time in the near future.

Source: Paul Grant, 7 July 2005, *Accountancy Age*,
**www.accountancyage.com**.

## Types of audit

### Types of financial statement audit

A financial statement audit (also referred to as a year-end audit, somewhat misleadingly, and/or a statutory audit and/or financial audit) is an examination (by an external auditor) of the records and reports of a company and an examination/assessment (by an external auditor) of the degree as to which a company's financial statements are in accordance with generally accepted accounting principles and practices.

As suggested earlier, a financial statement audit can – if so required – be sub-divided between:

- a balance sheet audit – which would include:
  - determination of both existence and ownership of all assets and liabilities,
  - confirmation that all assets and liabilities have been correctly and properly valued in accordance with UK GAAP,
  - confirmation that all assets and liabilities have been measured in accordance with UK GAAP, and
  - verification that the presentation and disclosure of all assets and liabilities is complete and consistent with the requirements of UK GAPP, and in particular the provisions of Companies Act 1985 Schedule 4,

- a profit and loss account audit – which would include:
  - verification that all income and expenditure has been correctly determined in accordance with UK GAAP,
  - confirmation that all profits and losses have been properly assessed in accordance with UK GAAP,
  - confirmation that all transactions have been appropriately measured in accordance with UK GAAP,
  - verification of the completeness of disclosure of all income and expenditure, and all profits and losses, and
  - verification that the presentation and disclosure of information is consistent with the requirements of UK GAAP, and in particular the provisions of Companies Act 1985 Schedule 4.
- a cash flow statement audit – which would include:
  - confirmation that all transactions have been appropriately measured in accordance with UK GAAP, in particular FRS 1 (as amended),
  - verification of the completeness of disclosure of all income and expenditure, and
  - verification that the presentation and disclosure of information relating to – company operating activities; returns on investments and servicing of finance; taxation; capital expenditure and financial investment; acquisitions and disposals; equity dividends paid; the management of liquid resources; and corporate financing – is consistent with the requirements of UK GAAP, and in particular the provisions of FRS 1 (as amended).

Clearly, the key features of such a financial statement audit are:

- primarily financial orientated,
- principally concerned with historical/static created representations, and
- orientated to/designed for external corporate stakeholders.

As such they are designed to substantiate, validate, verify and/or confirm the information contained within a company's financial statements and facilitate the formulation of an opinion on whether the financial statements of a company provide a true and fair view of the company's state of affairs as at the end of the financial year, and its profit and loss accounting for the year.

## Types of compliance audit

### Internal control/systems audit

Mainly systems-based, an internal control audit is an objective examination and evaluation of the effectiveness of a company's internal control procedures in the prevention and detection of potential security threats and/or other financially damaging events/occurrences. Such an audit would also seek to assess the adequacy of management feedback processes and procedures in identifying and eliminating potential threats and risks to the company's governance, present well-being and future survival.

An internal control audit is essentially an objective assurance/review process designed to:

- identify system requirements, procedures, processes and protocols,
- determine current compliance with existing system requirements, procedures, processes and protocols,
- determine areas of potential internal control weakness,
- provide a quantifiable risk assessment of any such internal control weaknesses, and
- recommend possible improvement to internal controls to eliminate possible financial/non-financial loss.

And as a consequence not only improve, but also add value to, the company's activities and operations.

Undertaken as part of a company's on-going internal audit function, such an internal control audit would:

- be mainly system-based, and
- aim to support the work of the company's external auditor.

### Management audit

A management audit is an evaluation of performance and compliance in relation to regulatory, process, economic and efficiency-based accountability measures at all management levels. Such an audit focuses on outputs and results (rather than merely process) and evaluates the effectiveness and suitability of controls by contesting the validity of extent processes and procedures, systems and methodologies. A management audit is not designed merely to test and identify conformity and/or non-conformity with existing system requirements, procedures and protocols. The key objectives are to:

- validate the need for existing system requirements, procedures and protocols, and
- identify key problems areas – or cause and effect patterns.

Management audits are generally performed internally – by internal auditors – and are essentially systems-based compliance audits.

### Corporate governance audit

The term corporate governance describes (for our purposes) the processes by which a company is directed, controlled and complies with relevant legislation, extant rules and codes of practice. It is, in essence, a broad framework of rules and relationships, systems, processes and procedures by which authority is exercised and controlled within a company, with the generally accepted contemporary principles of corporate governance including:

- the rights of shareholders,
- the interests of other stakeholders,
- the roles and responsibilities of the company directors and board members (including non-executive directors), and
- company disclosure policies and procedures.

A corporate governance audit would include an examination/assessment of:

- the general procedures involved in the preparation of a company's financial statements,
- a company internal controls procedures,
- the independence of the company external auditors,
- corporate remuneration arrangements for all executive directors, non-executive directors and senior managers,
- corporate procedures for the nomination of individuals on the board,
- the level of resources made available to directors in perusal of their fiduciary duties, and
- the company procedures for the management of risk.

The key objectives of a corporate governance audit are:

- to ensure openness and transparency,
- to promote integrity, honesty and trust, and
- to encourage responsibility and accountability,

and are generally undertaken by external auditors.

## Types of operational audit

### Risk audit

A risk audit is an examination of the effectiveness of company processes, procedures and protocols in:[19]

- identifying the nature and contexts of risk (risk identification),
- constructing an effective understanding of its origin and nature (risk assessment),
- developing an appreciation of its implications (risk evaluation), and
- designing effective strategies to manage its consequences (risk management).

Such a risk audit may relate to:[20]

- a category/group/subset of companies possessing common characteristics and/or sharing common attributes,
- a company and/or business type/sub-type within a category/group/subset,
- a cycle of operation within the company and/or business type/sub-type, and
- a system within a company's cycle of operations.

A risk audit may, for example, consider:

- the nature of company/cycle/system transactions (e.g. the volume of transactions, the value of transactions and the complexity of transactions),
- the adequacy of the company/cycle/system internal controls,
- the nature of the company/cycle/system operating environment,
- the nature of the company/cycle/system regulatory environment, and
- the level and adequacy of company/cycle/system resources (including human resources, tangible and non-tangible assets).

### Social audit

A social audit is an examination of the extent to which the operations of a company have contributed to social goals of the wider community. Social audits are concerned more with effectiveness rather than efficiency and can be seen as a means of assigning some influence over corporate activities to relevant external stakeholder groups such as employees, consumers and the local community. They provide a framework through which a company can:

- identify and qualitatively measure its social performance,
- account for its impact on the community, and
- report on that performance to its key stakeholder groups.

In a corporate context, social audits remain at a very early stage of development and remain difficult to perform because there exists no generally accepted measure of social performance.

### Environmental audit

An environmental audit is an independent assessment of the current status of a company's compliance with applicable environmental requirements and/or an evaluation of a company's environmental policies, procedures, practices and controls.

In essence, an environmental audit is an examination of a company's environmental 'friendliness' and is concerned primarily with a company's environmental management systems. Such an audit would review the company's:

- environmental policies,
- objectives and targets,

- performance procedures and monitoring protocols, and
- management review processes.

Where a company is registered with the European Eco-Management and Audit Scheme (EMAS)[21] it is required to appoint an external verifier . . . (usually an external auditor) . . . and to publish, annually, an externally verified (or audited) environmental statement (Porter *et al*, 2003: 541).

For a company, the benefits of EMAS registration[22] and of course an environmental audit may include:

- the possible development of marketing opportunities by demonstrating corporate awareness of environmental issues and concerns,
- possible access to new markets by demonstrating greater internal efficiencies through the active management of environmental risks, and
- the enhanced use (where the company (or organisation) is registered) of ISO 14001.[23]

### Value for money audit

A value for money audit is an examination of the manner in which assets and resources are allocated and utilised within the business, and as such is concerned primarily with three interconnected and interrelated concepts: economy, efficiency and effectiveness.

Although retrospective in nature, the primary objectives of a value for money audit will be:

- to provide an independent assessment and examination of how economically, efficiently and effectively resources and assets are being utilised, and
- to offer independent information and advice to companies on how to improve corporate services and competitive performance by adopting value for money policies and procedures.

Such a value for money audit may relate to:

- an identifiable cycle of operation within the company and/or business type/sub-type (e.g. the corporate expenditure cycle),
- an identifiable system within a company's cycle of operations (e.g. the purchasing system within the corporate expenditure cycle), or
- an identifiable activity within a system (e.g. the use of consultants in the purchasing systems within the corporate expenditure cycle).

Now we have briefly reviewed a few of the main types of audit within each of the three categories identified earlier, what about an accounting information systems audit?

## Accounting information systems audit – a context

As we have for the previous chapters of this text, we will continue to adopt what some may well consider an *alternative view* of a company's accounting information systems.[24] That is a holistic contextualisation of a company's accounting information systems that *prima facie* considers them to be an all-encompassing collection of politically constructed socio-economic networks.

As we have seen, there can be little doubt that in a contemporary context, accounting information systems and, more importantly, computer-based accounting information systems now play a central role in:

- portraying, evaluating and governing the extensive and expanding domains of economic and social life, and

■ enabling social and economic activities to be rendered knowable, measurable, accountable and manageable at a distance.

More importantly, as we have also seen, such accounting information systems possess no aesthetic qualities other than those assigned by human agency. They are politically contrived and socially constructed contextualisations that favour some groups rather than others. Reified as providing an all-encompassing representation of economic activity, accounting information systems are, in a contemporary context, socially, politically and economically significant. They are frequently mobilised in the adjudication of economic claims between competing constituencies by providing a mechanism through which selected aspects of a consciously constructed accumulation process – sustained as a particular system of social relations – can be defined, mediated, legitimated and utilised (clearly in a socio-political context):

■ to sustain and reinforce organisational operations – that is transaction processing management,
■ to support decision making by internal decision makers and ensure the objective transformation of economic/financial data into accounting information – that is information management,
■ to discharge obligations relating to stewardship and control the acquisition, management and disposal of organisational resources – that is internal systemic control,
■ to fulfil legal, social and political responsibilities and encourage alignment with extant regulatory requirements – that is external systemic control.

Remember these from Chapter 1?

Clearly then, if we consider/perceive a company's accounting information system to be an all-encompassing socio-political contextualisation of a company's processes, procedures and protocols (as we do!) we must also – as a consequence – consider an accounting information systems audit to be neither an element and/or component of, nor a feature/characteristic aspect of, any type of financial statement audit, compliance audit or operational audit. Indeed, quite the opposite!

Such an overarching contextualisation of a company's accounting information systems implies a hierarchical (audit) framework in which the latter – financial statement audit, compliance audit and operational audit – are themselves no more than constituent aspects of the former – an accounting information systems audit.

See Figure 15.3.

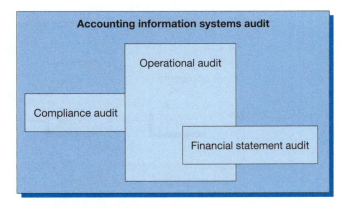

**Figure 15.3** Accounting information systems audit

It is, however, worth noting that for some academics and practitioners – often constrained by an over-reliance on *hard system* positivism – such a view of a company's accounting information systems as an all-encompassing contextualisation of a company's processes, procedures and protocols is not widely accepted. Indeed, for some – albeit mostly those of a positivistic[25] proclivity/functionalistic inclination clearly influenced by the evermore powerful priorities of capital – an accounting information systems audit does not, at least in an empirical context, exist! It is a delusional fallacy, an erroneous fabrication, a misleading constructed notion and a created terminology that is no more than merely another abstract description of or for a compliance audit. More specifically an internal control/systems type audit whose key aspects/objectives (as we have seen earlier) are very often concerned primarily with:

- the mechanistic, the technical and the functional aspects of accountability and internal control, and
- the quantification and measurement of *hard* systemic processes, procedures and protocols.

It is this positivist rejection of an accounting information systems audit – as no more than a constructionist charade – other than as a constituent aspect of an internal control/systems audit that continues to impose (and indeed continually reinforce):

- a narrow functionalism,
- an over-compartmentalisation of understanding, and
- an excessive reliance/emphasis on imposed quantification and abstract measurement,

in which:

- compliance type audits are viewed as primarily concerned with data/information relating to procedures and protocols associated with input/process activities and events,
- operational type audits are viewed as primarily concerned with data/information relating to procedures and protocols associated with process activities and events, and
- financial statement type audits are viewed as primarily concerned with data/information relating to procedures and protocols associated with process/output activities and events.

This continues to necessitate not only a very specific *imposed* structure to analysis and understanding, but also a particular politicisation of knowledge – a professional technocracy of protectionist fragmentation and guarded over-compartmentalisation.

See Figure 15.4.

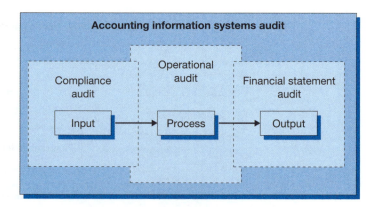

**Figure 15.4** Accounting information systems audit – systems view

So, what about the audit of computer-based accounting information systems? Before we continue it would perhaps be useful to consider:

■ the purpose of the audit, and
■ the audit techniques we can use.

Or, put more simply, what are we trying to do, how are we going to do it and exactly why do we audit?

Always remember the audit axiom: *'In God we trust. Everyone else we audit!'*

## Purpose of an audit

As suggested earlier, an audit is an inspection, examination and verification of a company's financial and accounting systems, supporting documents, records and financial statements. It is perhaps due to:

■ the growing complexity (and ever-increasing virtual nature) of transactions and transaction processing,
■ the increasing temporal and spatial remoteness of transactions and transaction processing,
■ the escalating possibility and consequence of error, fraud,[26] loss/theft of assets and breaches of security/acts of violence, and
■ the increasing possibility of conflicts of interest, resulting from transactions and transaction processing,

that accounting information systems audits are often purposefully viewed as being designed primarily to promote greater functional efficiency of capital markets, through:

■ increased information transparency,
■ greater information accuracy,
■ increased transaction/transaction processing security, and
■ enhanced corporate management accountability.

So what does the auditor (external and/or internal) seek to do? The auditor will seek to:

*obtain sufficient appropriate audit evidence to be able to draw reasonable conclusions on which to base an audit opinion* (SAS 400[27] para 2).

In this context:

■ sufficiency is the measure of the quantity of audit evidence,
■ appropriateness is the measure of the quality or reliability and relevance of audit evidence, and
■ audit evidence is *'any perceived object, action or condition relevant to the formation of a knowledgeable opinion,'* (Anderson, 1977: 251) or *'all the facts and impressions auditors acquire which help them form an opinion,'* (Porter *et al.*, 2003: 52).

Sufficiency of audit evidence – the quantity of audit information required – will be both influenced and determined by, for example:

■ the consequences, risk and materiality of any potential error and/or misstatement,
■ the nature of existing internal control systems, and
■ the source and reliability of evidence.

Appropriateness and dependability of audit evidence – the quality or reliability and relevance of audit evidence – will be determined by the origin/basis/foundation of the audit evidence. For example, whether such audit evidence has been obtained from:

- the inspecting of financial and accounting systems, supporting documents, records and financial statements,
- the undertaking of appropriate computational analysis,
- the making of enquiries and the obtaining of confirmation of the existence, ownership and valuation of assets/liabilities, and/or
- the observing of company procedures and processes, and the determining of the existence and effectiveness of internal controls.

Clearly, whilst such audit evidence needs to be:

- relevant,
- reliable,
- appropriate,
- timely, and
- cost effective,

from an (all encompassing) accounting information systems audit context, such audit evidence should seek to ensure the existence of adequate/efficient/effective internal controls *inter alia*:

- appropriate levels of segregation of duties in company procedures and processes,
- adequate physical controls in the acquisition, management and disposal of assets and liabilities,
- relevant and proper authorisation procedures in the acquisition, management and disposal of assets and liabilities,
- adequate management and supervision procedures in the acquisition, management and disposal of assets and liabilities,
- established and defined organisational/management/control structures,
- adequate arithmetic and accounting procedures in company procedure and processes, and
- approved personnel procedures for the recruitment, appointment, promotion, management and dismissal of staff members.

## Auditing techniques

There are of course a range of auditing techniques that auditors (both internal and external) regularly employ, to:

- gather data/information,
- obtain audit evidence,
- communicate findings and, of course,
- formulate and develop an opinion,

on:

- a system (or sub-systems),
- a group of procedures,
- a cluster of processes,
- a collection of regulations/protocol/controls, and/or
- a set of financial statements,

to determine the existence, adequacy, efficiency and effectiveness of internal controls – internal controls which are, in many cases, now IT-based.

Such auditing techniques would (within the context of an audit plan/programme)[28] include *inter alia*, for example:

- the use of narrative reports/descriptions,
- the use of flowcharts (including systems, program and document flowcharts),
- the use of Internal Control Questionnaires (ICQs),
- the use of statistical sampling, and
- the use of Computer Aided Audit Techniques (CAATs) (including the use of test transaction data and/or audit software/programs).

## Narrative reports/descriptions

Primarily used as a descriptive tool, an auditor's narrative description is essentially a detailed description of *how* a system/sub-system operates. It would include a detailed explanation and/or review of:

- all the documentation (physical and/or virtual) used in the system/sub-system under review,
- all the processes, procedure and protocols that exist as part of the system/sub-system under review, and
- all the internal control procedures and processes that are present within the system/sub-system under review, including details of relevant segregation of duties, physical controls and authorisation, management and supervision/control procedures.

Have a look at the following example narrative report/description:

Company:    EoNio Ltd
Type:       Small family owned manufacturing company
Location:   York
Date:       September 2006
System:     Purchasing system – paper-based with BACS payment interface

EoNio Ltd is a small manufacturing company located in York. The company purchasing systems operates with the following departments:

- a requisitioning department,
- a purchasing department,
- a receiving department,
- a stores department,
- a purchasing ledger (accounts) department, and
- a treasury department.

The general purchasing procedures are as follows. A requisitioning department raises a purchase request. This purchase request is forwarded to the purchasing department. The purchasing department then obtains a quotation from an approved supplier. Once the quotation has been received and approved, the purchasing department raises a purchase order (four copies). Two copies of the purchase order are sent to the supplier, one is sent to the receiving department and one is sent to the purchase ledger (accounting department).

Prior to delivery the supplier is requested to send one copy of the purchase order back to the purchasing department as acknowledgement of the purchase order receipt. When the goods are delivered a Goods Received Note (GRN) (three copies) is received. One copy is *filed in the receiving department, one is kept by the stores department and one is sent to purchase ledger (accounting department), where it is matched and filed with the appropriate purchase order.*

*The supplier retains a delivery note, authorised (signed) by an appropriate member of staff from the receiving department. When the invoice is received from the supplier the purchasing department matches the purchase order, GRN and invoice, and authorises payment.*

*All payments are made by BACS and require authorisation from the company cashier.*

The main advantages of narrative reports/descriptions for an auditor are:

- they can be written/prepared with little technical experience,
- they can record/portray a system, a program and/or a document flow in precise detail.

The main disadvantages of narrative reports/descriptions are:

- they are language specific and therefore lack international mobility,
- they do not readily describe the temporal flow and/or the sequencing of events and/or data/information flow in a system and/or sub-system, and
- they can be time consuming to prepare and to use, especially where excessive detailed narrative is used.

## Flowcharts (including system, program and document flowcharts)

Remember flowcharts? We discussed system, program and document flowcharts in some detail in Chapter 7.

A flowchart is merely a diagrammatic representation, a picture, of a system, a (computer) program and/or a document flow.

The main advantages of flowcharting for an auditor are:

- flowcharts can be drawn with little knowledge and/or experience,
- they can record/portray a system, program and/or a document flow in its entirety, and
- they eliminate the need for extensive narrative descriptive notes.

The main disadvantages of flowcharting for an auditor are:

- flowcharts are only suitable for recording/portraying standard systems,
- they are only useful when recording dynamic/active systems, and
- major amendment to flowcharts can be difficult.

The main types of flowcharts used in auditing are:

- a system flowchart – which provides a logical diagram/picture of how a system operates, and illustrates the system in a step-by-step fashion, from input to conversion process to output,
- a document flowchart – which illustrates the flow of documentation and information within a system – from origin to destination, and
- a program flowchart – which describes the processing stages within a computer-based system, for example:
  - batch processing system,
  - online (3 stage) processing system,
  - online (4 stage) processing system, and/or
  - distributed/remote processing system.

## Internal control questionnaires (ICQs)

An internal control questionnaire is a standardised questionnaire comprising of a series of questions, each of which seeks to enquire as to the existence, effectiveness and efficiency of internal control procedures within a company's transaction processing cycle, systems and sub-systems.

An internal control questionnaire would seek to ascertain/confirm/verify that internal controls established by the company to:

- ensure adherence to management policies,
- the safeguarding of assets, and
- the completeness and accuracy of accounting and financial records,

are functioning in an orderly and efficient manner, in terms of:

- separation of duties,
- definition and allocation of responsibilities,
- documentation of procedures, processes and transactions,
- authorisation, approval and security protocols, and
- supervision/management of operational transactions.

The following provides a sample list of questions/types of questions that would be included in a stock management ICQ.

### Physical/environment control

- Are stock item adequately safeguarded against damage from the weather, other accidental damage, unrecorded movement and/or unauthorised removal?
- Are stock items stored in a secure, controlled environment?
- Are stock items stored in an organised manner?
- Is adequate insurance cover relating to stock items available?
- How often is the stock insurance policy reviewed?
- Are all issues and receipts of stock recorded through the use of pre-numbered documents?
- Are the stock records up-to-date?
- Are detailed records kept for all stock items showing quantities/type, location, value, usage and selling price?

### Accounting

- Are general ledger control accounts reconciled with the stock records?
- Is the reconciliation independently reviewed?
- Are differences promptly investigated and corrective action taken?
- Are detailed accounting controls maintained?

### Stock management and stock control

- Are formal counts of major items of stock undertaken?
- Are all stock items counted at least once a year?
- Are annual counts carried out by employees independent of the stores?
- Do adequate formal procedures for the annual stock count exist?
- Are the stock count sheets pre-numbered and controlled?
- Is there an independent check on annual stock prices?
- Are the accounting records reconciled to the results of the annual stock count?
- Is there a written procedure to ensure that cut-offs are accurate?

- Are stocks reviewed periodically and a determination made of slow-moving items, obsolete items and excess stock items?
- Does the organisation monitor stock turnover?
- Is the disposal of written-off stock items adequately controlled and accounted for?

## Statistical sampling

In an audit context, sampling means:

> *the application of audit procedures to less than 100% of the items . . . to obtain and evaluate audit evidence about some characteristic of the items selected in order to form or assist in forming a conclusion concerning the population. Audit sampling can be used as part of a test of control or as part of a substantive procedure* (SAS 430[29] para 4).

Auditors use sampling to formulate conclusions and/or opinions about a population/universe of transaction data and/or procedures/processes based on the sample – usually because it would be either too costly and/or too time-consuming to examine an entire population/universe.

Such sampling techniques include *inter alia*:

- unsystematic sampling (or unrestricted random sampling) – random sample selection not based on any qualitative/quantitative characteristic,
- judgemental sampling – subjective sample selection based on a predetermined set of qualitative/quantitative characteristics, for example size, value and event date,
- block or cluster sampling – sample selection in which particular groups or jurisdictions comprising groups are randomly identified,
- statistical sampling[30] – sample selection determined by the application of probability theory and required confidence levels/levels of sampling risk,
- restricted random or systematic sampling – random sample selection followed by – for example – every *n*th item.

## Computers in auditing accounting information systems

There can be little doubt that the past 10 to 15 years has seen information technology and computer-based techniques invade (and indeed continue to infiltrate):

- conventional auditing procedures and processes, and
- established audit techniques used by auditors.

This has occurred in an unprecedented, unpredictable and often chaotic way – sweeping way and replacing years of established custom, convention and tradition with little more than passing concern.

In terms of audit procedures/processes, the invasion of computer-based information technology has been seen in areas such as:

- the creation/amendment/storage of audit working papers,
- the scheduling/monitoring of audit investigations/activities,
- data collection (e.g. computer-based ICQs/ICEs),
- information analysis/interpretation (e.g. computer-based flowcharting and narrative report writers), and
- audit report generation.

In terms of audit techniques, the invasion of computer-based information technology has been seen in areas such as:

- the development and facilitation of remote location audit (virtual auditing),
- the development of generic software testing programs,
- the promotion of computer-based statistical sampling techniques,
- the use of analytical review procedures,
- the development of decision support systems,

and perhaps most importantly of all,

- the development of computer assisted audit techniques (CAATs).

## Computer aided audit techniques (CAATs)

CAATs can be defined as any single, group and/or cluster of audit techniques that use information technology-based applications as primary investigative tools. Applications such as:

- generic audit software,
- embedded audit modules/facilities,
- utility software,
- test data,
- application software tracing and mapping, and
- expert audit software.

### Generic audit software

Specific purpose-related and/or function-related computer programs (e.g. data retrieval programs) designed to:

- examine specific computer files/records,
- select, manipulate, analyse, sort, and summarise data held in specified files/records,
- undertake examination and analysis of data held in specified computer files/records,
- select samples of computer files/records/data for analysis, and
- prepare format specific reports.

Such generalised audit software can include both:

- programs acquired or developed/created for audit purposes and,
- programs embedded in computer-based systems (including spreadsheets and databases).

### Embedded audit modules/facilities

Audit facilities/modules and/or audit applications are permanently embedded within a computer-based processing system and are generally used in:

- high-data volume computer systems/networks, and/or
- high-risk computer systems/networks.

### Utility software

Utility software/programs are provided by computer hardware/software manufacturers and/or retailers. They are usually add-on programs often utilised in the operational functioning of the computer system/network.

Such utility programs can be used to:

- examine processing activity,
- test programme activities,
- test system activities and operational procedures,
- evaluate data file activity, and
- analyse file data.

Although these utility programs are not specifically designed for auditing purposes, they can, and indeed often are, used in pre-processing procedures – that is manipulating record data into an auditable format by:

- extracting specific data items from a database, and/or
- sorting, merging or joining files, and/or specific data records within them.

### Test data

Test data can be:

- live test data – that used during normal computer-based processing cycles, and/or
- dead test data – that used outside normal computer-based processing cycles.

Test data can be used to test and assess:

- the validity of computer-based processing procedures,
- the efficiency of computer-based processing procedures,
- the effectiveness of computer-based control protocols, and
- the accuracy of computer-based analytical and computational processes.

Test data can be used to test and assess:

- any single, group and/or cluster of programs/procedures,
- any system/network component, and/or
- any system/network in its entirety.

Test data techniques include:

- Integrated Test Facilities (ITFs), and
- BaseLine Evaluations (BLEs).

### Application software tracing and mapping

Application software or specialised programs/tools can be used to:

- analyse data flow through specified software applications,
- assess the processing logic of specified software applications,
- validate and document the processing procedures, and
- evaluate software application controls, processing logic, paths and sequences.

Application software tracing and mapping includes program/system/network:

- mapping,
- tracing,
- snapshots,
- parallel simulations, and
- code comparisons.

### Expert audit software

Expert audit software and/or auditing decision support systems/programs are essentially auto-mated knowledge systems of experts in the field. Such expert systems can included *inter alia*:

- risk analysis programs
- transaction analysis protocols, and
- control objective testing packages.

We will discuss computer assisted audit techniques in more detail below.

# Auditing computer-based accounting information systems

As we have discussed earlier (see Chapter 4), there can be little doubt that the new world order of the mid-20th century and early 21st century in which the search for:

- sustainable profitability,
- wealth creating opportunities,
- greater flexibility and adaptability, and
- long-term commercial competitive advantage,

has become central to the turbulent global priorities of market-based corporate capitalism and its desire to forge institutional interdependencies consistent with its continued survival and expansion. A search that itself has become:

- increasingly dependent on evermore complex symbolic forms of knowledge,
- evermore reliant on ephemeral technologies and knowledge-based systems, and
- evermore dependent on transferable forms of information.

Founded on:

- the complex flows of increasingly fictitious capital,
- the temporal and spatial displacement of resources, and
- the transferability of knowledge and information,

there can be little doubt that whilst the continued rise of *contemporary* corporate capitalism was clearly facilitated by the expansion, development and increasing sophistication of information technology products, services and capabilities, the information revolution has nonetheless continued to remain a product of the increasing controversial priorities of global market-based capitalism.

Remember, information technology is just another increasingly competitive business within just another increasingly turbulent industry, within just another ever-expanding and evermore chaotic marketplace. Imagine what would have happened to Microsoft Inc. if Microsoft Windows-based software platform had not been commercially successful in the 1980s? Would Microsoft have still survived to become the same commercially successful company that it is today? Probably not!

It was the increasing pressures to:

- provide both internal and external users with more relevant/accurate information,
- support management decision-making/control processes, and
- facilitate external regulation and control,

as a consequence of the turbulent and ever-changing global priorities of market-based corporate capitalism that promoted the need for more efficient and effective information systems and the demand for increasingly computer-based accounting information systems. Computer-based/ information technology orientated accounting information systems that have now – without doubt – become the essential component of the corporate cache of competitive information orientated technologies.

As we have seen earlier in this chapter, accounting information systems whether computer-based/information technology orientated and/or otherwise which:

- contain financial files, records and/or data,
- process and/or analyse such financial files, records and/or data, and/or
- generate statutory financial information from such financial files, records and/or data,

are required to be audited. This is a mandatory requirement for UK companies enshrined in UK company law (see Companies Act 1985).

So how do you audit computer-based/information technology orientated accounting information systems? For an effective and efficient audit, an auditor needs to validate/verify the existence of:

- appropriate application controls – these will vary between individual applications and are required to ensure:
  - the completeness and accuracy of records, and
  - the validity of data,
- relevant general controls – these will *not* vary between individual applications, will relate to the environment and are required to ensure:
  - the proper development and implementation of applications, and
  - the integrity of program data files.

It is therefore common for auditors to adopt what we will regard as a *bi-lateral audit approach*, as follows:

- a content (or application) audit – assessing the functional/operational processes, procedures and protocols of the computer-based accounting information systems, and
- a context (or environment) audit – assessing the general controls/environment aspects of a company's accounting information systems architecture (see also Chapter 5), for example:
  - organisational controls,
  - development and maintenance controls,
  - access controls, and
  - sundry controls.

## Content (or application) audit

Historically, content/application auditing – assessing the functional/operational processes, procedures and protocols of the computer-based accounting information systems – was classified as follows:

- auditing around the computer,
- auditing through the computer, and
- auditing with the computer (using a range of Computer Assisted Audit Techniques (CAATs)).

However, this classification – whilst still enjoying some popularity (for whatever reason) in a number of contemporary accounting information systems texts, and indeed some auditing texts, is rather dated and in a contemporary context perhaps somewhat naïve, since it fails to recognise how current advances in information technologies have not only changed the nature, analytical ability and processing capability of many CAATs, but also increasingly distorted the boundaries between what were historically well-defined, independent and discrete CAATs.

For our purposes, we will adopt a more contemporary classification, as follows:

- non-CAAT-based auditing (auditing around the computer), and
- CAAT-based auditing (auditing through and/or with the computer using a range of computer assisted audit techniques).

Both of these are very relevant and extremely important to the effective and efficient auditing of computer-based/information technology orientated accounting information systems.

## Non-CAAT-based auditing (auditing around the computer)

Audit around the computer refers to an operational approach in which the computer (system and/or network) is considered a black box – a device, network and/or a system whose function and/or activities are known but whose internal design and/or operations/processes are not. As a consequence only externally identifiable behaviour, outcomes and/or inputs/outputs are visible and therefore measurable.

Such an approach entails circumventing the computer system and/or network and assessing/reviewing input and output data only. By using such an approach, no review of the computer system/network processing and/or application controls is undertaken.

Clearly, such an approach is only suitable where:

- complete documentation (either physical or virtual) is available and an audit trail of events, activities and/or procedures is complete and visible,
- audit evidence of the accuracy and occurrence of events, activities and/or procedures is available and verifiable, and
- events, activities and/or procedures are simple and identifiable.

## CAAT-based auditing (auditing through/with the computer)

As we saw earlier, computer assisted audit techniques can be defined as any single, group and/or cluster of audit techniques that use information technology-based applications as a primary investigative tool, such as generalised audit software, utility software, test data, application software tracing and mapping, audit expert systems and embedded audit facilities.

Although there are a number of CAATs that can and indeed are used for more than one purpose, in general they can be categorised as follows:

- CAATs used in the analysis of data/information, and
- CAATs used in the verification of (internal) control systems.

### CAATs used in the analysis of data

Although not necessarily confined to accounting data,[31] these CAATs are used to select, analyse/examine and summarise either permanent data and/or transaction data held/stored in specified files/records.

There are essentially two types of CAATs commonly used for the extraction, analysis and/or reviewing of computer-based file/record data. These are:

- the use of generic and/or expert audit software to undertake data file interrogation, and/or
- the use of embedded audit modules/facilities to monitor data file activity.

### Data file/record interrogation

Data file/record interrogation software/programs can be used to perform a variety of audit-related procedures, including:

- selecting files/records for assessment/examination (including the use of sampling procedures),
- testing the content and structure of selected files/record to ensure conformance to required/specified standards/formats,
- analysing file/record content by specified characteristic (called content stratification),
- searching for files/records for the existence of duplicate transactions,
- searching for files/records for the existence interruption/variances in processing sequences,
- comparing the content of two or more files/records (that should match/agree) for any inconsistencies, disparities and/or exceptions,

- comparing the content of two or more files/records (that should not match) for content equivalency and/or similarity,
- analysing, categorising and/or merging files/records for further audit testing, and
- summarising file/record content (including preparing control totals, etc.).

Whilst the use of generic audit software for data file/record interrogation is efficient and effective in terms of time and reliability, and generally easy to use, there is a need to ensure the compatibility of the generic audit software with the target system/sub-system and of course the computer system/network.

### Embedded audit modules/facilities

An embedded audit module/facility is an audit application (usually a cluster of related programs), that permanently resides in a processing system/sub-system within a system/network (see Figure 15.5). Such embedded audit modules/facilities are generally employed in:

- processing systems/sub-systems that process high volumes of data and, increasingly,
- processing systems/sub-systems that process high risk data (e.g. high value and/or confidential data records).

Although there are many variations to the use of embedded audit modules/facilities these can be classified into two distinct approaches:

- embedded data collection, and/or
- tagging.

In the former an embedded audit module/facility essentially monitors and examines all transactions that enter a processing system/sub-system. When a transaction arises that satisfies a pre-selected criteria/parameter, a record (an audit file) of the transaction details is created before the transaction is permitted to continue for further processing.

In the latter, specified records are merely tagged – an extra field is added to each specified/pre-selected data record – to facilitate/enable identification for future audit analysis. Again

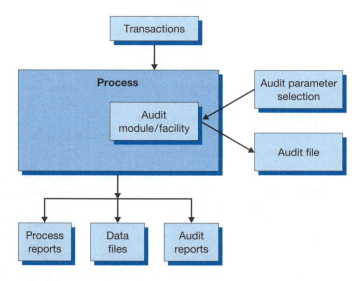

**Figure 15.5** Embedded audit module/facility

a summary audit file would be created recording the details of all data records tagged and processed.

Embedded audit modules/facilities are clearly a very powerful and potent audit technology. However it is important to ensure that:

- the interception of transactions occurs at the most appropriate processing stage within a system/sub-system stage,
- the operation of the embedded audit module/facility does not degrade system/sub-system performance,
- the audit selection criteria/parameters and created audit files are protected against unauthorised alteration.

### CAATs used in the verification of (internal) control systems

These CAATs are designed to examine, assess and verify a system/sub-system's internal controls to:

- determine the reliability of controls, and
- assess the accuracy/validity of accounting files and data records, and indeed other associated non-accounting files and data records.

There are (perhaps unsurprisingly) many alternative techniques that can be utilised to review and verify a systems/sub-systems internal controls. These include *inter alia*:

- the use of test data,
- the use of integrated test facilities,
- the use of parallel simulation, and
- the use of program code comparison.

### Test data

Test data can be used to test and assess:

- any single, group and/or cluster of programs/procedures,
- any system/network component, and/or
- any system/network in entirety.

But more importantly they confirm the operation of:

- existing programs whose processed output is unpredictable and/or random,
- existing programs whose processed output is irreconcilable with data input, and/or
- new and/or amended programs.

Test data can be either:

- live – that used during normal computer-based processing cycles, and/or
- dead – that used outside normal computer-based processing cycles.

They can be used to examine/assess the processing logic of programs and authenticate:

- input protocols,
- processing procedures,
- output routines, and
- error detection facilities.

Such test data can also be used to assess any associated non-computer-based processes, procedures and protocols.

The main advantages of using test data are:

- they are simple to operate,
- they are extremely cost effective, and
- they require limited technical knowledge/ability.

The main disadvantages/problems are:

- the use of test data only confirms/authenticates the programs tested at the time,
- where a new *in development* program is tested changes (whether authorised or otherwise) may occur/may be allowed to occur after testing but prior to *live* implementation, and
- the use of test data on either an *in development* program and/or a *live* program may not test all the combined unpredictable permutations of circumstances that may arise.

It is therefore extremely important to ensure that where test data are used:

- effective configuration management and/or change control protocols exist – to ensure that tested procured and/or developed software/programs are securely protected from any unwarranted and/or unauthorised amendment, and
- efficient test data design protocols exist to ensure that:
  - a wide range of programming functions/processes are appropriately exercised, and
  - a variety of program permutations are adequately assessed,
  and confirm that the tested program (whether *in development* or *live*)
  - does/will do what it is meant to do, and
  - does not/will not do what it is not meant to do.

### Integrated test facility

An integrated test facility is sometimes used in the audit of complex application systems. In essence it provides an in-built test facility through the creation of a fictitious system/sub-system (e.g. a subsidiary, a department or a branch within a company's live accounting information system). See Figure 15.6.

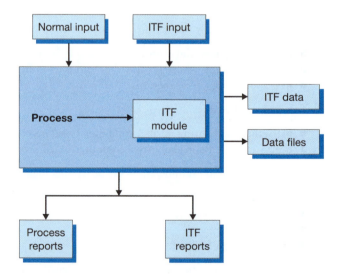

**Figure 15.6** Integrated test facility

Whilst there are clearly limited operational costs involved (once a test facility has been designed, developed and implemented), the main advantages of using an integrated test facility are:

- it provides comprehensive testing of a live system,
- it facilitates unscheduled, undisclosed and anonymous testing, and
- it provides *prima facie* and authenticable evidence of correct and proper program functions/operations.

More importantly, once such an integrated test facility is operational it can not only be used for program testing but also for user training, etc.

However, there are significant risks involved in using such test facilities. Where an integrated test facility is created – whether for auditing purposes and/or training purposes – it is important that any test data created during an audit is not allowed to corrupt the *live* accounting information system.

## Baseline evaluation

A baseline (systems and/or security) evaluation is the assessment, selection and implementation of systems procedures and/or security measures within a computer-based system based upon systems procedures and/or security measures and protocols used in similar computer-based systems in companies that are generally accepted to be well-run.

Such evaluations can take many forms including the use of test data to validate selected systems procedures/security protocols.

## Parallel simulation

Parallel simulation is the generation of an independent program to simulate/imitate part of an existing application program (see Figure 15.7). It is designed to test the validity and verify the accuracy of an existing program/cluster of programs.

The main advantage of using parallel simulation is that since any simulation program will normally be concerned with only a few discrete aspects of a live operational program within the accounting information system, such a simulation program will generally:

- be simple to operate,
- be not very complex,

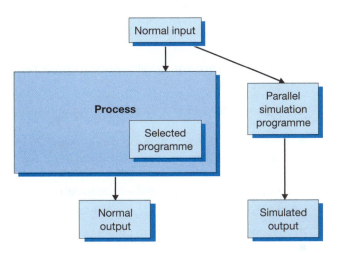

**Figure 15.7** Parallel simulation

- be cheap to design and implement, and
- require limited technical ability to use.

However as with test data (see above) the main disadvantage/problem with using parallel simulation is that its use as a test, will only confirm/authenticate the program(s) tested at the time they are tested.

## Utility programs – code comparators

These are utility programs that will:

- compare generational versions (definitive and amended versions) of the same computer program,
- identify changes and/or alterations made,
- ascertain and validate the source of such changes and/or alterations, and
- report on the impact of such changes and/or alterations.

For existing live programs, such utility programs are often used as part of an *authorisation audit* – to assess all variations between a definitive version of a *live* program and the amended currently-used version of a *live* program to determine an authorisation audit trail.

Alternatively, for newly installed developed and/or procured programs, such utility programs can be used as part of a *configuration audit* – to assess the validity of implementation control protocols and procedures by comparing the current version of a *live* program to its predecessor *development and/or procured* program to identify any unauthorised configuration changes that may have been made.

## Some guidelines on where to use CAATs

There is little doubt that the use of CAATs in both auditing and non-auditing (accounting information systems related)-investigations/activities has grown enormously over the past 10 years. Although this list is by no means exhaustive, some of the most popular areas are:

- financial statement audit – substantive testing,
- financial statement audit – compliance testing,
- financial statement audit – analytical review and predictive analysis,
- compliance audit – internal control audit,
- compliance audit – management audit/efficiency analysis,
- operational audit – value for money audit.

### Financial statement audit – substantive testing

CAATs are used to:

- sample test transactions files and data to ensure the accuracy and propriety of accounting transactions, and
- sample test transaction files and data to verify and validate asset and liabilities balances (using auditing software to reconcile balances).

### Financial statement audit – compliance testing

CAATs are used to:

- test controls/procedures which cannot be observed directly, and/or
- test procedures, processes and/or protocols for which no direct documentary evidence exists that internal controls are operating effectively.

*Financial statement audit – trend analysis and analytical review*

CAATs are used to test for trends/comparability of transactions/balances between:

- different accounting periods,
- different accounting locations (within the company), and/or
- different accounting types (e.g. debtors' balances within the debtors ledger).

*Compliance audit – internal control audit*

CAATs are used to:

- test and detect possible fraudulent transactions (sampling authorisation procedures and processes), and
- test network security using port scanning tools and/or network intrusion detection tools.

*Compliance audit – management audit/efficiency analysis*

CAATs are used to:

- test the efficiency of a client's computer system/network to ensure adequate cost-effective processing throughput of work is being achieved, and
- assess the effectiveness of resource allocation.

*Operational audit – value for money audit*

CAATs are used to test financial transaction data for trends.

## Some guidelines on planning the use of CAATs

Although CAATs can be used for a wide variety of audit purposes (and indeed some non-audit purposes), there is perhaps, not unsurprisingly, no clear definitive guide on *how* to use CAATs. This is because their use and application will vary depending on:

- the nature of client company being audited,
- the nature and structure of the target system/sub-system being tested,
- the structure and content of the files/data records being tested, and
- the CAAT application(s) being used.

However, in determining whether to use CAATs, the main decision factors that would influence using or not using CAATs include:

- the computer knowledge, expertise and experience of the auditor/audit team,
- the availability of suitable CAATs and information technology facilities,
- the cost effectiveness of using CAATs,
- the resource implications of using CAATs,
- the possible time constraints imposed on the audit and/or the use of CAATs,
- the integrity of the client's information system and information technology environment, and
- the level of audit risk associated with the audit.

In a general context, the following can be regarded as a broad guide:

- define aim and objective of the test(s),
- agree file/data retention protocols with the client company,
- analyse the client company's target system/sub-systems program operations,
- identify relevant file(s) and data records required,
- confirm the structure and location of relevant file(s) and data records,

- determine the criteria for selecting files and data records required,
- determine a sampling routine (if required),
- determine the level of file/data record interrogation required,
- identify the position within the processing cycle at which file/data record interrogation will be performed,
- specify the format of the data file and method of storage,
- ensure/confirm the correct version of *live* files are interrogated and, where appropriate, arrange for copies of these to be taken for use in the interrogation,
- present interrogation findings/evidence and determine an opinion.

The following are seven rules of best practice when using CAATs.

### Rule 1

Ensure background research is adequate and up-to-date and any deficiencies in knowledge and/or understanding are addressed, and information in the client company's target system/ sub-system, its relevant programs, files and data records, and the company's coding system/ structure is appropriate and relevant.

### Rule 2

Ensure all audit work is recorded and appropriately documented, including:

- audit objectives,
- the system (and programs) under audit,
- specifications of the files and/or data records being tested,
- information on relevant data records/types and recognition characteristics,
- the audit software (CAAT) being used, and
- the names of contacts and their designations within the company.

### Rule 3

Ensure all data retrieval programs, embedded facilities, test data, integrated test facilities and/or simulations are reviewed, assessed (independently if possible) and up-to-date – reflecting any changes that may have occurred in the client company's operation procedures, processes, protocols and programs.

### Rule 4

During the testing procedures ensure appropriate control records are created and reconciled to the client company's accounting information systems records. It is also important to validate and confirm that all specified data records have been identified, processed and appropriately tested.

### Rule 5

Accounting information systems are highly structured dynamic constructs whose evolution/ change for the better is inevitable – nothing stays the same. Changes imposed by external environmental factors and/or internal management decisions (usually prompted by external environment factors) often have significant impact not only on the structure and content of transaction file and/or data records but, more importantly, on the content and organisation of permanent files and associated data records.

A client company's target system/sub-system and associated programs rarely remain unchanged for very long. If a CAAT associated test is repeated, either as part of:

- an ongoing audit test, or
- a specific assessment test,

it is important to obtain confirmation (from appropriate client company personnel) that no system changes in the intervening test period have occurred that have altered:

- the system's/sub-systems' programs, procedures, processes and/or protocols,
- the structure and content of transaction/permanent files, and/or
- the content and structure of data records.

Where such confirmation is not forthcoming or unavailable, or where identified (and confirmed) changes have occurred that have affected:

- the system's/sub-systems' programs, procedures, processes and/or protocols,
- the structure and content of transaction/permanent files, and/or
- the content and structure of data records,

it may be necessary to:

- redesign the content,
- reconfigure the specifications, and/or
- reassess the parameters,

of any data retrieval programs, embedded facilities, test data, integrated test facilities and/or simulations that may be used.

### Rule 6

Always ensure written authorisation is obtained from appropriate client company personnel before any CAAT that requires interfacing with the company's operation computer system and/or *live* accounting information systems. Where connection to an online system is necessary ensure files and/or data records are accessed in *read only* mode to prevent possible data corruption.

### Rule 7

Ensure that the use of any CAAT is:

- time efficient, and
- cost effective.

We will now look at the context (or environmental) audit and, in particular, review the general environmental controls that should exist within a company's accounting information systems environment to ensure its secure and efficient operations.

## Context (or environment) audit

A context (or environment) audit is an assessment of the effectiveness of a company's accounting information systems architecture and related internal controls.

In a broad sense, the term accounting information systems architecture means the totality of surrounding conditions – the entirety of all the physical and other factors that can and do affect the effective and efficient operation of a company's system, sub-systems and/or network. It is, in essence, the combination of corporate procedures, processes, and protocols which facilitates the interface between:

- the computer system/network – as a physical entity,
- the accounting information system – as a virtual construct, and
- the corporeal reality of the *real world*.

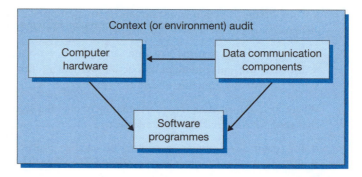

**Figure 15.8** Context (or environment) audit

It is the physical design and/or structural arrangements of:

- computer hardware,
- software programs, and
- data communications components,

within a company's accounting information system.
      See Figure 15.8.

## Accounting information systems architecture – general controls

Within a computer environment – in particular within a company's accounting information systems architecture – we can distinguish between four levels of general controls, as follows:

- organisational controls,
- system development and maintenance controls,
- access controls, and
- sundry controls.

See Figure 15.9.

### Organisational controls

As we discussed in Chapter 14, the cornerstone of a company's internal control procedures is the existence of an adequate and well-defined hierarchical separation of duties. Within a company's computer environment, at a minimum, there should be a distinct separation/division between:

- operational processes and procedures, and
- systems/network management, analysis and design.

Furthermore, within a company's computer environment/accounting information systems architecture, at a minimum – within computer associated operations – there should be a distinct separation of duties between:

- authorising events – that is procedures involved in the authorising and approving of defined phases of processing,
- executing events – that is procedures involved in the active processing of data,

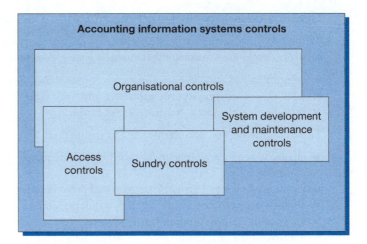

**Figure 15.9** Accounting information systems architecture

- managing events – that is procedures involved in the supervision and administration of data processing activities, and
- safeguarding events – that is procedures involved with the protection and security of physical assets and non-physical resources (e.g. data files, data records and structured output information).

In essence, separation of duties should exist between:

- data capture procedures,
- data entry procedures,
- data processing procedures, and
- processing authorisation protocols.

More importantly, sufficient internal controls should exist to ensure that:

- computer operations staff are *not* involved in, or responsible for:
  - data capture procedures, and/or
  - systems analysis and programming procedures,
- systems analysis and programming staff are *not* involved in or responsible for:
  - data capture procedures, and/or
  - computer operational procedures (data entry and data processing).

Indeed, from a functional/operational aspect such internal controls should ensure that:

- within a computer operations department adequate separation of duties exists between:
  - data administration processes,
  - computer operations procedures,
  - data control activities,
  - file library maintenance procedures, and
  - network control processes and protocols,
- within the systems analysis department adequate separation of duties exists between:
  - systems analysis procedures,
  - systems design processes,
  - systems maintenance and management activities, and
  - programming procedures.

## System development and maintenance controls

Within systems management, development and maintenance procedures, sufficient internal controls should exist to ensure that any new system does not:

- compromise existing live systems,
- conflict with existing security protocols, and
- introduce/create additional environment risks.

Sufficient internal controls should exist to ensure that:

- all new systems developments/acquisitions are adequately reviewed, tested and appropriately approved,[32]
- all (internal) control system[33] changes and program alterations are approved,
- all document procedures are regularly validated, and
- all systems and/or program specifications are reviewed and amended as required, and approved by management and user departments.

The existence of such internal controls should ensure that not only is data processed appropriately, completely and without prejudice, but also, where appropriate, an effective validation procedure exists for the efficient detection, location and correction of processing errors which will reduce the overall possibility of financial loss.

## Access controls

In Chapter 14, we explored three distinct hierarchical layers of control:

- physical security control layer,
- technical security control layer, and
- human security control layer.

It is these three layers of control that collectively comprise what are commonly referred to as access controls – inasmuch as:

- physical security controls are designed to prevent/restrict resource access and asset movement,
- technical security controls are designed to restrict/control user privileges, and
- human security controls are designed to enforce *an approved* control culture.

Such internal controls should ensure the active use of appropriate authorisation procedures to:

- control access to computer hardware/resources to authorised and approved personnel only,
- restrict access to software/programs to appropriately authorised personnel/users and control authorised personnel/user rights and privileges, and
- manage/control access to data files and data records.

This could be through the use (individually or in combination) of:

- personalised ID badges/security smart cards,
- security passwords and/or personalised biometrics,
- hardware/software security tagging and software/program encryption, and
- computer usage/data files access monitoring.

## Sundry controls

Sundry internal controls relate to:

- the safeguarding of assets and resources, and
- the secure protection of data and information.

They should ensure that appropriate systems and procedures exist for:

- the secure protection of data files, transaction data and programs (including protection from theft, breaches of security, acts of violence and/or the impact of natural disasters),
- the regular backup (secure copying) of data files, transaction data and programs, and
- the secure off-site storage of backup data files, transaction data and programs.

A key aspect of such sundry controls would of course be a disaster contingency recovery protocol to be used in the unlikely event of a significant and widespread disaster befalling the company (see also Chapter 14).

## Auditing computer-based accounting information systems – more issues

There can be little doubt that for the auditing of computer-based accounting information systems, 20th and 21st century advances in technology – in particular information technology – have metaphorically speaking been a double-edged sword. Whilst such advances have revolutionised the *modus operandi*[34] of many aspects of corporate accounting information systems, most noticeably by:

- fundamentally revolutionising data capture/data entry procedures,
- radically transforming data processing procedures,
- drastically expanding data/information storage capacities, and
- significantly enhancing information analysis and data/information transfer/communication,

they have also:

- transformed many of the traditional techniques used in auditing corporate accounting information systems – for example, IT-related/computer-based:
  - data collection (ICQs/ICEs),
  - data analysis (flowcharting and narrative report writers), and
  - narrative report writers, and
- introduced a vast portfolio of new computer assisted auditing techniques – for example, IT-related/computer-based:
  - generic software testing programs,
  - computer-based statistical sampling techniques,
  - IT-related analytical review procedures, and
  - computer-based decision support systems.

Such advances have nonetheless created a number of significant issues for auditors in the auditing of computer systems – in particular computer-based accounting information systems – of which the most important relate to:

- databases,
- online networks, and
- real-time (online 3 stage) systems.

### Databases

As an organised body of information or an information set with a regular structure or a collection of related information organised to facilitate complex interpretation and analysis, databases – in particular relational databases – are now a central feature of *all* computer-based accounting information systems.

Problems associated with the use of databases relate to:

- the recognition of inappropriate use,
- the identification of unauthorised access,
- the detection and prevention of unapproved content changes, and
- the detection and correction of improper database processing.

Clearly a failure to detect/identify inappropriate use, unauthorised access, unapproved content changes and improper processing would compromise:

- the security of the database,
- the integrity of the data contents,
- the validity of data records, and
- where personal data is recorded, processed and/or stored the confidentiality of data elements.

This is especially relevant in cases where a company's databases can be accessed remotely, either via a private and/or public network (e.g. over the internet).

Remember, a company has a legal duty under the Data Protection Act 1998 to ensure that any personal data is appropriately processed and securely maintained.

Appropriate internal controls should exist to ensure:

- the use of encryption facilities to protect highly sensitive database contents,
- the use of authorisation keys/passwords to restrict access to authorised personnel/users only,
- the use of appropriate separation of duties between database administration and database security management, and
- the use of access/performance logs to monitor/record database access/changes, and, where appropriate, prevent unauthorised access/changes to sensitive data elements.

### (Online) networks

A network is essentially a data communications system – a system enabling an organisation and/or company to share information and programs (see Wilkinson *et al.*, 2001), whilst an *online*[35] network is a computer system/network and/or facility/service that is accessed remotely via a dial-up connection through a public and/or private network.

Such communication networks can vary in terms of:

- network architecture,
- network topology (see Chapter 5), and
- network interconnection.

Whilst historically such communication networks were – indeed some continue to be – hard-wired networks (using copper and/or fibre optic cabling between network devices/facilities), the move toward wireless networking (WLAN) and the reliance on radio waves and/or microwaves to:

- establish network connections,
- maintain communication channels, and
- transmit/transfer data and information,

has become the major feature of early 21st century information technology development.

Wireless networking offers:

- greater networking mobility, and
- increasingly flexible connectivity.

Whilst there are clear disadvantages/problems such as:

- potential for interference due to adverse environmental and/or physical conditions,
- possible intrusion by other wireless devices/transmission, and
- potential interference by unauthorised users,

the popularity of wireless business networking appears due to:

- improved efficiency and effectiveness of wireless technology and, perhaps most importantly,
- the ever-reducing cost of wireless products/wireless networking.

Clearly, for all communication networks (both hard-wired and indeed wireless networks), in particular (for our purposes) network facilities which:

- capture (input) financial-related data and information,
- process/record/convert financial data and/or information, and/or
- transmit (output) financial-related data and information,

it is, from both an operational and management/administration aspect, essential that:

- regular vulnerability scans including network perimeter assessments,
- frequent penetration tests including security evaluations/assessments, and
- regular communication tests including network traffic efficiency/effectiveness assessments,

are undertaken, to ensure:

- the verification and validation of all appropriate network traffic,
- the identification and prevention of inappropriate use and unauthorised access/security breaches,
- the prevention of communication disruptions,
- the detection and correction of unapproved network amendments, and
- the correction of inappropriate network traffic.

## Real-time (online 3 stage) systems

As we discussed in Chapter 5, a real-time (online 3 stage) system is a computer system/network and/or facility/service that responds to prescribed environmental events *in the world* as they happen and in which the time at which output is produced is significant. That is for a real-time system, it is the input-to-output response time that is the key identifiable requirement of the system.

Such systems can be sub-divided into a number of alternative types, based on:

- the speed of response of the system, and
- the criticality of response of the system.

Using the speed of response, a system can be categorised as either a fast real-time system or a slow real-time system. Although there is no clear boundary/distinction between either type, generally:

- a system with a response time measured in seconds (or less) can be considered fast, and
- a system with a response time measured in minutes (or more) can be considered slow.

Clearly, this leaves an indeterminate area/period of response times in which a system could theoretically be categorised as either fast or slow! Using criticality of response, a system can be categorised as a hard real-time system and/or a soft real-time system.

A hard real-time system is a system where the response time is specified as an absolute value with the response time normally dictated/imposed by the external environment. In such systems, where a response is not generated, the system will be considered to be in error and will invariably require the performance of some form of error recovery procedure, whilst operating at either:

- a reduced level of functionality, or
- a zero level of functionality (shutdown).

A soft real-time system is a system where the response time is normally specified as an average value, with the response time normally dictated by the company and/or the business/industry within which the company operates. For any single response an acceptable range/time period for a response is defined. Where a response is not generated within such a defined range/period the system may be considered in error.

In essence, real-time systems can be categorised into four system types as follows:

- hard-fast real-time systems,
- hard-slow real-time systems,
- soft-fast real-time systems, and
- soft-slow real-time systems.

Examples of hard-fast real-time systems would be:

- embedded computer process control systems, and
- computer-based intrusion/inflection detection systems.

Examples of soft-fast/very fast real-time systems would be:

- ATM systems,
- EPOS systems,
- PIN and CHIP payment systems, and
- data streaming and/or online network communication systems.

Particular problems faced by auditors when auditing real-time computer-based accounting information systems/sub-systems which are becoming increasingly common in manufacturing but especially in retail and services companies, relate to:

- the verification of appropriate segregation of duties,
- the confirmation of hardware/software management protocols,
- the authentication of transaction verification procedures,
- the validation data file/data record security,
- the confirmation of program and communication security, and
- the verification of system/program update authorisation procedures.

Clearly, testing for the existence of appropriate segregation of duties, system administration and management processes, and security and control protocols within a real-time system will not only depend on:

- the configuration of the system/sub-systems,
- the purpose of the system/sub-systems,
- the level of activity of the system/sub-system,
- the criticality of the system/sub-system, and
- the network relationship (to other systems/sub-systems) of the system/sub-system,

but will also require the use of a range of content (application) audit techniques – probably CAATs-based – and a range of context (environment) audit techniques.

## Concluding comments

Whilst there can little doubt that the *nature* of the company audit as an independent inspection and examination of a company's accounting information systems has remained more or less unchanged certainly over the past 50 years, there can also be little doubt that:

- the ever-increasing and very often public demise of many highly respected, long-established and once enormously profitable companies, and perhaps as a consequence,
- the increasingly risk averse attitude of many market participants,

has clearly influenced the *emphasis/focus* of contemporary accounting information systems audits.

More importantly perhaps has been the enormous growth in and availability of computer-based technologies/IT-related facilities.

With the traditionalistic emphasis on bureaucratic paper-based processing systems now confined (thankfully) to the tattered and worn pages of corporate history and replaced by a vast array of increasingly complex and interactive computer-based processing systems/networks, it has been the almost overwhelming embrace of such technologies and the use of increasingly sophisticated computer-based/IT-related systems and facilities, that has:

- revolutionised the *process* of contemporary company audit, and
- transformed the role of the auditor.

A revolution that has catapulted auditors and auditing into a postmodern IT-dominated brave new world!

## Key points and concepts

Access controls
Accounting information systems audit
Audit evidence
Audit program
Base case systems evaluation
Cluster sampling
Compliance audit
Computer Assisted Audit Techniques (CAATs)
Content (applications) audit
Context (environment) audit
Embedded audit modules/facilities
External audit
Financial statement audit
Flowchart
Generic audit software
Integrated test facilities
Internal audit

Internal control questionnaire
Judgemental sampling
Narrative report/description
Operational audit
Organisational controls
Parallel simulation
Process management controls
Protocol management controls
Random sampling
Security controls
Sundry controls
Syntactic controls
Systems development and maintenance controls
Test data
Unsystematic sampling
Utility software

## References

Anderson, R.J. (1977) *The External Audit*, Croop Clark Pitman, Toronto.

Davies, T. and Boczko, T. (2005) *Business Accounting and Finance*, McGraw Hill, London.

Habermas, J. (1984), *The Theory of Communicative Action*, volume 1 and volume 2, (Trans. McCarthy, T.), Beacon Press, Boston.

Habermas, J. (1987) 'Excursus on Luhmann's Appropriation of the Philosophy of the Subject through Systems Theory,' in *The philosophical Discourse of Modernity: Twelve Lectures*, pp. 68–85, MIT Press, Cambridge.

Morris, J. (1977) *Domesday Book 20 Bedfordshire*, Philimore, Chichester.

Porter, B., Simon, J. and Hatherley, D. (2003) *Principles of External Audit*, Wiley, Chichester.

Wilkinson, J.W., Cerullo, M.L., Raval, V. and Wong-On-Wing, B. (2001) *Accounting Information Systems*, Wiley, New York.

## Bibliography

Bodnar, G.H. and Hopwood, W.S. (2001) *Accounting Information Systems*, Prentice Hall, London.

Gelina, U.J., Sutton, S.G. and Oram, A.E. (1999) *Accounting Information Systems*, South Western, Cincinnati, Ohio.

Hall, J.A. (1998) *Accounting Information Systems*, South Western, Cincinnati, Ohio.

Mosgrove, S.A., Simkin, M.G. and Bagranoff, N.A. (2001) *Core Concepts of Accounting Information Systems*, Wiley, New York.

Vaassen, E. (2002) *Accounting Information Systems – A Managerial Approach*, Wiley, Chichester.

Woolfe, E. (1997) *Auditing Today*, FT/Prentice Hall, London.

## Websites

### Useful auditing websites

www.iia.org.uk
Institute of Internal Auditors
www.ifac.org.
International Federation of Accountants
www.apb.org.uk/apb.
The Auditing Practices Board
www.emas.org.uk.
Eco-management and audit scheme
www.theiia.org/itaudit.
US Institute of Internal Auditors IT Audit Forum

## Self-review questions

1. Briefly explain the role of an auditor and distinguish between the role of an internal auditor and the role of an external auditor.
2. Distinguish between a financial statement audit, a compliance audit and an operational audit.
3. Define and explain the purpose of a content (application) audit.
4. Define and explain the possible use of a non-CAAT-based audit.
5. What factors should an auditor consider before using a CAAT?
6. Define and explain a context (environmental) audit.
7. Identify and describe five alternative auditing techniques.
8. Define and distinguish between each of the following terms:
   - generic audit software,
   - utility software, and
   - expert audit software.
9. Distinguish between a hard real-time system and a soft real-time system.
10. Briefly explain the main types of controls often used by companies to minimise the risks and problems associated with the use of EDI.

## Questions and problems

### Question 1

Describe and evaluate the primary role and function of an internal auditor, and explain how and why the role of an internal auditor has changed over recent years.

### Question 2

'The external auditor is a bloodhound whose sole purpose is the detection of fraud.' Discuss.

### Question 3

Real-time transaction processing systems are now far from unusual.

*Required*

(a) Explain what additional problems real-time transaction processing systems cause the auditor compared with a batch environment.
(b) Explain what steps the auditor needs to take to solve the problems identified above.
(c) Explain with reasons which CAATs could be used in this real-time environment.

### Question 4

(This question also requires knowledge and understanding of issues addressed in Chapters 4 and 14.)

The use of EDI is now common in a wide range of industries.

→

## Required

Explain:

- the main uses of EDI,
- the risks and problems associated with its use, and
- the main controls an auditor would expect in a large service company using EDI as part of its operational activities.

## Question 5

The business environment of the early 21st century continues to change with increasing vigour. The growth of e-commerce and e-retailing, and the use of the internet for the movement of goods, services and information has clearly promoted a greater interconnectivity. An interconnectivity that has not only opened up and created enormous business opportunities, but has also increased the exposure of UK businesses, in particular UK companies, to previously unknown levels of risks and security threats, the costs and consequences of which have been and indeed continue to be significant.[36]

## Required

Explain how such change has affected the role of external auditors in undertaking their duties as required by the Companies Act 1985.

# Assignments

## Question 1

You have recently been appointed internal (systems) auditor for NiTolm Ltd, an established FMCG company located in the north-east of England. The company has retail outlets in Hull, York, Scarborough, Newcastle and Durham. NiTolm Ltd has been operating successfully for many years and operates a networked computer-based accounting information system with a growing percentage of its transactions occurring through its web-based e-commerce facility.

## Required

Describe the alternative types of audit a company such as NiTolm Ltd could be subject to and distinguish between the following alternatives:

- non-CAAT-based auditing, and
- CAAT-based auditing.

## Question 2

(This question also requires knowledge and understanding of issues addressed in Chapters 9 and 15.)

You have recently been appointed as auditor for Bepelear Ltd, a small electrical accessories company. The company operates both an internet-based sales system and a retail outlet-based sales system.

For the previous five financial years the company has made average annual purchases of £18m (all purchases from UK suppliers), and average annual profits of approximately £9m. The company has approximately 50 employees working at six locations throughout the UK: Manchester, which is the company's head office, Birmingham, Leeds, Swindon, Bristol and Newcastle.

For the year ended 31 March 2006, approximately 75% of the company's sales were made through its internet-based sales system.

*Required*

Making whatever assumptions you consider necessary:

(a) Describe the control objectives of a company sales system and the general controls and application controls you would expect to find in an internet-based sales system.
(b) Describe the compliance tests you would undertake during the audit of Bepelear's internet-based sales system.

Note: You are not required to provide comment and/or discussion on Bepelear's retail outlet-based sales system.

## Chapter endnotes

[1] The term 'life-world' is used in the Habermasian context – meaning the shared common understandings – including values – that develop through contact over time within social groupings (see Habermas, 1984, 1987).

[2] The balance sheet and profit and loss account as defined in Schedule 4 Companies Act 1985, and cash flow statement as defined in FRS 1.

[3] The history of auditing – the heritage of auditing – is indisputably international. The need and desire for accountability for financial and business transactions undoubtedly has its roots in antiquity, and can perhaps be traced back to the ancient civilisations of Babylonia, Mesopotamia, Egypt and Central America, and indeed India.

In a UK context the contemporary role/function/context of audit whilst perhaps traceable back to the Domesday Book 1085 (see Morris, 1977) was more an emergent creation of changing socio-economic circumstances of the latter part of the 18th century and the early part of the 19th century (see Porter *et al.*, 2003).

[4] UK GAAP (United Kingdom Generally Accepted Accounting Principles) is the overall body of regulation establishing how company accounts must be prepared in the UK. This includes not only extant accounting standards, but also applicable UK company law.

[5] Undertaken in accordance with extant UK Auditing Standards.

[6] In the UK, for auditing purposes, the term 'qualified accountant' means an individual or firm that has a current audit-practising certificate and is a member of one of the five Recognised Supervisory Bodies (RSB) (as defined and recognised by the Secretary of State), these being:

- the Institute of Chartered Accountants in England and Wales,
- the Institute of Chartered Accountants of Scotland,
- the Institute of Chartered Accountants in Ireland,
- the Association of Chartered Certified Accountants, and
- the Association of Authorised Public Accountants.

Details of the requirements for recognition as an RSB are detailed in the Companies Act 1989, Schedule 11, Part 11.

[7] Not all companies are required to have an annual audit. If a company qualifies for exemption and chooses to take advantage of such an exemption (e.g. dormant companies and certain small companies) then they do not have to have their accounts audited.

To qualify for total audit exemption, a company (other than a dormant company) must:

- qualify as a small company,
- have a turnover of not more than £5.6m, and
- have a balance sheet total of not more than £2.8m.

To qualify for dormant company audit exemption, a limited company (together with a series of other criteria) must not have traded during the financial year.

[8] The term 'prepared properly' means in accordance with the Companies Act 1985.

[9] Available @ www.iia.org.uk/about/internalaudit.

[10] By ensuring:

- all assets of the company (or organisation) are being securely safeguarded,
- all corporate operations are conducted effectively, efficiently and economically in accordance with internal protocols, policies and procedure,
- all laws and regulations are complied with, and
- all records and reports are reliable and accurate.

[11] In May 2000 the original Cadbury Code (1992) and subsequent reports (including the 1998 Hampel Committee update of the Cadbury Code and the 1999 Turnbull Committee report *Internal Control: Guidance for Directors on the Combined Code* (published by the Institute of Chartered Accountants in England and Wales) were all consolidated by the Committee on Corporate Governance. (See Davies and Boczko, 2005)

[12] Following the EU Eighth Directive, the Companies Act 1989 introduced a framework for regulating the appointment of external auditors, to ensure that only appropriately qualified and properly supervised people are appointed as company auditors.

[13] Companies Act 1985, s385. Also note that where no external auditor is appointed, the Secretary of State may appoint an auditor (Companies Act 1985, s385, s387, s388).

[14] 'The financial statements must present a true and fair view of the company's state of affairs as at the end of the financial year and its profit or loss for the financial year, and must also comply with the form and content requirements of Schedule 4 of the Companies Act 1985 (CA 1985, s226)' (Porter *et al.*, 2003: 100).

[15] This list is by no means exhaustive and many other alternative industry, sector and/or company specific types of audit/definitions of audits may exist.

[16] See www.apb.org.uk/apb.

[17] See www.ifac.org.

[18] A list of IFAC member bodies is available @ www.ifac.org/About/MemberBodies.tmpl.

[19] See also the discussion on the precautionary principle in Chapter 14.

[20] See also the discussion on contemporary transaction processing in Chapters 8, 9, 10, and 11.

[21] EMAS (Eco-Management and Audit Scheme) is a voluntary initiative designed to improve corporate environmental performance and was established by EU Regulation 1836/93 (subsequently replaced by EU Council Regulation 761/01).

The aim of the scheme is to recognise and reward those companies (and organisations) that go beyond minimum legal compliance and continuously improve their environmental performance. In addition, it is a requirement of the scheme that participating companies (and organisations) regularly produce a public (and externally verified/audited) environmental statement that reports on their environmental performance. For further information see www.emas.org.uk/aboutemas/mainframe.htm.

[22] See www.emas.org.uk/why%20register/mainframe.htm.

23 ISO 14001 was first published in 1996 and specifies the actual requirements for an environmental management system. It applies to those environmental aspects over which the organisation has control and can be expected to have an influence.

The standard is applicable to any company (and organisation) that wishes to:

- implement, maintain and improve an environmental management system,
- demonstrate conformance with extant internal environmental policies, procedures and protocols,
- ensure compliance with environmental laws and regulations, and
- seek certification of its environmental management system by an external third party.

See www.iso14000-iso14001-environmental-management.com/iso14001.htm.

24 Remember that an accounting information system is:

- a cohesive organisational structure – a set of directly and indirectly interrelated processes and procedures, objects and elements, events and activities,
- an interconnected set/collection of information resources that share a common purpose and functionality,
- an interconnected set of systems and/or sub-systems whose purpose is the acquisition, capture, storage, manipulation, movement, interchange, transmission, management, control and analysis of data (and information) through which the (financial) consequences and the (financial) causes and effects – of not only social, but political and economic inputs/outputs – can be identified, processed, managed and controlled.

25 That is someone who emphasises observable facts and excludes any notion of the metaphysical.

26 Whilst not specifically required to search for fraud, external auditors undertaking a financial statement audit must have a duty of care to plan and perform their audits to obtain reasonable assurance that such financial statements are free from material misstatement, and to report to the company any evidence that they suspect may result in fraud (SAS 82 *Consideration of fraud in a financial statement audit* (1997)).

27 SAS 400 *Audit evidence*.

28 An audit programme is a procedural framework, a list and/or plan of audit procedures required to be followed during an audit. It is a series of structured steps necessary to achieve the audit objective. It is, in effect, the functional context of the audit itself.

29 SAS 430 *Audit Sampling*.

30 The most common approaches being:

- sampling for attributes (measuring the frequency with which a particular characteristic is or is not present), and
- sampling for variables (measuring/estimating the total value/number within a population/ universe).

31 These CAATs can also be used to select, analyse/examine and summarise data held/stored in non-accounting files/records – for example processing logs and/or access/security logs, which may be created when computer-based files and records are accessed and accounting data is processed.

32 Whilst the auditors should not – in any way – be considered part of any system/sub-system, any process and/or any procedure, since that would seriously jeopardise the auditors' independence, they should nonetheless be consulted (as should end-users) when significant new developments/alterations are being considered.

[33] Simple integral internal controls should always be preferred – essentially because they minimise bureaucracy and are therefore time efficient and cost effective. Such integrated internal controls should be part of a general strategy to detect and prevent fraud.

[34] Meaning mode and/or method of operation.

[35] Historically the term online referred to a system that allowed the computer systems/IT facilities to work interactively with its users. Clearly, not anymore!

[36] Information Security Breaches Survey (2006), PricewaterhouseCoopers/DTI – see Chapters 13 and 14.

# Accounting information systems development: managing change

## Introduction

For a company/organisation trading in today's business environment – an environment increasingly dominated by the politics of global competition and the volatile economics of the marketplace – an environment in which companies/organisations are increasingly preoccupied not only with the inevitability of change, but also the consequences such change may produce, the importance of knowledge and information – the importance of an adequate information system, in particular, an up-to-date and relevant accounting information system – cannot be underestimated.

Indeed, in today's evermore uncertain business environment – an environment in which companies/organisations are constantly engaged in a never-ending battle for new markets, new customers and new products, and a search for greater revenue – for increased profitability and greater shareholder wealth – the:

- development and adaptation of a company's/organisation's accounting information system, (as a component aspect of the company's/organisation's business information system), and
- integration and absorption of an ever-changing, ever-developing portfolio of information and communication technologies,

has become a prerequisite not only for competitive stability and long-term commercial success but, more importantly – for corporate survival.

This chapter examines the importance of accounting information systems development, in particular:

- the need for a cohesive accounting information systems development strategy,
- the socio-economic problems associated with accounting information systems development,
- the political nature of accounting information systems development, and

■ the processes and problems associated with the following key stages of the corporate accounting information system development life cycle:
- systems planning,
- systems analysis,
- systems design,
- systems selection,
- systems implementation, and
- systems review.

## Learning outcomes

By the end of this chapter, the reader should be able to:

■ consider and explain the socio-political context of accounting information systems development,

■ describe the major characteristics of the six key stages of the systems development life cycle,

■ illustrate an appreciation of alternative planning, analysis and evaluation techniques,

■ demonstrate a critical understanding of the risks associated with accounting information systems' development, and

■ illustrate an understanding of the need for an information and communications technology strategy.

## Accounting information systems – the need for change

*There is nothing permanent, except change* (Heraclitus of Ephesus).[1]

As we have seen in previous chapters, whether they operate as simple paper-based manual systems or as highly complex, highly integrated internet enabled computer-based systems, accounting information systems are essentially socio-political constructs. They exist as imposed unifying structures, employing both tangible and intangible resources to:

■ collect, store, process, and transform selected transaction data into accounting information (see Wilkinson *et al.*, 2001), and

■ provide constructed representations for decision-making purposes to both internal and external stakeholders (see Vaassen, 2002).

And yet, as semi-open, output orientated[2] systems, accounting information systems are neither permanent nor stable. They are, like many (if not all) artificially constructed organisational systems (including business and accounting information systems) – subject to almost constant change. This process of change is conditioned by the ever-chaotic interaction of an increasingly complex array of environmental factors.[3]

And yet, as suggested by Strebal (1996):

*(whilst). . . change may be a constant, . . . it is not always the same* (1996: 5).

Why? All organisational systems – both accounting and non-accounting – operate within a multi-dimensional environment – an environment comprising of many different interrelated layers.[4]

It is the interaction of the various macro and micro factors and characteristics that comprise each layer which creates what is often referred to as 'environmental turbulence'. And, it is this environmental turbulence that is the source/cause or the trigger for change within a system – whether that system is a company or organisation, or a sub-system within the company/organisation, for example an accounting information system. More importantly, it is the unique combining of these macro and micro factors and characteristics within the layers that comprise an environment which determines the nature and scope of any reaction to such environmental turbulence.

Broadly speaking, in a systems context, we can classify external environments into three categories[5] – based on the level/scale of environmental turbulence within the environment:

- a stable environment (also known as a closed change environment)[6] – that is a steady state environment in which there is little or no change, or an environment in which change is cyclical, repetitive and expected,
- a predictable environment (also known as a contained change environment)[7] – that is a dynamic environment in which change is intermittent, and whilst neither cyclical nor repetitive is nonetheless predictable and manageable, and
- an unpredictable environment (also known as a open ended change environment)[8] – that is a volatile environment in which change is turbulent, fast-moving, frequent and unpredictable.

In addition, Grundy (1993) suggested that within an organisational context (and remember accounting information systems are constructed organisational systems), there exist three varieties of change, these being:

- smooth incremental change – that is change which is slow, systemic, predictable and planned,
- rough incremental change – that is change which occurs periodically, or as described by Senior (1997): '*periods of tranquillity punctuated by acceleration in the pace of change,*' that are concerned more with realignment and readjustment rather than substantial change, and
- discontinuous change – that is change which occurs rapidly, sometimes unpredictably, and causes substantial change as a result of, for example, a new discovery and/or new development.

Within a stable environment change would generally be smoothly incremental with occasional periods of rough incremental change and with very few periods of discontinuous change. Within a predictable environment change would generally be smoothly incremental with increasing periods of rough incremental change and fragmented periods of discontinuous change. Within an unpredictable environment change would generally be roughly incremental (with limited periods or no periods of smooth incremental change) and extensive periods of discontinuous change.

See Figure 16.1.

There can be little doubt that the latter part of the 20th century and the (very) early part of the 21st century have – certainly in a business context – witnessed two key developments:

- a growing integration of social, political and economic systems – that is a movement towards a single global society . . . or single global marketplace, and
- an increasing use of and dependency on information and communications technologies – that is a movement towards a technology-based information society.

It is these two developments that have, above all else, acted, and indeed continue to act, as the main catalysts for the ongoing commercial development of the internet (and the web), the increasing use of which has, in a reciprocal context, further accelerated:

- the ever-growing sense of integration or 'global oneness,' and
- the ever-growing dependency on information and communication technologies.

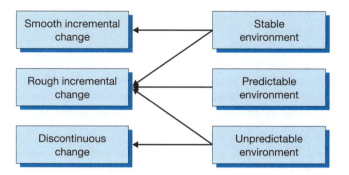

**Figure 16.1** Varieties of change

Perhaps therein lies the problem. Closer integration produces greater volatility. Greater volatility produces greater uncertainty. And, greater uncertainty produces a demand for even-greater integration, . . . which produces greater volatility and even greater uncertainty, . . . which produces an even-greater demand for even-greater integration, etc.

In essence, as systems become more unpredictable, they become increasingly uncertain – an unpredictability that is constantly fuelled by, for example:

- the changing needs and demands of users/stakeholders,
- the changing structure and content of finance-related regulations,
- the continuing impact of information and communication technology, and
- the increasing consequences of an evermore globally competitive business environment.

Indeed, as suggested by Stacey (1996):

- a stable environment (or closed change environment) has a tendency to be close to certainty, with change often being linear and planned, whereas
- an unpredictable environment (or open ended change environment) has a tendency to be far from certainty with change often being discontinuous and unplanned.

## Types of change

In an accounting information systems context, change can be defined as any amendment, alteration and/or modification to the structure and/or operation of a system or a component sub-system, and includes amendments, alternations and/or modifications to:

- data input procedures,
- data capture and filtering processes,
- data management protocols,
- internal documentation and control procedures,
- data processing procedures,
- information output procedures, and
- feedback/feedforward control procedures.

Change can be classified by:

- type (or nature), and/or
- level (or scale).

In terms of type (or nature), change can be divided into two sub-categories, as follows:

- hard change – that is change emerging from the introduction/integration of new information and communications technologies, and/or
- soft change – that is change resulting from organisations restructuring and/or procedural adaptations.

In terms of level (or scale) change can be divided into two sub-categories, as follows:

- minor change – that is change which has only a limited impact on a small number of components, procedures, processes and/or sub-systems within a system, and is commonly referred to as 'fine tuning' and/or 'incremental adjusting', and
- major change – that is change which has a substantial impact on a significant part of a system and/or number of systems and is also referred to as 'systems adaptation,' and/or 'process transformation'.

Have a look at the four quadrant matrix in Figure 16.2.

Using the four quadrant matrix (see Figure 16.2), we can classify change (within an accounting information systems context) into four different categories:

- soft-minor change,
- hard-minor change,
- soft-major change, and
- hard-major change.

### Soft-minor change

Soft-minor change can be defined as component, procedure and/or process change(s) resulting from organisational restructuring/procedural adaptation, and would include for example:

- the consolidation of data input procedures,
- the introduction of new documentation, or
- the introduction of minor software amendments/updates.

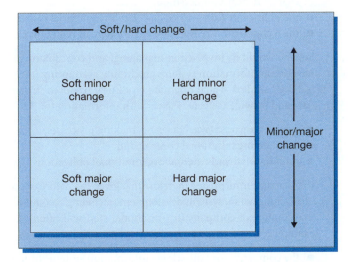

**Figure 16.2** Change matrix

### Hard-minor change

Hard-minor change can be defined as substantial technological change(s) resulting from organisational restructuring, and would include for example:

■ the introduction/addition of new network facilities, or
■ the extending of existing capabilities.

### Soft-major change

Soft-major change can be defined as a substantial modification/reorganisation of systems procedures, process and practices, and would include for example:

■ the introduction of new, wide-ranging internal control procedures, or
■ a change in company-wide data processing procedures – from batch to online/real-time processing.

### Hard-major change

Hard-major change can be defined as the widespread introduction of new information and communications technologies, and would include for example:

■ the development of web-based transaction processing facilities,
■ the introduction of chip and PIN payment systems, or
■ the introduction of new RFID[9] technologies.

## Change management

Clearly, whether change to an accounting information system constitutes a minor amendment, a fine tuning adjustment or indeed a major structural adaptation, it must be adequately planned, properly implemented and appropriately monitored and controlled. This is for four reasons:

■ the economic reason – to ensure adequate resource are available,
■ the social reason – to ensure that the consequences of any associated organisational/procedural change is clearly understood,
■ the political reason – to ensure that any potential resistance is minimised, and
■ the technological reason – to ensure that all regulatory consequences are understood.

So who would be involved in managing, and coordinating information systems change? As we have seen, information systems (including accounting information systems) are – in an organisational context – goal orientated, political resource structures, designed to process (selected) data and provide (selected) users with information to:

■ support organisational decision-making processes,
■ facilitate organisational control, and
■ fulfil internal and external organisational obligations.

It is perhaps unsurprising therefore that given the nature, scope and possible impact/consequences of any information systems development (including accounting information systems development), that a range of company/organisational staff will often be involved, including staff from, for example:

■ the company's/organisation's information systems function,
■ the company's/organisation's management and/or administration function,
■ the company's/organisation's human resource management function,

- the company's/organisation's financial management/accounting function and, where necessary,
- other functions/services and/or external agencies.

We will refer to such a coordinating team as a systems development team.

It is perhaps worth noting that whilst in some companies/organisations the information systems function is part of the management/administration function (department), in others it is part of the finance function (department), and in yet others it is an independent function (department). In the following discussion we will assume the latter to be the case.

### Information systems function

The information systems function is relevant where a systems development involves the introduction/integration of new information and/or communications technologies. It can be divided into four interrelated functions:

- information systems management,
- systems development management,
- applications management, and
- technical services management.

See Figure 16.3.

### Information systems management

Information systems management is concerned with the overall information technology architecture within a company/organisation, in particular the planning, acquisition, development and use of information systems including databases, operating systems and information and communication technology networks.

### Systems development management

Systems development management is concerned with:

- the development of new information processing systems,
- the development of user-support activities, and
- the maintenance of hardware and software facilities.

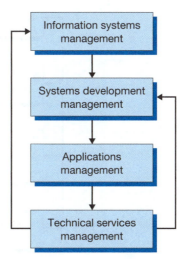

**Figure 16.3** Information systems function

### Applications management

Applications management is concerned with the provision and management of information systems applications, including the provision of appropriately licensed software and up-to-date intrusion detection/security software.

### Technical services management

Technical services management is concerned with the management of:

- data communications facilities,
- systems programming and systems security,
- technical support systems, and
- PC/server maintenance systems.

#### Management/administration function

The management/administration function is relevant where a systems development has a wider business context and/or a significant strategic implication on the company/organisation.

The management/administrative function can be divided into four key functions:

- administrative management,
- operations management,
- information management/data administration, and
- internal (systems) audit.

See Figure 16.4.

### Administrative management

Administrative management is concerned with providing overall strategic encouragement and support to:

- ensure alignment with existing strategies,
- establish systems goal/objectives,

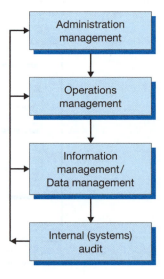

**Figure 16.4** Management/administration function

- review performance,
- establish policies.

## Operations management

Operations management is concerned with the processes and procedures that create goods and/or provide services, including the implementation of organisational policies and protocols to ensure the satisfaction of company objectives.

## Information administration/data management

Information administration/data management is concerned with controlling the manner in which any personal data are, or are to be, processed – a key function being:

- the management of data access, and
- the establishment of a data controller as required by the Data Protection Act 1998.

Section 4(4) of the Data Protection Act 1998 provides that:

> *it shall be the duty of a data controller to comply with the Data Protection Principles in relation to all personal data with respect to which he is the data controller.*

## Internal (systems) audit

Internal (systems) audit is concerned with:

- appraising the efficiency of operational activities of the company,
- assessing the effectiveness of internal administrative and accounting controls, and
- evaluating conformance with managerial procedures and policies.

### Human resources management

The human resource management function is relevant where a systems development involves/will involve:

- the recruitment of new employees,
- the reduction of existing employees,
- the retraining of existing employees, and/or
- the relocation/redistribution of existing employees.

### Financial management/accounting function

The financial management/accounting function is relevant where a finance/accounting context to a systems development is required and involves:

- the financial appraisal/evaluation of the capital expenditure costs associated with a systems development, and
- an analysis and assessment of the revenue cost and benefits of a systems development.

### Other internal services and/or external agencies

The use of other internal services – for example departmental representatives, employee representatives and/or external agencies (e.g. specialist consultants) may be relevant where:

- a systems development involves technical issues and factors on which additional specialist advice and/or information is required, and/or
- a systems development may have substantial organisational consequences (e.g. employee redundancies).

## Accounting information systems development – alternative approaches

There are many alternative approaches to information systems development – in particular accounting information systems development – the most common being the systems development life cycle approach. However a variation of this approach – the prototyping approach – is also widely used, especially where a systems development involves:

■ the introduction/development of new operational systems, and/or
■ the introduction/development of new information and communication technologies,

and requires the determination of end user requirements – that is an understanding of what end users want from the system/technology. We will look at this prototyping approach later in this chapter.

## The systems development life cycle approach

There can be little doubt that in a modern, commercially active company/organisation, a well-designed, user orientated information system(s) can contribute to/assist in:

■ increasing operational revenues,
■ reducing operational costs,
■ eliminating non-value added activities,
■ improving the coordination of organisational activities,
■ improving customer-related services, and
■ improving management decision making.

It is therefore perhaps unsurprising that information processing systems – in particular accounting information systems, are regarded as one of the most valuable assets a company/organisation can possess.

In essence, the systems development life cycle is a practical framework – a sequential multi-stage framework which provides a broad context for the pre-development stages, development stages and post-development stages of an information system – or for our purposes, an accounting information system.

The systems development life cycle involves six critical stages,[10] these being:

■ systems planning and the identification of systems and/or sub-systems within an (accounting) information system that requires further development, amendment, improvement, renewal or replacement,
■ systems analysis and the assessment of existing system or sub-system problems,
■ systems design and the development/formation of a blueprint/conceptual design or range of alternative blueprints/conceptual designs for a completed system or sub-system,
■ systems selection and the determination of how the system will be acquired/developed,
■ systems implementation/conversion and the implementation of the selected design and/or conversion of an existing system,
■ systems review and the operational maintenance, monitoring and evaluation of the selected system/sub-system performance.

See Figure 16.5.

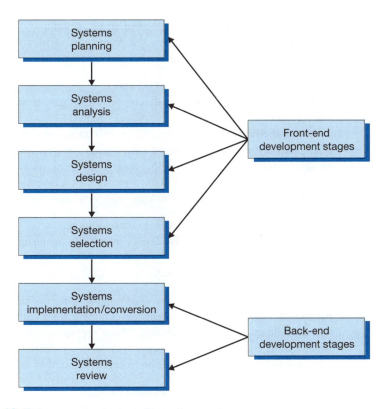

**Figure 16.5** Systems development life cycle

The first four stages (systems planning, systems analysis, systems design and systems selection) are often referred to as the *front end development stages* since they are mainly concerned with 'what' the system(s) will do, whereas the last two stages (systems implementation and systems review) are often referred to as the *back end development stages* since they are mainly concerned with 'how' the system(s) will accomplish its objectives.

Before we look at the systems development life cycle it would perhaps be useful to define what the term 'systems development' means?

For our purposes we will define the term systems development as the development of an information systems or systems (including an accounting information system) by a process of investigation, analysis, design, implementation and maintenance, the primary objectives of such a systems development being to ensure that:

- all company/organisation systems/sub-systems function effectively,
- all company/organisation systems/sub-systems resources are used efficiently,
- all company/organisation systems/sub-systems objectives are consistent and comparable,
- all company/organisation systems/sub-systems are adaptable, and
- all possible systems/sub-systems duplication is minimised.

A systems development project can involve for example:

- the construction of a new system or sub-system,
- an amendment to an existing system, or sub-system (e.g. a reduction in, addition to, and/or the redesign of a system's internal procedures/processes),

- an improvement to an existing system, or sub-system,
- the renewal of part of an existing system or sub-system, and/or
- the replacement of part of a system or sub-system,

or, indeed a combination of any of the above.

Before we look at the systems development life cycle, it would perhaps be useful to clarify four key points.

Firstly, the systems development lifecycle is an iterative framework, which can and indeed often does, involve the repeating of a stage and/or stages – possibly a number of times – until an agreed outcome/consensus to that stage is achieved. As a consequence, the time scale of a systems development, the cost and the resource commitment – from initial plan to implementation and post-development monitoring – can vary enormously, depending on:

- the nature and extent of the systems development,
- the size and complexity of the development team managing/coordinating the development, and
- the urgency of the development.

Secondly, (as suggested earlier) the wide ranging impact of many systems developments often necessitates the creation of a systems development team containing a wide selection of skills and capabilities from both inside and, where appropriate, outside the company/organisation. Although the responsibilities of such a systems development team would of course vary from company to company or organisation to organisation, they would include, for example:

- the reviewing of systems development projects,
- the prioritising of systems development projects,
- the allocating of funding to systems development projects, and
- the coordinating, management and controlling of systems development projects.

Invariably, given:

- the eclectic nature of the individuals that comprise the systems development team, and
- the wide-ranging portfolio of responsibilities of such a systems development team,

it is not surprising that in some instances the systems development process can become fragmented, disjointed and highly politicised, especially where development team members feel personally and professionally threatened by proposed development(s).

Thirdly, because of the increasing complexity of the marketplace and indeed the increasing variety of pressures faced by many companies/organisations, it is probable that a company/organisation may have a number of systems development projects in progress simultaneously – all at different stages of the development life cycle.

Fourthly, the complex and interrelated nature of business information systems – in particular accounting information systems – often means that changes to one system or sub-system may necessitate changes/amendments to another related system or sub-system: the so-called indirect development consequence. Clearly, it is important for a systems development team not only to possess a clear understanding of both how systems and sub-systems are interrelated/interconnected but how changes in a system/sub-system may affect other interrelated/interconnected systems/sub-systems.

Remember, while looking at each of the systems development life cycle stages in more detail we are primarily concerned with systems developments concerning accounting information systems.

# Systems planning

*Prior planning prevents poor performance* (Anon).

Systems planning involves the identification and prioritisation of system(s)/sub-system(s) that require/may require further development, amendment, improvement, renewal and/or replacement.

The systems planning stage is often divided into two distinct sub-stages, these being:

- a strategic planning stage, and
- a systems developing planning stage.

## Strategic planning stage

The purpose of the strategic planning stage is to provide a framework or context for any planned systems developments – a reference framework which for our purposes we will consider as comprising of three interrelated strategies, these being:

- the strategic mission and objectives of the company/organisation,
- the strategic information plan of the company/organisation, and
- the information and communications technology strategy of the company/organisation.

Note: Although strictly speaking the strategic planning stage is not really part of the systems development life cycle – because the systems development life cycle is concerned primarily with the development of specific systems and applications, whereas the strategic planning stage is concerned primarily with the corporate/organisational context of such developments – it nonetheless provides an important 'starting point' for all systems developments, whether such developments are:

- formal developments – that is developments which are timetabled and resourced as part of a company's/organisation's cyclical strategic review programme, and/or
- informal developments – that is developments which emerge as a result of:
  - an ad hoc request from a departmental manager, and/or
  - the identification of error/problems by a system(s)/sub-system(s) user.

## Systems developing planning stage

The purpose of the systems developing planning sub-stage is to ensure that any planned systems developments are appropriately identified, suitably defined, accurately evaluated, correctly prioritised and consistent with the company's/organisation's strategic mission. This stage is often referred as the systems development planning stage, which for our purposes we will consider as comprising of four interrelated phases:

- an *evaluation phase* in which the rationale for and feasibility of a systems development project is assessed,
- a *development phase* in which a systems development project proposal is prepared,
- a *prioritisation phase* in which systems development projects are prioritised, and
- a *design phase* in which a preliminary systems design for selected/accepted systems development projects is produced.

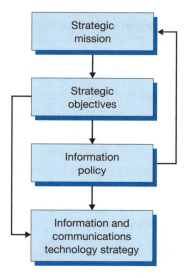

**Figure 16.6** Strategic planning stage

## The strategic planning stage in detail

As suggested earlier, the strategic planning stage can be divided into the following:

- the strategic mission and objectives of the company/organisation,
- the information policy of the company/organisation, and
- the information and communications technology strategy of the company/organisation.

See Figure 16.6.

### Strategic mission and objectives of the company/organisation

A strategy is essentially a mission-based, objective focused plan that within a corporate/organisational context can, and indeed does, exist at a number of different levels. For example, at a corporate level the organisational strategy is concerned primarily with the overall purpose and scope of the company/organisation and its ability to meet the expectations of stakeholders. Such an overarching strategy would comprise of a number of lower level functional strategies – all related to the various strategic business units within the company/organisation – for example product/service development strategies, human resource management strategies, financial strategies, legal strategies, information systems strategies and information technology management strategies – each of which would be comprised of a number of operational strategies concerned primarily with ensuring the efficient and effective use of corporate/organisational resources and processes.

In a broad sense then, a strategic mission can be defined as the overriding longer-term direction of the company/organisation – designed to fulfil/satisfy stakeholder expectations. Such a strategic mission is a multi-level hierarchy, often comprised of:

- corporate/organisation goal(s) which describes the aim/purpose of the company/organisation,
- corporate/organisational objective(s) which provides a quantification of any company/organisation goal, and
- corporate strategy which defines the broad actions required to achieve the company's/organisation's goals and objectives.

So how is a corporate strategy developed? Although there are many variations, there are essentially two alternative approaches:

- a reactive opportunistic approach, (sometimes referred to as freewheeling opportunism), or
- a proactive structured approach.

Whereas, the reactive opportunistic approach is often regarded as the 'high-risk strategy' strategy and, therefore, uncertain, hazardous and potentially very risky, the proactive structured approach is often described as the 'low-risk strategy' strategy. The latter is a formal and highly structured approach which would normally consist of the following stages:

- a strategic analysis stage – concerned with the environment of company/organisation resources and of stakeholder expectations,
- a strategic choice stage – concerned with the generation, evaluation and selection of alternative strategies, and
- a strategic implementation stage – concerned with a consideration of both resource and information requirements, and the practical implementation of the selected strategy and/or strategies.

Whilst most companies/organisations would prefer to pursue the proactive, structured approach and be seen as 'in control', strategically speaking, invariably in some instances the reactive opportunistic approach will have to be used, especially where excessive environmental turbulence exists.

### Information policy of the company/organisation

There can be little doubt that in a business context, the quality of any decision-making process within a company/organisation will be dependent upon the quality of information available on which to form a judgement and/or make a decision. That is there is a direct positive correlation between the quality of information and the quality of the decisions made – and therefore the quality of the decision-making process.

For a market-based wealth maximising company/organisation, the quality of information is often assessed using a range of qualitative features, for example relevance, reliability, accuracy, validity, timeliness and completeness, amongst others, whereas the quality of a decision is invariably measured using quantitative factors such as the political, economic and financial benefits judged to have accrued as a consequence of the decision. That is the wealth created or business value created as a consequence of the decision.

Clearly, it is important for company/organisation to ensure adequate guidelines or, more precisely, an adequate information policy exists to control and manage the provision, dissemination, communication and utilisation of information within the company/organisation.

This is for three reasons. Firstly, for corporate governance purposes to ensure that the company/organisation:

- maintains a visible balance between political, economic and social goals,
- promotes the efficient use of resources, and
- encourages accountability for the stewardship of those resources.[11]

Secondly, for management control purposes to ensure that appropriate levels of information are made available to the appropriate management/operational levels to ensure that the company/organisation:

- maintains adequate internal control of all its activities, and
- maintains adequate security to safeguard all its assets and resources.

Thirdly, for wealth maximisation purposes to ensure that the company/organisation derives the greatest net benefit from acquisition, possession and use of information.

In a broad sense, an information policy can be divided into five levels:

■ an operational level – concerned with the identification of information provision issues and information flow problems,

■ a planning level – concerned with the designing of improved information provision/ information flow within a company/organisation to minimise the impact of information provision issues and information flow problems,

■ a development level – concerned with the development and implementation of improved information provision/information flow within a company/organisation to minimise the impact of information provision/information flow problems,

■ an structural support level – concerned with the overall architecture/framework of information flow within a company/organisation and the management of information provision/ information flow within the different levels of a company/organisation, and

■ a strategic level – concerned with the identification of strategic information needs and requirements of the company/organisation.

Note: It is at the planning level and the development level that the information policy of a company/organisation has a direct influence on systems development and the systems development life cycle.

Clearly, the nature, structure and complexity of an information policy would differ from company to company or organisation to organisation. Issues/factors such as:

■ the size of the company/organisation,
■ the structure of the company/organisation, and
■ the complexity of the company/organisation,

would all influence a company's/organisation's information policy (see for example Vaassen, 2002). More importantly, such issues/factors would have a significant impact on the practical application of a company's/organisation's information policy, in particular the processes and procedures it uses to identify and determine information needs and requirements.

### Information and communications technology strategy of the company/organisation

We will consider issues related to information and communications technology strategy later in this chapter.

## Systems development planning stage in detail

As suggested earlier, it is likely that a company/organisation would have a number of systems development projects under consideration, all of which need evaluating, rationalising and prioritising owing to limited resources and capabilities.

### Evaluation

The evaluation phase is concerned with appraising the feasibility of a proposed system(s)/subsystem(s) development project and would consider three key issues:

■ economic feasibility – for example: What are the estimated potential costs[12] of the systems development and what estimated tangible[13]/intangible[14] benefits will accrue for the system once it is implemented?

■ technical viability – for example: What information and communication technologies will be required to realise the systems development, and are such information and communication technologies currently available?

■ operational/implementation capability – for example: What resources will be required to realise the systems development, and are such resources currently available – in particular human resources?

In addition to the above, it may also be necessary to assess the legal/regulatory aspects/consequences of a systems development – especially if additional costs may need to be incurred to satisfy legal/regulatory requirements (e.g. the Data Protection Act 1998).

Clearly, any evaluation/feasibility study would invariably be quantitative in nature and may involve the use of a wide selection of financial management/financial planning and analysis techniques, in particular investment appraisal/capital budgeting techniques including for example:

■ discounted cash flow – that is net present value and/or internal rate of return,
■ accounting rate of return – for example return on investment, and
■ payback – including discounted payback.

So, which investment appraisal/capital budgeting technique is the most used? Whilst most companies/organisations will use a discounted cash flow variant/measure and consider the longer-term net present value of a systems development, invariably liquidity and the conversion of any net benefits into actual cash flows will be a major concern. It is therefore uncommon for a company/organisation to use a return on investment variant and/or payback variant as primary evaluation measurements.

### Development

The development phase is concerned with the preparing of a systems development project proposal.

Following the completion of the systems development project evaluation, such a project proposal would provide a basis on which the systems development team can decide as to whether to proceed with the systems development project or abandon it, and would in general seek to:

■ establish a rationale for the systems development project and explain its relevance in terms of current operations and the company/organisation,
■ illustrate the potential contribution the systems development project (if accepted and implemented) would make to the overall strategic objectives of the company/organisation, and
■ summarise the net benefit/net cost of the systems development project.

### Prioritisation

The prioritisation phase is concerned with the prioritising of system(s)/sub-system(s) development projects, the key assessment criteria being an assessment of the potential strategic contribution of the proposed system to the company/organisation in terms of:

■ increased wealth creation,
■ improved resource utilisation,
■ improved information provision, and
■ enhanced decision making.

Whilst there are a number of alternative approaches that may be used to prioritise systems development projects – many of which would be company/organisation unique – it is likely that the majority of such approaches would seek to quantify any strategic contribution, possibly using a predetermined weighted scoring system in which a selected range of factors and issues would be considered.

### Design and scheduling

The design and scheduling phase is concerned with confirming a preliminary system(s)/sub-system(s) design for selected/accepted development project(s) and providing a definitive schedule of development. That is a development schedule for each stage of the systems development life cycle, detailing:

- a capital and revenue expenditure budget for each stage of the systems development project,
- an implementation time plan for each stage of the systems development project,
- a critical analysis of core activities (usually a critical path analysis) for the systems development project,
- an acquisition schedule for the systems development project, and
- a resource schedule for each stage of the systems development life cycle.

## Systems analysis

The systems analysis stage seeks to formally assess the functional attributes of current/existing system(s)/sub-system(s), the aim being:

- to identify any operational problems within the current/existing system(s)/sub-system(s), and
- to determine the precise nature of such operational problems.

Such an analysis is required because to solve a problem, it is important first to understand what the problem is and second to understand where the problem is!

The systems analysis stage involves the following phases:

- a survey of the current/existing system,
- an analysis of system requirements,
- an identification of user information needs and requirements, and
- the development and documentation of a systems requirement report.

See Figure 16.7.

### Survey the present system

This survey is designed to provide a fundamental understanding of the operational aspects of the target system(s), the aim being not only to identify problem areas within the current existing system(s) but to provide important data for modelling/design purposes and, more importantly, to establish a working relationship with system(s) or sub-system(s) stakeholders.

The success or failure of any system(s)/sub-system(s) development will, to a large extent, depend on:

- the quality of data collected,
- the relationship developed between the system(s) development team and system(s) stakeholders and, of course,
- the viability of the system(s)/sub-system(s) proposal.

However this survey approach is not without its advantages and disadvantages.

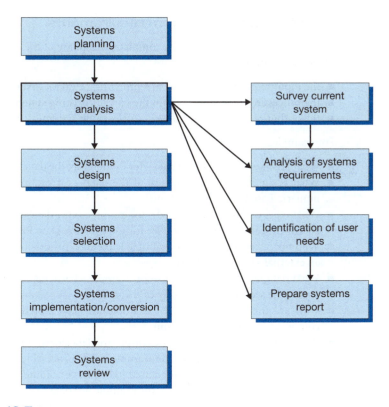

**Figure 16.7** Systems analysis

### Advantages of undertaking a systems survey

By undertaking a current/existing system(s)/sub-system(s) survey, the systems development team can:

- identify the root problem of the current/existing system(s)/sub-system(s),[15]
- identify which aspects of the current/existing system(s)/sub-system(s) may be retained within the new system(s)/sub-system(s) design, and
- identify what conversion processes would be required where a new system(s)/sub-system(s) is required.[16]

### Disadvantages of undertaking a systems survey

By undertaking a current/existing system(s)/sub-system(s) survey, the systems development team may concentrate too much on the detailed processes and procedures of the current/existing system(s)/sub-system(s), and as a consequence may:

- fail to understand/appreciate the bigger picture,
- fail to identify correctly the root problem of current/existing system(s)/sub-system(s), and
- produce a sub-optimal system(s)/sub-system(s) design that fails to address the root problems of the old system(s)/sub-system(s).

## Identify/determine system requirements

Once the systems survey has been complete, this phase of the systems analysis process seeks to identify/determine:

- the input requirements of the current/existing system(s)/sub-system(s),
- the processing procedures within the current/existing system(s)/sub-system(s), and
- the output requirements of the current/existing system(s)/sub-system(s).

For example:

- What are the main sources of data – for example are the data internally or externally generated?
- What is the nature and structure of the data – for example are the data narrative-based, numeric-based or a combination?
- What types of data are processed – for example is the data subject to disclosure requirements and/or processing restrictions (see for example the Data Protection Act 1998)?
- Who processes the data – for example is the data processing in-house or is it outsourced to an external service provider?
- What data input controls exist – for example what type of application controls are used to ensure the security and integrity of the data?
- How are the data stored – for example are data stored via manual documentation or computer-based documentation?
- Where are the data stored – for example are data stored on-site or off-site?
- How are the data processed – for example is data processing manual or computer-based, and if computer-based, are data processed in batches or online?
- What are the data flow trends – for example are data processing transaction levels seasonal significant and are any trends linked to any other identifiable activity?
- What data processing controls exist – for example what type of application controls are used to ensure data are processed accurately and securely?
- What are the data processing transaction levels – for example is the current/existing system(s)/ sub-system(s) operating at capacity or is spare processing capacity available?
- How efficient is the data processing systems – for example what are the current error levels within current data processing procedures and are such levels acceptable?
- How effective are data processing system – for example are there excessive delays in data processing procedures and are such delays acceptable?
- What are the current resource costs – for example are costs excessive when compared to other similar systems and if so are such costs justifiable?
- Do any redundant operations/processes exist – for example are all systems processes and procedures in use?
- Does any redundant documentation exist – for example is all system/processing documentation appropriate?
- What data output controls exist – for example what type of application controls are used to ensure data are output correctly, timely, accurately and securely?
- Who are the system(s)/sub-system(s) users – for example are users internal and/or external?

Such facts can be gathered in many ways, perhaps the most common being:

- by questionnaires,
- by personal interview,
- by observation,
- by participation, and
- by documentation review.

### Questionnaires

Questionnaires are a valuable method for the collection of data and information during the systems analysis stage. They can be used to obtain specific, detailed information about:

- the sources and nature of data collected and processed,
- the type and nature of specific procedures/process,
- the volume of transactions processed,
- the process control procedures, and
- the output destination of processed data.

It is however important that the questionnaire is constructed correctly, since:

- the inclusion of inappropriate questions,
- the improper ordering of questions (see the sandwich theory below),
- the inaccurate scaling of answers, and/or
- the incorrect formatting of a questionnaire,

could make the survey results valueless.

There are many types of questions that can be used, some of the most common being:

- closed-ended questions – that is questions where there are a limited and fixed set of answers,
- open-ended questions – that is questions where there is no predefined suggested answers,
- dichotomous questions – that is questions where there is a 'yes' or a 'no' answer,
- multiple choice – that is questions where there are several answers from which to choose,
- contingency questions – that is questions that are answered only if a particular answer was given to a previous question, and
- scaled questions – that is questions where answers are graded on a weighted scale for statistical analysis purposes.

There are no generic predetermined criteria for the use of the above types of questions or indeed any other types of questions. In general, their use is activity specific – that is it will depend on:

- the nature of the survey,
- the target audience of the questionnaire, and
- the type of data to be collected.

In general, however, there are three commonsense rules to the construction and use of questionnaires, these being:

- keep the questionnaire simple,
- keep the questionnaire short, and
- keep the questionnaire clear.

Where at all possible, adopt the three-stage questionnaire format:

- first stage (initial section of the questionnaire) questions should be of a screening type nature (e.g. who are you? what do you do?),
- second stage (mid-section of the questionnaire) questions should be of a system-specific nature (e.g. how does a specific process function? what control procedures exist?), and
- third stage (final section of the questionnaire) questions should be of an opinion obtaining nature (e.g. what do you think are the major problems within the current/existing system?).

The advantages of using questionnaires are:

- they are inexpensive to use,
- they are time efficient, and
- responses can be anonymous to protect respondents.

The disadvantages of using questionnaires are:

- can be difficult to develop,
- response rates can be very low, and
- conflicting responses can be difficult to clarify.

### Personal interviews

Personal interviews are a useful method for obtaining data/facts concerning:

- the operations of the current/existing systems, and
- user perceptions of the current/existing system.

Such personal interviews can be either:

- structured and formal – with the predominant use of closed-ended questions, or
- unstructured and informal – with the predominant use of open-ended questions.

The selection of interview type depends again (as with questionnaires) on:

- the nature of the survey,
- the target group of the questionnaire, and
- the type of data to be collected.

The advantages of using personal interviews are:

- in-depth and complex questions can be asked, and
- responses can be clarified.

The disadvantages of using personal interviews are:

- they can be time consuming,
- they can be very expensive, and
- personal bias/personal self-interest may affect interviewee responses.

### Observation

Observation can be defined as the passive and informal monitoring of a physical event, activity and/or procedure, and invariably involves appropriate forms of surveillance, inspection and/or examination.

Such passive observation allows the development team to determine directly:

- what processes and procedures take place,
- how the processes and procedures are managed/monitored,
- who is involved in the each of the processes and procedures, and
- how long each processing cycle/procedure takes.

An example of such passive observation would be where a member of the systems development team reviewing a company's/organisation's sales procedures observes the activities of members of the sales support team.

Where appropriate, such observations should not be limited to a single observation but should, where possible, occur over a number days/weeks. More importantly, such observations should if at all possible be undertaken unannounced, and/or at the very least without excessive notice, to ensure that representative activities and not a pre-manufactured version are observed.

The advantages of using observation are:

- it can produce an in-depth understanding of the system(s)/sub-system(s), and
- it can verify not only what system(s)/sub-system(s) functions occur, but more importantly how such system(s)/sub-system(s) functions occur.

The disadvantages of using observation are:

- it can be time consuming,
- it can be very expensive, and
- activities/responses can be difficult to assess/interpret.

### Participation

Participation can be defined as the active involvement in a physical event, activity and/or procedure, and occurs where a development team is keen to obtain a working knowledge of a set of processes and/or procedures within a system(s)/sub-system(s).

Such active participation allows the development team to directly determine:

- whether current documentations is efficiently designed,
- what processing/procedural problems exist,
- what types of data processing errors occur,
- why such data processing errors occur, and
- whether any redundant processes/procedures still exist.

An example of such active participation would be (using the example above) where a member of the systems development team reviewing a company's/organisation's sales procedures participates in the activities of members of the sales support team.

The advantages of using participation is it can produce an in-depth understanding of the system(s)/sub-system(s) and the problems associated with its procedures and activities

The disadvantages of using participation are:

- it can be time consuming, and
- it can be very expensive.

### Documentation review

Company/organisation documentation is of course an important source of information for a systems development team, and reviewing such documentation can provide an insight into not only what documents exist but, more importantly, where such documents are used and by whom.

Such documentation can be categorised as either:

- company/organisation generic documentation, or
- application specific (or system(s)/sub-system(s) specific) documentation.

Company/organisation generic documentation would include for example:

- historical records,
- organisation charts,
- company/organisation financial statements,
- company/organisation strategic mission statement, and/or
- company/organisation budgets/forecasts.

Application specific (or system(s)/sub-system(s) specific) documentation would include for example:

- organisational charts,
- operational documentation,
- systems and documents flowcharts,
- procedural manuals and systems narrative,

- accounting information databases,
- charts of account,
- system(s)/sub-system(s) performance reports, and
- system(s)/sub-system(s) transaction reports.

The advantage of using a documentation review is that it provides objective data on the system(s)/sub-system(s) under review and facilitates further study and examination.

The disadvantages of using documentation review are:

- documentation may not be available, and
- where documentation is available the review may be costly and time consuming.

## Identify user information needs and requirements

Based on the data/information collected earlier on:

- the physical nature/characteristics of the current/existing system(s)/sub-system(s), and
- the information requirements of current/existing system(s)/sub-system(s),

this phase of the systems analysis process seeks to assess:

- the current nature of user information needs and requirements,
- the current level and complexity of such needs and requirements, and
- their current format,

to determine:

- the appropriateness of such user information needs and requirements, and
- their continued relevance.

This is predominantly a cost/benefit-based rationalisation process designed to:

- evaluate the relative importance of user information needs and requirements,
- eliminate inconsistent and/or conflicting user needs and requirements, and
- minimise excessive duplication of information.

## Development and documentation of a systems report

Once the analysis of the current/existing needs has been completed and all appropriate facts have been collected, collated and assessed, it is important for the systems development team (or its representative) to prepare a formal report for the company/organisation management (or a delegated management committee/group).

Such a report should provide:

- a complete appraisal of the results of the initial survey,
- a detailed review of the problems/issues identified,
- a summary analysis of user needs/requirements, in particular information needs and system(s)/sub-system(s) requirements and, perhaps most importantly,
- a comprehensive report providing a detailed description of the suggested/recommended requirements of the new system(s)/sub-system(s).

## Systems analysis report

Whilst the systems analysis report is often viewed as the outcome of, and therefore the final phase of, the systems analysis stage, it is important that the detailed description contained within the analysis report only explains *what* the new system(s)/sub-system(s) should do. Such a detailed description should not seek to provide details of *how* the new system(s)/sub-system(s) should function – that is the systems analysis report should not specify a detailed design(s) for the new proposed system(s)/sub-system(s) by recommending for example specific processing methodologies, particular data storage media/facilities and/or data file structures.

Why? Because it is important that the systems analysis report remains impartial, unbiased, objective and, where at all possible, avoids influencing the design stage of the systems development life cycle.

Although the structure of such a systems analysis report would vary from company to company or organisation to organisation, in a broad sense it would contain some, if not all, of the following detail:

- a rationale for the study – explaining the background to the systems analysis,
- the scope of the analysis – detailing the parameters of the systems analysis,
- a description of overall problem/issues identified – detailing the results of the survey,
- a summary of system requirements and a specification of user requirements – detailing *what* the new system(s)/sub-system(s) should do,
- a summary of resource implications – net cost/net benefit (and proposed timescale) of the development, and
- recommendations – for example whether the development should continue and if so what priority should be assigned to it.

## Systems design

The systems design stage involves two key phases:

- a conceptual design phase, and
- a physical design phase.

Both could be undertaken by a sub-group of the systems development team. The conceptual design phase is concerned with developing a design (or a range of alternative designs) for the completed system(s)/sub-system(s) – that is an schematic outline or blueprint for how the system(s)/sub-system(s) will work. The physical design phase is concerned with establishing the physical design of the completed system(s)/sub-system(s) – that is what the system(s)/sub-system(s) will look like. See Figure 16.8.

### Conceptual design phase

In a broad sense, a conceptual design is a theoretical/abstract design that seeks to provide a representation of the structure of a system(s)/sub-system(s). In a systems development life cycle context, it is concerned with the nature of the relationships between process and flows – that is how such processes and flows are connected and how they interact. The purpose of the conceptual design stage is to develop a general framework within which the needs and requirements of users/stakeholders can be met.

There are many alternative approaches to the conceptual design phase, of which the function orientated approach (or the top-down approach) and the object orientated design approach (or the bottom-up approach) are perhaps the most common.

#### The function orientated design approach

The function orientated design approach (or the top-down approach), is also referred to as the structured design approach. It is an approach which commences with an overview of the

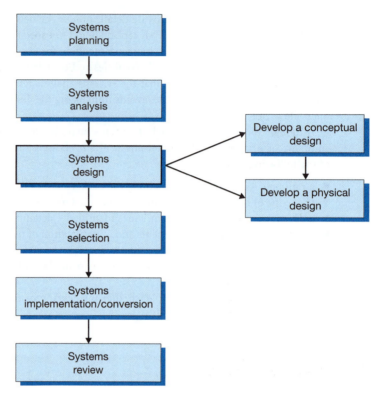

**Figure 16.8** Systems design

proposed system/process – that is the *primary or context level* – which is then separated/divided into its constituent sub-systems/sub-processes – that is the *transitional level* – which are then separated/divided into their constituent sub-systems/sub-processes – that is the *foundation level* – until the basic data components of each of the sub-systems/sub-processes within the proposed system/process are identified.

The advantages of the function orientated approach are:

- it can minimise fault replication, and
- it promotes flexibility.

However, the disadvantages are:

- it can be time consuming, and
- it can be costly.

Despite such disadvantages, the function orientated design approach is still widely used for information systems design – especially for accounting information systems.

### The object orientated design approach

The object orientated approach commences with an analysis of available standard system/process objects (or more appropriately system/process components and/or modules) and uses such objects as a basis for the conceptual design. Such an approach is widely used in software development projects.

The advantages of the object orientated approach are:

■ it can significantly reduce design time, and
■ it can reduce overall design costs.

In addition, because system/process components/modules are already available, it can:

■ improve system/process maintenance, and
■ improve user support.

The disadvantages of the object orientated approach are:

■ it can lead to problem inheritance – problems may be replicated for one system/process to another system/process, and
■ it can limit innovation – using existing components/modules may limit design possibilities, suppress creativity and restrain originality.

So, what design considerations would the conceptual design phase address?
   It would consider for example:

■ systems/process communication – for example:
  ● what communication configurations will be used,
  ● what form of communication channels will be used, and
  ● what type of communications network will be used,
■ data input – for example:
  ● what forms of data input will be used,
  ● what source documents will be required and how they will be structured,
  ● what input medium will be adopted/used, and
  ● how input data will be validated,
■ data storage – for example:
  ● what data storage medium will be used,
  ● how the data will be stored,
  ● what file format will be used,
  ● how the data files will be organised, and
  ● how access to data files will be controlled,
■ data processing – for example:
  ● how the data will be processed, and
  ● when and where the data will be processed,
■ data output – for example:
  ● what format of data output will be used,
  ● how frequently the data output will be produced,
  ● what data output medium will be used,
  ● how the data output will be validated, and
  ● how the data output will be scheduled.

Once a broad palate of design alternatives has been determined and agreed by the sub-group, it would be necessary to prepare a conceptual design specification for the systems development team, detailing the range of possible input, process, storage and output alternatives considered suitable/appropriate for the new system(s)/sub-system(s), the purpose being to provide the systems development team with a design template/design guide for the physical design phase of the systems development.

## Physical design phase

The physical design phase is primarily concerned with determining how the conceptual design can/will be implemented, and would involve identifying and determining the precise nature of:

- the data input(s),
- the system(s)/sub-system(s) process/procedure,
- the data files,
- the system(s)/sub-system(s) programs,
- the data output(s), and
- the system(s)/sub-system(s) internal controls.

Again such a task would more than likely be delegated to a systems development team sub-group – its role being to consider the 'real world' complexities of making the conceptual design a reality.

### Design considerations – data input(s)

Determining the precise nature and variety of data input(s) – for example:

- the source of data input(s),
- the format and medium of data input(s), and
- the type, volume and frequency of data input(s),

is often considered to be the most important design consideration of any physical design. This is especially important where it is likely that a number of alternative data input format/medium may be used in the new system(s)/sub-system(s).

Why? Primarily, to minimise the possibility of data input errors, but also to ensure:

- the cost effectiveness of each data input format/medium,
- the accuracy and uniformity of all data input(s),
- the appropriateness and relevance of all data input(s),
- the integrity and security[17] of all data input(s), and
- the compatibility of all data input(s).

Clearly issues of data source, data type and input volumes and frequencies will have a major influence on determining the medium used to collect/input data – that is for example, whether data is collected and/or input using:

- a hard document-based input (usually a physical paper document),
- a virtual document-based input (usually a computer-based input screen), or
- a combination of both.

For example a high-frequency, low-value data input such as customer-based ATM transactions[18] would of course be suited to a virtual document-based input procedure. However, low-frequency, high-value, high-risk data input would be more suited to a hard document-based input procedure.

### Design considerations – processing procedures

It is of course more than likely that the processing procedure selected will be either partly, if not completely, computer-based. Of the many alternative types of processing procedures available, for example:

- periodic (batch) processing (offline processing),
- immediate processing,
  - online (3 stage) processing,
  - online (4 stage) processing, and
- distributed processing,

the selection of the precise design nature of the system(s)/sub-system(s) processing procedure would normally be determined by the 5Ws criteria. These are:

- For *whom* is the data to be processed – for example, who are the users/stakeholders and what are their needs and requirements?
- *What* data is to be processed – for example is it predominantly quantitative or qualitative?
- *When* is the data to be processed – for example is it at a single scheduled time or at number of scheduled times?
- *Where* is the data to be processed – for example is it at a single location or a number of geographically separate locations?
- *Why* is the data to be processed – for example is the data processing for data collection/storage purposes or is it for data analysis purposes, for example for making decisions.

Answers to the above should not only provide an indication of:

- the overall complexity of the data processing procedures,
- the repetitiveness of the data processing procedures,
- the uniformity of the data processing procedures, and
- the frequency of the data processing procedures,

but also an indication of the possible limitations/restrictions that may exist – for example limitations of current processing abilities, communication capabilities and/or even technological resources.

## Key design criteria

Put simply, any selected processing procedure (or combination of processing procedures) should be:

- cost effective,
- compatible with existing processing procedures (if required/necessary),
- accurate,
- appropriate,
- relevant,
- secure, and
- minimise the possibility of data processing errors and/or data loss.

### Design considerations – files

In a design context the structure, content and storage of data files will invariably be influenced by a number of issues:

- the source and format of the data input(s),
- the procedure(s) adopted to process the data input(s),
- the destination and frequency of the data output(s), and
- the existence of external requirements (e.g. the requirements of the Data Protection Act 1998).

The aim is to maintain data integrity, maximise data security and minimise data errors, whilst ensuring the availability of and accessibility to data input(s) and data files.

### Design considerations – programs

Whether a program (software system) is developed either in-house or acquired (purchased) from an external supplier/developer should be influenced and determined by user/stakeholder needs and requirements, and not, as is often the case, by cost alone. Remember, a program (software system) that does not satisfy the needs/requirements of its users/stakeholders is a waste of money! We will look at both these alternatives in more detail later in this chapter but for now assume that the program (software system) is developed in-house. How would that process be undertaken?

There are, as you would probably expect, a number of alternative program (software system) development processes, some of the more common being:

- the waterfall approach,
- the prototyping approach,
- the synchronise/stabilise approach, and
- the spiral approach.

The waterfall approach is a sequential development approach which establishes goals and assessment targets for each development phase. The advantage of the waterfall model is that it simplifies the development process because there is no iteration, but the main disadvantage is that it does not allow for revision to take place.

The prototyping approach is one in which a prototype (or early approximation of a final program) is constructed, tested and reworked as necessary until an acceptable workable program is achieved.

The synchronise and stabilise approach is one in which a program is divided into individual application modules on which separate specialist teams work in parallel. The key to this approach is to ensure that the separate programming teams frequently synchronise their programming activities/coding activities to ensure that a stable final product/program will be produced.

The spiral approach is an approach in which the programme development combines the features of the prototyping model and the waterfall model. The advantage of the spiral approach is that there is/can be continuous revision/reviewing of development progress to date. The main disadvantages are that such an approach can be costly, resource intensive and time consuming. Nevertheless the spiral approach is an approach that is often used in large, complex, company/organisation-wide program (software system) developments.

In addition to the above, there are also the following:

- the Rapid Application Development (RAD) approach in which program developments are undertaken using workshops or focus groups to gather system requirements – the aim being to speed up the program development process, and
- the Joint Application Development (JAD) approach in which users/stakeholders are directly involved in the program (software) development usually through the use of collaborative workshops/development sessions.

Assuming that the spiral approach is adopted for the program (software system) development, what stages would be included in the development process? The main stages would be:

- an analysis of the feasibility of the program (software system),
- the identification and analysis of the program (software system) requirements,
- the preparation of a detailed design specification of the program (software system),
- the coding/programming of the software system,
- testing the program (software system), and
- maintaining the program (software system).

The key criteria are:

- functionality,
- accuracy,

- integrity,
- security,
- compatibility,
- usability,
- appropriateness, and
- relevance.

### Design considerations – data output(s)

The primary design consideration of any physical design phase is determining the precise nature and variety of data outputs – for example:

- the destination of data outputs,
- the format and medium of data outputs, and
- the type, volume and frequency of data outputs.

The main categories of data output(s) are:

- supply led output(s) or more appropriately scheduled output(s),
- demand led output(s),
- special purpose output(s), and
- exception reports.

As with data input(s), determining the precise nature of data outputs is especially important where it is likely that a number of alternative data output formats/medium may be used in the new system(s)/sub-system(s). Why? Primarily, to ensure:

- the cost effectiveness of each data output format/medium,
- the accuracy and clarity of all data output(s),
- the timeliness and relevance of all data input(s), and
- the integrity and security[19] of all data input(s).

Clearly issues of data destination, data type, data output trigger and output volumes and frequencies will also have a major influence on determining the medium used to issue/distribute output data. For example whether data is distributed and/or output using:

- a hard document-based output,
- a virtual document-based output, or
- a combination of both.

### Design considerations – internal controls

System(s)/sub-system(s) internal controls should *prima facie* be designed to ensure[20] the efficient and effective operations of all system(s)/sub-system(s) processes and procedures, and the security of assets and resources – that is:

- prevent and minimise the occurrence of errors, undesirable events and adverse threats,
- detect and identify any errors and adverse threats that have occurred, and
- correct and remedy the causes of adverse threats and/or undesirable events.

Such internal controls will invariably be influenced by:

- the source of the data input(s),
- the procedure(s) adopted to process the data input(s),
- the destination and frequency of the data output(s), and
- the existence of external regulatory requirements.

So, what types of internal control could be used? Such internal controls could comprise of:

- documentation checks (preventative internal controls),
- authorisation checks (preventative internal controls),
- validity assessments (preventative/detective internal controls),
- accuracy assessments (detective internal controls),
- security checks (detective internal controls),
- integrity checks (detective/corrective internal controls), and
- audit checks (detective/corrective controls).

## Systems selection

Once the blueprint/conceptual design specification of the system(s)/sub-system(s) has been completed, approved and adopted, and the underlying physical/operational design has been agreed, the systems selection stage – that is the process of selecting how the system(s)/sub-system(s) will be put together – can start.

There are essentially three possible alternative selection approaches, these being:

- an acquisition approach in which hardware/software components are purchased from an external supplier/developer – also known as an out-house acquisition,
- a development approach in which hardware/software components are developed internally – also known as an in-house development, and/or
- a combined approach in which some hardware/software components are purchased from an external supplier/developer and some are developed internally.

Within each approach there are of course a number of subsidiary issues that would need to be considered, for example:

- If the system(s)/sub-system(s) is to be purchased as a complete system:
  - how will the purchase be financed/arranged? and perhaps more importantly,
  - how will the supplier/developer be chosen?
- If the system(s)/sub-system(s) is to be developed in-house:
  - what resources and competencies will be required? and
  - how will the development be managed?
- If the system(s)/sub-system(s) is to be partly developed in-house and partly purchased from an external supplier/developer:
  - what hardware/software components will be developed internally? and
  - what hardware/software components will be acquired externally?

So, how would a company/organisation decide which approach to use?

In general, the decision would be made by the systems development team (in consultation with other relevant management representatives), and would be based on a combination of internal and external factors, perhaps the most important of these being:

- the net cost/net benefit of purchasing and/or developing the system(s)/sub-system(s),
- the levels of skills, competencies and capabilities available within the company/organisation,
- the availability of appropriate suppliers/developers for the hardware/software components, and
- the operational compatibility of any developed and/or acquired hardware/software component(s).

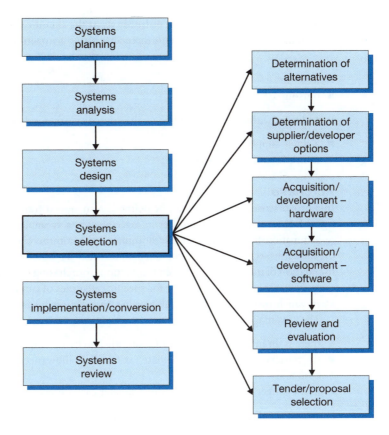

**Figure 16.9** Systems selection

Although it is difficult to say with any degree of certainty which of the above approaches is the most common, it is often the case that in large developments and/or projects involving company/organisation-wide systems/sub-system(s), that the combined approach is used.

So what are the main phases within the systems selection stage? The selection stage would involve the following phases:

- the determination of alternative selection options,
- the determination of supplier/developer options,
- the acquisition/development system components – hardware,
- the acquisition/development system components – software,
- the review/evaluation of alternative tenders/proposals, and
- the selection of successful tenders/proposals.

See Figure 16.9.

## Determination of alternative selection options

If a company/organisation chooses to pursue an acquisition approach, or indeed a combined approach, within which some hardware/software components are acquired from an external supplier/developer, what alternative acquisition options are available? Whilst the precise details of any acquisition would depend on the specific features of the systems development, the nature of the components and (as we have already seen) the extant capabilities of the company/organisation, in general there are perhaps three alternative acquisition options available, these being:

- purchase,
- lease, or
- outsource.

In addition, within each of the above, the company/organisation could use either:

- a single supplier/developer, or
- multiple suppliers/developers.

### Purchase

In a broad sense, a purchase can be defined as an agreed transfer of property and/or property rights from one person to another in exchange for a valuable consideration, and is a method of acquisition that has historically dominated the commercial activities of many companies/organisations. Whilst in a contemporary context such a method continues to form the commercial foundation of many revenue-based transactions, purchasing has – certainly since the late 1970s/early 1980s – become less popular for specific categories of capital assets, especially those capital assets which are subject to high levels of value depreciation due to rapid technological obsolescence.

The advantages of purchasing are:

- there is an immediate transfer of legal title and ownership,
- the purchaser can claim immediate tax (capital) allowances – sometimes up to 100% of the cost, and
- in the longer term, there is overall a smaller cash outlay.

However, the disadvantages of purchasing are:

- there is a large initial capital outlay – the full cost at purchase,
- there may be an increase in gearing if the purchase has to be financed through borrowing,
- all the risks related to the purchased asset(s) (e.g. risk of failure, risk of obsolescence) are borne by purchaser, and
- all the repair and maintenance costs related to the purchased asset(s) are borne by the purchaser.

Clearly, purchasing high-value capital assets which may need/require regular servicing and maintenance, constant upgrading and frequent replacing – in particular, capital assets (including both hardware and in some instances related software) relating to the provision of information and communication technology facilities/capabilities could place an excessively heavy strain not only on a company's/organisation's longer-term borrowing (if the acquisition is to be financed by debt), but perhaps more importantly, a company's/organisation's working capital.

An alternative to the purchasing of such a capital assets is, of course, to lease.

### Lease

A lease can be defined as a legal contract between the owner of the asset(s) (the lessor) and another party (the lessee), and relates to the transfer of possession and use of an asset(s) for valuable consideration for a specified period of time.

Whilst there are many named variations, in an accounting/finance context, there are essentially two types of leases:

- a finance (or capital) lease which involves a series of payments over the majority of the expected life of the asset(s) and for the majority of the cost of the asset(s), and in which the lessee acquires all the economic benefits and risks of ownership, and

- an operating lease[21] which involves a series of payments over a period (usually one to five years) that is less than the expected life of the asset(s), and in which the lessor remains responsible for all servicing and maintenance.

Mainly for fiscal reasons, the popularity of leasing grew enormously in the late 1970s/early 1980s for a wide range of assets. And, whilst during the latter part of the 1990s and the early part of 21st century leasing has become a much more asset focused industry, in a contemporary context, it is not uncommon for companies/organisations to lease a range of assets, for example:

- premises and buildings,
- plant, machinery and equipment,
- vehicles, and
- information and communication technology hardware/software.

The advantages of leasing are:

- there is a small initial cash outlay – it avoids large capital outlay,
- it can reduce/eliminate risks of ownership and can lessen the impact of technological obsolescence,
- it can help to conserve working capital and minimise cash outflows,
- it minimises the need for borrowing, and
- lease payments are a tax deductible expense.

The disadvantages of leasing are:

- the ownership of the asset(s) does not transfer from the lessor to the lessee, and
- the lease may involve a long-term commitment for the lessee and may therefore be expensive.

### Outsource
We will look at the issue of outsourcing in detail later in this chapter.

## Determination of supplier/developer options

Before deciding whether to use a single supplier/developer and/or multiple suppliers/developers, it is of course important to first determine whether those under consideration are appropriate and the type the company/organisation should deal with.

### Selecting a supplier/developer
There are many factors/issues a company/organisation should consider when selecting/approving a supplier/developer. Questions to consider would include, for example:

- Is the supplier/developer well established?
- Is the supplier/developer experienced in information and communications technology?
- Is the supplier/developer industry recognised/approved?
- Is the supplier/developer reliable?
- Are external third-party references available?
- Does the supplier/developer offer guarantees and/or warranties on the products/services it supplies/provides?
- Is the supplier/developer's products/services up to date?
- Does the supplier/developer provide finance for the purchase/development of hardware/software systems? If not does it provide alternative acquisition means (e.g. leasing)?
- Does the supplier/developer provide implementation and installation support/maintenance?
- Does the supplier/developer provide post-implementation and installation training and support?

In some companies/organisations this (pre)selection of a supplier/developer is often referred to as 'pre-qualification' inasmuch as potential suppliers/developers may be asked to demonstrate their financial, commercial and technical capabilities.

### Single supplier/developer

The advantages of using a single supplier/developer are:

- it can simplify the acquisition/supply process,
- it may ensure compatibility, and
- it may be a more reliable service.

The disadvantages of using a single supplier/developer are:

- it may limit product range, and
- it may increase risk (the supplier/developer stops trading, etc.).

### Multiple suppliers/developers

The advantages of using multiple suppliers/developers are:

- it may result in cheaper prices (due to competition),
- it may result in increased product range, and
- it can spread risk (supplier/developer stops trading, etc.).

The disadvantages of using multiple suppliers/developers are:

- it can be inconvenient,
- it can be complex,
- it may increase administration costs,
- it may be less reliable, and
- it may result in possible incompatibilities.

## The acquisition/development system components – hardware

Invariably information and communications technology hardware will be *bought into* the company/organisation – that is developed, constructed and supplied by an external third party. Because such acquisitions can have a significant cost – benefit implication, as well as representing a substantial long-term commitment, it is essential that:

- an appropriate hardware supplier is selected, and
- an appropriate hardware system is selected.

### Selecting a hardware system

The main factors/issues a company/organisation should consider when selecting a hardware system would include, for example:

- Specificity – what are the main features/capabilities of the hardware system?
- Technology – is the hardware system technology up-to-date and relevant?
- Comparability – are any external third-party evaluations of the performance of the hardware system available?
- Compatibility – if necessary can the hardware system be integrated into existing hardware systems?
- Availability – is the hardware system available now, and is it reasonably and competitively priced?
- Maintainability – what guarantees and warranties are available with the hardware system?

- Expandability – can the hardware system be expanded to include external facilities (e.g. external data storage)?
- Affordability – is financing available and/or are specific discounts available?

### The acquisition/development of system components – software

In a broad sense, software can be either developed or acquired (purchased). There are two alternative approaches to the in-house development of software, these being:

- the top-down approach (or management specific approach), or
- the bottom-up approach (or end user development approach).

There are two alternative approaches to the acquisition of software (where it is not developed in-house), these being:

- the acquisition of generic software, or
- the acquisition of commissioned software.

In addition, where software is acquired, it is important to ensure that an appropriate software retailer/supplier is selected.

### In-house development of software – top-down approach

The top-down development approach is an iterative process which commences with an overview of the development/design project, in which:

- the strategic objectives of the development are established,
- the critical development factors of the development are identified, and
- a broad design structure is formulated.

The emphasis is on establishing an understanding of the context of the development project/design.

Once a broad development/design structure has been established, a greater level of detail is introduced. The introduction of this further level of detail – in particular its impact on the development/design structure – is assessed and reviewed, and where necessary a refined overall development/design structure is produced. This assessment and review is repeated until a complete and detailed development and design specification is available – and the software design can be fully tested.

See Figure 16.10.

Such a process is of course not dissimilar to the function orientated conceptual design approach discussed earlier.

The advantages to the top-down approach are:

- the overall strategic context of the development/design minimises the risk of development/design errors and ensures/promotes compatibility with existing software systems, and
- the iterative reviewing and refining of the overall development/design structure results in better testing, less development waste and a reduction in bad documentation.

The disadvantages are:

- the development is often divorced from user needs and requirements – that is the development process may produce 'what we think you want' as opposed to 'what you really need',
- the process can be very time consuming and resource intensive,
- full testing of any development/design cannot be undertaken until a complete and detailed design specification is available, and
- end users may resist the imposition of newly developed software because of a lack of involvement in the development/design process.

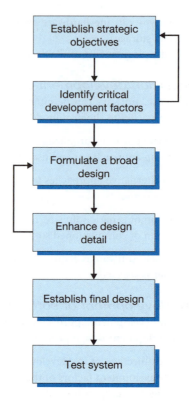

**Figure 16.10** In-house development of software: top-down approach

### In-house development of software – bottom-up approach

An alternative is a bottom-up approach (sometimes referred to as end user development). The bottom-up approach is a design process which focuses on the detailed aspects of individual parts/modules within a development/design, and emphasises early preliminary testing of individual parts/modules within a development/design specification. Once complete and fully tested, the parts/modules are then linked together with other parts/modules to form larger composite modules/structures, which are then linked to other composite modules/structures and the process repeated until a complete and detailed development and design specification is available. See Figure 16.11.

Such a process is of course not dissimilar to the object orientated conceptual design approach discussed earlier.

The advantages of the bottom-up approach are:

■ the development/design process is controlled by software end users ensuring that the development/design meets their needs, and
■ user software implementation and control procedures are managed by software end users producing greater flexibility, versatility and adaptability.

The disadvantages are:

■ development errors and logic issues may emerge when parts/modules are linked to other parts/modules,

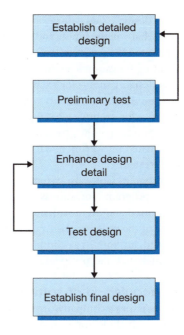

**Figure 16.11** In-house development of software: bottom-up approach

- development errors may result in incorrect or inconsistent documentation,
- poor development/design control may result in parts/modules being inadequately tested,
- parts/modules may be incompatible, and
- there could be excessive duplication and waste, resulting in increased costs and the inefficient use of resources

In reality, the modern approach to software development and design usually combines both the top-down and bottom-up approaches. Why? Put simply, whilst an understanding of the complete picture in terms of the strategic context of any development/design is considered by some to be a necessary, if not essential, prerequisite for good design – that is adopting a top-down approach – most software development/design projects often use existing software specifications as a base development platform (usually to aid integration with existing software) rather than start a development/design project from a zero base – that is adopting a bottom-up approach.

The main stages involved in this combined approach would be:

- analysis of the feasibility of the program (software system) – that is a detailed evaluation of the program (software system) development project and a determination as to whether it is feasible.
- identification and analysis of the program (software system) requirements – that is once the program (software system) feasibility has been confirmed detailed requirements should be established, in which variables and processes[22] are precisely identified and defined,
- preparation of a detailed design specification of the program (software system) – that is once its requirements have been established a design specification should be developed focusing on three key areas:

- high-level design issues – for example what specific programs (software system) will be required, what will the inputs and outputs be, and what will the relationship and/or inter-action between the program (software system) and existing programs (software systems) be (including for example existing/current operating systems),
- low-level design issues – for example how will the program (software system) function and what modular components will be used/required, and
- data design – for example what will be the structure of data inputs and outputs,
- coding/programming of the program (software system) – that is once the design is complete they are translated into a functional program – that is the program (software system) code needs to be created,
- testing the program (software system) – that is once the coding/programming is complete, the complete program (software system) will require testing to ensure that it functions as intended/required and on the intended platform(s), and
- maintenance of the program (software system) – that is once the program (software system) has been tested, authorised as complete and delivered to the users, it will inevitably require regular maintenance and/or updating.

### Out-house acquisition of software – generic software

The main factors/issues a company/organisation should consider when selecting a generic software system would include, for example:

- Specificity – what are the main features/capabilities of the software and is the software package well documented?
- Usability – is the software user friendly and are online enquiry facilities available?
- Controllability – does the software contain appropriate and adequate control features?
- Comparability – are any external third-party evaluations of the performance of the software available?
- Compatibility – is the software compatible with existing company/organisation software?
- Availability – is the software available now and is it reasonably and competitively priced?
- Maintainability – what guarantees and warranties are available with the software?
- Expandability – can the software system be expanded/amended/customised to meet specific company/organisational requirements?
- Affordability – is financing and/or are specific discounts available?

Purchased software is often referred to as *canned software*.

### Out-house acquisition of software – commissioned software

Commissioned software – also known as bespoke software – can be defined as software which is specifically created for a company/organisation to meet preagreed conditions and requirements. Such software can be either:

- newly developed software, or
- modified/amended generic software.

Where a bespoke software package is commissioned, it is important for the company/organis-ation commissioning the work to ensure an appropriate software developer is appointed. More importantly, it is essential that: a detailed development plan, a price/detailed costing and a detailed performance/delivery timetable are all agreed in advance with the software developer.

Where appropriate (especially for the larger development to be delivered in stages over a number of months) a contract detailing the nature of the development project and the rights and responsibilities of all parties to the contract should be agree and signed.

## Review/evaluation of alternative tenders/proposals

Where a systems development project represent a major undertaking for a company/organisation, it is likely that a number of suppliers/developers may be asked to submit a tender/proposal for some, if not all, of the development work.

A tender can be broadly defined as an unconditional offer to enter into a contract which, if accepted, becomes legally binding.

There are of course many alternative type of tendering, the most common being:

- open tendering,
- restricted tendering, and
- negotiated tendering.

Open tendering is essentially a single-tier bidding process, in which all interested suppliers/developers can submit a tender in response to a tender notice issued by the company/organisation. Normally such a tender notice would stipulate:

- the conditions that apply to the tender process,
- how the tender process will work,
- where tender documents can be obtained, and
- the last date by which tenders will be accepted.

Restricted tendering is a multi-tier bidding process in which suppliers/developers are initially requested to submit an 'expression of interest'. These expressions of interest are evaluated and a shortlist of appropriate suppliers/developers is then created. Those on the shortlist would then be invited to submit a formal tender, which would then follow the open tendering procedure discussed above. This restricted tendering procedure is most likely to be used where a large number of suppliers/developers are expected to submit tenders.

Negotiated tendering occurs where a company/organisation negotiates a tender with one or more approved suppliers following a pre-qualification process (see earlier). This negotiated tendering procedure is most likely to be used where:

- specialist services and/or components are required,
- where compatibility with existing services/components is crucial, or
- as a means of reducing the numbers of tenders – for example as part of the restricted tendering process.

Whatever tender process/procedure is used, once all tenders have been submitted and received, they need to be objectively reviewed and evaluated – and of course a selection made.

During this review and evaluation process, it is of course important that the integrity of the tender process as a competitive procedure is maintained, and essential that the evaluation of submitted tenders is undertaken fairly, objectively and impartially.

The review process would primarily consider how well the submitted tenders comply with all the requested criteria, and would usually be reviewed and evaluated using:

- a pre-determined set of criteria, and
- a pre-agreed scoring and weighting system,

to evaluate individual aspects/components of the tender. This would perhaps also incorporate benchmark performance measures and/or test simulation scores and evaluations for specific aspects/components of the tender.

Such pre-determined criteria could include for example:

- the price of the tender,
- the financial viability of the tender submission,

- the experience of the supplier/developer,
- the technical merit of the tender submission,
- the suitability and compatibility of the tender submission,
- the expandability and flexibility of the tender submission, and
- the projected completion time period of the development.

Clearly, whilst the precise nature of the award criteria would differ in each situation it is very unlikely that any tender would be successful on the basis of price alone. Rather a tender would be awarded to the supplier/developer based on value for money. And who would undertake this review/evaluation? It would probably be undertaken by a specialist subgroup appointed by and accountable to the systems development team. This sub-group may also include specialist consultant advisers from outside the company where appropriate.

## Selection of successful tenders/proposals

Once the objective review and evaluation had been completed by the specialist sub-group and reported to the systems development team, it would be the latter – in consultation with appropriate users/stakeholders – who would be responsible for taking one of three possible course of action:

- Where the specialist sub-group had identified a clear successful tender the systems development team would be responsible for *confirming* and *awarding* the tender to the successful supplier/developer.
- Where the specialist sub-group had identified a number of successful tenders the systems development team would be responsible for *selecting* and *awarding* the tender to the successful supplier/developer.
- Where the specialist sub-group had identified no successful tenders the systems development team would be responsible for *reviewing* the tender process, *assessing* the reasons for a lack of successful tenders and, where appropriate, *recommencing* the tender process.

## Systems implementation and conversion

Systems implementation/conversion involves the implementation of the selected design and/or the conversion of an existing system(s)/sub-system(s). The systems implementation stage would normally contain the following phases:

- the establishment of an implementation timetable,
- the allocation of system(s)/sub-system(s) responsibility,
- the development of appropriate monitoring control methodologies.
- the establishment of performance criteria,
- the preparation of location resources,
- human resource management – acquisition, training and education,
- the preparation of system(s)/sub-system(s) documentation, and
- the testing of system(s)/sub-system(s).

In addition to the above, where a systems development involves the changing/moving of an existing operational system to a new one, issues regarding:

- systems conversion – that is how the conversion will be managed, and
- data conversion – that is how/what data will be converted,

will also need to be considered. See Figure 16.12.

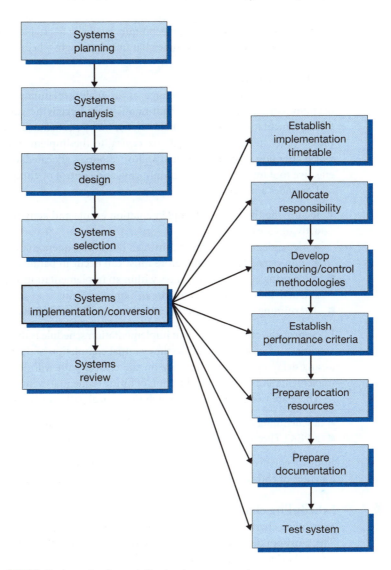

**Figure 16.12** Systems implementation/systems conversion

## Systems implementation

### *Establishment of an implementation timetable*

Clearly, the first phase of any implementation process is the establishment of an implementation schedule – a timetable of activities and events which will ultimately result in the installation of a fully operational system(s)/sub-system(s). Because such an implementation schedule will often contain a vast array of events and activities, it is critical that within the implementation schedule there is:

■ a prioritisation of the key implementation/development activities and events, and
■ an identification of the so-called critical path of the implementation schedule or, more precisely, a recognition of the sequence of activities that limit how quickly an implementation can be completed.

There are of course a number of techniques available to establish an implementation timetable/ schedule, the most – perhaps somewhat unsurprisingly – being critical path analysis.

## Critical path analysis

Critical path analysis can be defined as an analysis/planning technique that can be used to diagrammatically represent the continuous chain of activities and events critical to the successful implementation of system(s)/sub-system(s) by a scheduled completion date. By focusing on those events and activities which are critical to the implementation schedule, that is those to which attention should be devoted and/or resources allocated, critical path analysis provides an effective tool for the planning, monitoring and control of complex implementation schedules, and provides a means of:

- identifying the nature of implementation events and activities – that is whether events and activities are considered:
  - dependent and therefore must/can occur in sequence (that is 'one after the other'), or
  - non-dependent and therefore must/can occur in parallel (that is 'at the same time'),
- prioritising events and activities within an implementation schedule – that is whether events and activities are considered core or non-core, and
- determining the minimum duration over which such events and activities can be completed.

In essence, the critical path of an implementation schedule is the longest sequence of dependent activities and events, that lead to the eventual completion of the implementation plan inasmuch as any delay of any event/activity on the critical path will delay the system(s)/sub-system(s) implementation – unless the duration of future sequential events and/or activities can be reduced.

There are two main ways in which the critical path can be presented, using either:

- a scheduling chart – for example a Gantt chart, and/or
- a PERT (Project Evaluation and Review Technique) chart.

Both are equally useful and the selection of the most effective form of presentation is essentially a matter of choice, circumstance and, of course, personal taste.

## Scheduling chart

Scheduling charts are often used in the planning, development and implementation of a system. The most popular, and indeed the most widely used, scheduling chart is the Gantt chart. The Gantt chart is extremely useful in:

- assessing the maximum period of a development project,
- determining and prioritising resource requirements during a development project,
- establishing an order/timetable for development events/activities within a development project,
- identifying and managing interdependencies between development events/activities, and
- monitoring the progress of a development project.

Whilst it is possible to develop/draw a Gantt chart manually, most (if not all) development managers/systems development teams would use a charting software program (e.g. Microsoft Project available @ www.microsoft.com) to build, develop, amend and manage Gantt charts.

## PERT charts

PERT is a variation on critical path analysis that takes a slightly more sceptical view of time estimates made for each event/activity of the development project. For each event/activity time estimate, PERT uses a weighted average of:

- the shortest possible length of time each event/activity will take,
- the most likely length of time each event/activity will take, and
- the longest possible length of time each event/activity will take.

It then calculates the weighted average time for each event/activity using the following:

Shortest time + (4 × Likely time) + Longest time/6

## Allocation of system(s)/sub-system(s) duties and responsibilities

Within any systems development, whatever the size, it is inevitable that at some point during the implementation stage discussion regarding:

- the allocation of duties within the system(s)/sub-system(s), and
- the assignment of responsibilities within the system(s)/sub-system(s),

will need to take place. This is because often when a new system(s)/sub-system(s) is developed and introduced, duties and responsibilities, for example, for:

- data capture procedures,
- data security,
- data processing procedures,
- data storage facilities, and
- system(s)/sub-system(s) management

will invariably cut across a range of company/organisation departments. It is therefore import-ant that a suitable allocation occurs in order to ensure that sufficient separation of duties and responsibilities will exist post-implementation and ensure the existence of:

- adequate internal control within the new system(s)/sub-system(s), and
- appropriate security within the new system(s)/sub-system(s).

For example, within a company's/organisation's information systems – specifically within its accounting information system – it is important to ensure the existence (as a minimum) of at least the following separation of duties and responsibilities:

- user/stakeholder department – duties/responsibilities relating to data capture and data preparation,
- IT operations – duties/responsibilities relating to data processing, data management and data file library maintenance, and
- IT development – duties/responsibilities related to systems analysis, systems management and systems programming.

That is within the above:

- staff members of IT operations do *not* undertake duties/responsibilities relating to data capture and data preparation or to systems analysis, systems management and/or systems programming,
- staff members of IT development staff do *not* undertake duties/responsibilities relating to data capture and/or data preparation, or to data processing, data management and/or data file library maintenance,
- staff members of user departments do *not* undertake duties/responsibilities relating to data processing, data management and/or data file library maintenance, or to systems analysis, systems management and/or systems programming.

In many cases this process of allocation of duties, assignment of responsibilities and determin-ation of line accountabilities will emerge from, and be established by, reference to the structure and nature of the new system(s)/sub-system(s). It will therefore be a simple, if somewhat formal, routine exercise – an objective and apolitical systems development allocation/assignment exercise. In some cases, however, this process can become very political, divisive and disruptive, especially where:

- the nature, scope and impact of the new system(s)/sub-system(s) on the company/organisation (or a large segment of the company/organisation) will be significant,
- the manner in which the new system(s)/sub-system(s) is to be implemented is unclear and/or uncertain, and/or
- the impact and/or effect of the new system(s)/sub-system(s) on employees and/or groups of employees within the company/organisation will be substantial.

Clearly, it is in the best interests of the company/organisation to minimise any attempt at politicising the development and/or implementation process. Why? Because such politicisation (whatever its origin or cause) may provoke unwarranted resistance – resistance to the development and implementation of the new system(s)/sub-system(s) and the adoption/use of related information and communication technologies. A resistance which can, if left unresolved, become extremely costly in both a financial and business context.

We will look at the politics of accounting information systems development and the management of resistance later in this chapter.

### Establishment of performance criteria

As we will see later an essential part of the post-implementation assessment is a determination of the success or otherwise of the new system(s)/sub-system(s). A part of this post-implementation assessment is of course an assessment and measurement of the performance of the new system(s)/sub-system(s) the criteria for which will invariably be established during the systems implementation stage.

In establishing performance criteria, it is important to determine:

- What performance criteria will be used – for example qualitative or quantitative factors?
- How will performance be measured?
- When will performance be measured – for example every week, every month or every year?
- Who will perform/be responsible for performing the assessment?
- And perhaps most importantly, who will review the assessment results?

### The preparation of location resources

The preparation of location resources (often referred to as site preparation) involves ensuring that:

- adequate and appropriate location facilities are available for the installation of information and communication technology hardware,
- appropriate integrity and security measures will be implemented to control access to the installation facilities,
- sufficient power supply services will be available at the location,
- appropriate communications facilities will be available at the location, and
- appropriate environmental controls (e.g. humidity controls/temperature controls) will be implemented to protect the installed information and communication technology hardware.

Clearly, the costs of such preparation can be substantial, especially where such location preparation requires for example:

- the construction of new premises,
- the development of newly acquired premises,

- the refurbishment of an existing company/organisation-owned premises,
- the leasing of additional premises, and/or
- the acquisition/installation of specialist equipment/facilities (other than information and communication technology hardware) – for example:
  - backup power facilities – for example additional power generators,
  - property security facilities – for example CCTV systems,
  - environment management systems – for example air conditioning systems.

### Human resource management – acquisition, training and education

Resource preparation (often referred to as employee recruitment/employee orientation) involves ensuring that:

- the appropriate and timely recruitment of qualified and/or experienced staff is undertaken to satisfy any shortfall in employee skills and/or knowledge, and
- the appropriate and relevant levels of training and education are provided for those staff members to be involved in using and/or managing the new system(s)/sub-system(s).

Regarding this latter issue, it is important that:

- any training and education programme should include not only training and education on the system(s)/sub-system(s) hardware and/or software, but more importantly, training and education on the processes, procedures, policies and protocols developed to support the new system(s)/sub-system(s), and
- any training and education programme should cater for the level and status of its audience, and:
  - focus on their needs and requirements and, where appropriate,
  - combine both formal and informal activities as part of the training and education programme.

Whilst such resource preparation activities can be very expensive, and time consuming and disruptive, such resource preparation activities are vital to any system(s)/sub-system(s) development. An inadequate availability of skills and/or knowledge once the system(s)/sub-system(s) are operational could not only result in substantial operational problems but perhaps more importantly significant additional costs.

### The preparation of system(s)/sub-system(s) documentation

As part of the systems implementation process it is important that the systems development team ensures that appropriate system(s)/sub-system(s)-related documentation is available not only for management and for technical support staff, but perhaps most importantly for system(s)/sub-system(s) users and stakeholders.

Such documentation would include for example:

- a development narrative,
- an operational guide, and
- a user/stakeholder manual.

### A development narrative

This would normally include:

- a description of the development process,
- a description of the system(s)/sub-system(s) input, process and output procedures,
- a description of the system(s)/sub-system(s) data management procedures,

- a explanation of the information and communications interfaces,
- a listing of system(s)/sub-system(s) programs and coding structures, and
- a description of system(s)/sub-system(s) security.

It would also include, where appropriate, relevant flowchart charts and dataflow diagrams and, where necessary, example copies of systems documents. The purpose of such a development narrative is to provide a detailed technical specification of system(s)/sub-system(s).

## An operational guide

This would include for example:

- details of system(s)/sub-system(s) operating schedules/timetables
- details of system(s)/sub-system(s) hardware and software components,
- a description of the system(s)/sub-system(s) files and databases, and
- a description of system(s)/sub-system(s) users.

The purpose of such an operational guide is to provide detailed information on how to operate the system(s)/sub-system(s).

Note: For system(s)/sub-system(s) security purposes, it is important that the operational guide does not contain information such as systems flowcharts and program code because a system(s)/sub-system(s) operator should not, under any circumstances, have access to data/information that may reveal the system(s)/sub-system(s) internal logic.

## A user/stakeholder manual

This would include:

- a system(s)/sub-system(s) reference guide,
- an overview of the system(s)/sub-system(s) and its major functions,
- examples of data input procedures and data analysis tools,
- a comprehensive guide to error messages, errors codes and error descriptions,
- a tutorial guide,
- a training programme – usually task or topic orientated, and
- a help/problem referral guide.

The purpose of such a user/stakeholder manual is to describe how to use the system(s)/sub-system(s) and it is likely that much of the above would be provided as an online facility.

### Testing the system(s)/sub-system(s)

A final and perhaps crucial phase prior to any systems implementation, is the system(s)/sub-system(s) test. It is important that the system(s)/sub-system(s) is correctly tested to ensure that any faults and defects are appropriately rectified, any weaknesses and imperfections suitably repaired, and any limitations and inadequacies correctly resolved prior to implementation. Such testing would include,

- data capture/input tests,
- data processing tests,
- data/information output tests,

and would seek to determine:

- the appropriateness of system(s)/sub-system(s) documents,
- the reliability, integrity and security of user input processes and procedures,
- the availability of output information and the timetabling of system(s)/sub-system(s) reports,

- the processing capacity/ability of the system(s)/sub-system(s),
- the appropriateness of system(s)/sub-system(s) data processing procedures,
- the reliability and effectiveness of operating and control procedures,
- the appropriateness of data backup/data storage/data management procedures, and
- the suitability of disaster contingency recovery procedures.

A final testing of the system(s)/sub-system(s), often called an acceptance or transfer test, would involve users providing data (preferably actual data) for the final test phase of the new system(s)/sub-system(s). Such end-user-related testing is designed to confirm to the users the credibility and integrity of the new system(s)/sub-system(s).

## Systems conversion

Systems conversion can be defined as the process of changing/moving from an existing operational system to a new one.

There are essentially four approaches to systems conversion, these being:

- direct (or immediate) conversion,
- pilot (or modular) conversion,
- phased conversion, and
- parallel conversion.

### Direct (or immediate) conversion

Direct (or immediate) conversion is the most risky of all conversion processes/procedures and consists of an immediate switch over from the old system(s)/sub-system(s) to the one(s). Such a conversion process (also known as the *cold turkey approach*) is appropriate only where:

- the system(s)/sub-system(s) being replaced is of little or no value,
- the new system(s)/sub-system(s) is very different (operationally and/or technically) from the existing system(s)/sub-system(s),
- the existing system(s)/sub-system(s) and the new system(s)/sub-system(s) are simple, and/or
- the need for conversion from the old system(s)/sub-system(s) to the new one(s) is urgent.

The main advantage of the direct (or immediate) conversion is that the conversion process is immediate and inexpensive. The disadvantage is that the process can be very risky, especially where conversion problems occur. Such a failure could result in for example the incorrect processing and/or incorrect management of data as a consequence of a loss of system(s)/sub-system(s) integrity, and/or a failure of system(s)/sub-system(s) security.

### Pilot (or modular) conversion

Pilot (or modular) conversion occurs when a new system(s)/sub-system(s) is tested and introduced at either:

- specifically selected locations, or
- specifically selected functions/services.

If tests prove successful, then the new system is gradually introduced throughout the old system(s)/sub-system(s). Such a conversion process (also known as the *localised transition approach*) is suitable where both the old system(s)/sub-system(s) and the new replacement system(s)/sub-system(s) are crucial to the ongoing survival of the company/organisation.

The main advantage of the pilot (or modular) conversion is that such a conversion process allows for the testing of and training on a new system(s)/sub-system(s) in a live functioning environment, resulting in the identification, and correction of operational procedure/process errors (sometimes referred to as debugging).[23]

The main disadvantage of the pilot (or module) conversion is that such a staged/segmented introduction can extend substantially the time period of the conversion process and as a consequence increase the overall cost of conversion.

### Phased conversion

Phased conversion occurs when a new system(s)/sub-system(s) is gradually introduced and the old one(s) gradually removed. Such a conversion process (also known as the *incrementalist approach*) is suitable where:

- the new system(s)/sub-system(s) is very different (operationally and/or technically) from the existing one(s), and/or
- both the old system(s)/sub-system(s) and the new replacement one(s) are crucial to the ongoing survival of the company/organisation.

The main advantage of a phased conversion is there is a greatly reduced risk of systems/sub-systems failure because the transition is gradual, with resources and capabilities introduced/transferred in a programmed, coordinated and managed approach. However, the disadvantages of phased conversion are:

- the conversion process may take a considerable time,
- additional costs may be incurred as a result of creating temporary connections/interfaces to facilitate the gradual transfer of procedures and processes,
- incompatibilities may arise between the old system(s)/sub-system(s) and the new one(s),
- the timetabling of the conversion process, unless closely managed, may become problematic, especially where large complex transfers are involved.

### Parallel conversion

Parallel conversion occurs when both the new system(s)/sub-system(s) and the old one(s) are operated simultaneously for a period of time (e.g. days, weeks or months). Obviously, the longer the period, the greater the overall cost.

Such a conversion process (also known as the *dual approach*) is suitable where:

- the data processed and the information produced by system(s)/sub-system(s) being replaced is of substantial value to the company/organisation, and/or
- both the old system(s)/sub-system(s) and the new replacement one(s) are critical to the ongoing survival of the company/organisation.

The main advantage of a parallel conversion is there is a greatly reduced risk of conversion failure because the transition to the new system(s)/sub-system(s) only takes place once the parallel running has indicated no procedural/processing problems exist with the new system(s)/sub-system(s). However, the disadvantages of phased conversion are:

- the conversion process to the new system(s)/sub-system(s) may take considerable time,
- additional costs may be incurred as a result of parallel running of the two system(s), and
- operational problems may occur (e.g. employee resistance) as a result of the need to maintain two different system(s)/sub-system(s) simultaneously.

Finally we also consider data conversion.

### Data conversion

Where there is a system(s)/sub-system(s) conversion from the old to the new, there will invariably be a need to convert data from one to the other. This happens for a number of reasons, for example:

- the data structure used within the new system(s)/sub-system(s) may differ substantially from the old one(s),
- data file content used within the new system(s)/sub-system(s) may be significantly different from the old one(s), and/or
- the data storage medium used within the new system(s)/sub-system(s) may differ from the old one(s).

Such a conversion process can of course be time consuming, extremely repetitive, very tedious and enormously expensive, especially where a substantial amount of data and a substantial number of data files exist. So, it is not uncommon for a company/organisation facing a substantial data conversion task/activity to consider outsourcing it to an external company/organisation.

There are essentially three stages to the data conversion process, these being:

- data file selection,
- data file conversion, and
- data file validation.

## Data file selection

Data file selection involves:

- identifying the data files that require conversion to the new data file format, and
- evaluating the integrity of the data, contained in the data files, for example:
  - measuring the accuracy of the data,
  - determining the relevancy of the data, and
  - assessing the consistency of the data.

## Data file conversion

Data file conversion involves the adaptation/alteration of the data files – that is changing the formatting of a data file, and can be defined as the process by which data files created for the use in a system/application are modified and/or transformed to a data file format that can be used in another system/application.

## Data file validation

Data file validation involves:

- ensuring that all data/data files have been correctly converted,
- evaluating the accuracy of the content of the converted data files, and
- ensuring that no data/data files have been lost and/or corrupted during the data conversion process.

## Systems review

*There is no better teacher than history* (Anon).

Systems review involves the monitoring and evaluation of the selected system(s)/sub-system(s) performance, the primary aim of such a review being to determine the success (or otherwise) of the company/organisation systems development process.

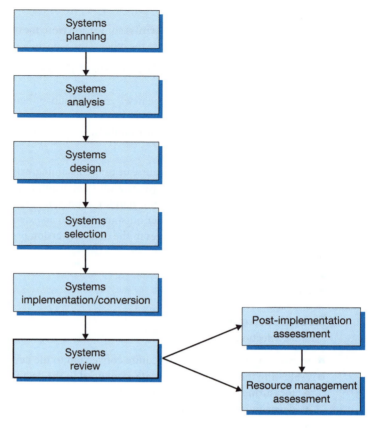

**Figure 16.13** Systems review

The systems review stage involves the following phases:

- a post-implementation assessment, and
- a resource management assessment.

See Figure 16.13.

## Post-implementation assessments

The post-implementation assessments will normally occur sometime after system(s) imple-mentation – the period and the frequency of the assessments obviously depending on the importance/criticality of the system(s) developed.

The aim of the post implementation assessment is to measure/assess the success or otherwise of the system(s) development process and determine whether the objectives of the system(s) development have been achieved. Often undertaken by the systems development team, such a post-implementation assessment would ask questions such as:

- Are users satisfied with the system(s) operations – if not why not?
- Are system(s) procedures functioning reliably and effectively?
- Are data input/capture procedures functioning correctly?

- Are data being processed accurately and appropriately?
- Are data output procedures functioning properly and in a timely fashion?
- Are processing errors correctly identified and resolved?
- Are there any ongoing intersystem(s) compatibility issues?
- Are control and security processes and procedures functioning efficiently?

In addition, the post-implementation review would also assess:

- the appropriateness of conversion/transfer/introduction procedures – for example:
  - Was the process clearly explained to users/stakeholders?
  - Was the conversion/transfer/introduction timetable appropriate?
  - Were any data and/or files lost during the conversion/transfer/introduction process?
- the effectiveness of user training provided as part of the system(s) implementation procedures – for example:
  - Was adequate and timely training available for users/stakeholders?
  - Was the conversion/transfer/introduction training documentation appropriate?
- the effectiveness of organisational/operational changes made as a consequence of the system(s) development – for example:
  - Were the organisational/operation changes appropriately timetabled?
  - Was the rationale for the changes clearly explained to users/stakeholders?
  - Was any consultation process with users/stakeholders undertaken?
- the appropriateness and usefulness of user documentation produced as part of the system(s) implementation procedures.

Where initial post-implementation assessments are positive – continuing post-implementation assessments by the systems development team may become unnecessary. In which case, the systems development team may transfer (or sign over) system(s) ownership to the company/organisation department responsible for the ongoing operational management of the system(s) and future assessments may become part of the company's/organisation's regular, planned monitoring process.

However, where post implementation assessments continue to identify operational problems and issues, the systems development team may need to or may be required to undertake remedial design/implementation action, in which case the system(s) ownership would remain with the team until all outstanding problems and issues are resolved.

It is perhaps worth noting that in terms of overall costs, it is not unknown for the post-implementation review costs/monitoring costs to exceed the actual planning, analysis, design, selection and implementation costs combined.

## Resource management assessment

The aim of the resource management assessment is to measure/assess the effectiveness of resource utilisation during the systems development process, and is sometimes regarded – perhaps somewhat unfairly – as a systems development team efficiency audit.

In an operational sense, the purpose of such an assessment is to determine how efficiently and effectively company/organisation resources were used during the planning, analysis, design, selection, implementation and review stages of the systems development life cycle, and as such would normally be undertaken by either an internal audit team or a senior management team where an internal audit section/department does not exist within the company/organisation. It may, in exceptional circumstances (e.g. where the assessment requires specialist knowledge), be undertaken by external consultants.

Such a resource management assessment would ask questions such as:

- Was the system(s) development process adequately coordinated and appropriately managed?
- Did any conflicts of interest arise during the system(s) development process and if so were they adequately/satisfactorily resolved?
- Were original system(s) development cost/benefit estimates accurate?
- Were there any significant departures from the original estimates/budget and, if so, were such departures assessed, approved and authorised?
- Were the system(s) development benefits fairly valued?
- Have the system(s) development benefits been realised?
- Was the system(s) development timetable realistic?
- Were there any significant departures from the system(s) development timetable and, if so, were such departures assessed, approved and authorised?
- Was the system(s) development process adequately communicated by the systems development team?

Clearly, where problems/issues are identified, remedial action by the company/organisation management would need to be taken, especially where such problems/issues are significant.

Again, the final outcome of the review stage would be a post-implementation review report.

## Systems review report

Once the post-implementation review has been completed and all appropriate facts have been collected, collated and assessed, it is important for the systems development team (or its representative) to prepare a formal report for the company/organisation management (or a delegated management committee/group).

Although the structure of such a post-implementation review report would vary from company to company or organisation to organisation, in a broad sense all reports would contain some, if not all, of the following detail:

- an overview and background of the systems development – explaining the background to the systems development,
- an evaluation of the systems development – for example were objectives achieved and were expected net benefits realised,
- an evaluation of user/stakeholder satisfaction/comments,
- an evaluation of the systems development team, and
- recommendations for future systems developments.

## The accountant/auditor and the systems development life cycle

Clearly in any systems development concerning a company's/organisation's accounting information systems, whether directly or indirectly accountants and/or auditors would need to be involved possibly as part of the systems development team. But what contribution would they bring to the systems development project?

During the various systems development life cycle stages, it is likely that the accountant/auditor would:

- provide financial/technical expertise during the planning stage,
- assist in the specification of system(s)/sub-system(s) documentation during the design stage,

- advise on internal control procedures during the design stage,
- provide financial advice during the selection stage,
- provide information of systems security procedure during the design and implementation stage,
- ensure adequate audit trails exist during the implementation stage, and
- confirm the existence and adequacy of internal controls during the post-implementation review stage.

## The prototyping approach

In an accounting information systems context, prototyping can be defined as the incremental development of new system applications and/or procedures using an interactive and iterative feedback process, the objective of the prototyping approach being to produce a system specification from which a fully functional system and/or systems can be developed (Emery, 1987). The basis premise of the prototyping approach is that end users find it easier to identify *what they do not want*, as opposed to *what they want*.

Note: Although the prototyping approach can be used as an alternative to the systems development life cycle approach, it can (and often is) used as part of it. For example it is often incorporated into the initial (or front end) stages of the systems development life cycle approach as a means of identifying and clarifying end user requirements.

The prototyping approach involves four stages, these being:

- the specification of user needs and requirements,
- the development of an initial prototype,
- the modification of the prototype, and
- the acceptance or rejection of the prototype.

See Figure 16.14.

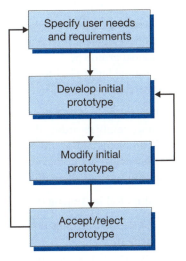

**Figure 16.14** Prototyping approach

## The specification of user needs and requirements

This specification stage will involve:

- identifying the systems and/or sub-systems requiring development,
- analysing and assessing the development need,
- specifying end user needs and requirements, and
- formulating a blueprint/conceptual design and/or range of alternative blueprints/conceptual designs.

## The development of an initial prototype

This development stage will involve determining an initial physical/operational design or prototype of the blueprint/conceptual design to be adopted.

## The modification of the prototype

This modification stage will involve:

- presenting the prototype to end users,
- obtaining end user feedback on the prototype, and
- changing/amending the prototype based on end user feedback.

As an iterative process, this modification process may be undertaken a number of times depending on the feedback offered by end users.

## The acceptance or rejection of the prototype

Where user feedback regarding the prototype system(s) is positive and constructive, and end user needs and requirements are well-defined and agreed, the prototype system(s) may after a number of modifications be developed into a fully functional system(s). This type of prototype is often referred to as an operational prototype. However, where significant and continuing disagreement exists over:

- the feasibility of the prototype system(s), and/or
- the definition of end user needs and requirements,

the prototype system may be discarded and the system development pursued using the traditional systems development life cycle approach. This type of prototype is often referred to as a non-operational prototype.

In general prototyping is used for developments that involve management-related and/or decision support-related systems. That is systems developments where there is or may be:

- a high level of ambiguity about the systems development,
- substantial uncertainty regarding the nature and/or structure of the system(s) processes,
- considerable problems and/or difficulties in defining system(s) requirements,
- significant uncertainty about the outcome of the systems development,
- a considerable number of alternative system(s) designs.

Prototyping is also ideal for system(s) developments which involve:

- experimental system(s)/investigational system(s),
- high-risk system(s),
- infrequently used system(s), and/or
- continual changing system(s).

For example, developments involving:

- strategic/executive information systems, and/or
- online data retrieval/information recovery.

However, prototyping is generally unsuitable for systems developments that involve:

- standard company/organisation-wide systems,
- large and/or complex company/organisation-wide systems,

especially system(s) that have limited design alternatives, well-defined system(s) requirements, and/or predictable processing procedures. For example, developments involving:

- a company's/organisation's debtor management system(s), and/or
- a company's/organisation's purchasing system(s).

## The advantages of prototyping

The main advantages of prototyping are:

- it can provide for an improved definition of end user needs and requirements,
- it can offer an increased opportunity for modification/change,
- it can facilitate a more efficient and effective development process, and
- it can result in fewer development problems and errors.

## The disadvantages of prototyping

The main disadvantages of prototyping are:

- it can involve a significant amount of end user commitment and may therefore result in a less efficient use of systems resources,
- the continuous modification of the systems specification and/or end user requirements may result in excess time delay and/or the development of:
  - an incomplete system,
  - an inadequately tested system, and/or
  - an inadequately documented system,
- the continuous revision of the systems specification and/or end user requirements may create negative behavioural problems.

## The politics of accounting information systems development – managing resistance

*There is nothing more difficult to carry out, nor more doubtful of success, nor more dangerous to handle than to initiate a new order of things* (Niccolo Machiavelli, *The Prince*, 1532).

In today's evermore chaotic, interconnected and technology orientated market environment, change (certainly in an accounting information systems context) is, it would appear, inevitable, especially change involving information and communication technologies. And yet, whilst such change may be seen as unavoidable – even perhaps inescapable – such change or, perhaps more appropriately, the consequences of such change – can and indeed often are perceived and understood in many different ways.

For example, for some, change may be seen as bad: that is its consequences may be seen as destructive and malevolent – the intention being to replace, even destroy, long and well-established practices and procedures. For others, such change may be seen as good: that is its consequences may be seen as beneficial and constructive – the intention being to break down traditional barriers, remove outdated and inappropriate practices and procedures, and engage with the 'brave new world'.

But how can such a diverse range of alternative understandings arise? Put simply, they arise because change (certainly within a corporate/organisational context) whilst motivated by an increasingly vast array of interconnected factors and issues, is invariably political in nature, with its consequences affecting different socio-economic groupings within a company/organisation in different ways. For example the introduction of 'Chip and PIN' technologies in many high street retail stores during 2003/04 affected lower-level operational employees differently to tactical-level junior/middle managers, who in turn were affected differently to strategic-level senior managers.

For example:

- lower-level operational employees, for example retail assistants, required an understanding of the operational aspects of the new technologies and the use of the new customer payment procedures,
- junior/middle managers, for example store managers, required an understanding of the control requirements and reconciliation aspects of the new technologies, and
- senior managers required an understanding of the longer-term cost–benefit impact of such technologies.

It is the potential impact of change (especially information and communication technology orientated change) on different socio-economic groupings within a company/organisation – the social and economic consequences on an individual and/or groups of individuals within the company/organisation – that will, if sufficiently negative and/or adverse, stimulate an agenda of defiance, opposition and non-cooperation from an individual and/or groups of individuals.

## Sources of resistance

Clearly, how an individual and/or a group of individuals perceive or understand a change/proposed change – whether it involves:

- the adoption of information and communication technologies, and/or
- the introduction of new/revised processes, procedures and/or protocols,

will of course determine their reaction to such change – in particular the level of opposition/resistance that may arise.

But why does such resistance emerge? Indeed, what are the sources of such opposition? Resistance to change – whether in the form of defiant opposition or merely non-cooperation from an individual and/or groups of individuals – will often emerge when:

- the nature, scope and context of the change/proposed change is ambiguous,
- the manner in which the change/proposed change is to be introduced and coordinated is unclear,
- the possible impact/affect of the change/proposed change on individuals/groups of individuals is uncertain, and/or
- the level of support (and reassurance) offered by those coordinating the change, to those affected by the change/proposed change (e.g. regarding training) is limited and/or vague.

That is resistance and opposition emerges where there exists:

- considerable bias/ambiguity, and
- significant fear and uncertainty,

regarding the change/proposed change. The intensity of any resistance and opposition offered is influenced by:

- the individual/personal characteristics/profile of those affected by the change/proposed change, and
- the level of personal loss that an individual and/or groups of individuals may incur as a result of the change/proposed change.[24]

## Types of resistance

Resistance can of course take many forms. It can range from:

- hostile aggression, to
- defiant opposition, to
- negative projection.

### Hostile aggression

Hostile aggression can be defined as an unprovoked violent act and/or hostile action designed to damage and/or possibly inflict injury. Examples of hostile aggression would be:

- the deliberate impairment of information processing hardware, for example the wilful destruction of input/output devices,
- the intentional sabotage and/or theft of data storage facilities,
- the theft of data and/or data storage facilities,
- the deliberate introduction of software viruses, and
- the intentional removal of control procedures and protocols.

### Defiant opposition

Defiant opposition can be defined as a deliberate act of avoidance and the wilful resisting of procedures and protocols. Examples of defiant opposition would be:

- the deliberate failure to follow appropriate internal control procedures,
- the intentional processing of transactions using incorrect/inappropriate documentation, and
- the purposeful (perhaps even fraudulent) omission of authorisation procedures.

Defiant opposition differs from hostile aggression inasmuch as there is no intention and/or deliberate act to damage, destroy and/or inflict injury or harm.

### Negative projection

Negative projection can be defined as the transference and/or allocation of blame or responsibility. It occurs when:

- the introduction of a new system or sub-system,
- the development of new procedures and processes, and/or
- the integration of new information and communication technologies,

is inappropriately blamed for errors and problems.

Examples of negative projection would be:

- where a new procedures and processes are blamed for excessive error levels in the processing of transactions, and/or
- where new information and communication technologies are accused of increasing time delays in the production of information.

Clearly, no matter how resistance emerges – no matter what its source or indeed what form such resistance takes – it needs to be effectively managed. Why? Because continued resistance to change, in particular continued opposition to change from different socio-economic groupings within a company/organisation may create unrest and escalate into internal conflict, which could if significant be politically and economically damaging for the company/organisation.

## Managing resistance and resolving conflict

Where resistance and opposition does arise it is important to:

- identify and define the nature of the resistance/opposition,
- identify and define the symptoms/reasons of the resistance/opposition, and
- develop a strategy to manage/contain such resistance.

Indeed, in managing change, it is important that those assigned with planning, developing and implementing any change, succeed in:[25]

- establishing a sense of importance and urgency about the change/change process,
- developing an acceptable rationale for any proposed change,
- creating a sufficiently powerful coalition to support any change/proposed change, and
- resolving any obstacles/hindrances to any proposed change at an earlier stage in the change process.

There are of course many strategies which can be adopted to assist in minimising resistance – although perhaps not fully eliminating such opposition. It is for example important to ensure:

- open communication and discussion takes place during the planning, development and implementation stage of any change/proposed change,
- adequate support (and reassurance) is offered to those affected by the change/proposed change,
- open and honest feedback is available at all stages during the planning, development and implementation stages of any change/proposed change, and
- user participation is encouraged during the planning, development and implementation stage of any change/proposed change.

## So resistance is futile?

Well not really! Indeed, not all resistance is bad. Whilst there can be little doubt that in some instances resistance to change, especially unprovoked and unwarranted hostile and aggressive resistance, can not only be socially harmful but more importantly economically damaging to a company/organisation, some resistance – whilst perhaps initially unwelcome and inconvenient – can be politically constructive and economically beneficial.

For example, such resistance may help to:

- focus attention on critical issues which may have been overlooked by the systems development team,
- identify operational faults within a proposal which the systems development team may have failed to recognise, and/or
- identify technical issues which may have a detrimental impact on operational control procedures.

As a consequence resistance could result in a more cost effective and operationally efficient system(s)/sub-system(s).

# Towards an information and communications technology strategy

As we have seen earlier, in a company/organisation context, the development of accounting information systems cannot be divorced from the *pull effect* of the ongoing integration of new information and communications technologies.

But why is it important for a company/organisation to develop and maintain both an information systems and an information and communications technology strategy? There are many reasons, perhaps the most important of these being:[26]

- information and communications technologies are socially, politically and economically important,
- they can involve high capital and revenue costs,
- they can (and often do) have an impact on all management levels within a company/organisation and involve many different stakeholders,
- they are enabling technologies, often involving leading edge technologies and/or high performance niche areas,
- they have a major impact on the creation, presentation and distribution of information, and
- they are often seen as a critical success factor and a major contributor in the development of sustainable competitive advantage.

We will consider this last reason in a little more detail.

## Information and communications technology as a source of competitive advantage

The term competitive advantage can be described as an advantage gained over competitors by offering consumers and clients greater perceived value, and arises from discovering and implementing sustainable ways of competing that are both distinctive and unique. Such competitive advantage can be achieved by, for example:

- developing barriers of entry to limit the bargaining power of buyers and the bargaining power of suppliers by, for example, establishing close interrelationships with both suppliers and customers,
- developing barriers of entry to prevent rival competitors entering the marketplace by, for example, maintaining a competitive pricing policy by minimising supply costs and/or increasing cost efficiencies, and/or,
- differentiating products/services from those of rival competitors in the marketplace.

There are of course a number of ways in which information systems and information and communication technologies can be used in developing and sustaining competitive advantage, for example:

- creating linkages between a company/organisation and its customers and/or suppliers – for example the use of electronic data interchange (EDI) facilities, and/or internet-based extranet facilities,
- integrating the use of information and communication technologies into the company/organisation value chain – for example the use of enterprise resource planning applications, data mining[27] and/or data warehousing[28] facilities, and
- enabling the development of new distribution channels/new retail services – for example the use of internet based e-commerce applications.

All of these would have an accounting information systems impact.

## Information and communications technology strategy – costs and benefits

There can be little doubt that information systems and indeed information and communications technologies have different degrees of importance in different companies/organisations, a difference of importance which managers often fail to understand fully. Indeed, many companies/organisations invest large amounts of money in information and communications technologies, for example in:

- developing extensive state-of-the-art computer networks,
- creating all-embracing web-based interfaces, or
- adopting advanced real-time information processing technologies.

Some of which may well be spent wisely and some carelessly, if not negligently. Foolish irresponsibly can be costly and disastrous.

In a financial context, the key to developing an intelligent information and communication technology strategy is a simple cost–benefit analysis – a balancing of the costs associated with an investment and the benefits that may accrue from any such investment. Put simply, it is not how much is spent that matters but how well it is spent.

So what are the costs and benefits associated with information and communications technology strategy?

### Information and communications technology costs

The socio-economic costs associated with information systems/information and communications technology spending would include a wide range of capital and revenue costs, for example:

- the cost of hardware equipment (capital costs),
- the cost of software and other program utilities (capital costs),
- installation costs – for example building refurbishment costs (capital and/or revenue costs),
- development costs (revenue costs),
- security costs – for example intrusion detection systems costs (capital and/or revenue costs),
- personnel costs – for example staff training and education costs (revenue costs), and
- operating costs (revenue costs).

### Information and communications technology benefits

The socio-economic benefits associated with information systems/information and communications technology would include, for example:

- a reduction in employee-related costs (revenue cost savings),
- a reduction in operating costs (revenue cost savings),
- a reduction in system maintenance costs (revenue cost savings),
- an increase in income from the disposal of information and communication, and technology equipment[29] (revenue income), and
- an increase in income from operational economies of scale (revenue income).

So how can a company/organisation develop an information and communications technology strategy?

## Developing and information and communications technology strategy

There are of course many ways in which a strategy for the continued investment in and integration of information and communications technology into corporate/organisational information systems (further details on an Information and Communication Technology Audit Grid are available on the website accompanying this text www.pearsoned.co.uk/boczko) – especially accounting information systems – can be developed, perhaps the most obvious and traditional starting point being to use a simplified form of gap analysis[30] or position analysis, to address two key questions:

- What is the company's/organisation's current information and communication technologies usage/requirement – that is what information and communication technologies do we need/ use now?[31]
- What is the company's/organisation's future information and communication technologies requirement – that is what information and communication technologies will we need/use in the future?[32]

In essence, the first question is essentially a *spatial* assessment of information and communications technology within a company/organisation. That is a determination of what the *current position* of information and communication technologies within a company/organisation actually is. The second question is essentially a *temporal* assessment of information and communications technology within a company/organisation. That is it is concerned with the *future position* of information and communications technology within a company/organisation.

### A spatial context: What do we do now?

There can be little doubt that in a contemporary sense, information and communication technologies can and indeed do play an eclectic variety of roles within a modern company/ organisation – a variety of roles that appears to increase day by day.

Indeed, as the pace/velocity of change in information and communication technology applications and capabilities continues to increase, so has the variety of organisational procedures, processes and activities affected by such technologies.

Nevertheless, despite the almost endemic presence of information and communication technologies in corporate/organisational activities – despite the growing multiplicity of roles which such technologies now play – we can, in a broad sense, identify a need/use hierarchy (a spatial framework) comprising of three interrelated levels of functional roles that information and communication technologies play within a company/organisation.

These roles can be categorised as:

- a peripheral (or supplementary) role,
- a companion (or intermediary) role, or
- a substantive (or principal) role.

### Peripheral (or supplementary) role

For a company/organisation within this category, information and communications technologies are seen as providing only a *supporting* role. That is such technologies are used to support marginal non-core/non-essential and non-value creating activities within the company/ organisation, and are often restricted to, for example:

- specific activities (e.g. payroll and/or financial accounting), or
- particular services (e.g. word-processing facilities, e-mail or even internet access), or
- particular technologies (e.g. a limited/fragmented network).

With the quality of the provision – that is the technical specification of the provision – often limited. More importantly, future developments in information and communications technologies are seen as having only a limited impact on the company's/organisation's overall commercial competitiveness.

### Companion (or intermediary) role

For a company/organisation within this category, information and communications technologies would be seen as providing a *facilitating* role in:

- supporting and enhancing marginal non-core activities within the company/organisation, and
- developing and improving principal core value-creating activities within the company/organisation.

This facilitating role can be either:

- a *maintenance* role, or
- a *development* role.

For a company/organisation within the former sub-category (*maintenance* role), information and communications technologies whilst currently a major factor in the company/organisation would not be expected to play a significant role in the future activities of the company/organisation. Whilst there is a current heavy dependency on information and communications technologies, technologies under development are unlikely to have a major/significant impact on the company's/organisation's future strategies and/or its overall commercial competitiveness.

For a company/organisation within the latter sub-category (*development* role), information and communication technologies, whilst not currently a major factor, are expected to play a significant role in the future activities of the company/organisation, with applications and technologies under development likely to produce a high potential contribution to the company's/organisation's future strategies, and have a major impact on its overall commercial competitiveness.

### Substantive (or principal) role

For a company/organisation within this category, information and communications technologies would be seen as providing a *strategic* role. That is such technologies – for example:

- internet-based services technologies,
- networking/relationship technologies, and/or
- information processing technologies,

play a major role in providing, developing and enhancing a wide range of core value creating activities within the company/organisation. Such technologies are seen as:

- possessing a high and significant business value, and
- providing substantial added value to the overall commercial activities of the company/organisation.

More importantly future developments in such technologies are seen as having a substantial and significant impact on the commercial activities of the company/organisation, with their expanded use being seen as a critical factor in the future development and success of its overall commercial activities.

#### *A temporal context: What do we need to do to get to where we want to be?*

In a temporal context, we can identify a three alternative but interrelated information and communication technology strategies, these being:

- a position consolidation strategy,
- a provision enhancement strategy, and
- a technology improvement strategy.

### Position consolidation

In an information and communication technology context, a position consolidation strategy is a *maintenance strategy*, and can be defined as a strategy designed to preserve current capabilities. Such a strategy would consist of renewing and/or updating existing information and communication technologies to sustain current capabilities, and is characterised by a reactive movement since it results from the pull effect of changes in, and/or enhancements to, information and communication technology applications and capabilities.

A position consolidation strategy would normally be associated with a minimal investment approach.

### Provision enhancement

In an information and communication technology context a provision enhancement strategy is a *development strategy* and can be defined as a strategy designed to maximise capabilities by enhancing the use and knowledge of information and communication technology-based applications. Such a strategy would consist of elevating the importance of existing information and communication technologies by, for example:

- providing additional training and education, and/or
- increasing or improving accessibility to information and communication technologies,

to enhance current capabilities and is characterised by a combination of:

- a reactive movement resulting from the pull effect of changes in and/or enhancements to information and communication technology applications and capabilities, and
- a proactive movement resulting from the push effect of changes in and/or amendments to company/organisational objectives and operational procedures, processes and activities.

A provision enhancement strategy would normally be associated with revenue spending strategy.

### Technology improvement

In an information and communication technology context, a technology improvement strategy is an *acquisition strategy*, and can be defined as a strategy designed to improve – through acquisition – the technical quality/technical specification of existing information and communication technologies.

Such a strategy would consist of replacing and/or updating information and communication technologies (including hardware and software) by, for example:

- the acquisition and installation of new network communication facilities, and/or
- the development/introduction of new improved software operating systems,

to improve current capabilities and is characterised by proactive movement resulting from the push effect of changes in and/or amendments to:

- the company's/organisation's objectives, and/or
- the company's/organisation's operational procedures, processes and activities.

A technology improvement strategy would normally be associated with a capital expenditure strategy.

## Towards a strategy context

In a broad sense, the business value (and strategic importance) of information and communication technologies is primarily (although not exclusively) a function of position enhancement so that merely improving the technical quality of information and communication technologies within a company/organisation will not on its own increase the business value of such technologies. A company/organisation is unlikely to invest in information and communications technologies where such technologies are unlikely to produce any identifiable net benefit and/or competitive advantage, or, positively impact on the overall business value of the company/organisation. Thus it is likely that:

- a company/organisation in which information and communications technologies play only a limited *peripheral or supplementary role* would most likely pursue a *position consolidation strategy* – although some provision enhancement activities would of course be necessary (minimal technology improvement would of course occur, but it is likely that such technology improvement would be as a result of external environmental pressure/demand),
- a company/organisation in which information and communications technologies play a *companion or intermediary role* would most likely pursue a *provision enhancement* strategy, together with an appropriately managed technology improvement strategy, and
- a company/organisation in which information and communications technologies plays a *substantive or principal role*, would most likely pursue a *technology improvement strategy* together with an appropriately managed proactive *provision enhancement strategy*.

Each of the above strategies would produce what is often called '*intra-role migration*'. That is migration which can be defined as movement within the boundaries of a single functional role. Such migration occurs when the organisational context of information and communication technologies within a company/organisation is marginally modified, but nevertheless continues to play the same role.

So what about changes in the role information and communications technologies play within a company/organisation? Is it possible that their role will change from being peripheral (or supplementary) to being companion (or intermediary), or from being companion (or intermediary) to being substantive (or principal).

Such a change is often called 'inter-role migration' and can be defined as cross migration to a different functional role. Such migration would occur when the organisational context of information and communication technology within a company/organisation is substantially modified.

## Outsourcing

Outsourcing (or contracting out) can be defined as the provision and management of internal company functions by an external company/organisation and consists of the delegation of non-core internal activities within a company/organisation (the client user) to an external agent (the service provider). It involves – perhaps unsurprisingly – a considerable degree of two-way information exchange, coordination and trust.

There are essentially two categories of outsourcing, these being:

- resource outsourcing in which a service provider agrees to provide and manage a set of organisational resources including, where appropriate, staff resources, a set of resources which comprise an organisational segment, and
- functional outsourcing in which a service provider agrees to provide a discrete service or facility, for example customer/client support services and/or customer/client call centre functions.

So what facilities, activities or indeed services are normally outsourced? Although outsourcing (as a contracting-out business process) has a long history dating back to the early 19th century[33] such outsourcing was normally related to production/manufacture-related facilities/activities either directly (e.g. product manufacture) or indirectly (e.g. raw material supply). In a contemporary context, outsourcing is now used in a vast range of company/organisational facilities/activities including:

- manufacturing and engineering facilities,
- human resources management,
- facilities and real estate management activities,
- accounting and internal audit functions and, of course,
- information and communications technology facilities.

It is perhaps worth noting that whilst many service orientated companies/organisations (e.g. banks and insurance companies) have relocated support services and/or call centre facilities, and many manufacturing companies/organisations have relocated production activities and/or distribution facilities, to other countries or geographical locations, such relocation is not necessarily outsourcing – it is off-shoring. Indeed, outsourcing and off-shoring, whilst often used interchangeably, are in fact very different.

Put simply outsourcing involves the transfer of an organisational function/activity to an external agent/third party, and means sharing company/organisational control with *another company and/or organisation, located either in the UK or in another country*. Off-shoring involves the transfer of an organisational function/activity to another country and *represents a relocation of an organisational function/activity to a foreign country*, and does not necessarily involve the transfer, sharing or control of an asset, function and/or activity.

## Outsourcing information and communications technology-related activities/facilities

Whilst there can be little doubt that many companies/organisations (including many UK FT250 companies) have at some time in the not to distant past outsourced some or part of their information and communications technology-related activities/facilities such outsourcing was historically restricted to operational non-core information and communications technology-related activities/facilities. It was rare – certainly up to the early 1990s (although not unheard of) – for a company/organisation to outsource strategic and/or core information and communications technology-related activities/facilities.

Today, however, mid-way through the first decade of the 21st century, many companies/organisations (including many UK FT100 companies) now outsource a range of core and non-core activities. This is to:

- maintain operational flexibility in an ever-changing marketplace,
- reduce overall costs, and
- maximise the use of resource.

So what information and communications technology-related activities/facilities are normally outsourced? Outsourced activities/facilities include for example:

- data processing and information management facilities – including:
  - data selection and capture facilities,
  - data storage/data management services,
  - data maintenance and processing facilities, and
  - information management and distribution services,

- network management services[34] – including:
  - installation and maintenance services,
  - desktop support services,
  - server support facilities,
  - server and network monitoring services,
  - server health check facilities, and
  - off-site storage facilities,
- software support services – including:
  - training and education services,
  - help desk support services, and
  - technical support facilities.

So how does outsourcing work? There are essentially three outsourcing models normally used in the outsourcing of information and communications technology related activities/facilities, these being:

- an on-site outsourcing model,
- an off-site outsourcing model, and
- blended outsourcing.

### On-site outsourcing

On-site outsourcing occurs when outsourced resources/facilities are provided by the service provider on site – that is at the outsourcing company's/organisation's location.

This type of outsourcing is often used where:

- specific resources are required for the outsourced activity,
- the outsourced activity requires high levels of security/confidentiality and constant monitoring,
- the outsourced activity is not for a defined period, and/or
- the outsourced activity is highly iterative.

### Off-site outsourcing

Off-site outsourcing occurs when outsourced resources/facilities are provided by the service provider off site – that is from a location other than the client user's location. This type of outsourcing is often used where:

- the requirements and specifications of the outsourced activity can be defined and agreed in advance,
- the client user's on-site resources/facilities are limited, and
- the service provider can provide a more efficient and effective service from a remote location.

Increasingly, where off-site outsourcing requires/entails the provision of services/facilities from and/or the undertaking of activities at a location other than in the country of the client user, such off-site outsourcing is – perhaps somewhat confusingly – often referred to as off-shore outsourcing.

So why outsource in a country other than the country where the client user is located? In general, the criteria for off-shore outsourcing are:

- the outsourced service/activity has a high information content,
- the outsourced activity is repeatable,
- the service provider does not require direct customer interaction with the client user,
- the service can be provided using web-based technologies,
- the infrastructures required to support the outsourced services/activities are simple to create, and
- there is a high wage differential between the client user's country and the off-shore location.

### Blended outsourcing

Blended outsourcing occurs where a service provider provides resources/facilities using a combination of on-site outsourcing and off-site outsourcing for example:

- the provision of front office support services on-site, and
- the provision of back office technical facilities off-site (and/or off-shore).

This is an increasingly popular outsourcing model, especially in for example network support/management, where a service provider can/will monitor network infrastructure from a remote location, but will – at regular intervals – undertake a network health check[35] on-site at the client user's location.

## Advantages and disadvantages of outsourcing

The main advantages for the client user are:

- lower overall costs,
- better asset utilisation,
- improved quality of service,
- greater access to expertise, and
- better access to advanced information and communications technology.

The main disadvantages are:

- possible poor service,
- loss of control of key resource,
- reduced competitive advantage, and
- limited flexibility.

## Minimising risk – using a service level agreement

Critical to the outsourcing of any information and communication technology-related activity/facility is of course an outsourcing agreement between the service provider and the client user – an outsourcing agreement which is often known as a service level agreement.[36]

Such an agreement exists as a result of:

- a simple oral understanding (the weakest form of service level agreement),
- a exchange of letter of agreement, or
- a legally binding sealed contractual agreement (the strongest form of service level agreement).

It should be used to define, for example:

- the nature of the service to be provided by the service provider (the supplying company/organisation),
- the legal relationship between the service provider and the client user,
- the quality/standard of service to be provided by the service provider,
- the level/nature of any compensation to be paid as a consequence of a failure by the service provider to achieve the standard of service required by the service level agreement, and
- the level/nature of any compensation to be paid as a consequence of a failure by the client user to comply with the remuneration conditions imposed by the service level agreement.

A service level agreement should cover (in detail) issues such as:

- the scope of service to be provided, including details of the quality standards/delivery procedures required under the service level agreement (e.g. data processing procedure/timetables, response times, data back-up procedures, etc.),

- the period over which the service(s) is to be provided,
- the location(s) at which the service(s) is to be provided,
- the procedures for the monitoring and reviewing of the service provider's performance (e.g. compliance assessment meetings),
- the duties and responsibilities of the service provider and/or the client user in controlling and managing service provider access to client's assets and facilities,
- the duties and responsibilities for the service provider and/or client user in:
  - maintaining the security of confidential data/information, and
  - protecting intellectual property rights,
- the processes and protocols to be adopted for changes to be made to the conditions/requirements of the service level agreement,
- the duties and responsibilities of the service provider and/or the client user for disaster recovery in the event of a systems failure, and
- the procedures and protocols to be adopted for the termination of the service level agreement by either the service provider and/or the client user.

Although all service level agreements will contain some requirements/conditions specific to:

- the service provider,
- the client user, and/or even
- the service type,

it is nonetheless important – for both the service provider and the client user that any service level agreement clarifies three key issues:

- the procedures for the monitoring, tracking and reviewing of the service provider's performance, and determining the service provider's compliance with the conditions/requirements of the service level agreement,
- the processes and procedures for resolving disputes, problems and issues arising out of the service provider's and/or client user's failure to comply with the requirements of the service level agreement, and
- the levels of compensation to be paid as a consequence of any breach of service level agreement obligations resulting in a failure by the service provider and/or the client user to comply with the requirements of the service level agreement.

See Article 16.1.

### Breach of agreement

Unless specifically agreed within the service level agreement, determining not only the existence of a breach, but more importantly, level of a breach or failure to comply with the requirements of a service level agreement can be problematic. It is perhaps not surprising, that many information and communication technology-related service level agreements provide for the use of some mutually agreed performance metric, for example:

- a positive assessment metric such as a performance scorecard system in which points are awarded for targets achieved, and/or requirements complied with, or
- a negative assessment metric such as a failure points system in which points are awarded when targets are not achieved, and/or requirements not complied with,

to determine the level and extent of any breach.

(See also the discussion on problem resolution later in this chapter.)

## Article 16.1

### Firms must get tough on hosts

*Users should ensure contracts include guarantees.*

Analysts are advising hosted software customers to ensure their contracts include guarantees against downtime. Such clauses could help to reassure firms as to the stability of hosted services in the wake of recent service interruptions.

Analyst Forrester Research last week called for Salesforce.com to offer a standard service-level agreement (SLA) with its hosted customer relationship management (CRM) subscriptions, and argued that customers need to tighten controls over performance levels of hosted software generally. 'Companies should review existing contracts to better understand what guarantees exist, and negotiate for additional clauses in new contracts that include compensation for unexpected downtime,' said Forrester's Liz Herbert. Firms should also involve IT staff to perform due diligence on service providers, monitor performance and 'get aggressive' with suppliers to ensure compensation is paid if necessary, Herbert suggested in a research note. Instead, some firms leave decisions to 'line-of-business [managers who] rarely have experience in negotiating application vendor contracts, and unfortunately . . . don't always push for a contractual agreement that reimburses them for unexpected outages'.

Salesforce chief executive Marc Benioff said his company offered private SLAs to customers who wanted them. 'We don't have 100 percent uptime but nobody else does,' he added. Salesforce has invested heavily to bolster failover, but Benioff said his firm has no definite plans to build a UK hosting facility. Forrester pointed out that rivals NetSuite and Salesnet offer standard SLAs based on 99.5 and 99.6 percent uptime respectively. Other analysts backed Forrester's recommendations for SLAs. In a blog entry this month, Butler Group's Teresa Jones wrote: 'Software as a service . . . means that the actual performance of the application is outside the control of the organisation using the service. One way to wrest back some control is to ensure that an SLA is defined at the outset, preferably with some recompense for SLA breaches.'

Meanwhile, Robert Bois of AMR Research said, 'The reality is that many companies running software behind the firewall experience outages all the time. It's just that Salesforce.com customers experience them all at once.' He advised prospects and customers to look carefully at SLAs, and potentially put terms in place to ensure that they are compensated if these are not met.

Source: Martin Veitch, *IT Week*, 30 January 2006,
**www.itweek.co.uk/itweek/news/
2149506/firms-tough-hosts**.

### Minor breach

Sometimes a failure/breach of service level agreement is not considered a fundamental breach (as defined in the service level agreement and/or measured by the pre-agreed performance metrics), that is the breach is considered to be of a minor nature and no more than a limited infringement either by the service provider and/or the client user, for example:

- the service provider:
  - fails to adhere to a predetermined data processing timetable,
  - fails to provide prearranged support facilities, and/or
  - refuses to comply with specific security procedure, or
- the client user:
  - fails to adhere to a predetermined payment/remuneration schedule, and/or
  - fails to provide appropriate access to assets and facilities,

an appropriate claim for compensation for losses incurred, and/or losses to be incurred as a result of a failure by the service provider and/or the client user to comply with the requirements of the service level agreement, would normally be agreed as stipulated in the service level agreement.

### Major breach

If a failure/breach of service level agreement is considered fundamental (as defined in the service level agreement and/or measured by the pre-agreed performance metrics) – that is the breach is considered to be a major nature, and representing a substantial failure, for example:

- the service provider:
  - fails to comply with confidentiality agreements,
  - repeatedly refuses to provide essential core services in accordance with the service level agreement, and/or
  - repeatedly fails to meet pre-agreed quality standards and/or target deadlines,
- the client user:
  - repeatedly fails to provide access data/information in accordance with the service level agreement, and/or
  - repeatedly fails to provide appropriate access to assets and facilities,

then termination of the service level agreement by the party not in breach of the service level agreement results. Where appropriate, a legal claim for damages and compensation for losses incurred and/or to be incurred as a result of the breach could follow.

### Force majeure[37]

It is perhaps worth noting that most information and communication technology service level agreements contain a *force majeure* clause – a clause which exempts both the service provider and the client user from any liability arising from a compliance failure and/or performance delay arising from events/occurrences *beyond their reasonable control*.

Such events/occurrences would include for example:

- acts of war,
- acts of God,
- acts of nature – including earthquakes, hurricanes and floods,
- civil riots, and
- government imposed trade embargos.

Put simply, such a *force majeure* clause provides explicit exemption from any liability for compensation where such liability has arisen from a failure/breach of agreement caused by one or more of the above events/occurrences.

### Problem resolution

Most information and communication technology-related service level agreements will contain a predefined and pre-agreed problem resolution protocol/clause containing details of the processes and procedures to be employed by either the service provider and/or client user in the event of a failure by the other party to comply with the conditions and requirements of a service level agreement.

Depending on the nature and seriousness of the alleged failure/breach of agreement, the problem resolution procedures could comprise of up to five interrelated stages, these being:

- an identification stage,
- an assessment stage,
- an escalation stage,
- an arbitration stage and, where necessary,
- a litigation stage.

## Identification stage

The identification stage is designed to ascertain the nature of the breach of agreement, that is for example:

- the type of failure(s) that has/have occurred,
- the time, date and location of each failure and, where possible,
- the cause of each of the failure,

with its single purpose being to gather factual evidence.

The identification stage will normally be part of the service level agreement monitoring and reviewing procedures and processes.

## Assessment stage

The assessment stage is designed to clarify the level of breach of agreement – for example, whether the breach constitutes a minor infringement or major failure. Indeed, it is at the assessment stage that any mutually agreed performance metric (as defined in the service level agreement) will be used to determine the level of the breach. As with the identification stage, the assessment stage will also normally be part of the service level agreement monitoring and reviewing procedures and processes.

Where a breach of agreement (by either the service provider and/or the client user) is deemed to be of a minor nature and agreed by both parties to have taken place, then compensation will be made by the party in breach of agreement to the other party – usually at an agreed tariff.

See Example 16.1.

## Escalation stage

Where agreement cannot be reached at the assessment stage – a stage which usually occurs at an operational/tactical management level – then escalation to a higher management level may be required. The escalation stage is designed to move an unresolved problem up to a higher tier of management, both at the service provider and the client user, and is usually used where:

- a breach of service level agreement is deemed by either the service provider or the client user to be a major breach, and/or
- a mutually agreed level of compensation for a minor breach of service level agreement cannot be reached.

The aim of the escalation stage is to elevate discussion to a more strategic level and consider the strategic context of the alleged breach of agreement and the potential consequences of a failure to achieve a mutually acceptable resolution.

In many cases, where alleged breach does reach this stage, it is usual that after minor political manoeuvring, discussion and a lot of negotiation, a resolution will normally be found – whether that resolution entails:

- making a financial payment at an agreed level as compensation for the breach of agreement,
- issuing a letter of apology or, even
- mutually agreeing to terminate the service level agreement.

## Arbitration stage

It is of course possible that a resolution may not be found – especially where a significant difference of opinion exists between the service provider and the client user regarding the nature and level of the breach of agreement. In such cases arbitration may be the final option.

Backup Direct™ (On Direct Business Services Ltd) is the UK based **online data backup** service provider for UK business. See www.backupdirect.net

The following is a copy of Backup Direct™ service level agreement (Business Users) available @ www.backupdirect.net/library-service-level-agreement.htm.

### *Service Level Agreement*

#### Backup Direct™ Service Level Agreement (Business users)

*This Service Level Agreement ('SLA') covers performance guarantees for our Business online backup service only, and is made between Backup Direct™ ('Backup Direct™', 'Provider', 'we', 'us', 'our') and you ('Client', Customer, 'you').*

*Clients are responsible for checking this document from time to time, as notifications of updates will not be made. This document will be located online at:*

*http://www.backupdirect.net/library-service-level-agreement.htm.*

*The following SLA Terms and Conditions apply only to Customers agreeing to a Minimum Service Period of one year or more for Backup Direct™ Business Services and only in respect of the provision of such services during such period and where Customer's accounts with Backup Direct™ are in good standing. The Terms and Conditions apply only where a Client is not in material breach of the Terms and Conditions of the Software and Service License Agreement which can be found at:*

*http://www.backupdirect.net/library-license-agreement.htm.*

*Availability of this SLA may be subject to further conditions or qualifications set forth in additional related agreements between Backup Direct™ and the Customer including the Software and Service License Agreement. All remedies set out herein shall not be cumulative, and shall be Customer's sole and exclusive remedy for non-performance under the relevant Agreement.*

#### Data Centre Configuration
*The Backup Direct™ Data Centre is architected to deliver the maximum system uptime, security and reliability.*

#### System Availability Guarantee
*We offer a 99.9% uptime guarantee. This means that for any given month, while unlikely, it is possible that we may experience an average downtime of up to 43.2 minutes per month excluding Scheduled Maintenance.*

#### File Restore Guarantee
*All files backed up on the Backup Direct™ System will be available for a period of 30 days from the date of backup. In the event of a Client wishing to restore a file or a group of files previously backed up on the Backup Direct™ System, Backup Direct™ guarantees that the file or files will be recoverable within four hours from the initial request.*

#### Application/Database recovery Guarantee
*Application and Database files backed up on the Backup Direct™ System will be recoverable within 24 hours from the initial request.*

#### Disaster Recovery Guarantee
*In the event of a major data loss by the client involving the loss of entire servers and their contents, where such servers and files are legitimately backed up on the Backup Direct™ System, we will make all reasonable efforts to provide expert guidance to the client in order to restore the system to its original operational state. We will provide such support as is necessary to work with the clients or its suppliers in order to ensure that system files and data files are restored to any replacement hardware subject to the condition that such replacement material is correctly configured, specified and available.*

#### Notification of non-performance
*To be eligible for compensation under any of the above Guarantees, the Client must notify Backup Direct™ of a possible incident. Upon opening a support ticket, we will ascertain whether the problem exists within our realm of reasonable control. We will make reference to system log files to confirm the appropriate breech of the performance Guarantee. In the event of a disaster, notification by telephone to the Support Team is acceptable, where the Support Team will validate the nature of the disaster.*

**Compensation Payments**
*In case of non-performance under this Agreement, the client will be compensated as follows:*

*System Availability Guarantee – if an outage exceeds 43.2 minutes, we will refund 5% (five percent) of the Client's base monthly recurring fee per hour of downtime, up to 100% (one hundred percent) of the base monthly recurring fee.*

*File Restore Guarantee – if a file or set of files is not recoverable within 4 hours of the initial request, we will refund the client 5% (five percent) of the Client's base monthly recurring fee for each MB (Megabyte) of non-restorable data, up to 100% (one hundred percent) of the base monthly recurring fee.*

*Application/Database Recovery Guarantee – if system and or database files or set of files are not recoverable within 24 hours of the initial request, we will refund the client 5% (five percent) of the Client's base monthly recurring fee for each MB (Megabyte) of non-restorable data, up to 100% (one hundred percent) of the base monthly recurring fee.*

*In all cases these Compensation Payments are non-cumulative and the highest amount for each category will be paid. In all cases the maximum payment in anyone month will not exceed 100% of the Client's base monthly recurring fee.*

**Refund Procedures and Exceptions**
*Clients must notify us via email to sla@backupdirect.net or via fax to 08701 417 437, indicating that they wish to pursue their rights as guaranteed by this SLA within 7 days of the incident. If a response from us is not received within 24 hours, the Client should assume that a technical difficulty has prevented us from receiving their request, and should contact our personnel via telephone at 08000 789 437.*

**Scheduled Maintenance**
*Scheduled Maintenance means any maintenance at the Backup Direct™ Data Centres, where the Customer is notified 48 hours in advance by telephone, email, fax and that is performed during a standard maintenance window Mondays through to Thursdays from 03:00 hours to 07:00 hours GMT.*

**Force Majeure**
*Except in respect of payment liabilities, neither party to this agreement will be liable for failure or delay in performance of its obligations under this SLA due to reasons beyond its reasonable control including: acts of war, acts of God, earthquake, flood, riot, embargo, government act or failure of the Internet, provided that the delayed party gives the other party prompt notice for such cause.*

*This document was last modified on 03/02/03.*

**Example 16.1** A service level agreement

Arbitration is merely an alternative form of dispute/problem resolution – often seen as an alternative to litigation, in which the parties to a dispute agree to submit their respective positions to a neutral third party[38] for resolution. For service level agreement disputes, the third party could, for example, be:

- an industry regulator,
- an independent company, or
- a government sponsored agency.

## Litigation stage
Where arbitration fails to provide a resolution agreeable to both parties, litigation may be the only remaining course of action. Clearly, where litigation is considered as a course of action, expert legal advice *must* be obtained prior to the commencement of any action – no matter how extensive the alleged failure/breach of contract. Litigation as a final course of action is not only very expensive in financial terms, it can also be very time consuming in business management terms and, potentially, very damaging to the name and market reputation of the company and/or organisation.

## Compensation

At any of the above stages, where an alleged failure/breach of agreement has been proven and agreed to have occurred by both the service provider and the client user, compensation may be awarded. In a broad sense, such compensation can be defined as financial reparation for loss or injury suffered as a consequence of the alleged failure/breach of agreement, with the level of compensation paid dependent on the nature of the alleged failure/breach of agreement and the extent of the loss/injury suffered as a result.

Whilst compensation for minor infringements/breaches of agreement will normally be based on a mutually agreed tariff, compensation for a major failure/breach of agreement can be much more difficult to establish/quantify. However it is perhaps worth noting that claims for excessive compensation – however justifiable they may appear – will generally be legally unenforceable, since they will be regarded as a penalty and not payment of compensation.

## Termination

Service level agreements do not last forever, especially those related to information and communication technology-related activities/facilities. Although some service level agreements may exist for many years, invariably a time will come when a service level agreement between a service provider and a client user will need to be renegotiated – a renegotiation which may or may not result in the appointment of a new service provider.

Whether such a decision is financially motivated – that is based on cost – or technology motivated – that is based on service quality/service delivery – when such a decision is made, it is important that:

- an orderly termination of service provision from the current service provider occurs and, where necessary,
- an organised migration from the current service provider system(s) to the newly appointed service provider system(s) occurs.

For information and communication technology-related activities/facilities, especially facilities-related service level agreements (e.g. network support and/or data storage), organised migration (often over an extended period) is critically important in order to minimise possible service disruption and/or possible data loss.

Whilst it is not unknown for such migration to take place over periods of up to 12 or 18 months, especially where the outsourced information and communication technology-related activity/facility is a major core activity with the client user's company/organisation, in general average migration periods of up to six months tend to be the norm. Clearly, in any migration it is important for the current service provider to provide all reasonable assistance to the client user in the migration to the newly appointed service provider's system, and whilst in the majority of transfers that will be the case, in a minority of cases problems can occur. Problems often result from a deterioration in the relationship between the current service provider and the client user once the appointment of a new service provider has been announced. Such problems can range from:

- the purposeful obstruction of transfer/migration activities,
- the deliberate distribution of confidential (and/or commercially sensitive) information,
- the premeditated corruption and/or infection of data/files, to
- the intentional destruction of network hardware.

Whilst most information and communication technology-related service level agreements contain specific conditions on and detailed requirements for the termination of a service provision and the migration to another service provider, such problems may, nevertheless, still occur. Where they do, and negotiation fails to resolve the situation, then litigation may be the only solution.

## Concluding comments

Change, especially in an information and communication technology context/accounting information systems context, is as we have seen, inevitable. Consequently it is important for a company/organisation to control such change by not only identifying the causes of such change but more importantly managing the impact/consequences of such change. A failure to do so could be disastrous – certainly in the longer term.

## Key points and concepts

| | |
|---|---|
| **Blended outsourcing** | **Parallel conversion** |
| **Bottom-up development approach** | **Peripheral role** |
| **Commissioned software** | **Phased conversion** |
| **Complimentary role** | **Physical design phase** |
| **Conceptual design phase** | **Pilot conversion** |
| **Data conversion** | **Position consolidation** |
| **Defiant opposition** | **Prototyping** |
| **Direct conversion** | **Provision enhancement** |
| **Discontinuous change** | **Rough incremental change** |
| **Function orientated design approach** | **Smooth incremental change** |
| **Generic software** | **Soft-major change** |
| **Hard-major change** | **Soft-minor change** |
| **Hard-minor change** | **Substantive role** |
| **Hostile aggression** | **Systems analysis** |
| **In-house development** | **Systems conversion** |
| **Information policy** | **Systems design** |
| **Negative projection** | **Systems development life cycle** |
| **Object orientated design approach** | **Systems implementation** |
| **Off-site outsourcing** | **Systems planning** |
| **On-site outsourcing** | **Systems review** |
| **Out-house development** | **Technology improvement** |
| **Outsourcing** | **Top-down development approach** |

## References

Ansoff, I.H. and McDonnell, E.J. (1990) *Implanting Strategic Management*, Prentice Hall, New Jersey.

Aseervatham, A. and Anandarajah, D. (2003) *Accounting Information and Reporting Systems*, McGraw Hill, Sydney.

Bagranoff, N.A., Simkin, M.G. and, Strand N.C. (2004) *Core Concepts of Accounting Information Systems*, Wiley, New York.

Cadbury, A. (2000) Global Corporate Governance Forum, World Bank, New York.

Earl, M.J. (1989) *Management Strategies for Information Technology*, Prentice Hall, London.

Emery, J.C. (1987) *Management Information Systems: The Critical Resource*, Oxford University Press, Oxford.

Grundy, T. (1993) *Managing Strategic Change*, Kogan Page, London.

Kotter, J.P. (1996) *Leading Change*, Harvard Business School Press, Cambridge, USA.

Kotter, J.P. and Cohen, D.S. (2002) *The Heart of Change: Real Life Stories of How People Change Their Organizations*, Harvard Business School Press, Cambridge, USA.

Machiavelli, N. (1532) *The Prince*, Translated by Marriot, W.K. (1916) Macmillan, London.

McFarlan, F.W. and McKenney, J.L. (1983) *Corporate Information Systems Management: the Issues Facing Senior Executives*, Dow Jones Irwin, Homewood, IL.

Romney, M. and Steinbart, P. (2006) *Accounting Information Systems*, Pearson Education Inc., New Jersey.

Senior, B. (1997) *Organisational Change*, Pitman, London.

Stacy, R. (1996) *Strategic Management and Organisational Dynamics*, Pitman, London.

Strebal, P. (1996) 'Choosing the right path', *Mastering Management*, Part 14, Financial Times, London.

Vaassen, E. (2002) *Accounting Information Systems – A Managerial Approach*, Wiley, Chichester.

Wilkinson, J.W., Cerullo, M.L., Raval, V. and Wong-On-Wing, B. (2001) *Accounting Information Systems*, Wiley, New York.

## Bibliography

Sadler, D. (1989) 'Management Development,' in Sisson. K., *Personnel Management in Britain*, Blackwell, Oxford.

## Self-review questions

1. Describe the six main stages of the systems development life cycle.

2. According to Grundy (1993) there are three varieties of change. Distinguish between the following:
   - smooth incremental change,
   - rough incremental change, and
   - discontinuous change.

3. Distinguish between the following:
   - soft-minor change,
   - hard-minor change,
   - soft-major change, and
   - hard-major change.

4. Explain the key stages you would expect to find in the systems analysis stage of the systems development life cycle.

5. Describe the four main stages of the prototyping approach to systems development.

6. Distinguish between the following types of resistance
   - hostile aggression,
   - defiant opposition, and
   - negative projection.

7. Explain the main factors/issues a company/organisation should consider when selecting a hardware system.
8. Distinguish between a top-down approach and a bottom-up approach to the in-house development of software.
9. Distinguish between the following types of outsourcing:
   - on-site outsourcing,
   - off-site outsourcing, and
   - blended outsourcing.
10. Describe the main details that would normally be covered in an outsourcing service level agreement.

## Questions and problems

### Question 1

Borlan plc is a UK listed and UK-based retail company. Because of significant data processing problems encountered during the 2004/05 and 2005/06 financial years, the managing director of the company launched a company-wide development review of its accounting information systems in late 2006.

*Required*

Assuming the company-wide development review recommends the introduction of a new accounting information system, describe and evaluate the key stages you would expect to find during the systems development process.

### Question 2

Learn-a-lot Ltd is a small but expanding Leeds-based retail company that provides computer-based educational facilities and equipment for a range of public and private sector colleges and universities specialising in post-graduate professional IT courses. As a result of a recent increase in demand for the courses offered by universities and colleges, the company is considering expanding its current retail facilities.

The company is seeking to establish a presence in both Hull and York in order to benefit from the high number of undergraduates studying IT and computer science-related degrees at the local universities.

The company is, however, aware that such an expansion would require not only a substantial capital investment, but also a significant change in the company's accounting information systems procedures, especially those concerned with the recording of sales income.

*Required*

As their recently appointed systems accountant, prepare a report for the management of Learn-a-lot Ltd on the importance for a company like Learn-a-lot Ltd to possessing a cohesive strategy for the development and implementation of information and communication technologies within its accounting information systems.

### Question 3

Describe and evaluate the main costs/benefits associated with information and communication technologies, and explain why it is important for a company to develop an effective information and communication technology strategy.

$\rightarrow$

## Question 4

During the systems development life cycle, it is not uncommon for a systems development team seeking to introduce new systems and procedures to face/encounter significant resistance.

### Required

Explain why such resistance may emerge, what forms such resistance can take and how such resistance can be managed and minimised.

## Question 5

Where an alleged breach of a service level agreement occurs, it is important that any such alleged breach of agreement is resolved as soon as possible. Depending on the nature and seriousness of the alleged breach, the problem resolution procedures could comprise of up to five interrelated stages, these being:

- an identification stage,
- an assessment stage,
- an escalation stage,
- an arbitration stage, and
- a litigation stage.

### Required

Describe and critically evaluate each of the above stages main stages.

# Assignment

## Question 1

In January 2006, Richard Houghton was appointed as group systems accountant for FIRST plc a UK-based retail company. Currently, the company has 18 retail outlets located throughout the UK. The company's head office is in Manchester. The company currently operates three alternative sales facilities; web-based sales, mail-order sales and over-the-counter sales.

All web-based and mail-order sales are processed at the company's head office in Manchester and despatched from its main distribution centre in Wigan. All over-the-counter sales are processed at each individual retail outlet. For the year ending 31 March 2006 the company retail sales were £87m and its net profits were £28m.

At a recent meeting with the company management board, Richard suggested that the company should explore the possibility of reviewing its over-the-counter sales procedures by introducing a new range of 'Pay by Touch technologies' to replace the existing chip and PIN technologies. Although many of the management board were not clear on exactly what 'Pay by Touch technologies' were, they were sufficiently intrigued by the idea of using biometrics as part of the company's revenue cycle that they suggested a feasibility study be undertaken on the possible advantages and disadvantages of introducing such technologies.

### Required

Making what ever assumptions are necessary prepare a feasibility report for the management board of FIRST plc detailing the possible advantages and disadvantages of introducing 'Pay by Touch technologies'.

## Question 2

In August 2006, following extensive discussion, the management board of FIRST plc, a UK-based retail company, approved the introduction of 'Pay by Touch technologies' in all its 18 retail outlets, and appointed Richard Houghton (group systems accountant) as chair of the project development team.

### Required

Describe and critically evaluate the main stages that would be involved in successfully introducing such technologies into the company's revenue cycle, and the problems that may be faced by the systems development team in their introduction.

## Chapter endnotes

[1] Heraclitus of Ephesus (approximately 535–475 BC) was known as 'The Obscure' and was a pre-Socratic Greek philosopher in Ephesus in Asia Minor.

[2] A demand/output orientated system is a system in which the functioning of the system and its sub-systems are primarily conditioned by external environmental pressures, whereas a supply/input orientated system is a system in which the functioning of the system and its sub-systems are primarily conditioned by internal management pressures.

[3] The term 'environmental factors' is used to describe all those factors which exist outside the system's boundary.

[4] If you recall, in Chapter 14 we considered this multi-dimensional layering when we explored the issue of *context filtering* – the process through which the priorities of capital (or the marketplace and its component institutions) impose their requirements though a complex hierarchy of macro and micro factors and characteristics.

[5] This is an adaptation of Ansoff and McDonnell's (1990) five level typology of environmental turbulence.

[6] See Stacy (1996).

[7] *Ibid.*

[8] *Ibid.*

[9] Radio Frequency IDentification (RFID) refers to the technologies that can be attached to an object (e.g. a retail commodity) that can be used to transmit data to an RFID receiver. In a commercial context RFID is often viewed as an alternative to bar coding.

[10] Some academics suggest that the systems development life cycle contains only four stages: systems planning, systems analysis, systems design and systems implementation (e.g. see Bagranoff *et al.* (2004)), whilst others suggest that the systems development life cycle contains only five stages: systems planning, systems analysis, systems design, systems implementation and systems review (e.g. see Aseervatham and Anandarajah (2003) and Romney and Steinbart (2006)), and yet others suggest that the systems development life cycle contain six stages: systems planning, systems analysis, systems design, systems selection, systems implementation and systems review (e.g. Wilkinson *et al.* (2001)).

[11] See Cadbury (2000).

[12] Such costs would include for example hardware/software acquisition costs, design costs, programming and testing costs, data conversion costs, training and education costs and hardware/software maintenance costs.

[13] Such tangible benefits would potentially include, for example, increased sales incomes, reduce payroll costs and better working capital management.

[14] Such intangible benefits would potentially include, for example, improved decision making, more efficient operations, improved communications and greater stakeholder satisfaction.

[15] It may be that the root problem of a system(s)/sub-system(s) is not a design issue but a management and/or employee issue which can perhaps be resolved without the need for expensive redesign.

[16] Where an current/existing system(s)/sub-system(s) is to be replaced, it is important to assess how such a replacement will occur – for example:

- what system(s)/sub-system(s) processes will be phased in,
- what system(s)/sub-system(s) processes will be phased out,
- what data/information will be transferred,
- how will the data/information be transferred, and
- what training and education requirements will be needed to ensure the new systems function correctly.

[17] Such security would also include restricting/confirming user access.

[18] Individual ATM withdrawals are normally limited by the account holding institution/bank. Although the precise nature of the restriction will differ from bank to bank or institution to institution, it is not uncommon for a restriction/limit of £200–£250 per day to apply to ATM withdrawals from an individual personal current account.

[19] Such security would also include restricting/confirming user access.

[20] See Chapter 14.

[21] Sometimes (somewhat incorrectly) referred to as a service lease or contract hire.

[22] A variable is data which change over time, whereas a process is an activity which in an information and communications technology context transforms data.

[23] Debugging can be defined as a process of detecting, locating and removing mistakes, defects and/or imperfections, in a system(s)/sub-system(s). Debugging tends to be harder when various sub-systems are tightly coupled, as changes in one may cause bugs to emerge in another.

[24] For example:

- a loss of financial rewards,
- a loss of power base, and/or
- a loss of utility.

[25] For an organisational context see Kotter (1996) and Kotter and Cohen (2002).

[26] See Earl (1989).

[27] Data mining can be defined as the process of analysing data to identify patterns or relationships, and refers to the use of information and communication technologies in either:

- generating new hypotheses (bottom-up data mining), or
- confirming existing hypothesis (top-down data mining).

[28] The term data warehouse refers to a collection of data gathered and organised so that it can easily be analysed and used for the purposes of further understanding the data.

[29] Although given the speed of change within information and communication technologies, such saving are likely to be very small.

[30] There are many definitions of the term 'gap analysis' but for our purpose we will use the term to mean a deficiency assessment. That is a process of determining and evaluating the difference between what is needed and what is available. Put simply, the difference between where 'we' are and where 'we' want to be.

31 For example using Earls's (1989) quality/value map – see the website accompanying this text www.pearsoned.co.uk/boczko for further details.

32 For example using McFarlan and McKenney's (1983) strategic grid of information systems – see Appendix 16.1 for further details.

33 For example, in the USA during the early 1800s the production of wagon covers and clipper ships' sails was outsourced to factories in Scotland, with raw material imported from India. See http://www.globalenvision.org/library/3/702.

34 For example see www.intrasource.co.uk.

35 A network health check can be defined as an assessment of the efficiency of the physical network in its active form as well as an assessment of the logical network connections.

36 Software management agreements, facilities management agreements, network management agreements and server support agreements are all examples of service level agreements.

37 *Force majeure* is French for greater force and can be defined as a force which cannot be controlled by the parties to a contract/agreement and which may prevent either party complying with the provisions and requirements of the contract/agreement.

38 Sometimes referred to as the arbitrator(s) or the arbiter(s).

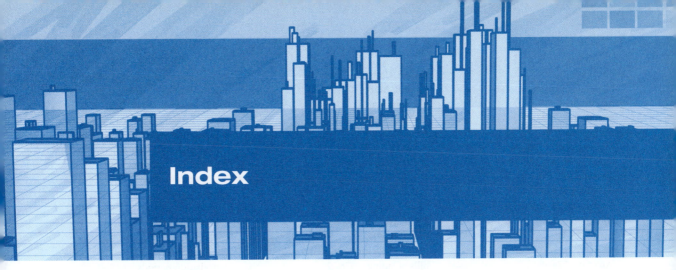

# Index